Macmillan 180.00 set

Mystery and Suspense Writers

Mystery and Suspense Writers

The Literature of Crime, Detection, and Espionage

Robin W. Winks
Editor in Chief

Maureen Corrigan
Associate Editor

VOLUME 2

*Ross Macdonald
to
Women of Mystery*

CHARLES SCRIBNER'S SONS
An Imprint of Macmillan Library Reference USA
NEW YORK

Charles Scribner's Sons
An imprint of Macmillan Library Reference USA
1633 Broadway
New York, NY 10019

Library of Congress Cataloging-in-Publication Data

Mystery and suspense writers : the literature of crime, detection, and
    espionage / Robin W. Winks, editor in chief ; Maureen Corrigan,
    associate editor.
        p.   cm.
    Includes bibliographical references and index.
    ISBN 0-684-80492-1 (set : alk. paper). — ISBN 0-684-80520-0 (v. 2
: alk. paper)
    1. Detective and mystery stories, English—Dictionaries.
2. Detective and mystery stories, English—Bio-bibliography—
Dictionaries. 3. Detective and mystery stories, American—Bio-
bibliography—Dictionaries. 4. Detective and mystery stories,
American—Dictionaries. 5. Spy stories, American—Bio-bibliography—
Dictionaries. 6. Spy stories, English—Bio-bibliography—
Dictionaries. 7. Spy stories, American—Dictionaries. 8. Spy
stories, English—Dictionaries. 9. Crime in literature—
Dictionaries. I. Winks, Robin W. II. Corrigan, Maureen.
PR830.D4M97   1998
823'.087209'03—dc21
    [B]   98-36812
                                                            CIP

1 3 5 7 9 11 13 17 19 20 18 16 14 12 10 8 6 4 2

PRINTED IN THE UNITED STATES OF AMERICA

The paper used in this publication meets the minimum requirements of American National Standard for Information Sciences—Permanence of Paper for Printed Library Materials. ANSI Z39.48-1992.

CONTENTS

CONTENTS

CONTENTS

ROSS MACDONALD

(1915–1983)

ROBERT F. MOSS

IN THE AMERICAN hard-boiled detective tradition, three authors stand out as masters. The first two, Dashiell Hammett and Raymond Chandler, got in on the ground floor, writing for *Black Mask* magazine and establishing the conventions of the genre. The third, Kenneth Millar—who wrote under the pen name Ross Macdonald—came slightly later. He adopted the form as created by Chandler and Hammett and modified it to reflect his own experiences, sensibility, and perceptions of human behavior. He softened the sharp, violent edge of the hard-boiled genre, toned down its language, and deepened its moral and psychological complexity. During his thirty-two-year career, Millar produced twenty-four novels and, after years of relative obscurity, achieved a commercial and critical success far greater than anything Chandler and Hammett saw during their lifetimes. Millar's mature novels—the twelve Lew Archer books written between 1959 and 1976—stand alone as a body of work unmatched in consistent quality and volume by any other American detective writer.

Life

Kenneth Millar was born in Los Gatos, California, on 13 December 1915. His parents, John Macdonald Millar and Annie Moyer Millar, were Canadian citizens who had come to California from Great Slave Lake in the Northwest Territories. The family soon moved to Vancouver, British Columbia, where John Millar took a job as a harbor pilot. When Kenneth was three years old, his father abandoned the family without warning. Annie Millar had worked previously as a nurse, but typhoid fever left her incapable of supporting herself and her young son. She went as far as taking Kenneth to the gates of an orphanage before deciding she could not abandon the boy. He spent the rest of his childhood moving from town to town in Canada, living almost as a charity case among various relatives. As an adult, looking back on his youth, Millar described himself as a boy who by the age of sixteen "had lived in fifty houses and committed the sin of poverty in each of them" (*Self-Portrait*, 1981, p. 51).

At the age of eleven, Kenneth Millar read Charles Dickens' *Oliver Twist* and felt an immediate identification with the novel's hero; from then on he wanted to be a writer. A year later, supported by his Aunt Margaret, he moved to Winnipeg and attended St. John's School, a semimilitary academy. There he came into close contact with wealthy children for the first time, "learned something about the Canadian class structure and . . . evolved a desire to rise in it—not always be at the bottom" (quoted in Tutunjian, p. 69). The stock market crash of 1929 ended Millar's stay at the school, but his two years at St. John's had instilled in him a sharp awareness of class and monetary inequities, an awareness that would stay with him the rest of his life.

In 1930 Millar moved to Kitchener, Ontario, where he lived with his grandmother and an aunt in an atmosphere of poverty and fundamentalist morality. He enrolled in the Kitchener-Waterloo Collegiate and Vocational School, where he spent hours in the school library reading Fyodor Dostoyevsky, Samuel Taylor Coleridge, Wilkie Collins, and Stephen Leacock. At night he stayed up late reading boys' pulp adventures about characters such as Falcon Swift, the Monocled Manhunter. One afternoon he discovered a copy of Dashiell Hammett's *The Maltese Falcon* in a lending library run out of a Kitchener tobacco shop. He read much of the book on the spot and felt that "the secret meanings of the city began to organize themselves around me like a second city" (*Self-Portrait*, p. 7). His school years were a time of anger and resentment, and his grades suffered, but Millar read steadily on his own and also began to write. He appeared in print for the first time in 1931 when "The South Sea Soup Co.," a parody of Sherlock Holmes, was published in *The Grumbler*, his school's literary magazine.

After graduating in 1932, Millar worked for a year on a farm, earning only room and board. He felt trapped in poverty and believed he would never be able to attend college. His mother had long encouraged him to think of himself as American by birth, and California remained in his mind as a sort of lost kingdom from which he had been exiled. These elements of his childhood—the abandonment by his father, his impoverished upbringing, his sense of disinheritance and exile—would provide the thematic groundwork for his mature fiction.

Millar was given a chance to escape his surroundings in 1932, when his father died and left him a $2,500 insurance policy. This money was put into an annuity and allowed Millar to attend the University of Western Ontario in London. He majored in English and history and published stories, poems, and sketches in the literary supplements of the *University of Western Ontario Gazette*. After his mother died in 1935, Millar left college and spent a year bicycling through Europe before returning to Ontario and completing his degree. In the public library he met Margaret Sturm, who had attended the same high school as Millar, and the two were married in June 1938.

Millar spent the next year at the University of Toronto, where he took graduate education courses and earned a teacher's certificate, then landed a job teaching English and history at the Kitchener Collegiate Institute. To earn enough money to live through the summer, he wrote children's stories for Sunday-school newspapers and contributed stories, poems, and humorous sketches to the Toronto *Saturday Night*—his first paid publications. His and Margaret's only child, Linda Jane Millar, was born in 1939. In September 1940 Margaret was confined to bed because of a heart ailment and while recuperating wrote *The Invisible Worm* (1941), which was accepted by Doubleday and launched her career as a mystery novelist. Through the 1960s she would remain a far more successful author than he.

In 1941 Kenneth Millar entered the graduate program at the University of Michigan and studied under W. H. Auden, who was there on a visiting professorship. Auden not only introduced Millar to authors such as Franz Kafka and Søren Kierkegaard but, as a noted mystery fan, helped convince him that the detective novel was a legitimate literary form. In 1943, while completing his doctoral course work, Millar wrote *The Dark Tunnel*, a spy novel published by Dodd, Mead in 1944.

The same year, Millar enlisted in the U.S. Naval Reserve and served as a communications officer on the escort carrier *Shipley Bay*. The ship was engaged in combat in May and June 1945, then served as a troop carrier after the Japanese surrender. While waiting out his term of duty, Millar completed his second novel, *Trouble Follows Me* (1946). He was discharged in March 1946 and, rather than returning to graduate school, settled with his family in Santa Barbara, California, the town that would become Santa Teresa in his Lew Archer novels. He quickly wrote two more books, *Blue City* (1947) and *The Three Roads* (1948), his first entries in the hard-boiled detective genre.

Although his first four novels received positive reviews, they were not commercial hits. Of the four, only *The Dark Tunnel* sold well enough to require a second printing; it was twenty years before one of his novels (*The Goodbye Look* in 1969) sold more than ten thousand hardback copies. Millar continued writing, however, and in 1949 reached the first turning point in his career with the publication of *The Moving Target*. The book introduced his series detective Lew Archer and was published under the pseudonym John Macdonald (Millar wished to reserve his own name for future nonmystery novels). The book sold only moderately, but it was selected for reprinting by the Mystery Guild and was his first novel to be published in paperback, the format that would earn much of his income in the 1950s and 1960s.

In the fall of 1948 Millar returned to the University of Michigan to complete his doctorate. He wrote his dissertation on Samuel Taylor Coleridge's psychological criticism and received his degree in February 1952, but he decided against a job in academia. Millar published eight novels during the 1950s, all but one—*Meet Me at the Morgue* (1953)—featuring Lew Archer as the detective. Because of potential confusion with fellow mystery writer John D. MacDonald, Millar changed his pseudonym first to John Ross Macdonald and finally to Ross Macdonald. He was still trying to find his own niche within the hard-boiled tradition and frequently struggled with editors at Knopf and Pocket Books, who expected him to write more in the mode of Dashiell Hammett and Raymond Chandler.

In February 1956 Millar's daughter, Linda, was involved in a vehicular homicide in Santa Barbara and, as a result, received eight years probation and was ordered to undergo psychiatric treatment. The crisis was a great blow to Millar and his family, and they moved for a

year to Menlo Park near San Francisco. There he began to confront for the first time the painful legacy of his Canadian childhood and underwent psychotherapy himself, which convinced him of the importance of Sigmund Freud's ideas. *The Doomsters* (1958) was written during this period and showed Millar's determination to break once and for all from the tradition of Raymond Chandler. The novel's sales were disappointing, and Millar—now saddled with substantial medical and legal bills—searched for new writing markets. He began writing verse again, tried to sell an idea for an atomic-era spy story to *The Saturday Evening Post*, and contributed more than forty book reviews to the *San Francisco Chronicle*. He also began working on a nondetective novel that drew heavily on his childhood experiences in Canada. After at least three false starts he abandoned the story. It was essential, though, for Millar to deal with this childhood material; Lew Archer and the detective form made such a treatment possible.

Although it received no special critical notice, *The Galton Case* (1959) was a breakthrough for Millar in terms of material and technique. Through the mediating character of Lew Archer, he could finally incorporate his most personal and distinctive themes: the inescapable past, the quest for identity, the corruption of money and power, the deadly influence of dreams. His technique steadily improved over the next decade as he formulated increasingly sophisticated plots and probed deeper into the social world of southern California.

Millar also began to experience critical and commercial success in the 1960s. In 1965 *The Far Side of the Dollar* received laudatory reviews from Anthony Boucher of the *New York Times Book Review* and Julian Symons of the *London Sunday Times*. The novel led to Millar's being awarded a Golden Dagger by the Crime Writers Association and his election to the honorary presidency of the Mystery Writers of America. The sale of film rights to *The Moving Target* (released as *Harper* in 1966) earned him enough money to purchase a home in the exclusive Hope Ranch section of Santa Barbara. The associated publicity stimulated interest in Millar's out-of-print novels, many of which were republished in paperback by Bantam.

During this period, Millar and his wife became increasingly active in environmental causes. In 1964 he was involved in the effort to preserve the nesting grounds of the California condor, and he wrote articles on the subject for *Sports Illustrated* and the *San Francisco Chronicle.* The same year, the Coyote Canyon fire nearly destroyed his house, and the blaze came to symbolize for him the intersection between moral and environmental concerns. In 1969 Millar helped lead protests following a massive oil spill off the coast of Santa Barbara and, subsequently, was a cofounder of the Santa Barbara Citizens for Environmental Defense. Environmental issues became an important part of his fiction, and he used the Coyote Canyon fire and the Santa Barbara oil spill as central events in *The Underground Man* (1971) and *Sleeping Beauty* (1973), respectively.

Although his 1960s novels were commercially successful, it was not until the publication of *The Goodbye Look* that Millar achieved his full popular and critical breakthrough. The novel was reviewed on the front page of the *New York Times Book Review* by William Goldman, who called the Archer stories, "the finest series of detective novels ever written by an American." *The Goodbye Look* was the first of Millar's novels to make the *New York Times* best-seller list, where it remained for fourteen weeks. His next book, *The Underground Man*, solidified this success. Eudora Welty praised the novel in a long front-page article in the *New York Times Book Review*; the book sold fifty-four thousand copies in the first six months and reached fourth on the *Times* best-seller list.

Millar had been writing at the top of his form since 1959, but it had taken over a decade for readers and critics to recognize him. Commercial success was important to him because he had long wanted to write "democratic" novels that would be read, enjoyed, and understood by a large audience. By 1971 he had achieved such an audience, with over five million of his books in print worldwide. Despite his new wealth, his and Margaret's life in Santa Barbara remained relatively unchanged. They lived frugally, eating plain food and wearing department-store clothes; when they dined out it was invariably at modest cafeterias such as the Copper Coffee Pot in downtown Santa Barbara. To a large degree, the poverty of Millar's childhood and the years it took for him to succeed as an author prevented his enjoying the money that came in at the end of his career. He distrusted wealth and believed it had a corrupting influence on those who possessed it. In a 1969 interview, Millar commented on purchasing his home at Hope Ranch, Santa Barbara: "I felt bad about it. I kept wondering what am I doing in a place like this and what will a place like this do to me?" (quoted in Leonard, p. 3).

After his breakthrough, Millar published two more novels, *Sleeping Beauty* and *The Blue Hammer* (1976), and several collections of his essays, reviews, and short stories. In 1974 his career was recognized with a Grand Master Award from the Mystery Writers of America. Not long after completing *The Blue Hammer*, Millar began experiencing memory lapses and temporary confusion; his condition was diagnosed as Alzheimer's disease in 1981. He died on 11 July 1983 at the age of sixty-seven.

The Early Novels (1944–1948)

Kenneth Millar's first four novels are competent but undistinguished thrillers. Traces of his mature themes and subject matter are evident, but Millar was still searching for his own form and technique. His first novel, *The Dark Tunnel*, draws heavily on his experiences at the University of Michigan and his travels in prewar Germany. The narrator/hero, Dr. Robert Branch, is a young English professor who stumbles upon a Nazi spy ring operating on his campus; the plot is complicated when he begins to suspect that a German girl he fell in love with years before is somehow involved in the conspiracy. The novel touches briefly on distinctive Millar themes: switched identities, the American need for happiness, and the distancing effect of money. Absent, however, is a sense of the complexity of evil and criminal motives. Peter Schneider, the primary villain, is depicted as a soulless killer. As in Millar's later novels, human sexuality lies behind the crimes, but in *The Dark Tunnel* it is portrayed as diseased and debased—particularly in Schneider's bisexuality, which reminds Branch "of the epicene white worms which change their sex and burrow in the bodies of dead men underground" and results in his feeling "sick with a moral sickness" (1972 ed., pp. 221, 86).

Millar's second novel, *Trouble Follows Me,* is also a wartime spy thriller, which draws on Millar's own navy experiences and involves an officer's cross-country pursuit of Japanese agents. He moved in a new direction with *Blue City,* entering the hard-boiled mystery genre—a form better suited for his thematic and psychological concerns. The novel, which shows a heavy indebtedness to Dashiell Hammett's *Red Harvest* (1929), details a discharged soldier's single-handed attempt to purge his hometown of crime and civic corruption. The plot allows Millar to introduce the themes of exile and return, class conflict, the corruption of wealth, and the dangers of dreamy idealism. The toughness of the story, however, is at odds with Millar's sensibility; both the narrator's improbable success at purging crime and his reformation of a hooker with a heart of gold strain the novel's credibility.

Millar's fourth novel, *The Three Roads,* has similar weaknesses. The plot is compelling: a soldier suffering from amnesia must solve the murder of his wife. But the structure involves awkward narrative shifts to explain the story's background, and the trick ending (which reveals that the narrator himself is the murderer) requires clumsy and unbelievable plot twists. The book nevertheless shows Mil-

lar exploring psychology and Freudian themes in depth for the first time. The narrator's quest to recover his memory and solve the murder highlights the inescapability of the past and its influence on the present. Millar had found his material, but he was still lacking the form and structure that would allow him to handle it successfully.

The Entrance of Lew Archer

Many of the weaknesses in Millar's first four books are the result of the narrative point of view. In each novel, the dominant consciousness is actively and personally involved in the events around him. This close relationship creates difficulties of development and explication: how to relate effectively the information that the narrator already knows (or should know). Millar wanted to push the boundaries of the hard-boiled novel and use it to comment on serious and personal issues, but doing so threatened to bog down the stories in excessive inner monologues and non-action sequences. Alfred A. Knopf, in fact, required Millar to cut some ten thousand words from *The Three Roads* in order to concentrate the action. Millar solved these difficulties in his fifth novel, *The Moving Target* (1949), which introduced Lew Archer as private investigator/narrator.

Archer became Millar's regular series detective, appearing in all but two of his next seventeen novels. In his foreword to the collection *Archer in Hollywood* (1967), Millar wrote that his creation occurred at a crucial time:

> I felt it was now my duty to write an autobiographical novel about my depressing childhood in Canada. I tried, and got badly bogged down in sloppy feelings and groping prose. . . . I was in trouble, and Lew Archer got me out of it. I resembled one of his clients in needing a character to front for me. Like many other writers . . . I couldn't work directly with my own experiences and feelings. A narrator had to be interposed, like protec-

tive lead, between me and the radioactive material. (p. vii)

It was ten years before Millar finally incorporated his childhood experiences into his fiction, but the introduction of Archer marked the first step toward Millar's maturation as a writer.

The novels provide few details of Archer's personal life, but they are enough to give a sense of the man. Archer is a native Californian who grew up in impoverished circumstances in Long Beach, the port city just south of Los Angeles. As a youth he—like Millar himself—was painfully aware of his low social status and the limitations it imposed. Archer was a troubled teenager, sharing "joyrides and brawls with the lost gangs in the endless stucco maze of Los Angeles" (*Find a Victim*, 1955 ed., p. 168). He was saved by an alcoholic cop who caught him stealing a car battery: "He stood me up against the wall and told me what it meant and where it led. He didn't turn me in" (p. 168). As an adult, Archer is always aware that he had been perilously close to becoming one of the criminal losers he encounters daily in his professional life. Instead, he joined the Long Beach police force in 1935. He spent five years as a cop but was forced out because he refused to participate in dirty political deals and would not accept payoffs from the local bosses.

At the opening of *The Moving Target*, Archer is thirty-five years old and has run a one-man private detective agency in Los Angeles for almost ten years, interrupted by army service during World War II, which involved him in the ground fighting on Okinawa. Since his discharge, his business has consisted primarily of "peeping on fleabag hotel rooms, untying marital knots, [and] blackmailing blackmailers out of business" (*The Drowning Pool*, 1970 ed., p. 11). It is not a lucrative line of work. Archer lives in a modest five-room bungalow on a middle-class residential street in Los Angeles, though he never goes home "till sleep is overdue." He is recently divorced from his wife, Sue, who left him because he devoted too much time to other people's problems. Although Archer—on rare occasions—does become romantically involved with women he meets during investigations, his life is essentially a lonely one, with few interests outside his detective work.

The details of Archer's life are less important than the role they allow him to play as the novels' narrator and mediating consciousness. With *The Moving Target*, Millar drew on the model of Raymond Chandler for an effective narrative technique. "Chandler," he wrote in his foreword to the *Archer in Hollywood* collection,

> had recently shown, in a brilliant series of novels, how a private detective could be used to block off over-personal excitements while getting on with the story. Archer in his early days, though he was named for Sam Spade's partner, was patterned on Chandler's Marlowe. Chandler's Anglo-American background and my Canadian-American one gave our detectives a common quality: the fresh suspicious eye of a semi-outsider who is fascinated but not completely taken in by the customs of the natives. (pp. vii–viii)

This semi-outsider status allows Archer to move through all strata of California society, from the homes of the wealthy families who often employ him to the poor neighborhoods where much of the stories' violence occurs. His isolated, lonely life lets him devote all his energies to the investigation without his being restricted by personal loyalties and responsibilities. Although Archer is the narrator of the novels, he is not the hero. His behavior is important for advancing the plot, but he functions more as a catalyst for the actions of the other characters. Above all, Archer is not a policeman interested in solving crimes and bringing the guilty to justice; he is, instead, a searcher who probes the complex relationships among people and attempts to discover the truth of what has happened and, more important, why it has happened.

Archer's narrative role allowed Millar to extend his technique and to begin developing his own themes and motifs. The advance is apparent in the opening pages of *The Moving Target*, in which Millar sets up a sharp contrast between wealth and poverty. Archer is hired by Mrs. Ralph Sampson to find her husband, a wealthy oilman who has been kidnapped. Archer describes Cabrillo Canyon, where the Sampsons live, by noting, "The light-blue haze in the lower canyon was like a thin smoke from slowly burning money. Even the sea looked precious through it, a solid wedge held in the canyon's mouth, bright blue and polished like a stone. Private property: color guaranteed fast; will not shrink egos" (1970 ed., p. 1). The contrast with the nearby town of Santa Teresa is stark: "We drove through a mile of slums; collapsing shacks and storefront tabernacles, dirt paths where sidewalks should have been, black and brown children playing in the dust. . . . After Cabrillo Canyon I felt like a man from another planet" (p. 12). In the Lew Archer novels, money causes its possessors to wall themselves off from the surrounding world, and the sheltered life is neither happy nor fulfilling. Ralph Sampson is so spiritually starved that he must search for excitement in extramarital affairs and astrological cults—involvements that apparently lead to his abduction.

The American dream of social mobility and self-improvement, embodied in the character of Albert Graves, is also an essential element of the novel. Graves, the Sampson family's lawyer, has worked his way up from an impoverished childhood and become a moderately successful attorney with ambitions to rise even higher. He has fallen in love with Ralph Sampson's daughter Miranda, who "was everything he'd dreamed about—money, youth, bud-sharp breasts, beauty on the way. He'd set his mind on her and had to have her" (p. 17). Graves's ambition causes him to kill his rival Alan Taggert so that he can marry Miranda, then, after the marriage, to murder Ralph Sampson so that he can inherit the Sampson wealth. Sex, money, ambition, and crime are intimately linked in *The Moving Target*, and this relationship of forces is the essential material of Millar's fiction.

Between 1950 and 1958 Millar published seven more novels, six of which feature Lew Archer, and he continued to introduce new elements to his fiction. In *The Drowning Pool*, the character of Cathy Slocum shows Millar's first treatment of concealed parentage and troubled teenagers trapped in an unstable family life. *The Way Some People Die* (1951), which is set largely in Long Beach and fictional Pacific Point, extends Archer's exploration of the world of poverty and the underclass. The plot begins with a missing person case but soon leads Archer into a series of murders involving drug peddlers, pinball racketeers, crooked wrestling promoters, and young amoral hustlers trapped by their surroundings. As early as *The Moving Target*, Millar had rejected the notion of black-and-white morality and inherent evil; in *The Way Some People Die*, he underscores the point. Archer's description of a professional wrestling match mocks the simplistic morality play that so easily hoodwinks the spectators. His conviction that evil is the product of circumstances is made clear when he says of a judgmental mother, "She lived in a world where people did this or that because they were good or evil. In my world people acted because they had to " (repr. in *Archer in Hollywood*, p. 227). The novel also marks the first appearance of a female murderer in Millar's fiction but, unlike the femmes fatales of Raymond Chandler and Mickey Spillane, Galley Lawrence is not a man-controlling sexpot. She is a woman who has been mistreated and victimized by men and lashes out in an almost instinctive defense. By the mid-1950s Millar had learned from and adopted many of the conventions of hard-boiled writers such as Hammett and Chandler, but he was beginning to move away from them in his own distinctive direction.

The Break from Chandler

Although profoundly important in shaping his fiction, the influence of Raymond Chandler had become a liability to Millar by the mid 1950s. Chandler had by then published five novels and was recognized as the leading practitioner of the American hard-boiled novel. The shift in Millar's technique and style since *The Moving Target* had received a lukewarm reception from his hardback publisher, Alfred A. Knopf, and the situation was compounded by the fact that the 1950s mystery market was heavily dependent on paperback sales. Before accepting Millar's ninth novel, *Meet Me at the Morgue,* Knopf submitted the story to Pocket Books for approval. Pocket's editor responded that the story lacked the normal punch of the hard-boiled genre and that "the sharp contrast between good and evil, so noticeable in Chandler's books and so important to this kind of story, is simply missing" (quoted in Bruccoli, 1984, pp. 47–48). Millar responded with a five-page letter to Knopf detailing his objections to Chandler and discussing the new direction in which he was trying to take his own fiction:

> Chandler's subject is the evilness of evil, and his highest achievement, the vivid scene of conflict between (conventional) evil and (what he takes to be) good. . . . I can't accept Chandler's vision of good and evil. It seems to me that it is conventional to the point of sadism. . . . My subject is human error. My interest is the exploration of lives. As Pocket Books points out, my stories lack a powerful contrast between good and evil, because I don't see things that way. (quoted in Sipper, pp. 37–38)

Chandler, who was a generation older than Millar, wrote stories about a fallen, corrupt world that had lost the values and gentlemanly code of his youth. Rather than seeking the cause of this assumed degeneration, Chandler focused on his detective Philip Marlowe's search for a personal code of conduct, a way to guide his own behavior within a corrupt society. Lew Archer is on a different quest, concentrating not on his own behavior but on that of the people around him, continually seeking to understand why they do what they do.

Although his written protest was aimed primarily at Chandler, Millar was also reacting strongly against the writing of Mickey Spillane. Spillane's *I, The Jury* (1947) and successive novels had achieved phenomenal sales by taking the most lurid features of Chandler—brutality, raw sexuality, and macho bravado—and magnifying them into sensational melodrama. "The old-line hardboiled mystery," Millar claimed in his letter to Knopf, "has been ruined by its own practitioners, including Chandler. Spillane pulled the plug. I refuse to follow it down the drain, because I'm thoroughly convinced that I'm writing something better" (quoted in Sipper, p. 39). Millar, ultimately, won his battle with Knopf and Pocket Books.

Millar's move away from Chandler involved more than his treatment of good and evil. As he matured as a writer, Millar became increasingly aware of plot and structure and how they could contribute to the novel as a whole. In his 1965 essay "The Writer as Detective Hero," collected in *On Crime Writing* (1973), Millar commented, "Chandler described a good plot as one that made for good scenes, as if the parts were greater than the whole. I see plot as a vehicle of meaning. It should be as complex as contemporary life, but balanced enough to say true things about it" (p. 303). After *The Moving Target*, Millar's novels become more carefully planned and more complex in structure. His technique involves multiple plotlines that ultimately converge, parallel characters and events, and surprising reversals at the conclusion of the stories. The reversal—generally, when one suspect is cleared and an unexpected character is identified as the murderer—is a standard device in the mystery genre, but Millar employed it for a more important purpose than merely catching the reader off guard. "The surprise with which a detective novel concludes," he argued, "should set up tragic vibrations which run backward through the entire structure" ("The Writer as Detective Hero," p. 303).

This effect can be seen clearly in the denouement of *The Barbarous Coast* (1956). Archer's investigation into a series of murders at a California beach club seem to point to Isobel Graff, the schizophrenic wife of a Hollywood studio mogul. Mrs. Graff, who has been in and out of a private sanitarium, apparently became a murderess out of jealousy over her husband's extramarital affairs—a rather standard detective story conclusion. In the last scene, however, Archer exposes the real murderer: Clarence Bassett, the mild-mannered manager of the beach club. Bassett, who has been having a long affair with Mrs. Graff, manipulated her into trying to kill her husband and, after that went awry, committed the other murders to keep the truth from coming out. Bassett was born into a wealthy, prominent family but was ruined by the stock market crash of 1929. Not long after, he fell in love with Isobel but, because of his impoverished state, lost her to Simon Graff, a low-born man newly rich from his rising career as a Hollywood producer. The revelation of Bassett's guilt challenges traditional assumptions about good and evil and reinforces Millar's belief in the power and destructiveness of sex, class, and money. Archer describes Bassett's face by saying, "It wasn't an unusual face. It was quite ordinary, homely and aging, given a touch of caricature by the long teeth and bulging eyes. Not the kind of face that people think of as evil. Yet it was the face of evil, drawn by a vague and passionate yearning toward the deed of darkness it abhorred" (repr. in *Archer in Hollywood*, p. 526). This type of reversal, which sheds tragic light not only on the plot of the story but also on Millar's view of human motivations, is a distinctive feature of the best Lew Archer novels.

During the 1950s Millar also shifted away from Chandler in his creation of character types. *The Moving Target* opens with a scene very similar to the beginning of *The Big Sleep:* the detective's interview with a wealthy client who has been paralyzed in a fall from a horse. The novel's characters—Claude the mystic cult leader, Puddler the thug, Miranda the young temptress—have much in common with Chandler's vivid, highly stylized creations. Over the next decade, however, Millar toned down his characterization. As he

explained in his letter to Knopf, "The characters are less remarkable but more lifelike. . . . none of my characters are familiar; they are freshly conceived from a point of view that rejects black and white classification. There is none, or a good deal less, of the Chandler phoniness" (quoted in Sipper, p. 40). Millar was consciously shifting mystery conventions away from a romantically charged underworld and toward the mundane, suburban world of middle-class America.

Related to Millar's use of character is his development of a distinct style, particularly in his dialogue and the voice of his narrative. Again, he was consciously moving away from Raymond Chandler, who deliberately incorporated into his novels as much "tough talk" and street slang as he could. Chandler's dialogue is sharp and rich, but highly stylized and artificially constructed. Millar tried to maintain the richness of vernacular language while avoiding the tough talk that had, particularly with Spillane and his imitators, become clichéd. "I've slightly purified the style," he claimed. "It's the vernacular, yes, but it's a purified vernacular. I don't think it's going to decay, as most vernacular stories do, for that reason. It's written with one ear to what people say and the other ear to the *Oxford English Dictionary* and the old English classics and American classics" (quoted in Tutunjian, p. 81). Millar's intention for his fiction can be seen in this statement about Chandler: "He wrote like a slumming angel, and invested the sun-blinded streets of Los Angeles with a romantic presence. While trying to preserve the fantastic lights and shadows of the actual Los Angeles, I gradually siphoned off the aura of romance and made room for a more complete social realism" (quoted in Bruccoli, 1971, p. xvi).

Turning Point: The Galton Case

When he completed *The Doomsters,* Millar presented it to his publisher as "the culminating book (though not the last) in the

Archer series. . . . My book is intended to close off an era—rather a big word, but I'm feeling my oats a little—in the 'hardboiled' field, and probably will. My longtime and ultimate project is to find a place to stand from which I can fling some tenderizing salt on the tail of, conceivably, a small new Canadian or North American Karamazov or Quixote" (quoted in Bruccoli, 1984, p. 55). Millar once again attempted to write a nonmystery novel drawing upon his Canadian youth, but after three abortive drafts he abandoned the story. Lew Archer, acting as a welder's mask or distancing device, allowed Millar to incorporate his autobiography into a detective story. The result was *The Galton Case,* the first of Millar's mature novels.

The novel begins when Lew Archer is hired to find Anthony Galton, the son of a wealthy Santa Teresa widow and heir to the family fortune. Galton had disappeared twenty-three years before (during the Depression), idealistically changing his name and leaving privileged life in order to live with "the common people." Archer soon discovers that Anthony Galton has been dead for two decades, the victim of a brutal murder. At the same time, a young man named John Brown, Jr., appears on the scene and claims to be Galton's son and heir. Archer exposes Brown as Theodore Fredericks, who spent a childhood of extreme poverty and physical abuse in Canada. Fredericks has been enlisted by the Galton family lawyer and a tough ex-con in a scheme to defraud Mrs. Galton of her estate.

Despite its bleakness, the novel has a fairytale ending. In a gimmicky reversal, John Brown, Jr., turns out to be the real son of Anthony Galton. When Nelson Fredericks—Theodore's putative father—killed Anthony Galton over twenty years before, Galton's wife went to Canada with Fredericks, who threatened to kill her baby, and "Theodore" was raised to believe he was Fredericks' son. The story of John Brown, Jr., has many parallels to Millar's own childhood, but it is not exact autobiography. "Fiction," Millar explained in his foreword to the *Archer at Large* (1970) collection,

when it is working well, lifts out of the writer's life patterns which tend toward the legendary. But the patterns are disrupted and authenticated by bits and pieces of the original life-stuff—names and places, scraps of conversation, old feelings and forces like spawning salmon working their way back up the stream of time. (p. ix)

Writing *The Galton Case* served as therapy for Millar, allowing him to confront and make sense of his painful childhood experiences. He credited the psychiatric treatment he underwent in 1956 and 1957 with making the novel possible and marking "the difference between my early and later books. There's no question that my work has deepened since then. Freud was one of the two or three greatest influences on me" (quoted in Solokov, p. 108). Millar's critics have made much of this admitted Freudian influence, but his novels cannot accurately be termed psychological. Apart from occasional, brief observations by Archer, Millar neither psychoanalyzes his characters nor details their mental processes. Rather, the characters define themselves through their behavior and speech. The Freudian influence lies behind the events of the stories; his theories of human behavior are reflected in the characters' deeds. Freud, Millar explained, "made myth into psychiatry, and I've been trying to turn it back into myth again in my own small way" (p. 108). The myth of Oedipus—both as told by Sophocles and as adapted by Freud—is particularly visible in Millar's fiction, though he is in no sense retelling or reworking the oedipal story. Instead, Millar takes many of the patterns present in the myth—exile and return, the question of identity, the search for parentage, the inescapability of fate and the past—and incorporates them into his hard-boiled novels.

Although it was greeted with little fanfare by reviewers, *The Galton Case* marked Millar's artistic maturation. Over the next sixteen years he wrote eleven more novels and with them established himself as the most respected and influential detective writer of his generation. The basic themes and patterns for his fiction were set; for the rest of his career he would continue to expand upon them, pushing his exploration of contemporary American life and his own past and present. Critics have debated which book is the best, but all eleven are superior examples of the hard-boiled form.

Themes and Patterns of the Mature Novels

The idea of time and the past lies at the heart of Millar's fiction. In the world of the novels, no understanding of present actions and situations is possible without taking into account what has happened in the past. Lew Archer understands this tenet, but other characters in the novels repeatedly try to cover up and forget what has happened years and even decades before. For Millar's murderers (such as Taps Tappinger in *Black Money* [1966] and Mrs. Bradshaw in *The Chill* [1964]) this desire to hide previous deeds is understandable: they must do so to avoid prosecution. Throughout Archer's investigations, however, he finds himself involved with characters who want to obscure or deny the past for less critical reasons: to protect a loved one, to forget painful experiences, to protect their reputations and social status, or merely to avoid unpleasant conversations. These characters usually include Archer's clients, who hire him to resolve a problem in the present but refuse to discuss their families' past with him. The problem inevitably leads Archer years backward in time, uncovering an elaborate web of cause and effect. As he puts it in *The Chill*, the cases open up "gradually like fissures in the firm ground of the present, cleaving far down through the strata of the past" (1965 ed., pp. 72–73).

In each of Millar's novels after *The Galton Case*, the crimes that Archer begins investigating in the present have been engendered by crimes committed as far back as two generations. Although the motives vary, the initial crimes always turn murderous and are fueled by improper sexuality (generally, adultery). Twenty or more years later, the hidden sins erupt from below the surface of the past and destroy the lives of the sons and daughters (and grandsons and granddaughters) of the initial sinners. In *The Ferguson Affair* (1960), this lesson is learned the hard way by Colonel Ian Ferguson, who fathered and abandoned an illegitimate daughter while in school at Harvard, and by his new wife Holly, who has tried to forget her impoverished upbringing and become a movie star. "I thought I could start a brand new life," Ferguson tells his lawyer Bill Gunnarson, "as if I hadn't already had a life. Holly was doing the same thing in her way. She tried to turn her back on everything, her family, the whole past. But the past has its revenges" (1963 ed., p. 213). The plots of Kenneth Millar's novels detail the revenges of the past on those who do not recognize its inescapable power.

Time and the past are not the only inescapable forces acting on Millar's characters. Equally important are the possession and influence of wealth. Poverty has a destructive effect on the novels' lower-class characters, instilling in them anger and despair and tempting them into criminal acts to escape their deprivations. Obtaining and possessing wealth, however, is no solution. Millar's novels portray money not as liberating or offering possibilities but rather as stultifying and corrupting. His descriptions of the expensive homes, clubs, and neighborhoods show money separating its possessors from reality and cutting them off from the life around them. When Lew Archer visits his client's home in *The Galton Case* he comments, "I got some sense of the guarded peace that walled estates like this had once provided. In the modern world the walls were more like prison walls, or the wire fence around a nursing-home garden" (1970 ed., p. 140). The characters in Millar's novels put great stock in money and its ability to buy them a vibrant, painless life. In the end, they find themselves in the position of Colonel Ferguson, who realizes, "I condemned myself. Condemned myself to the hell of money" (p. 139).

Millar's characters again and again fail to understand that money is more than a tool or a possession. Money causes its possessors to turn inward, to guard continually against losing their wealth; this defensiveness skews the way they view and treat other people. This effect is obvious in those who were raised in a privileged atmosphere, such as Peter Jamieson of *Black Money*, who is "in the habit of buying things and people" (1967 ed., p. 3). The corruption, however, is not restricted to those born into money. In *The Galton Case*, the values of John Brown, Jr., begin deteriorating within days of his claiming his inheritance. Brown sends Archer a note thanking him for his efforts. He adds at the end, "For what it's worth, I did persuade Grandmother to send you an additional check in token of appreciation." Archer observes, "It seemed to be pure gratitude undiluted by commercialism until I reflected that he was taking credit for the check [the Galton's lawyer Gordon] Sable had sent me" (p. 121). John Brown, Jr., a wealthy man for only a few days, is already adopting his grandmother's attitude that Archer is a mere "laborer" and should be rewarded when "worthy of his hire" (p. 141).

The effect is more extreme in *Black Money*. Pedro Domingo/Francis Martel, after finally achieving his lifelong dream of wealth and importance, immediately erects a veil of secrecy and seclusion. When Harry Hendricks, a bumbling operator investigating Martel's background, takes a snapshot of him, Martel's first response is to try to buy the camera and film. When this fails, he snatches the camera and crushes it beneath his heel. This cruelty is magnified when he catches Hendricks spying again and beats him to death. Domingo/Martel's brief exposure to wealth hardens him and instills in him the same corruption that is associated with the possessors of old money. Not even Lew Archer is immune. In *The Instant Enemy* (1968), Archer rescues oil heir and businessman Stephen Hackett from a kidnapper and is rewarded with a check for $100,000 from Hackett's mother. The money, far more than Archer has ever imagined possessing, immediately raises a red flag: "It excited me in a way I didn't quite like. Underlying the excitement was a vague depression, as if I belonged to the check in a way, instead of having it belong to me" (1991 ed., p. 138). At the end of the novel Archer saves himself by tearing the check into small pieces of confetti.

Money is a powerful force in the lives of Millar's characters, but it is connected to an even more dangerous influence: dreams and fantastic ambition. A recurring motif in the Archer novels is the pursuit of the American dream—discarding the past, remaking oneself, and achieving wealth and respectability. Millar was heavily influenced by the work of F. Scott Fitzgerald, whom he called "my dream writer" (Tutunjian, p. 76) and he reread *The Great Gatsby* once a year. The *Gatsby* version of the American dream is reflected in many of Millar's characters: John Brown, Jr., in *The Galton Case*, Larry Gaines and Holly May in *The Ferguson Affair*, Catherine Wycherly in *The Wycherly Woman* (1961), Carol Harley in *The Far Side of the Dollar*. The strongest adaptation of the myth is in *Black Money*, which is essentially a reworking of Fitzgerald's story with a Latin American dreamer in the role of Gatsby. Pedro Domingo was born the son of a Panamanian prostitute but has ambitions of greatness. He comes to the United States, gets a job as a pool boy at a tennis club, and falls in love with Ginny Fablon, the daughter of a wealthy club member. She becomes Domingo's Daisy, and he vows to return to Montevista a wealthy man and marry her. When Domingo sees the opportunity to get Leo Spillman, a Las Vegas gangster, out of a jam, he seizes the chance. Spillman takes Domingo under his wing and sends him to school in Europe. Now rich and calling himself Francis Martel, Domingo returns to Montevista and marries Ginny Fablon.

Like Gatsby, Domingo and his dream die violently at the hands of a murderer. There is, however, a crucial difference between Fitzgerald's and Millar's version of the American dream myth. Jay Gatsby's ambition and dreaming—his "heightened sensitivity to the promises of life"—is what redeems and humanizes him in Fitzgerald's eyes. For Millar, dreams and ambitions are destructive and deluding. As Archer notes, "Martel was one of those dangerous dreamers who acted out his dreams, a liar who forced his lies to become true" (p. 119). His dreams are ended by Professor "Taps" Tappinger, whose vision of "the luminous city of the mind" leads him to seduce two of his students—including Ginny Fablon—and to murder both Ginny's parents and Pedro Domingo when they get in the way of his romantic delusions. In Millar's fictional worlds, dreams—like money—pull people away from reality and lead not to greatness but to destruction.

The society depicted in Kenneth Millar's novels has denied the past, enthralled itself to wealth, and become deluded by fantasy. The victims of this delusion, ultimately, are the adolescents and young adults. All of Millar's mature novels begin with young people in trouble; often, he is hired to find a "normal" teen who has disappeared. The young people he encounters are "boys in adolescent storm" and girls experiencing "the growing pains of womanhood." Their parents' refusal to accept reality only heightens the normal pain and confusion of adolescence. In *The Far Side of the Dollar*, for instance, Ralph and Elaine Hillman have raised their son Tom as if he were their natural child; then, as he approaches maturity, they tell him that he was actually adopted. In reality, Tom is the illegitimate son of Ralph Hillman and a woman named Carol Harley. The Hillmans have lied because they wanted to protect Tom, but he disappears and, searching for the truth about his parentage, becomes entangled in a world of violence and murder. "Tom had felt betrayed by one world," Archer observes, "the plush deceptive world of Ralph Hillman . . . He had plunged blindly into another" (p. 207). Hidden parentage plays a similarly catalytic role in *The Wycherly Woman*, *The Zebra-Striped Hearse* (1962), *The Instant Enemy*, *The Goodbye Look*, and *The Underground Man*.

Kenneth Millar was writing in a genre that tended toward romanticism and melodrama, but he adapted the conventions of the detective form to create social realism. The Lew Archer novels are all set in southern California, and the region provides both a physical and a symbolic backdrop to the action. Millar's work is highly descriptive, capturing how it looked and felt to drive down the main streets of the bedroom towns scattered around Los Angeles, to enter the homes and beach clubs of the wealthy, to walk through the dirty alleys of slum neighborhoods. He was particularly sensitive to the changes taking place in southern California, and his novels capture a society out of touch with nature and reeling from unprecedented growth. In *The Wycherly Woman*, for example, Archer describes Boulder Beach College as

> one of those sudden institutions of learning that had been springing up all over California to handle the products of the wartime population explosion. Its buildings were stone and glass, so geometric and so spanking new that they hadn't begun to merge with the landscape. . . . Even the young people sitting around on the grass or sauntering with their books from building to building, didn't look indigenous to me. They looked like extras assembled on a set for a college musical with a peasant subplot. (1963 ed., p. 13)

Millar's fictional portrayal of Los Angeles depends heavily on the newness of the society. "Southern California," he said in a 1972 interview,

> is a recently-born world center . . . just in the last twenty-five years, since the war, on the basis of a new technology. It's become the center of an originative style. It differs from the other centers in that the others have been there for a long time and have more or less established a life-style and a civility which keep things pretty much under control. And they have established a relationship with the natural world, centuries old, which hasn't changed much. Here in California, what you've got is an instant megalopolis superimposed on a background which could be described as raw nature. What we've got is the

twentieth century right up against the primitive. (Carroll, p. 149)

This thin line between the modern and the primitive provides an ideal setting for Millar's stories of crime: even in the wealthy suburban neighborhoods, the impulse to murder is only barely hidden by a veneer of sophistication and respectability.

Since early in the twentieth century, southern California—with its mild climate, fertile land, miles of beaches, nearby mountains— had been promoted and mythologized as a land of dreams. The oil boom in the 1920s and the explosion of heavy industry (particularly aircraft manufacture) after World War II made many Californians rich and convinced millions of Americans that the West Coast offered unlimited opportunities for prosperity. The presence of Hollywood, with its glamour and glitz and tales of instant celebrities, only heightened the myth. From his semi-outsider position as a dual Canadian/Californian citizen, Kenneth Millar recognized the appeal but also saw through the illusion of the region. "If California is a state of mind," he wrote, "Hollywood is where you take its temperature. There is a peculiar sense in which this city existing mainly on film and tape is our national capital, alas, and not just the capital of California. It's the place where our children learn how and what to dream and where everything happens just before, or just after, it happens to us" (*Archer in Hollywood*, p. viii). California functions, in short, as a microcosm of the American dream.

Dreams, of course, are not reality. Millar's fiction repeatedly captures the failure of California as the land of opportunity. The opening of *The Wycherly Woman* makes the point explicitly:

Coming over the pass you can see the whole valley spread out below. On a clear morning, when it lies broad and colored under a white sky, with the mountains standing far back on either side, you can imagine it's the promised land.

Maybe it is for a few. But for every air-conditioned ranchhouse with its swimming pool and private landing strip, there are dozens of tin-sided shacks and broken down trailers where the lost tribes of the migrant workers live.

The Lew Archer novels are filled with characters who come to California with ambitions and high hopes and end up joining the ranks of the "lost tribes." Taken individually, they are merely hard-luck cases. Together, they add up to something more disturbing. Beneath Millar's novels—particularly the later ones— runs a powerful current of doom. Sometimes the sense comes across in wisecracks, such as Archer's comment, "The jukebox was playing rock—music for civilizations to decline by, man" (*The Ferguson Affair*, p. 150). More often, though, it is expressed in earnest. "You know, Archer," a police officer says in *The Wycherly Woman*, "whole strata of society seem to be breaking loose and running wild in this civilization—if civilization is the right word" (p. 120). This apocalyptic feeling is underscored by the natural disasters that frame the action of *The Underground Man* (a wildfire) and *Sleeping Beauty* (an oil spill). The California of Kenneth Millar's fiction is nothing less than a civilization on the edge of collapse.

Despite his vivid descriptions of the region's topography and his commentary on the problems of California society, Millar has drawn fire from critics who have accused him of not being in touch with contemporary life in the 1960s and early 1970s. Millar's mature novels were written during the height of the Cold War and the space race, the civil rights movement and the Watts riots, Vietnam and the antiwar protests. These momentous events surface in Millar's fiction only rarely and only in brief, offhand comments: Nick Chalmers in *The Goodbye Look* is "very critical of the war" and his father "considers that unpatriotic" (p. 16); five-year-old Ronny Broadhurst in *The Underground Man* picks up a toy telephone and says into it, "Calling Space Control. Calling Space Control" (p. 228); at the end of *The Instant Enemy*,

Archer tears up a check and watches it drift "down on the short hairs and the long hairs, the potheads and the acid heads, draft dodgers and dollar chasers, swingers and walking wounded, idiot saints, hard cases, foolish virgins" (p. 212). Apart from these glimpses, the Lew Archer novels indeed seem greatly distanced from the events of the 1960s.

Millar's fiction, however, is not really about the decade of hippies, soldiers, and civil rights marchers. His concern is elsewhere, with his own generation and their actions in the decades just before and after World War II. The troubled teenagers in the novels belong "to a generation whose elders had been poisoned, like the pelicans, with a kind of moral DDT that damaged the lives of their young" (*The Underground Man*, p. 226). Archer, though he tries to help the youths in his cases, is less concerned with analyzing their troubled lives than he is with coming to understand the poisoned generation that preceded them. And, though he strongly denounces black-and-white morality and simplistic views of good and evil, there is a strong moral element in Millar's work. The crimes in his novels are fueled by money, sex, and ambition, but these are not ultimately to blame for the social malaise. They are, rather, basic forces that—in absence of the corrective force of moral values—shape and distort human behavior. Millar articulated this idea as early as *The Moving Target*. Miranda Sampson, after learning about the crimes committed by Albert Graves in his quest to marry her, tells Archer, "I wish I had no money and no sex. They're both more trouble than they're worth to me." Archer replies, "You can't blame money for what it does to people. The evil is in people, and money is the peg they hang it on. They go wild for money when they've lost their other values" (p. 182). This emphasis on values forms the basis of his critique of American society after World War II—the event he repeatedly singles out as shaking loose the moral fabric of the country.

Millar was intensely concerned with human motivation and the influence of environment and psychological forces on individuals.

But, "the essential problem," he said in 1972, "is how you are going to maintain values, and express values in your actions, when the values aren't there in the society around you, as they are in traditional societies. In a sense, you have to make yourself up as you go along" (quoted in Carroll, p. 149). As the Canadian charity boy nurtured on the dream of returning to California and reclaiming his rightful inheritance, Millar very much believed in the importance of ambition, social mobility, and material achievement. As a sensitive observer of Californian life, however, he doubted the viability of the American formula of success because it lacked the necessary structure of values to control the evil impulses that all individuals share.

Because they lack a traditional moral compass, the characters in Millar's fiction fail to recognize that their actions have inescapable consequences. The complex web of crime in *The Wycherly Woman* is rooted in Carl Trevor's adultery two decades before, but he is blind to his own culpability, blaming the events instead on a malign fate. "You don't understand how a man's life can go sour," he tells Archer. "You start out with an innocent roll in the hay, and you end up having to kill people" (p. 274). Archer, of course, understands precisely what Trevor does not: that a roll in the hay is never innocent, that it creates ramifications and responsibilities that cannot be swept under the rug. This type of moral denial can also be seen in Frederick Kincaid of *The Chill*, a "frightened man who valued his status the way some previous generations valued their souls" (p. 92). When his son's new wife is charged with murder, Kincaid's response is to deny all involvement and attempt to have the marriage annulled. Archer tries, ineffectually, to set him straight:

> Somebody has to assume responsibility. There's a lot of it floating around loose at the moment. You can't avoid it by crawling into a hole and pulling the hole in around you. The girl's in trouble, and whether you like it or not she's a member of your family. (p. 91)

For the adults of Archer's generation, the denial of culpability is almost a mantra or refrain: "It's not my fault. I'm not responsible."

If there is a lesson offered by the Lew Archer stories it is that a society cannot function and thrive unless its members remove the ethical blinders of idealism, status, and simplistic morality and begin to accept personal responsibility for the things they do. Some of Millar's characters do come to this realization. Colonel Ferguson of *The Ferguson Affair* admits his culpability in having a child out of wedlock as a young man, goes to visit the mother of that child, and vows to stick with his new family no matter what happens in the future. For most of the guilty parties, however, it is too late for redemption. In *The Chill* and *The Underground Man*, the murderers are arrested and taken to jail, still denying their responsibility for the crimes. When there is self-realization, it is usually too late to make amends. In *The Wycherly Woman*, *The Far Side of the Dollar*, *Black Money*, *The Goodbye Look*, and *Sleeping Beauty*, the accused killers all commit suicide.

Despite their bleakness, Millar's books do hold out some hope for the future. The younger generation, though their lives are damaged by the "moral DDT" that poisoned their parents, are not irredeemably ruined. Near the end of *The Wycherly Woman*, Bobby Doncaster admits that he has made some terrible mistakes. "Twenty-one is a good age to make them," Archer tells him. "You don't have to go on compounding them" (p. 233). The young, unlike their elders, are growing impatient with pat answers and false appearances. "No phoniness," Archer observes in *The Far Side of the Dollar*, "was the code of the new generation, at least the ones who were worth anything" (p. 214). Davy Spanner in *The Instant Enemy* is "a serious boy" who "wants to grow up and be a real man and do something useful" (p. 24). Redemption will not be easy. No phoniness, Archer realizes, "was a fairly decent ideal, but it sometimes worked out cruelly in practice" (*The Far Side of the Dollar*, p. 214). Some, such as Davy Spanner, have inherited too much trouble and are destroyed by it. The strength and honesty Archer sees in the teenagers he encounters, nevertheless, leaves him with some encouragement—enough, at least, for him to say at the end of *The Underground Man*, "I hoped that Ronny's life wouldn't turn back toward his father's death as his father's life had turned, in a narrowing circle. I wished the boy a benign failure of memory" (p. 273).

Legacy

With his eighteen Lew Archer novels, Kenneth Millar successfully took the conventions of the hard-boiled detective novel and used them to create a literature that was complex, compelling, and deeply personal. In the process, he helped shape the future of the American detective story. Dashiell Hammett, to paraphrase Raymond Chandler's famous statement, took murder out of the drawing rooms and country manors of the English deductive mystery and dropped it in the mean streets of urban America, where criminals speak a genuine vernacular and commit murder for a reason. Chandler took up where Hammett left off, adding a vibrant style, sharp wit, and a rigid demand for values and codes of conduct. Writing as Ross Macdonald, Kenneth Millar took the form one step further.

Dennis Lynds, who writes crime novels under the name Michael Collins, has summed up Millar's legacy to the writers who followed him:

> Ross Macdonald brought the detective novel out of the mean streets and into our streets, or he showed us where our daily world and the mean street touched. He brought Lew Archer into the world of the reader. He gave the detective novel personal and psychological validity in a world the reader had to recognize as part and parcel of his own . . . What Ross Macdonald did was take murder and crime and put them back in the living room Hammett had taken them out of—but now it is a real living room, now the forces of vio-

lence inside the people are real forces that come from real causes in a real world the reader can, and must, understand. (Collins, p. 123)

In doing this, Kenneth Millar ensured his place alongside Chandler and Hammett as an American hard-boiled master.

Selected Bibliography

WORKS OF ROSS MACDONALD

NOVELS

Note: The first four novels were published under the author's given name, Kenneth Millar. *The Barbarous Coast* and subsequent novels were published under the pseudonym Ross Macdonald.

The Dark Tunnel. New York: Dodd, Mead, 1944; Bantam, 1972.
Trouble Follows Me. New York: Dodd, Mead, 1946.
Blue City. New York: Knopf, 1947.
The Three Roads. New York: Knopf, 1948.
The Moving Target. By "John Macdonald." New York: Knopf, 1949; Bantam, 1970.
The Drowning Pool. By "John Ross Macdonald." New York: Knopf, 1950; Bantam, 1970.
The Way Some People Die. By "John Ross Macdonald." New York: Knopf, 1951. Repr. in *Archer in Hollywood.* New York: Knopf, 1967.
The Ivory Grin. By "John Ross Macdonald." New York: Knopf, 1952.
Meet Me at the Morgue. By "John Ross Macdonald." New York: Knopf, 1953.
Find a Victim. By "John Ross Macdonald." New York: Knopf, 1954; Bantam, 1955.
The Barbarous Coast. New York: Knopf, 1956. Repr. in *Archer in Hollywood.* New York: Knopf, 1967.
The Doomsters. New York: Knopf, 1958.
The Galton Case. New York: Knopf, 1959. Repr. in *Archer at Large.* New York: Knopf, 1970.
The Ferguson Affair. New York: Knopf, 1960; Bantam, 1963.
The Wycherly Woman. New York: Knopf, 1961; Bantam, 1963.
The Zebra-Striped Hearse. New York: Knopf, 1962.
The Chill. New York: Knopf, 1964; Bantam, 1965.
The Far Side of the Dollar. New York: Knopf, 1965.
Black Money. New York: Knopf, 1966; Bantam, 1967.
The Instant Enemy. New York: Knopf, 1968; Warner Books, 1991.
The Goodbye Look. New York: Knopf, 1969.
The Underground Man. New York: Knopf, 1971.
Sleeping Beauty. New York: Knopf, 1973.
The Blue Hammer. New York: Knopf, 1976.

COLLECTIONS

Note: Collections are published under the pseudonym Ross Macdonald unless otherwise noted.

The Name Is Archer. By "John Ross Macdonald." New York: Bantam, 1955. Short stories.
Archer in Hollywood. New York: Knopf, 1967. Includes *The Way Some People Die* and *The Barbarous Coast.*
Archer at Large. New York: Knopf, 1970. Includes *The Galton Case.*
On Crime Writing. Santa Barbara, Calif.: Capra Press, 1973. Includes "The Writer as Detective Hero" and "Writing *The Galton Case.*"
Great Stories of Suspense. Edited by Ross Macdonald. New York: Knopf, 1974.
Lew Archer, Private Investigator. New York: Mysterious Press, 1977. Short stories.
Archer in Jeopardy. New York: Knopf, 1979.
A Collection of Reviews. Northridge, Calif.: Lord John Press, 1979. Book reviews.
Self-Portrait. Edited by Ralph B. Sipper. Santa Barbara, Calif.: Capra Press, 1981. Articles and essays.
Early Millar. Santa Barbara, Calif.: Cordelia Editions, 1982. Juvenilia by Kenneth and Margaret Millar.

BIBLIOGRAPHIES AND ARCHIVE

Bruccoli, Matthew J., *Kenneth Millar / Ross Macdonald: A Descriptive Bibliography.* Pittsburgh: University of Pittsburgh Press, 1983.
———. *Kenneth Millar / Ross Macdonald: A Checklist.* Detroit: Gale Research, 1971.

Ross Macdonald's manuscripts are housed at the University of California at Santa Barbara.

INTERVIEWS

Carroll, Jon. "Ross Macdonald in Raw California." *Esquire* 77: 148–149, 188 (1972).
Cooper-Clark, Dianna. "Interview with Ross Macdonald." In her *Designs of Darkness.* Bowling Green, Ohio: Bowling Green State University Popular Press, 1983. Pp. 83–100.
Grogg, Sam, Jr. "Ross Macdonald: At the Edge." *Journal of Popular Culture* 7: 213–222 (summer 1973).
Leonard, John. "Ross Macdonald, His Lew Archer and Other Secret Selves." *New York Times Book Review,* 1 June 1969: 2–19.
Solokov, Raymond A. "The Art of Murder." *Newsweek,* 22 March 1971: 101–104, 106, 108
Tutunjian, Jerry. "A Conversation with Ross Macdonald." *Tamarack Review* 62: 66–85 (1974).

BIOGRAPHICAL AND CRITICAL STUDIES

Barnes, Daniel R. " 'I'm the Eye': Archer as Narrator in the Novels of Ross Macdonald." *Mystery and Detection Annual* (1972): 178–190.

Bruccoli, Matthew J. *Ross Macdonald.* San Diego: Harcourt Brace Jovanovich, 1984.

Carter, Stephen R. "Ross Macdonald: The Complexity of the Modern Quest for Justice." *Mystery and Detection Annual* (1973): 59–82.

Collins, Michael. "Expanding the *Roman Noir:* Ross Macdonald's Legacy to Mystery/Detective Authors," *South Dakota Review* 24: 121–124 (spring 1986).

Goldman, William. Review of *The Goodbye Look. New York Times Book Review,* 1 June 1969: 2.

Grella, George. "Evil Plots." *New Republic,* 26 July 1975: 24–26.

Pry, Elmer B. "Ross Macdonald's Violent California: Imagery Patterns in *The Underground Man.*" *Western American Literature* 9: 197–203 (fall 1974).

Schopen, Bernard A. *Ross Macdonald.* Boston: Twayne, 1990.

Sipper, Ralph B., ed. *Inward Journey: Ross Macdonald.* Santa Barbara, Calif.: Cordelia Editions, 1984.

Skenazy, Paul. "Bring It All Back Home: Ross Macdonald's California." *South Dakota Review* 24: 68–110 (spring 1986).

Spier, Jerry. *Ross Macdonald.* New York: Ungar, 1978.

Steiner, T. R. "The Mind of the Hardboiled: Ross Macdonald and the Roles of Criticism." *South Dakota Review* 24: 29–54 (spring 1986).

Wolfe, Peter. *Dreamers Who Live Their Dreams: The World of Ross Macdonald's Novels.* Bowling Green, Ohio: Bowling Green State University Popular Press, 1976.

HELEN MACINNES
(1907–1985)

PRISCILLA L. WALTON

Women have different fantasies because they're trained to seek not power but a powerful man.

Ken Follett

HELEN MACINNES WROTE a steady stream of best-selling espionage thrillers over a forty-four-year period, yet today it is almost impossible to find any of her twenty-one novels. Despite MacInnes' Scottish birth, her books are completely out of print in the United Kingdom, although the works of her contemporaries Eric Ambler, Morris West, and Alistair MacLean are available, as are those of Ian Fleming, Len Deighton, and John le Carré. Theoretically, it is possible to order a handful of MacInnes' novels in North America—in practice, however, they are virtually nonexistent. Indeed, MacInnes' novels are most likely to be found in yard or rummage sales.

Curiously, the expected reasons for MacInnes' absence from bookstore shelves do not hold: her books sold in the millions and, in her day, she was called the "queen of the spy novel." Four of her novels were made into feature films, but only two have made the transition to video, and require special ordering. Since MacInnes' career—at least during her lifetime—was undeniably successful, why is obscurity the apparent fate of one of the first women ever to pen spy novels? Why can one find all of the "kings," but not the sole

"queen"? Speculations as to this "why" underpin the analysis that follows.

Helen Clark MacInnes was born in Glasgow on 7 October 1907. She earned her master's degree at Glasgow University, where she also met Gilbert Highet. MacInnes married Highet in 1932 and moved with him to Oxford, where he began his career as a classics scholar. Five years later Highet took up a position at Columbia University, and the couple moved to New York. In 1941 the author published her first novel, *Above Suspicion*, drawing upon her honeymoon trip to Bavaria and her diary entries regarding the rise of Hitler's Germany. MacInnes and Highet became American citizens in 1951 and made their permanent home in Manhattan, where Highet died in 1978.

In a 1978 interview quoted in the *New York Times*, MacInnes spoke about the political bent of her novels. She claimed, "If I can be labeled anything, I am a Jeffersonian Democrat." MacInnes continued to write until she suffered a stroke and died on 30 September 1985, at which time her editor, Julian P. Muller, remembered her as "the creator of acute, exciting novels set against backgrounds of meaningful present-day events. . . . Her purpose always was to strike at authoritarian governments. In the genre of highly literate suspense she is considered unrivaled" (*New York Times*, p. 6). Indeed, MacInnes' books sold more than twenty-three million copies in the United States alone and were translated into twenty-two languages.

Helen MacInnes in Context

Thrillers were relative latecomers to the world of mass-market genre fiction. The western had been established by the late nineteenth century and detective fiction by the 1930s; espionage novels did not emerge as a significant popular genre until the 1950s. MacInnes' first novel, *Above Suspicion* (1941), appeared at the beginning of World War II and, not surprisingly, concentrated on the machinations of the Nazi regime. But like other espionage fiction, her works found a new focus as the end of the war inadvertently laid the groundwork for the Cold War. In keeping with global events, the espionage genre commenced to articulate (and foster) public fears of secretive Communist takeovers; at the same time, it solidified itself as an important and best-selling formula. Spy fiction performs as a conduit to "connect and serve as a condensed expression for a series of ideological and cultural concerns that have been enduringly important since [its emergence as a genre in] the late 1950s, " contend Tony Bennett and Janet Woollacott (p. 18). Nonetheless, while the concerns addressed by the thriller may have risen to prominence during the Cold War, the genre itself did not originate there. Rather, espionage fiction has its roots in Victorian sensation writers, such as H. Rider Haggard and Robert Louis Stevenson, and more particularly in fin de siècle novelists like Rudyard Kipling and Joseph Conrad, whose novels also appeared at times of disruptive and radical change.

Kipling's *Kim* (1901) provides a virtual template for the ideological locus of the spy novel. Set in turn-of-the-century India, *Kim* details the story of a young Anglo-Indian, adopted by the army, who becomes a player in what the narrative calls "the Great Game." The Great Game comprises espionage efforts to maintain Her Majesty's empire—earlier works were more likely to focus on expanding the British Empire than on affirming it, for the simple reason that the empire was not yet under siege. Kim's background is of special interest here, for, as an Anglo-Indian, his hybrid status highlights the idea that the "outside" colonial subject is as desirous of British rule as his "inside" imperial counterparts.

Kipling's Great Game is reiterated in Conrad's *The Secret Agent* (1907), although in a less resplendent form. The pattern of the "outsider" working for the "inside" is concomitantly echoed in the author himself, since Conrad's Polish background rendered him, too, an "outsider." Again, this "outsider" can be seen as working to affirm imperialism and to stress the legitimacy of British empirical rule. In *The Secret Agent*, ragtag terrorists and anarchists plot to bomb the Greenwich Observatory and are stopped in the nick of time, although their machinations throw into relief the flagging morale of the British public.

The espionage novel, perpetuated by such authors as John Buchan and Graham Greene, continued to intrigue readers throughout World War I and its aftermath. By the end of World War II, however, and with the loss of India, the British Empire was crumbling, and the resulting Commonwealth no longer held its former status as the primary player in the Great Game. This state of affairs spawned the "golden age" of the spy genre: in a period of growing anxiety over Britain's status in the postwar period, thrillers worked to glamorize the empirical remnants, as they testified to the glory of British intelligence. As adventure novels, these texts are packed with action and suspense, detailing the perambulations of the agent (who is always male) and his efforts to root out threats to God and Country.

One of the chief proponents of the contemporary thriller, Ian Fleming, published his first novel, *Casino Royale*, in 1953, and set the tone of the espionage genre for the ensuing decades. Fleming, who was himself a former member of the British espionage agency, MI5, constructed the mythos of the handsome, romantic spy. Fleming's novels trace the adventures of his hero, James Bond (soon to become a household word), and his ruthless pursuit of even more ruthless enemy agents. As Umberto Eco suggests, Fleming's work is as "conservative as, basically, the fable—any fable—is conservative; his is the static, inherent, dogmatic conservatism of fairy tales and myths, which transmit an elementary wisdom, constructed and communicated by a simple play of light and shade, by indisputable archetypes which do not permit critical distinction" (p. 169). Accordingly, the Bond novels highlight and construct divisions between the "Free World" and the "Communist Threat," in that a good secret agent (like Bond) is a cool customer who nonetheless will risk his life for the sake of his country. Armed with various ingenious gadgets, Bond is rewarded for his efforts with the attentions of numerous gorgeous women (some counteragents, most not), whom he picks up and discards at will.

John G. Cawelti, in his study *Adventure, Mystery, and Romance* (1976), argues that genre or formula fiction fulfills four important functions. Formula works "affirm existing interests and attitudes by presenting an imaginary world that is aligned with these interests and attitudes"; they "resolve tensions and ambiguities resulting from the conflicting interests of different groups within the culture or from ambiguous attitudes toward particular values"; they enable their "audience to explore in fantasy the boundary between the permitted and the forbidden and to experience in a carefully controlled way the possibility of stepping across this boundary"; at the same time, they "assist in the process of assimilating changes in values" and "thus contribute to cultural continuity" (pp. 35–36).

Cawelti's contentions are crucial to understanding the cultural performance of genre works in general and espionage novels in particular. The dual movement of formula fiction, that is, the ways in which it both affirms

norms and values and enables readers to assimilate changes, means that the overall performance of a particular genre may work to endorse the ideological norms of its consumers, while subtle transformations within it reflect shifts in the social climate. Genre fiction, therefore, enables readers to work through various cultural anxieties in a "controlled fashion."

Hence, while Fleming's texts reiterate important conceits of the former empire as commonplace truisms, the espionage novel alters in the hands of novelists writing in a different period. John le Carré, for example, is far more critical of the espionage game than his precursors, although the question of honor and country continue to underpin his novels. More than Fleming, le Carré is openly aware of his imperial forebears like Kipling and Conrad. He reiterates the espionage world as the Great Game in the title of his 1996 novel, *Our Game,* and throughout the Smiley trilogy (although "the game" is generally lower-cased). Interestingly, Pym, the protagonist of *A Perfect Spy* (1987), describes himself as "one of us," and Smiley notes of a double agent that he "was of his own kind"; this is a term that resonates throughout Conrad's *Lord Jim* (1900), which concentrates on a man whose mystery lies precisely in the fact that he *is* "one of us." Just who "us" is, is never explicated, but one can draw some conclusions from what "us" is not.

If as Cawelti suggests, genre fiction in general helps its public to assimilate social change by emphasizing cultural anxieties, Bennett and Woollacott point to the concerns that spy fiction in particular addresses. For them, "the primary ideological and cultural co-ordinates" have been

first, representations of the relations between West and East or, more generally, between capitalist and communist economic and political systems; secondly, representations of the relations between the sexes, particularly with regard to the construction of images of masculinity and femininity; and, thirdly, representations of nation and nationhood. (p. 18)

Bennett and Woollacott's analysis illuminates the "us" versus "them" construction of the thriller, where without question, "them" is the Communist East, and "us" is the West, but representations of nation and nationhood are equally important. In British espionage fiction, "us" only ambivalently includes the United States, for if Britain is no longer the primary Western power, it deeply resents the country that has taken its place. Anti-Americanism peppers novels from Fleming's to le Carré's where the Americans are perhaps more hated than the Soviets. The traitor, Haydon, in *Tinker, Tailor, Soldier, Spy* (1975) "turns" because "he hated America very deeply." Notably, "Smiley, might, in other circumstances, have agreed" (p. 355).

Perhaps of most importance to a discussion of Helen MacInnes, however, is Bennett and Woollacott's suggestion that gender constructions and sexual relations are of pivotal concern to the thriller formula. On one level, the genre is riddled with intense homoerotic male bonding. Nonetheless, it is clear that the "us" of the novels is not openly gay, for the novels, concomitantly, reveal an intense homophobia. Invariably, the double agents are gay, bisexual, or sexually ambiguous. As one of Fleming's bureaucrats, in *From Russia with Love* (1957), declares: "I thought we were all agreed that homosexuals were about the worst security risk there is."

Of particular interest in contextualizing the novels of Helen MacInnes, however, is the fact that "us," in the spy thriller, is emphatically not female. Take, for instance, Fleming's misogynistic portrayals of women as ugly lesbians or as beauties who serve primarily as toys for sexual pleasure, to be discarded when their attractions diminish. Women are suspect in Fleming's texts, much as they are in those of Kipling, Conrad, and le Carré. Hence, given the ways in which thrillers act as conduits for gender anxiety, and given that the genre as a whole tends to be overwhelmingly male-focused, it is intriguing to explore what happens when a woman enters into the espionage milieu. While, certainly, the primary concerns outlined continue to pervade the genre, they also shift when the cultural location of the author changes. And such is the case with the works of Helen MacInnes.

MacInnes' Spy Novels: Redefining "Us"

MacInnes burst onto the thriller scene in 1941 with *Above Suspicion,* a novel so well received it launched her on a long career of espionage writings, which ended only in 1984, a year before her death. MacInnes' writing provides cultural markers of the prevalent ideologies and values of her time and falls, roughly, into three categories: the representation of World War II (1941–1950); the delineation of the postwar period, the rise of the Communist threat, and the Cold War (1951–1976); and the advent of various terrorist organizations and their relationship to the Cold War (1978–1984).

Above Suspicion was quickly followed by *Assignment in Brittany* (1942), *The Unconquerable* (1944; U.S. title, *While Still We Live*), *Horizon* (1945), *Friends and Lovers* (1947), and *Rest and Be Thankful* (1949). In the tradition of espionage novels, the texts of the "World War II" category are filled with action and suspense, but they are liberal in their politics. A common thread running throughout these works underscores the importance of loyalty, nationalism, and the imperatives of allied union. *The Unconquerable,* for example, traces a young Scot's stay in Poland during the Nazi invasion, dramatizing the Polish underground movement and the Allied help that fuels the lagging spirits of a conquered people. Passages like the following pepper the text and emphasize the necessity of certain subversive activities:

> Tomorrow the enemy may come. We have this day, by the grace of God. That is why I have called you together. Some of us have met before, some have only been recruited to our ranks in the last few weeks, some have been chosen to join us in the last few days to fill the gaps in our ranks caused by enemy

action. Our purpose is one, whoever we are, whatever we have been. We fight on. Poland will not die, while we still live. (p. 219)

The heroic actions of the Underground make up the bulk of this novel and point to the significance of collaborative action, which is an important recurrent theme in the author's works.

With the end of the war, MacInnes' focus, like that of her male counterparts, turned to the new threat emanating from the Soviet Union. The novels of this period include *Neither Five nor Three* (1951), *I and My True Love* (1953), *Pray for a Brave Heart* (1955), *North from Rome* (1958), *Decision at Delphi* (1960), *The Venetian Affair* (1963), *The Double Image* (1966), *The Salzburg Connection* (1968), and *Message from Malaga* (1971). Often, exemplars of novels in the "Cold War" category concentrate on returning soldiers surprised by the realization that the war they have fought and won still continues at "home," if in a different form. *Neither Five nor Three*, for instance, concentrates on a former journalist, who remained in occupied Germany after V-day in Europe, and arrives back in the United States to discover that his country is beset by secret Soviet networks. As a result, "good" Americans are called upon to counter the Communist propaganda found in the media:

> "There's no choice. . . . They've chosen the weapons. Infiltration and control of propaganda sources. We shall have to learn to know them for what they are. Or go down in history as the biggest boobs of all time. For the writing is on the wall, clear to see. It is up to people like you and me, Paul. It is up to people like us, who make our living in an information medium—the publishers, the writers, the producers and directors, the journalists, the columnists, the teachers and the preachers, the editors, the television and radio men. It's up to us. We ought to see the lies and guard against them. We've got to expose them." (p. 69)

These novels, like those of the earlier category, focus on value-motivated citizen action,

rather than on specific espionage organizations.

MacInnes' later texts continue to dramatize the Cold War, but they branch out to examine the emergence of terrorist groups. This last category encompasses works like *The Snare of the Hunter* (1974), *Agent in Place* (1976), *Prelude to Terror* (1978), *The Hidden Target* (1980), *Cloak of Darkness* (1982), and MacInnes' final novel, *Ride a Pale Horse* (1984). These writings often target Soviet efforts to fund terrorism, as in *Prelude to Terror*, which details the adventures of an art critic who is sent to purchase a masterpiece for a Texas millionaire, only to discover that he has walked into a Soviet plot. As it is explained to him:

> "Many [terrorist groups] are small, disjointed, irrational. . . . There are others, however—the real menace. Their aim? Dissension, terror, havoc, and always against the West. They have been well trained. Now, they are well directed. In some cases, they have been linked together. The threat is there. And increasing. Because of the money behind them."
> "Surely . . . subsidies like that can be traced to their origin."
> "Eventually, yes. That is why the Communist countries now find it more discreet to use indirect means."
> "Laundering the cash?"
> "It's more complicated, and much deadlier than that." (p. 69)

Interestingly, MacInnes' concern is for the West as opposed to one specific country or one person's individualistic heroics.

MacInnes' novels bear obvious similarities to other espionage writings, yet their focus on communal action, and (later) on NATO, renders them less directly nationalistic than those of male espionage writers. MacInnes rarely documents the doings of one country's particular secret service. As she documents the influx of terror into the West and efforts to stem the tide of the Communist movement, her novels are also less class oriented than others in the genre; in fact, they deliberately minimize the tensions generating from class conflict (although the protagonists are always of the middle to upper classes). In MacInnes' early works, the "people" are lauded: "The engineer was still the engineer; the lawyer remained the lawyer; the farmer and land-owner still belonged to the villages. But these differences were like salt and pepper in the flavour of a broth. The communal dish was all the better for the varied seasoning" (*Unconquerable*, p. 438). Later in *The Unconquerable*, the philosophy of an absent but major figure is extolled: "He doesn't believe in one class dominating. He believes in the best men of all classes being the leaders. He doesn't divide people into horizontal levels. He divides them vertically: good citizens, bad citizens. He believes there's a natural aristocracy among people: an aristocracy of courage and brains and human decency" (p. 527).

The spies that appear in MacInnes' works are less glamorous than those in male-authored texts and are characterized, more often than not, as people performing important and often unrecognized services. There are few fancy gadgets in MacInnes, and no secret machinations within clandestine organizations. Hence, MacInnes' novels are relatively straightforward in their efforts to document the ways in which governments—as the elected representatives of the people—work to protect their citizens and subjects.

MacInnes' focus on international collaborations, in its divergence from the nationalistic impetus of her male counterparts, might well arise from MacInnes' own international status as a Scot living in the United States. MacInnes' preoccupation, from *Above Suspicion* to *Ride a Pale Horse*, is with communal alliances. Her early works, like *The Unconquerable*, underscore the importance of collaborative action (as discussed above in relation to Polish underground networks), and her inclination to celebrate international cooperation continues throughout her oeuvre. In the middle works, which concentrate on Soviet machinations to destroy the West, her protagonists are usually disinterested citizens who become involved with either NATO efforts or unofficial citizen groups. Thus, in *Neither Five nor Three*, the text's protagonist, Paul Haydn, returns to the United States from his service abroad and discovers secret Soviet "disinformation" networks operating in his own country. When he resumes his former work as a journalist, his publisher tells him of problems encountered at the magazine as a result of certain articles printed by a previous editor: "The effect of those . . . articles was to make our readers think that America was run by cheats and crooks. . . . [In one of them] you were left with the feeling that a system such as ours would inevitably result in decadence. . . . In a way, I felt I was fighting shadows" (pp. 64–65). Paul decides to join a group established to counter this disinformation with positive accounts of American lifestyles. It is important to note that the group is a confederation of volunteers, driven to action by concerns for their country.

Similarly, in *North from Rome*, vacationing playwright Bill Lammiter stumbles onto Soviet espionage groups in the Italian capital. His concern for his former fiancée, who is unwittingly about to marry a Communist agent, motivates him to help NATO forces in their efforts to stem the tide of drug trafficking into the West: "The main target was America. The shipments of drugs were constantly being steered through western Europe toward the United States. . . . the whole thing is a campaign against the West, planned and carefully subsidized by its enemies" (pp. 80–81). Bill learns that the purpose of this drug trafficking is to demoralize Western citizenry, and that it comprises "a remarkably efficient organization, international in scope, with its key men all Communists. It can be turned to political uses when necessary. Meanwhile, it adds to the Communists' secret funds, helps to corrupt their enemies and gathers a list of future traitors—drug addicts can always be bribed by heroin, or blackmailed with threats of exposure. They'll be quislings, every one of them" (p. 83). Lammiter, bound both by his personal worry for his former fiancée and by his patriotic duty, agrees to help identify a key meeting of Communist agents from around the globe.

MacInnes has been accused of displaying a naively pro-American bias. The *Times* obituary that summarizes her career contends that MacInnes' "latter novels tended in a somewhat black and white manner, to pit a scheming and malign Soviet Union against a United States of candid and generous impulses." Yet, placed in context, MacInnes' novels are no more black and white than those of her male counterparts; the difference lies in her refusal to condemn the United States, manifesting a contrast to her British contemporaries. That is, where le Carré depicts the United States as bumbling and stupid, MacInnes spins this construction into a more positive image. Her writing, therefore, works in contrast to the negative portraits of Americans in most espionage novels. In MacInnes' texts, Americans are neither stupid nor rash: "all foreigners believed Americans were rash. If only they knew us properly. Rash? Ambitious perhaps. But not rash" (*North*, p. 60). Similarly, in *Message from Malaga*, the protagonist grates at the stereotype thrust upon him: "Why should these people think Americans don't have a pride of their own? Why the hell have I to pretend I'm stupid, easily manoeuvred, pushed around like a pawn on a chessboard?" (p. 79). The hero of *The Hidden Target*, Bill Renwick, returns to the United States from the United Kingdom and thinks:

No need to judge his country by the headlines any more; now he had a wider frame of reference—people in all their variety, with all their opinions and beliefs and pride in their jobs. Sure there were weaknesses here and there, even some rents and tears, worrying self-indulgences, but the main fabric was still strong. A good place to live, and worth a good fight. (p. 119)

MacInnes' portrayal of Americans might lend itself to charges of naïveté, but her characterizations work to counter the negativity that underscores so much espionage fiction. Further, her refusal to engage in a particular patriotic nationalism breaks down the tightly focused emphasis of most spy novels. The West, in general, is MacInnes' concern, not one particular country over another. Even her final novels, which follow one character, Bob Renwick, through *Prelude to Terror*, *The Hidden Target*, and *The Cloak of Darkness*, have a cross-border international locus. Renwick is an American who lives in London and works for the international organization he has established:

Interintell—or International Intelligence against Terrorism. It had been Renwick's brain child, conceived in Brussels, set up in London, staffed by ex–NATO intelligence men like Renwick himself. As an American, he would have been pleased to see Washington as Interintell's headquarters for shared information on terrorist conspiracies and connections. But he had decided on London for several valid reasons. Western Europe had been under savage attack by organized terrorism; the United States—so far—hadn't experienced the same intensity. Then there was the matter of co-operation between intelligence services, and that came more willingly from Europeans; they had felt the need. The United States—so far, again—had not. (*Cloak*, pp. 1–2)

As one character puts it: "D'you know what I like about your Interintell? Your care for the West. Much too good a civilization to be thrown away" (*Cloak*, p. 144).

On another level, MacInnes' refusal to rely on a single individual's actions works against common perceptions of an American emphasis on the unencumbered self. Interestingly, MacInnes' own "Americanness" does not advance individualism, a dominant strand of traditional American ideology. In fact, MacInnes' lack of an individualistic focus sits in marked contrast to her British counterparts, who frequently emphasize the doings of one particular spy.

MacInnes' portrayal of disinterested persons who get caught up in various intelligence operations—from the British couple on vacation in Bavaria in *Above Suspicion*, to the returning journalist in *Neither Five nor Three*, to Colin Grant, an art dealer inadvertently involved in Soviet money-laundering shenanigans in *Prelude to Terror*—constitute one of her bequests to the spy novel. Even her hero Bob Renwick, who is a professional, works for an organization that is somewhat unique in structure: "We don't pull rank. We began as friends—people who knew each other—and we keep it that way" (*Cloak*, p. 290). Hence, rather than depicting organizations that close ranks against the populace, MacInnes, in Jeffersonian fashion, dramatizes the concerned citizenry of a generalized West. Her interest in outsiders—again, perhaps a reflection of her own inside-outside status as a Scot living in the United States—as opposed to those inside secret organizations shifts the locus of the espionage genre and works in contrast to her male counterparts' professional and nationalistic spies. Furthermore, as a woman, MacInnes is consigned to a place outside the espionage business (both fictional and historical), and her cultural displacement lends itself to depictions of other outsiders.

When Women Write Spy Novels

As the bulk of spy novels suggests, most secret-service agencies are male dominated. When (or if) women appear, they are almost inevitably relegated to minor positions or, alternatively, constructed as enemy agents. MacInnes' fictions, through dramatizations of disinterested observers/actors, work to subvert the "closed-club" aspect of espionage fiction. Rendering that "inside" permeable, she upsets the polarized "us"-versus-"them" construction, which functions in relation to "the enemy," as well as to those outside the agency in question. In MacInnes' hands, these secret services lose their exclusive status and become agencies that act as representatives of the public.

MacInnes' novels do often feature male protagonists, yet unlike those of her counterparts, her male characters are generally involved in romantic relationships. This has led to charges that MacInnes is not a "real" es-

pionage writer. As the anonymous author of "Helen MacInnes: The Female Ludlum" protests, "critical reviews of MacInnes will begin by labeling her a spy writer, then before the end of the paragraph will tag her 'romantic suspense.' Why this fate does not also befall Robert Ludlum is inexplicable" (p. 82). The criticism illuminates some of the problems that have befallen MacInnes' works: conventionally, women's texts of suspense have been categorized as "romantic suspense" (whether they are or not), while novels by male writers enjoy "serious" labels such as "spy thriller" or "espionage fiction." But, unlike writers who more comfortably fit the "romantic suspense" category, like Daphne du Maurier, Victoria Holt, and Mary Stewart (although the latter two do, at times, pen thrillers), MacInnes adheres to the formula of espionage fiction. Ken Follett's assertion, in "Why Women Don't Write Spy Novels," that "when women write spy stories or general thrillers the plot is often just a channel through which a love story can flow" (p. 39), may shed light on the difference between the two subgenres, in that romantic suspense concentrates on relationships, where espionage fiction emphasizes action and intrigue. If such is the case, MacInnes is unquestionably a thriller writer. Her focus is espionage, although her depiction of female characters differs from those of her male counterparts. In MacInnes' hands, female characters are more than cardboard diversions, and the romantic relationships she portrays are successful. Indeed, the female partner in MacInnes' work is characterized as a tried, true, and intelligent female companion. These women are not the femmes fatales of Ian Fleming, nor the untrustworthy and deceitful female characters of John le Carré. Instead, they play important roles either as supportive mates or as active agents.

From *Above Suspicion* to *Cloak of Darkness*, MacInnes' novels feature happy couples who help each other through times of crisis. In *The Double Image*, for example, while the bulk of the narrative rests with John Craig—an American historian who becomes a key player in the identification of a Nazi-war-criminal-turned-Soviet-agent—his love interest, Veronica Clark, helps with the exposure. Although the plot tends to cast Veronica as a victim (she is used both by a group of Soviet agents and by NATO forces), she does not meekly accept her role: "I warn you I have a lot of questions. But I'll ask them when I feel sure I'll get some honest answers. In this last week, I've become very tired of lies," she advises a NATO agent (p. 289). In complement to Veronica's potential as a partner for John lies the marriage of John's sister, Sue, and her husband, George, an American diplomat. In this relationship, Sue is integral to the marriage's success, and when times are tough, she and George find comfort in each other.

While it would be misleading to construct MacInnes as an early feminist, her texts do spotlight the intricacies of female roles. Christine Gledhill's contentions about women in popular culture help to elucidate the operation of MacInnes' novels:

> Gender representation is at the heart of . . . cultural negotiation. . . . When popular culture forms . . . attempt to engage contemporary discourses about women or draw on women's cultural forms in order to renew their gender verisimilitude and solicit the recognition of a female audience, the negotiation between 'woman' as patriarchal symbol and woman as generator of women's discourse is intensified. (pp. 76–77)

As a complement to Cawelti and Bennett and Woollacott's assertions that the thriller, as a popular genre, acts as a conduit for cultural fears about social change, Gledhill's contentions nuance the ways in which formula works navigate female representations. For her, popular culture's portrayals make up a field of textual, cultural, and social negotiations (pp. 86–87), and her arguments are particularly significant in relation to MacInnes' depictions of womanhood, which, both celebratory and ambivalent, shift and vacillate over the years, providing markers of fluctuating gender constructions. Hence, the changes that occur in women's cultural roles throughout the latter half of the century,

along with the anxieties they evoke, are clearly evident in MacInnes' oeuvre.

In early novels, like *The Unconquerable*, the significance of women's roles during wartime are foregrounded. Here, protagonist Sheila Matthews works for the Polish underground, and, the narrative is quick to point out, so do other women: "The large room was a mass of dark shapes. . . . There were some women in the room. They sat on the few chairs. The men sat on the floor or stood beside the bookcases. All looked towards the desk, each with his own attitude of attention" (p. 218). Flipping back to a more conventional depiction, Sheila ultimately finds contentment as the wife of a heroic resistance leader and returns to England at his request. As she alternates between active agent and wife on-the-sidelines, Sheila performs as an exemplar of women's evolving roles during and after the war. Her transformation from a sort of Polish Rosie-the-Riveter into a Harriet Nelson character indicates how her shape shifts throughout the novel. By the novel's conclusion, Sheila is in England waiting patiently, "hoping for some more crumbs of good news. But that was all she was to be allowed" (p. 617). Sheila ends her adventures in the relative safety of her uncle's home, where she will bear her courageous husband's child.

The heroines of *Neither Five nor Three* also mirror the inconsistencies and contradictions inherent for women in the postwar status quo. This novel documents the development of career woman Rona Metford. When Rona runs into her former lover, Paul Haydn (the novel's hero), he queries her about her job: "What about your job at *Trend*? I heard you were practically running the Architecture Department. Good for you" (p. 25). Rona modestly underplays her role, although the text highlights her ambitions and her intelligence:

> "Just more gossip. I'm only an assistant to Mr. Burnett. I imagine what should go inside a room once he has decided its shape. I'm not fully qualified yet, you see."
>
> "You mean as an architect?" He was surprised. "Still following that idea? Then you got a college degree?"

"Yes, I made it. Part-time work and night classes. That sort of thing."

"Not as much fun as Vassar, I'd imagine."

"No." She smiled. "Still, it was either that way or nothing." (p. 25)

Despite her clear abilities, however, the novel (mirroring its postwar locus) details how Rona is quite happy to throw away her career and move on to that really important thing for women: marriage. After Rona's lover, Scott, announces their engagement, she looks forward to immersing herself in her new role as wife. In this scene, Scott proclaims: "I've been deciding one thing, to-night. We are getting married. We'll set a definite date for this summer. We've waited long enough. . . . Will you take a chance on my earning power?" Rona responds "Oh, Scott!" and throws her arms around him (pp. 48–49). Reminiscent of Laura Petrie's wail ("Oh, Rob!"), Rona's delight over her forthcoming nuptials infuse the text, and she later turns to her sister, Peggy, for confirmation of her life choices. Peggy, who was writing a doctoral dissertation on Marcel Proust when she decided to marry, provides a role model: Peggy now finds her intellectual satisfaction as the mistress of her husband's salons, where she modestly disclaims her accomplishments. One of her husband's students notes, "Professor Tyson, I didn't know your wife was an authority on Proust," to which Peggy "protests happily": "I'm not" (p. 87).

While Rona initially represents the independent career woman, and Peggy the domestic goddess, it is interesting that the two have a deep and meaningful relationship. Peggy believes it is the differences between them that engender this mutual respect. As she reflects on their closeness, she summarizes their history:

It's odd, she was thinking—Rona feels guilty because she can afford to buy more than I can. And I have guilt because I got a college education before father died, and Rona couldn't get a degree except by working in an office through the day and taking classes at night.

But perhaps that is why we are such good friends, each of us with our little sense of respect for the other. Now, if only Rona finds as wonderful a husband in Scott as I've found in Jon, everything will be all right. (p. 78)

Peggy, ever mindful of her sister's happiness, firmly believes that if Rona can "find a husband," she, too, in 1950s fashion, can enjoy the domestic bliss that accompanies marriage to the right man. Like Peggy, she can then devote herself to rewarding domestic and familial chores:

"Barbara [Peggy's daughter] looks like a butterball. An angelic butterball."

"If you had seen her slinging the suds around the bathroom to-night when I was trying to wash some of her clothes in the hand basin, you wouldn't think she was an angel." That reminded Peggy to look at the socks and vests and sweaters drying on the wooden stand near the open window. She put down the bowl of chopped eggs, and went over to turn the clothes around and keep them from ridging as they dried. (p. 73)

Contrarily, however, while Rona cannot wait to marry Scott, she insists on finishing the architectural degree for which she has worked so hard. She urges Scott to recognize the benefits of her educational choice, which, she incongruously contends, will help her to make a comfortable home for the two of them:

"What did you do last night?"

"Oh, very prosaic! I did some laundry. And I read up on that architecture test." She kept her voice cheerful, although it hadn't been exactly her idea of how to spend a Saturday evening.

"Still serious about becoming fully qualified?" he asked.

She dished the eggs neatly. She said, "Why not be qualified, anyway? I'm more than halfway through the course, you know. Or don't you want an architect in the family?"

"Might be useful," he said with a laugh, and carried the plates into the dining room.

Rona took off her apron, and brought the coffee and toast.

"Some day," she said, "I can design our own house, and then we needn't go apartment hunting any more. I'll do a study for you that will knock your eye out." (p. 116)

A field of contradictory negotiations, therefore, *Neither Five nor Three* documents the antithetical maneuverings of domestic ideology. Yet, even as the novel clearly stresses how a woman's happiness will be found in domesticity, it continues to emphasize the importance of women's abilities. One character observes:

I remember a Frenchman telling me during the war . . . that the biggest surprise to him in the whole campaign had been the women. They could take more punishment than men. He'd send a girl on a dangerous mission—they did a lot of night courier jobs—and she'd run into trouble, nothing too serious but just enough to fray a man's nerves into making a false move, and she'd not only get through her brush with the Gestapo, but next morning she'd be standing in her kitchen, trying to cook a dinner and blaming the Boches for the scarcity of vegetables. (p. 344)

Because MacInnes' career spans several decades, her works allow for a historical overview of women's fluctuating roles over the years, and, assimilating social changes, the author begins, by her middle novels, to portray female secret agents. Generally, these women work for NATO, although their service to the West tends to stem from personal loss, as is the case of Claire Connor in *The Venetian Affair*. When protagonist Bill Fenner chivalrously objects to the use of a female agent in the fiction's proposed mission, a NATO agent explains that Claire is "someone who got caught up in this whole business by a quirk of fate. She's like you, in many ways. Her life would be much more comfortable if she hadn't listened to me" (pp. 144–145). Claire had become involved in espionage because of the terrorist bomb that killed her

husband, and she discovered that working for NATO helped her to make sense of her husband's death. Nonetheless, Claire's remarkable abilities as a professional agent annoy Bill:

"Do you always think of everything?" . . .

He took her hand as they approached the large, ornate back door of the Vittoria. It was his way of saying he was sorry. She looked up in surprise, and smiled. He had chased some of the worry away, at least. "I wasn't much help to you there," he admitted, "Was I?"

She laughed in her relief. "You did let me get my own way," she reminded him. Kicking and screaming, she thought. What had made him so ornery all of a sudden?

"Do you get your way with every damned man you meet?" (pp. 185–186)

Bill and Claire fall in love during their "Venetian affair," and Claire gives up her espionage work to become Bill's wife. For a 1990s reader, however, much of the text's inadvertent humor arises from Bill's consistent tendency to underestimate Claire's skills.

As they document the shift in women's roles from active workers to domestics in the 1940s and 1950s, the texts also reflect the second wave of feminism in the 1960s and 1970s. The tenets of early liberal feminism move throughout MacInnes' later novels, which document how women become less inclined to throw away their careers to submerge themselves in domestic bliss. In *Prelude to Terror*, for example, the difficulties facing working women are foregrounded when Colin Grant falls in love with a NATO agent, Avril Hoffman. The two are happy together, but problems arise from Avril's job:

"We have years ahead of us to learn and keep on learning. But not if you are still sharing your love, dividing it between me and—." He pointed to the instructions lying under her hand. "It's me or Renwick," he said, his mouth set. (p. 278)

Ultimately, the couple work out a compromise—Avril agrees to return to NATO to finish her current assignments, at which time she will (reluctantly) quit the agency and join Colin in matrimony. The text seems uneasy with this premise, however, and provides an "easier" solution to the couple's potential problems by killing off Avril in a terrorist confrontation, during which she tries to save Colin.

In *The Hidden Target*, Bob Renwick, Avril's boss in *Prelude to Terror*, follows his love interest, Nina, across the globe. Nina has unwittingly become involved in a terrorist expedition, but, no one's fool, she becomes aware of the dangers of her position:

> "I know," she said. "You risked everything in order to shock me into leaving. You did shock me. But I can't leave. Not yet. . . ."
>
> He [Renwick's agent] stared at her in disbelief. "You really think you can go on, never let them know, never give your real feelings away? No, no. Now that you've learned so much, you're in double danger."
>
> "On the contrary. Now that I know—and it isn't so much, either—I'm on guard."
>
> "Not so much?" My God, he thought, when Renwick hears how I broke the rules tonight, he'll—no, perhaps Renwick wouldn't. He can guess what I'm dealing with here; he warned me about Nina. And I thought I could handle her. (p. 227)

In fact, no one can really "handle" Nina, because she is smart, savvy, and perceptive. She extricates herself from the terrorists, and ultimately agrees to marry Renwick. The text concludes with Nina learning from Gemma Gilman, who is married to Renwick's colleague, the secrets of being a good spy's wife:

> "Truth and confidences," Gemma mused. "Oh, you'll have plenty of them, don't worry. Provided you don't gossip. And you don't. It's a very private kind of life, actually. Rather nice, too: it draws you closely together. It has to. Or else it would all fly apart."
>
> *A very private kind of life* . . . "A lot must depend on the woman, doesn't it?" Nina asked hesitantly.
>
> "Of course. And very flattering it is," Gemma said cheerfully. (p. 317)

An intelligent woman, Nina learns her lessons well, and, in *Cloak of Darkness*, she has become the perfect espionage agent's companion. Ever quick-witted, in this novel she is able to save herself from her would-be attackers by disguising her appearance, a precaution that none of the men who are protecting her think necessary.

Yet, it is not until *Ride a Pale Horse* that a woman finds happiness blending career and marriage. Karen Cornell, the protagonist of MacInnes' final novel, is an investigative reporter for a prestigious Washington newspaper. While on assignment in Czechoslovakia, Karen is contacted by a would-be Soviet defector, and thus becomes a key component in NATO's efforts to obtain top-secret information. The difference in this novel lies in its conclusion, wherein Karen and her newfound love, Peter Bristow, replay the argument between Colin Grant and Avril Hoffman—to a quite different purpose. This time, there is no suggestion that Karen will cease to be a journalist, and when she insists that Peter include her in his adventures, he agrees: "If you must leave, then I leave, too. . . . I mean that." The novel ends: "She laughed and held out her hand. He grasped it firmly. Together, they mounted the steps and entered the house" (p. 369). *Ride a Pale Horse*, therefore, marks the first collaboration between lovers that ends in a professional partnership.

From Helen to Harriet: The Infantilization of the Female Spy

If MacInnes is instrumental in dramatizing the importance of women in espionage activities, her disappearance from bookshelves suggests that the pivotal contributions she made to the spy genre were deemed insignificant—at least temporarily. For a long time, one of the only popular female spies was to be found in Louise Fitzhugh's 1964 children's book, *Harriet the Spy*. Within the text, Fitzhugh portrays an active female agent, Harriet M. Welsch, an eleven-year-old "spy," who delights in documenting the activities of her friends and neighbors.

Harriet the Spy offers some interesting gender shifts: Harriet is bent on an espionage career; her friend, Janie, is a serious scientist, who is planning to blow up the world; and her male friend, Sport, who wants to be a ball player, spends most of his time cooking and cleaning for his father. But the text takes a curious turn when Harriet's spying begins to serve as a means of grooming her for "ladyhood." In one scene, Harriet refuses to take dancing lessons, since they are unbefitting a spy-in-training. Her nurse points out that Mata Hari's modus operandi was not guerrilla fighting in the woods but rather going to parties, where she picked up information while dancing with generals, for instance. Harriet is persuaded by this argument, and decides to funnel her skills into journalism, an arena that, at the time, proved more amenable to women.

Hope for Helen

Since the era of Fitzhugh's novel, however, several other female authors, like Marilyn Sharp and Evelyn Anthony, have entered the espionage milieu, although it was not until the late 1980s and early 1990s that women engaged with the genre in numbers sufficient to make a difference. Along with Evelyn Anthony now are writers like Carolyn Hougan, Wilma Riley, Linda Davies, and Dorothy Gilman. While Gilman's hero, the indomitable Mrs. Pollifax—New York matron and undercover CIA agent—provides for amusing plays on the thriller genre, the idea of a female spy seems to have attracted public attention, to such an extent that even Hollywood has begun to portray her. The French film *La Femme Nikita* (1990) was so popular that it spawned an American remake, *Point of No Return* (1993), and a television series, as well as movies like Geena Davis' *The Long Kiss Goodnight* (1997).

At the same time, with the dissolution of the Soviet Union and the collapse of the "us"-versus-"them" ideology that shapes early spy fiction, women writers have begun to bend the espionage formula in on itself. In their hands, the "enemies" are no longer Communist spies but rather longtime Western agents who have become disillusioned with contemporary "liberal" politics. Evelyn Anthony's novels, for instance, have moved from the detection of high-placed traitors in the Secret Intelligence Service (*The Legend*, 1968) to efforts to break a ring of former international agents, which turned terrorist for profit (*The Doll's House*, 1992). In turn, other authors are beginning to alter and subvert the tenets of the espionage form. Amanda Kyle Williams' *Club Twelve* (1990) features a lesbian protagonist, Madison McGuire, as an undercover agent. Gayle Lynds's 1996 *Masquerade* documents how hero Liz Sansborough uncovers a plot, devised by high-placed CIA officials (termed "cold warriors"), to manipulate currency prices in Europe in order to pad their own Swiss bank accounts.

Maureen Tan's 1997 novel, *AKA Jane*, profiles MI5 superagent Jane Nichols, who writes hard-boiled detective fiction as a means of catharsis after she has completed a mission. This twist offers interesting possibilities, for, although female spy writers are still relatively few in number, the nod, in *AKA Jane*, toward hard-boiled detective fiction bodes well. The hard-boiled genre is particularly relevant to women spy writers, since it has been revolutionized by female writers (Sara Paretsky, Sue Grafton, and Marcia Muller offer only a few of countless examples). If the same trend is emerging for women espionage novelists, the genre may be in for a major overhaul. One can only hope that such an overhaul might persuade publishers to reprint the novels of Helen MacInnes, who is, in fact, the foremother of them all.

Selected Bibliography

WORKS OF HELEN MACINNES

Note: Editions cited in the text are listed last.

Above Suspicion. Boston: Little, Brown, 1941; New York: Fawcett, 1978.

Assignment in Brittany. Boston: Little, Brown, 1942; New York: Fawcett, 1978.

The Unconquerable. London: Harrap, 1944; Glasgow: Fontana, 1990. U.S.: *While Still We Live.* Boston: Little, Brown, 1944.

Horizon. London: Harrap, 1945; Boston: Little, Brown, 1946; New York: Fawcett, 1979.

Friends and Lovers. Boston: Little, Brown, 1947; New York: Fawcett, 1979.

Rest and Be Thankful. Boston: Little, Brown, 1949; New York: Fawcett, 1978.

Neither Five nor Three. New York: Harcourt Brace, 1951; Glasgow: Fontana, 1985.

I and My True Love. New York: Harcourt Brace, 1953; Fawcett: 1978.

Pray for a Brave Heart. New York: Harcourt Brace, 1955; Fawcett, 1979.

North from Rome. New York: Harcourt Brace, 1958; Greenwich, Conn.: Fawcett, 1959.

Decision at Delphi. New York: Harcourt Brace, 1960. Repr. in *The Deadly Decisions.* New York: Harcourt, Brace & World, n.d. Pp. 3–403.

The Venetian Affair. New York: Harcourt Brace, 1963; Fawcett Crest, 1963.

Home Is the Hunter. New York: Harcourt, Brace & World, 1964. Two-act play.

The Double Image. New York: Harcourt Brace, 1966; Glasgow: Fontana, 1977.

The Salzburg Connection. New York: Harcourt, Brace & World, 1968.

Message from Malaga. New York: Harcourt Brace, 1971; Glasgow: Fontana, 1981.

The Snare of the Hunter. New York: Harcourt Brace, 1974.

Agent in Place. New York: Harcourt Brace, 1976; Ballantine, 1985.

Prelude to Terror. New York: Harcourt Brace, 1978; Glasgow: Fontana, 1981.

The Hidden Target. New York: Harcourt Brace, 1980; Glasgow: Fontana, 1982.

Cloak of Darkness. New York: Harcourt Brace, 1982; Ballantine, 1983.

Ride a Pale Horse. New York: Harcourt Brace, 1984; Ballantine, 1985.

BIOGRAPHICAL AND CRITICAL STUDIES

Bennett, Tony, and Janet Woollacott. *Bond and Beyond: The Political Career of a Popular Hero.* London: Macmillan, 1987.

Cawelti, John G. *Adventure, Mystery, and Romance: Formula Stories as Art and Popular Culture.* Chicago: University of Chicago Press, 1976.

Eco, Umberto. "Narrative Structures in Fleming." In *Gender, Language, and Myth: Essays on Popular Narrative.* Edited by Glenwood Irons. Toronto: Univ. of Toronto Press, 1992. Pp. 157–182.

Evans, Elizabeth. "Helen (Clark) MacInnes." In *Twentieth-Century Crime and Mystery Writers.* Edited by John M. Reilly. Chicago: St. James, 1991.

Follett, Ken. "Why Women Don't Write Spy Novels." In *Murderess Ink.* Edited by Dilys Winn. New York: Workman, 1979. P. 39.

Gledhill, Christine. "Pleasurable Negotiations." In *Spectators: Looking at Film and Television.* Edited by E. Deidre Pribram. London: Verso, 1988. Pp. 64–89.

"Helen MacInnes." In *Contemporary Authors.* New Revision Series, vol. 58. Edited by Daniel Jones and John D. Jorgenson. Detroit: Gale, 1997.

"Helen MacInnes: The Female Ludlum." In *Murderess Ink: The Better Half of the Mystery.* Edited by Dilys Winn. New York: Workman, 1979. Pp. 81–82.

Macdonald, Gina. "Helen MacInnes." In *British Mystery and Thriller Writers Since 1940.* Edited by Bernard Benstock and Thomas F. Staley. Detroit: Gale, 1989.

McDowell, Edwin. "Helen MacInnes." *New York Times.* 1 October 1985: B6.

"Miss Helen MacInnes." *The Times.* 2 October 1985: 12. Obituary.

NGAIO MARSH
(1895–1982)

BRUCE HARDING

DAME (EDITH) NGAIO MARSH was born in Christchurch, New Zealand, on 23 April 1895. Over a fifty-year span, from 1932 to 1982, Marsh wrote thirty-two classic English detective novels while simultaneously building a reputation as a distinguished theater director who specialized in the plays of Shakespeare. She also wrote a number of short stories, most of which involved detection.

Marsh's singular achievement was to capture international acclaim in literature and the arts while contributing to the cultural life of New Zealand.

While Marsh certainly loved all things English, she stayed rooted in New Zealand and always came back to her home and friends and to her role as the informal godmother of the New Zealand theater. She did not, however, confine her patronage, expertise, and vigorous support to theatrical matters. She was also a prominent figure in the promotion of all the arts in her home country. In 1967 a new playhouse, the Ngaio Marsh Theatre, was named in her honor at Canterbury University in Christchurch, New Zealand, in recognition of her work.

Life

Marsh was the only child of loving—if somewhat unconventional—parents. Her unusual first name (pronounced NIGH-oh) is a Maori word connoting cleverness and was chosen by her uncle, a lay missionary fluent in the Maori language. In later years, Marsh reflected on her childhood, describing herself as a little girl who "was obligingly introverted, delicate, solitary, fanciful, pig-headed and rather morbid." In 1910 Marsh attended a small independent girls' school called St. Margaret's College. It was here that she developed her great love of history and her commitment to the theater, writing and adapting several plays.

Marsh attended the School of Art at Canterbury University College full-time from 1914 to the end of 1919, studying painting. Her deeper impulse was toward words, however, and the visits of the Allan Wilkie Theater Company from 1916 introduced Marsh to live Shakespearean productions of a professional quality. She once described the opening night of their *Hamlet* as "the most enchanted I was ever to spend in the theater." Inspired by this, Marsh wrote the play *The Medallion*. Her mother encouraged her to show Allan Wilkie this script and, to her astonishment, he employed her for a tour of New Zealand in the autumn and winter of 1920.

Marsh taught speech craft at the School of Drama and Dancing in Christchurch, then spent much of the 1920s producing a series of traveling vaudeville shows and large-scale fund-raising charity pantomimes for an organization known as Unlimited Charities (*Blue-bell in Fairyland* [1924], *The Sleeping Beauty* [1925], and her own play, *Cinderella* [1926]). These productions moved her into the circle of a Canterbury gentry family, the Rhodes, whom she dubbed "the Lampreys" (*Death of a Peer* [1940]). She followed them to England in 1928, where she ran a gift and decorating shop in Knightsbridge.

Marsh brought with her to England the first three chapters of a novel set in New Zealand, but she abandoned the project, feeling herself "steaming busily down the well-worn rails of the colonial novel." Two years later her mother, Rose Elizabeth Marsh, arrived for a visit but soon became ill. One wet Sunday afternoon, Marsh was cooped up alone in their basement flat, reading a detective story (probably an Agatha Christie), and she decided to try her hand at the form. "I wondered if I could write detective fiction. It was as much to amuse my mother as anything else," she later asserted. In fact, Ngaio Marsh had seen *Alibi*, a play by Christie, within a few weeks of her arrival in London. Marsh wrote of this "detective drama" that "the play has much more quality than most of its kind, and the character drawing is firm and interesting" (*The Press*, 15 December 1928). Marsh wrote *A Man Lay Dead*, her first published detective novel, from 1931 to 1932. She then returned to New Zealand to attend to her mother, who died from liver cancer in November 1932.

Throughout the 1930s Marsh continued to paint occasionally, produced more detective novels on contract with Geoffrey Bles, traveled again to England and Europe, looked after her elderly father, and produced more plays for local repertory societies in New Zealand. She wrote a play, *Exit Sir Derek*, for Canterbury College's Drama Society (performed in October 1935) with the help of Dr. Henry Jellett. With Jellett she coauthored the novel *Death Follows a Surgeon*, which was published as her third crime novel, *The Nursing-Home Murder*, in 1935. During the war, Marsh undertook voluntary aid work at Burwood Military Hospital in Christchurch, driving repatriated soldiers in a hospital bus. It

was while performing these strenuous duties and writing more novels (such as *Death of a Peer, Death and the Dancing Footman* [1941], and *Colour Scheme* [1943]) that Marsh began a lengthy Shakespearean association. This association resulted in twenty productions, from her 1943 "*Hamlet* in Modern Dress" until *A Midsummer Night's Dream* (which starred Sam Neill) in 1969.

Throughout her long career, Marsh was associated with an aristocratic milieu. Writing to a fellow New Zealand writer in 1939, she made whimsical reference to the American dust jackets of her novels: "I colour up to the roots of my hair when I see them," Marsh observed. "I am represented as a bosom friend of royalty, famous statesmen, and the entire intelligentsia of Great Britain." This image of Marsh—which was largely the consequence of her long association with the aristocratic Rhodes family—has endured and may be described as a liability. Marsh is portrayed in the novel *Blue Blood* (Penguin Books, 1997), by the New Zealand author Stevan Eldred-Grigg, as a person stuck irretrievably in a groove of arrogance, social snobbery, frustrated homosexuality, and a stunted state of morbid psychopathology.

Marsh was unquestionably the product of what Samuel Hynes has called *The Edwardian Turn of Mind* (1968), being brought up "in an age dominated by King Edward VII and Queen Alexandra, joint symbols of the established order—rich, punctilious, and unoccupied—and behind them the past, a corridor of peace, sunlit and pastoral." Hynes describes the Edwardian age as "a long garden party on a golden afternoon—to those who were inside the garden." This indeed captures the prevailing spirit, assumptions, and ongoing appeal of Golden Age detective fiction, of which Marsh remained a devoted exponent across five decades and thirty-two novels (from *A Man Lay Dead* in 1934 to *Light Thickens* in 1982). She may be described as the last of the Golden Age practitioners, even though she modernized and enlivened the form. It is important to note that the garden party certainly ended for the young Ngaio Marsh with the tragic death of her childhood friend and fiancé in World War I. It is, in fact, entirely possible that the emotional trauma of that loss was a relevant factor in Marsh's later decision to work within the emotionally restricted confines of Golden Age literary conventions—what she called "this queer, circumscribed and isolated form of fiction." For while Anthony Berkeley Cox observed in 1930 that the detective story was developing into the novel with a crime theme, "holding its readers less by mathematical than by psychological tics," Jessica Mann reminds us that Marsh "never wrote anything which touched her emotions more deeply" (*Deadlier than the Male*, p. 224) and that she seemed "unable to force herself into the self-exposure which revealing more [about her characters] would entail" (p. 225).

Yet Marsh's popularity was enduring. In 1949 she was honored in London by the "Marsh Million," an event in which a million copies of her books were published in one day. From January to February 1950, she produced *Six Characters* for a short season at the Embassy Theatre in London. In 1951 Marsh published *Night at the Vulcan* and she was voted "one of the best active mystery writers by an international poll" (*Ellery Queen Mystery Magazine*, September 1951). That same year the British Commonwealth Theatre Company was established under her direction.

In 1962 Marsh's play for children, *A Unicorn for Christmas*, was turned into an opera by David Farquhar. That same year, Marsh delivered the Macmillan Brown Lectures on Shakespearean production (*Three-Cornered World*) and received an honorary doctoral degree from Canterbury University. In 1965 Little, Brown published Marsh's autobiography, *Black Beech and Honeydew*. In June 1966 she became Dame Ngaio Marsh in the Queen's Birthday Honours, and in July 1967 she produced *Twelfth Night* to open the new Ngaio Marsh Theatre in Christchurch. Her final full-scale production was of Shakespeare's *Henry V* in 1972, when she was seventy-seven years old. Her last theatrical effort, in 1976, was a one-man show, *Sweet Mr. Shakespeare*, which she wrote and produced in collabora-

tion with Jonathan Elsom. In March 1978 she received the Grand Master Award of the Mystery Writers of America, along with Dame Daphne du Maurier and Dorothy B. Hughes, at the Second International Congress of Crime Writers. In September 1978 her thirtieth detective novel, *Grave Mistake*, was published. That same year a New Zealand television company released adaptations of four of her novels as the "Ngaio Marsh Theatre." Marsh spent 1979 writing the bulk of her novel *Photo Finish*, which was published in 1980 to mark the fiftieth anniversary of the Collins Crime Club, underscoring the fact that she was indisputably the last of the original Golden Age "crime queens." She then tackled the novel that she had long wished to write: *Light Thickens*, which confronts the theatrical taboo surrounding "the Scottish play" and which provides a superb insight into how Marsh believed *Macbeth* should be staged. She completed this work just six weeks before her death on 18 February 1982.

The Mystery Novels of Ngaio Marsh

Together with Agatha Christie, Dorothy L. Sayers, and Margery Allingham, Marsh is considered one of the four "queens of crime" of British detective fiction. But in 1978 she noted that the genre "has not only proliferated, it has diversified" beyond the "pure" classic form typified by Edgar Allan Poe, Émile Gaboriau, Arthur Conan Doyle, Freeman Wills Crofts, R. Austin Freeman, John Rhode, and Agatha Christie—a format in which the characters, "however animated or enchanting are two-dimensional" ("Entertainments," p. 28). Marsh classified herself with Sayers and Allingham as a practitioner of what she dubbed the "impure" form:

Here the puzzle element is retained, but the author now seeks to present his characters in the round and the style is, or purports to be, sophisticated. This is . . . [impure] because, while the author can be honest, penetrating and exhaustive about all the characters except one, he is obliged to be devious and misleading in his handling of that one—the guilty person. It is this flaw, I think, that sets three-dimensional detective writing, however brilliant, in a minor category. ("Entertainments," p. 30)

Marsh wrote social mystery novels and British country melodramas in a highly literate idiom. John Chamberlain, writing in the *New York Times* in the 1940s, described Marsh as "a writer with a marvelous sense of comedy and a gift for crazy characterization that rivals the ability of the Aldous Huxley of *Chrome Yellow* days"—a judgment that Marsh would have found agreeable, given her admiration for Huxley.

Marsh constructed intricate plots and light, melodramatic, quasi-Wodehousean characterizations in order to parade some quite complex individual characters whose vigorous interaction often eclipses the central crime and its detection. The critic Jean White once observed that with a single phrase Marsh "can limn a character into the memory."

Ngaio Marsh had a very fine sense of humor and was probably first attracted by the comic possibilities of detective fiction. The genre also values civility and style, the disciplined observance of conventions, and a strict economy of expression, all of which are embodied in her own life.

Marsh was always a painstaking craftswoman who paid meticulous attention to detail, continually striving for procedural accuracy. Sir Harold Scott, the commissioner of London's Metropolitan Police from 1945 to 1953, once commented that she had "never put a foot wrong" in her accounts of police investigation. Marsh's concern for precision is also evident in the descriptions of her victims, usually rendered with the sober accuracy of a mortician. In one case, she describes the results of the ingestion of cyanide in a Jonestown-style cult:

> Her face twisted into an appalling grimace. Her body twitched violently. She pitched forward like an enormous doll, jerked twice and then was still. . . . The eyes, wide open and protuberant stared. . . . At the corners of the mouth were traces of a rimy spume. The mouth itself was set, with the teeth clenched and the lips drawn back in a rigid circle. . . . She may have been in a state of ecstasy but she was undoubtedly dead. (*Death in Ecstasy*, pp. 25, 28)

In addition, Marsh used her varied experience as an art student, a touring company actress, coproprietor of an interior decorating shop, and a producer of vaudeville, light pantomimes, revues, and drama. As she once asserted, "All that has been grist to my mill." But she was also a highly meticulous student of criminology, medical toxicology, and legal procedure. Over the years, Marsh amassed a library of reference books on medical jurisprudence, toxicology, police law, pathology, notable trials, and criminology.

As Maurice Richardson once wrote in "The Observer," Marsh led "the cultivated, zestfully characterised, drawing room school of crime fiction." On the other hand, as the English crime novelist P. D. James has observed, Ngaio Marsh sought, "not always successfully, to reconcile the conventions of the classical detective story with the novel of social realism." But classic detective fiction by its nature is not realistic: instead it often presents a very artificial and literary world, reminiscent of early works by P. G. Wodehouse, Evelyn Waugh, and Aldous Huxley. The emphasis is on the handling of facts within the broader framework of fantasy, enchantment, and romance. And, not surprisingly, Marsh's best novels are always markedly theatrical, in their tone if not in their setting.

Characters

As a formative figure in the evolution of the detective novel, Marsh made a small but distinctive contribution to world literature. Like Sayers, Marsh bequeathed to the form the use of a polished literary style; she also developed a more rounded and novelized characterization, particularly in her sustained depiction of her own principals, Roderick and Troy Alleyn.

Jennifer Dunning judged that a "good deal" of Marsh's enduring popularity may be attributed to the character of Roderick Alleyn: "Though more practical, Alleyn was as charming, imperturbable, scholarly and nearly as suave as Dorothy Sayers' Lord Peter Wimsey, that paragon of English detectives," but "Dame Ngaio's detective was more down to earth" (*New York Times* obituary, 19 February 1982).

Marsh frequently noted that the day before she began writing *A Man Lay Dead* she had visited William Cartwright's Dulwich College Picture Gallery in Camberwell. Her father had attended Dulwich, a public school founded by the Elizabethan tragedian Edward Alleyn (1566–1626). Looking for a name for her detective the following day, Marsh decided on "Alleyn" as a compliment to her father.

The novelist Susan Howatch has praised Marsh as "an elegant, disciplined writer" possessed of acute "outsider's insights into the heart of a vanished social world." In penetrating that largely "upper-crust" world, Marsh used her well-heeled sleuth, Roderick Alleyn, who possesses what Colin Watson calls the detective hero's "implicit instrumentality in restoring the rule of right over wrong" (*Snobbery with Violence*, p. 192). Alleyn also clearly conforms to Watson's notion of the Great Detective being "traditionally a somewhat priestly figure, utterly reliable, incorruptible and socially unsmirched" (p. 211). Murder may, in detective literature, be regarded as "a sort of inexcusable faux pas" (*Death in a White Tie*, p. 174), and Alleyn remarks ironically that it is indubitably "a crime in bad taste" (*Killer Dolphin*, p. 229). There is a memorable moment during World War II when Alleyn remarks to Inspector Fox:

"Does it seem odd to you, Fox, that we should be here so solemnly tracking down one squalid little murderer, so laboriously us-

ing our methods to peer into two deaths, while over our heads are stretched legions of guns? It's as if we stood on the edge of a crackling landside, swatting flies."

"It's our job."

"And will continue to be so. But to hang someone—now! My God, Fox, it's almost funny." (*Death and the Dancing Footman*, p. 342)

Alleyn has indeed vented much moral indignation over the death penalty, reflecting the fact that Ngaio Marsh became very strongly opposed to the practice after reading Gerald Gardiner's book *Capital Punishment as a Deterrent* (Gollancz, 1956), in which he advanced the thesis that while "there are a good many things to be said against capital punishment, the real point is that there is nothing whatever to be said *for* it" (p. 117). Such swirling crosscurrents of ethical argumentation are a noteworthy feature of Marsh's novels, focused upon Alleyn's rigorously self-analytical and moral posture. Alleyn often states that murder is the ultimate act of deviance and that the greatest social evil is to destroy a fellow human being.

Kathryne Slate McDorman reminds us that the moment when Marsh created Chief Detective-Inspector Alleyn was an era in England that saw "entrenched class attitudes having to retreat at every advance of professionalism" (Rahn, p. 122). Marsh cleverly made the transition between the aristocratic Lord Peter Wimsey and today's police procedural: "Only Marsh envisions an aristocratic cop whose right hand man is a working-class inspector struggling to meet the requirements to rise in the ranks of Scotland Yard" (p. 123). Indeed, in later books we discover that Roderick Alleyn lectures new recruits (*Clutch of Constables*, 1968) and is the author of a textbook on police procedure (*Vintage Murder*, 1937).

There is no evidence that the two world wars shook Marsh's faith in stable and established order. Rather, Marsh played her part in building what Evelyn Waugh termed "little independent systems of order" of her own, and it is no accident that she once described her chosen genre as a "queer, circumscribed, and isolated form of fiction." Erik Routley, one of Marsh's most perceptive critics, finds this noteworthy: "She is never oppressed by any sense of the evil which righteousness is at war with," and thus she "stays completely and obediently within the humanist tradition of human perfectibility," so that her fictions sail in calm waters "with no intrusions from ethical doubt" (p. 149).

The scholar Stephen Knight has suggested that, in crime fiction, "form and content together create the crucial realisation of a pleasing, comforting world-view" (*Form and Ideology in Crime Fiction*, p. 5). This is demonstrated in Marsh's conservative fictions by her distrust of ideology, whether religious or political. This pattern persists in her final novel in the anachronistic figure of Bruce Barrabell, the actor of "extreme leftist" views (*Light Thickens*, p. 46). Barrabell belongs, improbably, to an organization called the Red Fellowship, to which—even more improbably—this unreliable Equity representative "was asked to report on his tasks." Barrabell has tried to politicize the cast of the Dolphin Theatre, but they have been far too occupied by the challenge of staging *Macbeth* "to listen to new ideas," such as Barrabell's startling assertion that Shakespeare "was a very confused writer. His bourgeois origins distorted his thought-processes" (ch. 5, iv). This stock caricature of Marxism strikes a false note, but it is not Marsh's political ineptitude that is on display. Rather, this is a clue that it is Barrabell who has mental problems; his wife had been "beheaded by a maniac" called the Hampstead Chopper, as Alleyn explains to Fox (ch. 8, ii).

The paradigm of deviance is clearly central to detective fiction and its containment via such safe "oddballs" as Barrabell confirms Knight's thesis. In Marsh's work deviance is customarily split into two distinct streams: the criminally deviant (the killer or the spy, such as the traitor Sir Harold Lacklander in *Scales of Justice* [1955]) and the politically deviant (usually a Communist—a motif that made its first appearance in 1935 with Nurse Banks in *The Nursing-Home Murder* and that resurfaced in 1982 with Barrabell). The outsider per se is often a foreigner, such as Mrs. Anna Bünz (*Death of a Fool* [1956]), who could have been blamed for the homicide, inasmuch as she had suffered ill-treatment at the hands of William Andersen and, having observed the secret rehearsal of the Dance of the Five Sons, knew about the decapitation sequence well in advance. In the final analysis, however, anyone who may be described as antiestablishment is, by definition, "deviant" in the Marsh cosmos.

English County Settings

Though a colonial writer, Marsh received exposure to a refracted image of the English country house ideal via two grand country estates in her New Zealand homeland: Meadowbank, occupied by the Rhodes family, and the Mount Peel homestead, which was memorialized as "Deepacres" in the prologue to *Death of a Peer*. Once established in Buckinghamshire in 1928, Ngaio Marsh began to frequent a large number of English country homes—a practice that greatly helped her in constructing closed-circle puzzles in locales such as Dorset, South Devon, Cornwall, Suffolk, Kent, the Channel Islands, and the fictional "East Mardian" and "Swevenings."

Marsh eagerly followed the Sherlockian dictum that "the lowest and vilest alleys in London do not present a more dreadful record of sin than does the smiling and beautiful countryside" ("The Adventure of the Copper Beeches"). W. H. Auden, pondering on the attraction of an English village setting for writers of detective fiction, suggested that, because it most approximates an Eden in our world, "the greater the contradiction of murder."

The greatest advantage for a detective novelist in a country village lies in the fact that the author does not have to portray events, in Marsh's words, on "too wide a screen." With small groups, a restricted range of characters can be isolated. This principle is vividly exemplified in *Death and the Dancing Footman*. The combination of several volatile and competitive individuals in an isolated Dorset country house allows tensions and anxieties to surface, leading inevitably to a crime of violence.

It was not until her eighth novel, *Overture to Death* (1939), that Marsh actually wrote a traditional English village novel (set in the hill country of Dorset). Marsh's best village setting was offered in *Scales of Justice*, mainly in the form of the memorable Nurse Kettle's warm love of the countryside around the mythical Swevenings, in Barfordshire. It is significant that Marsh chose a Middle English word meaning a dream place for the name of the village. Alleyn informs Fox that the area has had a turbulent past, and yet the opening description of the place emphasizes the stark contradiction of murder in such an idyllic setting:

Nurse Kettle pushed her bicycle to the top of Watt's Hill and there paused. Sweating lightly, she looked down on the village of Swevenings. Smoke rose in cosy plumes from one or two chimneys; roofs cuddled into surrounding greenery. The Chyne, a trout stream, meandered through meadow and coppice and slid blamelessly under bridges. It was a circumspect landscape. Not a *faux pas*, architectural or horticultural, marred the seemliness of the prospect. (p. 3)

Little would Nurse Kettle suspect all the nasty undercurrents of the village, from a fishing rivalry for the mammoth local trout to Kitty Cartarette's murderous designs upon her unwary and honorable husband, which provide the book with its momentum. The plot of this work hinges on the notion of noblesse oblige, which acts as a dominant ethical criterion in Marsh's fictional universe. Lady Lacklander informs the doting Nurse: "You're an Elizabethan, Kettle. You *believe* in degree. You're a female Ulysses, old girl. But degree is dependent upon behaviour, I'd have

you know" (p. 57). The chief constable tells Alleyn that Lady Lacklander runs Chyning and Swevenings: "For some reason they seem to like it. Survival of the feudal instinct you might think" (p. 91). In chapter 12, Lady Lacklander administers her final rebuke to her oddball son, George, regarding his reckless flirtation with Kitty Cartarette, forthrightly scolding him for muddling his values: "You led a completely unscrupulous trollop to suppose that if she was a widow you'd marry her" (p. 293). The fact that such a flirtation led to an unpremeditated act of murder reinforces the seriousness of George Lacklander's dereliction of duty as a member of the gentry.

Marsh gave considerable prominence to drug-trafficking or drug-taking as a cause or motive for murder in novels as diverse as *Enter a Murderer* (1935), *Death in Ecstasy* (1936), *Swing, Brother, Swing* (1949), *Spinsters in Jeopardy* (1953), *Clutch of Constables*, *Last Ditch* (1977) and *Grave Mistake*. Blackmail, theft, and gambling also feature in the Marsh canon. Death by English ritual is central to *Death of a Fool*, occultism mixed with Shakespeariana imbues *Death of a Peer*, and the mafiosi make an unwelcome appearance in *Photo Finish*. P. D. James, surveying the range of criminal focus in Marsh's fiction, observed that this "gently-reared, fastidious lady, is surprisingly ruthless and robust in her dispatch of victims" (p. 2). Examples of this grotesquerie include being hacked with a sheep hook, suffocation in a wool bale followed by crushing in a wool press (*Died in the Wool* [1945]), an impaling and a draft of etching acid (*Artists in Crime* [1948]), a deadly miasma of "Slaypest" weedkiller in an atomizer (*False Scent* [1960]), thalium placed in milk of magnesia, death in agony, and the horrors of an exhumation in *Final Curtain* (1947). Earl Bargainnier recalls "the victim's defenestration after being hit with an iron poker in *Tied Up in Tinsel*, or the sleeping pills being forced into the suffocated victim's mouth in *Grave Mistake*," as late examples of Marsh's gothicism (*Ten Women of Mystery*, p. 97). As a New Zealand journalist wryly observed, "Rarely does Ngaio Marsh resort to bang bang you're dead!" Bargainnier explains what he calls Marsh's "penchant for such bizarre, even outlandish methods of murder" through her belief that the single act of violence that generates the plot dynamic must be striking and original so that "her characters will be shocked, frightened, puzzled and utterly unable to stop talking about it until Alleyn provides the final explanation" (p. 98).

It is a classic Golden Age convention that neither the victim nor the villain can be sympathetic characters for readers, and again Earl Bargainnier has written perceptively about Marsh's application of this principle. He notes that her victims "are either unlikeable—philanderers, rich and disagreeable elderly people, bitchy or neurotic women, blackmailers, etc.—or unknown, so that the reader feels nothing when they die, the major exceptions being *Death in a White Tie* and *Death at the Bar*" (p. 96). Bargainnier observes that Marsh's murderers are "a varied lot":

> With the exception of two spies and six crooks, three of whom have "respectable" covers, Marsh's murderers are amateurs. Their motives are most often greed or the desire to protect themselves from ruin. However, [four] are insane, and there are single examples of murder as the result of sudden anger, of religious mania, and even of a perverted kind of pity. (pp. 96–97)

Notwithstanding all this, it seems clear that Marsh, due to her sheltered upbringing, knew she could not get an authentic grasp of the rather raw contours of the New Zealand experience at that time and, wishing to impress the Rhodes entourage, chose to write in a genre that is itself genteel in both its values and its social assumptions. Knowing that her vision of life was rather circumscribed, Marsh therefore chose to work within a circumscribed literary form, and, as she gained in confidence with that form, she gingered it up. As H. Douglas Thomson wrote of the *roman policier*, "What is the detective story if not a grown-up nonsense rather proud of its education and logic?" (*Masters of Mystery*, 1931).

A classic instance of Marsh's engaging whimsicality as a novelist of manners is to be found in a comment she made in 1949: "I always make a point of keeping the most pleasant-sounding name for the murderer. As he or she is bound to come to an unpleasant end, it seems the very least the author can do" (*Australian Women's Weekly*, 29 January 1949, p. 9).

Theatrical Settings

Marsh's extensive knowledge and experience of theatrical milieux served her well in the scenic construction and brisk dialogue of her exercises in detection. She once expanded on her love of theatrical settings for her fiction: "Theatre people belong comfortably to detective fiction. They're larger than life. They dramatize everything; it's their business to do so." Indeed, detective novels may be said to consist of a series of "scenes," and like plays they have to be rigorously economical in their execution. Also, like stage drama, detective stories are based on linear, continuous plots. The dramatic parallels include an elaboration of the plot after the introduction of the key dramatis personae; incidental characters who may complicate the action for added variety and impact; a clash of personalities and hidden tensions, which find an outlet in the classical catastrophe (here, the dramatic climax of murder); additional drama as the investigation proceeds and meets with inevitable obstacles and resistance; and the standard resolution and denouement.

Indeed, this heightened sense of theatricality strongly inflects Marsh's portraiture of Roderick Alleyn: when he is first in New Zealand, Alleyn recognizes in himself "a kind of nostalgia, a feeling of intense sympathy and kinship with the stage" (*Vintage Murder*, p. 185). He also asks himself: "Is my mere presence in the stalls a cue for homicide?" (*Vintage Murder*, p. 151). It is explained years later in *Killer Dolphin*:

Alleyn was not altogether unused to the theatrical scene or to theatrical people. He had been concerned in four police investigations in which actors had played—and "played" had been the operative word—leading roles. As a result of these cases he was sardonically regarded at the Yard as something of an expert on the species. (p. 111)

The assistant commissioner of police once remarked to Alleyn: "You *are* the man for the job: what with your theatrical past and your dotage on the Bard" (*Killer Dolphin*, Little, Brown, p. 112).

The U.S. scholar Marilyn Rye has commented on Marsh's extensive use of "theatrical metaphors" in her fiction, noting that Alleyn often acts as an audience for criminal performances: "Marsh's detective is always aware of the construction of crime as an aesthetic act." Alleyn thinks very frequently of *Hamlet*, perhaps his favorite Shakespearean play. When eavesdropping on one occasion, he observes wryly to Inspector Fox, "Next stop, with Polonius behind the arras in a bedroom" (*False Scent*, p. 185). When asked to give advice by one Miss Meade, Alleyn thinks of himself as "a mature Hamlet" (*Killer Dolphin*, p. 259). Indeed, at the beginning of Alleyn's fictional appearance, he chided a journalist friend for his "theatricality" (*A Man Lay Dead*, p. 75). In Marsh's thirtieth novel, *Grave Mistake*, Sybil Foster's gardener (who is named, ironically, Gardener—the first possible hint of his falsity) is an exemplary specimen of the histrionic homicide. Alleyn tells Verity Preston that Gardener had long cultivated his air of "the pawky Scot" and that "by and large" he was "a loss to the stage. I can see him stealing the show in a superior soap" (p. 250). A recurrent feature in Marsh's fiction was the notion of murder as a performance event, shown in the classic deaths of Surbonadier (*Enter a Murderer*), Rivera (*Swing, Brother, Swing*), William Andersen (*Death of a Fool*), and Dougal McDougall (*Light Thickens*).

Jane Hipolito has observed that the "basis of Alleyn's enduring appeal and the secret of Ngaio Marsh's continuing success is a superb sense of style ... which seems directly informed by her lifelong attention to literature, art, and especially the theater" (*Mystery and Detection Annual 1972*, p. 233). Hipolito suggests that "the reason for Alleyn's invariable detection of the criminal has always been his dramatic knack of interpreting character" (p. 235). Alleyn, however, should not be considered the only thespian in the Marsh novels: on the contrary, there is a critical congruence of the detective and the criminal as actors—those who may not be what they seem. In this perspective, crime and its investigation are both conceived as games, albeit games in deadly earnest. Indeed, Hipolito astutely noted that for Marsh murder "is essentially histrionics," and that most of her novels are "absolutely concentric" in their design so that "the large drama, the plot of the entire book, is mirrored and concentrated by the smaller, interior drama staged by the characters, much as the play-within-a-play of *Hamlet* strengthens that work" (p. 234). Marsh explicitly worked her practical understanding of the live theater into her craft in the following works: *Enter a Murderer, Vintage Murder*, "I Can Find My Way Out" (1946), *Final Curtain, Killer Dolphin, Tied Up in Tinsel*, and *Light Thickens*.

Marsh's conception of the criminal was derived from her own peculiar sense of the theater and the theatricality of life and its stabilizing rituals. She has used this conceit in many of her works, from the specialized ritual of the jazz group (*Swing, Brother, Swing*); to the parish concert with its preordained "order of service" (*Overture to Death*); to the *Hamlet*-like graveyard ritual in *Grave Mistake*; to the pistol shot at a climax in the Unicorn Theatre play (*Enter a Murderer*); to the deathly, preplanned arrival of a weighty jeroboam at an on-stage birthday party (*Vintage Murder*); to the decapitation in a production of *Macbeth* (*Light Thickens*); and to, above all, the shared cultic experiences that provide suitable occasions for the ritualized murders in *Death in Ecstasy, Spinsters in Jeopardy, Death of a Fool*, and *Tied Up in Tinsel* (1972). As the New Zealand critic Joan Stevens usefully observed, all Marsh's stories are theatrical. "Their dialogue moves with an actor's sense of reaction and timing, the scenes are set with a producer's care for details of significant movement, and there are frequent quotations from dramatic literature" in them.

Critical Reception

Marsh received a generally favorable first notice for *A Man Lay Dead*, her first novel, in the *Times Literary Supplement*, albeit as "Mr. Marsh," whose "manipulation of motive and alibi is neat and effective and repays careful attention" (17 May 1934, p. 362). However, the reviewer did chide that "His [*sic*] methods of detection . . . are somewhat distracting. Detective-Inspector Alleyn is a 'most superior person,' expensively educated, a connoisseur of good living and rather tiresomely familiar." That reservation aside, Nicholas Blake (Cecil Day Lewis) referred to fictional sleuths being toned "down from the Holmes to the Roderick Alleyn type." Marsh's adoption of a more naturalistic detective led the way, as did her creation of Inspector T. R. Fox, who transcended the classical convention of the dull sidekick. "Teddy" Fox becomes the perfect confidant and, at worst, a comic foil—being a discreet, stolid, redoubtable colleague who, when rounding up suspects, reminds Alleyn "of a dependable sheep-dog" (*Hand in Glove* [1962], p. 229).

Not surprisingly, the anonymous reviewer of *Vintage Murder*, in *John O'London's Weekly* (21 May 1937), dubbed Alleyn "that likeable chap," which, Marsh later conceded, pleased her very much "because that was how I liked to think of him: a nice chap with more edge to him than met the eye" (*The Great Detectives*, p. 5). Erik Routley added that Alleyn is "the last romantic hero in detective fiction" and "a very satisfying and amiable kind of superman—the sort of person it is worth trying to keep on the right side of" (p. 147). A later reviewer of *Hand in Glove* described Alleyn as "that comfortably upper-class Scotland Yardbird" (*Life*, 22 June 1962). Yet, as P. D. James asserted, Alleyn, the son of a baronet, "is devoid of social or intellectual elitism," and in Marsh's books "it is the upper-class characters who are petty-minded, treacherous, delinquent or murderous and are judged accordingly," for "in her fiction she never assumed that they were morally superior to less privileged beings ("On Ngaio Marsh," p. 2).

Marsh's name was first linked competitively to Agatha Christie's during World War II, when her American publishers invented the slogan "She has Dorothy Sayers and Agatha Christie wondering if their crowns are on straight." In the years after Christie's death, Little, Brown adopted the words of Dilys Winn's 1977 review that Marsh "writes better than Christie ever did; she is more civilized, knows something about the arts, and her characterizations have more life than Christie's. . . ." Since Christie's death in 1976, it was inevitable that comparisons would be pressed further. What is usually overlooked is the fact that these "crime queens" knew one another personally. Marsh disliked the slogan "It's time to compare Agatha Christie to Marsh instead of the other way around," describing it as "silly" because Christie was too well established for a challenger. Also, Marsh believed that Christie wrote in an entirely different way, being the undisputed master of pure plot-driven puzzles. Marsh pointed out that Christie led the "classic" form and that neither should be compared with the other because of their individual approaches to the crime craft. Marsh always started with people: "I usually start with only the sketchiest idea of the plot and it grows with the book, and that always means an awful lot of rewriting." Marsh worked to transform detective fiction into more rounded, three-dimensional portraiture, noting that she was always more interested in people.

The plot is a chore to me [and] I simply start by thinking of a group of people, then I think, "Well now, which of these people is going to be capable of a crime of violence and under what given circumstances?" Therefore I have got to have a setting and a situation that would single out, as it were, this one character in a group. (interview with Bruce Harding, 1978)

Many of Marsh's minor or occasional characters fit the original meaning of *caricatura*—that is, an overloaded representation with elements of the burlesque—in keeping with her conformity to the game dimension of detective fiction. Thus, we meet Major Hamilton Sweet (*When in Rome*, 1970), who has "a savage white moustache and looked like an improbable revival of an Edwardian warrior," and the elderly lawyers, the Rattisbons, desiccated Dickensian embodiments of their arcane craft. It is this character development, presumably, that led an anonymous reviewer to laud Marsh's melodramas: "They come as a boon and a blessing to men, / The mystery stories from N. Marsh's pen" (*Sphere*, January 1945). All this should remind us that Ngaio Marsh often wrote in a spirit of compassionate deflationary farce, describing her modus operandi, which did not change with new fashions in the genre, as being "in the line of the original detective story, where a crime is solved calmly."

Reviewing *Final Curtain* in 1947, Samuel Marchbanks (the pseudonym of Canadian novelist Robertson Davies) lauded Marsh as "the New Zealander upon whom the mantle of Dorothy Sayers appears to have fallen." Earl Bargainnier has provided a crisp summation of Marsh's achievements as a late Golden Age novelist whose "own acutely clear eyed and sensitive nature have enabled her to incorporate elements of the novel of manners, of romance, of satire, of character and of her personal interests to create a distinctly individual body of work" (*Ten Women of Mystery*, p. 102). After Marsh's death in February 1982, the *Times* of London declared that she "was one of those writers who during the 1930s raised the detective novel to a high level of literary art." At the same time, the noted New Zealand playwright Bruce Mason wrote that her novels "were finely crafted,

richly erudite displays, yet [Marsh] never insisted on her virtuosity, letting one find it for oneself." Marsh would have fully assented to Evelyn Waugh's view that "properly understood style is not a seductive decoration added to a functional structure, it is of the essence of a work of art." The private and fictional worlds of Ngaio Marsh were above all elegant, quiet and refined. Bruce Mason called her a "queen of the spirit" who preferred the formal, the ceremonious, and the graceful in art. In the well-chosen words of the historian Kathryne Slate McDorman, Ngaio Marsh's commitment to excellence, "be it in popular fiction or classical theater, argues persuasively for recognizing her for what she was, a woman of letters" (*Ngaio Marsh*, p. 145).

Selected Bibliography

WORKS OF NGAIO MARSH

NOVELS

A Man Lay Dead. London: Geoffrey Bles, 1934; New York: Sheridan, 1942.

Enter a Murderer. London: 1935; New York: Pocket Books, 1941.

The Nursing-Home Murder (with Henry Jellett). London: Geoffrey Bles, 1935; New York: Sheridan, 1941.

Death in Ecstasy. London: Geoffrey Bles, 1936; New York: Sheridan, 1941.

Vintage Murder. London: Geoffrey Bles, 1937; New York: Sheridan, 1940.

Artists in Crime. London: Geoffrey Bles, 1938; New York: Furman, 1938.

Death in a White Tie. London: Geoffrey Bles, 1938; New York: Furman, 1938.

Overture to Death. London: William Collins, 1939; New York: Furman, 1939.

Death at the Bar. London: William Collins, 1940; and Boston: Little, Brown, 1940.

Death of a Peer. Boston: Little, Brown, 1940. U.K.: *Surfeit of Lampreys.* London: William Collins, 1941.

Death and the Dancing Footman. Boston: Little, Brown, 1941; London: William Collins, 1942.

Colour Scheme. London: William Collins, 1943; Boston: Little, Brown, 1943.

Died in the Wool. London: William Collins, 1945; and Boston: Little, Brown, 1945.

Final Curtain. London: William Collins, 1947; and Boston: Little, Brown, 1947.

Swing, Brother, Swing. London: William Collins, 1949.

U.S.: *A Wreath for Rivera.* Boston: Little, Brown, 1949.

Opening Night. London: William Collins, 1951. U.S.: *Night at the Vulcan.* Boston: Little, Brown, 1951.

Spinsters in Jeopardy. Boston: Little, Brown, 1953; London: William Collins, 1954. U.S.: *The Bride of Death.* New York: Spivak, 1955.

Scales of Justice. London: William Collins, 1955; Boston: Little, Brown, 1955.

Death of a Fool. Boston: Little, Brown, 1956. U.K.: *Off with His Head.* London: William Collins, 1957.

Singing in the Shrouds. Boston: Little, Brown, 1958; London: William Collins, 1959.

False Scent. Boston: Little, Brown, 1960; London: William Collins, 1960.

Hand in Glove. Boston: Little, Brown, 1962; London: William Collins, 1962.

Dead Water. Boston: Little, Brown, 1963; London: William Collins, 1964.

Killer Dolphin. Boston: Little, Brown, 1966. U.K.: *Death at the Dolphin.* London: William Collins, 1967.

Clutch of Constables. London: William Collins, 1968; Boston: Little, Brown, 1969.

When in Rome. London: William Collins, 1970; Boston: Little, Brown, 1971.

Tied Up in Tinsel. London: William Collins, 1972; Boston: Little, Brown, 1972.

Black as He's Painted. London: William Collins, 1974; Boston: Little, Brown, 1974.

Last Ditch. Boston: Little, Brown, 1977; London: William Collins, 1977.

Grave Mistake. Boston: Little, Brown, 1978; London: William Collins, 1978.

Photo Finish. London: William Collins, 1980; Boston: Little, Brown, 1980.

Light Thickens. London: William Collins, 1982; Boston: Little, Brown, 1982.

SHORT STORIES

The Collected Short Fiction of Ngaio Marsh. Edited by Douglas G. Greene. New York: International Palygonics Ltd, 1989.

"The Figure Quoted." In *New Zealand Short Stories.* Edited by O. N. Gillespie. London and Toronto: Dent, 1930.

"Murder at Christmas." *Grand Magazine,* December 1934. Repr. as "Death on the Air." In *Grand Dames of Detection.* Edited by Sean Manley and Sogo Lewis. New York: Lothrop, Lee & Shepard Co., 1973.

"Chapter and Verse: The Little Coppestone Mystery." *Ellery Queen Mystery Magazine* 61: 7–25 (March 1973). Repr. in *Ellery Queen's Murdercade.* New York: Random House, 1975.

"A Fool About Money." *Ellery Queen Mystery Magazine* 62: 114–118 (December 1974). Repr. in *Ellery Queen's Crime Wave.* New York: Putnam, 1976.

"Morepork." In *Verdict of Thirteen: A Detection Club Anthology.* Edited by Julian Symons. New York: Harper & Row, 1978.

NONFICTION BOOKS AND MONOGRAPHS

A Play Toward: A Note on Play Production. Christchurch, N.Z.: Caxton Press, 1946.

Play Production (with drawings by S. M. Williams). Wellington, N.Z.: NZ Education Department, School Publications Branch, 1948. rev. ed. 1960.

Perspectives: The New Zealander and the Visual Arts. Auckland, N.Z.: Auckland Gallery Associates, The Pelorus Press, 1960.

Black Beech and Honeydew. Boston: Little, Brown, 1965. (Marsh's autobiography)

ARTICLES AND ESSAYS

"The Background." *Press* (Christchurch, N.Z.), 22 December 1934.

"German Anecdote." In *Lady Newall's New Zealand Gift Book.* Wellington, N.Z.: P.E.N., 1943.

"Dialogue by Way of Introduction" (with Allen Curnow). In *First Year Book of the Arts in New Zealand.* Wellington, N.Z.: H. H. Tombs Ltd, 1945.

"Theatre: A Note on the Status Quo." *Landfall* 1 (March 1947): 37–43.

"Shakespeare in New Zealand." *Education* 1 (1948): 226–230.

"National Theatre." *Landfall* 3 (March 1949): 66–69.

"The Development of the Arts in New Zealand." *Journal of the Royal Society of Arts* 99, no. 4840 (9 February 1951): 246–259.

"A Note on a Production of *Twelfth Night.*" *Shakespeare Survey* 8 (1955): 69–73.

"New Zealand, Welfare Paradise." *Holiday Magazine* 28, no. 5 (November 1960): 102–108.

"The Hand in the Sand." In *The Mystery Bedside Book.* Edited by John Creasey. London: Hodder & Stoughton, 1960.

"When You Take Up Writing You Are On Your Own." *New Zealand Herald,* sec. I, 26 May 1962.

"Shakespeariana's Lunatic Fringe." *Press,* Christchurch, N.Z., 24 April 1964.

"Stratford-on-Avon." *Atlantic Monthly* (February 1967): 116–118.

"Achievement in Fine Arts." *Times,* 6 February 1963. New Zealand supplement: 6.

"The Quick Forge." *Landfall* 18 (1964): 32–40.

"Early Reading: Dame Ngaio Marsh on *A Noah's Ark Geography.*" *Education* 26, no. 7 (1977): 25.

"Birth of a Sleuth." In *Writing Suspense and Mystery Fiction.* Edited by A.S. Burack. Boston: The Writer Inc., 1977.

"Roderick Alleyn." In *The Great Detectives.* Edited by Otto Penzler. Boston: Little, Brown, 1978.

"Entertainments." *Pacific Moana Quarterly* 3, no. 1 (January 1978): 27–31.

"Portrait of Troy." In *Murderess Ink*. Edited by Dilys Winn. New York: Workman Publishing Co. 1979.

"Women on Women." *Landfall* 130 (June 1979): 101.

"Remembering John Schroder, 1885–1980." *Landfall* 136 (December 1980): 406–407.

PLAYS

Published:

The Christmas Tree. London: S.P.C.K., 1962.

Unpublished:

"Little Housebound." Produced 1922. New Zealand.

"Exit Sir Derek" (with Henry Jellett). Produced 1935. New Zealand.

"Surfeit of Lampreys" (with Owen B. Howell). Produced 1950. U.K.

"The Wyvern and Unicorn." Produced 1955. New Zealand. This play was the basis for the libretto written by Marsh for the opera "A Unicorn for Christmas," produced 1962, New Zealand.

"False Scent," revised (with Eileen Mackay). Produced 1961. U.K.

"Sweet Mr. Shakespeare" (with Jonathan Elsom). Produced 1976. New Zealand. Norwegian Television, 1985, as "Gentle Master Shakespeare."

TELEVISION SCRIPT

Slipknot. Directed by Brian Bell. NZ Broadcasting Corporation, 1967.

BIBLIOGRAPHY

Gibbs, Rowan, and Richard Williams. *Ngaio Marsh: A Bibliography*. Scunthorpe, U.K.: 1990.

BIOGRAPHICAL AND CRITICAL STUDIES

BOOKS

Lewis, Margaret. *Ngaio Marsh: A Life*. London: Chatto & Windus, 1991.

Lidgard, Carolyn, and Carole Acheson, eds. *Return to Black Beech: Papers from a Centenary Symposium on Ngaio Marsh*. Christchurch, N.Z.: The University of Canterbury, 1996.

McDorman, Kathryne Slate. *Ngaio Marsh*. Boston: Twayne Publishers, 1991.

Rahn, B. J., ed. *Ngaio Marsh: The Woman and Her Work*. Metuchen, N.J. and London: The Scarecrow Press, 1995.

ESSAYS OR SHORT ENTRIES

Acheson, Carole. "Cultural Ambivalence: Ngaio Marsh's New Zealand Detective Fiction." *Journal of Popular Culture* 19, no. 2 (fall 1985): 159–174.

Bargainnier, Earl. "Roderick Alleyn: Ngaio Marsh's Oxonian Superintendent." *Armchair Detective* 11 (January 1978): 63–71.

———. "Ngaio Marsh's 'Theatrical Murders.' " *Armchair Detective* 10 (April 1977): 175–181.

———. "Ngaio Marsh." *Ten Women of Mystery*. Ohio: 1981.

Harding, Bruce. "In Memoriam: Dame Ngaio Marsh." *Landfall* 142 (June 1982): 242–245.

———. "The New Zealand Stories of Ngaio Marsh." *Landfall* 144 (December 1982): 447–460.

———. "The Twin Sisters in the Family of Fiction: Pirandellian Praxis and the Dramatic Narratives of Ngaio Marsh." Paper presented to Popular Culture Association, 14 April 1995.

James, P. D. "On Ngaio Marsh." London: 1995.

Jones, Glenda. "Death and the Dame: Ngaio Marsh (1895–1982)." In *A Shot in the Dark*. Derbyshire: Amber Press, 1996.

Mann, Jessica. *Deadlier than the Male: An Investigation into Feminine Crime Writing*. Newton Abbot and London: David and Charles, 1981.

Rahn, B. J. "Ngaio Marsh: The Detective Novelist of Manners." *Armchair Detective* 28, no. 2 (spring 1995): 140–147.

———. "MWA's 50th—Ngaio Marsh's 100th." *Fiftieth Anniversary Mystery Writers Annual*. New York: Mystery Writers of America Inc., 1995.

———. "Ngaio Marsh's Dramatic Detective Novels." *Mystery Scene* 47 (May/June 1995): 15, 55.

Routley, Erik. *The Puritan Pleasures of the Detective Story*. London: Victor Gollancz, 1972.

Shadbolt, Maurice. "Dame Ngaio Marsh: Shakespearian Queen of Crime." *Reader's Digest* 101 (January 1973): 34–39.

Stevens, Joan. "Ngaio Marsh: Artist in Crime." *New Zealand Listener* 8 (May 1972): 13.

Sturm, Terry. "Popular Fiction." In *The Oxford History of New Zealand Literature in English*. Auckland: Oxford University Press, 1991.

Symons, Julian. *The Detective Story in Britain*. London: Longmans, Green, 1962; New York: The Mysterious Press, 1972.

Thompson, Mervyn. "On the Death of Ngaio Marsh." *Landfall* 142 (December 1982): 442–446.

Wilson, Edmund. "Who Cares Who Killed Roger Ackroyd?" 1945. Repr. in *Classics and Commercials: A Literary Chronicle of the Forties*. New York: Farrar, Strauss & Co., 1950.

MARGARET MILLAR
(1915–1994)

MARY JEAN DEMARR

MARGARET MILLAR WAS a mistress of her craft with a gift for the creation of both penetrating characterization and skillfully misleading plotting. Many of her novels are psychological studies of warped characters whose unhealthy views of their worlds impinge tragically on their relationships and on the lives of those with whom they come in contact. Often her novels establish what seems to be a truth about a character or a situation, gradually lead the reader ever deeper into that character or situation, and then, in revealing facts not presented or in reinterpreting those facts, force a radical shift in the reader's understanding of all that has preceded. Occasionally, several successive shifts occur in the last chapter of a novel, but when Millar was writing at her best she managed to create frameworks which made sense in all of the various if changing ways in which they are seen. Thus, her mysteries and novels of suspense may be described as both plot driven and character based. She was highly regarded as a mystery writer during her lifetime, but neither then nor since has she enjoyed the wide popularity merited by her impressive body of fine work.

Life

A Canadian by origin but a Californian by choice, Margaret Ellis Sturm Millar was born on 5 February 1915 in Kitchener, Ontario, to Henry William and Lavinia Ferrier Sturm. She was educated at the Kitchener-Waterloo Collegiate Institute from 1929 to 1933 and at the University of Toronto from 1933 to 1936, where she studied classics and developed the interest in psychiatry which came to strongly influence her crime fiction. In 1938 she was married to Kenneth Millar, who is better known under his pseudonym Ross Macdonald. They met while in high school, as members of a debating team. Her initial success at writing crime fiction suggested to him that he take up the same career; ironically he achieved more renown and acclaim than she. Their marriage, which combined separate and successful careers in the writing of crime fiction, endured until his death in 1983. She had one child, Linda Jane, who predeceased her.

Although she lived from 1942 to 1944 in Ann Arbor, Michigan, and found there the setting for several early novels, most of Millar's married life as well as her career were based in Santa Barbara, California, which, thinly disguised, appears frequently as a setting in her fiction, variously named Santa Felicia and San Felice. After the birth of her daughter, which was followed by complications which made her an invalid for some time, she read and began to write mysteries. She worked briefly as a screenwriter for Warner Brothers (1945–1946) and was a member of the Writers Guild of America West and the Mystery Writers of America, which she served as president in 1957–1958. She received the Edgar award in 1956 for *Beast in View* (1955) and in 1983 for *Banshee* (1983) and was also an Edgar runner-up for *How like an Angel* (1962) and *The Fiend* (1964). Named Grand Master by the Mystery Writers of America in 1982, she was also honored by the Los Angeles *Times* as Woman of the Year in 1965. In addition to her criminous interests, the major passions of her life were ecology and bird-watching. A non-crime publication, *The Birds and the Beasts Were There* (1968), sometimes described as an autobiographical work, is a series of essays and vignettes about her life as a bird-watcher. Although the great bulk of her work consists of novels in the mystery and suspense genres, she also published noncrime novels early in her career. She died in Santa Barbara of a heart attack on 26 March 1994.

Career

Millar began her career as one of the last writers of the Golden Age of crime fiction. Her early books, centering on Dr. Paul Prye and Inspector Sands, tend to fall into familiar Golden Age types, particularly her version of the English country-house mystery. The plots play fair and implicitly challenge the reader to solve each case before its clarification in the last chapter. These novels, then, are derivative, and though they are still readable, they are of interest today primarily for revealing the earliest stage of the career of a writer who was to do much better work later. Three Prye novels and three Sands books constitute most of Millar's apprenticeship, though it should be noted that the detectives appear together in one novel, *The Devil Loves Me* (1942) and that one nonseries book, *Fire Will Freeze* (1944), interrupts the Sands series. These novels were published in the early 1940s, while the second half of the decade was defined by her experimentation with three noncriminous novels—another, her last outside the genre, followed in 1954. *Fire Will Freeze* is, like the Sands

novels which preceded and followed it, a comic novel of the Golden Age type. These novels of the early 1940s were published at a rapid pace—all six books were issued between 1941 and 1945.

With *Do Evil in Return* (1950), Millar began the publication of the nonseries suspense novels which became characteristic of her work for the remainder of her career, and she entered the second major period of her creativity. In the years 1950 to 1964, all nine novels she published are unrelated and appeared less rapidly, usually at about two-year intervals. These books represent some of her best work, novels in which plotting remains strong and characterization takes on far greater depth than previously. After 1964, Millar's publication lapsed until 1970. The seven novels published from that year until the end of her career in 1986 constitute her final body of work. Her novels were by then being published more infrequently, but their quality remained high. Thematic issues tend to be somewhat more fully developed than in her second period, and the quality of plotting and characterization retains its excellence. Once again she creates a series detective, Tomas Aragon, who, like his predecessors, appears in three books. He is, however, a more rounded character than Prye or Sands, and the novels in which he appears are, like the other books written at this time, fine suspense novels.

Series Detectives

In her first period, when she was essentially writing in the tradition of the crime novels of the Golden Age of mystery fiction, Millar's novels show a clear kinship with the work of such authors as Agatha Christie and Dorothy L. Sayers. They are witty comic novels, more apparently plot driven than the finer fiction which followed. She began with the creation of a series detective, Dr. Paul Prye, a psychiatrist, who follows the path blazed by Christie's Hercule Poirot and Sayers' Lord Peter Wimsey. He might, in fact, be considered an

American Wimsey, as seen by a Canadian writer. He is a witty amateur, often detached and frequently making apparently irrelevant remarks which are actually deftly to the point. He detects by seeming not to detect, and he poses as a smart aleck, enabling him to lull suspects into ignoring him, not realizing that he is dangerous to them. His profession of psychiatry, using Millar's deep interest in that area, enables him to understand his suspects and to solve the sometimes very intricate crimes presented to him.

In *The Invisible Worm* (1941), at his first of three appearances, Prye is described as a man "dressed in immaculate white flannels topped with a navy-blue blazer, [who] looked like a man of the world, and the rather quizzical smile in his blue eyes suggested that he was also a man amused at the world" (p. 24). His mysteries are of the traditional type, with a limited number of suspects all pent up together in a single house. The setting of this first novel is the home of a wealthy family in a small town near Chicago, in which Prye is temporarily living as a consulting psychiatrist and observing the wife of the head of the family. In *The Weak-Eyed Bat* (1942), he is again acting as a consulting psychiatrist, this time in a vacation colony of summer cottages in Canada. Although the setting is broader than a single household, there is again a small and clearly limited group of suspects. This novel might be seen as Millar's version of Sayers' *Strong Poison*, for here Prye meets and falls in love with Nora Shane, whose name partly echoes that of Sayers' Harriet Vane, perhaps an indication that Millar was intentionally paying homage to Sayers. However, Nora lacks Harriet's scruples, and by the end of the novel her joke-filled courtship with Prye ends in their engagement. As is his habit, Prye babbles a lot, quotes poetry, and puns wildly. He finally gathers the suspects together in a confrontation scene and explains the truth in a revelation scene.

In the third Prye novel, *The Devil Loves Me*, the setting moves to Toronto but once again presents a closed circle of suspects, this time those in the household of Nora Shane's

family at the time of what was to have been her wedding to Prye. The wedding is interrupted by murder, which Prye investigates, and at the end of the novel Prye and Nora elope, in an ironic counterpoint to Sayers' *Busman's Honeymoon*, in which Lord Peter and Harriet have a traditional wedding and then together solve a murder. The novel does not serve as an introduction to married life for the couple and lacks the thematic depth of Sayers' much finer work. Even though Nora and Prye do compare notes occasionally, Prye's real companion in detection is a new detective, Inspector Sands, "An odd little man . . . the type who encourages you to talk by his very quietness, until you talk too much" (p. 143). In character he is therefore almost the exact opposite of Prye, though the two are similarly presented in that little background information is given about either. In Sands's case, however, this is more significant, because his isolation and detachment are pertinent to both his character and his methods of detection. Both Prye and Sands detect, and each separately is able to explain parts of the solution to the crime. Thus, their unintentional cooperation is necessary for a full solution. In marrying off Prye, this novel brings his detecting career to an end, and he appears no more. Sands, however, appears in two more novels, *Wall of Eyes* (1943) and *The Iron Gates* (1945). Both are psychological novels which study dysfunctional families, in each case with Sands acting as a detached observer who feels contempt for the people whom he must detect. Like the Prye novels, these books are typical of the Golden Age, though Millar's type of detective has changed from the comic eccentric to the detached outsider.

Tomas Aragon appears in three successively published late novels: *Ask for Me Tomorrow* (1976), *The Murder of Miranda* (1979), and *Mermaid* (1982). He reveals his creator's changes of interest by important differences from Prye and Sands. He has an ethnic Hispanic background, unlike Prye and Sands, about whose origins little is revealed but who are both clearly WASPs. He lacks the Golden Age features that defined Prye and, to a lesser extent, Sands. A young lawyer, very junior in his firm, he is married and much in love with his wife, Laurie MacGregor. They have a very modern and long-distance marriage, for she has retained her birth name and is a pediatrician serving her internship in a San Francisco hospital several hundred miles north of Aragon's home in southern California. In all three novels, he consults with her by telephone, conversations which mix laments for their enforced separation with discussions of his current case, on which she is often able to cast light because of her medical knowledge. Laurie finally appears in person at the end of *Mermaid*, when she hastens to Santa Felicia to care for her husband after his near drowning in the novel's climax. Her presence onstage, upsetting Millar's well-defined convention of keeping her in the wings, brings this series to a fitting conclusion. In plotting, characterization, and tone, these three Aragon novels belong with her other suspense novels, not with the earlier books centering on series detectives. These books are dark and far from comic, even when Millar is most sardonically funny. *Ask for Me Tomorrow* most sharply epitomizes this darkness; in it Aragon travels back and forth between Santa Felicia and Baja California, working out a convoluted story of drugs, fraud, vengeance, and obsessive love and eventually learning that, ironically, his very investigation has made him an unwitting accessory to murder.

Characterization

Millar's detectives, both the three series characters and those invented for individual novels, are always male. However, her protagonists are often female, and the majority of her most interesting characters are women. She created a variety of women, both strong and independent characters and weak and pitiable ones. Particularly in her early novels, her women tend to be unpleasant and driven by selfish concerns. In their world it is assumed that people are controlled by selfishness; the women seem to feel nothing outside themselves and to be aware of no possibilities for existence other than a parasitic dependence on or manipulation of others. A repeated motif which is related to the solipsism of these women is the desire to escape, illustrated strikingly by Juanita in *A Stranger in My Grave* (1960); women like Juanita have dreams of wanting to go elsewhere, vague and unrealizable notions that somewhere else there is a better place for them.

Millar's interest in psychology led her to the creation of fascinating characters with greatly varying mental conditions. She skillfully depicted women whose instability led to disasters. Family and other relationships, especially dysfunctional ones, are dissected in a number of novels. Many of these women are manipulative and dependent, and disaster follows their blindly cruel behavior. Some are cold and detached, unable to feel truly, and others are obsessed and passionate, unable to manage their emotions. A number of her most memorable female characters are weak and malleable, controlled by others. Particularly notable examples of this kind of character are Amy in *The Listening Walls* (1959) and Daisy in *A Stranger in My Grave*. Often praised for its psychological power is *Beast in View*, a study in split personality in which the protagonist, Helen Clarvoe; the detective, Paul Blackshear; and the reader are misled about the relationship between Helen, a reclusive and bitter heiress, and Evelyn Merrick, an elusive and malicious telephone stalker who is hounding Helen. Helen's old jealousy of Evelyn's prettiness and popularity as well as the emotional scars of her abusive childhood seem to balance against Evelyn's anger over the forced annulment of her brief marriage to Helen's homosexual brother. Evelyn's attempts to play on Helen's fears and insecurities appear at first to begin to humanize their intended victim, but the eventual outcome, revealed only after several dramatic and shocking twists, is calamitous. Isolation ultimately leads to disaster. Some readers may find this novel's denouement difficult to accept, because aspects of the relationship between Helen and Evelyn that must ultimately be reinterpreted are so firmly established early on.

A device that Millar used with frequency and skill is the pairing of female characters. *Beast in View*, in which Helen Clarvoe and Evelyn Merrick eventually are collapsed into each other, is one dramatic example. Other instances are the very early *The Iron Gates*, in which a deceased first wife and the present second wife are contrasted, with startling results. The device is also used conspicuously with such characters as Kelsey and Alice in *Wall of Eyes*, Mrs. Hamilton and Mrs. Loftus in *Vanish in an Instant* (1952), Thelma and Esther in *An Air That Kills* (1957), Amy and Wilma in *The Listening Walls,* and Daisy and Juanita in *A Stranger in My Grave.*

One of Millar's most interesting uses of paired women occurs in *Do Evil in Return,* her first mature novel. Dr. Charlotte Keating, a successful physician entangled in an illicit affair with Lewis Ballard, is contrasted with her patient, Ballard's wife, Gwen, a feminine woman and apparently a conventionally good wife. A third female character is Violet, young, weak, and pregnant, who comes to Charlotte for help. Charlotte is at first caught between these two other women, both of them tangled up with her lover (Lewis is responsible for Violet's pregnancy). Violet's portrayal is brief, for she soon becomes a murder victim, and Gwen, at first seemingly a sympathetic character, is gradually revealed as a manipulative woman who uses her apparent femininity and weakness to control others. Charlotte's strength is fallible, for it leads her to take risks which almost bring about disaster, and in the novel's conclusion her comfort in the face of the depths of evil she has seen comes from her increasing attraction to police investigator Easter. The contrast between Charlotte, the unconventional woman doctor, and Gwen, the conventional wife, reveals Gwen's hollowness and malice while suggesting that Charlotte's professional behavior, if sometimes foolish and risky, is emotionally normal.

Millar is also notable for her ability to create brief portrayals, little vignettes of characters who are not central to a novel's action but who become so real that the reader remembers them after other aspects of the book are forgotten. Among the most memorable are young Frederic Marshall Quinn III, the epitome of all bratty children, in *The Murder of Miranda. An Air That Kills* is replete with such passing portraits, among them two rascally little boys, a woman whose dog is killed by a car, and an eleven-year-old Mennonite girl who yearns to see the world and dreams of beauty that is forbidden to her by her religious heritage. One final example of many that might be cited is the veterinarian in *The Listening Walls,* who pities anyone who lacks the comfort and companionship of a pet.

Plotting

Millar's skill in plotting is remarkable. She is mistress of the sudden reversal which forces the reader to reevaluate all that has gone before, reinterpreting motive, characterization, and the meanings of events. Perhaps her most typical pattern, inherited from the Golden Age and established in early novels, is the revelation scene in the final chapter. Here, the detective explains the meanings of all that has gone before and reveals the identity of the guilty person. In some cases, this also means for Millar a revelation of identity, for the use of disguise is a repeated motif, as, for instance, in *Wall of Eyes, Rose's Last Summer* (1952), and *Vanish in an Instant.* The image of the web is an appropriate description of her plotting methods, a device she uses several times, notably in the title of her final novel, *Spider Webs* (1986), and as the controlling image (a "web of ropes") in *Vanish in an Instant.* She typically invents several sets of characters who are involved in separate plotlines, and as she gradually reveals more and more about both sets of characters and both lines of action, they draw closer and closer until, in the last chapter, a dramatic and unexpected plot twist brings them together and discloses that they have all along been one story. A good example of this method of plotting is *Vanish in an Instant.* In this novel, the use of a shifting point of view helps to mystify, as it moves between the main character and others surrounding her, gradually casting doubt on her, creating suspicion, and building suspense.

Particularly interesting is the plotting of *A Stranger in My Grave,* which weaves together three main plot strands: Daisy's attempts to recover a lost memory and discover the meaning of a particularly disturbing dream, the story of her father's irresponsible behavior over the years, and the narrative of her husband's infidelity and his child by Juanita. Events which seem at first to be related only through their varied and often indirect connections to Daisy are shown to have deeper and more ominous meanings. The revelations here come in two stages; the murder is explained in the next to last chapter, but the relationships and motives are clarified only in the final chapter. What makes this novel so powerful is the skillful way in which thematic material and characterization are woven together with the dramatic and suspenseful plot. Themes of child neglect in two generations, of racism, and, most centrally, of identity are prominent. Several characters need to find their identity by learning where they have come from. Deceptively a contentedly married "happy innocent" who knows that she is partly role-playing, Daisy becomes obsessed with learning the significance to her past of a mysterious Carlos Camilla, the "stranger in [her] grave." The detective she hires to assist her in her search is himself literally a man of no background, a foundling who was given the name Jesus Pinata by the nun who took him in on Christmas Eve. He later adopted the name Stevens because his original given name led him into too many fights. Unlike Daisy, who learns the identity of Carlos Camilla and his perhaps shocking relationship to her in the novel's last line, Pinata accepts his lack of background.

The plot examines Daisy's relationship with her largely absent father and compares two mother-daughter pairs—one white, wealthy, and comfortable (Daisy and her controlling mother) and one poor and Mexican (Daisy's husband's lover, Juanita, and her mother)—as well as setting Daisy and Juanita against each other. Daisy is rich, unassertive, married, and childless, while Juanita is Hispanic, promiscuous, and the mother of many children. Through these contrasts, a study is made of anti-Hispanic prejudice as well as of class differences. A technical device which first mystifies is the use of unexplained chapter headings, brief italicized passages with thematic connections to the chapters they open. They turn out to be excerpts from the letter which, given in full, constitutes the last chapter of the novel, a letter from Carlos Camilla which finally reveals the information Daisy has been seeking. This novel, because it so neatly weaves the ropes of plot, character, and theme together while also creating memorable and believable characters and well-motivated suspense about them, is a particularly satisfying example of Millar's craft.

Millar's plots cannot be forced into any easy pigeonholes. A number of the novels contain no murder until very near the end, their plots being used to set up the conditions which lead to the killing. In other cases, deaths not originally seen as murders must be reevaluated on the basis of later knowledge. Killings often take place offstage. In *An Air That Kills,* there seems to be no murder until the last chapter, in which the truth about guilt and obsessive love leading to murder is clarified in surprising plot reversals. *The Listening Walls* perhaps takes this practice to its highest degree, for the last line of the novel suggests, however ambiguously, a final twist on what may have been the suicide that opened the novel. Equally unusual, however, is *The Murder of Miranda,* in which there is no death until almost the end of the novel, and that death is a suicide. No murder actually occurs until after the book ends, and that is the presumed conviction and execution of an innocent person. In *Banshee,* again, there is no murder, for a child's death, which has been a catalyst for change in the lives of that child's family and neighbors, turns out to have been accidental. Justice is not always done in the world of these novels, and things are often not what they seem.

Twice, late in her career, Millar based a novel on legal process. Most of *Beyond This Point Are Monsters* (1970) consists of a court hearing. A young widow's petition to have her husband declared dead and his will probated so that she can resume a more or less normal life leads to elucidation of his disappearance. He had been believed murdered, but his body was never found. The court proceedings are clearly and believably depicted. The widow is a sympathetic protagonist, and other interesting characters are portrayed. Additionally, problems surrounding the use of Hispanic migrant workers in southern California are indicated. Similarly, *Spider Webs* follows the trial for murder of a black man accused of killing a white woman. The lives of those concerned in the trial—lawyers, clerk, reporter, witnesses, judge, and defendant—are followed concurrently with the process of the trial itself. The effects of the trial on its participants are studied, and interesting revelations of character—the racism of the prosecutor and the bisexuality of the defense attorney, for example—are made. An ironic verdict is followed by two sudden and unexpected plot twists. In this, her last novel, Millar was still fashioning surprising plots even while accepting the limitations imposed by the actuality of the legal process.

Thematic Concerns

While Millar has generally been most highly praised for her plotting and use of psychologically sound characterization, interesting uses of current social concerns are also present in her fiction. Their presence and the depth with which they are developed increased over time. Her novels, like much detective fiction, tend to mirror the attitudes of the period of writing, if only because the necessary attention to detail in this genre leads to social verisimilitude. The early novels, most obviously per-

haps those featuring Dr. Paul Prye, are set among wealthy people who have servants and are accustomed to a life of leisure and comfort. They seem anachronistic when read today, for both the people and their lifestyle appear mannered and artificial, and while cleverly dissecting their upper-class subjects, they lack the thematic depth of later books.

Among the social themes most obvious in Millar's fiction are such concerns as social class and classism in *Wall of Eyes* and *Do Evil in Return*, drug use in *Wall of Eyes*, dysfunctional families in *Wall of Eyes* and *The Iron Gates*, racism in *Spider Webs*, psychological isolation in *Beast in View*, pedophilia in *The Fiend*, women's concern about youth and beauty in *The Murder of Miranda*, child abuse or neglect in *A Stranger in My Grave* and *Banshee*, migrant workers and illegal immigration in *Beyond This Point Are Monsters*, religious cults in *How like an Angel* and *Ask for Me Tomorrow*, and homosexuality in *Beast in View*, *How like an Angel*, *Mermaid*, and *Spider Webs*.

Of particular interest is the theme of homosexuality, for Millar's attitude changed along with that of her society. In two relatively early novels, *Beast in View* and *How like an Angel*, homosexuality is presented negatively and perhaps even unthinkingly. The homosexual characters are not really examined with any care, and their sexual preference is used simply as a plot device. In *Beast in View*, Douglas Clarvoe's marriage has long ago been annulled because of his homosexuality, and his family's shame and the resentment of his former wife lead to unexpected results years later. The man destroys himself. His ineffectuality, perhaps connected to his "abnormal" sexuality, is emphasized by the fact that his death is accidental in the course of a botched suicide attempt. In *How like an Angel*, homosexuality is again used principally as a plot device. It is the motive for Patrick O'Gorman's murder and the reason for his widow's secrecy. Again, shame is the emotion most immediately associated with homosexuality.

Two late novels reveal how social attitudes

and Millar's assumptions changed. In *Mermaid*, a homosexual teacher, Roger Lennard, is sympathetically depicted. Embittered, he, like Douglas Clarvoe, kills himself. But he is not shown primarily as a weak and ineffectual man. Because he has been excommunicated from his church and is a teacher whose profession will be lost to him by the revelation of his sexual preference, his desperation and bitter defeat are understood and regretted by the novel's detective, Aragon, and by readers. The emphasis is on his victimization by society for his sexuality. And in *Spider Webs*, homosexuality is once again a theme examined briefly with some sensitivity. The defense attorney in this trial novel is a closeted bisexual man who contrasts sharply with the racist prosecutor. This is his last case, for, wearied, he intends to quit after it is concluded. His sexuality is but one aspect of his character and is not used to explain unfortunate behavior or to motivate crimes, as had been the case in the earlier novels which use the theme of homosexuality.

Millar's Worldview

Millar's work is impressive for its variety and its high quality in plotting and psychological examination of interesting characters. Her view of the world tends to be dark, and her examination of social themes does not always take them to great depth. Her early novels, particularly those apprenticeship books with Dr. Paul Prye as protagonist, are sardonically comic. Later books are often terrifying, in terms of both what the reader fears because of the author's skillful creation of suspense and what they reveal about the hidden recesses of the human soul. Justice is elusive, sometimes nonexistent, and people—even identities—are frequently impenetrable. Perhaps the central point of her fiction is that human beings have within them monstrous impulses. The title of *Beyond This Point Are Monsters* is emblematic. It refers to the legends on old maps which label unexplored places on the edges of the known world. The character who explains goes on to say,

> The rest of us have monsters, too, but we must call them by other names, or pretend they don't exist. . . . What a shock it is to discover the world is round and the areas merge and nothing separates the monsters and ourselves; that we are all whirling around in space together and there isn't even a graceful way of falling off (p. 144).

Each of Millar's novels reveals the monsters within which have led to disaster. And not all the books untangle the ropes of her webs, for sometimes in her worlds, after all the plot twists, monsters remain, still resisting exorcism.

Selected Bibliography

WORKS OF MARGARET MILLAR

CRIME NOVELS

The Invisible Worm. Garden City, N.Y.: Doubleday, 1941.
The Weak-Eyed Bat. Garden City, N.Y.: Doubleday, 1942.
The Devil Loves Me. Garden City, N.Y.: Doubleday, 1942.
Wall of Eyes. New York: Random House, 1943.
Fire Will Freeze. New York: Random House, 1944.
The Iron Gates. New York: Random House, 1945. Repr. as *Taste of Fears.* London: Hale, 1950.
Do Evil in Return. New York: Random House, 1950.
Rose's Last Summer. New York: Random House, 1952. Repr. as *The Lively Corpse.* New York: Dell, 1956.
Vanish in an Instant. New York: Random House, 1952.
Beast in View. New York: Random House, 1955.
An Air That Kills. New York: Random House, 1957. Repr. as *The Soft Talkers.* London: Gollancz, 1957.
The Listening Walls. New York: Random House, 1959.
A Stranger in My Grave. New York: Random House, 1960.
How like an Angel. New York: Random House, 1962.
The Fiend. New York: Random House, 1964.
Beyond This Point Are Monsters. New York: Random House, 1970.
Ask for Me Tomorrow. New York: Random House, 1976.
The Murder of Miranda. New York: Random House, 1979.
Mermaid. New York: Morrow, 1982.

Banshee. New York: Morrow, 1983.
Spider Webs. New York: Morrow, 1986.

OTHER WRITING

Experiment in Springtime. New York: Random House, 1947.
It's All in the Family. New York: Random House, 1948.
The Cannibal Heart. New York: Random House, 1949.
Wives and Lovers. New York: Random House, 1954.
The Birds and the Beasts Were There. New York: Random House, 1968.

BIOGRAPHICAL AND CRITICAL STUDIES

Bakerman, Jane S. "Margaret Millar." In *American Women Writers: A Critical Reference Guide from Colonial Times to the Present,* vol. 3. Edited by Lina Mainiero. New York: Ungar, 1981. Pp. 171–173.

Hale, Virginia S. "Margaret Millar (1915–). In *Great Women Mystery Writers: Classic to Contemporary.* Edited by Kathleen Gregory Klein. Westport, Conn.: Greenwood Press, 1994. Pp. 225–228.

Hoch, Edward D. "Millar, Margaret." In *St. James Guide to Crime and Mystery Writers,* 4th ed. Edited by Jay P. Pederson. Detroit: St. James Press, 1996. Pp. 749–750.

Lachman, Marvin. "Margaret Millar: The Checklist of an 'Unknown' Mystery Writer." *Armchair Detective* 3, no. 1:855–888 (1970).

Reilly, John M. "Margaret Millar." In *Ten Women of Mystery.* Edited by Earl F. Bargainnier. Bowling Green, Ohio: Popular Press, 1981. Pp. 225–249.

JOHN MORTIMER
(b. 1923)

SHARON VILLINES

A NOVELIST, PLAYWRIGHT, and former barrister, John Mortimer is known to mystery readers as the creator of Horace Rumpole, a cunning and rumpled old barrister firmly resisting retirement from his eloquent performances in London's famous courthouse, the Old Bailey. This humorous and satirical series, which first appeared in print in *Rumpole of the Bailey* (1978), consists of eleven collections of short stories that were written for adaptation to television Mortimer won numerous honors for his work, including writer of the year from the British Film and Television Academy in 1980 and Commander of the British Empire in 1986.

Mortimer's publishing career began with his novel *Charade* (1947). In the late 1950s, after publishing several relatively unsuccessful novels, Mortimer began writing for stage, radio, film, and television where he found a more appreciative audience. Two of his early plays, *The Dock Brief* and *What Shall We Tell Caroline?*, collected in *Three Plays* (1958), are precursors to his Rumpole series. *A Voyage Round My Father* (1971; radio broadcast, 1963) is an autobiographical account of his life with his father, a deeply formative figure for him. He has also written a humorous legal novel as Geoffrey Lincoln, *No Moaning of the Bar* (1957). Mortimer wrote six plays based on the life of Shakespeare and translated the plays of the French comic playwright Georges Feydeau. Aside from the Rumpole series, Mortimer is best known for his adaptations for television of *I, Claudius* (1972) from the novels of Robert Graves and *Brideshead Revisited* (1982) by Evelyn Waugh. By the early 1980s he had achieved international fame.

Mortimer's later novels are social satire and include *Paradise Postponed* (1985), a sequel, *Titmuss Regained* (1990), and *Dunster* (1992). His collections of interviews with notable men and women, *In Character* (1983) and *Character Parts* (1986), are considered some of the best interviews recorded. Originally published in the London *Sunday Times*, they are remarkable for the quality and sensitivity of the questioning. Mortimer also worked in Hollywood on several films including the adaptation of Henry James's story "Turn of the Screw" as *The Innocents* (1961).

In addition to his work as a writer, Mortimer retired in 1983 from a successful career as a barrister. He established several legal precedents in the area of freedom of speech by defending artists and publishers. His activities also contributed to the Theatre Act of 1968, which abolished government censorship of the stage in England. The Rumpole series is based on his own experiences at the bar, which he has recorded in two autobiographies: *Clinging to the Wreckage: A Part of Life* (1982) and *Murderers and Other Friends: Another Part of Life* (1994). In the late 1990s

Mortimer continued to write novels and to adapt his work and that of others for the stage and television. He lived with his wife and two of his daughters in Oxfordshire, England.

Biography

John Clifford Mortimer was born in Hampstead, London, on 21 April 1923, the only child of Kathleen May (Smith) Mortimer, a schoolteacher, and Clifford Mortimer, a barrister specializing in probate and divorce. His relationship with his mother was distant throughout his life, and his father seemed unaware of his existence during his first years. Mortimer spent his childhood playing in the elaborate family garden or in the kitchen with the maids. On vacations, he and his governess were placed in a boardinghouse away from his parents' hotel. At the age of five, he attended the prestigious Sloane Square school, arriving on the underground with his governess while other students arrived in Rolls Royces.

When Mortimer was ten, his father's vision began to fail as a result of glaucoma, and they started taking long walks together. His father would recite from memory all the Sherlock Holmes stories and choke with laughter as he retold the adventures of Bertie Wooster and his manservant, Jeeves. These walks became so pleasurable that the young Mortimer set his early ambitions on becoming a butler. By the time Mortimer was thirteen, his father was completely blind, a condition that was never discussed in the family. His mother became his father's companion, traveling with him to court each day where she read documents and took notes. Mortimer's father was not an easy person. He would spout poetry at odd times, invite argument by making outrageous statements, and thunder in rage when irritated.

Mortimer attended Harrow, a boarding school for the wealthy and socially elite young boys of England where some students were addressed as "Mister" and others, like himself, were not. In *Clinging to the Wreckage*, he describes living in cold drafty buildings, eating unfathomable food, and sitting through illogical lessons taught by eccentric and unpredictable masters. The only advantage of such an education was that "no subsequent form of captivity can hold any particular terror for you" (p. 33). Lacking athletic ability, he discovered the strategy of losing as quickly as possible or staying in the lavatory reading a book. Being elected to play Richard II in a school play was an early triumph.

Mortimer and his father maintained an unusually close relationship that greatly influenced his work as a writer. When they were together his father recited Shakespeare's plays so regularly that they became the basis for a code and secret family jokes. His favorite writers were Sir Arthur Conan Doyle, P. G. Wodehouse, Mark Twain, and H. Rider Haggard, all of whom can be seen as influences in Mortimer's work. When Mortimer read to his father his own attempts at writing, he received direct and less than encouraging criticism.

Mortimer's father also recounted stories from his days in court and discussed points of law with his son. As the author of the standard text on wills, *Mortimer on Probate*, he took great pride in his ability to challenge or prove the validity of a will by citing an obscure law. He also relished the chance to expose another's adultery by some clever means in order to secure a divorce for a client.

Although he had no desire to do so, Mortimer agreed to read law at Brasenose College, Oxford, as his father wished. World War II had started, and Mortimer believed he would never survive to practice; because of poor health, however, he was not accepted for combat duty. He graduated in 1942 with a bachelor of arts degree and took a job with the Crown Film Unit of the Ministry of Information, where he served for the duration of the war. As "fourth assistant" director, his duties required him to shout "Quiet, please!" at appropriate moments, a task for which he was ill suited but which allowed him to write between takes. Two of his short stories had been published, and he was working on a novel. As his inability to shout at the proper moments began to cut into the film unit's productivity, he was offered the job of scriptwriter. After listening to his first script, his father strongly suggested that after the war it would be a "wise precaution" to take the bar exams.

With the film unit, Mortimer learned to write dialogue, construct scenes, and turn ideas into visual drama. But his idea of drama was the Shakespeare of John Gielgud and Laurence Olivier and his favorite writers were Charles Dickens, Anton Chekhov, Ronald Firbank, Evelyn Waugh, P. G. Wodehouse, Raymond Chandler, and Lytton Strachey. After struggling daily with such memorable lines as "Roger and out!" and receiving several rejections of his novel, Mortimer returned to studying the law. His first novel, *Charade,* was finally published, but his writing commissions remained as stimulating as creating the captions for the Hall of Coal in the Great 1951 Exhibition. He was called to the bar in 1948.

During this time, Mortimer fell in love with Penelope Ruth Fletcher Dimont, a writer and neighbor who was married and the mother of four children. After hiring a private detective to prove their adultery so she could be divorced, they were married in 1949. At the age of twenty-six, Mortimer was suddenly supporting a family of six.

He began his law career by preparing cases for his father, gradually taking over his practice. When British law was reformed to allow divorces on grounds other than adultery, cases became simpler and shorter, and less remunerative. To supplement his income Mortimer continued writing and expanded his practice by "taking to crime."

In the late 1950s, in reaction to the severe loneliness he felt after his father's death and to what he felt were often whimsical decisions by judges, Mortimer decided to leave the bar. While his father enjoyed the obscure details of the law, Mortimer viewed it as a maze through which clients must be led to safety. Even the best laws could be intolerable when applied to individual situations. But then he was asked by Amnesty International to de-

fend a writer in Africa. He arrived to find the Nigerian playwright Wole Soyinka preparing for his university degree and reading P. G. Wodehouse while waiting to be tried for interference in an election in a country that was ill prepared to run a proper election.

The transposition of the absurd trappings of yellowing horsehair wigs, white neck bands, and baggy gowns to a region that was still establishing a democratic government made Mortimer acutely aware of the importance of the legal system and particularly the presumption of innocence. He returned to London with a new respect for the law and a greater commitment to the defense of free speech. Mortimer was named Queen's Counsel in 1966 and Master of the Bench in Inner Temple in 1975.

In 1971 Mortimer and his first wife obtained a divorce and in 1972 he married Penelope Gollop, a woman twenty-three years younger than himself. It was during this time that he began developing the character who became a classic in the field of mystery fiction.

Rumpole of the Bailey

Mortimer's first successful work was a one-hour radio play, *The Dock Brief,* which was broadcast by the British Broadcasting Corporation (BBC) in 1957. The story was based on a scene that Mortimer had witnessed in his early years at the bar, which he describes in *Clinging to the Wreckage.* Before the establishment of Legal Aid, if defendants, who sat in the "dock," were unable to pay they could choose any robed figure in the courtroom to defend them and the court would pay one guinea (less than five U.S. dollars). Busy barristers would exit the courtroom as quickly as possible when a "dock brief" was announced. The barristers who needed cases would sit on a long bench, as "wigged wallflowers" (*Wreckage,* p. 128), in hope of being chosen.

Using this image, Mortimer paired an unsuccessful barrister, Morgenhall, with an unsuccessful criminal. The barrister and the accused engage in a dramatic enactment of a successful defense that produces such an outrageous result that the defendant is acquitted because of the incompetence of his counsel. Both the defendant and the lawyer leave the court ecstatic with the illusion of their success.

The play was so well received that the BBC paid Mortimer an unprecedented extra twenty pounds. Even his father approved. In *Clinging to the Wreckage*, Mortimer explains that something about writing for voices coming through the air unconnected to a visible setting enabled him to "break the sound barrier of pure naturalism." By abandoning the search for literal models he had discovered "a new level of reality" and achieved a new satisfaction with his writing (p. 128).

Mortimer says in *Murderers and Other Friends* that when he was in his early fifties, he decided to write about a detective, "a Sherlock Holmes or a Maigret, to keep me alive in my old age" (p. 74). He made Rumpole a criminal-defense lawyer in honor of the Old Bailey hacks he had known and admired. Typical of the use of contrasts in Mortimer's comedy, the Old Bailey is a stately Edwardian palace with a dome, murals, marble statues, and underground cells for the best villains in London. Its official name is the Central Criminal Courts, and it was built on the site of the infamous Newgate Prison on Old Bailey Street. Serious crimes are generally not tried there because security is better at newer facilities.

Mortimer gave Rumpole many of his father's characteristics, including his habit of quoting poetry at odd moments, and his father's uniform: "a black jacket and waistcoat, striped trousers and cigar ash on the watchchain, although I left out my father's spats" (p. 74). He also added the early relationship between himself and his father in the scenes between Rumpole and his son. They walk in Hyde Park and Kensington Gardens, where the son plays Sherlock Holmes while Rumpole plays Watson. They try to deduce the private lives of the other strollers from their shoe shines and the handkerchiefs sticking out of

their sleeves. And later, still as Holmes and Watson, they dissect the proceedings of the day in court.

Like Mortimer's father, Rumpole quotes William Wordsworth, although in very bad moments he falls back on Lord Byron. Mortimer gave Rumpole a colleague's habit of calling impossible judges "old darling," and because he wanted him to have as hard a time at home as he had in court, he gave him a powerful wife, Hilda. "I began by writing some odd speeches for him and found that as soon as he stepped on to the page, he began to speak in his own voice, which is undoubtedly the greatest favour a character can do for you" (p. 74).

Although the Rumpole stories are conceived to be adapted as television plays and are generally broadcast before they are published, they are fully crafted as prose fiction. They benefit, however, from the television adaptation in that the character of Rumpole has been developed not only by the author but by the actor who plays him. In *Murderers and Other Friends*, Mortimer explains that he wanted Alastair Sim to play the part but "sadly Mr Sim was dead and unable to take it on" (p. 75). Both the producer and director suggested Leo McKern. For Mortimer, Leo McKern has become Rumpole and even enriched him. "Leo comes from Sydney, and Australians are born with one great advantage: they have almost no respect for authority. Rumpole's disdain for pomposity, self-regard, and the soulless application of the letter of the law without regard for human values, came naturally to him." McKern has played the part for over twenty years; "when Rumpole speaks in his own voice, it is always Leo's voice also" (p. 75).

Rumpole and the British Legal System

Like Mortimer and his father, Rumpole is a barrister. In the British legal system, there are two kinds of lawyers: "solicitors," who handle all legal matters except trials, and "barristers," who function solely as trial lawyers or "advocates before the courts." Solicitors choose and hire barristers for their clients as needed. Each time Rumpole defends one of the Timsons, a multigenerational family of unsuccessful but hardworking and principled petty thieves who provide Rumpole's only steady income, they are brought to him by their solicitor, Mr. Bernard.

Barristers receive "instructions" from the solicitor and the client in the form of "briefs," which include the plea and other stipulations about how the case is to be handled. In the early stories, Rumpole feels constrained by these instructions and argues over them. The later Rumpole just acts according to his conscience, particularly when he discovers he has been hired to lose a case because someone is being framed or because it is more politically expedient to be convicted and then martyred.

Though solicitors can choose to become barristers, or the reverse, the two professions have different governing bodies and preparations. Only barristers can become judges. While solicitors may form firms, barristers may only function independently. They usually share offices (chambers) and a clerk who manages the assignment of briefs, arranges fees with solicitors, and handles collections. Recurring themes in the Rumpole stories are suspicions that the clerk is pilfering coffee money and a debate over whether the clerk should be paid a percentage of fees or a salary. Rumpole regularly defends the clerk against the overly conscientious head of chambers who is elected to manage the office.

Barristers may represent clients in any of the countries under the rule of the Crown; thus Rumpole travels. Barristers may take both civil and criminal cases as either prosecution or defense. In court, the defense and the prosecution counsels sit side by side at one table facing the judge. Rumpole regularly mutters comments and objections to the opposing counsel at his elbow. Because Rumpole always defends, he and his associates often appear in cases against each other. Used as a plotting device, this increases the tensions between them and gives the reader a continued relationship with a few central characters.

In court, barristers are referred to as "counsel" and address each other as "my learned friend." Barristers address the judge by first saying "in my humble submission" or "with the very greatest respect." Rumpole's language can become even more flamboyant, particularly when he doesn't like the judge.

The courts of law are the Queen's (or the King's) Courts. The division between those who advocate in court and those who prepare and execute wills and contracts dates from 1340, when the role of advocate could be assumed only by someone who was considered appropriate to address the Crown. Barristers were wealthy and presumably educated nobility who were "giving their services" to the people. As a result, barristers dress elaborately in wigs and gowns in order to be "seen" or "recognized" by the court. Rumpole is often untidy in his dress, and court is stopped on one occasion because of his loose neck band.

As "descendants of nobility," barristers do not themselves negotiate or collect fees from clients and cannot sue if they are not paid. In "Rumpole and the Last Resort" (1983), Rumpole establishes an elaborate ruse to get a check from a solicitor who has not paid him for ten years. In fact, barristers are not well paid—particularly barristers like Rumpole who are not socially presentable, prefer criminal cases to lucrative civil cases, and do not publish on the fine points of law. He probably makes the salary of a very good secretary and has no pension.

Barristers are governed by four law societies called the Inns of Court: Gray's Inn, Lincoln's Inn, Inner Temple, and Middle Temple. To become a barrister, one must either have a law degree or pass qualifying exams. Students register with an Inn and when they pass their exams, the Inn "calls to the bar." At this point the student must do a pupilage, serving as an understudy (or a pupil) to a barrister for twelve months. The Inns of Court supervise the professional life of the barrister, including disbarment. The Inns are administered by their senior members, masters of the bench, called "benchers." Rumpole is a member of the Inner Temple and gains pupils by default when they do not work out elsewhere. Judges regularly threaten to report him to Inner Temple, usually for lack of respect.

All barristers are "junior counsel" until designated "Queen's Counsel" (QC), which requires at least ten years' experience. If there were a king, they would be King's Counsel. To become a QC, one applies to the lord chancellor who recommends to the queen (or king). Becoming a QC is referred to as "taking silk" because a QC wears a silk gown. QCs are barred from any sort of routine work and only appear in more important cases. They are known as "leaders" because they are followed into court by one or two assisting junior counsels. Rumpole often brags of the Penge Bungalow murder, which he won as a young barrister without a leader. He is sometimes expected to follow one of his younger associates into court, because some of them are QCs. Rumpole, to his ambitious wife's great disappointment, is repeatedly passed over.

Critical Analysis

In the character of Rumpole, Mortimer has fully achieved the goal he set for his writing in *Murderers and Other Friends*, where he says he hoped it would always be "about two feet above the ground, a little larger than life, but always taking off from reality" (p. 77). His work is characterized by a depiction of class consciousness as keen as that of Evelyn Waugh and by characters as eccentric as those of Charles Dickens. He uses a comedic structure as accomplished as that of Georges Feydeau and a humor as droll and loving as that of P. G. Wodehouse.

The first Rumpole stories are set in 1965 and told as memoirs in the first person: "I, Horace Rumpole, barrister at law, 68 next birthday, Old Bailey Hack . . . take up my pen . . . in order to write my reconstructions of some of my recent triumphs (including a number of recent disasters) . . ." (*Rumpole of*

the Bailey, p. 1). By 1983 in "Rumpole and the Sporting Life," Rumpole has caught up with himself, and the remaining stories occur in the present, unfolding as they progress.

At this point, Mortimer also begins playing with form, not always successfully. Rumpole begins telling parts of the stories in third person, explaining, sometimes laboriously, that he is reconstructing accounts as told to him by third parties. In "Rumpole and the Last Resort," the entire middle of the story is a first-person account by his pupil Fiona Allways, who is cleaning up Rumpole's papers when it is suspected that he has died.

Mortimer's most common plot structure presents three stories in counterpoint: a criminal trial, a conflict in chambers, and a long story told by Hilda that Rumpole tries to ignore. For instance, in "Rumpole and the Man of God" (1979), Rumpole is presented with the case of a cleric who is accused of shoplifting, Hilda insists that he help her with errands, and a colleague in chambers brings a woman to dinner whom Rumpole recognizes as a former client. After carrying a shopping basket for Hilda, and recognizing his friend's new love as a criminal, Rumpole realizes that the priest did not shoplift the items in his basket as he walked out of the department store. It was his sister, who had dragged him along on her shopping trip, who was the culprit.

Since Mortimer's stories are always written quite rapidly, he has accidentally had Rumpole living in different places. One character, a private detective named "Fig" Newton, has been given different names to account for the initials F. I. G. There are also repetitions that become tiresome when the stories are read consecutively. Characters are repeatedly reintroduced, and anecdotes and descriptions duplicated.

The early stories include almost poetic descriptions that are wonderfully apt and cleverly drawn but that sometimes distract from the whole. With *Rumpole's Return* (1980), the only novella-length work featuring Rumpole, the writing becomes much more fluid. Still rich with metaphorical description, this story is more than a set of clever observations linked to an answer. As the series progresses, Mortimer develops a smoother narrative and begins building more suspense by only partially revealing information or withholding it from the reader.

Although the Rumpole characters do not age noticeably, they do change. In the beginning, Rumpole is tormented daily by judges who disrespect him and clients who doubt his ability. Judge Bullingham is suspicious of all defense lawyers and decides against Rumpole's clients automatically. Rumpole is an embarrassment to his colleagues, who believe that criminal work is "downmarket." Rumpole's wife controls his home life, and while he mocks her behind her back, calling her "She Who Must Be Obeyed" after Queen Ayesha in H. Rider Haggard's *She,* he suffers in silent resentment. His son decides to become a dread sociologist and moves to America. The only place Rumpole feels safe is in Pommeroy's Wine Bar, where he drinks a cheap cooking claret he calls Chateau Fleet Street or Chateau Thames Embankment and tells himself old legal anecdotes.

Twenty years later Rumpole is still tormented by Judge Bullingham, but he spends more time outside the courtroom investigating and circumventing the power of the judge. He is now more in awe of Hilda, who has become a more sympathetic character and participates more actively in Rumpole's life, even in his cases. Rumpole even expresses his appreciation of Hilda who, he now recognizes, keeps him on course. Rumpole is still happy with Pommeroy's Wine Bar, where he is now joined by many associates. His disappointments over not becoming a fixture on *News of the World* or not becoming a QC fade, and he becomes a much stronger character by becoming legendary. Rather than the eloquent wooer of a jury, he becomes the eloquent defender of freedom and the "golden thread" of justice, which assumes innocence until guilt is proved beyond a reasonable doubt. He remains a down-in-the-heels, cunning, and not altogether aboveboard advocate, but he loves his work and has learned to subvert any forces he cannot control.

As the narratives become smoother, the comedic dialogues become stronger and are destined to become classics. In *Clinging to the Wreckage,* Mortimer discusses the nature of comedy and its role in his writing: "The world of farce is necessarily square, solid, respectable and totally sure of itself, only so it can be exploded. . . . It is impossible to be funny about funny people . . ." (p. 175). Adapting this principle to the artificiality and formality of the court set the stage for total hilarity. Mortimer's own experience had taught him that humor worked in a particular way in court. In freedom of speech cases, making the judge and jury laugh enabled him to win cases by questioning the obscene nature of the material found offensive. "Laughter is as much an enemy to the laws of censorship as it is to the heavy breathing and appalling humourlessness of most pornography" (p. 186).

As mysteries, the Rumpole stories evolve from humorous legal puzzles to investigations. In the early stories, Rumpole deduces the truth from courtroom testimony or his own superior knowledge, pieces together bits of information gained in seemingly disparate conversations, and traps witnesses into confessions through clever cross-examination. When this fails, he seduces the jury into believing the unbelievable. In the mature stories, when the action becomes more complex and the characters more human, Rumpole still relies on his well-developed abilities to manipulate people, but he also becomes more active in finding the information he needs and less reliant on simply observing.

"Rumpole and the Bright Seraphim" (1987) marks the point where he begins to take action. Sent to Germany to defend a Royal Air Force trooper accused of murder, Rumpole knows little of the laws of courts-martial and wonders why he was sent. The early Rumpole would have considered knowing too much about the law or actually reading briefs severely limiting in court, but this Rumpole questions the referring officer and details the information given in the official report. He then physically examines and reconstructs the scene of the crime. The solution is carefully detailed and accounts for the actions of several people. While the later stories still include discussion of legal principles and points of law, the structure is nearer that of more traditional detective stories with evidence presented, an investigation done, the criminal uncovered, and the story summed up.

Rumpole also begins to take a more active part in defending himself, however underhandedly. In "Rumpole and the Angel of Death," he encourages colleagues to take actions that will produce the opposite of their desired result but that will preserve his place in chambers or effect justice as he sees it. When an efficiency manager (and former caterer) wants Rumpole to plead guilty on more briefs to improve time-income ratios, Rumpole encourages him to propose a swinging singles party as a good-bye party for the old clerk the caterer is replacing. The head of chambers is Soapy Sam Ballard, president of the organization Lawyers as Christians, who Rumpole well knows is a complete prude. The caterer is never seen again. In other stories, Rumpole turns to blackmailing his colleagues on behalf of each other. He makes it clear, for example, that he knows that the same prudish head of chambers has falsified his tax statements but if he overlooks the suspicious handling of coffee money by the chamber's clerk, Rumpole will not report him. Many of the incidents that Mortimer attributes to Old Bailey judges, to clients, or even to Rumpole, seem exaggerated. But Mortimer insists that his major task in writing about the Old Bailey is a process of calming the truth until it has some degree of credibility. He insists that one incident in which Judge Bullingham breaks into one of Rumpole's final speeches to give a sports tournament score is taken directly out of a court proceeding in one of his major freedom-of-speech cases.

A great influence on Mortimer's practice of the law was his work in the theater. As he explains it in *Clinging to the Wreckage* (pp. 95ff, 181ff), he saw the advocate as an actor who must convince the audience of the validity of his story—a view his father taught him in their long discussions of the law. Mortimer considered his own style "distressingly flamboyant" (p. 97). Rumpole readily uses the tricks of ham actors to distract the jury from listening to opposing counsel's arguments and plans his dramatic closings and curtain lines carefully with a physical display of emotion.

For Rumpole, these histrionics are necessary in order to defend his clients from the excesses of the law and the whims of the judge. For him, the law is about people and their lives. Civil law is only about money. Rumpole loves criminal law because it goes to the heart of life, love, and liberty. While murder is the most serious of crimes, it is often the most understandable. People commit murder who would be incapable of embezzlement or exceeding the speed limit. In "Rumpole and the Younger Generation," Rumpole says, "A person who is tired of crime . . . is tired of life" (*First Omnibus*, p. 16).

Selected Bibliography

WORKS OF JOHN MORTIMER

THE RUMPOLE SERIES

The first Rumpole story was written for radio and broadcast as "Rumpole of the Bailey" by the British Broadcasting Corporation on 12 March 1975. It was first published as "Rumpole and the Confession of Guilt" in *Regina v. Rumpole* [*Rumpole for the Defence*] (1981). The regular television broadcasts of the Rumpole series began in 1978.

Rumpole of the Bailey. Harmondsworth, Eng., and New York: Penguin, 1978. Includes "Rumpole and the Younger Generation," "Rumpole and the Alternative Society," "Rumpole and the Honourable Member," "Rumpole and the Married Lady," "Rumpole and the Learned Friends," and "Rumpole and the Heavy Brigade."
The Trials of Rumpole. Harmondsworth, Eng., and New York: Penguin, 1979. Includes "Rumpole and the Man of God," "Rumpole and the Showfolk," "Rumpole and the Fascist Beast," "Rumpole and the Case of Identity," "Rumpole and the Course of True Love," and "Rumpole and the Age for Retirement."
Rumpole's Return. Harmondsworth, Eng.: Penguin, 1980; New York: Penguin, 1982.
Regina v. Rumpole: Rumpole for the Defence and Rum-

pole's Return. London: Allen Lane, 1981. Includes reprint of *Rumpole's Return* (1980) and a new collection of short stories as *Rumpole for the Defence:* "Rumpole and the Confession of Guilt," "Rumpole and the Gentle Art of Blackmail," "Rumpole and the Dear Departed," "Rumpole and the Rotten Apple," "Rumpole and the Expert Witness," "Rumpole and the Spirit of Christmas," and "Rumpole and the Boat People." The title *Regina v. Rumpole* was not repeated. *Rumpole for the Defence* was later published as a single title (London: Penguin, 1992).

Rumpole and the Golden Thread. Harmondsworth, Eng., and New York: Penguin, 1983. Includes "Rumpole and the Genuine Article," "Rumpole and the Golden Thread," "Rumpole and the Old Boy Net," "Rumpole and the Female of the Species," "Rumpole and the Sporting Life," and "Rumpole and the Last Resort."

Rumpole's Last Case. Harmondsworth, Eng.: Penguin, 1987; New York: Penguin, 1988. Includes "Rumpole and the Blind Tasting," "Rumpole and the Old, Old Story," "Rumpole and the Official Secret," "Rumpole and the Judge's Elbow," "Rumpole and the Bright Seraphim," "Rumpole and the Winter Break," and "Rumpole's Last Case."

Rumpole and the Age of Miracles. Harmondsworth, Eng.: Penguin, 1988; New York: Penguin, 1989. Includes "Rumpole and the Bubble Reputation," "Rumpole and the Barrow Boy," "Rumpole and the Age of Miracles," "Rumpole and the Tap End," "Rumpole and the Chambers Party," "Rumpole and Portia," and "Rumpole and the Quality of Life."

Rumpole à la Carte. Harmondsworth, Eng., and New York: Penguin, 1990. Includes "Rumpole à la Carte," "Rumpole and the Summer of Discontent," "Rumpole and the Right to Silence," "Rumpole at Sea," "Rumpole and the Quacks," and "Rumpole for the Prosecution."

Rumpole on Trial. Harmondsworth, Eng., and New York: Penguin, 1992. Includes "Rumpole and the Children of the Devil," "Rumpole and the Eternal Triangle," "Rumpole and the Miscarriage of Justice," "Rumpole and the Family Pride," "Rumpole and the Soothsayer," "Rumpole and the Reform of Joby Jonson," and "Rumpole on Trial."

Rumpole and the Angel of Death. Harmondsworth, Eng.: Penguin, 1995; New York: Viking Penguin, 1996. Includes "Rumpole and the Model Prisoner," "Rumpole and the Way Through the Woods," "Hilda's Story," "Rumpole and the Little Boy Lost," "Rumpole and the Rights of Man," and "Rumpole and the Angel of Death."

COLLECTED RUMPOLE STORIES

The First Rumpole Omnibus: Rumpole of the Bailey, The Trials of Rumpole, Rumpole's Return. Harmondsworth, Eng., and New York: Penguin, 1983.

The Second Rumpole Omnibus: Rumpole for the Defence, Rumpole and the Golden Thread, Rumpole's Last Case. Harmondsworth, Eng.: Penguin, 1987; New York: Viking, 1987.

The Best of Rumpole. Harmondsworth, Eng.: Penguin, 1993; New York: Viking, 1993. Introduction by the author. Includes seven stories chosen by the author: "Rumpole and the Younger Generation," "Rumpole and the Showfolk," "Rumpole and the Tap End," "Rumpole and the Bubble Reputation," "Rumpole à la Carte," "Rumpole and the Children of the Devil," and "Rumpole on Trial."

The Third Rumpole Omnibus: Rumpole and the Age of Miracles, Rumpole à la Carte, Rumpole and the Angel of Death. Harmondsworth, Eng.: Penguin, 1997; New York: Penguin, 1998.

SELECTED LONG FICTION

Several of Mortimer's works of long fiction contain story elements commonly found in the mystery genre. In *Paradise Postponed*, the story involves the mysterious contents of a will; in *Dunster*, alleged old war crimes lead to charges of libel; and in *Felix in the Underworld*, a mild-mannered writer of genteel novels is confronted with blackmail and involved in a reported murder. But while he uses criminal acts in his stories, most critics agree that his novels are more closely related to social satire and comedy, at which he is considered to be a master.

Charade. London: The Bodley Head, 1947; New York: Viking, 1986.

No Moaning of the Bar. By "Geoffrey Lincoln." London: Geoffrey Bles, 1957.

Will Shakespeare: The Untold Story. New York: Delacorte Press, 1977.

Paradise Postponed. Harmondsworth, Eng.: Penguin, 1985; New York: Viking Penguin, 1986.

Titmuss Regained. Harmondsworth, Eng., and New York: Penguin, 1990.

Dunster. Harmondsworth, Eng.: Penguin, 1992; New York: Viking Penguin, 1993.

Felix in the Underworld. New York: Viking, 1997; London: Penguin, 1998.

AUTOBIOGRAPHIES

Clinging to the Wreckage: A Part of Life. London: Weidenfeld & Nicolson, 1982.

Murderers and Other Friends: Another Part of Life. Harmondsworth, Eng.: Penguin, 1994; New York: Viking, 1995.

PLAYS

Mortimer has written extensively for stage, radio, film, and television and has done numerous adaptations for television and film. A list of these works as well as the dates on which they were first performed is available in *Contemporary Authors.* New Rev. Ser., vol. 21. Edited by Deborah Straub. Detroit: Gale, 1987. Pp. 315–316. A selected list follows.

Three Plays. London: Elek, 1958; New York: Grove, 1962.

The Innocents (with Truman Capote and William Archibald). 1961. Screenplay.

A Voyage Round My Father. London: Methuen, 1971. Radio broadcast, 1963. Produced, London, 1970.

I, Claudius. 1972. Teleplay.

Brideshead Revisited. 1982. Teleplay.

The Dock Brief. Harmondsworth, Eng.: Penguin, 1982. Includes *The Dock Brief, A Voyage Round My Father,* and *What Shall We Tell Caroline?*

OTHER NONFICTION

In Character. London: Allen Lane, 1983.

Famous Trials. Edited by Harry Hodge and James H. Hodge; selected and introduced by John Mortimer. London: Viking, 1984; New York: Penguin, 1984.

Character Parts. London: Viking, 1986; New York: Penguin, 1986.

The Oxford Book of Villains. Edited by John Mortimer. Oxford and New York: Oxford University Press, 1992.

ARCHIVES

Mortimer's manuscripts are collected at Boston University and University of California, Los Angeles.

BIOGRAPHICAL AND CRITICAL STUDIES

Each of John Mortimer's books and plays is reviewed extensively. Listings of those reviews are available in the major indexes of periodicals and newspapers.

Domnarski, William. "Will the Defendant Please Rise." *Virginia Quarterly Review* 59, no. 3: 523–531 (summer 1983).

Hartill, Rosemary. *Writers Revealed.* New York: P. Bedrick Books, 1989.

Hayman, Ronald. *British Theatre Since 1955: A Reassessment.* Oxford and New York: Oxford University Press, 1979.

Herbert, Rosemary. "Murder by Decree: An Interview with John Mortimer." *Armchair Detective* 20, no. 4: 340–349 (fall 1987).

"John Mortimer." In *Contemporary Literary Criticism,* vol. 28. Edited by Jean Stine. Detroit: Gale, 1984. Pp. 281–289.

"John Mortimer, 1923." In *Contemporary Literary Criticism,* vol. 43. Edited by Daniel Marowski and Roger Matuz. Detroit: Gale, 1987. Pp. 303–309.

Pritchett. V. S. "John Mortimer." *New Yorker,* 25 October 1982: 166, 169–171.

Ross, Jean H. "John Mortimer." In *Contemporary Authors.* New Rev. Ser., vol. 21. Edited by Deborah Straub. Detroit: Gale, 1987. Pp. 315–321.

Rusinko, Susan. "John Mortimer." In *Critical Survey of Mystery and Detective Fiction.* Edited by Frank N. Magill. Pasadena, Calif.: Salem Press, 1988. Pp. 1246–1251.

Strauss, Gerald H. "John Mortimer." In *British Dramatists Since World War II,* vol. 13 of *Dictionary of Literary Biography.* Edited by Stanley Weintaub. Detroit: Gale, 1982.

Taylor, John Russell. "In the Air: John Mortimer." In *The Angry Theatre: New British Drama.* Rev. ed. New York: Farrar, Straus & Giroux (Hill and Wang), 1969.

Thomas, Franklin. *The Liberty of Citizens.* London and New York: Granada, 1983. Lectures by Franklin Thomas, John Mortimer, Lord Hunt of Tanworth.

Wellwarth, George. "John Mortimer." In his *The Theater of Protest and Paradox: Developments in the Avant-Garde Drama.* New York: New York University Press, 1964. Pp. 253–257.

SARA PARETSKY
(b. 1947)

MARGARET H. KINSMAN

> I hadn't realized how tired I was until I got into my car. The pain in my
> shoulders returned in a wave that swept me back limply in the front
> seat. Little tears of hurt and self-pity pricked my eyelids. Quitters never
> win and winners never quit, I quoted my old basketball coach grimly.
> Play through the pain, not against it. (V. I. in *Blood Shot*, p. 209)

SARA PARETSKY, the author of the best-selling V. I. Warshawski detective series, is considered one of the pioneers of the contemporary female-private-eye novel. A strong, self-possessed, capable private investigator portrayed realistically and sympathetically in a vivid urban milieu, V. I.'s unconventional character broke new ground in the hard-boiled tradition of mystery writing when she debuted in the 1982 novel *Indemnity Only*. While women writers have consistently excelled in the mystery genre since its inception in the nineteenth century, female characters historically have been confined to stereotypical images of victim, femme fatale, loyal wife and sidekick, or amateur sleuth. Beginning in 1964 with Amanda Cross, who created the outspoken amateur detective Kate Fansler, and continuing in 1977 with Marcia Muller and her private investigator Sharon McCone, women writers of detective fiction, including Sara Paretsky, Sue Grafton, and Linda Barnes, have transformed the fictional woman detective.

Often created in the hard-boiled tradition of Dashiell Hammett's and Raymond Chandler's bourbon-swigging and womanizing urban detective heroes of the 1920s and 1930s, these sassy, stalwart female characters broke the mold. They also heralded an unprecedented explosion of mystery novels throughout the 1980s and 1990s featuring smart and capable female protagonists in the role of detective. No mere sacrificers of femininity in imitation of the male tradition, these are boldly conceived women of action and conviction, unafraid to take emotional and physical risks or to open their mouths and say what they mean. They have pushed the isolated omnipotence of the male-detective figure into a more complex, reflective, vulnerable, and humanistic characterization. In so doing, these fictional female detectives and their authors have proved both successful and popular, amassing an ever-growing international readership, winning critical acclaim, and irrevocably changing the form and content of contemporary crime and mystery fiction. As a result, it is no longer easy to subordinate, ignore, or exploit women characters in the genre.

Paretsky's achievement with her series of eight novels and collection of short stories featuring the compelling V. I. Warshawski, private investigator, is, in good genre tradition, in the dual creation of an unforgettable detective figure and an authentic representation of a city—in this case, Chicago. When identifying the distinctive features of the Paretsky oeuvre, theorists and critics such as Kathleen Gregory Klein, Sally R. Munt, Maggie Humm, Sabine Vanacker, Maureen T. Reddy, and Elizabeth A. Trembley consistently draw attention to her convincing portrayal of a professional single woman with feminist values and convictions; her affectionate and knowledgeable portrait of Chicago's historically pluralistic and blue-collar urban landscape; and her thematic concern with the arrogance and complexities of white-collar, corporate greed, corruption, and criminal activity.

Since V. I. Warshwaski's first appearance in 1982, she has attracted a wide readership of many ages, both sexes, and diverse backgrounds, including the V. I. Fan Club of Tokyo and residents of the White House. Fans of the best-selling author appreciate Paretsky's deep-rooted concern with social injustice, her placement of an outspoken woman character at the center of the mysteries, and her lively descriptions of Chicago. This introductory discussion of Paretsky's work focuses on the writer, her main character, and the city in order to discover features that distinguish the novels within the hard-boiled private eye tradition. The student reader attentive to layers of meaning in addition to the entertainment value of genre fiction will find much to reward him or her in the Warshawski series.

Life

For women to find a voice, a voice telling them that they may have adventures, that action is a woman's appropriate sphere, has been the difficult task of the last several centuries. (Paretsky, *The Independent*, 1997)

Paretsky, the only girl of five children, was born on 8 June 1947 in Ames, Iowa, "into a 'family where girls became secretaries and wives, and boys became professionals.' " (Blain et al., p. 830). Her father, David, was an internationally recognized microbiologist, and her mother, Mary, was a children's librarian in the Kansas public library system. Paretsky's paternal grandparents were Jewish immigrants who settled in Brooklyn; her maternal forebears were "mainline WASP" (Baker and Nietzel, p. 319). She attended small country schools in rural Kansas and played third base as a twelve year old for the school baseball team. Although she scribbled from an early age, there was little encouragement for her and no expectation that writing might be something she could pursue professionally. In a 1996 interview in *Crime Time* magazine, Paretsky said about her childhood:

In the whole time that I was growing up, I don't think anyone ever asked me what I wanted to do as an adult because it was just assumed that my destiny lay in the house. I wasn't encouraged to think I had a gift for writing, and I wasn't encouraged to think that it was something that I could aspire to any more than I might aspire to be a business person or a doctor. (Muller, p. 24)

While her brothers' higher education was planned and financed by the family as a matter of course, Paretsky had to pay her own way through college at the University of Kansas and later as a postgraduate at the University of Chicago. She graduated summa cum laude from the University of Kansas in 1967 with a double major in political science and Russian and an unofficial minor in the 1960s liberal and radical feminist ideologies being formulated on college campuses across the United States.

Paretsky spent the summer of 1966 in Chicago, where she did community service on the South Side. She remembers it as a formative experience:

It was just an extraordinarily vital and active time to be in Chicago. It was the summer that Martin Luther King was there organizing urban housing. Despite . . . the tremendous poverty and racial divisiveness, we had a lot of hope in that era to think that we might actually solve some of these problems. (Muller, p. 24)

A passion for social justice, political activism, and feminist values are part of the legacy Paretsky has passed on to her character V. I. Warshawski.

After graduating from college, Paretsky returned to Chicago to pursue a career in advertising, promotion, and public relations. In 1977, after gaining both an M.B.A. and a Ph.D. in history from the University of Chicago, she became a marketing manager for CNA Insurance in Chicago, one of the largest insurance companies in the United States. Here she gained knowledge of human foibles and the complexities of high finance. These experiences show up in her novels, where she expertly dissects greed and financial shenanigans in corporate Chicago. It was not until 1985, after the publication of three Warshawski novels and a lucrative sale of film rights, that Paretsky was able to leave the corporate world for a career as a full-time writer. That year, the Friends of American Writers honored her for the second V. I. novel, *Deadlock* (1984).

Other honors followed. In 1987 *Ms* magazine named her Woman of the Year. In 1988 Paretsky received the British Crime Writers Association's prestigious Silver Dagger award for her fifth novel, *Blood Shot* (U.K. title *Toxic Shock*), and was nominated to the University of Kansas Hall of Fame. Roosevelt University, Chicago, invited Paretsky to deliver the 1990 Friends of American Writers Lecture. In 1993, she received the German Crime Writers Association Marlowe Award for *Guardian Angel* (1992), and an Honorary Doctor of Letters from MacMurray College, Illinois. In 1996, Paretsky was honored with the Mark Twain Award for her distinguished contribution to midwestern literature.

Paretsky is a member of the Authors Guild, the Chicago Network, the Crime Writers Association, the Private Eye Writers of America, and the Mystery Writers of America (serving,

in 1989, as vice president). She is an effective and sought-after public speaker and a popular figure at crime- and mystery-fiction fan conventions, book signings, and publicity events. From April through June 1997, Paretsky was a visiting fellow at Wolfson College, Oxford University. In 1997 she was the featured guest at the annual Bouchercon Mystery Convention.

Paretsky was a founding member and first president of Sisters in Crime, a women's caucus inaugurated in 1986 and dedicated to "combat[ing] discrimination against women in the mystery field . . . and promot[ing] the professional advancement of women who write mysteries" (Sisters in Crime introductory leaflet, "A Brief History"). After twelve years, the movement had forty-five regional chapters and an international membership of over three thousand writers, readers, editors, agents, booksellers, and librarians and a Web site. Paretsky's galvanizing force and energy were crucial in the caucus's formative years and early successes in generating interest, calming people's fears about backlash, commissioning and publishing research on reviews of the work of women authors, and publishing a guide to books in print by women authors.

Paretsky's interest in women's issues is also evident outside her life as a professional writer. She is a longtime member of the Chicago National Abortion Rights Action League, serving as its director since 1987. She supports a host of causes aiding women, children, and the poor, having volunteered at health clinics, literacy programs, and domestic-violence programs and acted as a fund-raiser for women running for political office. Like her public-minded heroine Warshawski, Paretsky stays involved in social causes at a grassroots level, refusing to give in to what she has described as a national unwillingness to tackle today's crucial social issues, such as systemic racism, the poverty of the educational system, and homelessness. Paretsky established several scholarship funds to assist young people with interests in the creative arts, science, or sports. A University of Kansas scholarship is earmarked for young women who demonstrate leadership and have contributed to the understanding of women's issues.

The 1998 publication of Paretsky's novel *Ghost Country* marked a departure from the mystery genre and V. I. Warshawski, though the urban realism of the Chicago setting and the theme of homelessness remain close to the V. I. series. Publicity blurbs for *Ghost Country* took pains to reassure readers of Paretsky's plans to return to her popular detective. As of 1998, Paretsky, who is married to Courtenay Wright, a retired University of Chicago physicist, was still living in Chicago and writing full time.

V. I. Warshawski

You know me, Catherine: brave enough to try anything. . . . It all comes with practice, really. (V. I. Warshawski in *Killing Orders*, p. 263)

In a 1985 interview with *New York Times* columnist Marilyn Stasio, Paretsky said of her decision to feature a female detective: "I was determined to write a hard-boiled sleuth who was both a woman and a complete professional, someone who could operate in a tough milieu and not lose her femininity" (Stasio, p. 38). In a 1994 interview with the *Miami Herald*, she elaborated on the process of creating V. I., explaining how she had fantasized for years about creating a female private eye: "I didn't want Philip Marlowe in drag. What I really wanted was a woman who was like me and my friends. . . . The difference is that she didn't pull her punches. She didn't feel like she had to make nice" (Gressette, p. 41).

Paretsky endowed V. I. with attributes typical of detectives in the genre: loner status, a strong moral code, keen reasoning, imaginative and physical powers, and a healthy suspicion of entrenched power and privilege. In a departure from genre tradition, and particularly atypical for its female characters, V. I.

was also given feminist values, the ability and inclination to speak her mind, and an active (if intermittent) heterosexual life for which she is not made to pay the conventional female prices of remorse, guilt, or punishment. V. I.'s flaws—"I gave her the two that I knew best, which were sloth and anger" (Gressette, p. 41)—were included on the advice of an early editor, who thought Vic in danger of coming across as too perfect. As a woman short on housekeeping skills and long on acerbic repartee, the likable Victoria Iphigenia Warshawski (known variously as V. I., Vic, and rarely Vicki) made history in the first fifteen years of her literary existence.

V. I. Warshawski's introduction in *Indemnity Only* is typical of her activity in later novels: she is at the wheel of her car, navigating Chicago's Lake Shore Drive on a hot summer night. Through her use of the first-person voice, Paretsky establishes her character in the opening chapter of *Indemnity Only* as an active, energetic woman who can drive through a vivid urban landscape with purpose and confidence. V. I. is en route to her office in response to a message from a potential client who needs a private investigator. The narrative voice is no-nonsense, direct and wry, which suggests that V. I. is in charge of her life and able to make things happen. A typical self-reflective comment from V. I. illustrates the matter-of-fact way in which she accepts responsibility for her own actions and solves her own problems:

Even in the winter I try to run five miles a day. Although financial crime, my specialty, doesn't often lead to violence, I grew up in a rough South Side neighborhood where girls as well as boys had to be able to defend themselves. . . . so I work out and run to stay in shape. . . . I don't enjoy exercise, but it beats dieting. (*Killing Orders*, p. 19)

From the first glimpse of her driving through dark city streets and entering a dim, deserted office building, the reader senses V. I. can hold her own in a range of circumstances. Her narrative voice keeps the reader clued in to the ways she thinks, strategizes, and follows through on information she sees and hears. All of this adds up to a picture of a pro-active woman with great presence of mind and self-possession, striking a novel note in a genre traditionally given to stereotypical representations of women as passive and indecisive. When the prospective client (an aggressive and suspicious businessman) suggests his job is not one "for a girl to take on alone," V. I.'s response is utterly in keeping with her sense of self and of her profession and provides a blueprint for her characterization in subsequent novels: "I'm a woman, Mr. Thayer, and I can look out for myself. If I couldn't, I wouldn't be in this kind of business. If things get heavy, I'll figure out a way to handle them—or go down trying. That's my problem, not yours" (*Indemnity Only*, p. 9).

The multifaceted protagonist is also, in this debut novel, portrayed as a woman with humor, with an ability to reveal a vulnerable side (she admits to anxieties and fears and sometimes expresses them physically, for example by sweating or vomiting), and with intimate connections to other people. The personal life of the detective interacting with family, friends, and colleagues from varied walks of life becomes a subject of as much, if not more, interest to the reader as the crime under investigation.

In dramatic contrast to the portrayals of Golden Age hard-boiled detectives, such as Sam Spade and Philip Marlowe, about whom the reader learns very little in personal terms, Paretsky uses her female detective to reveal the complexity of a single woman's life in order to demonstrate the real and hidden costs for a woman following a trajectory that demands all of her attention and energies. With Paretsky, the single-minded detective, in many ways the antithesis of a typical adult, whose life is often fragmented and characterized by multiple demands and roles, rises to a new level as her problem-solving techniques encompass not only the solution to a crime but also a personal search for self. Being alert to the ways in which Paretsky configures the female search for self—the nonstop, tiring job

of asserting oneself in a world of male privilege—is key to understanding the originality and significance of the V. I. persona.

According to her creator, V. I. is an athletic, agile five-foot-eight, with short, light-brown curly hair, gray eyes, and olive skin that takes the sun well. She keeps in top physical condition through jogging, the occasional volleyball game, and exercising Peppy and Mitch, the golden retrievers she shares with her downstairs neighbor, the retired machinist septuagenarian Mr. Contreras. Over the course of eight novels, Vic ages from her early thirties to her fortieth birthday. Age mellows her, giving her an increasing understanding of her waning physical powers. In the later novels, she begins to worry about the implications for a private eye, who relies on physical agility and strength, of getting older.

As the series progresses, Vic's persona, ideals, and professional skills and abilities become more established, allowing her to develop a more introspective and gentle side and to reflect on both past and future. She needs to prove herself less often and becomes more able to show uncertainty and to give support and forgiveness to friends and family. One of V. I.'s great strengths is that she is not afraid to be wrong. While she does not always know what is best, she struggles to act in a moral way, consistent with the values of integrity and loyalty that she prizes. This is a characteristic that others value in her, as Louisa, an old friend of V. I.'s mother, Gabriella, demonstrates when she compares V. I. to her own daughter, Caroline: "She's honest and hardworking and she sticks up for what she believes in. And you're just the same. . . . Gabriella could see you now she'd be as proud as can be" (*Blood Shot*, p. 12). By the later novels, beginning with *Burn Marks* (1990), more balance is achieved, as Vic has less difficulty revealing weaknesses and exercising tolerance. By the end of the 1994 novel, *Tunnel Vision*, Vic is approaching her fifth decade with trepidation, meditating none too happily on her recent split up with policeman Conrad Rawlings, feeling less anxious about losing her closest friend and advocate, Dr. Lotty Herschel, and expressing uncertainty about her professional and personal direction.

Many of Vic's character traits—the stubborn streak, determination, a love of opera, frugality, a strong sense of social justice, the ability to handle a gun—are attributed to the strong and loving influences of her parents: her half-Jewish Italian-immigrant mother, Gabriella, and her Roman Catholic Polish-American policeman father, Tony. Both parents have died by the time Vic finishes law school and becomes an attorney in the public defender's office. Vic was a much-loved only daughter who never forgets her origins in blue-collar immigrant stock, even though her adult life resembles the classic American success story of second-generation assimilation, opportunity, and upward mobility. Now some geographical distance away from the working-class South Side neighborhood of her childhood, the adult Vic lives in a no-frills, but slowly gentrifying, area of Chicago close to Wrigley Field, home of her beloved underdog baseball team, the Chicago Cubs. Here, Vic's family of "consent" (Lotty, Mr. Contreras, the dogs, Lieutenant Bobby Mallory, Murray Ryerson, and Lotty's friend Max Loewenthal) mirrors—in terms of sturdy morals and ethics—the family of "descent" in which she grew up and was nurtured.

Emotionally and ideologically, Vic's identity is strongly determined by her roots. As more of her personal past and familial history is revealed over the course of the novels, it becomes clear just how present and influential her parents were and continue to be in V. I.'s life. Paretsky uses several devices to signal this continuing influence. One is a dream motif that gives free rein to Vic's subconscious in nighttime dreams and daytime interior monologues—both of which are reported back into the narrative. Thus, Vic makes frequent contact with Gabriella, often "remembering" in graphic detail the story of her refugee mother's flight from Mussolini's fascism to the United States. Sometimes Vic reports dreams of her own childhood experiences and memories. Other times, she "hears" Gabriella talk to her in present time—counseling her, reminding her of the values of hard work, determination, and steadfastness that were inculcated in her. Gabriella's voice also signals another kind of knowledge and wisdom that Vic can access in her dreams, an alternative to the reasoning and rational everyday voice that guides Vic through her investigations. In *Killing Orders*, a novel based on financial corruption and fraud in the Roman Catholic Church, an exhausted Vic surfaces from sleep, certain she has just missed an important message and "trying to reconstruct a dream I'd had. . . . Gabriella had come to me, not wasted as in the final days of her illness, but full of life. She knew I was in danger and wanted to wrap me in a white sheet to save me" (p. 213). Eventually understanding the import of this dream, Vic finds a way to move forward with her work of detection.

Another device linking Vic's identity to her roots is a small collection of material artifacts to which she is inordinately attached. She treasures her mother's diamond-drop earrings and the red Venetian wine goblets the young Gabriella carried from Italy to America. Vic preserves these glasses against careless guests, fire, and burglary with a passion that signals a deep love and respect for her mother and an abiding sense of her loss. Gabriella is also embodied in the print of the Uffizi gallery in Florence that hangs above the filing cabinet in Vic's otherwise utilitarian office and in the Olivetti typewriter to which Vic clings for years, before reluctantly entering the age of computers. Her father Tony's presence is evoked by the large oak office desk she bought at a police auction.

While her mother's voice surfaces frequently in Vic's conscious and unconscious thoughts, her father (a Polish cop who tried to make it in Chicago's predominantly Irish police force) lives most vividly in the memory and voice of Lieutenant Bobby Mallory. Tony's old police buddy Mallory is now a homicide cop, often involved in the cases V. I. investigates. Convinced that Tony, V. I.'s "gentle, good-humored father" (*Blood Shot*, p. 9), would be horrified by his daughter's profession and lifestyle, Bobby takes it as his personal mission in life to persuade V. I. (whom he calls Vicki, a nickname she allows to no one) to marry, settle down, have children, and "butt out of investigating." The uneasy relationship between V. I. and Bobby suggests, on one level, the traditionally troubled cop/private-eye dynamic characteristic of hardboiled detective fiction. The added dimension here is the personal, generational, and gendered conflict over values, the role of women, and the nature of professional and protective behavior, all of which are played out in a surrogate father/daughter relationship rooted in a shared past characterized by familial love and frustration.

Finally, the extended families of Tony and Gabriella link the past to the present in Vic's life. These relatives—some of whom are aging and have problems with indigence, alcoholism, and poor judgment—often provoke knotty questions for Vic to resolve about her own feelings as well as her filial duties and obligations.

Another pattern of past and present is found in Vic's network of women friends and colleagues, many of whom date back to her law-school days at the University of Chicago. The women Vic knows both personally and professionally represent the ways in which women have entered the public and private sectors of work since the 1960s (for instance, the worlds of corporate finance, local government, the arts, law, medicine, public health, entertainment) and the ways in which they associate with one another. Multigenerational, multiracial, and multiclass perspectives are brought to bear in each of Vic's investigations through this network of women, and the range of portraits of autonomous, professional women who value their work and their identities mirrors Vic's own position as a competent and self-sufficient member of society.

Most notable of these female characters is Dr. Lotty Herschel, a woman of great personal and professional stature. Lotty, some years older than Vic, is a Jewish Austrian refugee from Nazism who studied medicine in Lon-

don and then settled in Chicago to practice as a perinatologist. Lotty's role as both friend and mentor to V. I. provides continuity in the series, and allows Paretsky to give voice to another woman's life story. Lotty's prominence in her profession also gives Paretsky a further opportunity to explore and validate female achievement and agency. Both Lotty and V. I. value the high standards they set in their professional and personal lives. If V. I.'s guiding principles are integrity and loyalty, Lotty's are compassion and meaningful work. Between them, the two women demonstrate the importance of self-esteem, courage, and mental and physical stamina.

Lotty and Vic's relationship is founded in practical and emotional intimacy. Lotty patches up Vic when she gets hurt; Vic helps out at Lotty's public health clinic when she is short-staffed. Each is respectful of the other's privacy and often fiercely critical of the isolation and pigheadedness to which the other's strength of mind and purpose can lead. They demonstrate the value and importance of female relationships, reflecting the ways in which constructs of family and friendship have become more negotiable in late-twentieth-century culture. Vic and Lotty also share a history of political activism, having met and formed a friendship during Vic's law-student days, when both women worked as volunteers in an underground abortion-referral network.

Vic's most salient personality trait is her outspokenness. She is impatient, impertinent, rude, devastatingly frank, often very funny, and rarely apologetic. Determined not to be cowed, physically or socially, she is often read by women as inspirational because of her directness. Dealing, for example, with a scornful maître d'hôtel as he holds a door for her, she says, "Thank you, my good man. . . . Your contempt for women will bring you more pleasure than any paltry tip I could give you. Good night" (*Deadlock*, 1984, p. 230). Her courageous and targeted tongue is evidence of the mental toughness and stamina that often enable her to defuse potential violence in dangerous situations. Because she believes it is not a good idea to become overly reliant on a gun, wisecracking is one of her best weapons.

Vic operates on a self-confessed short fuse, regularly flying off the handle with varying results. One of her more endearing characteristics is the extent to which she is in touch with this aspect of her personality. She registers anger, much as she does fear, viscerally: "The pulse beside my right temple started throbbing" (*Blood Shot*, p. 91); "My eyes fogged and I felt my head buzzing" (p. 6). V. I. also understands her anger emotionally—"I opened my jacket to let the cool air flow through me and cleanse me"—and intellectually: "I started to say something rude, then thought better of it" (*Deadlock*, p. 5); "The next two hours put a formidable strain on my frayed temper" (*Deadlock*, pp. 5–6). Finally, she has an ability to turn a sharp mocking tongue on herself when she is on the verge of overdoing it: " 'Very well,' I said in cold anger, '. . . you can fire me, but you can't get rid of me.' I hung up. Beautiful, Vic: beautiful rhetoric . . . why be so full of female-chismo and yell challenges into the phone? I ought to write 'Think before acting' a hundred times on the blackboard" (*Indemnity Only*, p. 113).

Frequent expression of irritable feelings empowers V. I. and thus serves as an antidote to the cultural expectation that female rage be unexpressed and controlled. By the simple expedient of verbal expression and the mental catharsis of fantasy—"I restrained an impulse to brain her with her desk lamp" (*Indemnity Only*, p. 37)—Vic is cast as proactive and therefore a rewrite of the more predictable scripts for women in which anger is denied and suppressed. It is almost impossible for anyone to shame, humiliate, patronize, or victimize Vic, try as one might.

Taking responsibility for her feelings and impulses is one of the lifelong lessons Vic is engaged in learning. She understands that her rage stems from an illusion of helplessness. The domesticity and marriage that Bobby Mallory constantly urges on her, for example, represent for V. I. the habitat of helplessness. She remembers clearly the abandonment of self that she experienced during her brief marriage to the yuppie attorney Dick Yarborough and is determined not to repeat the mistake, even though this results in the risk of alienating Conrad Rawlings in the early stages of their affair in *Guardian Angel*: "Maybe [he] was so annoyed by my comments last night that he had withdrawn his protective arm" (p. 292).

Vic's private space, her apartment, represents, for the most part (excepting the occasional burglary or arson attack), a place of safety where she is answerable only to her own physical and spiritual needs—most of which are met with a long soak in the tub, a slug or two of Black Label, and any mold-free item the refrigerator might yield. It is important, indeed vital, that Vic steer clear of the traditional female role of servicing others, engaged as she is in breaking down barriers about what is acceptable female behavior. Marriage not only represents domestic servitude, but also entails an emotional and intellectual intimacy that V. I. finds threatening to her much-prized autonomy and self-reliance. V. I.'s frequently stated preference is to be accountable to no one: "I didn't like turning tail, handing my problems over to someone else to solve"; "All I could think was that I had run scared from my problems, . . . and now I was waiting like some good old-fashioned damsel in distress for rescue" (*Blood Shot*, p. 211, 212). She doesn't apologize to visitors for the messy state of her apartment. V. I. never makes a bed. She has an unshakable aversion to washing dishes. There is no mention of ironing. Paralleling the ways in which Vic breaks the rules on the mean city streets, she breaks the rules in her domestic sphere, where her domain is not the limited space of the kitchen, but the whole apartment. She lives alone, enjoys her solitude, and admits to being "messy, but not a slob" (*Indemnity Only*, p. 11).

It is fundamentally in keeping with the feminism, active social conscience, and wide net of friends of Paretsky's detective that genre convention is turned inside out in these novels. While on the surface the characterization of V. I. pays lip service to the stereotypical hard-drinking, wisecracking, cynical loner private eye with an entrenched suspicion of power and privilege, there is considerable complexity attached to each of these aspects. Where Marlowe and Spade are marked by hard living, the isolation of hotel rooms, and little personal or emotional history, V. I. Warshawski values the choices she has made in life, particularly in relation to her professional and marital autonomy, and is intimately involved in her urban and personal environments, with a strong sense of how the past connects to the present and points to the future.

The City

I never get lost driving in Chicago. If I can't find the lake or the Sears Tower, the L tracks orient me, and if all else fails, the x-y street coordinates keep me on target. (V. I. in *Bitter Medicine*, p. 39)

Chicago may be one of the most mapped, as well as written about, cities in the world. From its inception, the city has been home to large, often prosperous, and therefore influential, immigrant communities. Chicago as blue-collar, cosmopolitan, civically proud, multicultural, and divided by race, poverty, and ethnicity occupies a central position in the Paretsky novels, providing the context in which she explores her characters' lives and experiences and their various quarrels with its darker side of organized crime and systemic social injustice.

Under Paretsky's pen, the metropolis comes alive in all its paradoxical promise of possibility and mystery as well as the isolation, degradation, and danger inherent in the racial and economic divisions that mark Chicago's diverse demography. The observant reader will begin to recognize familiar Paretsky devices for signaling the plurality of the city. She uses geographical location, identifying a Greek restaurant here, a German one there, drawing attention to the way in which Chicago is still organized around small, eth-

nic neighborhoods like the Polish enclave of her South Chicago childhood. She refers to the sanitized elegance of the older suburbs (Hinsdale) and the gentrification of the near North Side. Characters' names (Gretzky, Aunt Helen Wojcik, Agnes Paciorek, Grafalk, Bobby Mallory, Rosalyn Fuentes) bear witness to the importance of the Middle European, Scandinavian, Irish, and more recently Hispanic communities in Chicago's industrial and political history. References to sports teams, architecture, food, rituals such as funerals, and leisure activities along the lakefront illustrate a large, powerful, self-confident city at work and at play. Chicago is portrayed as an unsentimental city, hardworking and without pretension.

Another familiar Paretsky device is the signaling of a historical framework for the city. In *Deadlock*, V. I. remembers her cousin Boom Boom's father, who was a stevedore on the docks in the 1930s and 1940s. Later in the same novel, Vic notes that a shop owned by a Pole during her childhood in South Chicago is now owned by a Mexican. The novel *Blood Shot* chronicles the deindustrialization of one of Chicago's largest blue-collar districts and the subsequent effects on the families and communities that worked the factories. The architectural legacy of the city, dating back to the nineteenth century, when wealthy Victorian industrialists put up homes and civic buildings, and continuing through the twentieth century, when skyscrapers were built, is frequently remarked on by Vic as she travels the streets of Chicago.

Paretsky also reveals the divisions between people that characterize a city where equal opportunity is still a dream for many sectors of the population and where prejudice can be easily justified. In *Bitter Medicine*, two characters with only a fragile claim to economic stability display a casual and endemic racism. Fabiano, a young Mexican with limited job prospects and an unwanted baby on the way, is anti-Semitic, referring to Lotty as "that Jew-doctor" (p. 50). Mrs. Kirkland, an admitting nurse at a suburban hospital faced with an emergency admission of Fabiano's young, pregnant wife, Consuelo, explains to Vic: "She's some Mexican girl who got sick on the premises. We do not run a charity ward here" (p. 22). Mrs. Kirkland has entered the word "Indigent" on Consuelo's admission form. Her unexamined bigotry is challenged by Vic, who points out that "Americans have never been very understanding of poverty, but since Reagan was elected it's become a crime almost as bad as child-molesting" (p. 23).

Paretsky further signals the racial and ethnic diversity of Chicago through Warshawski's own friends and family, who reflect the many places of origin of Chicago's six million citizens. In addition to the Irish, Polish, and Italian roots of Vic's own family, her longtime friend Sal Barthelme, owner of the Golden Glow Bar, and the cop Conrad Rawlings, who becomes her lover in *Guardian Angel*, are both African-American. Mr. Salvatore Contreras and Lotty's clinic nurse Carol Alvardo have names that suggest Hispanic forebears. The Chicagoans that Vic knows and loves, and many others she meets in the course of her adventures, are honest, hardworking people. Paretsky's sympathetic treatment of their struggles to build good lives for themselves and their families shows the other side of a city more famous for its criminals and corrupt elected officials.

In 1902, G. K. Chesterton published an essay titled "A Defense of Detective Stories," in which he suggested that detective fiction's cultural significance—that is, its appeal to the imagination of its readers—lies in its poetic treatment of the twentieth-century city. Detective fiction, he argued, shows the inherent paradox of the modern city: that it promises excitement and the possibility of adventure while at the same time harboring human misery and danger. As the detective, in this case V. I. Warshawski, ventures through the city streets, she meets both beauty and despair, and must accept the power of both. V. I. is moved by her city and its inhabitants, as well as exasperated and infuriated by its capacity for evil. In this quote from *Bitter Medicine*, V. I. illustrates the poetic paradox that Chesterton noticed so long ago: "The lake lay

to my left. The polished mirror surface was streaked with a light and color that would have inspired Monet. It looked at once peaceful and inviting. But its cold depths could kill you with merciless impersonality" (*Bitter Medicine*, p. 57).

A characteristic paragraph in a Warshawski novel places V. I. in the driver's seat of a beat-up car, sketching in and "mapping" a particular Chicago season and landscape, using accurate geographical and historical markers as well as the sight, sound, and smell of her city. The opening of *Bitter Medicine* shows Vic traveling out of the city into suburban mediocrity: "The heat and the tawdry sameness of the road drugged everyone to silence. The July sun shimmered around McDonald's, Video King, Computerland, Arby's, Burger King, the Colonel, a car dealership, and then McDonald's again. I had a headache from the traffic, the heat, the sameness" (p. 11). The sterility of the suburbs is a recurring motif in the novels, as is the shabbiness of Vic's South Loop office building, the Pultney. Located in the heart of Chicago's famous commercial and architectural district, the building reflects the gradual decline of the Loop over the last few decades: "At night it looked like a terrible place to have an office. The hall's mosaic-tiled walls were chipped and dirty. I wondered if anyone ever washed the scuffed linoleum floor" (*Indemnity Only*, p. 1). It is from this neglected, though once-proud, office building that Vic conducts her investigations into the sorrier aspects of life in Chicago. In the eighth V. I. novel, *Tunnel Vision*, the Pultney Building is finally pulled down, having served throughout the series as a constant reminder of Chicago's civic and architectural glories as well as its decaying underside.

Paretsky's characteristic attention to the changing economic and social conditions of Chicago can also be noticed in the neighborhood settings that she identifies with V. I.'s past. In *Blood Shot*, Vic returns to the blighted South Chicago of her childhood. Here she identifies the desolation of a once industrious, prosperous area overtaken by poverty and blighted by worn-out, rusting padlocked factories: "I could remember when eighteen thousand men poured from those tidy little homes every day into the South Works, Wisconsin Steel, the Ford assembly plant, or the Xerxes solvent factory. I remembered when each piece of trim was painted fresh every second spring. . . . But that was in a different life, for me as well as South Chicago" (p. 1).

In her introduction to *Windy City Blues* (1995; U.K. title, *V. I. for Short*), a collection of short stories, Paretsky guides the reader through the Chicago neighborhoods of her own experience and explains how and why she draws on this city to frame Vic's life and activities. Reflecting on the depressed South Chicago neighborhood whose steel mills traditionally provided a stopping place for new immigrants, Paretsky writes:

> It is the gallantry of this old neighborhood that made me take it for the home of my detective, V. I. Warshawski. The gallantry, on the one hand, and the racial and ethnic mix that turned it into a volatile soup on the other. . . . As each new wave of immigrants arrived, the previous ones, with a fragile toehold on the American dream of universal prosperity, would fight to keep the newcomers out. Girls . . . learned the basics of street fighting to protect themselves. (p. 7)

Chicago, then, provides a geographical, moral, and ethical landscape for Vic that she is utterly familiar with and against which she defines her purpose as a detective. Claiming the right to wander the city, unfettered and unmolested, her character transgresses traditional female restraint. She refuses to accept that there are places she cannot or should not go in the city. As Vic makes her way through her streets, on the move in her car or less frequently on foot, the city often functions as her compass, her source of direction, in much the same way that her past guides her. She always knows where she is going, her strong external sense of direction reflecting her steely inner purpose. It is only in the sterile, unmarked, and badly lit streets of the northwest suburbs that Vic needs to refer to a map: "I didn't know where I was going, and a dread I never felt in Chicago's traffic hit me in the stomach" (*Bitter Medicine*, p. 40).

Vic was also "lost" in the suburbs during her fourteen-month marriage to fellow law student Dick Yarborough, who, while seeming to support her as she agonized over leaving her job as a public defender, was really waiting for her to fill the traditional wifely role at home while he climbed his way up the legal profession. Both of them were mistaken in their youthful response to what the other represented. Part of Vic wanted to belong to the white Anglo-Saxon city establishment that claimed Dick and his aspirations; for his part, Dick was taken by Vic's independence and love of adventure. As Vic wryly observes when looking back at this part of her personal history, "Some men can only admire independent women at a distance" (*Indemnity Only*, p. 28).

Like the bodily discomfort she experiences on unfamiliar streets—"My hands were wet on the steering wheel" (*Burn Marks*, p. 24)—marriage and Dick's expectations stranded her in a place incompatible with her needs and aspirations. Choosing to leave in order to preserve and nurture her autonomy, Vic reminds herself and her lover Ralph Devereux, who verges on being overprotective, why she guards her autonomy: "I have some close women friends, because I don't feel they're trying to take over my turf. But with men, it always seems, or often seems, as though I'm having to fight to maintain who I am" (*Indemnity Only*, p. 160). V. I.'s struggles to claim her rights on her professional turf—the city streets—are effectively mirrored in her personal sphere, where she also breaks down barriers.

Major Themes

In the 1991 Hollywood film version of V. I., the detective, played with panache by Kathleen Turner, is asked, "What does it cost to hire you?" She replies, "A just cause." For Vic, the crimes of capitalist and patriarchal systems that operate against the interests of disenfranchised and powerless people at the bottom of the economic and social scales—the poor, ethnic minorities, women, and children—qualify as a just cause. White-collar crime in the institutions of Chicago; fraud and corruption in the Church; medical malpractice; graft in the corporate worlds of insurance, shipping, and chemical manufacture; child sexual abuse; violence against women; industrial pollution—all come under V. I.'s investigating eye.

Each of Paretsky's novels successfully integrates analysis of a larger social issue with the criminal investigation of some complex and labyrinthine aspect of city institutions. In *Burn Marks*, V. I.'s search for the killer of her aunt Elena's young friend Cerise is obstructed by politicians and police alike, both anxious to keep their corrupt control over public housing and real-estate developers secret. The plot of *Guardian Angel* (1992) revolves around a missing retired factory worker, Mitch, who knew something about his employers' illicit pension-fund looting. Mitch's plan to blackmail them to supplement his meager pension goes wrong and results in his murder. In order to unravel Mitch's story, Vic finds herself involved in a chase for closely guarded paper and computer trails locked behind office doors.

In each novel, Warshawski undertakes serious research, informing herself of the complexities of a subject and the people she is investigating. Her thoroughness and attention to detail act as a model for what could be an informed and alert citizenry were everyone to go to the lengths V. I. does. The reader, through V. I.'s catalog of detailed questioning and probing, comes to appreciate her tenacity in the face of frequent criticism from the police and corporate bureaucrats who often don't believe V. I. and negate her professional expertise. Even her friends sometimes berate her for being stubborn, opinionated, and determined to get to the bottom of things. Vic's chief modus operandi is to locate, reveal, and share information that is being kept secret by powerful institutions that put their own fi-

nancial and legal interests first. This, as Vic knows, usually works against the interests of the more disenfranchised sectors of society—the workers, the elderly, the ill, the poor. This notion of sharing information with the powerless in pursuit of social justice undercuts V. I.'s position as an isolated investigator and locates her instead in a context of teamwork, propelled by principles of affiliation, mutual support, and loyalty.

In this sense, it is clear that Paretsky's themes are to be found not only in her plot treatment of the machinations and results of white-collar urban crime. In addition, her thematic concerns include the construction of female identity and the various ways in which social justice and injustice are experienced in a racially diverse and divided city run by patriarchal systems and institutions. Paretsky's concern with the difficult social issues of modern life, such as homelessness, indigence, aging, child abuse, spouse battering, and random danger (street violence) suggests that her novels have an affinity with the nineteenth-century tradition of social realism, as well as their obvious connection to the hard-boiled detective tradition. Through V. I.'s heroic attempts to cope with the complexities of cases, which always involve difficult relationships between people faced with moral and philosophical dilemmas, the reader is reminded of the need to be attentive to the moral and ethical foundations of society and to examine these foundations when discrepancies occur.

The Critical Response

The breadth and diversity of the critical discussion around Paretsky and the larger subject of feminist crime fiction is testimony to the increasing seriousness with which genre writing is being treated, as well as an indication of the strong appeal of this particular subgenre to both readers and scholars of literature, popular culture, and gender studies. Paretsky's work is regularly and seriously reviewed in quality newspapers and journals on both sides of the Atlantic. She is increasingly the focus of scholars and academics writing from a variety of positions in a wide range of publications. The general acclaim she receives includes, inevitably, questions about feminism, gender, and genre.

The character of V. I. Warshawski challenges stereotypes of women and subverts a form that, particularly in the American hard-boiled subgenre, has been distinctly masculine. In a 1990s postscript to *Bloody Murder* (1972), his widely read and accessible history of the detective story, Julian Symons credits Paretsky with creating "a grittily impressive central character" and "complex story lines . . . well worked out." While Symons accepts that the mystery story is ideally suited for addressing social issues, he is critical of Paretsky's liberal political views as expressed through V. I.'s perspective on abortion rights, for example. His brief discussion of writers such as Marcia Muller, Sue Grafton, and Sara Paretsky underestimates the commercial and critical success and influence of the expanding hard-boiled female detective novel.

It is no surprise, then, that contemporary feminist cultural and literary inquiry, coming of age in the same decade as V. I.'s debut, provides the most illuminating and perceptive commentary on Paretsky's work. Kathleen Gregory Klein's *The Woman Detective: Gender & Genre* (1988) considers the detective novel as both a reflection of and a potential barrier to social change for women. Klein mitigates her conclusion that detective fiction is inherently conservative in its sexual politics with the example of Paretsky (among a few others) as a notable exception to authors who "maintain and reinforce a conservative political ideology toward sex/gender roles which accords with the conservative implications of the genre" (p. 223). Klein's detailed discussion of Paretsky's first four novels draws attention to how the "reader is always made aware of Vic as both a woman and a feminist, both in her positively attributed independent stance and in defensive responses appearing in dialogue, descriptions, and thoughts" (p. 212).

Sally Munt's *Murder by the Book? Feminism and the Crime Novel* (1994) offers a critical overview of the 1980s wave of feminist crime novels, exploring why the form proves so attractive a vehicle for oppositional politics, particularly for writers looking at gay and lesbian issues. She locates Paretsky's work in the "liberal feminist" tradition that asserts women's claim to the individual rights and freedoms guaranteed to each member of a democratic society and discusses the V. I. novels in the light of the ambivalences, strengths, and weaknesses Munt assigns to that position. What is a radical text for Klein is less so for Munt, who regards the lesbian thrillers of writers like Kathleen V. Forrest as more positive and transgressive examples of what feminism brings to the crime and mystery genre.

Positioned in between are discussions of Paretsky in Maggie Humm's *Border Traffic* (1991), where Humm notes her "oppositional stance to constraints of traditional detective fiction and to conventional gender scripts" (p. 210); and in Maureen Reddy's *Sisters in Crime* (1988), which focuses on female mystery writers who have created series protagonists. Reddy explains the new fictions in terms of a feminist aesthetic that envisions different lifestyles, gender roles, and kinds of social justice, a position with which Carolyn Heilbrun (the mystery writer Amanda Cross) concurs in her writings as a feminist literary theorist.

More recent discussions of the Paretsky oeuvre, which compare and contrast other representations of the single woman urban detective and consider the implications of the critical mass of such figures, are found in essays by Glenwood Irons, Anne Cranny-Francis, and Sabine Vanacker. In *The Naked City: Urban Crime Fiction in the USA* (1996), Ralph Willett discusses V. I. Warshawski in relation to the complexity of modern city life.

Conclusion

In a 1997 article for the *Independent*, Paretsky wrote: "My own heroine, V. I., is a woman of action. But her primary role is to speak. She says those things which I—which many women—are not strong enough to say for ourselves. . . . Her success depends . . . on her willingness to put into words things that most people would rather remained unspoken." In the boldly imagined figure of V. I. and in her representation of Chicago, Paretsky has made a distinctive and lasting contribution to the late-twentieth-century formulation of the urban American detective novel, offering the reader alternative blueprints for a woman's life and for concepts of justice and order in contemporary society. Both author and character are rule breakers—with substance.

Selected Bibliography

WORKS OF SARA PARETSKY

NOVELS AND SHORT STORY COLLECTIONS

Indemnity Only. New York: Dial, 1982; London: Gollancz, 1982.

Deadlock. New York: Dial, 1984; London: Gollancz, 1984.

Killing Orders. New York: Morrow, 1985; London: Gollancz, 1986.

Bitter Medicine. New York: Morrow, 1987; London: Gollancz, 1987.

Blood Shot. New York: Delacorte, 1988. U.K.: *Toxic Shock.* London: Gollancz, 1988.

Burn Marks. New York: Delacorte, 1990; London: Chatto & Windus, 1990.

Guardian Angel. New York: Delacorte, 1992; London: Hamish Hamilton, 1992.

Tunnel Vision. New York: Delacorte, 1994; London: Hamish Hamilton, 1994.

A Taste of Life and Other Stories. London: Penguin, 1995.

Windy City Blues. New York: Delacorte, 1995. U.K.: *V. I. for Short.* London: Hamish Hamilton, 1995. Short stories.

Ghost Country. New York: Delacorte, 1998; London: Hamish Hamilton, 1998.

ARTICLES AND ESSAYS

"Private Eyes, Public Spheres." *Women's Review of Books* (November 1988).

"Wild Women Out of Control." In *Family Portraits.* Edited by Carolyn Anthony. New York: Doubleday, 1989.

"Soft Spot for Serial Murder." *New York Times,* 28 April 1991: Sec. 4, 17.

"Protocols of the Elders of Feminism." *LAW/TEXT/CULTURE* (University of Wollongong) 1 (1994).

"The Hidden War at Home." *New York Times,* 7 July 1994: A19.

"It's No Trial to Watch 'Murder One.' " *Cape Cod Times,* 26 September 1995: C7.

"Property Rites: Women, Poverty, and Public Policy." *Illinois Issues* (summer 1996).

"Sexy, Moral, and Packing a Pistol." *Independent,* 18 June 1997: 22.

BOOKS EDITED BY PARETSKY

Beastly Tales: The Mystery Writers of America Anthology. New York: Wynwood Press, 1989.

A Woman's Eye: New Stories by the Best Women Crime Writers. London: Virago, 1991. Short stories.

Women on the Case. New York: Delacorte, 1996; London: Virago, 1996. Short stories.

MEDIA ADAPTATIONS

Indemnity Only. Audio collection. London: BBC Enterprises Ltd., 1991.

V. I. Warshawski. Film based on the V. I. Warshawski novels. 1991.

Deadlock. Radio IV BBC adaptations, 1995.

Killing Orders. Radio IV BBC adaptations, 1995.

When Danger Follows You Home. USA Network original film in association with Universal Television, 1997. Based on original characters created by Sara Paretsky.

BIOGRAPHICAL AND CRITICAL STUDIES

Baker, Robert A., and Michael T. Nietzel. *Private Eyes: One Hundred and One Knights: A Survey of American Detective Fiction, 1922–1984.* Bowling Green, Ohio: Bowling Green State University Popular Press, 1985.

Bakerman, Jane S. "Living 'Openly and with Dignity': Sara Paretsky's New-Boiled Feminist Fiction." *Midamerica* 12: 120–135 (1985).

Blain, Virginia Clements, et al. *The Feminist Companion to Literature in English: Women Writers from the Middle Ages to the Present.* London: Batsford, 1990.

Brandt, Kate, and Paula Lichtenberg. "On the Case with V. I. and Kinsey." *Hot Wire: The Journal of Women's Music and Culture* 10, no. 1: 48–50 (1994).

Cranny-Francis, Anne. *Feminist Fiction: Feminist Uses of Generic Fiction.* Cambridge: Polity Press, 1990.

Decure, Nicole. "V. I. Warshawski, a 'Lady with Guts': Feminist Crime Fiction by Sara Paretsky." *Women's Studies International Forum* 12, no. 2: 227–238 (1989).

Dudar, Helen. "Queen of the Gumshoes." *Lear's,* August 1991: 72–74, 96–98.

Emck, Katy. "Feminist Detectives and the Challenges of Hardboiledness." *Canadian Review of Comparative Literature* 21, no. 3: 383–398 (1994).

Gladsky, Thomas S. "Consent, Descent, and Transethnicity in Sara Paretsky's Fiction." *Clues: A Journal of Detection* 16, no. 2: 1–15 (1995).

Goodkin, Richard E. "Killing Order(s): Iphigenia and the Detection of Tragic Intertextuality." *Yale French Studies* 76: 81–107 (1989).

Gressette, Felicia. "Mystery Women." *Miami Herald*, 24 April 1994: 1J, 41.

Hileman, Monica. "V. I. Warshawski: A Macha, Feminist PI?" *Sojourner: The Women's Forum* 14, no. 7: 17 (1989).

Humm, Maggie. "Legal Aliens: Feminist Detective Fiction." In *Border Traffic: Strategies of Contemporary Women Writers*. Edited by Maggie Humm. Manchester, U.K.: Manchester University Press, 1991. Pp. 185–211.

Irons, Glenwood, ed. *Feminism in Women's Detective Fiction*. Toronto: University of Toronto Press, 1995.

———, ed. *Gender, Language, and Myth: Essays on Popular Narrative*. Toronto: University of Toronto Press, 1992.

Johnson, Patricia E. "Sex and Betrayal in the Detective Fiction of Sue Grafton and Sara Paretsky." *Journal of Popular Culture* 27, no. 4: 97–106 (1994).

Jones, Louise Conley. "Feminism and the P.I. Code: Or, 'Is a Hard-Boiled Warshawski Unsuitable to Be Called a Feminist?' " *Clues: A Journal of Detection*, 16, no. 1: 77–87 (1995).

Kaplan, Alice Yaeger. "On the New Hard-boiled Woman." *Artforum* 28: 26–28 (January 1990).

Kinsman, Margaret. "A Question of Visibility: Paretsky and Chicago." In *Women Times Three: Writers, Detectives, Readers*. Edited by Kathleen Gregory Klein. Bowling Green, Ohio: Bowling Green State University Popular Press, 1995. Pp. 15–27.

Klein, Kathleen Gregory. "Sara Paretsky." In *St. James Guide to Crime and Mystery Writers*. Edited by Jay Pederson. Detroit: St. James Press, 1996. Pp. 817–818.

———. "Watching Warshawski." In *It's A Print!: Detective Fiction from Page to Screen*. Edited by William Reynolds and Elizabeth A. Trembley. Bowling Green, Ohio: Bowling Green State University Popular Press, 1994. Pp. 145–157.

———. *The Woman Detective: Gender & Genre*. Urbana: University of Illinois Press, 1988.

Muller, Adrian. "Sara Paretsky Interview." *Crime Time* 6: 24 (1996).

Munt, Sally. *Murder by the Book? Feminism and the Crime Novel*. London: Routledge, 1994.

Reddy, Maureen T. *Sisters in Crime: Feminism and the Crime Novel*. New York: Continuum, 1988.

———. "The Feminist Counter-Tradition in Crime: Cross, Grafton, Paretsky, and Wilson." In *The Cunning Craft: Original Essays on Detective Fiction and Contemporary Literary Theory*. Edited by Ronald G. Walker and June M. Frazer. Macomb: Western Illinois University Press, 1990. Pp. 174–187.

Shapiro, Laura. "Sara Paretsky (*Ms* Magazine Woman of the Year)." *Ms.*, January 1988: 66–67, 92–93.

Stasio, Marilyn. "Lady Gumshoes: Boiled Less Hard." *New York Times Book Review*, 28 April 1985: 1, 38.

Symons, Julian. *Bloody Murder: From the Detective Story to the Crime Novel: A History*. London: Papermac, 1992 ed.

Szuberla, Guy. "Paretsky, Turow, and the Importance of Symbolic Ethnicity." *Midamerica* 18: 124–135 (1991).

———. "The Ties That Bind: V. I. Warshawski and the Burdens of Family." *Armchair Detective* 27, no. 2: 146–153 (1994).

Thompson, Jon. *Fiction, Crime, and Empire: Clues to Modernity and Postmodernism*. Urbana: University of Illinois Press, 1993.

Trembley, Elizabeth A. "Sara Paretsky." In *Great Women Mystery Writers: Classic to Contemporary*. Edited by Kathleen Gregory Klein. Westport, Conn.: Greenwood Press, 1994. Pp. 266–269.

Vanacker, Sabine. "V. I. Warshawski, Kinsey Millhone and Kay Scarpetta: Creating a Feminist Detective Hero." In *Criminal Proceedings: The Contemporary American Crime Novel*. Edited by Peter Messent. Chicago: Pluto Press, 1997. Pp. 62–86.

Wells, Linda S. "Popular Literature and Postmodernism: Sara Paretsky's Hard-Boiled Feminist." *Proteus: A Journal of Ideas* 6, no. 1: 51–56 (1989).

Willett, Ralph. *The Naked City: Urban Crime Fiction in the USA*. Manchester, U.K.: Manchester University Press, 1996.

Williams, John. *Into the Badlands*. London: Paladin, 1991.

ROBERT B. PARKER
(b. 1932)

MAUREEN CORRIGAN

THE HOME BASE of the traditional tough guy was a one-room dive outfitted with a rumpled Murphy bed, overflowing ash-trays, and a kitchenette stocked with liquor. Though it may have been less than elegant, it was the detective's sanctuary, and when un-invited visitors turned up, he could be down-right rude. Two-thirds of the way through Raymond Chandler's *The Big Sleep*, Philip Marlowe steps into his darkened apartment and finds a naked, giggling Carmen Stern-wood, who has duped the apartment manager into unlocking the door. Marlowe tosses her out, making it clear that he is repelled, not only by Carmen's kittenishly creepy behav-ior, but also by the fact that she has invaded his private space.

But, as the social revolution of the 1960s began to ring changes on the formula of de-tective fiction, a funny thing happened to the detective's bachelor pad: it began to look less like a low-rent version of Superman's Cave of Silence and more like a hippie commune where gumshoes, their friends, and adopted family members dwelt in hard-boiled har-mony. When Robert B. Parker introduced his sensitive male detective, Spenser, in *The Godwulf Manuscript* in 1973, he inaugurated a series that would earn him a place among the pantheon of great mystery writers. Indeed, Parker is generally acknowledged among crit-ics and scholars as the rightful heir to Dashiell Hammett, Raymond Chandler, and Ross Macdonald. Furthermore, Parker not only transformed the macho politics of the tradi-tional private eye but also the profession's preordained monkish lifestyle. Over the course of twenty-five novels (through early 1998), Spenser has constructed an alternative family, both multitudinous and multicultural.

For most of his series life, Spenser has maintained a committed, (mostly) monoga-mous relationship with Susan Silverman, a Jewish feminist therapist. Arguably even closer to Spenser's heart is his best friend, Hawk, a laconic African-American gun-for-hire. In *Early Autumn* (1981), the seventh novel of the series, Spenser became an adop-tive father to the teen-aged Paul Giacomin, who later becomes a professional dancer and choreographer. Other Spenser intimates in-clude Rachel Wallace, a radical lesbian femi-nist writer; Henry Cimoli, a gym owner who talks like Huntz Hall; straight-arrow cops, Frank Belson and Marty Quirk; a gay cop, Lee Farrell; a Chicano mob enforcer named Chollo; and Pearl, a hunting dog Spenser and Susan coyly refer to as their "baby." Strictly speaking, Spenser does not live with any of these folks (he and Susan alternate sleep-overs and Paul visits Spenser periodically) but, then again, how could he? The only space large enough to accommodate the Spenser clan would be one of those sprawling manor houses straight out of the pages of Golden Age mystery fiction.

The Spenser series is crucial to understand-ing the sea change that occurred in detective fiction during the early seventies: Spenser's evolution from an ersatz Philip Marlowe to a gun-toting Phil Donahue attests to the pliability of the hard-boiled formula and, in particular, to its capacity to revise hallowed codes of masculinity in response to the challenges of contemporary feminism. Simply stated, in Spenser, Parker created a paradigm for the contemporary American detective and helped revolutionize the politics of the hard-boiled form. Spenser began his detective career leering at big-breasted secretaries but quickly progressed to reading Simone de Beauvoir's *The Second Sex*. He once walked down life's mean streets alone, but he now jostles a mob of alternative family members for elbow room. Spenser is a man who is manly enough to kill yet womanly enough to cry—in short, he is America's first androgynous private eye.

Life

Robert B. Parker was born in Springfield, Massachusetts, on 17 September 1932, and he received a bachelor's degree from Colby College in Waterville, Maine, in 1954. He spent two years in the army and was discharged in 1956. He married his wife, Joan Hall, the same year; the couple first met at a birthday party when they were three years old and later ran into each other at a Colby College freshman dance. All of Parker's novels are dedicated to her, his sons (David, a choreographer, and Daniel, an actor), or all three. In 1957, he earned his master's degree in English from Boston University. After jobs as a technical writer and copywriter and as editor for Prudential Insurance Company, Parker briefly ran his own small advertising agency in Boston. With assistance from the G.I. Bill and a loan from his father, and with Joan's support, Parker went back to school full-time. He earned his doctorate at Boston University in 1971 with a dissertation on Raymond Chandler, Dashiell Hammett, and Ross Macdonald. In 1968, he began teaching at Northeastern University, where he be-

came a full professor in 1977. Despite his love for literature, Parker chafed at the constraints and pretensions of academia and yearned to make his living as a writer. Parker began work on the first Spenser novel, *The Godwulf Manuscript*, in November 1971 and finished it, writing about a page a day, in March 1973. Buoyed by the success of his early Spenser novels, Parker retired from academia in 1979 to write full-time. Practice brought his mature writing speed up to about five pages a day and four months per novel.

Parker acknowledges that he has mined his family and his experiences for his novels. Like Spenser's companion, Susan Silverman, Joan Parker is a child psychologist who regards the kitchen as alien territory. Spenser's adopted son, Paul Giacomin, is a dancer, modeled on Parker's oldest son, Daniel. Even the Parkers' German shorthaired pointer, Pearl, is identical to the dog that first makes its appearance in *Pastime* (1991). And Spenser's interests in cooking, weight lifting, carpentry, clothes, good liquor, and baseball mirror Parker's own. The Parkers' marriage went through a period of strain in the late 1970s, a separation reflected in the Spenser novels, particularly *The Widening Gyre* (1983) and *A Catskill Eagle* (1985). The Parkers found they could not live together—neither could they live apart. They solved their personal dilemma by dividing their large Victorian home in Cambridge, Massachusetts, into two dwellings where they each lead semi-independent lives. The Parkers, like their fictional counterparts, Spenser and Susan, date regularly and spend weekends together in a 1697 farmhouse they have restored in Concord, Massachusetts. The Parkers have founded Pearl Productions, a Boston-based independent film company named after their dog, Pearl.

The Spenser Novels

When *The Godwulf Manuscript* appeared in 1973, it was hailed as a witty, well-plotted mystery, but there was little to suggest that its wise-cracking, thirty-seven-year-old hero would transform American detective fiction. Before Parker began writing mysteries, of course, he had written his doctoral dissertation on Hammett, Chandler, and Macdonald, and his hard-boiled homework showed. As Spenser's name and his background as a Korean veteran and former heavyweight boxer indicate, Parker not only was using his own life for material but was attempting to fashion a warrior detective hero who would pay homage to Chandler's knightly preoccupations. Spenser also carries forward the genre's anti-authoritarian politics: readers learn that he has been bounced from the Massachusetts state police for insubordination. As *The Godwulf Manuscript* opens, Spenser has been called in by the president of a second-rate university in Boston to find an illuminated manuscript that has been stolen from the library. The culprits belong to one of those lunatic fringe organizations beloved of detective fiction—this one is called SCACE, Student Committee Against Capitalist Exploitation. About halfway through the novel, the manuscript turns up and Spenser is out of a job; but, like every self-respecting, autonomous detective before him, Spenser keeps plugging away at his personal crusade. "I'm not the cops," Spenser tells a sullen SCACE-ite, "I'm freelance, for crissake" (p. 64). Spenser wants to clear Terry Orchard, the girlfriend of a SCACE member, of murder charges. As usual, however, even that secondary plot is a cover story for investigations into American society. In this case, the investigation explores the worm-eaten core of traditional masculinity, which by the early 1970s was under assault by that familiar hard-boiled foe, female perversity, as well as by the new threat of feminism and the heady promises of the "male liberation" movement.

The male characters in *The Godwulf Manuscript* (Spenser, of course, excepted) are a parade of the walking wounded—victims of destructive roles who are too far gone even for the healing ministrations of the male liberation movement. Rolly Orchard, Terry's multimillionaire father, is an obsessive breadwinner who winds up being rejected by his ersatz hippie daughter and cuckolded by his wife. (In fact, Spenser seduces both Orchard's wife and daughter. Casing out the Orchard mansion before having his way with Mrs. Orchard, Spenser asks after the whereabouts of her husband. "At the office," sneers Mrs. Orchard. "Sitting behind his big masculine desk. Trying to feel like a man" (p. 103). English professor Lowell Hayden, who is the faculty advisor to SCACE and the mastermind behind the original theft, suffers from problems of a different sort. Because he has become involved with a group of hippies and has fallen under the sway of their androgynous, flower-power ethic, Hayden has mutated into a "girly-man," complete with long blonde hair and a slender build. To make matters worse, Hayden earns his living teaching medieval poetry. (Parker, having narrowly escaped from what he portrays as the emasculating maw of a university English department, is pitiless, here and in his other novels, in his treatment of academia. In fact, some of Parker's former colleagues at Boston University claim that Hayden strangely resembles the former head of the English department.) Hayden's wife, Judy, provides the conclusive evidence of his masculine deficiencies—recalling the mismatched couple from Ernest Hemingway's *The Sun Also Rises*, Judy is a lumpish Lady Brett to his fey Jake Barnes. Spenser describes every red-blooded American man's nightmare.

> A big hatchet-faced woman in her mid-thirties answered my ring. She was taller than I was and her blond hair was pulled back in a tight bun. She wore no make-up, and the only thing that ornamented her face were huge Gloria Steinem glasses with gold rims and pink lenses. . . . She wore a man's green pullover sweater, Levi's, and penny loafers without socks. . . . She was as lean and hard as a canoe paddle and nearly as sexy. (p. 149)

The Gloria Steinem glasses are a dead giveaway that Judy is one of those radical feminist types who eat men for breakfast.

Between Judy and an English department

secretary whom Spenser dubs "Mary Masculine," *The Godwulf Manuscript* did not garner Parker any consciousness-raising citations. Judy eventually proves to be a better man than her husband by taking a bullet for him; Hayden gets shipped off to jail; and society is once again safe in the hands of Spenser, who has proved himself immune to Judy's bluster and only momentarily susceptible to the Orchard women's charms. At this point in his development, Spenser is pretty much a vestigial figure—a flared-trousered version of the 1930s tough guy who is autonomous, physical, and emotionally guarded. The only hint that he may be susceptible to his society's changing definitions of masculinity is his hobby, gourmet cooking.

For its first few chapters, *God Save the Child* (1974), the second novel in the series, looks to be more of the same thing. Roger Bartlett, the client who hires Spenser to find his runaway son, Kevin, is a hen-pecked husband who performs suspiciously womanly chores like the laundry. His wife, Marge, is promiscuous and domineering. When Spenser visits the local high school to confer with Susan Silverman, Kevin's guidance counselor, he walks into her office and ogles a secretary. (This is a rerun of the opening scene in *The Godwulf Manuscript*, where Spenser charms the college president's secretary, Brenda Loring, whom he subsequently starts dating.) But, in an extraordinary moment in the history of American detective fiction, lust gives way to something more emotionally complex when Spenser meets Susan Silverman:

> Susan Silverman wasn't beautiful, but there was a tangibility about her, a physical reality, that made the secretary with the lime-green bosom seem insubstantial. . . . It was hard to tell her age, but there was a sense about her of intelligent maturity which put her on my side of thirty. (p. 36)

This surely is the first time in American detective fiction that a tough guy is smitten by the radiance of a woman's life experience, rather than the radius of her bosom. Spenser does not immediately throw over the bouncy Brenda for the good-looking, brainy Susan. In *God Save the Child* and throughout most of its successor, *Mortal Stakes* (1975), he divides his time between the two women, calling up Brenda when he wants "fun and wisecracks" (*Mortal Stakes*, p. 255) and Susan when he wants intelligent conversation combined with playful lovemaking. But the fact that Spenser is drawn to a woman like Susan signals that Parker has begun to overhaul the traditional hard-boiled romance formula, which dictated that the detective hero regarded attractive women either with fear and loathing (and rightly so, since they were almost always femme fatales) or with wistful longing for what might have been. Susan, on the other hand, is a sexually compelling, self-supporting, divorced career woman who identifies herself as a feminist. Susan stirs up Spenser's anxieties about intimacy and commitment, but, crucially, not his hatred. Over the course of ten years and twelve novels—from *Mortal Stakes* (1975) to *A Catskill Eagle* (1985)—Parker dramatizes Spenser's deepening, albeit conflicted, relationship to Susan, as well as to the key members of the alternative family he is assembling. In doing so, Parker invests the figure of the detective with a contemporary, emotionally vulnerable ideal of masculinity.

In *Mortal Stakes*, Spenser eschews the simple pursuits of missing manuscripts and spouses and, instead, explicitly tackles the knottier puzzle of trying to figure out what makes a man a man. Posing as a sportswriter, Spenser infiltrates the socially conservative milieu of professional baseball in order to determine whether Red Sox phenomenon Marty Rabb is on the take. He quickly learns that a sleazy sports announcer is pressuring Rabb to throw games by threatening to reveal that Rabb's wife, Linda, was once a prostitute. Forced to choose between his job or his family, Rabb makes the noble decision to shield his wife and young son, but his betrayal of the baseball brotherhood tears him apart. Several times throughout the novel, Rabb equates being a man with being a good husband, father, and ballplayer—to falter in any one of those categories endangers his sense of masculine selfhood.

Rabb's dilemma underscores why private eyes traditionally have avoided marriage: it is impossible to be wedded to both a job and a woman. What is remarkable about *Mortal Stakes*, however, is that Spenser does not flee further into his work and away from personal relationships despite what he sees of how such entanglements compromise Rabb's integrity. Instead, he becomes more and more drawn to the possibility of close connection with others. Arriving at Lieutenant Quirk's office to be questioned about his role in the murders of two hitmen, Spenser fixates on a clear plastic cube on Quirk's desk that contains pictures of his family. (The fact that Quirk displays such a family cube on his desk in the first place signals that he, like Spenser, is evolving into some new 1970s strain of "hard-soft" man.) As their conversation grows more heated, Quirk declares:

> "We've known each other awhile, Spenser, and maybe we got a certain amount of respect. But we're not friends. And I'm not a guy you know. I'm a cop."
>
> "Nothing else?"
>
> "Yeah," Quirk said, "something else. I'm a husband and a father and a cop. But the last one's the only thing that makes any difference to you."
>
> "No, not quite. The husband and father makes a difference too. Nobody should be just a job." (p. 294)

In 1926, Dashiell Hammett's Continental Op declared that, apart from work, he did not enjoy anything. For generations thereafter, every self-respecting gumshoe swore the same oath of obsessive-compulsive loyalty to his job. Now, along comes Spenser who, as his reply to Quirk indicates, is struggling to cast off the constricting old tough-guy trenchcoat of misanthropic machismo and is attempting to step into a roomier version of masculinity.

Toward the end of *Mortal Stakes*, Spenser turns away from good-time girl Brenda to the more emotionally demanding Susan. This shift occurs at the same time that Spenser's heretofore rigid code of good-guy behavior begins crumbling. Spenser's code required that he "never . . . allow innocents to be victimized and never . . . kill people except involuntarily" (p. 326). However, at the climax of the novel, Spenser must betray the second of those imperatives in order to preserve the first. In the last scene of the novel, Spenser reviews the case over dinner with Susan. This is another hard-boiled mystery milestone: traditional tough guys retreated to their rooms after a case was closed and nuzzled up to a bottle of bourbon. Spenser says:

> "I know what's killing [Rabb]. It's killing me too. The code didn't work."
>
> "The code."
>
> "Yeah, jock ethic, honor, code, whatever. It didn't cover the situation." (p. 327)

Note the uncertainty of that ending. Spenser is not sure what makes a man a man these days, and neither is Parker, nor the reader. What is clear, however, is that the old definitions of manhood are not adequate for the changing times. If Spenser's hard-boiled shell is cracked and compromised at the end of *Mortal Stakes*, by the end of *Promised Land* (1976) he is looking more like Humpty Dumpty than Humphrey Bogart. Once again, the novel showcases a spectacularly dysfunctional, upper-middle-class suburban family. Harvey Shepherd is a Cape Cod real estate developer whose latest project has gone belly-up. (As a rather heavy-handed commentary on the real estate industry's packaging of the American Dream, Parker calls Shepherd's doomed development the "Promised Land".) An unreconstructed type of guy, Shepherd believes he is fulfilling his primary responsibility toward his wife and kids by erratically providing for them. But, by the late seventies, wives with raised consciousnesses were demanding more of their bewildered husbands. Shepherd's wife, Pam, yearns for emotional intimacy and, when she cannot find it with her workaholic husband, she pursues it in a series of one-nighters at the local motel.

When the novel opens, Pam has run away and Harvey calls in Spenser to find her. Spenser soon learns that Pam has joined a radical feminist group headed by (what else?) a humorless, man-hating, slogan spouter and her bra-less lesbian bodyguard. These guerrilla Amazons, with Pam in tow, rob a bank to finance their evil plot to destroy the patriarchy and, in the process, kill an elderly bodyguard. Spenser subsequently decides that his mission is to liberate the gullible Pam from her wicked companions and to rid society of these trigger-happy she-monsters by sending them to prison. In *Promised Land,* Parker sets up the boundaries of what is permissible in terms of feminist politics: armed overthrow is out, but quiet revolution from within is a definite possibility.

The fact that feminists are the primary villains of this novel suggests Parker's—and Spenser's—continuing ambivalence toward the women's movement. Ambivalence is the word, rather than antipathy, because another woman who figures prominently in the novel identifies herself as a feminist; she also happens to be the woman with whom Spenser finds himself nervously falling in love. In a dramatically different reprise of Carmen Sternwood's infiltration of Marlowe's bachelor lair, Susan turns up unexpectedly in Spenser's motel room. When he enters, Susan is lying on the bed, not naked like the lamia-like Carmen, but clothed and reading a book by Erik Erikson. Instead of kicking this female interloper out and then destroying the befouled sheets, Spenser declares that he is thrilled to see Susan. But, later that day, Spenser has reason to regret his unguarded admission when Susan tells him that she loves him. Like Pam, Susan has been hungering for greater closeness and commitment from her man and, at first, she does not seem any more likely to get it. Spenser hems and haws and mutters moth-eaten lines about not wanting to complicate things. Then, after a marathon workout in the motel weightroom, a bourbon binge in the bar, and a solitary night in his room, Spenser faces Susan again and speaks to her the phrase that is to tough guys what

Kryptonite is to Superman: "I love you" (p. 99).

Toward the end of *Promised Land,* Spenser even proposes marriage to Susan, but fortunately she turns him down. The reason? Work. Susan does not want to give up her work as a guidance counselor in Smithfield, and Spenser surely is not about to relocate his office to some suburban mall. What Spenser and Susan fashion is a relationship (based on the real-life one of Parker and his wife, Joan) that also resembles the notorious open marriage of the political philosopher (and ur–detective fiction writer) William Godwin and the feminist writer Mary Wollstonecraft. Like their famous counterparts, Spenser and Susan maintain separate dwellings and occasionally enjoy separate relationships. (Early in the series, Spenser still holds on to vestiges of his hard-boiled manhood by engaging in sexual encounters on the side, as in his fling with reporter Candy Sloan in the Los Angeles–based mystery *A Savage Place,* 1981. This dubious double standard collapses when Susan runs off to California with another man in the 1985 mystery *A Catskill Eagle.* Ever since, a chastened Spenser has been monogamous.) Spenser and Susan's unconventional relationship, of course, depends on the necessary absence of children—an issue that arises later in the series.

As a product of the pre-sixties "masculine mystique," Parker himself clearly harbored some dread that turning his detective into a feminist might also turn him into a wimp. As *Promised Land* launches Spenser on his journey into the brave new world of sensitive manhood, it also expresses heightened anxieties about whether this journey of self-discovery will compromise his masculinity. Consequently, to reassure readers of Spenser's masculinity while also providing tangible evidence of his progress as a new man, *Promised Land* introduces Hawk, an African-American gun slinger whose name not only conjures up animalistic, predatory associations but also alludes to "Hawkshaw"—1920s slang for a detective. Hawk considers Spenser his masculine equal, even though he initially regards

Spenser's views on violence and women as soft.

When Spenser introduces Susan to Hawk (who has been hired by a big-time loan shark to put pressure on Harvey Shepherd), she is unnerved by the professional cordiality that exists between the two men and tries to draw moral distinctions between them:

> "But. . . ." Susan looked for the right words. "But [Spenser] does what he must, his aim is to help. Yours is to hurt."
>
> "Not right," Hawk said. "Maybe he aiming to help. But he also like the work. You know? I mean he could be a social worker if he just want to help. . . . Just don't be so sure me and old Spenser are so damn different." (p. 88)

Hawk's testimony reinforces Spenser's manhood at this critical juncture—real men do not become social workers. But, in his mercenary attitude to his work and his nonchalant attitude toward violence, Hawk here functions as Spenser's id—a negative example of what Spenser's aggressive instincts might turn him into if he does not keep them in check with the civilizing help of both Susan's companionship and literature. (One of Spenser's habits is to quote—and sometimes misquote—poetry for every occasion.)

Spenser not only acquires a best male buddy in *Promised Land* but also a steady female companion. Thus he has exceeded the quota, by two, of the number of intimate companions the traditional hard-boiled detective was allowed to have in his life. Tough guys like Mike Hammer might regularly butt heads with amiable police foils like Pat Chambers and play "palsy-walsy" with nice girls like his secretary, Velda, throughout the course of a series, but they never shared feelings, took vacations together, or hung out at each other's apartments. Spenser, in contrast, does not limit himself to Hawk or Susan but adds to his menagerie by acquiring a trusted friend in lesbian author Rachel Wallace, an adopted son in Paul Giacomin, and a "baby" in Pearl the hunting dog whose custody he shares with Susan. That is not even counting stand-up folks like cops Marty Quirk and Frank Belson or gym owner Henry Cimoli—all of whom have been with Spenser from almost the beginning of the series.

In *The Judas Goat* (1978), the more traditionally action-packed novel that followed *Promised Land*, Spenser and Hawk go to Europe together at the behest of multimillionaire Hugh Dixon to track down the revolutionaries whose random bombing of a London restaurant wiped out Dixon's family. Spenser frequently comments on Hawk's character throughout this novel and makes him sound much less human than the bomb-throwing zealots they are hunting. Midway through the novel, Spenser informs Susan that "Hawk has no feelings. . . . He's as good as anyone I ever saw at what he does. But he never seems happy or sad or frightened or elated. He never, in the twenty-some years I've known him, here and there, has shown any sign of love or compassion. He's never been nervous. He's never been mad."

"Are you a version of him?" the understandably anxious Susan then asks. "I got feelings," new man Spenser responds (though his uncharacteristic grammatical slip perhaps betrays the anxiety such an admission stirs up in Spenser). "I love" (pp. 166–167).

But Hawk's Zen combination of Star Trek's Mr. Spock and The Lone Ranger's Tonto was a hard act for Parker to sustain. First of all, some critics protested the inherent racism they saw in Parker's creation of a black sidekick who would carry out all the real dirty work. As the quintessential "other," devoid of emotion, Hawk is disturbingly similar to all those outlaw people of color who stirred up trouble in early hard-boiled fiction. Second, even Hawk was not immune to the influence of feminism on the culture. Around the middle of the Spenser series, he begins smiling and telling Spenser to give Susan his love.

After an intervening non-Spenser book (*Wilderness*, 1979), Parker wrote the fascinating novel *Looking for Rachel Wallace*, which was published in 1980. Rachel Wallace is a well-known radical feminist, out-of-the-closet lesbian author who has been receiving death threats. Her publishers insist that she hire Spenser as a bodyguard and what ensues, throughout the novel, is a series of sparring matches between the stereotypically humorless Wallace and Spenser about the nature of masculinity, feminism, and homosexuality. At the beginning of the novel, Wallace and Spenser are barely civil to each other, and his attitude toward her lesbianism would hardly pass as politically correct. Meeting Wallace's lover, a very attractive young woman, Spenser asks himself: "Was I a sexist? Was it ugly to think, *What a waste?*" (p. 60). But, in a variation of the old Hollywood plot where the potential lovers start out with mutual loathing and end the movie wrapped in each other's arms, Wallace and Spenser come to develop a deep regard for each other. Rachel is kidnapped toward the end of the novel and Spenser fears for her life. Fighting his way through a snowstorm that has paralyzed all of Boston, Spenser rescues Rachel from her captors, a dysfunctional family who hold her responsible for corrupting their daughter into a life of lesbianism. In a sobbing, hugfest of an ending, Rachel learns to respect, if not wholly approve, Spenser's macho code; Spenser, in turn, abandons some of his preconceptions and accepts a lesbian into his extended alternative family. Spenser's transformation into a new man has accelerated by the conclusion of *Looking for Rachel Wallace.*

The revised ideas about masculinity and the family that Parker had been working out in the early books came to fruition in *Early Autumn* (1981), his extraordinary seventh Spenser novel. *Early Autumn*, which contains only a faint suggestion of a mystery plot, really functions as a bildungsroman in which Spenser teaches the teen-aged Paul Giacomin how to be a man as they build a house together—even as Parker is building for Spenser a new kind of family grounded in elective affinities, not biology. Spenser first meets his future son Paul when the boy's mother, Patty, hires Spenser to kidnap him back from her ex-husband, Mel, who has violated their custody agreement. Mel and Patty constitute yet another textbook couple who illustrate the dan-

gers of unthinking adherence to traditional heterosexual roles. Mel, a former football hero, demonstrates a masculine affect as out of date as his body is out of shape. (We immediately know Mel is a macho mess because he is wearing a Ban-Lon shirt when Spenser first meets him. Sartorially savvy Spenser tells him, "You shouldn't wear a Ban-Lon shirt like that if you're going to scare people. It's a loser" [p. 20]. Subsequently, Mel gives up his son Paul without a fight—confirming Spenser's fundamental belief that clothes make the man.)

Patty espouses a muddled philosophy that combines "self-actualization" with total subservience to men. After Patty has subjected Spenser to a dose of her Stepford Wife thinking, he wonders aloud if Gloria Steinem makes house calls. (Spenser has noticeably warmed toward Steinem since that early crack about Judy Hayden's glasses in *The Godwulf Manuscript.*) " 'Oh, that's crap,' Patty Giacomin said. Her color was high. 'You probably mouth the liberal line like everyone else around here, but you know what's reality all right. Men have the money and power and if a woman wants some, she better get a hold of a man' " (p. 55).

Patty will do anything to hold on to her man of the moment, a slick lounge lizard whom Spenser dubs "Disco Steve." Consequently, when he threatens to tell Steve about Patty's monthly trips to a New York hotel where she has sex with strangers, Patty consents to hand over sole, unofficial custody of Paul to Spenser. At first, Paul looks like an unlikely candidate for the role of "son of Spenser." He is skinny and surly, indecisive and unkempt. Early in the novel, Spenser whisks the whining Paul away to a rickety cabin Susan owns in the Maine woods. Spenser ostensibly wants to protect the boy from the kidnappers his father has hired, but his ulterior motive is to give Paul a personality makeover.

Weeks pass and Paul learns how to lift weights, wield a hammer, and cook. He also comes to appreciate baseball and, with Spenser's bemused encouragement, nurtures his formerly forbidden passion for ballet. Most important, Paul learns how to be a new man like Spenser. On this extended "wild man" weekend, Spenser teaches Paul not to categorize people and tells him it's okay to cry sometimes. The most precious gift Spenser gives Paul is the quality that he himself holds most dear: autonomy. Spenser tells Paul that he needs to "get autonomous."

"Huh?"

"Autonomous. Dependent on yourself. Not influenced unduly by things outside yourself. . . . It's too early to ask a kid like you to be autonomous. But you got no choice. Your parents are no help to you. If anything, they hurt." (p. 123)

Ironically, in carrying out his mission to give Paul autonomy, Spenser abridges his own. This is the exquisitely tricky Scylla and Charybdis of gender behavior that new men like Spenser must navigate. To be a man (and a hard-boiled detective worth his license), Spenser needs to be able to stand tall and alone; but, to avoid turning into just another casualty of the masculine mystique (like Mel), Spenser also needs to create intimate connections with other people—which he does here by incorporating Paul into his alternative family. Consequently, by the time they return to civilization, Spenser has succeeded in spontaneously generating a son.

Spenser breaks away from the family theme in *A Savage Place* (1981), a novel set in Los Angeles, where he enjoys an extracurricular sexual relationship with reporter Candy Sloan. *A Savage Place* is one of Parker's fictional homages to Raymond Chandler—the key scenes and situations in *A Savage Place* have their origins in Chandler's masterpiece, *The Big Sleep*. (The title, *A Savage Place*, is a reference to the description of the fantastic kingdom of Xanadu in Samuel Taylor Coleridge's famous poem, "Kubla Khan":

A savage place! as holy and enchanted
As e'er beneath a waning moon was haunted
By woman waiting for her demon lover!

For Xanadu, read Los Angeles in Parker's novel. Throughout his career, Parker has gotten inspiration for his titles from canonical works by Shakespeare, Melville, Yeats, and, most recently, Spenser's namesake, the British Renaissance poet Edmund Spenser, author of *The Faerie Queene*.) *A Savage Place* distinguishes itself as a superior Spenser novel through its ending: Spenser is unable to prevent Candy from walking into a setup, and she is killed. Candy's death represents one of Spenser's few out-and-out failures. In *Ceremony* (1982), however, Parker returns Spenser to the dysfunctional family situations he excels at investigating. April Kyle, a student at the high school where Susan works as a guidance counselor, has dropped out and is working as a prostitute in Boston's Combat Zone. In an interesting, morally complicated ending, Spenser paternalistically rescues April from the streets but subsequently respects her refusal to be returned to her family. Instead, much to Susan's disgust, Spenser helps April fulfill her career ambitions by placing her in the care of Patricia Utley, a high-class madam.

The Widening Gyre (1983) is a comparatively formulaic novel about political corruption. Ronni Alexander, the fundamentalist Christian wife of Senate candidate Meade Alexander, turns out to have a weakness for sex and alcohol—a weakness that has been captured on videotape. Spenser steps in to repel the goons who are blackmailing Alexander to drop out of the Senate race. The novel, which contains strong echoes of the plot of *Mortal Stakes* (a good man being compromised by the flawed woman he married), is distinctive in the Spenser corpus for its Washington, D.C., setting and for its hints of a developing strain in Spenser's and Susan's relationship. That strain intensifies in *Valediction* (1984), which opens with Susan's graduation from Harvard (she receives a Ph.D. in psychology) and her surprise announcement that she has taken a job in San Francisco. Spenser spends much of the novel in a shell-shocked daze, cared for by Paul, Hawk, Henry Cimoli, and the rest of his extended family. Paul interests Spenser in a case involving the disappearance of one of the dancers performing with him in the Tommy Banks Dancers. Spenser's weakened state of mind accounts for the shocking ending of the novel, in which our invincible hero is nearly fatally injured by a hired gun—a situation that will occur again in *Small Vices* (1997).

Spenser's relationship problems, as well as the widespread political ramifications of the hard-boiled detective's adoption of an alternative family of mostly marginalized people, come to the fore in *A Catskill Eagle* (1985)—the novel Parker considers his magnus opus. In *A Catskill Eagle*, Spenser demonstrates that, in putting together his own multicultural tribe, he was doing much more than defending himself against a lonely old age. Instead, he was assembling a citizen militia in preparation for fighting an all-out culture war.

A Catskill Eagle begins with an outlandish premise. Though protesting that she still loves Spenser, Susan has left him (their estrangement, as noted, has been developing throughout the previous novels *The Widening Gyre* and *Valediction* as Susan has become more engrossed in her doctoral studies in psychology). She has moved to a small town near San Francisco to "find herself." Unbeknownst to Spenser, Susan has also become romantically involved with Russell Costigan, son of a wealthy industrialist. Since none of Spenser's romantic rivals are permitted to be as much of a man as Spenser, we quickly learn that Costigan is an emotionally unbalanced fellow with a serious Oedipal complex. When Susan belatedly begins to pull back from Russell, he orders his security goons to virtually hold her prisoner in her own apartment. Panicked, Susan phones Hawk and implores him to extricate her from this mess. But, since the Costigan family owns the town, Hawk is thrown in prison minutes after he arrives. Reluctantly, Susan then sends a note to Spenser, asking him to fly to the rescue.

Mama's boy Russell turns out to be a straw man; the real villain of this novel is Russell's father, Jerry, a white supremacist and "frontier radicalist" who believes in absolute individual freedom. Jerry makes a bundle fomenting revolutions in foreign countries and then selling arms to sustain the conflicts. For practical and symbolic reasons, Spenser cannot go up against this ultralibertarian alone. He must vanquish Jerry's ideology by calling upon his own coalition of rainbow warriors. Every single member of the Spenser clan—from lowly Henry Cimoli to Spenser's own personal Daddy Warbucks, Hugh Dixon from *The Judas Goat*—gather behind him to do battle with Costigan and his mercenaries. The stakes of the struggle are most clearly articulated by Spenser's friend, the lesbian feminist author Rachel Wallace. Called in to do research on the Costigan family, she tells Spenser and Hawk that Jerry Costigan is:

> "An anti-Semite. He seems to believe that America is in danger of being overrun by blacks and Jews and foreigners and"—she smiled again—"lesbians."
>
> "The lesbians are arming?" I said.
>
> "And gay men," she said, "and feminists and the IRS."
>
> "How about the worldwide Roman Catholic conspiracy," I said.
>
> "You get the idea," Rachel Wallace said. "Costigan appears to be fearful that America will be overrun by Americans." (pp. 260–261)

It is interesting to note that in *A Promised Land*, Spenser actually did encounter armed and dangerous lesbians. The rapid extent to which the politics of the series changed can be measured by the fact that only four years later, in *Looking for Rachel Wallace* (1980), lesbians such as Rachel were depicted as intelligent, attractive human beings with whom Spenser, albeit a wee bit uncomfortably, warmly connects.

Ostensibly, the Spenser-Costigan face-off is a battle over Susan, but it really turns into an apocalyptic confrontation between the forces of the liberal left and those of the pathologically nativist right over the issue of who gets to define America. In the surreal climax when Spenser, like some Dantesque hero, descends into Costigan's underground fortress and puts a bullet through Jerry's head, he is shooting down, once and for all, the status quo. Hard-boiled America is no longer the domain of socially conservative, wealthy, white, straight men; instead, it has been turned over to enlightened guys like Spenser and his rag-tag band of feminists, African-Americans, gays, and ethnics. Spenser emerges from his epic underground struggle in silence and returns to Boston with his exhausted but victorious troops.

Parker, too, seemed exhausted after *A Catskill Eagle*, turning out a series of thinner novels throughout the late 1980s and into the 1990s. Furthermore, some critics maintain that, after the emotional conflagration of *A Catskill Eagle*, the relationship between Spenser and Susan has lost its spark. Certainly, many of the novels that followed lacked the snappy dialogue that is one of Parker's strong points as a writer.

Taming a Sea-horse (1986) resurrects the character of April Kyle from *Ceremony*. April has left the care of her enlightened madam, Patricia Utley, and has begun turning tricks for the man she loves, a musician named Robert Rambeaux. When April disappears, Spenser snaps into action and discovers that Rambeaux is far from the starving musician he pretends to be; rather, he presides over a stable of hookers. Once again, Spenser returns April to comparative safety if not to moral salvation. *Pale Kings and Princes* (1987) is another medium-grade Spenser novel. Spenser is hired to investigate the brutal murder of a reporter named Eric Valdez. Valdez himself was investigating the drug trade in Wheaton, Massachusetts, a town that has become home to a large number of Colombian immigrants. While Spenser's probing into Valdez's death unearths his murderers, his efforts also result in the deaths of two people. Fortunately, Susan is on hand to help Spenser deal with the moral and psychological ramifications of his actions.

Crimson Joy (1988) takes readers further into Susan's professional world, as she is threatened by a lunatic who turns out to be a patient. As might be expected, the novel features many arguments between Susan and Spenser over the issue of her autonomy: since

Spenser and his compatriots, including Hawk, Frank Belson, and newcomer Lee Farrell (a gay cop) must camp out in Susan's home in order to apprehend her stalker, Susan justifiably feels crowded. *Playmates* (1989) returns Spenser to the sports world. This time, Spenser is called in to investigate why the best power forward in all of college basketball, Dwayne Woodcock, is shaving points. In still another replay of the *Mortal Stakes* scenario, Dwayne's girlfriend holds part of the answer. *Stardust* (1990) is, arguably, the most disappointing Spenser novel. Hailed as a "show biz thriller," it takes Spenser onto the set of a Boston-based show, *Fifty Minutes*, whose glamorous female star, Jill Joyce, is receiving anonymous threats. While Spenser works on finding Joyce's harrasser, Susan works on getting Joyce to confront her inner demons.

Mercifully, this run of mediocre Spenser novels was broken with *Pastime* (1991). *Pastime* returns readers to the Giacomin family as Paul seeks Spenser's help in finding his mother, Patty, who has disappeared. Paul is now in his early twenties and a struggling dancer, and Spenser's benevolent shaping influence on him is evident. In *Pastime*, Spenser also goes into more detail about his own upbringing. (Like Macbeth, Spenser is "not of woman born." According to the story that he belatedly shares with Susan in *A Catskill Eagle*, Spenser's mother died when she was pregnant, and he was delivered by Cesarean section and raised by his father and two maternal uncles in Wyoming. These guys, ur-new men, taught Spenser carpentry and cooking and an appreciation for literature—the very skills he passes on to Paul Giacomin. However, in some of the early novels, Spenser refers to his mother and claims he learned cooking from her. Obviously, Parker decided somewhere along the way that he wanted to emphasize the androgynous aspects of Spenser's all-male legacy.)

Double Deuce (1992), while not one of the best Spenser novels, is interesting because it focuses most intensely on Hawk. Hawk enlists Spenser's volunteer help in ridding a Boston housing project of its resident gang. Spenser soon discovers that Hawk's motivations are not completely altruistic: Hawk has been seeing a stunning, recently divorced childhood friend named Jackie who is the producer of a local *Hard Copy*–type television show. If Jackie can get footage of Hawk and Spenser flushing out the gang, her show's ratings will soar. Hawk obviously cares for Jackie—which represents a marked change from his earlier *Judas Goat* incarnation—but he does not allow himself to fully open up to her. Jackie complains, "He's fun to be with. He's funny. He knows stuff. He's a dandy lover. . . . But I can't seem to get at him" (p. 183). After he and Jackie break up, Hawk offers Spenser this terse explanation: "It never seemed a good idea to believe in [Love]. . . . Always seemed easier for me to stay intact if you didn't" (p. 218). While he is no rival to Spenser in the vulnerability department, Hawk's willingness to articulate his feelings (or lack of them) has grown dramatically over the years. Had he stayed stuck in that opaque, monosyllabic role that Parker originally created for him, he would have been as outmoded a male stereotype as Mike Hammer.

In *Double Deuce*, the relationship between Spenser and Susan also endures more stresses. Susan pressures Spenser into moving in with her and their "baby," the dog Pearl. For the space of a week, the domestically challenged Susan cooks dreadful dinners for Spenser and nags him about his whereabouts until, using her expensive doctoral training in psychology where it is most needed, she realizes that she has been engaging in a futile attempt to live up to her mother's example. Spenser then retreats back to his own lair and the couple resume their pattern of weekly sleep-overs. In the succeeding novels, up to *Small Vices* (1997), Spenser and Susan are renovating a colonial-era summer house, where they plan to eventually live together. The completion of this house, however, like Scheherazade's story cycle, seems destined to be indefinitely deferred. The dream of a shared house, as it turns out, will vanish in *Small Vices* (1997).

In *Paper Doll* (1993), another medium-grade novel, Spenser investigates crime in his own backyard. He is hired by the husband of Olivia Nelson, a woman who was bludgeoned to death on the streets of Beacon Hill, to find her killer. As is so often the case, in the course of his investigations Spenser also ferrets out the skeletons in the closet of the traditional family. *Walking Shadow* (1994), like the earlier *Double Deuce* and *Pale Kings and Princes*, is noteworthy because it takes Spenser out of his own community and drops him into unfamiliar ethnic and racial territory. A waterfront town in Massachusetts called Port City (echoes of Chandler's Bay City here) is home to a thriving and sometimes violent Chinese-American community. Spenser is called in to investigate the death of an actor who was shot dead on the stage of a local theater. The politics of *Walking Shadow*, however, are somewhat contradictory: while Parker attempts to vary the portrait of the Asian community in Port City, he also has Spenser do battle with an Asian dragon lady straight out of the pages of Sax Rohmer's Dr. Fu Manchu series.

Spenser's alternative family members, Boston detectives Frank Belson and Marty Quirk, come to the fore in *Thin Air* (1995). The middle-aged Belson has married a gorgeous young woman named Lisa St. Claire. Shortly after the marriage, she is kidnapped by a former lover who happens to be the kingpin of a Hispanic gang. As happens so often with the wives and girlfriends of primary Spenser clients and associates, Lisa has been hiding a sordid past, which Spenser uncovers in the course of rescuing her. Because it explores the mind of Lisa's abuser, *Thin Air* represents something of a regrettable foray into soft-core voyeurism for Parker. That Spenser becomes privy to the conjugal details of Belson's married life in this novel also signifies how close the two men have grown. *Chance* (1996), another one of the weakest Spenser novels, also embroils our detective in someone else's marital troubles. Boston mobster Julius Ventura hires Spenser and Hawk to find his daughter's missing husband, who, it soon becomes apparent, wants to stay missing. The novel takes Spenser and Hawk into the seamy netherworld of Las Vegas; it turns out to be less about a kidnapping than about a power struggle for control of Boston's mobs. While the Vegas setting is an intriguing change of scene for Spenser, the plotting and dialogue are mere shadows of the classic Spenser books.

Small Vices (1997) is a comeback novel for Parker: in this twenty-fourth Spenser outing, Parker's detective rediscovers his own inner wit. Moreover, characters are sharply drawn and moral situations are refreshingly complex. As an extra bonus, the plot (never a strong point of the Spenser series) is ambitious. Like the earlier *Valediction*, it involves an assassination attempt that nearly kills Spenser. The story opens when Spenser's pal, former assistant district attorney Rita Fiore, summons him to her office to discuss an old murder case that she successfully prosecuted. Four years earlier, a wealthy Pemberton College coed was murdered, and a known sex offender named Ellis Alves was convicted of the crime. Rita now works for a large private law firm where she has once again encountered Alves's public defender, who has remained convinced of his innocence. Now troubled by doubts herself, Rita persuades her law firm to foot the bill to have Spenser reinvestigate the case.

Soon after he begins snooping, he is threatened by a sinister "man in gray" whom Spenser instinctively recognizes as a lethal opponent. An anxious, bullet-ridden game of cat and mouse ensues—one that Spenser almost loses. His almost year-long recuperation from the assassin's best efforts requires all of Spenser's will power as well as the loyal ministrations of Hawk and Susan. The trio hide out in California in a rented house as Spenser regains his strength. The sojourn is paid for by the sale of Spenser and Susan's vacation home, thereby ensuring that the issue of Spenser and Susan moving in together will be indefinitely postponed.

The extended rehabilitation episode raises the disquieting issue that the aging Spenser may no longer have the muscle mass for his physically demanding job. Age is also an issue in the subplot here, which involves Susan's thwarted desire to adopt a child with Spenser. The corrosive effects of time are also felt in this novel in other ways. In the previous books, when Parker's erudite detective has been asked his name, he has favored the flippant tag "Spenser, like the English poet." In *Small Vices*, when he sidles up to a nubile college student at a bar and tries the line, she simply looks blank. As the doomsayers have been warning us, cultural literacy is declining. But for fans of the Spenser series, it is cheering to find that Parker has resurrected his own formerly high standards of writing in *Small Vices*. Like some ancient fertility god, Spenser here manages to emerge from his ritualistic burial, stronger and sharper than ever.

The snappy repartee that signaled a welcome return to the Spenser of old in *Small Vices* is also a distinguishing feature of *Sudden Mischief* (1998), the twenty-fifth Spenser novel. As in so many other Spenser novels, the fractured traditional family here is the source of trouble. Susan's ex-husband, who has given himself the new, non-Jewish last name of "Sterling," turns up after a long absence to ask for her advice. It seems that in the course of putting together a giant charity fundraiser named "Galapalooza," Brad came into contact with a few wealthy young matrons who found his manners offensive. Consequently, Brad is now being charged with sexual harrassment. A much-married loser (Susan was his first wife) who is behind in child support payments, Brad cannot pay for legal or investigative aid; naturally knightly Spenser tells Susan he'll be happy to come to the rescue. As soon as Spenser visits Brad to offer his pro-bono services, however, Brad protests that Susan overreacted and that things are fine. Of course, Spenser goes with his gut, trusts Susan, and persists in sniffing around Brad's fishy business dealings and personal life. That's when the bodies begin piling up.

Sudden Mischief represents a weak reprise of the themes of *A Catskill Eagle*. Brad, like Russell Costigan, is another feeble man to whom Susan was once (inexplicably) attracted. As a rival to Spenser, he's about as threatening as Barney the dinosaur. Everything about Brad, unlike Spenser, is inauthentic: not only his name, but his speech and clothing have the aura of the faux Wasp about them. Unlike Russell, however, Brad is exposed as a truly evil person by the end of the book. The mystery plot here (which contains, for Parker, some surprisingly graphic sequences) alternates with lugubrious chapters in which Susan explores her childhood and tries to puzzle out her historical problems with men, Spenser included. As in *Catskill Eagle,* only the combined forces of Spenser, Hawk, Rachel Wallace, and Henry Cimoli can save Susan from her worst instincts.

Other Novels

Occasionally, Parker has taken breaks from Spenser to explore other kinds of characters and genres. *Three Weeks in Spring* (1977), written with his wife, Joan, describes her fight with breast cancer and the couple's subsequent struggles with the disease's physical and emotional aftermath. *Wilderness* (1979) is a straightforward suspense story that is strikingly more violent than any of the novels in the Spenser series. *Love and Glory* (1983) is a *Great Gatsby*–like novel with heavy autobiographical overtones that opens at Colby College in the 1950s. The young, unprepossessing, would-be writer Boone Adams falls in love with golden girl Jennifer Grayle. The novel traces Boone's struggle to win Jennifer's heart and kick his dependence on alcohol; it stretches from the 1950s through Boone's service in the Korean War, his entrance into graduate school, and his first job as an English professor in the 1970s. To widespread critical acclaim in 1994, Parker published *All Our Yesterdays,* a multigenerational saga that traces the fortunes of an Irish-American family from the early years of the twentieth century.

Parker has also embarked on a couple of joint writing ventures with his idol, Raymond Chandler. In 1989, Parker completed Chandler's fragment of a Philip Marlowe novel, *Poodle Springs.* Chandler had written the first four chapters of the novel before his death in 1959; it is a novel that, no doubt, would have been difficult for him to complete even if death had not intervened. Chandler's *Poodle Springs* finds Philip Marlowe married to the beautiful heiress Linda Loring. Parker took that untenable situation and apparently decided that the only way a marriage would work for Marlowe would be if it were updated to resemble the autonomous, separate residence arrangement that he has forged with Joan and that Spenser, in turn, enjoys with Susan. It is a clever solution, but the novel, which also includes a mystery plot centered on the seamy underside of the resort town of Poodle Springs (Palm Springs), was published to predictably mixed critical reaction. Parker revisited Chandler's turf in *Perchance to Dream* (1990), a sequel to Chandler's 1939 classic, *The Big Sleep.* Critical reaction to this second collaboration with Chandler was largely negative, although many reviewers praised Parker's ear for Chandler's language. Parker was named by the Chandler estate to do the writing because of the skill with which he has managed to carry forward Chandler's themes and world view in the Spenser novels.

In the fall of 1997, Parker published *Night Passage,* a novel intended to be the first in a new mystery series starring thirty-five-year-old Jesse Stone. Jesse is a former Los Angeles police detective who has been fired for alcoholism. (After he and his wife split up, Stone hits the bottle, heavily.) Jesse is offered the job of chief of police in a small Massachusetts town called (deceptively) Paradise. He soon learns that the offer was something of a setup, as the town erupts in murders and mobsters.

Night Passage may represent Parker's attempt to solve the problems that Spenser's advanced age has introduced into those novels. Certainly, even though Jesse is flawed by his past troubles with drink and the failure of his marriage, he bears many similarities to Spenser: his belief in a code, his sense of autonomy, his sassy, antiauthoritarian humor. By the end of the novel, Jesse and his wife are discussing reconciliation, which introduces the possibility that they may be engaged in working out a relationship similar to that of Spenser and Susan in future novels. It remains to be seen, however, whether Jesse will develop the kind of multilayered personality and complex alternative family that has helped make the Spenser novels beloved by millions of readers.

Reception

By many estimates, Spenser is the most popular detective character in America today: he has appeared in twenty-five novels, all of them, since 1983, best-sellers. As of 1992, over eighteen million Spenser novels have been printed in the United States, and more than two million have been printed abroad. The novels have been published in virtually every European nation, and they are especially popular in Japan, where "Spenser" has appeared in television commercials and where the *Illustrated Encyclopedia of Spenser Novels* is a steady seller. Spenser has also appeared on-screen in sixty-five hour-long episodes of the *Spenser: For Hire* (1984–1989) television program, as well as a series of made-for-television movies for the Lifetime cable network. (Both the series and the movies starred Robert Urich as Spenser and the incandescent Avery Brooks as Hawk.) Although some of the plots of the television show and the movies were lifted from Parker's novels, Urich's on-screen characterization of Spenser, in particular, is much softer and "cuter" than that of the novels. Parker himself did not care for the casting of Urich as Spenser, nor was he pleased with the Avery Brooks spin-off, *A Man Called Hawk*. There is a Spenser cookbook, a Spenser fan club ("The Judas Goats"), a Spenser guide to Boston, and even "Spenser's Bookstore" (specializing, naturally, in mysteries) in Boston. Given that Spenser is a hard-boiled detective who would rather quote poetry than shoot lowlifes, his wide-ranging popularity is astounding.

Parker is generally acclaimed as the clearly deserving heir to his dissertation subjects: Hammett, Chandler, and Macdonald. His Spenser novels have set the standard for contemporary detective fiction. His gift for dialogue and characterization, especially, have been hailed. Plots, on the other hand, are recognized as secondary to Parker, particularly in the Spenser series. Over the past ten years, many critics and reviewers have noted a falling off in the series, although just when he has been judged to be resting on his laurels, Parker will manage to produce an ambitious and interesting novel, such as *Small Vices*, that restores the series to its place of prominence.

In the mid-eighties, Spenser was one of the targets of a widespread backlash against the new androgynous man. In a 1984 essay in the *New York Times Book Review*, George Stade blasted Spenser, along with the male protagonists of recent fiction by Philip Roth, Frederick Barthelme, and Leonard Michaels, for their wimpish behavior (12 August 1984). Three years later, critic George F. Will weighed in with a *Washington Post* column, decrying the fact that Spenser was becoming a sensitive crybaby (18 October 1987). Some feminist critics have voiced objection to Susan as a female character in need of rescue in the traditional hard-boiled mold. Other critics, however, find Susan—with her doctoral degree and her independent life—to be a refreshing and long-awaited change from the femme fatale–helpless maiden dichotomy that seems to adhere for women in the hard-boiled genre. In his early appearances in the series, Hawk was also portrayed by some critics as somewhat of a racial stereotype: a Jim to Spenser's Huck. As the series has developed and Hawk has grown more and more to resemble Spenser in his emotional affect and complexity, those criticisms have faded away.

A more benign, but potentially more damaging criticism of the Spenser novels is that they are not detective novels at all: rather, they are novels that feature a detective character, but which really concern themselves with issues about contemporary relationships. Scholars and critics of the genre continue to debate this question. Purists maintain that the hard-boiled formula is set in concrete, and that, ergo, the Spenser books are not hard-boiled at all but, rather, something else—a kind of soft-boiled, politically correct abomination of the form in which real pros, like the Continental Op or John "Flashgun" Casey, would never have deigned to appear. Fans of the post-sixties detective novel argue that Spenser and his descendants have rescued the genre from obsolescence.

Parker's astounding sales have put him in the enviable position of being able to ignore his critics. Among other honors, he was awarded the Edgar Award for best novel for *Promised Land* from the Mystery Writers of America in 1976, and he was the guest of honor at the 1982 Bouchercon in San Francisco.

Conclusion

Parker's introduction of a kind of "alternative family" for Spenser—a pattern that has been duplicated in the overwhelming majority of post-sixties detective novels—is, without doubt, one of the most significant changes in the hard-boiled formula since its creation in the early years of this century. Moreover, it is a development that is crucially connected to the genre's discarding of an outmoded, aggressive vision of masculinity. Early tough guys had to be alone in order to retain their precious autonomy; newer tough guys like Spenser have heeded their culture's call to become their own men by getting in touch with their emotions and opening up to others.

Instead of standing apart from the dysfunctional families who shuffle, in unbroken chain gang style, across the hard-boiled cityscape, contemporary detectives since Spenser create families of their own, uninfected by backstabbing, deceit, and internecine bloodshed. Everyone meaningfully connects; yet, everyone respects each other's space. The infinite superiority of these alternative families is confirmed by the fact that, in many contemporary hard-boiled mysteries, the detective's own family of origin makes an appearance to underscore the evils of biology. Though Spenser and Susan's respective clans are conveniently deceased, she is often propelled into yearnings for the normative (wanting marriage, wanting a child) by pressure from her mother from beyond the grave.

It is academic to argue whether Parker was the absolute first detective fiction writer to propose the creation of an alternative family for his hard-boiled detective, or whether that honor belongs to, say, Ed McBain, whose novels about the 87th Precinct, it could be argued, represent the saga of one big messy family. Marcia Muller, who created the Sharon McCone series in 1973, the same year Spenser debuted, also could be considered another competitor in the area of forging alternative families in detective fiction. Muller's detective heroine, until the most recent novels, lived and worked with her coworkers at the All Soul's Legal Cooperative in San Francisco, which certainly functioned as a ramshackle family. What is clear, however, is that Parker has most vividly elaborated the formation process of the detective's alternative family, as well as the political promise contained in such a culturally diverse family portrait. While certainly not every contemporary hard-boiled mystery writer has followed Parker's lead—the novels of Jonathan Valin and James Ellroy, among others, represent another strain in detective fiction writing that resolutely preserves the alienated lifestyle and conservative politics of the classic hard-boileds— Parker has crucially transformed the genre. Parker has updated that Norman Rockwell depiction of a typical American Thanksgiving by giving his readers an image of another kind of extended family gathering where there is room for everybody—whites and people of color, homosexuals and heterosexuals, feminists and mobsters—at the table.

The traditional hard-boiled detective was a man without a past, whose character was rigidly set and whose aversion to women and family life was simply a psychologically unexplained "given." In later hard-boiled mysteries, thanks to the widespread influence of

Parker's Spenser series, the detective is depicted as a creature with a past, which can be addressed therapeutically and, perhaps, overcome. (As Susan says to Spenser toward the end of *A Catskill Eagle*, "You can change what yesterday did to you" [p. 285].) For most detectives of the nineties, that past includes a family of origin whose members have frequently caused disappointment or pain or even death. Affected by the changes that Parker has wrought in the hard-boiled form, detectives no longer run away from the scary spectacle of family; rather they refashion it into an idealized vision of community that allows both autonomy and interdependence. Whereas early detective fiction put forward a utopian vision of work to give the detective's life meaning, novels since the advent of Spenser also propose a utopian vision of family to salve the detective's world-weary soul. Work and love—Freud said we needed them both in order to be happy. The original tough guys tried only for work; but, thanks to Parker, the new generation of post-sixties gumshoes wants to have it all.

Bibliography

WORKS OF ROBERT B. PARKER

NOVELS

The Godwulf Manuscript. New York: Dell, 1973.
God Save the Child. New York: Dell, 1974.
Mortal Stakes. New York: Dell, 1975.
Promised Land. New York: Dell, 1976.
Three Weeks in Spring (with Joan Parker). New York: Dell, 1977.
The Judas Goat. New York: Dell, 1978.
Wilderness. New York: Dell, 1979.
Looking for Rachel Wallace. New York: Dell, 1980.
Early Autumn. New York: Dell, 1981.
A Savage Place. New York: Dell, 1981.
Ceremony. New York: Dell, 1982.
The Widening Gyre. New York: Dell, 1983.
Love and Glory. New York: Dell, 1983.
Valediction. New York: Dell, 1984.
A Catskill Eagle. New York: Dell, 1985.
Taming a Sea horse. New York: Dell, 1986.
Pale Kings and Princes. New York: Dell, 1987.
Crimson Joy. New York: Dell, 1988.
Playmates. New York: Putnam, 1989.

Poodle Springs (with Raymond Chandler). New York: Putnam, 1989.
Stardust. New York: Putnam, 1990.
Perchance to Dream. New York: Putnam, 1990.
Pastime. New York: Putnam, 1991.
Double Deuce. New York: Putnam, 1992.
Paper Doll. New York: Putnam, 1993.
Walking Shadow. New York: Putnam, 1994.
All Our Yesterdays. New York: Putnam, 1994.
Thin Air. New York: Putnam, 1995.
Chance. New York: Putnam, 1996.
Night Passage. New York: Putnam, 1997.
Small Vices. New York: Putnam, 1997.
Sudden Mischief. New York: Putnam, 1998.

EDITED VOLUMES

The Personal Response to Literature. Edited by Parker with Harold DeLisle, et al. Boston: Houghton Mifflin, 1971.
The Craft of Prose. Edited by Parker with Peter L. Sandberg. New York: Wiley, 1973.

OTHER PUBLICATIONS

Sports Illustrated Training with Weights. Philadelphia: Lippincott, 1974.
"Marxism and the Mystery." In *Murder Ink: The Mystery Reader's Companion.* Edited by Dilys Winn. New York: Workman, 1977.
"What I Know About Writing Spenser Novels." In *Colloquium on Crime: Eleven Renowned Mystery Writers Discuss Their Work.* Edited by Robin W. Winks. New York: Charles Scribner's Sons, 1986.

MANUSCRIPTS

Manuscript Collection. Colby College, Waterville, Maine.

BIOGRAPHICAL AND CRITICAL STUDIES

Carter, Steven R. "Spenserian Ethics: The Unconventional Morality of Robert B. Parker's Traditional American Hero." *Clues* 1, no. 2: 109–118 (fall–winter 1980).
Casella, Donna. "The Trouble with Susan: Women in Robert B. Parker's Spenser Novels." *Clues* 10, no. 2: 93–105 (fall–winter 1989).
Eisman, Gregory D. "The Catskill Eagle Smashed: The Moral Demise of Spenser in Robert B. Parker's *A Catskill Eagle*" *Clues* 2, no. 1: 107–119 (spring–summer 1990).
Fiscella, Joan B. "A Sense of the Under Toad: Play in Mystery Fiction." *Clues* 1, no. 2: 1–7 (fall–winter 1980).
Geherin, David. *Sons of Sam Spade: The Private-Eye Novel in the Seventies.* New York: Ungar, 1982.
Gray, Russell. "Reflections in a Private Eye: Robert B. Parker's Spenser." *Clues* 5, no. 1: 1–13 (spring–summer 1984).

Greiner, Donald. "Robert B. Parker and the Jock of the Mean Streets." *Critique* 26, no. 1: 36–44 (fall 1984).

Hoffman, Carl. "Spenser: The Illusion of Knighthood." *Armchair Detective* 16, no. 2: 131–143 (spring 1983).

Kifner, John. "In the Kitchen with Robert B. Parker." *New York Times*, 11 June 1997, sec. C, p. 1.

Kurata, Marilyn J. "Robert B. Parker: An Interview." *Clues* 12, no. 1: 1–31 (spring–summer 1991).

Penzler, Otto. "Robert B. Parker." *Armchair Detective* 18, no. 3: 258–261 (summer 1985).

Ponder, Anne. "A Dialogue with Robert B. Parker." *Armchair Detective* 17, no. 4: 340–348 (fall 1984).

Presley, John W. "Theory into Practice: Robert Parker's Re-Interpretation of the American Tradition." *Journal of American Culture* 12, no. 3: 27–30 (fall 1989).

Robinson, Doug. *No Less a Man: Masculist Art in a Feminist Age.* Bowling Green, Ohio: Bowling Green State University Press, 1994.

Saylor, Louise V. "The Private Eye and His Victuals." *Clues* 5, no. 2: 111–118 (fall–winter 1984).

Svoboda, Frederic. "Hard-Boiled Feminist Detectives and Their Families: Reimagining a Form." In *Gender in Popular Culture.* Ridgemont, 1995.

Willis, Lonnie. "Henry David Thoreau and the Hard Boiled Dick." *Thoreau Society Bulletin* 170: 1–3 (winter 1985).

Zalewski, James W., and Lawrence B. Rosenfeld. "Rules for the Game of Life: The Mysteries of Robert B. Parker and Dick Francis." *Clues* 5, no. 2: 72–81 (fall–winter 1984).

EDGAR ALLAN POE
(1809–1849)

J. GERALD KENNEDY

EDGAR ALLAN POE was born in Boston on 19 January 1809, the second son of the actor David Poe, Jr., and the actress Elizabeth Arnold Hopkins Poe. Poe's father apparently deserted the family in late 1810 and died in December of the following year. Placing her elder son, Henry, with relatives in Baltimore, Eliza cared for Edgar and his younger sister, Rosalie, while continuing to perform theatrically. In declining health, she made her final stage appearance in October 1811 and died of tuberculosis on 8 December in Richmond. Rosalie went to live with the Mackenzie family, and Edgar found a home with John Allan and his wife, Frances Valentine Allan, a childless couple who raised the boy as their son but—significantly—never adopted him. Somewhat spoiled as a child, Poe visited nearby plantations and traveled to fashionable resorts with the Allans; he received an early schooling and reportedly could read a newspaper by age five. In 1815 Allan moved his family to London to open a branch of his mercantile firm. Edgar Allan (as he was known) attended boarding schools, where he studied Latin and Shakespeare and read contemporary authors like Sir Walter Scott. He likely browsed through magazines such as *Blackwood's*, reading sensational tales of the sort he later satirized in "How to Write a Blackwood Article."

The Making of a Poet

Financial reverses forced Allan to close his London establishment, however, and return to Richmond in July 1820. Edgar Poe—as he was again called—enrolled in Clarke's academy and there excelled in Latin and Greek, demonstrating a gift for satire and verse; he later studied classical literature and French. After long enjoying Allan's favor as a "very fine Boy," Poe began to play pranks and received a whipping for shooting "a lot of domestic fowls" at a nearby plantation (Thomas and Jackson, pp. 42, 49). In adolescence he wrote poems to local girls but most worshiped Jane Stith Stanard, the kindly mother of a friend; her death in 1824 so affected him that he often visited her grave. Yet he was not exactly the brooding introvert of myth. Proud of his athletic abilities, he engaged in footraces, boxing matches, and jumping contests; on a dare, he swam six miles down the James River on a blistering summer day. As a member of the Morgan Junior Riflemen, he formed part of the honor guard for the visiting Marquis de Lafayette. At fifteen, though, Poe increasingly irritated John Allan, who wrote that the boy was "quite miserable, sulky & ill-tempered to all the Family" (p. 61).

Allan's peevishness accompanied financial worries, but in 1825 he inherited three large plantations, together with "the slaves, stocks, and property of all kinds belonging thereto" (p. 64). This sudden wealth enabled Allan to buy a Richmond mansion and likely encouraged his ward to fancy himself the heir to a fortune. In his mid-teens, Poe fell in love with Sarah Elmira Royster, who lived across the street from the new Allan estate; the youth visited her house, sketched her likeness, and proposed to marry her when he returned from college. With his foster father's encouragement but with an insufficient living allowance, Poe enrolled at the University of Virginia in early 1826 and studied modern and classical languages. Drinking and gambling provided extracurricular amusement, ferocious fights were common, and many undergraduates carried dueling pistols. Thomas Jefferson's death on 4 July brought temporary solemnity to the campus—and prevented Poe from dining that autumn, as scheduled, with the author of the Declaration of Independence. The next semester Poe again distinguished himself in the classical languages and French, but gambling proved his undoing. Allan refused to cover his debts, estimated at two thousand dollars, and when Poe returned to Richmond, he learned that Allan would no longer support his studies.

He also discovered that, bowing to family pressure, Elmira had become engaged to another young man; Poe's love letters from Charlottesville had been intercepted by her father. The distraught Poe worked, probably without pay, in Allan's mercantile firm until a clash with Allan in March 1827 prompted the youth to leave home. Poe wrote two angry letters before his departure, accusing his foster father of lacking affection but also begging a loan to finance his travel. Allan rebuked Poe's lack of "perseverance & industry" and chided him for reading worthless books (p. 78). A few days later Poe left Richmond by ship, accompanied as far as Norfolk by an adventurous friend, Ebenezer Burling. After a stay in Baltimore to visit relatives, including his brother, Henry, he proceeded to Boston.

Little is known of his activities in Boston, but there Poe published his first volume of po-

etry, *Tamerlane and Other Poems* (1827). He enlisted in the U.S. Army as "Edgar A. Perry" and was stationed at Fort Independence, but when his unit was reassigned to South Carolina, Poe and the other members of the battery barely avoided shipwreck in a November gale off Cape Cod. After reaching Charleston, Poe performed military duty at Fort Moultrie on Sullivan's Island, later the setting of his tale "The Gold-Bug." In South Carolina, he also wrote poetry and extended his reading of Shakespeare and English verse. For a time he apparently flourished in the military, but longing for greater conquests, he sought to shorten his five-year enlistment. In December 1828, Poe's unit was reassigned to Fortress Monroe, Virginia, where he wrote a letter seeking Allan's consent to be discharged, alternately begging forgiveness and declaring that Allan's neglect fueled his own personal ambition. A subsequent promotion perhaps changed Poe's plans; while continuing to seek release from active duty, he also requested Allan's help in obtaining an appointment to the U.S. Military Academy. The merchant was then distracted by his wife's last illness, but when Poe arrived in Richmond in February 1829—too late for Frances Allan's funeral—he did achieve a temporary reconciliation with "Pa."

At twenty, Poe seemed on the verge of a more promising future; Allan bought him new clothes and wrote letters to secure an appointment to West Point. Upon his discharge, Poe went to Baltimore, where William Wirt, a U.S. Attorney General from Richmond, read his poem "Al Aaraaf" and enumerated the difficulties of getting published. Undeterred, Poe negotiated with a Philadelphia publisher, asking his foster father to subsidize a second volume of poetry. Although Allan refused, he did ask Secretary of War John Henry Eaton to approve Poe's application to the Military Academy. But he disclaimed Poe as his son, noting coldly: "Frankly Sir, do I declare that He is no relation to me whatever" (p. 92). Poe spent the next nine months mostly in Baltimore living with relatives, submitting poetry to various magazines, and arranging the publication of his second volume. In late 1829, Hatch & Dunning issued the collection *Al Aaraaf, Tamerlane, and Minor Poems*. Poe now regarded himself as "irrecoverably a poet" (*Letters*, p. 19), and even the irascible critic John Neal hailed his promise in the September and December 1829 issues of the *Yankee*.

The "Folio Club" Tales

Receiving an appointment to West Point in March 1830, Poe attended a summer bivouac and in September registered for courses in mathematics and French. He quickly gained a reputation as a satirist, dashing off doggerel that circulated among the cadets. Alternately studious and dissipated, jocular and morose, he one evening conspired with a cadet to simulate his own murder. He may have been dramatizing his own despair. Allan had again sent him to school without an adequate allowance, and Poe soon found himself in financial embarrassment. Meanwhile, Allan remarried in October 1830, an event that greatly diminished the cadet's prospects for inheritance. Because officers required independent wealth to maintain the trappings of rank, Poe began to neglect his duties and accused Allan of sending him to West Point "like a beggar" (*Letters*, p. 40). The breach with his foster father had become irreparable, and not coincidentally Poe's career in the military came to a swift, inglorious end. On 28 January 1831 he was court-martialed and dismissed for "gross neglect of duty" (Thomas and Jackson, p. 113). Yet in his final examinations Poe excelled in mathematics and French; despite his notoriety, the cadets raised funds to subsidize a new volume of poetry. Poe left the academy in February and went to New York, where publisher Elam Bliss issued *Poems by Edgar A. Poe* (1831), dedicated to the "U.S. Corps of Cadets."

Wretchedly ill, Poe languished in New York and then journeyed to Baltimore in the spring of 1831, where he found lodging on Wilks Street with his grandmother, Elizabeth Cairnes Poe, and Aunt Maria Clemm. The move reunited him with his brother, a bibulous sailor-poet afflicted by consumption; despite long periods of separation, the two brothers felt an uncanny bond and perhaps collaborated on certain poems. But the reunion was brief, for Henry died on 1 August. That summer Poe sought odd jobs but also pursued an important new line of literary activity. Responding to an advertisement in the Philadelphia *Saturday Courier* announcing a prize of one hundred dollars for the best original tale, he composed a handful of short fictional narratives, largely parodies of popular magazine genres. Although Poe did not win, the *Saturday Courier* featured his supernatural tale "Metzengerstein" just before his twenty-third birthday and by year's end published four other tales, all parodic pieces. Poe still had no income from his fiction, and although he continued to live with his grandmother, his aunt, and cousin Virginia, he seems to have had no regular employment.

His situation did not improve much during the next two years. He published a few poems in the Baltimore *Saturday Visiter* in early 1833, and that spring he moved with the family to Amity Street. He continued to write brief, exaggerated, often satirical prose tales and by late spring had completed eleven such pieces. About his personal life little is known; Poe apparently tutored Virginia, wrote flirtatious verses to another cousin, Elizabeth Herring, and for several months courted a girl named Mary Starr. He made a last appeal to Allan in 1833, presenting himself as "absolutely perishing for want of aid," but Allan apparently declined to reply (*Letters*, pp. 49–50).

In June the *Saturday Visiter* announced a literary competition to which Poe submitted a poem and six stories from a collection called "Tales of the Folio Club." He had contrived a brief, comic frame for the tales, introducing a fictitious club of eccentric storytellers. Dazzled by the "wild, vigorous" imagination of these pieces, the committee headed by John Pendleton Kennedy chose "MS. Found in a Bottle" for the premium in fiction, while

Poe's "Coliseum" placed second in poetry (Thomas and Jackson, p. 133). The story appeared in October, and the newspaper prepared to issue a "Folio Club" volume by subscription. But that plan collapsed, probably because Poe offended the editor, and instead Kennedy offered to recommend the manuscript to Philadelphia publishers Carey and Lea.

Still living in utter poverty, Poe published another story, "The Visionary," in *Godey's Lady's Book,* marking his first appearance in a nationally circulated periodical. Soon thereafter, worried that Allan's health was failing, Poe made an unannounced visit to his old home but was rebuffed by his foster father, who brandished a cane and ordered him to leave. Six weeks later, in March of 1834, Allan died, and his will made no mention of his foster son. Although he was discouraged, Poe doggedly continued to write tales and in November visited Philadelphia publisher Henry C. Carey, who expressed interest in the stories while doubting they would have commercial success. Advising Poe to place the tales in magazines and annuals, Carey soon washed his hands of the project.

Editorial Genius of the *Messenger*

Poe's disappointment was palpable, but Kennedy continued to encourage him; he probably wrote on Poe's behalf to Thomas W. White, the Richmond printer who, in late 1834, had founded the *Southern Literary Messenger.* Soon Poe made his first appearance in the journal: the March 1835 issue carried "Berenicë," a story so gruesome that Poe felt obliged to promise that he would "not sin quite so egregiously again" (*Letters,* p. 58). In succeeding months he contributed reviews and tales from the "Folio Club" series, and, exploiting local interest in balloon flights, he devised a burlesque science fiction tale, "The Unparalleled Adventure of One Hans Pfaall," depicting a voyage to the moon. Eager to

please White, Poe purchased supplies in Baltimore and traveled to Richmond in August to assist the publisher, little suspecting that his employment with the *Messenger* would emblazon his name in American letters.

The move to Richmond immediately complicated Poe's personal life. Losing the security and stability of family connections, he sought solace in drink. He quickly became attracted to Eliza White, the proprietor's daughter, and a romance ensued, even though White found Poe "rather dissipated" (Thomas and Jackson, p. 167). But in late August, Maria Clemm sent a disturbing letter reporting that in their destitution, she and Virginia were ready to accept shelter from Poe's detested cousin Neilson Poe. To Poe the news came like the thrust of a knife: he felt fiercely protective of Virginia (then thirteen), whom he called his "darling," "Sissy," and "little wifey" (*Letters,* pp. 69–71). He begged Mrs. Clemm and Virginia to join him immediately in Richmond and, to relieve his uncertainty, rushed to Baltimore in late September, perhaps even wedding his cousin in a private ceremony. White reported to a friend that Poe had "[flown] the track already" and judged him "a victim of melancholy" (Thomas and Jackson, pp. 170–171). Two weeks later, Poe arrived in Richmond with Mrs. Clemm and Virginia; White lectured him on temperance but reinstated him as editorial assistant.

Poe's growing influence in American letters may be gauged by editorial responses to the *Messenger.* Identified as White's assistant, Poe received much credit for the improved literary fare, and he touched off controversy by mocking Theodore Fay's *Norman Leslie* (1835), a novel "puffed" by the *New-York Mirror,* where Fay was associate editor. In the same issue Poe published his unfinished drama, *Politian,* based on the sensational Beauchamp murder case in Kentucky. Although he produced no new tales during his *Messenger* stint, Poe was inventive as a magazinist. Posing as a handwriting specialist, he analyzed signatures of various American writers in "Autography," and in "Maelzel's Chess Player" he delivered a pseudoscientific exposé of a touring automaton. When James Kirke Paulding praised his work, Poe promptly shipped him the "Folio Club" manuscript, entreating him to find a New York publisher. In correspondence, Poe called himself editor of the *Messenger*, and White published notices thus identifying him, but, significantly, the proprietor himself never acknowledged Poe's editorial authority.

In May 1836, perhaps to avoid local scandal, Poe married Virginia before several witnesses, including White and his daughter, Eliza. The bride, not yet fourteen, was still an immature girl, and it seems unlikely that the marriage initially involved conjugal relations. Presumably the couple later consummated the relationship, however, for an 1841 tale ("Eleonora") celebrates the passionate love between the narrator and his cousin-wife. Poe perhaps invited White to the wedding to allay doubts about his own steadiness and responsibility, for he had again lapsed into intemperance. In June he received discouraging news from Harper and Brothers, who declined to publish his "learned and mystical" tales, instead urging him to compose "a single and connected story" of book length (p. 212). By September, White had become so distressed by Poe's drinking and by his "cutting and slashing" reviews that he considered firing him (pp. 222, 236).

Fascinated by Jeremiah Reynolds' report to Congress on a proposed South Seas expedition, Poe began to compose a story narrated by a survivor of fantastic adventures near the South Pole. The *Messenger* carried two episodes of *The Narrative of Arthur Gordon Pym of Nantucket* (1838), tracing Pym's adolescent escape from "Edgarton" in terms reminiscent of Poe's flight from Richmond with Ebenezer Burling in 1827. The first installment in January 1837 coincided with White's dismissal of Poe's editorial "Tomahawk Man." In seventeen months, Poe had made the *Messenger* one of the most widely read journals in the country.

Shortly after his discharge, Poe left Richmond with Virginia and Mrs. Clemm and took up residence in New York to pursue an editorial offer. Little is known about Poe's year in the city except that he never received the expected position and published almost nothing. He attended a booksellers' dinner in March that included Paulding, Washington Irving, and William Cullen Bryant, and he labored to complete his sea novel, which was accepted for publication in May 1837. But that same month a bank crisis plunged the nation into a depression, forcing a publishing delay that left Poe once more in desperate financial straits.

Up and Down in Philadelphia

Early in 1838, Poe, nearly destitute, moved with his family to yet another publishing center, Philadelphia. He had virtually abandoned magazine writing and wrote in July to Paulding, then the new secretary of the navy, pleading for a "clerkship" to relieve him from "the miserable life of literary drudgery" (*Letters*, p. 681). The long-delayed novel, *The Narrative of Arthur Gordon Pym of Nantucket*, was published by Harper and Brothers in late July to mixed reviews; it appeared, not coincidentally, just as the Wilkes expedition (1838–1842) departed for the South Seas. From the publisher, Poe perhaps received some recompense, for by September he claimed to have "nearly" extricated himself from recent financial "embarrassments" (*Letters*, p. 112). He also corresponded with Nathan C. Brooks, whose *American Museum* magazine included in its inaugural issue Poe's mystical tale "Ligeia." He was beginning to recover the audacity and inventiveness that had marked his rise to national attention.

But Poe continued to live in poverty and beg loans from local acquaintances. About this time, he met William Burton, owner and editor of *Burton's Gentleman's Magazine*. Ironically, Burton had written a devastating review of *Pym*, but Poe swallowed his resentment, applied for work, and performed editorial odd jobs. He quickly assumed most of the work, and he resumed the caustic reviewing that was his trademark. Poe's developing sense of imaginative power soon produced "The Fall of the House of Usher" and "William Wilson." His growing literary renown encouraged Lea & Blanchard to publish his collected short fiction, *Tales of the Grotesque and Arabesque,* in December 1839. In the space of a year Poe had returned from near oblivion to claim a new and influential role in American letters.

About this time he also embarked on several audacious exercises as a magazinist. As a contributor to *Alexander's Weekly Messenger,* Poe challenged readers to send cryptograms and then displayed his cleverness by deciphering them. In early 1840, he also published in *Burton's* a serialized longer tale, "The Journal of Julius Rodman," a narrative of western exploration tracing the first expedition to cross the Rockies. Hoaxing the public, Poe lifted many passages from the history of the Lewis and Clark expedition (1814) and from Irving's *Astoria* (1836). Yet even as he perpetrated this deception, Poe attacked Henry Wadsworth Longfellow as a plagiarist, accusing him of stealing a poem from Alfred, Lord Tennyson. Dashing off hasty reviews, he felt overwhelmed by editorial work and resented Burton's offering prizes that he never awarded. In May, when Burton tried to sell the journal, Poe decided to start his own periodical, the *Penn Magazine,* and solicited subscriptions. Burton saw the prospectus and fired his assistant, provoking a warning from Poe: "If by accident you have taken it into your head that I am to be insulted with impunity I can only assume that you are an ass" (*Letters,* p. 130).

After the break with Burton, Poe dedicated himself to preparations for the *Penn.* The would-be publisher felt he must "do or die" (p. 152) and invited contributions from noted contemporary authors. When George Graham bought the *Gentleman's Magazine* and merged it with the *Casket* to create *Graham's Magazine,* Poe contributed a splendid tale, "The Man of the Crowd." Just as he was about to prepare the first issue of the *Penn,* however, he fell ill and remained bedridden a month,

postponing the debut until March. The delay was disastrous: a banking crisis in February 1841 dashed plans for launching the new journal and forced Poe to accept a temporary position with *Graham's.*

The new association proved important, however, for it furnished a steady income, elicited several remarkable tales, and restored Poe's status as a force in American letters. After he joined the staff, subscriptions to *Graham's* quadrupled. His first tale as a contributing editor, "The Murders in the Rue Morgue," introduced a new genre to prose fiction: the detective story. Reactions to the gruesome story had scarcely subsided when Poe inserted the horrific "A Descent into the Maelström." To stimulate popular interest, he also devised a cryptographic series called "Secret Writing" and a new handwriting series called "A Chapter on Autography." Impressed by Poe's originality, Graham offered his partnership in producing a new monthly, but Poe's frustration with the feminized *Graham's* format instead prompted him to seek a government appointment from President John Tyler. About this time he also composed "Eleonora," a prophetic tale about the narrator's quest for a second love after the demise of his cousin-wife.

The tale haunted Poe, for soon after its publication, Virginia suffered a pulmonary hemorrhage while singing and nearly died; Poe thus learned of the consumption that took her life five years later. Distracted and melancholy, Poe himself fell ill, lapsed into drinking, and neglected his magazine work—although he interviewed the young English novelist Charles Dickens. When Poe returned to *Graham's* one day, he found another man at his desk and resigned on the spot. Graham later offered the editorial position to Rufus W. Griswold, the anthologist who became Poe's nemesis. During this volatile period, Poe wrote a famous review of Nathaniel Hawthorne's *Twice-Told Tales,* introducing his theory that every word of a tale should contribute to the "outbringing" of a "single *effect*" (*Essays and Reviews,* p. 572). With Virginia battling a fatal disease, Poe composed and published "The Masque of the Red Death," a tale of deadly contagion.

His wife was still extremely ill when Poe visited New York in mid-1842, searching for editorial employment, and he went on a reckless drinking binge. He begged his friend Frederick W. Thomas to secure him a position in the Philadelphia Custom House, and on the literary front he prepared a new volume of tales. Also during that year he composed the horrific story "The Pit and the Pendulum," another detective tale, "The Mystery of Marie Rogêt," and the chilling murder story, "The Tell-Tale Heart," which appeared in James Russell Lowell's *Pioneer*.

Early in 1843, Poe formed a partnership with Thomas C. Clarke, who agreed to publish the long-postponed monthly magazine now called the *Stylus*. Seeking new subscribers—and a government post—Poe visited Washington, D.C., in March, went on a debauch, and embarrassed even his friends. He returned to Philadelphia penniless and humiliated, and two months later Clarke withdrew his support. But Poe finally received good news: his treasure-hunting tale, "The Gold-Bug," won a prize of one hundred dollars offered by the *Dollar Newspaper* and brought belated fame. In August another Philadelphia newspaper published "The Black Cat," but Poe was soon desperate for cash once more and in November began lecturing on American poetry in Philadelphia and nearby cities.

Doings and Undoings in Gotham

The lectures continued the following year and brought Poe a modest income. In early April, however, he moved back to New York with Virginia (Mrs. Clemm joined them later) and quickly created a public stir with "The Balloon-Hoax," a pseudojournalistic report about a transatlantic balloon flight. For an obscure Pennsylvania newspaper he next concocted a series on literary gossip called "Doings of Gotham," and he reported to Lowell that he was preparing a "Critical History of

Am. Literature" (*Letters*, p. 261). The *Dollar Newspaper* carried his tale "The Premature Burial" in July, and a few months later the *Gift* published his dazzling third Dupin story, "The Purloined Letter." By autumn Nathaniel Parker Willis hired him as an assistant at the *Evening Mirror*.

Poe became more active in the New York literary scene in 1845 and became a celebrity after the January publication of "The Raven," which was widely reprinted and parodied. A month later, he left the *Mirror* to join forces with Charles F. Briggs and John Bisco in publishing the *Broadway Journal*, where he resumed his indictment of Longfellow for plagiarism. A controversial February lecture at the Society Library contained stinging pronouncements on many contemporary American poets male and female. Poe nevertheless developed friendships with several literary women, attended their salons, and carried on a flirtation with Mrs. Frances S. Osgood. Thanks to Evert Duyckinck, editor at Wiley and Putnam, a new volume of twelve *Tales* by Poe appeared in June, and two weeks later he assumed editorial control of the *Broadway Journal*. But Poe's health was poor, thwarting his creative work, and he humiliated himself in October before the Boston Lyceum; instead of presenting a new poem as promised, he recited his arcane early poem, "Al Aaraaf," confounding listeners and eliciting hostile reviews. Returning to New York, he became proprietor of the *Broadway Journal* and struggled to keep it afloat, blaming "enemies" who plotted its destruction (*Letters*, p. 304). Wiley & Putnam brought out *The Raven and Other Poems*, and Poe created excitement by publishing "The Facts in the Case of M. Valdemar." But these developments did not enable him to save the only journal he ever owned; the *Broadway Journal* expired in January 1846.

Depressed and ill, Poe became entangled in a feud between two literary ladies—Mrs. E. F. Ellet and Mrs. Osgood—and scuffled with novelist Thomas Dunn English. Such episodes made Poe increasingly unwelcome at New York literary salons, and seeking rural tranquility, he moved his family that spring to a cottage in Fordham (now a section of the Bronx). His series on "The Literati of New York City" captured national attention in *Godey's Lady's Book*, and his brilliant revenge tale, "The Cask of Amontillado," appeared there in November. By then both Poe and Virginia were both "dangerously ill" with consumption (Thomas and Jackson, p. 672), dependent on Mrs. Marie Louise Shew, a volunteer nurse, and Mrs. Clemm for meals and nursing care. On 30 January 1847, Virginia Clemm Poe died of consumption, and Poe himself remained desperately ill. Mrs. Shew gradually nursed Poe back to health, and the poet responded by dedicating verses to her. The poet Sarah Anna Lewis also befriended Poe and Mrs. Clemm, providing welcome financial help, and in July he was well enough to journey to Philadelphia and Washington. One of the few works he completed in 1847 was the haunting poem "Ulalume," probably inspired by visits to Virginia's grave.

In a burst of new energy Poe began working in 1848 on a cosmological "prose poem" he titled *Eureka*; and rehearsing his argument, he lectured in February on "The Universe" before a New York audience. Soon thereafter he received a valentine poem from an admirer in Providence, Mrs. Sarah Helen Whitman, and reciprocated her attentions. About the same time that Putnam's published *Eureka*, he lectured on American poetry in Lowell, Massachusetts, and met Mrs. Nancy "Annie" Richmond, who swiftly became a confidante and soul mate. Upon his return, Poe traveled south to Richmond to seek support for the *Stylus*; among other social calls, he visited his first love, Sarah Elmira Royster Shelton, by then a wealthy widow. The delivery of a poem by Sarah Whitman, however, prompted him to depart immediately for New York. Acknowledging his need to find a new wife, he wrote Mrs. Shew that "unless some true and tender and pure womanly love saves me, I shall hardly last a year longer, alone!" (*Letters*, p. 373). In September he visited Providence, met Mrs. Whitman (a widow six years

his senior), and proposed to her in a cemetery. She declined, citing her age and poor health.

But Poe was undeterred, and in October he renewed his suit before going on to Lowell, where he unburdened himself to Annie Richmond, extracting a promise that she would come to his deathbed. Whether from unresolved grief about Virginia, thwarted love for Mrs. Richmond, or anxiety about marrying Mrs. Whitman, Poe swallowed an ounce of opium on 5 November in Providence, suffering a horrific overdose that was likely an unsuccessful suicide attempt. Although warned by friends and family against marrying Poe, Mrs. Whitman finally consented on the condition that Poe avoid strong drink. Days later, though, he wrote a passionate letter to Annie, claiming that he loved her "as no man ever loved woman" (p. 401). In December he returned to Providence and lectured before a crowd of nearly two thousand on the "Poetic Principle"; his performance thrilled Mrs. Whitman, whose family seemed prepared to accept the nuptials. But Poe's subsequent drinking prompted her to break off marriage plans, and her outraged suitor departed for New York.

In the new year Poe focused his fantasies upon Annie Richmond and wrote intimate letters confessing his hopes and "dark forebodings" (p. 438). In February he wrote "Hop-Frog," which appeared in a Boston weekly, the *Flag of Our Union*, and there he also published a poem, "For Annie," dedicated to Mrs. Richmond. Unexpectedly, a printer named Edward H. N. Patterson of Oquawka, Illinois, wrote to propose publishing the *Stylus* from that frontier outpost, and Poe took the offer seriously. He left for Richmond to raise funds and solicit subscriptions, but during a stop at Philadelphia he got drunk, landed in jail, and suffered terrible hallucinations. Publisher John Sartain cared for him until Poe could resume his travels, and perhaps in gratitude, Poe offered Sartain a new poem, "Annabel Lee." In Richmond, he resumed his attentions to Mrs. Shelton and in late July proposed marriage. Between drinking bouts, he there delivered his lecture on the "Poetic Principle," and in late August he joined the Sons of Temperance, possibly to reassure Mrs. Shelton. By late September, she consented to marry him, and Poe left for New York to bring Mrs. Clemm to the wedding. Just when he seemed on the verge of launching his magazine and wedding his first love, fate intervened. On a stop in Baltimore, coincidentally an election day, Poe apparently fell into the hands of political henchmen who, after plying him with drink, took him from precinct to precinct as a repeat voter. He collapsed and was taken to Washington College Hospital, where, after lingering in a delirium for four days, he died on 7 October 1849. His funeral took place the following day, and he was buried "without ostentation" in a nearby cemetery (Thomas and Jackson, p. 848). Reaction to Poe's death was mixed; Rufus Griswold, whom Poe had unwisely named his literary executor, published a scathing obituary in the New York *Daily Tribune*, while sympathetic tributes by George Graham and others appeared thereafter. For more than a century, Poe's work has excited admiration and scorn, as critics have pondered his works and debated his contributions to American literature. Generation after generation, his strange poems and disturbing tales continue to engage new readers, for they seem to plumb the most elemental uncertainties of human experience.

Poetry

From boyhood Poe aspired to be a poet, and his early enthusiasm for Lord Byron informs his first published volume, *Tamerlane and Other Poems*. The title poem presents the deathbed confession of a Turkish hero, who loses his first love while pursuing conquest and glory. Although Poe's conception of Tamerlane as a cursed and wandering figure is thoroughly Byronic, the Romantic plot barely masks the story of Poe's own ill-fated youthful romance with Miss Royster. The concluding poem, "The Lake," shows Poe's poetic development, for he portrays a brooding younger

self who, beside the "poison'd wave," experiences not "fright" but "tremulous delight." Finding beauty in the terrible, the fledgling poet inverts conventional values to make "an Eden of that dim lake" (p. 37).[1]

Poe's second volume, *Al Aaraaf, Tamerlane, and Minor Poems*, combined several works from the first collection with eight new pieces, including the esoteric "Al Aaraaf." Poe sets the action in 1574, when the star discovered by Tycho Brahe exploded, turned red, and then disappeared. The poet portrays a celestial dreamland presided over by the angel Nesace, who after thanking God for the creation of Beauty, visits the dying star Al Aaraaf—a place between heaven and hell—and commands Ligeia, a personification of nature's music ("Ligeia! Ligeia! / My beautiful one!"), to arouse the slumbering spirits before the star's extinction (p. 47). The lovers Angelo and Ianthe also inhabit Al Aaraaf, but because their hearts beat so wildly with passion, they ignore Ligeia and perish. This gem was the earliest version of "Sonnet—To Science," in which Poe accused Science of destroying earthly enchantment. Science at last (in the 1841 revision) deprives the poet of "the summer dream beneath the tamarind tree" (p. 38).

In his third collection, *Poems*, Poe gathered several new poems, of which "To Helen," stands as one of his greatest achievements. Inspired by his memory of Jane Stanard, the poem evokes the legendary Helen of Troy, whose beauty is like a vessel carrying the "weary, way-worn wanderer" to his "native shore." Her "hyacinth hair," "classic face," and "Naiad airs" transport the poet-seafarer back temporally "To the glory that was Greece, / And the grandeur that was Rome" (p. 62). "To Helen" represents an enduring treatment of obsessive attraction to a beautiful yet unattainable woman. Another remarkable poem was "Israfel," a verse celebrating the lyric genius of an angel. Poe compares his own plight, confined to "a world of sweets and sours," with the heavenly bliss of Israfel, who

---

1. All quotations from the works of Poe are taken from *Poetry and Tales* (1984).

despises "an unimpassion'd song" (pp. 63, 64). The poet asserts that were the angel to change places with him, "A stormier note than this would swell / From my lyre within the sky" (p. 64). "Irenë" (later, "The Sleeper") meditates on the strange slumber of the dead beloved, and "The Doomed City" (precursor to "The City in the Sea") tells how "Death has rear'd himself a throne" in a "strange city" surrounded by the sea (p. 67). Here Poe sketches a surreal scene that conveys death's terrifying, transformative power.

Apart from his unfinished verse drama, *Politian*, Poe sporadically composed occasional or lyric poems throughout the decade. Two works, "To One in Paradise" and "The Haunted Palace," were incorporated into prose tales. The latter, an eerie architectural allegory of the transition from reason to madness, apparently preceded by several months the composition of "The Fall of the House of Usher." "Sonnet—Silence," composed in late 1839, compares the "two-fold *Silence*" of "Body and Soul": while we need not dread the "corporate Silence" of physical death, we should "commend [ourselves] to God" if we encounter his "shadow," presumably the silence of spiritual death (p. 77).

Oddly, Poe wrote little poetry in 1840 and 1841, but in late 1842 he composed "The Conqueror Worm," an allegorical verse staging "the tragedy, 'Man,'" a "motley drama" whose hero is "the Conqueror Worm." For a tearful "angel throng," "mimes" perform a play about "Madness," "Sin," and "Horror," culminating in the arrival of a "blood-red thing" that feeds on "human gore" (pp. 77–79). One of Poe's most despairing visions of the human condition, he later inserted the poem into the tale "Ligeia." His much-quoted poem "Dream-Land" conjures up "a wild weird clime that lieth, sublime, / Out of Space—out of Time." Ruled by a phantom called "Night," this strange dreamland is populated by "Ghouls" and ghosts; only in death can its "mysteries" be apprehended (pp. 79–80).

During 1844, Poe also composed his most famous poem, "The Raven," a narrative of eighteen octosyllabic stanzas exploring the subject of mourning, here projected as a dialogue between the narrator and a bird that speaks but a single word. The narrator's melancholy breeds contradiction: he tries to suppress the memory of the "lost Lenore" by retrieving "forgotten lore"; he vows that she will be "nameless *here* for evermore" (pp. 81–82) and then speaks her name repeatedly. In his desire to recover his beloved, he ponders the raven's utterance and poses two fearful questions: whether there is "balm in Gilead" (spiritual salvation) and whether he will "clasp" Lenore in heaven (p. 85). But he already knows the answer, and the bird's "Nevermore" confirms his despair, pushing him toward madness. As an emblem of loss, the raven confirms the never-ending remembrance that is the narrator's fate; the poem thus brilliantly dramatizes obsessive melancholia. In "The Philosophy of Composition," Poe explained the poem's form and refrain, declaring that "the death . . . of a beautiful woman is, unquestionably, the most poetical topic in the world" (*Essays and Reviews*, p. 19).

The death of Virginia impelled the composition in 1847 of "Ulalume," a ballad of ten stanzas depicting a speaker's nocturnal ramble through "the ghoul-haunted woodland of Weir" with Psyche, his soul. When the planet Venus ("Astarte") emerges from behind a crescent moon, bringing the consolation of love, Psyche mistrusts its "pallor," although the narrator insists that its "gleaming" will guide them "aright" (p. 90). As they approach the "end of the vista," however, they are stopped "by the door of a tomb" (p. 91). Belatedly the speaker realizes that he has returned to his beloved's sepulchre exactly one year after her burial. He asks what "demon" has "tempted" him back and surmises that "merciful ghouls" have conjured up the "scintillant planet" to impede his return to "the thing that lies hidden in these wolds." If so, the power of the unconscious has been even stronger, leading him back to the physical impasse—the "door of a legended tomb"—that separates him from the "lost Ulalume" (p. 91).

Several distinctive poems emerged in Poe's final two years. The much-quoted "The Bells" uses alliteration and repetition in comparing different kinds of bells. The refrain, "the bells, bells, bells, bells, / Bells, bells, bells," manifests obsession and carries the poem to the brink of hysteria (pp. 92–95). "For Annie" refers to Poe's friendship with Annie Richmond and his 1848 suicide attempt. Having conquered "the fever called 'Living,' " the speaker consoles himself with "many / A dream" of Annie's care and tenderness. The enigma lies in the uncertainty of the speaker's condition—is he actually dead, having finished "living," or does he simply rest so "composedly" that he resembles a corpse? Much depends on how one interprets the "narrow" bed in the eighth stanza (pp. 98–99). Less puzzling is his late poem "Eldorado," inspired by the California gold rush but broadly reflective of Poe's tortured quest for fame. When the aging knight asks where to find Eldorado, the "pilgrim shadow" tells him to "Ride, boldly ride" "Down the Valley of the Shadow" (pp. 101). The language of Psalm 23 links this valley to death, but more generally the "shade" exhorts the knight to confront fear courageously. Poe's last poem, "Annabel Lee," reprises the theme of mourning and the compulsion to return to the tomb of the beloved. But Poe also evokes youthful happiness and affirms a love that survives death. Rather than memorializing Virginia Poe, "Annabel Lee" reflects plaintively on the universal experience that all love ends in loss.

Early Tales

Poe's apprenticeship as a magazinist began in 1831 with a handful of mostly comic stories. G. R. Thompson notes the often overlooked fact that nearly half of his sixty-odd tales display a penchant for satire, burlesque, or parody. "A Decided Loss" (later titled "Loss of Breath") finds him, for example, satirizing tales of premature burial by taking literally—and carrying to a ludicrous extreme—the colloquial expression "losing one's breath." Two notable early stories, "Metzengerstein" and "MS. Found in a Bottle," break the comic pattern; although both contain elements of exaggeration, Poe's solemn tone and sustained intensity appear to indicate creative seriousness (as Benjamin F. Fisher views the earlier tale). Establishing Poe's early interest in revenge and metempsychosis, "Metzengerstein" depicts the Baron's fatal encounter with a spectral horse embodying the spirit of his dead rival, Count Berlifitzing. Supernaturalism intrudes when the debauched Metzengerstein contemplates the figure in a tapestry of "an enormous, and unnaturally colored horse" (p. 136). When Metzengerstein's equerries later bring him a "gigantic and fiery-colored horse" that has escaped the burning stables of the nearby Castle Berlifitzing, we learn that a small portion of the tapestry has simultaneously disappeared (p. 137). The horse finally carries the Baron into the flames of the Palace Metzengerstein—a death attributable either to a supernatural curse or to the hero's "perverse attachment" to a "demon-like" creature (p. 140). At the crux of his interest in madness and self-destructiveness, *perverseness* became a major theme for Poe.

"MS. Found in a Bottle" tapped the vogue for sea stories, and Poe's achievement here (as Donald B. Stauffer has noted) lies in his shift from verisimilitude to fantasy. The prosaic details of the opening paragraphs give way to increasingly ominous images, borrowed from Samuel Taylor Coleridge's "Rime of the Ancient Mariner" and the Flying Dutchman legend. After various calamities, the narrator finds himself aboard a gigantic ebony ship manned by a spectral crew. With the ship caught in a powerful current, he feels torn between horror and curiosity, imagining himself "hurrying onwards to some exciting knowledge—some never-to-be-imparted secret, whose attainment is destruction" (p. 198). The frenzied last paragraph reveals that the story itself is the manuscript found in a bottle, a note composed on the brink of oblivion. With its interest in the mystery beyond death, the tale offers a prophetic metaphor for Poe's own journey as a writer.

One other early tale, "The Visionary" (later, "The Assignation"), invites greater critical attention. Set in Venice, the tale's melodramatic opening scene finds a famous Romantic poet diving into the canal to save an infant dropped by its mother, the Marchesa Aphrodite. The woman's unexpected encounter with the poet produces her cryptic vow: "Thou hast conquered—one hour after sunrise—we shall meet—so let it be!" (p. 203). After exhibiting his originality for the narrator, the poet declares himself "rapidly departing" for the "land of real dreams," drinks from a special goblet, and dies—just as a messenger arrives with news that the Marchesa has been poisoned (p. 211). Poe's treatment of the suicide pact raises as many questions as it answers, and the visionary's opinions and aesthetic preferences occupy much of the narrative. But here, as in "Metzengerstein" and "MS. Found in a Bottle," we see Poe's early striving to concentrate the force of the tale upon a final, shocking scene.

The Marchesa's demise marks the first appearance in fiction of a major motif, the death of a beautiful woman. Two other early stories are variations on the theme. "Berenicë" traces the narrator's peculiar obsession with the dazzling white teeth of his dying cousin, and in the lurid final paragraphs, Poe implies that the amnesiac narrator has in fact violated the tomb of Berenicë to extract the teeth from her "still breathing—still palpitating" body (p. 232). The story illustrates a significant technical development; although he had experimented with first-person narration in several early tales, Poe first introduced in "Berenicë" an agitated, unreliable narrator whose account reveals inadvertent evidence of his own delusions. As James Gargano has shown, Poe used this new method of narration to brilliant effect in several major tales, allowing the reader to perceive evidence of derangement to which the narrator is blind. In a sequel titled "Morella," the alienated narrator marries a woman of immense learning and watches irritably as she declines to death; on her death-bed she bears a daughter, who grows into the exact likeness of her mother. The suggestion of metempsychosis induces the narrator to name the child, perversely, after her mother, and when at last he bears his daughter to the tomb, he finds no trace of the first Morella in the crypt where he deposits the second. Poe's treatment of uncanny reincarnation, suggesting that the first Morella takes revenge on the alienated narrator, allowed the writer in late 1835 to rank "the tale" as his best story to date. Taken together, the early tales exhibit a maturing craftsmanship in their orchestration of sensational effects and exploration of the psychological dimensions of first-person narration.

Aside from a curious satire on dueling titled "Mystification," *The Narrative of Arthur Gordon Pym of Nantucket* was Poe's only new creative work during a bleak period of eighteen months. Dismissed by the author as "a very silly book" (*Letters*, p. 130), *Pym* represents a dizzying tour de force, a hoaxical potboiler charged with some of Poe's most shocking scenes, and a pseudo-autobiography that skates on the edge of sublimity and mystery. The scholar Joseph V. Ridgely has shown that *Pym* evolved as a patchwork narrative, reflecting changing intentions. Poe's ironic preface develops a strategy to pass off the novel as an authentic narrative of exploration: the fictional "A. G. Pym" claims authorship of a story first attributed in the *Messenger* to Poe. From the opening episode, Poe depicts his narrator caught in desperate circumstances, first impaled on the hull of a boat, then trapped in a ship's hold, and subsequently involved in a deadly counter-mutiny aboard the *Grampus*. Pym survives starvation, participates in cannibalism, and witnesses the death and instantaneous decomposition of his friend, Augustus, before being rescued, with a "half-breed" Indian (p. 1007) named Dirk Peters, by a British trading vessel bound for the South Seas. During several documentary chapters Poe's narrator metamorphoses from a callow youth into a learned naturalist and anthropologist. When Pym persuades the captain of the *Jane Guy* to investigate the polar region, they discover an island named Tsalal, inhabited by fierce-looking black natives. Just when the white men believe that they have placated the natives and prepared the way for commercial exploitation, the blacks massacre the crew. Pym and Peters (with a native hostage) flee the island in a canoe; for three weeks they paddle south into mild, milky seas. As they approach a vortex, a huge "shrouded" figure looms before them, and the narrative breaks off suddenly:

> And now we rushed into the embraces of the cataract, where a chasm threw itself open to receive us. But there arose in our pathway a shrouded human figure, very far larger in its proportions than any dweller among men. And the hue of the skin of the figure was of the perfect whiteness of the snow. (p. 1179)

Poe's puckish final "Note" reports that although Pym by an unexplained miracle returned from the South Seas, he has been killed in a subsequent accident before delivering his completed narrative.

Masterworks of Terror

If nothing else, the writing of *Pym* persuaded Poe that a tale's success depended upon brevity and unity of effect. That principle of composition was already guiding his writing in 1838 when he began work on "Ligeia." Here Poe stretched the limits of narratorial unreliability: his storyteller suffers from amnesia, takes opium, and experiences apparent hallucinations. He seems utterly dependent on Ligeia, a dying woman of consummate learning who plans to defy mortality by force of will. The narrator's reaction to her demise is curious; "with a child-like perversity" he refurbishes an abbey in funereal decor and "in a moment of mental alienation" (p. 270) weds a second wife, the blonde Lady Rowena. His palpable loathing for Rowena betrays evidence, as Roy P. Basler suggests, of an unacknowledged scheme to frighten her to death.

The "hideous drama of revivification" (p. 276) by which the apparently dead Rowena returns to life and assumes the appearance of Ligeia creates an electric moment virtually unparalleled in Poe's fiction. His use of calculated ambiguity—Do ruby drops fall into Rowena's wine? Does she then die?—heightens the radical uncertainty of what really happens in "Ligeia." The tale's outcome may indeed represent supernaturalism—metempsychosis or spiritual vampirism—or it may likewise be explained as narratorial delusion or even homicidal psychosis. Although he later added three paragraphs on Ligeia's death, along with the poem attributed to her, Poe justifiably considered "Ligeia" his best tale to date. Ending a creative drought, Poe entered the most productive period of his career. One month later he published "How to Write a Blackwood Article" and the pendant "A Predicament"—tales illustrating his irrepressible instinct for parody, even self-mockery. Before the end of 1839 he had written six more new tales, two of which—"The Fall of the House of Usher" and "William Wilson"—marked a great creative leap.

No other tale by Poe has attracted more critical discussion than "Usher," thanks to its psychological intensity and symbolic suggestiveness. Here Poe achieves an absolute unity of effect evoking melancholy and dread; from the opening sentence, every detail contributes to the foreboding atmosphere pervading the House of Usher. Visual analogies between Roderick Usher's face, the facade of the house, and the "Haunted Palace" of the embedded poem establish a complex analogy between the progressive derangement of the protagonist, the physical disintegration of the mansion, and the fate of rational thought, under assault by "evil things, in robes of sorrow" (p. 326). Usher's perverse relationship to his cadaverous sister, Madeline, drives the plot; once again the decline and apparent death of a beautiful woman pushes the protagonist toward madness. Usher suspects that in his "unnerved" condition, he must finally "abandon life and reason together" in a struggle with some incarnation of Fear (p. 322).

As in "Ligeia," the uncertainty of Madeline's condition produces an equivocal response. Conscious of her susceptibility to catalepsy, Usher decides to preserve her body within the house for a fortnight; yet upon viewing the "lingering" smile on her lips and the "faint blush upon the bosom and the face," he *screws down the lid* and places the body behind a heavy iron door (p. 329). He is both unwilling to concede that she is dead and unable to admit that she may be alive. The narrator, more baffled here than unreliable, has been summoned to comfort his old friend by rationalizing uncanny phenomena, but he finds himself increasingly unable to explain strange sights and sounds. Madeline's final horrific return suggests that she seeks revenge on her brother for burying her prematurely. As she embraces Roderick, he succumbs to the "terrors" (p. 335) he anticipated, and his simultaneous loss of life and reason seems literally to bring down the house in a grand cataclysm that the horrified narrator barely escapes. A half-century before the emergence of psychoanalysis, Poe developed an elaborate house-mind analogy to suggest that by entombing Madeline in the basement, Usher attempted to push her into the unconscious—that is, to repress the fear that she palpably represents. But as Freud later demonstrated, that which is repressed always, inevitably returns, and the final, fatal embrace in "Usher" is its sign and seal.

"William Wilson" introduces a new narrational strategy, a confession of perverse misdeeds by a remorseful storyteller. The narrator relates the enormities of his career, however, in a way that confuses repentance with rationalization. Explaining the strange antagonism between himself and his double (or doppelgänger), an identically named schoolboy who speaks only in a guttural whisper, the narrator reconstructs the rivalry to justify his hatred. Yet we also understand, from the opening inscription, that the second William Wilson represents the voice of conscience. When the narrator embarks on a life of debauchery and chicanery, the whispering Wilson mysteriously pursues him, exposing his deceptions. In the final encounter, set in Rome, Wilson confronts his counterpart and seems to dispatch him with a sword, but he finds himself gazing at his own reflection in a shattered mirror and hears a voice like his own say, "thou hast murdered thyself" (p. 357). Although Poe (reviewing Hawthorne) condemned allegory, his treatment of the killing of conscience in "William Wilson" is unmistakably allegorical. But his approach is altogether different from Hawthorne's: the story is more concerned with what Patrick Quinn regards as the psychology of divided consciousness than with an ethical dilemma.

Poe returned to the idea of doubling in "The Man of the Crowd" (1840), creating a gothic vision of London streets at night while a possibly unreliable narrator recounts his obsessive pursuit of an old man said to be "the type and the genius of deep crime" (p. 396) because he shuns solitude and seeks crowds. Representing the city as a lonely, terrifying place, this tale has seemed especially conducive to sociopolitical readings. Whether the old man is a monstrous deviant, the innocent object of relentless pursuit, or an emblem of alienation, the story's title seems finally to apply as much to the narrator as to his prey. Indeed, the story reverses the narrative logic of "William Wilson" to construct a doppelgänger relationship from the position of a dogged spectator. Although the narrator introduces himself as a rational observer, his perceptions reveal a morbid imagination as well as a blindness to the effects of his own stalking. He is a flawed prototype of the sleuth-hero, a would-be detective who claims to "read" the stranger's heart even as he declares it to be unreadable.

As Poe discovered in "The Man of the Crowd," the quest to solve a mystery could prove more fascinating than the mystery itself, and he shortly introduced the "tale of ratiocination" (to be discussed shortly). About the same time, his growing interest in analysis inspired the sea story "A Descent into the Maelström." Related by a Norse sailor, the narrative recalls "MS. Found in a Bottle" and *Pym* in its representation of a massive whirlpool. Drawing on encyclopedia articles to add verisimilitude, Poe superimposed upon the tale of terror—the sailor's experience in the whirling abyss—a display of reason, for the man's cool analysis of the geometry and physics of objects in the vortex finally saves his life. Unlike the horrific ending of "MS.," which culminates in the narrator's apparent death, "Descent" brings the sailor back to tell his story.

After Virginia Poe's 1842 hemorrhage, Poe published two tales reflecting his darkened mood and situation. "Life in Death" ("The Oval Portrait") again shows his attraction to allegory. In a Gothic chateau filled with paintings, a "desperately wounded" (p. 481) narrator takes shelter; one painting catches his fancy, the portrait of a young girl, whose "absolute *life-likeliness* of expression" (p. 482) startles him. In a bedside volume discussing the paintings he discovers the story of its creation: a passionate painter obsessed with his art has married the girl and then obliged her to pose for him, day after day, despite her pallid appearance, until he completes the portrait—said to be "Life itself" (p. 484). At that very moment, however, he sees that his beloved is dead, a tragedy that comments incisively on the parasitic relationship of Art to Life.

One month later, Poe published "The Masque of the Red Death," regarded as possibly the greatest of his short tales. Here the author accused of never writing a moral tale produced a profoundly ethical allegory concerned with human arrogance, social responsibility, and mortality. In the midst of a plague, Prince Prospero summons a thousand "hale and light-hearted" friends and seals off his castle, for "the external world could take care of itself" (p. 485). To divert himself from the misery outside, he stages a masked ball, but at midnight, a masked figure appears, "shrouded from head to foot in the habiliments of the grave" (p. 489) and daubed with blood. Prince Prospero draws a dagger to strike but suddenly falls dead; the revelers attack the specter but are horrified to find "the grave cerements and corpse-like mask . . . un-

tenanted by any tangible form" (p. 490). Thus they discover the presence of the Red Death and drop one by one in postures of despair. Although Poe narrates the story atypically in the third person, he achieves an impressive unity of effect, sustaining to the last sentence the "nameless awe" (p. 490) evoked by the mysterious figure.

In 1842 he returned to the formula of sensation satirized in "How to Write a Blackwood Article" to compose "The Pit and the Pendulum," a story recalling the 1808 suppression of the Spanish Inquisition after Napoleon's invasion of Spain. Sentenced to death, the narrator recovers from a swoon to find himself in total darkness, possibly buried alive. His captors have prepared an array of possible torments—a deep pit, a pendulum with a "razor-like crescent" (p. 501), and finally burning walls that contract, forcing him toward the abyss:

> At length for my seared and writhing body there was no longer an inch of foothold on the firm floor of the prison. I struggled no more, but the agony of my soul found vent in one loud, long, and final scream of despair. I felt that I tottered upon the brink—I averted my eyes—(p. 505)

Suddenly he hears the sound of voices, then of trumpets, as General Lasalle himself rescues him. Poe made no great effort here to achieve symbolic complexity; rather, in "The Pit and the Pendulum" he pushes to the limits the psychodrama of sensation resulting from deadly predicaments and hairbreadth escapes.

Reverting in late 1842 to the persona of an enervated, unreliable first-person narrator, Poe crafted "The Tell-Tale Heart." From its opening sentence, the tale conveys the derangement of a maniac who murders and dismembers an old man he professes to love—and who then recounts the story "calmly" as if to prove his sanity (p. 555). His narrative is a tissue of seemingly inadvertent revelations: first he says that the crime has been without motive, then he describes the oppressive effect of the old man's "vulture eye"; he tells of rehearsing the crime many nights, evoking in the old man the same terror that he himself has often felt "just at midnight" (pp. 556–557). After depositing the old man's remains beneath the floor, the narrator entertains three police investigators; his initial coolness gives way to panic when he hears a *"low, dull quick sound"* and in horror invites the police to pull up the floor to confirm the beating of the old man's "hideous heart" (p. 559). "The Tell-Tale Heart" was Poe's first story in a new key, making the narrator (as Max Byrd has noted) both the criminal and the detective.

Riding a surge of prodigious creativity, Poe then composed the ingenious narrative "The Gold-Bug." Evoking the legend of Captain Kidd, he combined cryptography with ratiocination to create a story of buried treasure set on Sullivan's Island, South Carolina. Entertaining the narrator, the eccentric William Legrand sketches a recently discovered gold beetle and unexpectedly notes a "hieroglyphical signature" on his scrap of parchment. When the narrator later returns, worried by his friend's entomological preoccupation, Legrand proposes an expedition, aided by his manumitted servant, Jupiter. Following Legrand's directions, Jupiter drops a line weighted by the gold bug through a skull in a tree, thereby marking the spot where the men unearth pirate treasure. For the astonished narrator, Legrand recounts how he recognized Captain Kidd's mark, chemically treated the parchment, and deciphered a coded message. By 1844, Poe considered "The Gold-Bug" his "most successful tale" (*Letters*, p. 253), and from the standpoint of sheer popularity it clearly was.

The author added a new study of homicidal fury in "The Black Cat." Following the method of "The Tell-Tale Heart," he adopted the first-person perspective of a condemned killer whose narrative represents an eleventh-hour confession. But here an important theme, "the spirit of PERVERSENESS," latent as early as "Metzengerstein," provides the key to the narrator's rage. This "unfathomable longing of the soul *to vex itself*—to offer violence to its own nature—to do wrong for the wrong's sake only" (p. 599) accounts for the impulsive execution of his beloved black cat, Pluto, and it likewise explains his adopting a new cat, identical to Pluto except for a white mark that prophetically resembles a gallows. When his wife prevents him from slaughtering the cat, the frenzied narrator instead "[buries] the axe in her brain" (p. 603) and walls up her corpse in the basement. During an investigation, the narrator brazenly raps on the wall where he has immured his wife; a feline howl prompts the police to pull down the wall, exposing the upright, decomposed body of the wife and the black cat—with a "solitary eye of fire"—sitting on her head (p. 606). Hinting of metempsychosis, the single eye suggests that Pluto has become the second cat. Written shortly after Virginia's hemorrhage, this narrative seems in context a shocking treatment of domestic relations, though as always we must avoid confusing Poe himself with his mad narrators.

In a much different vein, "Mesmeric Revelation" best reflects Poe's recurrent attraction to transcendental cosmology. The 1844 tale records the conversation between a mesmerist and a dying man named Vankirk, who under hypnosis explores "physical impressions" concerning mind, matter, God, and the "soul's immortality" (p. 718). Vankirk wishes to confirm his intuitions, and the mesmerist elicits the insight (reminiscent of Emerson) that "unparticled" matter "permeates" and "impels all things" and is thus "all things within itself" or "God" (p. 720). After revealing that "Divine Volition" created "rudimental" physical life so that "perfection" might be apprehended through contrast with "imperfection" (p. 725), Vankirk asks to be awakened, and with "a bright smile irradiating all his features," he instantly expires and exhibits rigor mortis (p. 726). The narrator suspects that Vankirk's final revelations arrived from the other side of death. Reflecting Poe's preoccupation with the soul's fate, Vankirk's happy death projects the transcendental optimism that the author labored to sustain against the dread that recurrently beset him.

Another tale of this period explores those darker fantasies, though in a way that turns panic to parody. "The Premature Burial" examines living entombment as verifiable fact, the most hideous fate that may befall a person. After a series of case histories, all drawn from contemporary periodicals, Poe's narrator acknowledges his own susceptibility to premature interment. Although he has taken precautions (securing a coffin with an escape hatch), he awakens one day in a tight, dark space and fears the worst. But he has merely fallen asleep aboard a ship, and the embarrassing episode prompts him to stop brooding on death. In a clever turn that exposes Poe's hoax, the narrator vows to read "no 'Night Thoughts'—no fustian about church-yards—no bugaboo tales—*such as this*" (p. 679). Poe relieves his anxiety about death and burial by mocking both the gullibility of the reader and his own inveterate morbidity.

In 1845, the annus mirabilis of "The Raven" and the *Broadway Journal*, Poe published three more important tales. "The Power of Words" extends the visionary speculation of "Mesmeric Revelation" by presenting a brief dialogue between two spirits. Agathos, the tutelary figure, explains to Oinos, a shade "new-fledged with immortality" (p. 822), that happiness derives not from knowledge but from the *quest* for knowledge; that God created actively only at the beginning of the universe; and that creation continues everywhere, for all causes produce endless effects. Agathos declares that no energy is ever lost: all motions have infinite consequences, and every word spoken creates "an impulse on the air" (p. 825) whose results are unimaginable. The tale thus reflects Poe's determination to construct a cosmological theory that would corroborate his intuitions about life after death and affirm the godlike power of the poet.

Moving in a radically different direction, Poe then returned to the problem of perverseness. In "The Imp of the Perverse," an odd hybrid of narrative and essay, the author casts doubt on efforts to interpret divine will by studying human nature and emphasizes instead a "primitive impulse" that impels forbidden acts (p. 827) and opposes the instinct for survival. The opening disquisition leads to the revelation by the previously undramatized narrator that, as a victim of this "imp," he stands condemned to death for committing the perfect crime—murdering an old man (whose estate he inherits) in a way that appears to be a natural death. After reveling in his cleverness, he gradually becomes tormented by an odd compulsion to blurt out a confession; amid a city throng, the "long-imprisoned secret bursts forth from [his] soul" (p. 831). Clearly the psychology of crime fascinated Poe, and "The Imp of the Perverse" marks one of his most penetrating studies, for he suggests that homicide may be displaced self-destruction. He also hints in the final sentence that dread itself may paradoxically inflame the perverse urge to do violence to the soul.

Uncertain whether the soul was immortal or simply an effect of consciousness that perished with the body, Poe wrote "The Facts in the Case of M. Valdemar" (1845). The tale returns to the theme of mesmerism and recounts another effort to place a dying man under mesmeric influence. Yet unlike Vankirk in "Mesmeric Revelation," M. Valdemar offers no "psychal impressions," only the sepulchral utterances of a man longing to die. Hypnotized on the verge of death, Valdemar loses all signs of vitality and defies the laws of language (as Roland Barthes has noted) by insisting that he is dead. He remains thus suspended for almost seven months, and when the narrator releases him from the trance, he decomposes instantly into "a nearly liquid mass of loathsome—of detestable putridity" (p. 842). Perhaps the most shocking conclusion Poe ever devised, this last paragraph rewrites the ending of "Mesmeric Revelation" as a gruesome spectacle devoid of transcendental optimism. "Valdemar" shows Poe publicly engaged in mystification while privately exorcising anxieties.

Only three prose texts from Poe's last years seem noteworthy. Clearly "The Cask of Amontillado" (1846) ranks among his greatest narratives, for its ironic treatment of revenge, condensed style, and disturbing conclusion intensify its dramatic effect. Montresor reconstructs a crime committed fifty years earlier, possibly as a deathbed confession to the nameless listener who "so well [knows] the nature of [his] soul" (p. 848). Yet as in "The Tell-Tale Heart" and "The Imp of the Perverse," the narrator also confesses in order to display his cleverness, and his scheme to entrap Fortunato reveals both meticulous planning and astute analysis of his adversary. Montresor plays on Fortunato's vanity as a wine connoisseur, then uses reverse psychology to lure him into the damp catacombs. After leading his nemesis to the supposed site of the Amontillado, Montresor walls up Fortunato to achieve what he supposes will be the vengeance with impunity desired at the outset. But his final call to Fortunato, his admission that his "heart grew sick," and his closing supplication ("*In pace requiescat*") suggest that for "half of a century," he has been plagued by guilt (p. 854). The etymological connection between family names (fortune/ treasure) implies that Fortunato and Montresor are ultimately doubles—and, indeed, Montresor buries his "friend" in his own family vault. Scholars have suggested sources for this tale in Poe's literary battles, but the deeper fascination of "The Cask of Amontillado" lies in the hint of self-persecution.

Making an audacious bid to reveal the ultimate nature of the universe—including the fate of the individual soul—Poe published his long, cosmogonical "prose poem," *Eureka*, in 1848. Whether his "Book of Truths" (p. 1259) is a brilliant elaboration of physical and spiritual insight or a confused, ultimately poignant effort to shore up his precarious sense of reality has long been debated. Presenting himself as an intellectual and visionary, Poe argues that the entire cosmos tends to return to a state of original unity. Critiquing the theories of Johannes Kepler, Sir Isaac Newton, Pierre-Simon Laplace, and others, he labors to construct rational proof of God's existence through the evidence of astronomy and physics. In his boldest response to the problem of death, which some critics regard as Poe's definitive pronouncement, he declares at the end of *Eureka:* "All is Life—Life—Life within Life—the less within the greater, and all within the *Spirit Divine*" (pp. 1358–1359).

Poe's last great tale, "Hop-Frog" (1849), culminates in a ghastly mass murder arranged by the title character, a dwarfish court jester. The tale exposes the king's cruelty when he forces the excitable jester to drink wine and tosses a goblet in the face of Trippetta, a dwarf girl who dances at court. Both Hop-Frog and Trippetta have been abducted from "some barbarous region" to serve the king as virtual slaves (p. 900). When the king humiliates Trippetta, however, Hop-Frog plots revenge by persuading the king and his seven ministers to masquerade in a "diversion" called "the Eight Chained Ourang-Outangs" (pp. 903–904). Posing as beasts, they plan to horrify guests at a masked ball, but Hop-Frog sets fire to their costumes, declaring that he now sees clearly "what manner of people these maskers are" (p. 908). The tale projects sympathy for the exploited, physically odd outsider and derives its force from an outrage that is both personal and political. The "ourangoutang" masquerade, trading on a familiar racial stereotype, strengthens the perception that Poe alludes to slavery in antebellum America. Unlike Montresor, the jester experiences no guilty conscience; indeed, he and Trippetta return to their homeland after effecting a thoroughly American revolt against tyranny.

The Tales of Ratiocination

During the 1840s, as a creative counterpoint to his tales of terror and perverseness, Poe invented the modern detective story. "The Murders in the Rue Morgue," his first concerted "tale of ratiocination" (*Essays and Reviews*, p. 573), in fact established its basic conventions. These consisted of a seemingly insoluble mystery, a supremely brilliant yet eccentric detective, an observant though less astute confidant, and an earnest yet inept police investigator. Nothing escapes the observation of C. Auguste Dupin, who demonstrates at the outset that he can read his friend's mind. Poe invented the less observant companion-narrator to defer the revelation of the mystery—which has in fact already been solved—by re-staging the detective's elucidation of the case for the benefit of his perplexed friend.

The author built his tale around the sensational Parisian murder of Madame L'Espanaye and her daughter, who have been attacked in a locked room. Citing conflicting newspaper sources, Poe deepens the confusion about the assailant until Dupin nonchalantly informs the narrator that he has solved the case, having deduced that the murderer was a primate able to climb a building and tear apart his victims. By inspecting the crime scene, he has also discovered a broken nail in a window frame (explaining the animal's route of escape) and a tiny ribbon that—in Dupin's dazzling analysis—links the beast to a Maltese sailor. Here the tale reaches its climax, for just as the detective concludes his explanation to the narrator, a sailor appears to claim his orangutan in response to a newspaper notice by Dupin. Realizing that he has been caught, the sailor compliantly provides the missing details that confirm the detective's solution. This scene of revelation, confirming Dupin's genius, is repeated before the Prefect of Police, who fails to solve the case because he is "somewhat too cunning to be profound" (p. 431).

Poe was somewhat less successful in devising the second Dupin case, "The Mystery of Marie Rogêt," which was based on contemporary accounts of the bizarre death in New York of a popular cigar salesgirl named Mary Rogers. Using newspaper reports, Poe attempts to have his fictional detective, C. Auguste Dupin, solve the real "murder," thinly disguised as a Parisian crime; while the story was in serialization, new evidence inconveniently suggested that the young woman had died after a botched abortion. The greater length of "Marie Rogêt" allows Poe to dilate on the sensational aspects of the case—the

hints of sexual molestation, the condition of the corpse, and the suspicion that a gang of ruffians had been involved. He again devotes much of the narrative to a meticulous analysis of conflicting accounts, and he hedges Dupin's final solution to avoid possible disconfirmation by the ongoing Mary Rogers investigation. Yet for some aficionados of the detective genre, the tale represents an intriguing exercise in extrapolation. At the end of a story obsessed with minute details, Poe mockingly (and perhaps self-mockingly) warns of the mistakes that arise when Reason seeks truth "*in detail*" (p. 554).

In "The Purloined Letter" C. Auguste Dupin in his last bow returns to solve the theft of a compromising letter. Paradoxically, the crime is intriguing because even the dull-witted Prefect of Police knows that the Minister D—— has stolen the love letter from the queen's boudoir and knows it to be in his possession. Complex game-playing thus pervades the tale: Dupin toys with the Prefect; he engages the Minister D—— in a battle of wits; and he playfully conceals his activities to astound the narrator as well. The climax occurs near the tale's midpoint: when the Prefect makes a second visit, Dupin asks the amount of the reward and instructs him to prepare a check; the "thunder-stricken" Prefect accepts the purloined letter and departs "without having uttered a syllable" (p. 688). Dupin then explains to the equally surprised narrator how he deduced that, because the Minister D—— is both a poet and mathematician (as is Dupin himself), he has audaciously hidden the letter in plain sight to evade the Prefect's search. Dupin has recovered the letter just as the Minister D—— obtained it: by substituting a worthless one. He further confesses that he has settled a score with D—— for an "evil turn" done to the detective once in Vienna. Few Poe tales have evoked more discussion in recent years: since Jacques Lacan and Jacques Derrida, respectively, probed the psychoanalytic dimensions of the tale's doubling and repetition and the implications of the letter as a sign of language and power, critics such as Barbara Johnson and John Irwin have added to the accretion of provocative commentary (Muller and Richardson).

About the same time he composed "The Purloined Letter," Poe also wrote " 'Thou Art the Man,' " a humorous backwoods murder mystery that evokes the classical origins of the detective story (the tragedy of Oedipus) while marking the end of Poe's formal experimentation with the modern genre he created. In 1846 he wrote to Philip Pendleton Cooke:

> These tales of ratiocination owe most of their popularity to being something in a new key. I do not mean to say that they are not ingenious—but people think them more ingenious than they are—on account of their method and *air* of method. In the "Murders in the Rue Morgue," for instance, where is the ingenuity of unravelling a web which you yourself (the author) have woven for the express purpose of unravelling? (*Letters*, p. 328).

As this self-deprecating comment implies, Poe little suspected the far-reaching nature of his achievement. Yet in just three years he had discovered most of the essential devices and strategies upon which innumerable detective writers of later generations would elaborate.

Conclusion

In the century and a half since Poe's death, his works have influenced writers as diverse as Stéphane Mallarmé, Flannery O'Connor, Vladimir Nabokov, and Joyce Carol Oates. His tales, in particular, have had an impact on three major mystery forms: fantasy and science fiction, horror stories, and detective fiction. In each case, later writers adapted Poe's ideas and methods to establish the conventions of a popular genre. Through the important French translation of Poe by Charles Baudelaire, for example, Jules Verne discovered in such high-flying stories as "The Unparalleled Adventure of One Hans Pfaall" and "The Balloon-Hoax" the strategies of verisi-

militude and technical extrapolation that characterized his early science fiction, which included *Five Weeks in a Balloon* (1869) and *From the Earth to the Moon* (1869). Three decades later he reached back to Poe's *The Narrative of Arthur Gordon Pym* for the inspiration that produced *Le Sphinx des glaces* (1897), a fantastic sequel to Poe's novel in which Pym explores the earth's interior after being sucked into the polar abyss. Often borrowing narrative devices from Poe, Verne's fabulous stories influenced H. G. Wells and a legion of twentieth-century authors of fantasy and science fiction.

Because the horror story derived from eighteenth-century gothic fiction and still earlier sources, Poe's contribution to that genre is not foundational, but his tales of terror have nevertheless provided an important model in this century. Perhaps his most conspicuous latter-day emulator was H. P. Lovecraft, whose discovery of Poe directly inspired his fictional juvenilia as well as several later works. "The Outsider" (1921), "The Rats in the Walls" (1923), and "Cool Air" (1926) figure as conscious responses to specific Poe tales, and Lovecraft's predilection for neurotic narrators, remote or archaic settings, and florid style suggests Poe's conceptual influence. Many contemporary exponents of the horror story Lovecraft helped to popularize acknowledge an ultimate debt to Poe. The prolific Stephen King, for example, seems to have drawn principally upon stories like "The Fall of the House of Usher" and "The Pit and the Pendulum" for the stunning claustrophobic intensity in novels like *The Shining* (1977).

Poe's contributions to later literature are most notable, however, in the domain of the detective story, and again Baudelaire's translation played a pivotal role. The Dupin stories apparently inspired journalist Émile Gaboriau to conceive a series of Poesque *Récits Etranges* that began and ended with "Le petit vieux de Batignolles," but his subsequent *L'Affaire Lerouge* (1866) introduced the *roman policier* (novel of police investigation) and launched a vogue sustained by Ponson du Terrail and Fortuné de Boisgobey, among others. Gaboriau's success in this form, along with the mystery novels of Wilkie Collins (who owed much to Poe), encouraged the writing of Sir Arthur Conan Doyle, who drew several key ideas from the example of Dupin—his minute observation, identification with the criminal, and ability to recognize paradoxes (such as clues hidden in plain sight). Doyle also adapted Poe's teaming of an eccentric, amateur superdetective with an admiring and often stupefied companion. The crime-solving adventures of Sherlock Holmes triggered a flood of twentieth-century detective fiction, and in many later works, such as E. C. Bentley's *Trent's Last Case* (1913) or John Dickson Carr's "That Gentleman from Paris" (1950), Poe's influence is palpable. John Irwin has lately shown that Jorge Luis Borges wrote his surreal detective stories in conscious, esoteric response to the three Dupin tales. Although Poe drew ideas for the detective story from Voltaire's *Zadig* (1748), Charles Dickens' *Barnaby Rudge* (1841), and the *Memoirs of Vidocq* (1828) (head detective under Napoleon I), his invention of what he called the "tale of ratiocination" finally launched a publishing industry. The Edgar Allan Poe awards presented annually by the Mystery Writers of America testify to his lasting influence on the form.

Selected Bibliography

WORKS OF EDGAR ALLAN POE

INDIVIDUAL WORKS

Tamerlane and Other Poems. By a Bostonian. Boston: Calvin F. S. Thomas, Printer, 1827.
Al Aaraaf, Tamerlane, and Minor Poems. Baltimore: Hatch & Dunning, 1829.
Poems by Edgar A. Poe. Second Edition. New York: Elam Bliss, 1831.
The Narrative of Arthur Gordon Pym of Nantucket. New York: Harper & Brothers, 1838.
Tales of the Grotesque and Arabesque, 2 vols. Philadelphia: Lea & Blanchard, 1840.
The Prose Romances of Edgar A. Poe. Philadelphia: William H. Graham, 1843.
Tales. New York: Wiley & Putnam, 1845.
The Raven and Other Poems. New York: Wiley & Putnam, 1845.
Eureka: A Prose Poem. New York: Putnam, 1848.

COLLECTED WORKS

The Works of the Late Edgar Allan Poe, 4 vols. Edited by Rufus Wilmot Griswold. New York: J. S. Redfield, 1850–1856.
The Complete Works of Edgar Allan Poe, 17 vols. Edited by James A. Harrison. New York: Thomas Y. Crowell, 1902.
Collected Works of Edgar Allan Poe, 3 vols. Edited by Thomas Ollive Mabbott. Cambridge: Belknap Press of Harvard University Press, 1969–1978.
Imaginary Voyages, vol. 1 of *The Collected Writings of Edgar Allan Poe.* Edited by Burton R. Pollin. Boston and New York: Twayne, 1981; New York: Gordian Press, 1994.
Poetry and Tales. Edited by Patrick F. Quinn. New York: Library of America, 1984.
Essays and Reviews. Edited by G. R. Thompson. New York: Library of America, 1984.

LETTERS

The Letters of Edgar Allan Poe, 2 vols. Edited by John Ward Ostrom. Cambridge: Harvard University Press, 1948; New York: Gordian Press, 1966.

BIBLIOGRAPHIES

Dameron, J. Lasley, and Irby B. Cauthen, Jr. *Edgar Allan Poe: A Bibliography of Criticism, 1827–1967.* Charlottesville: University Press of Virginia, 1974.
Hyneman, Esther F. *Edgar Allan Poe: An Annotated Bibliography of Books and Articles in English, 1827–1973.* Boston: G. K. Hall, 1974.

BIOGRAPHICAL AND CRITICAL STUDIES

Allen, Michael. *Poe and the British Magazine Tradition.* New York: Oxford University Press, 1969.
Asselineau, Roger. *Edgar Allan Poe.* Minneapolis: University of Minnesota Press, 1970.
Auerbach, Jonathan. *The Romance of Failure: First-Person Fictions of Poe, Hawthorne, and James.* New York: Oxford University Press, 1989.
Barthes, Roland. "Textual Analysis of a Tale of Poe." In *On Signs.* Edited by Marshall Blonsky. Baltimore: Johns Hopkins University Press, 1985. Pp. 84–97.
Basler, Roy P. "The Interpretation of 'Ligeia.'" *College English* 5: 363–372 (April 1944).
Bittner, William. *Poe: A Biography.* Boston: Little, Brown, 1962.
Bloom, Harold, ed. *The Tales of Poe.* New York: Chelsea House, 1987.
Bonaparte, Marie. *The Life and Works of Edgar Allan Poe: A Psycho-analytic Interpretation.* Translated by

John Rodker. London: Imago, 1949. With an introduction by Sigmund Freud.

Brand, Dana. "Reconstructing the 'Flâneur': Poe's Invention of the Detective Story." *Genre* 18: 35–56 (spring 1985).

Budd, Louis J., and Edwin H. Cady, eds. *On Poe.* Durham, N.C.: Duke University Press, 1993.

Byrd, Max. "The Detective Detected: From Sophocles to Ross Macdonald." *Yale Review* 64: 76 (October 1974).

Carlson, Eric W., ed. *The Recognition of Edgar Allan Poe: Selected Criticism Since 1829.* Ann Arbor: University of Michigan Press, 1966.

Cox, James M. "Edgar Poe: Style as Pose." *Virginia Quarterly Review* 44: 67–89 (winter 1968).

Davidson, Edward. *Poe: A Critical Study.* Cambridge: Belknap Press of Harvard University Press, 1957.

Dayan, Joan. *Fables of Mind: An Inquiry into Poe's Fiction.* New York: Oxford University Press, 1987.

Eliot, T. S. "From Poe to Valéry." *Hudson Review* 2: 327–342 (autumn 1949).

Elmer, Jonathan. *Reading at the Social Limit: Affect, Mass Culture, and Edgar Allan Poe.* Palo Alto: Stanford University Press, 1995.

Fiedler, Leslie. *Love and Death in the American Novel,* rev. ed. Normal, Ill.: Dalkey Archive Press, 1997.

Fisher, Benjamin F. "Poe's 'Metzengerstein': Not a Hoax." *American Literature* 42: 487–494 (January 1971).

———, ed. *Poe at Work: Seven Textual Studies.* Baltimore: Edgar Allan Poe Society, 1978.

Gargano, James W. "The Question of Poe's Narrators." *College English* 25: 177–181 (December 1963).

———. " 'The Cask of Amontillado': A Masquerade of Motive and Identity." *Studies in Short Fiction* 4: 119–126 (winter 1967).

Goddu, Teresa. *Gothic America: Narrative, History, and Nation.* New York: Columbia University Press, 1997.

Halliburton, David. *Edgar Allan Poe: A Phenomenological View.* Princeton: Princeton University Press, 1973.

Hammond, Alexander. "Edgar Allan Poe's *Tales of the Folio Club:* The Evolution of a Lost Book." *Library Chronicle* 41: 13–43 (1976).

Hoffman, Daniel. *Poe Poe Poe Poe Poe Poe Poe.* Garden City, N.Y.: Doubleday, 1972.

Howarth, William L., ed. *Twentieth Century Interpretations of Poe's Tales: A Collection of Critical Essays.* Englewood Cliffs, N.J.: Prentice-Hall, 1971.

Ingram, John H. *Edgar Allan Poe: His Life, Letters, and Opinions.* London: W. H. Allen, 1886; New York: AMS Press, 1965.

Irwin, John. *American Hieroglyphics: The Symbol of the Egyptian Hieroglyphics in the American Renaissance.* New Haven: Yale University Press, 1980.

———. *The Mystery to a Solution: Poe, Borges, and the Analytical Detective Story.* Baltimore: Johns Hopkins University Press, 1994.

Jacobs, Robert D. *Poe: Journalist and Critic.* Baton Rouge: Louisiana State University Press, 1969.

Kennedy, J. Gerald. *Poe, Death, and the Life of Writing.* New Haven: Yale University Press, 1987.

———. *"The Narrative of Arthur Gordon Pym" and the Abyss of Interpretation.* New York: Twayne, 1995.

———. "The Violence of Melancholy: Poe Against Himself." *American Literary History* 8: 533–551 (fall 1996).

Ketterer, David. *The Rationale of Deception in Poe.* Baton Rouge: Louisiana State University Press, 1979.

Kopley, Richard, ed. *Poe's "Pym": Critical Explorations.* Durham, N.C.: Duke University Press, 1992.

Levin, Harry. *The Power of Blackness: Hawthorne, Poe, Melville.* New York: Knopf, 1970.

Levine, Stuart. *Edgar Poe: Seer and Craftsman.* Deland, Fla.: Everett/Edwards, 1972.

Ljungquist, Kent. *The Grand and the Fair: Poe's Landscape Aesthetics and Pictorial Techniques.* Potomac, Md.: Scripta Humanistica, 1984.

Martin, Terence. "The Imagination at Play: Edgar Allan Poe." *Kenyon Review* 28: 194–209 (1966).

May, Charles. *Edgar Allan Poe: A Study of the Short Fiction.* Boston: Twayne, 1991.

Meyers, Jeffrey. *Edgar Allan Poe: His Life and Legacy.* New York: Scribners, 1992.

Miller, Perry. *The Raven and the Whale: The War of Words and Wits in the Era of Poe and Melville.* New York: Harcourt, Brace, and World, 1956.

Moss, Sidney. *Poe's Literary Battles: The Critic in the Context of His Literary Milieu.* Durham, N.C.: Duke University Press, 1963.

Muller, John P., and William J. Richardson. *The Purloined Poe: Lacan, Derrida, and Psychoanalytic Reading.* Baltimore: Johns Hopkins University Press, 1988.

Nelson, Dana. *The Word in Black and White: Reading "Race" in American Literature, 1638–1867.* New York: Oxford University Press, 1992.

Person, Leland S. *Aesthetic Headaches: Women and a Masculine Poetics in Poe, Melville, and Hawthorne.* Athens: University of Georgia Press, 1988.

Pollin, Burton R. *Discoveries in Poe.* Notre Dame, Ind.: University of Notre Dame Press, 1970.

Porte, Joel. *The Romance in America: Studies in Cooper, Poe, Hawthorne, Melville, and James.* Middletown, Conn.: Wesleyan University Press, 1969.

Quinn, Arthur Hobson. *Edgar Allan Poe: A Critical Biography.* New York and London: Appleton-Century, 1941; New York: Cooper Square, 1969.

Quinn, Patrick F. *The French Face of Edgar Allan Poe.* Carbondale: Southern Illinois University Press, 1957.

Regan, Robert, ed. *Poe: A Collection of Critical Essays.* Englewood Cliffs, N.J.: Prentice-Hall, 1967.

Reilly, John E. "The Lesser Death-Watch and 'The Tell-Tale Heart.' " *American Transcendental Quarterly* 2: 3–9 (2nd quarter 1969).

Renza, Louis. "Poe's Secret Autobiography." In *The American Renaissance Reconsidered,* edited by Walter Benn Michaels and Donald E. Pease. Baltimore: Johns Hopkins University Press, 1985. Pp. 58–89.

Reynolds, David. *Beneath the American Renaissance: The Subversive Imagination in the Age of Emerson and Melville.* New York: Knopf, 1988.

Riddel, Joseph. "The 'Crypt' of Edgar Allan Poe." *Boundary* 2: 117–141 (spring 1979).

Ridgely, Joseph V. "The Growth of the Text." In *Imaginary Voyages,* vol. 1 of *The Collected Writings of Edgar Allan Poe.* Edited by Burton R. Pollin. Boston and New York: Twayne, 1981; New York: Gordian Press, 1994. Pp. 29–36.

Robinson, Douglas. *American Apocalypses: The Image of the End of the World in American Literature.* Baltimore: Johns Hopkins University Press, 1985.

Rosenheim, Shawn. *The Cryptographic Imagination: Secret Writing from Edgar Allan Poe to the Internet.* Baltimore: Johns Hopkins University Press, 1997.

Rosenheim, Shawn, and Stephen Rachman, eds. *The American Face of Edgar Allan Poe.* Baltimore: Johns Hopkins University Press, 1995.

Rowe, John Carlos. *Through the Custom-House: Nineteenth-Century American Fiction and Modern Theory.* Baltimore: Johns Hopkins University Press, 1982.

Silverman, Kenneth. *Edgar A. Poe: Mournful and Neverending Remembrance.* New York: HarperCollins, 1991.

———. *New Essays on Poe's Major Tales.* New York: Cambridge University Press, 1993.

Stauffer, Donald B. "The Two Styles of Poe's 'MS. Found in a Bottle.' " *Style* 1: 107–120 (spring 1967).

Stovall, Floyd. *Edgar Poe the Poet: Essays New and Old on the Man and His Work.* Charlottesville: University Press of Virginia, 1969.

Thomas, Dwight, and David K. Jackson. *The Poe Log: A Documentary Life of Edgar Allan Poe 1809–1849.* Boston: G. K. Hall, 1987.

Thompson, G. R. *Poe's Fiction: Romantic Irony in the Gothic Tales.* Madison: University of Wisconsin Press, 1973.

———. "The Arabesque Design of *Arthur Gordon Pym.*" In Poe's *"Pym": Critical Explorations.* Edited by Richard Kopley. Durham, N.C.: Duke University Press, 1992. Pp. 188–213.

Walker, I. M. *Edgar Allan Poe: The Critical Heritage.* London and New York: Routledge & Kegan Paul, 1986.

Weiner, Bruce I. "Novels, Tales, and Problems of Form in *The Narrative of Arthur Gordon Pym.*" In Poe's *"Pym": Critical Explorations.* Edited by Richard Kopley. Durham, N.C.: Duke University Press, 1992. Pp. 44–56.

Whalen, Terence. "Edgar Allan Poe and the Horrid Laws of Political Economy." *American Quarterly* 44:381–417 (September 1992).

Wilbur, Richard. *Responses: Prose Pieces, 1953–1976.* New York: Harcourt Brace Jovanovich, 1976.

Williams, Michael J. S. *A World of Words: Language and Displacement in the Fiction of Edgar Allan Poe.* Durham, N.C.: Duke University Press, 1988.

Woodberry, George E. *The Life of Edgar Allan Poe, Personal and Literary,* 2 vols. Boston and New York: Houghton Mifflin, 1909; New York: Biblo and Tannen, 1965.

ELLERY QUEEN

FRANCIS M. NEVINS

ELLERY QUEEN was the joint byline of two first cousins who called themselves Frederic Dannay and Manfred B. Lee (and called each other Manny and Danny). They were born in Brooklyn's Brownsville district, nine months and five blocks apart. Lee was born Manford Lepofsky on 11 January 1905, and Dannay was born Daniel Nathan on 20 October of the same year. The Nathans moved upstate to Elmira when Danny was a baby, and he spent a childhood that recalls Mark Twain's Tom Sawyer, in a rural environment where he roamed the woods and fields and concocted elaborate business schemes like charging playmates two cents apiece to see the ghost of Long John Silver. His best friend during the Elmira years was named Ellery.

The Lepofskys remained in Brooklyn, and when Manny paid summer visits to Danny in Elmira, the boys would spend their time playing games of one-upmanship—a practice they continued during more than forty years of collaboration. In 1917 the Nathans moved back to Brooklyn, and that winter, while twelve-year-old Danny was in bed with an ear infection, one of his aunts loaned him a copy of Sir Arthur Conan Doyle's *Adventures of Sherlock Holmes*. The book so fired the boy's imagination that the next morning he got a public library card and stripped the shelves of every Holmes book he saw.

During their teens the boys became best friends. "We were cousins," Dannay said more than sixty years later, "but we were closer than brothers" (Behren). One of the interests that drew and kept them together was a common passion for detective fiction, and as early as 1920, while walking or riding the streetcar to and from Boys' High, they began, Dannay said, "to experiment with ideas, to play with the strings of plot" (*The Roman Hat Mystery*, 1979, p. iii). Manny Lee went on from high school to New York University, but Prohibition put an end to Meyer Nathan's liquor business and forced his son to quit Boys' High after his third year and go to work. In 1926 Dannay married Mary Beck, the first of his three wives, and two years later he was working as copywriter and art director for a New York advertising agency. Lee graduated from NYU in 1926, married for the first time in 1928, and found work in the Manhattan publicity department of the Pathé movie studio. The cousins' offices were only a few blocks apart, and they met for lunch almost every day.

American detective fiction in the late 1920s was dominated by the best-selling Philo Vance novels, written by art critic Willard Huntington Wright (1887–1939) under the pseudonym of S. S. Van Dine. Over their lunches Dannay and Lee discussed the idea of collaborating on a detective novel of their own in the same manner, complete with hyperintellectual sleuth and reams of erudite deduction. The announcement of a $7,500 prize contest, sponsored jointly by *McClure's* magazine and the publisher Frederick A. Stokes, catalyzed them into serious action. Over the next several months they worked frantically on evenings, weekends, and vacation time to complete a novel before the deadline. "I remember Manny Lee had to go to a wedding in Philadelphia during the time we were writing it," Fred Dannay said in a 1979 interview with *Playboy* magazine, "and I had to go with him, to the wedding of a complete stranger, just so we wouldn't lose the time it took to get there and back on the train" (p. 48). With their backgrounds in advertising and publicity they took great pains to give their protagonist a name that would be slightly unusual, easy to remember, and rhythmic in sound, and after a few false starts they hit upon Ellery Queen. To comply with the contest rule that every entry be submitted under a pseudonym, the cousins made the brilliant decision to use Ellery Queen not only for their protagonist—who is himself a detective novelist, presumably under his own name—but also for their joint byline. To avoid confusion, throughout this essay "Ellery" refers to the detective protagonist of the Ellery Queen novels and stories, and "Queen" refers to the byline.

The early months of 1929 put the cousins on an emotional roller coaster. The literary agency running the contest unofficially informed them that their submission had won, then a few days later told them that *McClure's* had gone bankrupt and its new owners had decided to award the prize to another entry. But Stokes liked their manuscript enough to make an offer for it anyway, though with a much smaller advance, and the result was the publication in August 1929 of *The Roman Hat Mystery*. In 1931, the pit of the Great Depression, after selling two more Queen books, Dannay and Lee gave up their day jobs and devoted full time to turning out a ninety-thousand-word detective novel every three months for the next few years.

What was each cousin's function in the Queen partnership? Through their long collaboration Dannay and Lee were asked this question countless times and always replied enigmatically, drawing a veil of secrecy over their division of labor as a sort of advertising stunt to keep readers intrigued. The truth in capsule form: Dannay created the skeletons and Lee put flesh on the bones. Each Ellery Queen novel began with a plot synopsis of about twenty-five thousand words in which Dannay would set forth the book's themes, plot, characters, clues, and deductions. As soon as Lee finished absorbing that synopsis the fur would begin to fly between the cousins. Lee's son Rand said that one time, after a heated argument over the phone, "Dad threw down a plot outline and exclaimed, 'He gives me the most ridiculous characters to work with and expects me to make them realistic!'" (Lee, p. 22). When the quarrels were settled, Lee would expand Dannay's synopsis into a novel of around one hundred thousand words and then the fighting would begin all over. "We are competitors and always have been," Dannay said. "We are always trying to out-top each other ("Case," *MD*, p. 204). And Lee once described a time when he and Dannay were working briefly as Hollywood screenwriters with an office directly under the studio's mimeograph department, whose duplicating machines clattered constantly. "*They* complained about the noise *we* were making!" (Shenker, p. 36).

Ellery I (1929–1935)

The cousins' first period runs from *The Roman Hat Mystery* through *The Spanish Cape Mystery* (1935) and encompasses nine novels as by and starring Ellery Queen, four more as by Barnaby Ross, and a number of short stories, most of which were collected as *The Adventures of Ellery Queen* (1934)—a title deliberately echoing that first book of Sherlock Holmes tales which had so changed young Dannay's life. Although superior in plotting, characterization, and style, the Queen novels of this first period were heavily influenced by the Van Dine blockbusters. The strict pattern of the titles, *The* adjective-of-nationality noun *Mystery*, comes from Van Dine's pattern, *The* six-letter-word *Murder Case*. Each running character in early Queen has a counterpart in Van Dine, with blockheaded Sergeant Velie, for instance, stemming from dumb Sergeant Heath in the Vance cases. Ellery's father, Inspector Richard Queen of the New York Police Department, calls on his brilliant son for help in difficult crime puzzles much as District Attorney Markham calls on that insufferable mandarin Philo Vance. Most important, it was from Van Dine that Dannay and Lee borrowed the concept of the super-intellectual detective, full of scholarly quotations, detached from people and the world, interested only in abstract problems, a Harvard-educated dilettante bibliophile who usually calls his father "pater" or "Inspector darling." Here is Ellery I as he walks on stage in *Roman Hat:*

> There was a square cut to his shoulders and an agreeable swing to his body as he walked. He was dressed in oxford grey and carried a light stick. On his nose perched what seemed an incongruous note in so athletic a man—a pince-nez. But the brow above, the long delicate lines of the face, the bright eyes were those of a man of thought rather than action. (1929 ed., pp. 15–16)

In their twilight years the cousins came to hate this version of the character, whom Manny Lee derided as "the biggest prig that ever came down the pike" ("Case," *MD*, p. 207). But those early novels are richly plotted specimens of the Golden Age deductive puzzle: bursting with bizarre circumstances, conflicting testimony, enigmatic clues (including that uniquely Queenian device, the dying message), alternative solutions, fireworks displays of virtuoso reasoning, and a constant crackle of intellectual excitement.

What makes Queen's novels stand out from the other detective fiction of the time is the cousins' insistence on playing fair: in Dannay's words, "the reader had to know everything that the detective knew, and therefore had an even chance of beating the detective before the solution was given . . ." (Dannay, interview, p. 2). And they did play the game

with scrupulous fairness, not only presenting all the facts honestly (albeit quite trickily on occasion) but stopping most of the novels at a certain point to issue a formal "Challenge to the Reader" to solve the puzzle ahead of Ellery. The odds, of course, were stacked in favor of the house, and when Dannay once boasted to an interviewer that Queen was always "completely fair to the reader," Lee cut in: "We are fair to the reader only if he is a genius" (Prescott).

Among the early Queen novels, perhaps the finest is *The Greek Coffin Mystery* (1932). Blind art dealer Georg Khalkis dies of heart failure in the library of his West Fifty-fourth Street brownstone. Three days later his coffin is taken to the church graveyard next door and lowered into the family crypt. When the burial party returns to the house, the attorney for the estate discovers that the steel box with Khalkis' will is missing from the wall safe. The police are summoned, but after two days the box is still missing. At a conference called to discuss the case are Inspector Richard Queen and a young, cocksure Ellery, who deduces that the box must be in Khalkis' coffin. An exhumation order is obtained, the coffin is opened, and inside is not the will but the decaying corpse of a second man, strangled, lying atop Khalkis' body. Inspector Queen and his men soon unearth a cornucopia of counterplots inside the Khalkis household and an assortment of intrigues outside, many rooted in the theft of a Leonardo da Vinci from a British museum.

Ellery proposes a devilishly ingenious solution based on the amount of tea water in a percolator and the color of a dead man's tie, but he soon learns that this version of events was prepared for him to find by the "player on the other side." This is the first of four solutions to the Khalkis case, each one radiating outward from those that went before and accounting for more of the total picture. The fourth and last explanation alone embraces the entire web of plot and counterplot (which Ellery describes as "a complex plan which requires assiduous concentration for complete comprehension" [p. 360]) and reveals, with total fairness to the superhumanly alert reader, a stunning surprise murderer. Although not flawless, *The Greek Coffin Mystery* is probably the most involuted, brain-crushing, meticulously constructed detective novel published in the United States during the genre's Golden Age.

The cousins next introduced a second joint byline, Barnaby Ross, and a new detective in the person of retired Shakespearean actor Drury Lane. Driven from the stage by total deafness, Lane has re-created an Elizabethan village community on his acreage above the Hudson, populating it with down-and-out theater people who earn their keep by sporting period costumes and Shakespearean names. But this power-driven tyrant wants more. "From obeying the jerk of the master's strings, I now have the impulse to pull the strings myself, in a greater authorship than created drama" (*The Tragedy of X*, p. 21). In a mad oedipal rivalry with Shakespeare's shade, Lane turns to intervening in real-world stories and, in a sense, rewriting them.

The Tragedy of X (1932) opens with a biographical sketch of Lane and his letter to the NYPD offering the solution to an unsolved murder case. When his deductions prove right, Inspector Thumm and District Attorney Bruno visit and thank the old man and ask his help on a problem even more bewildering. We flash back to four days earlier and visit a cocktail party thrown by the sadistic and lecherous stockbroker Harley Longstreet to celebrate his engagement to a much younger woman and make his guests squirm. Among those invited are Longstreet's browbeaten partner, his former mistress, a man who is in love with the woman Longstreet wants as his next mistress, a former lover of his present fiancée, and a corrupt politician who blames the brokers for ruinous losses in the market. After cocktails Longstreet insists that everyone go along with him to a dinner party in New Jersey. When a sudden thunderstorm makes it impossible to get a taxi for the trip to the ferry, they all board a crosstown trolley. The packed streetcar is lurching west toward the ferry slip when Longstreet reaches into his

pocket and suddenly keels over dead in the aisle, his hand pricked and bleeding in a dozen places.

Once on the scene, Inspector Thumm searches the dead man's pockets and finds a cork ball riddled with needles, each one coated at both ends with poison: pure nicotine. But there are too many suspects with motive and opportunity, and his investigation founders. When Thumm and Bruno have recounted these facts, Drury Lane announces that he believes he knows the murderer but, owing in roughly equal parts to his analysis of the situation and his lust to exercise power, refuses to say more. The next evening there is a second murder, the victim thrown from the upper deck of a ferry and crushed to pulp as the boat pulls into the Weehawken slip. Later come a spectacular murder trial, a disturbing conversation aboard a New Jersey commuter train, a third murder committed within a few feet of Lane himself, and finally, during another train ride, the unmasking.

The Tragedy of X introduced into the cousins' repertoire two motifs that were to become hallmarks. One, which they borrowed from Conan Doyle's *The Valley of Fear* (1915) and recycled throughout the novels of their first period, cannot be revealed completely without ruining several early Queen novels for those not yet familiar with them. The other, on which Dannay and Lee played variations for the rest of their careers, is the dying-message clue. During a night journey on the Weehawken local, which one commuter will not survive, Drury Lane and others involved in the case have a conversation about the last moments before death. This discussion is as central to the Queen canon as the locked-room lecture in *The Three Coffins* (1935) is to the works of John Dickson Carr. "There are no limits to which the human mind cannot soar," Lane declares, "in this unique, godlike instant before the end of life" (*The Tragedy of X*, p. 236). Not only does *The Tragedy of X* offer a superb puzzle and the rationale for dozens of future dying-message stories, it vividly re-creates a long-vanished time when America's cities and suburbs were linked by streetcars, ferries, electric interurban lines, commuter trains—in short, by a mass-transit system that worked and in this novel lives again.

In *The Tragedy of Y* (1932), Drury Lane visits Washington Square to probe a series of bizarre and imbecilic crimes in the doom-haunted Hatter household, which for the cousins seems to be a paradigm of American society: its members rotting with greed, sadism, and inertia, consenting for the sake of expected inheritances to be dehumanized in love-hate relationships with each other and with the bitch goddess of wealth and property who rules the roost. The identity of the murderer—a stunning surprise in the early thirties but far less so today—combines with the themes of Iagoesque manipulation and despair of human nature to make this one of the darkest detective novels ever written. Lane tackles his third puzzle in *The Tragedy of Z* (1933) and dies at the end of his fourth, which is aptly titled *Drury Lane's Last Case* (1933).

Ellery Queen remained active as both pseudonym and sleuth during the Drury Lane years. In *The Egyptian Cross Mystery* (1932), which may be the bloodiest pure detective novel ever written, Ellery and his father spend months on the trail of a multiple murderer who beheads and crucifies victims so as to turn them into embodiments of the letter T. As usual in Golden Age whodunits with a serial killer, the crimes are not random but connected. In *The American Gun Mystery* (1933), Ellery and Inspector Queen are among the twenty thousand spectators who have piled into the New York Colosseum for the opening night of a rodeo whose main attraction is the aging silent-Western film star Buck Horne, a character clearly modeled on William S. Hart. While Horne is supposed to be leading forty wild-shooting riders in a chase around the arena, someone fires a shot that is not in the script and the aged horseman falls to the tanbark where he is trampled to death.

The Siamese Twin Mystery (1933) leaves Ellery, his father, and the members of the household of Dr. John Xavier trapped by a forest fire in a mountaintop mansion. When Xavier is found shot to death in his study—with a game of solitaire laid out in front of him and a torn half of the six of spades clenched between his fingers—the Queens have to tackle the crime with no outside help. The climax is a blend of nobility and lunacy: the fire reaches the house, everyone left alive holes up in the cellar, and Ellery undertakes the absurd act of exposing the murderer while they await a horrible death. *The Chinese Orange Mystery* (1934) begins when an excruciatingly ordinary man is shown into a waiting room in the office suite of wealthy young publisher and stamp collector Donald Kirk, who happens to be a friend of Ellery. An hour later, when Kirk and Ellery enter the waiting room, it has been transformed into something out of Lewis Carroll: the rug turned upside down, pictures and clock facing the walls, and floor lamps standing on their shades. Lying on the overturned rug with his brains splattered and two African spears thrust up through his pants legs and under his jacket is Mr. Nobody from Nowhere, whose every article of clothing—collar, shirt, coat, trousers, shoes—is on him backward. The opening situation is so outré it is a shame the plot turns out neither credible nor all that complex.

Among the short stories collected in *The Adventures of Ellery Queen*, "The Glass-Domed Clock" and "The Bearded Lady" are notable for complex plotting and subtle dying-message clues. In "The Mad Tea Party," Dannay's favorite short tale from this period and another proof of his fondness for Lewis Carroll, Ellery is invited to a Long Island house party that is to feature a private performance of *Alice in Wonderland*, but festive spirits are dampened when the host vanishes the morning after Ellery arrives. Then comes the delivery of a series of packages containing pairs of shoes, cabbages, chessmen, and other bizarre objects. The tale indeed owes much to Carroll, but Ellery's psychological war against his adversary is inspired by Edgar Allan Poe's "Thou Art the Man!"

At the tail end of Queen's first period came "The Lamp of God," one of the finest detective novelettes ever written. A desperate phone call from an attorney friend takes Ellery to the raw January snowscape of Long Island. The patriarch of the maniacal Mayhew family is believed to have hidden a fortune in gold somewhere in the old mansion (reminiscent of a setting from Poe) where he had lived and recently died. The attorney, Thorne, suspects that certain of the old tyrant's relatives are bent on finding and taking the treasure before it can be turned over to the old man's long-lost daughter. After a raw-nerved evening with an obese doctor, a demented old lady, and an enigmatic young hired man, Ellery and the others got to bed but awaken to an event that convinces them the world has gone mad. The entire huge black house of old Sylvester Mayhew, next door to where they have been sleeping, has vanished in the night. This is one of the finest pieces of atmospheric writing in the genre, evoking chills that rise off the page into our bones. With images of light against darkness, sun against cold, and reason against absurdity, Queen summons up the terror of a universe abandoned to the demonic, then exorcises it through the rigorous use of the instrument given us by "chance, cosmos, God, whatever you may choose to call it": the enlightening human mind (*New Adventures*, p. 75).

Ellery II (1936–1940)

By the mid-1930s Dannay and Lee were making excellent money not just from books but from two lucrative media that had begun to buy their work: the slick-paper magazines, like *Redbook* and *Cosmopolitan,* and the movies. The demands of these markets led the cousins to reconfigure their principal character into Ellery II. In this second period, the Van Dine–patterned titles vanish and Ellery gradually trades in his intellectual priggishness for humanity. In Dannay's words: "We loosened the construction. . . . we put more emphasis on character development and background; we put more emphasis on

human-interest situations. . . . We turned to commercialism because we frankly wanted to make more money" (Dannay, interview, p. 4).

Compared with the classics of the first period, much of the cousins' output of the late 1930s suffers from thin plots, overdoses of tedious boy-meets-girl byplay, and characters tailored to please story editors at the slick-magazine suites and the studios. In the longer view, the exploits of Ellery II served at least in part to open up the deductive puzzle and make room within its cerebral rigor for more of the virtues of mainstream storytelling. In several short tales and in the novels *The Devil to Pay* and *The Four of Hearts* (both 1938), Ellery works as a Hollywood screenwriter, paralleling the cousins' brief stints at Columbia, Paramount, and Metro-Goldwyn-Mayer. Hoping to make their character more appealing to the mass media, Dannay and Lee had Ellery become involved with lovely gossip columnist Paula Paris, a prose amalgam of the heroines from Hollywood's screwball comedies of the time. And perhaps screwball is the best one-word description of Queen's take on movieland. "The place was filled with crazy people," Dannay said in 1979. "I told Manny even if I had to dig ditches for the rest of my life, I wasn't coming back" (Behren). *The New Adventures of Ellery Queen* (1940), which brought together all the short cases of Ellery II plus "The Lamp of God" and a few others from the early years, concluded this phase of the saga.

By 1940 Fred and Mary Dannay and their sons were living the suburban life in Great Neck, Long Island, and Fred was close to reaching his goal as a book collector: owning a copy of every volume of detective-crime short stories ever published. Manny Lee, divorced from his first wife, was sharing a Park Avenue apartment with his daughters. The cousins put in twelve-hour workdays at their respective homes and met once a week at a rented office to consolidate their material. Both men were chain smokers, and their workplace atmosphere tended to be on the thick side. On the office floor they kept a tattered brown envelope labeled "Ideas."

And at that time they needed every idea they could conjure up. Beginning in June 1939, when *The Adventures of Ellery Queen* series debuted on the CBS radio network, they had to turn out a sixty-minute script a week. Among the most complex of the early audio adventures is "The Last Man Club" (25 June 1939), in which Ellery (Hugh Marlowe) and his secretary and love interest Nikki Porter (Marian Shockley)—a new character created by the cousins to attract female listeners— witness a hit-and-run incident and are propelled by the victim's dying words into the affairs of a survivor-take-all group to which the dead man belonged. This is the first but far from the last death-plagued tontine (a joint financial arrangement whereby the participants contribute equally to a prize awarded to the sole survivor) in the Queen canon.

Ellery III (1940–1958)

Radio work gave Dannay and Lee a steady income but left them no time for any other writing. In September 1940 the show left the air, and the next fifteen months were among the most fruitful in the cousins' lives. Dannay, the historian and bibliophile of the duo, used his library of detective-crime short-story collections as the basis for editing *101 Years' Entertainment* (1941), the definitive anthology of short mystery fiction from Poe to Pearl Harbor. When he found countless first-rate tales for which that mammoth volume had no room, he persuaded publisher Lawrence E. Spivak to launch *Ellery Queen's Mystery Magazine* (*EQMM*), the genre's premier periodical, which Dannay actively edited from its first issue (fall 1941) until shortly before his death more than forty years later. It was also during these fifteen months that the cousins commenced their third and richest period as writers. Ellery III is not a detached Philo Vance clone but a human being scarred by the horrors he encounters, and the Queen books are no longer problems in deduction but much closer to mainstream novels.

Calamity Town (1942) opens on the afternoon of 6 August 1940, when Ellery steps off the train in Wrightsville, a small, tight-knit, vividly portrayed community that with the outbreak of war in Europe has become a boomtown. He needs a place to stay while he writes his next novel, but no hotel rooms or furnished houses are available except for one that has developed a reputation as a jinx. John F. and Hermione Wright had built a house next to their own as a wedding present for their daughter Nora and her fiancé, Jim Haight, but Jim had disappeared the day before the wedding and later a prospective purchaser had died of a heart attack in the house. Ellery rents the house and quickly bonds with the entire Wright family, especially with youngest daughter, Pat, whose steady is the county prosecutor. Then Jim Haight returns to town. He reconciles with and marries Nora. Ellery moves in with John F. and Hermione and Pat while the newlyweds move into the house built for them three years before. Day by day over months the marriage goes sour and the atmosphere thickens with hints that Jim is planning to kill his wife. At the Wrights' New Year's Eve party one of the drinks raised for a toast turns out to be poisoned, and Wrightsville's first homicide in years tears apart both the family and the town. The investigation, public reactions, sensational trial, and what follows are not just pieces of a puzzle (though a neat plot is hidden among them), but nightmares happening to people one cares about. Ellery, no longer the controlling mind but a man in a muddle, is powerless to affect events and contributes nothing until the final chapter.

Calamity Town, Dannay said, was "the best book that we thought we had written up to that time." But no national magazine made the offer for serialization rights that the cousins had expected, and no editor could explain why not. "We'd better find another basket for our eggs," Dannay told Lee. "If you can be turned down with no reason apparent on the best book you've ever written . . . then you've got to do something else" (Dannay, interview, p. 9). The obvious contender for "something else" was radio, and the cousins' agent soon found a new network and sponsor for the continued audio exploits of Ellery Queen. In January 1942 the series returned to the air and Dannay and Lee to the old grind of a script a week, although several of the "new" adventures were tighter rewrites of sixty-minute dramas from the program's first months. Manny Lee happened to visit the NBC studio during a rehearsal on 1 April and met actress Kaye Brinker, who was featured in the week's story. They began dating at once, were married on 4 July 1942, and stayed together until Lee's death almost twenty-nine years later. Except for summer rerun cycles and several hiatus periods, the series was heard weekly on one network or another until the spring of 1948. "A new plot every week knocked me out," Dannay said (Steinbrunner, p. 215). Even after mid-1945 when Dannay's function of providing a weekly plot outline was taken over by Anthony Boucher, the demands of *EQMM* left him little time for Ellery Queen novels.

The cousins had taken such care and pains over the creation of Wrightsville that it is no wonder they had Ellery go back there in *The Murderer Is a Fox* (1945). In the summer of 1944 a nerve-shattered war hero returns home after receiving some anonymous letters intimating that his wife was unfaithful during his service as a fighter pilot in Asia. Twelve years earlier Captain Davy Fox's mother had been murdered and his father sentenced to life imprisonment for the crime. The boy's adolescence had been a nightmare of failed attempts to escape the stigma and the fear of his own "tainted blood." As Davy wrestles with a growing compulsion to kill his wife, she goes for help to Ellery, who concludes that the only way to release Davy from the trap in which the past holds him is to reopen the old case and try to prove that his father did not kill his mother. Ellery's meticulous reconstruction of exactly what happened in the house of Bayard and Jessica Fox on 14 June 1932 is carried out with the intellectual tools of the historian and generates the sort of excitement that every conscientious historian feels while on the hunt for the truth of the past. Like many

Queen novels to come, this one ends with a false or partial solution followed by a second solution that is both final and shattering.

"In the beginning it was without form, a darkness that kept shifting like dancers" (*Ten Days' Wonder*, p. 3). With that echo of Genesis 1:2 we return yet again to Wrightsville in *Ten Days' Wonder* (1948). Howard Van Horn, sculptor son of a multimillionaire, comes in desperation to Ellery after a series of amnesiac blackouts that began on the night of his father Diedrich's marriage to the beautiful Sally whom Diedrich had raised from childhood. Psychiatrists have failed to free Howard from his obsessive fear that he has done or will do something horrible during a blackout. Ellery agrees to stay at the Van Horn mansion in Wrightsville and watch over this tormented young man, but before long he finds himself drawn into the hopeless trap in which Howard and Sally are caught. He reluctantly agrees to act as their go-between with an anonymous blackmailer and comes close to being jailed for grand theft. A missing necklace, a midnight chase through a storm-tossed graveyard, and a night-prowling religious fanatic combine with less theatrical elements to sustain the sense of menace among a cast of (excluding Ellery himself) only four central characters. In the final quarter of the novel there is a murder, followed by Ellery's virtuoso reconstruction of the crime, capped by an even more thunderous solution, revealed by Ellery to no one but the murderer, who will remind some of Drury Lane, others of Iago, and a great many of the biblical God. Beneath the mind-boggling plot, which Dannay spent years working out, *Ten Days' Wonder* is an audacious, ambitious attempt to re-create the cosmic drama of Western culture during its past few centuries: the penetration through the facade of infinite knowledge and love to the sadistic beast beneath, the demand of reason and decency for God's death.

At the start of the next and perhaps finest Queen novel, *Cat of Many Tails* (1949), Ellery has renounced his habit of intervening in others' lives: "Just let me be. . . . I've given all that up. I'm not interested any longer."

Racked with guilt over his responsibility for others' deaths and perhaps over his deicide victory in the Van Horn tragedy, he has detached himself. It is a scorching Manhattan summer a few years after the end of World War II, and the reminders of Hiroshima, the Nazi death camps, the Cold War, the division of Vienna, the first Arab-Israeli conflict, the anti-Communist witch-hunts, and the threat of nuclear annihilation generate an atmosphere thick with impending holocaust.

The world and national news headlines are nonetheless dwarfed by local headlines that convey the same message of mortality. A serial killer is loose in the city. Six people are strangled in less than three months, each victim different in every conceivable way from fellow victims: the faceless bachelor from the Gramercy Park district, the aging prostitute living above Times Square, the struggling shoe salesman from Chelsea, the madcap heiress who loved the subways, the bitter paralytic of East 102nd Street, the black girl from Harlem, and the later victims of the Cat seem to share only the cord of Indian tussah silk knotted about each one's neck. The bait of involvement is dangled before Ellery again with all its pain and risk, and once again he snaps at it. He immerses himself in the Cat hunt until, like his father, the police commissioner, the mayor, and everyone else, he is ready to drop in his tracks from the exhaustion and frustration of strategy conferences, press releases, radio addresses, coordination among agencies, liaisons with psychiatrists, confrontations with neighborhood self-defense committees, endless reviewing of files, and plodding up blind alleys. Then, suddenly and beyond human expectation, the obvious yet subtle link connecting all the victims and making sense of the carnage leaps into sight. Once again the apparent solution is topped by another, and once again Ellery is left shattered.

In key scenes at the beginning, middle, and end of this powerful novel, Ellery receives instruction from a father figure: first from Inspector Queen, who spurs him to involve himself again; then in a dream from the titan Prometheus, who in Greek mythology was the father of civilization; finally from the Viennese psychiatrist Dr. Seligmann, the "grandfather of the tribe," who has seen all the terrors in the world and the human heart. "I do not read newspapers since the war begins. I, I do not like to suffer. . . . For me there is today this room, tomorrow cremation, unless the authorities cannot agree to allow it, in which case they may stuff me and place me in the clock tower of the *Rathaus* and I shall keep reminding them of the time."

In *Cat of Many Tails*, Queen shows a fastidious contempt for humanity in the abstract but infuses life into countless individuals, including the Cat's victims who, though never seen alive, are brought to life in the words of others. From the interweaving of victims and survivors and bystanders and investigators, from the vivid pictures of where and how each one lives and what he or she thinks, hopes, and fears, there emerges a portrait of the city as a living character itself. Queen encompasses countless aspects of city life, from the racial turmoil to the struggle against the heat, from the chaos of a full-scale riot to the simple delights of radio programs like *The Shadow* and *Stella Dallas*. It is the most abundant book in the canon, offering permanent testimony to the potential of the mystery novel.

No Queen novel of the 1950s quite equals *Ten Days' Wonder* and *Cat of Many Tails* but many are worth exploring. In *The Origin of Evil* (1951), Ellery returns to Hollywood, no longer the goofy madhouse of the thirties but a grim place whose movie industry is under siege from television. His attempt to finish a novel is frustrated when nineteen-year-old Laurel Hill knocks on his door with the claim that her wealthy foster father was literally frightened to death two weeks earlier upon finding a dead dog on his doorstep. Roger Priam, the dead man's partner in the jewelry business, has also received some strange objects, and Priam's lush exotic wife quickly entangles Ellery in a household that includes an enigmatic secretary, a wandering philatelist, and a young man who lives in a treehouse. As Ellery probes more deeply into the Hill and

Priam households, the bizarre objects—a mess of dead frogs, an empty wallet, a portfolio of worthless stock certificates—keep popping up. Eventually he discerns the pattern, and his solution, followed as usual by a second that is even more breathtaking, ties plot and theme into an organic whole. The leitmotif of the book is Darwinian biology, and the answer to the implied question in its title is humankind. "People mean trouble. . . . There's too much trouble in this world" (p. 50).

As an editor Dannay had long believed that a mystery anthology should be held together by a central concept or theme, and he and Lee extended this tenet to their third collection of Ellery Queen short stories, *Calendar of Crime* (1952). Each of the twelve tales in this volume began life as a script for the Queen radio series, which Manny Lee later rewrote in prose form for publication in *EQMM*. Each adventure centers on an event or holiday associated with a particular month, from New Year's Day through Washington's Birthday and Memorial Day and Halloween to (of course) Thanksgiving and Christmas. The finest of the dozen are "The Inner Circle," in which Ellery investigates the deaths of several members of a survivor-take-all tontine among the 1913 graduating class of Eastern University, and "The Dauphin's Doll," an impossible-crime puzzle in which Ellery tries to protect a forty-nine-carat diamond crown from a master thief who has boasted that he will steal it while it is on display at a department store the day before Christmas.

Those tales, stemming as they do from radio plays of the middle forties, are rather light and amusing in tone. That the Queen novels from the late forties and early fifties are so much darker stems largely from events in the life of Fred Dannay. His first wife had died of cancer in 1945. Two years later he married again and bought a colonial house in Larchmont, a suburb forty minutes by train from Manhattan, and in 1948 Hilda (Wisenthal) Dannay gave birth to their first and only child.

[Stephen] was born prematurely at seven months and weighing less than two pounds.

He was the miracle baby of Doctors Hospital in New York City. We didn't realize for about a year that he—that the boy had had brain damage at birth . . . so severe that the child, who had an absolutely angelic face, never walked and never talked. . . . I was aware long before my wife that one of these days the tragedy would be capped by the death of that child. Actually he lived till he was six years old. (Dannay, interview, p. 8)

It is to the short unhappy life of Stephen Dannay that we owe the pervasive birth-death themes in several Queen novels beginning with *Cat of Many Tails*, which grew out of an anecdote told to Fred by one of the infant's doctors over dinner in the hospital cafeteria. In a sense, it is Stephen who inspired the only novel Dannay wrote without a collaborator.

The Golden Summer (1953), published under his birth name Daniel Nathan, was written as a kind of therapy against his son's impending death, a nostalgic reenactment of his own vanished childhood, and an exorcism of his anguished middle life. The setting is Elmira, New York, in the summer of 1915, and the story line deals with the business adventures of skinny, bespectacled, ten-year-old Danny Nathan, a physical weakling shrewd and nimble-witted enough to talk himself out of any spot and to manipulate his playmates out of their loose change. He displays the ghost of Long John Silver for a two-cent admission fee, raffles off a damaged copy of the latest Sherlock Holmes novel, and even adds a dime to his hoard through a splendiferous one-upmanship contest with his city cousin "Telford." *The Golden Summer* is at root a book-length double entendre: the season of innocent security and peace, the season when Danny tricked his contemporaries out of $4.73. Fred Dannay's brutally honest self-portrait provides the key to countless features of the Ellery Queen world, including the image of Ellery I as the weak-eyed young genius who dominates his environment by the force of his mind, and perhaps the Iagoesque quality of so many of the murderers Ellery, in all his incarnations, exposes.

The Glass Village (1954) is doubly unusual: it is one of only two Queen novels without Ellery and the other familiar series characters, and the only Queen book set in the midst of the cultural terror that marked the years of Joe McCarthy, the House Un-American Activities Committee, and the blacklist. In the withered New England hamlet of Shinn Corners live exactly thirty-six people, most of them embittered puritanical bigots. Judge Lewis Shinn is spending a week at his vacation home in the village where he was born, bonding with his nephew Johnny. A war veteran who had witnessed Hiroshima and was sexually mutilated in Korea, Johnny calls himself "a vegetable" and "the missing link between the flora and the fauna" (pp. 92, 93). What precipitates Johnny's slow journey back to the human race is the bludgeoning to death of ninety-one-year-old artist Fanny Adams in her studio one rainy afternoon. A foreign-looking tramp who had passed through the village shortly before the murder is instantly tagged as the perpetrator, hunted down, beaten, and almost lynched by the outraged citizens of Shinn Corners, who refuse to turn their prey over to the state police and insist on trying him themselves. To avert a gun battle Judge Shinn agrees to preside at that trial, a proceeding aswarm with legal gaffes, designed to placate the townspeople for now and be reversed by an appellate court later. Among the jurors is Johnny Shinn. Ten of the other jurors admit under oath that they are already certain the tramp is guilty. The bailiff, the court reporter, most of the jurors, and even the judge testify for the prosecution. Judge Shinn takes over as prosecutor while the prosecutor testifies against the defendant. Defense counsel fails to object to gross violations of his client's rights but fights loudly over the admissibility of trivia. The judge bangs the darning egg he is using as a gavel and hands down legal rulings he knows are dead wrong. This study in due process on the other side of the rabbit hole is also one of the finest Queen novels of the fifties, replete with bizarre clues, inspired misdirection, and even a sort of dying message, and with dark overtones like Johnny's reflection that "man was a chaos without rhyme or reason; that he blundered about like a maddened animal in the delicate balance of the world, smashing and disrupting, eager only for his own destruction" (p. 258).

In *QBI: Queen's Bureau of Investigation* (1954), the cousins brought together most of the Ellery Queen short-short stories (based on scripts from the Queen radio series) that had been published regularly in *This Week* since 1949 and reprinted just as regularly in *EQMM*. Among the best tales in the collection are "My Queer Dean!" in which an academic's linguistic spoonerisms help Ellery solve the theft of ten thousand dollars from a university administration building, and "Snowball in July," where an entire train apparently vanishes one summer morning on a straight stretch of track between two upstate New York whistle-stops six minutes apart.

Queen's third period came to an end with *The Finishing Stroke* (1958), in which the cousins nostalgically re-created the young manhood of Ellery himself. It is the winter of 1929, shortly after the publication of the author-detective's first novel—which happens to be titled *The Roman Hat Mystery*—and Ellery, along with a number of others, is invited to a twelve-day house party at the estate of his publisher's former partner. The holiday mood begins to dissolve when a costumed Santa distributes gifts and then vanishes. Then a series of bizarre objects pop up—a sandalwood ox, a toy house, a tiny lead camel—each accompanied by a piece of doggerel derived from "The Twelve Days of Christmas." An unidentified body is discovered in the library. More weird gifts turn up; blackmail, a love quadrangle, and a second murder enter the picture; and Ellery can shed no light until chance throws the case in his path again, twenty-eight years later. The characters in *The Finishing Stroke* are little more than line drawings, the prose is simple and unadorned, the plot elements are deadeningly familiar—the snowbound house party, the thirteenth guest, murder with an antique dagger in the lordly mansion's library, a seance, identical twins, mysterious clues dropped by an unseen hand—and the signals are clear throughout this reduction of the mystery genre to its bare fundamentals that, after completing their elegy to "the lovely past," Dannay and Lee would write no more.

And for the next several years they did not. Manny Lee, who had moved his family to a sixty-three-acre farm in Roxbury, Connecticut, became active in civic affairs, served a term as justice of the peace, and beat his playwright neighbor Arthur Miller in an election for a seat on the library board. Fred Dannay sold his huge collection of detective-story volumes to the University of Texas and spent two semesters on campus as a professor of creative writing.

If Dannay wanted to work on more Ellery Queen books, he was stymied by the fact that Lee was suffering a prolonged case of writer's block and literally could not do his share of the collaborations any more. In 1960 the cousins' literary agent came up with a scheme to expand Queen's readership beyond the slowly fading genre of pure detective fiction and into the booming field of original softcover crime novels without detection. Contingent on Dannay's and Lee's approval, the Scott Meredith literary agency arranged for a cycle of nonseries paperback suspensers, to be ghostwritten by other Meredith clients for a flat fee of around two thousand dollars per book, and published as by Ellery Queen, with royalties to be split by Dannay and Lee after the agency took its commission. Lee, who had eight children to support and was still plagued by writer's block, favored the proposal. Dannay was violently against it but felt that his cousin's financial and creative problems left him little choice but to go along. The manuscripts written by the various ghosts were submitted to Lee, who edited and sometimes heavily revised them as Dannay edited and sometimes heavily revised the stories he bought for *EQMM*. (Dannay refused to read any of the books published under this scheme and terminated the arrangement soon after his cousin's death.)

Ellery IV (1963–1971)

Five years after publication of *The Finishing Stroke*, the Meredith agency signed other writers, with no credits in the mystery field but high reputations in science fiction, to assume Lee's function and turn Dannay's complex synopses into new hardcover exploits of Ellery Queen. The Queen novels of this fourth and final period are marked by a zest for experiment within the strict deductive tradition and by a retreat from all semblance of plausibility into what Dannay liked to call "fun and games," that is, a potpourri of stylized plots and characters and dozens of motifs recycled from earlier Queen material.

First and by all odds best of the fourth-period novels was *The Player on the Other Side* (1963), written by Theodore Sturgeon from Dannay's lengthy outline. The setting is York Square, in Manhattan but surely not of it, an isolated pocket of the past at each corner of which stands a castle inhabited by one of four disparate cousins, with a diamond-shaped park in the square's center. The unifying image of course is chess: York Square is the board, each dwelling stands in the position of a rook, or castle, at the start of a game. The cousins are required to live in these castles by the terms of the will left by Nathaniel York, Sr., who has bequeathed to them his millions in equal shares after ten years of residence, with the share of any cousin who dies during the decade to be split among the survivors—our old friend the tontine redux. This time, however, we know the murderer from the outset. The person who is sending a paper polygon stamped with a cryptic initial to each York in turn before killing them one by one is Walt, the weak-brained and zombie-like handyman who serves as caretaker for all four cousins. But Walt is a simple soldier following orders, carrying out the detailed written instructions of someone signing himself as Y, who is using Walt the way Iago uses Othello, as a living murder weapon. In *Cat of Many Tails*, Inspector Queen prods Ellery out of guilt-haunted detachment by dangling the bait of involvement with the real world. In *Player*, he goads his son out of the real world into the chessboard of York Square. As the murders continue, as Ellery several times comes achingly close to the part of the truth we have seen from the beginning, as possibilities multiply and secrets are bared, the pattern of the web slowly becomes clearer until at last Ellery encounters the player on the other side—who is revealed to be not just a human being but symbolically the primal Y, YHWH, God, and whose death, as in *Ten Days' Wonder*, is witnessed by Ellery at the climax.

The next Queen novel, probably the most controversial book in the canon, was written from Dannay's outline by Avram Davidson. *And on the Eighth Day* (1964) is set in the war-ravaged spring of 1944. Ellery gets lost driving across the western desert, chances upon a religious-socialist community in the wilderness, and soon discovers that his coming had been foretold by the community's sacred book. All property in the valley of Quenan is held in common, no act of violence has been committed for generations, the word "war" is not in the lexicon, no one is alienated from the work he or she performs, the earth and humankind are in natural harmony—clearly we are in Eden before the Fall. Ellery's coming marks the beginning of a time of troubles foretold in the sacred book, and on the third night of his visit there is murder. The plot does not and, under the circumstances, cannot be expected to generate much intellectual excitement, but Queen structures his religious and historical analogies so as to create a sense of "the recurrence of the great and the famous across the shifting planes of space-time" and to generate an intuition of the presence of something that the human mind can never fathom. "It is too much. . . . it's more than reason can bear. Too much, an infinite complexity beyond the grasp of man. Acknowledge. Acknowledge and depart" (p. 190).

After Dannay wrote a few more books with Avram Davidson performing the Manny Lee

function, Lee overcame his writer's block and collaborated with Dannay on such late Ellery Queen novels as the excellent *Face to Face* (1967) and the well-meaning but awkward *The Last Woman in His Life* (1970). Most of Ellery's as yet uncollected short cases were assembled in *QED: Queen's Experiments in Detection* (1968). The book's last and finest tale is "Abraham Lincoln's Clue," which brings together bibliomania, philately, history, and the art of the riddle as Ellery tries to locate a lost first printing of Poe's "The Purloined Letter" autographed by both the author and the sixteenth U.S. president.

The Last Years

In the late 1960s Manny Lee suffered several heart attacks and, on doctor's orders, lost a great deal of weight. It did not save him. On 2 April 1971, Lee had another attack and died on the way to the Waterbury hospital. He never saw a copy of the last Ellery Queen novel. In *A Fine and Private Place* (1971), Ellery investigates a series of bizarre crimes in the household of the squat and bestial tycoon Nino Importuna, who was born on 9 September 1899, lives in a nine-story building at 99 East 99th Street, and in countless ways is obsessed with the number 9. The orgy of variations on this theme—including links between the conception and development of the murderer's byzantine scheme and the conception and development of a human fetus—is almost enough to make one overlook the unlikeliness of the plot.

At first Dannay planned to continue the series, either alone or with a new partner, but in 1972 his second wife died of cancer (as had his first twenty-seven years before), and with her death he began dying by inches. The only thing that kept him functioning was the inexorable work schedule that *EQMM* and the anthologies he continued to edit demanded of him. He abandoned all thought of writing more Ellery Queen novels, saying it would be disloyal to Manny's memory. Photographs of him taken in 1973 show the empty, devastated face of a man waiting for the dark to claim him.

In November 1975 he married for the third time, and it is not too much to say that Rose Koppel Dannay saved Fred's life. He had always been such a private person that, after almost thirty years, many of his closest Larchmont neighbors had no idea what he did for a living. Rose made it possible for him to enjoy the role of the genre's elder statesman, a role that time and the deaths of peers like Carr, Agatha Christie, and Rex Stout had bestowed on him.

In his eighth decade Dannay received more media exposure than in all his life previously. First came the sixty-minute television series (NBC, 1975–1976) starring Jim Hutton as Ellery and David Wayne as Inspector Queen. This was followed by guest lectures at the University of California, two appearances on the Dick Cavett show, superstar treatment at the 1978 International Crime Writers Congress, interviews with *Playboy* and *People* and countless other periodicals, a testimonial dinner celebrating the fiftieth anniversary of *The Roman Hat Mystery*, and an invitation to Tokyo for the premiere of a Japanese movie based on *Calamity Town*—it was a miracle he got any work done at all. But after he turned seventy-five, failing health forced him to curtail his activities. He was hospitalized three times, and on 3 September 1982 his heart stopped.

His death meant more than the end of a great tradition in detective fiction. Both separately and together, Frederic Dannay and Manfred B. Lee contributed so abundantly to so many different aspects of the genre—novels, novelettes, short stories, radio dramas, anthologies, magazines, bibliographic and scholarly studies—that Anthony Boucher, the founding father of intelligent and informed commentary on the field, needed just one short sentence to sum up their accomplishments: "Ellery Queen *is* the American detective story" (*Ellery Queen*, p. 11).

Selected Bibliography

WORKS OF ELLERY QUEEN

NOVELS PUBLISHED AS BY ELLERY QUEEN

The Roman Hat Mystery. New York: Stokes, 1929. Golden Anniversary Edition, New York: Mysterious Press, 1979.

The French Powder Mystery. New York: Stokes, 1930.

The Dutch Shoe Mystery. New York: Stokes, 1931.

The Greek Coffin Mystery. New York: Stokes, 1932.

The Egyptian Cross Mystery. New York: Stokes, 1932.

The American Gun Mystery. New York: Stokes, 1933.

The Siamese Twin Mystery. New York: Stokes, 1933.

The Chinese Orange Mystery. New York: Stokes, 1934.

The Spanish Cape Mystery. New York: Stokes, 1935.

Halfway House. New York: Stokes, 1936.

The Door Between. New York: Stokes, 1937.

The Devil to Pay. New York: Stokes, 1938.

The Four of Hearts. New York: Stokes, 1938.

The Dragon's Teeth. New York: Stokes, 1939.

Calamity Town. Boston: Little, Brown, 1942.

There Was an Old Woman. Boston: Little, Brown, 1943.

The Murderer Is a Fox. Boston: Little, Brown, 1945.

Ten Days' Wonder. Boston: Little, Brown, 1948.

Cat of Many Tails. Boston: Little, Brown, 1949.

Double, Double. Boston: Little, Brown, 1950.

The Origin of Evil. Boston: Little, Brown, 1951.

The King Is Dead. Boston: Little, Brown, 1952.

The Scarlet Letters. Boston: Little, Brown, 1953.

The Glass Village. Boston: Little, Brown, 1954.

Inspector Queen's Own Case. New York: Simon & Schuster, 1956.

The Finishing Stroke. New York: Simon & Schuster, 1958.

The Player on the Other Side. New York: Random House, 1963.

And on the Eighth Day. New York: Random House, 1964.

The Fourth Side of the Triangle. New York: Random House, 1965.

A Study in Terror. New York: Lancer, 1966.

Face to Face. New York: New American Library, 1967.

The House of Brass. New York: New American Library, 1968.

Cop Out. Cleveland: World, 1969.

The Last Woman in His Life. New York and Cleveland: World, 1970.

A Fine and Private Place. New York and Cleveland: World, 1971.

SHORT-STORY COLLECTIONS AS BY ELLERY QUEEN

The Adventures of Ellery Queen. New York: Stokes, 1934.

The New Adventures of Ellery Queen. New York: Stokes, 1940. Includes "The Lamp of God."

101 Years' Entertainment: The Great Detective Stories, 1841–1941. Edited by Ellery Queen. Boston: Little, Brown, 1941.

The Case Book of Ellery Queen. New York: Spivak, 1945.

Calendar of Crime. Boston: Little, Brown, 1952.

QBI: Queen's Bureau of Investigation. Boston: Little, Brown, 1954.

Queens Full. New York: Random House, 1965.

QED: Queen's Experiments in Detection. New York: New American Library, 1968.

The Best of Ellery Queen. New York: Beaufort Books, 1985.

NOVELS AS BY BARNABY ROSS

The Tragedy of X. New York: Viking, 1932.

The Tragedy of Y. New York: Viking, 1932.

The Tragedy of Z. New York: Viking, 1933.

Drury Lane's Last Case. New York: Viking, 1933.

AUTOBIOGRAPHICAL NOVEL
BY FREDERIC DANNAY

The Golden Summer. By Daniel Nathan. Boston: Little, Brown, 1953.

BIOGRAPHICAL AND CRITICAL STUDIES

Bainbridge, John. "Ellery Queen: Crime Made Him Famous and His Authors Rich." *Life*, 22 November 1943: 70–76.

Behren, David. *Transcript*, Norman (Oklahoma), 10 May 1979.

Boucher, Anthony. *Ellery Queen: A Double Profile*. Boston: Little, Brown, 1951.

————. "There Was No Mystery in What the Crime Editor Was After." *New York Times Book Review*, 26 February 1961: 4, 5, 50.

"A Case of Double Identity." *MD*, December 1967: 202–208.

Dannay, Frederic. Transcript of interview by author. Carroll College, Waukesha, Wis., 17 April 1979.

Fistell, Ira J. "Ellery Queen: The First Fifty Years." *West Coast Review of Books*, 12 November 1979: 82–86.

"Interview with Frederic Dannay." *Playboy*, June 1979.

Lee, Rand. "Dad and Cousin Fred Entered a Writing Contest." *TV Guide*, 11 October 1975.

Nevins, Francis M. *Royal Bloodline: Ellery Queen, Author and Detective*. Bowling Green, Ohio: Bowling Green State University Popular Press, 1974.

Nevins, Francis M., and Ray Stanich. *The Sound of Detection: Ellery Queen's Adventures in Radio*. Madison, Ind.: Brownstone Books, 1983.

Prescott, Peter S. "The Only Legal Way to Make Money from Murder." *Look*, 21 April 1970.

Shenker, Israel. *New York Times*, 22 February 1969.

Steinbrunner, Chris. "Challenges to the Listener." *Armchair Detective*, summer 1979.

MANUSCRIPTS

A vast amount of Dannay's papers are now held by the Rare Book and Manuscript Division of the Columbia University Library in New York. There is a collection of Dannay's and Lee's manuscripts at the Harry Ransom Humanities Research Center, University of Texas at Austin.

RUTH RENDELL

(b. 1930)

B. J. RAHN

RUTH BARBARA RENDELL, the daughter of Arthur and Ebba Elise (Kruse) Grasemann, was born in London on 17 February 1930. Her father, whose family came to England from Germany in the 1790s, was born in Plymouth. Her mother, who was born in Stockholm and grew up in Denmark, emigrated to England with her family when she was fourteen. Both parents were schoolteachers in east London; her father taught science and math in a grammar school, and her mother gave instruction to children between eight and eleven years of age in the senior part of a primary school. They were private people without much social life beyond the family circle. Ruth had a rather solitary childhood and was lonely but not unloved. Rendell's parents were avid readers, and each had a creative bent. They both painted, and Mrs. Grasemann also wrote poetry. Rendell is grateful to them for opening the door to the life of the imagination. As a child she began telling herself stories and later wrote some to entertain her cousins. She even completed a verse drama about the Celtic queen Boadicea by age fifteen.

Rendell attended an elementary school called Churchfields in the suburb of South Woodford, where she was born, until her parents moved to Loughton in Essex, where she entered the preparatory department of Loughton High School (for girls) at age seven and remained until she was eighteen. Upon leaving school, she chose not to attend university; later, while in her thirties, she studied English for a degree but did not complete it. Opting for a career in journalism instead, Rendell wrote for a local Essex paper, the Chigwell *Times*, for four or five years, rising to become chief editorial writer. From 1948 to 1952 she worked as a reporter and subeditor for the *Express and Independent* newspapers in West Essex. She admits that she was a bad reporter because facts were not enough for her. She was always trying to turn them into fiction, as when she enraged the owners of a house by stating it was haunted. She was better as an editor because it gave her more scope (Paterson, p. 40). At age twenty she married Donald Rendell, a fellow journalist. (They divorced in the early 1970s but remarried in 1975.) Rendell continued working until her son, Simon, was born in 1953. A devoted mother, Rendell gave up her job to raise her child. During his early childhood, she spent her spare time reading "all those things I would have read if I had gone to a university and taught myself French and classical Greek" (Rahn, 5 September 1997).

During this period she also served a self-imposed apprenticeship learning the craft of writing fiction. She wrote dozens of short stories, which she sent to women's magazines, but they were never published. At her husband's suggestion, she also experimented with longer fiction and tried her hand at a historical novel, a Jewish family saga, a comedy of manners à la Evelyn Waugh and Nancy Mitford, and a detective whodunit—just to see if she could do it. On the advice of the book editor at her husband's newspaper, she sent the drawing-room comedy to Harold Harris, the managing editor of Hutchinson at the time. Eventually, she was invited for an interview in the firm's London office and was told that they liked it and might publish it if she would rewrite it. When she refused, they asked whether she had done anything else. So she submitted the whodunit she had written "just for fun." Looking back, she was embarrassed at the unprofessional presentation of the manuscript: "I sent the draft to them exactly the way I had it with bits of cellotape stuck on here and there and notes scribbled in between the lines of the foolscap pages" (Rahn, 28 August 1980). Gerald Austen, who became her editor, suggested some revisions that she followed, spending the Christmas of 1963 rewriting, and in February of 1964 it was accepted for publication.

Thus, Rendell's career as a detective novelist began in November 1964 with the publication of *From Doon with Death*, featuring her team of police sleuths, middle-aged Detective Inspector Reginald Wexford and his younger assistant, Inspector Michael Burden. Although the framework of the police team is present, these books are not really police procedurals in which crimes are solved by police teamwork and routine; rather, they are whodunits in which the detectives happen to be policemen who perpetuate the conventional partnership so common in classic detective novels. During the ensuing years Rendell has written more than sixteen additional Wexford books, which have won her a firm footing in the field.

Almost simultaneously with the launching of her detective series, Rendell also began writing other novels in which crimes occurred, but which were not, strictly speaking, detective fiction. These books, typified by *To Fear a Painted Devil* (1965), *One Across, Two Down* (1971), and *The Face of Trespass* (1974), represent the second type of story for which Ruth Rendell has become famous, the tale of psychological suspense. They are centered in the consciousness of the main character— whether villain or victim—whose feelings of alienation, anxiety, fear, hatred, and anguish are experienced firsthand by the reader. Publication of these psychological thrillers has kept pace with the Wexford series; since the first, she has produced eighteen of them as well as two novellas and several collections of short stories.

In 1986 Rendell began writing a third type of mystery novel under the name of Barbara Vine. This pseudonym is composed of her middle name and her grandmother's maiden name. Rendell's interest in and knowledge of human psychology are evident here as well, but these works plumb the depths of the human psyche more in the manner of Henry James than Patricia Highsmith or Alfred Hitchcock. In these character studies Rendell simulates the gradual process of mental and emotional awareness growing over time, which results eventually in insight and sometimes in action. The novels are distinguished by subtle manipulation of the narrative viewpoint and complex patterning, which often produce startling ironic surprises.

Since 1964, Rendell's work has steadily gained recognition around the world. Her prizes and awards testify to her success. In the United States she has won three Edgar Allan Poe awards from the Mystery Writers of America (MWA), two for short stories—"The Fallen Curtain" (1974) and "The New Girlfriend" (1983)—and a third for *A Dark-Adapted Eye* (1986), written under the pen name Barbara Vine. In May of 1997 she was given the Mystery Writers of America's highest honor when she became a Grand Master.

In England she won a Crime Writers Association (CWA) Silver Dagger award for her novel *The Tree of Hands* (1984). She has also been presented with four Gold Dagger awards for the best novel of the year by the CWA: one for *A Demon in My View* (1976), another for *Live Flesh* (1986), a third for *A Fatal Inversion*

(1987, written as Barbara Vine), and a fourth for *King Solomon's Carpet* (1991, written as Barbara Vine). The last was also short-listed for the Whitbread Prize for best novel. Furthermore, in 1991 she earned the CWA's coveted Diamond Dagger, for lifetime achievement, which is the equivalent of the MWA's Grand Master award. Previously, she was awarded the Arts Council National Book award for the best work of genre fiction for *The Lake of Darkness* (1980) as well as some local awards in East Anglia—the Angel award for *The Killing Doll* (1984) and for *The House of Stairs* (1988, written as Barbara Vine). She received the *Sunday Times* award for Literary Excellence in 1990. Two titles by Barbara Vine were short-listed for the *Sunday Express* Book of the Year award: *Gallowglass* (1990) and *Asta's Book* (1993; U.S. title, *Anna's Book*).

Ruth Rendell is a Fellow of the Royal Society of Literature and holds honorary doctorates from the universities of Essex and East Anglia and from Bowling Green State University at Bowling Green in Ohio. In 1996 she was made a Commander of the Most Excellent Order of the British Empire in the Queen's Birthday Honors List, and in 1997 she became a working peer in the House of Lords when the Labour Party's Tony Blair took office as prime minister. Her title is Baroness Rendell of Babergh, named after a district in Suffolk where she lived for many years. Her coat of arms features two polar bears supporting a red lozenge decorated with white chevrons and a yellow Brimstone butterfly. The animals indicate her interest in wildlife and the environment.

As the last honor indicates, in addition to developing her writing career, Rendell has been active in politics for a number of years—first as a member of the Campaign for Nuclear Disarmament (CND; Paterson, p. 40), participating in demonstrations at Greenham Common in Berkshire and in Molesworth in Huntingdonshire. These concerns are reflected in her short story "Trebuchet" (*The Listener*, 18 July 1985). Long a Labour Party voter, when the nuclear threat was removed in 1991 at the signing of the Strategic Arms Reduction Treaty (START) between the Soviet Union and the United States, she became more active in Labour Party politics. She was an early member in the Thousand Club, whose members contribute one thousand pounds each year to the Labour Party, and she has been influential in recruiting many new members for the club. Rendell regularly attends the Labour Party Conference and campaigned vigorously for the Labour Party in the 1997 election (Rahn, 5 September 1997). She enjoys serving as a working peer and takes particular interest in such issues as literacy, libraries, battered women, and abused children: "I think the future of literacy in our children is very important, and I shall be a strong advocate for libraries. . . . I will also be campaigning for the rights of abused women" (Henderson, p. 2). Her maiden speech to the House of Lords, delivered on 16 December 1997, addressed problems of literacy.

An avid traveler, Rendell has visited most parts of the world with the exception of Russia, central Africa, and South America. She is keenly interested in America and has toured most of the fifty states. She has even done some travel writing, notably an essay on Alaska, "A Voyage Among Misty Isles," in the *New York Times Magazine*. Alaska is also the setting for one of her Barbara Vine novels, *No Night Is Too Long* (1994). In the essay she refers to herself as an amateur botanist and introduces the reader to the flora characteristic of the region as she hunts for the indigenous chocolate lily. The keen appreciation of landscape and evocative descriptions of the countryside—particularly of trees, shrubs, and uncultivated plant life in its natural habitat—displayed in this travel piece actually distinguish much of her work. She uses the natural environment, particularly woods and weather, to create mood and reveal character in many of her novels. Both *Kissing the Gunner's Daughter* (1992) and *Road Rage* (1997) embody fine examples of this technique.

When she is not roaming abroad, Rendell walks a great deal. Walking has always been part of her daily routine. After spending the morning writing, she takes a long walk and thinks about what she is going to write next. As she walks, she observes. The sense of place is always well defined in her fiction, as books such as *The Keys to the Street* (1996) reveal. More sedentary pursuits include listening to music, particularly the operas of Mozart and Handel. But her greatest pastime is reading. She reads at least five books a week: "I've read an enormous amount all my life. Reading is as much a part of it as eating and sleeping. I can't imagine what people who don't read do with their lives" (Paterson, p. 40).

Wexford Detective Series

As noted, Rendell's detective novels focus on Chief Inspector Reginald Wexford and his assistant, Inspector Michael Burden, who have earned an affectionate place in the hearts of whodunit readers everywhere. Linked uncomfortably at times in a traditional Holmes/ Watson partnership, these divergent personalities complement each other in a vital fashion that produces effective results. Wexford, a man in late middle age, epitomizes the type of detective most beloved by readers—the universal father figure—who is mature, responsible, dedicated, courageous, and totally incorruptible. He is also patient, tolerant, and compassionate as well as keenly perceptive, imaginative, and wise. Both his method of detection and his personality are reminiscent of George Simenon's Inspector Maigret and J. J. Marric's Commander Gideon—men of similar years doing similar jobs.

In nearly every case, despite Burden's diligent efforts in applying police procedures, the solution arises when Wexford follows up on some intuitive insight—often an inexplicable small factual detail that haunts him, or some peculiarity of a person's expression, glance, or intonation. Thus, success depends finally as much on unique personal gifts as on police methods. His intuitive perceptions foster unorthodox lines of approach and put him in conflict with his immediate superior, Chief Constable Griswold. Placed between the criminal classes and the bureaucratic hierarchy, Wexford represents the plight of imaginative modern man grappling with social machinery designed to dispense rough justice but not capable of the fine-tuning necessary for dealing with individual differences. As Wexford copes with opposition from above and below and walks the fine line between obeying regulations and exercising initiative, suspense builds in *Shake Hands Forever* (1975) and *Put On by Cunning* (1981; U.S. title, *Death Notes*).

Wexford's character is also developed through interaction with members of his family, who add color and texture to the fabric of the narrative and participate in important subplots. For example, in *A Sleeping Life* (1978), Wexford's daughter Sylvia realizes and rejects her second-class status as a woman in a man's world, while he investigates the perplexing murder of a woman who had been posing as a man in order to achieve success as a writer. The domestic crisis forms a kind of counterpoint to the main theme of the investigation, and ultimately Wexford attributes his successful deduction to his daughters, "One saying a woman would have to be an eonist to get a man's rights, and the other dressing as a man on the stage" (1980 ed., p. 171).

An obvious but necessary foil for Wexford, Mike Burden is a far cry from the pompous, fatuous, gullible, admiring Watson so common in classical detective fiction. Righteous, hardworking, and fastidious as well as obstinate, uncultured, and unimaginative, he is also logical, caring, and kind. In his capacity as alter-ego-cum-sounding-board, Burden revels in the roles of gadfly and devil's advocate. He and Wexford engage in a kind of acrimonious but rewarding dialogue that strengthens their friendship and contributes to their success. He also does much of the legwork and supervises routine aspects of the investigation.

Burden's personal life forms an additional center of interest and source for secondary action in *No More Dying Then* (1971), *Some Lie and Some Die* (1973), and, more recently, *The Veiled One* (1988). In the first, Mike Burden steps outside his official role to comfort an anguished woman whose small son has been abducted, and he finds a much needed outlet for his own emotional and physical needs, unfulfilled since the recent death of his wife. Although he is puritanical, Burden is a deeply passionate man who takes life's blows hard but grapples manfully with his problems. He is intensely sympathetic in his humanity. He subsequently remarries and develops considerably under his second wife's influence.

Although conforming to a conventional detective fiction formula, Rendell rises above it in the Wexford mysteries. Unlike many Golden Age writers who insisted that sex and crime do not mix in the detective novel, Rendell believes that sexual tension is the basis of a great many crimes and demonstrates it in her novels. However, sexual behavior is never gratuitous, and she never allows sexual matters to distract the reader from the principal focus on crime. Several plots are based on crimes of passion and reveal the atavistic urges governing human behavior in conflict with the constraints of civilization. Among other subjects, they deal with lesbianism and homosexuality (*From Doon with Death*), illegitimacy (*A New Lease of Death*, 1967; U.S. title, *Sins of the Fathers*, 1970), incest (*A Guilty Thing Surprised*, 1970), procreative instinct (*Murder Being Once Done*, 1972), transvestism and homophobia (*A Sleeping Life*), and adultery (*An Unkindness of Ravens*, 1985). Most of these books deal with problems that result when individuals either transgress deeply rooted sexual taboos or resort to violence in order to fulfill equally deeply rooted sexual yearnings. The most recent Wexford books have dealt with such social issues as racial prejudice (*Simisola*, 1994) and protection of the environment (*Road Rage*).

In *A Guilty Thing Surprised*, a brother and sister separated from each other during World War II meet as strangers and fall passionately in love. Each marries but the unions are loveless, for they are attracted only to each other.

Violence erupts when the jealous spouse of one of them discovers their secret. Other unorthodox sexual liaisons offer a kind of counterpoint to incest as Wexford and Burden investigate relationships to establish motive. Wexford discovers his own human limitations as he feels intense sexual desire for a young woman more than half his age, followed by the intense anger produced by the frustration of thwarted passion: "For the first time in his career he understood what impelled those men he questioned and brought to court, the men who forgot for a while chivalry and social taboo and sexual restraint, the rapists, the violaters" (p. 80). Wexford's ability to analyze his own behavior and relate it to that of his fellow men, to find the parallels in the human condition, is akin to the imaginative insight or intuition that enables him to solve the crime.

Murder Being Once Done—perhaps the best of the Wexford series—is about the intensity of the human need to nurture and the destructive powers unleashed when the procreative instinct is frustrated. It is secondarily concerned with the pain experienced during the waning of human potency and presents a mature study of male menopause, as Inspector Wexford, forced by a severe heart attack into unwelcome ease, regards the progress of a murder investigation from the sidelines.

Unable to accept his diminished physical strength and adjust to being replaced by younger, healthier men, Wexford struggles to prove his professional prowess because work has been his most vital activity. Professional rivalry reflects the Darwinian principle of natural selection, the survival of the fittest through intense competition for dominance among males of the species. During this compelling investigation of the murder of a young woman whose body was hidden in a mausoleum, the cemetery with its decaying vegetation and moldering tombs functions symbolically to remind the characters and the reader of mortality. This ever-present symbol of death forms a counterpoint to the ubiquity and intensity of the human procreative instinct.

Psychological Thrillers

Ruth Rendell's psychological mysteries offer riveting accounts of socially alienated people from various walks of life and provide clinically accurate studies of neurotic and psychotic personalities. The central character may be a villain, a victim, or both. In this group appear some of Rendell's most fully developed psychotic profiles: Arthur Johnson in *A Demon in My View*, Eunice Parchman in *A Judgement in Stone* (1977), Doreen (Dolly) Yearman in *The Killing Doll*, and Victor Jenner in *Live Flesh*. Wrought in vivid prose, these characters portray obsessive and compulsive behavior, anxiety neurosis, paranoid delusion, and persecution mania as well as psychopathic cutoff in terms that are comprehensible and to some extent sympathetic to the ordinary reader. Rendell's imaginative insights, emotional empathy, and interpretive talents combine to build a bond of understanding and compassion, however fleeting, for these less fortunate members of the human race.

In *A Demon in My View*, chance places two men with the same surname and the same first initial in a lodging house in north London. Arthur Johnson lives in a self-contained flat occupying the entire second floor, while Anthony Johnson rents a room and shares a bath on the ground floor. Apart from the similarity of their names, they have nothing in common. Although neither recognizes it at first, their lives will impinge upon each other with fatal consequences for one of them.

An illegitimate child brought up by his Auntie Gracie in very restrictive circumstances, Arthur is a psychopath who maintains rigid self-control but needs to break out of it periodically. Arthur, at fifty, answers correspondence and keeps the books for a local building contractor whose firm he entered upon leaving school at age fourteen. He regards himself as a normal man with "a small peculiarity" that he controls by not going out at night and by not drinking alcohol. He realizes that his "propensity" places his life and liberty at constant risk, but he projects the blame for his violent impulses onto "society." He feels "resentment against a society which had given him the need to commit such acts yet would condemn him with loathing for yielding to them" (1977 ed., p. 124).

His condition seems to have been produced by an extremely rigorous and repressive upbringing that has left him with feelings of acute anxiety, fear, guilt, and inadequacy. Arthur constantly strives to live up to the standards set by his deceased Auntie Gracie while knowing that he can never meet her expectations. "He had never reached those heights of perfection she had laid before him as fitting one who needed to cleanse himself of the taint of his birth and background" (p. 24). She bought him for one hundred pounds from her sister when he was two months old. He is compulsively neat and tidy and attempts to expiate his guilt by enslaving himself to a rigid regimen of household cleaning and domestic routine. He imposes the same need for order and control on his work at the office.

Arthur has no sex drive and no emotional relationships. He exists in a state of personal cutoff; he is incapable of affection or love. He relieves inner tensions with outbreaks of violence that give pleasure and make him feel empowered. As a child he experienced a feeling of tremendous power and pleasure from killing a mouse and later from jabbing a baby with a sharp pin. Arthur harbors intense feelings of hostility and aggression toward women, which he has released twice in the past by strangling women whom he met at random in the streets. Realizing that such behavior could result in imprisonment, he imposes self-discipline to protect himself, and he has also devised a therapy for himself. Arthur periodically relieves his intense inner pressure by pretending a dressmaker's dummy in the cellar is real while strangling her. She is his guardian angel, his safety valve. Thus, he releases his feelings of resentment and frustration through make-believe murder until the dummy disappears. Then Arthur must find a live victim on whom to vent his rage.

Anthony Johnson, "the other Johnson," enters Arthur's life when he moves to London to get his Ph.D. from London University. Anthony's secondary motive in moving to London is to force the married woman he has been having an affair with to choose between her husband and himself. Anthony believes that the separation will convince Helen that she loves him and should leave her husband. Arthur is annoyed at the coincidence of someone else with his name living in the same building, but is much more upset when he discovers that Anthony's window overlooks the entrance to the cellar where the porcelain-white lady awaits his renewed bouts of violence. Like the captain in Joseph Conrad's "The Secret Sharer" (1910) Arthur watches Anthony's every move and listens to every stray sound hoping to discover when Anthony will be absent in the evening so he can make a clandestine visit to the cellar. He is devastated when he realizes that Anthony spends most of his time at home studying.

A student at Radclyffe College in his mid-thirties, Anthony is writing his thesis on "Some Aspects of the Psychopathic Personality." Anthony's research notes offer an analytic commentary on Arthur's real thoughts and behavior. Anthony is interested in working with children, and when he can't get part-time work in a children's play center, he organizes a Guy Fawkes Day celebration for the neighborhood children on a strip of waste ground. When the landlord gives Anthony permission to collect rubbish for the bonfire from the cellar, he gathers up Arthur's mannequin for the effigy of Guy Fawkes. Arthur, in revenge for the disappearance of his scapegoat, confiscates Anthony's letters from Helen. This ploy backfires when Anthony writes to her and puts "A. Johnson" as the return address on the envelope.

Deprived of his passive partner in crime, Arthur strangles a live woman in an alley near his home to satisfy his internal demons. Knowledge that his guardian angel has disappeared increases Arthur's normal stress and leads him into the streets again looking for another victim. Mistaking a long-haired young man for a woman, Arthur attacks from

behind and receives a severe beating from his intended victim. Facial injuries mark him as the attacker, so he dare not leave home, especially after the police alert the public over the television news. When Anthony sees Arthur's face in the light while he is speaking on the hall telephone, he realizes the truth and debates whether or not to report Arthur to the police. Anthony's repugnance at being responsible for incarcerating a fellow human being for life is overcome by his reluctance to be indirectly responsible for other deaths if Arthur is not stopped. Ironically, before the police can apprehend him, Arthur is shot dead by Helen's jealous husband, Roger, who assumes Arthur is the writer of his wife's love letter when Arthur admits to the name "A. Johnson."

A Judgement in Stone portrays the social isolation and consequent paranoid delusion of an illiterate woman, Eunice Parchman, who was shifted about so often as a child during World War II that she never learned to read. When she was young she didn't want to learn, and when she grew older and wanted to read, she realized that finding a teacher would entail admitting her deficiency. In order to keep her secret, she began to withdraw from people. The habit of isolating herself became natural, and she forgot that it originated in a desire to avoid revealing her disability. "Illiteracy had dried up her sympathy and atrophied her imagination. That, along with . . . the ability to care about the feelings of others, had no place in her makeup" (p. 43).

Rendell asserts that literacy is one of the cornerstones of civilization and demonstrates in this novel the uncouth rage that has always motivated the violence of vandalism since the barbarian hordes sacked Rome. The devastation wrought is intensified by the role played by chance. Rendell's imaginative evocation of the limitations imposed by illiteracy are simultaneously illuminating and horrifying. "Literacy is in our veins like blood. . . . It is next to impossible to hold a real conversation . . . in which reference to the printed word is not made or in which the implications of something read do not occur" (p. 57). Eunice's inability to function in a literate society engenders loneliness, fear, resentment, and, finally, violent revenge. She is convinced that her employers "read to provoke her, for no-one, not even schoolteachers, could read that much for pleasure" (p. 50). And when they learn of her illiteracy, she has an acute paranoid reaction believing that they are telling everyone throughout the village about her. Her rage does not cool until they are all dead.

A strong vein of Marlovian irony shapes events in *The Killing Doll,* when, like Faustus, Peter (Pup) Yearman sells his soul to the Devil at age fifteen and seals the pledge with his blood, but he does not really believe the Devil has accepted the bargain. Shortly thereafter, he begins studying magic. He soon becomes infatuated with his new hobby, which he demonstrates to his sister, Dolly, a recluse whose sensitivity about a disfiguring facial birthmark prevents her from making friends and leading a normal life. When in jest Peter pretends to cast a spell on a doll that is a lookalike for their "wicked stepmother," and when the stepmother dies immediately afterward, Dolly is absolutely convinced Peter possesses magic powers. Peter continually denies it, and as time goes by and he achieves his personal and professional goals, he attributes his success to hard work or chance rather than to a supernatural silent partner.

At the end of the book, Peter congratulates himself on having achieved his ambitions—a thriving business, a successful career, a beautiful wife-to-be, and an expensive house—without having paid a horrendous price. He does not realize the price has been paid by his sister, who has become so isolated and alienated through his neglect that she has become a paranoid schizophrenic. She is plagued by the spirits of her dead mother and stepmother who chatter to her ceaselessly, and she has hallucinations of being haunted by Anubis, the jackal-headed god of the underworld, who follows her everywhere. As a kind of ironic auxiliary, Rendell includes a study of a second character, Diarmit Bawne, whose fear and alienation deepen because of the neglect of his rather large family. The novel ends as these two paranoid characters are about to meet their fate.

Another study of a psychopathic personality, Victor Jenner in *Live Flesh,* goes beyond the violent paranoid reactions of Eunice Parchman, Dolly Yearman, and Diarmit Bawne to create a character whose pathology involves resorting to violent sexual acts as a means of relieving hostility and asserting his identity. Victor's portrait is more complete and complex even than that of Arthur Johnson. Rendell admits,

One of the things I try to do . . . is present a person who is odious, has obvious emotional imbalance, but yet is pitiable. I don't want to portray characters who are wholly hateful. . . . [With Victor] I was consciously trying to push understanding as far as possible, to create someone who is as far as can be from our sympathy but who can yet command it. (Paterson, pp. 38, 40)

In addition to the splendid rendering of character, a finely honed sense of irony—akin to that fateful force encountered in Greek drama—pervades these novels. Often the plot structure pivots on some untoward event or unexpected coincidence by which characters are caught in snares of their own setting, as in *One Across, Two Down* and *The Lake of Darkness.* The role of chance in arranging the fates of these characters often produces a fine dramatic climax.

Victim-centered suspense novels, which trace their roots to the eighteenth century, have also been popular in the twentieth century and have attracted a large readership, especially since interest in and knowledge of the principles and practices of normal and abnormal psychology have become widespread. Some of these modern suspense novels have featured brilliant psychological character studies of victim mentality. Among them one could include Rendell's *The Face of Trespass, The Bridesmaid* (1989), and perhaps even *The Keys to the Street.*

In *The Face of Trespass,* everyman's nightmare of rejection and failure seems to come true as a young writer, deserted by his lover and his talent, faces the simultaneous disintegration of his romance and his career. His depression increases when, having refused to murder his mistress's husband, Graham (Gray) Lanceton suddenly finds himself accused of causing the man's untimely death because his rival's body is discovered at the foot of the cellar stairs at Gray's cottage. Gray's incrimination is made possible only because of his obsessive devotion to his lover, whose promises he believes and whose requests he obeys without question.

Like Gray, Philip Wardman in *The Bridesmaid* is another of many characters in Rendell's novels who is "lovesick." He becomes obsessed with his lover, Senta Pelham, with his own sexual needs and his fears of losing her, and with the extraordinary demands she makes upon him to prove his love. Philip is mesmerized by the surrealistic quality of their life together, and he begins to lose his ability to distinguish between what is real and what is illusory in the world that they share. This book is a splendid exploration of how an ordinary person can be influenced by another individual and his own passions to commit acts that go against the grain of his personality.

Barbara Vine

The Barbara Vine novels are distinguished by more complex plotting and characterization than either of the Rendell series. The plots of many of these books involve the retrieval of a secret from the past and its unraveling in the present, as in *A Dark-Adapted Eye, A Fatal Inversion, The House of Stairs, Anna's Book, The Brimstone Wedding* (1995), and *The Chimney Sweeper's Boy* (1998). In the others—*Gallowglass, King Solomon's Carpet,* and *No Night Is Too Long*—current action is determined by events in the recent past. So the influence of the past upon the present can be regarded as a theme in all of them. Usually Rendell chooses a personal narrative view-

point for the unraveling of intimate secrets. *A Dark-Adapted Eye* and *The House of Stairs* employ first-person narrators, and in *Anna's Book* and *The Brimstone Wedding*, two separate first-person accounts are alternated. Rendell conducts an interesting experiment with narrative viewpoint in *No Night Is Too Long*, which presents three first-person accounts of the same story in the style of Akira Kurosawa's *Rashomon* or Lawrence Durrell's famous *Alexandria Quartet*. The narrator's voice is alternately first person and third-person omniscient in *Gallowglass*. In *A Fatal Inversion, King Solomon's Carpet,* and *The Chimney Sweeper's Boy*, the third-person omniscient viewpoint prevails, perhaps because no single character predominates but rather the plot is focused on a group of characters. *Gallowglass* has much in common with the Rendell psychological suspense tales in that its chief narrator is psychologically damaged and has been classified and treated as a schizophrenic during four years in a mental hospital. Neurotic and psychotic characters also predominate in *King Solomon's Carpet*. When this parallel was mentioned to Rendell, she replied that such overlap was hardly surprising because, despite writing under two names, she was only one person.

A great admirer of Henry James, Rendell confesses to emulating his style when she writes as Barbara Vine. For example, *The House of Stairs* is a conscious reworking of *The Wings of the Dove* (1902). In addition, she often approaches psychological character study in a subtler manner, more in the Jamesian style. In the portrayal of personality, Henry James was intent on developing layers of accumulated rational and emotional perceptions and sensitive civilized responses for his characters to contemplate on the journey toward understanding of themselves and others, and he was content to conclude his novels with a final ironic observation on the joy and sorrow of the human condition. Rendell expands James's range to reveal not only how emotional needs can blind people to reality but also how intense passion nurtured by slow time can ultimately cause individuals to break through the restraints of civilized behavior into violence when they eventually apprehend the truth—or it is thrust upon them—and their illusions are destroyed.

Several of the Barbara Vine novels are stories told in retrospect, as if distance from the events were necessary for accurate assessment of their significance. Time is necessary for the mist to clear, for all the facts to emerge, for maturity to make sense of the mysteries and half-truths of youth. The narrators are prompted to embark upon a quest for greater understanding of people and circumstances through remembering and reinterpreting both events and the behavior of key participants in the light of fresh facts and/or more mature judgments of themselves and others. In these books Rendell employs a Jamesian approach in the careful manipulation of the dimension of time through narrative viewpoint.

The pattern of the narrative design is produced by a subtle interweaving of flashback and foreshadowing with the threads of the unfolding action in current time. Rendell uses various rhetorical devices to lead the reader along the path the narrator takes into the dark heart of the mystery and out again into the light of knowledge, from intriguing remarks about mistaken assumptions in the past ("I believed then") to remorse about not recognizing the significance of the moment ("Had I but known") to ominous hints of impending disaster ("The diaries lay waiting") to full insight in the present ("I realize now") to regret at not being able to see into the future ("I wish I knew"). As in real life, full understanding occurs only after time and experience have made dispassionate reflection and analysis possible.

In *A Dark-Adapted Eye,* the narrator is Faith Severn, the niece of both the murderer and the victim in the strange story of intense maternal love. A child at the time of the tragedy, she pieces together bits of the story thirty years later at the request of a journalist writing a book about her aunt. Faith agrees to assist the writer in his search for information partly because she herself is curious to learn what really caused her aunt to murder her own dearly beloved sister, an act that has tarnished the lives of all members of the family: "Murder reaches out through a family, stamping transfers of the Mark of Cain on a dozen foreheads, and though these grow pale in proportion to the distance of the kinship, they are there and they burn into the brain" (p. 243).

Thus, Faith plays the role of investigative reporter sifting through old family letters and photographs and interviewing as many of her relatives as will consent to cooperate. As she inquires into roles played by various family members and listens to their versions of incidents leading up to the murder, she compares what she hears with her own impressions of events at the time and makes the requisite adjustments enabled by further data and more mature judgment. She gains further insight into the tragedy, but only after taking all the family skeletons out of their cupboards, dusting them off, and examining them before returning them to their final rest.

In fashioning her plot, Rendell has taken an old adage—"It's a wise child that knows its own father," whose meaning seems so obvious and incontrovertible—and given it an ironic twist. The mystery in her tale is one of maternity, not paternity. It is the strange story of Vera Hillyard, who alienated her son by sending him to boarding school at a young age so she could devote herself to the upbringing of her younger sister, Eden, and who in later life dedicates herself to raising a second boy, Jamie, of whom she becomes obsessively fond. Her desperate need to love and be loved leads her into violence when her maternal rights are challenged.

In *A Fatal Inversion,* nineteen-year-old Adam Verne-Smith inherits an eighteenth-century manor house outside a small Suffolk village. When he goes to view his property before departing for Greece for the summer with his friend Rufus, the two decide to spend some time enjoying the unusually warm English weather. As golden day follows golden day, their sojourn extends, and they decide to cancel their trip to the Aegean. To help make ends meet, Adam wants to set up an informal commune. More by chance than design, Adam and Rufus are joined by a young female hitchhiker, Zosie, as well as Shiva, an Indian premed student, and Vivien, a self-styled student of Eastern religions. They settle into a heedless, hedonistic existence enjoying the lazy daze of summer at Wyvis Hall, which they rename Ecalpemos ("someplace" spelled backward) to sound like a Greek island.

As in *A Dark-Adapted Eye,* the thwarted passion that leads to madness and, indirectly, to death is frustrated maternal love. The overpowering need to nurture a child and be loved by it—"to come first" with someone—leads to kidnapping and finally to murder. Rendell creates a convincing portrait of a young woman who, having been rejected by her own mother, gives her illegitimate baby up for adoption and then suffers from postpartum psychosis, which leads her to steal another woman's child. Rendell follows her usual formula of providing the reader with two shocking surprises toward the end of the book. The ending also bears the characteristic Rendell ironic reversal as she flouts one of the most entrenched conventions of the genre: the principle of retributive justice is not invoked. Ironically, the character who seems to be the least able to function and whose behavior causes two deaths emerges unscathed with all dreams fulfilled at the end of the story.

Familiar Rendellian themes reappear in this work, including both child abuse, in the form of rejection by parents and its consequences, and the role of chance in ordaining a momentous chain of events. For example, if Rufus had not left London early to join Adam at Wyvis Hall, he would not have met Zosie and offered her the ride that led to her becoming a member of the commune. If Adam had taken a different turn and parked the van in a different place when they went into town to shop, then Zosie would not have seen the unattended baby and the whole chain of events ensuing from the kidnapping would not have occurred.

Interspersed throughout the narrative are the reveries of three male characters whose behavior is interpreted in part by themselves

and in part by an omniscient third-person narrator. Earlier episodes emerge through the recollections of these characters who participated in them, and all share in the guilt of complicity. Adam, who functions rather as Faith does in *A Dark-Adapted Eye* as the primary narrator, is the main character. He is the most involved, the most guilty, and the most damaged at the end. Of his companions, Rufus and Shiva, the latter is implicated more deeply and reacts more intensely to events. Of the three, Rufus changes least, hardly at all in fact.

Throughout the novel, the narrative viewpoint is carefully crafted to simulate the working of the human mind. Memory is stimulated by chance words, photographs, objects, aromas, in addition to deliberate effort to recall events. Adam is the most resistant to recollecting the past. Like Faith, as an adult he reassesses earlier behavior and gains a clearer perception of himself and others denied him previously by his youth and passions. As he remembers and reinterprets the past, he is compelled to confront his own ignorance, selfishness, and weakness. Adam is forced to grapple with his feelings of guilt and remorse. He realizes that he has loved only two people in his entire life, Zosie and his baby daughter, Abigail. His neurotic concern for Abigail's welfare alienates his wife.

In describing Adam's mental habits, Rendell employs a central metaphor comparing the processes of human memory to those of a computer's memory. This comparison comes naturally to Adam, a computer salesman. He imagines his conscious mind as a computer screen from which he can banish memories by striking an "Escape" key. As he resists random memories of particular past events or deliberately attempts to recall them, Adam extends the metaphor in describing his mental functions to include such computer terms as "key words," "files," and "RAM chips."

An important aspect of the handling of time is the careful differentiation of real time from the illusion of timelessness, the nevernever time of life at Ecalpemos. The former is achieved through careful dating of events throughout the summer; the latter is attained by not winding clocks and not keeping to a regular routine as well as through the use of hallucinogenic drugs and heavy indulgence in sex and alcohol. The patterning of the narrative is also carefully contrived so that there is no confusion between current time and remote time as the characters' vivid recollections are juxtaposed with contemporary conversation and action.

On one occasion the intensity of memory is so forceful as to cause Adam to lose the thread of conversation going on around him, but both he and the reader are deftly brought back to present time. On another occasion the return to reality causes him to stumble up the steps of a restaurant. Moreover, the arrangement of the sequence of events is very artful vis-à-vis the choice of which character tells what part of the story and which character tells it first—for example, who first mentions murder. The alternation between different characters' versions of events is very skillful, and changes of voice indeed occur even within the same chapter without a rift in the narrative.

In *The House of Stairs,* Rendell adapts the plot of Henry James's *The Wings of the Dove* to her own unique ends. In James's novel a young woman encourages a love affair between a dying young heiress and her own lover, hoping that after the death of the heiress her lover will inherit a fortune, which will enable them to marry and live comfortably. The plot is revealed to the heiress, who does die and leave a legacy to the young man, but the couple are prevented by ethical considerations from enjoying his newfound wealth as planned. Directly inspired by James's story, a similar conspiracy with significant ironic variations exists in Rendell's book, and here, too, the scheme fails, but for different reasons.

A young female novelist, Elizabeth Vetch, who may or may not be suffering from an incurable hereditary disease, finds herself attracted to a beautiful young woman, Bell, whom she introduces to her aunt and surrogate mother, Cosette, a wealthy middle-aged widow pining for her lost youth. Bell seduces

Elizabeth and later invites her brother, Mark, to a party given by Cosette, who delights in filling her large house with young people. As an ardent love affair develops between Mark and Cosette, both Bell and Elizabeth observe its progress with misgivings. When Mark and Cosette announce their wedding plans, violence is unleashed that scars all their lives.

Elizabeth, the narrator, embarks on a pilgrimage to find answers to questions of a psychological and factual nature by reconsidering and reevaluating previous events as well as by acquiring additional data. Her expedition is a journey toward truth—the revelation of her own role in fostering the relationships that ended in the tragedy of death and painful loss and the inevitable ensuing burden of her own guilt. At the end of the book she is as uncertain whether she has reached her destination as she is of her destiny.

The event that causes Elizabeth to begin her voyage of discovery is the shocking chance sighting in a crowded London street of the former friend and lover, who has just returned after spending fourteen years in prison. Elizabeth finds herself driven to make the effort to review and reappraise the painful past because of unresolved feelings and ambivalent attitudes toward her friend and their shared experience. She is troubled by questions only Bell can answer, and she wants Bell to complete the picture by supplying the missing pieces of the puzzle. The nature of events has separated Elizabeth from the other principal figures in the drama. Unlike Faith or Adam, she can appeal to only one other person for information and confirmation of her ideas. Like Adam, she must face her need-induced blindness to reality and accept the insult to her amour propre as she reviews her own role as dupe and pawn.

Elizabeth becomes obsessed with the process of recollection and reinterpretation in tranquillity—as Wordsworth would have it—so she writes an account of their personal history while she is supposed to be penning her latest novel. The design of the narrative is equal to the intricate patterning of a James novel. Murder is first mentioned at the halfway point, but the act is not recounted until the very end of the book. Elizabeth's narrative achieves what she never attempts in her own slick formula romances—a probing examination of the human heart in the manner of Henry James. Although no longer physically attracted to her, Elizabeth finds herself regarding Bell as an inescapable legacy from the past—a responsibility she must accept simply because they are bound by their unique and irrevocable shared experience. She discovers that her identity has been unalterably determined by the past because "the past is what we are."

Rendell pursues a familiar theme in *Anna's Book*, that of the compelling elemental role of family heritage in the sense of individual human identity. "Our need to know our origins is deep-seated, is at the root of personality" (1994 ed., p. 266). In returning to the theme at the heart of the mystery in *The Dark-Adapted Eye*, Rendell derives a more conventional but no less ironic interpretation from the aphorism: "It's a wise child that knows its own father." When Swanhild (Swanny) Kjaer née Westerby receives a poison-pen letter informing her that she is adopted and her origins unknown, she is deeply shocked and becomes obsessed with discovering her biological parents. Her dilemma is compounded when her "mother" refuses to explain the circumstances of her adoption, saying that it does not matter who her real parents were since she was so well loved by her adoptive family. Tormented by insecurity, Swanny begs, pleads, and demands, "I have a right to know who I really am, Mother" (p. 88), but Anna remains adamant in her refusal to enlighten Swanny. As a result, Swanny suffers from an identity crisis not only over her nuclear family but also concerning her racial origins, doubting whether she is even Danish. After Anna dies, Swanny discovers her diaries and decides to have them translated from Danish in hope of finding information about her adoption. Ironically, when the diaries are published and are a popular success, Swanny becomes a celebrity as her mother's daughter in the eyes of the reading public and develops a career as her mother's editor and spokesperson. However, she is still tormented by not knowing who she is.

In desperation, as she ages, Swanny identifies herself with a child in a notorious murder case who went missing from a neighboring street at the time Swanny was born. She has a stroke on the day following a visit to the home of the missing child, Edith Roper. Subsequently, she begins to manifest symptoms of split personality as she creates a second identity by imagining what Edith Roper might be like at her own age. The intensity of her despair—the depths of her tragedy—is revealed on her deathbed. As she dies, she utters the single word "nobody," echoing the term applied to her in the poison-pen letter twenty years previously. Swanny's peace of mind was destroyed by the envious, mean-minded malice of the anonymous writer. "That letter had damaged the last twenty years of Swanny's life. . . . From its arrival could be dated the beginning of that fruitless quest and the ultimate madness and destruction of everything she had once been" (p. 323). As it happens, Swanny's origins were not "tainted," and her foster mother's misplaced sense of discretion and selfish pride deprived Swanny, Swanny's natural father, and Anna herself of much happiness—which an acknowledged relationship would have provided—and instead quite literally drove Swanny mad. So Anna deserved as much of the blame as the poison-pen writer.

Another theme common to the Barbara Vine novels that appears in *Anna's Book* is the powerful role of chance in shaping human lives. Just as chance prevails at the time of Swanny's birth, facilitating her adoption and obscuring her identity, so, too, Anna's seemingly inconsequential act of tearing out a few pages from her diary with notes of a Danish sea disaster and details of the difficult birth of her fourth child, her giving them to a naval historian, and their fortuitous return after the historian's death thirty years later, also lead to the solution of Swanny's identity. The whimsical, capricious arm of chance has unforeseen far reaching consequences. "So

RUTH RENDELL

lightly and casually are great wrongs set in motion and tragedies precipitated" (p. 363).

Anna's Book resembles *A Dark-Adapted Eye* not only in theme but also in the character of the first-person narrator. As Faith embarks on a voyage of discovery about her aunt, so does Ann Eastbrook become intrigued by her Aunt Swanny's quest and endeavor to find the answer: "Since learning of the identity she's assumed, my own need to know had grown and grown" (p. 304). She identifies closely with Swanny, "I was Swanny's heir in more ways than one. Like her, I wanted to know" (p. 309). The narrative is composed of alternating excerpts from Anna's diary and Ann's account of her own involvement in Swanny's sad fate. Ann calls it a "double detective story, a quest for an identity, and a quest for a lost child" (p. 7). As she unravels the complex pattern of relationships in Anna's and Swanny's lives, her own history emerges with ironic links and developments.

This book does contain a second puzzle or subplot that is clearly linked to the main conflict. It is the story of another woman's desperate desire for a child, which leads to murder and kidnapping. In the subplot, Ann's old friend Cary Oliver is making a television documentary about an infamous murder in the past and enlists Ann's help because she hopes to find information in Anna's diaries. They visit the scene of the unsolved crime to assess its suitability for filming and interview the current tenants. Simultaneously, a young woman, motivated, as Swanny was, to trace her grandfather's origins, solves the murder and indirectly helps Ann toward her goal of identifying Swanny. Ironically, the grandchildren of the principal characters solve the puzzle their grandparents created. As in Rendell's other Barbara Vine novels, the characters see through a glass darkly while the truth is gradually disclosed in its entirety as the links between the past and the present are uncovered. Unfortunately, the truth emerges only after all the people whose lives were damaged by its suppression are dead.

In all of these novels, the youthful innocence and ignorance of the narrators are a handicap when important events occur in the past and cause them to make mistakes in interpreting people's behavior. Youthful passion also blinds Adam and Elizabeth, but perhaps not Faith or Ann. They all gain new insight into events and people by considering the past through a more mature contemporary perspective. In the cases of Faith, Elizabeth, and Ann, discussing past happenings with other participants elicits new information, which brings them closer to the truth. But a Jamesian ironic ambiguity pervades the endings of all these novels. Although much insight has been attained, total understanding is withheld—or comes too late—perhaps because partial awareness embodies the true nature of the human condition. This ironic ambiguity may also be an elliptical comment on the impossibility of capturing and representing reality in life and in fiction.

In *Gallowglass*, Rendell explores the implications of the idea that one's life belongs to the person who saves it. When Alexander (Sandor) Wincanton saves Joe Herbert from falling in front of a train in the London Underground, he tells Joe that his life belongs to him henceforth and Joe agrees. From that moment he becomes Sandor's gallowglass. "In ancient times, the gallowglass stood poised at the right hand of a Celtic chieftain. It was this warrior's duty to lunge in front of an axe or spear, to taste food and drink, to sacrifice his life, if required, to protect his chieftain." Joe is proud to fill this role and accepts without protest Sandor's right to punish him by "accidentally" cutting his upper lip with a razor or spilling bleach in his eyes. At the end of the story, Joe is grateful for the scars of a razor wound on his hand to remember Sandor by. When Sandor takes his own life by the same method Joe considered—jumping in front of an express train—Joe is overcome with grief and wonders whether their relationship would have been reversed if he had succeeded in preventing Sandor's death, that is, whether Sandor would have belonged to him. He identifies himself so much with Sandor that he hopes Sandor's mother will "adopt" him so he

786

will always feel close to Sandor, will become Sandor.

Sandor accepts Joe's love and loyalty as he would that of a faithful dog, as he has the slavish affection of his mother who has always been devoted to him. Although he despises both of them for their selfless blind devotion, Sandor behaves the same way with the woman he loves. Rendell's penchant for ironic reversal so evident in *A Dark-Adapted Eye* is apparent also in *Gallowglass.* Sandor became enamored of a woman he helped to kidnap a few years earlier in Italy. Instead of the captive identifying with the captor as has been described and documented in studies of the Stockholm Syndrome, in this case the captor formed an allegiance with the captive and abandoned his own values and agenda, even to the point of giving back his share of the ransom and trying to convince his colleagues to do the same. His ardor did not cool when the kidnap victim failed to keep promises to meet Sandor after she had been released. Instead, while serving a four-year prison sentence he formed a plan to kidnap her again because he was sure she reciprocated his affection and was being prevented from joining him by her husband. After meeting Joe, he kidnaps her a second time. When she rejects him absolutely of her own free will, he takes his own life. Common symptoms of the Stockholm Syndrome include cognitive distortion, depression, low self-esteem or loss of a sense of self, and love dependence typified by the feeling that one cannot survive without the partner's love.

In *The Chimney Sweeper's Boy*, Rendell reverts to a theme she has treated in both of her other series—the strong need felt by some men to procreate or to nurture children, an intense paternal love equivalent to maternal love. She explored this subject in *Murder Being Once Done* through the characters of Stephen Dearborn and John Lamont and in *A Demon in My View* through the character of Anthony Johnson. It reappears in Paul Garnet's behavior in *Gallowglass*; he cares more for his daughter than for his wife or his lover. In *The Chimney Sweeper's Boy*, Gerald Cand-

less, a well-known writer whose novels treat family life, marries an unsophisticated woman some fifteen years his junior who gives her heart to him completely. After she has produced two children—both girls—whom he dotes upon, he rejects her emotionally and physically and makes it quite clear that henceforth he will be her husband in name only. He is absorbed by the children and in effect becomes both father and mother to them. Ursula is terribly hurt but does not know what to do, so she does nothing. She is qualified only as a secretary/typist and cannot support herself if she were to get a divorce, but in any case she does not want to leave the children. So she remains in the family estranged from her children who love their father but treat her with indifference. As the years stretch on, Gerald becomes more famous, the girls grow up, and Ursula becomes more embittered in her loveless circumstances.

When Gerald dies unexpectedly of a heart attack, Ursula's life improves. While she is babysitting at a nearby hotel because she wants some contact with children, she meets a man and they become friends and then lovers. She hopes for a rapprochement with her daughters, but old habits die hard and they cannot learn to love her even in their father's absence. When the elder daughter decides to write her father's biography, she discovers that he had changed his name when he was twenty-five and had taken the name of a boy who died in childhood. Diligent research uncovers his real name and his nuclear family, but not the reason for his abandoning them and beginning a new life on his own. The truth emerges in an unfinished manuscript he entrusted to a fellow writer. He was a homosexual who loved being part of a large family, and he wanted children of his own. So he married Ursula only because she could provide him with the family he so longed for. The novel exposes the intolerant, brutal treatment of homosexuals before and after the British law decriminalizing homosexual activity between consenting adults was passed in the mid-1960s and Gerald Candless' pain because of it; at the same time it portrays the suffering he inflicted on hapless Ursula to fulfill his intense drive to nurture.

Social intolerance of alternative sexual orientation is a recurrent theme in Rendell's work and dates from her first published novel, *From Doon with Death*. The most probing examination of sexual orientation, however, occurs in *No Night Is Too Long*, in which a young man awakens to his own sexual needs and discovers his sexual identity through experience with partners of both genders. Unknowingly, the main character, Tim Cornish, falls in love consecutively with a man and a woman who are twins. His experience teaches him that the difference in degree and depth of passion is dependent on personality not gender. This book is in part about the thin line that divides homosexual and heterosexual passion, but it is also about the difference between sexual passion and love and their power to dictate human behavior. Driven by passion to commit murder, Tim's revulsion at his act prevents him from joining his beloved. He then embarks on a journey toward emotional and moral maturity.

Like *Anna's Book* this is a novel in which the act of writing or keeping a record of thoughts, feelings, and events is important. Writing forces the characters to reflect on events and analyze their feelings and refine their interpretations of experience. The act of writing provides the characters with insight into themselves and others, and it also offers a kind of release. The inclusion of multiple accounts of the same events allows the reader to gain a more accurate sense of objective reality than the subjective rendering of a single character could afford.

Conclusion

Whether written by Ruth Rendell or Barbara Vine, these murder mysteries do indeed fulfill their author's ambition: to write novels probing human character and exploring significant aspects of the human condition. In all three series the reader encounters deep awareness of the power of the sexual drive in determining human behavior—both erotic passion and the urge to procreate. Her characters reveal the human need to bond, to belong to someone, to love and be loved as well as the lengths to which people will go if these needs are frustrated. These books also register distress at the breakdown of responsible parenting, concern for abused children, and compassion for society's misfits. Rendell is a superb ironist whose work registers amusement and appreciation of the incongruities of life and an unrelenting exposure of man's inhumanity to man. In addition, a recognition of the role of chance informing people's lives is inescapable.

Ruth Rendell makes a unique contribution to the literature of crime fiction in the second half of the twentieth century in all three of her series. She extends the limits of the conventional whodunit in the Wexford books by revealing the relationship between sexuality and crime. Although other detective authors have written of the *crime passionnel* (or the "cream passionate" as Stanley Caspian calls it in *A Demon in My View*), no one else has treated so consistently and comprehensively the wide spectrum of sexual behavior, its diversity of expression and orientation, and the social intolerance of it beyond narrow prescribed limits as a basis of crime. The special province of many of the Rendell novels of psychological suspense is the relationship between mental illness and crime. These stories present the behavior of neurotic and psychotic characters empathetically so that their antisocial actions become understandable to the ordinary reader. But they go beyond description to address the conditions that produce aberrant behavior and, in many cases, to attribute blame to child neglect and child abuse. By employing more sophisticated literary techniques of narrative viewpoint and characterization to communicate theme in the Barbara Vine novels, Rendell has lifted the crime novel into mainstream fiction and earned profound respect from readers and critics alike.

Selected Bibliography

WORKS OF RUTH RENDELL
DETECTIVE SERIES

From Doon with Death. London: Hutchinson, 1964; Garden City, N.Y.: Doubleday, 1965.

A New Lease of Death. London: Long, 1967; Garden City, N.Y.: Doubleday, 1967. U.S.: *Sins of the Fathers.* New York: Ballantine, 1970.

Wolf to the Slaughter. London: Long, 1967; Garden City, N.Y.: Doubleday, 1968.

The Best Man to Die. London: Long, 1969; Garden City, N.Y.: Doubleday, 1970.

A Guilty Thing Surprised. London: Hutchinson, 1970; Garden City, N.Y.: Doubleday, 1970.

No More Dying Then. London: Hutchinson, 1971; Garden City, N.Y.: Doubleday, 1972.

Murder Being Once Done. London: Hutchinson, 1972; Garden City, N.Y.: Doubleday, 1972.

Some Lie and Some Die. London: Hutchinson, 1973; Garden City, N.Y.: Doubleday, 1973.

Shake Hands Forever. London: Hutchinson, 1975; Garden City, N.Y.: Doubleday, 1975.

A Sleeping Life. London: Hutchinson, 1978; Garden City, N.Y.: Doubleday, 1978; New York: Bantam, 1980.

Put On by Cunning. London: Hutchinson, 1981. U.S.: *Death Notes.* New York: Pantheon, 1981.

The Speaker of Mandarin. London: Hutchinson, 1983; New York: Pantheon, 1983.

An Unkindness of Ravens. London: Hutchinson, 1985; New York: Pantheon, 1985.

The Veiled One. London: Hutchinson, 1988; New York: Pantheon, 1988.

Kissing the Gunner's Daughter. London: Hutchinson, 1992; New York: Mysterious Press, 1992.

Simisola. London: Hutchinson, 1994; New York: Crown, 1995.

Road Rage. London: Hutchinson, 1997; New York: Crown, 1997.

CRIME NOVELS

To Fear a Painted Devil. London: Long, 1965; Garden City, N.Y.: Doubleday, 1965.

Vanity Dies Hard. London: Long, 1966; New York: Beagle, 1970. U.S.: *In Sickness and in Health.* Garden City, N.Y.: Doubleday, 1966.

The Secret House of Death. London: Long, 1968; Garden City, N.Y.: Doubleday, 1969.

One Across, Two Down. London: Hutchinson, 1971; Garden City, N.Y.: Doubleday, 1971.

The Face of Trespass. London: Hutchinson, 1974; Garden City, N.Y.: Doubleday, 1974.

A Demon in My View. London: Hutchinson, 1976; Garden City, N.Y.: Doubleday, 1977; London: Arrow Books, 1977.

A Judgement in Stone. London: Hutchinson, 1977; Garden City, N.Y.: Doubleday, 1978.

Make Death Love Me. London: Hutchinson, 1979; Garden City, N.Y.: Doubleday, 1979.

The Lake of Darkness. London: Hutchinson, 1980; Garden City, N.Y.: Doubleday, 1980.

Master of the Moor. London: Hutchinson, 1982; New York: Pantheon, 1982.

The Killing Doll. London: Hutchinson, 1984; New York: Pantheon, 1984.

The Tree of Hands. London: Hutchinson, 1984; New York: Pantheon, 1985.

Live Flesh. London: Hutchinson, 1986; New York: Pantheon, 1986.

Talking to Strange Men. London: Hutchinson, 1987; New York: Pantheon, 1987.

The Bridesmaid. London: Hutchinson, 1989; New York: Mysterious Press, 1989.

Going Wrong. London: Hutchinson, 1990; New York: Mysterious Press, 1990.

The Crocodile Bird. London: Hutchinson, 1993; New York: Crown, 1993.

The Keys to the Street. London: Hutchinson, 1996; New York: Crown, 1996.

BARBARA VINE NOVELS

A Dark-Adapted Eye. London: Viking, 1986; New York: Bantam, 1986.

A Fatal Inversion. London: Viking, 1987; New York: Bantam, 1987.

The House of Stairs. London: Viking, 1988; New York: Harmony, 1989.

Gallowglass. London: Viking, 1990; New York: Harmony, 1990.

King Solomon's Carpet. London: Viking, 1991; New York: Crown, 1991.

Asta's Book. London: Viking, 1993. U.S.: *Anna's Book.* New York: Harmony, 1993; New York: Onyx, 1994.

No Night Is Too Long. London: Viking, 1994; New York: Harmony, 1994.

The Brimstone Wedding. New York: Harmony, 1995; London: Viking, 1996.

In the Time of His Prosperity. London: Penguin, 1995.

The Chimney Sweeper's Boy. London: Viking, 1998; New York, Harmony, 1998.

NOVELLAS

Heartstones. London: Hutchinson, 1987; New York: Harper & Row, 1987.

The Strawberry Tree. London: HarperCollins, 1990.

The Strawberry Tree with *Flesh and Grass* by Helen Simpson. London: Pandora, 1991.

SHORT FICTION COLLECTIONS

The Fallen Curtain. London: Hutchinson, 1976; Garden City, N.Y.: Doubleday, 1976.

Three Cases for Chief Inspector Wexford. Helsinki: Eurographica, 1979.

Means of Evil. London: Hutchinson, 1979; Garden City, N.Y.: Doubleday, 1980.

The Fever Tree. London: Hutchinson, 1982; New York: Pantheon, 1982.

Matters of Suspense. Helsinki: Eurographica, 1983.

The New Girl Friend. London: Hutchinson, 1985; New York: Pantheon, 1986.

Collected Short Stories. London: Hutchinson, 1987; New York: Pantheon, 1988.

The Copper Peacock. London: Hutchinson, 1991; New York: Mysterious Press, 1991.

Blood Lines. London: Random House, 1995; New York: Crown, 1996.

Ginger and the Kingsmarkham Chalk Circle. London: Phoenix, 1996.

NONFICTION

Ruth Rendell's Suffolk. Photographs by Peter Bowden. London: Muller, 1989; London: Hutchinson, 1992.

Undermining the Central Line (with Colin Ward). London: Chatto & Windus, 1989.

"A Voyage Among Misty Isles." *New York Times Magazine,* 16 May 1993.

EDITED WORKS

A Warning to the Curious: The Ghost Stories of M. R. James. London: Hutchinson, 1987; Boston: Godine, 1989.

Introduction and notes to *Dr. Thorne* by Anthony Trollope. London and New York: Penguin, 1991.

Introduction to *Barchester Towers* by Anthony Trollope. London: Folio, 1989.

Introduction to *The Woman in White* by Wilkie Collins. London: Folio, 1989.

The Reason Why: An Anthology of the Murderous Mind. London: Cape, 1995; New York: Crown, 1995.

INTERVIEWS

Rahn, B. J. Unpublished recorded personal interviews: 28 August 1980; 7 October 1989; 5 September 1997.

BIOGRAPHICAL AND CRITICAL STUDIES

Alexander, Lynn M. "Ruth Rendell." In *Great Women Mystery Writers.* Edited by Kathleen Gregory Klein. Westport, Conn.: Greenwood Press, 1994. Pp. 295–299.

Bakerman, Jane S. "Ruth Rendell." In *Ten Women of Mystery.* Edited by Earl F. Bargainnier. Bowling Green, Ohio: Bowling Green State University Popular Press, 1981. Pp. 124–149.

———. "Ruth Rendell." In *St. James Guide to Crime and Mystery Writers.* Edited by Jay P. Pederson. Detroit: St. James Press, 1996. Pp. 877–879.

Boshoff, Alison. "Ruth Rendell Thrilled with Her New Title." *Daily Telegraph,* 2 August 1997: 1.

Budd, Elaine. "Ruth Rendell: Terror Times Two." In her *13 Mistresses of Murder.* New York: Ungar, 1986. Pp. 105–113.

———. "Women of Mystery." *Dynamic Years Magazine,* November 1983.

Carr, John C. "Ruth Rendell." In his *The Craft of Crime.* Boston: Houghton Mifflin, 1983.

Clark, Susan L. "A Fearful Symmetry." *Armchair Detective,* 22: 229–235 (summer 1989).

Cooper-Clark, Diana. "Ruth Rendell." In her *Designs of Darkness.* Bowling Green, Ohio: Bowling Green State University Popular Press, 1983.

de Bertodano, Helena. "The Unsolved Riddle of Mrs. Rendell." *Sunday Telegraph,* 29 May 1994.

Duncan, Andrew. "I've Never Been in a Police Station. I Just Make It Up." *Radio Times,* 23–29 March 1996: 20, 22.

Henderson, Mark. "Rival Queens of Crime." *Times,* 2 August 1997: 1–2.

Henry, William. "Dark Journeys." *Time,* 18 August 1986.

Hutchinson, Diana. "Murder's a Family Affair!" *Daily Mail,* 8 May 1984: 13.

"In Conversation with Ruth Rendell." *Fiction Magazine,* 3: 45–46 (spring 1984).

Jones, Nicolette. "Much Too Busy to Loiter in the Limelight." *Publishing News,* 16 December 1988: 9, 12.

Lyall, Sarah. "Mysteries, of Course, but Ruth Rendell Also Sees Real Evil." *New York Times,* 10 April 1995: C9, 13.

Paterson, Moira. "The Rewards of Crime." *Observer,* 16 February 1986: 38, 40.

Saunders, Kate. "Grim Deeds Perfected in the Depths of a Sunny Soul." *Sunday Times,* 19 August 1990: 3.

Stasio, Marilyn. "Investigating the Darker Corners of the Criminal Mind." *New York Times,* 4 February 1990, sec. 2.

Tallett, Dennis. *The Ruth Rendell Companion.* Calif.: Companion Books, 1995.

SAX ROHMER
(1883–1959)

R. E. BRINEY

FROM WORLD WAR I through the 1940s, the epitome of fictional international villainy—in magazines, books, movies, radio, comic strips, and eventually television—was the evil Dr. Fu Manchu, the creation of a British writer who used the name Sax Rohmer. During the 1920s and 1930s, Rohmer was one of the most widely read magazine writers in the English language. Although he is known today primarily as the chronicler of the supervillain Fu Manchu's exploits, his literary career was both longer and more varied than this association suggests.

Early Years and First Success

Sax Rohmer was born Arthur Henry Ward in the subdistrict of Ladywood, in Birmingham, England, on 15 February 1883 to parents of Irish extraction. His father, William Ward, was born in Clonmel, County Tipperary, and his mother, Margaret Mary Furey, was born in London, although her parents came from Athlone, Ireland. William and Margaret met in Birmingham, where both families had settled, and where William was employed as an office clerk. When Arthur was three years old, the family relocated to South London, where William eventually held the position of office manager in a firm of mechanical engineers. In spite of the long hours he spent at work, Wil-

liam provided what stability the family had. Home-educated, he probably taught his son to read, for by this time Margaret Ward, neurasthenic and increasingly dependent on alcohol, was spending her days reliving incoherent episodes from Irish legend and history, many of which she recounted to her son. Arthur received no formal schooling until he was nine or ten years old. It is not known what school or schools he attended (probably as a day student). The one most often mentioned is King's College School in Wimbledon, but the school's records for 1892–1902 do not list a pupil named Arthur Ward. Whatever formal education he received was supplemented by voracious reading: popular novels (many of them passed on to him by his mother), thrillers, ghost stories, the works of Bret Harte and Mark Twain, historical novels such as those of Alexandre Dumas père, the Sir Richard Francis Burton translation of *One Thousand Nights and a Night*, and accounts of Egyptian history and archaeology. During his teens, he began to write, drawing on his vivid imagination and the fund of obscure knowledge gleaned from his reading. These initial efforts produced nothing but rapid rejections.

Margaret Ward's health worsened, with tuberculosis compounding the effects of her alcoholism. She died in March 1901, a month after Arthur's eighteenth birthday. He completed his schooling during that same year and embarked on a series of short-term jobs. He worked briefly in a Spanish bank on Lombard Street, then as a clerk in a gas company, answering customer complaints, and as an errand boy and jack-of-all-trades at a small local newspaper. A more substantial newspaper job, as a reporter on the weekly *Commercial Intelligence*, was a result of a recommendation from the well-known editor T. P. "Tay Pay" O'Connor, who had been a friend of Margaret Ward's family. This job lasted little longer than Arthur's other attempts at employment. He next tried his luck as an illustrator, honing a natural talent by attending art classes. The black-and-white drawings that he submitted to assorted periodicals—of street scenes and buildings and landscapes, as well as cartoons—met the same fate as his fiction.

He turned back to writing, determined to make another assault on the fiction markets. At the same time, he adopted a new middle name. One of Margaret Ward's fancies was that her family was descended from the seventeenth-century Irish general Patrick Sarsfield, who served under James II. This possible genealogical connection, combined perhaps with Arthur's acquaintance with Billy Sarsfield, a pressman who worked on a number of small newspapers in the London area, led to the change: Arthur Henry Ward became A. Sarsfield Ward. Under this name he renewed his submissions to numerous fiction magazines. Finally, in the early autumn of 1903, two acceptance letters arrived in place of the half-expected rejections. "The Mysterious Mummy" had been accepted by *Pearson's Weekly*, where it appeared in the 1903 "'Xmas 'Xtra" issue published at the end of November, and "The Leopard-Couch" was bought by *Chambers's Journal* in Edinburgh, which published the story in its 30 January 1904 issue. "The Mysterious Mummy" is a clever and amusing account of a museum robbery, as told by the thief who carries it out. "The Leopard-Couch" deals with the supernatural properties of the titular object from Egyptian antiquity. Such uses of ancient Egyptian artifacts and deities would appear repeatedly in Rohmer's fiction throughout his career.

Five more stories—humorous, mystery, and historical adventure—sold in rapid succession and were published over the next three years. But Arthur had turned away from fiction again. He made a short trip to the Continent and upon his return renewed his acquaintance with a group of bohemian young men who supported themselves with miscellaneous jobs while hanging around on the fringes of the literary and theatrical worlds. It was at this time that he seems to have adopted the name by which he would be known for most of his career: Sax Rohmer.

The name Sax Rohmer may have been constructed with a deliberate meaning in mind, as Rohmer claimed in an interview in the *New Yorker*, 29 November 1947: "In ancient Saxon, 'sax' means 'blade'; 'rohmer' equals 'roamer.'" Or it may simply have been "made up" according to Rohmer's recipe for an author's name, as he told it to his friend and protégé Cay Van Ash (reported in private correspondence, 1989): the name should be exotic sounding, easy to remember, and short enough to fit on the spine of a book.

One evening in the early summer of 1905, while strolling with friends through Clapham Common, he met eighteen-year-old Rosie Knox. This encounter was the start of a highly unconventional courtship. Rose Elizabeth Knox was the youngest daughter of a theatrical family. Her father, George Thomas Knox, had been a well-known comedian in his youth. Her youngest brother, Teddy, became half of the vaudeville team of Nervo and Knox and later was a member of The Crazy Gang, which had a long career on the music-hall stage and in movies such as *Life Is a Circus, Alf's Button Afloat,* and *Gasbags.* When she met the newly minted Sax Rohmer, Rosie was already performing in a juggling act with her brother Bill. At the same time, Sax had music-hall connections of his own, which he kept secret. He had a talent for comic verse— something he preferred to hide from his readers in later years—and was busily producing songs and comedy sketches for an assortment of performers, including such established figures as George Robey and Harry Relph ("Little Tich"). This work, as well as forays into freelance journalism, provided only a precarious income. Nevertheless, Rosie eventually talked Sax, who had little regard for conventions, into marrying. They were married at the Lambeth Register Office on 14 January 1909. For almost two years they kept the marriage a secret from Rosie's family and from William Ward. Rosie continued to share a flat with her sister, while Sax lived with his father.

Before their marriage, at Rosie's urging, Rohmer had returned to writing fiction. Two short mystery stories appeared early in 1909 under the A. Sarsfield Ward byline (in one case altered by an editorial error to J. Sarsfield Ward), and a series of five cockney-dialect stories appeared anonymously, probably in the magazine *Yes & No*. These stories, dealing mainly with minor scams and get-rich-quick schemes that never come out as planned, feature a group of characters loosely based on Rohmer's bohemian friends. One character is called Digger, Rohmer's nickname among his friends. Many years later, the narrator of the Bernard de Treville stories would also be called Digger. The story "Narky" retained its popularity through the years and was reprinted in magazines (including *Ellery Queen's Mystery Magazine* in February 1953) and anthologies. Along with his return to fiction writing, Rohmer was fulfilling a commission from one of his music-hall friends. Based on themes and plot ideas suggested by George Robey, he wrote a collection of stories, dramatic monologues, and prose sketches, published anonymously under the punning title *Pause!* (1910; the book cover pictured a large hand). After this, he was done with anonymity and almost done with the A. Sarsfield Ward name. He had already been using the name Sax Rohmer for several years in his private life and on his music-hall work, and from now on it would be the byline on all but four of his published works. (His wife also modified her name: no longer Rosie, but Elizabeth. Some years later, when she published a few stories of her own, she used the byline Lisbeth Knox.)

Believing that success as a writer was not likely to be built only on short stories, early in 1911 Rohmer embarked on a more extended work: not a novel, but a series of connected stories featuring the same central characters, each story complete in itself but also forming part of a larger plotline. This format was much in favor with magazine editors of the time, and many of Rohmer's best-known books were originally written to this pattern. The first such series bore the title *The Sins of Séverac Bablon*. The title character is a descendant of the Royal House of Israel, the pure line of descent having supposedly been preserved in secret since the breakup of the kingdom after the time of Solomon. Once referred to by Rohmer as a "Jewish Robin Hood," Bablon possesses enormous wealth and secret influence and is served by hordes of silent henchmen. His victims are the rich and greedy, whom he coerces into donating much of their wealth to charities and worthy projects. His greatest achievement is the prevention of World War I: by frightening and blackmailing the Jewish financiers involved, he prevents a loan to Germany with which that country intended to wage war on Britain. As Bablon says at the end of his adventures, "For this will be forgotten all my errors, forgiven all my sins!"

The Bablon series was originally put aside unfinished. Arthur Greening, the publisher of *Pause!*, commissioned Rohmer to ghostwrite an autobiography of the comedian Harry Relph, which resulted in *Little Tich: A Book of Travels (and Wanderings)* (1911). This occupied Rohmer's attention throughout the summer. When the book was finished, he did not immediately return to the Séverac Bablon stories. Instead he turned to a character who was to become the foundation of his fame, the powerful and devious Oriental villain, Dr. Fu Manchu. Rohmer began writing the first Fu Manchu episode in the fall of 1911, but this series too was temporarily put aside. Greening's publishing business failed soon after the publication of *Little Tich*, leaving both the author and his subject without anything to show for their efforts. However, in an attempt at recompense, Greening introduced Rohmer to Newman Flower, the editor of *Cassell's Magazine of Fiction* and *The Story-Teller*. Flower commissioned Rohmer to complete the Séverac Bablon series, which began appearing in *Cassell's* in June 1912. As soon as he finished the Bablon stories, Rohmer returned to Dr. Fu Manchu and completed that series, which was also purchased by Flower and published in *The Story-Teller* beginning in October 1912. The last use of the Sarsfield Ward byline (without the *A.*) was on the story "The Secret of Holm Peel" in the December 1912 issue of *Cassell's*, which also carried the seventh Séverac Bablon episode. Over the next decade, three episodic series and twelve miscellaneous short stories by Rohmer were published under Flower's editorship.

At this point Rohmer, who was hopeless at record keeping of any kind, acquired a literary agent named Robert Sommerville to promote his work and handle his sales. Their association endured profitably for fifteen years but ended in the late 1920s with an acrimonious and expensive lawsuit.

Rohmer now found all of the major fiction magazines open to him and entered a period of remarkable productivity. The series "O'Hagan at Large" (which became the book *The Exploits of Captain O'Hagan*, 1916) began in *The London Magazine* in April 1913, and "The Methods of Moris Klaw" (later published as *The Dream Detective*, 1920) began that same month in *The New Magazine*. "The Quest of the Sacred Slipper" followed in the same magazine in September. Independent short stories also appeared, many of them commissioned to match cover illustrations already in stock. American magazine editors were not slow to catch on to Rohmer's popularity. His principal market in the United States was the weekly *Collier's*, beginning in February 1913. Over the next thirty-six years, no less than 208 issues carried Rohmer stories or serial installments. The *Collier's* connection was profitable for both Rohmer and the magazine. Rohmer's serials, particularly the

Fu Manchu stories, certainly contributed to the magazine's large circulation, which enabled it to weather the Depression. For periods during the 1920s and 1930s, Rohmer was one of the most widely read and most highly paid magazine writers in the English language, appealing to readers at all levels of society. (Longtime *Collier's* editor William Ludlow Chenery, in his 1952 book, *So It Seemed*, tells of how President Calvin Coolidge would send a White House messenger out to buy each new issue of the magazine as soon as it appeared, so he could keep up to date with the latest exploits of Fu Manchu.) Other U.S. magazines such as *Lippincott's*, *McClure's*, and *Short Stories* were also ready markets for Rohmer's work.

Book publishers quickly followed suit. Almost all of Rohmer's magazine work, beginning with the Fu Manchu stories, would appear in book form, sometimes almost simultaneously with the magazine publication, in other cases after a lapse of years. Methuen and Cassell became his regular hardcover publishers in Britain, while McBride and Doubleday issued most of his work in the United States.

Fiction did not occupy all of Rohmer's time. He was still producing work for the stage, now often with Near Eastern and Oriental themes—for example, a song called "The Camel's Parade" ("incorporating the original Bedouin melody 'The Mizmoune' ") and a verse monologue titled "The Pigtail of Li Fang Fu," with musical accompaniment written for Bransby Williams. Although Rohmer could not read music, he "composed" the tunes to several of his songs by humming them and having them transcribed by a collaborator. He also found time to pursue a nonfiction project related to his interest in mysticism and the occult, which may have developed out of his unconventional upbringing and wide-ranging early reading. It was certainly encouraged and focused by an older friend, Dr. R. Watson Councell, the physician who attended Margaret Ward during her final illness.

At Councell's urging, Rohmer joined the occult organization the Hermetic Order of the

Golden Dawn, whose membership at one time or another included such diverse people as Aleister Crowley, whom Rohmer knew and disliked, and William Butler Yeats. Rohmer also delved to a limited extent into theosophy. He was not a dedicated member of these organizations; once his initial curiosity had been satisfied, he moved on to something new. In the summer of 1913, his agent circulated among likely publishers a "Scheme for Large Illustrated Book on Sorcery and Sorcerers," with chapters on well-known proponents of the occult from Apollonius of Tyana to Cagliostro to Madame Blavatsky. The proposal was approved by Methuen, which had already published the first Fu Manchu book, and *The Romance of Sorcery* appeared in 1914. The book has been reprinted several times over the years and was in print as recently as the 1970s.

Rohmer's books were an immediate popular success, and most of them went through numerous editions both in England and in the United States. They were also translated into many languages, including Swedish, Dutch, Portuguese, Greek, and Indonesian. This success brought the Rohmers financial security, at least in the short term. They were able to travel in Egypt (a photograph of Rohmer aboard a dhow on the Nile was used for publicity purposes in 1913) and the Near East and move into much more comfortable housing. In later years they built a country house called Little Gatton, near Reigate, in the Surrey countryside. Rohmer was able to vacation in Madeira and indulge his interest in roulette at Monte Carlo. In the mid-1950s he estimated that he had earned nearly two million dollars from the Fu Manchu books alone. It is small wonder that he customarily signed his name using a dollar sign for the *S*. But his natural improvidence—when he had money, he spent it without regard to how long it would last—and some unwise business associations kept the Rohmers' fortunes in flux, and periods of affluence were punctuated by stretches in small flats.

Dr. Fu Manchu

The character that brought Rohmer his first fame could almost always be counted on to revive the exchequer. In later years, in articles and interviews, Rohmer left at least four accounts of the genesis of Dr. Fu Manchu. No two of these explanations agree in detail, and all clearly play on the audience's expectations from a creator of mysteries. Certainly the time was ripe for the introduction of such a character. Fascination with the superficial aspects of Chinese culture was linked with mystery in the public consciousness by popular entertainment figures such as the numerous stage magicians who adopted Chinese or pseudo-Chinese names (for example, Ching Ling Foo, a genuine Chinese, and Chung Ling Soo, the stage name of an American, William Ellsworth Robinson) and performed their illusions using Oriental costumes and stage settings. The Boxer Rebellion and its aftermath were fresh in the public's mind. The idea of the Yellow Peril—an invasion of the West by Asiatic hordes—raised in the sensational newspapers of the 1890s and reinforced by novels such as M. P. Shiel's *The Yellow Danger* (1898) and *The Yellow Wave* (1905), was still current. The activities of Chinese tongs in major cities of Europe and the United States were described daily in newspapers. Rohmer's inspiration, as reported by Cay Van Ash in chapter 10 of the Sax Rohmer biography, *Master of Villainy* (1972), was to pose the question: What if these local groups were in fact not independent but controlled by a single worldwide organization? Visualize a man powerful and intelligent enough to head such an organization, and you have Dr. Fu Manchu:

> Imagine a person, tall, lean and feline, high-shouldered, with a brow like Shakespeare and a face like Satan, a close-shaven skull, and long, magnetic eyes of the true cat-green. Invest him with all the cruel cunning of an entire Eastern race, accumulated in one giant intellect, with all the resources of science past and present. Imagine that awful being,

and you have a mental picture of Dr. Fu-Manchu, the yellow peril incarnate in one man. (*The Insidious Dr. Fu-Manchu*, chap. 2)

The first Fu Manchu series, consisting of ten stories, began publication in England in *The Story-Teller* in October 1912 and in the United States in *Collier's* on 15 February 1913. The series appeared in book form in Britain as *The Mystery of Dr. Fu-Manchu* (1913; U.S. title, *The Insidious Dr. Fu-Manchu*). The second Fu Manchu series began publication in June 1915, and the third in September 1916. Both were in book form before the magazine serials concluded as *The Devil Doctor* (1916; U.S. title, *The Return of Dr. Fu-Manchu*) and *The Si-Fan Mysteries* (1917; U.S. title, *The Hand of Fu-Manchu*). These three series were narrated by a London physician, Dr. Petrie (whose first name is never mentioned), and recount the battles of his friend Nayland Smith (later Sir Denis Nayland Smith), an agent of the British government battling Fu Manchu's plans for conquest or subversion of the Western world. Through the first-person narration, the reader gains occasional impressions of the thoughts and feelings of Petrie. Smith, on the other hand, remains a figure without a family or personal life. About him the reader learns only that he smokes a briar pipe, tugs on his earlobe when deep in thought, and "raps" and "snaps" his dialogue.

The Fu Manchu stories are cast as thrillers rather than as conventional murder mysteries. The identity of the culprit is never in doubt. The detection is concerned with explaining how the seemingly impossible crimes, such as thefts or murders in closely guarded settings, could have been carried out and with discovering the nature of Fu Manchu's deadly agents, who carry such intriguing names as the Zayat Kiss, the Coughing Horror, and the Flower of Silence. Each of the thirty original episodes (one of which appeared only in book form) follows one of three patterns: Smith and Petrie are menaced by one of Fu Manchu's exotic death traps, captured by his agents, or engaged in trying to foil a murderous attempt against someone who stands in Fu Manchu's way. The protagonists triumph either by good luck or (less frequently) their own wits, or else are rescued by the beautiful Kâramanèh, one of Fu Manchu's company who has fallen in love with Petrie.

Such episodic narratives may exert less of a hold on contemporary television-acclimated audiences than they did on the pre–World War I readership, and modern readers will be less inclined to pass over the casual ethnic stereotyping, which, as in much popular fiction of the period, is never far beneath the surface. The cookie-cutter nature of the episodes is mitigated by Rohmer's prodigality of exotic detail and his expert creation of atmosphere. The pace is fast, the settings well realized, and the menaces inventive. Opulence hides behind the most drab facade, and unexpected danger and adventure lurk around each corner. The books have seldom been out of print since their initial publication, and new editions appear periodically in Britain and the United States.

From the beginning, the Fu Manchu stories inspired a steady stream of imitations (such as the 1930s pulp magazine characters Dr. Yen Sin and Wu Fang), pastiches, parodies, and collateral descendants. Probably the most famous of the latter is Ian Fleming's *Doctor No* (1958).

At the end of each of the first three series, Fu Manchu is apparently disposed of: trapped in a burning building in the first, shot by Kâramanèh in the second, and drowned at sea in the third. It is likely that the third death was intended to be permanent. Like Arthur Conan Doyle with Sherlock Holmes, Rohmer did not want to be monopolized by his most famous character. It would be thirteen years before the public would see another Fu Manchu story. (And in these intervening years, Fu Manchu lost the hyphen from his name.) In *Daughter of Fu Manchu* (*Collier's* magazine, 1930; Doubleday, Doran, 1931), Fu Manchu's daughter, Fah Lo Suee, is the center of attention as she attempts to take control of her father's organization. She stirs up so much trouble that at last Fu Manchu himself, old and lame, emerges from retirement to join forces with Nayland Smith in defeating her. But the renewed taste of power revives Fu Manchu's ambitions, and his war against the West continues in another nine books spread out over the remainder of Rohmer's lifetime, plus one posthumous volume. The settings range from the Near East (*Daughter* and *The Mask of Fu Manchu*, 1932) to the French Riviera (*Fu Manchu's Bride*, 1933), London (*The Trail of Fu Manchu*, 1934), Haiti (*The Island of Fu Manchu*, 1941), New York City (*The Shadow of Fu Manchu*, 1948), and eventually mainland China itself (*Emperor Fu Manchu*, 1959). All of these books were plotted and written as book-length narratives rather than as collections of separate episodes. And unlike the early Fu Manchu series, which were set in a perpetual 1912, the later books join the real world and deal at least peripherally with such events as the upheavals in Europe in the 1930s, political and religious demagoguery in the United States, and Communist rule in China. But behind the scenes there is always Fu Manchu, pulling the strings, amassing secret weapons, and augmenting his power.

The later Fu Manchu books vary widely in quality, from tired retreads such as *The Drums of Fu Manchu* (1939) and *Re-enter Fu Manchu* (1957) to the high points of *Fu Manchu's Bride* and *The Trail of Fu Manchu*. The latter book is particularly interesting. Fu Manchu is again operating in England, headquartered in a system of abandoned tunnels beneath the Thames, where he is carrying out a particularly devilish alchemical process for manufacturing gold. The central portion of the book, in which Nayland Smith, Fah Lo Suee, and the narrator, Alan Sterling, are held captive in the tunnels and threatened with an agonizing death, is a set piece of sustained action and suspense, with a literally explosive conclusion. And in the surprising climax of the book, Dr. Petrie returns and plays a part that will have fateful consequences for everyone concerned. Because so many characters and settings from earlier books reappear in *Trail*, the book has an almost nostalgic air. Whether Rohmer intended it or not, the book

serves as a summing-up of earlier adventures, clearing the way for new stories to follow. And it stands by itself as a fast-paced and ingenious thriller well worth attention.

Other Detective Characters

Nayland Smith is an agent and troubleshooter for the British government, but he does not usually function as a traditional detective. Rohmer did, however, create several detective characters. In *The Sins of Séverac Bablon* (1914) there is a reference to "the three great practical investigators of the world." The greatest of these, M. Victor Lemage of the Paris Surcté, appears in the latter half of the book, while a second investigator, Mr. Brinsley Munro of Chicago, is merely mentioned. The third of the trio, Paul Harley of Chancery Lane, undertakes some offstage investigations in the book but later plays a central role in a series of novels, short stories, and a stage play. However, predictably enough in view of Rohmer's interest in the occult, the first of his detectives to take center stage in a series of stories is a "psychic detective," Moris Klaw.

Klaw is the proprietor of a musty curio shop near Wapping Old Stairs on the Thames, where entering customers are greeted by a shrill cry of "Moris Klaw! Moris Klaw! The Devil's come for you!" from a resident parrot. Like all of Rohmer's detectives, Klaw is a master of disguise and mimicry, to the point where no two of his acquaintances can agree on his true identity or personality. He generally appears as "a very old man who carries his many years lightly, or a younger man prematurely aged; none can say which" (*The Dream Detective*, 1925 ed., p. 12). Sometimes on his own and other times accompanied by his daughter, Isis, Klaw investigates cases of real or apparent haunting and possession, as well as more mundane but equally mysterious thefts and murders in a series of stories published in *The New Magazine* in 1913, which were collected in book form in 1920 as *The Dream Detective*. The stories range from

"The Headless Mummies," an amusing account of a man who has an eminently practical motive for beheading mummies in a museum, to "The Veil of Isis," an eerie and effective fantasy in which Isis Klaw plays a major role.

The first of Rohmer's detectives to have a book of his own was M. Gaston Max, originally of the Paris Sureté, who is introduced in *The Yellow Claw* (1915). Max makes ample use of his skill at disguise in his pursuit of the mysterious Mr. King, the agent of the Sublime Order that is suspiciously like Fu Manchu's Si Fan. In Max's second case, *The Golden Scorpion* (1919), the villain is revealed to be an agent of Fu Manchu, who makes a brief anonymous appearance in the book. Max reappears in *The Day the World Ended* (1930), one of Rohmer's few books in which a science-fiction element is dominant.

The action takes place in and near Germany's Black Forest, where a reporter named Brian Woodville has been sent to investigate rumors of supernatural events—bodies of men and animals drained of blood and giant bat-like figures flying over the countryside at night. The center of the mystery is at the ruined castle of Felsenweir, whose crumbling walls are patrolled by seven-foot men in armor. At this point Gaston Max appears, removing the disguise behind which he has been hiding for several chapters, and explains that the weird goings-on are not supernatural but the work of a mad scientist, complete with Buck Rogers–style flying suits, a death ray, and plans for world domination. This dismissal of the supernatural does not entirely dispel the creepiness of the early portions of the book, whose entertaining extravagance retains its appeal. Max's final appearance in print was in *Seven Sins* (1943), in which he pursues Nazi spies in wartime London. Max is also the central character in a series of six radio plays broadcast by the British Broadcasting Corporation in 1942, written by Rohmer, his wife, and his friend and protégé, Cay Van Ash.

Paul Harley was the next of Rohmer's detective characters to make an appearance. He is a private investigator and former Secret Service agent, clearly intended to be a Great Detective in the tradition of Sherlock Holmes, with an admiring journalist friend, Malcolm Knox, filling the Dr. Watson role. Harley's office in Chancery Lane is decorated with Oriental artifacts and an engraved portrait of Edgar Allan Poe and supplied with secret exits and a fully equipped theatrical dressing room in which Harley assumes and discards his numerous disguises. He is selective in his choice of client ("I have intimated to that distressed nobleman . . . that a laundry is the proper place to take his dirty linen" [*Bat-Wing*, Doubleday ed., p. 5]), but any touch of the strange or abnormal is certain to arouse his interest. In all, Harley does his detective work in nine short stories, two novellas, two novels, and a stage play. He first appears in "The House of the Golden Joss," a 1920 *Collier's* story included in the collection *Tales of Chinatown* (1922). His best-known cases are recounted in the novels *Bat-Wing* and *Fire-Tongue* (both 1921). In both books, the framework is that of a traditional murder mystery, but the trappings are exotic.

In *Bat-Wing*, Harley and Knox have been invited to Cray's Folly, a manor house in the Surrey hills. There have been attempts on the life of the new owner, Colonel Menendez, and, as a threat or warning, the severed head of a bat has been nailed to the manor house door. Colonel Menendez spins a tale of an encounter with a voodoo cult in the West Indies and of the cult's presumed desire to avenge an injury done to its leader. But, as John Dickson Carr would later do in such novels as *He Who Whispers* (1946), Rohmer used this fantasy episode as a red herring; there are sources of antagonism much closer at hand. When murder finally strikes, Harley employs a clever device to demonstrate how the crime was committed, but there remain other clues to be unraveled before the murderer is revealed. The solution to the crime was undoubtedly more novel in 1921 than it seems today, when so many other authors have used it in the interim. (Some years later, *Bat-Wing* took on an independent existence with which Rohmer was not involved: volume 217 in the Sexton Blake Library, New Series, titled *The Black Skull* [1929], uses Rohmer's plotline, and extended passages read like extracts from his book, with only minor rephrasing and, of course, Sexton Blake instead of Paul Harley as the detective.)

In *Fire-Tongue*, the better of the two Harley novels, the detective is in pursuit of a sect of Indian fire worshipers who have come to England to exact vengeance on an explorer who violated their sanctum and witnessed their secret rites. The interpolated fantasy sequence here is the explorer's first-person story, which has much the same atmosphere as one of Talbot Mundy's adventure stories of India. The main crime, however, is the murder of a man at his own dinner table, in circumstances that seem to rule out anything except natural causes. Rohmer was, in fact, so successful at closing off all possibility of foul play that he found himself without any explanation of how the murder could have been committed. Under ordinary circumstances this would not have been a problem, but in this case the situation was more than awkward. Unknown to the author, his agent had shown early chapters to the editor of *Collier's*, who had purchased the novel and begun publication before the remainder had been written. There was no possibility of going back and changing the account that had already been given. In later interviews, and in his own published memoirs, Rohmer credited his friend Harry Houdini with showing him a way out of the difficulty and thereby salvaging the novel, which was completed in marathon sessions from a New York hotel room, with the typescript pages sometimes going by messenger directly to the printer. It would be two years before Rohmer attempted another novel, and never again would he allow publication of a work-in-progress.

In the interim, Rohmer's theatrical connections came to his financial rescue. In collaboration with Julian and Lauri Wylie, he wrote the book and lyrics for *Round in 50*, a musical revue based loosely on Jules Verne's *Around the World in Eighty Days*. The show was de-signed as a vehicle for Rohmer's old friend George Robey; a young Sophie Tucker joined the cast late in its run. The revue opened at the London Hippodrome in March 1922 and ran for 471 performances.

Buoyed by the success of *Round in 50*, Rohmer next tried his hand at a full-length stage melodrama called *The Eye of Siva*. This is a Fu Manchu story—the residents of a country manor are under siege by agents of a mysterious, all-powerful figure—in all respects except the names. The villain is a Mandarin Yen Sun Yen instead of Fu Manchu, and the detective is Paul Harley instead of Nayland Smith. The production involved elaborate stage settings and lighting effects, and the cast included a live leopard named Kali. Arthur Wontner, later noted for his film portrayal of Sherlock Holmes, took the part of Paul Harley. The play opened at the New Theatre in London in August 1923 and, in spite of lukewarm-to-poor reviews, ran for eighty-six performances. It also had a brief revival five years later.

A prose version of the play, with some of the names and mysterious devices altered, was published under the title "The Voice of Kali" in *Short Stories* (10 December 1923). Rohmer was not quite done with Paul Harley, but the detective's best days were now behind him. The few Harley stories that appeared in the 1930s generally lacked the inventiveness and atmosphere of the earlier works.

The only police officer to serve as a main character in Rohmer's works is Daniel "Red" Kerry, Chief Inspector (and later Superintendent) of the C.I.D., who appears in two short stories ("The Daughter of Huang Chow" and "Kerry's Kid," both included in *Tales of Chinatown*) and two novels, *Dope* (1919) and *Yellow Shadows* (1925). All of these are set in London's Limehouse district. "The Daughter of Huang Chow" attempts, with only partial success, to be a slice of Chinatown life in the manner of Thomas Burke's *Limehouse Nights* (1917). The novels, particularly *Dope*, deal with drug use among London society, with roots leading to Chinatown, and have such standard trappings as opium dens, dope smuggling, and white slavery.

Two other detectives appear in a series of short stories. The first of these is Bernard de Treville, who started out as an updated version of an earlier Rohmer protagonist, Captain Bernard O'Hagan, but quickly metamorphosed into an adventurer, Secret Service agent, and tracker-down of lost treasures. Sixteen de Treville stories appeared in the Sunday supplement magazine *This Week* from 1937 to 1945; a seventeenth story, actually a variant of an earlier entry in the series, was published posthumously in *Edgar Wallace Mystery Magazine* in 1966. The *Myself and Gaston Max* radio plays of 1942 were adaptations of de Treville stories, with Max substituted as the central character. The stories are smoothly written and sometimes cleverly plotted but suffer from a sameness of subject—many of them deal with the search for a stolen jewel or other valuable item hidden in an unusual place—which may explain why they were never collected in book form.

The last of Rohmer's roster of detectives to appear in a book was Major Mohammed Ibrahim Brian Barûk, an Anglo-Egyptian. The ten stories about Barûk, most of them from *Collier's*, were collected in 1944 as *Bimbâshi Barûk of Egypt*. They are equally divided between straightforward detective stories with an English setting and stories of espionage and international intrigue in the Near East.

Fantasy and Supernatural Stories

For many readers, the most enjoyable of Rohmer's stories are those in which the mysterious and exotic elements are intensified to become overtly fantastic or supernatural. The fantastic elements range from devil worship and unnatural medical experiments (the short stories "Tchériapin" and "The Master of Hollow Grange") to ghostly phenomena ("The Haunting of Low Fennel") to supernatural romance ("The Curse of a Thousand Kisses") to ancient Egyptian sorcery ("In the Valley of the Sorceress"). The earliest of Rohmer's novels of this type, widely regarded as one of his best, is *Brood of the Witch Queen* (1918), in which an Egyptian mummy is revived to practice ancient sorcery in the modern world. In *Grey Face* (1924), a supposed reincarnation of Cagliostro plays equal havoc. The central character in *The Green Eyes of Bâst* (1920), is eventually revealed to be a were-animal. And the fantasy aspects of *Bat Wing* and *Fire-Tongue* have already been mentioned.

In *The Day the World Ended* the fantastic element is super-science rather than the supernatural. The same is true of *The Bat Flies Low* (1935), in which an ancient Egyptian secret suspiciously like atomic power is unleashed in modern New York City. *The Island of Fu Manchu* features not only Haitian voodoo but an invisibility machine. Finally, in one of his later novels, *The Moon Is Red* (1954), Rohmer again raises the theme of unnatural biology in the solution of a series of seemingly impossible and very brutal murders.

The New York Years

During World War II, Rohmer's British book markets were drastically curtailed, and magazine markets virtually ceased to exist. After the war, his attempts to reestablish his place in these markets were largely unsuccessful, so the Rohmers transferred their base of operations to the New World. They lived for a time in a small apartment in New York City (in the same building as another author, Jean Stafford, who wrote amusingly about their acquaintance). Rohmer had brought with him the script for a stage play about Fu Manchu. When this failed to find a backer, he converted the script into the novel *Shadow of Fu Manchu*. He did the same with an unproduced play titled *The Body's Upstairs*, which he and Elizabeth had written in the late 1930s; this became the novel *Hangover House* (1949). A third novel based on an earlier play was more significant. This was *Wulfheim*, based on a "masque with music," that Rohmer had written for Max Reinhardt in the 1920s but that remained unproduced. The book mixed theosophy, demonology, and hints of incest into a somber, mystical novel set in a make-believe medieval landscape and was published in England in 1950 under the pseudonym Michael Furey. A U.S. edition did not appear until 1972.

In order to qualify for permanent-resident status, the Rohmers had to leave the country temporarily. They relocated to the island of Jamaica, which they had visited in the 1930s, returned briefly to New York City and then moved to Greenwich, Connecticut, before finally settling in White Plains, New York.

This Week continued to be a market for short stories, and with Fawcett Publications' establishment of the Gold Medal line of original paperback novels, a new market for book-length works opened up. Rohmer began a new Fu Manchu story but found that, although the Gold Medal editors wanted mystery thrillers of the Fu Manchu type, they were leery of so overtly ethnic a villain. The Fu Manchu story, a long novella rather than a novel, found a home in the Toronto *Star Weekly* while something else had to be devised for Gold Medal.

At Elizabeth's suggestion, Rohmer resurrected a character and plot idea from the episodic 1929 novel *The Emperor of America*. In that book, Commander Drake Roscoe of the U.S. Navy battles an organization known as the Zones, which is intent on subverting the U.S. government. At the end of the book, the mastermind of the Zones is revealed to be a woman. Twenty-one years later, Roscoe is brought back to combat a worldwide organization headed by a woman, the Marquise Sumuru. Although her name, acquired through marriage, is Japanese, Sumuru is of no stated nationality or ethnic background. Her organization has a decidedly feminist attitude ("Women were designed by their Creator to be not men's mistresses but their masters") but otherwise functions much like Fu Manchu's organization. The Sumuru series extended to five paperback novels published between 1950 and 1956. At the time, hardcover edi-

tions appeared only in England; not until the 1970s did a small press in New York City issue U.S. hardcover editions for the collector market. The books are adequate popular entertainment, but the old inventive spark is rarely in evidence.

The Gold Medal editors were now receptive to a revived Fu Manchu, and in 1957 *Re-Enter Fu Manchu* was published. A follow-up novel progressed slowly, due mainly to Rohmer's accumulating health problems. By the time the manuscript was finished in early 1959, an assortment of heart and lung ailments had been compounded by a serious case of the flu. Rohmer now had no thought but to return to England, which he and Elizabeth did in early May, shortly after publication of *Emperor Fu Manchu*. After three increasingly uncomfortable weeks in a service flat in London, Rohmer entered University College Hospital, where he died on 1 June 1959 from a combination of pneumonia and stroke.

Coda

Sax Rohmer's name is inextricably linked with that of his most famous character, Fu Manchu, who, like Sherlock Holmes and Tarzan, has become an icon of popular culture, recognized and referred to by people who may never have heard of the original stories or their author. For good or ill, the Fu Manchu series and the other Chinatown novels are the longest lasting of Rohmer's works and have seldom been out of print since their original publication. The first three books form a sequence of thirty episodes of fast-paced popular fiction—no introspection, no character development, just headlong action in a perpetually foggy and mysterious Edwardian London. *Fu Manchu's Bride*, *The Trail of Fu Manchu*, and *The Island of Fu Manchu* are the best of the later entries. For those interested in going beyond this series, the novels *Brood of the Witch Queen*, *The Green Eyes of Bâst*, *Fire Tongue*, *Grey Face*, *The Bat Flies Low*, *Wulfheim*, and *The Moon Is Red* are all worth sampling, as are the short-story collections *Tales of Secret Egypt* (1918) and *Tales of East and West* (1932).

Selected Bibliography

WORKS OF SAX ROHMER

NOVELS

The Mystery of Dr. Fu-Manchu. London: Methuen, 1913. U.S.: *The Insidious Dr. Fu-Manchu.* New York: McBride, Nast, 1913.

The Sins of Séverac Bablon. London: Cassell, 1914; New York: Bookfinger, 1967.

The Yellow Claw. New York: McBride, Nast, 1915; London: Methuen, 1915.

The Devil Doctor. London: Methuen, 1916. U.S.: *The Return of Dr. Fu-Manchu.* New York: McBride, 1916.

The Si-Fan Mysteries. London: Methuen, 1917. U.S.: *The Hand of Fu-Manchu.* New York: McBride, 1917.

Brood of the Witch Queen. London: C. Arthur Pearson, 1918; Garden City, N.Y.: Doubleday, Page, 1924.

The Orchard of Tears. London: Methuen, 1918; New York: Bookfinger, 1969.

The Quest of the Sacred Slipper. London: C. Arthur Pearson, 1919; Garden City, N.Y.: Doubleday, Page, 1919.

Dope. London: Cassell, 1919; New York: McBride, 1919.

The Golden Scorpion. London: Methuen, 1919; New York: McBride, 1920.

The Green Eyes of Bâst. London: Cassell, 1920; New York: McBride, 1920.

Bat-Wing. London: Cassell, 1921; Garden City, N.Y.: Doubleday, Page, 1921.

Fire-Tongue. London: Cassell, 1921; Garden City, N.Y.: Doubleday, Page, 1922.

Grey Face. London: Cassell, 1924; Garden City, N.Y.: Doubleday, Page, 1924.

Yellow Shadows. London: Cassell, 1925; Garden City, N.Y.: Doubleday, Page, 1926.

Moon of Madness. Garden City, N.Y.: Doubleday, Page, 1927; London: Cassell, 1927.

She Who Sleeps. Garden City, N.Y.: Doubleday, Doran, 1928; London: Cassell, 1928.

The Emperor of America. Garden City, N.Y.: The Crime Club, 1929; London: Cassell, 1929.

The Book of Fu-Manchu. London: Hurst & Blackett, 1929. An omnibus containing *The Mystery of Dr. Fu-Manchu, The Devil Doctor,* and *The Si-Fan Mysteries.*

The Book of Fu-Manchu. New York: McBride, 1929. An omnibus containing *The Insidious Dr. Fu-Manchu, The Return of Dr. Fu-Manchu, The Hand of Fu-Manchu,* and *The Golden Scorpion.*

The Day the World Ended. Garden City, N.Y.: The Crime Club, 1930; London: Cassell, 1930.

Daughter of Fu Manchu. Garden City, N.Y.: Doubleday, Doran, 1931; London: Cassell, 1931.

Yu'an Hee See Laughs. Garden City, N.Y.: The Crime Club, 1932; London: Cassell, 1932.

The Mask of Fu Manchu. Garden City, N.Y.: The Crime Club, 1932; London: Cassell, 1933.

Fu Manchu's Bride. Garden City, N.Y.: The Crime Club, 1933. U.K.: *The Bride of Fu Manchu.* London: Cassell, 1933.

The Trail of Fu Manchu. Garden City, N.Y.: The Crime Club, 1934; London: Cassell, 1934.

The Bat Flies Low. Garden City, N.Y.: The Crime Club, 1935; London: Cassell, 1935.

President Fu Manchu. Garden City, N.Y.: The Crime Club, 1936; London: Cassell, 1936.

White Velvet. Garden City, N.Y.: Doubleday, Doran, 1936; London: Cassell, 1936.

The Golden Scorpion Omnibus. New York: Grosset & Dunlap, 1938; contains *The Golden Scorpion* and *Dope.*

The Sax Rohmer Omnibus. New York: Grosset & Dunlap, 1938; contains *The Yellow Claw* and *Tales of Secret Egypt.*

The Drums of Fu Manchu. Garden City, N.Y.: The Crime Club, 1939; London: Cassell, 1939.

The Island of Fu Manchu. Garden City, N.Y.: The Crime Club, 1941; London: Cassell, 1941.

Seven Sins. New York: McBride, 1943; London: Cassell, 1944.

The Shadow of Fu Manchu. Garden City, N.Y.: The Crime Club, 1948; London: Herbert Jenkins, 1949.

Hangover House. New York: Random House, 1949; London: Herbert Jenkins, 1950.

Nude in Mink. New York: Fawcett, 1950. U.K.: *Sins of Sumuru.* London: Herbert Jenkins, 1950.

Wulfheim. By "Michael Furey." London: Jarrolds, 1950; New York: Bookfinger, 1972.

Sumuru. New York: Fawcett, 1951. U.K.: *Slaves of Sumuru.* London: Herbert Jenkins, 1952.

The Fire Goddess. New York: Fawcett, 1952. U.K.: *Virgin in Flames.* London: Herbert Jenkins, 1953.

The Moon Is Red. London: Herbert Jenkins, 1954; New York: Bookfinger, 1976.

Return of Sumuru. New York: Fawcett, 1954. U.K.: *Sand and Satin.* London: Herbert Jenkins, 1955.

Sinister Madonna. London: Herbert Jenkins, 1956; New York: Fawcett, 1956.

Re-enter Fu Manchu. Greenwich, Conn.: Fawcett, 1957. U.K.: *Re-Enter Dr. Fu Manchu.* London: Herbert Jenkins, 1957.

Emperor Fu Manchu. London: Herbert Jenkins, 1959; Greenwich, Conn.: Fawcett, 1959.

Sax Rohmer's Collected Novels. Secaucus, N.J.: Castle Books, 1983. Repr. as *Fu-Manchu: Four Classic Nov-*

els. Secaucus, N.J.: Citadel Press, 1983; contains *The Hand of Fu Manchu*, *The Return of Dr. Fu-Manchu*, *The Yellow Claw*, and *Dope*.

The Fu Manchu Omnibus, Volume 1. London: Allison & Busby, 1995; contains *The Mystery of Dr. Fu-Manchu*, *The Devil Doctor*, and *The Si-Fan Mysteries*.

The Fu Manchu Omnibus. Volume 2. London: Allison & Busby, 1997; contains *The Daughter of Fu Manchu*, *The Mask of Fu Manchu*, and *The Bride of Fu Manchu*.

The Fu Manchu Onmibus. Volume 3. London: Allison & Busby, 1998; contains *The Trail of Fu Manchu*, *President Fu Manchu*, and *Re-Enter Fu Manchu*.

COLLECTIONS OF SHORT FICTION

Pause! London: Greening & Co., 1910. Published anonymously. Prose sketches and essays by Rohmer, based on ideas by George Robey.

The Exploits of Captain O'Hagan. London: Jarrolds, 1916; New York: Bookfinger, 1968.

10.30 Folkestone Express. Lloyd's Home Novels, no. 41, ca. 1917–1920.

Tales of Secret Egypt. London: Methuen, 1918; New York: McBride, 1919.

The Dream Detective. London: Jarrolds, 1920; New York: Doubleday, Page, 1925.

The Haunting of Low Fennel. London: C. Arthur Pearson, 1920.

Tales of Chinatown. London: Cassell, 1922; Garden City, N.Y.: Doubleday, Page, 1922.

Tales of East and West. London: Cassell, 1932.

Tales of East and West. Garden City, N.Y.: The Crime Club, 1933.

Salute to Bazarada and Other Stories. London: Cassell, 1939; New York: Bookfinger, 1971.

Bimbâshi Barûk of Egypt. New York: McBride, 1944. Published as *Egyptian Nights: Some Account of the Investigations of Bimbâshi Barûk*. London: Robert Hale, 1944.

The Secret of Holm Peel and Other Strange Stories. New York: Ace Books, 1970.

The Wrath of Fu Manchu and Other Stories. With an introduction by Robert E. Briney. London: Tom Stacey, 1973; New York: DAW Books, 1976.

NONFICTION

Little Tich: A Book of Travels (and Wanderings). By "Little Tich." London: Greening & Co., 1911. An autobiography of the comedian Little Tich (Harry Relph), ghostwritten by Rohmer.

The Romance of Sorcery. London: Methuen, 1914; New York: Dutton, 1915.

WORKS FOR THE STAGE

Round in 50. Opened 16 March 1922. Book and lyrics by Sax Rohmer and Julian and Lauri Wylie.

The Eye of Siva. Opened 8 August 1923.

Secret Egypt. Opened 4 August 1928.

The Nightingale. Opened 15 July 1947. Book and lyrics by Sax Rohmer and Michael Martin-Harvey.

SELECTED SHORT STORIES

"The Mysterious Mummy." By A. Sarsfield Ward. *Pearson's Weekly*, Xmas 'Xtra issue (24 November 1903).

"The Leopard-Couch." By A. Sarsfield Ward. *Chambers's Journal*, 30 January 1904.

"Narky." *Yes & No*, ca. 1910–1914. *Ellery Queen's Mystery Magazine*, February 1953.

"The Secret of Holm Peel." By Sarsfield Ward. *Cassell's Magazine of Fiction*, December 1912.

"The Headless Mummies." *The New Magazine*, November 1913.

"The Veil of Isis." *The New Magazine*, January 1914.

"The Haunting of Low Fennel." *The Story-Teller*, November 1915.

"In the Valley of the Sorceress." *The Premier Magazine*, January 1916.

"The Master of Hollow Grange." *The New Magazine*, June 1918.

"The Curse of a Thousand Kisses." *The Premier Magazine*, November 1918.

"Tchériapin." *The Sovereign Magazine*, April 1920.

"The House of the Golden Joss." *Collier's*, 7 August 1920.

"The Daughter of Huang Chow." *Detective Story Magazine*, 31 December 1921.

"Kerry's Kid." *Detective Story Magazine*, 8 April 1922.

"The Voice of Kali." *Short Stories*, 10 December 1923.

ARTICLES AND MUSICAL MONOLOGUES

"The Occult East." *Occult Review*, May 1914.

"The Music of Magic." *Occult Review*, October 1917.

"The Unwrapped Mummy." *Lloyd's Magazine*, January 1918; with seven drawings by Sax Rohmer.

"The Pigtail of Li Fang Fu." London: Reynolds, 1919. Musical monologue.

"White Slave Girls of East End Chinatown." *World's Pictorial News*, 8 October 1920.

Orange Blossom—A Chinese Tale. London: Reynolds, 1921. Musical monologue.

"Satan." *Daily Express* (London), n.d. (1930).

"Astral Voyages." *Nash's Magazine*, September 1935.

"Meet Dr. Fu-Manchu." In *Meet the Detective*. Edited by Cecil Madden. New York: Telegraph Press, 1935. Transcript of a radio talk.

"Pipe Dreams: Popular Novelist's Own Story." *Empire News* (Manchester, U.K.), 30 January–17 April 1938. Twelve weekly installments of reminiscences.

"Live Instruments of Villainy." *Empire News* (Manchester, U.K.), 20 March 1938.

"Death of the Jade Bride." *American Weekly*, 7 September 1952.

"The Curse of a Hundred Kings." *American Weekly*, 29 August 1954.
"How Fu Manchu Was Born." *This Week*, 29 September 1957.

INTERVIEWS

"The Doctor's Blade." *New Yorker*, 29 November 1947.
Goodwin, Geraint. "The Birth of Dr. Fu Manchu." *Daily Sketch* (London), 24 May 1934.

BIBLIOGRAPHIES

Note: The most complete Sax Rohmer bibliography compiled to date is not in print form but on a World Wide Web site, The Page of Fu Manchu (*http://www.njin.net /~knapp/FuManchu.htm.*) The page is maintained by Dr. Lawrence Knapp of Essex County College in New Jersey. New information is added at frequent intervals.

Day, Bradford M. "Sax Rohmer Bibliography." In *Bibliography of Adventure: Mundy, Burroughs, Rohmer, Haggard*. Denver N.Y.: Science Fiction & Fantasy Publications, 1964, pp. 33–66; lists books (alphabetically by title), magazine stories (chronologically), stories and articles in newspapers, and includes sections titled "A Short Biography" and "The Films of Sax Rohmer."

Goode, Greg. "The Oriental in Crime Fiction and Film: A Bibliography of Secondary Sources." *Armchair Detective* 15, no. 3: 203–211 (1982).

BIOGRAPHICAL AND CRITICAL STUDIES

Bleiler, Everett F. *The Guide to Supernatural Fiction*. Kent, Ohio: Kent State University Press, 1983; "Rohmer, Sax" (pp. 434–437) is a thumbnail biography and contains reviews of eleven Rohmer books; "Furey, Michael" (pp. 197–198) is a long review of the pseudonymous book *Wulfheim*.

Briney, Robert E. "Sax Rohmer: An Informal Survey." In *The Mystery Writer's Art*. Edited by Francis M. Nevins Jr. Bowling Green, Ohio: Bowling Green University Popular Press, 1970. Pp. 42–78.

Chang, Sue F. "From Fu Manchu, Evil Genius, to James Lee Wong, Popular Hero: A Study of the Chinese-American in Popular Periodical Fiction from 1920 to 1940."*Journal of Popular Culture* 10, no. 3: 535–547 (winter 1976).

Colombo, John Robert. "Sax Rohmer and His Yellow Shadows." *Tamarack Review*, no. 17: 43–57 (autumn 1960).

Goode, Greg. "The Oriental in Mystery Fiction: Part I: The Sinister Oriental." *Armchair Detective* 15, no. 3: 196–202 (1982).

Lane, Andrew. "The Crimes of Fu Manchu." *Million*, May/June 1991: 40–44.

Lowndes, Robert A. W. "The Immortal Enemy." *Is*, April 1971. Repr. in *The Rohmer Review*, August 1971: 1–10.

Poupard, Dennis, ed. "Sax Rohmer, 1883–1959." In *Twentieth-Century Literary Criticism*, vol. 28. Detroit, Mich.: Gale, 1988. Pp. 274–302; reprints much of Robert E. Briney, "Sax Rohmer: An Informal Survey," pp. 279–286, plus Rohmer commentary by many other critics.

Stafford, Jean. "Truth in Fiction." *Library Journal* 91, no. 17: 4557–4559 (1966).

Van Ash, Cay, and Elizabeth Sax Rohmer. *Master of Villainy: A Biography of Sax Rohmer*. Edited, with foreword, notes, and bibliography, by Robert E. Briney. Bowling Green, Ohio: Bowling Green University Popular Press, 1972.

Weinstein, Jay. "Fu Manchu and the Third World." *Society*, January/February 1984: 77–82.

Wu, William F. "Fu Manchu and Charlie Chan." In *The Yellow Peril: Chinese Americans in American Fiction, 1850–1940*. Hamden, Conn.: Archon Books, 1982. Pp. 164–182.

DOROTHY L. SAYERS
(1893–1957)

ROBERT ALLEN PAPINCHAK

BORN ON 13 JUNE 1893, in Oxford, England, Dorothy Leigh Sayers was the only child of Reverend Henry Sayers and Helen Mary Leigh. She had a comfortable childhood, first in Oxford and then in Bluntisham-cum-Earith. Her mother, the daughter of a solicitor and niece of the *Punch* humorist Percival Leigh, favored the city life of Oxford. Her father, a graduate of Magdalen College, had been appointed headmaster of Christ Church School and then, in 1897, was offered a prime position in Bluntisham, a village of just nine hundred residents. There, at the rectory, which one visiting missionary thought was a "gentleman's house," the young Dorothy lived with her parents, her paternal grandmother, Aunt Mabel Leigh, a cook, a manservant, and three maids. Over the years, a nurse was replaced in turn by several governesses. A local gardener; his wife, who was the laundry maid; and their son, who served as a houseboy, complemented the household staff.

The intellectual energy that defined the whole of Sayers' life was evident early on. Her father's musical talents in voice and instruments (particularly the violin) and her mother's literary aptitudes easily transferred to their daughter. She kept a lifelong interest in the violin. Able to read by the time she left Oxford at the age of four, with home schooling she learned Latin from her father when she was six. Her healthy imagination and vibrant creative mind led her to write poetry and fashion plays, complete with self-made costumes, sets, and properties, in her early teens. When she was thirteen, her favorite writer was Alexandre Dumas. She read *The Three Musketeers* in French and took on the part of Athos in full costume, outfitted with walking stick, ear-to-ear mustache, waist-length tresses, and feathered hat. Reluctant to leave the nurturing shelter of life in Bluntisham rectory, Sayers nevertheless came to realize that she was destined for one of the newly formed colleges for women and would need further preparation beyond what her governesses, her parents, and frequent excursions to London could offer.

Sayers was accepted at the Godolphin School in Salisbury and began her studies there in January 1909. She carried with her a crush on the actor Lewis Waller, whom she had seen with her parents in London performing in *Henry V.* He had "the most delicious voice you ever heard, and the most wonderful and glorious eyes ever seen" (*Letters*, 1995 ed., p. 13).[1] When a troupe of French actors visited the school, Sayers' excitement with the theatrical productions continued. She planned a Molière festival, but a measles epidemic that spread through the school and led to a bout with double pneumonia may have prevented her from following through with

1. All page references from *The Letters of Dorothy L. Sayers* are from the 1995 edition.

805

the celebration. Despite other health set-backs, she found kindred spirits with theatrical interests, excelled at scholarship in several areas (voice, violin, piano, French, and German), and won three distinctions on the Oxford and Cambridge Joint Board Higher Certificate Examinations of 1909. By 1911, she finished at the top in all England in the Cambridge Higher Local Examination. In 1912, she won the Gilchrist Scholarship to Somerville College.

Oxford broadened Sayers' horizons still further. The four years (1912–1916) she spent there presented her with another series of firsts. Like her childhood academic training in Bluntisham and her formal education at Godolphin, her scholarly pursuits at Oxford brought her closer to the consummate destiny of being an accomplished writer. It put her in touch with the prototype of her amateur detective Lord Peter Wimsey, her first flirtatious episode, her first publication, a subsequent first proposal of marriage, and her first job.

It was during the July 1913 degree-granting ceremony, the Encaenia, that Sayers first spotted the man who served as the model for her future detective. Maurice Roy Ridley, who was resident at Balliol College and eventually graduated from Oxford, like Wimsey, won the Newdigate Prize, which was given to an undergraduate for poetry. Dorothy thought his poem, "Oxford," was "not frightfully full of genius, and was very academic in tone and form . . . but there was an appealing sort of youthfulness and pathos and Oxford feeling about it that made it quite charming" (*Letters*, p. 79). Sayers was also charmed by Ridley's name, which she found reminiscent of a "hero of a six-penny novelette" (*Letters*, p. 79). Twenty-two years later, while she was seeking an actor to play Wimsey in the theatrical production of *Busman's Honeymoon*, Sayers was at Oxford to deliver a lecture on "Aristotle and the Art of Detective Fiction" and was startled by Ridley's "height, voice, charm, smile, manner, outline of features, *everything*" (*Letters*, p. 345). She recognized Ridley as the "perfect Peter Wimsey" (*Letters*, p. 345) but failed to remember that she had

seen him many years earlier. Ridley was not Sayers' only affair of the heart at Oxford. Her interest in music brought her in contact with Dr. Hugh Percy Allen, the organist at New College and the conductor of the Oxford Bach Choir. He was more than twice her age. He was also married, but that did not prevent flirtations. Like other young women before her, Sayers was often invited into the New College organ loft. Apparently she also held interest for men closer to her age, exchanging poems with some and talking about music with others.

Despite these romantic interludes, Sayers never gave up her fiercely independent spirit. She was the founding force behind the Mutual Admiration Society, a group of friends bound by common intellectual interests. (Many years later, in London, she was an initial member of The Detection Club, a group of fellow mystery writers.) She vowed never to marry, at least not a man she didn't care for. This commitment was the result of a marriage proposal from a theologian, the Reverend Leonard Hodgson. Hodgson's attention came as the direct result of his admiration of Sayers' first publication, a limited edition of poetry, *Op. I* (1916). Basil Blackwell, son of the well-known bookseller, printed the poetry collection as part of a series he envisioned to give attention to young poets. By mid-1917, after a brief, unsuccessful stint teaching French in Hull, she returned to Oxford as an editorial apprentice at Blackwell's. Sayers rarely found herself content with the tedium of sameness. The teaching assignment had bored her because of the rote learning her students seemed to accept. Being "afraid of getting into a rut" (*Letters*, p. 312) dulled her senses. No longer surfeited by office work and finding Blackwell's focus shifting to textbooks rather than literary endeavors, she left after two years to seek adventure abroad.

One of the residents at Sayers' Oxford set of rooms was Captain Eric Whelpton. He was also a contributing member to her weekly literary and musical salon. When he accepted a teaching position at L'École des Roches in Normandy, Sayers followed him, ostensibly to be a secretary at the school. Although Whelpton disavowed any romantic interest in her, she appeared to have a strong attraction to him. Finally, when it was apparent that Whelpton preferred someone else, she conceded and returned to England in 1920. During this interlude, it seems as though Sayers' imaginative processes began to create the character of Lord Peter Wimsey and other secondary characters found in her future novels. Wimsey and his gentleman's gentleman, Mervyn Bunter, coalesced from a composite of several people she encountered at Oxford and L'École des Roches. An ex-cavalry officer, Charles Crichton, tells of a former footman and batman whose relationship with him bore a resemblance to Bunter's relationship with Wimsey during Wimsey's war years. Wimsey's sartorial elegance, his gourmet tastes in food and wine, and his ancestral home and heritage may be an amalgamation of the characteristics of Crichton, Whelpton, and Roy Ridley.

Until the autumn of 1920, women were eligible for the title to a degree at Oxford University but were not officially graduates. Sayers was one of the first women to receive both bachelor's and master's degrees. Despite the fact that she was never particularly fond of teaching, when she found herself back in London in need of a job, she took temporary positions at Clapham High School and then in West London at a high school for girls. At the same time, the first novel in which Lord Peter Wimsey appeared, *Whose Body?* (1923), began to take shape. Professionally, Sayers then moved on to an advertising agency. In May 1922, she took a job on a trial basis as copywriter (for four pounds a week) with S. H. Benson. One month later, not knowing if she would "make anything of this business" (*Letters*, p. 191), she was employed permanently and stayed on for nine years. Her work there became a major source for the setting and plot of her ninth mystery novel, *Murder Must Advertise* (1933).

During this period (1921–1924), Sayers' personal life was also evolving. Two men— John Cournos and Bill White—left indelible marks. In the midst of her affair with the Russian émigré novelist Cournos, Sayers wrote to her parents that she did not know from one minute to the next if she was in "high spirits or the depth of gloom" (*Letters*, p. 177). While this might have been a comment on her lack of a job, it also acutely summarized the passionate intensity of her relationship with Cournos. Cournos was a freethinker who wanted a sexual involvement but no long-term commitment with a mystery novelist. He insisted on using contraceptives, which was opposed to Sayers' personal and religious credos. She wanted children and she wanted to be married to Cournos. The affair ended with ironic overtones. Cournos subsequently married American mystery writer Helen Kestner Sattenthwaite, aka Sybil Norton; Sayers had a child with a man she did not marry. Each achieved artistic vengeance in respective novels—Sayers with the character of Philip Boyes in *Strong Poison* (1930), Cournos in *The Devil is an English Gentleman* (1932).

Within two months after Cournos left England, Sayers met the man who became the father of her only child. Bill White, a motorcyclist and car salesman, was the exact counterpoint to Cournos. His intellect, Sayers wrote, wasn't "exactly his strong point" (*Letters*, p. 198). An unplanned pregnancy resulted from their affair. She kept the pregnancy a secret from friends, coworkers, and most of her family, including her parents. Her one confidante was her favorite cousin, Ivy Shrimpton. Ivy and her mother accepted foster children into their home near Oxford. It was there that Sayers took her son, John Anthony White, born on 3 January 1924. She did not abandon John Anthony. While Ivy was the caretaker of the child, Sayers supplied more than sufficient funds and contributed suggestions for his upbringing. She expressed continual concern for his health and intellectual well-being. In another curious irony, John Anthony eventually entered Oxford in Lord Peter Wimsey's college, Balliol, and his tutor was Roy Ridley, Lord Peter's physical model, whom his mother had met thirty-two years previously.

A little more than two years after John was born, Sayers married Atherton Fleming on 13 April 1926. He was twelve years her senior, divorced, and had two children. The Scot called "Mac" appeared to be a perfect match for her. He was a travel journalist for the *News of the World*, he exhibited interest in such popular entertainment as film and the theater, and he was an accomplished cook who later published a well-received *Gourmet's Book of Food and Drink*. Sayers continued working at Benson's; published *Clouds of Witness* (1926), *Unnatural Death* (1927), *The Unpleasantness at the Bellona Club* (1928), and *Lord Peter Views the Body* (1928) (a collection of short stories); and edited and wrote an important history of detective fiction in her introduction to the first volume of *Great Short Stories of Detection, Mystery, and Horror* (1928–1934; published in the United States as *The Omnibus of Crime*). Fleming and Sayers had future plans to adopt John Anthony as a couple, although they never did so. What Sayers later wanted for her alter ego, the mystery writer character Harriet Vane, she seemed to have found for herself, an equal partnership between like minds.

Two years after her marriage, illness and death tempered Sayers' life. Her father died of pneumonia in September 1928, and ten months later, in July 1929, her mother died. Like Wimsey, Fleming continually suffered from ill health, an after-effect of war. He and Sayers often spent vacations in accommodating climates like those of Cornwall or Kirkcudbright, Scotland (the site of *The Five Red Herrings*, 1931). With the death of her parents, Sayers' life changed again. The home in Witham that had been bought for her mother to live in after she left the rectory at Christchurch became the couple's new residence. More important, Sayers received a contract from an American publisher that guaranteed an income without having to wait for advance payments and royalties. This arrangement freed Sayers from her job at Benson's and gave her full time to devote to writing. In the next decade, she published eight novels that featured Lord Peter Wimsey; one significant non-Wimsey novel, *The Documents in the Case* (1930); and two more collections of short stories that included Wimsey and introduced another amateur detective, Montague Egg (*Hangman's Holiday*, 1933; *In the Teeth of the Evidence*, 1939).

In 1935, Sayers thought she was writing the last Wimsey novel, *Gaudy Night*. But the creative urges that were constantly searching for new challenges started to take her in a new direction with familiar parameters. While telling her lifelong friend Muriel St. Clare Byrne about the antics of a chimney sweep who had come to clean the Witham chimneys, Sayers developed the idea that he would be an entertaining stage character. Muriel agreed. Together they wrote and produced *Busman's Honeymoon*, the play that became the predecessor for the final Wimsey novel. Sayers' early love of the theater had returned. It was a short step from secular comedy to religious drama. Organizers of the Canterbury Festival (one of the best-known productions was T. S. Eliot's *Murder in the Cathedral*) invited Sayers to write a play. The result was *The Zeal of Thy House* (1937), based on an incident that had occurred during the burning and rebuilding of the choir at Canterbury at the end of the twelfth century.

The success of the play gave Sayers new vision. She abandoned Wimsey and devoted a large part of her writing life to theologically based endeavors. A radio nativity play for BBC Children's Programs led to a cycle of twelve plays broadcast monthly, published as *The Man Born to Be King* (1943). With a strong Christian faith and a belief in the triune structure of the Incarnation, Sayers proselytized for creativity based on her concept of a triumvirate of idea, energy, and power. She examined the premise fully in *The Mind of the Maker* (1941).

Having written all the mysteries she thought she would write, having achieved popular and critical success as a playwright and radio dramatist, and determined to stop writing and lecturing about religious subjects, at the age of fifty, Sayers sought another new venture. The last fourteen years of her life were taken up with an incomplete project, a new translation of Dante's *Divine Comedy.* During that period, she saw her son complete his education at Oxford. Fleming's ill health continued until he died of a cerebral hemorrhage in June 1950. Sayers was able to complete the first two books of Dante and was two thirds into the third volume, *Paradiso,* when she suddenly died from heart failure on 17 December 1957.

The Mystery Novels—The How of Whodunit

Dorothy L. Sayers' primary legacy to the world of detective fiction is the creation of Lord Peter Wimsey. He first appears as a secondary character in an unpublished short story, becoming involved in a cipher case after he loans his Piccadilly flat to a French politician. In a letter to her mother dated 21 January 1921, Sayers mentions an idea that became the impetus for the first novel, *Whose Body?,* in which Wimsey is the major character. The idea is to write a detective story that "begins brightly, with a fat lady found dead in her bath with nothing on but her pince-nez" (*Letters,* p. 174). What proceeds from these two instances is one of the most classic and memorable characters in the genre of mystery writing. In the handwritten manuscript "The Craft of Detective Fiction," Sayers lists six criteria for the basic detective hero. The detective must have a situation that provides him access to police, must be available at any time, must have wide-ranging knowledge, must be physically fit, must have an equal amount of leisure time and money, must have a character rich for development and not be too old, so that he can be developed gradually in a series of books. Wimsey fulfills these criteria. He has the advantages—money, contacts, free time—that his social status brings him. He is learned and adept at martial arts, and he carries emotional and physical wounds that begin to heal as he grows older.

In *Whose Body?,* Wimsey's first challenge is to solve the puzzle of the body in the bath. Returning to 110 Piccadilly Street to retrieve a sales catalogue of rare books, Lord Peter receives a call from his mother, the Dowager Duchess of Denver. A friend in Battersea, respected architect Alfred Thipps, has found a corpse. The lady Sayers envisioned in the letter to her mother has transmuted into a "tall, stout man of about fifty" (p. 21) wearing a pair of gold pince-nez. The body bears evidence of flea bites, smells of carbolic soap, and has tobacco-stained teeth. At the same time one body appears, another body disappears. This becomes an important clue for Wimsey. Lord Peter's professional companion in crime is Charles Parker (in later novels, Wimsey's brother-in-law). Parker visits Lord Peter's library, "one of the most delightful bachelor rooms in London [furnished in] black and primrose" (p. 26). Evidence of Wimsey's wealth and intellectual pursuits exists in the editions of rare books, a baby grand piano on which Wimsey plays Scarlatti sonatas, and Sèvres vases on the mantle. Parker brings news from Scotland Yard of the sudden disappearance of prominent financier, Sir Reuben Levy. Wimsey's nemesis at the Yard, the inept Inspector Sugg, is certain that the body in the bath is Levy.

To solve the case, Sayers introduces one of the key factors she utilizes in all of her mystery novels: the answer to how the murder was done. In the final Wimsey novel, *Busman's Honeymoon* (1937), Lord Peter enunciates his prime criteria, " 'Once you've got the How, the Why drives it home' " (p. 237). With the how and the why, the who easily reveals itself. The coroner's inquest in *Whose Body?* determines death by foul play as a result of a blow to the spine, but there is insufficient evidence to show how the blow was inflicted. It is left to Lord Peter to unscramble the mystery of the identity of the corpse and the disappearance of Sir Reuben. The novel finally turns on an identity plot with switched bodies, the specialized skills of a murderer who is a "cool and cunning fellow" (*Letters,* p. 174), and a familiar motive. The renowned neurologist Sir Julian Freke maintains a surgical practice for scientific experiments nearby Thipps's Battersea house. In fact, St. Luke's Hospital connects by a covered way to Freke's residence in a parallel line of houses in the back gardens. A woman Freke courted and expected to marry rejected him and eloped with Levy.

A macabre denouement puts Lord Peter's life in danger and leads to a Grand Guignol exhumation in a "raw fog" with "Dantesque shapes with pitchforks loom[ing] up" (p. 223). The last chapter of the novel provides the "how" with Freke's written confession, which supports Wimsey's sleuthing. In revenge for his lost love, Freke bludgeoned Levy to death, buried him, and then, annoyed at Thipps's "silly chatter about vivisection" (p. 248) and cursory dismissal of Freke's expertise, placed an unknown vagrant who bore a strong resemblance to Levy in Thipps's tub.

In addition to introducing Lord Peter Wimsey, this brief first novel established Sayers' ability to sustain suspense through ingenious plot devices. It also demonstrated her talent for creating compelling secondary figures. Several of the characters introduced in *Whose Body?* appear in future novels, chief among them, his manservant, Bunter; Parker; and the Dowager Duchess. Bunter's forensic skills include photographing the scene of the crime, lifting fingerprints, and chasing down clues. Parker gives Wimsey access to professional information and guidance. Lord Peter's mother provides maternal and moral support of Wimsey's undertakings.

Sayers' boldness as a mystery writer embarked on a crime series with an engaging protagonist is underscored by the second Lord Peter novel, *Clouds of Witness*. With Wimsey's basic character traits and intuitive and imaginative ratiocinative skills already established, Sayers made a courageous choice for the next book. The accused is a member of Lord Peter's family, his older brother, Gerald. The crime also involves his younger sister, Lady Mary Wimsey. Before it is resolved, the investigation reaches into the highest level of the House of Lords, where the trial is conducted. From its inception, Sayers saw the

new book as "much more complicated" (*Letters*, p. 201). She had to develop Lord Peter's character more fully, making him a "complete human being, with a past and a future, with a consistent family and social history, with a complicated psychology" ("Gaudy Night," p. 211). An attack on a member of Wimsey's family would be an attack on the center of his being. Although his mother supported his amateur detective work, his brother did not, finding Wimsey's involvement with other classes to be beneath his own class distinction. Gerald's disdain of Lord Peter's hobby would hinder elements of the plot during the investigative procedure.

Clouds of Witness begins one year after the events of *Whose Body?*. In the fall of 1920, Lord Peter, thirty-three years old, returns from a holiday in Corsica with a stopover in Paris. Bunter gives him a newspaper, which reports that his brother has been accused of shooting a "Byronic blighter" (p. 109), Denis Cathcart, Lady Mary's fiancé. Gerald has no apparent alibi for the time of the murder. To further complicate matters, Mary is implicated in the plot when she claims she heard shots at that hour. But a doctor testifies that the body had been dead well before that time. One further detail is significant. Gerald says that he received a letter from a friend, Tom Freeborn, claiming that Cathcart was a card cheat. Gerald confronted Denis to demand he end his involvement with Mary. Cathcart avers that he has already broken the engagement. But the letter cannot be found to support Gerald's testimony. This raises the unthinkable possibility of hanging an English peer for murder based only on circumstantial evidence.

When Lord Peter returns to the hunting lodge at Riddlesdale, he must unravel the mystery in order to clear his family's name. Sifting through clues with the help of Parker, Wimsey discovers the footprint of a size ten boot and a diamond cat charm with bright emerald eyes. Sayers' humorous comments about detective fiction in which "criminals . . . strew their tracks with little articles of personal adornment . . . for the benefit of the author" (p. 60) do not deter her from planting a series of additional artifacts (the belt of a Burberry is added to the pile of information) for Parker and Wimsey to follow along the trail to the solution of the crime.

Clouds of Witness is often considered one of the least satisfactory of Sayers' novels because the solution to the shooting (proved to be a suicide) depends on several coincidences and a melodramatic conclusion. Lord Peter locates the missing letter in a window as he tries to keep a sash from rattling. On an independent trip to Paris, Parker uncovers the source of the jeweled pin and its relationship to Cathcart's gambling and love life. And Lord Peter must take a dangerous eleventh-hour flight across the Atlantic and back in order to arrive at Gerald's trial in time to save him. If the novel appears to be structurally weak because of these matters, it does, nevertheless, contribute other factors to the Lord Peter Wimsey canon. Sayers develops her primary character by providing additional personal information about him. By choosing her protagonist's family as the target of investigation, Sayers ensures Wimsey's vested interest in the outcome of the case. He continues to suffer from the effects of the wounds he received in World War I. Nightmares haunt him. He is also haunted by the rejection of a love interest that was noted in *Whose Body?*, mentioned here and clarified by the end of the novel. The specific details of a trial in the House of Lords are as "unique in a detective story" (*Letters*, p. 223) as Sayers thought they would be, complete with three hundred British peers in scarlet robes and ermine and the need for a special Lord High Steward to conduct the inquiry.

The plot device of the next two novels—*Unnatural Death* (originally published in the United States as *The Dawson Pedigree*) and *The Unpleasantness at the Bellona Club*—revolves around subjects familiar to mystery novels: the administration of poison, the efficacy of last wills and testaments, and the crucial order of deaths. In her continued effort not to repeat herself from novel to novel, being sure that "each book . . . [has] a slightly different idea behind it" (*Letters*, p. 312),

Sayers invests these common elements with ingenious variations.

The bodies pile up in *Unnatural Deaths.* Sayers compounds the dilemma for her "noble sleuth" (as defined in the fictitious "Biographical Note" by Lord Peter's pretentious French cousin, Paul Austin Delagardie, which precedes the novel) by presenting him with three murders. Agatha Dawson is an ailing 72-year-old cancer patient cared for by her surviving grandniece, Mary Whittaker, when she dies. Bertha Gotobed, a former Dawson household maid, is found dead from unknown circumstances in a nearby forest. And Vera Findlater, one of Mary's constant companions, is bludgeoned to death. Early in the novel, knowing that Mary Whittaker is set to inherit from her aunt, Wimsey is certain that she is the murderer. In fact, he bets Parker "fifty to one that I bring it home to her within the year" (p. 64). What Wimsey is not certain of is how Mary killed Agatha Dawson. Apart from the prescribed morphine injection, an autopsy found nothing suspicious. Given the patient's ill health, the death is determined to be by natural causes.

Wimsey's suspicions are aroused, and he calls in one of Sayers' most endearing secondary characters, Alexandra Katherine Climpson. Miss Climpson is one of a group of women rendered redundant after the war. To Lord Peter, she is his "ears and tongue . . . and especially [his] nose" (p. 42). Along with other women in similar situations employed in his Cattery, ostensibly a typing service staff, she helps ferret out information, sometimes by less than legal means. Climpson makes several appearances in subsequent novels. In *Unnatural Death,* she is instrumental in finding pertinent information about the crime against Agatha Dawson. The key factor in Agatha Dawson's death is that she died intestate in November 1925, under an old property law. This means that Mary Whittaker, as the grandniece, was the legal heir. In January 1926, however, England endorsed the New Property Act. In that case, the inheritance would have gone to the Crown. If Wimsey can prove how Agatha's death was hastened in order to avoid the new law, then he would have a method to support his motive.

The remarkable solution Sayers provides to Lord Peter's dilemma is one of her most original ones. In fact, she draws the specifics of the method of murder from information she could have learned when she was involved with Bill White, John Anthony's father. Bill was an aficionado of motorcycles, and he may have given Sayers an understanding of an air lock in the gas feed. In *Unnatural Death,* Lord Peter and Parker encounter a young man with a problem with his motorbike. What appears to be an unimportant incident at the "Cross-Roads" becomes a central piece of foreshadowing that reveals the means of murder. Wimsey learns that Mary had formerly been a nurse. In her "greedy and heartless" manner, being as reprehensible as Sir Julian Freke in *Whose Body?,* Mary Whittaker had injected an air bubble into her aunt's main artery, creating an untraceable embolism. Bertha and Vera were murdered because they could incriminate Mary. Although she is finally arrested for an attack on Miss Climpson, Mary escapes legal punishment by hanging herself. In a final irony, the inheritance is divided between a formerly unknown cousin, and, if the New Property Act permits, a Whittaker next of kin.

Sayers' adept cleverness with plots continues in the next novel, which depends on poison, wills, and succession. The body in the library that causes *The Unpleasantness at the Bellona Club* belongs to the aged General Fentiman. His habit is to visit the club every morning at ten, read his newspaper, and stay in his favorite chair until evening. This time, on Armistice Day, Lord Peter encounters the weary, war-damaged Captain George Fentiman, the General's grandson, who views the club as a morgue. His perceptions seem accurate when he and Wimsey discover that the General is dead in his chair. Dr. Penberthy, a member of the club and an attending physician, declares that the General appears to have died in his sleep of natural causes. But there is something curious about the effects of rigor mortis—his left leg swings loose at the knee. At the same time, Wimsey learns that the General's sister, Lady Felicity Dormer, twelve years younger than he, has died, supposedly at half past ten.

Ten days later, the Fentiman family attorney, Murbles, presents Lord Peter with a conundrum. He needs to know who died first. Lady Dormer's fortune came from her husband's button business. According to her will, if her brother survived her, he was to receive the fortune. Twelve thousand pounds was left to a distant relative who lived with her as a ward and caregiver, Ann Dorland. Conditions were reversed, however, if General Fentiman predeceased Lady Dormer. Ann Dorland would receive the major portion of the estate and fifteen thousand pounds would be divided equally between Captain Fentiman and his older brother, Major Robert Fentiman. The sizable differences in the inheritances and the possible heirs prove to be enough incentive for Murbles to implore Wimsey to investigate the likelihood of murder.

Wimsey again draws on the aid of Parker. Their contrasting methods are defined. Parker is "cautious, solid, painstaking, his mind a blank to art and literature and exercising itself, in spare moments, with Evangelical theology, while Wimsey is "quick, impulsive, careless and an artistic Jack-of-all-trades" (p. 75). As partners, they balance each other out. Together, they collect the evidentiary clues to solve the case. The solution points to the curious circumstance of an out-of-order phone booth, the Armistice day tradition of two minutes of silence, and another incidence of false love. When Murbles, Parker, and Lord Peter uncover evidence that Major Robert Fentiman removed his grandfather's body from the phone booth during the two minutes of silence, the crime appears to be solved. An autopsy conducted after the exhumation, however, reveals that the General had swallowed a powerful dose of digitalin shortly before death. Now the finger points again to another possible primary heir, Ann Dorland, whose apartment reveals to Parker a supposedly inveterate interest in crime stories and chemical poisons.

When Wimsey attends a lecture by Dr. Penberthy, his ratiocinative skills come into play. He learns that Penberthy's experiments with sheep glands are meant to rejuvenate elderly patients. General Fentiman was supposed to be "another of Penberthy's miracles" (p. 4). Penberthy had romanced Ann with the assumption that she would receive Lady Dormer's money and he could use it to set up his clinic. Lord Peter deduces that Penberthy administered the deadly dose of digitalin. When he confronts Penberthy at the Bellona Club library at the conclusion of the novel, he offers Penberthy an honorable way out. Penberthy, like some of the criminals before him in Sayers' earlier novels, never goes to trial. Wimsey's habitual dislike for bringing criminals to justice established in *Whose Body?* prevails. His challenge is outwitting the criminal and solving the crime.

In 1930, Sayers published two novels. Before she moved on to the pivotal novel, *Strong Poison*, which introduced Harriet Vane to Lord Peter Wimsey and into the canon, she made an important departure in her next novel, *The Documents in the Case*. She collaborated with Dr. Eustace Barton, who wrote medical mysteries under the pseudonym Robert Eustace. She admired one of his short stories and suggested that they create a new detective who knew more about science than did Lord Peter. Although the novel carries a joint authorship, it is generally understood that Sayers created the characters, plot, and structure of the book and Barton contributed the medical information. Together, they produced a novel successful in discovering another original method of murder.

The method of composition of the novel and the choice of its final structure were also something new for Sayers. Having settled on a means for murder that involved symmetric and asymmetric molecules, Sayers needed characters, a plot, and a structure that could carry the scientific information. She settled on an epistolary form that she admired in the work of Wilkie Collins, particularly *The Moonstone*, which she deemed "the very finest detective story ever written" (*Great Short Stories of Detection, Mystery and Horror*, p. 25) and which she wanted to emulate. The series of first-person narratives in the letters help the plot unfold through multiple points of view, rather like a Rashomon enterprise, allowing for unreliable narrators as personalities are revealed to a number of different correspondents.

An introductory letter from Paul Harrison to Sir Gilbert Pugh, the Director of Public Prosecutions, registers concerns about the suspicious nature of the death of his father, George Harrison, head of the accounts department of electrical engineers. Paul is certain that the fifty-two documents he has collected six or seven months after his father's death question whether it was an accident, suicide, or murder. The basic story appears to be a simple one of domestic unrest. Fifty-two-year-old George Harrison and his second wife, Margaret, twenty years his junior, invite two male tenants to live above them. John Munting is a thirtyish "sallow [and] bilious-looking" (p. 20) poet; Harwood Lathom is a tall, dark, and thin painter in his mid-twenties. Together they represent the artistic side of the art/science continuum in the novel. Munting's fiancée, Elizabeth Bungie, is a novelist who supports the views of the modern woman. When Agatha Milsom, a maid for the Harrisons, writes to her sister, she sees an issue in the household dealing with the "virtues of the old-fashioned domestic woman and the perpetual chatter of the modern woman" (p. 15). She is sure that all men are self-centered and George Harrison is no different. Agatha observes what she thinks is neglect and abuse in the Harrison household. Munting, on the other hand, in a letter to Elizabeth, characterizes Margaret as a "suburban vamp . . . entirely wrapped up . . . in her own attractions" (p. 21). Lathom is more than sympathetic to Margaret.

Whoever has the more accurate perception of the Harrisons, the mood of the manor escalates to the point of George Harrison's painful death. It appears as though he died from eating poisonous mushrooms. Harrison's son is sure that his stepmother had something to do with the demise. The documents accumulate until the truth is resolved. In the process, Sayers introduces a discussion of the essential origin of life and death that is crucial to the complicated denouement. She and Eustace had worked out a plot dependent on the distinction between organic and inorganic matter. Munting attends a theological discussion that leads him to the conclusion that the murderer was "tripped up by a miserable asymmetric molecule" (p. 220). The devastating evidence is provided by a polariscope, a scientific instrument that looks like a small telescope vertically attached to a stand, which discriminates between organic and inorganic material. More particularly, the polariscopic examination reveals synthetic muscarine, the poison that killed George Harrison. Munting also knows that the murderer, Lathom, committed the crime at the instigation of Margaret Harrison, with whom he was conducting an adulterous affair.

Even though she was excited by the collaborative effort, it was a writing experiment she was not to repeat in the novel form. Later in 1930, she moved back to the Wimsey saga, introducing a new character who would turn the events of the canon toward an entirely new direction. From the outset of her mystery writing career, Sayers had established one clear objective for herself. Dissatisfied with the general level of detective fiction, she wanted her first Wimsey book to be "something 'less like a conventional detective story and more like a novel' " ("Gaudy Night," p. 208). Her ambition was to move crime fiction away from the novel of adventure and link it "more closely to the novel of manners" (*Great Short Stories*, p. 43). She thought *Whose Body?* "conventional to the last degree" ("Gaudy Night," p. 208) and saw *The Documents in the Case* well-received by readers and critics, as closer to her mark because of its "serious 'criticism of life' " ("Gaudy Night," p. 209). But it was *Strong Poison* that set her on a direct course toward achieving her goal.

Strong Poison created a double dilemma— for Lord Peter and for his creator. Sayers began

the novel "with the infanticidal intention of doing away with Peter" ("Gaudy Night," p. 210). This was to be Wimsey's last appearance in a novel. To ensure his demise, she was also going to marry him off. Her conviction was that "a detective married is a detective marred" (handwritten manuscript "How I Came to Invent the Character of Lord Peter," p. 2). Therefore, when he meets Harriet Vane and her smile turns his heart to water, both Lord Peter and Sayers have to make some decisions. Two pages after Wimsey meets Harriet, he proposes marriage to her. Sayers' choice was more complicated. First, her readers would not accept Wimsey's demise. More important, Sayers recognized that she "could find no words in which [Harriet] could accept [Peter] without loss of self-respect" ("Gaudy Night," p. 211). It would take several more novels before that could happen.

As with choosing Lord Peter's brother as the accused in *Clouds of Witness*, Sayers made another venturesome choice by making the future Lady Wimsey the accused in *Strong Poison*. Lord Peter is in the courtroom as a favor to Parker when he hears the judge's summing up of the charges against Harriet. She allegedly poisoned the thirty-six-year-old novelist Philip Boyes with arsenic. Harriet, a twenty-nine-year-old mystery writer, had been living with Philip for almost a year. They quarreled after he proposed, and she turned him down because she felt coerced into having to make a decision to adjust to his principles against her own. Harriet's independent nature, which is to be the sticking point in her relationship with Peter, is readily established. Her claim to innocence is that she had bought the arsenic and various other poisons to prove in one of her novels how easy it was to purchase them. The result of the trial is a hung jury. One of the three members of the jury to agree with Harriet's innocence is Miss Climpson. When a new trial is declared, Lord Peter, also convinced that Harriet is not guilty, has one month to prove his case.

At first he thinks that Boyes committed suicide. Then, based on evidence that Miss Climpson helps acquire, he realizes that an inheritance is the motive for the murder. Boyes has been left more than fifty thousand pounds. He dies three days after having dinner with his cousin, Norman Urquhart. Urquhart is the trustee for the estate of Boyes's great-aunt, Mrs. Rosana Wrayburn, an ailing nonagenarian who was once a successful actress, Cremorna Garden. Wimsey concludes that Urquhart, next in line to receive the inheritance, murdered Boyes. During the month left to him, he has to learn, as he had in the earlier novels, how Urquhart did it. Sayers' solution is another ingenious one. Urquhart and Boyes ate the same food during the dinner at which Boyes was supposedly poisoned. Having done research on arsenic poisoning, Sayers determines that Urquhart could have been building a tolerance to the poison by taking small doses over a period of time. When Wimsey researches the source and condition of the eggs used in the omelette, he finds the answer to vindicating Harriet.

As Wimsey is in the process of clearing Harriet's name, Sayers begins the process of establishing Harriet's identity for future novels. She makes few actual appearances in the novel. Her traits are defined by others. Collectively, she is characterized as intelligent, imaginative, high-spirited, of an independent nature. When she does appear, her exchanges with Lord Peter make her his perfect match. During his second visit with her in Holloway Prison, despite her dire situation, she manages to create a mock novel with him. Their equal wits are displayed in rapid repartee. At a Christmas dinner at Duke's Denver, Wimsey rises to defend Harriet when his imperious sister-in-law, Helen, defames her occupation and her character. He says that the detective stories she writes are "the purest literature we have" (p. 127). As for Harriet's character, in detective stories, "virtue is always triumphant" (p. 127). By the end of the novel, he vows his persistent pursuit of her toward the final prospect of marriage.

The Five Red Herrings (also published in the United States as *Suspicious Characters*) was an interlude for Sayers. Harriet Vane was established in the Wimsey canon, but Sayers was not completely satisfied with the couple. She had "landed [her] two chief puppets in a situation where, according to all the conventional rules of detective fiction, they should have had nothing to do but fall into one another's arms; but they would not do it, and for a very good reason. When [she] looked at the situation [she] saw that it was in every respect false and degrading" ("Gaudy Night," p. 211). She would have to abandon their story and come back to them in a later novel. Instead, she had Wimsey take a vacation to Scotland. In some ways, the book was a gift to Fleming. It was set in Gatehouse and Kirkcudbright, with "real places" and "real trains" (Foreword), in a landscape familiar to Sayers. She and Fleming, with his interests in fishing and painting, often vacationed in the villages.

The novel is a return to "pure puzzle" fiction, at which Sayers wanted to try her hand (*Letters*, p. 311). The experiment is not completely successful. Since the book turns on various characters' stories being repeated, the narrative often becomes tedious and repetitious. Sayers also built a gimmick into the novel—she leaves out an important clue, which would reveal the identity of the murderer early in the book. In place of the information, she leaves a blank page, expecting the clever reader to deduce the nature of the missing piece of evidence. The rest of the novel depends on Wimsey to reconstruct the crime until the murderer is arrested and confesses.

The opening sentence of the novel defines the nature of the area: "If one lives in Galloway, one either fishes or paints" (p. 1). All concerns revolve around these two activities. When Sandy Campbell, a landscape painter, is found dead under suspicious circumstances, there are six suspects to the crime: Michael Waters, Hugh Farren, Matthew Gowan, Jock Graham, Henry Strachan, and John Ferguson. All paint, all have been known to have quarreled with Campbell over one issue or another, and each has a motive for killing him. Conjecture becomes the structural focus of the book. The novel proceeds in step fashion to present each character's story. Details of the quarrels, possibilities of alibis, and suspicions of the crime are revealed in successive chapters. Despite the use of an authentic regional dialogue, which adds credence to the narrative, the routine presentation of information about the quarrels, possible lies and alibis, and suspicion of the crime dulls the pace of the novel. Nor is each of the suspects distinctive enough to rouse enthusiasm for his character. Even the professionals—a chief constable, an inspector, a sergeant, and two other constables—can't seem to settle on the same solution to the crime. Various hypotheses depending on timetables and charts point the finger to any of the suspects. Finally, Wimsey dismisses all the theories and provides his own, based on a reconstruction of the crime scene and his keen knowledge of painting. A missing tube of flake white paint, a stopped watch, and forged train tickets contribute to the final solution.

With her " 'time-table' puzzle problem" ("Gaudy Night," p. 209) experiment behind her, Sayers returned to the knotty issue of Wimsey's thorny courtship of Harriet Vane. This time it's Harriet who is on vacation, in *Have His Carcase* (1932). Eighteen months since she was acquitted of the murder of Philip Boyes in *Strong Poison*, she discovers a body on the beach near Wilvercombe on the southeast coast of England. Unlike the setting of *The Five Red Herrings*, Sayers notes that the "locality has been invented to fit the plot" (opening note to *Have His Carcase*). Committed to return to a "less rigidly intellectual formula . . . which will turn on an alibi and a point of medicine" (*Letters*, p. 312), Sayers again started with the how of the murder.

Harriet's grisly discovery of the corpse of Paul Alexis Goldschmidt occurs halfway through a planned sixteen-mile beach walk from Lesston Hoe to Wilvercombe. Fortified with a sandwich and a copy of Lawrence Sterne's novel *Tristam Shandy*, she sets off expecting a leisurely June morning. Instead, at the Devil's Flat-Iron rock formation, she encounters a man in a blue suit, brown shoes, mauve socks, and tie who appears to be asleep. Since he isn't moving, Harriet moves closer, and her examination reveals that his throat is cut. Following the precepts of her own detective creation, Robert Templeton, she surfs for clues, recovering an open cutthroat razor partially buried in the sandy water near the rock. In the next half hour, Harriet finds that the man is wearing gloves and carries a gold cigarette case. She retrieves a shoe, a hat, and a handkerchief. When she spots a fishing boat out at sea, she takes photos with her vest pocket camera. Then she sets off to report the crime.

Lord Peter, informed of the murder through Salcombe ("Sally") Hardy, his contact at the *Morning Star*, appears on the scene at the point when the deceased is identified as a twenty-two-year-old Russian named Alexis, a missing professional dancer from the local hotel. He had been engaged to a wealthy widow, fifty-seven-year-old Mrs. Weldon, whose son, Henry, disapproved of the age difference and the match. The novel is notable for developing the relationship between Harriet and Lord Peter. At the first instant of meeting her again, Wimsey proposes marriage, and Harriet turns him down. Instead, they turn their joint investigative skills toward solving the case. Dependency is still an issue. When Wimsey accidentally reveals the real reason he came to Wilvercombe—to protect Harriet—she is irate. Her retort is "I suppose you think I haven't been humiliated enough already, without all this parade of chivalry . . . I suppose every man thinks he's only got to go on being superior and any woman will come tumbling into his arms. It's disgusting" (p. 174). If Wimsey is "patronising, interfering, conceited, intolerable and all the rest of it," it is only because he wants "common honesty" from Harriet (p. 175). Even though he is aware that she doesn't want "ever again to have to depend for happiness on another person" (p. 175), he continues to make proposals several more times throughout the novel.

Meanwhile, they proceed with their joint task of solving the crime by drawing up a list of instructions of things to be noted, things to be done. They are certain that a series of coded letters discovered in Alexis' hotel room are the primary clues to understanding his murder. What they decipher is that Alexis has been the victim of a ruse. He has been led to believe that he is a direct descendant of Russian royalty, an heir of the Romanovs, and is entitled to a fortune. As was the case with others of her novels, Sayers introduced a unique fact to the crime by making hemophilia an important factor in the death of Alexis. After a series of aliases and alibis are uncovered, Wimsey summarizes the case as one of an "old fool [Mrs. Weldon] who wanted a lover and the young fool [Alexis] who wanted an empire" (p. 448).

Humor is a constant thread throughout the Wimsey novels. Witticisms prevail, puns are prominent, self-parody abounds, literary quotation tennis matches escalate. Nowhere is this more apparent than in *Murder Must Advertise.* The setting for the novel, an advertising agency, permits free reign for playing with language. The levity, however, is tempered by the seriousness of Sayers' concern for reaching her established goal of a novel of manners. She saw *Murder Must Advertise* as her "first real attempt at fusing the two kinds of novel [detective and manners] . . . in which, for the first time, the criticism of life was not relegated to incidental observations and character sketches, but was actually part of the plot" ("Gaudy Night," p. 209). Even so, she did not find the attempt completely successful; "the idea of symbolically opposing two cardboard worlds—that of the advertiser and the drug-taker—was all right; and it was suitable that Peter, who stands for reality, should never appear in either except disguised; but the working-out was a little too melodramatic, and the handling rather uneven" ("Gaudy Night," pp. 209–210).

When death comes to the advertising firm of Pym's Publicity, it comes in the guise of Death Bredon, also known as Lord Peter Wimsey. He has been hired anonymously by Mr. Pym under the pretense of being a new copywriter. Actually, he has been hired to discover the truth about Victor Dean's deadly fall down a well-lit steep spiral staircase. To go under cover, Lord Peter adopts his two middle names for his identity. He adjusts quickly to his new surroundings, hobnobbing with his colleagues, taking on copywriting assignments with fervor, turning out clever campaign slogans. One of them, the Whifflets cigarette campaign ("WHIFFLE YOUR WAY ROUND BRITAIN!"), mocks Sayers' own very successful Mustard Club ad campaign, devised at Benson's.

The serious side of Wimsey's assignment takes him into a milieu totally removed from the spirited world of advertising. He learns soon enough that Dean was not well liked and that he stole other people's ideas. He also finds out that Dean was involved with the shadow world of drugs, "sinning above his station in life" (p. 81). He cavorted with the Dian de Momerie crowd of "Bright Young People" (p. 42). Her parties were often the scenes of unbridled revelry. At one point in the novel, Wimsey masquerades as a harlequin and dives into a pool to gain Dian's attention. Later, to find out more information about a major drug distributor, Wimsey risks his life in a reckless driving challenge against Dian.

The two worlds of advertising and drug dealing come together when Wimsey breaks the code and learns how murder advertises. A cipher involving the first letter of an ad, the postman, and the names of pubs clues the drug dealers into where to make their drops. Parker, now Wimsey's brother-in-law, has been trying to crack the dope-smuggling ring for some time. He sees little difference between advertising and dope smuggling, declaring that "all advertisers are dope-merchants" (p. 251). Wimsey hastens to agree that the essence of advertising is to "tell plausible lies for money" (p. 76). Sayers manages to link the twin themes of the lack of ethics in advertising with the exploitation of drug trafficking. Parker does asseverate that drugs are perhaps more dangerous than slogans: "Dope-runners are murderers, fifty times over. They slay hundreds of people, soul and body, besides indirectly causing all sorts of crimes among the victims." He dismisses Dean's death: " 'slugging one inconsiderable pip-squeak over the head is almost meritorious' " (p. 252).

In her next work, Sayers firmly reached her goal of combining the novel of manners with a mystery. One of the most admired of Sayers' novels is *The Nine Tailors* (1934). Designed to be "a labour of love" about "a big church in the Fens, and a grave which is suddenly found to have an extra body in it" (*Letters*, pp. 320, 323), it was also much more than that. It was another step closer to Sayers's goal for the detective novel. She saw it as a "shot at combining detection with poetic romance, and . . . pretty nearly right, except that Peter himself remained . . . extraneous to the story and untouched by its spiritual conflicts. That was correct practice for a detective hero, but not for the hero of a novel of manners" ("Gaudy Night," p. 210). The novel is as firmly rooted in time and place as was *The Five Red Herrings*. It is also as dependent on specialized knowledge as was the information on the advertising world in *Murder Must Advertise*. Unlike those novels, *The Nine Tailors* succeeds in dealing with a grander scheme and larger theme. Lord Peter Wimsey confronts the forces of nature and the universe when he stumbles on circumstances of murder in the small village of Fenchurch St. Paul.

It's New Year's Eve when a heavy snowstorm strands Lord Peter and his manservant, Bunter, after their Daimler runs into a ditch. They walk to the nearby village, where the friendly rector, the Reverend Theodore Venables, and his wife, Agnes, offer them refuge. In addition to the winter storm, a flu epidemic is wreaking havoc with the community. The bell ringers at Venables' church had planned an all-night session, but one of the key participants, Will Thoday, has fallen ill with the flu. Lord Peter, with bell-ringing experience from his college days, offers to stand in for Thoday. His generosity eventually incriminates him in a murder with Poe-like overtones.

A second plotline involves the theft of an emerald necklace stolen more than twenty years earlier. The Wilbraham necklace was supposedly taken by a butler, Geoffrey Deacon, in collusion with a London thief, Nobby Cranton. Deacon was married to Mary Russell, but after his conviction, escape, and apparent death in a nearby quarry, Mary marries Will Thoday. The necklace was never found. The stories dovetail as the deadly flu strikes more villagers. First, the aged Lady Thorpe expires. Suddenly, in the spring, her husband, Sir Henry Thorpe, dies. When Lady Thorpe's grave is opened so that Sir Henry can be laid to rest with her, an "extra body" is discovered, its face smashed and its hands cut off. Lord Peter learns of the incident in a letter from Venables and is summoned to deal with the mystery because he was at the rectory when Lady Thorpe died and Venables thought the situation would interest him.

An inquest supplies few answers. The body is first identified as belonging to a transient garage mechanic and then to the thief, Cranton. What Wimsey and Bunter learn through a letter obtained by nefarious means is that Deacon is alive, had returned to retrieve the necklace, and was discovered by Will Thoday. Since Thoday and Mary could be declared illegally wed, causing a scandal, Thoday planned to hide Deacon in the bell tower and release him the next day. His bout with the flu kept him from doing that and resulted in Wimsey's taking his place as a bell ringer. The next day, Will's brother, Jim, discovers Deacon dead; it is he who disfigures the corpse and places it in the Thorpe grave. But Wimsey learns that neither Will nor Jim is guilty of murder.

The ingenious solution to the convoluted plot—practically unguessable but completely convincing—is one of the reasons *The Nine Tailors* receives recognition as a monumental achievement. Sayers had no personal experience with the English tradition of change ringing, but her extensive research into the art resulted in reams of documents with detailed information about bells and changes. She incorporated this material into the integral structure of the book, granting the novel its authenticity and its powerful denouement. Her scholarship earned her an invitation to be the vice president of the Campanological Society of Great Britain. *The Oxford Companion to Music* refers to *The Nine Tailors* as one source for an understanding of change ringing.

Other admirers of the novel note the use of setting as an important contribution to its value. The fen churches and the sense of village community are intrinsic to the plot and theme. The moral center of the community, the Reverend Venables, is recognized as a singular achievement in characterization. His genial nature combined with an eccentric absentmindedness almost overshadows Wimsey's personality with its Dickensian stature. Venables rallies the community for support of the historic bell-ringing ceremony, provides solace and compassion once the social fabric is challenged by the consequences of the discovery of Deacon, and endures the violent forces of nature during the destructive flooding of the fens at the conclusion of the novel. The novel culminates with a flood of biblical proportions. Almost a year after Wimsey's discovery of the hiding place of the emerald necklace and the identification of the extra body in the grave, one of the younger members of the village, Hilary Thorpe, asks him to return. He is reluctant to agree, but, as her sole trustee, he feels obligated to support Hilary, whose future education as a writer he has endorsed. This time, instead of a snowfall, he is greeted by torrential rains. When the sluice gates break, threatening the entire village, Wimsey climbs to the top of the belfry, the bells ringing in his ears. Almost driven mad by the sound "infinitely worse than any roar of heavy artillery," with "blood running from his nose and ears" (p. 390), he recognizes the source of Deacon's death as the tintinnabulation of the bells. Sayers' one extra body has led to an inexorable chain of events that reveals the character of an entire village. As the sluice keeper notes, "Dig up one thing and you got to dig up another" (p. 344). The power of this novel arises from the reader's realization that responsibility for the death in the bell tower rests with the entire community and with those individuals who are good or

benign. The death from tintinnabulation would not have occurred if Lord Peter had not good-naturedly agreed to fill in for the missing ringer. Or if Venables had not rallied the troops. Justice has been served by the rising waters—Will Thoday is among those lost in the flood. After the flood, it is as though the village has been absolved of its sins.

If *The Nine Tailors* is admired, *Gaudy Night* is revered. Generally regarded as the crowning achievement in Sayers' canon, it is the penultimate Wimsey novel. For Sayers, the challenge was to finally bring detective fiction in accord with the novel of manners. Character joins with plot, plot is related to setting, and all are united in theme. Harriet Vane returns to the center of *Gaudy Night*. It is three years since the events of *Have His Carcase*. Harriet is almost thirty-two years old, with a reputation for "keeping up a scholarly standard of English, even in mystery fiction" (p. 17), when she is invited to return to the fictional Shrewsbury College (based on Sayers' Somerville College) in Oxford for a Gaudy Night reunion (a gathering of alumnae). During the clamor of High Table (the meal at the faculty), former classmates and tutors seem more interested in her involvement with Lord Peter Wimsey than with her. At first disconcerted, she finds herself quickly defending him. She ruminates on "the marriage question" (p. 46), though she at first thought the trip to Oxford would grant her a respite from the ongoing romantic pursuit.

Sayers, on the other hand, found the setting the perfect place to explore the relationship between Harriet and Lord Peter. In the city seen as "the kingdom of the mind" (p. 467), she could reveal the true characters of each of her "puppets" ("Gaudy Night," p. 211) and finally resolve the five-year-long courtship. For Sayers, the life of the mind was the truest pursuit for an individual. A "real vocation and full emotional fulfillment were to be found in the creative life of the intellect" ("Gaudy Night," p. 212). In her own life, the "habit of intellectual integrity [was] at once the foundation and the result of scholarship" ("Gaudy

Night," p. 212). She had found her grand theme for *Gaudy Night:*

> By choosing a plot that should exhibit intellectual integrity as the one great permanent value in an emotionally unstable world I should be saying the thing that, in a confused way, I had been wanting to say all my life. Finally, I should have found a universal theme which could be made integral both to the detective plot and to the "love-interest" which I had, somehow or other, to unite with it. (p. 213)

Her solution for unifying the separate threads of her plot was to devise a parallel story line with a character who contrasts with the intellectual honesty evidenced by Harriet and others at Shrewsbury. She utilizes a "woman in whom the emotions had gained control over the reason" (*The Mind of the Maker,* p. 76). This drew Sayers' plot closer to the central theme of the novel, the "relation of scholarship to life" ("Gaudy Night," p. 217) examined through the twin themes of the heart versus the mind. The "whole theme of the Peter-Harriet complication [is] . . . that no relation can ever be sound that is not founded in faith to the fact. So that, unless the heart and mind are brought into this true relation, they must be kept apart or produce nothing but discord" (*Letters,* p. 353). Sayers' monumental task was to join Harriet and Peter and, by joining them, produce a unified work of art.

During the first night of the reunion, Harriet stumbles upon a "nasty, dirty and lunatic scribble" (p. 38) in the college quadrangle. She destroys it but "for all that, she wished she had not seen it" (p. 39). Before she leaves Oxford, she receives a note meant directly for her: "YOU DIRTY MURDERESS. AREN'T YOU ASHAMED TO SHOW YOUR FACE?" (p. 58). Then, back in London, months pass before she learns that the two incidents have escalated to a series of threats and other acts of vandalism. Dean Letitia Martin writes to Harriet about the campus "being victimized by a cross between a Poltergeist and a Poison-Pen" (p. 74) and beseeches Harriet to return to Shrewsbury to help solve the mystery.

Sayers is applauded for producing a mystery novel that sustains suspense despite the fact that there are no dead bodies. The tension in the plot relates completely to the identity of the malefactor who is writing notes, destroying manuscripts, leaving stabbed dummies in the chapel, creating blackouts, dropping false evidence in the science hall. More than a dozen incidents occur, including one that makes a direct attack on Harriet when a chess set Lord Peter bought for her is shattered. When the culprit is finally revealed, Sayers' main theme of intellectual integrity is discovered to be the source of the campus rampage. The disorder was predicated on revenge. Many years earlier, one of the newer teachers at Shrewsbury, Miss de Vine, had encountered a case dealing with academic integrity. A candidate for a master's degree, Arthur Robinson, had left a document out of his thesis because it would have contradicted and nullified his research. He changed his name, but because he was denied his degree and dishonored by the scholarly community, he was unable to find suitable employment and unable to support his family, and he subsequently committed suicide. His widow, Annie Wilson, took a job as a scout at Shrewsbury and sought vindication for her husband's humiliation. Annie's malice was "the product, not of intellect starved of emotion, but of emotion uncontrolled by intellect" ("Gaudy Night," p. 214).

Harriet and Lord Peter found themselves wrestling with a similar dilemma. They, too, were dealing with the conflict of the head versus the heart. The amateur detective Sayers had created in *Whose Body?* had matured to the age of forty-five. He had decided that he would make one more marriage proposal to Harriet. If she turned him down, then he would no longer pursue her. When the Dean recognizes the fact that she needs professional guidance to end the malevolent acts on campus, Harriet suggests Wimsey. He doesn't enter *Gaudy Night* (except for a flashback scene) until almost halfway through the novel.

When he is back in Harriet's life, she must confront her own confusion about their relationship. Miss de Vine had advised her, "Detachment is a rare virtue, and very few people find it lovable, either in themselves or in others. If you ever find a person who likes you in spite of it—still more, because of it—that liking has very great value, because it is perfectly sincere, and because, with that person, you will never need to be anything but sincere yourself" (p. 37). Later, she advises Harriet to marry Peter because he is "a very unselfish and a very honest man. . . . You needn't be afraid of losing your independence" (pp. 459–460).

During a long, idyllic picnic scene, as Harriet and Peter punt down the Cherwell, Peter's vulnerability is revealed, and Harriet makes her decision about marrying Peter. With his weaknesses exposed, she has a moment of illumination when she knows that "it has happened" (p. 300). She is startled by this epiphanic moment, which happens as she observes him while he quietly reads about the events at Shrewsbury. Later, when he drifts off into a contented sleep in the punt, she finds a copy of *Religio Medici* in his pocket and is unsettled by the passage she finds: "When I am from him I am dead till I be with him. United souls are not satisfied with embraces, but desire to be truly each other; which being impossible, these desires are infinite, and must proceed without a possibility of satisfaction" (p. 307). Harriet knows she has found both her intellectual and emotional equal. Hers would be a marriage of "two independent and equally irritable intelligences" (p. 460).

Sayers sees their marriage as a union of opposites. The "essential Peter is seen to be the familiar figure of the interpretative artist, the romantic soul at war with the realistic brain. Harriet, with her lively and inquisitive mind and her soul grounded upon reality, is his complement—the creative artist" ("Gaudy Night," p. 219). Together, they represent the unification of the themes she sought in *Gaudy Night*, the "exhibit [of] intellectual integrity as the one great permanent value in an emotionally unstable world" ("Gaudy Night," p. 213).

Busman's Honeymoon concludes the Wimsey saga. There are two forms of the story—the novel and a play with the same title written with Muriel St. Clare Byrne. Although the production of the play came before the novel, the texts were published at the same time. Sayers wanted it made "quite clear that the story was originally written as a Play, and that the novel was to that extent 'the book of the Play' " (*Letters*, p. 400). She didn't want audiences to think that the play was "the novel with all the best bits left out" (*Letters*, p. 400).

The subtitle and the dedication to the novel declare Sayers' other intentions. Since the story carried on the details of Harriet and Lord Peter's early days of marriage, its subtitle was a "love story with detective interruptions." As a play it was a detective comedy, as a novel, a "sentimental comedy [in which] the detective-interest might well seem an irritating intrusion upon their love-story." The organization of the novel illustrates these purposes. Between a prothalamion (a song celebrating a marriage) and epithalamion (a song in praise of the married couple) is the detective part of the story. The prothalamion section is a series of letters (snide ones from supercilious Helen, shocked ones from female friends) and diary entries (support and encouragement from the Dowager Duchess) about the preparations for the nuptials. The epithalamion provides information of the trial that follows the solution to the case, a glance at life with the Wimseys, and the reactions Lord Peter has to the verdict.

The Wimseys' honeymoon adventure makes up the major portion of the novel. They have bought an old farmhouse called Talboys in the village near Harriet's childhood home. Although preparations were supposed to have been made before their arrival, when they reach Talboys they encounter a misspelled note attached to the gate—"NO BREAD AND MILK TILL FUTHER NOTISE"—and the house is dark and locked. Bunter makes the best of the situation, and they all settle in for the night. The next morning, an idiosyncratic chimney sweep, Mr. Puffett, shoots soot from the chimney, dislodging what appears to be an unimportant piece of chain. Bunter, searching for libations, finds the body of William Noakes, the former owner, in the cellar. Death descends on the Wimsey household.

The solution to the crime includes another of Sayers' ingenious methods of murder, but one of her least convincing motives. Suspects include a niece who was in line to inherit, a young police officer who was party to blackmail, and the gardener who quarreled with the deceased. There appears to be no indication as to how Noakes could have sustained a blow to the head. Noakes's habits with a wireless radio, the position of a clock, and the height of a cactus connect in an explainable but slightly improbable way that also involves the physics of a pendulum. The crime was committed as revenge for the lack of repayment of the small sum of forty pounds.

In later years, Harriet remembered the early days of her honeymoon "as a long series of assorted surprises, punctuated by the most incredible meals" (p. 120); Lord Peter's impressions "were even less coherent; he said he had had, all the time, the sensation of being slightly drunk and tossed in a blanket" (p. 120). Regardless of the events surrounding their honeymoon, it was a suitable period of adjustment for the couple. Harriet recognizes that Lord Peter "carried about with him that permanent atmosphere of security. He belonged to an ordered society. . . . She was curiously excited. She thought, 'I have married England' " (p. 92). On Peter's side, following another discussion of possessiveness and independence and then during the closing segment of the epithalamion section, when his emotional vulnerability is thoroughly exposed, he willingly capitulates to Harriet's consoling arms. The Wimsey story concludes with the triumph of love, virtue, and equanimity.

Though Sayers finished her work on the Wimseys in *Busman's Honeymoon*, she left incomplete one other manuscript which focused on the couple. Jill Paton Walsh completed the novel, *Thrones Dominations*

(1998), returning to Lord Peter and Harriet three months after their marriage. As they settle into their new Audley Square surroundings, it is not long before they are involved in a mystery of blackmail, hidden identities, and several deaths. The theater milieu is a major focus of the plot. Laurence Harwell, a theater impresario who is the toast of the British public and an acquaintance of the Wimseys, finds his wife strangled in a country cottage, a haunting echo of a Grand Guignol production they had seen in Paris. Evidence points to Harwell as a prime suspect but Lord Peter and Harriet must reveal a number of unsavory relationships before a confession ensues. Meanwhile, as the Wimseys are continuing their period of marital adjustment, England, too, must learn to adjust to the death of one king, George V, and the ascension of another, Edward VIII, Prince of Wales. While London women shop for mourning costumes, making a run on black fabrics, some trim collars with white pleats, an important clue for part of the mystery. The novel is a commendable production, touching on previous Wimsey adventures and themes. Nor does it exclude other characters, like Bunter, who becomes engaged to photographer Mary Moles. The novel closes with news of Harriet's pregnancy, which precedes the evidence of the Wimseys' children in "Talboys." Overall it is a worthy addition to the Sayers canon.

The Short Stories—More Sinister Than Mysterious

Sayers is neither best known nor fondly remembered for her short stories. There are twenty-one Lord Peter Wimsey stories in four volumes—*Lord Peter Views the Body, Hangman's Holiday, In the Teeth of the Evidence*, and the posthumous *Lord Peter* (1972), which collects eighteen stories from the first three books and three additional stories. There are also eleven short stories that feature another detective, Montague Egg, and twelve more with neither Wimsey nor Egg. Among the forty-four stories, few demand attention. For the most part, they are brief brainteasers. What is appealing about several of the stories, however, is the introduction of a sinister and macabre element into the Sayers canon.

The Poe-like atmosphere of "The Abominable History of the Man with Copper Fingers" is shrouded with Hawthornean overtones. At the Egotists' Club in London, Varden, an American movie star handsome enough to serve as a model for the Apollo Belvedere, tells a tale of staying in New York with a respected sculptor, Eric P. Loder. Loder's mistress, Maria Morano, is a flawed beauty; the second toe on her left foot is shorter than the big toe. When she disappears, Varden suspects that she has become a living sculpture, ensconced in silver as a reclining nude on a Roman couch. When Varden is warned by a specter to leave or become Loder's next victim, he flees to Vancouver.

Lord Peter, hearing the tale at the club, intervenes to tell the second half of the story. Loder's intention was to fashion Varden into *The Sleeping Athlete*; then, because he bore a physical resemblance to Varden, he was going to leave New York with false papers and passport. When Lord Peter uncovers the ruse, he confronts Loder, who accidentally falls into a vat of cyanide and copper sulfate used for copper plating and ends up "poisoned . . . drowned and dead," his fingers transformed into the grisly image in the title.

Other stories in the same volume contain similar grotesque images. There is "The Fantastic Horror of the Cat in the Bag," a sordid "house that Jack built" story that follows two motorcyclists chasing each other to return a fallen bag, which hides the head of a victim whose torso resides in a locker in Paddington Station. In one of the longest stories, "The Undignified Melodrama of the Bone of Contention," sibling rivalry encounters the possibilities of supernatural specters as a phantom coach with four white headless horses and a headless coachman roams the New York countryside. The Hitchcockian image of a skewered spouse, evidence destroyed in a

baking chicken, is the result of a jealous husband's vengeance in "The Vindictive Story of the Footsteps That Ran." And diamonds turn up in a preserved stomach, the peculiar bequest in "The Piscatorial Farce of the Stolen Stomach."

As they were in more than one of Sayers' novels, wills are the focus of several short stories in this first collection. The false report of Lord Peter's death leads him to take on a disguised personality and infiltrate the inner sanctum of a secret criminal society in the melodramatic "The Adventurous Exploit of the Cave of Ali Baba." An adventuresome pursuit engages Lord Peter and his nephew, Viscount St. George, during a book shopping excursion in "The Learned Adventure of the Dragon's Head," when they uncover a perplexing will that sets them on the trail of monsters, dragons, and buried treasure. The ultimate puzzle fiction is a thorough exercise in "sustained frivolity" in "The Fascinating Problem of Uncle Meleeger's Will" (p. 46), when Lord Peter must solve the clues of a crossword puzzle hidden in the tiles of a small pool in order to locate a hidden second will.

The four remaining stories contribute in a minor way to the development of Wimsey's character in 1927, early in the Sayers canon. His gourmand palate for wine is demonstrated in "The Bibulous Business of a Matter of Taste," when not one but three Lord Peters appear, two of whom are impostors, and the true Wimsey is revealed by his identifying a Napoleon brandy. His gentleman's habit of discretion allows a diamond thief to go free if he returns the goods in "The Unprincipled Affair of the Practical Joker." During an episode of eavesdropping in a queue at the railroad station Gare Saint-Lazare, his acute ear for language eventually thwarts an attempted diamond heist because "The Entertaining Episode of the Article in Question" traps a thief whose grammar is incorrect. And though a reasonable deduction leads to an unsatisfying conclusion in "The Unsolved Puzzle of the Man with no Face," Sayers takes the occasion to remark on one of her favorite themes, an artist's relationship toward creative achievement.

Only four stories in *Hangman's Holiday* feature Wimsey. The least significant, "The Queen's Square," depends on a thin blackmail plot that hangs on costumed guests representing a variety of games and a trick of lighting focusing on the criminal. "The Image in the Mirror" is also slight, the story of an apparent doppelgänger that turns into the story of mirror twins separated at birth; this story is notable only for its references to H. G. Wells, the German film director Friedrich Wilhelm, Robert Wiene's *Cabinet of Dr. Caligari,* and the intriguing use of the fourth dimension as a plot device. Elements of wizardry weave their way through "The Incredible Elopement of Lord Peter Wimsey" when Wimsey steps in to aid a young wife who appears demented but is suffering from a "congenital thyroid deficiency." Edgar Allan Poe's "Purloined Letter" echoes in "The Necklace of Pearls" when the pearls' hiding place is discovered.

The major portion of this second collection of stories introduces another amateur detective, wine merchant Montague Egg. Egg is as middle class as Wimsey is upper crust. Despite his lack of sophistication, his deductive skills are nearly as keen as Lord Peter's. Contrasted with Lord Peter's literary quotations, Egg's endearing personality is supported by his constant aphoristic quotes from *The Salesman's Handbook.* His rules of the road include "Whether you're wrong or whether you're right, it's always better to be polite" ("The Poisoned Dow '08," p. 803), "A cheerful voice and cheerful look put orders in the order-book" ("Murder in the Morning," p. 123), and "The salesman's job is to get the trade—don't leave the house till the deal is made" ("Maher-Shalal-Hashbaz," p. 153).

In Egg's appearance in his first short story, the case of the poisoned corkscrew, he must clear the name of his employer because "The Poisoned Dow '08" is one he sold to a client. Like Wimsey, Egg's acute observation for details spots the chemist-murderer in "Sleuths on the Scent." His occupation helps him rec-ognize the discrepancy of time between real clocks and display clocks in "Murder in the Morning." Because he travels for Plummet and Rose of Piccadilly, he finds "One Too Many" identities on the train from London to Birmingham, sorts out "Murder at Pentecost" in Oxford when an irate student kills a master, and finds himself in the center of a series of horrific feline murders in "Maher-Shalal-Hashbaz."

Two stories without detectives complete *Hangman's Holiday.* The brutal irony of "The Man Who Knew How" occurs because of misconstrued information and a prank that goes awry. A stranger on a train, identified as Smith, tells another character, Pender, how sulfate of thanatol mocks heart attacks in hot baths. When a series of murders seeming to duplicate this information occur, Pender is certain Smith is a murderer. After he takes justice into his own hands, he learns that Smith is actually Bill Buckley, a respected crime reporter, who uses the tale to fool "boobs in railway carriages." A bizarre double irony and double instance of blackmail pervades "The Fountain Plays."

Two Wimsey stories and five Egg stories appear in *In the Teeth of the Evidence.* Neither Wimsey story is particularly inventive or contributory to Lord Peter's characterization. The title story starts at Wimsey's dentist's office, where he learns of a "corpse-in-blazing-garage" (p. 7), and proceeds to the mortuary, where the components of a tooth's crown disclose the clue to a fatal insurance fraud scheme. In the second story, a sixty-year-old moneylender is stabbed to death during an evening meal, but all suspects claim to have been "Absolutely Elsewhere." The Egg stories have the working-class sleuth continue to follow the precepts of *The Salesman's Handbook* through "A Shot at Goal," "Dirt Cheap," "Bitter Almonds," "False Weight," and "The Professor's Manuscript."

Among the ten remaining stories in the collection, one follows a news reporter who creates a mystery where none exists ("The Milk-Bottles"), another traces an ironic moral "Dilemma" faced when having to choose between a "martyr or a murderer" (p. 100), and a third outlines the misadventures of a struggling novelist and his secretary when they try to fabricate interest in his manuscript ("An Arrow o'er the House"). In "Scrawns," a house parlor maid is dismissed when she causes a disinheritance after she misconstrues some backyard digging by an artist and his young wife; a charade-like parlor game sweats out the guilty party in "Nebuchadnezzar"; a clever barber outwits a murderer by dying his hair green when he visits his shop in "The Inspiration of Mr. Budd"; and a husband harbors "Suspicion" of the wrong party when he thinks his new cook may be an arsenic poisoner.

"The Leopard Lady" and "The Cyprian Cat" are two more stories that carry bizarre, macabre elements reminiscent of Poe. In the first, Tressider is entrusted with his young orphaned nephew, Cyril, when he responds to a whisper he thinks he hears in a train station: "If the boy is in your way, ask at Rapallo's for Smith & Smith." He learns that Smith & Smith are in the "Removals" business and contracts with them to remove six-year-old Cyril from his life so he may inherit. A surreal element enters the story when Tressider envisions two leopards and a fairy lady with golden eyes in a neighboring garden. The mad voice of the narrator of "The Cyprian Cat" defends himself against the charge that he shot his friend's young wife because he "fired one shot and one shot only, and that was at the cat" (p. 209).

One short story in the collection, "Blood Sacrifice," deserves further attention because Sayers wrote it as an assignment to commit the perfect murder. For her, the "whole point of the story is that the only perfect murder is one in which the murderer can neither be charged nor even suspected" (Letters, p. 377). The scenario she creates relies on one of her familiar themes, the integrity of the writer. First-time playwright John Scales has phenomenal success with Bitter Laurel, starring actor-manager Garrick Drury. Scales objects when Drury alters the play and turns it into "sob-stuff" (p. 157). He is certain that his rep-

utation will be both established and ruined by the changes in the script. Scales writes his own dreadful irony when Drury is injured in a rainy-day car accident outside the theater. When a blood transfusion is needed, there appears to be an accidental mix-up of blood types, and Drury hemorrhages and dies. It's not completely clear, "except in the hidden chambers of [Scales's] heart," whether Scales was responsible. Sayers thought that "psychologically . . . the story is one of the best bits of work I've done" (Letters, p. 378).

In 1972, the eighteen previously published Lord Peter stories and three others appeared in a posthumous volume, Lord Peter. "Striding Folly," "The Haunted Policeman," and "Talboys," written in 1942, complete the Wimsey short-fiction canon. He appears only briefly in "Striding Folly," when he steps in to save Mr. Mellilow, accused of killing Creech, a neighbor and chess partner, over a grudge when he learns that Creech has sold the valley to the electrical company and that construction of a power plant would change the entire countryside. In "The Haunted Policeman," the early-morning birth of the Wimseys' first son leads Lord Peter to step outside for a cigarette at 3 a.m., when he encounters the new young police constable Alfred Burt. Wimsey invites him into the library for a drink, where Burt regales him with a strange story of a disappearing house at No. 13 Merriman's End complete with a body spied through the letter box. When Wimsey joins the investigation he uncovers a trompe l'oeil murder based on the "art of false perspective" (p. 428).

"Talboys" closes the Wimsey saga. Harriet, at work on a novel, and Lord Peter, now age fifty-two, have been married seven years and have three sons. The story skirts the parameters of infant psychology and corporal punishment when Lord Peter canes his son, Bredon, when he confesses to stealing two of a neighbor's prize peaches. A houseguest, Miss Quirk, objects to the caning with a lecture on the traumatic damage it could cause. The next day, the neighbor, Tom Puffett, claims that all of his peaches have been stolen the day before an important flower show. Once the culprits are revealed to be brothers who used another brother's fishnet to avoid leaving footprints, Lord Peter pulls a prank on Miss Quirk that proves her to be a hypocrite when she turns against her own psychologizing and spanks Bredon. The best of the short stories in the collections mimic in miniature Sayers' signal talents: a verisimilitude of settings and atmosphere that contribute to authenticity of place and time, a versatility of plots related to plausible solutions of ingenious methods of murder, and a variable catalogue of characters from the creative to the culpable.

After the Mysteries— Final Writings

After the mystery novels and short stories, the remainder of Sayers' writing career encompassed new forms and new visions. Her involvement with religious drama was activated by an invitation from the Canterbury Festival of Music and Drama. *The Zeal of Thy House* reiterates Sayers' themes of a character's relationship to fate and the integrity of the artist in relationship to his work. It is based on an incident that took place during the rebuilding of the cathedral after a fire in 1174. William of Sens, the chief architect hired for the project, misrepresents accounts, engages in illicit romances, is inattentive to his work, and, most egregiously, commits the sin of false pride, which leads to an accidental fall from the scaffolding. Since no one else was hurt, his injuries appeared to be the fated consequences of his actions. *The Devil to Pay* (1939) reinvents the Faust legend, giving Sayers the opportunity to investigate the problem of good and evil from her own perspective. Her contemporary character was a revolutionary seeking power as a dictator; his retribution is transformation into a black dog and relegation to Purgatory. For the Lichfield Cathedral, she based *The Just Vengeance* (1946) on a passage from Dante's *Paradiso* that focuses on the theme of atonement. A chronicle

play, *The Emperor Constantine* (1951) was produced for the Colchester Festival and culminates with the formulation of the Nicene Creed at the Council in Nicaea.

For the BBC, Sayers wrote *He That Should Come* (1939), a nativity play for their Children's Hour. Public clamor led to a monumentally successful play cycle, *The Man Born to Be King*, broadcast each month for a full year. Partly as a result of the acclaimed evangelical nature of this series of plays, the Archbishop of Canterbury offered Sayers the degree of Doctor of Divinity, which she declined on the ground that the nature of her Christianity was based more on an intellectual level than on a level of divinity.

The critical essay was another genre that commanded Sayers' attention. *Begin Here* (1939) began as a solicitation from her publisher to write a Christmas message that would encourage a nation at war to think positively about the future. *The Mind of the Maker* was the manuscript that buttressed her nomination for the Doctor of Divinity degree. Couched in terms of an examination of the creative process, Sayers draws a lengthy analogy based on the doctrine of the trinity. She postulates that all creative work derives from the creative idea, which begets the creative energy, which begets the creative power, all of which are one in the final product. *Creed or Chaos?* (1949) is a collection of seven essays originally presented as lectures that reaffirm Sayers' commitment to themes of Christian dogma and theology. Sayers's final, incomplete project was a translation of Dante's *Divine Comedy*. Her creative zeal and all-encompassing imagination were triggered by a book about Dante that had been written by Charles Williams, who had also recommended her to the committee for the Canterbury Festival. During an air raid in 1944, Dante's was the book she took with her into the shelter. As she had been obsessed by Dumas at age thirteen, at fifty-one she was entranced by Dante. The last years of her life saw her complete *Inferno* (1949) and *Purgatorio* (1955), but she died before she was able to finish *Paradiso*.

Selected Bibliography

WORKS OF DOROTHY L. SAYERS

NOVELS

Whose Body? London: Unwin, 1923; New York: Boni and Liveright, 1923.

Clouds of Witness. London: Unwin, 1926.

Unnatural Death. London: Benn, 1927. U.S.: *The Dawson Pedigree.* New York: Dial Press, 1928.

The Unpleasantness at the Bellona Club. London: Benn, 1928; New York: Payson and Clarke, 1928.

The Documents in the Case (with Robert Eustace). London: Benn, 1930; New York: Brewer and Warren, 1930.

Strong Poison. London: Gollancz, 1930; New York: Brewer and Warren, 1930.

The Five Red Herrings. London: Gollancz, 1931. U.S.: *Suspicious Characters.* New York: Brewer, Warren and Putnam, 1931.

The Floating Admiral (with members of The Detection Club). London: Hodder and Stoughton, 1931.

Have His Carcase. London: Gollancz, 1932; New York: Brewer, Warren and Putnam, 1932.

Ask a Policeman (with members of The Detection Club). London: Barker, 1933; New York: Morrow, 1933.

Murder Must Advertise. London: Gollancz, 1933; New York: Morrow, 1933.

The Nine Tailors. London: Gollancz, 1934; New York: Harcourt, Brace, 1934.

Gaudy Night. London: Gollancz, 1935.

Busman's Honeymoon. London: Gollancz, 1937; New York: Harcourt, Brace, 1937.

Double Death: A Murder Story, (with members of The Detection Club). London: Gollancz, 1939.

Thrones, Dominations. Completed by Jill Paton Walsh. New York: St. Martin's Press, 1998.

SHORT STORIES

Lord Peter Views the Body. London: Gollancz, 1928; New York: Payson and Clarke, 1929.

Hangman's Holiday. London: Gollancz, 1933; New York: Harcourt, Brace, 1933.

In the Teeth of the Evidence and Other Stories. London: Gollancz, 1939; New York: Harcourt, Brace, 1940.

Striding Folly. London: New English Library, 1972.

Lord Peter: A Collection of All the Lord Peter Wimsey Stories. Edited by James Sandoe. New York: Harper, 1972.

PLAYS

Busman's Honeymoon (with Muriel St. Clare Byrne). London: Gollancz, 1936.

The Zeal of Thy House. London: Gollancz, 1937; New York: Harcourt, Brace, 1937.

He That Should Come: A Nativity Play in One Act. London: Gollancz, 1939.

The Devil to Pay, Being the Famous Play of John Faustus. London: Gollancz, 1939; New York: Harcourt, Brace, 1939.

Love All. Pressmark: LC Plays. Department of Manuscripts, British Library, 1941; with *Busman's Honeymoon.* Kent, Ohio: Kent State University Press, 1984.

The Man Born to Be King: A Play-Cycle on the Life of Our Lord and Saviour Jesus Christ. London: Gollancz, 1943.

The Just Vengeance. London: Gollancz, 1946.

The Emperor Constantine: A Chronicle. London: Gollancz, 1951; New York: Harper, 1951.

ESSAYS

"Introduction." In *Great Short Stories of Detection, Mystery, and Horror,* 3 vols. London: Gollancz, 1928–1934. U.S.: *The Omnibus of Crime, The Second Omnibus of Crime,* and *The Third Omnibus of Crime.* New York: Coward, McCann, 1932–1935.

"How I Came to Invent The Character of Lord Peter." *Harcourt Brace News,* July 15 1936, pp. 1–2.

"Gaudy Night." In *Titles to Fame.* Edited by Denys Kilham Roberts. New York: Thomas Nelson & Sons, Ltd., 1937.

Begin Here: A War-Time Essay. London: Gollancz, 1940; New York: Harcourt, Brace, 1941.

The Mind of the Maker. London: Methuen, 1941; New York: Harcourt, Brace, 1941.

Even the Parrot: Exemplary Conversations for Enlightened Children. London: Methuen, 1944.

Unpopular Opinions. London: Gollancz, 1946.

Creed or Chaos? And Other Essays in Popular Theology. London: Methuen, 1947:

Introductory Papers on Dante. London: Methuen, 1954; New York: Harper, 1955.

Further Papers on Dante. London: Methuen, 1957; New York: Harper, 1957.

TRANSLATIONS

Tristan in Brittany, Being the Fragments of the Romance of Tristan Written in the Twelfth Century, by Thomas the Troubador. London: Benn, 1929; New York: Payson and Clarke, 1929.

The Divina Commedia, by Dante Alighieri. Cantica I: *Hell.* London, Baltimore: Penguin 1949, 1950. Cantica II: *Purgatory.* London, Baltimore: Penguin, 1955.

The Song of Roland. Harmondsworth, Eng.: Penguin, 1957.

BIOGRAPHICAL AND CRITICAL STUDIES

Brabazon, James. *Dorothy L. Sayers: A Biography.* New York: Scribners, 1981.

Coomes, David. *Dorothy L. Sayers: A Careless Rage for Life.* Batavia, Ill.: Lion Publishers, 1992.

Dale, Alzina Stone. *Maker and Craftsman.* Grand Rapids, Mich.: William B. Eerdmans Publishing Company, 1978.

————, ed. *Dorothy L. Sayers: The Centennial Celebration*. New York: Walker, 1993.

Durkin, Mary Brian. *Dorothy L. Sayers*. Boston: Twayne, 1980.

Hannay, Margaret P., ed., *As Her Whimsey Took Her: Critical Essays on the Work of Dorothy L. Sayers*. Kent, Ohio: Kent State University Press, 1979.

Haycraft, Howard, ed. *The Art of the Mystery Story*. New York: Simon & Schuster, 1946.

Hitchman, Janet. *Such a Strange Lady: A Biography of Dorothy L. Sayers*. New York: Harper & Row, 1975.

Kenney, Catherine M. *The Remarkable Case of Dorothy L. Sayers*. Kent, Ohio: Kent State University Press, 1990.

Reynolds, Barbara, ed. *The Letters of Dorothy L. Sayers: 1899 to 1936. The Making of a Detective Novelist*. London: Hodder and Stoughton, 1995; New York: St. Martin's Press, 1996.

————. *Dorothy L. Sayers: Her Life and Soul*. London: Hodder & Stoughton, 1993; New York: St. Martin's Press, 1993.

————, ed. *The Letters of Dorothy L. Sayers: 1937 to 1943. From Novelist to Playwright*. New York: St. Martin's Press, 1998.

GEORGES SIMENON
(1903–1989)

GEORGE GRELLA

In his long life and prodigious career Georges Simenon attained a unique place in detective fiction, modern French literature, and twentieth-century letters. His enormous body of work—surely nobody has read, or even located, all of his hundreds of books and stories, under all of his pseudonyms—and the accompanying bibliographical, biographical, and critical material would no doubt fill a library of more than modest size. Although he entitled one of his numerous autobiographical volumes, with a perhaps forgivable false modesty, *Un Homme comme un autre* (1975, A Man like Any Other), his life was as rich, varied, and singular as his monumental body of work: both exasperate, enrage, and sometimes even enchant his many critics and millions of readers. Whatever else he may have been, he was clearly neither a man nor a writer like any other. He created a special kind of novel, deservedly known simply as a "Simenon," as well as a special kind of detective story, the "Maigret," named after its central figure. Long after his retirement from writing novels and a decade after his death, despite endless critical and biographical discussions as well as the confessional nature of much of his fiction and nonfiction, Simenon remains for many a controversial and mysterious figure, as elusive and enigmatic as any character in his novels.

Early Years

Displaying the monumental narcissism of genius, Simenon has written extensively of his childhood and youth. Although he may seem, especially to a non-European, a quintessentially French figure, Georges Joseph Christian Simenon was born in Liège, Belgium, on 13 February 1903, the first son of Désiré and Henriette; from his parents the child inherited what Vladimir Nabokov calls in *Lolita* a salad of racial genes—in his case, French, Dutch, Flemish, and Prussian. His father worked as an accountant for an insurance company, just the sort of underpaid, lower-middle-class, white collar servitude that the author provided for many of his most desperate and pathetic characters. Weakened by a cardiac condition, Désiré suffered his first heart attack in 1918 and died in 1921 at the age of forty-four. Simenon adored his father, whom he always referred to as a sort of saint, and perhaps partly as a result, regarded his nervous, high-strung, complaining, often hysterical mother very differently. His complex feelings about her inspired numerous works of fiction and nonfiction, in which he attempted to come to terms with his family and his personal history. Despite her frequently harsh treatment; her outspoken preference for his brother, Christian; her consistent expressions of disappointment about his career and his choice of wives; and her resolute refusal to share his immense wealth or live in his grand mansion, she seems to have served as a strange sort of muse for Simenon, far more important than any of the women who obsessed him throughout his life. She appears in one guise or another in many of his works, and he devoted one of his volumes of reminiscence, appropriately entitled *Lettre à ma mère* (1974; *Letter to My Mother*, 1976), to their relationship.

Simenon was a talented and precocious student, and like many Catholic boys with intellectual abilities and interests and little money, he aspired to the priesthood. Observing that priests appeared to have quite a lot of free time, he economically decided to combine his devotion with his other ambitions— he would use that clerical leisure for writing, the career he claims to have decided on at the age of eleven (he also thought about training for another authoritarian institution, the military, for the same reason). However, when at the age of fifteen he learned of his father's precarious health, which meant that he would soon have to leave school and seek employment, he angrily renounced both his studies and his faith; Simenon called that moment the turning point of his life, his first recognition of the cruel workings of an indifferent fate, which became the subject of much of his writing. Perhaps another kind of fate was also at work, however, leading the young man through brief, unhappy periods of employment as an apprentice pastry cook—his mother's idea of an appropriate career—and a bookstore clerk, to his first introduction to his true vocation: only sixteen years old, through lucky chance, he landed a job as a cub reporter on the *Gazette de Liège*, ironically a conservative Catholic newspaper.

As it did for countless writers, particularly in American literature, working on a newspaper provided the young Simenon with the perfect apprenticeship. It instructed him in the discipline of deadlines and in a certain pared-down prose style, encouraged his extraordinary facility, and gave him access to the fascinatingly sordid place that became the world of his books. It enabled him to observe many strata of contemporary life, from the ineptitude and chicanery of politicians to the sordid cynicism of prostitutes and criminals. It showed him that he might be able to earn a living by his pen. His youthful experience in journalism influences all of his writing: people, places, and events of all sorts from those early years in Liège recur in fictional form throughout his work.

During that period he also began the course of behavior that defined his conduct throughout his life, both as a writer and "a man like any other." He joined a group of painters, writers, and dilettantes who called themselves La Caque (The Cask) and spent their time drinking destructively, trying drugs, occasionally sharing women, and arguing about the usual preoccupations of young aesthetes and intellectuals—life and death, heaven and hell, philosophy and art. He remembered the group and several of its members years later, in the novel *Le Pendu de Saint Pholien* (1931; *Maigret and the Hundred Gibbets*, 1963).

In those years in Liège, Simenon met a young artist, Règine Renchon (he always called her "Tigy"), whom he married in 1923; they had a son, Marc, in 1939. During that time he also began his notorious lifelong obsession with women, especially prostitutes, which he candidly and more or less accidentally revealed to the public many years later. He made several attempts at humorous and satirical fiction, and in 1921 published his first novel, *Au Pont des Arches* (At the Bridge of Arches). In that same year he entered the Belgian army for his compulsory military service, part of which he spent in occupied Germany but most in his native city, where he continued to write for the *Gazette.* He persuaded his superiors to permit him to continue his journalistic career and managed to avoid most of his military duties. He spent the majority of his time out of uniform and most of his leisure carousing with his fellow bohemians. The heavy drinking; the relentless pursuit of sexual excitement and fulfillment; the parallel and paradoxical desire for the stability of marriage and family; the discipline that allowed him to churn out newspaper stories, satirical columns, and short humorous fiction (under the name "Georges Sim") in the midst of numerous distractions; and even the charm and luck that kept him landing on his feet suggest the pattern of the decades to come, adumbrating the curious personal, domestic, and professional paths he followed for the next sixty years.

Paris and First Success

In 1922 the young writer journeyed to Paris, the obvious and logical step for anyone with his abilities and aspirations living in his time and place; although he travelled virtually all over the world and lived in many countries, he and his work were always associated with that city. The most vibrant artistic capital of the 1920s and 1930s, Paris beckoned artists and would-be artists of all kinds and degrees, from virtually every nation, contributing more than any other single place to the brilliant efflorescence of modernism: almost all of the most talented and accomplished musicians, dancers, painters, sculptors, poets, and novelists of the era lived and worked there at some point during that remarkable time; the young Belgian joined their ranks and ultimately, in effect, became one of them. It was a remarkable time, as exciting as the romantic and revolutionary era in France that Wordsworth celebrated in the eleventh book of his great poem *The Prelude:* "Bliss was it in that dawn to be alive, / But to be young was very Heaven!"

Simenon lived in France from 1923 to 1939, during which time he ascended to a success that in retrospect must have seemed improbable even to him; through his literary efforts he found there something rather like Wordsworth's very Heaven. While working as an office clerk for a right-wing writer, he assiduously studied the subject and style of various cheap magazines, called *revues galantes,* aimed at working-class women, and taught himself to write stories in the particular manner of each magazine. Displaying the facility and speed that marked his entire career, he wrote two or three stories a night, which he placed in a half-dozen different magazines. His good fortune continued when he was recommended for the job of secretary to a wealthy aristocrat, the Marquis de Tracy, for whom Simenon worked almost a year, traveling around France to his various houses; the two men became friends, and the marquis provided the writer with material for the French noble families and houses that sometimes appear in his novels.

While working for the marquis, Simenon continued writing short stories, submitting his more ambitious works to the daily newspaper *Le Matin,* whose literary editor was the celebrated and established French writer Colette. She systematically rejected his efforts but saw enough potential in them to summon him to a meeting and advise him to avoid a "literary" manner; he finally wrote something that pleased her and soon became a regular contributor. Still using his favorite pseudonym, "Georges Sim," as well as others, the young writer continued to turn out pulp fiction at a phenomenal rate, producing four or more stories a day and, beginning in 1924, various kinds of novels aimed at particular audiences—love stories, crime stories, travel stories, fantastic adventures, and so forth. His most recent biographer, Pierre Assouline, estimates that "[b]etween 1924 and 1931 he published about 190 pulp novels under at least seventeen pseudonyms" (p. 64). (The approximation is important and necessary—because of their subject's astonishing productivity, every Simenon scholar, critic, biographer, or bibliographer must deal in estimates and approximations.)

By 1925, Simenon had already become something of a cottage industry, supporting the unusual household that surrounded him most of his life—a secretary to type the eighty pages a day he produced, his wife to assist him in his artistic and social life, and their housekeeper, Henriette Liberge (whom he called "Boule"), with whom Simenon maintained an unusual and affectionate sexual relationship. In addition to his grueling work schedule and complicated domestic situation, he and his wife consorted with a large, varied crowd of artists and bons vivants, patronizing fashionable bohemian nightclubs. He also continued his obsessive pursuit of sexual gratification, especially of what might be called the commercial variety, which he professed to prefer, paying prostitutes and visiting whorehouses.

The bubbling ferment of Parisian artistic, cultural, and social life in the 1920s provided innumerable sources of delight for the young author, but surely none was more enchanting than the legendary Josephine Baker, who will forever be identified with the energy, excitement, and sensuality of the city in that remarkable era. Simenon first saw her dancing nude in the famous show, *La Revue Nègre*, in 1925 and, along with the rest of Paris, fell in love with the beautiful, sensual, exotic young black woman from St. Louis, Missouri; unlike the rest of Paris, however, he managed the enviable feat of having her fall in love with him. The two young artists—Simenon was twenty-three, Baker twenty—perfectly matched in temperament and appetite, immediately responded to each other and launched a torrid affair that lasted more than a year (apparently a long time for both of them). It may be a measure of Simenon's worldly success and even an indication of his self-confidence that at that young age he found one of the great passions of his life in so compelling a figure as Josephine Baker— that he loved and was loved by the woman who was the toast of Paris. Despite their compatibility and the intensity of the relationship, Simenon apparently realized that he could only play second fiddle to so extraordinary a personality; at considerable emotional cost to himself, therefore, he broke off the affair and left Paris to recuperate from the experience. The two remained close friends, however, maintaining their regard and perhaps even their passion for each other long after those heady days in Paris.

While conducting his affair with Baker, Simenon also displayed his ability and willingness to cultivate notoriety in other areas. In a publicity stunt that contemporary press agents would admire, he signed a contract to write a novel within a week (no great problem for a man who cranked out pulp fiction at the pace of a high-speed engine) while on public view inside a glass box. The stunt, orchestrated by the hustling publisher of a dubious newspaper, drove virtually all the major newspapers and magazines into paroxysms of commentary, most of it critical and satirical attack. Although nobody seems to remember that the whole enterprise ultimately was aborted, nevertheless, as Assouline points out, Simenon came to be known forever as "the man who wrote a novel locked in a glass cage" (p. 81). The incident, or at least the apparently sincere plans for it, seems typical of an author entirely willing to court public attention by any possible means.

An Inspector Calls

His recuperative period away from Paris may have revived his ambitions to write what he called "literature," or later, *romans durs*, "hard novels," as distinguished from his prodigious scribbling for the pulps. The beginnings of one of his greatest major accomplishments, the Maigret series, date back to his time away from the city and to his first journeys through the inland waterways of several European regions. In 1928 and 1929 he sailed the rivers and canals of France, Holland, and northern Europe with his unusual household, writing all the while. The experience proved central to his fiction in many ways, inspiring the locations, background, atmosphere, character, even motivation for many of his novels. But most of all, as he suggests in his *Mémoires intimes* (1981; *Intimate Memoirs*, 1984), it provided him with the character who made him rich beyond his youthful dreams and famous in a way even so assiduous a cultivator of fame probably could not have imagined. While sailing on the canals he created Commissaire (often translated as Inspector and promoted through the years to higher offices like Chief Inspector and Superintendent) Jules Maigret of the Police Judiciaire, writing the first novel to star the great detective, *Pietr-le-Letton* (*The Strange Case of Peter the Lett*, 1931). As he remembered it in *Intimate Memoirs*, "There appears one Maigret, who, I didn't know then, was to haunt me for so many years and turn my whole life around" (p. 29).

In fact, over the course of more than forty years and more than eighty novels, Maigret came to dominate the author's life, career, and reputation. Whatever the quality (and amplitude) of his work in all areas of fiction, from the innumerable pulp stories and romances to his "literature," Simenon's most profound and permanent achievement finally resides in those abbreviated, pithy, curiously static police novels about the investigations of the formidable Maigret. After 122 pulp novels published under his many pseudonyms, the first Maigret was also the first of his books to be published under his own name, which may indicate another aspect of its importance to the man and the author. (Initially, in fact, many readers were led to believe that "Simenon" was a pseudonym for the popular writer Georges Sim.)

Despite his great success with pulp novels, the author at first experienced problems finding a publisher for his new detective fiction. The publishers apparently objected to precisely those qualities that make Simenon's detective and his fictional investigations unique in the history of the form. The Maigrets differ completely from any detective, mystery, or crime novels preceding, surrounding, or following them; they are, quite simply, sui generis, a form unto themselves, novels that resemble no others, except perhaps some of the author's other works that deal not with detection but with the criminal possibilities and impulses within all of us. Their sheer number, their universal popularity, and, of course, their inherent quality placed the novels and their author in the forefront of literature; they essentially transformed his career. Inspector Maigret became one of the most famous fictional characters of the twentieth century and certainly one of its greatest detectives. Although he differed radically from the sleuths who preceded and surrounded him, for most students of the form he was promoted to the select rank of the great detectives.

Despite sterile and wearying negotiations with his publisher, complicated by contractual obligations to produce more pulp fiction, Simenon wrote four Maigrets in 1930. Always willing, indeed anxious, to promote himself and his work, he launched the series with a *bal anthropométrique* ("Anthropometric Ball"—the police used "anthropometric" cards to detail physical characteristics of suspects), employing an elaborate decorative motif of crime, detection, and punishment and attended by artists and aristocrats, editors and critics, nightclubbers and hangers-on. Although the more orthodox literary critics quite understandably and perhaps justifiably expressed disdain, the ball was a grand success, reaping an enormous amount of free publicity in the press, which was, after all, precisely the point; the new endeavor, as a result, began with the sort of accelerated start that most writers and publishers can only lust after, even in our age of nationwide book tours, television talk shows, media interviews, and tame reviewers. The author made himself available for stories in numerous newspapers and magazines, conducted widely advertised book signings, and was featured in a radio adaptation of a portion of *Maigret and the Hundred Gibbets*.

His youthful eagerness to pursue fame and fortune, coupled with the prematurity and magnitude of his success, no doubt inspired envy among Simenon's colleagues and critics. The heady wine of public acclaim at so young an age surely accounts for his constant self-promotion, his unabashed egomania, and the unashamed display of his overwhelming self-confidence. He hypocritically (or audaciously) even complained to interviewers about the burdens of notoriety, the impossibility of maintaining privacy and anonymity in Paris. His boasts about his international fame and his ambition to revive the moribund French novel, combined with his relentless self-advertising, stimulated the negative commentary of the critical community, who regarded his work with a certain skepticism throughout his career. His announcement in 1937 that he intended to win the Nobel Prize in ten years could hardly have endeared him to his fellow writers or the rest of the literary world, including the Nobel Committee, which never bestowed their award on him, perhaps in part because of that announcement.

Whatever the critical reaction, Simenon entered fully into his version of the life of a successful author, working and living at a pace and on a scale that most writers would not dare to imagine and thus perhaps supplying another reason for the hostility of the orthodox literary world. Today it seems incredible that he could accomplish so much memorable fiction while simultaneously conducting his constant self-promotion and enjoying a life of sybaritic luxury. His early success both nourished and stimulated his hunger for the good life, and he began to live very well indeed—his writing and his skill at marketing the product earned him deluxe accommodations, yachts, chauffeured limousines, and voyages to distant, sometimes wildly exotic, locations. Besides traveling around the globe, he moved frequently in his adopted country. In addition to his apartments in Paris, he lived in many houses throughout the 1930s—a small country estate near La Rochelle, a hunting lodge in the forest of Orléans, other luxurious dwellings in Neuilly and Porquerolles, then another house at Nieul-sur-Mer. In the same decade, in addition to his sailing trips on the inland waterways, he cruised the Mediterranean and journeyed to Lapland, Africa, and eastern Europe; he embarked on an around-the-world cruise, sailing west from the Hague in December 1934 and returning to Marseilles in May of 1935.

None of that frequent moving, traveling, and high living interfered with Simenon's writing; in fact, the decade of the 1930s proved a remarkably rich time for him. Main-

taining his usual amazing rate of speed, he published some sixty novels, among them nineteen Maigrets. The various trips fed both journalism and fiction: among other works, he wrote a series of articles about colonialism in Africa, and the world tour, for example, inspired six novels. Many of the "straight" novels from that period reflect his several voyages to exotic places, which in fiction he populated with wretched, desperate characters. His observations on those travels apparently both encouraged and exacerbated the negative experiences and emotions that he imparted to so many of his fictional people. Whether in Turkey, Russia, Africa, America, or Paris, his characters dwell in the dark landscape of Simenon, a sad, tense tropic of longing, pain, and defeat.

France During World War II

The end of the decade marked a new stage in the author's life and career and, more important, a new era for Europe and the world: Simenon's son Marc was born in April of 1939, and in September, Germany invaded Poland. France and England declared war, but Belgium, the nation of which he maintained his citizenship, remained neutral. Repeating the strategies of World War I, the German army invaded Belgium in May 1940, effectively destroying that neutrality. Simenon had been alerted in the general mobilization of the Belgian army in 1938, and after the invasion he expected to be drafted once again; when he reported to the Belgian embassy in Paris, he was appointed commissioner for Belgian refugees at La Rochelle, assisting the thousands of his countrymen fleeing their nation for France. He worked to provide them with the many needs of any displaced population, especially shelter, food, medicine, and temporary employment. He also betrayed an entirely ignoble anti-Semitism in his labeling of a group of Jewish diamond merchants from Antwerp as not Belgians but "stateless Israelites" (Assouline, p. 176).

Perhaps even less worthy, while his countrymen variously suffered, resisted, collaborated, or (mostly) just got along during World War II and the German occupation, after some initial anxiety and discomfort, Simenon thrived. When the German army invaded France itself and routed both the French and British troops, Simenon's job as commissioner ended, and he fled to a region of what became for a while Vichy France. He rented part of a large mansion in Fontenay and conducted himself, as he often did in his various rural retreats, like a combination of country gentleman and lord of the manor; he also, of course, continued writing and publishing, earning large sums from his books and film adaptations. Despite whatever inconvenience and vexation he may have endured (along with everyone else in France in that time), his career progressed with relative smoothness. One of his biographers notes that Simenon holds the record for the most film versions of literary works made during the occupation—nine to Balzac's seven—which indicates that his writing not only entertained millions but, possibly more important, did not offend the occupying forces. Those motion pictures, produced by Continental films, incidentally, were essentially German productions, underwritten through official funds, supervised by important German film people, and approved by the Nazi bureaucracy.

Despite the stirring myths of courageous resistance to the enemy, as numerous revisionist histories have pointed out and the Marcel Ophuls film *The Sorrow and the Pity* has most vividly documented, during World War II virtually the entire population of France, in effect, not only capitulated quickly to the German invasion but also collaborated eagerly with their conqueror. Simenon apparently believed mostly in his own survival, which may have made his personal neutrality and his accommodation to the status quo a relatively simple political and moral decision. Certainly numerous French intellectuals and alleged lovers of freedom and justice managed to cope relatively easily with the fact of defeat and occupation. Far from the agony of those who suffered most from the inhumanity of the German occupation—Jews, resisters, other sorts of "undesirables"—in the way of

imprisonment, deportation to concentration camps, torture, or execution, and whatever privation and discomfort the ordinary citizens of France might have endured, Simenon enjoyed an income and a freedom denied most of his fellow residents. He managed to acquire official permission to travel to Paris for both business and pleasure—he attended to contracts and meetings with publishers, dined as well as possible, and visited the better class of brothel. The ethical problems surrounding his comfortable personal life and his successful professional career seem never to have disturbed his peace of mind or interfered with his productivity.

On the other hand, the author also discovered firsthand something of what it was like for those people whom official German policy had designated as undesirable: some rabid anti-Semites and perhaps particular enemies of Simenon instigated a charge of racial impurity against him. He was, after all, an artist, which most conservative governments view as a highly suspicious occupation, and his accusers suggested that the name Simenon in fact derived from the Jewish name Simon. Fearful of deportation to a concentration camp, Simenon had to exert himself mightily to prove his acceptability to the German occupiers and their complaisant assistants in the Vichy government. He attempted to dig up the required birth and baptismal certificates of his ancestors, sought references from government servants and clergymen, implored well-connected acquaintances to authenticate his ethnic purity, pulled strings and curried favor, and through the support of influential friends was declared free of the fatal taint of Jewishness.

War's End

When the war finally ended, the frenzy of righteousness that welled up in a cowed populace of trimmers and collaborators, all busily exonerating themselves of their recent past, almost inevitably touched Simenon; he had lived entirely too well in every way during the war to escape suspicion and perhaps even punishment. His name appeared on a number of lists of those considered collaborators and was even mentioned over the radio as someone the Resistance had marked down for investigation or perhaps something more severe. After the Allied invasion of Europe, the Resistance forces grew stronger and bolder, and when British paratroopers landed near the remote hamlet where Simenon had relocated after the anti-Semitic inquiries, the author decided to revise his stance of neutrality. The Resistance members in his area happily and somewhat contemptuously accepted his propitiatory gifts of wine and food and promptly commandeered his Citroën automobile. When France was liberated and a number of people with scores to settle began the business of purges and retaliations, Simenon found himself vulnerable to charges of collaboration, some of them apparently the work of the same people who had earlier reported that he was Jewish. For a time he endured house arrest at yet another location while the authorities investigated his case, ultimately clearing him of active collaboration; as soon as he was free, he fled to Paris.

There he encountered new difficulties, the pressure of the purges then being conducted among the literary and cinematic community. Since he had prospered in both literature and film during the war, his name once again appeared on certain infamous lists. After some collaborationist journalists and editors whom he knew well were arrested, tried, and executed for their support of the occupation, his apprehensiveness about his fate naturally increased. If he was not in immediate danger of imprisonment or worse, some new decrees appeared directly aimed against people like him. The committees intent on purging French art of the collaborationist taint forbade the publication and distribution of the works and the payment of royalties to sanctioned writers; they also blacklisted certain filmmakers and banned their pictures. Although he escaped the worst of the retaliatory purges and punishments, Simenon was entirely aware of his dubious status and no doubt anxious about the possible loss of income; consequently, like so many of his fictional protagonists, he decided to embark on a new life in a new place. With his family he left France in 1945 and sailed to America.

The American Years

He traveled widely around the continent and resided in many different places—French Canada, Florida, Arizona, California, and Connecticut. At one time he considered becoming a citizen of the United States and began the necessary process, but changed his mind and moved back to Europe in 1955. In New York in 1945, while looking to hire a full-time, live-in secretary, he met a smart, accomplished, and bilingual young French-Canadian woman named Denyse (later called Denise) Ouimet, who immediately sparked a powerful attraction in him. The day they met they began a passionate relationship that rapidly blossomed into one of the great love affairs of his life. Strong, intelligent, and as sexually voracious as he, she responded to him fully; they began a typical Simenon ménage à trois, which, in 1948, after his housekeeper, Boule, finally arrived from France, became for a while a ménage à quatre.

The relationship with Denise, according to both of them, resembled his affair with Josephine Baker in its emotional fervor and in the equality and voracity of their sexual appetites. Its initial stages inspired one of his more highly regarded "straight" novels, *Trois Chambres à Manhattan* (1946; *Three Beds in Manhattan*, 1964), and their mutual giddiness may even influence the dreamy atmospheres of *Maigret à New York* (1947; *Maigret in New York's Underworld*, 1955), with the eccentric drunk who assists the Inspector, the circus performers, the psychic, and Maigret's own (occasionally alcohol-induced) sense of befuddlement. In 1950, Simenon obtained a Nevada divorce from Tigy; married Denise, who had given birth to a son, John, in September 1949; and moved his new family to Lakeville, Connecticut, where he lived for the next five years.

As usual, his traveling, his frequent relocations, his irregular personal life, and the peculiar circumstance of residing in a foreign country with the consequent necessity of learning another language did not prevent him from accomplishing his customary amount of work at his customary rate. Taking up residence in a new land, on the contrary, apparently provided a new impetus to his career. During his decade in North America he prospered both financially and artistically, acquiring significant wealth, fame, and honors. He published scores of stories and novels—twenty-six novels during his five years in Connecticut, for example—including dozens of Maigrets, attaining a world sales figure of three million copies a year. By 1951 he was the most frequently and widely translated French writer in the world, with, he estimated, at least one of his books published somewhere every week (Assouline, p. 284). He was profiled adoringly by Brendan Gill (who became a friend) in the *New Yorker*, interviewed in the excellent *Paris Review* series, named president of the Mystery Writers of America (1952, an honorary rather than an actual serving position), elected to the Belgian Royal Academy (1952), and made a knight of the French Legion of Honor (1955). As critical recognition began to catch up with financial success, he became not only a literary phenomenon and international celebrity but also a respected author. On his triumphant visit to Europe in 1952, crowded with parties, meetings, interviews, and press conferences, he revisited some of the scenes of his youth and enjoyed the many public displays of esteem from the literary community—publishers, editors, critics, and fellow writers.

Switzerland: Splendor and Sorrow

The productive and rewarding years in America, one of the most successful decades in Simenon's life, ended in 1955, when he moved his family back to Europe. He settled for a while in Cannes and then moved in 1957 to Switzerland, where he resided for the rest of his life. He lived for several years in a castle outside Lausanne before he moved in 1963 to an immense, luxuriously appointed house that he and Denise designed at Epalinges. There, established as an international figure, he spent the rest of his writing life. He settled with apparent ease into the role of distinguished international artist, celebrity author, and kindly paterfamilias. His family had increased, with the births of John (the immediate cause of his Reno divorce and marriage back in 1950); his only daughter, Marie-Jo (1953); and Pierre (1959); and in 1962 his son Marc's wife bore a child, making him a very happy grandfather.

Despite the grandeur and serenity of his surroundings and the many public displays of the great man at work and play in radio and television interviews, news stories, and photographic essays, his domestic life grew increasingly tense and unhappy. Beneath the appearance of a bustling business enterprise and the illusion of a happy household, his marriage was deteriorating and his family disintegrating. Alcoholic and hysterical, Denise had manifested a variety of pathological behaviors over the years, some of them perhaps induced by her relationship with a difficult, powerful, creative personality who was also a compulsive satyr. She was obsessively concerned about cleanliness and sanitized every room in which the peripatetic couple stayed; she insisted on an increasing number of secretaries and servants, from whom she demanded an increasing amount of time and effort; she took hours to compose long business letters on the most trivial matters; in the same manner, she occupied the telephone for extraordinary lengths of time; and she demonstrated a constant and almost frenzied need to control her entire environment. Always fascinated by psychiatry, Simenon attempted to understand her illness, studying texts, consulting experts, and coming up with a number of diagnoses on his own, including the most likely, manic depression. In 1962 she entered a psychiatric facility for treatment, including, most acutely, detoxification; in 1964 she reentered the clinic and, on the advice of several physicians, never returned to Epalinges: the marriage was effectively over.

Denise later revenged herself on Simenon with a candid memoir of their marriage, entitled *Un Oiseau pour le chat* (A Bird for the Cat, 1978); in 1981 she published a novel drawn from the same material, entitled *Le Phallus d'or* (The Golden Phallus); both books were apparently the work of a team of ghostwriters. The titles alone suggest something of her embittered interpretation of their relationship—herself as the innocent victim of the predatory, priapic Simenon. The author's own sorrows did not end with the separation from Denise, but increased with the growing unhappiness of his beloved daughter, Marie-Jo, a troubled young woman who began the first of several psychiatric treatments in 1966, when she was thirteen. In 1970 she suffered a nervous breakdown and spent several subsequent years of her short life undergoing one form of therapy or another and attempting one artistic career or another. Always obsessively fixated on her father, she embarked on a number of unsatisfactory romantic relationships, indulged in drugs and alcohol, suffered from anorexia, battled with a legion of inner demons, and ultimately committed suicide in 1978 at the age of twenty-five.

Simenon wrote the massive *Intimate Memoirs* as a long, sad love letter to his dead daughter, to examine his relationship with his lost child and to settle some scores with Denise, whom he blamed, with some justification, for Marie-Jo's death. The most controversial portion of that rambling, fascinating, often heartbreaking, sometimes unsatisfactory memoir involved his quotation of one of Marie-Jo's audiotapes; she recounted an incident that occurred when she was eleven years old, in which her mother masturbated in front of her, all the while telling her daughter that she would never please a man. According to Simenon, the bizarre incident, which Denise claimed never happened and which she managed to have censored from the book, appar-

ently left a deep and painful scar on Marie-Jo's psyche, which she could heal only by ending her life.

In 1961, Simenon had begun a sexual relationship with a new servant, Teresa Sburelin, who became one of his most loyal and devoted lovers. In a sense, she may have replaced Boule, the woman who spent her life serving him in every way; Boule left Epalinges in 1964, the same year that Denise departed for good. After a serious fall in 1966, when Simenon broke several ribs, Teresa became his nurse and something like his official companion. In 1970 his mother, Henriette, the woman who had dominated his life and work and for whom he would never feel adequate, died. Whatever their individual characters, the complexity of their relationships with Simenon, and the variety of emotions they aroused in him, the loss of wife, lifelong companion, beloved daughter, and domineering mother must have created seismic shocks in his own psyche. Certainly he took drastic steps and made profound changes in his life and art, surprising in a man and artist addicted to ritual and routine. He published his last "hard novel," *Les Innocents* (The Innocents, 1973), and the last Maigret, *Maigret et Monsieur Charles* (Maigret and Monsieur Charles, 1973), in 1972. In the same year he moved from Epalinges with Teresa, first to an apartment and then later to a small house in Lausanne. In 1973 he announced his retirement as a writer, going so far as to have the profession marked on his passport changed from "novelist" to "retired," an odd and somehow naively symbolic gesture of finality—as if an artist ceased being an artist when he stopped making his art.

In another symbolic gesture, he purchased a tape recorder and began to dictate what turned into twenty-one volumes of memoirs. That dictation and the consequent exercise in introspection and memory led to his *Letter to My Mother*, and the controversial *Intimate Memoirs*. In reality, however, just as he had announced, his career as an active writer was over. After so many years, so many journeys, so many houses, and so many words, he was ready to write the final chapter of his life. He became something of a European sage, a quasi-public version of the artist, the subject of admiring essays and profiles in the popular press, the era's notion of a great man. In one interview, conducted with his friend, fellow artist, and ardent fan, the great Italian film director Federico Fellini, he confessed to having had sex with ten thousand women, eight thousand of whom were professionals, as he called them. His biographers understandably regard the figure as something of an exaggeration, pointing out that it came from the man reputed to have written a novel while inside a glass box; like that falsehood, however, the confession apparently will cling forever to his name, so that he will always be known as the relentless satyr of his own invention. (It would be delightfully appropriate, of course, if the legends were somehow combined, so that he could be known as the writer who made love to ten thousand women in a week inside a glass cage!)

Throughout his last decades, Simenon continued to collect public honors from many sources. He continued to covet the Nobel Prize more or less openly in his maturity. It was, of course, the one great honor—richly deserved in the opinion of many readers and critics, including the present writer—that eluded him, one of the few major disappointments of his professional career.

In 1966 he was invited to the ceremonial unveiling of a statue of Commissaire Maigret, in Delfzijl, Holland, where the first Maigret was written. The event was attended by representatives of all his publishers and all the living actors who had played the detective in cinema and television productions. (Those many adaptations of his works, both hard novels and Maigrets, along with the options on others that were never actually produced, grew into an even larger source of income in his last years than the books themselves.) The Bibliothèque Simenon had opened in Liège in 1961, and he had been donating tapes of his dictation along with manuscripts, correspondence, clippings, articles, and French and foreign editions of his books to the University of

Liège since 1973; fittingly, the university established the Centre d'Études Georges Simenon in 1976. Despite his permanent self-exile from Belgium and the many places he had lived since he left his native country, he retained Belgian citizenship all his life; it was therefore appropriate that the most famous and successful Belgian writer in the world himself finally became, along with his most famous character, a sort of enduring public monument. Apparently desiring no other permanent memorial, he left instructions at his death that his body be cremated without any ceremony and that his ashes, mingled with his beloved daughter's, be scattered beneath a huge tree in the back garden of his last house in Lausanne. In a strange final gesture, he also directed that his children not be informed of his death, so that they would, as he said, learn of it on the radio. Georges Simenon died in his sleep in Lausanne on 4 September 1989.

The Work and the Reputation

In the world of letters, of course, Simenon has achieved a rather different kind of monumentality, together with a reputation and critical assessment as ambiguous as his personal history. A number of factors complicate the critical responses to Simenon throughout his career. To begin with, his early work in pulp fiction made it easy for many commentators to dismiss him as a mere entertainer of the masses. His widely publicized facility and fecundity always provoked doubts in the critical community, and to this day the one consistent negative view holds that no one who writes so much so fast could really be of any value. Simenon was also guilty of the related crime of immense popularity—millions of people all over the world read him in most of the modern languages, numerous motion pictures adapted from his works reached millions more, and from these endeavors he earned a very good living, which he allowed the world to know about. To put it simply, anyone who made so much money from so many books could not be considered a great artist by the critical community.

The author essentially developed two distinctive but related literary forms, commonly known as the Simenon and the Maigret, one, the *roman dur* or hard novel, the other, the *roman policier* or police novel. Working in his preferred short form, he seems to have found a mode and length perfectly suited to his spirit, intellect, temperament, perhaps even his physical powers and limitations. His characteristic brevity meshes with the terseness of his prose style to create an appropriate expression of both his ethic and his aesthetic, terms that would make so fervent a hater of abstractions most uncomfortable; his novels regard life in brief, bleak glimpses, impressionistic moments when more or less ordinary human beings react to some stress, some external alteration in their environment, some cruel happenstance. Almost invariably his protagonists react to that stress through a violent act—they hurt themselves or someone else, they abruptly change their lives, leave their homes, they even commit murder. Aside from the pain the characters share, their fates appear mostly to be sad and dismal, a series of consequences which some initial act or decision, however small, lays out as an inevitable chain of events proceeding from that initial point, generally ending in disaster.

Most of the people in the Simenons could very well appear in the Maigrets—in effect, they commit the crimes that Maigret, with his depthless understanding, must investigate. He provides at least a modicum of judgment for an author who seems never really to judge the misdeeds of his characters, finding them out, tracking them down, delivering them to what justice can be said to exist in this world. At the same time, because of his sympathy and understanding, his ability to enter wholly into a case, to understand fully the lives and personalities of its people, especially the victim, the detective also senses a powerful identification with the characters: he often feels profoundly sorry for them, he often expresses sadness at the results of his investigation, he even sometimes feels as if he had investigated himself and found nothing less than the criminal he seeks, the criminal in all of us. The detective in Simenon's Maigrets could very well serve as both another Simenon character and as a surrogate for Simenon himself, a perfectly appropriate representative of the author, unravelling a creation that someone else, his own creator, made—a murder, of course—and discovering that his task, as Simenon characterized writing in the *Paris Review* interview of 1955, is a "vocation of unhappiness."

In these days of repression and what has become generally known as political correctness, Simenon suffers a new kind of opprobrium: his remarkable sex life seems to offend more people than his books. Even Pierre Assouline writes of his subject with an occasional disapproving pursing of the lips or a hint of patronizing irony. He notes, for example, the numerous exotic places where the author managed to locate the best whorehouses, including the ice and snow of Lapland, and records Denise Simenon's perfectly valid complaints that although she and her husband made love three times a day, he still sought other women for sexual pleasure.

Any number of facile diagnoses could account for the author's powerful sexual appetite, including the theories of those psychiatrists whom Simenon, a devotee of medical texts and a reader of Freud and Jung, found so fascinating. Surely important connections exist, however, between sexuality and genius, the urge to create and to procreate, and the need to make love and to make art, which at some times may be exactly the same thing. After he completed a novel, Simenon would indulge in what one psychiatrist termed "a sexual outburst" (Bresler, p. 87). It hardly seems strange or unlikely that an artist so driven in his creative life would reveal himself equally driven in his sexual life. His incessant, casual, and apparently rapid copulations express the excessive energy that drove him all his life and enabled him to accomplish so much. Finally, perhaps as with his literary and commercial success, some of his detractors envy his sex life as well.

The sheer speed of Simenon's production, which accounts for its multitude, probably most offends his detractors. For many purists, a man who writes a detective novel in a week and a hard novel in eleven days simply cannot be composing great literature. Yet the discipline he imposed on himself throughout his career, adhering to a rigid routine almost military in its precision in the midst of the public events of a turbulent century and the private turmoil of a complicated domestic life, matched that of the most dedicated artists, even those who spend many years producing a small body of work—most notoriously Gustave Flaubert, but also writers in our century like James Joyce, E. M. Forster, F. Scott Fitzgerald, Henry Roth, J. D. Salinger, and Ralph Ellison.

The "state of grace," as he called it—note the religious phrase in a man who had long disavowed any faith—the trancelike condition that descended upon him in his fits of creation, the total absorption in his work that sometimes caused him physical problems or made him behave like his characters suggest an almost mystical approach to the act of composition, as if something larger and stronger than himself drove his writing. Both his methods and his production suggest something of the hallucinating artist, a creator who could not, even if he wished, stop himself from creating, a man possessed by powerful visions and driven to transform them into works of art. He often thought of himself as a successor to Honoré de Balzac, another prolific writer with a sexual appetite to match, but Simenon may more resemble those writers who dazzle through the opulence and profusion of their imaginations—Shakespeare, Charles Dickens, William Faulkner (a particular favorite of his), even Thomas Wolfe. Although he always wrote short books—in part because the creative act so completely exhausted his physical and psychic energy—and was a determined practitioner of a stripped, terse, chiseled style in the manner of such modern masters as Ernest

Hemingway, Dashiell Hammett, and James M. Cain, his genius, paradoxically, resembles more closely that of those exuberant, prolix masters of the dizzyingly hyperbolic.

Simenon frequently declared his uneasiness with intellectual speculation (and intellectuals themselves); his distrust of abstract ideas was perhaps an unwise attitude to hold in any literary community, but an almost fatal one in France, where theoreticians of all kinds traditionally dedicate themselves to exploring the outer reaches of the impalpably inane. A great many academically minded critical commentators simply cannot comprehend the notion of pure art or of a pure artist, whose chief activity and purpose is creation itself, the making of the work of art, which always, despite academic belief to the contrary, precedes ideas. His fiction grows not from the contemplation of a philosophical concept but from human stories, full of concrete events, real people, felt emotions. He did not write to advance ideas, preach sermons, argue ideology, convey advice; on the contrary, his writing reflects a man without any particular, identifiable convictions. He generally refused to discuss his work while he was engaged in it, forbade anyone from watching him while writing, and found it difficult to describe his novels after he had written them, all of which possibly suggests an involuntary compulsion to create beyond his own ability to articulate it, which might be called a pure devotion to his art.

Not only did Simenon adhere to a strict observance of both clock and calendar in his rigid writing routine, but he invariably also followed the same patterns to find his inspiration, the origins of his fiction. He would prepare himself by sharpening dozens of pencils and lining up his pipes already filled with tobacco, so that he could focus on the particular work and maintain his artist's trance. He kept meticulous files of the books he planned, each allotted a manila envelope with a few possible names of characters written on the outside, along with other notes and clippings inside. He drew his names and places from telephone directories, city maps, newspapers—the ordinary, available daily repositories of the real and the commonplace. Rumor suggested that he could visit a strange city and invent a novel merely by sitting in a hotel room and glancing through the names in the local telephone book. Even if his novels delve into the psychological and emotional depths of the human soul, they remain steadfastly on the observable surface of the actual.

The Maigrets

Despite his almost immediate success as a composer of pulp fiction and, consequently, a moneymaker for his publishers, as this essay notes earlier, Simenon initially had difficulty convincing them to accept his detective fiction. His novels featuring Jules Maigret of the Police Judiciaire first appeared during the period known among students of the form as the Golden Age of detective fiction; instead of providing a propitious environment for a new author with a new protagonist, however, that circumstance paradoxically worked against him. The spirits of Sir Arthur Conan Doyle and his great creation, Sherlock Holmes, still haunted this fertile period of the genre; Doyle, in fact, died in 1930, at just about the time Maigret was being born. In all the detective stories written and read in that rich time (most of them British in origin), the sleuth followed in the footsteps of Holmes and his friend, assistant, and chronicler, Dr. Watson. The classic English mystery novel, especially of that period, depends upon a complicated puzzle, a brilliant amateur investigator to solve it, a cast of recognizable characters drawn from the traditional comedy of manners, and the isolated, comfortable, frequently posh settings of country houses, tea parties, costume balls, village fetes, cruise liners, and first-class railway carriages. The detective in those stories was invariably a distinctive, often eccentric figure who solved difficult mysteries through superior powers of observation, analysis, and reasoning—following Sherlock

Holmes, characters like Agatha Christie's Hercule Poirot (another Belgian), John Dickson Carr's Gideon Fell and Sir Henry Merrivale, and Dorothy L. Sayers' Lord Peter Wimsey.

Simenon's books, as the reluctant publishers pointed out, bore no resemblance at all to any of the popular works of the classic tradition. Whether intentionally or not, the Maigret novels differ in virtually every detail from the most popular kinds of detective fiction of their time, almost as if the author consciously set out to break every rule, violate every convention, even challenge the very foundations of the form. In the creation of Inspector Maigret (despite the original French term and his various promotions, it is simpler to employ the English title he is most generally known by), Simenon ignored the contemporary context of the genre and consequently forsook the audience it had created. Ambitious to try something new and gifted with unusual self-confidence, he apparently decided to pioneer a boldly original invention, a new kind of detective story.

Inspector Maigret, to begin with, bears little resemblance to his colleagues in previous detective fiction. He is not a brilliant eccentric with a full complement of distinguishing characteristics and extraordinary powers of intellect and perception. Maigret instead is a very ordinary man, much more deserving than Simenon of the description "a man like any other." Although he begins fully fledged, so to speak, in his first appearance in *The Strange Case of Peter the Lett*, as the series progresses, sometimes moving back and forth in time, the history of his family, personal, and professional life gradually emerges, until he becomes a comfortable old friend to his readers. As the years and the cases pile up, we learn the details of his domestic and professional life, his favorite food and drink, his few friends, his limited amusements—that he does not drive a car, for example, that he spends his leisure moments attending the cinema and watching television. We learn something about his office at the Quai des Orfèvres, with its smoky coal stove, where sandwiches and beer are delivered during his interrogations. We learn a little about his colleagues, Lucas and Lapointe and Janvier, and about the various examining magistrates and the French system of jurisprudence, an accumulation of small facts that create the sense of a living world.

Of peasant origins—his father served as the steward or bailiff of a country estate—Maigret, as a professional policeman, resides in a stratum of the middle class, perhaps rising a notch or two through his promotions and his growing fame as a successful solver of criminal cases. Certainly his daily life and behavior seem crushingly commonplace, the existence of a happily humdrum and solidly bourgeois Frenchman. Thoroughly domestic and completely faithful, he lives with his pleasant, utterly devoted, and equally dull wife, Louise, in an apartment on the Boulevard Richard-Lenoir. Madame Maigret, as the authorial voice invariably refers to her, usually addresses him as "Maigret," as if they shared no particular intimacy or even friendship; sadly, they have no children, one of Maigret's few regrets. Although they behave toward each other with the affection of a long and happily married couple, they display almost nothing in the way of passion. In that, as in most other areas of his life, Maigret obviously differs as much from his creator as from other fictional detectives.

Although his name ironically suggests thinness ("*maigre*" is related to the English "meager"), the inspector is a large man—the early novels often describe him as "massive"—who eats heavily and eagerly throughout his novels; he pays close attention to his appetite, frequently specifying favorite dishes his wife makes especially for him. Madame Maigret often prepares heavy, hearty peasant fare—cassoulet, calves' liver, and his favorite, *choucroute* (sauerkraut), which he either consumes or thinks about consuming in almost every novel. His size and solidity, whatever the effects of his diet, also express a palpable gravitas, a sort of psychological dignity and massiveness, which constitutes one of his best weapons in dealing with criminals.

Maigret's attention to food, which may characterize the French anyway, and his frequent heavy drinking throughout the novels combine with his pipe smoking to provide one major connection with other fictional detectives, who usually display a powerful orality—eating, drinking, smoking, talking, and boasting a good deal. Many readers notice the particular alcoholic beverages that Maigret consumes in his investigations—quantities of wine, of course, along with Calvados, an apple brandy, and endless glasses of beer, which most often accompany his notorious marathon interrogations. Maigret's size now and then becomes a problem and demands moderation in eating and drinking, not always a successful endeavor. In *Maigret et le marchand de vin* (1970; *Maigret and the Wine Merchant*, 1971), for example, though suffering from one of his frequent colds and attempting to cut down on his drinking, in one short day Maigret drinks two glasses of rum before going home for lunch and two glasses of red wine with the meal and then washes his aspirin down with a shot of sloe gin before going back to the office; the combination and quantity are hardly unusual for him.

If the detective differs from his fictional predecessors, so the crimes that occupy his attention defy the usual conventions of the mystery story. Like the investigator, the criminals seldom resemble the fascinatingly intelligent adversaries of the usual fictional detectives; they employ no careful stratagems, clever devices, or elaborate deceptions. The people Maigret brings to justice throughout his career belong to virtually every social class, from the rural peasantry to the affluent bourgeoisie to the hereditary aristocracy, but they share a democratic sameness in the drab humanity of their personalities and actions. They are ordinary people who commit the extraordinary act of murder, with the usual limited range of motives—fear, lust, jealousy, greed, even, occasionally, love. Throughout his long career, when Maigret investigates murder, he invariably discovers the sad humanity of all those touched by crime, even the killers themselves; very often, a central figure in the act—victim, murderer, witness, survivor—is very like himself, indeed like one of us.

Providing another initial source of discomfort for Simenon's original publishers, Inspector Maigret solves most of his cases through his own special methods, entirely different from the brilliant deductions of Sherlock Holmes and all his fictional progeny. Although he is a professional policeman with the resources of a large, modern investigative machine behind him, Maigret rarely resorts to the magnifying glass or the microscope, the examination of fingerprints and fabrics, the recondite conclusions of medical examiners and laboratory chemists—in fact, unlike most cops in most books, he shrinks from dead bodies and grisly murder scenes and does not attend autopsies. Even the gifted amateur Sherlock Holmes prided himself on his scientific knowledge and published a "trifling monograph" on the different varieties of tobacco ash, yet Maigret exhibits almost no interest in the science and technology of detection.

Perhaps his most striking departure from the traditional detective of fiction could serve as the riposte to one of Sherlock Holmes's famous reiterated utterances, "You know my methods, Watson." In answer to the frequent inquiries of reporters and colleagues, Maigret always insists, on the other hand, that he follows no method. (The 1949 novel *Mon Ami Maigret* appeared in America under the ironically apt title, *The Methods of Maigret*, 1957.) Of course, he does proceed through his investigations in a particular manner, solving his cases in his own peculiar style, which differs radically from the techniques of both actual and fictional criminal investigation. Maigret's method involves a process of osmosis and absorption, which works in two ways—he absorbs and at the same time allows himself to be absorbed. Like a sponge, he soaks up the major and minor details of a case, yet he also sinks utterly into the investigation, becoming in a sense a part of it, as if he were constantly investigating himself, which may actually be the great and ultimate truth of his novels.

The typical atmosphere, both physical and psychological, that Maigret absorbs usually resembles the dark, seedy, cheerless world of one of his distinguished English colleagues, also a writer of thrillers, Graham Greene. While generally less specifically detailed and lacking the explicitly moral content of "Greeneland," Simenon country shares its physical and spiritual climate of sorrow, despair, and pity. Even when he investigates a crime in the countryside in *Maigret et les témoins récalcitrants* (*Maigret and the Reluctant Witnesses*, 1959), for example, the weather behaves according to the usual Simenonian meteorology—cold, damp, gray, overcast with the human tragedy. Although many Americans tend to believe that the French spend their time energetically discussing philosophical questions in cafés, enjoying gourmet meals, drinking wonderful wine, and having terrific sex, in Simenon's France—as in his Holland, Belgium, Turkey, Russia, and America—life is a monochrome pageant of pain, suffering, and unhappiness.

An artist of crime, once he begins his immersion, Maigret works through the irrational methods of intuition and imagination, trusting such illogical means as instinct, emotion, and sensitivity to create his solution. He does not so much reason or analyze as grope and feel his way down the dark path to truth. He responds to a questioner in *Maigret in New York's Underworld*, "I never reason. . . . I never think," and a few pages later, "I am not intelligent" (pp. 150 ff.). In almost all his investigations, he examines the personalities involved, their past lives, and their habits and tastes much more closely than whatever clues may exist. He frequently eats the local fare and drinks the local wine, along with his usual beer and Calvados, in the locale of a murder, trying to put himself inside the psyches of the people he studies; above all, he seeks to know and become a part of the atmosphere, which he considers all-important—once he absorbs that, he can understand everything else. In *M. Gallet, décédé* (1931; *The Death of M. Gallet*, 1933), he articulates his need to know the dead man as he was when alive—"I want to breathe the air he breathed . . . rub shoulders with the people he lived with. . . . I want to picture this man as a living being, not only in space but in time" (*Maigret Stonewalled*, p. 114).

Sometimes he even takes up residence in the area of a crime, quite literally becoming a character in his own investigation. In *The Strange Case of Peter the Lett*, for example, he stays in the posh hotel where his quarry, a master of disguise, occupies a suite. In a later case—the title, *Maigret en meublé* (1951; *Maigret Takes a Room*, 1960), indicates his method—he moves into a neighborhood to solve a murder. In one of the purest, truest, most characteristic and essential Maigrets, *Maigret et le corps sans tête* (1955; *Maigret and the Headless Corpse*, 1967), he simply returns over and over again to the same low bar near one of those favorite Simenon canals, gradually coming to understand the life and personality of the woman who runs it. The whole pathetic case, all of its people victims of one kind or another, opens itself up to him in a typically sad epiphany, all the more astonishing because it occurs exactly as he anticipated: nothing is more surprising than the expected.

Maigret often succeeds through a direct personal experience of the people, the situation, the events he investigates; at times he identifies in some way with a particular person or finds the person familiar because of his own past. In *Maigret chez le ministre* (1955; *Maigret and the Minister*, 1969), he pursues a missing government report and a case of blackmail because the cabinet minister who asks for help, an honest countryman among a gang of political scoundrels, reminds him of his own background and family. When he arrives at the ambiguous and unhappy truth of the affair, he recognizes himself in the man he has attempted to help: "Their eyes met. Once again the Superintendent had the impression that the man beside him resembled him like a brother. Both looked at each other with the same sadness of defeat, their shoulders hunched" (*Maigret and the Calame Report*, p. 183). That peculiar identification,

even with some unlikely people, occurs in one way or another in a great many of his novels.

Maigret rarely enjoys the triumph of bringing a criminal to justice; rather, he most often finds himself saddened by yet another revelation of human weakness, yet another insight into the common pain of ordinary life. Because of his vast sympathy, the inspector frequently cares more deeply for the people he must arrest than he does for their victims, who sometimes richly deserve their fates. In many novels he regrets the necessity of properly carrying out his duty, of serving as the instrument of judgment and punishment for people whose actions may grow from a perfectly justifiable motive; crime and guilt, he knows, are a complex affair. He is more repelled by the vicious intended victim than by her would-be killers in *Les Scrupules de Maigret* (1958; *Maigret Has Scruples*, 1959); in *Maigret Takes a Room* he must arrest the devoted lover of an invalid, solving a case that therefore causes him more grief than triumph. In *Maigret and the Wine Merchant*, he sympathizes deeply with the poor clerk, who is oppressed in his marriage and brutalized and humiliated by his rich, cruel boss until he is finally driven to murder.

From his earliest appearances the detective expresses compassion for almost all the people he must track down, most of it rooted in his constant attempts to find out their histories, the sequential accumulation of actions and decisions that led them to the crisis that brings him into their lives. When he discovers that he understands the people and thus solves the crime, the most unfortunate result is the permanent residue of the crime, his capacity to pity people precisely because he understands them. In one of his first cases, *Le Charretier de la "Providence"* (1931; *The Crime at Lock 14*, 1934), set along the banks of those canals the author sailed, he can feel nothing but an immense pity for the sad, silent, gentle man who kills because he discovers he cannot escape his past and himself. In *The Death of M. Gallet*, the inspector grapples with an apparently puzzling crime, which turns out to be a horribly botched suicide, again involving a man with another name, another life, who finds himself trapped in the prison of his own deceptions.

That reiterated theme of the double life, based on the situation of men who, for reasons they do not always fully understand, flee their families, homes, occupations, and themselves, preoccupies Simenon in both the Maigrets and the hard novels. Maigret's cases sometimes seem like new approaches to books that Simenon has written, from the opposite perspective, as if the detective were called upon after the fact to investigate the protagonists of hard novels like *L'Homme qui regardait passer les trains* (1938; *The Man Who Watched the Trains Go By*, 1945), *Bergelon* (1941; *The Delivery*, 1981), or *La Fuite de M. Monde* (1945; *Monsieur Monde Vanishes*, 1967). The subject, which John Raymond has discussed in his most useful *Simenon in Court*, deserves additional study, worthy of a book in itself. For untold reasons, the author seems fascinated by the existence of the inner, the buried, the other life, the possibility of an alternate self, perhaps even the doppelgänger of so many great nineteenth-century novels. Maigret's approach may represent something like a judgment or at least a commentary on the stories his creator tells in an entirely different context, another aspect of that fantastic creative imagination.

A spiritual atmosphere of sadness and defeat often overwhelms the Maigret novels, quite naturally affecting the detective, who has immersed himself in the world he examines and imbibed its miasma of desperation and fatality. In one of his most dismal cases, *Maigret and the Headless Corpse*, the absolute passivity of the woman he investigates, her pathetic vulnerability to sexual exploitation, and her melancholy indifference to fate instruct him most poignantly in the mystery of unhappiness, the one mystery he can never solve. As in *Maigret Takes a Room*, a hopeless love overwhelms the people involved, and the murder seems almost the only logical outcome of the unhappy emotional entanglement. If he enters the case, becomes one with the people he investigates, then surely he must suffer their anguish, feel their motives, know their despair, perhaps even act with their criminal intention. To identify wholly means not only that the detective must experience the lives of the people in the case but also that he cannot fully detach himself from the crime, its origins, its aftermath. Once again, he inevitably, if unconsciously, investigates himself—if he both immerses himself in a case and absorbs it into himself, then, in effect, he reconstructs it out of his own spirit. No wonder his investigations, no matter how successful, so often end in a sense of disappointment and defeat—even if he tracks down and arrests a criminal, he realizes that we are all criminals and all victims as well, that too often no one can ever really solve anything.

Given the people and the crimes they commit, in the jagged landscape of defeat in Simenon's dark country of the tortured human heart, it is no wonder that Maigret thinks of himself as very different from the usual policeman or the usual fictional detective. As several commentators notice, over and over again in his books, when he reflects on his life and his career, he frequently imagines an ideal vocation; in *La Première Enquête de Maigret* (1949; *Maigret's First Case*, 1958), for example, he thinks of a sort of spiritual consultant, whose counsel troubled people would seek: "In a manner of speaking he would have been a repairer of destinies. Not only because he was intelligent. Maybe he wouldn't have needed to be exceptionally intelligent? But because he was able to live the lives of every sort of man, to put himself in everybody's mind" (in *Maigret Cinq*, p. 360). For Maigret, the ideal policeman is a combination of physician and priest, who would hear, understand, forgive, and ultimately heal everyone and everything; Inspector Maigret is a very unusual cop indeed.

Finally, one of the best ways of understanding Maigret's career is the delightful book, *Les Mémoires de Maigret* (1951; *Maigret's Memoirs*, 1963). It really should have appeared at the end of Maigret's distinguished career as a sort of summing up, rather than in 1951, when Maigret still had a great deal of crime and detection ahead of him. As the title suggests, the volume consists of Maigret's rather sketchy reminiscences of his life and career in his own voice. Maigret recalls his childhood in the country, his youthful medical studies, the death of his father (at the age of forty-four, like Simenon's father), his first meeting with the woman who became his wife, his early years as a policeman, and so forth, illuminating other sides of the man who dominated so many novels. The major invention of the book, however, comes when a young journalist and novelist named Georges Sim enters Maigret's life in order to study him and his cases for a series of novels. Maigret reluctantly discusses his profession with the rather silly, self-important young man, revealing most of those thoughts and feelings that occupy all his novels. He points out differences between himself and "Simenon's Maigret," complaining about misreadings and exaggerations. He notices, however, that the writer comes to resemble his model, adopting certain of his habits and gestures; this turns the book into a complex literary work.

The *Memoirs* quite wonderfully show a fictional character commenting on his creator: the very notion of a novelist writing about his character writing about the novelist suggests the extent and quality of Simenon's wit and creativity. While allowing Maigret to tell Sim and us much about himself, he also accomplishes a remarkable tour de force, the sort of work that these days might be called metafictional or postmodern in its pioneering experimentalism. The novel indicates the graceful brilliance of Simenon's imagination and suggests, better than the huge and growing library of articles and books, biography and criticism, the apparently effortless artistry of a genius in full command of his powers; it is an entertaining proof of the quality of his achievement.

Simenon's reputation will rest forever on the immensity of his accomplishment, the monumental achievement of an unparalleled body of work. That corpus exemplifies the remarkable variety he extracts from a seemingly limited range of characters, situations, and motives and the power he imparts to so many brief excursions into the dark arena of the human spirit. Whatever controversies surround his life and art, whatever critical dialectic engages his achievement, his fiction places him among the great literary geniuses of the twentieth century—no writer of detective stories, no novelist of any kind, approaches him. He was an artist quite unlike any other.

Selected Bibliography

WORKS OF GEORGES SIMENON

This bibliography includes a list of the first publication, with the original French titles, of the Maigret novels, arranged chronologically, along with a much more limited selection of his writing in other genres. The initial English translations are included, citing both the first American and first British editions.

THE MAIGRETS

Au Rendez-vous des terre-neuvas. Paris: Fayard, 1931. Translated as *The Sailors' Rendezvous* by Margret Ludwig. In *Maigret Keeps a Rendezvous.* London: Routledge, 1940; New York: Harcourt Brace, 1941.

Le Charretier de la "Providence." Paris: Fayard, 1931. Translated as *The Crime at Lock 14.* In *The Triumph of Inspector Maigret.* London: Hurst and Blackett, 1934. Translated as *Maigret Meets a Milord.* Baltimore: Penguin, 1963.

Le Chien jaune. Paris: Fayard, 1931. Translated as *A Face for a Clue* by Geoffrey Sainsbury. In *The Patience of Maigret.* London: Routledge, 1939; New York: Harcourt Brace, 1940.

Un Crime en Hollande. Paris: Fayard, 1931. Translated as *A Crime in Holland* by Geoffrey Sainsbury. In *Maigret Abroad.* London: Routledge, 1940; New York: Harcourt Brace, 1940.

La Danseuse du Gai-Moulin. Paris: Fayard, 1931. Translated as *At the "Gai-Moulin"* by Geoffrey Sainsbury. In *Maigret Abroad.* London: Routledge, 1940; New York: Harcourt Brace, 1940.

M. Gallet, décédé. Paris: Fayard, 1931. Translated as *The Death of M. Gallet* by Anthony Abbott. In *Introducing Inspector Maigret.* London: Hurst and Blackett, 1933. As *Maigret Stonewalled* by Margaret Marshall. Harmondsworth, Eng.: Penguin, 1963.

La Nuit du carrefour. Paris: Fayard, 1931. Translated as *The Crossroad Murders* by Anthony Abbott. In *In-*

spector *Maigret Investigates.* London: Hurst and Blackett, 1933. As *Maigret at the Crossroads.* Harmondsworth, Eng.: Penguin, 1963.

Le Pendu de Saint Pholien. Paris: Fayard, 1931. Translated as *The Crime of Inspector Maigret* by Anthony Abbott. In *Introducing Inspector Maigret.* London: Hurst and Blackett, 1933. As *Maigret and the Hundred Gibbets.* Baltimore: Penguin, 1963.

Pietr-le-Letton. Paris: Fayard, 1931. Translated as *The Strange Case of Peter the Lett* by Anthony Abbott. In *Inspector Maigret Investigates.* London: Hurst and Blackett, 1933. As *Maigret and the Enigmatic Lett.* Baltimore: Penguin, 1963.

Le Relais d'Alsace. Paris: Fayard, 1931. Translated as *The Man from Everywhere* by Stuart Gilbert. In *Maigret and M. l'Abbé.* London: Routledge, 1941; New York: Harcourt Brace, 1942.

La Tête d'un homme. Paris: Fayard, 1931. Translated as *A Battle of Nerves* by Geoffrey Sainsbury. In *The Patience of Maigret.* London: Routledge, 1939; New York: Harcourt Brace, 1940.

L'Affaire Saint-Fiacre. Paris: Fayard, 1932. Translated as *The Saint-Fiacre Affair* by Margret Ludwig. In *Maigret Keeps a Rendezvous.* London: Routledge, 1940. As *Maigret Goes Home.* Baltimore: Penguin, 1967.

Chez les Flamands. Paris: Fayard, 1932. Translated as *The Flemish Shop* by Geoffrey Sainsbury. In *Maigret to the Rescue.* London: Routledge, 1940; New York: Harcourt Brace, 1941.

Le Fou de Bergerac. Paris: Fayard, 1932. Translated as *The Madman of Bergerac* by Geoffrey Sainsbury. In *Maigret Travels South.* London: Routledge, 1940; New York: Harcourt Brace, 1940.

La Guinguette à deux sous. Paris: Fayard, 1932. Translated as *Guinguette by the Seine* by Geoffrey Sainsbury. In *Maigret to the Rescue.* London: Routledge, 1940; New York: Harcourt Brace, 1941.

"Liberty-Bar." Paris: Fayard, 1932. Translated as *Liberty Bar* by Geoffrey Sainsbury. In *Maigret Travels South.* London: Routledge, 1940; New York: Harcourt Brace, 1940.

L'Ombre chinoise. Paris: Fayard, 1932. Translated as *The Shadow on the Courtyard.* In *The Triumph of Inspector Maigret.* London: Hurst and Blackett, 1934. As *Maigret Mystified.* Harmondsworth, Eng.: Penguin, 1965.

Le Port des brumes. Paris: Fayard, 1932. Translated as *Death of a Harbor Master* by Stuart Gilbert. In *Maigret and M. l'Abbé.* London: Routledge, 1941; New York: Harcourt Brace, 1942.

L'Écluse no. 1. Paris: Fayard, 1933. Translated as *The Lock at Charenton* by Margret Ludwig. In *Maigret Sits It Out.* London: Routledge, 1941; New York: Harcourt Brace, 1941.

Maigret. Paris: Fayard, 1934. Translated as *Maigret Returns* by Margret Ludwig. In *Maigret Sits It Out.* London: Routledge, 1941; New York: Harcourt Brace, 1941.

Cécile est morte. In *Maigret revient. . . .* Paris: Gallimard, 1942. Translated as *Maigret and the Spinster* by Eileen Ellenbogen. London: Hamilton, 1977; New York: Harcourt Brace Jovanovich, 1977.

Les Caves du Majestic. In *Maigret revient. . . .* Paris: Gallimard, 1942. Translated as *Maigret and the Hotel Majestic* by Carolyn Hillier. London: Hamilton, 1977; New York: Harcourt Brace Jovanovich, 1978.

La Maison du juge. In *Maigret revient. . . .* Paris: Gallimard, 1942. Translated as *Maigret in Exile* by Eileen Ellenbogen. London: Hamilton, 1978; New York: Harcourt Brace Jovanovich, 1979.

Signé Picpus. Paris: Gallimard, 1944. Translated as *To Any Lengths* by Geoffrey Sainsbury. Harmondsworth, Eng.: Penguin, 1944.

L'Inspecteur cadavre. Paris: Gallimard, 1944. Translated as *Maigret's Rival* by Helen Thomson. London: Hamilton, 1978; New York: Harcourt Brace Jovanovich, 1980.

Félicie est là. Paris: Gallimard, 1944. Translated as *Maigret and the Toy Village* by Eileen Ellenbogen. London: Hamilton, 1978; New York: Harcourt Brace Jovanovich, 1979.

Les Nouvelles Enquêtes de Maigret. Paris: Nouvelle Revue Française, 1944. Short stories.

Maigret à New York. Paris: Presses de la Cité, 1947. Translated as *Maigret in New York's Underworld* by Adrienne Foulke. Garden City, N.Y.: Curtis Books, 1955.

Maigret se fâche. Paris: Presses de la Cité, 1947. Translated as *Maigret in Retirement.* London: Routledge, 1947.

La Pipe de Maigret. Paris: Presses de la Cité, 1947.

Maigret et l'inspecteur malchanceux. Paris: Presses de la Cité, 1947. Translated as *The Short Cases of Inspector Maigret.* Garden City, N.Y.: Doubleday, 1959. Short stories.

Maigret et son mort. Paris: Presses de la Cité, 1948. Translated as *Maigret's Special Murder* by Jean Stewart. London: Hamilton, 1964. U.S.: *Maigret's Dead Man.* Garden City, N.Y.: Doubleday, 1964.

Les Vacances de Maigret. Paris: Presses de la Cité, 1948. Translated as *Maigret on Holiday* by Geoffrey Sainsbury. London: Routledge & Kegan Paul, 1950. U.S.: *No Vacation for Maigret.* Garden City, N.Y.: Doubleday, 1953.

La Première Enquête de Maigret. Paris: Presses de la Cité, 1949. Translated as *Maigret's First Case* by Robert Brain. London: Hamilton, 1958. Published in *Maigret Cinq.* New York: Harcourt Brace, 1965.

Mon Ami Maigret. Paris: Presses de la Cité, 1949. Translated as *My Friend Maigret* by Nigel Ryan. London: Hamilton, 1956. As *The Methods of Maigret.* Garden City, N.Y.: Doubleday, 1957.

Maigret chez le coroner. Paris: Presses de la Cité, 1949. Translated as *Maigret at the Coroner's* by Francis Keene. New York: Harcourt Brace Jovanovich, 1980.

Maigret et la vieille dame. Paris: Presses de la Cité, 1950. Translated as *Maigret and the Old Lady* by Robert Brain. London: Hamilton, 1958. Published in *Maigret Cinq.* New York: Harcourt Brace, 1965.

L'Amie de Madame Maigret. Paris: Presses de la Cité, 1950. Translated as *Madame Maigret's Friend* by Helen Sebba. London: Hamilton, 1960. U.S.: *Madame Maigret's Own Case.* Garden City, N.Y.: Doubleday, 1959.

Les Petits Cochons sans queues. Paris: Presses de la Cité, 1950.

Maigret au "Picratt's." Paris: Presses de la Cité, 1951. Translated as *Maigret in Montmartre* by Daphne Woodward. In *Maigret Right and Wrong.* London: Hamilton, 1954. As *Inspector Maigret and the Strangled Stripper* by Cornelia Schaeffer. Garden City, N.Y.: Doubleday, 1954.

Maigret en meublé. Paris: Presses de la Cité, 1951. Translated as *Maigret Takes a Room* by Robert Brain. London: Hamilton, 1960. U.S.: *Maigret Rents a Room.* Garden City, N.Y.: Doubleday, 1961.

Maigret et la grande perche. Paris: Presses de la Cité, 1951. Translated as *Maigret and the Burglar's Wife* by J. Maclaren-Ross. London: Hamilton, 1955. As *Inspector Maigret and the Burglar's Wife.* Garden City, N.Y.: Doubleday, 1956.

Les Mémoires de Maigret. Paris: Presses de la Cité, 1951. Translated as *Maigret's Memoirs* by Jean Stewart. London: Hamilton, 1963.

Un Noël de Maigret. Paris: Presses de la Cité, 1951. Translated as *Maigret's Christmas* by Lawrence G. Blochman. Garden City, N.Y.: Doubleday, 1959. Short stories.

Maigret, Lognon et les gangsters. Paris: Presses de la Cité, 1952. Translated as *Inspector Maigret and the Killers* by Louise Varèse. Garden City, N.Y.: Doubleday, 1954. Republished as *Maigret and the Gangsters.* London: Hamilton, 1974.

Le Revolver de Maigret. Paris: Presses de la Cité, 1952. Translated as *Maigret's Revolver* by Nigel Ryan. London: Hamilton, 1956.

Maigret el l'homme du banc. Paris: Presses de la Cité, 1953. Translated as *Maigret and the Man on the Boulevard* by Eileen Ellenbogen. London: Hamilton, 1975. As *Maigret and the Man on the Bench.* New York: Harcourt Brace Jovanovich, 1975.

Maigret a peur. Paris: Presses de la Cité, 1953. Translated as *Maigret Afraid* by Margaret Duff. London: Hamilton, 1961; San Diego: Harcourt Brace Jovanovich, 1983.

Maigret se trompe. Paris: Presses de la Cité, 1953. Translated as *Maigret's Mistake* by Alan Hodge. London: Hamilton, 1954.

Maigret à l'école. Paris: Presses de la Cité, 1954. Translated as *Maigret Goes to School* by Daphne Woodward. London: Hamilton, 1957.

Maigret et la jeune morte. Paris: Presses de la Cité, 1954. Translated as *Maigret and the Young Girl* by Daphne Woodward. London: Hamilton, 1955. U.S.: *Inspector Maigret and the Dead Girl.* Garden City, N.Y.: Doubleday, 1955.

Maigret chez le ministre. Paris: Presses de la Cité, 1955. Translated as *Maigret and the Minister* by Moura Budberg. London: Hamilton, 1969. U.S.: *Maigret and the Calame Report.* San Diego: Harcourt Brace Jovanovich, 1987.

Maigret et le corps sans tête. Paris: Presses de la Cité, 1955. Translated as *Maigret and the Headless Corpse* by Eileen Ellenbogen. London: Hamilton, 1967; New York: Harcourt Brace, 1968.

Maigret tend un piège. Paris: Presses de la Cité, 1955. Translated as *Maigret Sets a Trap* by Daphne Woodward. London: Hamilton, 1965; New York: Harcourt Brace, 1972.

Un Échec de Maigret. Paris: Presses de la Cité, 1956. Translated as *Maigret's Failure* by Daphne Woodward. London: Hamilton, 1962. In *A Maigret Trio.* New York: Harcourt Brace Jovanovich, 1973.

Maigret s'amuse. Paris: Presses de la Cité, 1957. Translated as *Maigret's Little Joke* by Robert Brain. London: Hamilton, 1957. U.S.: *None of Maigret's Business.* Garden City, N.Y.: Doubleday, 1958.

Maigret voyage. Paris: Presses de la Cité, 1958. Translated as *Maigret and the Millionaires* by Jean Stewart. London: Hamilton, 1974; New York: Harcourt Brace Jovanovich, 1974.

Les Scrupules de Maigret. Paris: Presses de la Cité, 1958. Translated as *Maigret Has Scruples* by Robert Eglesfield. London: Hamilton, 1959. In *Versus Inspector Maigret.* Garden City, N.Y.: Doubleday, 1960.

Maigret et les témoins récalcitrants. Paris: Presses de la Cité, 1959. Translated as *Maigret and the Reluctant Witnesses* by Daphne Woodward. London: Hamilton, 1959. In *Versus Inspector Maigret.* Garden City, N.Y.: Doubleday, 1960.

Une Confidence de Maigret. Paris: Presses de la Cité, 1959. Translated as *Maigret Has Doubts* by Lyn Moir. London: Hamilton, 1968; New York: Harcourt Brace Jovanovich, 1982.

Maigret aux assises. Paris: Presses de la Cité, 1960. Translated as *Maigret in Court* by Robert Brain. London: Hamilton, 1961.

Maigret et les vieillards. Paris: Presses de la Cité, 1960. Translated as *Maigret in Society* by Robert Eglesfield. London: Hamilton, 1962. In *A Maigret Trio.* New York: Harcourt Brace Jovanovich, 1973.

Maigret et le voleur paresseux. Paris: Presses de la Cité, 1961. Translated as *Maigret and the Lazy Burglar* by Daphne Woodward. London: Hamilton, 1963. In *A Maigret Trio.* New York: Harcourt Brace Jovanovich, 1973.

Maigret et les braves gens. Paris: Presses de la Cité, 1962. Translated as *Maigret and the Black Sheep* by Helen Thomson. London: Hamilton, 1976; New York: Harcourt Brace Jovanovich, 1976.

Maigret et le client du samedi. Paris: Presses de la Cité, 1962. Translated as *Maigret and the Saturday Caller* by Tony White. London: Hamilton, 1964.

La Colère de Maigret. Paris: Presses de la Cité, 1963. Translated as *Maigret Loses His Temper* by Robert Eglesfield. London: Hamilton, 1965; New York: Harcourt Brace Jovanovich, 1974.

Maigret et le clochard. Paris: Presses de la Cité, 1963. Translated as *Maigret and the Dossier* by Jean Stewart. London: Hamilton, 1973. U.S.: *Maigret and the Bum.* New York: Harcourt Brace Jovanovich, 1973.

Maigret et le fantôme. Paris: Presses de la Cité, 1964. Translated as *Maigret and the Ghost* by Eileen Ellenbogen. London: Hamilton, 1976. U.S.: *Maigret and the Apparition.* New York: Harcourt Brace Jovanovich, 1976.

Maigret se défend. Paris: Presses de la Cité, 1964. Translated as *Maigret on the Defensive* by Alastair Hamilton. London: Hamilton, 1966; New York: Harcourt Brace Jovanovich, 1981.

La Patience de Maigret. Paris: Presses de la Cité, 1965. Translated as *The Patience of Maigret* by Alastair Hamilton. London: Hamilton, 1966. U.S.: *Maigret Bides His Time.* San Diego: Harcourt Brace Jovanovich, 1985.

Maigret et l'affaire Nahour. Paris: Presses de la Cité, 1966. Translated as *Maigret and the Nahour Case* by Alastair Hamilton. London: Hamilton, 1967.

Le Voleur de Maigret. Paris: Presses de la Cité, 1967. Translated as *Maigret's Pickpocket* by Nigel Ryan. London: Hamilton, 1968; New York: Harcourt Brace Jovanovich, 1968.

L'Ami d'enfance de Maigret. Paris: Presses de la Cité, 1968. Translated as *Maigret's Boyhood Friend* by Eileen Ellenbogen. London: Hamilton, 1970; New York: Harcourt Brace Jovanovich, 1970.

Maigret à Vichy. Paris: Presses de la Cité, 1968. Translated as *Maigret Takes the Waters* by Eileen Ellenbogen. London: Hamilton, 1969. U.S.: *Maigret in Vichy.* New York: Harcourt Brace Jovanovich, 1969.

Maigret hésite. Paris: Presses de la Cité, 1968. Translated as *Maigret Hesitates* by Lyn Moir. London: Hamilton, 1970; New York: Harcourt Brace Jovanovich, 1970.

Maigret et le tueur. Paris: Presses de la Cité, 1969. Translated as *Maigret and the Killer* by Lyn Moir. London: Hamilton, 1971; New York: Harcourt Brace Jovanovich, 1971.

La Folle de Maigret. Paris: Presses de la Cité, 1970. Translated as *Maigret and the Madwoman* by Eileen Ellenbogen. London: Hamilton, 1972; New York: Harcourt Brace Jovanovich, 1972.

Maigret et le marchand de vin. Paris: Presses de la Cité, 1970. Translated as *Maigret and the Wine Merchant* by Eileen Ellenbogen. London: Hamilton, 1971; New York: Harcourt Brace Jovanovich, 1971.

Maigret el l'homme tout seul. Paris: Presses de la Cité, 1971. Translated as *Maigret and the Loner* by Eileen

Ellenbogen. London: Hamilton, 1975; New York: Harcourt Brace Jovanovich, 1975.

Maigret et l'indicateur. Paris: Presses de la Cité, 1971. Translated as *Maigret and the Flea* by Lyn Moir. London: Hamilton, 1972. Published as *Maigret and the Informer.* New York: Harcourt Brace Jovanovich, 1972.

Maigret et Monsieur Charles. Paris: Presses de la Cité, 1972. Translated as *Maigret and Monsieur Charles* by Marianne A. Sinclair. London: Hamilton, 1973.

SELECTED NONMYSTERY NOVELS

Au Pont des Arches. By "Georges Sim." Liège: Bénard, 1921.

Les Gens d'en face. Paris: Fayard, 1933. Translated as *The Window Over the Way* by Geoffrey Sainsbury. London: Routledge & Kegan Paul, 1951; New York: British Book Service, 1951.

Les Fiançailles de M. Hire. Paris: Fayard, 1933. Translated as *Mr. Hire's Engagement* by Daphne Woodward. London: Hamilton, 1956.

La Maison du canal. Paris: Fayard, 1933. Translated as *The House by the Canal* by Geoffrey Sainsbury. London: Routledge & Kegan Paul, 1952.

L'Homme qui regardait passer les trains. Paris: Gallimard, 1938. Translated as *The Man Who Watched the Trains Go By* by Stuart Gilbert. London: Pan, 1945; New York: Reynal & Hitchcock, 1946.

Chez Krull. Paris: Nouvelle Revue Française, 1939. Translated as *Chez Krull* by Daphne Woodward. In *A Sense of Guilt.* London: Hamilton, 1955.

Bergelon. Paris: Gallimard, 1941. Translated as *The Delivery* by Eileen Ellenbogen. New York: Harcourt Brace Jovanovich, 1981.

La Fuite de M. Monde. Paris: Editions de la Jeune Parque, 1945. Translated as *Monsieur Monde Vanishes* by Jean Stewart. London: Hamilton, 1967.

Trois Chambres à Manhattan. Paris: Presses de la Cité, 1946. Translated as *Three Beds in Manhattan* by Lawrence G. Blochman. Garden City, N.Y.: Doubleday, 1964.

La Neige était sale. Paris: Presses de la Cité, 1948. Translated as *The Snow Was Black* by Louise Varèse. New York: Prentice-Hall, 1950. Translated as *The Stain on the Snow.* London: Routledge & Kegan Paul, 1953.

Pedigree. Paris: Presses de la Cité, 1948. Translated as *Pedigree* by Robert Baldick. London: Hamilton, 1962.

Les Frères Rico. Paris: Presses de la Cité, 1952. Translated as *The Brothers Rico* by Ernst Pawel. In *Violent Ends.* London: Hamilton, 1954. U.S.: *Tidal Waves.* Garden City, N.Y.: Doubleday, 1954.

La Mort de Belle. Paris: Presses de la Cité, 1952. Translated as *Belle* by Louise Varèse. In *Violent Ends.* London: Hamilton, 1954. U.S.: *Tidal Waves.* Garden City, N.Y.: Doubleday, 1954.

En Cas de malheur. Paris: Presses de la Cité, 1956. Translated as *A Case of Emergency* by Helen Sebba. Garden

City, N.Y.: Doubleday, 1958; London: Hamilton, 1960.

Le Petit Homme d'Arkhangelsk. Paris: Presses de la Cité, 1957. Translated as *The Little Man from Archangel* by Nigel Ryan. London: Hamilton, 1957; New York: Harcourt Brace, 1966.

Strip-Tease. Paris: Presses de la Cité, 1958. Translated as *Striptease.* London: Hamilton, 1959.

Les Anneaux de Bicêtre. Paris: Presses de la Cité, 1963. Translated as *The Patient* by Jean Stewart. London: Hamilton, 1963; New York: Harcourt Brace, 1965.

La Chambre bleue. Paris: Presses de la Cité, 1964. Translated as *The Blue Room* by Eileen Ellenbogen. New York: Harcourt Brace, 1964; London: Hamilton, 1965.

Le Petit Saint. Paris: Presses de la Cité, 1965. Translated as *The Little Saint* by Bernard Frechtman. New York: Harcourt Brace, 1965; London: Hamilton, 1966.

Novembre. Paris: Presses de la Cité, 1969. Translated as *November* by Jean Stewart. London: Hamilton, 1970; New York: Harcourt Brace Jovanovich, 1970.

Les Innocents. Paris: Presses de la Cité, 1972. Translated as *The Innocents* by Eileen Ellenbogen. London: Hamilton, 1973; New York: Harcourt Brace Jovanovich, 1973.

AUTOBIOGRAPHIES

Je me souviens . . . . Paris: Presses de la Cité, 1945.

Quand j'étais vieux. Paris: Presses de la Cité, 1970. Translated as *When I Was Old* by Helen Eustis. London: Hamilton, 1972; New York: Harcourt Brace Jovanovich, 1971.

Lettre à ma mère. Paris: Presses de la Cité, 1974. Translated as *Letter to My Mother* by Ralph Manheim. London: Hamilton, 1976; New York: Harcourt Brace Jovanovich, 1976.

Un Homme comme un autre. Paris: Presses de la Cité, 1975.

Mémoires intimes. Paris: Presses de la Cité, 1981. Translated as *Intimate Memoirs* by Harold J. Salemson. San Diego: Harcourt Brace Jovanovich, 1984.

ARCHIVES

The Centre d'Etudes Georges Simenon (Liège, Belgium) holds correspondence from 1932–1980, manuscripts, working notes (the famous manila envelopes), research material, many original editions of both fiction and non-fiction works, a photo archive, and thousands of reviews and articles on Simenon from all over the world. The Simenon Center at Drew University houses first editions, manuscripts, some correspondence, and secondary materials.

BIOGRAPHICAL AND CRITICAL STUDIES

Assouline, Pierre. *Simenon: A Biography.* Translated by Jon Rothschild. New York: Knopf, 1997.

Becker, Lucille Frackman. *Georges Simenon.* Boston: Twayne, 1977.

Bresler, Fenton, *The Mystery of Georges Simenon: A Biography.* New York: Beaufort Books, 1983.

Collins, Carvel. "The Art of Fiction IX: Georges Simenon." *Paris Review* 8: 71–91 (1955).

Eskin, Stanley G. *Simenon: A Critical Biography.* Jefferson, N.C.: McFarland, 1987.

———. "Georges Simenon." In *Dictionary of Literary Biography: Yearbook 1989.* Edited by J. M. Brook. Detroit: Gale, 1990.

Gill, Brendan. "Profile." *New Yorker,* 24 January 1953.

Grindea, Miron, ed. *ADAM International Review* 34, nos. 328–330 (1969). Simenon issue.

Marnham, Patrick. *The Man Who Wasn't Maigret: A Portrait of Georges Simenon.* New York: Farrar, Straus, Giroux, 1992.

Raymond, John. *Simenon in Court.* London: Hamilton, 1968.

Young, Trudee. *Georges Simenon: A Checklist of His "Maigret" and Other Mystery Novels and Short Stories in French and in English Translations.* Metuchen, N.J.: Scarecrow Press, 1976.

MAJ SJÖWALL AND PER WAHLÖÖ

(b. 1935) and (1926–1975)

NANCY C. MELLERSKI
ROBERT P. WINSTON

WHEN MAJ SJÖWALL and Per Wahlöö spoke of their purpose in writing the Martin Beck police procedurals, they used a metaphor suggesting a surgeon and a patient: the authors would wield a "scalpel" in order to lay open the soft "belly" of the "morally debatable" bourgeois welfare state, exposing the cancer that was eating away at Swedish society (quoted in Lundin, *Twentieth-Century Crime and Mystery Writers*, p. 1553). In asserting this explicitly ideological aim for their series, Sjöwall and Wahlöö reconceived the crime novel as a progressive genre, rather than a fundamentally conservative one. Earlier detective fiction had often articulated a society's anxieties precisely in order to defuse them and thus reassure the reader; Sjöwall and Wahlöö, on the other hand, intended their novels as a polemical contribution to an ongoing political debate within Swedish society over the future of social democracy within a capitalist framework. Such a plan should not be surprising, coming from a pair of authors whose leftist sympathies were well known.

Critics who have placed Sjöwall and Wahlöö in the tradition of Swedish detective fiction suggest that there were a number of influences on their work. One of these was Stieg Trenter, whose mystery novels of the 1950s foregrounded a Stockholm setting. Another was Vic Suneson, the inventor of the Swedish police procedural, who, while he did not engage in social commentary per se, broadened the range of social classes from which his central figures were drawn, moving beyond the bourgeoisie who were the focus of earlier English mysteries. Critics also point to the detective fiction of Hans Krister Rönblom which, though set in rural Sweden, presented some of the same cynical criticisms of Swedish self-satisfaction. Sjöwall and Wahlöö combined their interest in these Swedish predecessors with the burgeoning interest in American hard-boiled and procedural detective fiction in the 1960s in order to redefine the police procedural for their own purposes.

Biography

Per (Peter Fredrik) Wahlöö was born in Goteborg, Sweden, on 5 August 1926. After graduating from the University of Lund in 1946, he worked as a journalist covering criminal and social issues for a number of prominent Swedish newspapers and magazines. In the 1950s Wahlöö engaged in radical political causes, activities that resulted in his deportation from Franco's Spain in 1957. He published his first two novels, *Himmelsgetan* (Heaven's goats) and *Vinden och regnet* (Wind and rain) in 1959 and 1961, respectively, but remained unknown outside Sweden until the appearance and translation of his third and fourth novels, *Lastbilen* (1962; later published in the United States as *A Necessary Action* [1969] and in Great Britain as *The Lorry* [1968]) and *Uppdraget* (1963; translated into English as *The Assignment* [1965]). These two novels, as well as *Generalerna* (1965; *The Generals* [1974]), deal with resistance to Fascist dictatorships in Spain and Central America. Wahlöö's sociopolitical concerns in these early novels foreshadow those explored fully in the Martin Beck series. In a similar vein, Wahlöö published two procedural thrillers featuring a police detective in an unidentified northern European country; these novels create an allegorical vision of Sweden as a future dystopia, a place where the "individual [is] physically looked after, but . . . spiritually incapacitated" (*The Steel Spring*, New York ed., p. 111). Chief Inspector Jensen appears in *Mord på 31: A våningen* (1964; *Murder on the Thirty-first Floor* [1966]) and later in *Stålsprånget* (1968; *The Steel Spring* [1970]), both of which target the shortcomings of the welfare state as the cause of the anomie that haunts Swedish society. Wahlöö's literary production also includes several radio and television plays and film scripts, as well as translations into Swedish of some of Ed McBain's 87th Precinct procedural novels.

Maj Sjöwall, born on 25 September 1935 in Stockholm, studied journalism and graphics there before finding employment as a reporter and art director at a series of newspapers and magazines. From 1959 to 1961 she was an editor with Wahlström and Widstrand, a publishing house in the capital. In 1961, she met Wahlöö while they were both writing for the same magazine publisher; over lunch in a restaurant they began discussing an idea for a way out of magazine work. After their marriage a year later, they started to outline the Martin Beck series, which they conceived to be an epic novel of three hundred chapters, divided into ten books of thirty chapters each; one book would be published each year. With careful research and attention to authentic detail, the series would exploit the concept of the crime novel as a mirror of dysfunction within Swedish society by following ten years in the career of the chief of the National Homicide Squad. Beck, the hero, would thus serve as the barometer of a changing atmosphere in Sweden, reflecting shifts in the political, economic, and social climate. The Beck epic was, according to its authors, more popular in the United States and in France than in Sweden, where the police procedural had been a relatively unappreciated genre until Sjöwall and Wahlöö published the first novel in the series.

They collaborated on other projects as well, writing a comparative study of police methods in Europe and the United States and editing the literary magazine *Peripeo.* They worked together until Wahlöö's death from pancreatic disease on 22 June 1975. Sjöwall did not publish another novel until 1990, when she coauthored *Kvinnan som liknade Garbo* (The woman who resembled Garbo) with Tomas Ross.

Sjöwall and Wahlöö's writing habits were remarkable: they worked from a detailed outline on alternate chapters at the same time, and Wahlöö claimed that their prose was interchangeable. No doubt their journalistic backgrounds made such a seamless collaboration possible, skilled as they both were in a style that demanded brevity, concision, and attention to detail. Living in Malmö in southern Sweden with their children, in an apartment with a view of a cemetery, they customarily wrote late at night after putting the children to bed. They called these quiet moments their most productive ones, as they sat facing each other at a table, writing out chapters of the Beck series in longhand. This serene domestic scene belies both the unsparing treatment of violence and the bitter parody that mark their fiction.

The Martin Beck Series

The opening of the first Martin Beck novel, *Roseanna* (1965), typifies much of their writing, combining a starkly understated, matter-of-fact description of the discovery of a corpse with a drily comic rehearsal of bureaucratic bumbling and procrastination. The body of Roseanna McGraw is found by chance in the canal locks at Borenshult in the jaws of a dredger, and the discovery sets off a systematic, if frustrating, investigation into her death by First Detective Inspector Martin Beck of the Homicide Bureau of the National Police and his colleagues. In this first novel, Beck appears not especially ambitious, though he has spent more than half his life on the police force, moving up through the ranks from patrolman; he is likely to achieve the rank of superintendent unless "death or some very serious error in his duties" intervenes to stop him (p. 10).[1] He lives in a small apartment in Stockholm with his wife, Inga, and his two children, Ingrid and Rolf. His marriage, apparently like the rest of his life, has settled into a dull routine that offers him little in the way of reward.

The portrayal of the first investigation is typical of the genre: Beck and his colleagues proceed methodically, through a lengthy inquiry ostensibly focusing on routine matters. As Beck himself thinks,

> Remember that you have three of the most important virtues a policeman can have. . . . You are stubborn and logical, and completely calm. You don't allow yourself to lose your composure and you act only professionally on a case, whatever it is. Words like repulsive, horrible, and bestial belong in the newspapers, not in your thinking. A murderer is a regular human being, only more unfortunate and maladjusted. (pp. 36–37)

Beck's musings foreshadow the solution to the crime, since the murderer proves to be a lonely and colorless middle-aged Swede who is finally betrayed by his singular inability to deal with female sexuality in any socially acceptable fashion.

While the Roseanna case is nominally routine, Sjöwall and Wahlöö prefigure the in-

creasingly political direction of their series by introducing an American colleague, Lieutenant Kafka of the homicide squad in Lincoln, Nebraska, who supplies them with crucial background information on the victim. Roseanna McGraw, though she appears to be a plain, clean-living librarian, is in fact an aggressive and sexually predatory female. She helps to bring about her own death by piercing the protective armor that her killer, Folke Bengtsson, has donned in order to cope with life in contemporary Stockholm. What begins as a difficult but ordinary investigation turns out to be unsatisfactory: Bengtsson can be arrested only after the police have entrapped him, so provoking him that he attempts to kill a policewoman who is being used as a lure. As Beck reflects, "They had all sat in their offices in Motala and Stockholm and Lincoln, Nebraska, and solved this case by means that could never be made public. They would always remember it, but hardly with pride" (p. 201).

Although *The Man Who Went Up in Smoke* (1969) appeared in English as the third Martin Beck novel, in fact it is the second in the original series (*Mannen som gick upp i rök*, 1966). Like its predecessor, it permits Martin Beck to make contact with police officers beyond the borders of Sweden and thus allows the authors to compare techniques of maintaining order in two cities under vastly different systems. Part of the authors' agenda is clearly to redeem police forces in socialist Eastern Europe from KGB-like stereotypes and to endorse the kinds of policework that gave Budapest "the lowest crime rate of any large city in the world," according to Wahlöö (quoted in "Copology," p. 28). When Beck arrives in Budapest and begins asking questions about the disappearance of Alf Matsson, a Swedish journalist, he quickly comes under surveillance, which he wrongly assumes is official. In fact, he has become the target of a drug ring organized by two West German tour guides. It is, rather, Beck's own investigation of Matsson's disappearance that reeks of political interference and central control.

Beck's Hungarian counterpart, Major

1. All references to the Martin Beck series are to the Vintage paperback editions.

Szluka, is not only efficient but urbane and witty as well. Although Szluka expresses the same sort of dissatisfaction with his job that we hear from members of the Swedish squad, the point here is that the quality of policing is in fact superior in Budapest. As Szluka puts it, "We don't often need to shoot, but when it's necessary, we shoot accurately" (p. 89). This claim contrasts with the litany of complaints about the brutality of Swedish police (and jibes about their marksmanship) that will be explored in greater detail later in the series. The net effect of the investigation in Budapest is the discovery that the Swedish journalist Beck has been seeking was actually a drug smuggler who had never even arrived in Hungary. In other words, in spite of the journey beyond Sweden's borders, the source of the crime lies, as it did in *Roseanna*, in Stockholm.

Matsson turns out to have been a colossal boor whose contempt for women provoked his own death at the hands of a drunken fellow journalist whose fiancée he had insulted. Although Beck and his squad discover the identity of Matsson's murderer, the solution to the mystery is once again unsatisfying. The murder was essentially an accident, according to both the killer, Åke Gunnarsson, and Martin Beck, so the consequence will only be more lives ruined once Gunnarsson and his fiancée are separated by prison walls. The novel ends with Beck sitting alone in a bar drinking to escape both his complicity in what essentially amounts to a state-sponsored crime and the prospect of a disappointing summer holiday with his family.

In *The Man on the Balcony* (*Mannen på balkongen*, 1967), Martin Beck and his squad undertake a two-pronged investigation. They seek a mugger who preys on the elderly and a serial killer who attacks young girls. Ironically, these assaults on the most helpless Swedish citizens occur in what ought to be refuges from the harshness of urban living, the parks of Stockholm. The investigations take place during early summertime; throughout the authors underscore the incongruity between the pleasant, sunny parks of Stock-

holm and the violence and criminal activity that occur within. Beck's colleague, Lennart Kollberg, "thought of the repulsiveness of the crime itself and he thought of the people who had been so hard hit by its blind meaninglessness. He had been through all this before, how many times he couldn't even say offhand, and he knew exactly how horrible it could turn out to be. And how difficult" (p. 29). As the Homicide Squad fans out through the entire city, attempting to prevent the murderer from striking again, it becomes clear that the green spaces of the city have been transformed into hunting grounds in which both police and a vast array of criminals stalk their prey; just as disturbing are the activities of well-meaning citizens who form vigilante squads to assist the police, but who are actually as threatening as those they pursue. By the end of the novel, then, any distinctions among the police, Stockholm's "good" citizens, and its criminals have virtually collapsed; as a result, the solution to the serial murders is grimly comic and wholly unsatisfactory to Beck and his colleagues. The murderer, at one time a gardening laborer in Stockholm's park system, is finally accidentally captured by the two least skilled "hunters" on the force, patrolmen named Kvant and Kristiansson. These two will, over the course of the next few books, provide a kind of comic counterpoint to the depressing investigations in which Beck and his colleagues become involved.

The Man on the Balcony identifies the parks as an institution perverted by the changing quality of life in Sweden; they are a microcosm of the kinds of illegitimate behavior—assault, robbery, alcoholism and drugs, vagrancy—that for Sjöwall and Wahlöö constitute daily existence in Stockholm. Potentially, the authors suggest, all Swedish institutions will be damaged by different forms of moral and social pollution. Even in these early novels, then, the series' direction is quite clear: it will record the decay of Sweden's social fabric.

By the time of the third novel, most of the series' characters have been introduced and their idiosyncrasies cataloged. Although

Sjöwall and Wahlöö's publishers refer to their books as the Martin Beck series, it is crucial to note that, like many police proceduralists, the two authors in fact create a corporate hero, the homicide squad. While it is true that Beck is (more or less) in charge throughout the books, he is not always the most prominent—or even the most productive—investigator, and, equally important, he is not always the key voice articulating what is wrong with Swedish society.

While the early entries in the series highlight the character of Martin Beck, we also meet a number of colleagues who share to varying degrees their chief's nascent disillusionment with the job of policing Swedish society. At first glance, Lennart Kollberg's outlook on life appears to be more cheerful and optimistic than that of his best friend and chess partner, Martin Beck. Overweight, a sensualist, Kollberg has waited twenty years to find the perfect wife for himself. In so doing, he seems to have escaped the conjugal problems that accentuate Beck's generally gloomy nature. In fact, Sjöwall and Wahlöö use Beck's and Kollberg's marriages to highlight their connections to society at large: Beck's deteriorating relationship with his wife, which becomes a leitmotif even in these early novels, intensifies the darkening picture of Swedish culture. Kollberg's happy marriage, on the one hand, provides him with a refuge from work, but on the other, makes him even more alarmed about the disintegration of Swedish community. For example, in *The Man on the Balcony*, Kollberg is particularly anxious about catching the killer of small children because his wife, Gun, is pregnant with their first child. Although Martin Beck and Lennart Kollberg work together like true partners, not even needing to articulate their thoughts about an investigation, Beck's relations with the rest of his squad are far more distant.

Gunvald Larsson is to some extent the obverse of Kollberg: Beck views him as impulsive and brutish, more inclined to burst through a door with a gun in his hand than to rely on sanctioned routine. What lies behind this behavior, we come to see, is his complete rejection of his comfortable bourgeois origins, what he calls in *Polis, polis, potatismos!* (1970) "that whole damn upper-class riffraff" (*Murder at the Savoy*, p. 99), in favor of an indignant socialism. This does not, however, prevent him from buying expensive, well-tailored suits and silk pajamas and driving a luxury car, albeit a product of Eastern Europe. Fredrik Melander is "a tall, lean man of grave appearance and methodical disposition. . . . He was known never to forget anything" (*The Laughing Policeman*, p. 22). Melander's reputation within the squad as a "human computer" reinforces to some extent the picture of policemen as automatons rather than caring human beings. Einar Rönn, the diminutive and soft-spoken northerner, is the least imaginative member of the squad:

> Rönn was not one of the shining lights of the age and he didn't pretend to be particularly well informed. He was quite content with himself and with life in general, and thought that things were pretty good as they were. It was these qualities, in fact, that made him a useful and capable policeman. He had a simple, straightforward attitude to things and had no talent for creating problems and difficulties which did not exist. (*The Laughing Policeman*, p. 64)

Rönn's plodding investigative technique and cramped, virtually illegible handwriting suggest the narrow, though hardly malicious, policeman whom Sjöwall and Wahlöö see as all too typical. His runny nose and constant head cold suggest the low-level irritation most citizens feel when they come in contact with the force. Although Sjöwall and Wahlöö clearly have an ideological agenda in mind, they endow characters as disparate as Larsson, Melander, and Rönn with enough human qualities to present a complex picture of a police squad attempting to do its best under difficult conditions.

Beyond the squad, however, Sjöwall and Wahlöö are less sympathetic to the Swedish police. The opening of the fourth novel in the series, *The Laughing Policeman* (*Den skrattande polisen*, 1968), brings back the duo of Kristiansson and Kvant, the unlikely heroes of *The Man on the Balcony:* "Both were 6 feet 1 inch tall, fair, broad-shouldered and blue-eyed. But they had widely different temperaments and didn't always see eye to eye." Kristiansson is "lazy." Kvant is "incorruptible. He never compromised over things he saw, but on the other hand he was an expert at seeing as little as possible" (p. 8). While these characters possess some of the worst qualities of Swedish policemen, Sjöwall and Wahlöö present them comically, using parody as a vehicle to underscore what they see as shortcomings in the force. This use of comic distance is no small feat, since Wahlöö once said to an interviewer that calling the Swedish police "pigs" would be "very mild . . . it is more common to hear them referred to as Gestapo swine" ("Copology," p. 28).

The Laughing Policeman revolves around a massacre on a bus, thus continuing the escalation of violence from single murders in the first two books through serial killings in the third. This novel is true to the archetype of the police procedural; every member of the squad investigates a particular aspect of the crime, and together they constitute the clearest example of the corporate hero in the Beck series. The novel also introduces an explicitly American theme. Since Sweden has no history of mass murder, the police turn to the United States for psychological profiles of such killers, assuming that the "disease" is contagious. As the profile provided by American experts turns out to be wholly wrong, Sjöwall and Wahlöö appear to suggest that the socialist state looks all too often to the capitalist one for explanations of inappropriate forms of behavior.

Ultimately, the murders in *The Laughing Policeman* are rooted in a sex crime that is sixteen years old. The investigation, then, takes two paths, exploring the present to find the murderer and the past to find the motive. Such a description, though, belies the frustration that dominates this novel. Dead end follows dead end, and the investigation grinds to

a halt. The authors indicate the futility of the squad's efforts by devoting a great many pages to decrying the commercialization of Christmas and the waste of police resources on protecting the American ambassador from demonstrations against the Vietnam War. The mystery is ultimately solved because one of the victims was a policeman, Åke Stenstrom, and the "inside case," the investigation into Stenstrom's life and work, provides the crucial clues. The murderer turns out to be a successful businessman with a shady past who offers a strikingly misguided claim of self-defense for the massacre: "I was defending myself and my family and my home and my firm" (p. 218) from public scandal. Gunvald Larsson is given the task of offering the authors' rejoinder:

> I feel for nearly everyone we meet in this job. They're just a lot of scum who wish they'd never been born. It's not their fault that everything goes to hell and they don't understand why. It's types like this one who wreck their lives. Smug swine who think only of their money and their houses and their families and their so-called status. Who think they can order others about merely because they happen to be better off. . . . We only see their victims. This guy's an exception. (pp. 218–219)

As with the earlier novels, then, there is no real satisfaction at the end; a murderer has been caught and condemned, but nothing fundamental has changed in Swedish society. In this case, though, the ills that continue to gnaw at the social fabric are explicitly rooted in class consciousness rather than in individual morality.

Beck's family life still functions as a marker for the relationship between the police and the people they nominally serve. Just as Beck provides the reader with a barometric reading of the state of Swedish society, the ups and downs of Beck's personal life mirror the difficulties of coping with the pressures of his profession and that profession's relationship to society at large. For example, he recalls a conversation with his daughter, with whom he is very close: "As a child she had said she could boast and be proud of the fact that her father was a policeman, but now she preferred to keep quiet about it" (p. 14). This meditation is embedded in the same paragraph in which Beck contemplates the police's handling of an anti–Vietnam War demonstration outside the U.S. embassy and wonders how it will be reported. Beck is certain that the police's behavior will be described as either "clumsy and inept or as brutal and provocative. In any case the opinions would be critical. Since he was loyal to the force and had been so for as long as he could remember, Martin Beck admitted only to himself that the criticism was often justified, even if it were a bit one-sided" (p. 14). Thus, the same stresses that alienate Beck from most of his family and much of the police force also cut him off from those whom he is meant to protect and serve. Only two relationships console him in his personal and professional life: his relationship with his daughter and his partnership with Lennart Kollberg.

Book five, *The Fire Engine That Disappeared* (*Brandbilen som försvann*, 1969) focuses on the mystery of how and why three people die in a house fire. What seems at first to be an accident turns out to be arson directed at a small-time member of a gang of thieves, smugglers, and pimps operating across national boundaries. This internationalization of crime continues the theme first articulated in *The Man on the Balcony*: Kollberg "thought too of the swift gangsterization of this society, which in the last resort must be a product of himself and of the other people who lived in it and had a share in its creation." He reflects on the "meaninglessness" of the crime and "how the new investigation methods" will offer little consolation to either the victims' families or the police themselves (p. 29).

With the intrusion of foreign assassins on Swedish soil, Sjöwall and Wahlöö once again raise the stakes for Beck's squad. Not only are the murders multiple, but they are wholly mercenary, and they reveal a network of criminal activity that threatens to undermine what little the police can do to maintain the security of the Swedish populace. This notion is reinforced by continuing commentary on the harsh policing of antiwar demonstrators (which began in *The Laughing Policeman*) and the lack of socially constructive engagement with those who could be helped, like young runaways or old pensioners. Sjöwall and Wahlöö thus reproduce a local version of the Vietnam War, fought at home in the neighborhoods of the city, which seem more and more like the jungles of Southeast Asia transplanted to a cooler climate. In this regard, *The Fire Engine That Disappeared* is a turning point in the series, since from this book forward the notion of urban warfare becomes increasingly important.

Two visions of policing bracket this novel. It opens with Gunvald Larsson's heroic rescue of eight people from a burning house, and it closes with the stabbing of Lennart Kollberg by a Lebanese hit man at Arlanda Airport. In between, the investigation is dominated by the disembodied voice of Hjelm, the forensic scientist, whose smug superiority contrasts sharply with the daily grind of routine police affairs. Humanity is displaced by technocracy, and the novel is replete with musings by squad members and their families on the definition of a good policeman, as well as ruminations on why anyone would choose a profession held in low repute by the public and marked by internecine jealousies within the force.

Once again, problems of family life point to those of the larger society. For example, the book opens with Martin Beck visiting his mother on her name day in an "old people's home" where she has gone so that she will not be a burden to him. Her thoughtfulness apparently does not carry over to Beck's wife, and their marriage is clearly unsalvageable by the end of this book. Life in the house has become so unpleasant that Beck's daughter, Ingrid, decides to move out even before she finishes high school, thus removing Beck's only ally in the home and foreshadowing the dissolution of his professional partnership with Kollberg in the final books of the series. Even more important, Ingrid enables Beck to envision a different life when she says, "I know I shouldn't really say this, but I'm going to all the same. Why don't you do the same? Move out?" (p. 150). Beck's questioning of the reasons for staying in his unhappy marriage in turn provoke larger questions about why he—or anyone—should stay in police work. The answer to that question will ultimately be given by Lennart Kollberg, in *Cop Killer* (1975), when he resigns. If Beck can liberate himself from what he sees as an oppressive marriage, and Kollberg can free himself from what he regards as an oppressive job, how, Sjöwall and Wahlöö ask, can the rest of the citizens liberate themselves from a society depicted as equally stifling and dispiriting.

This struggle is the main focus of *Murder at the Savoy*, in which an utterly unscrupulous businessman from Malmö, Viktor Palmgren, is murdered as a result of the control he exercises not only over a business empire but also over the lives of individuals caught up in that machine. As the murderer reveals in his final confession, Viktor Palmgren was "the bloodsucker . . . who lined his purse at the expense of other human beings, the big shot . . . who didn't give a damn about the welfare of his employees or tenants. He began to hate this man as he'd never thought it possible to hate any human being. . . . He didn't regret what he'd done" (p. 198). Viktor Palmgren lived behind an "impenetrable hedge and gate" in an old mansion which he "rebuilt and modernized for a million or two" (p. 42) and which contains on its grounds a sauna, a pool, magnificent gardens, and a lawn that is "very large and green, as well kept as an English golf course" (p. 43).

It is no wonder that Per Månsson, the Malmö cop who was born in a working-class section of the city, contemplates the mansion with a sense of disbelief and incomprehension: he remembers the neighborhood from his childhood, with its servants and chauffeurs "and upper-class children in tulle dresses and sailor suits. He'd felt so utterly outside of all that; the whole environment had appeared incomprehensible, like a fairy tale to him. Somehow it still felt the same way . . ." (p. 40). Månsson is ultimately disgusted; other investigators have the same reaction when they visit the overpriced, shoddy, and rundown apartments of both Palmgren and real estate developers like him.

Palmgren's original business began modestly enough in the import and export of fish but has expanded so that its tentacles encompass "more than herring" (p. 78). While the home office controls the core business in Malmö, other activities including real estate and stock trading are located in Stockholm, and an air freight business operates out of Copenhagen. The real estate company specializes in housing projects that resemble

> far too many of the rent traps built during recent years—an isolated group of high-rise apartments, slapped together quickly and carelessly, whose sole purpose was to make as large a profit as possible for the owner while at the same time guaranteeing unpleasantness and discomfort for the unfortunate people who had to live there. Since the housing shortage had been kept alive artificially for many years, even these apartments were in great demand, and the rents were close to astronomical. (p. 83)

The air freight company nominally flies canned fish to foreign countries but is suspected of flying smuggled arms to Africa and elsewhere. In both cases, the immorality of Palmgren's capitalist enterprises is abetted by the welfare state itself, which does nothing to remedy the housing shortage and apparently facilitates the shady traffic in weapons. Thus, according to *Murder at the Savoy*, the state is complicitous in a war on its own citizens as well as in wars abroad, spreading misery within its own borders as well as on far-flung continents.

The downhill spiral of the Svensson family, which culminates in Palmgren's murder itself, demonstrates the link Sjöwall and Wahlöö see between capitalism and the welfare bureaucracy. After Bertil Svensson is laid off at one of Palmgren's businesses and begins to drink as a result of his despair, a series of domestic "disturbances" provoke the intervention of, successively, the Temperance Board, the Bureau of Child Welfare, the Unemployment Office, the Vocational Training Board, the Department of Public Health, and, finally, the Rent Control Commission, which terminates the family's lease in a Palmgren-owned apartment. Thus the novel insists, sometimes quite stridently, that institutions meant to improve the quality of Swedish life work hand in hand with agents of Palmgren's empire intent only on boosting the profits of private property. For Sjöwall and Wahlöö this is the grand conspiracy that marks contemporary Sweden, and criminal capitalism is the root cause of the perversion of Sweden's socialist experiment. It is no wonder that at the end of the novel, Martin Beck says of the killer, "Hope he gets a light sentence" (p. 198). After all, Svensson is the only person who will suffer, since all of Palmgren's business associates will continue to prosper in their reprehensible enterprises; only the "shipyard janitor" will "have to rot away the best years of his life in a prison cell" (p. 204).

Dissatisfaction with the state of Sweden comes home to the members of the Homicide Squad, most forcefully to Lennart Kollberg, who best understands that he is a victim of "the policeman's occupational disease": the inability to "think like a normal human being" and to maintain "sensible relations with the rest of the world" (p. 102). Unfortunately, though, not all members of the Swedish police comprehend that they have been infected with this disease, and by ignoring their symptoms, they sometimes bring about their own deaths. Such is the case with Chief Inspector Stig Nyman, the victim in the next novel, *The Abominable Man* (*Den vedervärdige mannen från Saffle*, 1971). The links between this novel and its predecessor are clear, since the latter opens with Nyman in Mount Sabbath Hospital, suffering great pain from a cause no one seems able to diagnose, despite extensive testing. This transition from *Murder at the Savoy* to *The Abominable Man* is almost seamless and shows how clearly Sjöwall and Wahlöö understood themselves to be writing

not ten discrete books but a single coherent work that, for the sake of convenience, appeared in ten thirty-chapter installments. Nyman's violent death at the hands of a bayonet-wielding assassin is an act of revenge, related directly to Nyman's Fascist policing methods, his sadism, and his hostile attitude toward the general public.

Nyman is seen from multiple points of view in the course of the novel. To one of his trusted underlings, Harald Hult, Nyman is a "real man, and the best boss you could imagine" (p. 65). Although never guilty of brutality, says Hult, Nyman was "the best" at maintaining order; however, despite all his superior's efforts, even a policeman like Hult is disenchanted by the job:

How many times have people puked on me? How many times have people spit at me and stuck their tongues out at me and called me a pig or a swine or a murderer? . . . They always say us policemen are supposed to protect society. . . . And now there's hardly anything left to protect anymore. But you put up with it, because the morale on the force has been good. And if there'd been more men like Stig Nyman, then things wouldn't be the way they are today. (pp. 68–69)

Members of the public who have encountered Nyman perceive him quite differently, as their letters to the Justice Department Ombudsman reveal. Here Nyman is criticized for gratuitous brutality on a regular basis, so often that even an unimaginative policeman like Einar Rönn acknowledges the validity of the charge. Kollberg, who was taught hand-to-hand combat by Nyman during his military service, is even more critical. In his view Nyman is "a bastard," "a goddamned lousy policeman," a "disgrace to the force," a "sadist"; he is "The abominable man from Säffle" (pp. 56–61). In short, Kollberg, like the authors, sees Nyman and policemen like him waging nothing less than all-out war on the citizenry they have pledged to protect.

Ironically, the killer in *The Abominable Man* is himself an ex-policeman whose life was destroyed by Stig Nyman. When Åke Eriksson's diabetic wife was picked up by two policemen who believed she was intoxicated, Nyman left her in the "drunk tank," where she died of insulin shock. With the help of perjured testimony by younger colleagues, Nyman denies all responsibility for the death and escapes punishment. He then uses the bureaucracy to punish Eriksson for his series of complaints about both Nyman and the police force in general. Worn down, Eriksson is finally dismissed from the force after walking away from his post at the American Embassy during an antiwar demonstration. When Nyman contributes directly to the removal of Eriksson's little daughter by the Child Welfare Department, he ensures Eriksson's descent into a state of despair that leads to murder. This, then, is one possible, horrific outcome of the "policeman's occupational disease."

It is only fitting, then, that the novel end with a vision of domestic warfare when the Police Commissioner insists on sending in helicopters, specially trained police commandos, and "stormtroopers" (p. 165) to capture Eriksson. He responds by adapting his police training to guerrilla tactics, and the novel effectively reproduces the Vietnam War, against which so many citizens have protested throughout the series. The analogy makes clear the moral bankruptcy of the official "war on crime." But such a war necessarily has personal consequences, and so Martin Beck, who feels vaguely responsible for Eriksson's situation, tries to apprehend him alone, only to be gravely wounded before being rescued by Lennart Kollberg, who also acts out of a feeling of individual responsibility for Beck, his friend and colleague. Eriksson is finally captured by Gunvald Larsson and a citizen with an unlicensed handgun, two individuals who stand clearly outside the bureaucratic mainstream. In this book more than any other, Sjöwall and Wahlöö underline the incongruity between the members of Beck's Homicide Squad, who put a sometimes fallible but fundamentally humane face on policing and the "rats of fascism pattering about behind the wainscoting" (*The Locked*

Room, p. 52) of the new National Police Headquarters, intent on bringing about public "order" at any cost.

In *The Locked Room* (*Det slutna rummet*, 1972), Sjöwall and Wahlöö decry the nationalization and subsequent centralization of the Swedish police, which went into effect at the beginning of 1966. An ongoing symbol of what the authors see as the wrongheaded approach to keeping order is the

immense hole in the ground—out of which the gigantic showy building of the National Police Board would in due course rise up and obscure the view. From this ultramodern colossus in the heart of Stockholm the police would extend their tentacles in every direction and hold the dispirited citizens of Sweden in an iron grip. At least some of them. After all, they couldn't all emigrate or commit suicide. (p. 130)

The unfinished nature of the future headquarters suggests that there is still time to prevent the police from asserting power "of a totalitarian type" and creating a locked "fortress" designed to keep police activities secret from "the prying eyes and ears of persons having no business there—which meant, in this case, the entire Swedish nation" (p. 130). From the authors' point of view, the real danger is that the right will transform the police into a political force that wields power from within a "Ministry of Terror" (p. 131).

To underscore this point, Sjöwall and Wahlöö create a series of metaphoric locked rooms within each of the three related plots in *The Locked Room*. The novel opens with a bank robbery committed by an unemployed single mother, Monita, who is desperate to find a new life for herself and her young daughter. She leaves her depressing apartment, the locked room in which she finds herself trapped, in order to make a forcible withdrawal of funds from another locked room, the bank's vault, and thus free herself from the largest prison of all, a country that appears to have no future for her. The novel raises the question of robbery as a radical political act, though Monita would certainly qualify as an unconscious revolutionary. The second plot, Sjöwall and Wahlöö's nod to the Golden Age detective story, revolves around Karl Edvin Svärd, a retired warehouseman whose blackmailing of a petty criminal eventually leads to his death in a locked room. Beck undertakes the Svärd investigation alone, as a transition back to work after recovering from his gunshot wound in *The Abominable Man.*

Beck's inquiry serves as counterpoint to the novel's third strand, "Bulldozer" Olsson's direction of a special squad formed to deal not only with Monita's heist but also with a rash of similar crimes; after all, "To violate society's banks was to commit an outrage against its very foundations" (p. 49). Olsson's special squad has all the advantages of high-tech equipment, but in spite of their gear, they make complete fools of themselves. All their meticulous preparation ends in failure when they carefully safeguard the wrong bank in the wrong city. In every plot line of the novel, the refrain from the chain of command is: "Nothing of this must get out" (p. 47). Whatever else happens, the public must never laugh at the police. This sort of misguided thinking leads to a perceived need for "a more militant and homogeneous police force, for greater technical resources in general, and for more firearms in particular" (p. 50). The escalation in police firepower then leads to overreaction and brutality until "people were going about being scared of each other and Stockholm had become a city containing tens of thousands of terrified individuals. And frightened people are dangerous people" (pp. 50–51).

The outcomes of all three related investigations are ironic, even absurdist. Martin Beck's investigation, as careful and thorough as those of his Golden Age predecessors, leads him to discover the identity of Svärd's killer, Filip Mauritzon, but Olsson's "Bulldozer" tactics undermine Beck's careful work. Mauritzon is convicted for a crime he did not commit, the shooting of a bystander during the bank robbery, and the real killer, Monita, is

last seen lounging on a beach in Yugoslavia. Sjöwall and Wahlöö look back at an earlier form of detective fiction to reveal their nostalgia for an earlier, more humane, form of policing, embodied in the low-tech work of their protagonist. The book endorses Beck's approach by rewarding him in his personal life; he begins a satisfying and healthy relationship with Rhea Nielsen, who frees him from his self-imposed isolation. The book still ends on a cynical note, however, with two police bureaucrats discussing not only Beck's unsuitability for promotion but the potential scandal created by his accurate investigation.

Beck's "scandalous" behavior, that is, his good police work, is likewise the hallmark of the small group of colleagues who remain attached to the Homicide Squad in *Cop Killer* (*Polismördaren,* 1974), the ninth novel in the Beck series. The novel's two plots divide the squad: while Martin Beck pursues the murderer of Sigbrit Mård in rural Anderslöv, the others hunt a professional criminal, the "Breadman," and a teenager, Ronnie Casparsson, who is accidentally caught up in the death of a policeman.

Sigbrit Mård's death occurs "in the farthest corner of Sweden" (p. 197) and confirms that the violence and immorality of Stockholm have spread throughout the countryside. The Mård plot furnishes an occasion for Sjöwall and Wahlöö to reprise four previous novels: the discovery of Mård's body during a nature hike in a tranquil woodland echoes the serial killings in parks in *The Man on the Balcony;* the primary suspect in the apparent sex crime is Folke Bengtsson, the murderer from *Roseanna,* now released and living quietly in "the farthest corner of the Malmö Police District" (p. 197); the motive for the crime, the slaying of a mistress by a businessman afraid that his quiet life will be disturbed by her demands, recalls *The Laughing Policeman;* and the return of Åke Gunnarsson as a now sober and responsible journalist suggests the rehabilitation of the murderer from *The Man Who Went Up in Smoke.*

These reprises help tie together the series as a whole and remind the reader of Sjöwall and Wahlöö's original plan to create a ten-volume epic. Thematically, they reinforce key ideas already seen in the series. Folke Bengtsson is, in Kollberg's view, "insane" but "innocent" of Mård's murder (p. 163). The unsatisfactory investigation in *Roseanna* led to prison rather than a hospital, indicating the state has failed to address the underlying causes of that earlier crime. On the other hand, Åke Gunnarsson repeatedly tells Kollberg, "You saved my life" (p. 163), and his transformation reaffirms Sjöwall and Wahlöö's notion that humane policing can effect change. While the murderer in *The Laughing Policeman* was arrogant in his belief that he had a right to kill the mistress who importuned him, here the businessman is just as exploitative, but his weakened physical condition and his death from a coronary before he can be brought to justice are emblematic of the social and spiritual illness Sjöwall and Wahlöö see in Sweden's bourgeoisie.

The Casparsson plot focuses on the way in which the police have become a force for violence in Swedish society rather than a guarantor of order and justice. Ronnie Casparsson is not a "cop killer" (the only policeman to die in the book does so of a wasp sting); he is yet another in a long series of troubled adolescents who, alienated from their families and unaided by the welfare state, turn to petty thieving to survive. When the national police bureaucracy deliberately underplays the fact that the "slain" policeman actually died accidentally, Casparsson becomes the object of a nationwide manhunt, the unspoken goal of which is his death rather than his capture. Ironically, it is Gunvald Larsson, apparently the squad's most aggressive member, who saves Casparsson from "a massacre" (p. 302).

Every member of Beck's squad who plays an important role in these two investigations is alienated from the national police bureaucracy and culture. Beck is forced to arrest Bengtsson despite his belief that the latter is not guilty of this crime; Larsson and Rönn intervene to prevent the slaughter of two suspects by Stig Malm's "so-called main force . . . a hundred men, two helicopters, and ten dogs" (p. 302). The novel culminates in Lennart Kollberg's resignation from the force, an action he has been contemplating since the middle of the series.

Kollberg's "decision is in no way a political action, even though many people will see it in that light." Although Kollberg objects to the fact that "the police establishment has been increasingly politicized over the last few years, and the police force itself has been exploited for political purposes more and more often," it is the increase in violence that leads him to the conclusion that he "cannot feel any sense of solidarity with the kind of organization the police department has become. . . . The great increase in the number of violent crimes over the last decade is . . . largely due to the fact that policemen invariably carry firearms." The police rely on violence rather than "psychology," and the net effect is that Kollberg finds himself "so ashamed of [his] profession that [his] conscience will no longer permit [him] to practice it" (pp. 294–296). Sjöwall and Wahlöö underscore the immorality of policing as urban warfare by having an ex-paratrooper skilled in hand-to-hand combat resign from a civilian police force on the grounds of conscientious objection. As Kollberg turns away from public life and retreats to his home and family, the authors adopt an elegiac tone, mourning the loss of conscientious public servants overwhelmed by unthinking bureaucrats.

Martin Beck, though, cannot bring himself to resign, precisely because he is "simply too conscientious" (p. 189), as Sjöwall and Wahlöö describe him in the final book in the series, *The Terrorists* (*Terroristema*, 1975). Here Beck is chosen by the National Police Commissioner to lead a "preventive murder investigation" (p. 110), a security detail for a visiting right-wing American senator who resembles Barry Goldwater. In this assignment Beck must outwit the forces of ULAG, an international terrorist group that does not seem to discriminate politically among its victims. Beck is selected for the job for the cynical reason that, should anything go wrong, he will be easy to blame.

This is not, however, the only focus in this multiplot work. Beck is also called to testify in the case of eighteen-year-old Rebecka Lind, who was arrested and manhandled by the police when she naively tried to borrow money from a Swedish bank, and bank employees interpreted her request for funds as an attempted robbery. Rebecka is an innocent, a flower child totally unadapted to living in the urban jungle of contemporary Sweden. One of the ways young women can be exploited is through the burgeoning pornographic film industry, and Rebecka has in fact tried out for a part in a film by Walter Petrus, the novel's embodiment of this form of exploitation. In the third plot Petrus is murdered by his gardener, Sture Hellström, whose daughter, Kristina, has become a drug addict and prostitute as a result of her contacts with the filmmaker. While Kristina has fled to Denmark to await her death, Rebecka has attempted to work within the Swedish system. What she discovers is how and why it has completely failed her: school, work, welfare, and child services should all enable her to live a full life according to the welfare state's plan, but none of these institutions has encouraged or supported her. In the final pages of the novel, Rebecka's despair leads her to assassinate the prime minister of Sweden, an act that Martin Beck is powerless to predict or to prevent.

These three apparently disparate plots are linked in several different ways. The most obvious, of course, is Martin Beck's involvement, inspired at least in part by his fatherly concern for both Rebecka Lind and Kristina Hellström, who quite obviously remind him of his own daughter, Ingrid, who is still living on her own. If Beck is the good father, Petrus and the deliberately unnamed prime minister, a figure clearly modeled on Olof Palme, who in fact was assassinated some ten years later in 1986, represent exploitative, paternalistic figures who betray the trusts they hold for personal gain—Petrus for money and the prime minister for political power. The immediate motive for Lind's assassination of the prime minister is the deportation of the American Vietnam War deserter who is the father of her

child, and this links the plotline to a recurrent motif, present in the series from at least as early as *The Laughing Policeman.* America's despoliation of Vietnam serves as a metaphor for the ruin of Swedish political and social culture, a point confirmed by the presence of the American senator at the assassination.

As in their use of the title *Cop Killer,* which has a double significance, Sjöwall and Wahlöö deliberately blur the identity of the titular terrorists of the final novel in the Martin Beck series. While the government and SEPO, the security police, concentrate on ULAG, the foreign threat, and the national police concentrate on those who commit crimes against property, as Rebecka Lind supposedly did, Sjöwall and Wahlöö suggest that the true terrorists are businessmen like Walter Petrus (and all his predecessors in the previous novels) and the politicians who do their bidding. As "Crasher" Braxén, Lind's public defender, states at her arraignment,

> for as long as I can remember large and powerful nations within the capitalist bloc have been ruled by people who according to accepted legal norms are simply criminals, who from a lust for power and financial gain have led their peoples into an abyss of egoism, self-indulgence and a view of life based entirely on materialism and ruthlessness toward their fellow human beings. (p. 286)

These are precisely the people who will go unpunished, however, because the powers of the state are always directed at the disenfranchised who threaten to disturb public order.

This is an appropriate end to the series, since one of its major tasks has been to trace the consequences of the nationalization of the Swedish police, which reorganized "the old local ... system into a centrally directed, paramilitary force with frightening technical resources" (p. 188). The nationalized police force is itself a symptom of the government's desire to ensure its own power by ensuring social control. Sjöwall and Wahlöö again embody the surveillance of the citizens of Sweden in the building of the National Police

Headquarters, whose construction is first noted in *The Man Who Went Up in Smoke* and which, in *The Terrorists*, looms over the Stockholm landscape like an "almost completed colossus" (p. 318).

At the end of *The Terrorists*, Martin Beck is deeply ambivalent about remaining a policeman since he, like Kollberg before him, fears that he is contributing to the violent nature of Swedish society rather than preventing it. His half-articulated doubts are thus a counterpart to the half-finished police headquarters. Readers are left with the image of a noble squad, but also one that is mentally, if not physically, exhausted. For ten novels, the men and women who surround Martin Beck articulate their dissent from uncaring and proto-Fascist models of policing emanating from the highest ranks of the bureaucracy. Even figures like Gunvald Larsson, who begins as an almost parodic figure of strength and impassivity, or Einar Rönn, who seems to spend half his life "polishing" his runny red nose, understand the gulf between the police and the citizenry they nominally serve; they come to embody what ought to be the humanity of public service. They speak, of course, with multiple voices, creating an intricate fabric of dissent that pictures Sjöwall and Wahlöö's dismay at the increasing barrenness of contemporary Sweden, at the sterility predicted by Per Wahlöö in books like *Murder on the Thirty-first Floor* and *The Steel Spring* even before he began his successful collaboration with Maj Sjöwall.

Conclusion

Reviewers have generally been kind to the Martin Beck series; it has been published and discussed in over twenty countries. While *Roseanna* was not acclaimed initially, the second volume of the series began to spark the interest of American reviewers, who noted with particular approval the excellent characterizations, intricate plots, realistic details in the investigations, and the absorbing descriptions of the Swedish settings. They also praised the authors for the ways in which the novels reveal the pressures facing urban police everywhere. *The Laughing Policeman* garnered the Sherlock Award from the Swedish newspaper *Expressen* in 1968, the 1971 Edgar Allan Poe Award from the Mystery Writers of America for the best mystery novel of 1970, and the Italian Gran Giallo Città di Cattolica Prize in 1973. This same novel was turned into a motion picture by Twentieth Century Fox in 1973, although the setting was transposed to San Francisco and all the characters transformed into American cops; Walter Matthau and Bruce Dern starred. *The Abominable Man* was filmed as *The Man on the Roof* by Bo Widerberg in 1977.

Scholars have also been positive in their view of the novels. They have, for example, accepted that the Martin Beck series fulfills Sjöwall and Wahlöö's aim, the creation of a ten-volume epic. While some have argued that the first three novels are relatively apolitical, others have traced the critique of Swedish society back to the opening chapter of *Roseanna*. A few have complained that the last books in the series diverge from the tradition of the police procedural and lapse into farce or polemics, but others argue that the series consistently challenges the boundaries of the genre in new and interesting ways.

In this view, the novels succeed in Wahlöö's aim of taking a "scalpel" to the "belly" of the welfare state in order to identify the diseases that infect Swedish society. The series chronicles the gaps between rich and poor which lead to actions that society at large deems criminal; the authors disagree and use these behaviors to indict Sweden's political system rather than its alienated citizenry. Instead of reinforcing the most conservative values in a society, a charge often levelled at popular fiction in general and detective novels in particular, the books of the Martin Beck series become vehicles by which Sjöwall and Wahlöö can intercede on behalf of the disenfranchised, playing much the same role that an ombudsman would play in countering the abuses of state power. Many of their Swedish successors adopt this same approach, shunning the apolitical and embracing a more socially aware style. Among these authors are K. Arne Blom, Olov Svedelid, Kennet Ahl, and Leif G. W. Persson.

Selected Bibliography

WORKS BY MAJ SJÖWALL AND PER WAHLÖÖ

NOVELS BY PER WAHLÖÖ

The following were all originally published by Norstedt in Stockholm.

Himmelsgetan (Heaven's goats). 1959. Reprinted as *Hövdingen* (The Chieftain). 1967.

Vinden och regnet (Wind and rain). 1961.

Lastbilen. 1962. Translated by Joan Tate as *The Lorry*. London: Joseph, 1968. Translated by Joan Tate as *A Necessary Action*. New York: Pantheon, 1969; London: Pan Books, 1972.

Uppdraget. 1963. Translated by Joan Tate as *The Assignment*. London: Joseph, 1965; New York: Knopf, 1966.

Mord på 31: A våningen. 1964. Translated by Joan Tate as *Murder on the Thirty-first Floor*. London: Joseph, 1966. New York: Pantheon, 1972. Translated by Joan Tate as *The Thirty-first Floor*. New York: Knopf, 1967. *Kamikaze 1989*, a film based on *Mord på 31: A våningen*, starring Rainer Werner Fassbinder, is available from MGM/UA Home Video. 1984. German with English subtitles.

Stålsprånget. 1968. Translated by Joan Tate under the title *The Steel Spring*. London: Joseph, 1970; New York: Delacorte, 1970.

Generalerna. 1965. Translated by Joan Tate under the title *The Generals*. London: Joseph, 1974; New York: Pantheon, 1974.

SHORT FICTION BY PER WAHLÖÖ

Det växer inga rosor på Odenplan (Roses don't grow on the Odenplan). Stockholm: Norstedt, 1964.

MARTIN BECK SERIES, BY MAJ SJÖWALL AND PER WAHLÖÖ

The following were all originally published by Norstedt in Stockholm.

Roseanna. 1965. Translated by Lois Roth. New York: Pantheon, 1967; Vintage, 1976; Vintage Crime/Black Lizard, 1993.

Mannen som gick upp i rök. 1966. Translated by Alan Blair as *The Man Who Went Up in Smoke*. New York: Pantheon, 1969; Vintage, 1976; Vintage Crime/Black Lizard, 1993.

Mannen på balkongen. 1967. Translated by Alan Blair as *The Man on the Balcony: The Story of a Crime*. New York: Pantheon, 1967; Vintage, 1977; Vintage Crime/Black Lizard, 1993.

Den skrattande polisen. 1968. Translated by Alan Blair as *The Laughing Policeman*. New York: Pantheon, 1968; Vintage, 1977; Vintage Crime/Black Lizard, 1992.

Brandbilen som försvann. 1969. Translated by Joan Tate as *The Fire Engine That Disappeared*. New York: Pantheon, 1970; Vintage, 1977.

Polis, polis, potatismos! (Police, police, mashed potatoes!). 1970. Translated by Amy Knoespel and Ken Knoespel as *Murder at the Savoy*. New York: Pantheon, 1971; Vintage, 1977.

Den vedervärdige mannen från Säffle. 1971. Translated by Thomas Teal as *The Abominable Man*. New York: Pantheon, 1972; Vintage, 1980.

Det slutna rummet. 1972. Translated by Paul Britten Austin as *The Locked Room*. New York: Pantheon, 1973; Vintage, 1980; Vintage Crime/Black Lizard, 1992.

Polismördaren: roman om ett brott. 1974. Translated by Thomas Teal as *Cop Killer: The Story of a Crime*. New York: Pantheon, 1975; Vintage, 1978.

Terroristema. 1975. Translated by Joan Tate as *The Terrorists*. New York: Pantheon, 1976; Vintage, 1978.

FILM VERSIONS OF THE MARTIN BECK SERIES

The Laughing Policeman. Twentieth Century Fox, 1973. Produced and directed by Stuart Rosenberg. With Walter Matthau and Bruce Dern.

The Man on the Roof (from *The Abominable Man*). Svensk Filmindustry and Svenska Institutet, 1977: Directed by Bo Widerberg With Carf Gustaf Lindstedt.

In addition, six books in the series were adapted for television in Sweden, starring Gösta Ekman as Martin Beck.

NOVEL BY MAJ SJÖWALL

Kvinnan som liknade Garbo (The woman who resembled Garbo). With Tomas Ross. Stockholm: Norstedt, 1990

CRITICAL STUDIES

Bannon, Barbara A. "Authors and Editors." *Publishers' Weekly* 200, no. 10: 13–15 (6 September 1971).

Becker, Jens Peter. "The Mean Streets of Europe: The Influence of the American 'Hard-Boiled School' on European Detective Fiction." Translated by Ian E. Oliver, in *Superculture: American Popular Culture and Europe*. Edited by C. W. Bigsby. Bowling Green, Ohio: Bowling Green University Popular Press, 1975. Pp. 152–159.

Benstock, Bernard. "The Education of Martin Beck." In *Art in Crime Writing: Essays on Detective Fiction.* Edited by Bernard Benstock. New York: St. Martin's Press, 1983. Pp. 189–209.

Binyon, T. J. *Murder Will Out.* Oxford and New York: Oxford University Press, 1990. Pp. 111–112.

Blom, K. Arne. "Polis! Polis!" In *Murder Ink: The Mystery Reader's Companion.* Edited by Dilys Winn. New York: Workman, 1977. Pp. 334–335.

"Copology." *New Yorker* 47: 28 (22 May 1971).

Dove, George. *The Police Procedural.* Bowling Green, Ohio: Bowling Green University Popular Press, 1982.

Duffy, Martha. "Martin Beck Passes." *Time,* 106, no. 6: 58–59 (11 August 1975).

Lesser, Wendy. "Kungsholmsgatan Blues." *Threepenny Review*: 18–19 (summer 1983).

Lorenz, Janet E. "Maj Sjöwall and Per Wahlöö." In *Critical Survey of Mystery and Detective Fiction,* Authors Index 4. Edited by Frank N. Magill. Pasadena and Englewood Cliffs, N.J.: Salem, 1988. Pp. 1495–1501.

Lundin, Bo. "Wahlöö, Per (1926–75) and Maj Sjöwall (1935–)." In *Twentieth-Century Crime and Mystery Writers.* Edited by John M. Reilly. New York: St. Martin's Press, 1980. Pp. 1553–1554.

———. *The Swedish Crime Story/Svenska Deckare.* Translated by Anna Lena Ringarp, Ralph A. Wilson, and Bo Lundin. N. p.: Tidskriften Jury, 1981.

Maxfield, James F. "The Collective Detective Hero: The Police Novels of Maj Sjöwall and Per Wahlöö." *Clues* 3, no. 1: 70–79 (1982).

Mellerski, Nancy C., and Robert P. Winston. "Sjöwall and Wahlöö's Brave New Sweden." *Clues* 7, no. 1: 1–17 (1986).

Occhiogrosso, Frank. "The Police in Society: The Novels of Maj Sjöwall and Per Wahlöö." *The Armchair Detective* 12, no. 2: 174–177 (1979).

Phillips, McCandlish. "Writers' Collaboration Is a Marriage of Plots." *The New York Times*, p. 56, 5 May 1971.

"Sjoewall [sic], Maj." In *Contemporary Authors,* Vols. 65–68. Edited by Jane A. Bowden. Detroit: Gale, 1977. Pp. 547–548.

"Sjöwall, Maj, and Per Wahlöö." *World Authors 1970–1975.* Edited by John Wakeman. New York: H. W. Wilson, 1980. Pp. 761–764.

Van Dover, J. Kenneth. *Polemical Pulps: The Martin Beck Novels of Maj Sjöwall and Per Wahlöö.* Brownstone Mystery Guides, Vol. 11. San Bernadino, Calif.: Brownstone, 1993.

Van Gelder, Lawrence. "Per Wahloo, Author with Wife of Detective Beck Series, Dies." *New York Times,* p. 36, 24 June 1975.

"Wahloo, Per." In *Contemporary Authors,* Vols. 61–64. Edited by Cynthia R. Fadool. Detroit: Gale, 1976. Pp. 579–580.

"Wahlöö, Per." In *Contemporary Literary Criticism,* Vol. 7. Edited by P. C. Mendelson and D. Bryfonski. Detroit: Gale, 1977. Pp. 501–502.

"Wahlöö, Per." *Encyclopedia of Mystery and Detection.* Edited by Chris Steinbrunner and Otto Penzler. New York: McGraw-Hill, 1976. P. 406.

White, Jean M. "Wahlöö/Sjöwall and James McClure." *New Republic* 75: 27–29 (31 July 1976)

Williams, Thomas E. "Martin Beck: The Swedish Version of Barney Miller Without the Canned Laughter." *Clues* 1, no. 1: 123–128 (1980).

Winks, Robin W. *Modus Operandi.* Boston: Godine, 1982. Pp. 41–42.

Winston, Robert P., and Nancy C. Mellerski. "Brave New Sweden." In *The Public Eye: Ideology and the Police Procedural.* London: Macmillan, 1992; New York: St. Martin's Press, 1992.

Wizelius, Ingemar. "Literature." [In "The Arts in Sweden."] In *Sweden in the Sixties.* Edited by Ingernar Wizelius. Translated by Rudy Feichtner. Stockholm: Almqvist & Wiksell, 1967. Pp. 242–245.

MICKEY SPILLANE
(b. 1918)

MAX ALLAN COLLINS

MICKEY SPILLANE—adored and reviled, influential and resented—is a paradoxical figure in American crime and mystery fiction. One of the most widely translated authors of all time, and among the best-selling mystery writers worldwide, Spillane is famous for bringing to the hard-boiled mystery novel a degree of sex and violence previously unknown in the genre. Yet in his private life, he belongs to a conservative sect—the Jehovah's Witnesses—and, for all his household-name fame, he has been less than prolific in a mystery-writing career that began in 1947 with his enormously successful *I, the Jury*, which introduced his private-detective character, Mike Hammer.

Four distinct intervals characterize Spillane's career as a writer: 1947 through 1952, during which the initial six Mike Hammer novels and the non-Hammer *The Long Wait* (1951) were published; 1953 through 1960, an inactive period where novels were concerned but a productive one for shorter fiction (none of it featuring Hammer); 1961 through 1973, a fertile period during which Spillane published thirteen novels (five featuring Hammer); and 1979 through the late 1990s, a rather leisurely period, which began with two young-adult novels—*The Day the Sea Rolled Back* (1979) and *The Ship That Never Was* (1982)—and continued with the 1989 publication of *The Killing Man* and the 1996 publication of *Black Alley*, both Hammer novels.

Black Alley marks the fiftieth anniversary of the detective's first appearance, yet is only the thirteenth Mike Hammer novel and one of only two in a twenty-six-year period. Despite this rather modest list of novels featuring so popular a protagonist, Spillane is erroneously viewed as a prolific author in the vein of Erle Stanley Gardner (who wrote eighty-two Perry Mason novels).

This misperception is in part due to the success of the individual books—the first six Hammers are among the best-selling mystery novels of all time—but also hinges on Spillane's curious position in popular culture, a position he has nurtured and exploited to the point of highly profitable self-parody.

Early Years and Comic-Book Work

Frank Morrison Spillane was born in Brooklyn, New York, on 9 March 1918, the only child of working-class parents. The nickname Mickey came from his bartender father, John; his mother Catherine Anne's affectionate designation, Babe, would have made a less than appropriate byline for mystery fiction's most infamously hard-boiled practitioner.

Spillane was raised in Elizabeth, New Jersey, and if any hardships were attached to his growing up in a rough blue-collar neighborhood during the Depression, he has never reported them. He was a good student, cheerful and well behaved, and small for his age, though he displayed a talent for sports, including football and swimming; his summer job, which he looked back on fondly, was that of lifeguard.

Around summer beach campfires and in other social situations, young Spillane displayed a facility for spinning ghost stories and gleefully recalled "scaring hell out of the other kids," taking particular pleasure in giving the shivers to bigger, stronger boys. He began writing in high school or before and claimed his first publication came shortly after graduation, though what that story was or where it was published cannot be ascertained. Spillane said that throughout his college years and shortly thereafter he wrote stories for the "slick" magazines—*Saturday Evening Post, Collier's,* and others of their ilk, whose pages were frequented by the top fiction writers of the day—but this assertion has never been confirmed; he claimed he wrote under pseudonyms that were later forgotten.

He attended Fort Hays State College in Kansas briefly, in pre-law, but he concentrated more on football and fiction writing. Soon he was back on the East Coast, working as a clothing clerk in the basement of Gimbel's department store in New York City.

Spillane liked to brag good-naturedly that he began at the top of the fiction market and worked his way down—starting with the slicks, moving to the pulps, and, finally, entering the comic-book industry. Comic books play an important role in his career. On the one hand, they encouraged his visual sense and nurtured a boyhood love for adventure stories (his favorite writers were Alexandre Dumas and Anthony Hope, his favorite novels *The Count of Monte Cristo* and *The Prisoner of Zenda*). On the other hand, his appreciation for comic books unintentionally provided critics with a cudgel: throughout Spillane's career, facile, condescending critics would dismiss him as a "comic-book writer." Even an author Spillane admired, the cur-

mudgeonly mystery-fiction genius Raymond Chandler, invoked this phrase of damnation in dismissing his young competitor. (Chandler was influenced by Spillane, however: his character Philip Marlowe did not sleep with a woman until Hammer had paved the way.)

Spillane went to work in a so-called comic-book shop, where writers and artists toiled in anonymity. Various hands would work on a given story, with the art, from pencil layouts to finished pencil drawings, divided among as many as five or six illustrators, with one artist inking backgrounds, another figures, possibly another doing faces, and yet another providing the lettering; the writers, however, usually worked alone. It was a factory of sorts, and Spillane, whose previously published work had apparently been under pseudonyms, suddenly craved a credit line. He volunteered to write one- and two-page short stories, fillers designed to satisfy certain arcane postal requirements. These appealed to him, he often said, because on the prose fillers writers received a byline.

Many of these very short stories prefigure the later Spillane; they are action packed and occasionally feature a private eye, such as the 1941 tale "Trouble . . . Come and Get It!" published in *4-Most Comics.* But Spillane also wrote comic-book stories for such famous characters as Captain America, the Human Torch, and Submariner; he also adapted novels into comics for the *Classics Illustrated* series, including, perhaps, works by his heroes, Dumas and Hope. Sometimes working in an editorial capacity, Spillane outlined his stories simply, using a sentence or two to represent each picture.

Artist and comics historian James Steranko labeled Spillane "an extremely graphic [comics] writer as time would later prove. He wrote for the artist with explicit clarity. . . . Each sentence told precisely enough for the artist to draw just the right panel. This laconic and punchy delivery was the backbone of Spillane's later writing style."

World War II intruded on Spillane's thriving comics career, and the young writer enlisted in the U.S. Army Air Force, eagerly pursuing a childhood interest in aviation. His dream was to spend the war as a fighter pilot, but his outstanding communications skills and his flying abilities convinced his superiors to relegate him to training other pilots. Spillane spent most of the war in Greenwood, Mississippi, although some sources indicate he may have received a fighter assignment near the end of the war. He met and married his first wife, Mary Ann Pearce, in 1945 in Greenwood; they had four children—Kathy, Ward, Michael, and Caroline.

Achieving the rank of captain by the time he left the service, in 1946 Spillane returned with his young wife to the New York City area, where he found the comic-book industry in a slump. He had developed a new comic book (the beginnings of which probably predated the war) about a hard-boiled private detective named Mike Danger; he and several comic-book artists had put together a first issue, speculatively. Comic books had thrived during the war, with massive sales at military-base post exchanges; GIs, some of them barely literate, found the illustrated booklets cheap, fun, and easy entertainment. With the war over, however, sales were down, and Mike Danger could not find a home.

In the meantime, Spillane and his wife needed a home as well; he had acquired four acres near the Hudson River community of Newburgh, New York, where he hoped to build his own house. The failure of Mike Danger, and the general lack of work in the comic-book trade, frustrated this plan only temporarily. He announced to friends that he would write a mystery novel, based around the Danger concept, and get the money he needed—around a thousand dollars—for building materials for the house. "Mickey will tell you what seems like the most outrageous lie," longtime Spillane crony Ray Gill said, "and then, after you've laughed at him, he hits you over the head by making it come true." Mike Danger became Mike Hammer in Spillane's first novel, *I, the Jury*, which sold a few thousand copies. In the meantime, Spillane used his thousand-dollar advance to con-

struct a four-bedroom cinder-block house, with garage, and moved in with Mary Ann.

Soon Spillane had written a second novel, *For Whom the Gods Would Destroy*, which was rejected by Dutton, the publisher of his first novel, because its premise, according to the author, was deemed "too far-fetched"; however, the mediocre showing of *I, the Jury* in hardcover may have had something to do with the rejection.

Mike Hammer, a New Kind of Hero

The January 1948 paperback publication of *I, the Jury* initiated a publishing phenomenon that was to go far beyond Spillane's own career. Spillane's potent mix of sex and violence was an extension of the hard-boiled fiction that appeared in such 1920s, 1930s, and 1940s pulp magazines as *Black Mask* and *Dime Detective*. Dashiell Hammett and Raymond Chandler, among others, had graduated from those pulpwood pages to respectable publication by Alfred A. Knopf. Spillane's role model, however, was neither Hammett nor Chandler (though both affected his fiction) but Carroll John Daly, now little read and seldom republished but in the 1930s and 1940s a mainstay of *Black Mask* and other top pulps. Daly's hard-hitting detective Race Williams—who shot first and asked questions afterward—set the Wild West–like pattern for Spillane's urban cowboy Mike Hammer. Spillane's out-of-the-corner-of-the-mouth first-person style in the Hammer novels was patterned (though a great improvement) on Daly's style in the Race Williams stories.

Daly was an innovative writer—he is considered by many scholars to have created the private eye of fiction—but he lacked Spillane's talent and skills. A better storyteller on every level—plot, characterization, and style—Spillane upped the ante on not only Daly but also Hammett and Chandler by bringing to the tough detective story a new degree of frank sexuality and combat-gritty scenes of hyper-realistic violence.

Spillane was not a more realistic writer than his hard-boiled precursors. His novels, on the whole, are less grounded in reality than Hammett's certainly and Chandler's probably. Spillane writes with speed, and the rough-hewn poetry of his narrator creates a fantasy city, a New York of myth and dream, populated by the same character types as those found in the work of Daly, Hammett, and Chandler—good girls, black widows, thugs, frustrated cops, gang lords, corrupt society leaders—but delivered with a unique fever-dream fervor.

As a World War II veteran well aware of the loss of innocence his generation of men had suffered in combat and otherwise, Spillane sensed that popular fiction needed to be taken up a notch; he felt that hard-bitten ex-GIs would respond well to a no-holds-barred style of entertainment. In the postwar world Hammer inhabits, men and women sleep together, and like it; and when somebody gets shot, he bleeds—profusely.

In addition, Spillane crafted in Mike Hammer a new type of hero. To call Hammer the first mystery fiction antihero is probably correct in that he was the first popular hero of series fiction to behave as badly as the bad guys. Like Chandler's Philip Marlowe, Hammer is a modern-day knight, but he is a world-weary knight who has fought in the Pacific, battling "Japs" from foxholes and seeing buddies lose limbs and die. He is a knight every bit as brutal and fire-breathing as any dragon he might come up against. (The villain in Spillane's 1962 novel, *The Girl Hunters*, is called "the Dragon," and Hammer sarcastically refers to himself as "St. George.")

Spillane's contribution to popular storytelling extends well beyond mystery fiction. Virtually any contemporary loner hero of novels, film, or television who takes the law into his or her own hands can be traced back to Mike Hammer. Whether his name is James Bond or Dirty Harry, Billy Jack or Mack Bolan, his heritage includes Hammer. Hammer's heritage, of course, includes the western hero—the gunfighter of history and legend, particularly as popularized in Hollywood films by John Wayne, Randolph Scott, Audie Murphy, and others. But what sets Hammer apart, and makes the character a benchmark of sorts, is Spillane's post–World War II, urban setting. The suggestion, of course, is that the big city—specifically, New York—is as much a frontier town as Dodge City was in the 1880s; the city is not completely civilized, and the innocent townsfolk are prey to the urban variety of rustlers and outlaws.

In *I, the Jury*, Mike Hammer—called to the scene by Captain Pat Chambers of homicide—swears vengeance over the corpse of his dead friend, Jack Williams (an apparent nod to Daly's Race Williams). In combat in the Pacific, Jack had given an arm to save Hammer. The private detective will not trust a corrupt system that cares more about the murderer's rights than the victim's; Hammer will find the killer—whoever it is—and execute him or her. This dramatic opening sets the stage for a fast-moving but fairly conventional detective novel, as Hammer runs into numerous attractive, willing females and the occasional nasty male; he survives scuffles with both. Moving primarily through high-society circles, the lowborn detective falls in love with his late friend's psychiatrist, the blonde and beautiful Charlotte Manning.

What sets *I, the Jury* apart from the hard-boiled detective novels that preceded it is the denouement, in which Hammer tells Charlotte that he suspects she is the murderer; as she listens, Charlotte does a sexy striptease (described in loving detail through parenthetical, italicized interruptions to Hammer's soliloquy). Finally, a naked Charlotte falls into Hammer's arms, and the detective shoots her in the stomach with his .45 automatic. In her dying gasp, Charlotte asks how he could have done this to the beautiful woman he loved. And Hammer, in one of the most famous last lines in popular fiction, merely says, "It was easy."

This scene, more than anything else in *I, the Jury* (or in any of the novels that followed), outraged critics and social commentators.

Spillane in the next several Hammer novels did not stint on sexual situations and bone-cracking violence, both of which he described lovingly. Typical of the critical response to these early Mike Hammer novels was that of Malcolm Cowley in *The New Republic*, who labeled Spillane "a homicidal paranoiac," as well as a sadist and masochist (11 February 1952); James Sandoe in *The Saturday Review* dismissed Spillane as "an inept vulgarian."

Popular Success, Critical Condemnation

Not including translations and hardbound editions, *I, the Jury* sold more than eight million copies as of 1998. In 1984 Spillane's book sales were calculated at 160 million. The success of *I, the Jury* in paperback—followed by similar successes for the next three Hammer novels, *My Gun Is Quick* (1950), *Vengeance Is Mine!* (1950), *The Big Kill* (1951)—sparked the creation of the so-called paperback original (most paperback editions until this time had been reprints of hardcover books). Fawcett Publications—the distributor of Spillane's paperback publisher, Signet—created Gold Medal Books to help satisfy the demand for Spillane-style "product." The mainstays of the Gold Medal Books paperback-original publishing list were John D. MacDonald, whose early success, *The Damned* (1952), bore a supportive Spillane cover blurb, and Richard S. Prather's best-selling Shell Scott series, which added tongue-in-cheek humor to a Spillane-style sex-and-sadism mix.

From his first popular success in 1948, Spillane struck a chord with a wide audience, joining a short list (that includes Erle Stanley Gardner and Robert B. Parker) of mystery writers who have reached a mainstream audience. But for more than the first decade of Spillane's career as a mystery novelist, critics and social commentators were nearly unanimous in their vilification of him and his hero. Spillane was blamed for the "decline and fall" of the mystery novel, and *Parent's Magazine*

linked him to juvenile delinquency; it is no surprise that Spillane's alma mater, the comic book, was coming under similar fire from the same quarters.

"I don't give a hoot about readin' reviews," Spillane said in one interview. "What I want to read is the royalty checks." Laughing the harsh critical response off, Spillane encouraged his publishers to quote bad reviews to comic effect in advertising and for a number of years worked next to a bulletin board teeming with negative quotes from reviewers.

For all his bluster about "jerks who think they're critics," Spillane demonstrated in his work that he was sensitive to such criticism: in *One Lonely Night* (1951), he tackled the critics head-on, answering their questions and denunciations in this, his wildest, most violent novel; in later novels—starting with *The Deep* (1961)—he subdued his tendency toward overstated sex and violence.

A sort of hysteria, perhaps endemic to the McCarthy era, which coincided with the publication of many of Spillane's novels, colored critical reaction to his work. A later reappraisal (led by the writer of this piece and his frequent collaborator on the subject, James L. Traylor) acknowledged Spillane as an innovative storyteller and stylist who maintains a grip on the reader by the commanding presence of his protagonists, usually via an intense use of first-person narration (only one Spillane novel, *The Last Cop Out* [1973], is told exclusively in the third person).

Traylor has noted in Spillane "an instinctive, moralistic understanding that America itself was changing." Commenting on the loss of national innocence brought on by the assassination of President John F. Kennedy in 1963, Traylor continues:

Spillane revealed the darkness underneath that 1950s Norman Rockwell surface, particularly the darkness inherent in the archetypal frontier hero of which Mike Hammer was a modern urban extension.... [He] painted an America whose post-war world did not live up to expectations; whose returning war heroes were passionate, righteous, yet flawed, even disturbed. Spillane's novels have always concerned themselves with political corruption, lust for money and the evils of drugs. Spillane's vision is of a post-modern America, after World War II had destroyed her innocence. (unpublished essay)

Despite the ongoing reappraisal, Spillane remains the most misunderstood and under-appreciated major writer of hard-boiled detective fiction, and Hammer is often dismissed as immoral or even amoral. In Dashiell Hammett's seminal hard-boiled novel *The Maltese Falcon* (1930), private detective Sam Spade "sends over" his lover to the police for possible execution in an extension of the personal code he has developed to maintain sanity and order in an insanely violent, chaotic world. Part of Spade's code is, "When a man's [detective's] partner is killed he's supposed to do something about it," and even when his lover turns out to be his partner's killer, Spade accepts this self-designed rule with cool detachment. In *I, the Jury*, Hammer executes his lover in an extension of his personal code, which represents an effort to bring righteous order to that insanely violent, chaotic world; Hammer's code is a code of duties—one of which is that, when a man's best buddy is killed, he *has* to do something about it—and he deals with the world not with Spade's cool detachment (although he feigns this at times: "It was easy") but with intensity and passion.

The personal codes of Spade and Hammer are poles apart, although the end result is the same: a lover is sacrificed because she is a murderer. Spade sees the universe as a place devoid of meaning and civilization and its rules as absurd and arbitrary. Hammer sees the world as Eden after the fall, where the innocent victims of corrupt, evil men are failed by a society whose laws are unresponsive to the demands of a higher morality. Sam Spade does not believe in God; Mike Hammer not only believes in God, he considers himself God's traffic cop.

Where Sam Spade's code requires him dispassionately to turn his lover over to an executioner, Mike Hammer's code demands that he himself act as executioner. Spade is an amoral man who chooses a conveniently moral path; Hammer is a moral man who chooses what may seem an amoral path. As a holy avenger, Hammer must fight evil with evil; if brutal men define the battlefield, then brutality is called for in response—just as in World War II, when young Americans like Mickey Spillane (and Mike Hammer) enlisted in a war against such modern-day monsters as Adolf Hitler, Benito Mussolini, and Emperor Hirohito.

Critics tracing the decline and fall of the mystery novel have frequently presented the disparaged Spillane as an unpleasant distortion or even perversion of the respected Hammett; *Time* magazine (in a negative July 1966 review) termed Spillane the "direct literary descendent of Dashiell Hammett." But the authors have little in common beyond their genre and considerable skills. Hammett, an advocate of left-wing causes who spent time in jail for refusing to cooperate with the House Un-American Activities Committee, tells cold-blooded Sam Spade's story in the objective, understated third-person manner it requires. Spillane, a political conservative whose views border on the reactionary, tells hot-tempered Mike Hammer's story in a subjective, passionate first person that often approaches the surreal.

Reworking Stereotypes in a Surreal, Complicated World

Although Spillane considers characterization the most important element of fiction writing, his novels are largely populated with stereotypes, however vividly portrayed; but even the most critically acclaimed writers in the hard-boiled detective genre, Chandler and Hammett not excepted, also rely on stereotypes. The only fully rounded characterization in Spillane's work is Mike Hammer himself (and such Hammer surrogates in later novels as Johnny McBride in *The Long Wait* [1951] and Morgan the Raider in *The Delta*

Factor [1967]). The convincing, compelling voice of the storyteller makes the improbable Hammer vivid and real, which transforms the stereotypes with whom he associates.

Little background, other than his wartime service in the Pacific and vague references to police work prior to the war, is provided about Hammer, and his physical appearance is never described, other than throwaway self-denigrations relating to his size and ugliness. Occasionally, characters, particularly women, wax eloquent about his distinctive eyes, which "watch you," though the color of those eyes is never given.

The tactic of leaving Hammer undescribed grew from Spillane's desire to make his hard-hitting hero an everyman of sorts, to allow male readers to identify with Hammer. Similarly, Hammer's best friend, Captain Pat Chambers, is never described in any detail. Chambers serves as the detective's sounding board and information source and as a reminder that Hammer is a regular guy with buddies and a social life outside the violent cases of the novels. Chambers also represents the hamstrung authorities, a good man caught in a bad, ineffective system; Chambers rails on about the frustrations of his job, and, for all his warnings to Hammer to stay within the law, the police detective largely comes off as approving of and even envying Hammer, his alter ego unbound by society's rules and answering only to a higher authority. Only in *The Girl Hunters* does the characterization of Chambers vary from this pattern, when he reveals that he has long been in love with Hammer's secretary and soul mate, Velda.

Velda's last name is never given, although, unlike Hammer and Chambers, she is lovingly described; "leggy," her dark hair in a pageboy, Velda is Hammer's idealized woman—which is to say, essentially a female version of himself. She is physically powerful and a licensed private eye. In the earlier novels, Velda fits the pattern of loyal secretary longing for her boss, a private-eye-novel convention established in *The Maltese Falcon* with Sam Spade's secretary, Effie Perrine. But by *One Lonely Night* she is playing Jane to

Hammer's Tarzan, packing a gun in her garter belt, punching out bad guys, eager to join Hammer in his righteous crusades.

Hammer, Chambers, and Velda constitute the recurring cast in the Mike Hammer novels. Various district attorneys and their assistants turn up; each new book seems to feature another reporter (often retired) who is an old friend of Hammer's. Bad guys with whom Hammer has a long-standing grudge show up with alarming frequency but never recur in a second book. A secondary Chambers type of character, government agent Art Rickerby, appears twice, in *The Girl Hunters* and its sequel, *The Snake* (1964); so does real-life gossip columnist Hy Gardner, a Spillane crony. It is as if, in the surreal, film-noir-ish nightmare city that is Mike Hammer's world, the detective is always encountering old friends and enemies with new faces; the conflicts and problems he encounters are similarly old and new at once; and the dream landscape and its denizens subtly reinvent themselves from tale to tale, shifting but not really changing.

While the basis of Mike Hammer's philosophy is black-and-white—absolute good versus absolute evil—the surreal world he inhabits is complicated, even complex. Hammer is a good man who fights evil with evil, emerging gray in a world he has defined as black-and-white. The paradox of gray solutions for black-and-white problems is a continuing theme in the Hammer canon. For books that readers and reviewers describe as "action packed," the Hammer novels are rife with introspection.

In *My Gun Is Quick* Hammer tries to find redemption by aiding a prostitute in her attempt to enter the straight life; when his efforts cause her death, Hammer blames himself, feeling he brought destruction to a woman who did not deserve it.

In *Vengeance Is Mine!* Hammer is tormented by the memory of *I, the Jury*'s Charlotte and vows never to kill another woman; fortunately, the murderer—a near doppelgänger of Charlotte—is revealed to be a transvestite, allowing Hammer again to take the easy route. The trick ending of *Vengeance Is*

Mine! touches on several key but seldom explored aspects of Spillane's craft: the tongue-in-cheek black humor that reveals an authorial awareness of his tale's inherent absurdity; and an O. Henry–like zest to build to a joke-like, surprising punch line. Spillane takes glee in constructing stories that will not work without the final paragraph or even sentence, or in this case—and that of *The Deep*—word.

In *One Lonely Night*, the most blatantly surreal of his novels—considered his peak by admirers and his nadir by detractors—Spillane presents a Hammer tormented by his conscience, possibly contemplating suicide on the George Washington Bridge between New York and New Jersey on a gloomy night. His dark mood has been spurred by memories of a judge who earlier reprimanded him for, ironically enough, manipulating the system, when Hammer claimed self-defense to justify wholesale murder and vigilante actions.

In this novel—punctuated by Hammer's reveries of self-doubt—Spillane first exchanges gangsters for Communists as the object of his hero's venom; but those who identify Spillane with the notorious Senator Joseph McCarthy should note the author's use of a McCarthyesque figure to represent corruption, deceit, and venality. In the end Hammer comes to the frenzied conclusion that he is God's messenger of death, living "to kill the scum . . . so that others could live." The fever-dream climax in an abandoned paint warehouse combines sadomasochistic images—a kidnapped Velda is hanging nude from the rafters, for purposes of torture—with a Hammer-spawned bloodbath, the likes of which popular fiction had not seen before. (Hammer, mowing down Commies with a machine gun, literally ripping limbs from bodies with his gunfire, invokes a savagery worthy of that Greek "tough guy," Odysseus.)

In *The Big Kill* (1951) Hammer, for the first but not last time, does not execute the evil one himself; in effect, God does, through the innocence of a baby fondling a weapon to deadly results. In *Kiss Me, Deadly* (1952),

Hammer considers himself "getting old in the game," murdering the villain with less than his old exhilaration and striking out at the female accomplice only in self-defense. Hammer is left, apparently dying, shot in the stomach (as he had shot Charlotte), while a building burns around him.

A Nine-Year Hiatus and the Return of Hammer

Kiss Me, Deadly initiated a nine-year silence from Spillane, and readers and reviewers began to assume Hammer had died in that blaze. Some commentators attributed the best-selling novelist's inactivity to his widely publicized affiliation with the conservative religious sect the Jehovah's Witnesses (Spillane converted from Roman Catholicism sometime in 1952 or before). This is neither confirmed nor denied by Spillane, who will discuss religious matters privately—Jehovah's Witnesses are characteristically eager to be missionaries, after all—but declines to speak about these deeply held beliefs in public in the context of his commercial career.

It is true that the most sexually explicit novels of his career—*The Erection Set* (1972) and *The Last Cop Out* (1973)—were written when Spillane was "disenfranchised" from the Witnesses and that such later novels as *The Killing Man* (1989) and *Black Alley*, which are much more restrained in their sexual content and even in the use of profanity than Spillane novels of the 1970s, were written when Spillane was extremely active with the Witnesses. But it would be a glib overstatement and an unfounded assumption to say that Spillane's religious beliefs have led to the periods of inactivity in his career. Spillane has frequently stated that his motivation for writing is "an urgent need for money," and during flush periods of his career—when motion-picture and television licensing of the Mike Hammer character was generating income, for example—he felt no motivation to write.

Spillane is an energetic person who is inactive on one front—novel writing, for example—only because his vitality has been directed elsewhere. In the mid-1950s he performed in a circus act as a trampoline artist and as a human cannonball—an unusual career path for a best-selling writer to veer onto—and pursued stock-car racing, fencing, flying, deep-sea diving, and even undercover police work. He also appeared as himself in *Ring of Fear* (1954), a motion picture produced by John Wayne's company Batjac from a screenplay that Spillane rewrote; supervised a comic-strip version of Mike Hammer (doing some of the writing himself); was involved in radio, recording, and television projects; and wrote several unproduced screenplays.

During the nine-year break between novels, Spillane continued to write hard-boiled mystery fiction in the form of short stories and novellas (none featuring Hammer), usually publishing one a year, as if he were an athlete keeping in shape. Paradoxically, Spillane—for all his talk of writing for money—chose to do business with editors at low-paying men's magazines such as *Cavalier* and *Saga* out of loyalty to old friends who dated back to his comic-book days. The importance of friendship is a recurring theme not only in Spillane's work but also in his life.

His first novel after this hiatus—*The Deep*—did not feature Hammer, either. The bittersweet story of a former gang member returning to his old Brooklyn neighborhood to settle an old score, *The Deep* seems a metaphor for Spillane's return to the crime novel, a legendary tough guy returning home to mean streets. That the protagonist seems to be a bad guy but turns out to be a good guy—not a hoodlum, but a cop—is another telling indication of Spillane's view of himself.

In *The Deep*, Spillane creates a mood of menace without resorting to the extremes of violence in his early novels, and the sexual content is subdued as well. Whether this new, restrained Spillane was listening to the Jehovah's Witnesses, or to the critics, is impossible to say; perhaps *The Deep* merely represented the work of an older, more mature artist.

"There was a time when wild, gory scenes of violence were stock items in a story," Spillane said at the time of the novel's release. "I certainly went all out myself when that was the trend. Now times have changed." He did not mention that the trend toward violence was one that he had virtually initiated.

The absence of Hammer in Spillane's comeback novel was noted by many reviewers and readers. The next year, *The Girl Hunters* marked the private detective's return; apparently, he had not died in that burning building. Still, Hammer was not quite the same. Since readers had seen him last, he had been on an extended bender, drunk in the gutter, a victim of his own remorse for having sent his beloved Velda out, unadvisedly, on a dangerous assignment.

And fourteen years after "executing" his lover, Charlotte, Hammer is still haunted, saying, "It was a very long time ago. But it could have been yesterday. I could see her face, the golden tan of her skin, the incredible whiteness of her hair and eyes that could taste and devour you with one glance . . . Charlotte was still there" (p. 43).

With a prod from his now former friend Captain Pat Chambers, Hammer crawls out of the gutter and quickly detoxes when Velda is rumored to be alive; a familiar theme of later Hammer novels (resurfacing as late as 1996's *Black Alley*) is explored throughout *The Girl Hunters*: the formerly superhuman Hammer is older and not as tough as he once was. Since Hammer represents a fantasy version of Spillane, it is useful to keep Hammer's awareness of his own limitations in mind when considering the author's later works. No longer a hothead, the older Hammer of *The Girl Hunters* remains just as ruthless (he nails a bad guy's hand to the floor of a barn as a makeshift handcuff) but more clever and calculating, shrewder, smarter. His reputation as a legendarily murderous hard case is often enough to back a punk down; in the film version of the novel, co-scripted by Spillane, Mike Hammer stares down a saloon bully, forcing him through only words and a glimpse of the .45 in its "speed rig" to "eat" a bullet.

From *One Lonely Night* onward, Spillane and Hammer are clearly troubled by the detective's penchant for punishing murder with murder. Both writer and protagonist finally come to grips with this moral dilemma in *The Girl Hunters*. Rather than resort to a means as vile as the villain's, the hero must trick the villain into destroying himself—or herself, as when in *The Girl Hunters* Hammer rigs a shotgun to explode should the evil beauty he suspects try to kill him; she does, blowing off her own head, as Hammer turns away to retrieve his beloved Velda from hiding. Spillane relishes these blackly humorous finales and clearly is aware of the inherent absurdity of his hero and his hero's nightmare world.

That nightmare world of Mike Hammer's, however he might wish to define it, is not black-and-white but gray. The villains wear masks of social concern or lurk among the beautiful people—a psychiatrist, a senator, a senator's wife, a philanthropist, a famous actress, a doctor, a United Nations delegate. Only the victims, often beautiful women whose deaths ignite the proceedings, are truly innocent; but beautiful women can also represent evil.

The Hammer of the later novels—*The Body Lovers* (1967), *Survival . . . Zero!* (1970), *The Killing Man, Black Alley*—is no longer an executioner of evil ones. The character mellows, even as Spillane improves as a craftsman; these are polished, professional works, with Hammer's distinctive voice intact, as is Spillane's ability to move a narrative forward with energy and momentum. But the psychotic tone of the first six Hammer novels, which reflect a gifted young writer whose natural storytelling abilities and choice of a troubled, tortured hero make for irresistibly compelling popular fiction, is largely missing.

Perhaps the later Hammer novel that found the most enthusiastic acceptance from readers and critics was *The Twisted Thing* (1966). Spillane even received a glowing review from Anthony Boucher, the respected *New York Times Book Review* mystery-fiction columnist.

Boucher wrote,

For almost twenty years I have been one of the leaders in the attacks on Spillane; but of late I begin to wonder whether we reviewers, understandably offended by Spillane's excesses of brutality and his outrageously anti-democratic doctrines, may not have underestimated his virtues. . . . I suggest that [Mike Hammer's] creator is one of the last great storytellers in the pulp tradition, as he amply demonstrates in *The Twisted Thing*. (Collins and Traylor, p. 27)

The novel is first-rate, vintage Spillane, with the evil one revealed to be a child genius who had seemed the epitome of innocence. Ironically, *The Twisted Thing* is a retitled version of *For Whom the Gods Would Destroy*, the "too far-fetched yarn" that had been rejected by Dutton as the follow-up to *I, the Jury* in 1948. Spillane claims his story of a boy genius who has traded in his childhood, and innocence, for accelerated learning grew from a real incident reported in *Life* and other magazines. Pulling *For Whom the Gods Would Destroy* off the shelf and rewriting it only to the extent of changing the year and model of an automobile or two, Spillane demonstrated with the publication of a 1948 novel in 1966 that Hammer's world has a timeless noir quality. On the other hand, a book that would have seemed as shocking in 1948 as *I, the Jury* had in 1947—positing a child as a murderer well before William March's fine suspense novel, *The Bad Seed* (1954)—was regarded as just another, if excellent, Mike Hammer novel in 1966, indicating how widespread the public and critical acceptance of Spillane-style "sex and sadism" in detective fiction was, following his taboo-breaking early novels.

The Non-Hammer Novels

Spillane's Hammer novels are clearly his major contribution to mystery fiction, though even such non-Hammer titles as *The Deep* and *The Delta Factor* (1967) have been best-sellers. The only non-Hammer title of the seven books published in his most popular, significant period, 1947 to 1953, *The Long Wait* (1951), chronicles amnesiac Johnny McBride's search for his identity and, of course, a killer; violent but lower-key than the other Spillane books, with a tongue-in-cheek whimsy where the hero's irresistible appeal to women is concerned, *The Long Wait* trades Spillane's trademark New York City and a grim finale for a well-realized small-town setting and a happy ending.

The Tiger Mann series is an effort by the author to meet a competitor head-on: Spillane's paperback publisher, Signet, was doing extremely well in the mid-1960s with reprint editions of Ian Fleming's James Bond novels. Initially, Fleming had been presented to readers as "the British Mickey Spillane," but the popularity of his novels did not soar until President John F. Kennedy spoke highly of Fleming's work and the popular series of motion pictures began.

Spillane responded by writing his own series of spy novels, but predictably his protagonist—the improbably named Tiger Mann—was patterned not on Bond but on Hammer. Mann is complete with his Velda—Rondine—and works for a private spy agency with right-wing backing; Spillane ignores the globe-hopping aspect of Fleming's novels and has his secret agent rarely leave New York City. The United Nations comes under frequent ideological attack in the Mann novels, but the spies Mann encounters are very much like the gangsters Hammer comes across. The first Mann novel, *Day of the Guns* (1964), is generally considered the best and includes an interesting variation on the striptease finale of *I, the Jury.*

An uncharacteristically good-natured Spillane hero turns up in *The Delta Factor.* Morgan the Raider is a modern-day swashbuckler, in the manner not so much of Leslie Charteris' the Saint as of the heroes of Spillane's boyhood favorite, Alexandre Dumas. Spillane's enthusiasm for airplanes and his love of the sea—rarely touched on elsewhere in his novels, though fairly frequent visitors to his shorter fiction—turn up in *The Delta Factor,* which—with its passionate love story and cliff-hanger ending—promises a sequel that as of 1998 had not yet appeared.

In his longest, and most ambitious, novel, *The Erection Set,* Spillane attempts to break free of the mystery genre and enter the world of such best-selling writers as Harold Robbins and Irving Wallace. Updating one of his childhood favorites, *The Count of Monte Cristo,* Spillane follows Hammer-like hero Dogeron Kelly into the world of big business and includes science-fiction elements (specifically, an antigravity machine) that echo the author's comic-book background. A mysterious figure with a criminal background making a belated homecoming, Dogeron brings to mind the hoodlum character the Deep from the novel of the same name; and Sharon Cass is a typical larger-than-life Spillane heroine, though drawn in a more dimensional fashion than Velda or Rondine. The novel contains graphic sexual content, and the violence is hard-hitting; but the boldness of Spillane's unconventional literary technique—mixing first and third person as he chooses—indicates his potential as a writer of larger-landscape, mainstream popular fiction that as of 1998 he had not pursued.

Further indication that Spillane's potential as a popular novelist has not been entirely fulfilled in his shorter mystery novels can be found in *The Last Cop Out.* In this novel Spillane replaces his more typical subjective first-person narrative with an objective third person, and dialogue provides the engine for the novel, which consists of short, cinematic scenes. Spillane characteristically writes with a rough-hewn urban poetry that at its best is eloquent, at its worst purple; but in *The Last Cop Out,* Spillane's prose is so lean that characters have virtually no physical description. Perhaps in response to Mario Puzo's best-seller *The Godfather* (1969), Spillane centers on the Mob and an assassin who is executing top mobsters. A rogue cop, Gil Burke, returns to police ranks to help contain a gang-war bloodbath; he is a suspect as well, and the use of third-person narration deprives the reader of Burke's thoughts, rendering his innocence or guilt ambiguous, a clever narrative touch. *The Last Cop Out* is Spillane's most explicitly sexual book and also contains his most graphic, grisly scenes of violence. The author uses acts of sexual perversion to characterize his mobsters, while his hero and heroine prefer a romantic, gentle (that is, normal) variety of lovemaking.

Spillane's first young-adult novel, *The Day the Sea Rolled Back* (1979), marked a major change of pace. The book, winner of a Junior Literary Guild Award, is a lyrical adventure story reflecting the writer's interest in the sea; on a day when the tide goes out and does not come back, leaving a vast expanse of the ocean floor for exploration, Spillane's protagonists—a Hardy Boys–like pair named Josh and Larry—encounter secrets, treasures, and surprises. A second Josh and Larry story, *The Ship That Never Was* (1982), is even more fanciful, mixing spy elements out of Ian Fleming and swashbuckling adventure out of Anthony Hope, as the boys discover a longboat dating to 1791 that leads them to an island where a princess awaits. A third Josh and Larry young-adult novel, "The Shrinking Island," had not yet been published as of 1998.

Spillane's Work in Other Media

Spillane's popularity as a writer has been fueled by his high visibility as a celebrity and by the translation of his work to other media, particularly motion pictures and television. In 1953, against a backdrop of publicity, the producer Victor Saville initiated a much-publicized series of motion pictures based on Spillane novels.

I, the Jury (1953) was beautifully photographed by John Alton, widely considered the dean of film noir cinematographers in the then-popular 3-D process; the writer and director Harry Essex, however, was forced to soften the elements of sex and violence so associated with Spillane, including omitting the striptease at the end. The newcomer Biff Elliott was energetic and emotional as Hammer but perhaps too inexperienced an actor, and too small in stature, to meet the public's expectations for the embodiment of such a popular, larger-than-life character. Spillane's tactic of not describing Hammer, which so personalized the character for readers of the novels, backfired on the screen; and the first-person intensity and dreamlike quality of the narration were similarly difficult, if not impossible, for a filmmaker to capture. After all, Spillane has often described Mike Hammer as "a state of mind," and the literalism inherent in film worked against that idea.

The non-Hammer mystery, *The Long Wait* (1954), presented an effective Anthony Quinn in a rather pedestrian adaptation. For all of Spillane's phenomenal popularity among readers, movie audiences were not responding to Saville's films. But *Kiss Me Deadly* (1955) was at least marginally more successful at the box office and has gone on to become one of the most respected of films noir.

The director Robert Aldrich and the screenwriter A. I. Bezzerides brought their left-wing sensibilities to Spillane's right-wing material, with the intention of subverting it. The Hammer of the film *Kiss Me Deadly* (the title of which lacks Spillane's distinctive punctuation) is a successful but sleazy "divorce dick," driven not by revenge but by self-interest. Portrayed by Ralph Meeker, Hammer is a coldly ruthless near-thug, with only brutality linking him to Spillane's passionate urban knight. New York City has been exchanged for Los Angeles, as Hammer and a nebulous "they" seek the same valuable box, which turns out to contain a radioactive material that signals a symbolic end of the world. (A censored ending to the film, which seemed to echo Spillane's leaving Hammer to die in a burning house, was later replaced with additional footage consistent with Aldrich's original vision of Hammer and Velda escaping even as the apocalyptic nature of the box's contents is emphasized.)

What Aldrich and Bezzerides succeed in doing, however, is making the definitive 1950s Spillane film. Political differences aside, *Kiss*

Me Deadly presents a genuinely savage Mike Hammer (whose motivation eventually does shift to revenge) and a loving, loyal co-detective Velda, in a bizarre, nightmare world populated by beautiful, willing women and ugly, sinister gangsters, with an atmosphere of rampant, disturbing paranoia punctuated by brief but shocking scenes of violence—in other words, vintage Spillane. In their attempt to put Spillane down, Aldrich and Bezzerides have—in creating so influential and artistically successful a film—further bolstered his importance in American popular culture.

A final, mediocre Saville-produced film featuring Hammer followed in 1957—*My Gun Is Quick*—with Robert Bray as a physically imposing but colorless Hammer in an adaptation that ignored most of the source material, substituting instead a tepid reworking of Hammett's *The Maltese Falcon*. After a "pilot" episode starring Brian Keith as Hammer was rejected on grounds of violence, two seasons of a syndicated *Mickey Spillane's Mike Hammer* television series began in 1958, featuring an affable but rugged Darren McGavin; Hammer's trademark .45 was replaced by a .38 and Velda was missing, but a certain gritty Spillane flavor came through, enhanced by McGavin's flavorful first-person narration.

The films and TV series—as well as a radio show, the aforementioned comic strip, and a long-playing record album—joined with steady paperback reprint sales to keep the names Mike Hammer and Mickey Spillane in front of the public during the so-called drought between *Kiss Me, Deadly* and *The Deep*. But Spillane was unhappy with the way his detective had been portrayed on screen and how his novels had been "butchered by Hollywood," so, in 1962, he took matters into his own hands.

Having played himself in *Ring of Fear* and in several television commercials, as well as performing in skits on variety shows, Spillane decided to star as Hammer in a motion-picture version of *The Girl Hunters* that he would script himself. The author's aversion to Hollywood manifested itself in the film's production on the Metro-Goldwyn-Mayer lot at Elstree Studios outside London; only some minor, second-unit footage, specifically of street scenes, was shot in New York City. Assembling a largely British cast, including actress Shirley Eaton just prior to her appearance in the James Bond film *Goldfinger*, Spillane took center stage as Hammer, an ambitious move for a nonprofessional, untrained actor. The production was somewhat troubled—planned for color, the film was shot in black-and-white when some of the financial backing fell through; Spillane helped shore up the financing of the beleaguered production by selling several collections of short fiction to his British paperback publisher, Corgi.

Spillane the actor received some of the best reviews of his career, and his convincing, somewhat tongue-in-cheek performance is regarded as the strong suit of a conventionally made film, as directed by Roy Rowland. The script—written by Spillane in collaboration with Rowland and his longtime friend, the producer Robert Fellows—is the most literal translation of Spillane's work in the motion-picture medium. The problem of voice-over narration is bridged in the screenplay by removing it except in those moments when Hammer is ruminating about the past (specifically, his missing Velda) or pondering what he intends to do to the bad guys when he catches up with them. The feature was poorly distributed in the United States and frustrated Spillane's intention to produce a follow-up feature of *The Snake*, again with himself as Hammer. Spillane's production company tried again, in 1970, with *The Delta Factor*, without Spillane's participation as an actor; the low-budget, routine feature, starring Christopher George as Morgan the Raider, was barely released.

A 1982 feature film of *I, the Jury* with a brooding Armand Assante as Hammer suffered a similar fate; Spillane disavowed the production—a well-made, violent R-rated update of his book that included the execution of a nude Charlotte—the rights to which had been acquired from the estate of Victor Saville by the feature's screenwriter, Larry Cohen. In

October of 1981, Spillane began an association with the producer Jay Bernstein that proved much more successful: five *Mickey Spillane's Mike Hammer* television movies; and three versions of a series starring Stacy Keach as Hammer, two on the Columbia Broadcasting System and one in syndication. Keach became highly identified with the character and recorded audio books of a number of the Hammer novels.

Despite Keach's association with Hammer, Spillane himself—in part due to the frequent airing of *The Girl Hunters* on television—remains even more closely identified with Hammer, and "Mike Hammer" and "Mickey Spillane" are often used interchangeably, as if both were fictional characters.

Throughout the 1970s and 1980s, in one of the longest-running commercial campaigns in television advertising history, Spillane appeared as himself—often in tandem with actress Lee Meredith as the Doll, a blonde showgirl who loomed comically above the bantam author—for Miller Lite Beer. The campaign primarily centered around retired sports figures, particularly from the worlds of professional basketball, football, and baseball, and Spillane's presence as a famous mystery writer in such company suggested the macho nature of his image. Spillane, frequently appearing in Hammeresque trench coat and porkpie hat, seemed as much Hammer as Spillane, further melding the creator with his character in the public's mind.

Spoofing himself good-naturedly, Spillane was advertising himself and his books through these commercials (and print ads) as much as Miller Lite. His years as a beer salesman—which included many personal appearances with Meredith and at least one nightclub appearance in an act concocted by Spillane—were among his least prolific as an author; but his presence in such a high-profile advertising campaign kept him in the public eye and helped keep his books in print. During this period, Spillane viewed his work with Miller as "his job," and the time it took and the income it generated explain the accompanying dearth of fiction.

In addition, Spillane frequented the television-talk-show circuit—including such highly rated programs as Johnny Carson's *Tonight Show* and *Late Night with David Letterman*—and even appeared on variety and game shows, sometimes with his second wife, actress Sherri Malinou (Spillane and Mary Ann divorced in 1962). An attractive blonde, Sherri posed for Spillane's book covers (often in tandem with Spillane portraying Hammer), most notoriously in the nude for *The Erection Set* and *The Last Cop Out*. Though they briefly shared a Manhattan penthouse, Spillane and his second wife (they wed in 1964) spent most of their marriage living in separate residences, Sherri Spillane preferring Hollywood and New York City, Spillane staying in his unpretentious beachfront home near Myrtle Beach, South Carolina. The marriage ended acrimoniously in 1982.

Professional Storyteller and "Grand Master"

On 30 October 1983, Spillane married Jane Rodgers Johnson, a former Miss South Carolina twenty-eight years younger than he. The Spillanes have a low-key lifestyle that the writer has said includes "dinner at five o'clock every day and . . . bed generally between nine and ten. We eat seafood, pork chops, meat loaf, and—oh yes—Southern fried chicken. . . . That's us, biscuits and gravy every night." Though he has not entirely lost his clipped New York accent, Spillane refers to Northerners as "Yankees" and professes to hate New York City, although he loves rural New York State and in 1995 purchased a second home there. A new, rambling beachfront multistoried house replaced the oversize cottage Spillane lost in Hurricane Hugo in 1989; most of his writing, however, takes place in a carport office on stilts that somehow survived the storm. In the mid-1990s, he returned to comic books by co-creating a futuristic rendition of Mike Danger; although he did not do the comic-book script writing, Spillane has completed a draft of a Mike Danger sci-fi novel. In 1997, he was at work on two novels, a sea adventure titled *Something's Down There* and a final Mike Hammer in which Velda and her private eye at last marry.

"There's a big difference between an author and a writer," Spillane told *Writer's Digest* interviewer Jerry Cassidy in September 1976. "Writers are professionals who make money. Authors usually have one or two books to tell. . . . I was always a good storyteller. This is what makes a good writer. You have to be a good storyteller."

John G. Cawelti in *Adventure, Mystery and Romance* (1976) confirmed the writer's self-opinion: "Of all the hard-boiled writers, Spillane's art is closest in its mythical simplicity to folktale." Cawelti also pointed out that Spillane expresses a "hostility toward the sinful city and its corrupt men of wealth, its degenerate foreigners, and its Scarlet Women," although it should be noted that Spillane stories set in smaller-town and rural settings find no shortage of the first two categories, and, as for the third, Hammer and other Spillane protagonists count members of ethnic groups among their friends (and among the innocents evil preys upon). Those who feel Spillane's conservative religious beliefs are at odds with his violent morality plays are not considering the evangelical zeal of Mike Hammer's hatred for evil; and those who do not understand his appeal to a large reading audience disregard the fable-like attraction of Mike Hammer's simple solutions for the complex problems of post–World War II America.

"The only reason that all of these people read you," Spillane said of best-selling authors, including himself, "is because you're good—you give them a product that satisfies their desires" (unpublished interview).

All his protestations that he writes for money not art ("If Thomas Wolfe would sell, I'd write like Thomas Wolfe") simply indicate that Mickey Spillane—weathering the slings and arrows of critics, social commentators, and occasionally his fellow Jehovah's Witnesses—has found a sanctuary in viewing himself as a professional. His lifestyle is mod-

est, and he does not love money at all—it's against his religion.

In 1995 Spillane—after many years of denunciation from a good number of his fellow mystery writers—was finally acknowledged by his peers, when the Mystery Writers of America presented him with their most honored award, the Grand Master.

Selected Bibliography

WORKS OF MICKEY SPILLANE

NOVELS

I, the Jury. New York: Dutton, 1947.
My Gun Is Quick. New York: Dutton, 1950.
Vengeance Is Mine! New York: Dutton, 1950.
The Big Kill. New York: Dutton, 1951.
The Long Wait. New York: Dutton, 1951.
One Lonely Night. New York: Dutton, 1951.
Kiss Me, Deadly. New York: Dutton, 1952.
The Deep. New York: Dutton, 1961.
The Girl Hunters. New York: Dutton, 1962.
Day of the Guns. New York: Dutton, 1964.
The Snake. New York: Dutton, 1964.
Bloody Sunrise. New York: Dutton, 1965.
The Death Dealers. New York: Dutton, 1965.
The By-Pass Control. New York: Dutton, 1966.
The Twisted Thing. New York: Dutton, 1966.
The Body Lovers. New York: Dutton, 1967.
The Delta Factor. New York: Dutton, 1967.
Survival . . . Zero! New York: Dutton, 1970.
The Erection Set. New York: Dutton, 1972.
The Last Cop Out. New York: Dutton, 1973.
The Day the Sea Rolled Back. New York: Windmill, 1979. Juvenile.
The Ship That Never Was. New York: Bantam, 1982. Juvenile.
The Killing Man. New York: Dutton, 1989.
Black Alley. New York: Dutton, 1996.

COLLECTIONS

Me, Hood! London: Transworld Publishers, 1963; New York: New American Library, 1969.
The Flier. London: Corgi, 1964.
Return of the Hood. London: Transworld, 1964.
Killer Mine. London: Corgi, 1965.
The Tough Guys. New York: New American Library, 1969.
The Mickey Spillane Omnibus. London: W. H. Allen, 1973.
Vintage Spillane. London: W. H. Allen, 1974.
Tomorrow I Die. New York: Mysterious Press, 1984.

OTHER

Rowland, Roy, and Robert Fellows. *The Girl Hunters.* United Artists, 1963. Screenplay.

———. *The Delta Factor.* Spillane-Fellows, 1970. Screenplay.

Mickey Spillane's Mike Hammer: The Comic Strip. Park Forest, Ill.: K. Pierce. 2 vols., 1982–1984.

BIOGRAPHICAL AND CRITICAL STUDIES

Barson, Michael S. "The Apocalyptic Vision of Mickey Spillane." M.A. thesis, Bowling Green State University, 1976.

Cawelti, John G. *Adventure, Mystery and Romance: Formula Stories As Art and Popular Culture.* Chicago: University of Chicago Press, 1976.

Collins, Max Allan, and James L. Traylor. *One Lonely Knight: Mickey Spillane's Mike Hammer.* Bowling Green, Ohio: Bowling Green State University Popular Press, 1984.

Van Dover, J. Kenneth. *Murder in the Millions: Erle Stanley Gardner, Mickey Spillane, Ian Fleming.* New York: Ungar, 1984.

REX STOUT

(1886–1975)

DAVID R. ANDERSON

R EX STOUT—writer, entreprencur, and political activist—is one of America's most
important detective novelists, best known for
his series of thirty-three novels written between 1934 and 1975 featuring the overweight genius Nero Wolfe and Archie Goodwin, his irrepressible assistant. In the Nero
Wolfe saga, Stout artfully melded the conventions of the classic detective novel, such as a
cerebral but idiosyncratic detective and an
emphasis on the deductive process, with the
conventions of the American hard-boiled detective novel, including a streetwise detective
noted for his quick fists, his even quicker
mouth, and his sexual appeal, into a new form
of detective fiction that drew upon the
strengths of each existing form. Stout also
used the detective novel as a forum for ideas,
and his treatment of serious themes elevated
the genre, as did his crisp and witty prose. The
result was an enduring series that captured a
wide readership and changed the course of detective fiction.

Life

Rex Todhunter Stout was born 1 December
1886 in Noblesville, Indiana, but he grew up,
the sixth of nine children, in and around
Topeka, Kansas. His father, John Stout, hot-
tempered and overly disciplining, was by

turns a newspaper publisher, farmer, county
superintendent of schools, and traveling salesperson. His mother, Lucetta Todhunter Stout,
a brilliant but detached woman, lived by the
rule "Never praise or blame anyone, including
yourself" (McAleer, 1977, p. 44). With his father often absent and his mother at home but
isolated (a child who wished to speak with her
when she was reading had first to submit to a
face washing from a bowl of cold water she
kept at her elbow), Stout developed self-
reliance at an early age. He claimed to have
read all 1,126 of the books in his father's library by the age of eleven and to have mem-
orized Shakespeare's sonnets by the age of
twelve. He toured Kansas schools as a child,
exhibiting his mental ability to add long columns of numbers.

After graduating from Topeka High School,
Stout attended the University of Kansas only
briefly, after which he joined the navy, where
he served as pay-yeoman on Theodore Roosevelt's presidential yacht, the *Mayflower*,
from 1905 to 1907. From 1912 to 1917 he
served his first apprenticeship as a writer.
Paid by the word, he sold more than thirty
short stories to such pulp magazines as *All-
Story Weekly* and the *Black Cat* and published four novels serially in pulp magazines.
Dissatisfied with the quality of the fiction he
was producing while writing for money, in
1917 Stout stopped publishing fiction, concentrating instead on earning the financial in-

dependence that would enable him to improve his craft. With his brother he founded the Educational Thrift Service, a school savings program that worked through local banks and school administrators to encourage schoolchildren to save regularly. The venture was so popular, and profitable, that in 1926 Stout sold his share of the business and took time off to begin his second apprenticeship as a writer, this time as a "serious" novelist. The result was four psychological novels, *How like a God* (1929), *Seed on the Wind* (1930), *Golden Remedy* (1931), and *Forest Fire* (1933), and a political thriller, *The President Vanishes* (1934). With the psychological novels, which experiment with point of view and narrative time, Stout sought to take his place alongside William Faulkner and Ernest Hemingway. They were respectfully, but not enthusiastically, received; they have not found a place in the modernist canon.

Stout was searching for his niche not only as a writer but also as a person. In December 1916 he had married Fay Kennedy of Topeka. That marriage ended in divorce in 1931, and in 1932 he married Pola Weinbach Hoffmann, a distinguished designer of wool fabrics, also recently divorced. During this period he also built High Meadow, a house straddling the New York and Connecticut border where he lived with Pola for the rest of his life. Stout found his niche as a writer with the publication in 1934 of *Fer-de-Lance*, the first Nero Wolfe novel. It was followed by seven other Wolfe novels—*The League of Frightened Men* (1935), *The Rubber Band* (1936), *The Red Box* (1937), *Too Many Cooks* (1938), *Some Buried Caesar* (1939), *Over My Dead Body* (1940), *Where There's a Will* (1940)—and ten other novels, including some that feature other detectives Stout created, such as Tecumseh Fox, Alphabet Hicks, and Dol Bonner, a woman detective. At this point World War II intervened; Stout did not publish another book for five years.

During World War II, Stout served his country as a propagandist. As a member of the Fight for Freedom Committee, he lobbied for an early American entry into the war. This committee in turn led to the founding of Freedom House, dedicated to propagandizing for democracy, with which he remained associated for the rest of his life. Stout also served on the Writers' War Board, which produced scripts, advertisements, speeches, and other materials in support of the war effort. On 17 January 1943, he published in the *New York Times Magazine* a controversial essay called "We Shall Hate, or We Shall Fail," which attempted to place the blame for Hitler on the German people themselves. This essay elicited protests from Stout's colleagues on the War Board as well as from the magazine's readership and resulted in his resignation from Freedom House for a time. After the war Stout chaired the Writers' Board for World Government, an organization formed on the model of the Writer's War Board but intended to lobby for world government.

At the conclusion of the war, Stout returned to the life of writing with another Nero Wolfe novel, *The Silent Speaker* (1946). He settled into a pattern of writing one new Wolfe novel and one or two novellas a year from that point on. With a combination of a keen interest in politics and ample free time, he was not likely to avoid controversy, and he did not. Among the causes he championed in the postwar years was reprint royalties for authors—Stout argued that publishers were not paying adequate royalties to authors from sales of paperback reprints of hardcover books. He was both a fierce anti-Communist and a foe of McCarthyism. He deplored attempts to squelch challenges to governmental authority by labeling them as unpatriotic, and in *The Doorbell Rang* (1965) he attacked the Federal Bureau of Investigation for, among other things, unauthorized use of security checks to rein in dissent.

At the same time that he was attacking the FBI, however, he was vigorously defending the American war in Vietnam. He supported both President Nixon's and President Johnson's war policies, and as with his anti-German polemic after World War II, he found himself increasingly isolated in his hawkish position. He followed the unfolding of the Watergate investigation closely, and he took the opportunity in his last novel to attack Richard Nixon as a "phony statesman" (*A Family Affair*, 1975, p. 69). Stout spent his last years at High Meadow reading, gardening, writing, and enjoying the company of family and friends. As he aged he declined in physical vigor, but he remained intellectually vigorous and socially active into his eighty-ninth year. Rex Stout died at High Meadow on 27 October 1975.

Themes, Character, and Setting

Rex Stout wrote about order—the various kinds of psychic, social, and ethical order that we manage to fashion for ourselves as individuals and as a society—and the threats posed to that order by the complex of motives and emotions that, individually and collectively, make us human. Stout identified reason as the main source of personal and social order, and he saw emotion as the greatest threat to order. Thus, from his earliest pulp fiction to his last Nero Wolfe novel, he dramatized the tension between reason and emotion both within and among his characters. Taken as a whole, his detective novels dramatize the quest for order through the following narrative pattern. Typically his works begin with an ordered world, usually Nero Wolfe's office; then disorder in the form of violence enters that world and threatens it. There is a conflict, during which the detective seeks and identifies the source of disorder in the criminal, and then order is reestablished by the removal of the criminal. But this reestablished order is provisional. Violence can threaten again at any time, and even its temporary presence may have changed the ordered world. The grand questions posed by Stout's detective fiction are whether, ultimately, the quest for order can ever succeed and, if it does, whether that order can ever be made permanent.

Detective fiction before Rex Stout had been typically both socially and politically conservative. Detectives found the criminals, and the police collared them and took them away for punishment. The best interests of society and government were preserved. Stout's detective fiction adopts a much more individual vision of order. The criminals in his detective novels do not escape, but often the police do not collar them. They are removed another way: they may commit suicide or be forced into suicide, or they may be murdered by someone else, occasionally with the detective's tacit approval. Stout focused his attention on the forms order took in individuals and among families more than on the welfare of states and nations. For Stout the question was not "Are the streets safe?" but rather "Have we found a way to live with ourselves?"

In pursuit of these themes, Stout created two enduring detectives: Nero Wolfe and his assistant Archie Goodwin. An immigrant from that Balkan nation of Montenegro, Wolfe weighs over two hundred and fifty pounds. He loves fine food, grows orchids, reads voraciously—and he is a genius. At the same time, he is clearly neurotic. Wolfe follows a rigid daily schedule: at eight he breakfasts in his room, from nine until eleven he tends his orchids in the greenhouse on his roof, from eleven to one he works in his office, at one he has lunch, after lunch he works until four, from four to six he tends orchids, and at seven-thirty he has dinner. He never leaves his home on business. He never discusses business at mealtime. His prejudices are perhaps even more numerous than his rules. Most famously, he distrusts women and machines because of his conviction that both are likely to go arbitrarily and wildly out of control at any moment.

In the early novels of the saga, Nero Wolfe repeatedly applies to himself the label "romantic." He believes in elevated standards of human dignity and worth, in the existence and value of truth, in the power of reason, in permanent and stable standards of conduct. But his occupation presents him with daily threats to his romantic notions. Thus, Wolfe lives in constant tension between the ideal and the real. His eccentric rules and elaborate rituals, like the layers of fat that insulate him from his environment, constitute one line of his defense against a world in which human life is held cheap, murderers lie to prevent detection, emotion controls reason, and people behave abominably. He compensates for the disorder around him by insisting on an overly regulated and ordered home.

His other line of defense against disorder is detection. Unlike many other fictional detectives, Wolfe does not go to the crime scene to investigate clues. Indeed, he is not particularly interested in the facts of the case; rather, he focuses on the "phenomena." In a famous passage in *The Golden Spiders* (1953), he asserts: "Science in detection can be distinguished, even brilliant, but it can never replace either the inexorable march of a fine intellect through a jungle of lies and fears to the clearing of truth, or the flash of perception along a sensitive nerve touched off by a tone of a voice or a flicker of an eye" (p. 13). Wolfe calls his sensitivity to phenomena, his flashes of perception, "genius," and that genius complements his romanticism. Just as his ideal vision of human life aspires beyond the murk of passions and violence that he encounters every day as a detective, his methods of detection rise above the gritty details of the case. Part theologian, part philosopher, part psychologist, Wolfe inhabits the gulf between an ideal, ordered vision of humanity and the anarchic, disordered world around him. He finds refuge in the ideal environment created by the rules of his home.

Archie Goodwin, Wolfe's confidential assistant and the first-person narrator of the novels, represents Wolfe's link to the world outside the home they share. No romantic, Archie focuses on the practical and the everyday. "I do read books," he admits in *The League of Frightened Men*, "but I never yet got any real satisfaction out of one; I always have a feeling there's nothing alive about it, it's all dead and gone, what's the use, you might as well try to enjoy yourself on a picnic in a graveyard" (p. 2). Where Wolfe deals in phenomena, Archie deals in facts. He is the one who visits the crime scene, strong-arms the criminals, picks the locks, lifts the fingerprints, and romances the women in the Wolfe novels. Like the reader who races through a detective novel to find out who did it, Archie is in detection for the thrill of the chase. He goads Wolfe into accepting cases, pesters him to complete them, and punctures Wolfe's pomposity and self-centeredness.

But Archie Goodwin is also a romantic, in his way. By sharing Wolfe's home and table, he tacitly endorses Wolfe's aspirations for profound and rigorous thinking, noble behavior, and pure but regulated emotion. *The Doorbell Rang* emphasizes the extent to which Wolfe and Archie share values. During a debate on how to make use of sensitive information they have just received, Archie says, "Making a deal with a murderer isn't your style. Have I got it straight?" Wolfe responds, "I don't like your pronouns," and Archie concedes, "All right, make it 'we' and 'us.' It's not my style either" (p. 48). Later in the same novel, when they are arguing about the next step of the investigation, Archie reminds Wolfe, "You have no obligation except to investigate and use your best efforts." Wolfe responds, "Your pronouns again." And again Archie concedes, "All right 'we' and 'our'" (p. 76). In the end, Wolfe and Archie complement each other. Wolfe feels phenomena, and Archie discovers facts. Wolfe is a genius and Archie a man of action. Wolfe is subtle and Archie direct. Together, they form a complete detection team and a complete person, anchored in a shared idealism and tested by their shared investigations.

The Nero Wolfe series rests upon Wolfe and Archie, but a cast of supporting characters completes their world. Along with Archie, Fritz Brenner, Wolfe's cook, and Theodore Horstmann, his gardener, constitute Wolfe's intimate family. Fritz lives in Wolfe's New York City brownstone; Horstmann comes in during the days. Together, they complete Wolfe's romantically ordered home. Totally disconnected from criminals and detection, Fritz and Horstmann represent the domestic, nurturing arts. As if to insist that he can control his own environment, Wolfe's most adamant rules apply to their domains: two inviolable sessions a day with the orchids, no business discussed at table, rigid mealtimes.

Wolfe's professional family consists of Archie and three freelance operatives whom he hires from time to time when he needs extra help: Saul Panzer, Orrie Cather, and Fred Durkin. Saul Panzer is the best freelance operative in New York, and Wolfe saves him for the most important and difficult tasks. Of the members of Wolfe's professional family, Orrie Cather most closely resembles Archie. He is young, handsome, persuasive, and attractive to women. He lacks Archie's stability, however; more than once Wolfe has to rescue Orrie from a scrape involving a woman. Fred Durkin is neither as smart as Saul Panzer nor as young and glib as Orrie, stolid and dependable, he is one of the best "tailers" in New York.

The conventions of the detective novel include a testy relationship between the detective and the police, and Stout followed that convention in the Wolfe novels. Inspector Cramer of the New York police department and Wolfe have a cooperative but also occasionally adversarial relationship. Wolfe respects Cramer's integrity and his abilities; at the same time, he has little use for the normal routine of law enforcement. Because Wolfe investigates crime on his own terms, he and Cramer end up at odds in nearly every Wolfe novel. But Cramer also respects Wolfe's integrity, and he cannot ignore Wolfe's results. The two manage to negotiate grounds for a working relationship throughout the series, but the tensions between their functions and their personalities bar friendship.

Perhaps the most problematic area of Stout's Nero Wolfe stories is his treatment of women characters. Archie Goodwin has a girlfriend, Lily Rowan, who first appears in *Some Buried Caesar* and remains in the series until the end. Independently wealthy, Lily is not dependent upon Archie either financially or emotionally. She is intelligent, witty, and resourceful, and even Wolfe admires her, in his way. Julie Jaquette, from *Death of a Doxy*

(1966), is another strong, independent, and resourceful woman whom both Wolfe and Archie admire. For the most part, however, women in these novels are either dangerous or dependent. From the obsessive Dora Chapin in *The League of Frightened Men* through the sleepy-eyed murderer Dina Laszio in *Too Many Cooks* (1938), the heartless Cecily Pine of *Too Many Women* (1947) (who forces her husband to commit suicide), the vicious and demented Marjorie Ault of *A Right to Die* (1964), the hysterical Stella Fleming of *Death of a Doxy* to Lucile Ducos in *A Family Affair* (1975), who tries to blackmail her father's murderer rather than give Wolfe the information that would identify him, women in the Wolfe novels are dangerous because they are—paradoxically—either controlled by their emotions or coldly calculating. Wolfe apparently does not feel sexual desire; Archie does, but the novels represent it as a dangerous power that blurs good men's judgments and tempts bad men to violence.

The fundamental questions about women in the Wolfe novels revolve around the issue of control. *A Family Affair* offers an example of one side of the control issue. Lucile Ducos' father is murdered in Wolfe's house. When Archie goes to her apartment to talk with her, he sees books on her shelves by various feminists, from Betty Friedan to Simone de Beauvoir. In Archie's words, that "tagged her good" (p. 25) as a feminist. When he meets Lucile a few pages later, he observes, "Up to a few inches above her knees, she had good legs. A pity" (p. 33). Reporting on her to Wolfe, Archie calls Lucile a "phony." "A woman who has those books with her name in them wants men to stop making women sex symbols, and if she really wants them to stop she wouldn't keep her skin like that, and her hair, and blow her hard-earned pay on a dress that sets her off. Of course she can't help her legs. She's a phony" (p. 36).

Archie finds Lucile problematic because he cannot control her sexually. The result is violence. When Wolfe, Archie, Saul, Fred, and Orrie are discussing how to proceed with the investigation, Saul asks Archie for a suggestion on how to approach Lucile. Archie replies, "If I were a male chauvinist pig in good standing I'd say you might try raping her. As I said, she has good legs" (p. 91). The novel does not permit that kind of violence toward Lucile Ducos, but like many other difficult women in fiction, she experiences another form of violence: she is murdered by the blackmailer whose name she hid inside the endpapers of her copy of Friedan's *The Feminine Mystique.* Other attractive young women in the Wolfe novels are too easy to control. In *The Second Confession* (1949), Archie interrupts his detecting to study the swimming suit worn by Madeline Sperling, daughter of the man who has hired Wolfe.

> She had been doing some fast swimming but wasn't out of breath, and her breast, with nothing but the essentials covered, rose and fell in easy smooth rhythm. Even with her eyes closed for the sun she seemed to know where I was looking, for she said complacently, "I expand three inches. If that's not your type I'll smoke more and get it down." (p. 120)

Lily Rowan is the ideal woman of the series because she offers Archie the right combination of independence and susceptibility. Their courtship in *Some Buried Caesar* is essentially a negotiation over whether Lily will control Archie. Early in the novel Miss Pratt warns Archie away from Lily: "I used to think the talk about some woman being dangerous, you know, really dangerous, was romantic hooey, but it isn't. Lily Rowan is one. If she wasn't too lazy to make much of an effort there's no telling how many men she might ruin" (1963 ed., p. 36). Archie finds Lily too attractive to ignore, but he regards her cautiously. The eleventh chapter concludes with Lily slipping her arm through Archie's, and they enter the house that way—even though, as Archie points out, "it is a form of intimacy I don't care for, since I have a tendency to fight shy of bonds" (p. 105).

At lunch at the North Atlantic Exposition in Crowfield, Lily commits another proprie-

tary act. "Her eyes moved up me and over me, up from my chest over my face to the top of my head, and then slowly traveled down again. . . . I wanted to slap her, because her tone, and the look in her eyes going over me, made me feel like a potato she was peeling" (p. 60). Not only is Lily proprietary, she is also independent. A few pages later, she observes, "I don't suppose I'll marry. Because marriage is really nothing but an economic arrangement, and I'm lucky because I don't have to let the economic part enter into it. The man would be lucky too—I mean if a man attracted me and I attracted him." Archie, having first been peeled and now having heard a woman assert her independence, wonders, "which would be more satisfactory, to slap her and then kiss her, or to kiss her and then slap her" (p. 62). Attracted by her independence and repelled by her proprietary behavior, Archie suddenly sees across the way a development in the case and abandons Lily. This gives him the opportunity to assert his own independence: "Understand once and for all that I am a workingman and I only play with toys at odd moments" (p. 63).

In the novel's last chapter, Archie lays down the ground rules for their relationship when Lily calls to ask him to attend a wedding with her. Archie refuses. She offers cocktails and dinner. Archie counteroffers an evening at the Strand watching two men play pool. Lily agrees and again offers dinner. Archie refuses, and Lily agrees. Attending a wedding together, followed by dinner, becomes a meeting at a hotel to watch a pool match; Archie has preserved his independence and tamed a proprietary woman. By 1975, in *A Family Affair*, the Wolfe novels had found a place for a mutual relationship between Archie and Lily. After a telephone conversation, they hang up, and Archie comments: "We hung up. That's one of the many good points: *we* hung up" (p. 52). The Nero Wolfe series as a whole, however, tends to fear, and therefore to demonize, women.

Setting typically plays an important role in detective fiction, from the moor in Arthur Conan Doyle's *The Hound of the Baskervilles* to the mean streets of San Francisco in Dashiell Hammett's *The Maltese Falcon*. Setting also plays an important role in the Wolfe stories, but Stout focuses not upon the scene of the crime but rather upon the home of the detective. Setting becomes not the context for evil, as in *The Hound of the Baskervilles*, but rather the emblem of order and stability. Wolfe's home, a brownstone building on West Thirty-fifth Street in New York, doubles as his office. The novels typically begin and end in Wolfe's home (an exception is *Some Buried Caesar*, which begins with Wolfe and Archie in an auto accident) because they tend to put forth an aura of order, threaten that order with violence, and then confirm the strength and endurance of that order by returning to its emblem, the brownstone.

The Early Wolfe Novels: Intimate Violence

Stout's early Nero Wolfe novels focus upon intimate violence. *Fer-de-Lance* tells the story of an attempted murder that had its roots in the Argentine pampa, where a man came home to find his wife in bed with his best friend. He murdered her and left their infant child playing in her blood. As a grown man, that child seeks to avenge his mother's death by murdering his father, but he accidentally murders instead an innocent man who had himself once been the target of an attempted murder by his wife. When Wolfe is hired to investigate that accidental murder, he solves the crime by uncovering the bloody history of the murderer's family.

The League of Frightened Men portrays an obsessive love that drives a man to marry his former fiancée's maid so that he can get articles of her intimate clothing to keep in a treasure box. It is a fierce love that almost leads his wife to murder in his defense.

The Red Box tells the story of a murder the roots of which trace back to a penniless widowed man who sold his infant daughter to a woman whose own daughter had died and

who needed a child in order to inherit a fortune. This woman raised the child as her own, but ultimately she was forced to murder the child's natural father to preserve her secret and her fortune. Once again, in order to solve the crime, Wolfe must uncover a bloody family history.

In *Too Many Cooks*, the novel in which Wolfe travels to West Virginia to deliver an address to an audience of master chefs on American contributions to fine cooking, desire and greed prompt a man to murder so that he can have the victim's unfaithful wife. In Stout's favorite of his own novels, *Some Buried Caesar*, two families, riven with conflict both within and between each other, provide a turbulent backdrop for the action of the novel.

In these early novels, at the same time that he is establishing Wolfe's domestic and professional families with their routines, habits, and rules and portraying their brownstone as representative of order and stability, Stout pierces their ideal with one story after another of the intimate violence that occurs between parents and children, spouses and lovers, brothers and sisters. Far from an emblem of order, the family in these early novels is the site of masking, deception, treachery, and guilt. Understanding the present usually involves learning about a complex web of past relationships. The man who is killed by his son in the last chapter of *Fer-de-Lance* was actually killed, as Wolfe puts it, "by the infant son whom he deserted sitting on the floor among his toys in a pool of his mother's blood" (p. 311) The detective in these early novels works much more with "phenomena" than facts; indeed, by reading Paul Chapin's books rather than investigating the crimes themselves, Wolfe decides that Chapin in *The League of Frightened Men* did not murder his Harvard classmates. Detection almost becomes family therapy, for Wolfe, by naming murderers, not only solves crimes and earns his fee but also puts an end to the intimate violence born from the family.

But the early novels do not resolve the tension created between their representations of order and refuge and their vivid depiction of the arbitrary or the unexpected. The novels begin in Wolfe's office, the emblem of order; the plot folds out of the house and into the world from which Wolfe insulates himself in layers of fat behind brownstone walls. Ultimately, it returns to the office and to the order it represents, though even then, as in *The Red Box*, which ends with the murderer committing suicide in front of Wolfe's desk, that order has been compromised by the very actions required to assert it.

The Postwar Nero Wolfe Novels: Politics and the Family

From 1940 to 1946, Stout stopped publishing Nero Wolfe novels, focusing his efforts instead on generating propaganda for the U.S. war effort and on organizing other writers to support the war as well. He led a public life during the war years, and his involvement with a wide variety of politicians and government officials seems to have changed the direction of his fiction for a time, for when the Nero Wolfe novels resumed, they revealed a new interest in politics. When Stout took up the series again after the war, he alluded to Wolfe's and Archie's wartime experiences working for the U.S. government—Wolfe taking on special assignments in espionage and counterintelligence and Archie serving stateside in military intelligence. Their work took both of them away from their carefully ordered home and their overly regulated lives, and even though they took up their former patterns of living after the war, the series reflects a heightened awareness of the instability of the world outside.

The plot of *The Silent Speaker* (1946), for example, revolves around the murder of the director of the U.S. Bureau of Price Regulation just before a speech to the National Industrial Association. The novel bristles with the acronyms of agencies and bureaus, and one of its key tensions exists between the entrepreneurial industrialists and their regulators in government. As Wolfe explains to the directors of the NIA who attempt to hire him: "Everyone knows that your Association was bitterly hostile to the Bureau of Price Regulation, to Mr. Boone, and to his policies" (p. 31). Solving this crime plunges Wolfe and Archie into policy debates and politics rather than the family histories that characterized the prewar novels. At the end, Archie even accuses Wolfe of letting his politics interfere with his detecting: "Your opinion of the NIA coincides roughly with some other people's including my own, . . . and you knew the stink about the murders was raising cain with the NIA, and you wanted to prolong it as much as possible" (p. 306).

Politics also informs *The Second Confession* (1949). In this novel, James U. Sperling, a wealthy industrialist, worried that his daughter, Gwen, has fallen in love with Louis Rony, whom he believes to be a Communist, hires Wolfe to prove that Rony is in fact a Communist. That will be enough to end the relationship, because the daughter regards communism as "intellectually contemptible and morally unsound" (p. 9). Wolfe assures him: "We agree with your daughter." Archie seconds that, commenting that "a Commie is a louse" (p. 9). It turns out that there is a Communist in the Sperling circle, but it is not Gwen Sperling's boyfriend. By arranging to publish secret documents of the American Communist Party in the newspaper, Wolfe exposes one of Sperling's best friends as a Communist and the boyfriend as a member of a criminal organization. The novel ends with a murderer found and American communism discredited.

The distinction between the public and private is crucial to the Nero Wolfe series, for Wolfe and Archie have constructed a very private and idiosyncratically ordered world. They are able to live according to their "romantic" notions of ideal behavior mainly by excluding or avoiding threats to it. Like Stout himself, they are individualists. However, also like Stout himself, who during the war years had to abandon the secluded country home he had built himself to return to New York, and had to relinquish the niche he had found for himself as a writer to immerse himself in the public acts of propaganda and administration, Wolfe and Archie return from war to a changed world. Their clients bring cases about governmental agencies, lobbying organizations, and political parties. The emergence of a powerful criminal organization in New York forces upon them the problem of policing their city. This engagement with politics and policy became a permanent feature of the Wolfe series: *The Doorbell Rang* and *A Family Affair* are among Stout's most political novels.

Stout's postwar engagement with politics did not, however, completely alter the themes and structure of the Nero Wolfe series, for the postwar novels continue the focus on intimate violence that characterized the early Wolfe novels, and even the novels that turn to politics embed their political themes in family issues. In *Too Many Women* (1947), Jasper Pine, the president of Naylor-Kerr, Inc., wants to hire Wolfe to investigate the death of an employee. A department head at the firm has claimed that the employee was murdered, and this report is distracting the staff. The department head, Kerr Naylor, son of one of the founders of the company and named for the other founder, is Jasper Pine's brother-in-law. Immediately, family issues take center stage in the novel, not only because of the complex politics of a company where the president is at odds with the son of the founder, who also happens to be the brother of the president's wife, but also because of a "coolness" in Wolfe and Archie's family.

Too Many Women is one of the few Wolfe novels where much of the action takes place outside the brownstone. Wolfe and Archie have been getting on each other's nerves, so when Wolfe decides to take Pine's case, he suggests that Naylor-Kerr pretend to hire Archie as a personnel consultant. This would take Archie out of the house entirely while he investigates the crime. The solution to Naylor-Kerr's problems, and to the crime, turns out to be intimately connected to the web of

family relationships in the novel. Like the early novels, it is a study in intimate violence; crime, even in the corporate setting, turns out to spring from intimate relationships. The crime solved, Wolfe and Archie patch up their quarrel. Their family survives, but the coolness between them presages pressures that will finally separate Wolfe and Archie for a time.

And Be a Villain (1948), *The Second Confession* (1949), and *In the Best Families* (1950) form a trilogy, a complete narrative spread over three novels, in which Stout's familiar themes and his new engagement with politics merge. It is also a gesture toward one of the conventions of the detective novel, the detective's struggle with one supreme enemy. Sherlock Holmes's battle with Moriarty, the head of a criminal gang, defines this convention, and Stout uses this trilogy to offer a modern revision of it.

The trilogy begins with *And Be a Villain*, an allusion to Hamlet's bitter observation in the Shakespeare play that "one may smile, and smile, and be a villain" (act 1, scene 5). (The allusion to *Hamlet* is appropriate, since that play, too, is about intimate violence in the family and its repercussions.) Wolfe agrees to find the murderer of Cyril Orchard, who died dramatically by poison as a guest on a radio show. Unfortunately, he was poisoned by a bottle of the sponsor's soda, Hi-Spot, and the sponsor urgently wants the murderer caught. It turns out that the husband of the program's host, Madeline Frasier, was the brother of her producer, Deborah Koppel, and that he died of cyanide poisoning just as Orchard did. Wolfe discovers who would have a motive to kill Frasier's husband, and he discovers the link between that murder and the murders of Cyril Orchard and a woman named Beulah Poole, both of whom turn out to be blackmailers working for a criminal organization. The crime is connected to family history and intimate violence, but the most dramatic moment of the novel occurs not at the revelation of the identity of the murderer but rather when a cold, precise voice calls Wolfe ordering him not to investigate the murder of Beulah Poole. That voice belongs to Arnold Zeck, mastermind of a criminal organization. Wolfe refuses to back off the case, but it is solved before he and Zeck come into conflict.

Wolfe's next case, *The Second Confession*, brings him into conflict with Zeck again. Wolfe discovers that Louis Rony, though not a Communist as James Sperling has thought, is a lieutenant in Zeck's criminal organization. Wolfe characterizes Zeck's operation this way: "He has varied and extensive sources of income. All of them are illegal and some of them are morally repulsive. Narcotics, smuggling, industrial and commercial rackets, gambling, waterfront blackguardism, professional larceny, blackmailing, political malfeasance—that by no means exhausts his curriculum" (p. 57). Zeck again orders Wolfe off the case, and Wolfe again refuses. As a result, Zeck has the orchid-sheltering greenhouse on top of Wolfe's brownstone machine-gunned. But Rony is murdered, and Wolfe's investigation results in the naming of Rony's murderer, so again he and Zeck avoid a confrontation.

The third novel in the trilogy, *In the Best Families*, finally brings Wolfe and Zeck into open warfare. A wealthy older woman hires Wolfe to find out where her handsome, young, and penniless husband has been getting money. Shortly after she visits Wolfe's house, Zeck orders Wolfe off the case. He refuses, and his client is murdered. Without a word to any of his "family," Wolfe disappears from his home, travels to California, loses a huge amount of weight, grows a beard, and returns to New York to infiltrate Zeck's organization. The final showdown between Wolfe and Zeck, unlike the struggle at Reichenbach Falls between Sherlock Holmes and Moriarty, ends in a decisive victory for Wolfe.

From its beginning, the Nero Wolfe series was centered around the home Wolfe and Archie occupied on West Thirty-fifth Street. The family they established there embodied and protected both their individual and professional values. Their fussy schedules and their arbitrary rules imposed order on their domestic lives, just as their "romantic" values imposed order and coherence upon their professional and moral lives. By contrast, the families they encountered in their investigations, though apparently ordered and controlled by social convention, were in fact staging grounds for cruelty, deception, and intimate violence. This rhythm of excursion and return, from the brownstone out into the world and back again, held fast until the postwar novels.

As if his own experiences in public life during the war had changed his vision of the world, Stout returned from war to new rhythms in the Wolfe novels. Although the postwar novels preserve a focus on the family, they also engage with public affairs. The solidity of Wolfe and Archie's world cracks in the postwar novels. Stout does not make it clear whether that new public engagement causes the crack or whether Wolfe and Archie's romantic notions of the family finally succumb to the pressure of the real world.

Either way, the Zeck trilogy portrays the temporary disintegration of Wolfe's world. Mainly, the trilogy tests Wolfe's strategy of nonengagement. It denies him the possibility of withdrawing from the world and—insulated by his fat, his rules, his schedule, his will—living life on his terms. In three successive cases he cannot avoid engagement with a master criminal, until finally he must break every rule in order to regain his ordered home. The period of chaos during the middle portions of *In the Best Families*—with Wolfe gone, Archie on his own, the brownstone for sale, and everyone at odds—does finally end, but it introduces a note of uncertainty from which the series does not recover.

The Final Novels: No Place like Home

The last two decades of Nero Wolfe novels carry on the established themes of the series by continuing to focus on the family as both the source of order and its greatest threat.

Wolfe and Archie continue their engagement with public issues and events, from the behavior of the FBI to the Watergate scandal. The final period of the Wolfe series is marked by a gradual darkening of tone. The verities that had been challenged by the Zeck trilogy weaken further, until the series ends on a dark and equivocal note.

In *The Final Deduction* (1961), Mrs. Althea Vail hires Wolfe to ensure her kidnapped husband's safe return after a ransom of five hundred thousand dollars has been paid. Her husband is safely returned, but in the meantime Wolfe discovers that the ransom note had been typed by Mrs. Vail's secretary, Dinah Utley, who is murdered shortly after Jimmy Vail's release. Vail himself is the next to die, and Wolfe—who has been promised part of the ransom if he can find it—locates the ransom and identifies the murderer of Dinah Utley and Jimmy Vail. The crime, it turns out, is all in the family. Wolfe uncovers the familiar mix of greed and denatured love that lies at the bottom of so many crimes in these novels.

A Right to Die addresses the problem of relations between blacks and whites in America, a topic Stout had first addressed in *Too Many Cooks*. Paul Whipple, who as a young black waiter at Kanawha Spa in West Virginia had supplied Wolfe with the information he needed to name the murderer of Philip Laszio and clear Jerome Berin of a murder charge, now a middle-aged anthropologist at Columbia, asks Wolfe to investigate the white woman Whipple's son intends to marry in the hope that he will find something that will end their relationship. Wolfe normally does not touch domestic disputes (though so many of his cases involve them), but he makes an exception for Whipple, to whom he owes a debt. Archie barely begins to investigate, however, before Susan Brooke, Whipple's son's fiancée, is murdered, and Whipple's son is the prime suspect. Wolfe proves that Whipple's son is innocent by naming the murderer, a demented white racist who worked for a civil rights organization in order to be near Susan, whom she blamed for her son's death by suicide.

As with all of the Wolfe novels that embrace a political theme, *A Right to Die* shows how difficult it is for Wolfe and Archie to avoid engagement in policy and politics despite their elaborate rituals and defenses; however, the novel also locates the political in the context of the personal. It is difficult to say whether the murderer was prompted more by her racism or by twisted love for her son, but by placing the murderer at the heart of a civil rights organization, Stout cast doubt upon the possibility of peaceful relations between the races even as the novel portrays the respect between Whipple and Wolfe.

In *The Doorbell Rang*, Stout attacks the FBI. Despite his wartime labors for the government and his lifetime of involvement with political organizations, in his fiction Stout exhibits a deeply cynical attitude toward political organizations and institutions, from political parties to governmental agencies. *The Doorbell Rang* begins with a request from a wealthy widow who had sent ten thousand copies of an exposé on the FBI to influential people across America. She asks Wolfe to make the FBI stop harassing her. This novel constitutes a 1960s parallel to the Zeck trilogy of the 1940s, for Wolfe is again pitted against a seemingly invulnerable opponent with a much larger organization and more resources. As with Zeck, Wolfe refuses to be circumscribed by anyone else; the only reason not to take Mrs. Brunner's job would be the conviction that the FBI is too powerful to tackle, and Wolfe refuses to admit that. Against Archie's advice he takes on the case.

Wolfe manages to entrap the FBI in an illegal break-in, and he uses the threat of exposing their activities to leverage a promise that they will stop harassing Mrs. Brunner. There is a murder in the novel, but it is a secondary feature. *The Doorbell Rang* focuses on institutional deception and disregard for individual rights. When Inspector Cramer of the New York police and the head of the FBI's New York office are wrangling over a piece of evidence at the end of the novel, Wolfe breaks in with "Save your posing for audiences that will appreciate it. This one isn't sufficiently naive" (p. 153). That remark exemplifies the tone of the novel. The family as a source of stability and order becomes increasingly destabilized as the Wolfe novels progress; this novel offers little hope that government can take its place.

Death of a Doxy is one of the important novels about Wolfe's family in the series, along with the Zeck trilogy and *A Family Affair*. Orrie Cather, one of Wolfe's operatives, asks Archie to help him get out of a scrape with a woman. Orrie had been having an affair with Isabel Kerr, the mistress of a wealthy man, until Orrie becomes engaged to Jill Hardy, a flight attendant. But Isabel refuses to disengage, and she is threatening to go to Jill Hardy with intimate articles of Orrie's in an attempt to break off the marriage. Orrie wants Archie to go to Isabel's apartment when she is not there and pick up those articles. When he arrives at the apartment, Archie finds Isabel Kerr's corpse. She kept a diary in which she recorded her affair with Orrie, so before long the police arrest him on suspicion of murder, and Wolfe and Archie resolve to clear him of the charges because he is one of the family. As Wolfe explains, "If he didn't kill her I have an obligation I can't ignore. I am constrained not only by his long association with me but also by my self-esteem. You must know that I have no affection for him; he has frequently vexed me. . . . But if he didn't kill that woman, I intend to deliver him" (p. 24).

There are family issues on the other side of the case, too. Isabel's sister, Stella, raised her after the death of their mother, and Stella, ashamed of her sister's mode of living, will do anything to keep that information from the press. The investigation reveals the murderer, and Orrie is set free, but not before Archie begins to view Orrie with a more cautious eye than before. It is as though all the tensions from other families in the novels have finally infected Wolfe's own family. This novel contains one of the few strong and independent female characters that Stout created in the Wolfe novels, Julie Jaquette.

A Family Affair concludes the Wolfe series. One of Stout's best novels, it responds to the concerns raised by *Death of a Doxy*. The novel opens with Pierre Ducos, a waiter from Wolfe's favorite restaurant, calling at the brownstone at one o'clock in the morning and asking to speak to Wolfe because he believes someone is going to kill him. Archie gives Pierre a room for the night at the brownstone; moments later an explosion rocks the building. Someone had given Pierre a bomb in a cigar tube. He had opened it in his bedroom in Wolfe's home and blown his head away. Outraged by the intrusion of violence into his own home, Wolfe grimly vows to find the murderer. Before the investigation has gone very far, however, an extraordinary thing happens: Wolfe withdraws into silence. He refuses to talk about the case to Archie or to the police or to his lawyer. He and Archie are both taken to jail for their refusal to talk, and still Wolfe stands mute. It is an eerie echo of Wolfe's sudden disappearance from home in *In the Best Families*. There, he left to prepare himself for his battle with Arnold Zeck; in this novel, there is another bitter battle to fight, but the enemy lies much closer to home.

The Wolfe series concludes on a disillusioned note. However, in many ways the conclusion of the series represents a logical development of its themes. Wolfe and Archie persist to the last novel in their romantic notions of order. Similarly, they hold to the strictly regulated structure of their family life, as though surrounding themselves with rules and schedules could insulate them from all the forces of disorder that they encounter outside their home and office. But as it develops, the Wolfe series tests and probes Wolfe's romantic order. The war forces him out of his routine into a job with military intelligence; his battle with the master criminal Arnold Zeck forces him completely out of himself, his home, and even his moral orbit as he infiltrates Zeck's organization in order to destroy him. In the end, disorder does more than take Wolfe from his home: it infiltrates that home, until at last even that safe haven is compromised by the very human emotions from which Wolfe has sought to insulate himself.

Death of a Doxy first introduces the serious possibility that Wolfe's family may harbor disorder. When Archie discovers the corpse of Isabel at the beginning of the novel, his first thought is that Orrie may have set him up:

> As you know, Orrie, and as I know, you think it would be fine if you had my job. That's all right, there's nothing wrong with ambition. But what if you had got *too* ambitious? What if you knew there was nothing there to point to you? What if you had arranged for one man, me, to go there at a quarter past four, and for another man, maybe a cop on an anonymous tip, to arrive a few minutes after? It wouldn't have hooked me for murder, since the ME would set the time, but I would have the keys on me, not only yours, and the rubber gloves, and that would have been good for at least a couple of years. (p. 9)

It turns out that Orrie is not the murderer in *Death of a Doxy*, nor was he setting Archie up for a fall; however, in *A Family Affair* a member of Wolfe's family does turn bad. That act of treachery calls all the verities into question. As Archie puts it:

> Nero Wolfe, the great detective, the genius, is hogtied. He can't make a move. If he goes by the book, collects the pieces and hands Cramer the package, he will have to get on the witness stand and answer questions under oath about a man he has used and trusted for years. He wouldn't do that, he would rather spend ten years behind bars than do that. You know damn well he wouldn't and I'm glad he wouldn't. All of us would have to answer questions in public about a guy we have worked with and played pinochle with. (p. 135)

Archie and other members of the family devise a solution that removes the murderer from their midst, but the effects of this case linger. The novel ends with Wolfe and Archie trying to find peace.

The Nero Wolfe saga asks whether it is possible in a world riven by greed, lust, jealousy, hatred, and revenge to find order. The novels argue that order cannot be found in the family, government cannot guarantee it, and the police cannot enforce it. For a time, the novels suggest that individuals can create their own order locally by insulating themselves from the forces that disorder the world, but finally Stout conceded that even that was not possible. Nero Wolfe's romantic attempt to construct his own world fails.

Legacy

Asked what he thought his own reputation as a writer would be, Stout answered:

> Obviously the books I've written have got something in them that distinguishes them from the ordinary run of books. . . . What I don't know is what the books have in them that lots of books don't have. I don't know whether it's the characters, or the ingenuity of the stories, or something about my basic attitude toward people and life that comes out in them. . . . I'm very curious about it but I doubt if I'll ever find out before I die. (John McAleer, 1983, pp. 72–73)

There are no doubt many reasons for the lasting appeal of the Nero Wolfe novels, including those named by Rex Stout himself. More than twenty years after the last novel in the series, it is now possible to at least begin to understand the legacy of the series in terms of the genre of detective fiction. Stout's Nero Wolfe novels constitute a landmark in the history of detective fiction. After a career writing for money for pulp fiction magazines and another stint as a "serious" novelist, he found a niche in detective fiction. From 1934 until 1975, he published one of the longest and most fully developed series of novels and novellas about one detective in the history of American detective fiction.

In the Nero Wolfe series, Stout produced an important variation in the conventions of the detective novel by teaming a sedentary, intellectual detective with a detective whose origins lay with hard-boiled action fiction. The result was a new kind of detective fiction that embraced two traditions that had until then remained largely separate. Stout also enriched the detective novel by emphasizing the domestic setting of the detectives as a way of talking about the values they embody. A remarkable individualist himself, Stout wrote detective fiction that focused upon the values of the detectives; even though the Nero Wolfe novels engage public issues even as the trajectory of his own life brought Stout into the public sphere, the series remains fundamentally the testing of an individual ideal of order against the arbitrariness and randomness of life. In the final analysis, that ideal proved impossible to sustain, so that the Wolfe novels end in conflict and disillusionment rather than triumph. But the importance of the issues addressed in the Wolfe novels and the honesty of their treatment of those issues mark them as mature writing and earn Rex Stout his place in the history of writing.

Selected Bibliography

WORKS OF REX STOUT

Stout published many of his novels in abridged form in magazines before book publication; where applicable, dates given throughout this section are for first publication of the work in complete form as a book.

Her Forbidden Knight. All-Story Magazine 26: 855–878 (August 1913); 27: 117–142 (September 1913); 27: 415–433 (October 1913); 27: 652–675 (November 1913); 27: 935–950 (December 1913).

Under the Andes. All-Story Magazine 28: 241–380 (February 1914).

A Prize for Princes. All-Story Weekly Magazine 31: 111–142 (2 May 1914); 31: 369–404 (9 May 1914); *All-Story Cavalier Weekly* 32: 67–92 (16 May 1914); *All-Story Cavalier Weekly* 32: 315–348 (23 May 1914); *All-Story Cavalier Weekly* 32: 583–609 (30 May 1914).

The Great Legend. All-Story Weekly 53: 255–261 (1 January 1916); 53: 444–473 (8 January 1916); 53: 717–745 (15 January 1916); 54: 138–171 (22 January 1916); 54: 342–360 (29 January 1916).

How like a God. New York: Vanguard, 1929.

Seed on the Wind. New York: Vanguard, 1930.

Golden Remedy. New York: Vanguard, 1931.

Forest Fire. New York: Farrar and Rinehart, 1933.

The President Vanishes. New York: Farrar and Rinehart, 1934. (Published anonymously.)

O Careless Love! New York: Farrar and Rinehart, 1935.

Mr. Cinderella. New York: Farrar and Rinehart, 1938.

Mountain Cat. New York: Farrar and Rinehart, 1939.

NERO WOLFE NOVELS

Fer-de-Lance. New York: Farrar and Rinehart, 1934.

The League of Frightened Men. New York: Farrar and Rinehart, 1935.

The Rubber Band. New York: Farrar and Rinehart, 1936.

The Red Box. New York: Farrar and Rinehart, 1937.

Too Many Cooks. New York: Farrar and Rinehart, 1938.

Some Buried Caesar. New York: Farrar and Rinehart, 1939; New York: Pyramid Books, 1963.

Over My Dead Body. New York: Farrar and Rinehart, 1940.

Where There's a Will. New York: Farrar and Rinehart, 1940.

The Silent Speaker. New York: Viking, 1946.

Too Many Women. New York: Viking, 1947.

And Be a Villain. New York: Viking, 1948.

The Second Confession. New York: Viking, 1949.

In the Best Families. New York: Viking, 1950.

Murder by the Book. New York: Viking, 1951.

Prisoner's Base. New York: Viking, 1952.

The Golden Spiders. New York: Viking, 1953.

The Black Mountain. New York: Viking, 1954.

Before Midnight. New York: Viking, 1955.

Might As Well Be Dead. New York: Viking, 1956.

If Death Ever Slept. New York: Viking, 1957.

Champagne for One. New York: Viking, 1958.

Plot It Yourself. New York: Viking, 1959.

Too Many Clients. New York: Viking, 1960.

The Final Deduction. New York: Viking, 1961.

Gambit. New York: Viking, 1962.

The Mother Hunt. New York: Viking, 1963.

A Right to Die. New York: Viking, 1964.

The Doorbell Rang. New York: Viking, 1965.

Death of a Doxy. New York: Viking, 1966.

The Father Hunt. New York: Viking, 1968.

Death of a Dude. New York: Viking, 1969.

Please Pass the Guilt. New York: Viking, 1973.

A Family Affair. New York: Viking, 1975.

OTHER DETECTIVE NOVELS

The Hand in the Glove. New York: Farrar and Rinehart, 1937. (Features a female detective, Theodolinda Bonner.)

Double for Death. New York: Farrar and Rinehart, 1939. (A Tecumseh Fox mystery.)

Red Threads. In: *The Mystery Book.* New York: Farrar and Rinehart, 1939. (A mystery featuring Inspector Cramer but not Wolfe.)

Bad for Business. In: *The Second Mystery Book.* New York: Farrar and Rinehart, 1940. (A Tecumseh Fox mystery.)

The Broken Vase. New York: Farrar and Rinehart, 1941. (A Tecumseh Fox mystery.)

Alphabet Hicks. New York: Farrar and Rinehart, 1941. (An Alphabet Hicks mystery.)

Justice Ends at Home and Other Stories. Edited by John McAleer. New York: Viking, 1977. (Collects the best of Rex Stout's early stories written for the pulps.)

INTERVIEW

McAleer, John. *Royal Decree: Conversations with Rex Stout.* Ashton, Md.: Pontes Press, 1983.

BIBLIOGRAPHY

Townsend, Guy M., John J. McAleer, Judson C. Sapp, and Arriean Schemer, eds. *Rex Stout: An Annotated Primary and Secondary Bibliography.* New York: Garland, 1980.

BIOGRAPHICAL AND CRITICAL STUDIES

Anderson, David R. *Rex Stout.* New York: Ungar, 1984.

Barzun, Jacques. *A Birthday Tribute to Rex Stout.* New York: Viking, 1965.

Beiderwell, Bruce. "State Power and Self-Destruction: Rex Stout and the Romance of Justice." *Journal of Popular Culture* 27, no. 1: 13–22 (summer 1993).

Edel, Leon. "The Figure Under the Carpet." In *Telling Lives: The Biographer's Art.* Edited by Marc Pachter. Washington, D.C.: New Republic Books, 1979.

Gerhardt, Mia I. "Homicide West: Some Observations on the Nero Wolfe Stories of Rex Stout." *English Studies* 49: 107–127 (August 1968).

Jaffe, Arnold. "Murder with Dignity." *New Republic* 177: 41–43 (30 July 1977).

McAleer, John. *Rex Stout: A Biography.* Boston: Little, Brown, 1977.

Miller, Don, ed. *The Mystery Nook #9* (August 1976). (The Rex Stout Memorial Issue.)

Nickerson, Edward A. " 'Realistic' Crime Fiction: An Anatomy of Evil People." *Centennial Review* 25, no. 2: 101–132 (1981).

Rauber, D. F. "Sherlock Holmes and Nero Wolfe: The Role of the 'Great Detective' in Intellectual History." *Journal of Popular Culture* 6: 483–495 (spring 1973).

Wilson, Edmund. "Why Do People Read Detective Stories?" *New Yorker* 20: 73–75 (14 October 1944).

JULIAN SYMONS
(1912–1994)

H. R. F. KEATING

FROM THE DETECTIVE story to the crime novel: these words, the subtitle for Julian Symons' history of mystery fiction, *Bloody Murder* (1972; U.S. title, *Mortal Consequences*) can be seen as describing his own career as a writer of crime fiction. For almost the whole course of that career from his first book, *The Immaterial Murder Case* (1945), subsequently disowned as "appallingly bad" (Walsdorf, p. 3), to *A Sort of Virtue* (1996), written when he knew he had an inoperable cancer and posthumously published, the plot-dominated detective story and the people-dominated novel jostled in his pages.

Julian Gustave Symons was born on 30 May 1912, in London, England, to Minnie Louise and Morris Albert Symons. The youngest of five children, he was educated in various state schools. Symons did not attend university but took advantage of his employment as a shorthand typist and secretary to educate himself, reading a wide range of literature and focusing primarily on verse. In 1937 he founded *Twentieth Century Verse*, intended to provide a forum for young poets outside the circle of W. H. Auden. He ran the magazine single-handedly until the war.

His eldest brother was the dandy, gourmet, and bibliophile A. J. A. Symons, author of *The Quest for Corvo* (1934), a life of Frederick William Rolfe, self-styled Baron Corvo, a book that in recounting its author's difficulties in unearthing the truth about its subject brought a new approach to the art of biography. Julian greatly admired "A. J.," as his brother was called, and in 1950 wrote his biography, *A. J. A. Symons: His Life and Speculations*.

The Immaterial Murder Case came into existence shortly before World War II in light-hearted talk with Symons' fellow poet, Ruthven Todd. Written down by Symons, it languished in a drawer until Symons' wife, Kathleen (Clark), whom he had married in 1941, read it and suggested it might add some useful cash to his earnings as an advertising copywriter. Its eager reception by the upmarket crime publisher Victor Gollancz, coupled with inheriting from his friend George Orwell a weekly books column in the *Manchester Evening News*, soon enabled him to become a full-time writer of mystery fiction, biographies, and social and historical studies. *A Man Called Jones* (1947), also later disavowed, was the second of the crime fiction books that, he said, allowed him to write works that required prolonged research.

His career proper in mystery fiction may be said, then, to have made a start with the appropriately titled *Bland Beginning* (1949), putting at center stage the Inspector Bland, who had been a detective in the two previous books, with the half-formed intention of using him as a series detective. It was, however, something of a false start. Symons, looking back, did not think much of the book. More importantly, when he began thinking of the next, *The Thirty-First of February* (1950), a story which was eventually to combine experiences in advertising and reading Dostoyevsky (its detective bears some relation to the Grand Inquisitor of *The Brothers Karamazov*), he saw that though a series detective had advantages (mostly of a commercial nature), such a figure was not for him. To quote from his notes in *Julian Symons: A Bibliography*, the advantages were outweighed by "the fact that if you want to write a story showing people involved in emotional conflict that leads to crime a detective of this kind is grit in the machinery" (p. 9). In *The Thirty-First of February*, too, he saw that it was not in fact necessary even to have a murder. A detective's unceasing pursuit of a guiltless hero is enough to hold the reader.

So here, at the start, is Symons' desire to add to books inheriting something of the detective story in the Agatha Christie mode—her plotting was a lifelong pleasure to him—a considerable amount of the psychological study of the mainstream novel. His next book, *The Broken Penny* (1953), attempted to get even further away from what one of the characters in *A Man Called Jones* labeled the essential unlifelike fantasy of the classic detective story (a shrewd, if disguised, observation from the future historian of the genre) by attempting the pure thriller. That subgenre, however, was not wholly suited to Symons' talents. "Few people," he wryly notes, "shared my fondness for the book" (Walsdorf, p. 19). In *The Narrowing Circle* (1954), he reverted to a story with a murder mystery element—here his delight in plot is perhaps too obtrusive—which he darkens with an overspreading view of life as a grim, ever-narrowing circle of possibilities. This scarcely relenting distrust of appearances pervades almost all his fiction. He was not one to balk at harsh truths.

Indeed, he advocated in the strongest terms mystery fiction's right to contain any facts from life. "To exclude realism of description and language from the crime novel when it has been accepted as normal in other fiction is almost to prevent its practitioners from at-

tempting any serious work," he wrote in his 1966 collection of essays, *Critical Occasions* (p. 152). Although he was not the first serious crime writer to pioneer this freedom—Dashiell Hammett (whose biography Symons wrote in 1985) perhaps deserves that honor—certainly Symons' example over the years contributed not a little to allowing other crime writers to say things that once arbitrarily had been decreed unsayable.

Getting to the Truth

Setting aside *The Paper Chase* (1956; U.S. title, *Bogue's Fortune*, 1957), about which its author notes only, "The first page is the best!" (Walsdorf, p. 29), we come to *The Colour of Murder* (1957). In this book Symons threads a murder mystery through a story which he tells in two parts, first the protagonist's statement to a psychiatrist and then an account of his trial. This latter reflects Symons' sharp interest at that time and for much of his later career in the way justice may be done or not done in, in particular, the English legal system. It is here that we first meet Magnus Newton, the brilliant but humanly idiosyncratic barrister who appears (unlike a series detective) here and there in a number of trial scenes. *The Colour of Murder* gained the Crime Writers Association Gold Dagger, an award judged by a panel of critics. Symons has remarked that at this period he seemed to alternate between books that were successful and ones that were, in his words, very poor (but in which the prose was, as ever, precise and lethal). *The Gigantic Shadow* (1958; U.S. title, *The Pipe Dream*, 1959) falls into his second category, as another attempt at what is largely a thriller. Symons felt he had succumbed to an attention-grabbing opening without having a plausible plot to support it. However, his next, *The Progress of a Crime* (1960), is a book he considered among his half-dozen most successful. It won the Mystery Writers of America Edgar Allan Poe award for 1960.

Before writing he spent some weeks shadowing a junior reporter on a provincial morning paper, and at the start of the novel just such a young man is seen sitting in a bus reading Arnold Bennett's *Anna of the Five Towns* and admiring the author's unfussy directness, brisk humanitarianism, and eager appetite for life. It is, in fact, just these qualities that mark out the more hidden, other face of Symons the realist cynic. But the realist is still much to the fore, as exemplified by such acute observations as "the militant laughter of those protected by beer and warmth" (p. 10)[1] or the more sweeping words given to a world-weary editor: "There's always a sex angle. Lift the stone and sex crawls out from under" (p. 24). It is Symons' cool appraisal of the facts of existence that, in all his novels, gives to the sexual impulse its full weight.

The Progress of a Crime is as good an example as any of Symons' driving desire to get at the truth of things. Its story is just that, attempts to get at underlying truth. Hugh Bennett, the young reporter, attempts it by trying to find out what actually happened in a fatal knifing at a bonfire celebration, although before long he becomes imbued with the suspicion that he will never penetrate beyond the outer skin of reality, never be able (it is a typically illuminating phrase) "to twitch it aside as one takes the skin off custard" (p. 115). Similarly, the not particularly sympathetic Detective Superintendent Twicker, as single-mindedly determined as the Grand Inquisitor–like detective in *The Colour of Murder*, carries within himself still some remnant of his early missionary zeal for justice, for all that he admits he has to use the tough methods of unjust lower-ranking officers to unearth the facts. In this he is an embryonic Detective Chief Superintendent Hilary Catchpole, of Symons' two final books.

It is a hardened London crime reporter, significantly named Fairfield, who goes beyond the call of duty to find evidence that frees the apparently innocent youth eventually put on

[1]All pages refer to the British editions of Symons' works.

trial. But we as readers are not in Fairfield's hands. We are in the hands of Julian Symons, digger for the ultimate answer, which, in a final plot twist brought off with the adroitness of an Agatha Christie, is that the young man, found not guilty in part by the cunning advocacy of Magnus Newton, did in fact use the fatal knife at the bonfire. So simultaneously a murder mystery is finally resolved, and an unyielding point is made about the unjustness of justice systems.

Targeting Hypocrisy

Keeping to Symons' perceived pattern, such as it is, of successful-unsuccessful, the next book, *The Killing of Francie Lake* (1962; U.S. title, *The Plain Man*) was eventually characterized by its author as "a nice idea," portraying a character much like the arch-swindler Horatio Bottomley (whose biography he wrote in 1955), in the end "not [really] carried through" (Walsdorf, p. 56). Still, the setting, a catchpenny magazine that had started out as a genuine crusading journal, gave him plenty of opportunities for the sharp social comment, the twitching up of the outward all's-well custard skin, which he saw as his novels' primary aim. Thus the book's tenth chapter begins almost magisterially: "It is part of the deep hypocrisy of the English that they condemn nobody until they have been in prison" (p. 75).

We get too, however, Symons' equally laid-down description of Superintendent Nevers as "unimaginative but shrewd, a man with great feeling for tradition, authority, and what he would have called the decencies of life" (p. 93). It gives us a faint foreshadowing, once more, of the Hilary Catchpole of the last books. It is, too, an acknowledgement perhaps of how far toward a bourgeois outlook on life the fifty-year-old author had moved since his earliest working days as a clerk contriving to move in the world of bohemian writers and editing on a shoestring his own magazine. If Symons has not altogether made the change he postulates for himself in the dedicatory poem to *Bland Beginning* ("... the transverse alchemies/Corroding the bright Radicals to Tories"), he is at least showing the first signs, in his analysis of Nevers, of acknowledging the virtues of the bourgeois.

But hypocrisy is still squarely in his sights. So it is not surprising that his next book, *The End of Solomon Grundy* (1964), should be set in a particularly cozy and pretentious housing estate, the Dell, peopled with such contemporary figures as advertising men, architects, and actors. Disruptive Grundy himself is half of a team producing a classy, radicalish comic strip. Before long there is a murder to be solved, but this is not murder simply to puzzle the reader. It is murder committed to provide a story—one beguilingly readable—around which cling the facts of its times, the much-hailed sixties, set there to be excoriated, principally by the utterly unhypocritical, bulky, red-haired Sol Grundy.

Yet the story does present a puzzle, and a skillfully elaborated one. Part of that success is due to Symons' eschewing of the running detective. Not being tied to the eyes of one individual enabled him to further the did-he, didn't-he aspect of his story by such devices as, on one occasion, giving unrelatedly the possibly ambiguous text of a letter (p. 152), rather than describing the thoughts of either writer or recipient. More, the lack of a central focus means that Symons was able to approach his subject, his theme, from various oblique angles. In doing this he removes himself further and further from his story, the very opposite of what happens with a writer who tells a tale through one central character. Symons, for almost all his writing life, appeared to want to look on at a distance, dispassionately.

A Change of Strategy

Following the good–less good pattern, the next novel, *The Belting Inheritance* (1965), was a comparative failure. A modernization of the famous Tichborne Claimant case of the 1850s, in which a butcher from Australia asserted he was heir to a large British estate—Symons reviewed at length a book about it, found in *Critical Occasions*—it may be seen as another attempt at distancing himself from the actual and immediate in order to point to current hypocrisies. This was something he was to do again more than once. It comes in his harking back to Sherlock Holmes in *A Three-Pipe Problem* (1975), and yet more in the Victorian murder mysteries: *The Blackheath Poisonings* (1978), *Sweet Adelaide* (1980), and *The Detling Murders* (1982; U.S. title, *The Detling Secret*). But before these books came a trilogy of novels each with a title beginning *The Man Who . . .*

They represented a different new strategy. Symons felt at this stage, in the semi-obscure manner a writer feels about his future books, that he should try to write crime fiction even less attached to the rigidities of plot. He hoped that by interweaving his people more casually than before, he would be able, without a puzzle to be solved, to go into them more deeply. This brought about something of a change of style. In these three books there is less dialogue advancing the story and more long passages of analysis, delving into the psychology of characters, such as the sympathetic murderer of *The Man Who Killed Himself* (1967), Arthur Brownjohn. But the humor that runs like a cherry-red thread through all the books is still present. I myself well remember listening to him reading the passage in which Brownjohn, disguised as "Major Easonby Mellon," fails miserably to shoot his wife ("What are you doing in those ridiculous clothes?" p. 91), to an audience convulsed in mirth.

Disguises and masks run throughout Symons' work. In *The Man Whose Dreams Came True* (1968), we have a protagonist, Tony Jones, who is first seen "being" Anthony Scott-Williams and who in the course of the book becomes several other smart young men, personalities achieved rather than crude disguises. Masks both. And as such to be firmly, even cruelly, torn away. From the title of the book one knows that the dreams are going to come true only to prove disastrous to the dreamer. And so they do. In the final somber pages Jones is not only callously murdered in an alley but also stripped of all his identities, assumed and real. Although the book is a character study in which Symons gets convincingly inside his dubious protagonist, to tell its story he produces a fine plot. It is, however, not the sort of clues-weaving plot he has retained from the detective story in such books as *The Progress of a Crime* (and will later make use of again). It is, rather, the type of plot, the significant ordering of events, that mainstream novelists use. Where striking events occur, such as Tony's second encounter with the predatory middle-aged Violet Harrington, they are, however unexpected, perfectly plausible in terms of the real world.

The third of these novels that set out to expose the social ironies of their time, *The Man Who Lost His Wife* (1970), abandoned decisively the near-tragic world Symons had plunged con man Tony Jones into. Instead, using a milieu I described in the *Times* of London in reviewing it as "Upper colour-supplement [glossy world] Britain 1970," he produced a finely comic thriller largely set in holiday Yugoslavia and, again, filled with suspicions that people are not what they seem. But there is in it, too, a new note. It ends as happily as any such standard thriller, if with a hint of irony. Its publisher hero, Gilbert Weldon, finds his firm reestablished on a sound financial basis and his fears over his wife's fidelity set at rest. This almost banal rounding-off shows, perhaps at its clearest in Symons' career up to this point, the guarded heart forcing a way through the carapace of the wary pessimist.

Back to the Dark

As if shocked at his own admission, Symons turned next to as dark a subject as he could perhaps find. *The Players and the Game* (1972) is based on the folie à deux child torturing and killings known in Britain as the Moors murders, with some input from the Lonely Hearts murders in America. (In the latter case, Raymond Fernandez and Martha Beck were executed in 1951 following their conviction for twenty killings.) The novel was intended to show the horrors beneath the apparent tranquillities of everyday life, but Symons confesses, "I couldn't bring myself to write about the torture of children" (Walsdorf, p. 79). Instead, he made the driving force of the book a puzzle in more or less the classic detective-story form, with the mystery (most ingeniously contrived) being who among the characters are the two murderers, seen until the end only in the mask identities of "Dracula" and "Bonnie Parker."

But it is more than the puzzle that lures the reader forward. It is the account of the extinction of a weak mask-wearer, Paul Vane (he may or may not be "Dracula"), who tests his adopted persona against the hypocrisies and petty jealousies of a suburban environment not so different from the Dell of *Solomon Grundy*. Furthermore, "Dracula" is a disciple of Nietzsche, who is seen not only as the licenser of the unrestrained Superman but also as the philosopher of antihypocrisy. It is only in the last pages that he gets his comeuppance.

As if yielding once more to the fascination of plot construction, Symons followed this novel with *The Plot Against Roger Rider* (1973), which is indeed largely concerned with laying out a murder plot against the tycoon of the title, a man with, significantly, "a surface of aimless good humour" (p. 95). The plot, however, with the ingenuity Symons readers had come to rely on, turns out to reverse all expectations. But there is, as ever, more to the book than plot. Rider's wife is a former actress, always putting on funny voices, that is, one habituated to wearing varied masks. Rider's daughter, Sheila, starts comically obsessed with finding herself a "Natural Man," one she sees as free of all hypocrisy, although she ends engaged to the principal narrator, by no means such an ideal figure. An old schoolfellow of Rider's, despised and patronized and eventually given a paper-tiger job in his firm, is not only kept in play as the possible organizer of the plot, but in the last pages is seen as much removed from harsh reality as the edge-of-serene-lunacy Arthur Brownjohn, of *The Man Who Killed Himself.* Sex, too, the factor Symons never forgot, is shorn of its false romanticism in one brief aside here: "I'll tell you something a great writer said about it, H. G. Wells. He said it was no more important than sneezing" (p. 205). It is a happy Sheila (another almost concealed Symons acknowledgment of the upside) who says at the end, "It's hard to know what anybody's really like, isn't it?" (p. 205). Finally, when all becomes clear, it is after a long journey up an inhospitable hill to a hidden Sardinia castle, a journey that is echoed at the end of a book equally twisting with plot reversals, *The Criminal Comedy of the Contented Couple* (1985; U.S. title, *A Criminal Comedy*).

Harking Back

At this stage Symons tried the strategy of harking back to periods well before his own times, with the likely aim of guarding his heart while continuing to hammer away at truth-hiding hypocrisies as they have existed ever since human beings became civilized. In *A Three-Pipe Problem*, Symons pays tribute to Sir Arthur Conan Doyle, the writer he had admired since boyhood. He had earlier put Holmes into a collection of short stories, or inventions, *The Great Detectives* (1981), and he wrote a short biography of Holmes's creator four years after he had put onto the pages his Sherlock actor-cum-accidental-sleuth, Sheridan Haynes. He even resurrected Haynes thirteen years later in *The Kentish Manor Murders* (1988).

Encouraged by the success of *A Three-Pipe Problem*, he wrote a second novel removed from the contemporary scene, *The Blackheath Poisonings*, accepting a casual challenge from a fellow writer claiming (foolishly it may be thought in the 1990s) that it was

impossible to write a successful period crime story. The Victorian setting certainly gave opportunities for exposing hypocrisies, especially those of a sexual nature, and its speech patterns ring beautifully true to their times, as might be expected of a Sherlock Holmes enthusiast.

Cheered by the enjoyment he had experienced in the final writing of the book, he produced another Victorian story, *Sweet Adelaide.* To the straight story of *The Blackheath Poisonings* and its turning-over of the pretences of the times he added more than a slight resemblance to the early-twentieth-century Croydon poisonings (written about in his 1960 collection of possible miscarriages of justice, *A Reasonable Doubt*). He used details of the famous Adelaide Bartlett poisoning case of 1886, where after her acquittal an onlooker is said to have exclaimed that "in the interests of science she should now tell us how she did it." Much of the interest lies in what might be thought of as Symons' extra-literary answer to that question from the past, and it should be added it is extremely plausible. He felt the book was successful enough in artistic terms to move on to yet another Victorian mystery, *The Detling Murders.* But the fire may have gone out for him, and he found himself unsatisfied with it.

Still seeking an oblique approach, Symons made the following book something of a meditation on the art of Edgar Allan Poe, to whom he devotes a considerable section of *Bloody Murder* as well as writing a study of Poe's life and work, *The Tell-Tale Heart* (1978). *The Name of Annabel Lee* (1983) also draws on his experience teaching for a year at Amherst College and on his better acquaintance with other aspects of American life, enabling him to point to our universal hypocrisies with such incidental touches as having his "Graham College" gain a lavish drama hall by accepting as students the children of a dubious millionaire.

The book also includes a considerable amount of fantasy, often of a sexual nature, which appears sporadically all through Symons' novels. The trashy books "factory" of

The Narrowing Circle is an early example. Here, in keeping with the hallucinatory Poe-like tone, is the highly unlikely way Annabel Lee settles in at a moment's notice with the mild British lecturer, Dudley Potter (Symons is nearly as cunning with names as his admired Conan Doyle). All through the book, too, there is switching between the probing novel and the teasing detective story, although evidently the novel, the study of Annabel, is the main thrust.

Perhaps with a need to make the next book different—something many novelists feel—Symons embarked on a heavily plotted story, to which he insisted on giving the appropriate lengthy title *The Criminal Comedy of the Contented Couple.* (His American publisher insisted on *A Criminal Comedy.*) Looking back, Symons was pleased with the book, "thinking it among the best and sharpest" of his later work (Walsdorf, p. 112). But the characters most involved in the sheer plot are not altogether well realized, tending to have names hard to distinguish one from the other, while the characters who carry the novel strand of the book, its consideration of life as play, are much more realized. In the main narrator's description of a suburban party—"Was he right in feeling that Derek and Sandy were playing at being host and hostess, and the whole thing was a colour supplement luncheon" (p. 39)—we see Symons' move from exposing hypocrisy to seeing societies as widespread networks of cooperative self-delusion. But when, at the top of a mountain on Elba, there comes the final revelation—as startling as anything in Agatha Christie, or more so—there is a sense that what the novel aspect of the book has been saying about that wide hypocrisy has been pushed too much into the background.

Enter the Author

In 1990, after the somewhat unsuccessful book *The Kentish Manor Murders,* came *Death's Darkest Face.* This, too, is a harking back. Not to Sherlock Holmes or any imagined Victorian era, but instead to a time in Symons' own life, to an imaginary poet of the 1930s, Hugo Headley, whose body (if he has been murdered) has never been found. The book takes the form, too, of a fictional "Julian Symons" being asked to look at the papers of an unsuccessful amateur investigation. The book's half-recollections of true-life figures was echoed the next year in *Portraits of the Missing* (1991), a series of imaginary biographies bearing some relation to people Julian Symons had known in his early days.

The curious form *Death's Darkest Face* takes goes so far as to have "Julian Symons" propose, but only propose, a final answer to the question of how Hugo Headley died. In this new acknowledgment of the involvement of the author in the lives he has chosen to describe, we see Symons, in his last years, allowing something of his long-guarded heart to peep from behind the cool mask. It does so, more than in any previous book perhaps, in the authentic Symons voice, a voice with an easiness that freshens the long paragraphs of psychological analysis that before had tended to be as hard-going as if they were from a textbook. The onward drive is reinforced, too, by the cunning back-and-forth arrangement of the book's materials, a cunning not so much of detective-story plotting as of clever ordering. This method of telling the story does more than simply trick the reader into believing that, for instance, the writer of a quoted letter is a real person. It has the effect of validating the truth of the fictional character the reader is necessarily aware is so many words on paper.

Something of the same technique is also apparent in the next book, *Something Like a Love Affair* (1992). In it Symons gathered together many of the strands that had threaded through his other stories. There is corruption in public life, wrongdoing hidden beneath a surface of respectability. There are the almost inevitable (in Symons' eyes) deceptions of love. There is, too, a sudden-reversal murder plot, as astonishing as that of *A Criminal Comedy.* There is a young man who talks of "my dreams or fantasies or whatever you call 'em" (p. 126) and the heroine's feeling of "the dreamlike quality of my experience" (p. 158). There is a stranger who turns out to be wearing the mask of a paid hit man. There are references to the wider evils of the world: "She read every week of murder squads who went round killing stray children on the streets in Brazil" (p. 156). There is the half-dream when the heroine asks, "Is it a game, I can make it a game, is it a game or not?" (p. 139). But there is also something else, something that has only peeped up before: the character of Patty, the young home help, is quite simply a nice person, however much she brings with her traces of a nasty world.

And the people of the next book, *Playing Happy Families* (1994), also have many attributes of niceness, despite the fact that one knows, again from the very title, that all will not be happiness, and soon enough the happy-go-lucky daughter disappears (a case borrowed from the headlines of the immediate past). But there is too, most prominently, Detective Chief Superintendent Hilary Catchpole. To him and to his wife Symons devotes a long, warmly written passage, a life history that would have had no place in any Golden Age detective story. It has its truthful downside, but in the main it is a hymn, nothing less, to the good man, the good policeman, the honest bourgeois. "Everyone says you're a cold fish, Mr Catchpole," his wife says. "Funny you're so warm in bed" (p. 65). The guard on the heart is lifted, at least momentarily. Here again is a lively, warmhearted girl, a model, a witness in the investigation. She is called not Patty but Patsy, and she is a pleasure to read about. The optimism is washing inexorably in.

So we come to the last book, *A Sort of Virtue*, written under medical sentence of death. It is subtitled *A Political Crime Novel*, something Symons, always concerned by left-wing politics, had long wanted to try. Doing so allowed him to comment on the larger issues, to put forward a harsh but just indictment of his times, and thus to reiterate the theme that had run, more strongly and less, through all his fiction. It is summed up by the epigraph

he used from W. H. Auden: "The General Public has no notion / Of what's behind the scenes." But, more to the fore, is what at last Symons saw was not behind the scenes but, here and there, in the open. A sort of virtue.

This virtue appears in such peripheral characters as the half-honest fence, Moshe Davis, who wears a neat blue blazer and cravat ("the gentleman mask") and says about some young criminals, "They're not like you and me, Mr Catchpole, they're not gentlemen" (p. 85). Symons in the end has used a series hero, the personal authorial voice he drew back from for so long. Catchpole asks to have the words "He had a sort of virtue" (p. 131) put on his tombstone. They are perhaps an acknowledgment of what Symons, who died in Walmer, Kent, on 19 November 1994, came at last to feel might be a hope for our dirty world.

The Critic

Julian Symons was both a longtime newspaper reviewer of crime fiction (as well as novels and works of nonfiction) and author of a number of penetrating critical and critical-biographical books in the crime fiction field. Of these, *Mortal Consequences* (1972) and its several updatings as *Bloody Murder* (its British title) is the most important, a history of the genre from the end of the eighteenth century to 1992, tracing out what Symons saw as the progress of this sort of fiction "from the detective story to the crime novel." It was a pioneering work and may be said to mark the coming-of-age of crime fiction as a genre worthy of the highest consideration. It is, however, as Symons says in his preface to the 1992 edition, "the work of an addict, not an academic." It shines with his enthusiasms and is occasionally clouded by his disappointments and even scorn. These same qualities are to be found in his individual studies, his consideration of Edgar Allan Poe, *The Tell-Tale Heart*, his slight but interesting *Dashiell Hammett* (1985) and, not much less slight but a warm tribute, *Conan Doyle: Portrait of An Artist* (1979).

As a weekly reviewer Symons was without parallel in Britain. (It is almost impossible to compare his work to the different conditions of American reviewing, though Anthony Boucher provides some sort of comparison.) Anthony Berkeley, who was reviewing as "Francis Iles" at much the same period in Britain, came near him but was less acute. Dorothy L. Sayers, who preceded him by some years on the *Sunday Times,* was more flourishingly vigorous but could not rival his rapier stabs of insight and was altogether less judicious. Symons did not hesitate to say what was bad about a book, but he was tellingly exact in saying what was good.

Selected Bibliography

WORKS OF JULIAN SYMONS

MYSTERY FICTION

The Immaterial Murder Case. London: Gollancz, 1945; New York: Macmillan, 1957.

A Man Called Jones. London: Gollancz, 1947.

Bland Beginning. London: Gollancz, 1949; New York: Harper, 1949.

The Thirty-First of February. London: Gollancz, 1950. U.S.: *The 31st of February.* New York: Harper, 1950.

The Broken Penny. London: Gollancz, 1953; New York: Harper, 1953.

The Narrowing Circle. London: Gollancz, 1954; New York: Harper, 1954.

The Paper Chase. London: Collins, 1956. U.S.: *Bogue's Fortune.* New York: Harper, 1957.

The Colour of Murder. London: Collins, 1957; New York: Harper, 1957.

The Gigantic Shadow. London: Collins, 1958. U.S.: *The Pipe Dream.* New York: Harper, 1959.

The Progress of a Crime. London: Collins, 1960; New York: Harper, 1960.

The Killing of Francie Lake. London: Collins, 1962. U.S.: *The Plain Man.* New York: Harper, 1962.

The End of Solomon Grundy. London: Collins, 1964; New York: Harper, 1964.

The Belting Inheritance. London: Collins, 1965; New York: Harper, 1965.

The Man Who Killed Himself. London: Collins, 1967; New York: Harper, 1967.

The Man Whose Dreams Came True. London: Collins, 1968; New York: Harper, 1969.

The Man Who Lost His Wife. London: Collins, 1970; New York: Harper, 1970.

The Players and the Game. London: Collins, 1972; New York: Harper, 1972.

The Plot Against Roger Rider. London: Collins, 1973; New York: Harper, 1973.

A Three-Pipe Problem. London: Collins, 1975; New York: Harper, 1975.

The Blackheath Poisonings. London: Collins, 1978; New York: Harper, 1978.

Sweet Adelaide. London: Collins, 1980; New York: Harper, 1980.

The Detling Murders. London: Macmillan, 1982. U.S.: *The Detling Secret.* New York: Viking, 1983.

The Name of Annabel Lee. London: Macmillan, 1983; New York: Viking, 1983.

The Criminal Comedy of the Contented Couple. London: Macmillan, 1985. U.S.: *A Criminal Comedy.* New York: Viking, 1985.

The Kentish Manor Murders. London: Macmillan, 1988; New York: Viking, 1988.

Death's Darkest Face. London: Macmillan, 1990; New York: Viking, 1990.

Something Like a Love Affair. London, Macmillan, 1992; New York: Mysterious Press, 1993.

Playing Happy Families. London: Macmillan, 1994; New York: Mysterious Press, 1995.

A Sort of Virtue. London: Macmillan, 1996.

OTHER FICTION

The Great Detectives. London: Orbis, 1981; New York: Abrams, 1981. Short stories.

Portraits of the Missing. London: Deutsch, 1991. Imaginary biographies.

NONFICTION

A. J. A. Symons: His Life and Speculations. London: Eyre and Spottiswoode, 1950. With an afterword. London and New York: Oxford University Press, 1986.

Horatio Bottomley. London: Cresset, 1955.

A Reasonable Doubt. London: Cresset, 1960.

Critical Occasions. London: Hamish Hamilton, 1966.

Bloody Murder: From the Detective Story to the Crime Novel. London: Faber, 1972. U.S.: *Mortal Consequences.* New York: Harper, 1972. Rev. ed. published as *Bloody Murder.* London and New York: Viking, 1985; New York: Mysterious Press, 1993.

The Tell-Tale Heart. London: Faber, 1978; New York: Harper, 1978.

Dashiell Hammett. San Diego: Harcourt Brace, 1985.

Conan Doyle: Portrait of an Artist. London: Whizzard, 1979; New York: Mysterious Press, 1988.

EDITED WORKS

Twentieth Century Verse. London, 1937–1939.

The Modern Crime Story. Edinburgh: Tragara, 1980.

ARCHIVES

Manuscript Collection: Humanities Research Center, University of Texas, Austin.

BIBLIOGRAPHY

Walsdorf, John J. *Julian Symons: A Bibliography.* New Castle, Del.: Oak Knoll, 1996.

BIOGRAPHICAL AND CRITICAL STUDIES

Bargainnier, Earl F., ed. *Twelve Englishmen of Mystery.* Bowling Green, Ohio: Bowling Green State University Popular Press, 1984.

Carter, Steven. "Julian Symons and Civilization's Discontents." *Armchair Detective,* January 1979.

Cooper-Clark, Diana. *Designs of Darkness: Interviews with Detective Novelists.* Bowling Green, Ohio: Bowling Green State University Popular Press, 1983.

Craig, Patricia, ed. *Julian Symons at Eighty. A Tribute.* Helsinki: Eurographica, 1992.

Herbert, Rosemary. *The Fatal Art of Entertainment: Interviews with Mystery Writers.* Boston: G. K. Hall, 1994.

Julian Symons Remembered: Tributes from Friends. Council Bluffs, Iowa: Yellow Barn, 1996.

Woodcock, George. "Julian Symons." In *Twentieth-Century Crime and Mystery Writers.* Edited by John M. Reilly. Chicago: St. James, 1991.

JOSEPHINE TEY
(1896?–1952)

ALEXANDRA VON MALOTTKE ROY

JOSEPHINE TEY'S REPUTATION rests primarily on her latter-day investigation of Richard III's alleged murder of the princes in the Tower of London, *The Daughter of Time* (1951), which is regularly listed among the most popular, widely read mystery novels. Tey's conclusions inspired heated controversy and raised significant issues in terms of historical research. Other Tey works have been turned into movies (*A Shilling for Candles*, 1936, and *The Franchise Affair*, 1948) and television specials (*Brat Farrar*, 1949), and Tey's novels remain popular. Although she wrote during the so-called Golden Age of detective fiction, in the company of famous authors such as Agatha Christie and Dorothy L. Sayers, Tey's sensitive characterization and often controversial subject matter set her apart from her contemporaries. Familiar with all levels of English society as well as the arts, she was able, with a few words of dialogue, to delineate individuals and focus their salient characteristics. Frequently, her wit and humor show through as she pokes fun even at herself, as in her portrayal of Miss Easton-Dixon, the writer of fairy tales in *To Love and Be Wise* (1950), who has a lifestyle similar to Tey's.

Although all of her mysteries remain in print, to Tey, these novels were merely "yearly knitting," as she once told John Gielgud. Her true loves were historical dramas and novels, which she wrote under the pseudonym Gordon Daviot. In fact, her obituary in the *Times* of 15 February 1952 devoted three long paragraphs to a discussion of her plays and described her as "best known as a playwright" (Roberts, p. 468). Ironically, although she was best known for her plays during her lifetime, it is her "knitting" that established her reputation.

Life

The author known as Josephine Tey was born Elizabeth Mackintosh on 25 June 1896 (or possibly 1897), in Inverness, Scotland. She was the oldest of three daughters of Josephine Horne Mackintosh, a former teacher, and Colin Mackintosh, a greengrocer. Along with her sisters, she attended the Royal Academy at Inverness. Refusing to go to either the university or art school, she chose to attend the Anstey Physical Training College in Birmingham beginning in 1914. The curriculum was filled with strenuous physical training as well as difficult classes in physiology, psychology, pathology, and physiotherapy. She used her experiences as the basis for her 1946 novel *Miss Pym Disposes*; an incident that occurred during her subsequent career as a physical education teacher provided the method of murder. According to Jessica Mann in *Dead-*

lier Than the Male, Mackintosh was injured when some of her students dropped a gymnasium boom on her face (p. 211); the unpleasant Miss Rouse who receives the much-coveted teaching assignment in *Miss Pym Disposes* is killed in the same way.

Mackintosh taught in schools in both Scotland and England before being called home in 1923 to nurse her mother, who was dying of cancer. Josephine Mackintosh died on 24 June, leaving her daughter Elizabeth to care for the now widowed Colin. Little more is known of Tey's personal life. She was a recluse and did not participate in town activities. A very private, rather shy person, she always avoided the press and photographers. Her amusements apparently revolved around solitary activities such as frequent trips to the movies, reading, fishing, and following the horse races. To keep household duties from becoming too tiresome, she began writing: first a few poems, short stories, and sketches, then two novels, *Kif: An Unvarnished History* and *The Man in the Queue,* both published in 1929 under the name "Gordon Daviot." Apparently, she wished to keep her identity as a writer a secret from her neighbors; Daviot is the name of a village where the Mackintosh family spent happy vacation times during the writer's childhood. In *Kif,* she portrayed a young man who could best be described as an honest rogue, a character type she used again in *Brat Farrar.* Kif's war experiences and his postwar problems, which leave him poor, jobless, and near starvation, reflect his inability to control the circumstances of his life or to master his internal conflicts. The novel is surprisingly contemporary in plot and theme.

The Man in the Queue was her first detective novel. Yet, despite the success of this book (it won the Dutton Mystery Prize), she chose not to publish another mystery novel until 1936. Instead, she concentrated her efforts on the theater. Her first play, which did not reach production, was turned into a novel, *The Expensive Halo* (1931). This was probably Tey's only attempt at writing a love story. Although it was not favorably received as a

novel, it provided her with practice using the doubling motif that appears in *Brat Farrar.* No doubt, she also learned that sentimental love stories did not lend themselves well to her style of writing. The reader can only make assumptions about the lack of a romantic relationship in her life since no information is available. In his foreword to Tey's collected *Plays* (1953), John Gielgud suggests that she may have lost a loved one in World War I, but this is mere speculation (p. x).

In 1932, *Richard of Bordeaux,* starring Gielgud, was produced at the Arts Theatre and later transferred to the New Theatre. This, her most successful play, established the reputation of "Gordon Daviot" as a serious dramatist. Two more of her plays were produced in 1934: *The Laughing Woman,* describing the life of a sculptor, and *Queen of Scots,* a play about the unfortunate Queen Mary, featuring Laurence Olivier. Neither was as successful as *Richard.* Stubborn, strong, and independent, Tey often refused to rewrite any part of her dramas, and because of this obstinancy, some were never produced. When she did rewrite, as in *Queen of Scots,* she blamed the rewrites for the play's modest success.

In all, she wrote ten more full-length plays, thirteen short plays, and seven radio plays. Most of her plays reflect her interest in English and biblical history. Haunted by charges of plagiarism (mentioned by Gielgud in the foreword to *Plays*), she had little faith in her own ability to create unique plots, and her best works have history as a basis.

A Shilling for Candles, published in 1936, was the first novel written under the pseudonym Josephine Tey; she probably did not want the Daviot name, which was connected with the theater, to be associated with the popular mystery genre. ("Josephine Tey" was the name of a Suffolk great-great-grandmother on her mother's side.) But as if the structure of the mystery novel was still too confining, she did not immediately return to it. For the next ten years she continued to write under the Daviot name, and next produced her first and only nonfiction biography,

Claverhouse, published in 1937. Here, the reader can see groundwork being laid for the later *Daughter of Time.* History, Tey believed, had libeled John Graham of Claverhouse, the man who led the rebellion against William of Orange in an effort to return James II to the throne. She portrayed Claverhouse as a clever, diplomatic, and kind person, a victim both of historical lies perpetuated by the church and of flaws in the Scottish character.

Claverhouse was followed by *The Stars Bow Down* (1939), a play based on the biblical story of David, and *Leith Sands,* a radio drama that was performed in 1941. In 1946 "Daviot" published a volume of short plays, *Leith Sands and Other Short Plays.* In the same year, *The Little Dry Thorn,* another biblical play, was performed in April at the Citizens Theatre in Glasgow, and *Valerius,* a play about Roman Britain, was also produced. Both received polite critical attention but were far from the smash hit of *Richard of Bordeaux.* During Tey's entire writing career, six of her plays were produced in London.

By the end of 1946, she had returned both to the Tey pseudonym and to mystery novels. She wrote six out of her eight mysteries in the last six years of her life. Her first novel during this period was *Miss Pym Disposes,* followed by *The Franchise Affair.* In 1949 she published *Brat Farrar,* a novel of doubles and impersonation. *To Love and Be Wise,* a story about transvestism, impersonation, and revenge, followed in 1950. *The Daughter of Time,* which appeared in 1951, is without question Tey's most famous work. The book was published just weeks before her death. Although she had been suffering from cancer for a year, she had bravely kept the fact hidden from her friends and acquaintances, choosing instead to withdraw and endure alone. She spent most of her last year in Scotland but returned to London shortly before her death on 13 February 1952, leaving behind two manuscripts: *The Singing Sands* and *The Privateer.* In 1953, *Plays,* a three-volume collection of the Daviot works, was published with a foreword by John Gielgud.

Mystery Novels

Tey writes about the fragility of reality: Neither people nor situations are what they seem. Appearances are deceptive. Life, Tey seems to say, is illusory. In her novels, people are often impostors, pretending to be what they are not. This reality is inherently lonely, as closeness, when it occurs between two individuals, leads to violent and dangerous excesses, even murder. It is impossible "to love and be wise" in Tey's world. Victims, innocent and guilty alike, lead lonely lives. Furthermore, clues pointing to a criminal are likely to be misinterpreted, resulting in the suffering of an innocent person.

Tey's criminals act from a variety of motives. Some kill out of love: Mrs. Wallis kills to protect her self-centered daughter in *The Man in the Queue,* Leslie Searle plans to avenge her beloved cousin's death in *To Love and Be Wise,* and Beau Nash kills for her best friend in *Miss Pym Disposes.* Not one of these killers receives any serious punishment. Others of Tey's criminals commit crimes that reflect their own self-interest. Her younger criminals often act out of survival instinct, or in the case of Simon Ashby in *Brat Farrar,* pure greed. Lydia Keats (*A Shilling for Candles*), Henry VII (*The Daughter of Time*), and Heron Lloyd (*The Singing Sands*) attempt to preserve or enhance their careers. Tey's criminals, with the exception of Brat, tend to be egoistic, self-centered, and even arrogant, tendencies clearly portrayed in their eyes and faces. Tey firmly believed in the depravity of the criminal mind and seemed to share with Agatha Christie a belief that an individual's personality could be deduced by a careful analysis of his face or handwriting.

The Man in the Queue, initially published under the Gordon Daviot pseudonym but later reissued as a Josephine Tey novel, introduces the character of Inspector Alan Grant. Privately wealthy, well dressed, witty, intelligent, and unmarried, on many counts this new detective fits the stereotype of the classic detective of the Golden Age. Externally, at least, Grant resembles Ngaio Marsh's Roderick Alleyn. However, both Tey's detective and the crimes he investigates are very different from standard Golden Age fiction. Tey focuses on the mechanism of Grant's mind and allows the reader to get inside his confusion and discomfort. Grant is not infallible, and in fact has a regrettable tendency to arrive at the wrong conclusion. (It is possible that Colin Dexter derived the fallible Inspector Morse from Grant.) While Grant appears to be the quintessential detective of the Golden Age, underneath he suffers from nagging self-doubt, basic insecurities, and lack of trust in his own judgments. This is also true of Miss Pym and Brat Farrar, the "detectives" in later novels. Only Robert Blair in *Franchise Affair* escapes the self-critical pain and overdeveloped conscience. All Tey's detectives are honest, sincere, sensitive, very much alone in the world, and prone to snap judgments that are inevitably wrong. Not a one has any personal attachments or serious love relationships.

The Man in the Queue begins in London where people are waiting in line to see a play starring Ray Marcable, a popular, beloved actress. A fat woman protests being crowded, and as she steps away from the offender, he slips to the ground, dead, with a thin dagger in his back. Grant, assigned to the case, discovers that the unidentified victim was carrying a loaded revolver. Grant chauvinistically concludes that the murderer has to be a foreigner, probably a Levantine, since no Englishman would use such a weapon or method of murder. In fact, the murderer is neither male nor foreign, and Grant's spontaneous conclusions, based on intuition rather than deduction, are completely erroneous.

An anonymous letter arrives containing burial money for the unidentified victim and the sender's character is deduced by the handwriting: "Not well off. Not used to writing much. Clean. Smokes. Depressed" (p. 38). The dead man, later identified as a bookmaker named Albert Sorrell, knew Jerry Lamont, a man who resembles a "Levantine." Tey, a devoted follower of horse racing, was apparently well acquainted with bookies and describes

the milieu with great perception. Tey's burgeoning interest in the theater comes through in her descriptions of Ray Marcable, the self-centered, cold, yet appealing actress.

Grant chases the suspect, Jerry Lamont, across London and later follows him to Scotland, indulging in a fishing expedition while waiting for Lamont to emerge from hiding. Lamont is given shelter by a kindly, motherly woman, a character type that reappears in other Tey novels. The chase ends when Grant rescues the injured Lamont from certain death by drowning. Grant, however, begins to doubt Lamont's guilt. Pursuing a series of dead ends, he finally concludes that he should "believe what I see and know, and not what I feel" (p. 209). Suddenly, Mrs. Wallis, the fat woman from the queue, confesses to the crime. Sorrell, a disgruntled former boyfriend of Mrs. Wallis' daughter, Ray Marcable, had planned to murder the actress and then kill himself. Mrs. Wallis, it is predicted, will not be convicted of the crime. She acted from the best of motives, which apparently excuses her crime. Tey closes the novel asking the reader if there was indeed a villain.

Critics generally liked *The Man in the Queue*, but they did balk at the murder method, finding it unlikely that a man could be killed in a crowd with no one noticing. Some complained about the in-depth analyses of Grant's mental processes. Yet, that probing of Grant's reasoning is exactly what accounts for the continued success of the novel.

A Shilling for Candles, published under the new pseudonym Josephine Tey, almost immediately became the basis for a film directed by Alfred Hitchcock (*Young and Innocent*, 1937; released in the United States as *The Girl Was Young*). Critics insisted that the plot was simply a reworking of John Buchan's *The Thirty-Nine Steps*, thus reinforcing Tey's lack of faith in her ability to create original plots. The plot, similar to *The Man in the Queue*, involves an unknown victim, a definite connection with the theater, and an accused but innocent character who is hounded into illness by the misguided Inspector Grant. Again, Tey contrasts appearance and reality. The suspect appears guilty, yet is really a misunderstood victim.

This novel is much more finely tuned, with sharper dialogue and with more of the expected elements of a mystery novel—red herrings, clues, and foreshadowing—it more closely resembles the Golden Age formula.

An unidentified woman's body is discovered on the beach. A young man, Robert Stannaway Tisdall, arrives suddenly and collapses, weeping, although he does not know the victim's name and admits to stealing her car. The victim is Christine Clay, a well-known actress whose death produces no outpouring of grief. Tey also introduces "Jammy" Hopkins, ace reporter, who appears in several other novels and through whose eyes we view the inquest. Tey's ability to easily change point of view involves the reader more deeply in the personalities of the characters, making each one more individualized.

Grant confronts the distraught Tisdall with serious evidence—a button from an overcoat, presumably his, was found tangled in the victim's hair. Tisdall faints and is revived by Erica Burgoyne, the chief constable's daughter. Erica is one of Tey's ingenues—bright, creative, articulate, interesting, and above all intuitive. Like Teresa Desterro in *Miss Pym* and Jane Ashby in *Brat Farrar*, she is capable and honest and has mature insights that one would expect from someone years older. She immediately points out that Tisdall seems incapable of murder, even though he is a very recent beneficiary in Clay's will and seems to be an obvious suspect.

Again, Grant pursues someone who is protected by a kindly female—in this case Erica, who is determined to prove Tisdall innocent. She finds the missing overcoat and Grant must reconsider the case. A prominent psychic, Lydia Keats, announces in a public lecture that she knows the identity of the murderer. A sudden inspiration leads Grant to unearth sufficient evidence to arrest Lydia Keats for murder.

In *A Shilling for Candles*, Grant's personality is even more finely articulated than in his first appearance. Again he is often wrong,

but his tendency to make foolhardy, rash, and even dangerous assumptions makes him seem sympathetic to the reader. The novel's minor characters, such as Miss Pitts, Clay's cook, or Kindness, the head groom employed by Erica's father, are also lifelike. In a distinctive voice, each expresses differing opinions of the situation in a way that provides insights into individual characters as well as the victim and the accused. For example, we understand that Sergeant Williams, who sees Clay as admirable because she is a former factory worker who worked her way up in the world, undoubtedly has similar ambitions.

In *Miss Pym Disposes*, Tey abandons Inspector Grant, at least temporarily. Here the detective is Miss Lucy Pym, a retired French teacher who has written a best-selling book on psychology. Apparently, Tey had as little patience with psychology as she did with historians: the standard psychology books are ridiculed as idiotic, silly, and written in jargon, and Miss Pym's commonsense rebuttal has made her an instant celebrity. No violence occurs until near the end of the novel, and again we discover that the killer, like Mrs. Wallis, will escape without punishment and the murdered person is not the only victim.

The setting for *Miss Pym* is a physical-training institute. Miss Lucy Pym, teaching at the school as a guest lecturer, is naive and kindhearted. She wrongly assumes that the young women she meets at the school are the same. The lovely Mary Innes, Mary's devoted friend Beau Nash, and the unpleasant Miss Rouse are all members of this Eden-like atmosphere. The "Nut Tart," Teresa Desterro, is the only character who recognizes the intense, abnormal pressure of the college. This Eden is really a hell. Henrietta Hodges, the principal, plans to award Rouse the plum teaching assignment that Innes has her hopes set on. While proctoring an exam, Lucy strongly suspects Rouse of cheating. Yet she says nothing, thus beginning a chain of events that leads to murder. Lucy persistently acts out of kindness, which inevitably makes matters worse. When Rouse is discovered seriously injured in the gymnasium, Lucy has two clues persuading her that the "accident," which results in Rouse's death, was indeed murder. She accuses Mary Innes, who makes a stumbling, half confession and agrees to spend the rest of her life atoning for the crime by abandoning her career hopes. Just before leaving the college, Lucy realizes to her horror that Nash, not Innes, murdered Rouse. Noting that Nash's eyes are cold and shallow, Lucy wonders how she could have missed that vital physical clue.

The Franchise Affair, undoubtedly one of Tey's best mystery novels, is based on the eighteenth-century story of Elizabeth Canning, but it offers a very modern explanation for the disappearance of a teenager. Alan Grant reappears in this novel but is relegated to a background role, and the "crime" is really one of perjury, although initially it appears to be kidnapping. The detective, Robert Blair, is a small-town solicitor who falls in love with the accused, a not uncommon situation in mystery novels. Tey, however, underplays the love interest in favor of an in-depth probing of character.

"Franchise" is the name of a dilapidated, ugly house, which serves as the home of Marion Sharpe and her mother. Betty Kane, an attractive fifteen-year-old who had been missing for a month, accuses the Sharpes of kidnapping, imprisoning, and beating her. Regrettably, a newspaper specializing in "sensationalist" journalism picks up the story and all England learns of the girl's accusations. Blair, in an effort to help Marion, to whom he is increasingly attracted, sets out to prove Kane's story wrong. He discovers that the girl, raised by foster parents, is bright, spoiled, and oversexed. Her biological mother was of low moral character. Like mother like daughter, Tey implies.

While Blair tracks down the truth, the town turns into an ugly mob, terrorizing Marion and her mother. Grant is prepared to arrest the women based on the testimony of two witnesses. Fortunately, a hotel keeper in Copenhagen finally identifies Kane as the woman who spent four weeks at the hotel with her "husband," a traveling salesman. The Sharpes are vindicated.

Throughout the novel, the Sharpes, Scotland Yard, and, in fact, nearly everyone involved in the unfortunate situation express a deep hatred toward Kane, and Tey's own attitude toward Betty Kane (and, presumably, the historical Elizabeth Canning) is bitter and angry. The innocent victim is not innocent at all but a lying, conniving little trollop. She merely impersonates an abused teenager. Once again, the appearance is not the reality. The true victims are the Sharpes, who suffer horribly and whose pain can never be redressed. The perjury of the ingenue causes great agony for the older mature women.

In a Tey novel, the suspects are almost always the real victims, innocents who are persecuted wrongly and who suffer physically as well as emotionally. Murder victims are only moderately important. In fact, in two novels, the murders occurred in the distant past, and in two others, no murder occurs at all. Sometimes the supposed victims are in fact the criminal perpetrators. However, nearly everyone in a Tey novel suffers, with perhaps the exception of self-centered actresses and writers. Frequently, the detective, in spite of his or her own personal agony over the situation, causes the suffering of others. Grant harasses two suspects into illness, and Lucy Pym contributes to the suffering of an innocent and the freedom of the murderer. The cruelty of society causes pain as well. Marion Sharpe loses her home and possessions, probably due to arson. Even Richard III, as Tey points out, has suffered extremely through the loss of his good name in historical accounts. In all, innocence has been gravely victimized, a situation that society cannot and does not remedy.

Brat Farrar, another novel without Inspector Grant, continues the theme of impersonation. The main character is unusual—he is a criminal, an impostor come to swindle a family whom Tey characterizes as likable and sympathetic. Yet the reader becomes interested not so much in the crime as in the impostor, hoping that he emerges from the situation with at least some modicum of dignity and perhaps only a minor criminal record. (Again, Tey's influence on other writers is evident; Patricia Highsmith's amoral hero Tom Ripley appears derived from Brat.)

The motherly female character this time plays a more significant role. Aunt Bee has nurtured her brother's children, including two sets of twins. The oldest male child, logical heir to the family fortune, died. The complications involved with two sets of twins and an identical distant cousin is the sort of material so loved by Shakespeare for his comedies. However, here the results are far from comic. Patrick, the dead twin, had been kind and good and died an apparent suicide, his body never found. Simon Ashby, the survivor, is selfish and dangerous, a vicious enemy when aroused. Brat had been a foundling, with his sense of identity formed by working with horses. When approached to impersonate the dead Patrick, the lure of inheriting the family horse farm persuades him to accept. As Brat becomes increasingly involved in the affairs of the family, he begins to investigate the death of Patrick. He learns that Simon did indeed murder his twin. In a struggle between Simon and Brat, Simon is injured and, as a result, eventually dies. Uncle Charles later identifies Brat as the obvious offspring of cousin Walter. All ends happily enough, with Brat convalescing; Eleanor, the only nontwin, resolving to marry him; and Uncle Charles in charge of the family fortunes.

Brat Farrar was a critical and technical success for Tey. In this novel of doubling, Tey analyzes her characters by presenting them in terms of their opposites. Simon is wicked; Patrick was good. Brat is a combination of both. He may be a criminal impostor, but he is nonetheless likable and genuine in many respects. Jane and Ruth, the other twins, are versions of the ingenues Erica Burgoyne and Teresa Desterro—opposite types, yet both totally appealing. Another sort of contrast is manifested in the fact that Tey has George Peck, the rector, destroy evidence—although having a religious person closely involved in the resolution of a crime belongs to a long and honorable tradition that includes authors like Agatha Christie and Emma Lathen.

To Love and Be Wise deals with the theme of transvestism. Inspector Grant returns, as-

sisted by his friend, but not lover, Marta Hallard. At a party, Grant meets Leslie Searle, a handsome photographer who somehow makes most people feel uneasy. Tey makes full use of her theatrical experiences by portraying creative characters with wit and humor. Walter, a popular radio commentator, is quite taken with Searle, as is his fiancée, Liz. Throughout, Tey hints that something is "wrong" about Searle who, after an argument with Walter, disappears, never to be seen again. Grant, ignoring his instincts, jumps to the wrong conclusions. Ultimately, after many false clues, Lee (Leslie) Searle admits to impersonating a man. Her motives were twofold; she found more artistic freedom, and she could exact revenge for her cousin's suicide, which she assumed was caused by Walter's insensitive actions. Discovering the selfish personality of her beloved cousin, she abandons the plan and resumes her previous identity.

Critics were not kind to this novel, and it is frequently ignored in favor of *The Daughter of Time*. Yet, again, Tey has provided us with a work that has contemporary overtones. Lee Searle, realizing early in her career that it offers limited opportunities for a woman, disguises herself as a man. Her transvestism is suspected only in terms of feeling "uncomfortable" in his/her presence. Furthermore, Tey strongly hints at homosexual relationships between Searle and her cousin Marguerite and between a playwright, Toby Tullis, and a male dancer, Serge Ratoff. Same-sex relationships, she seems to imply, are so intense and involve so much devotion that it is impossible "to love and be wise." Beau Nash's devotion to Innes in *Miss Pym Disposes* is another example of intense love that results in murder. Tey never portrays this sort of concentrated devotion in a male-female relationship.

In 1951, shortly before her death, Tey published *The Daughter of Time*, her most popular and also her most controversial work. Favorably received by the critics at first, the novel has recently been both attacked and defended with great passion. Tey has been accused of writing a bad novel as well as a poor summary of history. Defenders of the novel note that she anticipates Paul Murray Kendall in his 1955 biographical approach to Richard III, placing emphasis not just on recorded evidence, but on the investigator's evaluation of human character and responses. The theme was one of her favorites: Richard III was a misunderstood individual defamed by Shakespeare and historians. She explores the idea in *Richard of Bordeaux* and in the play *Dickon* (1953), where he is portrayed as a firm, compassionate, loving victim who was cruelly betrayed, and even alludes to his innocence in *Miss Pym Disposes.*

The Daughter of Time is not a historical research paper, nor is it an unrestrained attack on historians. Tey questions interpretation of events, a variant of the appearance-versus-reality theme present in her other works. Searching original sources (including some that Tey herself invents for the novel), Inspector Grant comes to conclusions that challenge those of traditional history. This is hardly surprising, as a police detective's view of evidence would differ from that of most traditional historians. Tey believed history was often rewritten to suit current beliefs and prejudices. In *The Daughter of Time,* she focuses on personal interpretations of history—appearance—as opposed to what actually occurred—reality. Dilys Winn comments; "Grant's reconstruction of events is not only plausible, but so highly probable that *Daughter of Time* has been used in university history courses" (p. 96).

In *Daughter of Time,* Grant is confined to a hospital bed because of an injury incurred in the line of duty. Cranky and bored, he is intrigued by pictures of historical personages brought to him by his friend Marta Hallard. Richard III, Grant thinks, was a man who suffered greatly, a man whose main fault was that of being too kind. The portrait upon which Grant bases his opinion is in the British Museum and does indeed show a sad man. Since villains, after all, do not suffer, it is unlikely that Richard was guilty of murdering his two nephews in the Tower of London, or so Grant reasons, in a fashion that once again reflects Tey's insistence that psychological characteristics are mirrored in the face: Richard III simply does not "look" like a murderer. With the help of Brent Carradine, an American who acts as a research assistant, Grant determines that Richard was slandered and that, from a police point of view at least, no case against him existed. After determining that Henry VII was, in all likelihood, the murderer, Grant and Carradine are somewhat dismayed to discover that the theory is not a new one.

The Daughter of Time breaks all the rules of detective fiction. Action as such does not exist; the conflict is primarily between Grant and historians who are not present. Richard's character is portrayed through description and inference, not action and dialogue. Here Grant does not assume the guilt of an innocent person, nor does he so blatantly mistrust his instincts. In her reconstruction of events, Tey expresses her distrust of the press, past and present, as well as her distaste for "tonypandy," the term she uses to describe events that are reported historically but that either never took place or that occurred in a far different manner. She questions the reliability of "hearsay" evidence as well as accepting historical assumptions as correct. By combining history and detection, Tey presents us with her real thesis: history is as much a matter of personal perception as it is of written records. People view events through their own systems of belief, through the hearsay evidence of others, and through the filtering lens of the governing elements, all of which can distort the facts.

Manuscripts for *The Singing Sands* and *The Privateer* were discovered among Tey's papers after her death. She did not complete the final editing of either, and thus some weaknesses are present. Nonetheless, *The Privateer,* a fictional study and vindication of Henry Morgan, a well-known pirate, stands out as one of her most suspenseful, colorful works. Significantly, Morgan is a man with a loyal, loving wife and devoted friends for whom he would happily sacrifice himself. Tey, suffering and alone in the final stages of cancer, must have quietly yearned for this sense of devotion and community.

The Singing Sands again features Alan Grant, but this time, instead of a physical injury, he is suffering from emotional strain, nearing a breakdown, as evidenced by extreme claustrophobia. A train trip to his cousin's to recuperate provides Grant with the sort of medicine he needs. At first, he walks away from the discovery of a body on the train. Later, he finds an odd verse tucked in the newspaper he had inadvertently picked up and which clearly belonged to the dead man. Following clues in the poem, Grant begins to track the real solution to the murder across the Highlands of Scotland. Although he again makes the wrong conclusions, he eventually discovers that the victim was a pilot who had discovered an important historic ruin in Arabia, and the murderer is a vain explorer who wished to take sole credit for the find.

The Singing Sands is notable not only for its descriptions of the Scottish Highlands and the Hebrides, as well as the urban landscapes of Marseilles, London, and Paris, but also for its characterization. The focus is on Grant and, later, on Heron Lloyd, the murderer; women, who in previous novels had played significant and central roles, are in this novel relegated to the background. Grant's cousin provides a brief moment of comfort, Zoë Kentallen a very brief flirtation, and Marta Hallard a quick meal. No ingenue is involved.

In this last Grant novel, Tey reiterates her familiar themes of criminal vanity and the inaccuracies of assumptions: For instance, Grant assumes the poem describes Scotland; in fact, it refers to a ruin in the Arabian desert. Kenrick, the most likable of Tey's murder victims, is assumed dead from alcohol when in fact he was murdered. And again, Tey deals with doubles, most notably the dead man, who is at first assumed to be a French mechanic because of his misleading identification.

Conclusions

Tey's plots are uncomplicated and can generally be condensed into a few short sentences.

In only three of the novels are corpses discovered at the very beginning. In others, the crimes are old, while two novels deal instead with perjury and transvestism. Her breaks with traditional Golden Age detective novels are thus clear.

Tey's female characters can be classified into rather tidy little groups. The adults are unmarried and happy in that state; some have career obligations and others are "motherly" and protect or care for weak males, another of Tey's favorite character types. The talented and sophisticated actress, self-centered, more than a bit cold, and devoted to her career, appears frequently, as does the kindly, supportive woman—who plays a lesser role and in later novels becomes a kindly aunt or meticulous spinster. The male characters are often in need of care. They have the potential to love, but prefer to go fishing. Others are self-centered and cruel.

Catherine Aird has said that Tey "gave us a very real world, a world in which the reader can believe" (p. 62)—perhaps it is a world that somewhat reflects Tey's personal experiences caring for her father and working with people in the theater. No modern mystery writer would argue the importance of Tey's contributions to the craft. Her plots are not twisted, intricate affairs, but her characters stand out as memorable, carefully drawn individuals who are often delineated with a few words of dialogue. Her training in the theater influenced her style as well as the structure of her works. Furthermore, her focus on the conscience of the detective, the doubts, the anxieties, and the wrong conclusions, makes her writing more influential today than at the time of her death.

Selected Bibliography

WORKS OF JOSEPHINE TEY

A Shilling for Candles: The Story of a Crime. London: Methuen, 1936; New York: Macmillan, 1954.
Miss Pym Disposes. London: Davies, 1946; New York: Macmillan, 1948.

The Franchise Affair. London: Davies, 1948; New York: Macmillan, 1949.

Brat Farrar. London: Davies, 1949; New York: Macmillan, 1950. Published as *Come and Kill Me.* New York: Pocket Books, 1951.

To Love and Be Wise. London: Davies, 1950; New York: Macmillan, 1951.

The Daughter of Time. London: Davies, 1951; New York: Macmillan, 1952.

The Singing Sands. London: Davies, 1952; New York: Macmillan, 1953.

Three by Tey. New York: Macmillan, 1954. Contains *Miss Pym Disposes, The Franchise Affair, Brat Farrar.*

WORKS OF GORDON DAVIOT

NOVELS

The Man in the Queue. London: Methuen, 1929; New York: Dutton, 1929. Later published under the name "Josephine Tey" as *The Killer in the Crowd.* New York: Spivak, 1954.

Kif: An Unvarnished History. London: Benn, 1929; New York: Appleton, 1929.

The Expensive Halo. London: Benn, 1931; New York: Appleton, 1931.

The Privateer. London: Davies, 1952; New York: Macmillan, 1952.

STAGE PLAYS

Richard of Bordeaux. London: Gollancz, 1933; Boston: Little, Brown, 1933. First produced in London, 1932.

Queen of Scots. London: Gollancz, 1934. First produced in London, 1934.

The Laughing Woman. London: Gollancz, 1934. First produced in London, 1934.

The Stars Bow Down. London: Duckworth, 1939. First produced in Malvern, Worcestershire, 1939.

The Little Dry Thorn. In *Plays I.* London: Davies, 1953. First produced in London, 1947.

Valerius. In *Plays I.* London: Davies, 1953. First produced in London, 1948.

Dickon. In *Plays I.* London: Davies, 1953. First produced in Salisbury, 1955.

Sweet Coz. In *Plays 3.* London: Davies, 1954. First produced in Farnham, Surrey, 1956.

BIOGRAPHY

Claverhouse. London: Collins, 1937.

COLLECTED WORKS

Leith Sands and Other Shorts Plays. London: Duckworth, 1946. Includes *The Three Mrs. Madderleys, Mrs. Fry Has a Visitor, Remember Caesar, Rahab, The Mother of Masé, Sara, Clarion Call.*

Plays. 3 vols. London: Davies, 1953–1954. Includes the radio plays *Leith Sands* (broadcast in 1941), *Mrs. Fry Has a Visitor* (1944), *Remember Caesar* (1946), *The Three Mrs. Madderleys* (1944), *The Pen of My Aunt* (1950), *The Pomp of Mr. Pomfret* (1954), and *Cornelia* (1955).

BIOGRAPHICAL AND CRITICAL STUDIES

Aird, Catherine. "Josephine Tey." *The Armchair Detective,* 2: 156–157 (1968–1969).

——. "The Irreproachable Miss Tey." In *Murderess Ink.* Edited by Dilys Winn. New York: Workman, 1979. Pp. 61–62.

Arndt, Frances. "Josephine Tey." In *British Women Writers: A Critical Reference Guide.* Edited by Janet Todd. New York: Continuum, 1989. Pp. 661–662.

Aydelotte, William O. "The Detective Story as a Historical Source." In *The Mystery Writer's Art.* Edited by Francis M. Nevins. Bowling Green, Ohio: Bowling Green State University Popular Press, 1971. Pp. 306–325.

Blain, Virginia, et al., eds. "Josephine Tey." In *The Feminist Companion to Literature in English: Women Writers from the Middle Ages to the Present.* New Haven, Conn.: Yale University Press, 1990.

Bloom, Harold, ed. "Josephine Tey." In *Modern Mystery Writers.* New York: Chelsea House, 1995. Pp. 188–201.

Charney, Hanna. *The Detective Novel of Manners: Hedonism, Morality, and the Life of Reason.* Rutherford, N.J.: Fairleigh Dickinson University Press, 1981.

Davis, Dorothy Salisbury. "On Josephine Tey." *New Republic,* 20 September 1954: 17.

Furr, Grover. "Richard the Third and Stalin." 2 February 1996. Available at http://www.shss.montclair.edu/english/furr/rich3rd.html

Huttar, Charles A. "Elizabeth Mackintosh." In *An Encyclopedia of British Women Writers.* Edited by Paul Schlueter and June Schlueter. New York: Garland, 1988. Pp. 303–304.

Kendall, Paul Murray. *Richard the Third.* London: Allen & Unwin, 1955; New York: W. W. Norton, 1956.

Klein, Kathleen Gregory. "Josephine Tey." In *St. James Guide to Crime and Mystery Writers,* 4th ed. Edited by Jay P. Pederson. Detroit, Mich.: St. James Press, 1996.

——. "Josephine Tey." In *Twentieth-Century Crime and Mystery Writers.* Edited by John M. Reilly. New York: St. Martin's Press, 1985. Pp. 838–839.

Kunitz, Stanley, ed. "Elizabeth Mackintosh." In *Twentieth-Century Authors: A Biographical Dictionary of Modern Literature.* 1st supp. New York: H. W. Wilson, 1955. Pp. 620–621.

Mann, Jessica. "Josephine Tey." In her *Deadlier Than the Male.* New York: Macmillan, 1981. Pp. 210–217.

Morris, Virginia B. "Josephine Tey." In *British Mystery Writers, 1920–1939.* Edited by Bernard Benstock and

Thomas F. Staley. Detroit, Mich.: Gale, 1989. Pp. 284–296.

Pronzini, Bill, and Marcia Muller. *1001 Midnights: The Aficionado's Guide to Mystery and Detective Fiction.* New York: Arbor House, 1986. Pp. 777–779.

Roberts, Frank C., comp. *Obituaries from the* Times, *1951–1960.* Westport, Conn.: Meckler Books, 1979.

Rollyson, Carl E., Jr. "The Detective as Historian: Josephine Tey's *The Daughter of Time.*" *Iowa State Journal of Research* 53, no. 1 (August 1978): 21–30.

———. "Josephine Tey." In *Critical Survey of Mystery and Detective Fiction.* Edited by Frank N. Magill. Pasadena, Calif.: Salem Press, 1988.

Roy, Sandra. *Josephine Tey.* Boston: Twayne, 1980.

Simpson, Penny. "An Appreciation: Josephine Tey's Mystery Novel *The Daughter of Time.*" 1995. Available at http://www.sfu.ca/~psimpson/Tey.htm.

Smith, M. J. "Controversy: Townsend, Tey, and Richard III: A Rebuttal." *The Armchair Detective,* October 1977. Pp. 317–319.

Steinbrunner, Chris, and Otto Penzler, eds. "Josephine Tey." In *Encyclopedia of Mystery and Detection.* New York: McGraw Hill, 1976. Pp. 384–385.

Stewart, Ralph. "Richard III, Josephine Tey, and Some Uses of Rhetoric." *Clues* 12: 93–95 (spring/summer 1991).

Talburt, Nancy Ellen. "Josephine Tey." In *Ten Women of Mystery.* Edited by Earl F. Bargainnier. Bowling Green, Ohio: Bowling Green State University Popular Press, 1981. Pp. 42–76.

Townsend, Guy M. "Richard III and Josephine: Partners in Crime." *The Armchair Detective* 10: 211–224 (summer 1977).

Vickers, Anita Marissa. "Josephine Tey." In *Great Women Mystery Writers, Classic to Contemporary.* Edited by Kathleen Gregory Klein. Westport, Conn.: Greenwood Press, 1994. Pp. 332–335.

Winn, Dilys, ed. "Once upon a Crime." In *Murder Ink.* New York: Workman, 1984. P. 96.

S. S. VAN DINE
(1887–1939)

JOHN LOUGHERY

THE AUTHOR OF some of the most popular detective novels of his era—*The Benson Murder Case* (1926), *The "Canary" Murder Case* (1927), and ten other books featuring the erudite sleuth Philo Vance—S. S. Van Dine was, by any standard, an unlikely candidate for the important role he played in American popular culture during the Jazz Age and the Great Depression. The man credited with revitalizing a genre of questionable reputation in the United States (and long dominated by British authors), whose achievement paved the way for more durable talents such as Rex Stout and Dashiell Hammett, Van Dine in his youth scorned detective stories as making "their strongest appeal to children, divinity students, savages, stenographers, and other people of inferior intelligence and faulty education" (*Los Angeles Times*, 8 August 1909). A book reviewer for the *Los Angeles Times*, he wrote, "The woods are full of detective stories—most of them bad. In fact, any serious detective story is of necessity bad. It appeals to the most primitive cravings within us" (28 August 1910). This aesthete with little tolerance for mass entertainment was the same individual whose mysteries sold more than one million copies between 1927 and 1930, a writer credited by his editor, Max Perkins, with helping to keep Scribners afloat in the first months after the stock market crash. Indeed, the story of S. S. Van Dine's metamor-phosis from "highbrow" art critic and literary editor to best-selling novelist is as interesting as the crime solving of his sleuth and his romantic depictions of Manhattan in the age of the flapper and the speakeasy.

Early Days: Aspirations to Greatness

"S. S. Van Dine" was born of economic necessity in 1926, a last-ditch effort to salvage a floundering career. Willard Huntington Wright—the man behind the famous pseudonym—was born on 15 October 1887 in Charlottesville, Virginia. Typical of his snobbish values, already in place by adolescence, Wright referred to his birth in the South as "an unfortunate accident." A more suitable starting point for the genius he envisioned himself to be would have been New York City, the London of Oscar Wilde, or Guy de Maupassant's Paris. But Virginia it was, where Wright was raised first in Charlottesville and later in Lynchburg, before his parents, Archibald Davenport Wright and Annie Van Vranken—hotel proprietors—moved with their two sons, Willard and Stanton, to California at the time of the turn-of-the-century land boom.

As precocious boys and as hotel children, Willard and Stanton Wright lived a privileged life. This was entirely appropriate, in the eyes of their indulgent parents, because the children's gifts had been evident from the start: Stanton as an artist (he later became one of America's first abstract painters and a major presence in the art world of southern California) and Willard as a writer. Devouring the works of Honoré de Balzac, Charles Baudelaire, Arthur Rimbaud, and Wilde in their teens and getting into a fair amount of mischief with the law, the Wright brothers walked the beaches of Santa Monica outside their father's hotel and contemplated a future that would take them far from the middle-class expectations of their neighbors and peers.

The path to greatness in the arts was not a smooth one for either young man, however. Stanton had the good sense to marry a woman of wealth, at the age of eighteen, and to decamp for the studios of Montmartre and a course of self-study at the Louvre. Willard Wright's route to fame and fortune was more circuitous. Bouncing from school to school, Wright finally talked his way into Harvard in 1906, where he studied psychology with the brilliant Hugo Münsterberg and composition with Charles Townsend Copeland, whose pupils in that decade included T. S. Eliot, Walter Lippmann, and John Dos Passos. Before his expulsion the next year for failure to attend those classes he considered unworthy of his time, Wright discovered in Boston a milieu that appealed to him as more cosmopolitan than anything he had known in Santa Monica. The world of poets, museums, theaters, cafés, and brothels was for him, he told his parents upon his return to California, and his goal thenceforth was to establish himself in the east as a major presence in urban artistic circles. En route home, Wright met an impoverished young woman, Katharine Belle Boynton, in Seattle who was appropriately taken with his Byronic aura, and—with characteristic impetuosity—he married her on 13 July 1907 after a scant two weeks' acquaintance.

Wright senior attempted to set his wayward elder son up in business, but his best efforts did not amount to much. Willard Huntington Wright had no flair for sales or real estate and promised, at the age of twenty, to be a perpetual drain on his father's finances. The incompatibility of the newlyweds and the unplanned birth of a daughter the next year complicated an already awkward situation. Only a chance meeting with a reporter for the *Los Angeles Times* rescued Wright from the menial jobs he was forced to take to support his wife and child. Trading on his alleged Harvard education, he was hired as a book reviewer and occasional features writer. It was a good match: Harrison Gray Otis' paper, one of the most commanding and vitriolic publications in the state, appreciated strong opinions and strong language. Wright assured his editor that he could provide both.

Making use of George Bernard Shaw's observation that the critic who is modest is lost, Wright threw himself into his new life as a literary journalist with all the energy and ego he could muster. Within a few months of taking up his post at the *Times*, he was reviewing dozens of books a month in a scathing and often comic style and with a self-confidence that belied his age and lack of a college degree. Hallowed reputations meant nothing to him: Charles Dickens was a purveyor of "bourgeois humor" and Horace Walpole no more than "a superficial poseur." Best-sellers like Booth Tarkington and Mrs. Humphrey Ward were beneath contempt, politically minded novelists on the order of Upton Sinclair and Charlotte Perkins Gilman were lambasted as tired propagandists, and even local heroes such as Ambrose Bierce and Gertrude Atherton were picked apart for their "cacophonies of style" and intellectual bankruptcy. It was the probity of Theodore Dreiser, Frank Norris, and Stephen Crane; the dramatic innovations of Henrik Ibsen, Maxim Gorky, and August Strindberg; and the poetic vision of J. M. Synge, Arthur Schnitzler, and Hermann Sudermann that appealed to Wright and whose virtues his columns regularly extolled. Described by a colleague as "the most uncompromising and zealous literary critic the West ever saw . . . [a man who] had all the local authors scared to come out from under the bed" (*Los Angeles Times*, 18 March 1931), Wright used the largest-circulation paper in southern

924

California as his bully pulpit, preaching a gospel of modern realism, aesthetic rigor, and disdain for all commercialization.

Much as he liked to think of himself as sui generis, Wright had certain worthy models to ponder and emulate. Beginning in the 1890s, James Gibbons Huneker and Percival Pollard made names for themselves as advocates of the best of the new European literature and music. California poet and playwright John McGroarty believed in the critic's mission to advance America's cultural coming-of-age and welcomed Wright's contributions to his art nouveau journal, the *West Coast Magazine*, in the form of essays on "The Sex Impulse in Art" and "Estheticism and Unmorality." Most influential of all, however, was a Baltimore journalist only seven years older than Wright whose columns were as clever and strategically irreverent as anything ever seen in American journalism. In H. L. Mencken, Willard Wright recognized a kindred spirit as well as a potential mentor, and their friendship—based on a desire to rile the bourgeoisie as much as their shared passion for Friedrich Nietzsche and Dreiser—was to be one of the most meaningful relationships Wright ever enjoyed. In fact, it was through Mencken that Wright was finally able, in 1912, to make the transition from "West Coast bad boy" to East Coast mover and shaker. The trendy Manhattan magazine the *Smart Set* was in need of a new editor in chief. Mencken, the *Smart Set*'s book reviewer, had no intention of leaving Baltimore for New York, he told the publisher who offered him the position, but he knew exactly the right man for the job—arrogant and ambitious, but discerning, erudite, and ready for new challenges.

From the *Smart Set* to the Birth of Philo Vance

In many ways, Wright's year at the helm of the *Smart Set* was a replay of his year at Harvard. Caught up in the excitement of life in a major city and thrilled by the daily contact with intellectually stimulating people, he became almost antagonistic to practical considerations. Exceeding his publisher's goals, Wright decided that the *Smart Set* would be a vehicle for the raising of American journalism to new heights and the emancipation of American literature. He solicited daring new fiction from Theodore Dreiser and Floyd Dell, poetry from William Butler Yeats and Ezra Pound, and essays from James Gibbons Huneker and H. L. Mencken. Paying no attention to the magazine's ledgers or to subscribers' anxieties about how many stories in the monthly periodical dealt with sexual themes, Wright pursued his own course. Warnings from his nervous publisher went unheeded. Having traveled east sans wife and child, the twenty-five-year-old literary editor was too busy having a good time and fashioning a reputation as a bon vivant and eligible bachelor. As a friend of Mencken's, the writer Ernest Boyd, noted, "[Wright looked] as if he had just left the Café de la Paix . . . a Right-Bank American, if ever there was one." He also accurately observed that Wright was a man who "made no appeal to the affections, save those of certain members of the opposite sex." In the end, Boyd later summarized, Wright was "the most interesting and attractive unlikable man I have ever met" (p. 8).

Wright was fired from the *Smart Set*, to no one's surprise but his own, in January 1914, but not before he had wrangled from his employer an all-expense-paid trip to Europe, ostensibly to find material for the magazine but in reality to reunite with his brother, Stanton, and learn more about what was happening in painting and sculpture on the eve of World War I. In the following months, Stanton became for Willard the same kind of guide in the visual arts that Mencken had been in the fields of journalism and cultural criticism. The result of the brothers' intellectual collaboration was a landmark in art criticism: *Modern Painting: Its Tendency and Meaning*, published in 1915. In this influential (if idiosyncratic) tome, Willard Wright discussed modern art as a form of creativity evolving away from its roots in illustration, praised the investigations of Paul Cézanne and Henri Matisse, and predicted the coming ascendancy of abstract painting, in particular, the school of painting Stanton had developed, a style of color abstraction known as "synchromism."

The next few years were both an ecstatic and an excruciating time for Wright. Back in New York, following the German invasion of France, he curated exhibitions of the new painting styles he believed in; wrote some of the best art criticism of his day; co-authored a witty travel book with Mencken, *Europe After 8:15* (1914); and published an autobiographical novel, *The Man of Promise* (1916). His volume of aesthetic philosophy, *The Creative Will* (1916), was lauded by William Faulkner as one of the most thought-provoking books on the creative life he had ever read, and the anthology of Nietzsche's writings Wright edited, *What Nietzsche Taught* (1915), was recognized as an important educational text. The problem was that none of these endeavors made much money. Wright's debts accumulated, and he found himself living in genteel poverty. His circumstances became more dire during those periods when various drug addictions acquired in Europe—to marijuana, opium, and heroin—got the better of him. By 1917 Mencken, Dreiser, and other friends had become wary of their former colleague. His fits of temper, tall tales, and requests for loans he was in no position to repay were too numerous.

The coup de grace took place six months after the United States had entered the war in Europe. A Germanophile in his tastes in literature and music, Wright was never able to take seriously the Allied cause or the hyperpatriotic fervor that gripped the country after President Wilson's declaration of war in April 1917. Some undiplomatic remarks led to accusations of spying for the Kaiser, which made the headlines, and Wright found himself blackballed by every newspaper and magazine editor in the east in the autumn of 1917. He suffered a nervous breakdown and returned to California in disgrace. There he was supported by his widowed mother and nursed back to health by the wife he had not seen in years, both of whom he abandoned once again as soon as he was on his feet and able to head east. In the east, however, Wright was nothing more than a has-been whom critic Edmund Wilson referred to in 1925 as "a man who once gave the impression of being someone important." In art and publishing circles, no one in New York expected ever to hear from him again.

Wright had other plans, though. If America would not support a cultural commentator or take him seriously as an art or book critic, he determined he would make it on just those terms his homeland seemed to understand best: as an icon of popular culture. For a period of three years, while barely keeping ahead of the loan sharks and other irate creditors, Wright devoted himself to the study of detective fiction. Aided by two friends—Jacob Lobsenz, his doctor, and Norbert Lederer, a chemist by vocation and criminologist by avocation—Wright overcame his antipathy to the genre as a waste of time for serious thinkers. His experiment in "light reading" soon turned into a binge and ultimately, in Wright's usual manner, an obsession. H. C. Bailey, Eden Phillpotts, Arthur Conan Doyle, Ronald Knox, R. Austin Freeman, A. E. Fielding, J. S. Fletcher, Arthur Morrison, A. E. W. Mason: the authors Wright was drawn to were a varied, largely British, group, though he also devoured the complete works of Émile Gaboriau and Gaston Leroux, the Jacques Futrelle stories, and all the novels of Anna Katharine Green—in short, anything that was readable, talked about, and available in Lederer's vast private library.

In its initial stages, Wright's plan to write detective fiction of his own was a secret he wanted to keep from both family and friends. He worried about attempting something blatantly commercial and then falling short of the level of success he craved. His greatest fear was that he would be the same failure as a popular novelist that he felt he had been as an intellectual and aesthete. Wright was also nervous about the reactions of those former associates who had not abandoned the world of high culture—Alfred Stieglitz and Georgia O'Keeffe, George Jean Nathan, Mencken,

Dreiser, and especially his brother, Stanton. In time, however, his clandestine project took an unexpected turn. Wright became fascinated with the conventions and possibilities of a genre he had once derided, just as he became convinced that he could write a series of books that would be as original as anything yet published. The use of a pseudonym—"S. S. Van Dine"—promised some measure of protection should his plan fail.

In the first weeks of 1926, Wright was ready to emerge from his self-imposed exile and try his luck. He approached an old Harvard acquaintance, the already legendary Scribners editor Max Perkins, with plot outlines for three novels, which would be published at one-year intervals—the Benson, the "Canary," and the Greene murder cases, as he called them. Although not a great reader of detective novels himself, Perkins had the feeling that Wright was proposing a kind of fiction that might appeal to the new mass readership of the 1920s, an audience that no longer found Dreiser shocking and readily accepted a more amoral, or less sanctimonious, postwar ethos. Certainly he recognized that, in Philo Vance, Wright had created a sleuth as distinctive as Sherlock Holmes or Hercule Poirot. The smugness and erudition of this connoisseur-detective were a little overdone, some of the staff at Scribners felt, and the suggestion was broached that Vance's more outlandish mannerisms and exclamations might be toned down. Wright's reply was succinct. There was no need for Philo Vance to be likable, he explained. That never really mattered. It was enough—it was everything—that he should be modern and memorable.

Reinvigorating the Genre

American detective fiction was not a particularly strong commodity in the mid-1920s, neither intellectually nor commercially. The genre may have originated in the United States, with Edgar Allan Poe, but few American writers had kept pace with their British counterparts in devising effective tales of mystery, crime, and detection. Quality detective stories by native writers published between Reconstruction and World War I were few and far between. Anna Katharine Green's barrage of novels in the 1880s and 1890s, like the later works of Melville Davisson Post or Mary Roberts Rinehart, was more the exception than the rule. For ingenious plots, entertaining sleuths, and at least a modicum of craft in the writing, readers on this side of the Atlantic looked to the British. Hackwork was expected from the Americans, not great flair or originality.

Moreover, the form was not yet considered entirely respectable. Wright's own fulminations against the genre in the pages of the *Los Angeles Times* ("any serious detective story is of necessity bad") were perhaps more extreme than most, but the stigma of quasi-literacy, of low-level escapism, was an ongoing problem. The Philo Vance novels appeared at the right moment to help change that perception. It was Willard Huntington Wright's achievement to legitimize detective fiction in the minds of many Americans, even as he opened doors for others who surpassed him in talent and popularity.

One element of the appeal that the first three S. S. Van Dine novels held for readers in the 1920s was their highly contemporary, even topical, feel. Even though Wright's sleuth cultivated the aura of a fin de siècle aesthete—a Wildean dandy—the city outside his East Thirty-eighth Street apartment was relentlessly energetic and immediately recognizable. The speakeasies, gambling dens, restaurants, and art galleries Philo Vance alludes to, or visits, were actual landmarks of the day, and the real-life spirit of urban indulgence and moneymaking was all-pervasive. Equally important to the sense of authenticity, for his first two stories Wright used unsolved crimes of recent memory. The plot of *The Benson Murder Case* was based on the Joseph Elwell murder of 1920, in which a wealthy stockbroker and noted bridge player was found shot to death in his locked brownstone with no signs of forcible entry. *The "Ca-*

nary" *Murder Case* brought to mind the 1923 death of Dorothy King, the "Broadway Butterfly," a promiscuous beauty with expensive tastes and dangerous boyfriends. The third book, *The Greene Murder Case* (1928), was not based on an actual crime, but it evoked the world of Old New York that was quickly fading from view. A family torn apart by sibling rivalry, the Greenes inhabit one of the pseudo-Gothic mansions on the East River that still existed in the 1920s—a potent reminder of the new Gotham in the making.

Intricate plots and clever banter were other factors in the popularity of the Van Dine series, but the method of deduction, described by Philo Vance in the first book and evident in most of the later novels, was an even more distinctive feature of Wright's style. Echoing Wright's Harvard psychology professor, Hugo Münsterberg, Vance liked to explain to the Manhattan district attorney who regularly sought his help that "the only real clues [in criminology] are psychological, not material." A generation accustomed to popularized versions of Freud was a ready audience for the notion that the usual police process of accumulating evidence—which prompted a dry, last-minute revelation of the murderer's identity—was passé. The new method, Vance claimed, called for a subtle attention to the details of the crime, leading in turn to a theoretical portrait of the individual most likely to have committed the crime in that particular fashion. Suspects were then matched against the circumstances of the crime, in contrast to the traditional practice of abstractly following clues and alibis back to the guilty party. Like an art expert examining a painting to determine its authorship, Vance looked for "the creative personality, the unique élan" of the culprit. The true connoisseur will know a real Rembrandt from a forgery by its brush strokes and chiaroscuro, Vance theorized on more than one occasion, and the best modern detective will ascertain that one person, and one person only, could have murdered in the manner he or she did.

Whether or not every Van Dine fan bought this precious idea, it was clear that the voice behind the words was authoritative enough to allow for a willing suspension of disbelief. Indeed, Wright's true creative accomplishment had, in the end, nothing to do with plot, suspense, theory, or even milieu. The cultural labors of Willard Wright's early years and the long dark night of his breakdown had brought forth a character of great interest to Americans: not a benevolent sleuth or an emissary of justice, on the order of G. K. Chesterton's Father Brown or Dorothy L. Sayers' Lord Peter Wimsey, but a pampered, cynical man who solves brilliantly devised crimes more for the thrill of the chase than from any interest in morality and good citizenship. An emotional detachment from the plight of the victims, a willingness to bend the law for his own purposes, a skeptical view of authority, a healthy respect for money, and a Nietzschean sense that the world belongs to those clever enough to leave the old pieties behind—the values of Philo Vance were those of a generation molded by World War I, the disillusionment that followed the war, the new mores, and a stock market boom of unprecedented proportions. Vance's polysyllabic lectures and esoteric learning, his love of Cézanne and classical music were only so much icing on the cake. Wright had brought to life a fantasy version of his inner, idealized vision of himself, a bachelor art-lover with an ample private fortune whose services are desperately needed by the world at large. Where the men of practical affairs stumble, the bookish Philo Vance succeeds.

The best-seller status of the *Benson*, "*Canary*," and *Greene* novels surprised both author and publisher. Not only did the combined sales of the novels swiftly cross into the six-figure range, reaching the one million mark in the early 1930s, but the nature of the critical press they received was also unusual. Literary journals and intellectual monthlies paid attention to the advent of S. S. Van Dine, remarking on the new level of sophistication he had brought to American detective fiction, and public figures like President Calvin Coolidge and Secretary of Commerce Herbert Hoover readily acknowledged to reporters

S. S. VAN DINE

their own interest in the crime solving of Philo Vance. Isolated objections were heard from the start—Dashiell Hammett complained in the *Saturday Review of Literature* of 15 January 1927 that Vance "had the conversational manner of a high school girl who has been studying the foreign words and phrases at the back of her dictionary"—but annoyance at the character's egotism and prissiness was a minority response until the end of the decade. For a period of more than three years, S. S. Van Dine was a media darling.

Wright's success promptly brought him to the attention of the Hollywood studios, and in 1928 he returned to southern California in triumph to observe the filming of The *"Canary" Murder Case*, starring William Powell and Louise Brooks, and to be feted as a celebrity. Doing his best to spend as little time as possible with his brother, wife, and daughter, he hobnobbed with stars and directors who knew little about his earlier work as a spokesman for modern painting and literary realism. Yet even at the peak of his newfound fame and economic security, Wright was aware that the glory could not last and, in any event, could be redeemed only if he planned someday to return to that more "serious" work. In a jocular essay entitled "I Used to Be a Highbrow, but Look at Me," published in *American Magazine*, September 1928, he concocted his own version of the genesis of the Philo Vance novels that made a calculated, painstaking process seem like a sudden, almost fate-driven decision precipitated by a breakdown and overnight recovery. In subsequent interviews, Wright told of his plans to kill off his sleuth after the sixth book of the series in order to become, once again, a man of letters. Neither the studio heads who optioned his succeeding novels before they were completed nor his publishers took Wright seriously. Those who were themselves making money off S. S. Van Dine were content to see him pour his frustrated erudition into his detective fiction. *The Bishop Murder Case* (1929), a macabre story in which the killings are cleverly based on nursery rhymes, includes digressions on mathematics and physics and an all-important clue

from a play of Henrik Ibsen's. *The Scarab Murder Case* (1930) tells the story of the murder of Gramercy Park art patron Benjamin Kyle, bludgeoned with a statuette from his own Egyptian collection, but offers a pedagogical underpinning—footnotes about Egyptian history and notations on hieroglyphic transliterations—that borders on the absurd. To judge by the sales figures, Van Dine's audience was unfazed by the scholarly trappings. They were simply part of the game. But all that was soon to end.

The Thirties: Changing Tastes

Three years passed between the publication of *The Scarab Murder Case* and the next Van Dine novel (far too long a wait, in the view of everyone at Scribners). It was time that Wright used working on screenplays for Warner Brothers' "Vitaphone Shorts" and spending most of his fortune, after his divorce from Katharine in 1930, on a new young wife, Claire de Lisle (whom he had married on 24 October 1930), and a spectacular penthouse apartment. The appearance of *The Kennel Murder Case* in August 1933 and *The Dragon Murder Case* three months later rekindled some of the excitement in S. S. Van Dine that had been in danger of dying out during the hiatus. Yet it was also time for Wright to acknowledge that the field was becoming a good deal more competitive: Dashiell Hammett's *Thin Man* won accolades that year; Agatha Christie added a respectable volume to an already sizable canon; and *Murder Must Advertise*, the eighth Peter Wimsey novel, was attracting as eager an audience in the United States as it had in Great Britain, much to Wright's annoyance. There was no possibility now of honoring his pledge to kill off Philo Vance. In the fourth year of the Depression, Wright had only to look at the breadlines and panhandlers on the streets of New York and reflect on his own very different late—thirty-four thousand dollars in film rights for the *Kennel* and *Dragon* stories, hefty fees for their

929

magazine serialization, and substantial royalties. More than ever, he wanted a buffer between himself and the poverty he had known earlier in his life, and such protection could be achieved in the 1930s only by keeping his popular character alive at all costs.

The conflict between his economic need and his intellectual ambitions showed in the writing, by degrees. *The Kennel Murder Case* and *The Dragon Murder Case* are the last Van Dine books in which it is possible to detect even the faintest energy in the development of the plot, and whatever élan the novels possess can be attributed to their origin in Wright's two new passions. *The Kennel Murder* was a detective story that came from the dog-loving Wright, the man who owned his own kennels, entered his terriers in all the major dog shows, and amassed a library of books on breeding and grooming. *The Dragon Murder Case* was a product of Wright the fanatic ichthyologist, whose collection of exotic fish filled sixty-eight aquariums in his apartment. While both novels enjoyed generous reviews and brisk sales, they suggested that Wright had been correct when, in the late 1920s, he aired the theory that most detective novelists had only six strong books in them. *The Dragon Murder Case* was also the last of the Van Dine novels to be either a critical or a commercial success.

When Scribners announced the publication of the eighth novel the following year, Wright dealt with his inability to live without Philo Vance in a variety of ways. First, more carefully than ever, he avoided anyone he knew from the art and literary worlds who might remind him of the supposedly loftier goals of his youth, and he devoted himself to those new friends who appreciated the splendor of the penthouse parties and did not care where the money came from. Second, he pretended to have lost more in the stock market crash than had in fact been the case. Given the unexpected turn of economic events, he rightly assumed that few people would blame him for taking the safe route and giving the public what it wanted. Finally, Wright turned with more fervor than ever to romanticizing his past, making the mundane present bearable by inventing a history that was more glamorous than the reality. In this version, Wright gave himself a new birthdate (1888 instead of 1887), making it appear as if he had started his career at the *Los Angeles Times* at nineteen rather than twenty; presented himself as a mentor to Mencken and Ezra Pound; and spoke to interviewers about apocryphal friendships with Pablo Picasso, Igor Stravinsky, and Gertrude Stein. The aura of Wright's past life was such that those who had not known him then were not quite sure which anecdotes were true and which were fabrications.

The fear that he was not taken seriously any longer was exacerbated for Wright by the Hollywood treatment of his books, especially that of the eighth novel, *The Casino Murder Case* (1934). On the face of it, this was the least likely novel of the series to require rewriting for cinematic purposes. Vance's expostulations have to do with gambling rather than the fine arts, and they take second place to the momentum of the poisonings, false clues, and final unraveling of a taut story set among the fast-living gaming set of Manhattan. After-hours clubs, Park Avenue town houses, and a last-minute rescue in an eerie, abandoned casino suggest that Wright had his 1934 Metro-Goldwyn-Mayer (MGM) contract in mind when he devised his settings. Yet the script of the dreadful B movie that resulted, starring Paul Lukas and Rosalind Russell, kept only a bare minimum of the original material. Even Russell, then only a starlet who should have been grateful for any work, expressed her dismay at being associated with such a sorry product.

By the mid-1930s, Wright could see that he had reached an impasse. The hard-boiled school of detective fiction spoke more effectively to the times, and the affectations of an acerbic dandy were out of place. With *The Garden Murder Case* (1935) and *The Kidnap Murder Case* (1936), Wright nervously abandoned some of his own earlier principles of character and plot development—a true mystery is an intellectual puzzle with no room for romance or derring-do—in a last-ditch effort to retain his audience. *The Garden Murder Case* dramatizes family entanglements among a circle of racing enthusiasts and features Vance as the unrequited lover of one of the young female characters and a veritable acrobat whose staged leap from a balcony tricks the murderer into making an attempt on Vance's life, thereby unmasking himself.

In *The Kidnap Murder Case,* Vance is described as weary and easily distracted, although he rouses himself by the end of the book to become a model of tough talk and virile action. The problem is that a midnight stakeout in Central Park and the self-defense shooting of three men are antithetical to the spirit of Wright's sleuth—as artistically false as the thought of Miss Marple engaged in a car chase with guns blazing or Father Brown involved in a drunken fistfight. Yet the compromises of the ninth and tenth Van Dine novels were nothing to the self-parody of *The Gracie Allen Murder Case* (1938). The brainchild of Paramount, this book was simply a novelization of a synopsis prepared by Wright for a screenplay (for which the author had been paid a munificent twenty-five thousand dollars), with Gracie Allen acting as Vance's comic assistant. Allen's character, who calls her boss "Fido" Vance, is no more respectful of the detective than she needs to be.

Wright began his final detective novel in the fall of 1938 in a fatalistic mood. He was bitter at what he saw as the prostitution of his talents and his seduction by what William James called "the bitch-goddess SUCCESS" in a 1906 letter to H. G. Wells. He questioned America's mania for light entertainment even as he acknowledged that he had contributed to the process and handsomely benefited from it. Wright's doctors warned that his heavy drinking was straining an already damaged heart, but the need to make money to support his lifestyle forced Wright to push himself to create a twelfth Philo Vance novel, which in turn led to more self-doubt and more drinking. Stung by Paramount's insinuations that his ideas for *The Gracie Allen Murder Case*

had not been commercial enough, he made certain that every twist of the new story was committed to paper only after consultation with the studio. Sonja Henie had been optioned to play the lead, and the suggestion that the book might be titled *The Sonja Henie Murder Case* led to Wright's single demand: the four-word pattern that had been established twelve years earlier with *The Benson Murder Case* and broken with *The Gracie Allen Murder Case* would be restored or he would not lend his name to the project. Having sunk to the level in recent years of appearing in promotional advertisements for tire companies, board games, and several brands of liquor—anything that would pay enough to cover his extraordinary bills—Wright decided that he would draw the line at preserving that small tie to the happier time of Philo Vance's debut.

The Winter Murder Case was completed as a twenty-thousand-word draft in February 1939, but Wright did not live to revise it. He suffered a heart attack that month, and on 11 April 1939, six months short of his fifty-second birthday, he died in his penthouse apartment of coronary thrombosis. Like most newspapers in the country, the *New York Times* printed a lengthy and appreciative obituary. "He who had killed so many harmlessly knew how to live with enjoyment," the paper noted, unaware of the fears and tensions that had consumed America's best-selling detective novelist in his last years. In the editor's preface to *The Winter Murder Case*, published that fall, Max Perkins hinted at the complex pressures brought to bear on "a gallant, gentle man" in an era that was "turbulent and crude," but there was, Perkins felt, little point in saying more. Postcrity's harsh judgment was already making itself known. No American writer of comparable fame and wealth in his day suffered so abrupt an eclipse in the public mind as did Willard Huntington Wright—defender of literary realism, advocate of modern art, and creator of that least realistic of modern sleuths, the outlandish Philo Vance.

Selected Bibliography

WORKS OF S. S. VAN DINE

PUBLISHED AS WILLARD HUNTINGTON WRIGHT

Europe After 8:15 (with H. L. Mencken and George Jean Nathan). New York: John Lane, 1914.
What Nietzsche Taught. New York: Huebsch, 1915.
Modern Painting: Its Tendency and Meaning. New York: John Lane, 1915.
The Creative Will. New York: John Lane, 1916.
The Man of Promise. New York: John Lane, 1916.
The Future of Painting. New York: Huebsch, 1923.
The Great Detective Stories: A Chronological Anthology. New York: Scribners, 1927.

PUBLISHED UNDER PSEUDONYM S. S. VAN DINE

The Benson Murder Case. New York: Scribners, 1926.
The "Canary" Murder Case. New York: Scribners, 1927.
The Greene Murder Case. New York: Scribners, 1928.
The Bishop Murder Case. New York: Scribners, 1929.
The Scarab Murder Case. New York: Scribners, 1930.
The Kennel Murder Case. New York: Scribners, 1933.
The Dragon Murder Case. New York: Scribners, 1933.
The Casino Murder Case. New York: Scribners, 1934.
The Garden Murder Case. New York: Scribners, 1935.
The Kidnap Murder Case. New York: Scribners, 1936.
The Gracie Allen Murder Case. New York: Scribners, 1938.
The Winter Murder Case. New York: Scribners, 1939.

ARCHIVES

The Willard Huntington Wright Scrapbooks are at the Princeton University Library. The Willard Huntington Wright Papers (correspondence) are at the University of Virginia Library.

BIOGRAPHICAL AND CRITICAL STUDIES

Bartlett, Randolph. "A Man of Promise." *Saturday Review of Literature,* 2 November 1935: 10.
Boyd, Ernest. "Willard Huntington Wright." *Saturday Review of Literature,* 22 April 1939: 8.
Loughery, John. *Alias S. S. Van Dine: The Man Who Created Philo Vance.* New York: Scribners, 1992.
Lounsbery, Myron. "Against the American Game: The 'Strenuous' Life of Willard Huntington Wright." *Prospects* 5: 507–555 (1980).
Smith, David R. "S. S. Van Dine at 20th-Century Fox." In *Philo Vance: The Life and Times of S. S. Van Dine.* Edited by Jon Tuska. Bowling Green, Ohio: Bowling Green State University Popular Press, 1971. Pp. 48–58.
Tuska, Jon, ed. *Philo Vance: The Life and Times of S. S. Van Dine.* Popular Writers series no. 1. Bowling Green, Ohio: Bowling Green State University Popular Press, 1971.
———. *The Detective in Hollywood.* New York: Doubleday, 1978.

ROBERT H. VAN GULIK
(1910–1967)

WILT L. IDEMA

To the general public Robert van Gulik is known as the author of the Judge Dee novels, which feature a seventh-century Chinese official as their protagonist. Van Gulik wrote these books in his leisure hours as a career diplomat with the Netherlands Ministry of Foreign Affairs. While steadily rising through the ranks, van Gulik, who was trained as a sinologist, continued to pursue his academic interests, and his Judge Dee novels were both a by-product of his encyclopedic scholarship and a stimulus to him to research hitherto neglected areas of Chinese culture. His Judge Dee novels, which were based on a Chinese model and made use of much Chinese material, were not only popular in the West, but were also translated into Chinese.

Van Gulik's Early Youth and Student Days

Robert Hans van Gulik was born on 9 August 1910 in Zutphen, Netherlands, to William Jacobus van Gulik and Bertha (de Ruyter). His father was a medical officer in the Dutch colonial army, and served in the Dutch East Indies (present-day Indonesia), but had temporarily returned to his home country. When he returned to the East in 1915, he took his family with him, and van Gulik spent his primary-school years on Java, the main island of the Indonesian archipelago. When his father retired from active service, the family returned to the Netherlands and lived in the village of Beek near Nijmegen, a favorite location with returned expatriates, where van Gulik attended the gymnasium (high school).

During his high-school days van Gulik set out on both his literary and his scholarly careers. He published some reminiscences of his years in the tropics in the national periodical of gymnasium students, and assisted the eminent linguist C. C. Uhlenbeck in his lexical studies on the language of the Blackfoot Indians. Uhlenbeck's studies were published by the Royal Dutch Academy of Sciences, and van Gulik was listed as coauthor. Uhlenbeck also introduced him to the study of Sanskrit and of comparative linguistics.

When van Gulik entered Leiden University in 1930, he chose sinology as his subject. Leiden already had a long tradition as a center for oriental studies. The primary motivation in the establishment of the sinology department was not the pursuit of academic knowledge but the training of colonial officials who would be able to deal with the local populations in their native tongue. Following their studies in the Netherlands, future officials of the Ministry of Colonial Affairs were sent to China for one year of practical training. Chinese studies in Leiden combined a sound philological basis with an awareness of China's living traditions and its place as a modern nation. Moreover, in order to attract students to this demanding field, the Ministry of Colonial Affairs made special scholarships available to those students who were willing to sign a contract to serve in the colonies following the completion of their studies. This arrangement appealed to van Gulik, who wanted to be financially independent as early as possible.

In 1932, after obtaining his bachelor's degree in Chinese and Japanese, as well as his bachelor's degree in colonial law, van Gulik continued his studies at the University of Utrecht. He obtained his master's degree in oriental studies in 1934 with a thesis on Mi Fu's twelfth-century treatise on inkstones, and defended his doctoral dissertation at the University of Utrecht on 7 March 1935. This work, published as *Hayagriva: The Mantrayanic Aspect of Horse-Cult in China and Japan* (1935), deals with the fortunes of a horse-headed Indic deity in the Far East. During his student days van Gulik also remained active in the literary field: he published some Dutch translations of Chinese poetry in a variety of periodicals and also produced a Dutch translation of one of Kālidāsa's classical fifth-century Sanskrit plays.

Diplomatic Career

After he had obtained his doctorate, van Gulik entered the Ministry of Foreign Affairs, and was posted as assistant interpreter in Tokyo. Van Gulik left the Netherlands on 3 May 1935, traveling on the Trans-Siberian Railway. While he adapted with some difficulty to the rigid life of a bureaucrat, van Gulik's official duties in Tokyo left him ample time to pursue his academic interests. He became a member of various learned societies and established contact with numerous leading Japanese and Chinese scholars in Tokyo. He traveled frequently to Peking, where he made friends with local scholars. He did not limit

himself to the academic study of Chinese culture but also practiced the gentlemanly arts of calligraphy, seal cutting, painting, and zither playing. All these pursuits resulted in studies that are still consulted today.

When war broke out in the Pacific in 1942, van Gulik left Japan as he and other interned diplomats of the Allied powers were exchanged for their Japanese counterparts. Following some adventurous months in eastern Africa and Egypt, where he was trained as a secret agent, he was dispatched to New Delhi, and from there to Chungking, the wartime capital of Nationalist China, where he joined the Dutch legation. There, in 1943, van Gulik married Shui Shifang. Her father had been mayor of Tientsin and she worked at the time as a secretary in the Dutch embassy. Their eldest son was born in Chungking in 1944; he was later followed by two brothers and one sister. Chungking provided van Gulik with many opportunities to pursue his applied and academic studies, as many of China's finest minds, fleeing the Japanese invaders, had fled to this hot and humid town.

When the war was over, van Gulik was recalled to the Netherlands and posted to The Hague. In 1947 the Ministry of Foreign Affairs sent him to Washington, D.C. In 1948 he was again posted to Tokyo, where he remained three years. During this stay he published *Dee Goong An: Three Murder Cases Solved by Judge Dee* (1949), a translation of an anonymous Chinese novel of the Qing dynasty (1644–1911) dealing with the career of an official of the Tang dynasty, Di Renjie (630–700). This work provided the model for his own Judge Dee novels, the first two of which he wrote in the same years.

Following a short stint in New Delhi, van Gulik once again returned to the Netherlands. By now he had advanced to the highest ranks in the diplomatic service. From 1956 to 1959 he served as the Dutch representative to Lebanon, and from 1959 to 1962 he lived in Kuala Lumpur as Dutch ambassador to the Federation of Malaya (present-day Malaysia). He spent the years 1962–1965 in the Netherlands, and was posted to Tokyo a third time in 1965, as Dutch ambassador to Japan. He did not serve out his term, however. In 1967 van Gulik was diagnosed with lung cancer and he died in The Hague on 24 September 1967.

Van Gulik's Sinological Scholarship

Following the completion of his dissertation, van Gulik began work on a translation of the writings ascribed to the ancient philosopher Guiguzi (Master Ghost Valley). This project was representative of the philological scholarship dominant in European sinology during the 1930s. Van Gulik's manuscript was destroyed during World War II, and he did not return to the subject. He preferred to pursue topics that were close to his personal predilections rather than follow the academic fashion of the moment. As a result, he produced a number of highly original studies, most of which are still in print.

His interest in Chinese calligraphy and painting resulted in works such as *Mi Fu on Ink-stones: A Translation of the Yenshih, with an Introduction and Notes* (1938), *Chinese Pictorial Art as Viewed by the Connoisseur: Notes on the Means and Methods of Traditional Connoisseurship of Pictorial Art, Based upon a Study of the Art of Mounting Scrolls in China and Japan* (1958), and *Scrapbook for Chinese Collectors: A Chinese Treatise on Scrolls and Forgers. Shu-hua shuo-ling* (1958). His interest in the Chinese zither or "gugin," the preferred solo instrument of the traditional Chinese gentleman—van Gulik preferred the translation "lute"—led him to write a study of the instrument and its place in Chinese culture, entitled *The Lore of the Chinese Lute: An Essay in Ch'in Ideology* (1940), as well as a translation of a long third-century descriptive poem on the instrument by Xi Kang (223–262), published as *Hsi K'ang and His Poetical Essay on the Lute* (1941).

Van Gulik returned to the topic of Indian influences on Far Eastern culture in *Siddham: An Essay on the History of Sanskrit Studies in China and Japan* (1956). He also edited rare Chinese manuscripts he had found in Japan. During the last years of his life, both in Kuala Lumpur and Tokyo, van Gulik kept gibbons as pets, a hobby that encouraged him to study the role of the animal in traditional Chinese culture. The resulting monograph, *The Gibbon in China: An Essay in Chinese Animal Lore* (1967), included a recording that documented the animal's mournful cries.

Many of these subjects found their way into the Judge Dee novels. At the same time, van Gulik's work on the novels led him to explore new fields of inquiry. Hunting through Chinese sources for usable crimes and plots, he came across an early guide for magistrates, which he translated as *T'ang-yin pi-shih, "Parallel Cases from under the Pear-tree": A Thirteenth Century Manual of Jurisprudence and Detection* (1956). Searching for suitable models for his own illustrations of the Judge Dee novels, he came across various sets of pornographic prints from the final decades of the Ming dynasty (1368–1644). He had these reprinted privately—during the prudish 1950s—in a limited edition of fifty copies under the title *Pi-hsi t'u-k'ao, Erotic Colour Prints of the Ming Period, With an Essay on Chinese Sex Life from the Han to the Ch'ing Dynasty, B.C. 206–A.D. 1644* (1951).

Van Gulik later reworked his study of Chinese sexual behavior and sexological literature in *Sexual Life in Ancient China: A Preliminary Survey of Chinese Sex and Society from 1500 B.C. till 1644 A.D.* (1961). This monumental work has been translated into Chinese and, together with his Judge Dee novels, has made him one of the best known western sinologists in China. In the course of his research, van Gulik collected an extensive library of Chinese books containing many rare materials; eventually the collection was acquired by the Sinological Institute of Leiden University.

Traditional Chinese Crime Fiction

China has a long tradition of crime fiction. Even more important than the anthologies of exemplary cases compiled for the benefit of acting magistrates were the collections of spectacular cases of famous judges, which were written and read as fiction. The latter collections began to appear in the late–sixteenth century and were composed either in very simple classical Chinese, or in the vernacular language of the time. The most famous judge of them all was Judge Bao. As *Longtu gong'an* (Court Cases of Judge Bao) gained in popularity, the late–sixteenth century collections of cases of other judges were forgotten.[1]

The historical Judge Bao, Bao Zheng (999–1062), served as a local and metropolitan official in the first half of the eleventh century. He established a reputation as a cunning judge and, more important, as a fearless magistrate. In the traditional Chinese crime tale the full facts of the case are narrated right at the start. The question is not whether the magistrate will discover the true circumstances and the real culprit, but whether he will see to it that justice is done when a crime is committed by rich persons who may want to bribe him, or by powerful people who may appeal to their high connections. Judge Bao shows himself incorruptible, willing to stand up even to the emperor and his relatives. In the popular imagination Judge Bao became a god, who judged the living by day in his office on earth, and the dead by night in the underworld. Wronged ghosts did not hesitate to appeal to him in this world, informing him where their corpses had been buried and giving him incontrovertible evidence, even when the culprit had silenced all witnesses.

The cases of Judge Bao were already popular with professional storytellers in the capital during the twelfth and thirteenth centuries. When Chinese drama came into its own dur-

ing the thirteenth and fourteenth centuries, the stories were immediately adapted for the stage. They have remained favorites ever since, and in modern times have been repeatedly adapted for cinema and television. From the fifteenth century we have a number of long ballads that treat selected cases of Judge Bao, and near the end of the sixteenth century an enterprising editor combined his many cases into a novel of one hundred chapters. Editors in the seventeenth century rearranged the materials into a collection of sixty-four independent cases. This collection, the above mentioned *Longtu gong'an*, was immensely popular.

In the nineteenth century the cases were again reworked by a professional storyteller into long ballads, in which the stories were developed further. His performances were so successful that booksellers reworked the storyteller's version into a long novel, *Sanxia wuyi* (1879; Three Heroes and Five Gallants), which was followed by many sequels, in which the underlings of Judge Bao play an increasingly important role. During the same period an endless number of novels devoted to the activities of famous magistrates of the early decades of the Qing dynasty appeared, such as Shi Shilun (d. 1722) and Peng Peng (1637–1704), entitled, respectively, *Shi gong'an* (1798, 1893, 1903; The Cases of Judge Shi) and *Peng Gong'an* (1891–1894; The Cases of Judge Peng).

Dee Goong An

Van Gulik, a great admirer of the classic whodunit, was at first rather disappointed when he read traditional Chinese crime fiction: "The Chinese conception of the requirements a crime story should answer differs so much from our own, that such novels cannot be of interest to those of us who read detective novels for their relaxation values," he stated in the preface to *Dee Goong An*, and he proceeded to detail "the five main characteristics that are foreign to us." (These elements in-

[1]See the anthology by Leon Comber, *The Strange Cases of Magistrate Pao: Chinese Tales of Crime and Detection.* Rutland, Vt.: Charles E. Tuttle, 1964.

clude a lack of suspense, since the identity of the criminal is known; the ample use of supernatural elements; a passionate interest in irrelevant details; a bewildering number of names; and explicit descriptions of the final punishment of the criminal.) Nevertheless, the *Wu Zetian sida qi'an* (Four Strange Cases during the Reign of Empress Wu Zetian) sparked van Gulik's enthusiasm, although he declared the second half of the book a forgery. *Dee Goong An*, his translation of this work, accordingly limits itself to the first thirty chapters of the novel.

The *Wu Zetian sida qi'an*, an anonymous novel of the Qing dynasty, presents a fanciful and utterly ahistorical narrative of the career of Di Renjie. In traditional China, Di Renjie was revered as a staunch opponent of the notorious Empress Wu, the only woman in Chinese history who ascended the dragon throne in her own name. Following the death of her husband, Emperor Gaozong of the Tang dynasty (618–907), Empress Wu had first allowed her sons to occupy the throne, but in 690 she banished the reigning emperor and declared her own dynasty. Di Renjie was traditionally believed to have convinced her that in the end she could not transmit the throne to a member of her natal family but would have to transmit it to a son, as a married woman and mother can only receive ancestral offerings together with her husband.

As is quite common in Qing dynasty fiction, the *Wu Zetian sida qi'an* consists of two contrasting halves. In the first part we encounter Di Renjie (Judge Dee) as a local magistrate; he is very much the detective who discovers the truth behind outward appearances, for example, he finds out that a woman who has a reputation as a chaste widow actually uses this reputation as a cover, for she has murdered her husband and keeps a lover. In all these cases, Di Renjie sees to it that justice is done.

In the second part of the novel, Di Renjie as metropolitan official has no qualms about bending the law for the higher goal of opposing the empress and her cronies in order to preserve the dynasty. For example, the lover

of the empress wants to have easier access to the inner apartments of the imperial palace; Di Renjie suggests to him that he should dress as a eunuch so he can go in and out without any hindrance. But as soon as the scoundrel has dressed up as a eunuch, Di Renjie has him arrested and castrated so as to make reality fit the disguise. In the end Di Renjie participates in the return of the deposed emperor to the capital, a narrative that runs contrary to historical fact.

The *Wu Zetian sida qi'an* portrays a complete official who, out of concern for the people and loyalty to the dynasty, must act in different ways depending upon the circumstances. If the Chinese title of the novel may be taken as an indication of the intentions of its anonymous author, he probably saw in Di Renjie's devious dealings as a metropolitan official his crowning achievements. Van Gulik, however, on the lookout for an equivalent of the Western detective novel in traditional Chinese literature, noticed only a glaring contradiction between the two halves of the novel. Accordingly, he declared the second part, in which Di Renjie appears not as an honest detective but as a scheming plotter, an inept sequel to a brilliant beginning, although he could not produce any evidence for his case beyond the contents of the novel itself. It was only the amputated first half of the Chinese novel that served as a model for his own Judge Dee novels. While these have been praised for their "Chineseness" it should be borne in mind that in his preface, van Gulik praised this model as an exceptional combination of "a maximum of undiluted detection..., with a minimum of the peculiarly Chinese features discussed earlier."

The Judge Dee Novels

As in the *Dee Goong An*, van Gulik fused in his own works the political situation of the late seventh century and the social and cultural conditions of the last century of the Ming dynasty. His magistrate is aided by a number of private assistants, such as an elderly secretary and some former highwaymen, and is confronted by a number of cases at the same time. Also, one feels, Judge Dee—the perfect art connoisseur, the expert zither player, the efficient official, and the happy master of a harem of three contented wives—is portrayed very much as the perfect Chinese gentleman van Gulik himself would have wanted to be.

In his Judge Dee novels, van Gulik relied heavily on Chinese plots, which he adapted to his own taste. His first attempt at writing a Chinese mystery novel was *The Chinese Bell Murders* (1958). He began work on this novel in 1948 and revised it in 1951 after *The Chinese Maze Murders*, first published in English in 1956, had appeared in Japanese in 1950. The English text, he later claimed, "was meant only as basis for a printed Chinese and/or Japanese version, my aim being to show modern Chinese and Japanese writers that their own ancient crime-literature has plenty of source materials for detective- and mystery-stories" (Gotlieb, p. 71). He revised the novel once more in the years 1953–1956.

In *The Chinese Bell Murders* Judge Dee is confronted with three unrelated cases. The first concerns the murder of a butcher's daughter. This girl has a relationship with a student, whom she lets into her room at night. One night a mendicant monk sneaks into her room and kills her, whereupon the student is brought in for murder. This case is derived from the very first item in the popular editions of the *Longtu gong'an*, where Judge Bao eventually scares the villainous monk into a confession by having his lictors impersonate devils, while a prostitute plays the part of the ghost of the murdered girl. Van Gulik, however, solves the crime by tracking down the fence who bought the girl's jewels from her murderer. The name of the fence comes from the fifth item in the *Longtu gong'an*.

The second case concerns the rivalry between two prominent families, the Lins and the Liangs. This rivalry was the subject of the novel *Jiuming qi'an* (1904–1905; The Strange Case of Nine Victims) by Wu Woyao (1866–

1910), a major Chinese novelist of the early twentieth century. Hailed as China's first original detective novel because it opens in medias res, *Jiuming qi'an* is itself an adaptation of an earlier novel, in which the rivalry of two Kwantung clans over the geomantic position of a grave results in the killing of nine people. However, van Gulik added many details of his own invention, such as the element of Lin's salt-smuggling and his murder of his own son (because his wife, née Liang, has led him to believe the boy is his enemy's son). The detail of murdering someone by suffocating him under a heavy bronze temple bell was derived from the *Longtu gong'an*.

The third case in *The Chinese Bell Murders* deals with the abbot of a Buddhist monastery where women stay overnight in order to pray to the Bodhisattva Guanyin for offspring. The abbot enters the women's closed apartments through secret entrances and rapes them. This case is based on a vernacular novella of the early seventeenth century. The abbot is unmasked when prostitutes pose as women praying for the blessings of the goddess. Judge Dee recruits the prostitutes from a neighboring district and has them stay with his wives in the inner apartments of his own house. Whereas in the original tale the women who have visited the monastery all commit suicide once the case has been broken, and their husbands murder the children that were born following visits to the monastery, van Gulik's Judge Dee averts such a terrible outcome by declaring that some of the apartments where the women stayed did not have secret entrances. The case was of special relevance in the late forties and early fifties, because the Communists had revived the traditional lore about the lechery of monks, using it to discredit the religious elite.

In general, one cannot escape the impression that van Gulik's depiction of the Buddhist clergy in this novel is at least as much indebted to the scurrilous anti-Catholic pamphlets of eighteenth- and nineteenth-century Europe as to the situation of Buddhism in any period of China's history. Also, the relatively high status of the heads of the local guilds, and of merchants in general in *The Chinese Bell Murders*, more closely reflects urban society in the Dutch Republic than Chinese society as depicted in traditional Chinese fiction. Furthermore, the architecture of the Buddhist monastery and the mansion of the Lins, with their secret passageways and trapdoors, is reminiscent of the castles of horror of European gothic fiction. We also encounter in this novel the stereotypical descriptions of the seamy side of urban life, which reoccur in many of van Gulik's later novels.

Van Gulik completed his last Judge Dee novel, *Poets and Murder*, in 1967; it appeared posthumously in 1968. While the earlier Judge Dee novels tried to imitate many of the formal elements of traditional Chinese fiction, the later Judge Dee novels (beginning with *The Lacquer Screen*, 1962) are much simpler in this respect. Judge Dee is usually assisted by only one of his many underlings. Also he deals with one case at a time or with a number of cases that turn out to be interrelated. The latter is the case in *Poets and Murder*. The three cases confronting Judge Dee at the outset of this novel turn out to be closely connected: both the murder of a student and the murder of a female dancer turn out to have been committed by the same person, a former president of the Imperial Academy, who is also involved in the third case, the poetess Yoo-lan's murder of her servant girl.

The poetess Yoo-lan is modeled on the mid–ninth century female poet Yu Xuanji, who started out as a courtesan, became a concubine, and ended her short life as a Taoist nun. She is believed to have had an affair with the famous poet Wen Tingyun (812–870). She was condemned to death and executed after she had beaten her servant girl to death in a fit of jealousy. Van Gulik has embellished this tale in many ways, including turning the poetess into a professed lesbian. Her lesbianism is explained by her disappointments in heterosexual love, as she has been rejected by the only man she ever truly loved, the former president of the Imperial Academy. Her lesbian involvement with her female pupils re-

minds one of some of the fanciful descriptions of Sappho and her charges.

Van Gulik also adds the element of sadism (which he claimed to be absent from China in his *Sexual Life in Ancient China*). The former president of the Imperial Academy is characterized as perversely enjoying his own criminality—he exits the novel by committing suicide. In the characters of Yoo-lan and of the man who rejected her one may detect the echoes of van Gulik's readings in early–twentieth century Western sexology.

Behind the court poet Chang Lan-po, who doubts the value of his poetry and wonders whether his poems are sufficient to justify his life, one may discern the image of the Dutch poet J. C. Bloem (1877–1966), one of whose most famous lines runs: "Is dit genoeg, een stuk of wat gedichten, / Voor de rechtvaardiging van een bestaan?" (Is this enough, a handful of poems, / For the justification of an existence?). At the same time, one may see in him an alter ego of van Gulik, who had spent his life as a government official and knew his end was approaching.

Judge Dee in the West and in China

Van Gulik wrote all of his novels in English. He usually provided a postscript in which he explained relevant aspects of Chinese traditional culture. He also prepared his own Dutch translations of his works, and published a Chinese translation of *The Chinese Maze Murders* in 1952. The first two Judge Dee novels appeared in Japanese translation (in 1950 and 1951) before they were published in English. Starting in the 1960s his Judge Dee novels enjoyed great international success, with all of his novels translated into French and German. One of the many renditions into other languages is the Spanish translation of *The Chinese Gold Murders* by His Royal Highness Prince Bernhard of the Netherlands, which appeared in 1965 in Madrid as *Fan-*

tasma en Fu-lai. Van Gulik also cooperated in the adaptation of his novels as comics.

All of van Gulik's Judge Dee novels were eventually translated into Chinese. The Chinese translators often took great liberties with the texts. They often omitted as superfluous those passages in which the author explains details of Chinese life to his Western audience, and they had problems with the more sexually explicit passages. Perhaps the most interesting phenomenon is that the various independent novels were later reorganized into one long novel on the many cases of Judge Dee, after the model of the late–nineteenth century novels of famous officials.

For this purpose the individual novels were arranged in chronological order, not according to the date of composition, but according to the date of the events in the career of Judge Dee. This Chinese rearrangement was published as *Di gong'an* (The Cases of Judge Di). As van Gulik's own Judge Dee was modeled on an incomplete vision of his Chinese predecessor, it is a fitting retribution that his own works were refashioned by his Chinese translators into a mammoth novel of the type he disliked. Furthermore, his chronological survey of the career of his own Judge Dee, *Judge Dee at Work* (1967), provided the basis for the return of his protagonist to his own literary tradition.

Selected Bibliography

WORKS OF ROBERT H. VAN GULIK

NOVELS

The Chinese Maze Murders. The Hague: W. van Hoeve, 1956. Written in English in 1950 and first published in Japanese translation the same year and in Chinese in 1953. Later English-language editions are London: Michael Joseph, 1962, and Chicago: Univ. of Chicago Press, 1997.
The Chinese Bell Murders. London: Michael Joseph, 1958; New York: Harper, 1959.
The Chinese Gold Murders. London: Michael Joseph, 1959; New York: Harper, 1961.
The Chinese Lake Murders. London: Michael Joseph, 1960; New York: Harper, 1960.
The Chinese Nail Murders. London: Michael Joseph, 1961; New York: Harper, 1962.

The Red Pavilion. Kuala Lumpur, Malaya: Art Printing Works, 1961; New York: Scribners, 1970.
The Haunted Monastery. Kuala Lumpur, Malaya: Art Printing Works, 1961; New York: Scribners, 1969.
The Lacquer Screen. Kuala Lumpur, Malaya: Art Printing Works, 1962; New York: Scribners, 1970.
The Emperor's Pearl. London: Heinemann, 1963; New York: Scribners, 1964.
The Willow Pattern. London: Heinemann, 1965; New York: Scribners, 1965.
Murder in Canton. London: Heinemann, 1966; New York: Scribners, 1967.
The Phantom of the Temple. London: Heinemann, 1966; New York: Scribners, 1966.
Necklace and Calabash. London: Heinemann, 1967; New York: Scribners, 1971.
Poets and Murder. London: Heinemann, 1968; New York: Scribners, 1972.

COLLECTED SHORT STORIES

The Monkey and the Tiger. London: Heinemann, 1965; New York: Scribners, 1966. Two stories: "The Morning of the Monkey" and "The Night of the Tiger" (1963).
Judge Dee at Work. London: Heinemann, 1967. Seven stories: "The Coffins of the Emperor" (1959), "The Two Beggars," "The Wrong Sword," "The Murder on the Lotus Pond," "The Red Tape Murder," "Five Auspicious Clouds" (1961), "Murder on New Year's Eve" (1958).

TRANSLATION

Dee Goong An. Tokyo: privately printed, 1949. Repr. as *Celebrated Cases of Judge Dee*. New York: Dover, 1976. English translation of *Wu Zetian sida qi'an*.

BIOGRAPHICAL AND CRITICAL STUDIES

Alford, William P. "Robert van Gulik and the Judge Dee Stories." *Orientations* 12:50–55 (November 1981). "The Robert Hans van Gulik Issue."
Barkman, C. D., and H. de Vries-Van der Hoeven. *Een man van drie levens. Biografie van diplomaat/schrijver/geleerde Robert van Gulik* (A man of three lives. A biography of diplomat/author/scholar Robert van Gulik). Amsterdam: Forum, 1994. This book quotes extensively from the voluminous autobiographical notes prepared by R. H. van Gulik for the firm of William Heinemann. It is available in a French translation as *Les Trois Vies de Robert van Gulik*. Paris: Christian Bourgois, 1997.
Chen Zhimai, *Helan Gao Luopei* (Holland's Robert van Gulik). Taipei: Chuanji wenxue chubanshe, 1969.
Gotlieb, H. B. *Bibliography of R. H. van Gulik (D.Litt.)*, compiled for the benefit of the Boston University Libraries. Mugar Memorial Library "Robert van Gulik Collection." Boston: Boston University, 1969.

Hulsewé, A. F. P. "Nécrologie: R. H. van Gulik (1910–1967)." *T'oung Pao* 54:116–124 (1968).

Idema, W. L. "The Mystery of the Halved Judge Dee Novel. The Anonymous *Wu Tse-t'ien ssu-ta ch'i-an* and its Partial Translation by R. H. van Gulik." *Tamkang Review* 8: 155–170 (1977).

Lawton, Thomas. "Robert Hans van Gulik, Ambassador Extraordinary." *Orientations* 12: 12–22 (November 1981). "The Robert Hans van Gulik Issue."

McMullen, David. "The Real Judge Dee: Ti Jen-chieh and the T'ang Restoration of 705." *Asia Major*, 3d ser., vol. 6: 1–81 (1993).

Sarjeant, William Antony S. "Robert van Gulik and the Cases of Judge Dee." *The Armchair Detective* 15: 292–304 (1982).

Spence, Jonathan D. "Chinese Fictions in the Twentieth Century." In *Asia in Western Fiction*. Edited by Robin W. Winks and James R. Rush. Honolulu: University of Hawaii Press, 1990. Pp. 100–116.

Van de Wetering, Janwillem. *Robert van Gulik: His Life, His Work*. Miami: Dennis McMillan, 1987.

Walravens, Hartmut. "Richter Di bei der Arbeit. Zu Robert van Guliks Chinesischen Kriminalromanen." *Oriens Extremus* 36: 223–234 (1993).

EDGAR WALLACE
(1875–1932)

RICHARD BLEILER

DURING THE 1920S AND 1930S, the English writer Edgar Wallace was the world's foremost writer of crime and mystery thrillers and was hailed as "the king of thrillers." His compositional speed was extraordinary, the stuff of popular legend: he routinely wrote more than 10,000 words a day, and he could when pressed write 36,000 words in fifteen hours and draft 80,000-word novels and entire plays over weekends; in one four-day span, he wrote a serial of 120,000 words. A joke making the rounds during the 1920s had an American telephone caller attempting to reach Wallace at his home in England; when told that Wallace had just started a new play and had left word that he must not be disturbed until it was finished, the caller responds, "I'll hold." At his death in early 1932, Wallace had to his name 173 novels, 24 plays, 61 sketches, more than 2,000 short stories, and an enormous quantity of miscellaneous journalism; in addition, he had adapted many of his works for motion pictures, writing the screenplays himself.

Today Wallace is generally out of print and largely unstudied; when he is remembered it is for his first novel, *The Four Just Men* (1905), and for writing the original screenplay of *King Kong* (1933). The reasons for this neglect lie partially in Wallace's reputation, for though they tend to be neither his best nor his most interesting books, his thrillers have overshadowed his other works. Furthermore, most of Wallace's fiction promulgates attitudes that contemporary readers are likely to find distasteful, however innocently they are displayed. Despite some youthful dissatisfaction, Wallace accepted wholeheartedly the beliefs and mores of the middle classes of late Victorian and early Edwardian England; his work espouses the maintenance of a comfortable status quo. Wallace's contemporaries noted this; in a review of *The Gunner* (1928), Arnold Bennett states that "Edgar Wallace has a very grave defect, and I will not hide it. He is content with society as it is. He parades no subversive opinions. He is 'correct.' " This observation echoes Wallace's introduction to his autobiography, *People* (1926):

> This little autobiography is in itself a tribute to the system under which we live. There cannot be much wrong with a society which made possible the rise of J. H. Thomas or Edgar Wallace, that gave 'Jamie' Brown the status of a king in Scotland and put Robertson at the War Office as Chief of the Imperial General Staff. (pp. vii–viii)

Paradoxically, Wallace's stories are riddled with accounts of social, legal, and political injustices, and Wallace's protagonists often act as vigilantes in order to remedy these problems. These conflicting attitudes lend much of Wallace's work a curious tension: he advocates a societal status quo, yet depicts as heroic those who ignore laws and operate outside society—in order to punish those who have ignored laws and operated outside society.

Questions of values aside, Wallace's thrillers tend to be repetitive, cliché-ridden, and formulaic; the world they are set in is "a reassuring world, for the hero always wins in the end, crime never pays, love finds a way, and the heroine is always saved from worse than death" (Lane, 1939 ed., pp. 289–290). Early in his career Wallace found a formula for his plots: he would start a story, stop at a climactic point and start another, apparently independent story; story chains would alternate until a resolution occurred. As Margaret Lane has noted,

> despite the apparent variety of Wallace's thrillers, the plan of construction and the dramatis personae are nearly always the same. Unlike most writers of mystery stories, who have to devote the last couple of hours to sorting out the tangle, he set and then solved new problems all the way through the book, keeping only his basic mystery unexplained until the end. Inside the frame of the principal mystery, minor mysteries, slightly overlapping, are started like hares and pursued for a short distance, each new problem being set immediately before the solution of its predecessor. (p. 292)

The stories told with this formula are frequently of but two kinds: a mysterious and lethal organization threatens a group of people (or London or the world) before being exposed and stopped, or a mysterious and lethal person (or a group of people) behave as vigilantes, threatening and destroying those they feel merit punishment.

Wallace occasionally used women as protagonists, but the majority of his thrillers have male protagonists, and Wallace knew but two kinds of male protagonist: the civilian and the policeman. Although his civilians were introduced in roles ranging from fops to tramps, they invariably revealed themselves to be intelligent, hardworking, decisive, well informed, unmarried, and middle class in their values, if not their birth; following World War I, many of them were decorated veterans. Wallace's policemen are invariably capable and professional, unafraid of decisive action. In virtually all instances, the actions of the protagonists embody the political values described above: they became vigilantes to restore a societal status quo or to battle those from whom society must be protected. They may discuss their actions with their friends and colleagues, but they never experience regret or horror at having taken life. Above all, they are not complex personalities. (It is worth mentioning that when Wallace uses policemen as secondary characters, they are readily baffled by the villain and need guidance and purpose from the incredibly well informed hero. Never do the policemen question whether they should be taking orders from a civilian or how and why the civilian knows what he knows. Never does the story flag while the policeman completes paperwork.)

The villains of Wallace's thrillers tend also to be of but two kinds: the disreputable nobleman or financier, motivated by a need for money and its accompanying power, and the criminal genius, whose intelligence has often led him to madness but whose resources, malice, and capacity for lurking in disguise are almost limitless. Often the last chapter of the novel reveals the villain as the least likely character. Frequently, these villains have a male sidekick and, sometimes, a female assistant; these characters occasionally see the error of their ways and flee their employer, stealing needed funds that will enable them to lead middle-class lives far from the action. A subset of Wallace's villains are those characters who are introduced as criminals but whose nefarious actions serve a noble cause; often they seek to recover stolen inheritances via illegal methods.

The heroines of nearly all of Wallace's thrillers are unmarried, chaste, attractive, have grey eyes, and participate actively in the stories. Almost invariably, they act independently and, as a result, need to be rescued from the clutches of villains. A significant percentage of Wallace's heroines are heirs to fortunes they do not know about but which motivate villains to pursue them.

Despite their repetitive nature, many of Wallace's thrillers can still be enjoyed as period pieces. The characters are comfortably familiar, and the situations are well presented; Wallace told a lively story and could create and sustain suspense in the most unlikely situations. In addition, Wallace was a capable writer of dialogue and had a good ear for speech patterns; many of his works make effective use of lower-class slang. Finally, the backgrounds to the works are frequently well presented, providing concrete and interesting detail about subjects as varied as horse racing, the theater, English criminal classes, drug smuggling, and life in colonial Africa.

Life

Wallace's friend, secretary, and biographer Robert Curtis begins his account of his life with Wallace with the assertion that "Edgar Wallace did not write his most thrilling story; he lived it" (p. 13), but there is little that could be called exceptional about Wallace's early years. He was born Richard Horatio Edgar Wallace in Greenwich, England, on 1 April 1875, the illegitimate son of actors Mary Jane (Polly) Richards and Richard Horatio Edgar. His mother gave him up for adoption, paying Billingsgate fish porter George Freeman five shillings a week for his keep. Raised as Richard Freeman, Edgar Wallace did not know his parentage until he was ten years old. Although he was a voracious reader of popular fiction—*People* contains glowing references to the tales of the Arabian Nights and to Deadwood Dick—Wallace received little formal education, having quit school at twelve. Much of his childhood and early adolescence consisted of working odd jobs, either for relatives or neighboring tradesmen; he ran errands, served printers, worked in factories, and in December 1890 he forged George Freeman's signature and went to sea as a cabin boy

and cook on a trawler. He was constantly seasick, miserably cold, and wholly unsuited to the life of a fisherman. When the trawler docked at Grimsby in February, he ran away; his walk home took three weeks, and he survived by stealing clothes and food. Following this, he briefly assisted Harry Hansford, a relative of the Freemans, in the delivery of milk, after which he held an additional series of jobs. In no line of menial employment was Wallace successful; he retained a lifelong aversion to physical labor and left Hansford's milk business rather than scrub milk cans.

Most of the Freeman family were alcoholics, and perhaps the most important and long-lasting event of Wallace's adolescence was his signing the pledge at age sixteen. He joined a temperance lodge, the Sons of the Phoenix, serving as lodge secretary, and he remained a complete teetotaler for many years, drinking only sparingly in later life. Perhaps unfortunately, the youthful Wallace never took a similar pledge against gambling; he was an apparently compulsive frequenter of race tracks, dropping fortunes in the mistaken belief in his ability to handicap horses. When he became successful, he owned a stable and lost heavily on its consistently unsuccessful members.

At age eighteen Wallace enlisted in the Royal West Kent Regiment. He had previously worked in the St. John Ambulance Brigade, and his experiences in first aid stood him in good stead when he applied for permission to transfer to the Medical Staff Corps in Aldershot. He was successful as a medical orderly and enjoyed his work among the sick and dying, for his job gave him time in which to read, educate himself, and write verse. An interest in the theater led him to write songs, and when the music-hall performer Arthur Roberts accepted them, Wallace went AWOL for five days to hear Roberts' performance. Upon his return, Wallace received ninety-six hours of hard labor, and two months later was transferred to Simonstown, South Africa. There he made the acquaintance of a Wesleyan minister, the Reverend William Shaw Caldecott, whose Simonstown Wesleyan Mission Room had a small library. The Caldecott family practiced temperance; Mrs. Marion Caldecott was a writer and willing to assist Wallace in his writing; furthermore, the Caldecotts had a number of daughters, one of whom, Ivy Maud, married Wallace in 1901 after a protracted engagement. It was a union opposed by the Reverend Mr. Caldecott.

Wallace became known as the "Soldier Poet" after one of his verses, "Welcome to Kipling," appeared in the *Cape Times* in 1898; it led to an unremarkable meeting with the touring Rudyard Kipling. Wallace's first two books, *The Mission that Failed!* (1898) and *War! and Other Poems* (1900), were Kiplingesque collections of verse published to mixed reviews in South Africa. Wallace had high hopes for his third collection of poetry, which received English publication, but the verses about army life and Tommy that appeared in *Writ in Barracks* (1900) were almost universally excoriated.

In order to earn enough money to marry Ivy, Wallace had left the army in 1899 to begin a career as a journalist. He served as a military correspondent for Reuter's, reporting on the Boer War to an English readership; although the military censors attempted to thwart Wallace in his coverage, he devised ingenious means of circumventing them and on several occasions emerged with scoops involving the British field marshal Horatio Herbert Kitchener and the peace process. These infuriated Kitchener, whose influence was such that Wallace was banned as a war correspondent until World War I. Wallace's fourth book, *Unofficial Dispatches* (1901), collects a number of these columns and despite occasional jingoism show him to be a talented and lively journalist.

In 1902 Wallace became the first editor of the *Rand Daily Mail* in Johannesburg; he was dismissed in 1903 following a conflict with the newspaper's owner and charges of personal extravagance. He went to London with a pregnant Ivy and a half-completed play about Cecil Rhodes, *An African Millionaire* (1904), and found employment with the *Daily Mail*. Wallace believed firmly that the play would make his fortune, but it closed in Cape Town after only six nights. Wallace nevertheless retained an interest in the theater, ultimately achieving a measure of success with such plays as *The Ringer* (1926), *The Terror* (1927), *The Squeaker* (1928), *The Calendar* (1929), and *On the Spot* (1930); the last starred a young Charles Laughton.

By 1907 Wallace's relationship with the *Daily Mail* had become irrevocably strained. In 1905 he had self-published his first novel, *The Four Just Men*, and offered a prize of five hundred pounds sterling to the reader who guessed its solution, which would appear in the *Daily Mail*. More contestants than Wallace had anticipated solved the mystery and, because Wallace had not limited his prizes, he found himself facing certain bankruptcy: he had sold thirty-eight thousand copies of his book and lost fourteen hundred pounds. Alfred Harmsworth, owner of the *Daily Mail*, had to advance Wallace one thousand pounds to prevent a scandal being linked with his newspaper. This alone did not make Wallace persona non grata, but he was dismissed after the newspaper lost several libel suits because he had not adequately checked his facts before submitting stories.

In the two years following his employment with the *Daily Mail*, Wallace freelanced unsuccessfully, dodging bill collectors while losing his meager earnings at the tracks. His fortunes began to change in 1909, when he was commissioned to write a series of racing articles for George Beech of Shurey's publications. Following a meeting with the fiction editor Isabel Thorne, Wallace realized he could fictionalize his African experiences, and the result was the creation of Mr. Commissioner Sanders, an African representative of Great Britain's Foreign Office. "Sanders of the River" was immediately popular, and Wallace wrote numerous additional stories using his African experiences as background. He discovered too that successful characters could be reused indefinitely.

Wallace began dictating his work in 1914. Robert Curtis, a champion typist, became a fixture in Wallace's life, working exclusively for him following service in World War I. In 1915 young Ethel Violet King came to work for Wallace as secretary. Although he and Ivy had two sons and a daughter, their marriage was failing; Wallace separated from Ivy in 1918, divorced her in 1919, and married Violet in 1921. His pet name for her was Jim; they had one daughter, Penelope.

With the efficient Curtis transcribing his Dictaphone cylinders and the equally efficient and loving Jim handling his family and servants, managing his plays, and also transcribing dictation, Wallace's output became staggering. He began dictation between five and six o'clock in the morning and worked throughout the day; he and Jim had an active social life, but he would often dictate after dinner parties, telling his stories into the small hours of the morning and revising as fast as Curtis and Jim could transcribe his prose. If financial pressures or contractual obligations necessitated—and Wallace consistently spent more than he earned and enjoyed procrastinating—he dictated until the story was completed. He rarely got more than five or six hours of uninterrupted sleep and often catnapped during the day. In addition, he relied on stimulation from tea and cigarettes, using for the latter a ten-inch cigarette holder that he believed kept the smoke from his eyes. Curtis recalls that "thirty or forty cups of tea daily was his [Wallace's] average consumption; and I imagine he smoked about eighty or a hundred cigarettes [per day] through the famous ten-inch holder" (p. 69).

In 1930 Wallace ran for a seat in the House of Commons. Though an affable speaker, he knew nothing about politics, and his attempts at flippancy—he told an audience that "a writer of crook stories ought never to stop seeking new material"—badly backfired; he lost by more than thirty-three thousand votes (Lane, p. 373). In November 1931 the RKO studios of Hollywood offered him a contract of six hundred pounds sterling a week, and Wallace, who was at times directing motion pictures and acting as chairman of the British Lion Film Corporation, needed the money and accepted. He rented a house in California,

wrote daily to Jim, went to the races, and worked on the screenplay that was filmed as *King Kong* in 1933. On 7 February 1932, he collapsed and was diagnosed as a diabetic, a condition aggravated by overwork, poor physical condition, and years of drinking enormous amounts of heavily sweetened tea. He died on 10 February 1932; his letters and cables to Jim were published in May as *My Hollywood Diary* (1932). Despite his enormous earnings, Wallace died in debt, forcing Jim to sell her jewelry and move to smaller quarters with Penelope; Jim died fourteen months after her husband's death, "from worry and overwork," according to publisher George H. Doran (p. 279). Wallace's literary estate was not profitable until 1934.

Contemporary readers are likely to find Wallace an often unsympathetic figure, a driven spendthrift whose obsessive gambling left his money at the race track and his staff unpaid, a man who so came to believe in his own infallibility that he became domineering and obsessively jealous in his desire to control the lives of others: he disinherited his son Bryan in 1928 because the twenty-four-year-old wished to remain in Switzerland and race bobsleds rather than return to England. (Upon Bryan's penitent return, Wallace readmitted him to the family circle.) The published accounts of Wallace's contemporaries, on the other hand, are unanimous in praise. Numerous accounts recall Wallace's occasionally extravagant generosity; Robert Curtis' account of his life with Wallace is more encomium than biography; and Jim's account of her seventeen years with Wallace, *Edgar Wallace by His Wife* (1932), in a loving tribute, recognizing and consistently forgiving Wallace's faults.

Works

The majority of Wallace's writings contain elements of mystery and crime, and there are numerous series that consist of only a few books. Falling into this category are the stories featuring young Henry Arthur Milton, better known as the Ringer (*The Gaunt Stranger*, 1925; U.S. title, *The Ringer*, 1926; and the short story collection, *Again the Ringer*, 1929; U.S. title, *The Ringer Returns*, 1931); the Squeaker (*The Squeaker*, 1927; U.S. title, *The Squealer*, 1928); Inspector Wade (*The Feathered Serpent*, 1927); and the elderly eccentric Superintendent Minter, also known as "The Sooper" (*The Man from Morocco*, 1926; U.S. title, *The Black*, 1930; *Big Foot*, 1927; and *The Lone House Mystery*, 1929). Wallace's significant thrillers, however, comprise just three series: the Just Men, Superintendent Elk, and Mr. J. G. Reeder.

The Four Just Men, Wallace's first novel, is the first of six books to feature George Manfred, Raymond Poiccart, and Leon Gonsalez; the fourth Just Man, Merrell, died shortly before the story opens. It is immediately established that the Just Men are vigilantes, unhesitatingly ready to kill when their demands are not met. Their motivation, however, is not monetary but a desire to bring retribution to people who have escaped the law either through their cleverness or through miscarriages of justice; the Just Men strive ruthlessly to maintain a social equilibrium. Early in the novel, Manfred explains himself to Miguel Thery, a criminal assisting him: "You kill for benefit; we kill for justice, which lifts us out of the ruck of professional slayers. When we see an unjust man oppressing his fellows; when we see an evil thing done against the good God . . . and against man—and know that by the laws of man this evil-doer may escape punishment—we punish" (p. 12).

The premise that activates *The Four Just Men* is, somewhat surprisingly for Wallace, one that advocates acceptance. Sir Philip Ramon, the English secretary of state for foreign affairs, is sponsoring a bill that will return resident aliens to certain death in their politically volatile homelands. Recognizing that the bill is pernicious, the Just Men threaten Ramon. Their warnings, in handwriting "of the flourishing effeminate variety that is characteristic of the Latin races" (p. 22), tell Ramon that "unless your Government withdraws this Bill, it will be necessary to remove you, and not alone you, but any other person who undertakes to carry into law this unjust measure" (p. 23). Even after the Just Men introduce bombs into public places, Ramon remains unyielding, and he is found dead in a locked room, a mysterious stain on his right palm. Thery too is found dead, a similar stain on his right palm; Manfred, Poiccart, and Gonsalez have vanished.

The first edition of *The Four Just Men* concluded with an appendix praising Wallace and providing readers with a form upon which they could submit solutions to the mystery. Later editions include neither editorial nor form and are revised to reveal that Ramon's telephone had been hooked into a power line. Ramon was electrocuted when he answered his telephone; Thery bungled the connection and died through his carelessness.

In *The Council of Justice* (1908), the Just Men battle the anarchist group entitled the Red Hundred, thwarting the anarchists' bombing of London by using trained falcons to rip apart the fabric of the bomb-carrying balloons. Manfred, however, is betrayed to the police, and he is tried and sentenced to death. He vanishes in a puff of black smoke while on the gallows, saved by the wizardry of Poiccart and Gonsalez, who have tunneled beneath the gallows. The Just Men had communicated with the imprisoned Manfred via colored flags, a method similar to that Wallace employed to obtain confidential information during the Boer War.

The third novel in the series, *The Just Men of Cordova* (1917), is the weakest; it appears that Wallace added the Just Men to an already extant story, expanding a novelette to novel length. The story begins in Cordova, introducing a mysterious Dr. Essley and a poison whose touch is death, then moves to England and describes the nefarious activities of the murderous, stock-swindling Colonel Black, who in reality is Dr. Essley. The Just Men appear only sporadically in the novel and are less than successful in the destruction of Black/Essley; he is finally apprehended by

Lord Francis Ledborough, a handsome young policeman who has been present throughout the story as Constable Fellowe.

The last novel to feature the Just Men, *The Three Just Men* (1925), is one of the liveliest and appears to have been written with Wallace's tongue firmly in his cheek. The story concerns the activities of a Swedish scientist, the elderly Dr. Eruc Oberzohn, who collects snakes and has invented a device that leaves its victims with what appears to be a snake bite. Dr. Oberzohn needs money, for his illicit arms trade has failed; the general who formerly ordered weapons was "placed against an *adobe* wall and incontinently shot to rags by the soldiers of the Government against which he was in rebellion" (pp. 29–30). In addition, Dr. Oberzohn's beloved brother Adolph has been killed by the Just Men. Unaware that the Just Men are now monitoring him, Dr. Oberzohn plots to steal the fortune of his secretary, young Mirabelle Leicester, by marrying and murdering her. The Just Men rescue Mirabelle frequently, deal death to Oberzohn's gang efficiently and promptly, and after a pitched battle destroy Oberzohn with his own invention, a device akin to a lengthy cigarette holder that shoots spikes of frozen snake venom.

There is an engaging element of self-parody in *The Three Just Men*. The mad scientist/criminal mastermind genres are spoofed, as is the fast-moving, episodic, and melodramatic story for which Wallace had become known. In addition, *The Three Just Men* is cheerfully self-referential, and a significant portion of the novel takes place during a performance of Wallace's play *The Ringer*: " 'I've been looking up the reviews of the dramatic critics,' states Gonsalez, 'and as they are unanimous that it is not an artistic success, and is, moreover, wildly improbable, it ought to be worth seeing. I always choose an artistic success when I am suffering from insomnia' " (p. 229).

The Just Men also appeared in two collections of short stories, *The Law of the Four Just Men* (1921; U.S. title, *Again the Three Just Men*, 1933) and *Again the Three Just Men* (1928; U.S. title, *The Law of the Three Just Men*, 1931). Though repetitive, the tales of retribution, cheerfully, mercilessly, and occasionally lethally applied, are lively and fast moving: blackmailers are revealed and arrested, white slavers are whipped, crooked gamblers are ruined, and a drug dealer is led to think he has committed murder and is about to be hanged.

Uneven though its stories are, the Just Men series is far from static, and in the initial presentation of the Just Men there is an intriguing element of projection, for the Just Men probably embody the ideals of the youthful and impoverished Wallace: Manfred, Poiccart, and Gonsalez are enormously rich, highly intelligent, thoroughly educated, socially well connected, and physically active; their skills include fluency in languages ranging from Spanish to Arabic and expertise in foods, wines, chemistry, gardening, criminal classification, pistols, airplanes, and fast cars. They know what to do and have the wherewithal to do it; they are not afraid to act, for there is no ambiguity in the choices facing them. Furthermore, although the Just Men begin the series as outlaws, they are at its conclusion respected private detectives, for the British government pardoned them for their heroic behavior during World War I; it is possible to equate the increased acceptance of the Just Men with Wallace's success as a writer. It is equally possible that the mature Wallace realized that the line between a bomb-throwing seeker of justice and a bomb-throwing political terrorist is an ethically fine one, and that the most palatable vigilantes are those who leave their victims alive but undone by their own treachery.

There are five books in the series featuring Superintendent Elk, who is introduced in *The Nine Bears* (1910; U.S. title, *The Other Man*, 1911) as "a detective officer chiefly remarkable for his memory. A tall, thin, sad man, who affects a low turned-down collar and the merest wisp of a black tie. If he has any other pose than his desire to be taken for a lay preacher, it is his pose of ignorance on most subjects" (p. 39). The stories in which Elk appears tend to involve would-be criminal masterminds determined to obtain money: *The Nine Bears* describes the activities of Gregory Silinski, a murderous, swindling Pole whose attempts at naval world domination fail and lead to his capture by policeman T. B. Smith. *The Fellowship of the Frog* (1925) was apparently Wallace's favorite among his books; its twisted plot describes the eventual capture of the deadly master criminal known as the Frog, who "studied bank robberies as a doctor might take up the study of anatomy" (p. 279). *The Joker* (1926; U.S. title, *The Colossus*, 1932) describes the activities of Stratford Harlow, an unscrupulous multimillionaire. The titular character in *The Twister* (1928) is Anthony Braid, a well-to-do young Englishman; the story involves the machinations of the murderous and sexually obsessed Dutchman, Rex Guelder. The criminal in *White Face* (1930) is one whose crimes, initiated out of his desire for his past to remain hidden, escalate, ending with multiple murders; though his situation is convincing, Wallace's treatment of it is anticlimatic.

Elk only rarely achieves significant life of his own, and often seems to exist only to react to those around him. He nevertheless prefigures one of Wallace's most successful characters, Mr. John Gray Reeder, a former banker who works as chief investigator for the Public Prosecutor's Department in London. J. G. Reeder, as the character is known, is first introduced as a secondary character in *Room Thirteen* (1924), a cheerfully implausible story of intrigues among crooks. Reeder does not appear until nearly a third of the way through the volume, when he is introduced as a sad-faced, middle-aged man; other characters consider him a police mastermind. In the last chapter, Reeder is revealed to be a secret-service man named Golden, and John Gray, the dashing young crook present throughout the story, is revealed to be J. G. Reeder. It is a climax that fails to satisfy, and Wallace evidently felt that the middle-aged man was the more interesting character, for in the following collection of stories, *The Mind of Mr. J. G. Reeder* (1925; U.S. title, *The Murder Book of*

J. G. Reeder, 1929), the young man ceases to exist, and the descriptions of Reeder become vivid:

> Mr. Reeder was something over fifty, a long-faced gentleman with sandy-grey hair and a slither of side whiskers that mercifully distracted attention from his large outstanding ears. He wore half-way down his nose a pair of steel-rimmed pince-nez, through which nobody had ever seen him look—they were invariably removed when he was reading. A high and flat-crowned bowler hat matched and yet did not match a frock-coat tightly buttoned across his sparse chest. His boots were square-toed, his cravat—of the broad chest-protector pattern—was ready-made and buckled into place behind a Gladstonian collar. The neatest appendage to Mr. Reeder was an umbrella rolled so tightly that it might be mistaken for a frivolous walking cane. Rain or shine, he carried this article hooked to his arm, and within living memory it had never been unfurled. (pp. 13–14)

Reeder also appears in one novel (*Terror Keep*, 1927), and seven novelettes collected into two books (*Red Aces*, 1929; and *The Guv'nor and Other Stories*, 1932; U.S title, *Mr. Reeder Returns*, 1932). Taken collectively, they reveal Reeder as a formidable character: his thinness masks great strength, his numerous statements about having "a criminal mind" reveal an enormous cunning and a substantial understanding of human character, and his seeming isolation is tempered by the raising of chickens (buff Orpingtons and leghorns) and his ability to care for the much younger Margaret Belman, a struggling typist who accompanies him on several adventures. Furthermore, frail, eccentric, and old-fashioned though J. G. Reeder appears, he is one of Wallace's deadlier heroes: " 'Don't be rude,' said Mr. Reeder mildly, 'or I'll trip you on to your back and push the ferrule of my umbrella into your right eye—or left eye, whichever is most convenient' " ("The Man Who Passed," *The Guv'nor* p. 132).

The best of the works featuring Reeder is *Terror Keep*, which begins with the escape from prison of maniacal John Flack, a criminal genius of the highest order. (Wallace was fascinated by criminal geniuses and hoped vainly to meet one.) Recognizing that Margaret is in danger from Flack, Reeder sends her to take a job in a remote hotel; he remains in London, casually evading attempts on his life from airguns and poisoned milk. The latter half of the novel takes place in the hotel, which is built over secret caverns, is riddled with secret passages, contains secret stairs and stores, and is a deathtrap, the headquarters of Flack's gang. Reeder consistently demonstrates implacable courage, mental acuity, and great resourcefulness, and he reveals a merciful side of his character by refusing to shoot Flack in cold blood. The novel ends with his engagement to Margaret. Though *Terror Keep* is thoroughly implausible, the story is lively, vivid, cheerful, and shows Wallace at the top of his form.

Several of Wallace's nonseries thrillers deserve mention. *The Crimson Circle* (1922) is one of many novels that inverts the situation established in the Just Men series: the apparently unstoppable and well-informed Crimson Circle gang is killing those who will not pay protection, and it is up to the police (the seemingly stolid Inspector Parr), a private detective (Derrick Yale), and the hero (Jack Beardmore) to stop the gang. There is an element of the fantastic in the character of Yale, who has a mild psychometric ability, and Beardmore agonizes because Thalia Drummond, the secretary he loves, is apparently in league with the Crimson Circle. The characterization of Drummond is well handled, and the gallows speech of the leader of the Crimson Circle echoes Wallace's belief in temperance: "Never drink. Drink was my ruin! If it were not for drink I should not be here!" (1929 ed., p. 300).

The Face in the Night (1924) involves stolen diamonds, a jewel thief, rival detectives, and several murders. In addition, there is occasional incidental information about South Africa and the diamond trade, presented with convincing detail: "The man was from abroad, probably South Africa . . . he was

wearing *veltshoen*, a native-made boot, very popular among the Boers, and the tobacco in his pouch is undoubtedly Magaliesberg. There's no other tobacco like it" (p. 29). Though the writing is occasionally dreadful (" 'It is true—it is true!' stormed Dora in a harsh whisper" [p. 53]), it is also occasionally witty; the characterizations can be equally sharp.

The protagonists in the short story collections *The Brigand* (1927) and *The Mixer* (1927) are Anthony Smith and Anthony Newton, respectively. They are men who live by their wits, con men whose prey is other con men; the police know this and, by not pursuing Smith and Newton, they express at least tacit approval. The central conceit of criminals undone by other criminals is not new, but Wallace handled it with aplomb, and such was his influence that elements of his work can be seen in the creation of Hugh Cave's the Eel, Leslie Charteris' the Saint, John Creasey's the Toff, and enormous numbers of similar characters who appeared in the pulp magazines from the 1930s forward.

The nine linked stories in *Four Square Jane* (1929) describe the exploits of a female criminal, a small woman far more intelligent than the police who pursue her. In the early chapters, she successfully steals from the rich, in particular the unpleasant Lord Claythorpe. As her character develops, Jane—whose real name is Joyce Wilberforce—becomes a seeker of justice, her robberies serving ultimately to assist her in recovering a stolen inheritance. The book is unexceptional in the telling, weak as prose, and improbable in the plotting, but it is exemplary in providing demonstrations of Wallace's narrative formulae.

The Devil Man (1931) is arguably not a work of fiction, as it recounts the life and death of Charles Peace (1832–1879), a Victorian criminal notorious for numerous burglaries and two murders. Peace passed as a respectable man, operating in disguise by blackening his complexion and concealing a disfigured arm with one made of gutta-percha; he nearly escaped the police by jumping from a moving train. Peace was far from a criminal master-mind, but he was a melodramatic figure:

> [Peace] was a clear, incongruous figure of a man. His height could not have been more than five feet; the big, dark, deep-set eyes were the one pleasant feature in a face which was utterly repulsive. They were the eyes of an intelligent animal. The forehead was grotesquely high, running in furrows almost to where, at the crown of the head, a mop of gray hair rolled back. The unshaven cheeks were cadaverous, deeply lined and hollow. (p. 22)

Much of *The Devil Man* is realistic, however, and the introductory melodrama is soon replaced by an almost journalistic recounting of Peace's actions:

> The little man with the dark face was popular in the neighbourhood; attended a local church; made and mended kites for small boys; manufactured toys of all kinds and distributed them gratuitously. He had a kindly word for everybody. His neighbours said of him that he was quite the gentleman, which had been said before by witnesses who had a better opportunity of testing his gentility. (p. 250)

The Devil Man appeared late in Wallace's career and is one of his best works, combining Wallace's fast-moving story with convincing factual detail and material from the transcript of Peace's trial. Its 80,000 words were written between a Friday night and a Monday morning.

Finally, although they are only marginally thrillers, the twelve books in the series featuring Mr. Commissioner Sanders, African representative of the Foreign Office of Great Britain, deserve mention. Sanders operates somewhere in Africa—Wallace is vague as to his exact location, providing the impossible geographic coordinates of latitude 2° N, longitude 46° W—and governs somewhere between sixteen and twenty-three tribal nations on the Ochori River. The first story in the "Sanders of the River" series is "The Education of the King" (1910), in which Sanders settles a tribal dispute by threatening the king of the aggressor tribe, establishes a boy of nine as a puppet king, sends packing several annoying missionaries and do-gooders, and must stop trouble when the puppet king is misled by scheming natives. The boy is whipped, learns obedience, and sacrifices himself when the scheming natives attempt to kill Sanders.

"The Education of the King" is not particularly well written, and its ending is sentimental. It is explicit in its expression of English attitudes toward Africans and empire: the Africans are "children" and "childlike," and like children, they are fickle, often dangerous, and need constant guidance. Sanders is prompt to hang miscreants, for "hesitation to act, delay in awarding punishment, either of those two things would have been mistaken for weakness amongst a people who had neither power to reason, nor will to excuse, nor any large charity" (*Sanders of the River*, 1930 ed., p. 3). If one dismisses the narrative flaws, racism, and imperialist ideology, the story is a basic statement about duty, love, responsibility, and maturity; it contains several humorous exchanges that develop Sanders' character, and it has a good sense of detail and place.

Although Sanders initially operates by himself, other characters are introduced and remain to help. Over the course of the series Sanders is assisted by Captain Patrick George Hamilton, who commands the approximately one hundred native troops—Houssas—that assist the English in the collection of taxes and protect the other natives from swindlers, slave traders, and each other. Also assisting is Lieutenant Francis Augustus Tibbetts, known as Bones, and (later in the series) Captain Hamilton's lovely sister Patricia. Most important, Sanders receives assistance from Bosambo Krooboy, chief of the Akasava tribe, a consummate thief and political schemer whose every seemingly benevolent action has repercussions unanticipated by Sanders.

Bosambo first appears in "Bosambo of Monrovia" (1910), the third story in the series, and with his presence the Sanders stories frequently change tone and become superficially lighter, though their subtexts remain dark and bloody. Bosambo, who has casually murdered his way to a tribal kingship, is clearly superior to Sanders in intelligence and is so remarkably devious that he can be seen as a trickster figure. Though the colorless Sanders is nominally more powerful, Bosambo consistently subverts the power of the white man to his benefit: on their first meeting, Bosambo steals binoculars from the unsuspecting Sanders, then tells his people that he is Sanders' son. Soon after, he successfully sells an Englishman lands and goods that are not his, then gives the Englishman hemp and convinces him that he has the sleeping sickness. At the conclusion of *Sanders of the River*, Bosambo is Sanders' willing instrument of revenge on a tribe that has slain a white woman. Though Bosambo does not figure in all of the Sanders stories, those in which he appears are more often than not the better stories.

Conclusion

So popular was Wallace that publisher George H. Doran claimed that in 1928 one of every four books printed and sold in England, apart from Bibles and textbooks, was written by Wallace. During the three decades following Wallace's death, his characters and narrative techniques were actively copied. Hundreds (if not thousands) of writers wrote stories in which clones of the Just Men killed those who would corrupt society, master criminals were firmly thwarted by active young heroes, and justice was administered by determined vigilantes rather than through the courts. Wallace has been linked to writers as diverse as Thomas Burke and Roy Vickers, to the creation of the pulp characters the Shadow, Doc Savage, the Saint, and the Spider, as well as to numerous lesser pulp characters; it has been claimed that "Robert Wallace," the house name used on the novels published in the pulp magazine *Phantom Detective*, was created to remind readers of Edgar Wallace. Furthermore, what with reprint and paperback editions, Wallace's work influenced writers publishing during the 1950s and 1960s. Ian Fleming's James Bond has been linked to Wallace's influence, and Friedrich Dürrenmatt's

crime novel *Die Panne* (1955) pays homage to the Just Men. An *Edgar Wallace Mystery Magazine* published a total of thirty-five issues in England from 1964 to 1967.

From this high point, Wallace's influence diminished to the point where he is almost forgotten and is read only by historians and the occasional fan. Nor is this situation likely to change. Although Wallace's individual works frequently have elements that can be praised, there are simply too many individual works for praise to mean anything: he wrote too much, glibly repeating himself in works that were stylistically flat, formulaically plotted, repetitively characterized, and thematically undistinguished. It is probable that Wallace would be the first to agree with such an assessment, for although he possessed a streak of vanity, he was sufficiently self-critical to realize that his abilities lay chiefly in the telling of exciting stories that appealed to the segment of the reading public that did not care for remarkable stylists, original plots, profound characterizations, and a wide variety of themes. By reading Wallace, this audience made it known that their tastes ran to plain tales, plainly told; and in the facile creation of stories to satisfy this readership, Wallace reigned supreme.

Selected Bibliography

WORKS OF EDGAR WALLACE

NOVELS

The Four Just Men. London: Tallis Press, 1905; rev. ed., 1906. Boston: Small Maynard, 1920.

The Council of Justice. London: Ward Lock, 1908.

The Nine Bears. London: Ward Lock, 1910. Rev. ed. published as *The Other Man*. New York: Dodd Mead, 1911. Also published as *Silinski, Master Criminal*. Cleveland: International Fiction Library, 1930; *The Cheaters*, London: Digit, 1964.

The Just Men of Cordova. London: Ward Lock, 1917.

The Crimson Circle. London: Hodder and Stoughton, 1922; Garden City, N.Y.: Doubleday, 1929.

The Face in the Night. London: Long, 1924; Garden City, N.Y.: Doubleday, 1929.

Room Thirteen. London: Long, 1924.

The Fellowship of the Frog. London: Ward Lock, 1925; Garden City, N.Y.: Doubleday, 1928.

The Gaunt Stranger. London: Hodder and Stoughton, 1925. U.S.: *The Ringer.* Garden City, N.Y.: Doubleday, 1926.

The Three Just Men. London: Hodder and Stoughton, 1925; Garden City, N.Y.: Doubleday, 1930.

The Joker. London: Hodder and Stoughton, 1926. U.S.: *The Colossus.* Garden City, N.Y.: Doubleday, 1932.

The Man from Morocco. London: Long, 1926. U.S.: *The Black.* Garden City, N.Y.: Doubleday, 1930.

Big Foot. London: Long, 1927.

The Feathered Serpent. London: Hodder and Stoughton, 1927; Garden City, N.Y.: Doubleday, 1928.

The Ringer. London: Hodder and Stoughton, 1927. Novelization of the 1926 stage play.

The Squeaker. London: Hodder and Stoughton, 1927. U.S.: *The Squealer.* Garden City, N.Y.: Doubleday, 1928.

Terror Keep. London: Hodder and Stoughton, 1927; Garden City, N.Y.: Doubleday, 1927.

The Gunner. London: Long, 1928. U.S.: *Gunman's Bluff.* Garden City, N.Y.: Doubleday, 1929.

The Twister. London: Long, 1928; Garden City, N.Y.: Doubleday, 1929.

The Calendar. London: Collins, 1930; Garden City, N.Y.: Doubleday, 1931.

White Face. London: Hodder and Stoughton, 1930; Garden City, N.Y.: Doubleday, 1931.

The Devil Man. London: Collins, 1931; Garden City, N.Y.: Doubleday, 1931.

SHORT STORY COLLECTIONS

Sanders of the River. London: Ward Lock, 1911; Garden City, N.Y.: Doubleday, 1930.

The Law of the Four Just Men. London: Hodder and Stoughton, 1921. U.S.: *Again the Three Just Men.* Garden City, N.Y.: Doubleday, 1933.

The Mind of Mr. J. G. Reeder. London: Hodder and Stoughton, 1925. U.S.: *The Murder Book of Mr. J. G. Reeder.* Garden City, N.Y.: Doubleday, 1929.

The Brigand. London: Hodder and Stoughton, 1927; Chicago: Academy, 1985.

The Mixer. London: Long, 1927.

Again the Three Just Men. London: Hodder and Stoughton, 1928. U.S.: *The Law of the Three Just Men.* Garden City, N.Y.: Doubleday, 1931.

Again the Ringer. London: Hodder and Stoughton, 1929. U.S.: *The Ringer Returns.* Garden City, N.Y.: Doubleday, 1931.

Four Square Jane. London: Readers Library, 1929; New York: World Wide, 1929.

The Lone House Mystery. London: Collins, 1929.

Red Aces. London: Hodder and Stoughton, 1929; Garden City, N.Y.: Doubleday, 1930.

The Guv'nor and Other Stories. London: Collins, 1932.

U.S.: *Mr. Reeder Returns.* Garden City, N.Y.: Doubleday, 1932.

STAGE PLAYS

An African Millionaire. London: Davis Poynter, 1972. Produced South Africa, 1904.

The Ringer. London: Hodder and Stoughton, 1929; New York: French, 1929. Adaptation of Wallace's novel *The Gaunt Stranger.* Produced London, 1926.

The Terror. London: Hodder and Stoughton, 1929. Adaptation of Wallace's novel *Terror Keep.* Produced Brighton and London, 1927.

The Squeaker. London: Hodder and Stoughton, 1929. Adaptation of Wallace's novel *The Squeaker.* Produced London, 1928; produced as *Sign of the Leopard,* New York, 1928.

The Calendar. London: French, 1932. Produced Manchester and London, 1929, with Wallace as director.

On the Spot. Produced London and New York, 1930.

OTHER WORKS

The Mission That Failed! A Tale of the Raid and Other Poems. Cape Town: Maskew Miller, 1898. Includes "Welcome to Kipling" as "A Tommy's Welcome."

War! and Other Poems. Cape Town: Eastern Press, 1900.

Writ in Barracks. London: Methuen, 1900. Poems.

Unofficial Dispatches. London: Hutchinson, 1901.

People: A Short Autobiography. London: Hodder and Stoughton, 1926; Garden City, N.Y.: Doubleday, 1929.

My Hollywood Diary. London: Hutchinson, 1932.

King Kong. Grosset & Dunlap, 1933. From an idea by Edgar Wallace and Merian C. Cooper. Screenplay completed by James Creelman and Ruth Rose.

BIOGRAPHICAL AND CRITICAL STUDIES

Bennett, Arnold. "I Read a 'Thriller'—and Startle My Friends." *Evening Standard,* 19 July 1928.

Cook, Michael L. *Monthly Murders. A Checklist and Chronological Listing of Fiction in the Digest-Size Mystery Magazines in the United States and England.* Westport, Conn.: Greenwood Press, 1982.

———, ed. *Mystery, Detective, and Espionage Magazines.* Westport, Conn.: Greenwood Press, 1983.

Curtis, Robert. *Edgar Wallace: Each Way.* London: Lane, 1932.

Doran, George H. *Chronicles of Barrabas, 1884–1934.* New York: Harcourt, Brace, 1935.

Edgar Wallace Mystery Magazine. Published in England from August 1964 until June 1967. With the exception of issue for May 1965 (vol. 2, no. 10), each issue reprinted one of Wallace's short stories. In addition to reprinting Wallace, the magazine reprinted stories by such writers as Agatha Christie, G. K. Chesterton, George Bernard Shaw, Sax Rohmer, Barry Perowne,

Mrs. Gaskell, and Roy Vickers. Original stories were in a minority, but the authors of these included Victor Canning and Penelope Wallace, daughter of Edgar.

Kiddle, Charles. *A Guide to the First Editions of Edgar Wallace.* Motcombe, Dorset, Eng.: Ivory Head Press, 1981.

Kiddle, Charles, and Richard Williams. *Edgar Wallace: First American Editions.* Scunthorpe, South Humberside, England: Dragonby Press, 1992.

Lane, Margaret. *Edgar Wallace: The Biography of a Phenomenon.* London: Heinemann, 1938; Garden City, N.Y.: Doubleday, Doran, 1939. Rev. ed., London: Hamilton, 1964.

Lofts, W. O. G., and Derek Adley. *The British Bibliography of Edgar Wallace.* London: Howard Baker, 1969.

Sampson, Robert. *Yesterday's Faces,* vol. 5 of *Dangerous Horizons.* Bowling Green, Ohio: Bowling Green State University Popular Press, 1991. Includes a checklist of works by and about Wallace.

Wallace, Ethel V. *Edgar Wallace by His Wife.* London: Hutchinson, 1932.

Williams, Richard. *Edgar Wallace British Magazine Appearances (Fiction).* Scunthorpe, South Humberside, England: Dragonby Press, 1988.

———. *Edgar Wallace: A Filmography.* Scunthorpe, South Humberside, England: Dragonby Press, 1990. Second edition.

———. *The Edgar Wallace Index (Books and Fiction).* Scunthorpe, North Lincolnshire, England: Dragonby Press, 1996.

DONALD E. WESTLAKE
(b. 1933)

LAWRENCE BLOCK

DONALD EDWIN EDMUND Westlake was born in New York City on 12 July 1933. His parents, Albert Joseph Westlake and Lillian Margaret née Bounds, were natives of Albany, New York, and the family moved there when he was six years old. He was educated in Catholic schools in Albany and attended Champlain College in Plattsburgh, New York (1950–1955), and, after two years in the U.S. Air Force (1954–1956), Harpur College (1956–1957), now the State University of New York at Binghamton. By the time he enrolled at Harpur, Westlake had written an unpublished novel about the air force as well as a slew of short stories, some of which he had managed to sell. He had chosen his career much earlier:

I knew I was a writer when I was eleven. It took the rest of the world about ten years to begin to agree. . . . Neophyte writers are always told, 'Write what you know,' but the fact is, kids don't know *anything*. A beginning writer doesn't write what he knows, he writes what he read in books or saw in the movies. And that's the way it was with me. I wrote gangster stories, I wrote stories about cowboys, I wrote poems about gold prospecting, I wrote the first chapters of all kinds of novels. The short stories I mailed off to magazines, and they mailed them back, in the self-addressed stamped envelopes I had provided. (*Note:* Throughout this article, the author's sources include personal knowledge and reminiscences of the subject.)

One year short of graduation from college, Westlake moved from Binghamton to New York City in 1958. There, like no end of young men who would spend their lives in writing or publishing, he became a fee reader for Scott Meredith, the literary agent. He read "sixty short stories or eight novels or some mix thereof every week," writing letters over Meredith's signature "about how *this* story doesn't quite make it but shows really amazing talent and do try us again with another story and another check."

The work was both an education and an apprenticeship for an emerging writer. Reading slush submissions taught the budding writer what did and didn't work on the page, and his presence in the office led to frequent assignments. Westlake wrote confession stories and magazine articles on assignment and was able to give up his job altogether for steady freelance work writing fifty-thousand-word softcore paperback sex novels. His first real novel, *The Mercenaries*, was published in 1960. Speaking about that period of time Westlake said,

The stories that were getting published were more and more frequently mystery stories, and I think it's a natural tendency to go where you're liked, so the next time I tried to write a novel it was a mystery novel. That's when I began to describe myself as a writer disguised as a mystery writer, a remark I continued for ten or fifteen years, until the face grew to match the mask.

Westlake moved to Brooklyn in 1958 and then to New Jersey in 1960, and in the late 1990s continued to live in and around New York. In 1979 he married the writer Abby Adams; his two earlier marriages ended in divorce. In addition to some fifty novels, almost all of them touching at least peripherally the genre of mystery and suspense, he has written reportage, essays, book reviews, and a children's book. He has also written successfully for the screen and was nominated for an Academy Award for his adaptation (1989) of Jim Thompson's *The Grifters* (1963). In 1992 he was named a Grand Master by the Mystery Writers of America.

A computer could have written the foregoing biography and would very likely have had an easier time of it than I. Objective journalism has never been either my strong suit or my predilection. How, indeed, am I to be objective about Don Westlake? He has been my friend for almost forty years. I made his acquaintance in print before I met him in the flesh. In early 1959 I was in Yellow Springs, Ohio, working as a writer for Midwood Books. I had worked the previous year for Scott Meredith, the same literary agent for whom Westlake read. I read other Midwood titles when I found them, in a spirit of professional curiosity. One such volume, "Backstage Lore," led me to write a note to Henry Morrison, my (and Don's) agent at Scott Meredith at the time. "This one's pretty good," I observed. "Who wrote it?"

In the summer of 1959 I met the author. We introduced ourselves at the Scott Meredith office, where we'd both come to pick up checks or drop off manuscripts, or both. I went back with him to his apartment on West Forty-sixth Street between Ninth and Tenth Avenues. I met his wife and their infant son, and we had dinner and talked for hours. I've been his friend ever since, and I've been his enthusiastic reader as well. There was a period in the late sixties when we didn't speak, and even then I went on reading his books. (I was occasionally mean-spirited enough during that brief span to hope I wouldn't like his latest work, but I always did.)

Moreover, there have been startling parallels in our careers. We both worked for and were subsequently represented (and misrepresented) by the same agent. We sold stories to the same magazines and sex novels to the same purveyors of schlock. We both wound up as mystery writers without having consciously chosen the field early on. We both wrote voluminously under pen names and were intermittently neurotic about keeping our true identities a secret. And each of us, in a world that reveres brand names, has stubbornly insisted on writing more than one sort of book. "How can you write some books that are so funny and others that are so hard-boiled and serious?" I am asked that question all the time, and so is Westlake.

Sometimes people confuse us and our writings. "I remember the first book I read about Matthew Scudder," a fan told me a while ago. "It was an early one, and he was spending all his time building a wall in back of his house." It was a very early one, I agreed; Scudder's name was Mitch Tobin at the time, and he was a character in a book by Tucker Coe, a pseudonym of Westlake's. More recently, a woman asked me if my novelettes about that Jewish cop with a bad heart would ever be published in book form. "The book was *Levine*," I told her. "It was published in 1984, and I used the pen name Donald E. Westlake on it." So how can I be objective about either the man or his work, when I have been uncommonly fond of both for so many years? I won't even try. What I can and will do is discuss the tissues and organs in his remarkable body of work. I'm not sure this needs doing—one of the work's most remarkable qualities, after all, is its sheer accessibility—but that's what they want me to do, so I'll do it.

Hard-boiled Mysteries

Westlake's first novel, *The Mercenaries*, was bought by Lee Wright at Random House, whom Westlake calls "the best editor I've ever had." The narrator is essentially a mid-level corporate executive, but the corporation employing him is an organized criminal enterprise. There's a murder, and he has to solve it, using the skills he's acquired on the job and the resources (bought cops, criminal informants) available to him. No one had written anything quite like this at the time, and Wright was sufficiently impressed with its novelty to ballyhoo the book in a manner that helped and harmed it in the same breath. She heralded it as "the first new direction in the tough mystery since Hammett." That guaranteed the book a certain amount of attention and also virtually ensured that a great many people's responses would fall somewhere between "Oh, yeah?" and "Sez who?"

The book doesn't live up to its billing, but it's difficult to see how it could. For one thing, there had been several new directions since Dashiell Hammett; for another, *The Mercenaries* wasn't that great a departure. It was (and is) a terse, tough-minded mystery with a lead character who, while by no means unsympathetic, is the sort who could be called amoral. The novel received a fair amount of attention and was given an Edgar nomination from the Mystery Writers of America as best first mystery of the year. (It didn't win, coming in second to a book by Jack Vance, which, even though it was arguably a first mystery and thus technically eligible for the award, was not a first novel.) With the publication of *The Mercenaries* and Random House's acceptance of his second mystery, *Killing Time* (1961), Westlake began to feel secure as a writer. I can vividly recall sitting in his up-stairs flat in Canarsie while he confided to me that he thought he had it made. The way things were shaping up, he said, he could count on being able to make ten thousand dollars a year as a writer, year in and year out.

No one would have called *Killing Time* the first new direction since Hammett. It was, on the contrary, very much a turn *toward* Hammett. Westlake has always admired Dashiell Hammett enormously, but he is considerably more restrained in his enthusiasm for the

other putative founder of the hard-boiled school, Raymond Chandler. His second book—*Killing Time*, the title of the first of two novellas published as *$106,000 Blood Money*—is very much an homage to Hammett, with persistent echoes of *Red Harvest* (1929) and *Blood Money* (1927). ("Homage," according to Westlake, is the French word for plagiarism.) A hard, fast, nasty book, it was a good sequel to the author's first novel and seemed to confirm him as an heir to the Black Mask tradition.

Nowadays, "sequel" is almost always taken to mean the next book in a series, but the genre was different back then. Publishers were not nearly so inclined to urge writers to produce a series of books about a single character. The feeling persisted that a book in a series amounted to rather less artistically than one that stood alone. A full-fledged novel, it was assumed, ought to use up its lead character by its end, either providing him with a catharsis or killing him or both. Readers might prefer series, but so what? Since a mystery novel was presumed to have an audience of four to six thousand, what difference did it make what readers liked?

Times have changed, and a young Westlake today would find himself keeping his lead character, Clay, alive at the end of *The Mercenaries* and writing a dozen books about him. They might have been interesting books, but fortunately for Westlake's development, he was instead encouraged to write varied books and find his own way as a writer. He followed *Killing Time* with *361* (1962), my personal favorite of his hard-boiled period and, to my mind, the first book in which he found a voice that was uniquely his. The title, *361*, is the numerical heading for "killing" in *Roget's Thesaurus*, and that entry is the epigraph, with its host of synonyms for slaughter. It concerns the two sons of a gangster and their efforts to help him regain power after his release from prison. Someone once said that all American crime fiction is about the search for one's father; this novel, too, is about the narrator's search for his father, and it derives unmistakably from the author's personal mythology. (The interested reader might refer to Westlake's fascinating and immensely readable essay in the *Contemporary Authors* autobiography series.)

Westlake's early hard-boiled period, if you will, concluded with *Killy* (1963), the story of a labor union troubleshooter, and *Pity Him Afterwards* (1964), a suspenseful tour de force about a psychopathic killer at a summer theater. (Westlake hammered out *Pity Him Afterwards* in four or five days to overcome a siege of writer's block; it's probably a better book than he realizes.) During this time, he wrote what we then called a "serious" novel. (We used the word to indicate a mainstream novel with literary aspirations; it would, in fact, be hard to explain why *361*, say, was anything other than serious.) Westlake called the book "Memory" and describes it thus:

> At the beginning of the novel, an actor on tour is hit on the head and hospitalized. His brain is damaged, so that his long-term memory goes; his memory loss is accelerated; last month is lost to him. By the time he comes out of the hospital, the touring company is long gone and so is his past, though he has enough memory to function in normal ways, and has fitful glimpses of a brighter and more interesting yesteryear. The book is about the functions and uses and glories of memory, and about the slow despair of the hero.

I read "Memory" in manuscript, which, as it turned out, was the only way anyone ever read it. I sat up all night with it, certain I was reading a great novel, unquestionably worthy of being mentioned in the same breath with the best existential fiction. It was never published. Virtually all the editors who saw it turned "Memory" down in terms more glowing than they would have dared apply to the books they accepted. They all loved it, they all praised it, and they all said they couldn't figure out how to sell it. They compared it to the works of Fyodor Dostoyevsky, Franz Kafka, Mark Twain, and Thomas Wolfe, and they said they were confident someone else would figure out how to publish it successfully.

I remember this when I hear people whining about how difficult it is now, how the fabled midlist book no longer has a chance. I read "Memory" almost thirty-five years ago, in publishing's kinder, gentler era. The book was important and of the highest quality— and, incidentally, an edge-of-the-chair read— and nobody could summon up the gumption to get it into print. Things may be not so great now, but don't try to tell me that was a golden age back then. I don't think so. Years later, Westlake read "Memory" after an agent told him it would probably be publishable, only to decide against trying to market it. His feeling was that the book was too much a creature of its time. Would I be similarly sanguine about publishing an early book that had never seen print? I have such a book; it was unpublishable then, and I'd prefer it stay unpublished now. But that's different, it seems to me. "Memory" wasn't unpublishable, and no one ever called it unpublishable. It was simply unpublished.

Another thing to wonder about—and we can wonder all we want because we will never know the answer—is what Westlake would have gone on to write if "Memory" hadn't been consigned to the dustbin of literature. Throughout his career, Westlake has written the books he's wanted to write. While his intent has always been commercial, he has been led more by artistic considerations than commerical ones. If, the failure of "Memory" notwithstanding, he'd been overtaken by an idea for another novel of the same sort, I don't doubt for a moment that he would have written it. As he has said, however, it is a natural tendency to go where you're liked. And the subconscious, the part of the self from which literary ideas flow, is no less inclined to steer clear of doors that have been slammed in its face and to close a few doors of its own. If "Memory" had been a success, who can doubt for a moment that Westlake would have had ideas for other serious literary fiction? But it wasn't, and he didn't.

The Comic Mystery Novels

"Use the accident" is a catchphrase in the visual arts. What it generally means is that one ought to be guided, even inspired, when something other than what one intended emerges on the canvas. Whether it is a slip of the brush or a bubbling up of the unconscious, don't obliterate it precipitously. Maybe there's a way to make use of it. The accident that Westlake has used, more than once, is humor. His sixth novel for Random House was designed to be one more variation on a hard-boiled theme, an innocent on the run, but it started to become funny. Westlake was worried and called his agent, who reminded him that there had been no funny mysteries since the death of Craig Rice and told him to stop what he was writing and do something else.

The advice struck him as eminently sound, but he was fortunately unable to take it. The book demanded to be written, and he decided to give in, get it out of his system, and then go back to being serious. He recalls:

> The fact is it had never occurred to me that I could write funny. [In childhood] I wasn't the funniest kid around, I was the funniest kid's best friend. So what this book was trying to do I had no idea, but I followed it, and it kept on being funny.

The book was published as *The Fugitive Pigeon* (1965), and it confounded everybody by doubling the author's sales domestically and doing very well abroad. In the years that followed Westlake produced one comic novel after another, all of them the sort of work we have come to call "Westlakean." Before *The Fugitive Pigeon*, there was no such thing as a comic mystery novel; within a few years such a category did in fact exist, and Westlake essentially owned it.

In one book after another, Westlake pitted his hero, an imperiled innocent, against an all-powerful but inept system. The world reflected in books like *The Busy Body* (1966), *The Spy in the Ointment* (1966), *God Save the Mark* (1967), and *Somebody Owes Me Money* (1969) is a far different place from the setting for Westlake's earlier work. It is filled with criminals, and they perpetrate felonies and occasionally kill one another, but good always triumphs, and nothing too terrible ever happens to anyone we care about.

The most casual reading of his work makes it quite clear that neither the serious nor the comic novels can claim exclusive title to the "real" Donald Westlake. Both provide accurate reflections of their author. I would contend that he (like everyone else) has a light side and a dark side and that he (unlike the great majority of writers) is equally capable of writing from either of these sides. And, of course, there is dark in light and light in darkness. His hardest, toughest work is not without the leavening of humor, nor is his lightest, airiest confection entirely devoid of substance. With *The Fugitive Pigeon*, Westlake seems to have gone over entirely to his light side and to have remained there but for such anomalous later works as *Kahawa* (1982), *Sacred Monster* (1989), *Humans* (1992), and *The Ax* (1997). In point of fact, he never ceased to produce darker work as well, but he did so under pen names.

Mitch Tobin, the guilt-ridden, depressive ex-cop who is the hero of five novels written under the name Tucker Coe, provides an ideal window onto Westlake's darker side. The source of Tobin's anguish is that while he was cheating on his own wife in the bed of the wife of a criminal he had previously arrested, his partner was shot dead by another crook—and Tobin was not there to back him up. This is enough to make Tobin severely dysfunctional and to turn him into a pariah in the New York Police Department. (This does strain credibility a bit. While I'm willing to believe Tobin might agonize over his role in his partner's death, he'd never get such an extreme reaction from his fellow cops. But never mind.)

Tobin more or less mends things with his wife, though a little couples therapy might not be amiss. And he devotes the greater portion of his energies to building, slowly and meticulously, a concrete wall around the perimeter of his backyard, walling himself in and walling the world out. This is a wonderful metaphor, and Tobin's character, quite perfectly realized, fits it superbly. He is drawn reluctantly away from his wall, and back into the world, by the cases he has to take in order to make ends meet. As a de facto private eye, Tobin works in areas of the demimonde a cop would regard from a distance and with contempt—homosexuals in *A Jade in Aries* (1971), hippie kids in *Don't Lie to Me* (1972). An outcast himself, Tobin is sympathetic to the people he meets, in spite of his prejudices. Over the course of five books, Tobin gradually began to heal, even as his wall neared completion. What helped him as a human being made him no longer compelling as a dark hero, and Westlake stopped writing about him.

The Richard Stark Novels

"When the shit hit the fan, Parker threw himself in front of it." No, none of the Richard Stark novels opens that way, though I live in hope. Westlake began writing about Parker in 1960 and produced sixteen books about him (and four about his colleague, Grofield) in the space of fifteen years. I remember reading the first chapter of what came to be the first Parker book, *The Hunter* (1962). Parker, walking across the George Washington Bridge into New York, is offered a lift by a motorist and tells the guy to go to hell. I read the chapter through and asked Westlake if he knew where the book was going. He answered that he didn't. He found out as he wrote it. Parker, a professional thief, has escaped from custody and is looking to get even with the people who betrayed him and to recover money that is rightfully (or, since he stole it in the first place, wrongfully) his. The book was never intended as the first volume of a series, and, in fact, Parker was back in police custody at the book's end; he was set free when an editor at Pocket Books said he'd publish *The Hunter* if Parker were to escape and reappear in three books a year. Westlake agreed at once; he'd

only had Parker recaptured because he thought he had to, that villains had to die or get caught at the end.

Parker's concern—to get back the money he's owed—drives the first three books. (This is a recurrent theme in Westlake's fiction; for a lighter treatment, see *Somebody Owes Me Money*.) The books that follow are caper novels. In book after book, Parker plans a job, assembles a crew, and pulls it off—and then something goes wrong, and he has to mend his fences and salvage what he can. There is even a standard formal structure for the books. They are written in four parts, like a symphony, three of them narrated from Parker's point of view. The second or third section is told from the point of view of one of the other characters. The minor characters—some turn up in more than one book, some are heard from but once, and some, of course, are killed off in these harsh and violent books—are brilliantly realized and economically sketched. The bits of color—Parker buys a stolen truck, Parker arranges financing for a job—are clever, vivid, and engaging. But it is Parker himself, a coldly logical but not inhumane sociopath, who is eternally fascinating.

It is impossible to guess what will or will not be read years hence. (And does it really matter? Why should we value posterity's ill-informed judgment more highly than our own?) That said, it's my opinion that the Parker novels will prove to be Westlake's most enduring work. I base this judgment not on their merit, which I think is considerable, but on the special hold they have on readers. People don't just read the Parker books; they reread them, over and over and over. And if any quality makes a book last over time, I think that may be it: not that the book cries out to be read but that it insists upon being read again and again.

In 1974, Westlake wrote the sixteenth Parker novel, *Butcher's Moon*. It was longer than the others, and in it he brought back surviving co-conspirators of Parker's from throughout the series, all assembled to help Parker rescue Handy McKay, his closest friend. If the series had to end, that was a good book to end it on, and it looked as though Westlake had done just that. He made several attempts to write further about Parker, and it didn't work. Westlake has said that he doesn't know why Richard Stark retired.

> I tried several times to put him back to work, but he was tired and leaden. His imagination was gone, the simplicity of his prose was gone, the coldness of his view was gone. It never worked. On the other hand, I've learned from embarrassing experience never to make absolute statements about the future.

Indeed. Parker returns in *Comeback* (1997), and it's as if he had never been gone. He hasn't lost a step.

Several years before Richard Stark's extended temporary retirement, Westlake ran into problems trying to write about Parker. In the story idea he was developing, Parker was called upon to steal the same thing over and over, and there was something inherently antic in the premise. If this had happened in Parker's initial appearance in 1960, Westlake would have either abandoned the book as a bad idea or simply allowed it to be funny, as he would do a few years later in *The Fugitive Pigeon*. But he had already written enough books about Parker to have established beyond doubt that Parker was not a funny guy.

Handed a lemon, he made lemonade. He recast the book and created John Dortmunder, a sort of anti-Parker—not a bumbler, but a supremely unlucky fellow who inhabits a kinder, gentler criminal universe and whose jobs go horribly wrong in unfailingly amusing ways. Dortmunder was never intended as a series character; he was just the solution to that lemon. Neither had Parker been so intended, and a couple of years after *The Hot Rock* (1970) was published, Westlake saw a bank temporarily housed in a mobile home and thought an enterprising person could back a truck up to the bank and drive it away. *Bank Shot* (1972) was the result, and since then he has written a whole string of books about Dortmunder and Kelp and Murch and the

gang. Although all of them are good, some are better than others. *Drowned Hopes* (1990) is the strongest book to date, though *Jimmy the Kid* (1974) can claim to be the most interesting; in it, Dortmunder's men steal the plan for their caper from a (fictitious) book by Richard Stark.

I haven't said anything much about Westlake as a screenwriter, and I don't think I will—not that there's nothing to say, but that I'm not at all the person to say it. I haven't seen many of the productions, and film and television writing lie well outside my area of interest, let alone expertise. I can say that I thought his work on *The Grifters* was superb and would have made Jim Thompson himself happy, if anything could have that unlikely effect. In recent years Westlake has made a substantial portion of his income from screenwriting, and what is remarkable is not what he has or hasn't done for Hollywood but that he has managed to touch pitch without being defiled. Hollywood ruins most of the writers who go anywhere near it. Many stop writing prose fiction after a few years, and those who make the effort generally find out that they have lost the knack.

Perhaps Westlake's secret lies in the fact that he has kept his distance from the place while getting wholly (and happily) involved in the work. He doesn't go out to California, except for the occasional meeting. He stays in New York City or in his house upstate, and he works on screenplays the same way he works on novels, batting them out on his manual typewriter. He continues, after so many years, to be as productive and as wonderfully unpredictable as ever. In the late 1990s he produced *Smoke* (1995), a savage indictment of the tobacco industry in the guise of a rollicking invisible man comedy; *The Ax*, a taut, hard-edged novel about a victim of corporate downsizing who assures himself a job by killing off all the better-qualified prospects; and *Comeback*, Parker's long-awaited return. He has always written rapidly and well, and he has never written better or faster than he's writing now—after all those years and all those books.

Selected Bibliography

WORKS OF DONALD WESTLAKE

NOVELS

The Mercenaries. New York: Random House, 1960. Also published as *The Smashers.* New York: Dell, 1962.
Killing Time. New York: Random House, 1961. Also published as *The Operator.* New York: Dell, 1964.
361. New York: Random House, 1962.
Killy. New York: Random House, 1963.
Pity Him Afterwards. New York: Random House, 1964.
The Fugitive Pigeon. New York: Random House, 1965.
The Busy Body. New York: Random House, 1966.
The Spy in the Ointment. New York: Random House, 1966.
God Save the Mark. New York: Random House, 1967.
Who Stole Sassi Manoon? New York: Random House, 1969.
Somebody Owes Me Money. New York: Random House, 1969.
The Hot Rock. New York: Simon & Schuster, 1970.
I Gave at the Office. New York: Simon & Schuster, 1971.
Bank Shot. New York: Simon & Schuster, 1972.
Cops and Robbers. New York: Evans, 1972.
Help I Am Being Held Prisoner. New York: Evans, 1974.
Jimmy the Kid. New York: Evans, 1974.
Two Much. New York: Evans, 1975.
Dancing Aztecs. New York: Evans, 1976. Also published as *A New York Dance.* London: Hodder & Stoughton, 1979.
Enough. New York: Evans, 1977.
Nobody's Perfect. New York: Evans, 1977.
Castle in the Air. New York: Evans, 1980.
Kahawa. New York: Viking, 1982.
Why Me? New York: Viking, 1983.
High Adventure. New York: Mysterious Press, 1985.
Good Behavior. New York: Mysterious Press, 1985.
Trust Me on This. New York: Mysterious Press, 1988.
Sacred Monster. New York: Mysterious Press, 1989.
Drowned Hopes. New York: Mysterious Press, 1990.
Humans. New York: Mysterious Press, 1992.
Don't Ask. New York: Mysterious Press, 1993.
Baby, Would I Lie? A Romance of the Ozarks. New York: Mysterious Press, 1994.
Smoke. New York: Mysterious Press, 1995.
What's the Worst That Could Happen? New York: Mysterious Press, 1996.
The Ax. New York: Mysterious Press, 1997.

THE PARKER NOVELS BY RICHARD STARK

The Hunter. New York: Pocket Books, 1962. Also published as *Point Blank.* London: Hodder & Stoughton, 1967.
The Man with the Getaway Face. New York: Pocket Books, 1963. Also published as *The Steel Hit.* London: Hodder & Stoughton, 1971.
The Outfit. New York: Pocket Books, 1963.
The Mourner. New York: Pocket Books, 1963.
The Score. New York: Pocket Books, 1964. Also published as *Killtown.* London: Hodder & Stoughton, 1971.
The Jugger. New York: Pocket Books, 1965.
The Seventh. New York: Pocket Books, 1966. Also published as *The Split.* London: Hodder & Stoughton, 1969.
The Handle. New York: Pocket Books, 1966. Also published as *Run Lethal.* London: Hodder & Stoughton, 1972.
The Rare Coin Score. New York: Fawcett, 1967.
The Green Eagle Score. New York: Fawcett, 1967.
The Black Ice Score. New York: Fawcett, 1968.
The Sour Lemon Score. New York: Fawcett, 1969.
Slayground. New York: Random House, 1971.
Deadly Edge. New York: Random House, 1971.
Plunder Squad. New York: Random House, 1972.
Butcher's Moon. New York: Random House, 1974.
Comeback. New York: Mysterious Press, 1997.
Backflash. New York: Mysterious Press, 1998.

THE GROFIELD NOVELS BY RICHARD STARK

The Damsel. New York: Macmillan, 1967.
The Dame. New York: Macmillan, 1969.
The Blackbird. New York: Macmillan, 1969.
Lemons Never Lie. New York: World, 1971.

THE MITCH TOBIN NOVELS BY TUCKER COE

Kinds of Love, Kinds of Death. New York: Random House, 1966.
Murder Among Children. New York: Random House, 1967.
Wax Apple. New York: Random House, 1970.
A Jade in Aries. New York: Random House, 1971.
Don't Lie to Me. New York: Random House, 1972.

COLLECTED SHORT STORIES

The Curious Facts Preceding My Execution and Other Fictions. New York: Random House, 1968.
Once Against the Law (edited with William Tenn). New York: Macmillan, 1968.
Levine. New York: Mysterious Press, 1984.
Tomorrow's Crimes. New York: Mysterious Press, 1989.

UNCOLLECTED SHORT STORIES

"Arrest." *Manhunt,* January 1958.
"Everybody Killed Sylvia." *Mystery Digest,* May 1958.
"The Devil's Printer." *Mystery Digest,* September 1958.
"Sinner or Saint." *Mystery Digest,* December 1958.
"Decoy for Murder." *Mystery Digest,* March 1959.
"Death for Sale." *Mystery Digest,* April 1959.
"The Ledge Bit." *Mystery Digest,* September/October 1959.
"Knife Fighter." *Guilty,* November 1959.

DONALD E. WESTLAKE

"Anatomy of an Anatomy." *Alfred Hitchcock's Mystery Magazine*, September 1960.

"An Empty Threat." *Manhunt*, February 1960.

"Friday Night." *Tightrope*, June 1960.

"A Time to Die." *The Saint*, January 1962.

"A Toast to the Damned." *Off Beat Detective Stories*, April 1962.

"Lock Your Door." *Alfred Hitchcock's Mystery Magazine*, August 1962.

"The Letter." *Mike Shayne Mystery Magazine*, August 1965.

"The Method." *Alfred Hitchcock's Mystery Magazine*, October 1965.

"The Spoils System." *Alfred Hitchcock's Mystery Magazine*, December 1965.

"Stage Fright." *The Saint*, September 1965.

"Cool O'Toole." *Alfred Hitchcock's Mystery Magazine*, September 1966.

"Teamwork." *Shell Scott Mystery Magazine*, February 1966.

"Ask a Silly Question." *Playboy*, February 1981.

"Re Porter." *Ellery Queen's Mystery Magazine*, June 1981.

"A Good Story." *Playboy*, October 1984.

"Breathe Deep." *Playboy*, July 1985.

"Horse Laugh." *Playboy*, June 1986.

"Too Many Crooks." *Playboy*, August 1989.

"The Dortmunder Workout." *New York Times Magazine*, 29 April 1990.

"A Midsummer Daydream." *Playboy*, May 1990.

"Love in the Lean Years." *Playboy*, February 1992.

"Party Animal." *Playboy*, January 1993.

BIOGRAPHICAL AND CRITICAL STUDIES

DeAndrea, William L. "Westlake, Donald E(dwin)." In his *Encyclopedia Mysteriosa*. New York: Prentice Hall, 1994. Pp. 371–372.

Nevins, Francis M. "Westlake, Donald E(dwin Edmund)." In *St. James Guide to Crime & Mystery Writers*. Edited by Jay P. Pederson. Detroit: St. James Press, 1996. Pp. 1039–1041.

CORNELL WOOLRICH
(1903–1968)

FRANCIS M. NEVINS

OF ALL THE AUTHORS who have tried their hands at turning readers' spines to columns of ice, the one most often considered the supreme master of the art—in a phrase, the Hitchcock of the written word—was Cornell Woolrich. His full name was Cornell George Hopley-Woolrich and he was born in New York City on 4 December 1903 to parents whose marriage collapsed in his youth. His mother, born Claire Attalie Tarler, was the daughter of George Tarler, a Russian Jewish émigré who had made his fortune in the import trade with Mexico and Central America. His father, Genaro Hopley-Woolrich, was English by birth, Latino by ethnicity. Very little is known of him, but he seems to have been a happy-go-lucky adventurer, attractive and susceptible to women. In 1907 he and Claire left New York with three-year-old Cornell to resettle in Mexico. The marriage did not long survive the move. Claire returned to the Tarler household on West 113th Street near Morningside Park, and the child stayed with Genaro below the border. His schooling was punctuated by holidays whenever another revolutionary leader captured the town where they lived, and as a hobby he collected the spent rifle cartridges that littered the streets beneath his windows.

When Cornell was eight, Grandfather Tarler took him to Mexico City's Palace of Fine Arts to see a traveling French company perform Giacomo Puccini's then new opera *Madama Butterfly*, an experience that gave the boy a sudden sharp insight into color and drama and his first sense of tragedy. Three years later, on a night when he looked up at the low-hanging stars from the valley of Anahuac, he understood that someday, like Cio-Cio-San, he too would have to die. From that moment he was haunted by a sense of doom. In his autobiography, *Blues of a Lifetime* (1991), he writes, "I had that trapped feeling, like some sort of a poor insect that you've put inside a downturned glass, and it tries to climb up the sides, and it can't, and it can't, and it can't" (p. 16).

During Woolrich's adolescence he returned to New York City and lived with his grandfather, aunt, and mother in George Tarler's house on 113th Street. In 1921 he enrolled at Columbia College, a short walk from home. He chose journalism as his major but dreamed of a more romantic occupation, like being an author or a professional dancer. In his junior year, while immobilized with either an infected foot or a bad case of jaundice (his own accounts of the incident are at odds), he began the first draft of a novel. When it sold a few months later, he quit Columbia to pursue the dream of bright lights.

Pre-Suspense Fiction, 1926–1934

The main influence on Woolrich's early work was F. Scott Fitzgerald, the literary idol of the 1920s, and Woolrich's first novel, *Cover Charge* (1926), chronicles the lives and loves of the Jazz Age's gilded youth, child-people flitting from thrill to thrill, conversing in a mannered slang that reads today like a foreign language. But several motifs from his earlier and later life and his later suspense fiction can be detected in this rather amateurish debut: the fascination with dance halls and movie palaces; the use of popular song lyrics to convey mood; touches of vibrantly colorful description; a long interlude in Mexico City complete with performance of *Madama Butterfly*; romance between Alan Walker, the ballroom dancer protagonist, and two women, each of whom is old enough to be his mother; an extravaganza of coincidence to keep the story moving; and a despairing climax with Alan alone in a cheap hotel room contemplating suicide, his legs all but useless after an auto smashup, abandoned by the women he at various times loved. "I hate this world. Everything comes into it so clean and goes out so dirty" (p. 280).

Children of the Ritz (1927), which may have been suggested by his mother's marriage to a man beneath her social class, is a frothy concoction about a spoiled heiress who impulsively marries her chauffeur. The book won a first prize of ten thousand dollars in a contest co-sponsored by *College Humor* magazine, which serialized it, and First National Pictures, which filmed the story in 1929. Woolrich was invited to Hollywood to help with the adaptation and stayed on as a staff writer, although he never received screen credit for whatever contributions he made. One of the dialogue and title writers employed by First National at about this time was named William Irish. In 1942, Woolrich inexplicably took this name as a pseudonym.

With novels, movie chores, and an occasional article or story for magazines like *College Humor, College Life, McClure's,* and *Smart Set,* Woolrich must have been a busy young man indeed. By the time of his gritty and cynical third book, *Times Square* (1929), he had begun to develop the headlong storytelling drive and the concern with the torments and the maniacal power of love that came to mark his later suspense fiction. The first half of his autobiographical novel, *A Young Man's Heart* (1930), is set in Mexico around 1910, and the viewpoint is that of a young boy during and after the collapse of his parents' marriage.

In December 1930, while still working in Hollywood, Woolrich suddenly married twenty-year-old Gloria Blackton, a daughter of the pioneer movie producer J. Stuart Blackton, who had founded Vitagraph Studios in 1897. The marriage was never consummated. A graphic diary he kept but later destroyed (although not before it had been found and read by Gloria and her family) indicates that he had been homosexually active for some time prior to the marriage, which he had entered as a sort of sick joke or perhaps for cover. In the middle of the night he would put on a sailor outfit that he kept in a locked suitcase and prowl the waterfront for partners. The marriage ended within three months, and Woolrich fled to New York and mother. "I was born to be solitary," he says in his autobiography, "and I liked it that way" (p. 4). But the pages of his novels and stories are haunted by the shadow of his desperate need for a relationship with a woman who never was and never could have been.

After the breakup of his marriage, Woolrich and his mother traveled extensively in Europe. His sixth novel, *Manhattan Love Song* (1932), is the best of his youthful books and the only one that, if published a few decades later, would have been called a crime novel. It begins with a quintessential Woolrich moment.

First she was just a figure moving toward me in the distance, among a great many others doing the same thing. A second later she was a girl. Then she became a pretty girl, exquisitely dressed. Next a responsive girl, whose eyes said "Are you lonely?", whose shadow of a smile said, "Then speak." And by that time we had reached and were almost passing one another. Our glances seemed to strike a spark between us in mid-air. (p. 5)

Wade, the narrator, soon becomes a helpless slave to his passion for the enigmatic Bernice. Under her spell he abandons his job, assaults and robs a homosexual actor for money to spend on her, and treats his wife, Maxine, who still loves him desperately, like filth. Although Bernice in some mysterious way is controlled by unseen powers in the city, she responds so passionately to Wade's abject passion for her that she is ready to sacrifice everything and risk the powers' vengeance in order to start life over again with him. As usual in Woolrich's stories, however, love opens the door to horror, and those who manage to survive have nothing left but to wait for the merciful release of death.

For the next two years Woolrich sold next to nothing. He had moved out of the house on 113th Street and into a cheap hotel, determined to make it as a writer without his mother's help, but he was soon deep in debt and reduced to sneaking into movie houses by the fire doors for entertainment. Frantically he tried to complete and find a publisher for a novel he had begun two years earlier, a story of ballroom dancers in 1912 Paris (as he described the plot some thirty years later in *Blues of a Lifetime*) for which he hoped some Hollywood studio would pay him enough to liberate him from the Depression. No one was interested in the book, and finally Woolrich tossed the entire manuscript of "I Love You, Paris" into the garbage. But at that moment he was on the brink of a new life as a writer, one so different from his earlier literary career that decades later he said it would have been better if all his pre-suspense fiction "had been written in invisible ink and the reagent had been thrown away" (*Blues of a Lifetime*, p. 12). He was about to become the Edgar Allan Poe of the twentieth century and the poet of its shadows.

Pulp Crime Stories, 1934–1940

"There was another patient ahead of me in the waiting room. He was sitting there quietly, humbly, with all the terrible resignation of the very poor" (*Somebody on the Phone*, 1943, p. 166). Woolrich's first crime story, "Death Sits in the Dentist's Chair" (*Detective Fiction Weekly*, 4 August 1934), offers a vivid picture of New York City during the worst of the Depression, a bizarre murder method (cyanide in a temporary filling), and a race against the clock to save the poisoned protagonist—elements that soon became Woolrich hallmarks. His two other mystery tales of 1934 are equally characteristic. "Walls That Hear You" (*Detective Fiction Weekly*, 18 August 1934) opens with the invasion of nightmare into the viewpoint character's workaday existence when he finds his younger brother with all ten fingers cut off and his tongue severed at the roots. And "Preview of Death" (*Dime Detective*, 15 November 1934) has a Hollywood moviemaking background and another unusual murder method—setting fire to an actress in a flammable Civil War hoopskirt—which Woolrich had first used as a method of accidental death in *Times Square*.

The ten crime stories Woolrich published in 1935 were of uneven quality but stunning variety, embodying most of the motifs, beliefs, and techniques at the core of his fiction. "Murder in Wax" (*Dime Detective*, 1 March 1935) is his earliest attempt at first-person narrative from the viewpoint of a woman. "The Body Upstairs" (*Dime Detective*, 1 April 1935) is marked by casual police brutality and intuition that passes for detection. In "Kiss of the Cobra" (*Dime Detective*, 1 May 1935), demonic nightmare once again invades everyday life, but this time in rather absurd form— the narrator's widowed father-in-law brings home as his second wife a Hindu snake priestess complete with reptiles. "Red Liberty" (*Dime Detective*, 1 July 1935) anticipates the police-procedural genre with its simple story about the finding of a body inside the Statue of Liberty, the first of many New York landmarks that figured in his pulp stories. "Dark Melody of Madness" (*Dime Mystery*, July 1935), better known as "Papa Benjamin," deals with a jazz bandleader who learns too much about a New Orleans voodoo cult and reintroduces the theme of the evil power whose prey is man.

In "The Corpse and the Kid" (*Dime Detective*, September 1935), better known as "Boy with Body," a boy finds that his father has killed his promiscuous new wife. The son desperately tries to cover up the crime by carrying the woman's body, wrapped in a rug, out of the New Jersey seaside town where the family lives and over to the roadhouse rendezvous where her current lover is waiting for her. The account of the boy's journey is Woolrich's first set piece of pure nail-biting suspense, and the psychological overtones suggest some of the horrors in the author's relations with his own parents.

"Dead on Her Feet" (*Dime Detective*, December 1935), which was heavily influenced by Horace McCoy's classic *They Shoot Horses, Don't They?* (1935), tells of a murder at a marathon dance contest and a cop who forces the dead girl's lover to dance with her corpse until he confesses, driving the innocent man insane just before the real killer is caught. The dominant influence on "The Death of Me" (*Detective Fiction Weekly*, 7 December 1935) was clearly James M. Cain's *The Postman Always Rings Twice* (1934), from which Woolrich borrowed—not for the last time—the motif of the man who gets away with the murder he did commit but is nailed for the one he didn't. "The Showboat Murders" (*Detective Fiction Weekly*, 14 December 1935) is Woolrich's first rapid-action whizbang, with a thin plot but whirlwind pace. And "Hot Water" (*Argosy*, 28 December 1935), about a movie star and her rough-diamond bodyguard, gives further evidence of Woolrich's intoxication with Hollywood.

Between 1936 and 1939 Woolrich sold at least 105 more stories as well as two book-length magazine serials. By the end of the decade he had become a fixture in mystery pulps of all levels of quality, from *Black Mask* and *Detective Fiction Weekly* to cheapies like *Thrilling Mystery* and *Black Book Detective*. He also appeared in Whit Burnett's prestigious literary magazine *Story*. His genres include historical adventures, Runyonesque comedies, gems of Grand Guignol, even an occasional tale of pure detection, ranging in quality from magnificent to abysmal. But very few lack the unique Woolrich mood, tone, and preoccupations. Typically, they take place in a seedy hotel, a cheap dance hall, a precinct station back room, a rundown movie house; the recurring themes are the corrosion of love and trust and the entrapment of innocent people by uncontrollable powers.

One of the most characteristic types of Woolrich story is the oscillation thriller. Two central characters share a close relationship—lovers, husband and wife, father and son, roommates. A crime is committed, slowly mounting evidence compels or comes within an inch of compelling one of the two to believe that the other is guilty, and the suspense builds as the viewpoint character oscillates between doubt and trust and doubt again. In "The Night Reveals" (*Story*, April 1936), insurance investigator Harry Jordan learns that his wife, Marie, has been slipping out of their Lexington Avenue apartment in the hours before dawn. He begins following her through the ghostly city streets and soon comes to suspect that something has turned her into a pyromaniac. Is he right? The reader joins the protagonist in his dark night of the soul. In some oscillation stories the suspected person is innocent, and the damning evidence comes from wild coincidence or a frame-up, but in others the person is indeed guilty, and in still others neither the characters nor the reader ever learns the truth. Because Woolrich has no series characters or ground rules, the suspense is real, and our own uncertainty matches that of the people on the page.

Another Woolrich specialty is the heart-in-the-throat noir race against time and death. "Johnny on the Spot" (*Detective Fiction Weekly*, 2 May 1936) is set in the depth of New York's night. Hunted by the mob because he knows too much and wants out,

Johnny Donovan is cornered in an all-night cafeteria and about to be taken away for torture and death when his eighteen-year-old wife, Jean, comes into the hash joint for a furtive rendezvous with him. She sees that the hit men have him. For the rest of the story we race with Jean through the darkness on a mad quest to kidnap the top mobster's wife and swap her for Johnny—or, if it's too late for that, to kill her too.

Among Woolrich's fast-action whizbangs, one of the most suspenseful is "You Pays Your Nickel" (*Argosy*, 22 August 1936). Subway guard Delaney is bored stiff at his job until the morning his train is taken over by a homicidal maniac and he's suddenly part of a hair-raising underground duel as the cars carrying the two of them, hundreds of screaming commuters, and a bag with fifty thousand dollars in stolen money careen out of control through the tunnels. This superb action story, usually reprinted as "Subway," is so vividly written that the reader is thrust into the volcano and trapped there until Woolrich melts everything down.

In "The Corpse Next Door" (*Detective Fiction Weekly*, 23 January 1937), Woolrich pushes us into the skin of a man with a guilt-flayed conscience and, as in Poe's "The Tell-Tale Heart," makes us live his torments. A faceless nonentity scratching out a bare white-collar existence amid the quiet despair of the Depression is driven mad with fury by the invisible thief who has been stealing his bottle of milk from the stoop of his drab apartment before he and his wife get up in the morning. He sets a trap for the thief, kills him in a fit of wrath, hides the body inside the closeted Murphy bed in the vacant apartment next door, and slowly but inevitably is driven over the edge.

"Murder at the Automat" (*Dime Detective*, August 1937) offers not only a vivid picture of 1930s New York but also a lovely puzzle resolved with total fairness to the reader. Homicide detective Nelson tackles the case of Leo Avram, an old skinflint who comes into the Automat every night for coffee and a bologna sandwich, until the night the sandwich behind the coin slot he chooses turns out to be laced with cyanide and kills him. It is typical in Woolrich's world that when the police cannot figure out how anyone could have poisoned precisely the sandwich Avram selected, they threaten to frame the prime suspect. Woolrich powerfully evokes the Automat and the seedy night people who call it home.

"Goodbye, New York" (*Story*, October 1937) takes place in Manhattan's streets, subways, and railroad tunnels and is told in the first person from the viewpoint of a young woman whose husband has killed his corrupt ex-boss and stolen just enough to let the couple start life over. This edgy, feverish heartbreaker of a tale follows their frantic attempts to evade the police net closing around them and get out of the city. "Two doomed things, running away. From nothingness, into nothingness. . . . Turn back we dare not, stand still they wouldn't let us, and to go forward was destruction at our own hands" (*Violence*, 1958, pp. 36–37). This is a perfect image of life in the Woolrich world.

In "Dusk to Dawn" (*Black Mask*, December 1937), we live with yet another hunted and doomed protagonist running headlong through the nightscape. Jobless and penniless, Lew Stahl sneaks into a New York movie palace without a ticket, as Woolrich had often done in the lean years. He tries to lift the wallet of a sleeper in the deserted mezzanine to take out one dollar to buy a meal and discovers that the man isn't asleep. He's dead, with a knife in his back. A woman several rows behind them in the dark is convinced that she saw Lew wield the knife and runs for the police. Stalked and desperate, fleeing through the night-bound city, he steals a gun, then uses it, and his fate is sealed.

"Dime a Dance" (*Black Mask*, February 1938) is the first of several Woolrich tales in which a female first-person narrator is staked out as bait to trap a psychotic murderer of women. Taxi dancer Ginger Allen is taken from work one night by homicide cop Nick Ballestier and told that her only friend among the dancers has been strangled and then stabbed repeatedly by a serial killer who dances with his victims' corpses (as in "Dead on Her Feet") to the jazz tune "Poor Butterfly" (as in Puccini's opera). A month later a strange new customer shows up at Joyland and asks Ginger to dance with him. The climax is a suspense classic.

"I Wouldn't Be in Your Shoes" (*Detective Fiction Weekly*, 12 March 1938) combines a powerful picture of scratching for survival with a dark picture of the human condition. We enter the quietly wretched life of Tom Quinn, who works for a miserable salary and every day dreads being laid off. One stifling August night he loses control and throws a pair of his shoes out the open bedroom window at a pair of cats yowling on the back fence. Months later those shoes lead to his arrest, conviction, and death sentence for the murder of an old miser in a shack a few blocks away. The haunted and lonely plainclothesman Bob White meets Quinn's wife, Ann, and the two of them race the clock to find another murderer. The man they track down, however, insists that he's innocent too, and it seems impossible that either he or Quinn is guilty. But one of them must be, and by the story's end both are left in ruin. Life is a trap, malevolent and beyond reason. To anyone unlucky enough to be born, Woolrich says: "I wouldn't be in your shoes, buddy," knowing he's in them too.

"Mystery in Room 913" (*Detective Fiction Weekly*, 4 June 1938) is an episodic novella that takes place in a New York hotel. Over a long stretch of the Depression, three different men check into Room 913 and unaccountably jump out the window into the street during the night. House detective Striker refuses to accept the deaths as coincidental suicides and becomes obsessed to the point of psychosis with proving they are something else. He finds a Bowery derelict, sets him up in 913 as bait, and becomes responsible for the man's death; he then goes jobless for months and changes his appearance beyond recognition until he can check into 913 himself and force a confrontation with the specter, which is the naked face of death and of the world's malevolence.

The protagonist of "Three O'Clock" (*Detective Fiction Weekly*, 1 October 1938) is Paul Stapp, the nondescript owner of a small clock and watch repair shop. After an unexplained concussion he becomes convinced that his wife, Fran, is entertaining a lover in their house while he's at work. Rather than confront her, he decides to blow up her, the lover, the house, and everything in it. Over time he smuggles into his basement the raw materials for a bomb. Then, one afternoon at the hour when Fran is shopping, he comes home, goes down to the basement, and sets the bomb to explode at three o'clock. But this is the same afternoon two moronic daylight burglars have picked to break into Stapp's house. When he encounters them on his way out, they knock him unconscious, bind and gag him in the basement, tie him to a thick pipe, and make their getaway, unaware that they've immobilized him within a few feet of a bomb set to explode in ninety minutes. For those minutes Woolrich makes us live in Stapp's flesh, unable to speak or move or make a sound anyone can hear, his frozen eyes fixed on the clock as its hands run on toward three. The suspense and anguish are so intense in this quintessential Woolrich story that one can hardly read it without dying a little.

"Men Must Die" (*Black Mask*, August 1939), better known under its reprint title "Guillotine," is set in France and broken down into a large number of short scenes. The events of the present, as condemned murderer Robert Lamont is ritually prepared for execution, alternate with chronologically ordered flashbacks so that we see what Lamont did and why he hopes he won't have to die for it. His lover, Babette, has contrived to meet the headsman, an old loner whose pride is his status as the only man in France with a license to kill. Babette dines with M. de Paris on the night before he is to decapitate Lamont, hoping desperately that she will be able to slip poison into his meal and thus invoke the national tradition (which Woolrich apparently invented) that when the executioner dies the next prisoner set to be guillotined receives a pardon. The narration is so objective and detached that we get no hint which of these two, the private murderer or the state murderer, we are supposed to wish dead. And by the time the flashback scenes have caught up to the present and Lamont is brought step by step closer to the scaffold while the old man is journeying across predawn Paris with the guillotine blade in his bag and his own death churning inside him, the tension in this grotesque classic has become all but unbearable.

What was the man like who spun out these bleak visions? The best physical description comes from Woolrich's pulp contemporary Steve Fisher (1912–1980), who used him as the model for the brutal and love-tormented homicide detective Cornell in *I Wake Up Screaming* (1941):

> He had red hair and thin white skin and red eyebrows and blue eyes. He looked sick. He looked like a corpse. His clothes didn't fit him. . . . He was frail, grey-faced and bitter. He was possessed with a macabre humor. His voice was nasal. You'd think he was crying. He might have had TB. He looked like he couldn't stand up in a wind. (p. 51)

As for his lifestyle, the reminiscences of colleagues picture him as a painfully introverted man, living in hotels with his mother and going out almost never, the tortured patterns of his work reflecting the strangler grip in which Claire Attalie Woolrich held him.

The "Black" Novels and Later Short Stories, 1940–1948

In 1940 Woolrich joined the migration of pulp detective writers from lurid-covered magazines to hardcover books. In his first overt crime novel, *The Bride Wore Black* (1940), he writes in cool, unemotional prose of a mysterious woman named Julie who enters the lives of various men and, for reasons never explained until the climax, murders them.

Woolrich divides the book into five free-standing episodes, each built around a symbolic three-step dance. First there is a chapter showing Julie, each time in a new persona, preparing the trap for her current target; then comes the execution of her plan, each victim being ensnared in his own romantic image of the perfect woman; finally, several pages deal with Wanger, the faceless homicide cop who's stalking the huntress through the years. At last, in part 5, they meet, and we discover the untold back story: Julie's husband was killed on the church steps moments after their marriage, and she has devoted the rest of her life to tracking down and systematically murdering the drunk driver and his four cronies whom she blames for her loss. What Julie learns at the denouement is that, just like the men she killed, she, too, has been victimized by a perverse, malignant, and unknowable power; that a tangle of grotesque and credibility-defying coincidences has ruined her precisely as she in turn ruined her prey, for no reason whatsoever. When she understands this and says, "It's time for me to go," clearly she means that it's time for her to die as well.

This first in Woolrich's so-called Black Series was followed by *The Black Curtain* (1941), the masterpiece on the overworked subject of amnesia. Frank Townsend recovers from a three-year memory loss, becomes obsessed with learning who and what he was during those missing years, and finds love, hate, and a murder charge waiting for him behind the curtain. In the book's first two sections Woolrich evokes with desperate urgency the feeling of being without an identity and the prey of unseen forces. The third and final section, rooted in his pulp action tales of the 1930s, lacks the intensity of the earlier parts and leaves all sorts of nagging questions unanswered, but, like so much of Woolrich, the book is impossible to lay down unfinished.

Black Alibi (1942) is a terror novel about a killer jaguar menacing a South American city while a lone Anglo hunts a human murderer who may be hiding behind the jaguar's claws. This time Woolrich dropped his quintessential themes of loneliness and despair and concentrated on pure suspense, and the result is a thriller with menace breathing on every page. The five long set pieces, in each of which a vividly characterized young woman is stalked through the nightscape by unspeakable horrors, are among the finest sequences he ever wrote.

Woolrich's most sustained piece of first-person narration by a woman, *The Black Angel* (1943), deals with a terrified young wife's race against time to prove that her convicted husband did not murder his girlfriend and that some other man in the dead woman's life is guilty. Like Julie in *The Bride Wore Black*, she enters the lives of several such men, of whom one at most is the killer she is looking for, and in one way or another destroys them all and herself too. Writing in the first person from the wife's viewpoint—a huge risk for an introverted loner who never knew a woman intimately—Woolrich makes us feel her love and anguish, her terror and desperation, her obsessions that grow to madness inside her like a cancer as she flails the world like a destroying angel to save her man from Mister Death.

The Black Path of Fear (1944) tells of a man who runs away to Havana with an American gangster's wife. The vengeful husband follows them to Cuba, where he kills the woman and frames the lover, leaving him a stranger in a strange land, menaced on all sides and fighting for his life. The climactic chapters with their dope dens and sinister Orientals, secret passages and hairbreadth escapes are exciting and action-crammed enough. But it is the earlier chapters, with their evocations of love discovered and love destroyed, their sense of what it must be like to be alone and hunted through a nightmare city of the mind, that demonstrate why Woolrich is revered as the Alfred Hitchcock of the written word.

In *Rendezvous in Black* (1948), grief-crazed Johnny Marr holds one among a small group of people responsible for his fiancée's death. He devotes his life to entering the lives of each of that group in turn, finding out whom each one most loves, and murdering these loved ones so that the person who killed his fiancée will live the grief he lives. This is *The Bride Wore Black* with the sexes reversed and the structure as it should have been—with the explanation of the serial murders at the beginning so that we have some clue how to respond, with a genuine noir cop instead of a cipher in the role of hunter stalking the killer through the years, with a wealth of heart-stopping suspense and anguish instead of cool objective narration, with the forces of chance and fate kept in perfect balance, and with a strong climax lacking *The Bride*'s monkey tricks of plot manipulation. Woolrich, as usual, punches ridiculous holes in the continuity, but on the visceral level where his work stands or falls this is a masterpiece.

In the early 1940s he continued to turn out stories and novellas for the pulps in diminishing quantity but with no shortage of classics. His annihilation stories "All at Once, No Alice" (*Argosy*, 22 March 1940) and "Finger of Doom" (*Detective Fiction Weekly*, 22 June 1940) share one of the most powerful premises in noir literature, and in both tales Woolrich wrings that premise dry of emotional torment and existential dread. A lonely young man has miraculously found the one right woman, but just before they are to marry she vanishes into nothingness. Everyone who apparently had known or seen the woman denies she ever existed, and the police to whom the man frantically appeals for help cannot find the slightest proof she walked the earth. Convinced that she is a figment of his lunatic imagination, they kick him out with contempt and abandon him to despair—all but one lone-wolf cop who is willing to believe that the young man just might be telling the truth.

The living nightmare stories "C-Jag" (*Black Mask*, October 1940) and "And So to Death" (*Argosy*, 1 March 1941), better known respectively under their reprint titles "Cocaine" and "Nightmare," form another matched pair of noir classics. The protagonist comes to consciousness after a blackout episode and is haunted by the memory of having done something horrible while out of himself.

Back in the waking world he tries to shrug off the memory as the residue of a bad dream, hangover, drug dose, or whatever. Then he finds on his person an objective fragment from the nightmare, and then another, and before long he is on the edge of madness. Desperately, he appeals to his brother-in-law, who is a cop and, like most Woolrich cops, as ready to hang those in need of aid as to help them. The two men go back together into the shadows, hunting for the answer.

Perverse, malevolent, and hopeless are the words for the image of life Woolrich offered in "Three Kills for One" (*Black Mask*, July 1942). Like so much of his fiction, this novella begins with the last hours of someone marked for destruction. Gary Severn picks the wrong moment to walk down to the corner newsstand for a midnight paper and winds up charged with the murder of a cop during a robbery. Ruthlessly pressured by the police, all the witnesses identify Severn. Also convicted for the same crime is Gates, a small-time hoodlum who, literally while sitting in the electric chair, confesses to a priest that he is guilty but that his partner was a fellow hoodlum, Donny Blake, not Severn. Gates rejects the priest's spiritual ministrations and although it is already too late, demands that the padre try to save Severn's body rather than Gates's soul. After the double execution, Blake is arrested, tortured under a surgeon's watchful eye, and confesses.

Then word comes from "upstairs" that in order to cover up their having railroaded an innocent man to the chair, the police will let Blake go free. Plainclothesman Eric Rogers reacts to Blake's release like "a true believer who has just seen his scripture made a mockery of" (William Irish, "Two Murders, One Crime," *If I Should Die Before I Wake*, 1945, p. 97). He resigns from the force and spends the next three years stalking Blake, carrying on the quest like Julie in *The Bride Wore Black*, without money or visible means of support, as if his rage for "justice" were all the food and drink he needed. The parallels with Javert and Jean Valjean in Victor Hugo's *Les Misérables* (1862) are not coincidence. In time

Blake is so terrorized he tries to kill himself, but Rogers refuses to let him take the easy way out and saves his life. The stalking goes on until chance or fate allows Rogers to frame Blake for another death that he knows wasn't murder at all.

Woolrich's dwindling output of short fiction in the 1940s was due at least in part to the discovery of his huge backlog of stories by the entrepreneurs of dramatic radio. Dozens of his pulp tales were naturals for audio adaptation, and his material was purchased in dizzying quantities for broadcast on series like *Suspense* and *Molle Mystery Theatre*. The thirty-minute version of "The Black Curtain" (*Suspense*, 2 December 1943, starring Cary Grant), which may have been scripted by Woolrich himself, ranks among the most powerful radio dramas ever written:

> I tried to put it all behind me, to resume my life where it left off over three years ago. . . . I don't want to find out anything anymore. I want it all to die away and be still. And it will. All except Ruth. *Because somewhere behind that black curtain I was loved, and loved someone!* We must have known a love I'll never know again. (emphasis added by author)

The Pseudonymous Novels, 1942–1952

As if all this activity were not enough, Woolrich continued to write more novels, too many for publication under a single byline. When he needed to come up with a pseudonym, the name that he and *Story* magazine editor Whit Burnett hit upon was William Irish. Had Woolrich known that obscure First National title writer back in the 1920s, and had he been carrying the man's name in the back of his mind ever since?

The first novel published under the Irish byline was *Phantom Lady* (1942). Scott Henderson quarrels with his wife, goes out and picks up a woman in a bar, spends the evening with her, and comes home to find his wife dead and himself accused of her murder. All the evidence is against him, and his only hope is to find the woman who was with him when his wife was killed. But she has vanished into thin air, and everyone in a position to know swears that no such woman ever existed. He is sentenced to die, and as the hours rush toward execution day, the woman who loves him and his best friend frantically search for the phantom. The plot is so involuted that final explanations require two dozen closely printed and none too plausible pages, but the emotional torment and suspense are unforgettable.

Deadline at Dawn (1944) takes place on a single night in the bleak streets and concrete caves of New York as we follow a desperate young couple who have until sunrise to clear themselves of a murder charge and escape the web of the city. The story line is loose and relaxed, with many characters and incidents in no way connected to the main plot. But the cliff-hanging crosscutting between Quinn's and Bricky's searches through the night streets keeps tension high, and the two-pronged quest is punctuated by touches of the deepest noir. Woolrich evokes New York after dark and the despair of those who walk its streets with a pathos unmatched in the genre.

Of all his novels the one most completely dominated by death and fate is *Night Has a Thousand Eyes* (1945), which was published under the pseudonym George Hopley (Woolrich's middle names). A simpleminded recluse with apparently uncanny powers predicts that millionaire Harlan Reid will die in three weeks, precisely at midnight, in the jaws of a lion, and the tension rises to unbearable pitch as the doomed man's daughter and a sympathetic cop struggle to avert a destiny that they suspect, and soon come to hope, was conceived by a human power. Woolrich makes us live the emotional torment of this waking nightmare until we are literally shivering in our seats.

Waltz into Darkness (1947), under the William Irish pseudonym, is set in New Orleans around 1880 and begins as much of Woolrich

begins, with a man being eaten alive by loneliness. "Any love, from anywhere, on any terms. Quick, before it was too late! Only not to be alone any longer" (p. 10). Enter the femme fatale, the nameless woman who is Louis Durand's destiny, whom he comes to love with such maniacal intensity that for her he will degrade himself to any extent, cheat, kill, endure torture and even death. "Louis," he is asked at the end, "is this what it's like? Does it always hurt so?" "It hurts," he replies, "but it's worth it. It's love" (p. 308). Like several Woolrich men before him, Louis is an acolyte worshiping at the altar of love, and the woman is his goddess. Woolrich describes her in overwhelmingly religious and maternal language: she is God the Mother, unknowable and cruel as life. Louis is caught in her as in a whirlpool, and we are trapped in his skin. In the cold light of reason the book is ludicrous, but no one can read Woolrich and be reasonable.

In *I Married a Dead Man* (1948), another William Irish novel, a woman with nothing to live for and in flight from her sadistic husband is injured in a train wreck. She wakes up in a hospital bed surrounded by luxuries because, as she eventually realizes, she has been wrongly identified as another woman, one who had had everything to live for but had died in the train disaster. Helen grasps what seems to be a heaven-sent chance to start over and even falls in love again, but her new life proves to be a gift from the dark god who rules the Woolrich world. At the climax she and we are confronted with two and only two possibilities, neither of which makes the least sense, each of which will destroy innocent lives. "I don't know what the game was. . . . I only know we must have played it wrong, somewhere along the way. . . . We've lost. That's all I know. We've lost. And now the game is through" (p. 254). Woolrich's last major novel is one of the finest and bleakest of his works.

The success of his novels led to publication of several collections of his shorter work in hardcover and paperback volumes that are extremely rare today. Woolrich's stories were staple items in the endless anthologies of short mystery fiction published during the 1940s. In addition to the dozens of radio plays adapted from his work, fifteen movies were made from Woolrich material between 1942 and 1950 alone. And his influence pervaded the culture of the 1940s so extensively that many film noir classics of that period give the sense of having been adapted from his work even though he had nothing to do with them.

The Last Long Years, 1948–1968

Woolrich published little after 1948, apparently because his long-absent father's death and his mother's prolonged illnesses, as well as his own progressing alcoholism, paralyzed his ability to write. That he was remembered during the 1950s is largely due to Ellery Queen (Frederic Dannay), who reprinted in his magazine a host of Woolrich pulp tales, and to Alfred Hitchcock, whose film *Rear Window* (1954) was based on a Woolrich story. Woolrich's magazine work proved as adaptable to television as it had to radio a decade earlier, and series like *Mirror Theater, Ford Theatre, Alfred Hitchcock Presents*, and *Schlitz Playhouse of Stars* frequently presented thirty-minute filmed versions of his material. Even the prestigious *Playhouse 90* made use of Woolrich, presenting a ninety-minute adaptation of "Rendezvous in Black" (CBS, 25 October 1956) starring Franchot Tone, Laraine Day, and Boris Karloff. The finest adaptation of Woolrich in any form is Hitchcock's sixty-minute version of "Three O'Clock," starring E. G. Marshall and broadcast on the series *Suspicion* (NBC, 30 September 1957) as "Four O'Clock." It is pure Hitchcock, pure Woolrich, and perhaps the most totally suspenseful film the master ever directed.

Woolrich's personal situation remained wretched, and more than once he sank to passing off slightly updated old stories as new work, fooling book and magazine publishers as well as readers. Not long after his mother's death in 1957 came *Hotel Room* (1958), a collection of nonsuspenseful tales set in a single room of a New York City hotel at various times from the building's years of sumptuous fashionableness to the last days before its demolition. The Saint Anselm was an amalgam of the desiccated residential hotels in which mother and son had lived, and the stories set there mark the beginning of Woolrich's end. Yet once in a while he could still conjure up the old power. "The Penny-a-Worder" (*Ellery Queen's Mystery Magazine*, September 1958) is a wry downbeat tale of a pulp mystery writer of the 1930s desperately trying to crank out a complete novella overnight. And "The Number's Up" is a bitter little account of gangland executioners mistakenly taking an innocent couple out to be shot.

Diabetic, alcoholic, wracked by self-contempt, and alone, Woolrich dragged out his life. He would come to a party, bringing his own bottle of cheap wine in a paper bag, and stand in a corner the whole evening. If someone approached and tried to tell him how much he or she admired his work, he would growl, "You don't mean that" and find another corner. In 1965 he moved into a comfortable if spartan suite of rooms on the second floor of the Sheraton-Russell, at Park Avenue and Thirty-seventh Street, and continued the slow process of dying by inches. He wrote a little, leaving unfinished much more than he completed, but publishers continued to issue collections of his stories. *The Ten Faces of Cornell Woolrich* (1965), with a glowing introduction by Ellery Queen, was of high quality, but seven stories of the ten came from earlier Woolrich collections.

The Dark Side of Love (1965) brought together eight of the author's recent "tales of love and despair," but the only one that ranks with his best work is the dark gem "Too Nice a Day to Die." A desperately lonely woman turns on the gas in her apartment one morning, ready to end her life. The phone rings. From force of habit she picks up the receiver. It's a wrong number, someone wanting Schultz's Delicatessen. The absurdity gives her the will to live one day longer. She goes out, walks about the city, and, thanks to the long arm of chance or fate, meets in Rockefeller Plaza a man who seems to be as right for her as she seems to be for him. As they are on their way to her place for dinner, she is run down while crossing the street and dies. The world according to Woolrich has rarely been rendered in such fitting form.

During 1967 his slow march to the grave quickened into a fast walk. He developed a bad case of gangrene in one leg but put off seeing a doctor for so long that, in January 1968, the leg had to be amputated above the knee. He returned to the Sheraton-Russell with an artificial leg on which he could never learn to walk and spent his final months in a wheelchair, alone and immobilized, much like the protagonist of his 1926 novel *Cover Charge*. But the best of his late stories still hold the magic touch that chills the heart, and his last two suspense tales are among his finest. "For the Rest of Her Life" (*Ellery Queen's Mystery Magazine*, May 1968) follows a young woman whose husband has turned out to be a sadistic abuser of women. She meets another man and confesses the truth; together they try to escape. Every move they make throughout this excruciating story is precisely the wrong thing to do, and Woolrich keeps tightening the screws until we are screaming at them to change their course before it's too late. But each wrong move has also been foreordained in the womb of destiny, and Linda and Garry are the last of the doomed couples whose shattered remains fill the Woolrich world.

In "New York Blues" (*Ellery Queen's Mystery Magazine*, December 1970), a nameless man who has killed the woman he loves, or thinks he killed her, or perhaps killed no one at all, sits in the dark of a room on the second floor of a New York hotel and looks out at the night, waiting in terror for those who are death personified to take him. Within this minimalist framework Woolrich manages to reprise virtually every motif, belief, and device that had permeated his fiction for decades: flashes of word magic, evocative song lyrics, love and loneliness, madness and

death, amnesia, paranoia, and despair. "Each man dies as he was meant to die, and as he was born, and as he lived: alone, all alone. Without any God, without any hope, without any record to show for his life" (p. 20). If this was the last story he completed, he couldn't have ended his career more fittingly.

In the late 1960s Woolrich had plenty of money, and his critical reputation was secure not only in America but also in Europe, where François Truffaut had filmed both *The Bride Wore Black* and *Waltz into Darkness*, but his physical and emotional condition remained hopeless. He died of a stroke on 25 September 1968, leaving unfinished two novels (*Into the Night*, 1987, and "The Loser," unpublished), an autobiography (*Blues of a Lifetime*), a collection of short stories ("I Was Waiting for You," unpublished), and a long list of titles for stories he had never begun, one of which captures his bleak world in a single phrase: "First You Dream, Then You Die." He left no survivors, and only a handful of people attended his funeral. His estate was willed in trust to Columbia University for the establishment of a scholarship fund for students of creative writing. The fund is named for Woolrich's mother.

Conclusion

In Woolrich's crime fiction there is a gradual development from pulp to noir. The earlier a story, the more likely that it stresses pulp elements: one-dimensional macho protagonists, preposterous methods of murder, hordes of cardboard gangsters, dialogue full of whiny insults, blistering fast action. But even in some of his earliest crime stories one finds aspects of noir, and over time the stream works itself pure.

For the mature Woolrich the great world is an incomprehensible place where beams happen to fall, and are predestined to fall, and are toppled over by malevolent powers—a world ruled by chance, fate, and God, the malign thug. But the everyday life he portrays is just as terrifying and treacherous. The dominant economic reality is the Depression, which for Woolrich is usually personified by a frightened little guy in a run-down apartment with a hungry wife and children, no money, no job, and desperation eating him like a cancer. The dominant political reality is a police force made up of a few decent cops and a horde of sociopaths licensed to torture and kill, whose outrages are casually accepted by all concerned, not least by the victims. The prevailing emotional states are loneliness and fear. Events take place in darkness, menace breathes out of every corner of the night, the bleak cityscape comes alive on the page and in our hearts.

Woolrich had a genius for creating types of story perfectly consonant with his world: the noir cop story, the clock-race story, the waking nightmare, the oscillation thriller, the headlong-through-the-night story, the annihilation story, the last-hours story. These situations and variations on them are paradigms of our position in the world as Woolrich sees it. His mastery of suspense, his genius (like that of his spiritual brother Alfred Hitchcock) for keeping us on the edge of our seats and gasping with fright, stems not only from the nightmarish situations he conjures up but also from his prose, which is compulsively readable, cinematically vivid, and high-strung almost to the point of hysteria. It forces us into the skins of the hunted and doomed, where we live their agonies and die with them a thousand small deaths. In his finest work every detail serves this purpose, even the chapter headings. Chapter 1 of *Phantom Lady* is entitled "The Hundred and Fiftieth Day Before the Execution," so that even before Marcella Henderson is strangled the countdown to the day of her innocent husband's electrocution for the murder has begun. In *Deadline at Dawn*, Woolrich replaces the customary chapter titles or numbers with clock faces so that like Quinn and Bricky we feel in our bones the coming of the dreaded sunrise.

But suspense presupposes uncertainty. No matter how nightmarish the situation, real suspense is impossible when we know in advance that the protagonist will prevail (as we would if Woolrich had used series characters) or will be destroyed. This is why, despite his congenital pessimism, Woolrich manages any number of times to squeeze out an upbeat resolution. Precisely because we can never know whether a particular novel or story will be light or dark, *allegre* or *noir*, his work remains hauntingly suspenseful.

The viewpoint character in each story is usually someone trapped in a living nightmare, but this doesn't guarantee that we and the protagonist are at one. In fact, Woolrich often makes us pull away from the person at the center of the storm, splitting our reaction in two, stripping his protagonist of moral authority, denying us the luxury of unequivocal identification, drawing characters so psychologically warped and sometimes so despicable that a part of us wants to see them suffer. Woolrich also denies us the luxury of total disidentification with all sorts of sociopaths, especially those who wear badges. His noir cop tales are crammed with acts of police sadism, usually committed or at least endorsed by the detective protagonist. To take two examples from stories published in 1935, in "The Body Upstairs" the cops investigate a woman's murder by poking lighted cigarettes into her husband's armpits until, though innocent, he's about to confess, at which point the detective in charge berates the husband as a weakling who can't take punishment. And in "Dead on Her Feet," as already described, the policeman Smitty drives the dead woman's innocent lover insane by forcing him to dance with her corpse. These monstrosities are explicitly condemned almost never, and the moral outrage we feel has no internal support in the stories except the objective horror of what is shown, so that one might almost believe that a part of Woolrich wants us to enjoy the spectacles. If so, it is yet another instance of how his most powerful novels and stories are divided against themselves so as to evoke in us a divided response that mirrors his own self-division.

Even on the subject of love he tends to divide our reaction. Often, of course, he identifies unambiguously with whoever is lonely, whoever is in love, or needs love, or has lost it. From the absence of love in his own life springs much of the poignancy with which he portrayed its power and joys and risks and pains and much of the piercing sadness with which he described its corrosion and loss. There is a haunting moment in *Phantom Lady* when the morgue attendants are carrying out the body of Scott Henderson's wife. "Hands riveted to him, holding him there. The outer door closed muffledly. A little sachet came drifting out of the empty bedroom, seeming to whisper: 'Remember? Remember when I was your love? Remember?'" (p. 37). On the other hand, several Woolrich classics are precisely about protagonists—Julie in *The Bride Wore Black*, Alberta in *The Black Angel*, Johnny Marr in *Rendezvous in Black*—who destroy their own lives and the lives of others in a mad quest to save a loved one from death or avenge one who has already died.

Woolrich does invariably unite himself and us with his people at one moment. In the face of the specter of Anahuac nothing matters anymore: saint or beast, sane or mad, if any person is on the brink of death Woolrich becomes that person and makes us do likewise. In "Three O'Clock," we sit bound, gagged, and paralyzed with the morally warped Stapp while the bomb ticks closer and closer to the moment of destruction, and Woolrich punctuates the unbearable suspense with language and imagery clearly echoing the story of the crucifixion of Jesus, whose agony also ended at three o'clock. During the brief electrocution scene of "Three Kills for One," the cold steel hood falls over the head of the murderer Gates, and he whispers: "Helen, I love you." No character named Helen ever appears in the story. At the point of death we are forgiven much, and if we love we are forgiven everything.

The intense, feverish, irrational nature of the Woolrich world is mirrored in his literary faults. As a plot craftsman he is sloppy beyond endurance. His output abounds in outlandish contrivances, outrageous coincidences, "surprise" developments that require us to suspend not only our disbelief but also our knowledge of elementary real-world facts, chains of so-called reasoning that a two-year-old could pull apart. But in his most powerful work what would ordinarily be gaffes become functional elements that enable him to weave contradiction and existential absurdity into his dark fabric. Long before the theater of the absurd, Woolrich discovered that an incomprehensible universe is best reflected in an incomprehensible story. This same sloppiness holds true for his style, which purely on its merits as prose is often undisciplined, hysterical, sprawling with phrases and clauses crying out to be cut, sentences without subjects or predicates, rhyme or reason, and words that simply do not mean what Woolrich guesses they mean. Many (by no means all) of these features are functional in Woolrich's doom-shrouded world, just like many (by no means all) of his plot flubs. Without the sentences rushing out of control across the page like his hunted characters across the nightscape, without the manic emotionalism and indifference to grammatical niceties, the form and content of the Woolrich world would be at odds. Between his style and his substance Woolrich achieved the perfect union that he never came within a mile of in his private life.

"I was only trying to cheat death," he wrote in a fragment found among his papers. "I was only trying to surmount for a little while the darkness that all my life I surely knew was going to come rolling in on me some day and obliterate me. I was only trying to stay alive a little brief while longer, after I was already gone" (from the dust jacket of *Nightwebs*, 1971). Trapped in a wretched psychological environment and gifted or cursed with an understanding that being trapped is par excellence the human condition, he took his decades of solitude and shaped them into a haunting body of work. He tried to escape the specter of Anahuac, and he couldn't, and he couldn't, and he couldn't. The world he imagined, will.

Selected Bibliography

WORKS OF CORNELL WOOLRICH

NOVELS

Cover Charge. New York: Boni & Liveright, 1926.
Children of the Ritz. New York: Boni & Liveright, 1927.
Times Square. New York: Liveright, 1929.
A Young Man's Heart. New York: Mason, 1930.
The Time of Her Life. New York: Liveright, 1931.
Manhattan Love Song. New York: Godwin, 1932.
The Bride Wore Black. New York: Simon & Schuster, 1940.
The Black Curtain. New York: Simon & Schuster, 1941.
Black Alibi. New York: Simon & Schuster, 1942.
The Black Angel. New York: Doubleday, 1943.
The Black Path of Fear. New York: Doubleday, 1944.
Rendezvous in Black. New York: Rinehart, 1948.
Savage Bride. New York: Fawcett, 1950.
Hotel Room. New York: Random House, 1958.
Death Is My Dancing Partner. New York: Pyramid, 1959.
The Doom Stone. New York: Avon, 1960.
Into the Night (completed by Lawrence Block). New York: Mysterious Press, 1987.

SHORT STORIES

Nightmare. New York: Dodd, Mead, 1956.
Violence. New York: Dodd, Mead, 1958. Includes "Goodbye, New York" (under the title "Don't Wait Up for Me Tonight").
Beyond the Night. New York: Avon, 1959. Includes "The Number's Up."
The Ten Faces of Cornell Woolrich. New York: Simon & Schuster, 1965. Includes "Finger of Doom" (under the title "I Won't Take a Minute").
The Dark Side of Love. New York: Walker, 1965. Includes "Too Nice a Day to Die."
Nightwebs. New York: Harper & Row, 1971. Includes "Dead on Her Feet," "The Corpse Next Door," "Murder at the Automat," "The Penny-a-Worder," and "Dusk to Dawn."
Angels of Darkness. New York: Mysterious Press, 1978. Includes "For the Rest of Her Life."
The Fantastic Stories of Cornell Woolrich. Edited by Charles G. Waugh and Martin H. Greenberg. Carbondale: Southern Illinois University Press, 1981. Includes "Kiss of the Cobra."
Rear Window and Four Short Novels. New York: Ballantine, 1984.
Darkness at Dawn. Carbondale: Southern Illinois University Press, 1985.
Blind Date with Death. New York: Carroll & Graf, 1985.
Vampire's Honeymoon. New York: Carroll & Graf, 1985.

NOVELS BY WILLIAM IRISH

Phantom Lady. Philadelphia and New York: Lippincott, 1942.
Deadline at Dawn. Philadelphia and New York: Lippincott, 1944.
Waltz into Darkness. Philadelphia and New York: Lippincott, 1947.
I Married a Dead Man. Philadelphia and New York: Lippincott, 1948.
Strangler's Serenade. New York: Rinehart, 1951.

SHORT STORIES BY WILLIAM IRISH

I Wouldn't Be in Your Shoes. Philadelphia and New York: Lippincott, 1943. Includes "I Wouldn't Be in Your Shoes," "Three O'Clock," "And So to Death" (under the title "Nightmare"), and "Dark Melody of Madness" (under the title "Papa Benjamin").
Somebody on the Phone. Philadelphia and New York: Lippincott, 1943. Includes "Death Sits in the Dentist's Chair," "Johnny on the Spot," "Mystery in Room 913," and "The Corpse and the Kid" (under the title "Boy with Body").
After-Dinner Story. Philadelphia and New York: Lippincott, 1944. Includes "The Night Reveals."
If I Should Die Before I Wake. New York: Avon, 1945. Includes "Three Kills for One" (under the title "Two Murders, One Crime").
The Dancing Detective. Philadelphia and New York: Lippincott, 1946. Includes "Dime a Dance" (under the title "The Dance Detective").
Borrowed Crime. New York: Avon, 1946.
Dead Man Blues. Philadelphia and New York: Lippincott, 1948. Includes "Men Must Die" (under the title "Guillotine").
The Blue Ribbon. Philadelphia and New York: Lippincott, 1949. Includes "You Pays Your Nickel" (under the title "Subway").
Six Nights of Mystery. New York: Popular Library, 1950.
Eyes That Watch You. New York: Rinehart, 1952. Includes "All at Once, No Alice."
Bluebeard's Seventh Wife. New York: Popular Library, 1952.

NOVELS BY GEORGE HOPLEY

Night Has a Thousand Eyes. New York: Farrar & Rinehart, 1945.
Fright. New York: Rinehart, 1950.

AUTOBIOGRAPHY

Blues of a Lifetime: The Autobiography of Cornell Woolrich. Edited by Mark T. Bassett. Bowling Green, Ohio: Bowling Green State University Popular Press, 1991.

ARCHIVES

Only a small number of the Woolrich manuscripts survive. These can be found at the Rare Book and Manuscript Division of Columbia University Library.

BIOGRAPHICAL AND CRITICAL STUDIES

Bassett, Mark T. "Cornell Woolrich: Dance and the Detective." *Journal of Popular Literature* 3: 22–34 (spring–summer 1987).

Gruber, Frank. *The Pulp Jungle.* Los Angeles: Sherbourne Press, 1967.

Lacassin, Francis. "Cornell Woolrich: Psychologist, Poet, Painter, Moralist." Translated by Mark T. Bassett. *Clues* 13: 41–78 (fall–winter 1987).

Malzberg, Barry N. *The Engines of the Night.* Garden City, N.Y.: Doubleday, 1982.

Nevins, Francis M. *Cornell Woolrich: First You Dream, Then You Die.* New York: Mysterious Press, 1988. The comprehensive checklist of Woolrich's writing printed at the end of this book includes detailed information on all his magazine stories and on the countless adaptations of Woolrich's work in movies, radio, and television.

Sandoe, James. "Dagger of the Mind," *Poetry* 68: 146–163 (June 1946).

Todorov, Tzvetan. *The Poetics of Prose.* Translated by Richard Howard. Ithaca: Cornell University Press, 1977.

THE ARMCHAIR DETECTIVE

B. J. RAHN

If an armchair traveler is a person who never stirs from home, but satisfies a longing to visit exotic faraway places vicariously by reading travelogues, then, analogously, an armchair detective is an individual who prefers to solve crimes by exercising analytical powers while sitting comfortably at home. This term has commonly been applied to readers of the genre who are considered detectives manqué when they pit their wits against those of the fictional sleuth in attempting to solve the crime before he or she does. Awareness of this role is manifested in Ellery Queen's explicit challenge to the reader. However, the phrase also refers to the fictional character of the armchair detective, who has existed since the inception of the genre. Like Hercule Poirot in *The ABC Murders* (1936), he disdains running around the countryside like a bloodhound upon a scent to collect fingerprints and cigar ash. The extent to which the sleuth relies on someone else to gather information is directly related to the purity of his role as armchair detective.

There seem to be two sorts of armchair detectives: those who are not actually involved in the investigation and are content to draw upon the data gathered by official investigators as a basis for their own theories and those who conduct their own investigation through agents without leaving their chairs. Instead of interviewing witnesses and examining physical evidence at the crime scene, like Sherlock Holmes or Dr. Thorndyke, the first type of armchair detective leaves that work to others but uses the data presented in newspapers and police reports and at inquests or trials as the basis for analysis and solution of the crime. The second type of armchair sleuth employs assistants who report observations of sites and objects, interviews with witnesses and suspects, and research findings. The sleuth forms a hypothesis on the basis of secondhand data but directs its collection rather than relying on someone else to shape the inquiry. The detective is in charge even while staying at home.

The degree of the sleuth's involvement affects the narrative structure of the story. As E. F. Bleiler notes in the *St. James Guide to Crime and Mystery Writers* (p. 810), with the first type of armchair detective there is no ongoing action; the denouement preempts the investigation itself and becomes the central narrative focus. Thus, in tales featuring the first type of armchair detective, the story is told in retrospect by a nonparticipant, so the author must rely on the unraveling of the puzzle alone rather than the excitement of developing events to generate suspense and compel the reader's interest. But stories with the second type of armchair sleuth are closer to classic detective fiction, wherein the narrative begins after the most dramatic event—the murder—has occurred and the majority of the tale is devoted to its unfolding investigation; thus there are many opportunities for exciting action and interaction leading to the dramatic unmasking and confrontation of the villain at the climax of the story.

Origins

Edgar Allan Poe established the concept of the armchair detective in his short story "The Mystery of Marie Rogêt" (1842), wherein Chevalier C. Auguste Dupin forms a hypothesis based on newspaper accounts and police reports concerning the brutal murder of a young woman whose body has been found floating in the Seine. Although Poe disclaims anything but coincidence, this case is remarkably like the actual murder of Mary Cecelia Rogers near New York in 1842. The first-person narrator is the same "I" as in "The Murders in the Rue Morgue" (1841) who reports what Dupin says and does. In eliminating errors to get at the truth, Dupin focuses more on exposing the logical flaws in the various printed reports than on building his own chain of evidence. This oblique emphasis on the quality of thinking results in a narrative that is more of a logical disquisition than a murder mystery, although all the elements of the latter are present. Moreover, the narrative lacks a conventional ending, and so there is no sense of the closure so important in a murder mystery.

Three weeks after the crime occurs, Dupin is consulted by the Prefect, who is stymied. After the Prefect gives a brief oral account of the case, the narrator is deputed to collect copies of police evidence as well as copies of the newspaper accounts of the tragedy. The first thirty pages are devoted to recounting the facts and confirming the identity of the corpse by disputing alternative theories involving whether or not dead bodies float, the length of time needed for a submerged body to float, and the time the body was placed in the water. After eliminating a middle-aged friend of the family and Marie's fiancé as suspects, Dupin proposes to strike out in a new direction. Knowing the importance of accidental, chance, collateral events in the general his-

tory of human knowledge, he proposes to reread the newspapers concerning contemporary circumstances that surround the event in the hope of discovering a fruitful new path of inquiry outside the established channels of investigation. As a result, Dupin excerpts six passages and then speculates about their content. He analyzes the facts to form a hypothesis. In doing so, he employs logical deduction based on circumstantial evidence and common sense.

In the three pages before his valediction, Dupin concludes that the murder of Marie Rogêt was committed by the swarthy man, probably a naval officer of her acquaintance, who was seen with her on the fatal day she vanished. Dupin calls for a full investigation of his whereabouts at the time of the crime. Moreover, he urges comparison of the writing style and script of the officer with those of the communications sent to the newspapers attempting to inculpate a gang as well as those of earlier letters averring the guilt of an exonerated suspect, M. Mennais, implying that the missing swarthy seafarer had attempted to cast blame on others. Dupin recommends additional interviews with an innkeeper and coach driver in order to get more information about the man seen with Marie on the Sunday she disappeared. Finally, he advises tracing an abandoned boat from which Marie's body may have been dumped into the river—a clue that he is confident will lead to the killer. Ultimately, Dupin does not present a solution to the crime but rather suggests a series of steps that he believes will lead to a conclusion of the case. Dupin's hypothesis is based on written records rather than firsthand observation of the crime scene and personally conducted interviews, thus establishing the prototype for the armchair detective.

Fifty-three years later, in 1895, the British writer Mathew Phipps Shiel published three short tales under the title *Prince Zaleski*. In the three stories, "The Race of Orven," "The Stone of the Edmundsbury Monks," and "The S. S.," the narrator consults a reclusive sage, Prince Zaleski, in his secluded mansion for answers to compelling mysteries. The Prince solves the first two without stirring from his exotic, luxurious apartment. To supplement his oral reports, the narrator provides letters written by the principals in the first case and a diary in the second case. On the basis of these data, Zaleski produces accurate analyses of the problems. The purported murder of the head of the house of Orven turns out to be suicide prompted by motives of family honor, and the strange death in the second story, brought on by exacerbated nerves, is ancillary to the mystery of a precious turquoise that seems to disappear but really only changes color. Zaleski's solution in the first case is facilitated by his acquaintance with the family's history and in the second by his knowledge of Persian gems, but in both he relies on logical deduction to explain the detailed execution of the crimes.

Popular Success

Emmuska, Baroness Orczy (1865–1947), an émigré to England from Hungary, is often erroneously given credit for creating the first armchair detective in her Old Man in the Corner series published in *The Royal Magazine*. Instead, just as Sherlock Holmes established the detective as a popular figure in fiction, so Baroness Orczy's Old Man created a taste for the armchair detective in the public mind. Certainly, Orczy's stories were widely read and more influential than those of her predecessors. In particular, by introducing a sedentary character whose milieu was a tea shop, they encouraged women to write crime fiction by demonstrating that to be successful, a detective did not need the education, professional training, physical prowess, and social mobility that was displayed by the high-profile sleuths in the period but which was commonly outside women's experience. After Orczy's character appeared early in the twentieth century, many other writers created memorable examples of this figure.

Orczy published three series of detective stories in *The Royal Magazine* between 1901 and 1904, which were collected in book form in *The Case of Miss Elliott* (third series, 1905) and *The Old Man in the Corner* (first and second series, 1909). A fourth series, which was less successful, appeared as *Unravelled Knots* (1925). Although Orczy preserves the device used by Poe and Arthur Conan Doyle of the two-character partnership, she pairs a cranky old man with an attractive young female journalist, whom he meets in a tea shop near the Strand in London. The Old Man is certainly an unprepossessing specimen whose name, Bill Owen, is revealed only once in "The Mysterious Death in Percy Street." Polly Burton, a reporter for London's *Evening Observer*, is a breath of fresh air relieving the men's club atmosphere prevailing in the genre at the time. By mismatching age and gender, Orczy creates a very odd couple indeed. What they have in common is an overwhelming interest in contemporary crimes.

Polly first encounters the Old Man at a corner table in an ABC (Aërated Bread Company) tea shop when he strikes up a conversation without an introduction because he observes her reading an account of a mysterious crime in the newspaper. Amused by his appearance and startled by his opening remark, which seems a direct answer to her unspoken thoughts à la Dupin or Holmes, Polly gives a sarcastic rejoinder designed to discourage him. However, he continues to talk and registers unconventional attitudes that intrigue her. Not only does he have contempt for the police and little reverence for the law, but more often than not, he also admires the clever criminal who outwits the police. With long, pale, trembling fingers, he nervously ties and then unravels intricate knots in a piece of string—as an adjunct to thought—while discussing puzzling crimes. In reply to her scornful invitation to explain a mystery that had baffled the police for the past year, the Old Man first relates the case in detail and then propounds his solution before disappearing quickly out the door, leaving a stunned Polly and his bit of string behind him. Without exception, the ensuing tales conform to this two-part narrative pattern of retrospective summary followed by elucidation.

As the precursor of subsequent armchair detectives, the character of the Old Man as well as his methods deserve scrutiny because they established precedents. The Old Man is not officially involved in investigating any of the criminal happenings he discusses. He tackles cases for the pure pleasure of the mental exercise, but he is not confined to his tea shop corner. Although he leaves his armchair to collect information, his role is always that of passive observer. He gathers information not only from newspapers but also from inquests and trials he attends as a member of the public. And in "The York Mystery" he visits a crime scene after the event to verify his theory by observing physical details of spatial relations. He also makes notes, conducts research, and takes photographs of the principals involved in various cases. In some instances, he does not disclose his sources, so Polly (and the reader) must be content with such explanatory phrases as "I found out . . .," "I took the trouble to make certain inquiries . . . ," and "I have since ascertained . . ."

Blind Sleuth

The epitome of the armchair detective would seem to be represented by a blind man prevented by his disability from actively gathering evidence and forced to draw inferences from facts supplied by others. But the gifted amateur English sleuth Max Carrados, introduced by Ernest Bramah in 1914, moves about with the ease and agility of his sighted companions. In fact, many people who observe him refuse to believe he is blind. Carrados has tuned his other senses to a hypersensitive pitch so that he often perceives the physical world more fully than others who depend principally upon visual impressions. If one accepts the premise that the more sedentary the armchair detective is, the purer a specimen he presents, then Carrados is not a particularly fine example because he is quite active. He

visits crime scenes to collect physical evidence and interview witnesses; hence, he employs the standard investigative techniques of any gifted amateur detective and does not rely solely on secondhand data. He also employs an assistant to be his "eyes"; Carrados has trained his butler, Parkinson, to be a first-class observer. Louis Carlyle, a former schoolmate who runs a detective agency, refers cases to him.

"The Coin of Dionysius" and "The Mystery of the Vanished Petition Crown" show Carrados at his best as an armchair detective in that he solves both cases without leaving his study. Both involve the theft of a rare coin. In the former, Carrados recognizes a forgery of a coin that he had handled two years previously, when its owner displayed it to a group of experts. He is able to identify the villains and their methods partly because he detected and defeated their attempt to make counterfeit copies of coins from his own collection. In the tale of the Petition Crown, a young woman suspected of stealing a valuable coin at an auction is referred to him by Mr. Carlyle. While telling her story, she realizes that she dropped the missing coin into the wrong tray when she was startled by a man staring at her. Later, she was sitting in a chair previously occupied by the same gentleman; when he requested that she vacate "his" seat, she refused, indicating several empty chairs nearby. Placing his hand on the chair back, he also paused to speak with her upon a pretext as he was leaving. On the basis of her account of events, Carrados infers that the man noticed her inadvertent misplacing of the coin, that he bought the tray containing the valuable coin and switched it for one more like its fellows, that he hid the booty in his chair, and that he planned to return to retrieve it. To prove his theory and exonerate Carlyle's client, Carrados goes to the auction house, locates the hidden coin, and sets a trap that the malefactor obligingly falls into. Although Carrados solves the case while sitting in his armchair, he arranges a dramatic confrontation with the culprit in the style of Dupin or Holmes.

Female Armchair Detective

Toward the end of the 1920s, Agatha Christie's Miss Jane Marple began her career as an armchair detective in a half dozen short stories that Christie published in *The Sketch*. Augmented with seven more tales, they appeared in 1932 as *The Thirteen Problems* (also published as *The Tuesday Club Murders*, 1933). In the first six stories, a group of friends meets on Tuesday evenings in the home of Miss Marple. Each, in turn, tells a story disclosing a criminal problem that the others try to solve. The six members of the group include four professional men—the novelist Raymond West (Miss Marple's nephew); a clergyman, Dr. Pender; a solicitor, Mr. Pethrick; and Sir Henry Clithering, retired Commissioner of Scotland Yard—and two women —an artist, Janet Lempriere, and Miss Marple. All relate mysteries of which they have firsthand knowledge and that reveal their personalities and expertise. Although various members of the group propose plausible solutions, nonetheless, it is Miss Marple who supplies the correct answer as she counts stitches while knitting something white and soft and fleecy by the fire. The narrative pattern is the same in the latter seven stories, but the setting and characters are different. The characters are gathered at the home of Colonel and Mrs. Bantry, where they amuse themselves after dinner with the same parlor game. In addition to Arthur and Dolly Bantry, the party includes Miss Marple, at the behest of Sir Henry Clithering, plus a middle-aged medico, Dr. Lloyd, and a beautiful-but-dumb young actress, Jane Helier.

In both groups of stories Miss Marple is clad in remarkably Victorian attire for the 1930s. "Miss Marple wore black lace mittens; an old lace fichu was draped round her shoulders and another piece of lace surmounted her white hair" ("The Blue Geranium," p. 85). She shed this dated costume and the persona of armchair detective in favor of a more active investigative role in the later novels. She is characterized as a diffident, deferential elderly spinster with a ruthlessly unsentimental penetrating insight into human nature derived from observation of village life. In fact, she is able to unravel the cases under discussion because the individuals described remind her of villagers who have committed similar indiscretions. She admits that she has had a very uneventful life, but she claims that people are very much alike everywhere. In "The Tuesday Night Club," when her nephew patronizes her with his man-of-the-world superiority and exclaims that he doesn't understand how she does it, she puts him in his place by stating: "No, dear, but you don't know as much of life as I do" (p. 13).

Armchair Private Eye

In *Fer-de-Lance* (1934), Rex Stout introduced Nero Wolfe, one of the few armchair detectives who earns his living by solving crimes. Wolfe is a professional investigator employing full-time and part-time staff members. In fact, Stout adapts the armchair sleuth to the private investigator formula. Because of his extreme corpulence—his weight is estimated at one-seventh of a ton—Wolfe, who may have been modeled on Sherlock's brother, Mycroft Holmes, rarely leaves his house on West Thirty-fifth Street between Tenth and Eleventh Avenues in Manhattan. Wolfe's town house includes plant rooms on the glassed-in roof, which contain his extraordinary orchid collection. One of the top seven orchid breeders in the United States, Wolfe has won acclaim for the new varieties he has developed with the aid of his skilled gardener Theodore Horstmann, who lives on the premises. Wolfe also employs a full-time chef, Fritz Brenner, a French-speaking Swiss who has an apartment in the basement. In order to finance his ruling horticultural passion; indulge his tastes for books, food, and wine; and support the household, Wolfe undertakes criminal cases for high fees. He is inordinately lazy, however, and has to be goaded to work by his assistant-cum-secretary, Archie Goodwin. Even at times when the bank balance is dangerously low and a substantial infusion is needed, Wolfe has refused lucrative commissions because either the problem or the client didn't appeal to him. When he does undertake a case, he concentrates the full force of his remarkably analytical mind on the problem and through a combination of thoroughness, perseverance, and patience achieves astonishing results. Like any other private investigator, Wolfe begins with the puzzle presented by his client and tries to shed light on it by gathering more information, but instead of venturing out into the mean streets himself, he sends his assistant.

In addition to functioning as Wolfe's chauffeur, accountant, stenographer, typist, general office manager, and bodyguard, Archie performs investigative chores of information gathering assigned by Wolfe, which include observation, interviewing, and research. Archie is a well-trained observer and an accomplished interviewer; moreover, he has a prodigious memory for details and faces. Sometimes Archie brings a witness or suspect home for Wolfe to interview personally. Periodically, gathering the information that Wolfe requires places Archie in jeopardy, and so he has to fight his way out or, occasionally, even shoot his way out of a dangerous situation. When Archie's eyes and ears, arms and legs are insufficient, Wolfe hires additional freelance helpers, namely Saul Panzer, Fred Durkin, and Orrie Cather, according to the nature of the tasks at hand. Although Panzer is the best "eye man" in the business, no one can surpass Durkin for surveillance or Cather for interviewing.

Wolfe likes to be actively involved in the conclusion of a case. After he has analyzed the information supplied by his operatives and formed his theory, Wolfe summons the principal figures to his office to present the solution and/or extract a confession from the guilty party in what the reader recognizes as the conventional final confrontation scene of most detective stories. At this dramatic climax, which is carefully orchestrated by Wolfe from behind his desk with the other characters seated facing him, violence may occur, which the ever-alert Archie must quell. While Wolfe doesn't leave his chair, he nonetheless prompts the action with his remarks. Because he is sedentary, Wolfe seems to behave like the second type of armchair detective, but he does interact with the individuals at the center of the case and influence their behavior. Although he directs the entire investigation from a sitting position, Wolfe's active participation at the conclusion of a case represents a departure from the usual formula for the armchair detective.

Anthony Boucher (William Anthony Parker White, 1911–1968), celebrated reviewer for the *New York Times* and inspiration for Bouchercon, the most venerable annual mystery fiction convention, wrote a novel and short stories featuring armchair sleuths. In addition to Nick Noble, an alcoholic retired cop who appeared in several short stories, Boucher also created Dr. John Ashwin, a professor of Sanskrit at the University of California at Berkeley, who really relished his role as armchair detective. In *The Case of the Seven of Calvary* (1937), Boucher plays by the rules in that Ashwin remains strictly behind scenes. Information is brought to him by Martin Lamb, a graduate student who functions as Watson to his Sherlock. Lamb is intimately involved with characters at the heart of the action and even witnesses one of the murders. He supplies useful reportage, serves as a sounding board as Ashwin develops a hypothesis, and even does valuable independent research that advances the investigation. He also acts as a conduit of Ashwin's views, which proves crucial in developing the plot. On the basis of facts supplied by Martin and the newspapers about the first murder, Ashwin concludes that the wrong person was killed and predicts a second murder. His theory alerts the intended victim, who disposes of his would-be killer before he can strike again. When the first murderer dies violently and the second murderer's life is then threatened by a third person, Ashwin is forced to revise his hypothesis. In a conventional resolution, Ashwin recounts his solution step by step, eliminating false leads one by one until he confronts the second murderer with the truth. His explication is a model of logical deduction.

Mid-Century Developments

The mid-twentieth century witnessed the appearance of two of the most ideal armchair detectives in the genre. Two normally active men are forced by illness to pursue detective investigations from the sickroom—one at home, the other in the hospital. Each story is a tour de force in its own right. In 1944, Cornell Woolrich, writing as William Irish, published his famous short story "Rear Window" in an anthology titled *After Dinner Story*. (It had previously appeared two years earlier as "It Had to Be Murder" in *Dime Detective*, an American pulp magazine.) The mobility of Hal Jeffries, whose leg is encased in plaster, is limited to a few feet as he alternates between his bed and his armchair by the window. In this first-person narrative, he explains that he can't read or sleep and therefore spends hours sitting by the window to relieve his boredom. As he keeps his lonely vigil seeking distraction to pass the long hours, he watches the lives of his neighbors through the rear windows of their apartments like so many television soap operas. He is amused by the harum-scarum teenagers who go out partying every night; he is saddened by the young widow who puts her child to bed before putting on her makeup and leaving every evening; and he feels compassion for the out-of-work husband and his sick wife.

He becomes curious when Mrs. Thorwald in the fourth-floor flat directly opposite his upstairs bedroom window fails to appear one day after the light in the bedroom has remained on all night behind the drawn shade. His curiosity changes to suspicion when her husband begins acting oddly. The husband makes a careful survey of the courtyard windows both at dawn and in the evening of the same day; moreover, he fails to greet his wife

upon his return. When he lowers the shades in the kitchen and living room windows, lights spring on behind them but not in the bedroom. Later the kitchen shade is raised while the man packs his wife's dresses in a trunk and then surveys the surrounding windows for a third time. At dawn, when the husband's head pops up in the living room window, Jeffries deduces that he must have spent the night on the sofa, which means he hasn't been near his wife for two nights. After porters remove the trunk the next morning and the husband finally raises the bedroom shade on an empty room, the narrator is struck by the conviction that the husband has murdered his wife.

Jeffries depends on his finely honed observational skills and his ability to draw logical inferences from them to ascertain that a murder was committed and that the body was stowed in the trunk. A police search of the apartment reveals nothing. When the police trace the trunk to a country address and a woman claiming to be Mrs. Thorwald unlocks it with her own keys in their presence—proving its contents harmless—they abandon the case, but Jeffries does not. He is more determined than ever to prove his point and devises stratagems to force Thorwald to divulge the location of the body. He sends the husband an anonymous threatening letter, makes menacing anonymous phone calls, and attempts to unnerve him by having an easily detected search of the premises conducted while he is absent—but all to no avail. The solution comes to him in a Platonic flash as the analytical part of his brain finally interprets puzzling visual images noted earlier in the day as he observed a house agent showing the remodeled flat on the fifth floor directly above that of his suspect. Hence he is able to help the police produce the corpus delicti literally without leaving his chair.

In Josephine Tey's *Daughter of Time* (1951), Inspector Alan Grant is flat on his back with a fractured leg and a concussed spine, having fallen through a trap door while chasing one of the less savory specimens of London's criminal classes. Bored with staring at the cracks in the ceiling, Grant becomes intrigued by the disparity between Richard III's humane countenance displayed in his official portrait from the National Portrait Gallery and his vicious behavior in murdering his young nephews in the Tower, as recorded in popular history books. Grant pursues his subject from historian to historian, trying to glean as much information about Richard as possible, advancing from school texts to the acknowledged authority of Sir Thomas More's *History of Richard III*, to modern scholarly accounts. When Grant realizes that More's famous account of Richard's life was written relying on secondhand reportage during a Tudor regime, the policeman in him rejects it as "hearsay evidence" and decides to investigate the four-hundred-year-old murders strictly following the rules of evidence of a police inquiry. He enlists the aid of Brent Carradine as research assistant to search fifteenth-century records for facts to use in assessing Richard's character and deciding whether he was guilty of murdering the young princes in the Tower. Grant gives assignments to Carradine as he would to a junior officer.

The investigation has two parts. First they investigate Richard's behavior from his accession to the throne upon the unexpected death of his brother, Edward IV, in April 1483, evaluating all his acts for traces of violent ambition, because the standard explanation of Richard's motive in murdering his nephews was his need to eliminate rivals to the title. When his brother died, Richard was appointed guardian to Edward's elder son, who was a minor. His claim as Protector was never challenged. Moreover, on the basis of testimony given two months later by Robert Stillington, bishop of Bath, that the marriage of Edward IV to Elizabeth Woodville was invalid, on 25 June Parliament passed a bill called Titulus Regius, which proclaimed Edward's children illegitimate and declared Richard to be king. There was no overt opposition to his coronation and no need to do away with the boys. Even if Richard had removed the boys, there were five sisters between him and the throne.

Having found no evidence on which to base a charge, Grant exonerates Richard. Then he tries to find the real culprit. Following police procedure, Grant instructs Carradine to ascertain who would benefit most from the deaths of the princes and the whereabouts, at the time of the boys' deaths, of the principal persons involved.

After Henry VII succeeded to the crown in 1485, he repealed the Act of Titulus Regius. Henry had married Elizabeth, Edward IV's eldest daughter, and by revoking Titulus Regius he made her legitimate, but by the same pen stroke he legitimized her siblings and made the elder boy king of England. Further investigation reveals that Henry systematically eliminated the adult males in the York line by trying and convicting them of capital crimes on trumped-up charges and rendered many of the females powerless through marriage with loyal Lancastrians.

Next they investigate the confessed assassin, Sir James Tyrrel of Gipping, and discover that he was appointed Constable of Guisnes in France by Henry in 1486 and lived abroad on his estates until May 1502, when he was recalled to England and beheaded without trial in the Tower. His confession of murdering the young princes in 1483 at Richard's behest was declared after his death, but no signed confession existed. Subsequently Grant and Carradine learn that Tyrrel was granted two general pardons a month apart in the summer of 1486, shortly before he left for France. General pardons were common and exonerated an individual from responsibility for adverse consequences of acts committed during a previous term of office, rather like an act of indemnity. Two general pardons separated by only a month were unprecedented and give rise to the question of why the second was needed. Perhaps the murders had been planned before the date of the first pardon but could not be executed till later so Tyrrel demanded a second pardon.

Grant and Carradine conclude that the actual murders probably took place in the month between the pardons. Henry's motives in allowing Tyrrel to live undisturbed for sixteen years and then deciding to eliminate him are not explained.

Based entirely on inferences drawn from fifteenth-century records, Grant solves the case. He clearly belongs to the second category of armchair detective, as he directs the investigation of these historical murders while bedridden by posing questions for an assistant to answer.

Ethnic Sleuth

In the 1940s, two American writers who subsequently earned recognition for introducing Jewish detectives published short stories featuring nonethnic armchair sleuths. Although both James Yaffe and Harry Kemelman are best known to readers for novels displaying the shrewd human insight and impeccable logic of authority figures from the domestic and religious spheres of the Jewish community, the Jewish mother and the rabbi, their early efforts presented more conventional characters.

Paul Dawn, James Yaffe's first detective, appeared in a few short stories that Yaffe wrote and published between the ages of fifteen and eighteen. Dawn was a professional policeman heading the Homicide Squad's Department of Impossible Crimes; however, he acts the role of the armchair sleuth in "The Problem of the Emperor's Mushrooms" (*Ellery Queen Mystery Magazine*, 1945) as he solves the murder of the Emperor Claudius I by his wife Agrippina in 54 B.C. while sitting in an easy chair sipping coffee and chatting with the historian Professor Bottle.

In the 1950s and 1960s Yaffe created one of the genre's purest examples of an armchair detective when he introduced Mom, a middle-aged Jewish housewife living in the Bronx whose only son, David, is a policeman in New York's homicide squad. Yaffe retained the mixed gender partners introduced by Orczy but reversed their ages in pairing a young man

with an old woman. Furthermore, he modified their roles. Dave, the male narrator and titular detective, professes mystification, and Mom, instead of being merely a passive female listener, is actually the problem solver. Like Miss Marple, Mom is able to interpret seemingly inscrutable human conduct because a suspect's behavior reminds her of that of a relative or neighbor. Unlike Miss Marple, Mom's eccentricity resides in her ethnicity; she is a stereotypical domineering Jewish mother whose malapropisms, misuse of prepositions, mispronunciation, and incorrect syntax reveal her immigrant youth on New York's Lower East Side.

Dave and his wife, Shirley, have dinner with Mom every Friday evening. Over dinner, between the matzo ball soup and the apple strudel, Dave reports on the latest case perplexing his department, and Mom solves it through logical deduction based on her knowledge of human nature. After Dave has presented the details of the crime, Mom asks three or four seemingly irrelevant questions and then produces her solution like a rabbit out of a hat. While Mom fetches the coffee, Dave calls headquarters. Mom is at her best in "Mom Remembers" and "Mom in Spring."

Mom and Dave also appear in four novels written in the 1990s. After Dave's wife dies, he takes a job as investigator in the Public Defender's office in Mesa Grande, a small city at the foot of the Rocky Mountains. It isn't long before Mom joins him. The formula doesn't change much in the extended narrative. Mom stays at home while Dave goes to work, but he brings his problems home with him after work and discusses them with her. Mom listens, asks questions, and makes suggestions that Dave acts on. The investigations develop step by step in *A Nice Murder for Mom* (1988) and *Mom Meets Her Maker* (1990) as Dave delivers information piecemeal and follows Mom's advice at each stage.

Harry Kemelman's Nicholas (Nicky) Welt, Snowden Professor of English Language and Literature at an unnamed university in New England, made his debut in "The Nine Mile

Walk" (*Ellery Queen Mystery Magazine*, 1947). This story garnered immediate widespread admiration among aficionados. It became so widely known that it was reissued with other Nicky Welt stories, including "The Straw Man" and "End Play," in a collection titled *The Nine Mile Walk* (1967). In the introduction, Kemelman stated, "The Nicky Welt stories attracted attention . . . because they were the epitome of the armchair type of detective story. The problems were solved by pure logic, and the reader was given the same clues that were available to the detective hero" (p. 10).

Kemelman follows Poe in pairing Welt with a nameless friend who serves as sounding board, assistant, and narrator. Although they are age peers (late forties), Nicky always treats his assistant condescendingly—rather like a schoolmaster with a backward pupil. Nicky is introverted and reclusive, while the narrator is extroverted and gregarious. Formerly on the law school faculty, Nicky's friend ran for the office of County Attorney on the Reform Party ticket and won. He therefore has useful connections within the various departments of criminal investigation in the town, and he can obtain the latest information on current cases and is routinely involved in them. He often encounters a problem in his work and receives Nicky's advice in solving it. Sometimes they are both drawn in through shared activities, such as chess at the university, or through common acquaintances ("Time and Time Again"). The narrative format is the same in almost all of the stories. The narrator listens to a detailed description of a case and usually a possible explanation; he may even posit a theory himself, as in "End Play." Then Nicky will point out logical flaws in the theory and propose an alternative solution, often supported by circumstantial evidence, which proves to be true. His deductions are based only on the data presented in the account of the problem.

In "The Nine Mile Walk," after the assistant has embarrassed himself by drawing incorrect inferences from statements by a political opponent, Nicky attempts to demonstrate that most inferences may be logical and yet not true. He challenges his friend to provide a sentence of ten to twelve words so he can demonstrate his premise. From the simple sentence "A nine mile walk is no joke, especially in the rain," Nicky draws inferences about time and distance in relation to local public transport and the local topography of Fairfield County that lead to the solution of a murder and apprehension of the culprits. The narrator, however, has the last laugh because Nicky's inferences are all too true.

Rabbi David Small, Kemelman's other sleuth, is not really an armchair detective. In fact, the novels, published from the mid-1960s through the mid-1990s, do not contain much detection because Small is more rabbi than sleuth and he merely undertakes a case in order to help a member of his congregation and/or a friend. Instead, these books portray problems of Jewish life, including crime, in a small Massachusetts suburban community, Barnard's Crossing.

Fin de Siècle

Isaac Asimov's Black Widowers series was published in the *Ellery Queen Mystery Magazine* intermittently from the 1970s to the 1990s and was also collected in anthologies. Although essentially an adaptation of the Christie formula in "The Tuesday Night Club," this series offers one of the purest examples of the form. The armchair detective is Henry Jackson, a waiter whose full name is revealed only in the first story, "The Acquisitive Chuckle," in which his character and background are sketched. Henry listens as members of the Black Widowers club discuss and posit solutions to a problem at their monthly meetings held at the Milano restaurant in New York City. They call themselves Black Widowers because their club was founded as a refuge from disapproving wives; of course no women are allowed at their meetings. The group is composed of six members: a writer, Emmanuel Rubin; an artist, Mario Gonzalo; a cryptographer, Thomas Trumbull; an organic chemist, Paul Drake; a patent attorney, Geoffrey Avalon; and a high school mathematics teacher, Roger Halsted. None of the club members or Henry is involved directly as an investigator in any of the cases debated, very few of which involve murder. After they have rejected most of the hypotheses presented, Henry then suggests his own simple solution, with the modest disclaimer that he merely states what is left after their "labors had eliminated so many false trails."

Asimov described these stories as very cerebral, which implies that they focus on the puzzle. Indeed, characterization is minimal. Beyond basic physical description and a few mannerisms and attitudes to distinguish one from the other, the reader learns nothing about these men. Even Henry, the main character, is repeatedly referred to by the same phrase, which emphasizes his lack of individuality by calling attention to his nondescript unlined, sixtyish face. Henry is staid, reticent, diffident, and scrupulously honest. Justice for him involves retribution. As for the plots, the club meetings, and hence the narrative structure, follow a rigid and unvarying formula: conversation over preprandial drinks, during which a theme is introduced as well as the evening's guest; more conversation over dinner, during which the theme is explored further; and then the "grilling" of the guest over coffee and brandy. The guest is assured of absolute confidentiality, including that of Henry, who is an ex-officio club member. The guest presents a puzzle during his grilling, which the Black Widowers try to fathom—to no avail. As a last resort, they turn to Henry, who sorts out the problem. In "The Obvious Factor" (*Ellery Queen Mystery Magazine*, May 1973), wherein Henry unmasks the guest as a liar, he demonstrates the truth of Sherlock Holmes's precept that "when the impossible has been eliminated, then whatever remains, however improbable, is the truth" (*Tales of the Black Widowers*, p. 91). Actually, all the stories illustrate this principle.

Conclusion

The armchair detective has endured over the 150 years of the genre's history. This convention has been adapted to a variety of character types, including the gifted amateur sleuth, the private investigator, and the professional policeman. Armchair sleuths have been drawn from both genders, as have their creators, and their ages have spanned the decades from youth to advanced age. As noted by Bleiler, these stories focus primarily on the unraveling of a tightly constructed puzzle. In addition to contriving the puzzle, the challenge for the writer is to generate suspense despite the absence of exciting events. To compensate for the lack of ongoing action, many writers have inspired interest by creating detectives with vivid eccentricities. The principal pleasures for the reader are satisfaction in the elucidation of the complex puzzle and delight in the vividly wrought eccentric sleuth. There seems little doubt that this type of character will survive beyond the millennium.

Selected Bibliography

Asimov, Isaac. *Banquets of the Black Widowers*. Garden City, N.Y.: Doubleday, 1984.

———. *Tales of the Black Widowers*. Garden City, N.Y.: Doubleday, 1974. Includes "The Obvious Factor."

Baring-Gould, William S. *Nero Wolfe of West Thirty-Fifth Street*. Harmondsworth, Eng.: Penguin, 1969.

Bleiler, E. F. "Baroness Orczy." In *St. James Guide to Crime and Mystery Writers*, 4th ed. Edited by Jay P. Pederson. Detroit: St. James Press, 1996.

Boucher, Anthony. *The Case of the Seven of Calvary*. London: Zomba Books, 1984.

Bramah, Ernest. *Best Max Carrados Detective Stories*. Edited by E. F. Bleiler. New York: Dover Publications, 1972. Includes "The Coin of Dionysius" and "The Mystery of the Vanished Petition Crown."

———. *Max Carrados Mysteries*. Harmondsworth, Eng.: Penguin, 1964.

Christie, Agatha. *The ABC Murders*. London: Collins, 1971.

———. *The Thirteen Problems*. New York: Berkley Books, 1984. Also published as *The Tuesday Club Murders*. New York: Dodd, Mead, 1933. Includes "The Blue Geranium" and "The Tuesday Club Murders."

Kemelman, Harry. *The Nine Mile Walk.* New York: Putnam, 1967. Includes "The Nine Mile Walk," "The Straw Man," "End Play," "Time and Time Again."

Orczy, Baroness Emmuska. *The Case of Miss Elliott.* London: Unwin, 1905.

———. *The Man in the Corner.* Edited by Burke N. Hare. New York: International Polygonics, 1977; New York: Dodd, Mead, 1909. Includes "The York Mystery."

———. *The Old Man in the Corner: Twelve Mysteries.* Edited by E. F. Bleiler. New York: Dover Publications, 1980. Includes "The Case of Miss Elliott" and "The Mysterious Death in Percy Street."

———. *Unravelled Knots.* London: Hutchinson, 1925.

Poe, Edgar Allan. "The Mystery of Marie Rogêt." In *Great Tales and Poems of Edgar Allan Poe.* New York: Washington Square Press, 1940.

Shiel, Mathew Phipps. *Prince Zaleski.* Boston: Robert Brothers, 1895. Includes "The Race of Orven," "The Stone of the Edmundsbury Monks," and "The S.S."

Stout, Rex. *Fer-de-Lance.* New York: Bantam Books, 1992.

Tey, Josephine. *The Daughter of Time.* New York: Collier, 1988.

Woolrich, Cornell. *Rear Window.* By "William Irish." New York: Ballantine Books, 1984.

Yaffe, James. *Mom Meets Her Maker.* New York: St. Martin's Press, 1990.

———. *My Mother, the Detective: The Complete "Mom" Short Stories.* Norfolk, Va.: Crippen & Landru, 1997. Includes "Mom Remembers" and "Mom in Spring."

———. *A Nice Murder for Mom.* New York: St. Martin's Press, 1988.

———. "The Problem of the Emperor's Mushrooms." Norfolk, Va.: Crippen & Landru, 1996.

BLACK DETECTIVE FICTION

STEPHEN SOITOS

AFRICAN AMERICAN WRITERS have written detective fiction since the beginning of the twentieth century. From the first serialized detective novels published in African American periodical literature, black writers adapted the usual conventions of detective fiction to their own ends by altering the detective persona; infusing their novels with black vernaculars, such as language and music; and using the popular culture form to examine issues of race, class, and gender. Authors such as Pauline Hopkins, J. E. Bruce, and Rudolph Fisher wrote novels featuring black detectives that established a tradition of black detective writing with which African Americans could transform a Eurocentric popular art form. Black detective fiction became especially well known and popular in the 1980s and 1990s. With the emergence of writers like Walter Mosley and Barbara Neely (alternatively written BarbaraNeely), books with black detectives written by black authors gained mainstream recognition and readers as well known as President Bill Clinton, who is a big fan of Mosley's work.

The Birth of Black Detective Fiction

The long tradition of African American detective fiction began with Pauline Hopkins' *Ha-gar's Daughter*, which was serialized in the *Colored American Magazine* from 1901 to 1902. Hopkins introduces Venus Johnson, a black female detective, in this novel about a black woman "passing" as white in the Civil War–era South. This novel established important attributes of African American detective writing, including the use of a black detective persona, black vernaculars, double-conscious detection, and hoodoo. ("Double-conscious" is the term W. E. B. DuBois used to describe African Americans' awareness of themselves as second-class citizens within a racially prejudiced society; "hoodoo" refers to syncretic religions of African Americans in the New World.) These themes were elaborated on by several African American writers before Chester Himes began his post–World War II series of Harlem detective novels. J. E. Bruce's *Black Sleuth* (1908–1909) features an African-born detective who brings a black nationalist perspective on American society to the detective genre. Bruce successfully extended African American self-identity beyond the confines of America and in the process showed ways in which black writers could use the detective persona to illustrate the inherent intelligence, nobility, and pride of the black race. Rudolph Fisher's *The Conjure Man Dies* (1932) was the first black detective novel set in Harlem with all black characters. His variation on the locked-room murder mystery uses the classic format of an amateur detective helping the police and has elements of the modern police procedural in its use of forensic evidence. He cleverly demonstrates how hoodoo elements could be used to reinforce black pride, the shared cultural identity and independent religious practices of black Americans connected to an African past. He also introduces themes from the Harlem Renaissance—a black literary, intellectual, and cultural movement that occurred in Harlem, New York City, between 1919 and 1929—to black detective fiction.

Chester Himes

Chester Himes (1910–1984) proved to be the most prolific black writer in crime and mystery fiction. He published ten detective novels—*For the Love of Imabelle* (1957), *The Crazy Kill* (1959), *The Real Cool Killers* (1959), *All Shot Up* (1960), *The Big Gold Dream* (1960), *Cotton Comes to Harlem* (1965), *The Heat's On* (1966), *Run Man Run* (1966), *Blind Man with a Pistol* (1969), and the posthumous *Plan B* (1993). Himes restructured the traditional hard-boiled detective narrative by introducing a simultaneous time frame (a narrative structure that shows actions in different episodes happening at the same time) while creating a mythical landscape of Harlem that is both satirical and absurd. Seen as a group, his ten novels provide a wide-ranging review of changing African American behavior and development in the black community.

Himes is a good example of how a black detective writer uses the detective genre for specific agendas while criticizing the form, or "signifies on" the detective genre, to re-create it with an African American difference. First of all, he created his own version of the detective persona. He relied, in part, on some of the accepted conventions of the classic and hard-boiled traditions—violence, sexism, critique of corruption on all levels—but also forged new images of the detective with his Harlem detectives, Coffin Ed Johnson and Grave Digger Jones. Coffin Ed and Grave Digger work as a team, whereas most hard-boiled detective novels project single, loner protagonists. Also, by writing his novels in the third person, Himes broke with the conventional hard-boiled first-person narration. He gave more background information about his detectives than earlier authors of hard-boiled fiction. A good portion of their characters derives from their social conscience, which has them fighting crime in the black world but unable to do anything about the direct causes of the poverty that necessitates the crime.

Overall, Coffin Ed and Grave Digger represent a volatile blend of black pride, anger, and frustration. These qualities are often manifested in their ability to understand the tricksters of the Harlem milieu, as well as in their use of signifying asides indicting the white power structures that control them. For example, Grave Digger says to Anderson, his white superior:

> We got the highest crime rate on earth among the colored people in Harlem. And there ain't but three things to do about it: Make the criminals pay for it—and you don't want to do that; pay people enough to live decently— you ain't going to do that; so all that's left is let'em eat one another up. (*Cotton Comes to Harlem*, p. 18)

But Coffin Ed and Grave Digger, unlike other detectives of the hard-boiled school, are unable to expose or radically alter the corruption and crime that permeate Harlem. Part of the reason lies in the fact that Harlem is a city within a city, and any effectual change relies on a substantial alteration of the racial social climate, which does not occur in these books. The detectives' blackness is an integral ingredient to the success of their investigations because they are directly connected to the black community. They use both ratiocination and violence to solve their cases, but rather than focusing simply on the crime and capture of the suspect, they are interested in the social and political atmosphere, often to the exclusion of detection.

Himes's two detectives are double-conscious in the sense that they are often trickster figures; they use their blackness in conning their witnesses and their superiors to solve crimes. This double-consciousness comes into play consistently in white-black relationships. It suggests that blacks share a sociopolitical consciousness or worldview that carries forward into their cultural creations. Himes further expands double-conscious detection by giving masking and trickster qualities to a wide range of characters in the novels. Himes's vision becomes increasingly darker as the tricksters dupe fellow blacks and often themselves. Harlem manifests a carnival atmosphere in the early novels, but as the books progress, the spectacle turns more and more ominous. The last novel, *Plan B*, ends in total chaos and violence, instigated by the ultimate trickster of the armed black revolution, Tomsson Black.

Black vernaculars and, to some extent, hoodoo or alternative religious practices are major factors in differentiating black detective texts from other detective novels. Black vernaculars are expressive arts of black Americans that are derived from folk traditions and form part of African American culture. References to music and dance, black language, and black cuisine are laced into the detective text, forming a "blackground" that is specific to black detective fiction. Himes embroiders his descriptions of Harlem with blues and jazz. He also uses black vernacular speech, for example, in *The Real Cool Killers* " 'Wait a minute, you big mother-raper, till ah finds my arm!' he yelled. 'It got my knife in his hand.' " (p. 8). Vernaculars in this sense create their own subtext and extend the parameters of the black detective tradition as they are repeated from novel to novel.

Himes did not start as a detective novelist—he wrote many short stories and novels before he focused on the genre. He was born in the United States to the third generation of black Americans out of slavery; his father was a college professor. Himes's early years were marred by disruptive behavior, and he spent seven years (1929–1936) in the Ohio State Penitentiary for armed robbery. It was in prison that Himes taught himself how to write. He published short stories such as "To What Red Hell" (1934) and "The Night's for Cryin'" (1937) in *Esquire* magazine. Many of his early stories featured white protagonists.

After his prison stint, he married, and he worked and wrote on both the West Coast and the East Coast of United States. His first four novels garnered him little critical or financial success, but while working in a cafeteria in Harlem he gathered much of the background he later used in his detective novels. Owing to racial tension and prejudice and financial problems, Himes left the United States in 1953 to live in France. Like other black writers, including Richard Wright and James Baldwin, he chose expatriation in an attempt to find relative social peace.

With the publication of his first detective novel, *For the Love of Imabelle*, Chester Himes initiated his unique contribution to the African American detective tradition. Broke and in Paris, Himes wrote this novel at the urging of Marcel Duhamel, the editor of the *Série Noire*, a French publication of hard-boiled detective stories devoted to such American authors as Dashiell Hammett, Raymond Chandler, Cornell Woolrich, and Horace McCoy. Duhamel offered Himes an advance to write a detective novel, which in France enjoyed a high literary status, and it was Duhamel who persuaded Himes to add Coffin Ed Johnson and Grave Digger Jones to his narrative. These two Harlemites became the most famous black detectives in detective literature, appearing in all but one of Himes's crime novels.

Himes wrote all of his Harlem detective books in Europe. Mining his memory and using his natural bent toward absurdist fiction, Himes created an imaginary cityscape of Harlem that was never meant to be real. His ten novels substantiate an achievement in detective fiction unmatched by any other African American writer. Himes took the hard-boiled detective novel and transformed it with African American sensibilities, extending the use of detective personas, double-conscious detection, black vernaculars, and hoodoo as previously presented in the works of Hopkins, Bruce, and Fisher. Himes also elevated the depiction of violence, one of the primary facets of detective fiction, to a new plane of expression. The evolution of the use of violence in Himes's detective novels both reflects an increased aesthetic awareness of this common hard-boiled motif and constitutes a thematic statement. In his detective novels, Himes presents a social critique that unequivocally demonstrates the effects of racism and poverty in Harlem. The violence develops throughout the works as he portrays a community in turmoil, tilting toward chaos and erupting into anarchy. Finally, in the last works, violence becomes a root of revolt as well as an expression of despair.

The detective story plot, melded with the social, religious, and political background of Harlem, provided a perfect marriage of imagination and reality, well suited to Himes's episodic style, racial consciousness, and satiric sensibilities. The Harlem detective series makes important commentary on race and class in both white and black worlds, while thrilling and delighting the reader with chases, fights, and outlandish scams. Himes transforms traditional detective fiction by using its conventions in a number of experimental ways, altering the narrative, using parallel stories, and creating a changing cast of black characters caught in absurd situations.

This absurd vision depicted so well in the detective novels harbors within it the seed of a bitter truth. The extreme behavior of Himes's black characters, while outrageous in a slapstick fashion, is predicated on the simple but serious fact that racism completely controls their lives. This vision of absurdity as a direct result of racism figures prominently in all of his detective novels. Harlem becomes a microcosmic testing ground for his portrayal of African American existence. Himes's two detectives, Coffin Ed and Grave Digger, fully understand the social injustice and poverty that lie at the root of Harlem's problems.

In a number of novels Himes uses the narrative device of simultaneity, in which parallel actions take place at the same moment. This suggests an Afrocentric worldview in that circularity, simultaneous visions, and time travel are aspects of African religions. (Ishmael Reed explored this in his novels by destroying linear and historical time). Along with reworking the linear time frame, Himes alters another important facet of traditional detective fiction. The natural order of society is no longer restored by solving the crime and punishing the criminal. The themes of Himes's later novels suggest that moral order is impossible in a culture so damaged by racism. As Coffin Ed and Grave Digger progress toward ineffectuality, frustrated idealism, and eventual death, Himes's plots mirror the disintegrating social fabric of the community around them. His fractured plots pitch white against black and black against black in an increasingly chaotic world of exaggerated political dimensions. In some ways, Harlem itself becomes as important as plot and character in the detective novels since it represents all the isolated and segregated black communities throughout the United States. In powerfully descriptive prose, Himes uses a combination of black vernaculars to depict the black urban atmosphere of African American folk culture as it is lived in America's largest black community. As a unit, the novels express a definitive achievement in black detective fiction in the use of the main elements of black detective fiction. Furthermore, the progression from *Love of Imabelle* to *Plan B* presents an overview of African American social and political conditions in the United States during that period.

Coffin Ed and Grave Digger's use of double-conscious social satire in the early novels grows increasingly bitter and vituperative in the last few works. Violence becomes less comic and more politically motivated until *Plan B*, when black revolution erupts and catapults the community into total upheaval. From his first detective novel, Himes showed how the detective plot could be used for political satire. Perhaps his most important discovery was that violence, usually used for dramatic effect in hard-boiled detective fiction, might be applied to African American political ends. All of the novels pinpoint racism as lying at the root of the disorder in the black community, a racism so diffuse and debilitating that blacks end up fighting blacks as whites continue the racist practices that threaten black existence.

In *Blind Man with a Pistol*, Coffin Ed and Grave Digger are incapacitated by a systematic repression engineered by their white superiors. In *Plan B*, they are simply useless tools who end up being killed. No longer can they keep the peace in Harlem. And while they are reduced to ineffectual characters in the text, the politically violent wing of an obscure black nationalist group plunges Harlem into violent revolution.

Himes is often considered to be merely a hard-boiled detective writer who wrote entertaining detective thrillers. This is hardly the case. He transformed the detective novel handed down to him from the American masters Hammett and Chandler and established the black detective novel as a vehicle for social critique, depicting madness in Harlem that cannot be cured except by a radical realignment of moral values in the United States. In the process, Himes further demonstrated how important "blackground" was to African American detective fiction. His descriptions of Harlem illustrate the sociopolitical themes of his novels, while his fascinating views of the interiors of bars, nightclubs, and soul-food restaurants depict the exotic and culturally specific environs of the black community. In the end, the double-conscious method of his two detectives proves fruitless in solving crimes. Himes's last works end up being parodies of detective novels in that nothing gets resolved while the detectives themselves become the victims.

Himes presented African American culture in a unique way and through the detective genre created a new appreciation for the complexity and diversity of black America. The political and moral message behind the wild escapades in Himes's narratives suggests a radical sensibility not previously seen in the black detective tradition. Himes successfully changed the way blacks came to deal with the detective form, opening up the field for further creative experimentation by black writers.

Ishmael Reed and Clarence Major

Himes proved to be a valuable predecessor to Ishmael Reed (*b.* 1938) in his reinterpretation of the detective novel. Reed acknowledged that Himes showed him the way to use the detective format for African American themes, but Reed went much further than Himes in his experimental use of the form. Reed virtually abolished the classic hard-boiled variety of the detective novel (with its linear narrative, recognizable detective, and resolved ending), retaining only the useful structural and iconic portions of detective fiction (a search for missing clues, an atmosphere of danger and darkness, and the use of guns and jargon from detective films) for his satirical novels *Mumbo Jumbo* (1972) and *The Last Days of Louisiana Red* (1974). Reed's interest in social satire and historical revisionism displaces the traditional detective format, leaving only the armature of the detective formula on which he hangs a sophisticated exploration of African American themes. He uses the detective formula to present his neo-hoodoo vision as an affirmative re-creation of African American identity.

As the head of a private detective agency, the Neo-HooDoo Kathedral, the character PaPa LaBas represents the double-conscious trickster detective. Reed effectively employs neo-hoodoo—his term for raised black consciousness combined with hoodoo magic and African American spirit—to represent the black perspective while at the same time using the four primary themes of black detection in a postmodern novel of experimentation. Continuing the motif of detective transformation, Reed's PaPa LaBas uses neo-hoodoo to confound white attempts to destroy the black race. His far-ranging powers connect him spiritually to ancient hoodoo while presenting a revisionist interpretation of history along Afrocentric lines. Reed confirms the importance of black vernaculars to the healthy creation of black culture. His greatest contribution to the black detective novel lies in showing how African American hoodoo can be innovatively transformed to support social and political ends.

Whereas Reed almost abolishes the detective formula through his alteration of traditional detective themes, Clarence Major (b. 1936) effectively continues the transformation by writing a novel that critiques the very process of writing. In *Reflex and Bone Structure* (1975), Major retains only the barest minimum of detective allusions in his novel while forging new connections between reader and text. As an antidetective novel, *Reflex and Bone Structure* challenges conventional notions of time and history while continuing postmodern experimentation. Like Himes and Reed before him, Major contradicts the primary detective conventions, particularly in his refusal to have a positive resolution to the story.

Harking back to Edgar Allan Poe's theory of ratiocination, Major writes a metafictional novel that suggests the mind cannot solve all mysteries. He uses the detective format for a book about perception and language that also critiques the novelistic conventions of characterization, plot, and predictable motivation. With his background in modern art and his interest in the poetics of prose, Major infuses his complex postmodern novel with African American sensibilities against a backdrop of indeterminant chaos. The black detective novel in this case questions the nature of reality and the function of the written word with narration shifting from first person to third person and by having no plot or detective, having unreliable characterization, using surreal images, abolishing linear time, and having magical reinventions of time, place, and action. Major complicates the objective

stance of traditional hard-boiled first-person narration with a highly subjective, self-referential, postmodern experimental format. Major's book is written by a nameless narrator whose depiction of crime and detection questions the very nature of perception itself (Can the world be perceived in any objective fashion, or do we construct reality out of our subjective imagination?) and in the process reworks the substance of African American detective fiction. Both Reed and Major use double-conscious hoodoo narrative and structural ploys in self-reflexive novels that signify on the black detective tradition.

The Female Black Detective

Since 1975 a revival of interest in detective novels by black writers has created a growing field of new work. Furthermore, black detective authors have gained a measure of respectability and recognition as the readership and acceptance of black detectives have become more diverse. This is especially true with regard to black female authors, who have continued a tradition by maintaining an African American cultural viewpoint. Some detective books by black women writers include Dolores Komo's *Clio Browne: Private Investigator* (1988); Barbara Neely's *Blanche on the Lam* (1992), *Blanche Among the Talented Tenth* (1994), and *Blanche Cleans Up* (1998); Eleanor Taylor Bland's *Dead Time* (1992), *Slow Burn* (1993), and *See No Evil* (1998); Nikki Baker's *In the Game* (1991), *The Lavender House Murder* (1992), and *Long Goodbyes* (1993); Nora Deloach's *Mama Solves a Murder* (1994) and *Mama Stalks the Past* (1997); Valerie Wilson Wesley's *When Death Comes Stealing* (1994) and *Where Evil Sleeps* (1996); Charlotte Carter's *Rhode Island Red* (1997); and the works of Grace F. Edwards, who has been compared to Chester Himes for her use of Harlem as a setting, especially in *If I Should Die* (1997).

After the publication of Pauline Hopkins' *Hagar's Daughter*, which introduces an ama-

BLACK DETECTIVE FICTION

teur black female detective, we do not know of any African American women writing novels with black female detectives until the publication of Dolores Komo's *Clio Browne*. It is important to note that black female detectives have appeared in print almost concurrently with the renewed interest in female detectives as a whole. Contemporary African American female detective writers work out of two traditions—the extended tradition of male and female detective writing and the narrower tradition of black detective writing.

Clio Browne revises the white male model of the private investigator by introducing a contemporary African American female who inherits a detective agency, the Browne Bureau of Investigation, from her father, who started it in 1947. Clio calls him the first black private investigator in the city of St. Louis and perhaps in the whole country. Her pride in her family is evident from the first pages of the novel. She informs us that she kept her maiden name while she was married, that she has a son who is a fighter pilot in the navy, and that she lives with and is deeply attached to her mother. Her husband, one of St. Louis' first black police officers, was killed in the line of duty. Clio Browne is highly educated, and she displays her bachelor's and master's degrees proudly on the walls of her small midtown office. She mentions more than once her desire to write a definitive history of the black investigator in the United States.

The novel is a comic blend of mishaps and coincidences that echoes variations on the hard-boiled novel. Like other hard-boiled detectives, Clio Browne has a private practice and accepts cases as a paid professional. But unlike other hard-boiled detectives she carries no gun and has no pernicious vices except a desire for ice cream and other fatty foods and a fashion and money consciousness that she tries to keep in check. The issues of money, class, and race enter the story early on when she accepts the case of Serena Scutter-Paschal, a white society matron whose diamond ring has been stolen. The contrasts between the two women and their families are alternately obvious and subtle.

As a private investigator, Clio has a small and shoddy but clean office and an often absent secretary. She also has a highly developed sense of morality that prevents her from becoming involved in domestic cases. Clio solves the case of the ring through a combination of coincidence, dogged determination, and good luck. The important aspects of this mystery novel lie in the establishment of the detective persona; the black female detective continues in many ways a tradition in black detective writing as a whole. For example, Clio uses her blackness as part of her detective trade. She often masks herself as a maid to gain entry into houses, and she lapses into black dialect when the occasion demands. She is well aware of her differences from detective heroes of the past, such as Sherlock Holmes, to whom she often contrasts herself. She does not use the ratiocination of classic male detectives; instead, she works from gut responses, like Agatha Christie's Miss Marple and many white female detectives. Like other black detectives, Clio works with a group that includes white male detectives who help her out. *Clio Browne* is a women-centered novel that mildly critiques male behavior, both black and white, but saves its strongest criticism for white privilege and prejudice. Clio believes that, in cases of police investigation, the color of one's skin often determines who is believed. As the first black female detective novel in the contemporary period, *Clio Browne* introduces us to a black female perspective that is independent and assimilationist. References to black food and black music and language are made throughout the novel.

Barbara Neely (b. 1941) has written several novels featuring Blanche White as an amateur detective. Both *Blanche on the Lam* and *Blanche Among the Talented Tenth* are murder mysteries in which the protagonist becomes involved by circumstances. Blanche is a domestic who cleans and cares for white families. In both novels she is not a professional detective, although she feels that her job has given her the occupational skills of one. The two novels show the development in Blanche's consciousness as she moves from a southern environment in the first novel to a sheltered and elite black community in Maine in the second. *Blanche on the Lam* provides a contemporary counterpoint to *Hagar's Daughter* in that here, too, the female protagonist uses her position and her blackness for purposes of detection. The novel gives an important viewpoint in the black detective novel because it tells the whole story from the black maid's perspective.

There are many interesting similarities between the black female detective figures of Clio Browne and Blanche White. Like Clio, Blanche finds herself pitted against a southern white aristocracy. Clio and Blanche are both closely connected to their families and unabashedly express their love and emotional bonds in the first pages of the novel. Both are single women with family ties and close girlfriends, but neither has a permanent relationship with a male. Clio and Blanche, coming out of working-class environments, express knowledge of black culture, African history, and women's rights that is predominately self-taught.

In *Blanche on the Lam*, Blanche hides out from the police by posing as a domestic in a white household. In the next novel of the series, Blanche visits an exclusive black aristocratic resort where issues of class and gender play a major role. There are no white people in the novel, but the gradations of skin color among the vacationers provide ample opportunity for an insidious internal prejudice, and the resort is a microcosm of the class and color antagonism in black society at large. Along with this critique of class consciousness based on color, the novel provides a running commentary on relationships between black males and females. Blanche is much less interested in assimilation than Clio Browne. She devotes her attention to the black community and leans toward a black separatist viewpoint. She also voices strong support for black culture and believes in the power of hoodoo and its spiritual connection to ancestors and Africa.

Blanche actually earns a living as a domestic and sees a connection between her domestic status and the folk tradition of African culture. It is this pride in her background and black skin that provides the anchor for her personality as well as the fulcrum for her investigative behavior. In *Blanche Among the Talented Tenth*, murder and blackmail provide the motivations for plot development in the novel, but the story has more to do with social frictions among African Americans in an insular and intense environment. The novel skewers false behavior among blacks, both male and female, who see a hierarchy of social position based on skin color and occupation. From her position at the bottom of the social totem pole, Blanche provides a sweeping perspective and incisive social commentary, which indicates new ways that the detective novel can be used to explore contemporary issues of African American culture.

Both Dolores Komo and Barbara Neely continue the African American detective tradition by altering and extending the detective persona with black female consciousness. Their novels also use black vernaculars liberally, constantly apply double-conscious detective techniques, and make some use of hoodoo awareness in rounding out an African American perspective. Three other black female novelists—Nikki Baker, Eleanor Taylor Bland, and Valerie Wilson Wesley—are not quite as successful in this capacity, for they include very little specific African-American cultural reference. Although these authors are supportive of African American culture, their novels are more concerned with female identity in the changing sociopolitical climate of the contemporary United States.

Nikki Baker (b. 1962) has written three detective novels featuring Virginia Kelly, a proud African American lesbian, as an amateur detective. The three stories take place in Chicago, Provincetown, Massachusetts, and the small Midwestern town of Blue River, Indiana, where Virginia was brought up. Virginia lives in the fast lane of contemporary urban life and works as a well-paid investment options broker for a Chicago firm. Her first-person narratives are told from a distinctive viewpoint that outlines topical issues of sexuality and class for a well-educated and ambitious black woman. Virginia is a liberated black female involved in an on-again, off-again relationship with Emily, a white accountant. Amid numerous affairs and interactions with other women and a few men, Virginia struggles to define her place in American society, first as a lesbian and then as a black woman. She leans toward a lesbian separatist attitude, yet hides her sexuality in her workplace and fights with her parents, who cannot accept her sexual orientation.

Virginia is an amateur detective whose personal life is in chaotic change. The crimes of the first three novels function as plot devices, backgrounded against the more important issue of her intense identity quest. The mysteries loosely follow the pro forma constructions of murder and investigation usually adhered to by mystery novelists and established by such classic detective writers as Arthur Conan Doyle and Agatha Christie. Instead of reinterpreting established forms of the genre, however, Nikki Baker has redefined the first person in the detective tradition and made it one of marginalized difference in that the detective narrator found in Baker is in continuous struggle with herself and the larger world. Baker has reversed the typical hard-boiled approach. Rather than presenting a detective persona consciously adapting the world to her viewpoint and thereby establishing ultimate control, Baker gives us a detective who more often than not questions herself and the viability of her frame of reference. Less crime novels than social critiques, Baker's three novels explore the insular world of lesbian politics in explicitly sexual and gay terms. At the same time, they present an interesting picture of the corporate world and contemporary materialism from a unique viewpoint.

Eleanor Taylor Bland's two novels feature Marti MacAlister, a Chicago homicide detective. Marti is a liberated black female, a widow with two children, who has struggled to attain recognition and appreciation from her professional associates as well as from the

people she deals with as a homicide detective. She has a white male partner who provides an effective counterpoint to her black female perspective. Both novels are written in the third person and reinterpret police procedural formats by introducing social themes filtered through the consciousness of an African American policewoman. Likewise, Valerie Wilson Wesley's *When Death Comes Stealing* concerns a single mother, Tamara Hayle, who is a private investigator in Newark, New Jersey. This murder mystery deals with urban African American society from a black female perspective.

Walter Mosley

Walter Mosley (*b.* 1952) has emerged as the most influential and widely hailed black writer of detective fiction. His *Devil in a Blue Dress* (1990), *A Red Death* (1991), *White Butterfly* (1992), *Black Betty* (1994), and *A Little Yellow Dog* (1996) confirm the continuity of the male black detective tradition and provide the best example of how that tradition has developed in the last quarter of the twentieth century. These five novels feature the detective Easy Rawlins and take place predominantly in Watts, a black area of Los Angeles. Mosley has consciously set out to write a series of detective novels that span a historical period of African American history and development in the United States. Each novel takes place in a specific year—1948, 1953, 1956, 1961, and 1963—and depicts the changing historical and cultural milieu. At the same time, each novel shows the progression of Easy Rawlins' self-development, as the detective reveals more and more about himself and his growing black consciousness. In some ways, his personality and social development mirror the changes in society around him.

The first novel, *Devil in a Blue Dress*, sets the tone for the rest of the series. We are introduced to Easy, a single black man scarred by his experiences in World War II and his reception back in the States as a lower-class citizen, even after he risked his life for his country. Set upon by the arbitrary whims of his white boss in an aircraft factory, where he works as a mechanic, Easy is fired from his job. This racial environment and particular locale had already been mined by Chester Himes in one of his early protest novels, *If He Hollers Let Him Go* (1945). Mosley's intent is to use the detective form to show aspects of black existence in this period while at the same time writing a mystery story that involves the issue of passing as white, another common theme used previously by black detective writers, such as Pauline Hopkins.

Easy Rawlins is part of the black southern migration to the West Coast. Although the mystery novels pick up his life as he lives it in Watts, Mosley published a prequel called *Gone Fishin'* (1997) that features Easy's early life in East Texas in 1939. In this novel, Easy is shown as a man caught in a dilemma revolving around his best friend's killing of his stepfather. Easy witnesses the crime but accepts money to keep quiet, and this moral quandary infects his conscience to the degree that it is referred to in *Devil in a Blue Dress*. In *Gone Fishin'*, we learn much background information about Easy only hinted at in the mystery novels, such as his having been raised on a sharecropper's farm and having been deserted by his parents. Many of the characters from this time and place, like the best friend, Mouse, and Mouse's wife, figure in the later mystery novels. Moreover, much of Easy's characterization as a marginally employed, semiliterate victim of many incidents of racism is carried forward into the mystery novels.

Easy's detective persona illustrates many of the changes that black detective writers used to signify on the white detective form. For example, he is to some degree a reluctant private eye who is drawn into his cases by circumstance. Easy becomes a detective because his blackness allows him entry into certain areas of society where whites have little access. He is also a trickster whose life is full of duplicity and ambiguity.

Throughout the five books, Easy maintains a series of manual labor jobs, and in the last, *A Little Yellow Dog*, he is working as a janitor at a school, a position that allows him a secret intelligence of the crime in that novel. There is an evolution of this conceit from Venus Johnson, the slave detective in *Hagar's Daughter*, through *The Black Sleuth* and Barbara Neely's novels. Easy takes this one step further because he is actually a man of property who owns his own house. He is very secretive about this aspect of his private life. By forcing the world to see him as a typical poor black man, Easy lives an increasingly dangerous life that threatens to destroy his private and public personas. The effects of this secrecy take a toll on his personal life. Easy's double existence is further complicated by his relationship with his best friend, Mouse, who pops up in the novels at the most crucial moments. Mouse represents the unrepentant black outlaw who lives outside the constrictions of society and abides no insult, whether from white or black. He might be called Easy's alter ego in that he is a dangerous man with a hair trigger who is ready to act instinctively and usually violently in any situation. Mouse lacks Easy's rational ability to think through a situation. He often assists Easy in his detective investigations and provides the strong arm that Easy needs.

Easy's loyalty to Mouse runs through all the novels. They almost function as a detective team, a partnership that we have seen in other African American detective novels. With one foot in the streets with Mouse and the other in a more sedate middle-class existence, Easy evidences a complicated double-sidedness to his character. His double existence plays out on a number of levels. Easy pursues education and reads books, yet he insists on speaking in black dialect to establish his credentials as a black man of the streets. Like other detectives, he is conscious that social position and class are evidenced by one's use of language, and he makes this his advantage when dealing with white and black police.

Easy Rawlins' depiction as the black Everyman, a man of the people, bears analogy to Raymond Chandler's private eye Philip Marlowe. In his series of detective novels, Chandler helped define the hard-boiled tradition, which was typically white, male, and prejudiced. In *Devil in a Blue Dress*, Mosley cleverly reinterprets Chandler's famous opening scene from *Farewell, My Lovely* (1940), in which Marlowe is dragged up to the black bar on Central Avenue in Watts by Moose Malloy to look for Malloy's old girlfriend, Velma. In this scene Chandler's description of the bar and its inhabitants is told from the white viewpoint, laced with disdain and racist imagery. The blacks are described by Chandler as "dinges," a race apart, aliens in Los Angeles, inferior and strange.

Mosley writes a revisionist interpretation of this scene from the black perspective and thereby continues the black detective tradition—this time with an African American viewpoint. Now it is the blacks in the bar, including Easy, who are in control, and it is the white man, Albright, who is put at a disadvantage. Easy is hired by Albright because he is black and he will be able to penetrate the black areas of Los Angeles looking for Daphne Monet. This scene establishes the basic points about the black detective tradition further reinterpreted by Mosley's five novels. Easy is not a private eye by training. Like other black detectives (Blanche White, for example), he assumes the role of detective as a means of survival and an attempt to help other members of the black community. His detective status is thrust upon him by the circumstances of his life. Easy comes to detection as a way to help his friends and solve mysteries that threaten the well-being of the black community, and he often finds himself as the center stabilizing point when crimes destroy the fabric of the society he inhabits.

Easy is an amateur detective who turns semiprofessional as the books progress. He works for money but does not retain an office, nor does he have any official status as a detective. His first-person narration harks back to the heyday of hard-boiled detective fiction, yet his character retains important elements of the black detective tradition. Contrary to most hard-boiled fiction, Easy's personal life and connection to the black community are integral to the progression of the plot. As we have seen, this is a theme that runs through black detective novels. His personal life is not static, as is the case with most early hard-boiled detectives. Easy is a black man who ages and evolves. In the first novel he is a bachelor with a shady past and a drinking habit. By the third story he is married with a daughter and son. At the end of the novel Easy has separated from his wife, and his former affair with the wife of one of his best friends has become an important part of the plot.

In *White Butterfly*, Easy has a baby daughter, Edna. Three years later, in *A Little Yellow Dog*, he has two illegally adopted children, Jesus and Feather. Easy's marriages disintegrate and his affairs multiply to complexity, but his human qualities create a sympathetic and recognizable person who is maturing and growing in the difficult environment around him. The murders and disappearances are the plot motivations of Mosley's books, but the real purpose of the detective series is to illustrate the continuing tensions between everyday black citizens and the white and powerful economic superstructure in which they must live.

The racial tension of Los Angeles is amply demonstrated throughout these books by the depiction of covert and overt prejudice. Some of these incidents turn violent. Others are just continual reminders of the difficult lives that black citizens live. However, an undercurrent of racism permeates the series, and Easy's outlook is unquestionably influenced by the racial prejudice that he has endured and that he has witnessed among his friends and community. Indignation at injustice is not a new phenomenon to hard-boiled detective fiction, but Mosley carries his detective series into new moral territory with his continuous indictment of the racism that permeates the lives of his characters.

Easy is the outsider on the path of truth. His brutal treatment by the police is another convention lifted from the white detective genre, but in this case it is amplified by the fact that Easy is black and therefore treated much worse. We see the Watts of 1948, a close-knit community of African Americans who share a lifestyle and worldview, fragment and disintegrate in the passage of years to 1963. As in other hard-boiled detective novels, Easy is drawn into a conspiracy of corruption that reaches to the highest level of wealth and politics in Los Angeles. Depicting class and cultural conflict is perhaps the greatest asset of hard-boiled detective fiction. Easy follows in the tradition of the black detective because he uses his double-consciousness in perceptive ways to solve cases. As W. E. B. DuBois first implied in his concept of double-consciousness, Easy realizes the world first as a black person and then as a person, which gives him special insight into behavior and crime both black and white.

Mosley also has an acute eye for black vernacular detail. His descriptions of the bars and clubs of Watts are reminiscent of Himes's interiors while they concentrate the reader's attention on such vernacular elements as language, food, music, and religion. With these expressions of African American culture, Mosley's books continue the tradition of using the detective form to reveal and explore the lives of blacks in the United States. Black vernaculars such as music and language specify an African American cultural achievement and are woven into the plots as part of the cultural cityscape. Special language, idiomatic expressions, and particularly tone establish examples of black language use. Easy's struggle for identity through social and political associations in the black community becomes a running theme in the novels. Easy moves through a well-described milieu of clubs, church organizations, street scenes, and jazz bars that give the background atmosphere of Watts.

Mosley's extension of the black detective persona continues a tradition. He effectively comments on the flux of black American life without sacrificing important elements of the detective tradition. Like the work of Chester Himes, Mosley's series adds up to more than a sum of its parts. Himes's series followed a path of decreasing optimism and humor to-

ward chaos and disintegration with both his detectives and the surrounding black community. Mosley's novels also show a world growing increasingly angry and dark. Easy has his friends and his family to help support him in his struggle, but as the novels progress it is Easy's detective status that gives him the greatest meaning in life.

Other Black Detective Fiction

Black detectives are found in Australian, English, West Indian, and African fiction as well. And there are black detectives created by writers who are not themselves black. Arthur Upfield's Inspector Napoleon Bonaparte, a part-aboriginal detective whose beat is Australia, is an example of both and is the subject of a separate discussion in this volume, in the essay on the ethnic detective. Many present-day critics of black detective fiction would find Upfield's work racist and his series figure, "Bony," unconvincing and at times condescending, but the fact that Upfield wrote of a black detective as early as 1929, beginning with *The Barrakee Mystery*, and continued to do so for nearly four decades no doubt influenced subsequent writers. John Ball's *In the Heat of the Night* (1965) launched a series about a black policeman, Virgil Tibbs, that led to a long-running television series. Whether the fact that neither Upfield nor Ball was black influenced their work, or destined them to write from the outside in, is an appropriate subject for exploration, though not in the space permitted here. Both wrote well before the height of the civil rights movement; perhaps the question is better put to a more recent series, written by an English author, Reginald Hill, best known for his Dalziel and Pascoe novels. In the 1990s, Hill launched a new series featuring a black detective of West Indian origin, Joe Sixsmith, who frequently reflects on the meaning of being black in contemporary Britain. Hill's titles, such as *Born Guilty* (1995), speak of his point of view. Black writers who write of black protagonists are multiplying in Australia—Philip McLaren, who is a Kamilaroi, or aborigine, has won a significant award for his work, of which *Scream Black Murder* (1995) is representative—and one can confidently expect more black writers of West Indian or African origin coming out of Britain, such as Mike Phillips, writer of the Sam Dean series, exemplified by *An Image to Die For* (1995).

Conclusion

The growing number of black detective writers in the last half of the twentieth century indicates a new energy and achievement in the detective genre. Black female authors apply new varieties of expression to the detective novel, making it a vehicle influenced by both a feminist and an African American consciousness. In the best of these books, the authors emphasize the survival skills of black females in contemporary culture. New authors, such as Penny Mickelbury and Gary Phillips, have recently entered the genre.

These black authors demonstrate that male and female black detective personas continue to have meaning to contemporary readers. The idea of the black detective was initiated by Pauline Hopkins and J. E Bruce at the beginning of the twentieth century. Chester Himes expanded on the role of the black detective and showed how detective conventions could be used by black writers to critique social and racial conditions in the United States. The continuing popularity of black detective fiction indicates the usefulness of the detective genre to African American creative exploration and cultural definition.

Selected Bibliography

PRIMARY WORKS

WORKS OF NIKKI BAKER

In the Game. Tallahassee: Naiad Press, 1991.
The Lavender House Murder. Tallahassee: Naiad Press, 1992.

Long Goodbyes. Tallahassee: Naiad Press, 1993.
The Ultimate Exit Strategy. Tallahassee: Naiad Press, 1996.

WORK OF JOHN BALL

In the Heat of the Night. New York: Harper & Row, 1965.

WORKS OF ELEANOR TAYLOR BLAND

Dead Time. New York: St. Martin's Press, 1992.
Slow Burn. New York: St. Martin's Press, 1993.
See No Evil. New York: St. Martin's Press, 1998.

WORK OF J. E. BRUCE

Black Sleuth. Serialized in *McGirt's Magazine*, 1907–1909.

WORK OF CHARLOTTE CARTER

Rhode Island Red. New York: Serpent's Tail, 1997.

WORKS OF NORA DELOACH

Mama Solves a Murder. Los Angeles: Holloway House, 1994.
Mama Stalks the Past. New York: Bantam, 1997.
Mama Saves a Victim. Los Angeles: Holloway House, 1997.
Mama Stands Accused. Los Angeles: Holloway House, 1997.

WORKS OF GRACE F. EDWARDS

If I Should Die. Garden City, N.Y.: Doubleday, 1997.
A Toast Before Dying. Garden City, N.Y.: Doubleday, 1998.

WORK OF RUDOLPH FISHER

The Conjure Man Dies. 1932. Rpt. New York: Arno Press, 1971.

WORKS OF REGINALD HILL

Born Guilty. New York: St. Martin's Press, 1995.
Pictures of Perfection. New York: Dell Books, 1995.
On Beulah Height. New York: Delacorte Press, 1998.

WORKS OF CHESTER HIMES

If He Hollers Let Him Go. Garden City, N.Y.: Doubleday, Doran, 1945.
For the Love of Imabelle. New York: Fawcett, 1957. Also published as *A Rage in Harlem.* New York: Avon, 1965.
A Jealous Man Can't Win. New York: Avon, 1959. Rpt. as *The Crazy Kill.*

The Real Cool Killers. New York: Avon, 1959.
All Shot Up. New York: Avon, 1960.
The Big Gold Dream. New York: Avon, 1960.
Cotton Comes to Harlem. New York: Putnam, 1965.
The Heat's On. New York: Putnam, 1966.
Run Man Run. New York: Putnam, 1966.
Blind Man with a Pistol. New York: Morrow, 1969.
Plan B. Jackson: University Press of Mississippi, 1993.

WORK OF PAULINE HOPKINS

Hagar's Daughter: A Story of Southern Caste Prejudice. 1901–1902. Rpt. in *The Magazine Novels of Pauline Hopkins* by Pauline E. Hopkins. New York: Oxford University Press, 1988.

WORK OF DOLORES KOMO

Clio Browne: Private Investigator. Freedom, Calif.: Crossing Press, 1988.

WORK OF CLARENCE MAJOR

Reflex and Bone Structure. New York: Fiction Collective, 1975.

WORK OF PHILIP MCLAREN

Scream Black Murder. Sydney, Australia: HarperCollins, 1995.

WORKS OF WALTER MOSLEY

Devil in a Blue Dress. New York: Norton, 1990.
A Red Death. New York: Norton, 1991.
White Butterfly. New York: Norton, 1992.
Black Betty. New York: Norton, 1994.
A Little Yellow Dog. New York: Norton, 1996.
Gone Fishin'. Baltimore: Black Classic Press, 1997.

WORKS OF BARBARA NEELY

Blanche on the Lam. New York: St. Martin's Press, 1992.
Blanche Among the Talented Tenth. New York: St. Martin's Press, 1994.
Blanche Cleans Up. New York: Viking Press, 1998.

WORK OF MIKE PHILLIPS

An Image to Die For. London: HarperCollins, 1995; New York: St. Martin's Press, 1997.

WORKS OF ISHMAEL REED

Mumbo Jumbo. Garden City, N.Y.: Doubleday, 1972.
The Last Days of Louisiana Red. New York: Random House, 1974.

WORK OF ARTHUR UPFIELD

The Barrakee Mystery. London: Hutchinson, 1929.

WORKS OF VALERIE WILSON WESLEY

When Death Comes Stealing. New York: Putnam, 1994.
Where Evil Sleeps. New York: Putnam, 1996.

BIOGRAPHICAL AND CRITICAL STUDIES

Lewis, Diane E. "Whodunit? Not the Maid." *Boston Globe Magazine,* 26 March 1998: 24–25, 33–38.
McGee, Patrick. *Ishmael Reed and the Ends of Race.* New York: St. Martin's Press, 1997.
Soitos, Stephen. *The Blues Detective: A Study of African American Detective Fiction.* Amherst: University of Massachusetts Press, 1996.
Woods, Paula. *Spooks, Spies, and Private Eyes: Black Mystery, Crime, and Suspense Fiction.* New York: Doubleday, 1995.

CRIME NOIR

CHARLES L. P. SILET

J IM THOMPSON'S NOVEL *The Killer Inside Me* (1952) concludes with the dying Lou Ford, torn apart by a fusillade of police bullets, wondering if "our kind," who started the game with a crooked cue and wanted so much but got so little, who meant to do so well and did so badly, will get another chance in the "Next Place." Lou Ford's fading questions could stand as the epitaph for all those characters who people the stories written in the "crime noir" tradition. Crime noir fiction memorialized the losers, the misfits, and the wayward wives who stumbled into crime through their greed, insanity, or just plain stupidity and paid the price. It is a style of crime writing that, as a definable subgenre, has received scant attention and remains underappreciated, yet it is one of the most powerful and evocative in crime fiction.

The term "crime noir" designates a brand of American fiction that has never been properly defined. "Noir" brings to mind the French terms *roman noir*, *film noir*, and *série noire*, which are related to types of cinema or literature that deal with the darker side of life, the noir world associated with gangster and crime films, mystery and detective novels—those popular arts (and even on occasion high arts) that explore the underside of culture. Crime noir is a type of crime fiction that exceeds the boundaries of the conventions set by the traditional definitions of mystery and detective stories. It is fairly well determined by a time frame, beginning in the early 1930s

and ending in the late 1950s; a set of writers, especially James M. Cain, Cornell Woolrich, and Jim Thompson; and a consistent range of themes. In addition, three properties are central to the understanding of noir fiction: its relationship to the historical moment in which it was written, the working-class orientation of most of the central characters (Lou Ford's "people"), and the almost unendurable bleakness of the stories.

To work toward a definition of crime noir, this essay includes a detailed description of the various elements and parameters of crime noir as a subgenre of crime fiction; a decade-by-decade analysis of crime noir writers, with some remarks on film noir; and a highly select bibliography of both primary and secondary sources for further study of the form. This format is designed not only to define crime noir but also to explore the factors that gave rise to it.

The Parameters of Crime Noir Fiction

Although crime noir grew from the same roots as hard-boiled detective fiction, the narratives do not feature a detective, or at least not a series detective, nor are the stories themselves a series. Crime noir novels tend to be, as the British say, "one-off" works. While the lack of a series, like the various

Sam Spade stories by Dashiell Hammett or Robert B. Parker's Spenser books, tends to restrict the fiction's marketability, it allows authors a greater freedom, the freedom, say, to dispose of characters, especially the central character, in more creative ways. This freedom also permits crime noir writers to produce a more unstable kind of fiction, one that can dig deeper into the country's problems and explore to greater depths its ailing psyche.

Furthermore, lacking the central detective figure who usually shapes the narrative voice and often the perspective of the fiction—frequently in rather conventional ways—crime noir stories potentially extend the range of protagonists. The detective is a professional and therefore has certain skills that help him survive in an uncertain world—characteristics that noir characters usually lack. Detective stories also are by nature investigations with the attendant clues and a solution to the mystery at the end that motivates the plot of the narrative. Crime noir fiction avoids such a trajectory and relies more on an accumulation of incidents that resolve themselves into a conclusion, but one that is usually tragic in outcome.

Like the hard-boiled tradition, crime noir fiction began during the 1920s in the pulp magazines and grew to fruition during the hard days of the Depression. But unlike hard-boiled fiction, which tends to use the social and economic realities of the times as background against which the problem-solving detective works his skills, noir writing foregrounds the social and economic conditions and those trapped in them in the main thrust of the plot. And while the detective always manages, even if only marginally, to rise above the defeats of those whom he serves—often the wealthier members of society (who else could afford to hire a detective in the first place?)—the typical noir protagonist usually is swept under by social forces he or she is unable to control. The detective also usually holds to a "code" that affords him a nobility of sorts and elevates him, if only slightly, above the criminal elements among whom he plies his trade. In contrast, noir fiction centers on the frequently unwitting criminals themselves and explores the depths of their moral descent into a personal and social hell. There is little to redeem the typical noir character, who, unlike the detective hero, usually does not save anybody, even himself, in the course of the action of the plot and rarely exhibits any adherence to what might be considered a code, let alone conventional morality.

In brief, crime noir describes a type of crime story—not a mystery proper, which suggests a "whodunit"—that presents everyday people, not usually detectives or police officers or professionals of any sort, whose lives become extraordinary because they become caught up in a web of criminal activity, often as a result of personal compulsions or environmental forces beyond their control. Such characters are usually, but not always, working class or lower middle class and are not criminals by trade or initial intent. Noir characters typically fall into crime, especially for money, out of desperation, ignorance, or fear, particularly fear for their own well-being. They often do not appear to understand the final consequences of their criminal actions or seem only dimly aware of them.

Since these characters are frequently driven to crime by compulsions or obsessions over which they seem to have no or at most minimal control, their lives appear to be governed by some malevolent fate. Male noir protagonists habitually lust after a female temptress with "black widow," that is, destructively sexual, tendencies. Less often the reverse is true, although women also may be drawn to equally dangerous male figures. Noir characters live desperate lives that seem destined to fail, and, indeed, very few survive the consequences of their actions. In addition, they have few resources—financial, social, or psychological—with which to combat the world's aggression, manipulations, or indifference. Consolations are few, pleasures fleeting, opportunities scant. As a result, crime noir fiction presents a very bleak look at life from the bottom of the barrel. To borrow a title from one of the better-known plays of the

French existentialist writer Jean-Paul Sartre, it is a world with "no exit."

The settings for noir crime fiction are usually also rather prosaic; they are set in ordinary daily life and not the extraordinary world of conventional mystery, the details of the fiction avoid exotic locales, and the plots do not rely on overly dramatic events. Noir fiction tends to be socially oriented and more often than not contains a sharp critique of the culture in which it takes place. Most crime fiction is socially conscious and at least by indirection presents social criticism; noir fiction just does so more overtly.

A good deal of crime noir is written in the pulp fiction tradition—as were the original hard-boiled detective stories—with a fast-paced, direct style that often eludes even minimal literary overtones. Even though the requirements of popular fiction demanded a readily accessible prose style, it is remarkable how poetic some of the noir work is, how evocatively the writers could paint the prosaic lives of their characters and settings. Noir prose more closely resembles the clipped style of Dashiell Hammett than the pseudoliterary prose of Raymond Chandler, who frequently appeared to be slumming among the pulps. Many of the most famous noir novelists, Cain, Woolrich, David Goodis, and Thompson among them, also wrote for the movies, and the effects of film-scripting techniques are imprinted on noir stylistics as well. In the end, despite the scarcity of literary overtones, noir authors did evolve a real style, one that was both hard-hitting and evocative and suited the purposes of their fiction.

World War II added to the disjunctions of the Depression, and the reentry of veterans into civilian life became a theme of much noir fiction. GIs, who had been taught to kill, had to be redomesticated into a world in which there was less room for violent, direct action. Mickey Spillane's Mike Hammer novels fall outside the noir definition, but their sadism and violence reflect the frustrations faced by recently demobilized troops in an increasingly complex and alien civilian world. The success of Spillane's series helped reconfigure the use of realism in crime fiction.

As the crime noir tradition developed during the 1940s and 1950s, the plots became darker, the characters nastier, and the social situation more desperate. The fiction often featured physical grotesques, as in Jim Thompson's *Savage Night* (1953), or alcoholics, prostitutes, petty grifters, hit men, and assorted psychopaths. Noir fiction gave new meaning to the old saw that life is brutish and short.

The Cold War and the claims of a conformist society also contributed to the paranoia and violence of the noir fictional environment. In a world made uncertain by the presence of the atomic bomb, destabilized by changing ethnic and gender demands, and increasingly defined by conventional middle-class consumerist values, the possibilities for alienation expanded. While socially abnormal behavior may have seemed an understandable and perhaps a normal reaction to the dislocations of the Depression, in the postwar economic boom and amid the conformist political attitudes of anticommunism fostered by McCarthyism, such behavior was perceived as increasingly aberrant, if not un-American. For such politically active writers as Jim Thompson the repressions of the postwar world became ever more intolerable, and their fiction grew disaffected and shrill.

Furthermore, as the democratization of literature, especially fiction, was carried apace by the growth in paperback publication of an increasing number of works, there was a backlash on the part of the literary establishment that further marginalized writers of crime fiction and especially noir authors. The popular arts came under intense scrutiny during the 1950s and were blamed for everything from the decline of patriotism to the increase in juvenile delinquency. The pressures to censor comic books, television, movies, crime fiction, even rock and roll grew amid a proliferation of congressional investigative committees bent on discovering the sources of the moral decline in postwar America. Literary critics, religious leaders, and moralists of all stripes called for a crackdown on what they felt were unacceptable forms of popular expression, and noir authors, among others, withdrew increasingly into a dark world of repression and sublimation that was reflected in their novels, especially those of Thompson and Goodis, and the early work of Charles Willeford.

In the 1960s, American culture broadened to include an ever-wider acceptance of ethnic and gender diversity and of political protest. Out from under the constraints of political and social repression characterized by McCarthyism, the arts also expanded. In 1961 Barney Rosset, the publisher of the Grove Press, challenged the obscenity laws in the United States by issuing an American edition of Henry Miller's *Tropic of Cancer*, which was first published in 1934 in Paris by the Olympia Press, and which had been banned for sale in the United States by customs officials on the grounds of its "obscenity." Although there was no federal prosecution, some individual booksellers were challenged in local courts (apparently on the advice of the Justice Department) for selling the book. With the assistance of the Grove Press these local cases were gradually settled. Along with previous challenges on behalf of D. H. Lawrence's *Lady Chatterly's Lover* and John Cleland's *Fanny Hill*, the *Topic of Cancer* court cases opened literature to more explicit material. The American movie industry copied international film cultures and began to deal with more adult subject matter, including more graphic depiction of sexuality and violence. Popular music revolted from the blandness of the 1950s and became more political and socially aggressive. The economics of the book trade helped paperbacks achieve respectability as more and more of the classics were reprinted in soft cover and began appearing in college classrooms. In addition, university courses in the study of popular culture began to erode traditional notions of high and low values, and crime fiction slowly gained respectability as a subject for academic study.

Although the heyday of crime noir passed with the 1950s, remnants of the form persist today in the fiction of such diverse writers as James Ellroy, Andrew Vachss, Elmore Leonard, Carl Hiaasen, Shane Stevens, and others who continue to write single crime books that focus on the criminal mind and the underside of American life. Even though these new writers are energized by their social commitment, they write from a different perspective, and the voice of Lou Ford's people, if not their pleas, has undergone a significant change. Much of the territory of crime noir has been usurped by traditional crime writers who have folded crime noir's issues into other, more contemporary genres, like the hardboiled detective novel, the thriller, and the serial-killer novel.

The 1930s and James M. Cain

The birth of crime noir fiction can be traced to the 1930s and grew out of the Great Depression, the consequences of which undermined Americans' confidence in their social, economic, and cultural institutions. The collapse of the American Dream for so many people turned writers toward the plight of those least protected from the dislocations, particularly economic, that the Depression produced, and mainstream American literature rediscovered the downtrodden. Authors like Mike Gold and Richard Wright explored their ethnic backgrounds and wrote about American cultures previously largely ignored. Clifford Odets wrote about labor unions, as did John Steinbeck, who launched his career writing about the down-and-out, most successfully the rural poor from Oklahoma. Erskine Caldwell fashioned his two most famous novels, *Tobacco Road* (1932) and *God's Little Acre* (1933), out of his experience with southern rural poverty. Even Ernest Hemingway tried his hand at fictional social commentary in *To Have and Have Not* (1937).

Crime fiction writers, who had always been attracted to the lower depths of American life, also became more socially aware and produced a growing number of works that sought to capture the effects of the Depression on everyday life. S. S. Van Dine and his ilk continued to be popular, and interest in their upper-class detectives remained strong, at least during the early years of the decade. The hard-boiled detective novel flourished as well. But the real energy in crime fiction was being generated by a group of writers who fashioned a new type of crime story, crime noir, which chose as its focus the mind and psyche of the criminal and the restricted lives that such figures led.

In many ways James M. Cain's work serves to define crime noir writing and represents the form at its most typical. Cain grew up in a cultured American family: his father was an academic administrator and later president of Washington College, and his mother was a classically trained coloratura. After Cain graduated from college in 1910, he studied to become an opera singer, but he soon gave up his singing aspirations and decided to become a writer instead. He returned to Washington College to teach math and English while learning the craft of writing. He also earned a master's degree in drama at the same time. Academic life did not suit Cain, and he worked briefly as a newspaper reporter before joining the army. He served overseas during World War I, where he edited the divisional newspaper, the *Lorraine Cross.*

After the war Cain sold articles to H. L. Mencken's *American Mercury,* and he began work on the editorial staff at the New York *World* under the tutelage of Walter Lippmann. He also continued to write, mostly drama, and brought out a collection of his plays in 1930. After serving as the managing editor of the *New Yorker* for nine months, he moved to Hollywood to work for Paramount Pictures. On and off over the years, Cain wrote scripts for a number of the Hollywood studios: Metro-Goldwyn-Mayer (MGM), Warner Brothers, Twentieth Century-Fox, and Universal. There is a certain irony that Cain never was successful in adapting his own fiction for the screen in spite of the fact that he was an experienced dramatist and skillful adapter of other writers' fiction. The publication of

The Postman Always Rings Twice (1934), his first crime novel, was a commercial and critical success and established him as a fiction writer. Cain turned out crime-based stories throughout his life, eventually publishing a dozen novels for which he is remembered today.

Although he shared a middle-class background with Dashiell Hammett and Raymond Chandler, Cain's style of writing took him in a different direction from that of the two hard-boiled authors. In fact, Cain publicly dissociated himself from the "tough guy" school of writers, which included not only Hammett and Chandler but also Hemingway and John O'Hara, claiming that his novels were striving for something else. Despite his protests, however, literary history has placed Cain with the tough guys. David Madden, in his *James M. Cain,* called him "the twenty-minute egg" of the hard-boiled school.

Cain's academic background in drama unquestionably influenced his fiction, and many of his best stories feature elements associated with classical drama, especially the role of hubris, or overweening pride, in the hero's rise and eventual downfall. Despite his interest in tragedy, however, Cain avoided classical drama's upper-class bias, and the best of his novels feature lower-class characters who struggle to live out lives warped by the American dream of success. The typical Cain protagonist always falls just short of achieving the promise that appears is his due. It is in the lives of Cain's characters that noir fiction came into its own and established its place among the varieties of American crime writing.

The Postman Always Rings Twice is a prototypical noir novel and an example of what is most typical of Cain's own writing. The story is a quintessential Depression tale, told in the first person by a drifter, Frank Chambers. His fate is sealed in the novel's opening pages when he stops by chance at a wayside gas station-cum-restaurant run by a Greek immigrant, Nick Papadakis, and his midwestern-born wife, Cora. Frank, who has a nose for human unhappiness, senses at once that Cora is dissatisfied in her marriage and wants out. She quickly confirms his suspicions.

Frank's overwhelming sexual attraction to Cora provides his initial motivation to help her escape from the loveless entanglement. The pot is sweetened by Nick's business, the gas station and restaurant, which has the potential to be fairly profitable and to satisfy Frank's dream of financial security, which so far has eluded him. Like insurance agent Walter Huff in Cain's later novel *Double Indemnity* (1936), Frank is persuaded by his greed and sexual attraction to help a femme fatale (Cora) murder her unwanted spouse. Although the murder is carefully planned and executed, the protagonists become entrapped in the legal fallout from Nick's death and quarrel over the insurance money. Eventually, Frank kills Cora as well. He is caught by the police, tried and found guilty, and sentenced to die. The novel concludes as he awaits his imminent execution.

All of the elements of a noir crime story are contained in *The Postman Always Rings Twice*. The central male character falls into a situation by accident and against his better judgment commits the crime compelled by his unchecked sexual passion. The narrative is then driven to its tragic conclusion by the mutual suspicion between Cora and Frank created by equal amounts of guilt and fear. Although Frank possesses a sharp native intelligence, he overreaches himself, and the events of his life simply get out of control. Eventually, he must pay the penalty for his libidinal excesses. By centering the novel on working-class characters (especially Cora) who are driven by their obsession with money and security—both of which elude them in the end—Cain has written a tragic Depression-era story, one in which the "little guys" become pawns in a larger game whose rules have been set by corporate America. As in *Double Indemnity*, the couple relies on the windfall of an insurance payoff, and they run afoul of the insurance company's investigation that eventually unravels their well-laid plans.

The lack of the traditional mystery elements of either the classic British or the American hard-boiled detective genres pulls this story out of the context of the action of a detective or the accumulation of clues. There is no gunplay or exotic poison here, just the daily routine of frying hamburgers and pumping gas, buying neon signs and feeding busloads of tourists. Even the murder of Nick is rigged to look like an automobile accident, one of the most prosaic kinds of American death. The extraordinary is banished in favor of the ordinary, and the novel plays out its action amid these petit bourgeois circumstances.

The lack of suspense about who killed Nick also shifts the emphasis from the traditional concerns of the mystery story onto the motivation of Frank and Cora and the emotional drives that promote the crime. The story also relies on a fictional world that emphasizes the sordid without any knightly figure to relieve it. The ending of the novel, too, reminds us that such noir stories seldom have an uplifting denouement. Frank is going to be executed according to the laws of California, and unlike the classic mystery tale, in which at the end everything is restored to an emotionally satisfying equilibrium, the world of *Postman* will continue on its rather indifferent way without him.

The Postman Always Rings Twice is not, then, a conventional mystery. The emphasis is on the criminal's financial and sexual motivations, however banal, and on the social forces that shape them and finally determine the fate of the characters. It is as if, given these circumstances, this historical moment, Cora and Frank have little to do with their actions aside from playing out the hand dealt them by fate. Also lacking is any carefully delineated moral code outside the conventional legal one established by the state of California. There is no voice of Sam Spade to enunciate an ideal that can transcend the everyday and elevate the moral lesson of the narrative beyond the mere criminality of the characters' actions. All that remains at the end of the novel is Frank's panicked voice as he asks the prison priest to pray for him, and his hope that he will be reunited with Cora in an afterlife, wherever that may be.

In another of his early noir novels, *Mildred Pierce* (1941), Cain moves away from the original first-person, tough-guy style, which focuses on a male protagonist who in some measure is destroyed by a classic femme fatale. *Mildred Pierce* is written in the third person with a woman as its focus; it covers a wider time period and social frame; it deals as much with the protagonist's history as her present; it is a more leisurely paced book; and there is no crime. More like a Woolrich novel, *Mildred Pierce* is about obsession and the slow decay of personality brought about when it is unchecked.

Mildred Pierce, like *The Postman Always Rings Twice* and *Double Indemnity*, later became a highly successful film. The adaptation of these three Cain novels during the 1940s— *Double Indemnity* in 1943, *Mildred Pierce* in 1945, and *Postman* in 1946—virtually outlined the subgenre of film noir that reached the height of its popularity during the late 1940s and early 1950s. In fact, Michael Curtiz's film *Mildred Pierce* is now so much better known than Cain's book that it is easy to confuse the two, but it is important that they not be conflated because the book differs in many significant ways from the film. The major departures concern a shift from third- to first-person narrative, the use of the flashback, a move up in social scale—Joan Crawford's rendition of Mildred is much classier than Cain's—and the presence of a murder that opens and closes the movie narrative. Furthermore, Cain's Mildred ends up fat and alcoholic and does not walk into the sunrise with her husband as Joan Crawford does at the end of the film. These changes made for a good film but were bitterly opposed by Cain himself, who brought out all of his anti-Hollywood feelings in a series of pointed letters he wrote to the film's producer, Jerry Wald.

Cain's novels of the 1930s and *Mildred Pierce* provided the basic elements of the crime noir story. The shift of the elements of the novel away from the traditions of the classic and the hard-boiled detective stories established a new subgenre, one that was carried on by other writers for the next two decades. Chandler's remark about giving crime back to those who actually commit it applies less to the hard-boiled detective fiction as he was writing it and more to the less consciously dramatic yet increasingly "realistic" crime noir fiction of Cain.

The Great Depression proved to be a fertile period for crime fiction in general and noir fiction in particular. Authors who had been writing in other genres became interested in tough-guy fiction and the effects of the environment on people's lives. Erskine Caldwell, for instance, wrote two such novels before he turned to the Georgia back country. Unlike the writings of many other authors who worked in the noir tradition, Caldwell's first stories were published in the pages of such avant-garde small magazines as the *New American Caravan*, *Pagany*, *Hound and Horn*, and *Transition*. His first two novels— actually novelettes—were also published by small presses and at his own expense. *The Bastard* (1929) and *Poor Fool* (1930) were big city novels in the tradition of literary naturalism, and like the drifter from *The Bastard*, who is subjected to random violence of the urban jungle, the characters of these books were at the mercy of uncontrollable environmental and hereditary forces. In his early novels Caldwell's protagonists were more in the style of Dashiell Hammett than William Faulkner.

Two other minor masterpieces from the 1930s in the noir tradition also deserve mention: Horace McCoy's *They Shoot Horses, Don't They?* (1935) and Edward Anderson's *Thieves like Us* (1937). McCoy's novel is firmly planted in the milieu of the Depression and concerns an erstwhile actress and a fledgling movie director who team up in the hope of winning a few bucks in a local dance marathon. The novel traces their gradual disintegration as they are worn down both physically by the dance and emotionally by their growing sense of futility. McCoy's seedy setting on the edge of Hollywood's glamour world undercuts the myth of instant stardom and fame held out by the fantasy of the film world. It is a hard, cruel novel, one that ends as the director awaits his execution for the mercy killing of his partner, Gloria.

Anderson's *Thieves like Us* is also a quintessential novel of the 1930s, featuring a Bonnie and Clyde–like pair caught up in a murder and robbery spree that sends them fleeing across the country in an unsuccessful attempt to elude the law. The main characters, Keechie and Bowie, are an attractive young couple in love, but as a consequence of his criminal past and the psychotic behavior of the other members of the gang, the hardened criminals Chicamaw and T-Dub, Bowie cannot free himself to live peacefully with Keechie, and the couple is destroyed by the unyielding workings of the law. Throughout the novel, Anderson subjects his readers to the realities of the poverty and social convulsions of the Depression. *Thieves like Us* is a work of unrelieved naturalism, one in which the characters can find only momentary respite from the overwhelming forces of their environment and history.

Cornell Woolrich and the 1940s

By the early 1940s the world was once again at war. Crime writers responded to the war and its aftermath in various ways. Mickey Spillane, for example, used the problems of the returning GIs to reshape his fiction. Crime noir writers, such as Woolrich, W. R. Burnett, Fredric Brown, William Lindsay Gresham, and Cain opted to ignore the times and plunged their novels and characters underground into psychotic worlds of time and space, dreamscapes hazy with fear and shrouded in uncertainty.

Between 1940 and 1948, Cornell Woolrich, writing under his own name and under the pseudonym William Irish, published six novels now referred to as the Black series—all of the books had the word "black" in the title, as in *The Bride Wore Black* (1940), *The Black Curtain* (1941), *Black Alibi* (1942), and *The Black Angel* (1943)—in which he explored a fatalistic world of betrayal and fear. He also plumbed the dark and deviant personalities of his characters, which were hidden under a thin veneer of respectability and needed only the right circumstance to erupt into violence and death. If Cain's world was marked by indifference and his characters motivated by commonplace greed and lust, Woolrich's world is more ambiguous, and the ruling passions of his major figures seem to be anxiety and fear. As Cain had done in his fiction, Woolrich focused on ordinary people, although not necessarily from the working class, who became caught up in circumstances beyond their control. In their helplessness, his characters often retreated into a kind of internal hell that at times became so intense that they lost their sense of self. It was through such disintegrating personalities that Woolrich established his milieu and portrayed an unstable and dangerous world.

One of his most memorable and most successfully realized novels was *Phantom Lady* (1942). The story is structured around a simple time scheme: a countdown to the execution of the central character, who has been convicted of killing his wife. Each chapter starts with a heading that counts the number of days remaining before his death, and the declining number of days provides the novel with its basic suspense. As the days tick by, there is an intense investigation, by the police, a private investigator, and the main character's girlfriend, to find the elusive "phantom lady" who can provide the alibi that will clear him of the murder of his wife. Although the investigation is reminiscent of the traditions of other crime fiction, Woolrich keeps the tension centered on the increasing panic of his main character.

In Woolrich's fiction, random events, often a death, play a central part, and these unexpected blunders of fate change forever the lives of his characters. For example, in *The Bride Wore Black*, a freak accident results in the death of the groom at a wedding, and his widow becomes obsessed with finding his killers. In *I Married a Dead Man* (1948), a pregnant, unmarried woman takes on the identity of a new bride she has met on a journey after both the woman and her husband die in a train wreck. The pregnant woman is able to pull off this charade because the husband's family has never met their son's wife. The story revolves around the character's ability to assume another's identity after only a few hours' social conversation on the train. This is an unstable fictional world, where the personalities of the characters are subject to radical dislocation and the environment offers little help to them in fashioning a new one.

There is also something about the uncertainty of life, a fatalism Woolrich recognized even as a youth, that permeates the writing. For no matter how the story turns out, there is little to redeem either the characters or the society in which they live. Is the human personality so fragile, so easily unsettled, that to assume any sort of individual stability in it is an illusion? What about the fickle world in which we live? Is it also so shifting that life is finally like walking on quicksand? Woolrich never conclusively answers these questions, and his readers are left with the queasy feeling that reality is so elusive that the human personality will always be off balance and fragmentary.

A noir writer from the 1930s who also was popular in the 1940s, both in fiction and film, was W. R. Burnett. The novel that launched his career was the gangster classic *Little Caesar* (1929), which as a movie also launched Edward G. Robinson's film career. Although Burnett's novels of the 1930s dealt with predictable criminal subjects, it was *High Sierra* (1940) that became his noir classic. The story focuses on the criminal loner Roy Earle and traces his tragic life from his release from prison until his death in an automobile crash in a clash with the police. In typical noir fashion Earle is basically a good person whose life has taken a dreadfully wrong turn. Humphrey Bogart played Roy in a finely nuanced performance in one film version.

In a later novel, *The Asphalt Jungle* (1949), Burnett again used the narrative device of the manhunt around which to construct his story. Dix, the central character, spends the novel vainly attempting to escape from his life of crime to return to his boyhood home in rural Kentucky. The circumstances and futile life of Dix mark *The Asphalt Jungle* as a noir novel in the truest sense of the genre. In the movie version, Sterling Hayden, who plays Dix, poignantly dies just as he reaches the farm. *The Asphalt Jungle* was the first novel of a trilogy, along with *Little Men, Big World* (1951) and *Vanity Row* (1952), in which the writer explored the corruption of big-city politics.

Another writer in the noir tradition of the 1940s deserves mention — Fredric Brown. After a career spent writing for such pulps as *Street and Smith's Detective Story Magazine*, *Dime Mystery*, and *Weird Tales*, Brown produced a series of novels during the 1940s and 1950s. His most famous were *The Fabulous Clipjoint* (1947), which won the Edgar in 1948, and *The Screaming Mimi* (1949), Brown's only novel to be made into a movie. The protagonist of *The Screaming Mimi* is an unsavory Chicago newspaper man with a drinking problem. The plot features a reworking of the Jack the Ripper story, in which a serial killer brutally kills young women of doubtful reputation and the reporter swears off booze in order to find the killer. Like other noir fiction, Brown's novel takes his reader through the big-city underworld and is peopled with lowlifes struggling against heavy odds in a hostile environment. *The Screaming Mimi*, like so many other noir stories, avoids a happy conclusion, and after its twist ending, we find the reporter back on the street and on the bottle.

Finally, there is William Lindsay Gresham's strange tale *Nightmare Alley* (1946), which in some ways is both the most individual and the most extended example of noir fiction of the 1940s. From the epigraph taken from T. S. Eliot's "Waste Land" (1922) about Madame Sosostris, "the famous clairvoyant," to the tarot cards that adorn each chapter heading, the novel oozes an atmosphere of the weird and unworldly. Its setting in the world of a carnival also contributes to its place on the fringe of normal society. The central figure is a charismatic hustler, whose rise and fall the book traces in excruciating detail as he makes his way from headliner to ultimate denigration as a sideshow geek. It is a story of greed, chicanery, violence, and, finally, self-destruction—in other words, the perfect vehicle for the noir sensibility.

After World War II, Woolrich's fiction, along with Burnett's and Brown's and Gresham's, became popular sources for the noir movies that promoted such unease in postwar movie audiences about the state of American life. The films made from his novels and stories both at the time and subsequently have remained of interest to film scholars and film viewers alike. This may suggest that the nervous preoccupations of Cornell Woolrich and other 1940s noir authors have remained to haunt us even in the last decades of the century.

Film Noir

The connection between crime fiction and the movies has long been widely recognized, but only recently has it been carefully examined. Crime films appear early in the history of the American cinema. D. W. Griffith's *Musketeers of Pig Alley* (1912) was not the earliest, but it certainly is one of the most important early silent movies to treat the subject of urban crime. In the 1930s, Warner Brothers produced a memorable series of gangster films that launched the careers of Humphrey Bogart, James Cagney, and Edward G. Robinson. But it was not until the 1940s that films based on crime noir subjects established a subgenre of their own, and interestingly enough it was the French who first discovered these films and called them film noir.

A group of young French film critics writing for cinema journals during the late 1940s spotted what they perceived as a newly emerging film style from the glut of low-budget, Hollywood B films that swamped the European market just after the war. The young critics called these atmospheric movies about the underside of American life "film noir" after the crime fiction books published by Gallimard, which were called *séries noires*. Motivated both by political conviction—many of the writers were left-leaning—and by their fascination with style, these cineasts were mesmerized by the darkness of the look of the films and by the gloominess of their subject matter. The name stuck, and since then dozens of books and scores of articles have examined the noir film as a discernible style containing the reflection of American postwar disillusionment.

Although the time frame is flexible, noir movies date roughly from 1941 and John Huston's atmospheric remake of Hammett's classic tale *The Maltese Falcon* (1930) to 1958 and Orson Welles's *Touch of Evil* based on a Whit Masterson pulp novel, *Badge of Evil*, published in 1956. The definitions of film noir are varied, but most of them include the stylized use of lighting, especially in black-and-white films, and the reliance on the themes of violence, greed, and sex. Noir films were made fast with low budgets and largely avoided casting Hollywood stars, relying instead on the second-rank players under contract to the studios at the time. The femme fatale, or "spider woman," who preyed on the male protagonist was also a staple of the noir movie. During this period the work of all the major noir novelists was adapted for film, and many of those movies have become American classics or at least have a cult following.

A case in point is Cornell Woolrich, whose novels and stories were widely adapted by Hollywood throughout the 1940s and 1950s, which produced films that were thematically dark, intensely personal, and tightly structured. Some of those films are Robert Siodmak's *Phantom Lady* (1944), Harold Clurman's *Deadline at Dawn* (1946), John Farrow's *Night Has a Thousand Eyes* (1948), and Mitchell Leisen's *No Man of Her Own* (1950), which was made from *I Married a Dead Man*. One of his short stories became the basis for Alfred Hitchcock's classic suspense thriller *Rear Window*, filmed in 1954. In addition, like that of other noir authors, Woolrich's fiction has proved quite popular with European directors, especially the French, and François Truffaut adapted his first crime novel, *The Bride Wore Black*, into a Hitchcock-inspired noir film, *La Mariée était en noir* (*The Bride Wore Black*) in 1968.

Other noir classics proved attractive to European directors as well. The 1942 Italian film *Ossessione* (*The Obsession*), directed by Luchino Visconti, was based on Cain's novel *The Postman Always Rings Twice* and became the first neorealist film, a film style that had widespread influence over cinema worldwide. Noir fiction and movies influenced other European films and filmmakers as well. Such movies as Henri-Georges Clouzot's *Diabolique* (1955); Jean-Luc Godard's first new-wave film, *A Bout de souffle* (1959, *Breathless*), with its Bogart-like character played by Jean-Paul Belmondo; and Truffaut's 1983 rendition of Charles Williams' *The Long Saturday Night* (1962), *Vivement Dimanche* (*Confidentially Yours*), employ an atmosphere of noir pessimism, obsession, and self-destruction.

Although traditional film noir remains firmly associated with the postwar period, one in which Western societies were experiencing large-scale social and economic realignments, the film style has proved to be surprisingly resilient and survives today on cinema screens around the world. That film noir owes its origins to the traditions of noir fiction is uncontested, but the reasons for its current popularity remain unclear.

Jim Thompson and the 1950s

Like the Depression era and the immediate postwar years, the 1950s had their defining characteristics as the United States desperately tried to return to a semblance of normality. Even though the period was a time of unprecedented prosperity and opportunity for the white middle classes, it was also a time of

strain. The war conditions had promoted an equality of sorts between genders and among ethnic groups. Women and minority workers were employed in large numbers to fill the ranks of those in the services. When the war was over and the soldiers returned to civilian life, Americans tried to return to the old social patterns. There was, however, no going back, and the 1950s became a time of growing unrest as both minorities and women demanded a larger role in American life.

Accompanying these social pressures came the rise of anticommunism with its ongoing efforts to impose conformity of thought and political affiliation in the name of national defense. The House Un-American Activities Committee examined "Communist" infiltration of the motion picture business; senate hearings organized by Joseph McCarthy went after subversives in the State Department; eventually, there was even a governmental committee that investigated comic books, which were said to corrupt the traditional values of American youth and promote juvenile delinquency, teenage sex, and an increase in urban violence. The decade became obsessed with security, both national and personal, and anything or anyone that appeared different or threatening was attacked for being "subversive." Paradoxically, winning World War II abroad seemed to increase tensions at home, and during the 1950s the whole country became paranoid.

The crime writer who most prominently captured the feel of the immediate postwar years was probably Mickey Spillane, whose comic-book hero Mike Hammer, war vet and private eye, exemplifies the fear and incipient violence that underlay the surface quietism of the period. A more sophisticated and interesting writer to look at, however, was the author of a series of crime noir paperback originals, Jim Thompson. In the pages of his uncompromising novels, Thompson explored the downside of American life by focusing on characters who had been deformed by the pressures of living on the margins of capitalist society: petty crooks, corrupt law officers, small-town dropouts, and unsuccessful cons. His fiction examined the lives of criminals and dissected how their quirky approach to life warped their view of society at large.

Thompson's life was by all accounts an unsettled one. When he was a child, his family moved often as they followed the quixotic career of his father, who apparently made and lost several fortunes in the oil business. An inability to achieve order or any kind of mental or emotional serenity in his life haunted the author and most certainly contributed to the alcoholism he constantly battled. Although Thompson briefly attended the University of Nebraska, he never graduated. He married early, and in order to support his wife and growing family—he eventually had three children—Thompson worked at a number of jobs: in the oil fields, as a vegetable picker, and for a collection agency. After the publication of his first story at age fifteen, however, Thompson was able to earn extra money writing, particularly with sketches about the down-and-out characters he worked among. During the 1930s he was appointed director of the Oklahoma Writers project, and in the 1940s his first two novels appeared. Disappointingly, both *Now and on Earth* (1942) and *Heed the Thunder* (1946) were financially unsuccessful. The novel *Nothing More than Murder*, published in 1949, became the first of an impressive series of crime books, mostly paperback originals, that Thompson wrote between 1952 and 1954.

Always broke and frequently drunk, Thompson worked for whatever market was open to his talents; he worked fast and often, and his efforts were largely forgotten as quickly as they appeared. In the mid-1950s he collaborated with Stanley Kubrick on two of the director's early films, *The Killing* (1956) and *Paths of Glory* (1957). Thompson wrote television scripts, short stories, and more crime novels throughout the rest of the decade and into the next. He kept writing until several strokes stopped him. Sadly, none of his books was in print at the time of his death in 1977. A decade later readers and critics rediscovered his work as more and more of his novels were reissued.

Thompson's fiction also had a strong attraction for the film industry. In 1972 Sam Peckinpah directed the first version of *The Getaway*, starring Steve McQueen and Ali MacGraw, and proved to be the perfect director to film Thompson's most action-packed book. Peckinpah's rough style also managed to capture something of the novel's sleaze as well as its exhilarating prose. Director Roger Donaldson remade the film in 1995 with Alec Baldwin and Kim Basinger, but it had lost something of the Thompson feel. In 1990 both Stephen Frears's *The Grifters* and James Foley's *After Dark, My Sweet* were released, and a host of Thompson-like knockoffs have continued to appear.

Thompson's fiction is characterized by a stubborn nihilism, and his preoccupation with the criminal mind, often portrayed in first-person narratives, did much to extend the crime noir tradition. Furthermore, Thompson's environment appears to be more actively malevolent, unlike Cain's or Woolrich's more or less neutral settings. This may be due in part to his Marxist politics and in part to unstable personal circumstances. In any event, the typical Thompson character exhibits more actively developed traits of paranoia, fear, and psychosis than was evident in the fiction of his predecessors. Through a succession of social outcasts, maimed and twisted by fate and circumstance, Thompson depicted a fictional world of unrelieved rage and self-destructiveness, full of sadomasochistic relationships, that erupts into outbursts of staggering violence. For example, in his 1953 novel *Savage Night*, Charlie ("Little") Bigger, a dwarfish hit man, is hacked to death by his ax-wielding girlfriend. Such savage extravagance gives Thompson's writing a hard edge missing from much other crime noir, and it signaled a shift in fictional tone that came to mark the noir writing after him.

In Thompson's stories even conventional characters with commonplace values and stereotyped views of the world harbor homicidal lusts that can, in the right circumstances, boil over into vicious reprisals. In his fiction, insanity is the norm. Thompson creates a particularly frightening view of life, one that remains unsoftened or unmitigated by love or understanding. By placing the criminal at the center of his work, Thompson filtered the perspective of the world in an especially nasty way and shifted the moral perspective of the fiction off center. There is no innocence in Jim Thompson's fiction, and clichéd platitudes about right and wrong, good and evil, become meaningless as guides for behavior. This is especially evident when the protagonist is a lawman gone bad, as with Lou Ford in *The Killer Inside Me*—one of Thompson's most remarkable novels.

Told in the first person, *The Killer Inside Me* traces the gradual mental disintegration of a small-town sheriff whose uncontrollable lust for murder haunts his life. As a child, he was sexually abused, and later he also sexually abuses others. His "sickness," as he describes it, has produced such an overwhelming disregard for human life that by the end of the novel Ford welcomes death as an escape from his compulsions. What is especially chilling about the book is its matter-of-fact style, through which Thompson exposes the horrors Ford commits and his distorted vision of life. Although he is driven by compulsions beyond his control, Lou Ford is fully conscious of them, and he uses his position as a small-town law officer to manipulate those weaker and more vulnerable then he in order to hide his misdeeds. The sheriff kills repeatedly, and though he is devastated by the deaths, he seems to relish them at the same time. Fully aware of the consequences of the murders, Ford's indifference in committing them is what makes his actions so frightening.

Perhaps Thompson's most action-driven narrative is *The Getaway* (1959). The novel follows newly paroled Doc McCoy and his dangerous but sexy wife, Carol, as they blast their way across the Southwest racing for the sanctuary of Mexico. Doc's easy charm masks his penchant for violence and death, and the novel's nervous, hard-driving prose mirrors the edgy relationship between the couple and their hostile reaction to the world. Before the novel is over, it is strewn with bodies, but nei-

ther Doc nor Carol gets caught by the authorities. Their escape puts a twist on such 1930s crime-spree novels as *Thieves like Us*, which Thompson's novel resembles at least in outline. No one ever really gets away in a Jim Thompson novel—although Carol and Doc elude the law, they still have each other to contend with. If hell is other people, as Sartre claimed, then Thompson's ending suggests that Doc and Carol will be living in hell, locked in a relationship of mutual distrust that neither can ever completely overcome. In the novel's suggestive last lines, the couple toast each other on their freedom. Carol drinks to him and their getaway, Doc to her and "another such victory." In this context, the novel's title becomes double-edged. They have escaped the law but not each other. This is Thompson's fiction in its most sardonic form.

Of course, Jim Thompson was not alone in writing novels that examined postwar paranoia and fear. The paperback original provided a starting point for the careers of many authors who later moved on to other venues in their writing, including Kenneth Millar, who gained fame with the highly successful Lew Archer series, which he wrote under his pseudonym Ross Macdonald; Donald Hamilton in his pre–Matt Helm years; and John D. MacDonald before the Travis McGee books. All these authors began their careers working in the paperback noir tradition.

While he was still writing under his real name, Kenneth Millar, a Canadian transplanted to southern California, wrote several stand-alone novels that explored the troubling underworld of crime. His first two books, *The Dark Tunnel* (1944) and *Trouble Follows Me* (1946), were spy novels, but in *Blue City* (1947) and *The Three Roads* (1948), Millar covered the same ground as other noir authors. For example, in *Blue City*, which reworked the terrain of Hammett's *Red Harvest* (1929), a young man returns to his hometown to avenge the death of his father, who was involved in underworld corruption that the son knew nothing about. In typical noir fashion, although the hero eventually exposes the town's corrupt and criminal society, he receives scant moral reward for his efforts.

Donald Hamilton first made his name as an author with two novels published in the 1950s—*Line of Fire* (1955) and *Assignment: Murder* (1956). Both books feature unconventional protagonists who possess considerable skill at killing. In *Line of Fire*, a suicidal character who has been emasculated in a hunting accident is hired to fake an assassination attempt in order to gain sympathy and votes for a political candidate. Needless to say, the job goes awry. In *Assignment: Murder*, an atomic weapons researcher is shot while out hunting and kills his attacker before passing out. When he awakens he must clear himself of a murder charge without any memory of the events. In both books, Hamilton explored a number of modern issues through the rather unconventional mind-set of his heroes.

Another writer who began in the originals was John D. MacDonald, a prolific author who worked in many genres, including the hard-boiled detective story and science fiction. In the late 1940s his early stories appeared in such pulp magazines as *Doc Savage* and *Dime Detective* and later in such "slicks" as *Liberty* and *Cosmopolitan*. His early novels, such as *The Damned* (1952), *Border Town Girl* (1956)—which has a distinctly Jim Thompson–sounding title—and *The Empty Trap* (1957), were clearly noirlike in setting and plot. Set on the U.S. border with Mexico, the books examine the tensions between American nationals who have a penchant for crime and the simple, innocent Mexicans whom they try to exploit.

If proof were needed of MacDonald's indebtedness to the noir tradition, he provided it in a review of Cain's novel *The Institute* (1976), which appeared in the *New York Times Book Review* (22 August 1976, pp. 18, 20). There he acknowledged his special debt to Cain and other earlier crime authors. MacDonald observed that these writers had cut unnecessary ornament from their fiction, moved the plots along with a "spare, ruthless vigor," and achieved "a dreadful, and artistic, inevitability." Cain and the others, he noted, changed the definitions of suspense for both

writers and readers and forced fiction to "get on with it" (p. 18). MacDonald obviously learned this lesson well, because although he went on to write the very successful Travis McGee series, the traces of his noir beginnings lingered even in his later, more accessible novels.

During the 1950s, crime fiction, like other forms of writing, became more expansive, and the elements of violence and sex, previously handled more tentatively, became more explicit. But it was Jim Thompson who substantially upped the ante of crime noir during that decade with a string of novels that lashed out at the platitudes and conventions of American life with a fierceness seldom experienced in literature. As a result, the latent qualities of crime noir fiction surfaced in a particularly brutal way and changed forever the frame of the genre, opening it to the flood of novels filled with serial killers, child molesters, and assorted other psychotics that have been with us ever since.

The 1960s and Beyond

Although Jim Thompson continued to write into the 1960s and his characters have appeared on the screen ever since, his fiction does seem to mark the end of traditional crime noir. In part this may be due to the fact that the Depression, World War II, and the paranoid 1950s produced the cataclysmic social dislocations that crime noir authors used in such a dramatic and focused way. Moreover, the conventions of the crime novel in general have changed, and all the genres now routinely include crime noir themes and characters. Hard-boiled detective writing has become more violent and sexual than it was in the days of Hammett and Chandler, and even the cozy mystery novel frequently exhibits traces of the macabre absent in the world of the gentlemen detectives Hercule Poirot and Lord Peter Wimsey.

Locales have also expanded, and it is just as likely that a mystery will occur in the small-town Midwest as in Los Angeles. Codes of conduct for crime characters have changed too. The contemporary private investigator, once a knight in armor—even if slightly tarnished—is as likely now to be far more flawed and venal than was Sam Spade or Philip Marlowe. As the endings of crime novels have become more problematic, the convention of a world put to rights by the solution of the crime and arrest of the criminal, so much a part of the traditional mystery and detective story, has weakened. Even the focus on the downtrodden and criminal, once largely marginalized in traditional crime writing, is no longer reserved for crime noir fiction.

Like film noir, the cinematic relative of crime noir, new versions of the old tradition still appear in contemporary popular culture, however, and such authors as Elmore Leonard, Carl Hiaasen, Andrew Vachss, James Ellroy, and Shane Stevens have adapted the tradition in their contemporary neo-noir crime stories. Although these contemporary writers for the most part live and work in quite a different literary environment, they still push deeply into the American psyche to explore the unpleasant depths of our lives. Their characters often are subject to the same emotional and environmental constraints that warped Lou Ford, Cora Papadakis, and Cornell Woolrich's denizens of the night as they search for new ways to explore darker aspects of the modern world.

Noir writing has changed since the days of Jim Thompson. For one, it has become more graphic in the depiction of sex, violence, and the environment; for another, it is funnier. Of the new developments in modern crime writing, perhaps the most distinctive is the extensive use of comedy—often twisted and morbid to be sure, but comedy nevertheless. Two of the best of the writers to use noir humor are Leonard and Hiaasen, whose novels are often macabre and whose characters are as grotesque and twisted as Little Bigger, Doc and Carol McCoy, or Lou Ford. Both Leonard and Hiaasen are masters at creating an absurd plot, frequently of rococo complexity, and eccentric crooks, who are as often mild-mannered and polite as wacky.

Vachss, Ellroy, and Stevens have driven noir fiction to the limits of graphic expression. There is no harder-hitting social critique than Vachss's disturbing examination of child abuse in the more rancid sections of modern New York City. Ellroy's writing is probably, at its most extreme, the hardest-driven prose in the crime novel, but, then, very few authors have ever experienced the trauma of having their mothers murdered when they were ten. It was an event that left him emotionally crippled for years. He became a teenage junkie and alcoholic living in abandoned houses before he turned his life around and began his career as a writer. And Stevens simply wrote three of the most intense and chilling psychological thrillers ever. A closer look at the novels by these modern writers may help establish more concrete examples of how traditional noir elements have been incorporated by the contemporary crime novel.

Elmore Leonard began his writing career with westerns before shifting his attention to modern-day Detroit, a sort of lawless frontier, where he wrote a series of novels about the underworld with uncanny detail and insight. The characters who inhabit such novels as *52 Pick-up* (1974), *Swag* (1976), *Unknown Man No. 89* (1977), *The Switch* (1978), and *City Primeval* (1980) are deftly drawn, and Leonard's dialogue proves him a master of the northern urban dialect. Although the settings are grim and the action often very violent, the novels themselves are quite funny, and many of his characters are more hapless than mean or cruel. His humor, however, does not obscure the social impact of the books. Leonard's Detroit is a very nasty place, and the characters living there are unpleasant figures.

In the 1980s Leonard moved his fictional locale to Florida, and most of his books since then have taken place in the Sunshine State, even though the events of his fiction are often far from sunny. Beginning with *Gold Coast* (1980), Leonard's characters have taken on more psychological depth, and since then he has given us a series of con men, petty grifters, and psychopaths who charm and bully their way through life, exploiting everyone and everything in their path. In the process, Leonard has turned his considerable talent for social satire toward the poolsides and palm trees of the sand-and-surf world of this demiparadise that has been so exploited and despoiled over the past fifty years. Like Hiaasen, Leonard has worked to expose the dreamworld of Florida for the haven of scoundrels and scalawags that it has become.

Carl Hiaasen's first southern Florida crime book, *Tourist Season* (1986), set the tone for those that have followed. Bent on relieving Florida of those he feels are responsible for its environmental devastation, an ecoterrorist decides that killing tourists—the title *Tourist Season* is a double entendre—is the best way to slow the real estate developments that are creating much of the ecological waste. He starts murdering those who are drawn by the state's natural wonders and enviable climate, and he does so in spectacular ways in order to attract the attention of the news media in the hope that the adverse publicity will keep visitors back in Wisconsin.

In all of Hiaasen's novels there is an ever-widening gap between the once paradiselike environment of his native state and the human exploitation of those natural wonders that is driven by human greed and stupidity. Hiaasen once incurred the wrath of every high-minded publicist in the state when, on a national television program, he was asked about his solution to this crisis and responded that there wasn't anything wrong with southern Florida that couldn't be put right by a force-five hurricane.

Stormy Weather (1995) may provide a more detailed version of his answer. In that novel he traces the social chaos that follows the devastation caused by a large storm. This time the migration of outsiders is primarily motivated not by the search for sun and warm weather, but rather by cash. The scramble for the easy money to be had by repairing the broken houses left in the hurricane's wake becomes a metaphor for the accelerated economic despoliation of the state over the past fifty years. It all seems so logical: unscrupulous builders construct expensive houses with cheap materials to provide the influx of new residents with inferior dwellings. The opportunity will come to do it all over again when the houses fall apart under the normal fluctuations of the environment.

Hiaasen's novels feature an all-star cast of weird, often bumbling characters. They provide proof of what happens to humans when they live in such a meretricious world. In *Skin Tight* (1989), for example, Hiaasen's target, among others, is the plastic surgery industry. His set of characters includes a shaky surgeon, an ambulance-chasing shyster, a hit man with severe skin problems, and an in-your-face television talk-show host whose program is named—what else—"In Your Face." These are the kinds of people who help create the devastation of the environment that, in turn, helps condition such people to become who they are. Like mutants from some toxic dump, the denizens of Hiaasen's books often seem to slither from a social ooze, trailing behind them the detritus created by their wanton self-destructiveness.

Like Leonard, Hiaasen's social critique may seem muted by his humor, but underneath it he is providing a sharply honed attack on those who would victimize both the tourists and the environment in the name of progress and market forces. In Carl Hiaasen's world, the rhetoric of hucksterism is exposed for the sham that it is, and the brochure-perfect picture of the Florida good life is peeled away to reveal its costs and consequences. Like the noir writers before him, he writes of exploitation and the lost American dream, of those disappointed or broken by the struggle against odds so overwhelming that the chances of their ever succeeding remain always elusive.

Andrew Vachss has been writing a series of books featuring Burke, a special kind of private eye, who spends as much time avenging the exploited children of his city as he does solving the cases he is hired to investigate. His world is a battle zone so dangerous that his extraordinary personal caution, which under normal conditions would be paranoid, seems only good sense. It is a world peopled by the worst collection of child molesters, creeps, psychopaths, and deviants ever to have hit the pages of crime fiction. There is "Mole," an electronics expert who lives in a junkyard guarded by dogs of incredible fierceness. Burke gets his phone messages at Mama's, a Chinese restaurant run by a female Fu Manchu, and he consorts with, among others, a cross-dressing hooker who is saving his money to get a sex-change operation in Denmark.

In *Blue Belle* (1988), the third in the series, Burke is after deviants who are operating a "ghost van," in which they pick up teenage prostitutes in order to kill them. He is hired by a consortium of pimps to ferret out the killers before they ruin the trade in underage sex. Written with graphic detail, Vachss's prose is peppered with observations on the evils of the modern city and its odd assortment of predators and prey. In no uncertain terms these asides condemn a modern society so preoccupied with money and power that it is unconcerned with the fate of its most vulnerable citizens. As in the work of other crime noir authors, the theme of vulnerability focuses attention on the failures of American life and on those excluded from its glittering rewards.

Although Vachss's world appears cartoonlike in its exaggeration of depravity, this is merely an extension of the realities that create our urban environment. Burke's anger at a system so incompetent and uncaring throws into high relief the large-scale inconsistencies of an end-of-the-century megalopolis. Even the stylization of his characters contributes to this bizarre portrait of a universe gone terribly wrong. Andrew Vachss's vision, and there is no other word for it, is terrifying and, in its terror, provides a social critique uniquely savage in modern crime writing.

James Ellroy began his career with a series of conventional cop novels, the "Hopkins in Jeopardy" books, before writing a quartet of police novels set in postwar Los Angeles, *Clandestine* (1982), *The Black Dahlia* (1987), *The Big Nowhere* (1988), and *L.A. Confidential* (1990). These novels reprise the atmosphere of both noir fiction and movies of the period. Perhaps most devastating, because most clearly personal, is *The Black Dahlia*, a story based on a notorious, unsolved, real-life case of the brutal murder of a young woman not unlike the one from Ellroy's own past. The mood of these novels is uniformly dark, and although the writing style, language, and characters have been modernized, they evoke the insistent brutality of Jim Thompson and the unnerving fear of Cornell Woolrich. Ellroy's Los Angeles is decidedly not Chandler's nor, for that matter, the southern California of Ross Macdonald's later work. These novels come from streets less sanitized than before.

What is particularly noteworthy in Ellroy's fiction is his insistent, driving prose. Characters are swept along, hurled headlong toward various forms of annihilation and death. Events unfold rapidly, often outpacing his heroes' ability to understand them. The plots are mazelike and frequently promote a dazed feeling in his readers as well as his characters. Like Jim Thompson, whose novels always appear to slide downward from their opening pages, Ellroy fashions a world as inexorably determined.

Since the early 1970s, Shane Stevens has written several intensely interior crime books in which he has exhumed the criminal consciousness. *Dead City* (1973) traces the brief and violent career of a couple of hapless muscle men who try desperately to gain a foothold within the world of organized crime. Set in the inverted world of a criminal organization, the novel twists the traditional Horatio Alger trajectory—the road to success is paved by hard work and pluck. No matter how diligently these witless characters try, they never seem to get it right, and they eventually pay for their failure when their lifeless bodies are unceremoniously dumped into an oil-slicked bay in New Jersey. *By Reason of Insanity* (1979) follows across the country the murderous career of the serial killer Thomas Bishop, who thinks he is the illegitimate child of Caryl Chessman and who is obsessed with avenging his father's execution. The novel presents a dual consciousness, both that of the lunatic murderer and that of his pursuer, who attempts to track him down and stop the killing. Equally chilling is Stevens' portrait of an ex-Nazi in *The Anvil Chorus* (1985), a novel that burrows into the mind of a mass exterminator on the run from the authorities.

In his work Stevens achieves a level of intensity reminiscent of the best of the noir writers, who tried to convey the savage lunacy of criminal psychosis. His characters appear ordinary enough, but they commit acts of horror that are especially terrifying because, to the perpetrators, they appear so unexceptional. Of the many writers who have tried to portray the banality of criminal behavior alongside its terrors, Shane Stevens has been among the most successful.

Conclusion

Although the characteristics of crime noir fiction appear in other forms of crime writing, in its purist form it still remains primarily restricted by the period from the 1930s to the 1960s. The specific combination of character, setting, theme, and style that originally designated crime noir belongs to history and in the books of James M. Cain, Cornell Woolrich, Jim Thompson, and the dozens of other authors who for profit or out of conviction wrote about the downside of American life. The presence of noir elements in contemporary crime and mystery fiction only attests to the continuing importance of the plots and characters and subjects that these writers first articulated.

In the 1980s, Black Lizard Books, a small publishing house in Berkeley, California, began reissuing some of the classic noir titles. They reprinted not only the works of Thompson, Cain, and Goodis but also that of many of the lesser-known writers in the tradition, such as Harry Whittington, Paul Cain, Helen Neilson, and Dan J. Marlowe. Black Lizard was eventually taken over by Random House, and many of their titles are now being published along with more traditional detective writers, among them, Hammett and Chandler. Still, Black Lizard helped resurrect many forgotten writers who had slipped into oblivion.

Contemporary films, too, have reintroduced the noir sensibility to American culture in what film critics have called "neo-noir." As has already been mentioned, many of the newer noir films have been reworkings of old movies, such as Bob Rafelson's *The Postman Always Rings Twice* (1981), with Jack Nicholson and Jessica Lange; Robert Altman's *Thieves Like Us* (1974), a remake of Nicholas Ray's *They Live by Night* (1949); and Tamra Davis' *Guncrazy* (1992), reminiscent of the Joseph H. Lewis 1949 cult film *Gun Crazy*. This darkening of American cinema, however, has also produced its own contemporary noir stories, most notably those of the enfant terrible Quentin Tarantino, whose *Pulp Fiction* (1995) set new standards (if that is the right word) for modern crime cinema. Since the phenomenal success of his films, dozens of Tarantino knockoffs have appeared on American movie screens.

In spite of the boom in neo-noir movies, fictional noir is a problematic literary form even today. Unlike their contemporaries in hardboiled detective fiction and in the variations on the classic mystery story, crime noir writers remain on the periphery of the genre. Perhaps the books are just too grim, too uncompromisingly tough-minded, and the characters too unredeemed to attract a sympathetic readership or to provide the average escapist fare mystery readers have come to expect. The social critique may also seem excessive for Americans brought up to believe that their system is somehow open to all and that the morality of hard work and fair play continues to define it. In spite of everything that mitigates against it as a fictional style, however, crime noir in its various guises continues, even if on a subterranean level, to haunt American literature.

Selected Bibliography

CRIME NOIR

WORK OF EDWARD ANDERSON

Thieves like Us. New York: Frederick A. Stokes, 1937.

CRIME NOIR

WORKS OF FREDRIC BROWN

The Fabulous Clipjoint. New York: Dutton, 1947.
The Screaming Mimi. New York: Dutton, 1949.

WORKS OF W. R. BURNETT

Little Caesar. New York: Dial Press, 1929.
High Sierra. New York: Knopf, 1940.
The Asphalt Jungle. New York: Knopf, 1949.
Little Men, Big World. New York: Knopf, 1951.
Vanity Row. New York: Knopf, 1952.

WORKS OF JAMES M. CAIN

The Postman Always Rings Twice. New York: Knopf, 1934.
Double Indemnity. In *Three of Kind.* New York: Knopf, 1943. Previously published in *Liberty Magazine* (1936).
Serenade. New York: Knopf, 1937.
Mildred Pierce. New York: Knopf, 1941.
The Institute. New York: Mason Charter, 1976.

WORKS OF ERSKINE CALDWELL

The Bastard. New York: Heron Press, 1929.
Poor Fool. New York: Rariora Press, 1930.
Tobacco Road. London: Secker & Warburg, 1932.
God's Little Acre. New York: Modern Library, 1933.

WORKS OF JAMES ELLROY

Clandestine. New York: Avon, 1982.
The Black Dahlia. New York: Mysterious Press, 1987.
The Big Nowhere. New York: Mysterious Press, 1988.
L.A. Confidential. New York: Mysterious Press, 1990.

WORK OF WILLIAM LINDSAY GRESHAM

Nightmare Alley. New York: Rinehart, 1946.

WORKS OF DONALD HAMILTON

Line of Fire. New York: Dell, 1955.
Assignment: Murder. New York: Dell, 1956. Also published as *Assassins Have Starry Eyes.* New York: Fawcett, 1966.

WORKS OF CARL HIAASEN

Tourist Season. New York: Putnam, 1986.
Double Whammy. New York: Putnam, 1989.
Skin Tight. New York: Putnam, 1989.
Stormy Weather. New York: Knopf, 1995.

WORKS OF ELMORE LEONARD

52 Pick-up. New York: Delacorte, 1974.
Swag. New York: Delacorte, 1976. Also published as *Ryan's Rules.* New York: Dell, 1976.
Unknown Man No. 89. New York: Delacorte, 1977.
The Switch. New York: Bantam, 1978.
City Primeval. New York: Arbor House, 1980.
Gold Coast. New York: Bantam, 1980.

WORKS OF JOHN D. MacDONALD

The Damned. New York: Fawcett, 1952.
Border Town Girl. New York: Popular Library, 1956.
The Empty Trap. New York: Popular Library, 1957.

WORK OF HORACE McCOY

They Shoot Horses, Don't They? New York: Simon & Schuster, 1935.

WORKS OF KENNETH MILLAR (Ross Macdonald)

The Dark Tunnel. New York: Dodd, Mead, 1944.
Trouble Follows Me. New York: Dodd, Mead, 1946.
Blue City. New York: Knopf, 1947.
The Three Roads. New York: Knopf, 1948.

WORKS OF SHANE STEVENS

Dead City. New York: Holt, Rinehart, and Winston, 1973.
By Reason of Insanity. New York: Simon & Schuster, 1979.
The Anvil Chorus. New York: Delacorte, 1985.

WORKS OF JIM THOMPSON

Now and on Earth. New York: Modern Age, 1942.
Heed the Thunder. New York: Greenberg, 1946.
Nothing More than Murder. New York: Harper, 1949.
The Killer Inside Me. New York: Lion, 1952.
Savage Night. New York: Lion, 1953.
A Hell of a Woman. New York: Lion, 1954.
After Dark, My Sweet. New York: Popular Library, 1955.
The Getaway. New York: New American Library, 1959.
The Grifters. Evanston, Ill.: Regency, 1963.

WORKS OF ANDREW VACHSS

Blue Belle. New York: Knopf, 1988.
Hard Candy. New York: Knopf, 1989.
Blossom. New York: Knopf, 1990.

WORKS OF CORNELL WOOLRICH

The Bride Wore Black. New York: Simon & Schuster, 1940. Also published as *Beware the Lady.* New York: Pyramid, 1953.
The Black Curtain. New York: Simon & Schuster, 1941.
Black Alibi. New York: Simon & Schuster, 1942.
Phantom Lady. By "William Irish." Philadelphia: Lippincott, 1942.
The Black Angel. New York: Doubleday, 1943.
Night Has a Thousand Eyes. By "George Hopley." New York: Farrar, 1945.
Deadline at Dawn. By "William Irish." Philadelphia: Lippincott, 1947.
I Married a Dead Man. By "William Irish." Philadelphia: Lippincott, 1948.
Rear Window and Four Short Novels. New York: Ballantine, 1984.

ANTHOLOGY

Crime Novels. 2 vols. New York: Library of America, 1998.

BIOGRAPHICAL AND CRITICAL STUDIES

Bassett, Mark T., ed. *Blues of a Lifetime: The Autobiography of Cornell Woolrich.* Bowling Green, Ohio: Bowling Green State University Popular Press, 1991.

Cawelti, John G. *Adventure, Mystery, and Romance: Formula Stories as Art and Popular Culture.* Chicago: University of Chicago Press, 1976.

Collins, Max Allan, and James L. Traylor. *One Lonely Knight: Mickey Spillane's Mike Hammer.* Bowling Green, Ohio: Bowling Green State University Popular Press, 1984.

Davis, Kenneth C. *Two-bit Culture: The Paperbacking of America.* Boston: Houghton Mifflin, 1984.

Docherty, Brian, ed. *American Crime Fiction: Studies in the Genre.* New York: Insights, 1988.

Fine, Richard. *James M. Cain and the American Authors' Authority.* Austin: University of Texas Press, 1992.

Gruber, Frank. *The Pulp Jungle.* Los Angeles: Sherbourne Press, 1967.

Hamilton, Cynthia S. *Western and Hard-boiled Detective Fiction in America: From High Noon to Midnight.* Basingstoke, Eng.: Macmillan, 1987.

Haut, Woody. *Pulp Culture: Hardboiled Fiction and the Cold War.* New York: Serpent's Tail, 1995.

Hoopes, Roy. *Cain.* New York: Holt, Rinehart, and Winston, 1982.

Klein, Marcus. *Easterns, Westerns, and Private Eyes: American Matters, 1870–1900.* Madison: University of Wisconsin Press, 1994.

Landrum, Larry N., et al. *Dimensions of Detective Fiction.* Bowling Green, Ohio: Bowling Green State University Popular Press, 1976.

Lehman, David. *The Perfect Murder: A Study in Detection.* New York: Free Press, 1989.

McCauley, Michael J. *Jim Thompson: Sleep with the Devil.* New York: Mysterious Press, 1991.

MacDonald, John D. "A Mystery and a Romance," *New York Times Book Review,* 22 August 1976: 18, 20.

Madden, David. *James M. Cain.* New York: Twayne, 1970.

———. *Cain's Craft.* Metuchen, N.J.: Scarecrow Press, 1985.

———, ed. *Tough Guy Writers of the Thirties.* Carbondale: Southern Illinois University Press, 1968.

Marling, William. *The American Roman Noir: Hammett, Cain, and Chandler.* Athens: University of Georgia Press, 1995.

Nevins, Francis M., Jr. *Cornell Woolrich: First You Dream, Then You Die.* New York: Mysterious Press, 1988.

Nolan, William F. *The Black Mask Boys: Masters in the Hard-boiled School of Detective Fiction.* New York: William Morrow, 1985.

Panek, LeRoy Lad. *Probable Cause: Crime Fiction in America.* Bowling Green, Ohio: Bowling Green State University Popular Press, 1990.

Polito, Robert. *Savage Art: A Biography of Jim Thompson.* New York: Knopf, 1995.

Roberts, Thomas J. *An Aesthetics of Junk Fiction.* Athens: University of Georgia Press, 1990.

Skenazy, Paul. *James M. Cain.* New York: Continuum, 1989.

Symons, Julian. *Bloody Murder. From the Detective Story to the Crime Novel: A History.* New York: Viking, 1985.

Winks, Robin W., ed. *Modus Operandi: An Excursion into Detective Fiction.* Boston: Godine, 1982.

———. *Detective Fiction: A Collection of Critical Essays.* Woodstock, Vt.: Countryman Press, 1988.

Woeller, Waltraud, and Bruce Cassiday. *The Literature of Crime and Detection: An Illustrated History from Antiquity to the Present.* New York: Ungar, 1988.

THE ETHNIC DETECTIVE
Arthur W. Upfield, Tony Hillerman, and Beyond

RAY B. BROWNE

ETHNIC CRIME FICTION—like literature in general—is by one definition all-inclusive. Regardless of differences in heritage, behavior, and culture, we are all (to paraphrase Franklin Delano Roosevelt's 1938 speech to the Daughters of the American Revolution) ethnics or descended from ethnics. Anyone, therefore, writing fiction about the friction in crime and punishment between one culture and another is an ethnic crime writer. A representative list of ethnic crime writers and their investigators might include Edgar Allan Poe (M. Dupin, French); Stuart M. Kaminsky (Inspector Porfiry Rostnikov, Russian); John P. Marquand (Mr. Moto, Japanese); Sara Paretsky (V. I. Warshawski, Polish American); Claire McNab (Carol Ashton, lesbian, Australian); George Baxt (Pharoah Love, gay, black American). The list could go on and on, including virtually every nationality and ethnic group in the United States and abroad.

In the 1980s and 1990s ethnic crime fiction blossomed for at least three distinct and specific reasons. First, authors of crime fiction always look for new fields in which to present different and exotic material; variety in setting, character, and plot are a much-desired spice. Bill Pronzini and Martin Greenberg, in their introduction to *The Ethnic Detectives*, call this a "handle." For ethnic crime writers this "handle" is especially useful because it provides their readers with an economical and comfortable form of geographical and cultural tourism, a traveling to exotic societies and strange people, with exposure to but safety from danger. The unusual venues and people with exotic beliefs and practices provide new and exciting adventures.

A second reason for the rapid growth of ethnic crime fiction is that several writers began writing about ethnic groups to correct misconceptions and ignorance. Some of these writers have ethnic backgrounds different from the groups they depict. Such fiction uses the gentle art of persuasion to change the sentiments of the general reader. The more we know about a people the less hostile or indifferent we become.

Finally, at its best, ethnic crime fiction can provide great cultural insight. It dramatizes conflicts between cultures, reveals the fears of the dominant society, provides humor, and, finally, covertly or overtly reestablishes the reader's feeling of safety from and superiority over other peoples or groups of people. It is good politics as well as justice to give every minority group a fair hearing. So ethnic crime writing becomes a kind of affirmative fiction, demonstrating remorse and atonement for former and present social injustices.

For our purposes, then, ethnic crime fiction is literature about crime, usually murder, involving people of at least two ethnic groups. Generally, though not always, the official or private investigator is of a dominant group and the people being investigated belong to a minority group within the dominant culture.

Such fiction is usually much less stylized and "literary" than hard-boiled detective fiction and uses frank direct language in a realistic way. Sex, for example, is more often named and approached directly, not indirectly by suggestion and metaphor; it is physical, not poetic. Ethnic crime fiction differs most dramatically from so-called Golden Age or "cozy" detection fiction in being more lifelike. It has none of the hothouse atmosphere of the older form.

Perhaps ethnic crime fiction most closely resembles that of feminist crime writers. Both have essentially the same goals, and in fact ethnic crime fiction may involve strong female characters. But feminist crime fiction centers on the woman character, who is generally in a familiar setting, while ethnic feminist crime fiction emphasizes the unfamiliar atmosphere and cultures. Dana Stabenow (b. 1952) perhaps illustrates this characteristic in describing the attitude and role of her heroine, Kate Shugak, a small, sturdy Aleut woman who is "a loner by preference, an echo of the independent and nomadic existence of her ancestors. In the future I see her being dragged kicking and screaming into a leadership role in her tribe" (letter to the author).

American Nisei—that is, Americans of Japanese descent—have been represented in ethnic crime fiction by E. V. Cunningham, pseudonym of the American author Howard Fast (b. 1914), who also wrote under his own name and under the pseudonym Walter Ericson. Cunningham's fiction takes the attitude that the world is evil because people have departed from humanity, but that its ultimate reclamation lies in a return to the common person. His ethnic crime novels concern Masao Masuto, detective sergeant of the Beverly Hills Police Force. Cunningham is keenly aware of other oppressed minorities in the Los Angeles area, especially Mexican women and children, whom he includes in his novels. As a member of one minority group, he speaks for all. His works are at best interesting but not top-quality.

Ethnic crime fiction is fast catching on and developing in Alaska. Among the several Alaskans turning out such fiction, none is more typical or effective than the above mentioned Dana Stabenow, who was raised in a half Aleut, half Filipino family in Sidonia, in south central Alaska. She has written six crime novels featuring Kate Shugak, an Aleut who is five feet tall and 110 pounds, is retired from the Anchorage D.A.'s office, and has a scar running from one side of her throat to the other from a cut she received in a fight with a man. Stabenow is strong on adventure, and her books carry the sharp imprint of life among the Native Americans of Alaska.

The Native American is forcefully represented in ethnic crime fiction by Jean Hager, who is one-quarter Cherokee and lives in Tulsa, Oklahoma. Hager's writing strength lies in her expert and sensitive chronicling of the conflict between the Cherokee community and the white majority surrounding it. She has written four novels featuring the half-Cherokee Chief Bushyhead, head policeman of the sleepy Oklahoma town of Buckskin, and four featuring Molly Bearpaw, chief and only employee of the northeast Oklahoma office of the Native American Advocacy League. *Spirit Caller* (1997), featuring Molly Bearpaw, demonstrates that Hager's position as recorder of Cherokee folklore and culture is secure.

Tony Hillerman

Among the most accomplished of ethnic crime writers is Anthony Grove Hillerman (b. 1925), who focuses on the Navajo of the American Southwest. His works are the high-water marks against which others are compared. His endorsement is sought by publishers on at least half a dozen manuscripts a week on all kinds of writings. Hillerman has himself turned to anthologizing various types of ethnic stories and western fiction in general. He is the dean of advocacy literature on Native rights today.

Tony Hillerman was raised among Pottawatomie and Seminole Indians and for eight years attended an Indian school for girls, where he learned his compassion for the downtrodden and unenfranchised. A veteran of World War II, he has worked as a reporter and editor for several newspapers, and as a professor and assistant to the president of the University of New Mexico.

To Hillerman ethnic crime novels are the ideal way to teach the cultures and life values of a people. An effective writer of such fiction must use genuine settings and personalities. He began by studying the ethnic crime stories of the Australian author Arthur W. Upfield, whose work consciously or unconsciously resonates throughout his writings, as Hillerman suggests in his introduction to Upfield's *A Royal Abduction*:

> I cannot honestly say that when I set about to write my own version of the mystery novel, Arthur Upfield was consciously in my mind. Subconsciously, he certainly was. Upfield had shown me—and a good many other mystery writers—how both ethnography and geography can be used in a plot and how they can enrich an old, old literary form. When my own Jim Chee of the Navajo Tribal Police unravels a mystery because he understands the ways of his people, when he reads the signs left in the sandy bottom of a reservation arroyo, he is walking in the tracks [Upfield's detective] Bony made fifty years ago.

Hillerman has been influenced by other masters in crime fiction. In *Talking Mysteries* he names Eric Ambler "because he never wrote the same book . . . twice"; Raymond Chandler, "a master of setting scenes which engage all the senses and linger in the mind"; Graham Greene; Ross Macdonald, who "taught every one of us that, given enough skill with metaphorical language, one plot is all you ever need for as many books as you want to write"; George V. Higgins; and Joan Didion with her "superb journalism" (pp. 27–28).

Hillerman learned his craft well and moved on to his own territory. He has tried to develop an authentic background with careful cultural analysis. As an experienced journalist he has an eye for details, as avid amateur anthropologist he searches for the essence of cultures, and as storyteller he knows how to weave details of experience. Against the harsh dry and yellow Navajo landscape, Hillerman depicts the intricacies, subtleties, and differences of various Native American cultures—Navajo, Hopi, Zuni, and others—as well as the Spanish and Southwest Anglo cultures, though he works most thoroughly in Navajo. He is proud of the fact that both Navajo and Zunis have "recognized themselves and their society" in his books, which have been "heavily used in school and on reservations and . . . throughout the Indian world by other tribes." Hillerman disclaims that his ethnological material is "intended to meet scholarly and scientific standards," but tries to make it realistic and authentic enough to be credible.

Native American experts agree that Hillerman sometimes misses the details of Indian culture. In his introduction to *Talking Mysteries*, Ernie Bulow, formerly employed at the Bureau of Indian Affairs, says that when he first heard Hillerman reading from *The Dark Wind* (1982) he recognized that the author knew nothing about how to pronounce Hopi words and did not realize that there are not and probably never will be Navajo policemen like Leaphorn and Chee. He also notes that Hillerman frequently gets details wrong, as in *The Ghostway* (1984), when he has Chee take a sweat bath by pouring water over hot rocks when he should have known that Navajo take their sweat baths dry. But Bulow acknowledges that, details aside, Hillerman is an excellent storyteller.

In picturing the ancient home of the Navajo, Hillerman emphasizes the age and harshness of the land, in contrast to mankind's pitiable newness and weakness. People of different generations and cultures adjust to nature in different psychological, physical, emotional, and religious ways. Although his Native American characters are caught in the struggle to reconcile old-fashioned and new ways of dealing with life, Hillerman is perhaps more concerned with the ways whites despise Native American cultures, particularly their spiritual connection to their homeland. In one of his many nonfictional statements on the subject, "Why Not Religious Freedom for All Americans?" Hillerman points out that the guarantee of religious freedom for all Americans, "a source of patriotic pride," extends to religions imported from Europe and Asia but does not cover Native American beliefs and practices, as it should. There are specific reasons for this deficiency. "Protection of tribal shrines presents a unique problem. Most are natural landmarks: mountains, lakes, springs, salt deposits, eagle nests high in mesa walls. They are never buildings," he says, and they usually involve beliefs and practices that seem alien and outlandish to the dominant culture. But these natural objects cry out for recognition. "There are ways to grant full First Amendment rights of religious freedom to all Americans," he insists (*Tony Hillerman Companion*, pp. 305–307). For example, he calls for an end to "the harassment of the Pueblo people and others who make ritual use of eagle feathers (and eagles) in some religious rites."

Hillerman's fiction moves with the rhythm of Indian attitudes and life. The reader must accommodate to Indian time. The sun rises and traverses the heavens at its own leisure. The Indians have adjusted. Even in a life-threatening emergency Jim Chee and Joe Leaphorn, Hillerman's detectives, question a Navajo patiently while the Native approaches his answers indirectly. That is the Indian way, which Chee and Leaphorn understand and respect, as they carefully police the 25,000 square miles of the Navajo reservation in Arizona, Utah, and New Mexico.

Hillerman writes of the soul of the Indians' civilization and culture. Because he is more concerned with the spirit of his characters than with their appearance, their physical descriptions grow incrementally, one part here, another there. It takes half a dozen books before readers know what the characters look like, whereas we have long since understood them psychologically. Less important and peripheral characters, who are not so complicated, are often described graphically.

Hillerman downplays dramatic prose. He is a steady and clear stylist who allows his fictional world to develop at its own pace and on its own terms. Therefore, frequently the reader must accept some aspects of the plot on trust. Eventually the ends will come together despite the fact that those ends are sometimes moved by people who seem to have insufficient motivation for their actions.

Joe Leaphorn was first introduced in *The Blessing Way* (1970), and is also featured in *Dance Hall of the Dead* (1973) and *Listening Woman* (1978). Hillerman develops his character gradually throughout the series. When we first meet him, Leaphorn has been married to Emma, a woman of the Bitter Water family, for some thirty years. Through the years he gets noticeably older, puts on weight, grays a little, and grows stiff in the back. For several reasons he is disinclined to trust Jim Chee, as well as FBI agents, and generally gets the reputation of being hard to get along with. Janet Pete calls him "Grouchy Joe" (*Talking God*, 1989). He suspects the motives of nearly everyone, including some Navajo. Life and experience have dried up the well of his compassion.

The Blessing Way, thick with Navajo superstition and folklore, has anthropologist Bergen McKee and Leaphorn searching for two aspects of the truth—Leaphorn for a murderer, McKee for an explanation of rumors of a wolf in the neighborhood. Action switches from Leaphorn to McKee so quickly that the reader must be alert to avoid getting lost. The book smells of the library. Many Native American readers agree with Ernie Bulow that many details are askew. In *Talking Mysteries*, Bulow says the "ethnography of the book was shaky," and that Hillerman had "never slept in a hogan with fifteen other people or stood in the cold until dawn three nights running to follow an Enemy Way, smelling piñon smoke and feeling the throb of the drum" (pp. 13–14). Even Hillerman, in later years, acknowledged that the book has its shortcomings. Hillerman has some difficulty in leaving the campus of the University of New Mexico, with which he has been associated since 1965. He frequently includes professors and other campus folk as major characters, but they generally are not his strongest characters. He admires academics but they often fall short of more "natural people."

In *Dance Hall of the Dead*, Hillerman is unusually passionate in his study of Navajo lore. He still has the university in mind. An anthropologist whose theory about the disappearance of an Indian tribe is being threatened by later research is out with a disciple searching for proof of his long-held belief. When he is unsuccessful, he plants false evidence in the digs. Some Navajo and Zuni kids discover the deception, and the anthropologist kills them to protect his secret.

Listening Woman is more of an action novel than its predecessors. But it is also concerned with religion and morality. Margaret Cigaret, a blind medicine woman, visits Hosteen Tso to treat his illness. Instead of getting well, Tso is murdered. Though it looks like the work of a Navajo, authorities believe it was done by an outsider. The murder was in fact committed by a man everyone calls Goldrims because of his glasses. So there is no religious involvement. But throughout the novel, Leaphorn demonstrates that he cannot completely shake off Navajo beliefs in witchcraft.

After three books featuring Leaphorn, Hillerman introduced his second detective in *People of Darkness* (1980). Jimmy (Jim) Chee, probably the more appealing of the two detectives, is also featured in three novels. Through the series we learn that he began his police work when he was about twenty-five years old. He had passed all the tests and been accepted at the FBI Academy in Virginia but was hesitant to attend because he really wanted to become a Navajo singer like Hosteen Frank Sam Nakai, his mother's brother. From the beginning Chee recognizes that he is a Navajo country boy who knows little of the world, about which he is curious but apprehensive.

He does not want to pay too high a price for sophistication. He develops some affection for Mary Landon, who is introduced in *People of Darkness* as a young teacher of fifth-grade English and social studies at Crownpoint Elementary School. She understands kids and men. Mary, a graduate of the University of Wisconsin, moves back to Milwaukee and has Jim visit her there, but apparently decides that although she loves him he does not conform to her stereotypical picture of Indians, and she gradually cools the relationship. Because of his naïveté, Chee is suspicious of the world, of Jim Leaphorn, and of most other aspects of life outside his immediate associates and clan. Chee's mother's clan is the Slow Talking People, his father's, who is dead, is the Bitter Water Dinee.

In *People of Darkness*, Chee is asked by a rich lady to find a stolen box of "keepsakes" that belong to her husband. The local Navajo will not work for her because they think the husband, hunter Benjamin J. Vines, is a witch. Chee, somewhat chary, agrees only to think about taking the job. He is told by Vines himself that the stolen box is not missing. The whole episode is tied in with a hired gunman named Colton Wolf who is trying to find his long lost brother and mother. Wolf is demented and remorseless, willing to kill anyone and everyone either casually or for cause. When Wolf goes into the hospital room where Chee is a patient, Chee manages to escape through a hole in the ceiling. Wolf then shoots Chee's hospital roommate and a nurse out of pique. It is a study of motivated madness. In 1994, Jon L. Breen called it Hillerman's "best novel to date" (*The Tony Hillerman Companion*, p. 23).

In *Skinwalkers* (1986), Hillerman brings Leaphorn and Chee together for the first time, to the advantage of both. Leaphorn and Chee develop characteristics that were only hinted at in their individual stories. Chee is more doubtful that anything will ever come of his relationship with Mary Landon, and has now met Janet Pete, a lawyer for the Navajo Nation's Legal Aid Society. Leaphorn is becoming more human and agreeable. But the tension between the two, hinted at or stated explicitly in earlier novels, now comes to a head. The older lieutenant thinks sergeant Chee is young, excitable, and unobservant, and doubts the direction of Chee's investigation into Navajo religion. Chee will stop if directly ordered to do so, but Leaphorn is reluctant to order him to cease inquiries into religious matters.

A Thief of Time (1988), Hillerman's favorite and most popular work, is complicated. It begins with an image of the peace of Southwest nature being broken by the invasion of human beings, and ends, that invasion corrected, with the harmonious song of two individuals perfectly at peace with themselves and the world. The introductory paragraph is especially bucolic:

> The moon had risen just above the cliff behind her. Out on the packed sand of the wash bottom the shadow of the walker made a strange elongated shape. Sometimes it suggested a heron, sometimes one of those stick-figure forms of an Anasazi pictograph. An animated pictograph, its arms moving rhythmically as the moon shadow drifted across the sand. Sometimes, when the goat trail bent and put the walker's profile against the moon, the shadow became Kokopelli himself. The backpack formed the spirit's grotesque hump, the walking stick Kokopelli's crooked flute. Seen from above, the shadow would have made a Navajo believe that the great *yei* northern clans called Watersprinkler had taken visible form. If an Anasazi had risen from his thousand-year grave in the trash heap under the cliff ruins here, he would have seen the Humpbacked Flute Player, the rowdy god of fertility of his lost people.

The novel plays on the idea of two people searching for Anasazi pots in a cliff dwelling, one legitimately though illegally, the other illegally and illegitimately. Eleanor Friedman-Bernal, a Jewish anthropologist, discovers that the dig she wants to explore has been despoiled by someone else who is obviously recovering the priceless treasures to convert into cash. Out by the dig in the middle of the night she is approached by a "humped shape that was coming out of the moonlight into this pool of darkness" (p. 16). Ellie, though armed with a .25-caliber pistol, is terrified, as she has a right to be. As a result of this encounter, she disappears and is missing for two weeks before Leaphorn and Chee are called in to investigate. Indians report that she has been destroyed by the Devil.

When the detectives arrive, Leaphorn is ready to retire from the police force because Emma has died needlessly from a blood clot formed during an operation for a brain tumor. Chee, meanwhile, is off larking with Janet Pete, who is interested in buying a used Buick. Out testing it for Janet after a mechanic friend has told him it is a lemon, Chee meets a wanted suspect on the highway, makes a U-turn to chase him, and winds up in the sagebrush in a considerably damaged Buick. Pete then claims that car dealers always mislead women about automobiles.

Leaphorn and Chee get together at a revival meeting of the Navajo evangelist Slick Nakai, a known dealer in Anasazi pots. Chee abandons his research in used cars and helps Leaphorn investigate the disappearance. Perhaps because Leaphorn is on terminal leave and will abandon the force in ten days, Chee does not have to defer to the older man's authority, and they work well together, without their usual suspicions and tensions. Leaphorn decides not to leave the police force and the book ends in beautiful closure as their professional association becomes spiritual.

> Jim Chee noticed Leaphorn was watching him.
> "You all right?" he asked.
> "I've felt better," Leaphorn said. And then he had another thought. He considered it. Why not? "I hear you're a medicine man. I heard you are a singer of the Blessing Way. Is that right?"
> Chee looked slightly stubborn. "Yes sir," he said.
> "I would like to ask you to sing for me," Leaphorn said.

In a final evaluation of Hillerman's works, what conclusion can we draw? First, he is a master storyteller, sympathetic with ethnic groups outside the main power structure. He is poetic, religious, sensitive, and understanding. Although he writes in the vernacular, his mode of expression is neither crude nor sexual. He is especially noted for his peaceful tone and incremental presentation of detail.

Finally, Hillerman is an observant, careful spinner of tales that both entertain and teach. He is unexcelled as an ethnic crime writer and is the model—the touchstone—for many other Native American ethnic crime writers.

H. R. F. Keating

Henry Reymond Fitzwalter Keating (b. 1926), one of Britain's leading ethnic crime writers, is also a well-known scholar of mystery and crime writing. He has been chief reviewer of mysteries for the London *Times* (1967–1983), author of *Sherlock Holmes: The Man and His World* (1979), and editor of *Crime Writers: Reflections on Crime Fiction* (1978), *Whodunit? A Guide to Crime, Suspense, and Spy Fiction* (1982), and *The Bedside Companion to Crime* (1989). Keating was born and reared to be a writer of crime fiction. He has said his mother read detective stories to him when he was eleven or twelve years old, and he declared to himself that he could "never *not* write a detective story, with a murderer to be discovered" (Salwak, p. 82). Although he has written many kinds of crime fiction, Keating is best known to readers as the creator of Inspector Ganesh Ghote (pronounced Go-tay) of the Bombay Criminal Investigation Department (CID).

Keating was driven to the Ghote series by necessity. He had already published three crime novels when he confided to a friend that he was unable to support himself on his crime fiction. Although he had the highest sales in Britain, he felt he had to break into the American market. Keating thought that both British and American readers would be fascinated by the exotic setting of India and decided to introduce them to the Indian crime scene

through a bumbling, alternately proud and servile Indian who spoke fractured English. Keating had never been to India but realized he could gather enough geographical and cultural information from books and from people who *had* visited India, to create his own atmosphere and personality. Keating did not visit India until ten years after his first successful Ghote novel, but when he did view the scene of his action he was satisfied with the authenticity of his depiction.

Keating is directed by his philosophy that "the ethnic crime story is . . . a crime novel which considers some aspect of life by looking the contrast between how people live in its country of origin and how they live in some very different parts of the world" (*Crime and Mystery: The 100 Best Books*). Crime novels are also characterized by humor. "Why do we read crime stories?" he asks. "Short answer: for fun" (*The Bedside Companion to Crime*, p. 7). Beyond the entertainment value, however, Keating admits, "On a still lesser plane crime writing today is a notable source of straightforward social comment and criticism" and a voice for one's philosophy (*Whodunit?* p. 18). Though he continues to write conventional Golden Age detective stories because he admires Sherlock Holmes and Hercule Poirot, Keating's greatest accomplishment lies in his Ghote novels at their best. Throughout the series he investigates the complicated social, political, and linguistic world of India, which can be complex and confusing to the non-native. It is a world of castes, colors, and subtleties that keeps the non-Indian at arm's length, but Keating adds elements of humor in order to provide the "outsider" with a sense of safety and superiority.

The Perfect Murder (1964) was the perfect way to launch Ghote into the British and American markets. The reader is thrown immediately into the swirl of a very complicated Indian society, where color and status are all-important. Ghote is only an inspector in the CID and the case he is assigned deserves someone of higher rank. The scene is Bombay, where many people speak broken English.

Ghote's English is more wretched than most. He himself is bumptious, bumbling, and either humble or arrogant depending on the people with whom he associates. Keating's rendition of Indian culture and speaking patterns, which he knew only at second or third hand, was integral to the success of this venture into a foreign world. Indian literary critic Meera T. Clark attests to Keating's authenticity: "Besides having a canny eye for the intricacies of Indian politics, Keating also has a remarkable ear for the curious linguistic mutation, Indian English" (Salwak, p. 3).

Keating's best works place Ghote in Bombay, where he can be played against other Indians and the British. When he is in Britain or America, Ghote is deprived of his dignity and self-respect, and must become servile. More importantly he is out of the element that allows him to be both comic and dignified. In *Inspector Ghote Hunts the Peacock* (1968) Ghote is forced to go to London to deliver a speech on behalf of his superior. Although he dreads the speech, Ghote looks forward to meeting other Indians in London and getting to know the people of his favorite foreign country. The idea of reading his boss's message makes Ghote feel inferior. When he gets to London, however, the fame of Inspector Ghote has preceded him in the Indian community. The Indians force him to look into an affair that is monopolizing their attention. Ghote discovers to his chagrin that in London the caste system is deeply embedded. The Indians in their community and he, therefore, are treated as inferior to the British. He is somewhat elevated, however, after he has completed his talk and can play his usual role as superior to other Indians and inferior only to the British.

Keating doesn't seem to know when to avoid subjects that are beyond his realm. *Filmi, Filmi, Inspector Ghote* (1976), takes Ghote to India's version of Hollywood, known as Bollywood, home of the native film industry, where he considers the absurdities of the film business. Although Ghote is able to track down the murderer of a movie star, Keating seems as uncomfortable writing about the artificial world of filmmaking as he is in describing the fake world of beauty contests in *Is Skin-Deep, Is Fatal* (1965). Unable to control his disdain, *Filmi, Filmi* is a largely unsuccessful effort.

Keating is most successful when he allows Ghote to be a dignified caricature and generally unsuccessful when he spoofs the caricature, because the portrait that emerges is grotesque. Such is the case in *Go West, Inspector Ghote* (1981). A rich Bombay magnate's daughter has been sent to California and has fallen in with the wrong people. Ghote is sent to investigate. Bumbling Ghote does not fare well in California, and Keating's attitude and purpose are unclear. He seems to hate and be uncomfortable in the everyday culture of California, and is unable to have Ghote live in it naturally. Thus California, its inhabitants, India, and Ghote are twisted to the breaking point and the novel falls off its unnatural underpinning.

In most of the Ghote novels Keating demonstrates an unwavering affinity for democracy and the common people. In *The Sheriff of Bombay* (1984) he is inclusive and explicit. The sheriff of Bombay can be any famous or well-known citizen. Here he is one of Bombay's most famous movie stars and a frequenter of local whorehouses. Keating is concerned with the power of the rich to drive poor girls to prostitution and then to abuse and murder them. It is they who possess the power of the everyday and ordinary, the important aspects of life, as the narrator remarks about Ghote: "Not for the first time in his career he was grateful for the powers of observation to be found in the common man or woman of Bombay, powers undulated by the fatal gift of being able to read, of being able to see only in preordained patterns." The murderer, when discovered, is quite an unexpected perpetrator. Concerning the injustice of Indian society, Ghote speaks for Keating: "Some of us are born with more active consciences than others. I've worried about things ever since I can remember. Am I doing right? In some ways it's a good thing, and in other ways it's a bad thing. It hampers you from doing things perhaps; but that's the way one is, and it comes out in the writing." "Inside him [Ghote] is a lot of me," Keating said in a London Radio Times interview headed "Inspector Ghote, C'est Moi" (quoted in Salwak, p. 85).

Keating's highly developed sense of the absurdities of the human comedy continues to inform. In *Asking Questions* (1996), his twenty-first Ghote novel, he reaches out to new concerns, in what may be his strongest novel to date. His study is about Indian scientists, who feel inferior to their American and British counterparts, and will do almost anything to draw success to themselves. One woman fakes her data on an experiment and publishes her results prematurely because she is afraid an American will prepublish and take the glory from her. She is guilty of the sin of personal and national ambition. She freely admits her scientific sin. Keating condemns her soundly.

In his ethnic novels, Keating is consistent in developing a point of view but inconsistent in expression. One of the strengths of the books is in Ghote's ability to mix with and react to the complex Indian society, with its castes and complicated politics and attitudes. Keating is especially skilled in reproducing the several kinds of English spoken by the various peoples of Indian society. Throughout, the unidiomatic English gives the British or American reader a feeling of ascendancy over the characters in the book, especially over Ghote, the supposed exemplar in the books. The reader's "comfort zone" over such "outsiders" as Hercule Poirot and Ganesh Ghote accounts for a good deal of the feeling of closure that an effective crime novel provides. At his best, Ghote is one of the most amusing ethnic crime fighters in the genre.

James McClure

Ethnic crime fiction faces powerful obstacles in an authoritarian, closed society, since criticism of the dominant society and its execu-
tion of laws can quickly bring the wrath of those in power. But such fiction flourished in South Africa with the work of James McClure, who managed to satisfy his own strong convictions about apartheid while offending neither the oppressed nor the oppressor. McClure's pictures of South African society are so realistic and accurate that they seem to please everyone—white advocates of apartheid because they reveal a system that worked, and opponents because they catalog an institution rotten with discrimination, abuse, and violence. Apparently readers see in the books what they want to see. Nevertheless, McClure's novels about society and crime during apartheid distinguished him as an important social critic and as the most significant South African author of ethnic crime fiction.

James Howe McClure (b. 1939), South African author of police procedurals, was born in Johannesburg and educated in Pietermaritzburg, Natal. He was a commercial photographer, an English teacher, and a reporter and subeditor for newspapers in Edinburgh and Oxford before turning to crime fiction, a medium he thought would best transmit his message about South Africa. After moving to Britain in 1965, McClure published nine books featuring Afrikaner Lieutenant Tromp Kramer and his Zulu assistant, Sergeant Mickey Zondi. McClure chose "Trekkersburg" (Pietermaritzburg) as the locale for his police procedurals. McClure's fiction is direct and real, developed through a lot of action accompanied by economical vernacular dialogue. Some scenes seem gratuitously graphic, as with the brief introductory chapter of *The Caterpillar Cop* (1972), a seduction scene in which two naive teenagers romp amid the trees around the Trekkersburg Country Club. Frightened by his audacity, the boy jumps up and runs away. The girl follows, finds a body on the ground that she assumes is his, bares her breasts and places his hand on one breast, then feels blood on the limp and cooling hand. Terrified, she calls out his name and he answers from behind a nearby tree. And thus the crime scene is introduced!

In order to walk the razor edge of South African apartheid, white Kramer and black Zondi each must live life on two levels—one level for the closely observant dominant white society and another for their private attitudes toward each other. This private life is a close and important one. They have saved each other's lives on numerous occasions and have deep mutual love and respect, though often they must disguise their feelings. In a world of tension, where the line is likely to snap at any moment, McClure introduces grim humor, laughter, and double entendre to turn away violence and disaster. Kramer and Zondi speak a double language, part of the system that allowed South African apartheid to last so many years. It was a system of hidden laughter. McClure suggests, "Apartheid wouldn't have stood a chance without, as it were, taking advantage of the resilient good humor of a most dignified people" (Wall, p. 28).

The Steam Pig (1971) is an extraordinary first novel. It concerns the murders of a white woman and a black gangster by the same gruesome method—driving a bicycle spoke through the ribs under the arm until it ruptures the aorta and causes slow death. Both murders are investigated concurrently. The importance of the double investigation varies according to the officials and the color of the victim's skin. Whites are more important than blacks, even in death.

Snake (1975) is a most powerful example of McClure's approach to and resolution of the apartheid question. It begins with a white showgirl named Eve who titillates the locals twice a night by having a giant python slither between her naked breasts and down between her thighs. After a late Saturday night show she is approached in her dressing room by one of her many fans, a movie star. She teases him until he murders her. Murder number one. Number two is of a black man named Lucky. The same police force has to investigate both murders concurrently. But they are not of equal importance. Kramer reminds Zondi that although Eve is "a *girl* girl" (p. 25) she is more important than the black victim, any

black. This is demonstrated when the police chief upbraids Kramer for sending Zondi to question whites about the murders. "I resent the fact," he says, "that one of my senior officers saw fit to send an inexperienced subordinate in his place to conduct a most delicate inquiry" (p. 163). When Zondi has had to kill the white murderer, Kramer mockingly chastises him: "Just wait till the Colonel hears what you've done this time," he says (p. 197).

Throughout the series, Zondi increasingly demonstrates his equality with Kramer, perhaps even his superiority. In *The Sunday Hangman* (1977) a man is found hanged on the limb of a tree, apparently a suicide. Though all the officers find it hard to believe that the man took his own life, it is Zondi who confirms their suspicions of murder. Zondi hears and believes a bit of Zulu folklore recounted to him by three Zulu boys who had detected the hanging corpse early on. They remind him that a hanging suicide urinates on the ground and ants will move their eggs away from under such a corpse. Since ants were still under this body, it obviously had been hung there after death.

Again and again McClure's fiction minimizes the differences among the four classes. In *Snake* Kramer describes white society's attempt to ignore the interrelatedness of white and black society, "thinking it's two worlds apart. What happens in one doesn't mean anything in the other. They actually *touch*, don't they?" (p. 54). But to deny the appearance of touching, official society goes to extreme measures, as McClure shows in *The Sunday Hangman*, even so far as to build two gallows: one for whites, one for blacks.

Stylistically, McClure is direct, grim, economical, and unrelenting, with descriptions and figures of speech that raise the hair on the reader's head. In *The Sunday Hangman* he describes a rock: "Like a skull on a dunghill, the great white stone shone in the moonlight" (p. 186). In *The Blood of an Englishman* (1980) a man lying on an autopsy slab is described: "He lay unzipped from pubic arch to jaw bone, and looked as though he was passing through

Customs" (p. 198). It is hard not to be impressed with such graphic writing, and it is easy to be caught up in McClure's description of the grim reality of life in South Africa during apartheid.

Arthur W. Upfield

Ethnic crime fiction in Australia reached its greatest achievement in the works of a transplanted Briton, whose career was never recognized and rewarded as it should have been. Arthur (William) Upfield (1888–1964) came to love his adopted country with passion. He was born in Gosport, near Portsmouth, the eldest of five boys. The Upfield house was crowded, and young William, as he was called, was something of a troublemaker, restless practical joker, and nonconformist, always following his own star. In 1911, at the age of twenty-two, Upfield was sent to Australia, where, it was hoped, he would become a respectable farmer or at least stay out of jail. His father's words to his departing son were that he would never amount to any good, and Australia, with a population of four million inhabitants, was so far away that Arthur could never save enough money to get back to England. This parental attitude and act of expulsion cut deeply into Arthur's personality and psyche and left lasting scars. Upfield became abrupt, independent, an enigmatic wanderer. Through the years in Australia he tried his hand as boundary rider, cattle drover, sheepherder, rabbit tracker, opal gouger, grape picker, cook, and station manager. Of this lifestyle Upfield once said, "I clung to it till my teeth fell out." Upfield volunteered for European military service in 1914, returned to Australia in 1919, and stayed put thereafter.

Upfield seems to have been made for Australia, and Australia for him. He needed a large and free land to let his roaming instinct develop. He found such a place in the new continent that had originally received Britain's outlaws and prisoners. For fifty-four years Upfield loved and spoke for Australia.

When he died he was still thinking about the bettering of his adopted land. Upfield was always sickly and asthmatic, and his health declined in his last years, but when he died in 1964 he was writing his thirty-fourth novel. He apparently was still a frustrated, individualistic man not willing to accept the world on its own terms. He was an Australian in his own strange and alien world.

Upfield's Australia was not always peaceful. Tension between Aborigines and whites occasionally exploded in violence, and peace was tenuous. Upfield saw in the conflict between the two races a drama played out between primitivism and civilization, with an obvious potential for disaster but also with some hope. With such a point of view Upfield was the earliest self-conscious author of ethnic crime fiction in Australia. Unlike other well-known Australian authors, such as Colleen McCullough (*The Thornbirds*), and Nevil Shute (*A Town Like Alice*), Upfield was not interested in the epic, in the vital struggle for the political control of man. He threw his strength into defending the Aborigines.

In a thoughtful essay in the *New Republic*, critic John Cawelti observes that detective fiction is ordinarily biased with "certain presuppositions about the society, law, and morality from the Anglo-American tradition." Upfield's works, Cawelti says, "illustrate the power of the detective story formula to bring out distinctive qualities of morals and manners," but also demonstrate the inability of the genre to address the deeper, more complex issues of culture and society. In fact, Upfield's fiction was the expression of his whole life and philosophy. He was too big to contain in a narrow genre. His works are really studies in cultural and philosophical anthropology, which use crime fiction only as their modus operandi. While their artistic accomplishment is uneven, Upfield's works are some of the most ambitious in ethnic crime fiction.

Upfield's working area is the whole of Australia, but especially the Outback. His antagonists are man and nature; in Australia, nature, often more terrible than man, demands heroic reaction. Upfield's protagonist—the

1039

half-breed Napoleon Bonaparte, also known as "Bony"—faces deserts hundreds of miles across, sand spouts fifty miles wide, rabbits in the millions, renegade camels, flooding rivers, and lakes that dry up in summer, water spouts that blot out the sun, and the loneliness of a country where one's nearest neighbor may live a hundred miles away. "Common to all," Upfield says in *The Man of Two Tribes* (1956), is the force of opposition to man: "the country will get any man who goes into it alone" (p. 30). This is Upfield's reason for trying to instill compassion and communality among all Australians.

The books are conventionally heroic. Bony is a superman, with a classic birth that is mysterious and unusual. In *The Man of Two Tribes*, Bony gives his most succinct description of his origin, which is paraphrased in all the other novels: "I never knew my father . . . I never knew my mother either. She was found dead under a sandalwood tree, with me on her breast and three days old. . . . In spite of my parentage I am unusual. Or is it because of my parentage?" (p. 20). Upfield explains the strength of the mixture that produced Bony in *The Sands of Windee* (1931):

> He walked the soft tread of the Australian aboriginal. . . . By birth he was a composite of the two. His mother had given him the spirit of nomadism, the eyesight of her race, her passion for hunting; from his father he had inherited in overwhelming measure the white man's calm and comprehensive reasoning; but whence his consuming passion for study was a mystery. . . . [He] was the citadel within which warred the native Australian and the pioneering, thrusting Britisher. He could not resist the compelling urge of the wanderlust any more than he could resist studying a philosophical treatise, a revealing autobiography, or a ponderous history. He was a modern product of the limitless bush, perhaps a little superior to the general run of men in that in him were combined most of the virtues of both races and extraordinary few of the vices. (pp. 1–2)

Such a person pushed hard against the boundaries of genre fiction and was instrumental in the development of ethnic crime fiction. Unlike most fictional detectives, Bony prefers crimes that are old. For him, time is an ally. He does not like to witness violence and does not particularly care if criminals are punished for their crimes. Like Sherlock Holmes and Hercule Poirot he likes to solve crimes because they provide him with mental exercise. In that respect he is a standard cerebral detective.

Upfield's fictional world differs from those of H. R. F. Keating and James McClure in its focus on the heroic and the tragic. When Upfield emphasizes the ethnic aspects of Bony or his society he does so to raise the higher goals of the salvation of human society, certainly not for any condescending humor that a reader might see. He is first of all a writer of heroic literature that, since he lives among aboriginals in need of a champion, centers on Australia's ethnic dispossessed and raises them to noble stature.

Upfield's books are reminiscent of the works of James Fenimore Cooper and Herman Melville, though he apparently never read either. In Bony, as in Cooper's Chingachgook and Hawk-eye, we see the universal theme of the frontier hero caught between civilization and nature. At his strongest, Upfield reminds us of Melville's preoccupation with aboriginals ground under the conventions of civilization. Upfield parallels Melville's broad humanistic goals in his notion of brotherhood of all men and women, in his rhetoric, and in his symbolism.

Upfield cared little for literary niceties. He was careless in construction and indifferent to his words once they were on the page. In *Crime and Mystery*, H. R. F. Keating says Upfield's *Sands of Windee* is a masterpiece of authenticity, but written in "leadenly ponderous prose." In *Bloody Murder*, Julian Symons calls Upfield's characters "wooden" (p. 124), and Stephen Knight in *Continent of Mystery* (1997) calls Upfield the "classic tourist thriller writer" (p. 158). But some critics have seen the merit of the novels beyond the prose. John Ball calls Upfield's work "a notable achievement in the structure of Australian literature" in his introduction to the Mystery Library edition of *The New Shoe* (1951).

In Upfield's obituary, dated 14 February 1964, the London *Times* recognized that popular fiction had lost a major writer and described his accomplishments approvingly:

Upfield, by pedantic literary standards, wrote rather badly; his grammar was liable to slip. But in Bony he created a unique and memorable character, in his approach to crime he shared some of Simenon's sadness and sympathy, and he had real descriptive power. Few other writers have brought a seemingly lifeless desert more colourfully to life or been more successful in communicating the unexpected beauty of Australia's hills and forests and rocky coasts.

Upfield was interested in writing only for everyday readers, and he wrote in a style best suited for them, as he recorded in *An Author Bites the Dust* (1948):

In this country literature is a piece of writing executed in schoolmasterly fashion and yet so lacking in entertainment values that the general public won't buy it. Commercial fiction—and this is a term employed by the highbrows—is imaginative writing that easily satisfied publishers and editors because the public will buy it. (p. 73)

Independent in literary judgment as in everything else, Upfield followed his own muse. He felt that the mechanics of presentation were less important than the story he told: "Better a good story with plenty of errors than a piece of prose perfectly done and having no story," he said (p. 74).

The resulting prose is heroically Melvillian, though lacking the biblical sonority of *Moby-Dick*. Both authors thought of nature as a symbol, both conceived comically, and both were powered by great outbursts of rhetorical flourish. Upfield sounds Melvillian, for example, in one passage where he addresses and describes nature: "Old Man Drought was dead, battered and bludgeoned by the drops of water. The beaten Earth, ravished and scarred,

bedraggled and weary, conceived, and the womb prepared to give forth its fruit" (*Bony and the Black Virgin*, 1965, p. 121). For Upfield, as with Melville, nature is a Bible: "The print of the Book of the Bush doesn't quickly vanish" (*Virgin*, p. 178).

At times Upfield peoples his stories with characters and humor reminiscent of both Melville and Charles Dickens, whom Upfield had read as a child and to whom he frequently makes reference. The broadest and most effective use of humor comes in *The New Shoe*, where Mr. Penwarden, an old artisan, builds coffins for the people around him. The purchasers try them out before their final use just to make sure they are comfortable. Mr. Penwarden philosophizes: "Life is a Forge. Sorrow is the Fire and Pain the Hammer. Comes Death to cool the Vessel." He coaxes Bony to lie down in a coffin to test it and says: "You'd fit nicely. Take off your shoes . . . might scratch." Bony agrees: "I couldn't be more comfortable in bed." On another occasion, Penwarden tells Bony:

"I'll tell'e what . . . sir. . . . There is no one now wantin' a first-class coffin, and as you just tole me, I must keep me hand in or go sort of stale on the junk. What about one for you, now? A good one to keep out the cold and wet for two or three hundred years?" (p. 54)

Penwarden philosophizes to Bony: "We all want a corrector . . . sir, and there's nothin' like the sight of a coffin to melt away pride and vanity."

One of Upfield's strongest novels, *Bony and the White Savage* (1961; U.S. title, *The White Savage*), concerns the return of a giant man who had been imprisoned for numerous counts of assault, rape, and various other crimes. He is a "psychopath as well as a paranoiac" a "gorilla" and a "throw-back to a prehistoric monster" (p. 19), yet the people in the small community where he was born and reared look upon him as an intellectual and good boy. The point of the novel is the need to educate the naive, to bring them out of their Alice in Wonderland state of mind, and to get them to recognize evil. The writing style in this book is unusually hard, stark, and harsh, but at the same time metaphoric and heroic, the description graphic:

> The eye of the wind, having circled toward the Antarctic, had worked on the sea with spectacular results. The Front Door of Australia was now being savaged by all the white ghosts from the South, tearing at the feet of this monolith, leaping high as though to clutch the hair of a giant and pull him down for the later attackers to devour. (p. 211)

Upfield's strongest books, in fact, concern various aspects of the supernatural. In *Bushranger of the Skies* (1940; U.S. title, *No Footprints in the Bush*, 1944), the symbol is an airplane, a common aspect of Australian bush life. Impelled by a demonic agency, the mad pilot is determined to destroy the people on the ground. In *The Will of the Tribe* (1962) a crater called "Lucifer's Couch" is a fearful supernatural place that must be invaded if a murder is to be solved, but the Aborigines will not go near it. Another element of the supernatural is caves, which appear in five books. In *A Royal Abduction* (1932) caves constitute a womb, a haven, a maze of safety, and in *The New Shoe* the cave blends into the symbol of a coffin.

Perhaps the most important symbol to Upfield is clothing, which represents restraint and civilization, and dramatizes the struggle between the Aborigine and the "civilized." Nakedness is natural, wearing clothes is civilized and unnatural. In all his books, when he contrasts natives with whites, Upfield uses the figure of the undressed and the dressed. Aborigines wear feathers for clothes, and the fewer the better.

In *The Will of the Tribe* Tessa, an Aboriginal girl, has been adopted by a white family and brought up as if she were one of their white children. She always wears white. She wants to become a schoolteacher and work among the whites. Another Aborigine on the farm, Captain, though not adopted, is loved by the whites and treated as a member of the family. He, too, wears white clothes, but he is determined to work among the Aborigines. He encourages Tessa to give up her ambitions for teaching white children and instruct her own people instead. She is torn between the two traditions and styles of life. Although always immaculately dressed in the style of a white woman, she cannot give up the Aboriginal custom of suggestively swinging her hips when she walks. One afternoon Captain turns a gun on her in an attempt to change Tessa's way of thinking. As Tessa flees from him, she sheds the clothes of white civilization, which impede her speed. After she has pulled off her blouse and bra, she feels free. "She knew she had regained what they said was her second wind," and by doing so she had outrun Captain and achieved independence. Realizing that she has escaped danger, Tessa remembers "her mother's force, and the voices of all women in the world. Now you know what to do if you are caught away from camp by a strange Aborigine, they said." Tessa, hearing this admonition, reaches down and pulls off her "beautiful green silk panties" and then collapses upon "the sandy ground and clawed the sand over her breasts and between her thighs." She decides she cannot avoid being an Aborigine. But she is an Aborigine of a new order, free and independent.

Upfield did not believe that woman's place was on the reservation. He did not even believe in separate but equal lifestyles, though he felt white interference caused most of the Aborigines' troubles. He was a cultural gradualist, who believed that it would take several generations for the Aborigines to be assimilated into the dominant culture. Because of this attitude, Upfield has suffered an ironic fate among the people he loved and tried to help. Joe Kovess reports that Upfield's works have been declared off-limits by the Aborigines:

> All of Upfield's novels were withdrawn from school libraries about 10 years ago. While he presented aboriginals in a favorable light at a time when they were considered to be infe-

rior to whites, Upfield is now considered to have been guilty of stereotyping mental traits when he says that Bony has "inherited the white man's ability to reason more clearly and more quickly than aboriginals" and that "once an aboriginal is thoroughly aroused he is a terrible person." So Bony had to go. (*The Bony Bulletin*, 1 [Nov. 1981], 3.)

Thus Arthur Upfield, who has been read in American anthropology classes and whom Ernest Hooten of Harvard called "a shrewd anthropological observer," is a name not to be found in the liberal Australian literature.

Upfield's fate in Australia shows the price that art and anthropology must pay when an outraged ethnic people is awakened. But condemning and censoring Upfield for not writing with a vision of the future seems short-sighted and unwise, as well as anachronistic. His books were not science fiction, not visionary, not futuristic, not utopian. They were realistic and accurate depictions of the Australia of his day—of the people, the ways of life, of attitudes and mores as he understood them. Upfield's works have had a lasting though perhaps subtle effect on all Australians. His books spread the picture of Australian culture far and wide. They did more to teach Americans about Australia than all the chambers of commerce and travel literature of the 1940s. American GIs who served in Australia and the Pacific theater during World War II read Upfield, brought him back with them, and introduced a new author to the United States. Although banned by the Aborigines, Upfield stands as a jewel among Australian ethnic writers, and his Bony is one of the outstanding crime investigators of all time.

Upfield's fate in writing about a minority culture illustrates the possible outcome pioneers can suffer. Writing early about a society that had not achieved the sophistication it now has, he has been criticized for picturing the society as it was rather than as it would become. Such is the danger for all writers of ethnic crime fiction who choose not to romanticize their subjects. But the best ethnic crime writers dedicate themselves to presenting their subjects as they see them, unvarnished. Experience has shown that—for writers in all genres—reality presented with respect and dignity provides the best approach.

Selected Bibliography

PRIMARY WORKS

WORKS OF E. V. CUNNINGHAM

Sylvia. New York: Doubleday, 1960.
Phyllis. New York: Doubleday, 1962.
Alice. New York: Doubleday, 1963.
Lydia. New York: Doubleday, 1964.
Shirley. New York: Doubleday, 1964.
Penelope. New York: Doubleday, 1965.
Helen. New York: Doubleday, 1966.
Margie. New York: Morrow, 1966.
Sally. New York: Morrow, 1967.
Samantha. New York: Morrow, 1967. Masuto.
Cynthia. New York: Morrow, 1968.
The Assassin Who Gave Up His Gun. New York: Morrow, 1969.
Millie. New York: Morrow, 1973.
The Case of the One-Penny Orange. New York: Holt, Rinehart, 1978. Masuto.
The Case of the Russian Diplomat. New York: Holt, Rinehart, 1978. Masuto.
The Case of the Poisoned Eclairs. New York: Holt, Rinehart, 1979. Masuto.
The Case of the Sliding Pool. New York: Delacorte, 1981. Masuto.
The Case of the Kidnapped Angel. New York: Delacorte, 1982. Masuto.
The Case of the Murdered Mackenzie. New York: Delacorte, 1984. Masuto.

WORKS OF JEAN HAGER

Terror in the Sunlight. New York: St. Martin's Press, 1977.
The Grandfather Medicine: An Oklahoma Mystery. New York: Worldwide, 1989. Bushyhead.
Night Walker. New York: St. Martin's Press, 1990. Bushyhead.
Ravenmocker. New York: Mysterious Press, 1992. Bearpaw.
Ghostland. New York: St. Martin's Press, 1992. Bushyhead.
The Redbird's Cry. New York: Mysterious Press, 1994. Bearpaw.
Blooming Murder. New York: Avon, 1994.

Seven Black Stones. New York: Mysterious Press, 1995. Bearpaw.
Fire Carrier. New York: Mysterious Press, 1996. Bushyhead.
Death on the Drunkard's Path. New York: Avon, 1996.
Spirit Caller. New York: Mysterious Press, 1997. Bearpaw.

WORKS OF TONY HILLERMAN

The Blessing Way. New York: Harper, 1970. Leaphorn.
The Fly on the Wall. New York: Harper, 1971. Only novel not featuring Navajo Tribal Police.
Dance Hall of the Dead. New York: Harper, 1973. Leaphorn.
Listening Woman. New York: Harper, 1978. Leaphorn.
People of Darkness. New York: Harper, 1980. Chee.
The Dark Wind. New York: Harper, 1982. Chee.
The Ghostway. New York: Harper, 1984. Chee.
Skinwalkers. New York: Harper, 1986. Leaphorn and Chee.
A Thief of Time. New York: Harper, 1988. Leaphorn and Chee.
Talking God. New York: Harper, 1989. Leaphorn and Chee.
Coyote Waits. New York: Harper, 1990. Leaphorn and Chee.
Sacred Clowns. New York: Harper, 1993. Leaphorn and Chee.
The Fallen Man. New York: Harper, 1996. Leaphorn and Chee.

HILLERMAN COLLECTIONS

The Joe Leaphorn Mysteries. New York: Harper, 1989.
The Jim Chee Mysteries. New York: Harper, 1990.
The Mysterious West. Edited by Tony Hillerman. New York: Harper, 1994.

WORKS OF H. R. F. KEATING

Death and the Visiting Firemen. London: Gollancz, 1959; New York: Doubleday, 1973.
Zen There Was Murder. London: Gollancz, 1960.
A Rush on the Ultimate. London: Gollancz, 1961; New York: Doubleday, 1982.
The Dog It Was That Died. London: Gollancz, 1962.
Death of a Fat God. London: Collins, 1963; New York: Dutton, 1966.
The Perfect Murder. London: Collins, 1964; New York: Dutton, 1965.
Is Skin-Deep, Is Fatal. London: Collins, 1965; New York: Dutton, 1965.
Inspector Ghote's Good Crusade. London: Collins, 1966; New York: Dutton, 1966.
Inspector Ghote Caught in Meshes. London: Collins, 1967; New York: Dutton, 1968.
Inspector Ghote Hunts the Peacock. London: Collins, 1968; New York: Dutton, 1968.

Inspector Ghote Plays a Joker. London: Collins, 1969; New York: Dutton, 1969.
Inspector Ghote Breaks an Egg. London: Collins, 1970; New York: Doubleday, 1971.
Inspector Ghote Goes by Train. London: Collins, 1971; New York: Doubleday, 1972.
Inspector Ghote Trusts the Heart. London: Collins, 1972; New York: Doubleday, 1973.
Bats Fly Up for Inspector Ghote. London: Collins, 1974; New York: Doubleday, 1974.
A Remarkable Case of Burglary. London: Collins, 1975; New York: Doubleday, 1976.
Filmi, Filmi, Inspector Ghote. London: Collins, 1976; New York: Doubleday, 1977.
Inspector Ghote Draws a Line. London: Collins, 1979; New York: Doubleday, 1979.
The Murder of the Maharajah. London: Collins, 1980; New York: Doubleday, 1980.
Go West, Inspector Ghote. London: Collins, 1981; New York: Doubleday, 1981.
The Lucky Alphonse. London: Enigma, 1982.
The Sheriff of Bombay. London: Collins, 1984; New York: Doubleday, 1984.
Under a Monsoon Cloud. London: Century Hutchinson, 1986; New York: Viking, 1986.
Dead on Time. London: Century Hutchinson, 1988; New York: Mysterious Press, 1989.
Inspector Ghote, His Life and Times. London: Century Hutchinson, 1989.
The Iciest Sin. London: Century Hutchinson, 1990.
The Rich Detective. London: Gollancz, 1993.
Cheating Death. London: Gollancz, 1994.
The Good Detective. London: Gollancz, 1995.
Asking Questions. London: Gollancz, 1996.

WORKS OF JAMES McCLURE

The Steam Pig. London: Gollancz, 1971; New York: Harper, 1972.
The Caterpillar Cop. London: Gollancz, 1972; New York: Harper, 1973.
Four and Twenty Virgins. London: Gollancz, 1973.
The Gooseberry Fool. London: Gollancz, 1974; New York: Harper, 1974.
Snake. London: Gollancz, 1975; New York: Harper, 1976.
Rogue Eagle. London: Macmillan, 1976; New York: Harper, 1976.
The Sunday Hangman. London: Macmillan, 1977; New York: Harper, 1977.
The Blood of an Englishman. London: Macmillan, 1980; New York: Harper, 1981.
The Artful Egg. London: Macmillan, 1984; New York: Pantheon, 1985.
Imago. London: Macmillan, 1989; New York: Mysterious Press, 1988.

WORKS OF DANA STABENOW

A Cold Day for Murder. New York: Berkley, 1992.
Dead in the Water. New York: Berkley, 1993.

A Fatal Thaw. New York: Berkley, 1993.
A Cold-Blooded Business. New York: Berkley, 1994.
Play with Fire. New York: Berkley, 1995.
Blood Will Tell. New York: Putnam, 1996.

WORKS OF ARTHUR W. UPFIELD

The House of Cain. London: Hutchinson, 1928; New York: Dorrance, 1929.

The Barrakee Mystery. London: Hutchinson, 1929. U.S.: *Lure of the Bush.* New York: Doubleday, 1965.

The Beach of Atonement. London: Hutchinson, 1930.

The Sands of Windee. London: Hutchinson, 1931.

A Royal Abduction. London: Hutchinson, 1932; San Diego, Calif.: Macmillan, 1984.

Gripped by Drought. London: Hutchinson, 1932.

Wings Above the Diamantina. Sydney: Angus and Robertson, 1936. U.S.: *Wings Above the Claypan.* New York: Doubleday, 1943.

Mr. Jelly's Business. Sydney: Angus and Robertson, 1937. U.S.: *Murder Down Under.* New York: Doubleday, 1943.

Wind of Evil. Sydney: Angus and Robertson, 1937; New York: Doubleday, 1944.

The Bone Is Pointed. Sydney: Angus and Robertson, 1938; New York: Doubleday, 1947.

The Mystery of Swordfish Reef. Sydney: Angus and Robertson, 1939; New York: Doubleday, 1943.

Bushranger of the Skies. Sydney: Angus and Robertson, 1940. U.S.: *No Footprints in the Bush.* New York: Doubleday, 1944.

Death of a Swagman. New York: Doubleday, 1945.

The Devil's Steps. New York: Doubleday, 1946.

An Author Bites the Dust. New York: Doubleday, 1948.

The Mountains Have a Secret. New York: Doubleday, 1948.

The Widows of Broome. New York: Doubleday, 1950.

The Bachelors of Broken Hill. New York: Doubleday, 1950.

The New Shoe. New York: Doubleday, 1951.

Venom House. New York: Doubleday, 1952.

Murder Must Wait. New York: Doubleday, 1953.

Death of a Lake. New York: Doubleday, 1954.

Sinister Stones. New York: Doubleday, 1954.

The Man of Two Tribes. New York: Doubleday, 1956.

Bony Buys a Woman. London: Heinemann, 1957. U.S.: *The Bushman Who Came Back.* New York: Doubleday, 1957.

Bony and the Mouse. London: Heinemann, 1959. U.S.: *Journey to the Hangman.* New York: Doubleday, 1959.

Bony and the Kelly Gang. London: Heinemann, 1960. U.S.: *Valley of Smugglers.* New York: Doubleday, 1960.

Bony and the White Savage. London: Heinemann, 1961. U.S.: *The White Savage.* New York: Doubleday, 1961.

The Will of the Tribe. New York: Doubleday, 1962.

Madman's Bend. London: Heinemann, 1963. U.S.: *The Body at Madman's Bend.* New York: Doubleday, 1963.

Bony and the Black Virgin. New York: Collier, 1965.

The Lake Frome Monster. Completed by J. L. Price and Dorothy Strange. London: Heinemann, 1966.

Breakaway House. Sydney: Angus and Robertson, 1987.

ANTHOLOGY

Pronzini, Bill, and Martin H. Greenberg, eds. *The Ethnic Detectives: Masterpieces of Mystery Fiction.* New York: Dodd, Mead, 1985.

BIOGRAPHICAL AND CRITICAL STUDIES

Bakerman, Jane. "Joe Leaphorn and the Navajo Way: Tony Hillerman's Indian Detective." *Clues* 2: 1 (1981).

Ball, John. Intro. to *The New Shoe* by Arthur Upfield. San Diego, Calif.: University Extension, 1976.

Browne, Ray B. *Heroes and Humanities.* Bowling Green, Ohio Popular Press, 1986.

———. *The Spirit of Australia: The Crime Fiction of Arthur W. Upfield.* Bowling Green, Ohio: Bowling Green State University Popular Press, 1988.

Bulow, Ernie, and Tony Hillerman. *Talking Mysteries: A Conversation with Tony Hillerman.* Albuquerque: University of New Mexico Press, 1981.

Cawelti, John. *New Republic,* 30 July 1977, 39–41.

Clark, Meera T., "Detective Fiction and Social Realism: H. R. F. Keating." *Clues* 2: 1 (spring/summer 1981).

———. "H. R. F. Keating: An Interview." *Clues* 4: 2 (fall/winter 1983).

Coale, Samuel. "Hillerman and Cross: The Reinvention and Mythic Re-Modeling of the Popular Mystery." *Clues* 16: 2 (fall/winter 1995).

Donaldson, Betty. "The Novels of Arthur Upfield." *Armchair Detective* (November 1974).

Erisman, Fred. *Tony Hillerman.* Boise, Idaho: Boise State University Press, 1989.

Freese, Peter. *The Ethnic Detective: Chester Himes, Harry Hemelman, Tony Hillerman.* Essen: Verlag Die Blaue Eule, 1992.

Greenberg, Martin, ed. *The Tony Hillerman Companion.* New York: HarperCollins, 1994.

Hawke, Jessica. *Follow My Dust! A Biography of Arthur Upfield.* London: Heinemann, 1957.

Hillerman, Tony. Intro. to *A Royal Abduction* by Arthur Upfield (see above).

Keating, H. R. F., ed. *Blood on My Mind.* London: Macmillan, 1972.

———, ed. *Agatha Christie: First Lady of Crime.* London: Weidenfeld and Nicolson, 1977; New York: Holt Rinehart, 1977.

———, ed. *Crime Writers: Reflections on Crime Fiction.* London: British Broadcasting Corporation Publications, 1978.

———. *Sherlock Holmes: The Man and His World.* London: Thames and Huson, 1979; New York: Scribners, 1979.

———, ed. *Whodunit? A Guide to Crime, Suspense, and Spy Fiction.* London: Windward, 1982; New York: Van Nostrand, 1982.

———, ed. *Crime and Mystery: The 100 Best Books.* London: Xanadu, 1987; New York: Carroll and Graff, 1987.

———. *The Bedside Companion to Crime.* London: O'Mara, 1989; New York: Mysterious Press, 1990.

Knight, Stephen. *Continent of Mystery: A Thematic History of Australian Fiction.* Melbourne: Melbourne University Press, 1997.

Reilly, John M. *Tony Hillerman: A Critical Companion.* Westport, Conn.: Greenwood Press, 1996.

Salwak, Dale. "An Interview with H. R. F. Keating," *Clues* 5: 2 (fall/winter 1984).

Symons, Julian. *Bloody Murder.* New York: Mysterious Press, 1992.

Tamaya, Meera. "Interview with H. R. F. Keating," *Clues* 12: 2 (fall/winter 1992).

———. *H. R. F. Keating: Post-Colonial Detection, A Critical Study.* Bowling Green, Ohio: Bowling Green State University Popular Press, 1993.

Wall, Don. "The Achievement of James McClure." *Clues* 10: 1 (spring/summer 1989).

THE FEMALE DETECTIVE
From Nancy Drew to Sue Grafton

MAUREEN T. REDDY

WHEN EDWARD STRATEMEYER, writing under the name Carolyn Keene, created Nancy Drew in 1929, he invented a character so new in mystery fiction that she ought to be seen as the founding figure in what is now an important strain of the genre. While Nancy was certainly not the first female detective nor even the first female series detective, this "girl detective" had little in common with her predecessors or her contemporaries in crime novels, who were mostly nosy, older spinsters like Agatha Christie's Miss Marple or secondary, helpmate characters in series featuring male detectives, such as Dorothy Sayers' Harriet Vane in the Peter Wimsey novels. Although she was invented by a man, Nancy Drew owes her continued existence to a woman, Stratemeyer's daughter, Harriet S. Adams, who took over both the series and the pseudonym with the fourth book and wrote at least one new installment annually for more than five decades.

From its first appearance, the Nancy Drew series was hugely popular with adolescents, especially girls, and is remembered fondly by many contemporary women writers, several of whom credit the books for their continued interest in reading and, eventually, writing mysteries. A Nancy Drew conference in Iowa in the early 1990s drew some of the most prominent creators of female detectives, including Susan Dunlap and Nancy Pickard.

It's not difficult to understand Nancy Drew's appeal. She is smart, pretty, wealthy, and—most important—free and independent. Most of her adventures take place in the summer, so we do not see her negotiating the world of school, a location of anxiety for many girls. Nancy's mother, conveniently, is dead before the series begins, her place partly taken by a dedicated housekeeper, Hannah Gruen, who has less power than does Nancy in the household. Her father allows her extraordinary freedom, trusts her completely, respects her intelligence so much that he often asks for her help with his law practice, and is endlessly willing to indulge her every whim, few questions asked. His confidence in Nancy never wavers, despite his having to rescue her at the climaxes of several of her more than 130 adventures. Nancy has two loyal girlfriends, Bess and George, who function as sidekicks, helping her with her mystery solving and offering admiring comments on her abilities, but contentedly playing second bananas to her starring role in their adventures. Her boyfriend, Ned, is as accommodating as Mr. Drew, helping, rescuing, or just staying out of Nancy's way, depending on her wishes of the moment.

From the perspective of the average preteen girl, Nancy lives an entirely charmed life. In addition to the uncritical regard of friends and father, she has an extensive wardrobe (carefully described in most of the books), her own car (a sporty roadster in the earlier books), a large and comfortable house, few onerous household duties, and evidently unlimited vacation time and funds. She also has power. In book after book, adults hasten to do Nancy's bidding, including the police, who are always grateful for her help and willing to act on her say-so alone. Nancy is even the perfect age: sixteen in the first few books, then perpetually eighteen for the rest of the series.

Although a number of the early books in the series have been updated, not much other than obvious period details has changed in Nancy's world in nearly seventy years. That the Nancy Drew series has waned in popularity in the 1980s and 1990s may be attributed in part to the influence of the series itself. Its huge popularity, of course, spawned many imitators, but only two really caught on with the Nancy Drew market of young teen and preteen girls: the *Babysitters' Club* series, in which a group of young girls sometimes solve mysteries, and *Goosebumps,* the R. L. Stine series of mystery-horror books.

Grown-up Problems

Whereas Nancy Drew is forever eighteen, her readers are not forever twelve. As the first few generations of preteen and teen readers grew beyond Nancy Drew, they found no other fictional series character fully able to take her place. While there were plenty of women writers of mystery fiction, most of these writers' series featured male protagonists, as did virtually all series written by men. The few series that did focus on adult female sleuths in the years 1929 to 1971 for the most part followed the traditions of the nosy spinster (e.g., D. B. Olsen's Rachel Murdock) or the helpmate of a male detective. The few writers to flout those conventions—such as Margaret Tayler Yates with "Davvie" McLean (a news correspondent, whose first appearance was in *The Hush-Hush Murders* in 1937) and Amanda Cross with Kate Fansler (an English

professor who first appeared in *In the Last Analysis* in 1964)—generally invented amateur detectives.

Nancy Drew is also an amateur, but that status seems temporary, dictated by her youth; the books leave the strong impression that once she's truly an adult, she will either give up detecting entirely or become a professional private eye. Characters like Davvie McLean, a world traveler and professional writer, and Kate Fansler, wealthy, independent, and intelligent, match for adult women some of the fantasy elements met for teens by Nancy Drew, but their right to investigate, their authority, is always at issue in a way that Nancy's is not. Moreover, authors of mystery fiction focusing on unpaid amateur detectives must always struggle to establish a plausible explanation for the protagonist's involvement in crime solving, an especially difficult struggle when the protagonist is a woman at a time when women's roles are circumscribed. In contrast, the professional private detective needs no motive to investigate other than the desire for money. *Female* private investigators in the years preceding the second wave of the feminist movement—which began, roughly, around 1965—need a motive to hold any paid employment at all, perhaps especially a type of work whose requirements are at odds with traditional gender-role expectations for women.

This tension between role requirements for women and for detectives is palpable in the books featuring female professional private investigators in the years between 1880 and 1971, and it often results in plots that deny "these characters either as detectives or as women," in critic Kathleen Gregory Klein's estimation (p. 1). For instance, in the chapter of *The Woman Detective: Gender and Genre* that focuses on women protagonists in dime novels, Klein notes that each of the seven books she considers, all written by men, includes a secondary plot—about marriage, about male detectives, or about the female detective as unwomanly in some striking way—that ultimately overwhelms the main plot. The very few series written by women with female private eyes as their protagonists in these years vary little from the texts written by men. Anna Katharine Green's Violet Strange, for instance, is an upper-class belle whose motive for detecting is to earn money for a disinherited sister's education and whose detecting is subordinated to a marriage plot. Kay Cleaver Strahan's seven novels about detective—"crime analyst," in Strahan's formulation—Lynn MacDonald (published 1928–1939) weirdly subordinate the detective herself, making her something of a background figure even though the book jackets announce that these are "Lynn MacDonald" mysteries. The 1960s saw the emergence of female private eyes evidently meant to appeal to male sexual fantasies, such as G. G. (pseudonym for Gloria and Forrest) Fickling's Honey West books, all of which foreground sexual adventures, leaving crime solving in the background, and Henry Kane's Marla Trent, whose first appearance is titled *Private Eyeful* (1959), which gives a good idea of the book's tone and main interest.

Dorothy Sayers' 1946 critique of women detectives in *The Art of the Mystery Story* identifies some of the central problems. Noting that the few women detectives created by that point have "not been very successful," Sayers complains that these detectives tend to be "irritatingly intuitive" or else foolishly "active . . . walking into physical danger and hampering the men engaged on the job" (p. 79).

> Marriage, also, looms too large in their view of life; which is not surprising, for they are all young and beautiful. Why these charming creatures should be able to tackle abstruse problems at the age of twenty-one or thereabouts, while the male detectives are usually content to wait till their thirties or forties before setting up as experts, it is hard to say. (p. 79)

Sayers concludes that women are more believable as amateur detectives than as professionals, saying that "better use has been made of women" in non-private-eye books (p. 79).

The chief reason that women were more believable as amateurs than as professionals

lies outside fiction, in women's social position. Although there have always been women who worked outside their homes (popular mythology notwithstanding), the range of jobs available to them was sharply limited before second-wave feminism's impact began to be felt in the 1970s. Certainly few women could be found working as police officers—the most common training ground for private eyes in fiction, as in life—or as private investigators before the 1970s. Rooted as it is in realist traditions, and in common with other forms of popular fiction, mystery fiction tends to reflect prevailing social conditions and to present at least a surface verisimilitude. Readers of mystery fiction are likely to experience problems suspending disbelief when they encounter characters who correspond neither with the ordinary world outside the novel nor with the conventions of the genre—hence the scarcity of female police or private investigators before women moved into a broad range of occupations in the 1970s and thereafter.

The amateur detective of either gender, of course, presents problems of verisimilitude, but these problems tend to be muted by firmly established genre conventions. Despite rising homicide rates in the second half of the twentieth century, murder remains uncommon, and ordinary citizens in the United States and in Britain—the countries in which most mystery series are set—are unlikely ever to be even tangentially involved in a suspicious death. Creators of series featuring amateur detectives must invent plausible reasons for their characters' repeated involvement in murder investigations, and readers, prepared by genre conventions to suspend disbelief fairly readily for the series novel's premise, must be willing to accept these reasons without intense scrutiny. Placing a woman in the position of detective creates a further barrier to suspending disbelief, one exacerbated when the woman holds a job that readers are used to associating only with men. In short, women detectives in nontraditional occupations make inordinate demands on readers. The majority of jobs that women were likely to hold up until the late twentieth century—factory-line workers, clerks, secretaries, nurses, teachers, domestic workers—offered little scope for the independent action and contact with a large population needed for amateur detectives' repeated encounters with murder to be at all credible. It should come as no surprise, then, to learn that many female amateur detectives in mystery fiction were academics, as women entered the academy earlier and in larger numbers than they did other professions.

A popular choice of venue for mystery fiction in general, the academy serves as a version of the country house of Golden Age mysteries, presenting a limited number of suspects with byzantine relationships that produce motives for murder galore, hidden behind a veneer of civility. Scholarly training imparts investigative skills and, at least in theory, inculcates veneration of truth and reason, both central values in traditional mystery fiction.

One of the most important figures in the development of the female detective is Amanda Cross, the pseudonymous creator of English professor and amateur detective Kate Fansler and, under her own name, Carolyn Heilbrun, an important feminist theorist. The first Kate Fansler book, the Edgar Award–winning *In the Last Analysis*, appeared in 1964, just before Betty Friedan's *The Feminine Mystique* (1963) jump-started the second-wave feminist movement by analyzing the dull oppression of middle-class white women's lives in the United States. In this first novel, Kate is something of an "honorary member of a male club," Heilbrun's own term in *Reinventing Womanhood* for women who find success in male-dominated professions by following and identifying with male examples and doing nothing to alter the existing hierarchy or to enable other women to follow in their footsteps (p. 39). The solution to the murder in *In the Last Analysis* turns on what Kate calls her "recipe for integrity": "Find the man who loves his work and loves the cause he serves by doing it" (1966 ed., p. 63). She gets involved in a murder case when she

agrees to help find the real culprit in order to clear a friend's name; she doubts that the suspect actually committed the murder because the accused is a man who loves his work. The real killer turns out to be someone who does not value work and who indeed has no real work of his own. The plot and structure of *In the Last Analysis* are both highly traditional, as is the conception of the amateur detective's role—to right wrongs the official system of justice either perpetrates or cannot fix. Cross's major contribution is to move an adult woman into the position of detective without subordinating her detecting to a romance plot. Particularly important is Kate's insistence on the value of work for *both* men and women—a still unusual position in 1964—which is also illustrated in Cross's nonstereotypical depiction of Kate as a woman who loves her work and who finds a central meaning in her life through that work.

The second Kate Fansler novel, *The James Joyce Murder* (1967), also emphasizes the importance of intellectual work to Kate, but it moves Kate out of the traditional position of detective and into an oddly passive, supporting role reminiscent of earlier mysteries with female protagonists. In this novel, two men solve the mystery without Kate, who merely listens to their reconstruction of the crime. Significantly, the murder victim was a woman who is represented as deserving to die, with her death considered by all "an act of sanitation" (1982 ed., p. 75). This second book in the series turns out to be a bridge between the mostly traditional conception of both women and detectives found in the first book and a feminist reconsideration of the woman as detective that begins in the third book, *Poetic Justice* (1970), and continues through the rest of the novels in the series, which as of this writing number eleven. Beginning with *Poetic Justice*, Cross reinvents the female detective, increasingly incorporating feminist themes and critiques in her novels and focusing on issues of concern to women. Whereas the first two novels in the series share the traditional mystery's interest in restoring order, the remaining novels question the implications of social order and social justice themselves, exposing that order's dependence on the oppression of women. Kate's role as detective diverges ever more sharply from male models as the series continues. Cross's interventions in the genre laid the groundwork for the female detectives who have forever changed the world of mystery fiction.

Early Hard-Boiled Women

In 1972, P. D. James published *An Unsuitable Job for a Woman*, her first book to feature professional private investigator Cordelia Gray. As this novel opens, twenty-two-year-old Cordelia inherits both a failing detective agency and a gun after the suicide of her ineffectual partner, Bernie Pryde, who had hired her as a typist but began teaching her about investigative work and took her on as a partner. *An Unsuitable Job for a Woman* traces Cordelia's growth into a professional detective, suggesting along the way the character traits and life experiences that might enable a young woman to become both a self-sufficient adult and a self-confident professional. With Bernie's death, Cordelia is left entirely on her own, a condition already familiar to her: her mother died when Cordelia was just one year old, and her father, a small-time revolutionary, consigned her to a series of foster homes and boarding schools until she became useful to him as an errand-runner for his political cronies. The father has died not long before the novel's opening, but Cordelia has no reason to miss him much. Cordelia, then, is radically solitary, a condition very close to that of the American male heroes of hard-boiled detective novels. James's novel owes a considerable debt to the hard-boiled tradition, and *An Unsuitable Job for a Woman*'s placement of a woman in the position of private eye triggered an extensive reconsideration of that subgenre.

The male hard-boiled private eye, as created by Dashiell Hammett and further refined by Raymond Chandler, is defined by his isolation. His loner status marks both his separateness from the corrupt society his (usually first-person) tales expose and his connection to the solitary, romantic heroes of quest tales. Numerous critics have remarked on the direct line of descent between American frontier romances—a genre established in large measure by James Fenimore Cooper in the early nineteenth century—and hard-boiled detective fiction. In thinking about the evolution of the female detective, it is worth remembering the intensely masculine code embodied in private-eye novels, especially the relationship between such figures as Cooper's Natty Bumppo, or Hawkeye, and the heroes of hard-boiled novels, such as Sam Spade and Philip Marlowe. Sam Spade and his literary progeny are urban cowboys, fantasy figures dedicated to a quest for truth and governed by their own private codes of honor and morality.

Although Hammett's depiction of Sam Spade in *The Maltese Falcon* (1930) is widely considered the definitive portrayal of a hard-boiled private eye, it was Raymond Chandler who expressly articulated the private eye's essential characteristics in *The Simple Art of Murder*:

> Down these mean streets a man must go who is not himself mean, who is neither tarnished nor afraid. The detective in this story must be such a man. He's the hero. He's everything. He must be a complete man and a common man, yet an unusual man. He must be, to use a rather weathered phrase, a man of honor. He is neither a eunuch nor a satyr. I think he might seduce a duchess, and I'm quite sure he would not spoil a virgin. If he is a man of honor in one thing, he's that in all things. He is a relatively poor man, or he would not be a detective at all. He is a common man or he could not go among common people. He has a sense of character or he would not know his job. He will take no man's money dishonestly, and no man's insolence without due and dispassionate revenge. He is a lonely man, and his pride is that you will treat him as a proud man or be very sorry you ever saw him. (pp. 20–21)

As Kathleen Gregory Klein points out, Chandler's repetition of "man" and "he" in this definition is not merely conventional usage; substituting "woman" and "she" results in absurdity (p. 126). Similarly, substituting a woman for a man in the position of detective in a hard-boiled novel's plot exposes the subgenre's gender limitations. Creating a female detective requires a reworking of the subgenre's conventions, as even the title of James's first Cordelia Gray book indicates. Detecting, as conventionally defined, is indeed an "unsuitable job for a woman," and Cordelia has to struggle against male resistance to her doing her job throughout that novel. While all hard-boiled private eyes encounter resistance, only for female detectives is that resistance specifically related to gender.

Unfortunately, P. D. James did not rework the subgenre's gender conventions entirely and did not return to Cordelia Gray for ten years after *An Unsuitable Job for a Woman*, when she published the second—and, apparently, last—book in this series, *The Skull Beneath the Skin* (1982). The Cordelia we meet in this novel is a greatly diminished version of the Cordelia that the end of *Unsuitable* seemed to promise. Instead of the fully adult, competent, calm professional detective we see in the first novel's final scenes, the Cordelia of *Skull* makes foolish choices, fails to solve the central mystery, is nearly killed by the murderer, and, by the end of the book, has retreated to a specialization in finding lost pets, realizing that detecting murderers is an unsuitable job for her, if not for all women. Nicola Nixon reads in Cordelia's failure both the trace of P. D. James's own turning away from early seventies feminism and the author's desire to squash fans' persistent clamoring for a return of Cordelia, when James herself clearly prefers her main series character, Adam Dalgliesh.

The deliberate diminishing of Cordelia in *Skull* and fans' disappointment together account for the current near-invisibility of the first novel. Discussions of the proliferation of female private eyes in the 1980s for the most part ignore James's character, and there seems to be general critical and popular agreement that the first female private eye is Marcia Muller's Sharon McCone, who made her first appearance (five years after James created Cordelia) in *Edwin of the Iron Shoes* (1977). Certainly Muller, who is cited often by other women mystery writers as an important inspiration, has done more to alter the genre than did James with Cordelia, but the fact remains that Sharon McCone is not the first modern female detective in mystery fiction. She is, however, the first modern female detective to remain at the center of an ongoing series and also the first modern American female detective. Like the male hard-boiled detective, the female version seems particularly American, which may be another reason for fans' and critics' tendency to credit Muller with inventing this new form of detective fiction. Certainly most of the writers working in this subgenre in the 1980s and 1990s have been themselves American, including Liza Cody, the American expatriate creator of the British Anna Lee and Eva Wylie series.

In order to understand fully Muller's early contributions to the development of the female detective, the first Sharon McCone book ought to be put in several larger contexts. When *Edwin of the Iron Shoes* was published, liberal feminist ideas had already seeped into public consciousness, while more radical varieties of feminist thought continued to be distorted in the press and were perceived as ridiculous or frightening (or both) by large numbers of Americans. The late seventies began the era of such statements as "I'm not a feminist, but . . . ," followed by "I believe in equal pay for equal work" and similar sentiments. Even as survey after survey showed broad endorsement of basic liberal feminist demands—for equal pay, for equal opportunity in work and in education, and so on— comparatively few women, and even fewer men, identified themselves as feminists. Liberal feminists proposed an agenda of reform, not revolution, essentially asking that women be added in to existing power structures and institutions without demanding that those structures and institutions be dismantled.

Radical feminists, in contrast, shared a commitment to revolution, seeing equality of opportunity as impossible in what they perceived as an inherently unequal social system and as, in any case, beside the point: Why clamor to be added to a system one believes to be corrupt and corrosive?

Edwin of the Iron Shoes appeared in 1977 at the same time as the first book to feature a radical feminist detective, M. F. Beal's *Angel Dance*. The contrast between the two detectives, the plots in which they feature, their public reception, and their subsequent fortunes is instructive. Even their publishers contrast: Muller's book was published by the small but mainstream David McKay (with later books in the series published by St. Martin's Press), while Beal's was published by the feminist Crossing Press. Muller's novel introduces Sharon McCone, an investigator for the All Souls Legal Cooperative in San Francisco. The mystery plot of *Edwin* is paralleled by a romance plot, as Sharon develops an uneasy relationship with a police lieutenant, Greg Marcus, during the course of the book. This first Sharon McCone book is more soft- than hard-boiled, although Sharon shares some characteristics with hard-boiled heroes; for instance, she is something of a loner, but her solitariness is mitigated by her connection, both personal and professional, with the other All Souls people and by her budding relationship with Marcus. Sharon expresses mild liberal-feminist leanings, as, for instance, when she describes another character as "my kind of woman, one who made her way on her own steam and refused to be held back" (p. 106), but never expressly identifies herself as a feminist.

In contrast, M. F. Beal's detective, Kat Guerrera, is hired as a detective to guard feminist writer Angel Stone precisely because she herself is a radical feminist; because of her revolutionary activities, she is seen by her employer as able to negotiate and to understand the world from which threats to Angel's safety come. Unlike Sharon McCone, who cooperates with the police and even becomes personally involved with one cop, Kat holds herself entirely aloof from all government systems. Where Sharon is heterosexual, Kat is bisexual and prefers women; she is in fact attracted to her client, Angel. Where Sharon successfully repels attempts to frighten her off the case and suffers only minor physical violence, Kat is brutally battered and raped. Most important, *Edwin of the Iron Shoes* demonstrates that a woman can function as a fictional private detective without imposing vast changes in the genre; *Angel Dance* shows that the form cannot accommodate a radical feminist detective. While Muller succeeds in pushing the genre boundaries a bit with Sharon McCone, similar to the liberal feminists' agenda of reform, Beal's novel explodes the genre and stands finally outside it, like radical feminists in society. It's unsurprising, then, to note that Sharon McCone has since appeared in eighteen more novels, while Kat Guerrera had just the one outing.

The mild feminism of the first Sharon McCone novel looks downright radical, however, in contrast to some of the other series featuring women professional detectives that began in the 1970s, such as Lillian O'Donnell's Norah Mulcahaney. A New York Police Department detective, Norah first appeared in *The Phone Calls* (1972); by the time of Muller's first Sharon McCone novel, there were five books in O'Donnell's series. The wild popularity of police procedurals in print, in films, and on television from the 1970s through the 1990s suggests a widespread public interest in the workings of law and order and in the usually invisible machinery of a mysterious and closed system, an interest that a number of women writers have exploited since O'Donnell first created Norah.

O'Donnell does not challenge the boundaries of police procedurals and does not seriously examine the implications of a woman's entering an almost exclusively male occupation. Norah is highly conventional, both in her dedication to the law-and-order ideals of policing and in her private life as well. One critic, Jane Pennell, remarks that Norah is "more feminine than feminist" (p. 92); in fact, although there are hints of a superficial brand of liberal feminism in Norah's musings early in the series (on male officers' prejudices against women officers), the plots and themes of the series are profoundly antifeminist. For example, several of the villains in O'Donnell's series are male dupes of manipulative women, in a pattern reminiscent of male hard-boiled detective fiction. These novels offer implicit justification for male domination and for the existing status quo of gender inequality. While some women writers after O'Donnell did indeed turn to police procedurals, O'Donnell seems to have been less of an influence than has been Marcia Muller, judging from the ways in which these female detectives have developed and the difficulties they are shown as struggling against.

The Female Hard-Boiled Detective in the 1980s

While Sharon McCone was created in the 1970s, she is really a creature of the 1980s—Muller did not produce a second book until *Ask the Cards a Question* (1982), with further installments in the series appearing more or less annually from then on. Sally Munt notes that the 1980s were the heyday of feminist crime novels, which she sees as an expression of a "decade of Thatcherism and Reaganism which reified an individualist, urban culture" (p. 201). Munt argues that novels—mostly liberal feminist—featuring female private detectives offer women "a fantasy of individualized power and control" (p. 201), understandably attractive when many women feel a lack of either power or control. Whatever the reasons, which are likely to be more complex than Munt's formulation allows, the early 1980s saw a huge increase in the numbers of women writers of mystery fiction with strong women protagonists, as well as the continuation of earlier series such as Muller's and Cross's. In 1981 and 1982, for instance, first novels in series were published by, among others, Liza Cody (*Dupe*, featuring Anna Lee), Sara Paretsky (*Indemnity Only*, featuring V. I.

Warshawski), and Sue Grafton (*"A" Is for Alibi*, featuring Kinsey Millhone). Although some male writers also created female detectives during this period, the greatest developments in the evolution of the female detective are attributable to women writers.

In the years since their first novels appeared, Paretsky and Grafton between them have remapped the terrain of the fictional private eye. Two more different writers working within a single subgenre are difficult to imagine. Paretsky is highly educated (she holds a doctorate in history from the University of Chicago), self-consciously feminist, and politically active within the field of crime fiction. After deciding she wanted to leave the insurance industry, for which she had worked for a long time, Paretsky chose the mystery genre for her first attempt at fiction writing because she was a fan and wanted to try a form she knew well. She has said that she made "a lot of false starts" before inventing Warshawski:

> In 1979, I realized that I was trying to create a character who was aping the Raymond Chandler tradition, only in female form, and what I really wanted was a woman who was doing what I was doing, which was trying to make a success in a field traditionally dominated by men. With that realization, I was able to find V. I.'s voice. (*Contemporary Authors*, p. 335)

Outspoken about what she saw as inequitable treatment of women mystery writers by reviewers, publishers, and award committees, Paretsky was the founding president of what has come to be the international organization Sisters in Crime. Established in 1986, Sisters in Crime's express purpose, as stated on the group's web page, is to "combat discrimination against women in the mystery field, educate publishers and the general public as to inequalities in the treatment of female authors, and raise the level of awareness of their contribution to the mystery field." An early Paretsky-organized Sisters in Crime effort involved examining reviews: Were books by women featuring women reviewed less frequently than were those by men? They were, and the organization proceeded to work to redress this imbalance. Counting all the reviews in the mystery column of the *New York Times Book Review* in 1987, Sisters in Crime determined that only 10 percent of the books reviewed were written by women. They wrote to the editor to point out the bias and also publicized their study's findings. By 1989, 25 percent of the books reviewed in that same column were by women. Surveys focusing on local papers around the United States achieved similar results. Other projects included producing a booklet that offers members advice for promoting their books (dubbed "Shameless Self-Promotion for Brazen Hussies"). Paretsky was named a Woman of the Year by *Ms.* magazine in 1987 in recognition both of her efforts with Sisters in Crime and of her detective fiction.

Grafton, on the other hand, came to mystery writing via writing for film and television. When Sisters in Crime was established, she expressed a lack of interest in joining and has mentioned in various interviews her discomfort with being categorized as a woman writer. Yet Grafton, too, asserts that she is feminist, saying in a 1989 interview, "I am a feminist from way back" (Taylor, p. 11). In that same interview, Grafton explains, "When I decided to do mysteries, I chose the classic private eye genre because I like playing hardball with the boys" (p. 12). Paretsky and Grafton evidently operate on quite different understandings of feminism, with Paretsky seeing feminism as a collective project and Grafton perceiving it as women's exercising the right long enjoyed by men to assert their autonomy and individuality.

Grafton's and Paretsky's protagonists and the plots in which they figure reflect their creators' different stances, yet share significant similarities. For example, in contrast to Muller's Sharon McCone and Cody's Anna Lee, both are independent, self-employed investigators, answering to no one but themselves for longer than it takes to solve a single case. All four of these detectives are cut off from their families of origin: Sharon (at least in the early books in the series) and Anna are es-

tranged from their families, who object to their choice of work and independent ways of living. V. I. and Kinsey are orphaned; Kinsey actually has been orphaned twice, once when her parents were killed in a car accident and again when the aunt who raised her died, ten years before the events in *"A" Is for Alibi*. All are in their early thirties as their respective series begin, and none of these detectives is married. Warshawski has been married and divorced once and Kinsey twice; ex-husbands crop up in several of the series' novels to further complicate the detectives' lives. Most strikingly, given the statistical likelihood that women in their thirties will have borne children, none of these detectives has children, and only V. I. gives the possibility much thought, often wondering in the early books in Paretsky's series what having children would be like.

In their solitariness—parentless, spouseless, childless—these detectives resemble their male counterparts, but that similarity serves to throw profound differences into sharper relief. Solitariness for a woman has a far different meaning in Western societies than does solitariness for a man: a woman choosing autonomy over connection, a single life over marriage, independence over interdependence or actual dependence acts contrary to gender-role expectations, while a man making the same choices fulfills those expectations. That is, the solitary woman is perceived as "unwomanly," while the solitary man's "manliness" is affirmed. Further, in all of the novels in these series, the protagonists are shown as actively seeking connection with others; however, for the detectives to maintain their independence, the novels suggest, these affectional bonds must fall outside the bounds of conventional family relationships. Feminists in the 1970s pointed out that the family has often been the site of women's oppression, an insight that works itself out in the detective novels of the 1980s.

With the exception of Muller, whose detective's emotional needs are satisfied by serial romantic interests and by coworkers, creators of hard-boiled female detectives in this period invent chosen families for their heroes, who establish enduring bonds with a few friends. These relationships are often with older characters, who may by virtue of age and sex seem to fill parental roles and therefore to substitute for the detective's dead or absent parents. The actual functions of these parental-substitutes, in the detectives' lives, however, do not fit neatly into any predetermined, nuclear-family roles. Kinsey, for instance, grows close to her elderly landlord, Henry Pitts, much as Anna Lee is close to her downstairs neighbors, Bea and Selwyn Price. In both cases, though, the relationships are fluid and egalitarian; the older friends do not exert power over the detectives, the relationships exhibit an unscripted mutuality, and—most important—there is no tangled family history to overdetermine every interaction. In *"F" Is for Fugitive* (1989), Kinsey is staying in Henry's house after the bombing of her apartment at the end of *"E" Is for Evidence* (1988) and beginning to feel "emotional claustrophobia" (p. 11). In earlier books, Kinsey occasionally worries that Henry wants to play a fatherly role toward her, but in this novel she comes to understand that he wants to mother her. She tells him to stop fussing, because "I don't need a mother," to which Henry replies, "You need a *keeper*" (p. 14). Kinsey eventually decides that she can accept his mothering: "Instead of viewing him with suspicion, I think I'll enjoy him for the time we have left, whatever that may be. He's only eighty-two, and God knows, my life is more hazardous than his" (p. 261).

V. I. Warshawski's most significant relationship is with Lotty Herschel, who sees the detective as both daughter and friend; with Lotty—who is more of a mother substitute than are any other characters in these texts—V. I. gets to work out a more mature and less romanticized mother-daughter connection than she had with her own mother. Her downstairs neighbor, Mr. Contreras, sometimes tries to act as her father, usually with disastrous results, but for the most part he imagines a role for himself as V. I.'s assistant detective. V. I. pointedly comments that she

gets along better with women than with men, "because I don't feel they're [the women] trying to take over my turf. But with men, it always seems, or often seems, as though I'm having to fight to maintain who I am" (*Indemnity Only*, 1982 ed., p. 141).

Of the "big three" female hard-boiled detective fiction writers—Grafton, Muller, and Paretsky—Muller seems the most deeply interested in providing an ongoing romantic relationship for her detective and the least interested in exploring the implications of gender-based conflict within romantic relationships. In the first three McCone novels, we see Sharon becoming involved with Greg Marcus, a relationship that ends painfully but that does not stop her from entering into a romantic entanglement with Don, a radio personality, in the fourth book, *Games to Keep the Dark Away* (1984). That relationship also eventually ends, but it leads to another that continues into the current Sharon McCone books. It is fair to say that all of Muller's Sharon McCone books in some way incorporate romance plots and that those plots often threaten to overwhelm the mystery, in the pattern Kathleen Gregory Klein notes as typical of earlier series featuring female detectives.

Paretsky and Grafton, in contrast, demonstrate much less interest in romance plots, but they also show the difficulty of breaking free of social codes that govern heterosexual romances. Sexual involvement for their detectives almost invariably poses threats to independence, as many of the men with whom these detectives form romantic or sexual relationships eventually perceive the detective's job as an obstacle or feel compelled to try to protect the detective in some way. V. I. Warshawski at one point tells a new lover a cautionary tale about the end of her marriage, but he fails to heed the implicit warning. She says that her ex-husband wanted her to be available to attend social functions important to his job and otherwise to subordinate her work to his. He imagined "he'd fallen in love with me because I'm so independent; afterwards it seemed to me that it was because he saw my independence as a challenge, and when he couldn't break it down, he got angry" (*Indemnity Only*, p. 141). In *Blood Shot* (1988), the fifth Paretsky novel, V. I. struggles to establish a more adult understanding and a more mutual relationship with Caroline, a teenager who is her surrogate little sister. At the end of the book, Caroline says that she hopes V. I. will always be her sister, and V. I. replies—in the book's final line—"Till death do us part, kid" (p. 328). This double parody, of the marriage service and of hard-boiled language, underscores the novel's theme of the centrality of women's friendships and also implies that such friendships take precedence over heterosexual marriage or romance in V. I.'s life.

For much of the series thus far (now at "M"), Sue Grafton's Kinsey Millhone deliberately avoids romantic entanglements, which create too many problems, in her view. For the most part she limits herself to involvements that are more physical than emotional, at least in the books published in the 1980s. She asserts in *"C" Is for Corpse* (1986), "I like my life just as it is" (p. 13), and explains that once or twice a year, "I run into a man who astounds me sexually, but between escapades, I'm celibate, which I don't think is any big deal. After two unsuccessful marriages, I find myself keeping my guard up, along with my underpants" (p. 13). Kinsey reflects occasionally on what she learned from the aunt who raised her, who was herself single and childless but for Kinsey; often these lessons emphasized female independence. In *"D" Is for Deadbeat* (1987), for instance, Kinsey recalls her aunt advising, "Rule Number One, first and foremost, above and beyond all else, was financial independence. A woman should never, never, never be financially dependent on anyone, especially a man. . . . Any feminine pursuit that did not have as its ultimate goal increased self-sufficiency could be disregarded. 'How to Get Your Man' didn't even appear on the list" (pp. 107–108). Kinsey's view of marriage is jaded in the extreme; at one point, she reads a restraining order on a secretary's desk that says in part, "And he is enjoined and restrained from annoying, molesting, threatening, or harming petitioner," and comments that "given the average marriage these days, this sounded like pre-nups" (*"F" Is for Fugitive*, p. 150).

The plot of *"A" Is for Alibi* merges the physical dangers of Kinsey's job with the emotional and psychological risks of romance, but in a plot that is emphatically not a romance, as Kinsey has a brief affair with the man she later realizes is the murderer she seeks. This plot pattern is familiar from male hard-boiled novels: the detective ignores suspicions, becomes sexually involved with a person eventually revealed to be the killer or closely linked to the killer, discovers the truth, and kills the betraying, dangerous lover. Grafton here indeed plays "hardball with the boys," as the gender reversal alters the meaning of the plot pattern and suggests that men are far more dangerous to women than vice versa, the tradition of the dangerous woman in male hard-boiled novels notwithstanding. Unfortunately, however, Grafton's challenge to stereotypes does not go beyond mere gender switching in this first novel, in which all the male characters are one-dimensional and potentially dangerous but all the female characters are allowed individuality and subjectivity. Happily, Grafton's subsequent novels break that pattern.

The plots of novels featuring these female hard-boiled detectives in the 1980s tend to link a particular investigation to large social problems and to the wider feminist project of examining women's social position itself. Many of the crimes Kinsey, Anna, Sharon, and V. I. investigate—which in the cases of the latter three are often not the crimes they were hired to investigate—turn out to be elaborately interwoven with the social oppression of women and with larger patterns of crime and corruption. This pattern parallels that of male hard-boiled novels, in which the detective generally uncovers a huge, previously hidden web of crime and deceit, reinforcing his justifiably paranoid view of society, but its focus on women's position reveals an interest definitely not shared by the creators of the male hard-boiled detectives. A number of the plots turn on child sexual abuse; for example, in *Blood Shot* Paretsky links that abuse to murder and to fraud, as one man arranges one murder and plans but fails to carry out several others, all in an attempt to keep his insurance fraud and past sexual abuse of his niece secret. In *Killing Orders* (1985), V. I.'s investigation turns up connections among big business, the Roman Catholic church, and the Mafia. The novel suggests that all three systematically victimize women, either by enlisting them as enforcers of the institution's own masculine power or by crushing them entirely. When the villains are female, they are often motivated by a desire to end or to avenge their own victimization, as in Grafton's *"F" Is for Fugitive.*

Like the male hard-boiled dicks, the female detectives operate in a violent world, where they encounter danger and must endure violence directed at them because of their jobs. Also like the men, the women frequently meet violence head on, using their wits, fists, and weapons, especially guns, to overcome the threats against them. Much as a male loner acts within gender-role expectations while a female loner violates them, a man who fights back with whatever weapons he can command further proves his manliness, while a woman further undermines her womanliness, as conventionally defined. Switching the gender of the detective requires a reconsideration of the meaning of violence and of the value of fighting back. A number of critics have remarked that one of the pleasures women readers find in the female hard-boiled novels is a vicarious feeling of power, as the detective successfully fights her way out of dangerous situations. However, the female detectives frequently express ambivalence about violence and seldom take pleasure in that violence, as their male counterparts often do. For the most part, the detectives resort to violence only when they are left with no alternative to preserve themselves, but there are occasional exceptions. In *Killing Orders,* for instance, V. I. sets up the murder of a character who she knows is responsible for her friend's death. Paretsky's novels tend to be

much more graphically violent than the other series considered here. In *Blood Shot,* for example, V. I. is beaten, kidnapped and left for dead, attacked by a thug with a gun, and threatened by a shady businessman; she manages to overcome all these assaults and threats, mainly by using her wits but also by using her gun.

Sometimes the detective honestly acknowledges the sheer fun of behaving violently, of defying all social controls and demands for civilized behavior. In *"F" Is for Fugitive,* Kinsey is attacked by another woman with a tennis racket; she describes the ensuing battle in minute detail, and then comments:

I felt giddy with power, happiness surging through me like pure oxygen. There's something about physical battle that energizes and liberates, infusing the body with an ancient chemistry—a cheap high with a sometimes deadly effect. A blow to the face is as insulting as you can get, and there's no predicting what you'll garner in return. I've seen petty barroom disputes end in death over a slap on the cheek. (p. 167)

In the Grafton and Paretsky novels of the 1980s, the detective's attitude toward violence finds its clearest expression in her attitude toward guns. In the hard-boiled tradition, the pen is to the writer as the gun is to the detective. When the writer and her detective are both women, however, the symbolic values of both the pen and the gun shift: V. I. taunts a hired thug who has beaten her up and wants to shoot her by mocking the gun's phallic symbolism: "You big he-men really impress the shit out of me. . . . Why do you think the boy carries a gun? He can't get it up, never could, so he has a big old penis he carries around in his hand" (*Indemnity Only,* p. 203). For V. I., a gun is just a gun—a deadly weapon in the hands of either men or women—but she understands its other possible meanings. Kinsey Millhone uses her gun in self-defense in *"A" Is for Alibi,* killing a man who is trying to kill her. The shooting haunts her, forcing her to consider her position in the world; she says at the end of that novel, "The shooting disturbs me still. It has moved me into the same camp with soldiers and maniacs. . . . I'll be ready for business again in a week or two, but I'll never be the same" (1987 ed., p. 215). In later books in the series, Kinsey uses the gun again, but sometimes other weapons are more useful. For instance, in *"E" Is for Evidence,* she has better luck fending off an attacker with her purse and a toilet tank lid than with her gun.

In the male hard-boiled tradition, the novels are usually narrated in the first person by a man whose voice is cool, detached, and matter-of-fact; equal descriptive weight is given to crucial plot elements and to surface details of dress, food, and setting. Similarly, the novels considered here are narrated in the first person by the detective, whose voice is also cool, detached, and matter-of-fact. Paretsky and Grafton seem to revel in giving exhaustive catalogs of urban street directions, meals prepared and eaten (often peanut butter and pickle sandwiches for Kinsey, more elaborate gourmet concoctions for V. I.), and clothing (Kinsey's all-purpose black dress is a recurring motif, while V. I. is fond of expensive, well-made clothes and shoes).

Hammett originated a powerfully bare style of narration, relying on flat, declarative statements punctuated by the occasional metaphoric flight. Critics have described that style as well suited to conveying both a "sense of physical and temporal immediacy" and an impression of "the sheer gratuitousness of life," in which "events just happen" (O'Brien, p. 71). Warshawski's tough talk in the face of danger—her taunting of the armed hit man— is typical of both Paretsky's and Grafton's series. Although detectives' voices are as cool and their styles, especially Grafton's, as bare as Hammett's, these voices are certainly not what the critic James Naremore describes as "the voice of Male Experience," nor are they necessarily representative of female experience. Instead, they are atypical, idiosyncratic, personal voices, expressing individual experience that is not necessarily representative of

gender. Their characteristic ways of speaking connect Kinsey and, to a lesser extent, V. I. to a particular worldview that becomes detached from gender assumptions through these novels. Both Kinsey and V. I. are aware of the fictional tradition from which they spring, and their narratives include ironic, genre-related self-reflections in which they compare themselves with their male predecessors. In *Killing Orders,* V. I. wishes she had a bodyguard and then thinks, "Of course, a hard-boiled detective is never scared. So what I was feeling couldn't be fear. Perhaps nervous excitement at the treats in store for me" (1985 ed., p. 215). Similarly, in *"B" Is for Burglar* (1985), Kinsey enlists the help of an elderly woman, who tells the detective, "I'm going to start reading Mickey Spillane just to get in shape. I don't know a lot of rude words, you know" (1986 ed., p. 103).

"Getting in shape" is very much to the point, if we think of the detective's "rude words" as reflections of her self-perception of physical and mental toughness. Scott Christianson identifies Grafton's use of hard-boiled language as a way of appropriating traditionally male power, noting that Kinsey's "use of tough talk and wisecracks . . . transforms the classic private eye genre into a place from which a woman can exercise language as power" (pp. 128–129). Christianson argues that language is the distinguishing feature of the hard-boiled genre, noting such typical elements of hard-boiled prose remarked upon by earlier critics as a preponderance of active verbs that create a swiftly moving narrative, tough talk, wisecracks, and crude or vulgar colloquialisms. The hard-boiled detective's language, especially the wisecrack, is typical of wise guys, people who do not respect "authority, wealth, power, social standing, or institutions" (p. 131). Certainly this description precisely fits both V. I. and Kinsey.

Christianson sees an important connection between Kinsey's tough talk and her willingness to use her gun; her tough talk reflects her tough-mindedness, and is "an exercise of power—the power to express her emotions and sensibilities, and power over situations and circumstances" (p. 130). Kinsey talks tough to suspects and to cops, to her readers, and even to herself, like a mental exercise, just to keep in shape. She is most likely to break into wisecracks when dealing with a pompous or excessively sentimental person. And this can include herself. Thinking that a man is attracted to her and therefore is disappointed when she leaves for the night, she pulls herself up short and thinks that she "might have been kidding myself. Martinis bring out the latent romantic in me. Also headaches, if anybody's interested" (*"F" Is for Fugitive*, p. 181). Kinsey, like V. I., is most likely to talk tough when she's frightened, as a way of throwing off the person scaring her and also of bucking up her own courage. When she is awakened by a threatening phone call and feels terrified—heart pounding, disoriented—she says to the caller, "Listen, asshole. I know what you're up to. I'll figure out who you are and it won't take me long, so enjoy" (*"F" Is for Fugitive*, p. 192).

By the end of the 1980s, Grafton's series had reached "F"; Paretsky's and Cody's each numbered five and Muller's ten. Numerous other series featuring female private detectives had also begun, but Grafton, in particular, remained the most important—and popular—writer of female hard-boiled fiction. At the same time, there were many new series with female amateur detectives as their protagonists as well as a few with female police officers. The hard-boiled writers, especially the "big three," were important in establishing a readership for female detectives in general and also in pushing back the boundaries of what is possible to do with female protagonists in mystery fiction.

Police and Amateur Detectives in the 1980s

So many series featuring female amateur detectives or police officers began or continued in the 1980s that it is impossible to discuss them all here. Instead, this section simply points to several trends in such series while attending closely to just a few representative books, particularly those most clearly related in style or in theme to the female hard-boiled detective series discussed previously.

At the same time that she was publishing the first ten books in her Sharon McCone series, Marcia Muller also created two other series, one featuring a female amateur detective, Elena Oliverez (three books, 1983–1986), and one about an international art investigator, Joanna Stark (three books, 1986–1989). The Stark books straddle a line between the professional-private-eye tradition, although certainly not hard-boiled, and the amateur-detective tradition. Stark is a professional investigator, but her specialization in art fraud limits the possibilities in these books. Elena Oliverez is a Latina curator of a Mexican arts museum in Santa Barbara (interestingly enough, Kinsey Millhone's home turf, dubbed Santa Teresa in Grafton's series), one of the very few female minority detectives in series in the 1980s. The Oliverez series is set almost entirely within a Mexican-American community, and Elena's cultural background is a central element of these books; Muller incorporates a minicourse in Mexican-American arts and culture into the three books in the series, which is interwoven with plots centering on the arts museum. What is perhaps most interesting about this series is its exploration of mother-daughter relationships from something other than a critical or even downright hostile perspective—the mutual regard of Elena and her mother plays an important role in each book. Rather than enjoying "playing hardball with the boys," in Grafton's memorable formulation of her reasons for writing crime fiction, Muller here expresses pleasure in female-centered activities.

Other important mystery series featuring female amateur detectives in the 1980s include Carolyn Wheat's Cass Jameson books (Cass is a criminal lawyer in Brooklyn); Sharyn McCrumb's series about forensic anthropologist Elizabeth MacPherson; and

Nancy Pickard's enormously popular Jenny Cain series. The first Jenny Cain book was *Generous Death* (1984), which introduced Jenny as the director of a foundation in a small Massachusetts seaside town, Port Frederick. Of the five Jenny Cain books Pickard published in the 1980s, only the first was not nominated for an Anthony, Agatha, or Macavity award. Jenny comes from one of the wealthiest families in her little town, but she is burdened by guilt because her family handled dishonorably the closing of Cain's Clams, once the town's largest employer. Her family background is fraught with pain and difficulty, much like Sharon McCone's, and this background frequently features in the novels' plots. In a pattern now familiar to readers of mysteries with amateur protagonists, in the first books in the series Jenny is involved with a police lieutenant whom she eventually marries, Geof. Like many books with female amateur detectives, Pickard's series melds detection and romance plots, sometimes to the detriment of the mysteries; however, the popular success of these well-written books and their repeated acknowledgment by groups dedicated to advancing mystery writing suggest that the combination of romance and mystery is one many readers enjoy.

Susan Dunlap, like Paretsky and Pickard a founding member and past president of Sisters in Crime, began series in each of the three dominant mystery subgenres—private eye, amateur detective, and police procedural—in the 1980s. Her first series detective is Jill Smith, a Berkeley beat cop turned homicide detective. In contrast to Lillian O'Donnell's Norah Mulcahaney series, the Jill Smith series pushes the boundaries of the form in ways parallel to Grafton's and Paretsky's reinvention of the hard-boiled novel. Dunlap skirts many of the problems a woman might experience in joining a traditional, heavily masculine police force by setting her series in Berkeley, whose police force she depicts as unconventional, and, in the first book, giving Jill an African-American commanding officer

who is as far from traditional centers of (white male) power as is Jill. In the first book, *Karma* (1981), Jill insists on the Berkeley police's difference from other forces by reflecting on events in the late 1960s: "To residents they were a different breed, better educated, more liberal, as much 'Berkeley' as police. . . . Now, years later, it was still a police force I was pleased to be a part of" (p. 1). By portraying the Berkeley police as unusual and as more of an open system than a closed "fraternal order," Dunlap obviates the necessity of explaining, or even exploring, possible conflicts in a woman's dedication to law and order.

Jill is depicted as joining the police force nearly by chance, while looking for a job that would let her support her husband in graduate school. Jill soon learns, however, that she both enjoys and is good at her job, which leads to a divorce from her husband and a determination to move up the ladder at work. The conflict between work and home, career and romance, that Jill experiences is a familiar one for women, which had no parallel for men in the 1970s and 1980s. Jill's resolution of that conflict—choosing her job over her husband when her husband reveals his sexist attitudes toward her and his own boundless self-regard—is a resoundingly feminist and antiromantic choice. Nevertheless, many of the Jill Smith books incorporate romance plots, as Jill becomes involved with a fellow police officer, Howard, to whom she is initially attracted precisely because of their mutual love of policing in Berkeley.

Aside from this romance plot, Dunlap's Jill Smith series has more in common with the female hard-boiled novels than with police procedurals. Jill, like Kinsey and V. I., tells her own story in a voice that is tough and humorous; like Kinsey, Jill loves to crack wise, a fondness that occasionally gets her into trouble. In the later books in the series, Jill often operates like a private investigator as opposed to a police officer, as she cultivates informants and contacts outside the department and investigates cases independently. Jill does sometimes run into trouble with the internal politics of the department, but for the most part those conflicts are not specifically related to her gender. Despite intriguing shifts in the focus of the police procedural, Dunlap does not so much revise the genre as she does reform it a bit, mainly by setting her books in a nontraditional police department and by creating plots that focus on Berkeley's zany characters.

In 1984, Katherine V. Forrest published the first of her Kate Delafield novels, *Amateur City*, thereby beginning a thoroughgoing revision of the police procedural. Although Kate is the most conventional of the lesbian detectives created in the 1980s, she is the least conventional of the female police officers in fiction of this period precisely because she is a lesbian. Forrest's plots follow familiar lines— each begins with a crime and then follows Kate's procedure as she assembles clues and solves the crime, with the suspect's arrest coming as the conclusion to the novel. During the course of the investigations, however, Kate reflects frequently on her position within the Los Angeles Police Department as she tries to reconcile her personal values with the hierarchical, masculine, homophobic department for which she works; reminded of her anomalous position, she feels "the familiar heavy weariness at being reminded of her singularity" (*Amateur City*, p. 25)

Kate believes deeply in the ideals of law and order and sees her job as helping people, but in the second novel in the series, *Murder at the Nightwood Bar* (1987), several other lesbian feminists confront Kate about the meaning of her work. They tell her she has sold out to her oppressors by working to protect the interests of rich white men, and Kate believes there is some truth in their accusations. Yet what we also see is that Kate alone is able to stop a kidnap attempt by several men who attack the bar's patrons with lead pipes and taunt them ("make me puke, dykes," p. 102). She beats one man badly and uses her gun to hold off the rest. This novel suggests that police departments with lesbians are better than police departments without them; Kate provides an important service for the wider lesbian community by joining the LAPD. Moreover, the power she wields through her position enables her to help precisely those people she cares most about.

The other lesbian detectives to come into print in the 1980s—enough to constitute a trend—were either amateurs or, in a very few cases, private eyes, and most of the first novels in which they appear are combinations of mysteries and coming-out stories, the latter a popular genre for lesbian novels of the 1970s and 1980s. Several of these novels, such as Barbara Wilson's *Murder in the Collective* (1984), directly question mystery-novel conventions. In the second novel in her Pam Nilson series, *Sisters of the Road* (1986), Wilson violates the implicit limits on endangering the detective when she has Pam raped. The rape is described in the first person in horrifying detail; Pam's death is narrowly averted by another woman's coming to her rescue at the last possible moment. Rape is the violent crime women most fear, according to surveys; reading about this rape is likely to be much more disturbing than reading about the various beatings hard-boiled detectives endure, no matter how harrowing the detail. Wilson forces readers to confront the reality of rape through the consciousness of a woman with whom we have learned to identify. The only other female mystery writer to address rape through her detective's experience is M. F. Beal, in *Angel Dance.*

In the 1980s, 207 new mystery series by women were begun, most of them featuring female protagonists; an average of 79 new titles were published in those series annually. Roughly half of those series were begun in the last three years of the decade. By the end of the 1980s, then, the situation for readers wanting to move from Nancy Drew to adult female detectives had changed utterly from what it had been when the Nancy Drew series began in 1929. Instead of having trouble finding mystery books with female detectives, readers were likely to find it difficult to keep up with the sheer volume of such books published. The 1990s have continued this trend.

The Female Detective in the 1990s: Voices from the Margins to the Center

At the end of the 1980s, lesbian detectives represented the group farthest from the traditional centers of power then found in crime fiction. Although some white writers had created female detectives of color—most notably Marcia Muller, with Elena Oliverez and Sharon McCone, who is part Native American—there were no books in print by black women writers with black female detectives. In the 1990s, however, women writers began creating detective series that challenged not only mainstream mystery conventions but also the conventions of white feminist mysteries. Four series by black women writers can stand as examples: Barbara Neely's Blanche White novels, about a domestic worker who is an amateur detective; Eleanor Taylor Bland's police procedurals featuring Marti MacAlister; Valerie Wilson Wesley's Tamara Hayle series, about a professional private eye; and Nikki Baker's Ginny Kelly books, which are set in a middle-class lesbian milieu, depicting a professional woman with a master's degree in business administration who works at an investment company and acts as amateur detective. These writers are not the first or the only black women writers of detective fiction; they are, however, the first to enjoy popular success and critical acclaim as crime writers. All four of these series directly address issues of race and class as well as gender, question the conventional crime plot's movement from disorder to order and injustice to justice, and collectively redraw the borders of the genre. These series treat racism as a fundamental fact of U.S. culture, suggesting that the culture is in fact based on racism and showing how racial injustice masquerades as justice. Together, these series by black women writers expose the limits of the challenges that both white women and black men writers pose to the mystery genre.

With the exception of Bland's police procedurals, these series take the distrust of the police typical of hard-boiled novels much further than do other crime writers. Neely's Blanche comments on police as the natural enemies of ordinary black people like herself in *Blanche Among the Talented Tenth* (1994). After a man hits Blanche, a younger black woman tries to persuade her to call the police by making a feminist solidarity argument, but Blanche "wasn't about to betray herself or lie" (p. 228). She asks her friend, "How do you think I'll be treated? How seriously do you think the police would take me? . . . It scares me half to death to think of ever having someone do something to me that I can't avoid going to the police to get fixed" (pp. 228–229).

Although white female detectives' plots often include discussions or illustrations of ways in which gender bias works against them, they never reflect upon the ways in which their race offers them privileges and thereby complicates gender discrimination. Gender works in much more complex ways in the series by black women writers. In *Slow Burn* (1993), Bland has Marti, the only woman and one of just two characters who are black, think about the double jeopardy of race and gender and the "special rules" that require her to be "twice as good, twice as smart" and to "work twice as hard" as anyone else (p. 42). Baker and Bland create work situations for their detectives—black women working in predominantly male, predominantly white institutions—that cause them to be both hypervisible and invisible. That is, we are shown that whites often cannot see them as individual people—Ginny Kelly's boss, tellingly, cannot remember her name—because they are so fixated on the women's race. The plot of Neely's *Blanche on the Lam* (1992) makes much of this invisibility; when Blanche goes "underground," she hides in plain view, working as a domestic in the home of wealthy whites. She can hide so easily, stay on the lam in her own town, because the white powers-that-be do not really see her. They see a maid's uniform, a "domestic," not Blanche in her individuality. This invisibility constitutes Blanche's special power as a detective, as white people speak too freely in front of her, let too many secrets drop. While all four series considered here discuss issues seldom, if ever, raised by white writers of crime fiction, many of these discussions seem to assume a white audience. Indeed, in all four series there are direct commentaries on race matters that only make sense if read as directed at whites, as scenes of instruction on race.

Most strikingly, in contrast to the loners or near-loners who populate much detective fiction by white women, most of the black women detectives are deeply connected to community and perceive themselves as implicated in, and to some degree created by, that community's history. All of the detectives except Ginny Kelly are depicted as having intense, long-lasting friendships with other black women; these relationships are both personal and political and never fraught with the kind of suspicion of intimacy and interdependence seen in the series featuring white female detectives. Furthermore, while few white women detectives are depicted as having primary responsibility for children during the course of the series in which they feature, with the exception of a few "cozy" series in the 1990s, the reverse is true in mystery fiction by black women. Neely's Blanche is raising her niece and nephew on her own; Bland's Marti has two children and an informal co-mothering arrangement with her housemate and friend, Sharon; and Wesley's Tamara Hayle has a teenage son who figures largely in the first novel of the series. Hardboiled novels in which the detective is a black female single parent are truly something new, and they are far more radical in their reconsideration of the detective's role, character, and voice than any of the white female hardboiled books.

In addition to the reworking of detective fiction from an African-American female detective's position, several white women writers have begun experimenting further with the genre. The most notable of these is Liza Cody, who has put her Anna Lee series aside after six books and invented an extraordinary character, Eva Wylie, the likes of whom has not been seen before in detective fiction.

While many of the other women detectives share a few conventionally feminine characteristics—such as physical attractiveness, sex appeal, and the like—Eva is absolutely devoid of the feminine. She is huge, totally unladylike, and ugly. Her career goal is to be the foremost female wrestler in Britain, and in the first book focusing on her, *Bucket Nut* (1993), she fights as the London Lassassin. A member of the underclass, Eva lives on the farther reaches of society, working as a night security guard for an auto yard, where she lives in a borrowed trailer, and as a runner for a small-time gangster. Her mother is a sometime prostitute who gave her children to her own mother to raise and who had no objection when they were taken by the state at their grandmother's death.

Eva grew up in, and frequently ran away from, a number of foster homes and detention centers. Eva's first-person narratives detail her often illegal activities in a distinctive voice. For instance, she quite enjoys participating in a bar melee that begins with a police raid and a bar patron's throwing a can of gas: "Well, you can imagine, can't you? Everyone screaming, and coughing and weeping and running every which way. Tables and chairs sent flying, broken glass. Now that's what I call anarchy. 'Nobody move!' the Fueherer [police] yelled at the seething mob. How stupid can you be? . . . Laugh? I thought I'd never stop" (*Bucket Nut,* 1993 ed., p. 37). Eva sees Anna Lee herself (who plays a minor role in the series) as the enemy, no different from the police and the other authority figures she hates. The three Eva Wylie books published thus far suggest ways in which the more mainstream female detectives meet precisely the gender requirements that their narratives suggest they violate.

At the same time as these new voices entered the ranks of female detectives, a number of the important series begun in the 1980s continued. Muller's Sharon McCone series by the late 1990s included eighteen novels, and the detective had changed considerably in the novels published in the 1990s. She had established what appears to be an enduring romantic relationship with an ecological activist, Hy Ripinsky, who is also a pilot, an experienced investigator, and a man with a past shrouded in mystery. Several of these McCone novels trace her movement out of the All Souls legal cooperative and into a business of her own, her becoming a pilot, and her attempts to reconcile with her extended family. The Sharon McCone of the 1990s was quite different from the detective Muller first created: older, more socially conservative, more business-oriented, less tough in voice and in stance. Sara Paretsky's V. I. Warshawski had not changed as much, and the novels in that series tended to link a particular crime to broader social conditions, but her voice, too, had altered somewhat. Novels of the 1990s, such as *Tunnel Vision* (1994), tended to be more densely written than the earlier books, with V. I. less prone to wisecracks and more given to extended, philosophical reflections.

In contrast, Kinsey Millhone had changed little from *"A" Is for Alibi* to *"M" Is for Malice* (1996), although readers certainly learned more about her and some of her circumstances had changed. In *"J" Is for Judgment* (1993), Kinsey began to find out more about her extended family, after a cousin got in touch with her, and this family connection—an extremely troubled one—continued as a plot element in later books. The later books also trace a romance, albeit not one involving Kinsey: instead, her landlord's brother, William, falls in love with and eventually marries Rosie, the owner of Kinsey's neighborhood restaurant and bar. Kinsey herself developed an ongoing—with a long interruption—relationship with Robert Dietz, a security consultant she hired to protect her from a contract hit in *"G" Is for Gumshoe* (1990). The books in which Dietz figures were few, however, and the romance was quite muted; still very much in the foreground was the mystery plot.

The moods of Grafton's novels in the 1990s varied considerably from one another, with only Kinsey's distinctive voice unifying the series. The contrast in mood and tone between *"K" Is for Killer* (1994) and *"L" Is for*

Lawless (1995) is especially striking. To date, *"K"* is the darkest, most disturbing of the Kinsey Millhone books, concerned with family betrayals and with what happens to the survivors when a death goes unavenged. It includes, as Kinsey's client, a mother obsessed with her daughter's murder. Kinsey's own actions in this novel are disturbing, to readers and to herself. At the end of the novel she sets up a murderer to be killed, much as V. I. Warshawski does in *Killing Orders,* but she instantly regrets her decision. *"K"* ends with Kinsey's question, "Having strayed into the shadows, can I find my way back?" (p. 285).

"L" suggests that the answer is yes, because, as yet, this is the only entirely light-hearted caper in the entire series. There is no murder until the very end, which is quite unusual for Grafton; also unusual is that this novel focuses on an investigation that Kinsey takes on as a favor for a friend (her landlord, Henry) and for which she is not paid. What begins as a seemingly simple attempt to obtain death benefits on behalf of a veteran's survivors turns into an odyssey across much of the United States, with Kinsey hanging around with a pair of criminals who think they are Bonnie and Clyde but who act like members of the gang that couldn't shoot straight. *"L" Is for Lawless* seems like an experiment in a slightly different genre for Grafton and includes many elements not found in other books in the series. Even in these two very different books, Kinsey's voice remains the same as ever; wisecracking, tough, and spare.

One of Kinsey's most marked personality traits is her ease with lying. In *"K" Is for Killer*, she gets a confession out of a young woman by implying that their conversation is confidential and then makes it clear that she plans to reveal what the woman said. The woman is furious at this betrayal and says, "You said you wouldn't *tell*," to which Kinsey responds, "I didn't actually say that, but if I did, I lied. I'm really a wretched person. I'm sorry you didn't understand that. Now get out of my car" (p. 258). Kinsey is, of course, not a wretched person. She is no lady, either, nor an honorary man, but a funny, smart, tough, independent female detective. With her, Grafton provides readers with a worthy successor to the male hard-boiled detectives and to Nancy Drew; Kinsey is what Nancy might have been had she been born later and allowed to grow up.

Selected Bibliography

FEMALE DETECTIVE WRITERS

WORK OF M. F. BEAL

Angel Dance. Freedom, Calif.: Crossing Press, 1977.

WORK OF ELEANOR TAYLOR BLAND

Slow Burn. New York: St. Martin's Press, 1993.

WORKS OF LIZA CODY

Dupe. New York: Scribners, 1981; Warner 1983.
Headcase. London: Collins, 1985; New York: Scribners, 1986.
Under Contract. London: Collins, 1986; New York: Scribners, 1987.
Bucket Nut. New York: Doubleday, 1993; Warner, 1995.
Musclebound. New York: Mysterious Press, 1997.

WORKS OF AMANDA CROSS

In the Last Analysis. New York: Macmillan, 1964; Avon, 1966.
The James Joyce Murder. New York: Macmillan, 1967; Ballantine, 1982.
Poetic Justice. New York: Knopf, 1970; Avon, 1972.

WORKS OF SUSAN DUNLAP

Karma. New York: St. Martin's Press, 1981.
Too Close to the Edge. New York: St. Martin's Press, 1987.
A Dinner to Die For. New York: St. Martin's Press, 1987.
Pious Deception. New York: Villard, 1989.
Diamond in the Buff. New York: St. Martin's Press, 1990.
Death and Taxes. New York: Delacorte, 1992.
Time Expired. New York: Delacorte, 1993.
High Fall. New York: Delacorte, 1994.

WORKS OF KATHERINE V. FORREST

Amateur City. Tallahassee: Naiad Press, 1984.
Murder at the Nightwood Bar. Tallahassee: Naiad Press, 1987.
Murder by Tradition. Tallahassee: Naiad Press, 1991.

WORKS OF SUE GRAFTON

"A" Is for Alibi. New York: Holt, Rinehart, and Winston, 1982; Bantam, 1987.
"B" Is for Burglar. New York: Holt, Rinehart, and Winston, 1985; Bantam, 1986.
"C" Is for Corpse. New York: Henry Holt, 1986.
"D" Is for Deadbeat. New York: Henry Holt, 1987.
"E" Is for Evidence. New York: Henry Holt, 1988.
"F" Is for Fugitive. New York: Henry Holt, 1989.
"G" Is for Gumshoe. New York: Henry Holt, 1990.
"H" Is for Homicide. New York: Henry Holt, 1991.
"I" Is for Innocent. New York: Henry Holt, 1992.
"J" Is for Judgment. New York: Henry Holt, 1993.
"K" Is for Killer. New York: Henry Holt, 1994.
"L" Is for Lawless. New York: Henry Holt, 1995.
"M" Is for Malice. New York: Henry Holt, 1996.

WORKS OF P. D. JAMES

An Unsuitable Job for a Woman. London: Faber, 1972.
The Skull Beneath the Skin. New York: Scribners, 1982.

WORKS OF MARCIA MULLER

Edwin of the Iron Shoes. New York: David McKay, 1977.
Ask the Cards a Question. New York: St. Martin's Press, 1982.
The Tree of Death. New York: Walker, 1983.
Games to Keep the Dark Away. New York: St. Martin's Press, 1984.
The Cavalier in White. New York: St. Martin's Press, 1986.
There's Something in a Sunday. New York: Mysterious Press, 1989.
Where Echoes Live. New York: Mysterious Press, 1991.
The Broken Promise Land. New York: Mysterious Press, 1996.
Both Ends of the Night. New York: Mysterious Press, 1997.

WORKS OF BARBARA NEELY

Blanche on the Lam. New York: St. Martin's Press, 1992.
Blanche Among the Talented Tenth. New York: St. Martin's Press, 1994.
Blanche Cleans Up. New York: St. Martin's Press, 1998.

WORKS OF LILLIAN O'DONNELL

The Phone Calls. New York: Putnam, 1972.
No Business Being a Cop. New York: Putnam, 1979.
Ladykiller. New York: Putnam, 1984.

WORKS OF SARA PARETSKY

Indemnity Only. New York: Dial, 1982; Ballantine, 1983.
Killing Orders. New York: Morrow, 1985; Ballantine, 1986.
Blood Shot. New York: Delacorte, 1988.
Tunnel Vision. New York: Delacorte, 1994.

WORKS OF NANCY PICKARD

Generous Death. N.p., 1984; Arlington Heights, Ill.: Dark Harvest, 1992.

But I Wouldn't Want to Die There. New York: Pocket Books, 1993.

Confession. New York: Pocket Books, 1994.

Twilight. New York: Pocket Books, 1995.

WORKS OF BARBARA WILSON

Murder in the Collective. Seattle: Seal Press, 1984.

Sisters of the Road. Seattle: Seal Press, 1986.

The Dog-Collar Murders. Seattle: Seal Press, 1989.

Gaudi Afternoon. Seattle: Seal Press, 1990.

Trouble in Transylvania. Seattle: Seal Press, 1993.

WORK OF MARGARET TAYLER YATES

The Hush-Hush Murders. New York: Macmillan, 1937.

BIOGRAPHICAL AND CRITICAL STUDIES

Campbell, Sue Ellen. "The Detective Heroine and the Death of Her Hero: Dorothy Sayers to P. D. James." *Modern Fiction Studies* 29, no. 3: 497–510 (1983).

Chandler, Raymond. *The Simple Art of Murder.* New York: Ballantine, 1972.

Christianson, Scott. "Talkin' Trash and Kickin' Butt: Sue Grafton's Hard-Boiled Feminism." In *Feminism in Women's Detective Fiction.* Edited by Glenwood Irons. Toronto: University of Toronto Press, 1995.

Grella, George. "The Hard-Boiled Detective Novel." In *Detective Fiction: A Collection of Critical Essays.* Edited by Robin W. Winks. Englewood Cliffs, N.J.: Prentice-Hall, 1980; Woodstock, Vt.: Countryman Press, 1988.

Heilbrun, Carolyn. *Reinventing Womanhood.* New York: Norton, 1979.

Heising, Willetta L. *Detecting Women 2: A Reader's Guide and Checklist for Mystery Series Written by Women.* Dearborn, Mich.: Purple Moon Press, 1996.

Klein, Kathleen Gregory. *The Woman Detective: Gender and Genre.* Urbana: University of Illinois Press, 1988; rev. ed., 1995.

Mason, Bobbie Ann. *The Girl Sleuth: A Feminist Guide.* Old Westbury, N.Y.: Feminist Press, 1975.

Munt, Sally R. *Murder by the Book? Feminism and the Crime Novel.* New York: Routledge, 1994.

Nixon, Nicola. "Gray Areas: P. D. James's Unsuiting of Cordelia." In *Feminism in Women's Detective Fiction.* Edited by Glenwood Irons. Toronto: University of Toronto Press, 1995.

O'Brien, Geoffrey. *Hard-Boiled America.* New York: Van Nostrand Reinhold, 1981.

"Paretsky, Sara." In *Contemporary Authors,* vol. 129. Edited by Susan M. Trosky. Detroit: Gale, 1990. Pp. 334–337.

Pennell, Jane. "The Female Detective: Pre- and Post-Women's Lib." *Clues* 6, no. 2: 85–98 (1985).

Reddy, Maureen T. *Sisters in Crime: Feminism and the Crime Novel.* New York: Continuum, 1988.

Sayers, Dorothy L. "Introduction." *The Art of the Mystery Story: A Collection of Critical Essays.* Edited by Howard Haycraft. New York: Simon & Schuster, 1946; New York: Biblio and Tannen, 1976.

Stowe, William W. "Hard-Boiled Virgil: Early Nineteenth-Century Beginnings of a Popular Literary Formula." In *The Sleuth and the Scholar: Origins, Evolution, and Current Trends in Detective Fiction.* Edited by Barbara A. Rader and Howard G. Zettler. New York: Greenwood Press, 1988.

Taylor, Bruce. "G Is for (Sue) Grafton." *Armchair Detective* 22: 4–13 (winter 1989).

INTERNET RESOURCE

The Sisters in Crime web page can be accessed at www.books.com/sinc/home.htm

GAY AND LESBIAN MYSTERY FICTION

ANTHONY SLIDE

IN 1970, A NEW-STYLE private detective was introduced in the tall, lean, blond-haired, blue-eyed frame of Dave Brandstetter. Brandstetter is well educated, well dressed, worldly-wise, witty—and gay. But there is no similarity between Brandstetter and the stereotypical homosexual characters to be found in most earlier mystery novels. He is masculine, a hard drinker (Glenlivet whiskey preferred), a heavy smoker, and distasteful of such brazen homosexual traits as effeminacy, love of Judy Garland, and S&M.

Mainstream Publishers and the "New" Gay Detective

Dave Brandstetter was the creation of Joseph Hansen, at the time a closeted gay man, who had cofounded a homosexual periodical, *Tangents*, and authored nine gay novels under the name "James Colton." One of those early works, *Known Homosexual* (1968), reprinted in 1984 as *Pretty Boy Dead*, is a murder mystery concerned with a young white man, leading a double or triple life, implicated in the death of his African-American male lover. It is patently aimed at the gay market and far removed from the Brandstetter novels, which were written with a mainstream audience in mind and with a singular lack of explicit ho-

mosexual love scenes. The novels may have gay themes, often involving men leading duplicitous lives, but Brandstetter and the novel's other gay characters could easily be cast as heterosexual without the plotlines losing any of their originality.

At the same time, Joseph Hansen does not shy away from providing his hero with lovers. The first Dave Brandstetter novel, *Fadeout*, published by Harper & Row in 1970, does not reveal the hero's sexual preference until the sixth chapter, but once exposed, much is made of Brandstetter's sex life. We learn that his former lover, Rod Fleming, whom he met in 1945, has died of cancer. For the first, and almost only, time in any of the novels, Brandstetter has a one-night stand—with a Mexican kid infatuated with the investigator—but at *Fadeout*'s close, Brandstetter has a new lover, Dave Sawyer, a Rod Fleming substitute, who remains with him through the fifth novel, *Skinflick* (1979). In the next book, *Gravedigger* (1982), Brandstetter begins a relationship with a young black television journalist, Cecil Harris, whom he met in the fourth novel, *The Man Everybody Was Afraid Of* (1978), and, despite some bumpy patches, the two remain together to the end.

The twelve novels and one collection of short stories, *Brandstetter and Others: Five Fictions* (1984), featuring Dave Brandstetter form a collective whole. The supporting players, including Captain Ken Barker and Lieutenant Jefferson Leppard of the Los Angeles Police Department, attorney Abe Greenglass, restaurateur Max Romano, and Brandstetter's best friend, lesbian Madge Dunstan, remain the same. Brandstetter works as an investigator for his father's insurance company until the latter's death forces him to set up business on his own in *Skinflick*. The Los Angeles of the novels is Chandleresque, often dark and dangerous, and yet Brandstetter regularly escapes from that ambience to the security of his Laurel Canyon home, to good food, good music, good company, and good whiskey.

Homosexuality, often closeted, is a primary focus of the plotlines. A radio personality is apparently shot by his lover in *Fadeout*. A gay son is behind the murder of his book-dealer father in *Death Claims* (1973). A mother returns home to find her son's body—and his gay lover holding a gun—in *Troublemaker* (1975). A gay activist is accused of the murder of a homophobe in *The Man Everybody Was Afraid Of*. Brandstetter investigates the death of a right-wing bigot in *Skinflick*. A gay father claims his daughter is the victim of a mass murderer in *Gravedigger*. An elderly gay man with a penchant for female attire is the central character in *Nightwork* (1984). The serial killing of AIDS sufferers is the subject of *Early Graves* (1987). Only in *The Little Dog Laughed* (1986), *Obedience* (1988), *The Boy Who Was Buried This Morning* (1990), and *A Country of Old Men* (1991) does homosexuality play a secondary role.

Like his creator, Dave Brandstetter was born in 1923. He grows old with the novels but never, apparently, loses his sexual attraction to other gay men. Throughout the series, Brandstetter is constantly confronted by scantily clad or naked young men, often—a favorite expression with Hansen—"kicking into their pants." Even in his sixties, Brandstetter is propositioned by naked men in their twenties. In *A Country of Old Men*, a naked young musician attempts a seduction of the hero, only to be rejected with "a light kiss on his mouth" (p. 163). By this last novel, Brandstetter's energies are fading. He is approaching

seventy, and his lover, Cecil Harris, notes, "We don't do a lot of loving any more, do we?" (p. 133). As Hansen has commented, a writer must pay for allowing his character to age naturally, and the price in the Brandstetter series is the hero's death from a massive heart attack at the close of *A Country of Old Men*. That both gay and straight readers can feel sorrow at such a parting is indicative of Joseph Hansen's ability to create and nurture a gay hero whose lifestyle is acceptable and nonthreatening to all.

A decade after the appearance of Dave Brandstetter, another gay private eye, Don Strachey, was introduced to a mainstream readership by Richard Lipez (b. 1938), writing as Richard Stevenson. Strachey is based in Albany, New York. Like Brandstetter, he is in his forties when the series begins, and, like his creator, Strachey had been married prior to coming out. As with Brandstetter, Strachey has a lover, the long-suffering Timothy "Timmy" Callahan, who must deal not only with the physical dangers his partner insists on facing but also with Strachey's wandering penis, which is brought fully under control only in response to the threat of AIDS.

The central theme of all the Don Strachey novels is homophobia, which, the author notes, does such awful things to people, straight and gay. In the first novel, *Death Trick* (1981), published by St. Martin's Press, Strachey is hired by a homophobic couple to locate their gay son, implicated in the murder of another gay man. In *On the Other Hand, Death* (1984), Strachey must contend with threats against two aging lesbians and the kidnapping of a fanatical gay-rights organizer and his lover. The complex plot of *Ice Blues* (1986) involves the theft of two-and-a-half-million dollars by a gay man intent on buying votes in order to bring about a liberal political climate in Albany. Outing, an activity of which Strachey does not approve, is the subject matter of *Third Man Out* (1992), while the murder of one gay man by another is the topic of *Shock to the System* (1995). When a liberal-minded family decides to sell the family newspaper in *Chain of Fools* (1996), Strachey becomes involved, influenced by Timmy's having been the lover of one family member back in high school and another family member's being a lesbian.

Unlike Joseph Hansen, Richard Stevenson does not avoid sexual encounters in his novels—Strachey has a well-described one-night stand with an aging drag queen in *Death Trick*—but throughout, the primary sexual theme is the relationship between Strachey and Timmy. Timmy wants their commitment to be permanent and monogamous, which Strachey feels may result in the pair's playing Ozzie and Harriet. Despite the serious issues raised in his books, Stevenson never loses his sense of humor, and he demonstrates a unique ability to write erotic love scenes without getting into detail or description of body parts. He forces the reader, gay or straight, to confront issues affecting the gay community, from AIDS to activism, and to realize that there is often no easy, convenient, politically correct response. A gay character is often in the wrong, and, for example, in *Ice Blues*, Strachey and Timmy accept that stolen money cannot be used to influence politics, no matter how worthy the objective (not that the source prevents their donating it to a good cause—in this case, an AIDS fund-raising organization).

Humor was a major factor in the original popularity of the four novels—*Vermilion* (1980), *Cobalt* (1982), *Slate* (1984), and *Canary* (1986)—written by Michael McDowell (b. 1950) and the late Dennis Schuetz under the pseudonym of Nathan Aldyne and published by Avon Books. The central character here is a Boston-based barman, Daniel Valentine, who teams up with a straight real-estate agent, Clarisse Lovelace, to become the Nick and Nora Charles of gay mystery fiction. The pair, who had a brief sexual liaison before Valentine discovered his true sexual identity, inhabit a witty if cynical gay world, in which drug use and casual sex are the norm in a pre-AIDS era.

In the compelling first novel, *Vermilion*, Nathan Aldyne featured a straight police lieutenant who is introduced to the gay S&M scene—and who thus discovers what it is like to be on the receiving end of brutality. Such sophistication and outrageous plotlines are singularly lacking in the work of two more-recent gay writers of gay mystery fiction, Grant Michaels and Mark Richard Zubro. Although the Boston police lieutenant in Grant Michaels' initial novel, *A Body to Die For* (1990), would appear at first to be the answer to a gay man's dreams, the character fails to develop. A gay Chicago police officer, Paul Turner, is the likable—and refreshingly non-promiscuous—central figure in one series of novels by Zubro, beginning with *Sorry Now?* (1991). Zubro's main body of work, however, beginning with *A Simple Suburban Murder* (1989), stars hero Tom Mason, who, like his creator, is an Illinois schoolteacher, and who lives out every gay man's fantasy by cohabiting with a professional football player. The couple are at least nonstereotypical, which is more than can be said for Grant Michaels' hero, Stan Kraychick, an effeminate women's hairdresser.

The best of the new gay, mainstream mystery writers, and a worthy successor to Joseph Hansen, is Michael Nava (b. 1954). A sensitive and inventive novelist, Nava is not unwilling to take on a controversial issue such as pedophilia, as he does in *How Town* (1990), and the tragedy of a slow, painful death from AIDS in *The Hidden Law* (1992). Nava has worked as a deputy city attorney in Los Angeles and as a lawyer in private practice, and his central character, Henry Rios, is a young, gay, Hispanic lawyer, introduced in *The Little Death* (1986) as a lawyer with the public defender's office in Los Angeles.

Nava is concerned as much with characterization as with plot, and his stories are heavily influenced by the hero's personal life and by his past sexual encounters. The short-term lover of Henry Rios is murdered in *The Little Death*. In *Goldenboy* (1988), Rios is hired to defend a young man accused of murdering a coworker who threatened to expose his homosexuality, and he takes a fellow coworker of his client, a dozen or more years his junior, as a lover. In *How Town*, Rios defends a childhood friend and convicted child molester on a murder charge. Rios had a childhood crush on the accused man's brother, and he must come to terms not only with his earlier life, but also, and more important, with the issue of pedophilia. Just as the pedophile is attracted to children because "they taste different, they smell different" (p. 54), so must Rios acknowledge that his sexual interest in a bodybuilding policeman is based as much on the man's childlike, round, pretty face as his physique and personality. "They taste different, they smell different—" six words that separate men from boys—or do they?

With *The Hidden Law*, Michael Nava allows the plotline, involving a Chicano state senator, to take a secondary role to the relationship between Rios and his young lover dying of AIDS. The lover cannot live with someone who is not diseased as he is, who cannot understand the pain and suffering he is experiencing, and so leaves Rios for a fellow AIDS sufferer and ACT-UP activist. In many respects, *The Hidden Law* is a transitional novel, moving Nava away from the mystery genre to the personal, testamentary novel.

The past again intrudes on Henry Rios as *The Death of Friends* (1996) begins with an earthquake. His life is further shaken by the death of an old friend, Supreme Court judge Chris Chandler, with whom Rios had an affair while the two were at law school, but whose past is hidden from his wife. At the novel's conclusion, Rios discovers that the judge had AIDS and sees his former lover die.

Incubators: Small Presses and Gay Mystery Fiction

Nava has commented that "my first two books were more subconsciously for a gay audience. . . . Now I'm writing books for people who want to identify with what I write about, regardless of what they call themselves" (Slide, p. 131). Prior to making the jump to a mainstream publisher (Harper & Row) with *How Town*, Michael Nava was one of a select group of gay authors published by Boston-based Alyson Publications. Founded in 1980 by Sasha Alyson, the company has helped find an audience for gay writers of both fiction and nonfiction.

In 1989 Nava edited an anthology of short stories of mystery and suspense for Alyson, *Finale*, which highlighted a number of writers whose work was aimed strictly at the gay or lesbian market. The collection includes work by Samuel M. Steward (1909–1993), who also wrote as Phil Andros; Steward is the author of two mystery novels for Alyson, *Murder Is Murder Is Murder* (1985) and *The Caravaggio Shawl* (1989), both featuring a gay American college professor, presumably based on the author, who serves as a "legman" for the unlikely sleuthing team of Gertrude Stein and Alice B. Toklas. The Alyson mysteries offer graphic sex aplenty, including a murder clue of a unique double-condom device for positioning on two men at the same time in *The Butterscotch Prince* by Richard Hall, the pen name of Richard Hirshfeld (1926–1992), who also contributed to *Finale*. The central character of *The Butterscotch Prince* (first published in 1975 and reprinted by Alyson in 1983), is a black, gay, New York schoolteacher, and the novel has much to do with the coming-out process, well told against a background of New York gay culture.

Katherine V. Forrest (b. 1939) is the only other writer of book-length fiction included in *Finale*, but, aside from Nava, she is the most important. Beginning with *Amateur City* (1984), Forrest has authored a series of mysteries featuring Los Angeles police detective Kate Delafield. She is a lesbian who has studied law and served with the military in Vietnam, and, like Dave Brandstetter, her lover of many years has recently died. A cold woman, Delafield has little to do with the lesbian activist scene. Her first major introduction to it occurs in the second novel, *Murder at the Nightwood Bar* (1987), in which Delafield investigates the killing of a nineteen-year-old woman in the parking lot of a lesbian bar. The novel is, as Forrest has written, the cornerstone of the series, in which a number of emotional issues facing lesbians are discussed openly and with sincerity, and in which Delafield comes to terms with her own sexuality.

The Hollywood blacklist and its impact form the background to Forrest's third novel, *The Beverly Malibu* (1989), in which the author takes time out to honor Lillian Hellman. "Gay bashing" in its most insidious form— the rationalization that one man is justified in killing another because he is gay and supposedly coming on to the murderer—is the subject of *Murder by Tradition* (1991). It is also the novel in which Delafield takes a lover, Aimee Grant, whom she met at the Beverly Malibu apartment building. Aimee persuades Delafield to face up to her past, and to the war years in Vietnam, by attending a reunion in Washington, D.C., in *Liberty Square* (1996). Writing with assurance and the skill of a first-rate novelist whose sexual preference is an irrelevance, Katherine V. Forrest turns out her finest work to date, delving into the past to discuss the issue of gays and lesbians in the military—and more precisely, in Vietnam, where they were more welcome than in the America of the Clinton administration. Delafield and Forrest more than hold their own outside of the familiar milieu of Los Angeles, and the final chapter at the Vietnam Memorial is one of the most poignant to be found in gay and lesbian fiction.

Liberty Square was written for the crime fiction imprint of a mainstream publisher, Berkley. Katherine V. Forrest's other mystery novels, as well as her many books outside of the genre, were published by the Naiad Press, where for many years she was senior fiction editor. Founded in 1973 by Barbara Grier and Donna J. McBride, the Naiad Press is the largest publisher of mystery fiction for the lesbian market. Its writers and their novels are indicative of a national and international lesbian readership. Nikki Baker (b. 1962) is a black lesbian mystery writer whose Virginia Kelly novels, beginning with *In the Game* (1991), illuminate the problems of being a gay woman of color in the 1990s. The issue of being lesbian and a Native American was ad-

dressed by Jeane Harris (b. 1948) in her second novel, *Delia Ironfoot* (1992). Maine is the setting for the novels of Karen Saum (b. 1935), beginning with *Murder Is Relative* (1990) and praiseworthy for their skillful, thoughtful rendering of the main character, a fifty-two-year-old lesbian who is also a recovering alcoholic.

Vicki P. McConnell was Naiad's first lesbian writer of lesbian mystery fiction, introducing her heroine, Nyla Wade, in *Mrs. Porter's Letter* (1982). The settings vary, but the plotlines are invariably silly and heavily influenced by the gothic romance. Similarly, the mystery novels of Pat Welch, beginning with *Murder by the Book* (1990), are contrived, although the author uses her Berkeley, California, setting to advantage.

Old-fashioned in construction but as substantial as the best of the mainstream mystery novels are the books of Jaye Maiman (b. 1957), who introduced her New York–based heroine, Robin Miller, in *I Left My Heart* (1991). The central figure in *Introducing Amanda Valentine* (1992), by Rose Beecham (b. 1958), is a former member of the New York police department, currently living and working in Wellington, New Zealand. While searching for a serial killer, Valentine proves a likable heroine, one with potential appeal to a mainstream audience. Also from the same part of the world is Inspector Carol Ashton of Sydney, Australia. Introduced by Claire McNab in *Lessons in Murder* (1988), Ashton meets her lover, Sybil Quade, when Sybil is a suspect in the brutal murder of a schoolteacher. Like all of the books from the Naiad Press, the Claire McNab novels are heavy in explicit sexual situations. Nonetheless, with Katherine V. Forrest, Claire McNab is the best mystery writer developed so far by Naiad.

Other lesbian publishing houses also have their mystery writers. New Victoria Publishers, founded in 1975, is responsible for a series of novels by Sarah Dreher, featuring travel agent Stoner McTavish, introduced in a book of that name in 1985. Another New Victoria writer is J. M. Redmann (b. 1955), whose heroine, a lesbian and self-described "fuck-up" named Michele "Mickey" Knight, is a New

Orleans private investigator who speaks in the manner of a hard-boiled detective from the 1930s or 1940s. Knight was introduced in *Death by the Riverside* (1990) and is also featured in *Deaths of Jocasta* (1992) and *The Intersection of Law and Desire* (1995).

In 1976 the Seal Press was founded by Faith Conlon and Barbara Wilson, and Seal has published two series of mystery novels by Wilson. The central character in the first series is Pamela Nilsen, who, like her creator, lives in Seattle; she is introduced in *Murder in the Collective* (1984) as the owner of a printshop; Nilsen and Wilson are at their best in *The Dog Collar Murders* (1989), which takes on the heavy subjects of S&M and pornography. The second series features Cassandra Reilly, whose work as a translator permits her to travel around the world. In *Gaudí Afternoon* (1990), she is in Barcelona, Spain, and in *Trouble in Transylvania* (1993), she is waylaid in Budapest while on her way to catch the Trans-Mongolian Express in China.

Banned Books, founded in 1985 by Benjamin Eakins, has published a series of mysteries by Antoinette Azolakov (b. 1944), all starring a self-described "butch dyke" named Cass Milam. Ms. Milam, who likes "a dyke who looks like a dyke," is not perhaps every reader's cup of tea, but she certainly gets results far more quickly than Miss Marple.

Canadian novelist Eve Zaremba was published by a variety of small presses before signing with Second Story for *Uneasy Lies* (1990), which was followed by *The Butterfly Effect* (1994). Her books are tightly worded and constructed, and all feature Helen Keremos, a Vancouver, British Columbia–based lesbian private investigator. Keremos was introduced—hired by a Manitoba professor to find his missing gay son—in *A Reason to Kill* (1978), which is perhaps most remarkable for its puzzling reluctance to clearly label the heroine as a lesbian.

Canadian publisher Gynergy Books has brought out four novels by Jackie Manthorpe (b. 1946), featuring a rather stereotypical lesbian gym teacher from Montreal named Harriet "Harry" Hubley. The first book, *Ghost Motel* (1994) has more to do with metaphysics than mystery. Both Hubley and her lover, Judy, have affairs on the side, while "Harry" investigates the death of an elderly, lesbian motel keeper. *Ghost Motel* was followed by *Deadly Reunion* (1995), *Last Resort* (1995), and *Final Take* (1996).

Firebrand Books, founded in 1984 by Nancy Bereano, publishes Shirley Shea (b. 1924), writing as Marion Foster. Her lesbian heroine, Mrs. Harriet Fordham Croft, is a Canadian attorney of indeterminate age, introduced in *The Monarchs Are Flying* (1987). There is more than a touch of Perry Mason to be found in Mrs. Croft, who discovered her own sexuality late in life, and *The Monarchs Are Flying* includes a major courtroom trial in which Croft defends a young lesbian reporter accused of murdering her ex-lover.

Felice Picano (b. 1944), who created the Gay Presses of New York in 1980, is the author of the mainstream novel *The Lure* (1979), in which a supposedly straight sociology professor is persuaded to pose as a gay man in order to help the police trap a homosexual killer. The basic notion is absurd—why did not the police use a gay man?—and the plotline typifies many gay mystery novels written for a specialist audience in which a gay man's fantasies are fulfilled. In a similar vein, the heroes of Mel Keegan's *Ice Wind and Fire* (1990) are captured by modern-day slave traders in the West Indies, stripped, physically examined, and consigned to the auction block. The mystique of the cowboy is the central theme in *Cowboy Blues* (1985) by Stephen Lewis, in which a Los Angeles private detective is hired to find the missing boy-lover of a rodeo rider. A psychiatrist active in the S&M world is the hero in *Masters' Counterpoints* (1991) and *One for the Master, Two for the Fool* (1992) by Larry Townsend (b. 1935). In the first, he investigates the kidnapping of various heterosexual young men, all of whom are sexually tortured.

Also intended for a gay audience, but at a more intellectual level, are two novels by Jack Ricardo (b. 1940): *Death with Dignity* (1991), which deals with homosexuality in relationship to the Catholic Church, and *The Night G.A.A. Died* (1992), in which a CIA-FBI investigator infiltrates the Gay Activists Alliance in 1971 and recognizes his own homosexuality. British television personality Jeremy Beadle lives a double life as the author of a series of accomplished mystery novels for the Gay Men's Press. Both *Death Scene* (1988) and *Doing Business* (1990) provide a vivid portrait of London's gay scene, with the latter demonstrating a grim fascination for London's rent boys (hustlers) and the Soho pubs they frequent. The lengths to which gay men in prominent positions will go in order to hide their sexuality is the subject of British author W. Stephen Gilbert's *Spiked* (1991), another first-rate "gay" mystery novel, again with a rent boy playing a prominent part.

First Glances: Early Gay and Lesbian Images

The earliest documented mystery story with a lesbian character is "La fille aux yeux d'or" ("The Girl with the Golden Eyes") by Honoré de Balzac (1799–1850), one of the linked stories in *Histoire des treize* (1834; published in English as *The Thirteen*, 1901). Set in the Paris of the early 1800s, where "everything is tolerated," the story has as its central character Henri de Marsay. He becomes infatuated with Paquita Valdès, "the girl with the golden eyes," only to discover at her death that she is the lover of his half-sister Euphémie. The story also contains a hint of male homosexuality, with Henri described as "the prettiest boy in Paris" and enjoying a close relationship with another young man, "a giddy youth," named Paul de Manerville. The gay connotation may be questionable, if somewhat influenced by the suggestion that Balzac was homosexual, but there can be no argument, as critic Jacques Barzun has noted, that "The Girl with the Golden Eyes" is "a brilliant study of lesbianism combined with predatory instincts" (Barzun and Taylor, p. 29).

The earliest gay character on record in a mystery novel is possibly John Jasper in *The Mystery of Edwin Drood* (1870) by Charles Dickens (1812–1870). Critic Eve Kosofsky Sedgwick has identified an "erotic triangle" between the three principal characters, Jasper, Edwin Drood, and Rosa Bud, pointing out that "there are passages between the two men that sound like outtakes from Shakespeare's Sonnets" (p. 181). Certainly there are clues pointing to the homosexuality of Jasper, a choirmaster who enjoys the company of young men. Many early mystery writers link drugs with homosexuality, and Jasper is an opium addict. Dickens describes Jasper's devotion to Drood as "womanish," and the writer's failure to complete the novel leaves open the possibility that Edwin Drood was killed by John Jasper out of jealousy of the boy's love for Rosa Bud.

Of course, this homoerotic interpretation of *Edwin Drood* is subject to dispute. Furthermore, a strict constructionist might consider it an unwarranted invasion of privacy to contemplate a homosexual relationship between Sherlock Holmes and Dr. Watson, and find it equally outrageous to suggest that the relationship between the misogynistic Nero Wolfe and his handsome assistant Archie Goodwin in the novels of Rex Stout was anything other than platonic. A reader intent on defiling the realm of classic mystery fiction might infer improper behavior between Margery Allingham's Albert Campion and his manservant Lugg, between Dorothy L. Sayers' Lord Peter Wimsey and his faithful servant Bunter, between Agatha Christie's Hercule Poirot and his friend Captain Hastings; or question the nonmarital status of Christie's Miss Marple or Heron Carvic's Miss Seeton.

Nonetheless, Arthur Conan Doyle (see also separate essay on Doyle) did unequivocally contribute to the gay and lesbian mystery genre with one short story, "The Man with the Watches," first published in the *Strand* magazine, and reprinted in book form as the initial entry in *Round the Fire Stories* (1908). On a train from London to Manchester, a couple refuse to sit in the first compartment to which they are shown because the sole occupant is smoking a cigar. On the journey north, all three seemingly disappear. In their place is a young man with six watches on his person, shot to death. An American named James provides the solution to the mystery. The murdered man is his brother Edward, "one of the most beautiful creatures that ever lived," a spoiled mama's boy who had come under the influence of a criminal named Sparrow McCoy and had taken to wearing female attire in the pursuance of various illegal activities. The couple boarding the train were Edward and McCoy. The cigar-smoking passenger was James. James confronts his brother, telling him he will never make "a Mary Jane" of himself. McCoy and James fight, and Edward is accidentally shot. James permits McCoy to escape after the latter tells him, "You loved your brother, I've no doubt; but you didn't love him a cent more than I loved him, though you'll say that I took a queer way to show it." Although the story makes heavy use of euphemisms, there are more than enough clues to identify its two homosexuals.

John Buchan (1875–1940; see separate essay) uses a similar suggestiveness to label a homosexual character in the second Richard Hannay novel, *Greenmantle* (1916). The captive Hannay is taken by the German villain, Colonel Stumm, to his room. Hannay writes, "At first sight you would have said it was a woman's drawing-room. But it wasn't. I soon saw the difference. There had never been a woman's hand in that place. It was the room of a man who had a passion for frippery, who had a perverted taste for soft delicate things. . . . I began to see the queer other side to my host, that evil side which gossip had spoken of as not unknown in the German army" (p. 101). To his credit, Buchan does not embrace the obvious and dress his homosexual in female attire. He presents the reader with a nonstereotypical gay man who is ugly, violent, and strong, someone of whom Hannay can say at his death, "He was a brute and a bully, but, by God! he was a man" (p. 342).

To Englishman Richard Henry Sampson (1896–1973), writing as Richard Hull, goes the credit for introducing a gay leading man in a mystery novel. Unfortunately, his creation, Edward—who is the narrator as well as the lead in *The Murder of My Aunt* (1934)—is also repulsive, fat, greasy, self-indulgent, a would-be murderer, and, in the words of his Aunt Mildred, "a namby-pamby little pansy boy" (p. 193). Sampson himself was a confirmed bachelor, spending much of his life in the security of his all-male London club.

One generally looks in vain for a positive depiction of a gay or lesbian character in the mystery novels of the 1930s and 1940s. If mentioned at all, homosexual characters are generally disdained, and presented in as offensively stereotypical fashion, as are Jewish characters. *A Bullet in the Ballet* (1937), by Caryl Brahms (1901–1983) and S. J. Simon (d. 1948), notably departs from this tendency. The novel's two gay men are both murder victims, but the "homosexual" atmosphere in the novel is exceptionally relaxed and friendly, as befits the urbane and witty, if somewhat dated, style of its British coauthors—who, quite possibly, use the term "homosexual" for the first time in a mystery novel. Gore Vidal (b. 1925), who wrote three mystery novels under the pen name of Edgar Box, also viewed the ballet as a logical place to find gay men: *Death in the Fifth Position* (1952) has a ballet background, contains an amusing sequence at a gay bathhouse, and is arguably the first mystery novel to call a gay a gay. A gay ballet director is the murder victim in Haughton Murphy's *Murder Takes a Partner* (1987), and there is also a gay murder victim and other gay characters in Murphy's Reuben Frost mystery *A Very Venetian Murder* (1992).

The Pharaoh Love trilogy by George Baxt (b. 1923)—*A Queer Kind of Death* (1966), *Swing Low, Sweet Harriet* (1967), and *Topsy and Evil* (1968)—has historical importance not only in that it features an openly gay New York police detective, but also because this group of mainstream mystery novels is filled with gay jargon, puns, and witticisms. The initial offering is the best of the group, with its extraordinary ending, in which Pharaoh Love allows the murderer to go free on the promise that he will become his lover. (It is also perhaps the first work of mystery fiction with a Native American gay character.) The other two books are frankly ridiculous, with Pharaoh Love reappearing in *Topsy and Evil* as a transsexual.

After writing a number of mystery novels with Hollywood themes and often gay allusions—*The Tallulah Bankhead Murder Case* (1987), *The Talking Pictures Murder Case* (1990), and *The Greta Garbo Murder Case* (1992)—Baxt reintroduced Pharaoh Love in *A Queer Kind of Love* (1994). The flamboyant characterization was gone, and, mysteriously, Love was restored to his original male form. True to fashion, however, he does end the novel in bed with his homophobic detective partner.

Gay and Lesbian Portrayals by the Classic Mystery Writers

One of the grandes dames of British mystery writers, Gladys Mitchell (1901–1983), is responsible for introducing a major lesbian character to the modern mystery. *Speedy Death* (1929) marks the debut of the eccentric detective-heroine Mrs. (later Dame) Beatrice Adela Lestrange Bradley, who here must deal with the murder of a houseguest of the Bing family. The guest is engaged to the daughter of the household, Eleanor—and, at death, turns out to be a woman. It does not take long for Mrs. Bradley to determine what is going on. "Have you ever heard of sexual perversion?" she asks the chief constable (1988 ed., p. 105). When it becomes apparent that Eleanor is the murderess, Mrs. Bradley takes the law into her own hands and kills her. Apparently, such an outcome was reasonable, from the novel's point of view: Mrs. Bradley is acquitted at a trial where she is defended by her son. During her long and active writing career, Mitchell's draconian attitude toward gays and lesbians remained unchanged, as did the oblique language she used to make her

way around the subject. As late as *The Death-Cap Dancers* (1981), a detective-inspector comments on the relationship between an older and younger man, "There's a lot of that sort of thing about in these days, especially since the law was changed."

Gladys Mitchell's sisters in crime were equally homophobic. In *Flowers for the Judge* (1936), Margery Allingham (1904–1966) lets Albert Campion indulge in a spot of queer bashing when he encounters an unsavory young man (one of whose flaws is that he has no interest in women) tampering with evidence. A man who acts homosexual but proves to be a woman, and possibly a lesbian, appears to be a murder victim in *To Love and Be Wise* (1951), written by Elizabeth MacKintosh (1896–1952), under the pen name of Josephine Tey. "A queer set-up," as an investigating sergeant comments.

Agatha Christie (1890–1976; see separate essay) is less virulent in her prejudices than some of her sister writers, with her gay or lesbian characters generally unimportant or inexplicit. The occasional gay character can be found in the earlier novels; a retired antiquarian, Mr. Pye, in *The Moving Finger* (1942) is obviously homosexual, and two aging spinsters, Miss Hinchcliffe and Miss Murgatroyd, are most certainly a lesbian couple in *A Murder Is Announced* (1950). In *Nemesis* (1971), middle-aged Clotilde Bradbury-Scott murders her niece and lover, Verity Hunt, when she discovers that Verity plans to marry. In a curious confrontation, the unmarried and childless Miss Marple speaks to Bradbury-Scott of "the happiness of normality," pointing out that "a different kind of love" came into Verity's life when she met a young man, and that "she wanted to escape—to escape from the burden of the bondage of love she was living in with you. She wanted a normal woman's life" (p. 243).

The most homophobic of the female British mystery writers was Ngaio Marsh (1895–1982; see separate essay). Marsh basically ignored lesbians, but the male homosexuals who occasionally appear in her novels are equated with female impersonation and drug addiction. This dangerous stereotyping by Marsh links homosexuals directly to criminal elements in her society. Thus, she identifies gay men as what they were in the Britain of which she writes, an element of society that could be imprisoned for its behavior. A gay man into drugs is a supporting player in *When in Rome* (1971), but Marsh is at her queer-baiting best in *Singing in the Shrouds* (1958), wherein a ship's steward—described by Inspector Roderick Alleyn as "a queer little job"—enjoys dressing up as a woman, a foible that leads to his death. Oddly, many of the men in the books of Ngaio Marsh speak in such precious tones that it would be relatively easy to label most of them gay.

Ngaio Marsh is, however, hoisted with her own petard. Just as she perceives homosexuality in every drug user, a gay man can find inadvertent homosexual references throughout her texts. Just what is the reader to make of Alleyn's relationship with journalist Nigel Bathgate, with the two men talking to each other in such high camp fashion; of the two young, decidedly effeminate men with the darling names of Peregrine Jay and Jeremy Jones, living together in *Killer Dolphin* (1966); or of Alleyn's son, who is so affected in *Last Ditch* (1977) that he is accused of making a gay pass at another man.

Dorothy L. Sayers (1893–1957; see separate essay), by contrast, deserves limited credit for her depiction of lesbians, including murderess Nurse Mary Whittaker, in *Unnatural Death* (1927), published the following year in the United States as *The Dawson Pedigree*. The worst criticism that Sayers can summon up for lesbians, delivered by the heterosexual Miss Climpson, is that "It is natural for a school-girl to be shwärmerisch—in a young woman of twenty-two it is thoroughly undesirable."

There are no gay characters per se, but there is a strong homoerotic quality to be found, in the novels of J. I. M. Stewart (b. 1906), who also writes as Michael Innes (see separate essay). In *The Man from the Sea* (1955), the hero discovers a naked young man on the beach and races through the sand with him. The author writes of "a golden torso and a ripple of muscle under a fine skin" in describing a semi-nude young man in *The Case of Sonia Wayward* (1960). In *Mungo's Dream* (1973), two young male students at Oxford take a nude midnight swim together and then wrestle equally naked, with the dialogue clearly indicating the couple had taken hold of each other's "private parts."

Julian Symons (1912–1994; see separate essay) offers an ambivalent representation of homosexuality in novels written from the 1950s through the 1990s. A gay couple in a relationship similar to that of Casper Gutman and Wilmer in Dashiell Hammett's *The Maltese Falcon* (1930) are supporting players in *Bogue's Fortune* (1956). The leading lady in *The Man Whose Dreams Come True* (1968) ponders if she is a lesbian, while the central character in *Death's Darkest Face* (1990) wonders if "by nature" he is homosexual. The husband of the main figure in *Something Like a Love Affair* (1992) is gay and masochistic, his secret exposed when his wife finds photographs of him naked and handcuffed, being disciplined by two toughs. In *The Name of Annabel Lee* (1983), however, the S&M is primarily heterosexual.

The American hard-boiled private-detective school of mystery writers has not been kind to gay men. Dashiell Hammett (1894–1961; see separate essay) includes three gay characters, Joel Cairo, Casper Gutman, and Casper's sidekick Wilmer, in *The Maltese Falcon* (1930), but none could be considered role models. Wilmer is identified as gay when Sam Spade refers to him as a "gunsel" (slang for catamite), while in a cryptic conversation between the two men, Spade calls Gutman "the fairy." In *Serenade* (1937) by James M. Cain (1892–1977), opera singer John Howard Sharp loses his voice as a result of the trauma brought on by his homosexual relationship with conductor Stephen Hawes. Only a night of heterosexual passion restores the singer to his full vocal power. In this drama of heterosexuality versus homosexuality, there is no doubt as to where the author stands—he fully believed the basic premise of his story, and includes homosexual stereotypes and situations, including a party at which gay men appear in drag.

A number of critics have suggested that Raymond Chandler (1888–1959; see separate essay) was a latent homosexual, providing as evidence the author's close relationship with his mother and his strong aversion to gay men. Chandler's first published story, "Blackmailers Don't Shoot," which appeared in a 1933 issue of *Black Mask*, includes an intriguingly limp-wristed bodyguard, and there is a strong suggestion that the relationship between Walter and Harry is homosexual in the 1939 *Dime Magazine* short story, "Pearls Are a Nuisance." The attraction that Philip Marlowe feels for men is obvious in *Farewell My Lovely* (1940) and *The Long Goodbye* (1953).

If Chandler was a latent homosexual, Cornell Woolrich (1903–1968; see separate essay) was one filled with self-loathing. That sorrowful feeling is evident in those few short stories in which gays prominently appear. In *Manhattan Love Song* (1932), narrator Wade allows himself to be picked up by a gay actor, whom he beats up and robs. When it was first published in the May 1963 issue of the *Saint Mystery Magazine*, "Story To Be Whispered" did not make it clear why a young man in the San Francisco of the 1920s would beat a prostitute to death at the moment of sexual climax, but missing from the original printed version were lines indicating the prostitute was, in reality, a transvestite. There are subtle, often well-hidden, gay references in Woolrich's novels *Cover Charge* (1926) and *The Black Path of Fear* (1944) and in the short stories "Death Sits in the Dentist's Chair" (1934), "The Night I Died" (1936), "Round Trip to the Cemetery" (1937), and "It Only Takes a Minute to Die" (1966).

Milton Propper (1906–1962) is one of the few mystery writers from the 1930s and 1940s known to have been gay. Propper wrote fourteen novels featuring a Philadelphia police detective and bachelor named Tony Rankin. There are no acknowledged homosexual or lesbian characters in the books, but in a number the murderer is found out to be a man who had lived for a time as a woman.

Frederic Dannay (1905–1982) and Manfred B. Lee (1905–1971), writing as Ellery Queen, confuse transvestites with gays in *The Last Woman in His Life* (1970) but do devote the last two pages of the novel to a discussion by Queen with his father as to the number of gay historical characters and how to recognize a homosexual (or as they are decribed here, "deviates").

Columnist Waldo Lydecker has a waspish quality that brands him as gay in *Laura* (1943) by Vera Caspary (1899–1987). An Austrian nobleman and a Nazi war criminal are very obviously gay and, unfortunately, offensively evil, in Caspary's *A Chosen Sparrow* (1964). The Nazi is fond of female attire and ultimately escapes capture by dressing as the heroine-narrator Leonora Neumann. While the latter tells of her suffering in a concentration camp, no reference is made to the fate of homosexuals in the Nazi death camps.

With *Strangers on a Train* (1949; filmed by Alfred Hitchcock in 1951), Patricia Highsmith (1921–1995) became a mystery writer of international repute. Of the two men, Charles Anthony Bruno and Guy Haines, who accidentally meet on a train ride through Texas and plan the perfect murders, it is obviously Bruno who is gay, a mother's boy who develops an obsessive love for Haines. At the same time, Haines is fully aware as to how the relationship is developing, at one point acknowledging that "he might have been Bruno's lover." Highsmith has frequently written of gays and lesbians. An American writer in Tunisia develops a friendship with a gay Scandinavian in *The Tremor of Forgery* (1969). A mentally unstable New Yorker is protective of the innocence of a lesbian in *Found in the Street* (1987).

Patricia Highsmith (see separate essay) is at her best in the series of novels featuring Tom Ripley, who is both amoral and perhaps asexual. He most certainly displays an ambivalent attitude toward sex, participating in what would appear to be a gay relationship, which he denies, with the man he later murders in

The Talented Mr. Ripley (1955). In *The Boy Who Followed Ripley* (1980), a sixteen-year-old American teenager becomes infatuated with Ripley, whose wife wonders if the boy is *tapette,* or homosexual. Tom introduces the young man to the gay nightlife of Berlin and even visits a gay bar in drag. "No wonder Berliners like disguises," muses the supposedly straight Ripley. "One could feel free, and in a sense *oneself* in a disguise." The ambiguity of the relationship between Ripley and the boy is emphasized by Highsmith's detached writing style. The two share a room and, on three occasions, a bed. But do they sleep together? No definite answer arises from the pages of *The Boy Who Followed Ripley.*

Among mystery writers, Patricia Highsmith is unusual in that she was also active in other fields of fiction. As Claire Morgan, she published *The Price of Salt* (1952), which she described as the first lesbian novel with a happy ending. In her own lifetime, *The Price of Salt* was reprinted under Highsmith's own name, and at the end of her career, she published *Small g: A Summer Idyll* (1995), with a central gay character and set around the comings and goings at a Zurich gay bar.

Changing Sensibilities

In the 1940s, gay characters had begun cropping up more often in cameo roles. Morna Doris Brown (b. 1907), writing as E. X. Ferrars in *Murder Among Friends* (1946; U.S. title, *Cheat the Hangman*), has her heroine visit a London pub during World War II. The customers include "gentle-faced young men in very pretty clothes who were earnestly interested in one another" (p. 165), and one particularly moving characterization is of a young man looking for his lover.

A major breakthrough for lesbian characters came in 1947 with publication of Hilda Lawrence's *Death of a Doll.* The plotline concerns the death of a young woman who falls from a window at a New York female residential facility, managed by a couple who are very

obviously lesbian but never identified as such. The younger of the two proves to be a murderess, but, for once, her sexual preference is unrelated to the killing.

A marvelous irony propels the short story "Love Lies Bleeding" by Philip MacDonald (1896–1980), included in the anthology *Something to Hide* (1952). A playwright is accused of the murder of a female set designer, but while he is in custody two similar killings occur, and the man is released. The reader learns that the playwright is indeed a murderer, and the two additional murders were engineered by his male lover in order to save the playwright. The cleverness of the plot is only equaled by the ingenuity of the author in detailing a homosexual relationship without once resorting to specifics.

From supporting characters whose sexuality is discreetly conveyed, gays and lesbians progressed to murder victims. In *The Feathers of Death* (1960), by Simon Raven (b. 1927), a British officer in Africa takes an enlisted man as his lover, is responsible for his death, but is acquitted; he is then killed by one of his lover's buddies. There is little criticism of the officer's sexual activities; his colleagues are only concerned that homosexuality should be kept between men of their own class. Other gay and lesbian murder-mystery victims include the young policeman in Frank Branston's *Sergeant Ritchie's Conscience* (1978), a lesbian games mistress in a British public school in Polly Hobson's *A Terrible Thing Has Happened to Miss Dupont* (1970; first published in the U.K. in 1968 as *Titty's Dead*), a lesbian who sexually molests her daughter in B. M. Gill's *The Twelfth Juror* (1984), a gay judge with a penchant for dresses in Gregory McDonald's *Flynn's In* (1984), and the wife of a Mafia figure involved in a lesbian affair in Lillian O'Donnell's *A Good Night to Kill* (1989). A gay CIA agent forces the hero to strip naked in Pete Hamill's *Dirty Laundry* (1978)—he is, of course, killed. Although they do not die, two homosexuals are brutalized several times in the mythical country of Brabt, created by Julian Rathbone (b. 1935) for *Watching the Detectives* (1983). The author has one of his heroes refer to one gay man as "a nastly little faggot," "queer," and "probably a Jew too."

If not serving as the murder victim, the homosexual plays against stereotype as a vicious killer. Two gay men shoot and kill a pair of policeman who interrupt their lovemaking in James Dillinger's *Adrenaline* (1985). In a novel remarkable for its accurate depiction of the hustler scene in Hollywood, Arthur Lyons's *Hard Trade* (1981) includes a gay killer, a gay murder victim, and a closeted gay governor of California. When a teenager is discovered in bed with his younger brother by his parents in Teri White's *Bleeding Hearts* (1984), he murders them; escaping from jail, he embarks on a series of savagely vicious killings of gay men. An effeminate, obese, gay hairdresser in Brian Cleve's *Vote X for Treason* (1965) is remarkably adept with a razor and also happens to be a member of British Intelligence. The gay S&M scene forms a backdrop to a number of mysteries, and Philip Caveney's extraordinary *Skin Flicks* (1995) is also concerned with gay snuff films. The British inspector investigating the crimes in *Skin Flicks* is gay and, at the book's conclusion, becomes a transsexual, while the straight hero admits that the best kiss he ever received was from the inspector in drag. Dennis Smith's *Glitter and Ash* (1980) has as its villain an aging, waspish, bitchy homosexual who firebombs a New York discotheque, killing more than forty inside. It does not take long for the fire marshals to identify this as a crime perpetrated by "faggots."

The Savages (1980) by Peter Hill would have us believe that a gay killer became homosexual as the result of a childhood rape by his stepfather. When the man's lover dies of a heart attack after seeing his pet poodle savaged by fox-hunting hounds, he takes revenge on the animals' owners, feeding one victim to a starving pig and cutting open another from his chin to his crotch. Hill's detective hero is the handsome, heterosexual Leo Wyndsor; in *The Hunters* (1976), Wyndsor gets his sexual comeuppance when he presents himself nude

in the bedroom of a former girlfriend, only to be told that she is now a practicing lesbian.

A gay serial killer mutilates his young victims in Wendy Hornsby's *Half a Mind* (1990). The amusing high spot is a courtroom scene in which a Marine, questioned about his murdered buddy, reveals his presence at a gay bar, but insists, "There are no homosexuals in the Marines" (p. 71). In Bill James's *Halo Parade* (1992), an English police constable goes undercover as the lover of a gay gangster. When the latter discovers lipstick on the man's penis, he kills him.

Despite changing sensibilities within the mystery genre and within society at large, through the 1960s and 1970s, pejoratives about homosexuality remained in common usage, and many major writers maintained the old tradition of ignorance and homophobia. In *Fantasy and Fugue* (1956), the British poet and intellectual Roy Fuller (1912–1991) had advised the reader that "the hallmark of the psychopath is homosexuality," and at the novel's close, the central character's brother is revealed as guilty of two murders, as responsible for the hiding of "a little pansy deserter" from the British Army, and as homosexual. In Chester B. Himes's *All Shot Up* (1960), police brutalize the customers at a gay nightspot in Harlem: "They want to be treated rough; brings out the female in them," explains the novel's hero, Coffin Ed Johnson. (See discussion of Hines in essay on "The Black Detective.") And a number of contemporary American mystery writers continue to present similarly phobic gay images, as with Donald E. Westlake (b. 1933), writing as Tucker Coe in *A Jade in Aries* (1970), Evan Hunter (b. 1926), writing as Ed McBain in *The House That Jack Built* (1988), and John D. MacDonald (1916–1986), in *Dress Her in Indigo* (1969). (See separate essays on Westlake, Hunter, and MacDonald.) Frank King introduces a gay NYPD detective-hero in *Down and Dirty* (1978) but then has him break another gay man's arm while the two are having sex, use the term "faggot" as an insult, and describe himself as an "incidental gay." As late as 1995, Jonathan Valin's *Missing*, in which a bisexual man disappears and is murdered, contains not one sympathetic gay character and concludes with the killer allowed to go free.

Bill Pronzini (b. 1943) and Collin Wilcox (b. 1924) combined writing talents for *Twospot* (1978), with chapters written alternately by their respective heroes, the Nameless Detective and Lieutenant Frank Hastings. Among the novel's characters is a gay hit man, killed by Hastings. It is the Nameless Detective who makes some pointed comments on the rights of individuals to be gay. Wilcox introduces a number of gay characters in *Aftershock* (1975). Pronzini's Nameless Detective faces a group of gays and bisexuals in *Deadfall* (1986) and is reasonably sympathetic, although admitting, "I was still old-fashioned enough to feel uncomfortable with some of the more open and iconoclastic attitudes of the homosexual community" (p. 26). In *Shackles* (1988), the Nameless Detective becomes the prisoner of a mystery man who, it transpires, was sent to Folsom Prison on the evidence of the Nameless Detective. At Folsom, he was raped, became the "private property" of two different prisoners, and is now dying of AIDS. Collin Wilcox tackles the issue of AIDS in *Calculated Risk* (1995), in which both a murder victim and his lover are HIV-positive. Clearly neither Wilcox nor his fictional hero Frank Hastings are sympathetic toward gays.

Other writers could use gay epithets with surprising warmth and affection, as does Bob Cook (b. 1951) in *Paper Chase* (1990). A group of retired MI5 men gather to mourn a deceased colleague, whom they describe without animosity as "a nancy," "one of the brown-hat brigade," "a pillow-chewer," and "an arse bandit." As early as John le Carré's *A Murder of Quality* (1962), the gay brother of a colleague of George Smiley is described by his students as "a queer," but to Smiley, "he's not quite the man his brother was." The whole issue of gay men as British spies—Guy Burgess, Anthony Blunt, and Donald Maclean—is well investigated in Tony Cape's *The Cambridge Theorem* (1989), in which "gay" is described as a "short, abused word."

In *Not One of Us* (1971), June Thomson captures the isolation that most homosexuals feel living in a small, unsympathetic community. Because he is aloof and nonconformist, "John Smith" is the primary suspect in the murder of a teenage girl. As the novel progresses, however, "Smith" finds a friend in the investigating inspector and the relationship between the two men is cemented at the novel's close: "John Smith" moves on, leaving behind his sole companion, his dog, in the inspector's care.

The benevolence of a policeman toward a gay man appears again in John Bardy's *Unholy Ground* (1992): regarding the murder in Ireland of an aging, reclusive Englishman—known by British Intelligence to be not only a courageous allied spy during World War II but also a "pooftah" or "a bum boy"—only a Dublin policeman has the audacity to comment that "the sin of being a sodomite outweighed the virtue of saving what remains of civilization from people like Hitler." The detective in Jill McGown's *Murder Movie* (1991) helps engineer a love affair between a male screenwriter and a film's leading man. The New York police detective in Joseph Trigoboff's *The Bone Orchard* (1990) displays a healthy attitude toward gays, while investigating the murder of two male strippers. Inspector Ben Jurnet, the brilliant creation of S. T. Haymon (1918–1995), is no less sensitive to homosexuals as he is to anyone else in *Death of a God* (1987) and *Death of a Hero* (1996).

Clearly, through the 1970s and 1980s the visibility of gay and lesbian characters had increased and outlooks on sexuality had broadened. For example, if Patricia Highsmith's character Ripley is bisexual, he was not alone in gay and lesbian mystery fiction. Mary F. Beal (b. 1937) featured a bisexual feminist in the 1977 novel *Angel Dance.* Tim Heald (b. 1944) is the author of two mystery novels with major bisexual characters: The Earl of Maidenhead is the bisexual murder victim in *Blue Blood Will Out* (1974), although his sexuality is less bothersome to the other characters in the novel than his being Jewish. In

Deadline (1975), a bisexual gossip columnist is murdered; his lover is the young Lord Wimbledon, who is heckled as a "fairy" while playing rugby.

Writing as Dan Kavanagh, Julian Barnes (b. 1946) is responsible for a series of novels featuring a bisexual ex-cop named Duffy, who was thrown out of the London police force on a trumped-up charge of having sex with an underage male teenager. Things get little better for the hero in the introductory novel, *Duffy* (1980). In a remarkably explicit sequence, a Soho gangster, anxious to stop Duffy's investigation of his operations, has the private investigator stripped and photographed with a naked seven-year-old boy masturbating him. Duffy survives to resurface in *Fiddle City* (1981), in which, through a pickup at a gay club, he gets a job investigating drug smuggling at Heathrow. Despite the premise that Duffy is bisexual, he is portrayed as impotent with his girlfriend, and all the sex in the novel is homosexual. As Duffy explains it, he prefers to pick up men rather than women, because at the end of the evening, a man is less likely to say no.

Favorite Themes of Gay and Lesbian Mystery Fiction

HOLLYWOOD

"Being a homosexual in Hollywood sure didn't seem to hurt anybody," says the personable gay secretary to a murdered Beverly Hills agent in *Final Cut* (1981) by Pamela Chais (b. 1930). Show business in general and Hollywood in particular have played prominent roles in many mystery novels with gay or lesbian content. Both abound in David Galloway's *Lamaar Ransom, Private Eye* (1981), including the lesbian title character and a gay black man who talks in a way that imitates Butterfly McQueen in the movie version of *Gone with the Wind*. The murder victim is a female impersonator in Terence Kingsley-Smith's *The Murder of an Old-Time Movie*

Star (1983). Paul Monette (1945–1995) is the author of the screwball comedy *Taking Care of Mrs. Carroll* (1978), in which a lesbian film star and chanteuse, reminiscent of Marlene Dietrich, impersonates the title character, and *The Gold Diggers* (1979), wherein a wealthy gay couple uncover the secret stash of artwork stolen by a silent-film producer. A Hollywood agent investigates the murder of a gay man whose body is discovered hairless and covered in cigarette burns in Donald Ward's comic mystery *Death Takes the Stage* (1988). The unsolved 1922 murder of director William Desmond Taylor, with many gay connotations, forms the background to *Thirteen Castle Walk* by DeWitt Bodeen (1908–1988), while the murder of the bisexual actor is investigated and solved in *Who Killed Sal Mineo?* (1982) by Susan Braudy (b. 1941).

HISTORICAL FIGURES

Among other gay historical figures to be located in mystery novels are J. Edgar Hoover and his lover, Clyde Tolson, who appear pseudonymously in William M. Green's *See How They Run* (1975). While Emmeline Pankhurst was not a lesbian, a number of her sister suffragists are so identified in Gillian Linscott's *Sister Beneath the Sheet* (1991). Why homosexuals, or *pédés*, such as Oscar Wilde, were tolerated in France at the turn of the century is explained in Richard Grayson's *Death en Voyage* (1986). Oscar Wilde is propositioned by Doc Holliday in Walter Satterthwait's *Wilde West* (1991). Wilde meets Sherlock Holmes in the amusing *Sherlock Holmes and the Mysterious Friend of Oscar Wilde* (1988) by Russell A. Brown, after the detective's pageboy, Billy, is lured into a male brothel. Holmes lectures Wilde on family values, but is told that his and Dr. Watson's bachelor life hardly sets an example. Upon being told that war hero General Gordon was gay, Watson removes his portrait from the wall of 221B Baker Street. Wilde's mysterious friend, who visits a male brothel, is not identified, but based on clues, he must be Alfred Bernhard Nobel.

RECURRING GAY AND LESBIAN CHARACTERS

As gays and lesbians have come to be accepted in some areas of society, so have they become recurring characters in a number of series of mystery novels. On the police front, Trevor Barnes (b. 1955) has a gay and black Scotland Yard detective in the procedural novels that began with *A Midsummer Night's Killing* (1992). Sergeant Ray Sussock is consistently humiliated by his gay son in Peter Turnbull's novels featuring the officers of Glasgow's P Division. Reginald Hill (b. 1936) has made a significant contribution to the presentation of positive gay characters in mystery novels with his Sergeant Wield, first introduced in *A Pinch of Snuff* (1978), but whose homosexuality is not revealed until the next book, *A Killing Kindness* (1981). Wield comes out in *Child's Play* (1987). Strong gay characters can also be found in Hill's *Ruling Passion* (1973), *Fell of Dark* (1991), and *Another Death in Venice* (1987). Jonathan Kellerman (b. 1949) has followed Hill's lead and offers his gay LAPD sergeant Milo Sturgis, who has all the stellar qualities to be found in a heterosexual police hero, in the novels featuring clinical psychologist Alex Delaware.

Stan Cutler (b. 1925) has authored three novels—*Best Performance by a Patsy* (1991), *The Face on the Cutting Room Floor* (1991), and *Shot on Location* (1993)—featuring straight private eye Rayford Goodman and gay ghostwriter Mark Bradley, all with a Hollywood theme, and all leaving the impression that the author is not completely comfortable around his gay characters. The musicians making up the Antiqua Players in the novels of James Golin include one gay man, Ralph Mitchell, but his homosexuality seems an irrelevancy. Similarly, actor Barnaby Gill is gay in the novels of Edward Marston, set in fourteenth-century London, but except for his occasional efforts at seducing underage players, Gill's homosexuality has no part in the plotline.

A very witty and gay New Orleans businessman is Matthew Arthur Sinclair, the hero of *The Glory Hole Murders* (1985) and *The Closet Hanging* (1987). The scrapes into which author Tony Fennelly (b. 1945) gets her hero are quite outrageous. Equally shameless is Kinky Friedman, who stars as himself in a series of novels set in New York and costarring his lesbian neighbor Winnie, whom he describes as a "gaplapper." Shelley Singer's Berkeley private eye, Jake Sampson, also has a lesbian neighbor and helper, Rosie, and both were introduced in *Samson's Deal* (1983). The best, and most prominent, of lesbian sidekicks operates a pet-washing establishment in New York and works with used-book seller and burglar Bernie Rhodenbarr in the mystery novels of Lawrence Block (b. 1938). Block's other main protagonist, Matthew Scudder, has been confronted by gay issues and characters in *The Sins of the Fathers* (1976), *Eight Million Ways to Die* (1982), *A Ticket to the Boneyard* (1990), and *A Dance at the Slaughterhouse* (1991).

Laurie R. King and Val McDermid are each responsible for two series of mystery novels, and in each case one features a straight and one stars a lesbian detective. Mary Russell, introduced in King's *The Beekeeper's Apprentice* (1994), assists and eventually marries Sherlock Holmes. King's other heroine is a San Franciso–based lesbian homicide detective, Kate Martinelli, introduced in *A Grave Talent* (1993). The novel is almost two-thirds finished before the author chooses to reveal her heroine's sexual preference. If it were not for Martinelli's lover, psychiatrist Lee Cooper, being nearly killed by a sociopath, her sexuality would be irrelevant. Of the three books in which Martinelli has appeared to date, the best is *To Play the Fool* (1995), a fascinating look at the "fool" in modern society.

British author Val McDermid has written one series featuring private investigator Kate Brannigan—set in the northern English city of Manchester and beginning with *Dead Beat* (1993)—and a second starring Glasgow-based journalist Lindsay Gordon, self-described as "a cynical socialist lesbian feminist." Lindsay Gordon was introduced in *Report for Murder* (1987). The Lindsay Gordon novels feature an entertaining group of lesbian characters and are refreshingly unpolitical in approach, but while the Kate Brannigan series has been picked up by a major U.S. publisher, Scribners, it took three years for the first Lindsay Gordon novel to find an American publisher, and the later books are available only from lesbian publishing houses.

The most recent and engaging of gay leading men to appear on the scene is Todd Mills, a Minneapolis television journalist, introduced by R. D. Zimmerman. Mills makes his debut and is outed in *Closet* (1995), which begins with the murder of his lover. In *Tribe* (1996), Mills has begun a relationship with the police officer he met investigating his lover's death, and helps his lesbian lawyer and former girlfriend protect their mutual grandson from religious fanatics. In *Hostage* (1997), a homophobic congressman is kidnapped by three AIDS sufferers, who intend to inject him with contaminated blood, and Mills learns that his lover, Steve Rawlins, has tested HIV-positive.

The Present and Future

A handful of American women writers have helped gay and lesbian characters come of age in the mystery novel. Carolyn G. Heilbrun (b. 1926), writing as Amanda Cross, has intellectualized the role of the gay and lesbian in society, beginning with the short story "Once upon a Time," in a 1987 issue of *Ellery Queen's Mystery Magazine*. "I know nothing about women loving women, except that I feared it; we had been taught to fear it," says an associate professor, the recipient of a pass from a female undergraduate student. The academic community and AIDS were dissected in *Nemesis* (1990), written by Joyce Carol Oates (b. 1938), writing under the pen name of Rosamond Smith, a perturbing novel that begins with a male rape. Sandra Scoppettone (b. 1936) introduced her forty-something lesbian private investigator, Lauren Laurano, in *Everything You Have Is Mine* (1991) and sen-

sitively handled the issue of her lover's gay brother with AIDS.

Elizabeth George (b. 1949) has introduced gay elements in *Payment in Blood* (1989), *Well-Schooled in Murder* (1990), and *In the Presence of the Enemy* (1996). Lesbian private investigator Lil Ritchie first came to attention in *Switching the Odds* (1992) by Phyllis Knight, her sexual preference of little relevance. There is no moralizing about lifestyles in P. B. Shaw's *The Seraphim Kill* (1994), in which there are three gay murders. All these female novelists follow in the honorable footsteps of Margaret Millar (1915–1994); the central character in her *Spider Webs* (1986) is a defense attorney who decides to come out of the closet.

Among popular contemporary American male writers, Robert Eversz (b. 1954) does well by lesbians in *False Profit* (1990), as does Robert B. Parker (b. 1932; see separate essay) in *Looking for Rachel Wallace* (1980), in which Boston private investigator Spenser is hired to protect an author who is a lesbian and a radical feminist.

Among Britain's favorite male mystery writers, both Robert Barnard (b. 1936; see separate essay) and Simon Brett (b. 1945) are comfortable with gay themes and characters. Barnard's Superintendent Perry Trethowan encounters gay men at a royal palace in *Death and the Princess* (1982) and, not surprisingly, among bodybuilders in *Bodies* (1986); in the latter, Trethowan also notes there are many gay men at Scotland Yard. As early as *The Disposal of the Living* (1985), Barnard points out that there are gay undercurrents to be found in a small Yorkshire town, where nothing is quite what it seems, and where a sign in a public toilet advises soldiers that they can earn five to ten pounds in "a simple and undemanding way." There is a gay murder victim, a strong gay theme, and a surprising and positive gay ending in Barnard's *A Scandal in Belgravia* (1991).

Simon Brett's generally out-of-work actor-investigator Charles Paris encounters gays in *Not Dead, Only Resting* (1984), *What Bloody Man Is That?* (1987), and *Corporate Bodies*

(1992). Paris had no problem in infiltrating the gay world in the first novel, but, as an example of the difference in attitudes between the United States and Britain, the American publisher chose to describe Paris' activities as "finding out all about perversion." The central female character in Brett's *Singled Out* (1995) has a gay man as her best friend and eventually discovers that her son is gay—and well adjusted.

John Harvey and Ian Rankin both offer gay situations to match the raw and brutal quality of their writing styles. Harvey's third novel, *Cutting Edge* (1991), has a gay character, and the next, *Off Minor* (1992), a lesbian. When a fellow detective inspector is murdered and found to be gay, Harvey's Detective Inspector Resnick welcomes to his team a black and gay detective constable in *Easy Meat* (1996). The novel's astoundingly brutal ending has the loutish, womanizing Detective Constable Divine raped, lying in hospital in a traumatized state, and with the gay constable trying to break through his silence.

Rankin's Edinburgh detective John Rebus relives his past in *Knots and Crosses* (1987), when, as a trainee with the Special Air Service, he and another man were imprisoned naked together in a small cell, and Rebus rejected the other's sexual advances. Rent boys, or male prostitutes, figure prominently in *Hide and Seek* (1994): they are paid to beat each other to a pulp in the boxing ring for the entertainment of wealthy, closeted homosexuals.

Minette Walters demonstrates the danger of judging individuals by appearance, as she furnishes a country house in a small English village with, apparently, three lesbians at the start of *The Ice-House* (1992). If nothing else, her plotline helps educate a detective sergeant, who jokes, "I've nothing against dykes . . . I just wouldn't stick my finger in one," early in the text and later finds himself sleeping with one. A male London journalist must fend off the increasingly fervent advances of an unappealing, drunken latent homosexual in Walters' *The Echo* (1997); at the novel's

close, the latter is the only central character facing an unhappy ending.

Caroline Graham's Sergeant Troy comes up against gays in *The Killings at Badger's Drift* (1988) and *Death of a Hollow Man* (1989) and displays prejudices that are easily identifiable as failings. Lesbians are central characters in *The Chief Inspector's Daughter* (1980) and *Cross My Heart and Hope to Die* (1992) by Sheila Radley (pseudonym of Sheila Mary Robinson, b. 1928), with the latter providing a poignant picture of the loneliness of an isolated lesbian in a small English village. The London barristers created by Sarah Cockburn, writing as Sarah Caudwell, are witty and urbane and should be featured in more than three novels. In the first, *Thus Was Adonis Murdered* (1981), the killing of one gay man by another is handled with good taste; not once does the author find it necessary to use a sexually descriptive term in reference to either the killer or his victim. In the second, *The Shortest Way to Hades* (1985), one of the barristers, Julia Larwood, spends a night with a lesbian without concern to herself or her colleagues.

The change in attitude toward gays and lesbians is in no small part due to the sympathetic characterizations to be found in the works of Britain's finest, and best-loved, mystery writers, P. D. James and Ruth Rendell (b. 1930). James, who scrupulously avoids the word "gay" as much as she tries not to categorize her characters, has gay men in *The Black Tower* (1975) and *Devices and Desires* (1989), with the former containing, arguably, the most elegantly written passage concerning gay relationships to be found in any mystery novel. Rendell's liberal Chief Inspector Wexford serves as counterpoint to the intolerance of his assistant, Mike Burden. The two men investigate a lesbian murder in *From Doon with Death* (1965), a gay murder in *Murder Being Once Done* (1972), and a killing by a gay man with AIDS in *Kissing the Gunner's Daughter* (1992). There are stronger gay and lesbian characters to be found in the novels written by Rendell as Barbara Vine, with such characters fully integrated into the stories of

Gallowglass (1990), *King Solomon's Carpet* (1991), and *No Night Is Too Long* (1994).

The mystery genre has covered homosexuality in ancient Rome in Joan O'Hagan's *A Roman Death* (1988), in medieval England in Paul Harding's *The Nightingale Gallery* (1991), and in the twenty-first century in Philip Kerr's *A Philosophical Investigation* (1992). In the last, we learn that gays and lesbians are accepted within society, but as the female chief inspector with lesbian tendencies tracking down a killer of gay men discovers, not necessarily in the London police force. We have come a long way, as gay men and lesbians, in the pages of the mystery novel, but just as in society, we have a long way to go and an uncertain future.

Selected Bibliography

GAY AND LESBIAN MYSTERY FICTION

The following listing includes both novels with gay and lesbian themes and characters and novels written for a gay and lesbian audience. Titles have been selected both on the basis of historical importance and literary worth.

Aldyne, Nathan. *Vermilion.* New York: Avon, 1980.

Azolakov, Antoinette. *Cass and the Stone Butch.* Austin, Tex.: Banned Books, 1987.

Baxt, George. *A Queer Kind of Death.* New York: Simon & Schuster, 1966.

Beadle, Jeremy. *Doing Business.* London: Gay Men's Press, 1990.

Block, Lawrence. *The Sins of the Fathers.* New York: Jove, 1976.

Box, Edgar. *Death in the Fifth Position.* New York: Dutton, 1952.

Brahms, Caryl, and S. J. Simon. *A Bullet in the Ballet.* Garden City, N.Y.: Doubleday, Doran, 1937.

Brown, Morna Doris. *Murder Among Friends.* By "E. X. Ferrars." London: Collins, 1946. U.S.: *Cheat the Hangman.* Garden City, N.Y.: Doubleday, 1946.

Brown, Russell A. *Sherlock Holmes and the Mysterious Friend of Oscar Wilde.* New York: St. Martin's Press, 1988.

Buchan, John. *Greenmantle.* New York: Grosset & Dunlap, 1916.

Cain, James M. *Serenade.* New York: Knopf, 1937.

Cape, Tony. *The Cambridge Theorem.* Garden City, N.Y.: Doubleday, 1989.

Caspary, Vera. *A Chosen Sparrow.* New York: Putnam, 1964.

Caudwell, Sarah. *Thus Was Adonis Murdered.* New York: Scribners, 1981.

Caveney, Philip. *Skin Flicks.* London: Headline Feature, 1995.

Christie, Agatha. *Nemesis.* New York: Dodd, Mead, 1971.

Fennelly, Tony. *The Glory Hole Murders.* New York: Carroll & Graf, 1985.

———. *The Closet Hanging.* New York: Carroll & Graf, 1987.

Forrest, Katherine V. *Amateur City.* Tallahassee, Fla.: Naiad Press, 1984.

———. *Murder at the Nightwood Bar.* Tallahassee, Fla.: Naiad Press, 1987.

———. *The Beverly Malibu.* Tallahassee, Fla.: Naiad Press, 1989.

———. *Liberty Square.* New York: Berkley, 1996.

Foster, Marion. *The Monarchs Are Flying.* Ithaca, N.Y.: Firebrand, 1987.

Gilbert, W. Stephen. *Spiked.* London: Gay Men's Press, 1991.

Hall, Richard. *The Butterscotch Prince.* Boston: Alyson, 1983.

Hammett, Dashiell. *The Maltese Falcon.* New York: Knopf, 1930.

Hansen, Joseph. *Known Homosexual.* North Hollywood, Calif.: Brandon House, 1968. Reiss. as *Pretty Boy Dead.* San Francisco: Gay Sunshine Press, 1984.

———. *Fadeout.* New York: Harper & Row, 1970.

———. *A Country of Old Men.* New York: Viking, 1991.

Harvey, John. *Easy Meat.* New York: Henry Holt, 1996.

Haymon, S. T. *Death of a Hero.* New York: St. Martin's Press, 1996.

Highsmith, Patricia. *Strangers on a Train.* New York: Harper & Bros., 1949.

———. *The Boy Who Followed Ripley.* New York: Lippincott & Crowell, 1980.

Hill, Reginald. *Child's Play.* New York: Macmillan, 1987.

Hornsby, Wendy. *Half a Mind.* New York: New American Library, 1990.

Hull, Richard. *The Murder of My Aunt.* London: Faber, 1934.

James, Bill. *Halo Parade.* New York: Countryman Press, 1992.

James, P. D. *The Black Tower.* New York: Scribners, 1975.

Kavanagh, Dan. *Duffy.* London: Jonathan Cape, 1980.

Kellerman, Jonathan. *Over the Edge.* New York: Atheneum, 1987.

King, Laurie R. *To Play the Fool.* New York: St. Martin's Press, 1995.

Lawrence, Hilda. *Death of a Doll.* New York: Simon & Schuster, 1947.

McBain, Ed. *The House That Jack Built.* New York: Henry Holt, 1988.

McDermid, Val. *Report for Murder.* New York: St. Martin's Press, 1987.

MacDonald, Philip, "Love Lies Bleeding." In *Something to Hide.* Garden City, N.Y.: Doubleday, 1952.

McGown, Jill. *Murder Movie.* New York: St. Martin's Press, 1991.

McNab, Claire. *Lessons in Murder.* Tallahassee, Fla.: Naiad Press, 1988.

Maiman, Jaye. *I Left My Heart.* Tallahassee, Fla.: Naiad Press, 1991.

Mitchell, Gladys. *Speedy Death.* London: Gollancz, 1929; Hogarth Press, 1988.

———. *Death-Cap Dancers.* London: Joseph, 1981.

Monette, Paul. *Taking Care of Mrs. Carroll.* Boston: Little, Brown, 1978.

Nava, Michael. *The Little Death.* Boston: Alyson, 1986.

———. *How Town.* New York: Harper & Row, 1990.

———. *The Death of Friends.* New York: Putnam, 1996.

Pronzini, Bill. *Deadfall.* New York: St. Martin's Press, 1986.

Queen, Ellery. *The Last Woman in His Life.* New York: World, 1970.

Radley, Sheila. *The Chief Inspector's Daughter.* New York: Scribners, 1980.

Rankin, Ian. *Hide and Seek.* New York: Otto Penzler, 1994.

Raven, Simon. *The Feathers of Death.* New York: Simon & Schuster, 1960.

Rendell, Ruth. *From Doon with Death.* Garden City, N.Y.: Doubleday, 1965.

Ricardo, Jack. *The Night G.A.A. Died.* New York: St. Martin's Press, 1992.

Scoppettone, Sandra. *Everything You Have Is Mine.* Boston: Little, Brown, 1991.

Singer, Shelley. *Samson's Deal.* New York: St. Martin's Press, 1983.

Smith, Rosamond. *Nemesis.* New York: Dutton, 1990.

Stevenson, Richard. *Death Trick.* New York: St. Martin's Press, 1981.

———. *Third Man Out.* New York: St. Martin's Press, 1992.

Steward, Samuel M. *Murder Is Murder Is Murder.* Boston: Alyson, 1985.

Thomson, June. *Not One of Us.* New York: Harper & Row, 1971.

Vine, Barbara. *The House of Stairs.* New York: Harmony, 1989.

———. *No Night Is Too Long.* New York: Viking, 1994.

Ward, Donald. *Death Takes the Stage.* New York: St. Martin's Press, 1988.

Wilson, Barbara. *Murder in the Collective.* Seattle: Seal Press, 1984.

Wilson, Colin. *Ritual in the Dark.* London: Granada, 1960.

Zaremba, Eve. *Uneasy Lies.* Toronto: Second Story, 1990.

Zimmerman, R. D. *Closet.* New York: Dell, 1995.

Zubro, Mark Richard. *A Simple Suburban Murder.* New York: St. Martin's Press, 1989.

———. *Sorry Now?* New York: St. Martin's Press, 1991.

BIOGRAPHICAL AND CRITICAL STUDIES

Baker, Jim, "Gay Novels: A Genre Redefined," *Los Angeles Times Calendar,* 2 January 1983: 74.

Barzun, Jacques, and Wendell Hertig Taylor. *A Catalog of Crime.* Rev. and enl. ed. New York: Harper & Row, 1989.

Klein, Kathleen Gregory. *The Woman Detective: Gender and Genre.* Urbana: University of Illinois Press, 1988.

Mason, Michael, "Marlowe, Men and Women." In *The World of Raymond Chandler.* Edited by Miriam Gross. London: Weidenfeld & Nicolson, 1977.

Morris, John, "No Dick Like an Old Dick," *LAMBDA Book Report,* vol. II, no. 5: 29 (June/July 1990).

Ponce de Leon, Juana, "Gay and Lesbian Publishing." *Publishers Weekly,* 8 December 1989: 14–23.

Sedgwick, Eve Kosofsky. *Between Men: English Literature and Male Homosocial Desire.* New York: Columbia University Press, 1985.

Slide, Anthony. *Gay and Lesbian Characters and Themes in Mystery Novels: A Critical Guide to Over 500 Works in English.* Jefferson, N.C.: McFarland, 1993.

White, Edmund, "Out of the Closet, onto the Bookshelf," *New York Times Magazine,* 16 June 1991: 22, 24, 35.

Young, Ian. *The Male Homosexual in Literature: A Bibliography.* Metuchen, N.J.: Scarecrow Press, 1982.

THE HISTORICAL MYSTERY

ROBIN W. WINKS

"THE PAST IS a foreign country; they do things differently there." So goes about the only aphorism still known from the work of the English writer L. P. Hartley. Perhaps he provides one clear reason—or, in fact, several reasons—why historical mysteries are so popular. This is the most rapidly growing subfield in the genre of mystery fiction, at a time when educators commonly report a decline in interest in history. But historical mysteries have little to do with history as it is taught in the schools and universities or as practiced by professional historians. These stories do, however, have many elements in common with more traditional mystery fiction. They help readers to escape from the present, into Hartley's other country. They provide a sense of seeing behind the scenes, much as detective novels that purport to reveal to the reader how a great hospital runs, how a fried chicken franchise works, or how the police carry out their routines. They can carry a rich and often unthreatening language, for though there have always been vulgarisms, the contemporary reader who is offended by scatalogical four-letter wordplay is not likely to be upset by medieval oaths, *forsooth*s, or even a string of *bloody*s. If a villain does not come through the door with a gun in his hand to resolve the next plot twist, as Raymond Chandler admitted to doing, he can enter with a broadsword. While the arcana of forensic science as it is known today may not be part of the story, life in a monastery, science and magic as under-

stood in the fourteenth century, and what today would be dismissed as superstition can play vital roles. Many readers are in love with the past, provided it does not make too many demands upon them and is not too difficult to understand.

There, of course, lies the problem for the trained historian. As one reviewer said in praise of a perfectly decent mystery, Kate Sedley's *The Plymouth Cloak* (1992), about Roger the Chapman in the fifteenth century, the author had written a "charming period piece: The scenery, occupations, and finery are medieval, but the foibles are of a contemporary nature." This is precisely the problem: while the scenery and the costumes are changed, human relations in *The Plymouth Cloak* are much as they are in the twentieth century. The reader is not, in fact, in another country but merely looking upon a stage set, suspending disbelief as actors play their roles upon the world stage as we believe we know it.

If it does not matter when a Robert Ludlum gets simple facts wrong, facts that could be corrected by reference to an atlas or a French dictionary, why should it matter more because the author of a "historical mystery" invents outlandish diction, lets figures strut upon that stage a decade after their death, or introduces a buckle or a fork half a century before it existed? The answer is simple: one knows that a modern thriller is a demand that we suspend disbelief and be entertained for an hour or so, while the very claim to be "historical" carries with it the implication of achieving the rich particularity of fact, in all its complexity, accuracy, and interrelatedness that we associate with, or should be able to attribute to, historians.

History is three things: what actually happened in the past; what people believe happened in the past; what historians say happened in the past. The first will never be fully recovered. The second may well be the most important, for people act upon what they believe about the past: they hate, love, celebrate, commemorate, and mourn a past in which they truly believe. Historical novelists, whether of mysteries or of an allegedly more serious kind of writing, are fundamentally engaged with the second definition: all mystery writers wish to make readers believe *x* in order to surprise them with *y*, and historical mysteries share this urgency. Thus, the writer of a historical mystery cannot be writing as a historian writes, cannot ask questions as a historian asks them, cannot lay out evidence as a historian would, for the goals are quite different. The reading public little understands this, or it would not praise so poor a novel as Josephine Tey's *The Daughter of Time*, a book anathema to many historians yet taken by most readers to describe what a historian does. (See separate essay on Tey.)

A crime takes place at a specific time, in a specific setting, and for motives mad or rational. A good mystery grows out of place and time and character. So, too, does a good work of history—for example, Garret Mattingly's classic reconstruction, *The Armada* (1959), of that moment in 1588 when the greatest navy ever assembled sailed from la Coruña in Spain to sweep the English fleet from the seas, only to be battered by a "Protestant Wind" and dashed upon the wave-tossed shores of Ireland. There is suspense in abundance as Mattingly tells his story of the triumph of Elizabethan England; his exacting descriptions of dress, armor, how soldiers stand in ranks, can be taken over almost whole into a work of fiction, though he was a professional—indeed, an academic—historian. When the work of fiction forces the scene to a different purpose,

not to speak of a different conclusion, it ceases to be history. Fiona Buckley's *To Shield the Queen* (1997), set in Elizabeth's court, and the work of P. F. Chisholm (pseudonym of Patricia Finney), especially *A Famine of Horses* (1995) and *A Surfeit of Guns* (1996), nicely capture the tone of the time but fall short of Mattingly's evocation of its meaning.

Historical mysteries must appear to be history without being so. They will be set in the past, a past imagined in part though, most likely, also carefully reconstructed through research into material culture: what dwellings looked like and were made of; what people of diverse positions wore and how they smelled; oddities to the modern reader: how they used dried moss as toilet paper; social relations, habits of mind, political tensions, and (though seldom well done) economic over- and undertones; how people of differing classes and castes spoke among themselves, to others from above or below, within professions and without, as Christians, Jews, atheists, as members of a counterculture when the term meant, if it meant anything, something other than it means now. The problem here, of course, is that all this research may drag the novel down. Anne Perry's heralded historical mysteries set in Victorian Britain often smell of the lamp, little social facts, small points of etiquette, inserted simply (it would seem) because they have been learned. A medieval mystery in which individuals speak as they would have spoken would prove unreadable to most readers today; how many readers consult Chaucer "in the original" or have any stomach for Piers the Plowman? One knows, all of the time, that the book in one's hand represents a game of compromises; so, too, does a book about a 1990s serial killer's spree, yet because the language is that of the headlines we read daily, we are far less aware of the compromises.

This is not to say that there cannot be good historical mysteries, or that a historical mystery cannot entertain and please despite inaccuracies. Does it matter that Steven Saylor, in *Arms of Nemesis* (1992), introduces a Lucretian oration seventeen years before it occurred? Perhaps the best historical mystery written is Iain Pears's *An Instance of the Fingerpost* (1998), and its recency may suggest that better talent is turning to the genre. But there is no accounting for public taste. Who would have anticipated the great popular success of a complex novel by a professor of semiotics such as Umberto Eco's *The Name of the Rose* (in English, 1983)?

From Tey to the "Counterfactuals"

No statement about the historical mystery can avoid the centrality of Josephine Tey's *The Daughter of Time,* in which she takes on the mystery of the princes in the Tower of London. This is not a crime story in a period setting; indeed, it is not truly a historical mystery at all, for all the detecting takes place in the present, though the crime to be solved occurred in the past. Is it not true of all mysteries, however, that to some degree they are about solving a crime that took place in the past, whether yesterday, last month, a decade ago, or in another century?

Published in London in 1951, *The Daughter of Time* was Tey's (a.k.a. Elizabeth Mackintosh) seventh novel and the fourth to feature Inspector Alan Grant. Laid up in a hospital, Grant entertains himself examining a series of depictions of faces of the famous; based on a picture of Richard III, he decides the much-maligned monarch cannot have been the evil figure described by Sir Thomas More and triumphalist Tudor historiography. "History taught"—always a suspect phrase—that the evil and hunchbacked Yorkist king, Richard III, had ordered the murder of his two nephews in the Tower of London in 1483, two years before he was meted out justice at the battle of Bosworth Field, where the crown of England was found on a bush and passed to the first great Tudor, Henry VII. Grant undertakes an investigation from his bed; a young American researcher, Brent Carradine, digs through archives and produces evidence that

Richard was not so bad after all and may well have been framed. Along the way Tey discourses on how easily the public is misled, points out some more recent parallels—the "Tonypandy massacre" in the Rhondda Valley of Wales in 1910, in particular—and demonstrates that people will go on believing what they wish to believe, whatever good gray historians (or an inspector from Scotland Yard) may say about the matter.

For a historian, Tey's book presents serious problems. Research is not done as she depicts it in the hands of her callow and cardboard American. A political reinterpretation of the events in the Tower or at Tonypandy would need to be infinitely more complex than Tey's, and she chooses the wrong villains. There can be few serious scholars who believe that character can be read from a picture (though this was a more common belief in Tey's childhood). Her nationalism gets in the way of the story. Worst of all, she withholds evidence from the reader, and in the end lets Grant and the reader learn quite casually that his interpretation of Richard's actions had been anticipated in 1901 by an author whom, had Grant or his researcher so much as skimmed a card catalog, they would have encountered at the outset of their investigation. The whole so misrepresents research, and so confuses research with simply looking things up, as to baffle historians. And because it depicts their work as a combination of luck and browsing, it leaves them dismayed. This reaction can be attributed in part, of course, to any professional group's annoyance that someone deemed amateur is treading on their turf or seeks to own history to a purpose different than the third definition cited above, but there is no gainsaying that *The Daughter of Time* is both a bad book and a deeply influential one.

There have been other historical mysteries about the presumed murders in the Tower. One takes Tey on directly: Guy M. Townsend's *To Prove a Villain* (1985), in which a professor of history tries to show how Tey's fallacies are related to misreading of evidence in a contemporary campus murder. Less effective are P. C. Doherty's *The Fate of Princes* (1990) and Robert Farrington's *The Killing of Richard III* (1971), which too dutifully marches forward to Bosworth Field. On a different order of writing is Elizabeth Peters' (pseudonym for Barbara Mertz) *The Murders of Richard III* (1974), which like *The Daughter of Time* is not set in the past but which does get most of its sums right, in a story about a librarian who joins a group of Richardists (or Ricardians) at a weekend house party during which the guests are attacked as they act out roles from Richard III's time. These attempts to resolve the mystery of the Tower run the gamut representative of most historical mystery fiction.

What, then, is a historical mystery? Need such a mystery be accurate in its portrayal of history? To the second question the only answer can be No, not slavishly so, else there would be no historical mysteries. Indeed, there would be no fiction of any kind, for a fundamental difference between fiction and fact is, reductio ad absurdum, that one is not "true" and the other is as much so as human endeavor can arrange. The question will always be, rather, does the quotient of error matter? Indeed, are there errors or simply manipulations on behalf of plot? Arabists have long pointed out errors and impossibilities in Lawrence Durrell's famed *Alexandria Quartet*; scientists detect frequent errors of hard science in much (but by no means all) science fiction; and while the child-in-peril novels of Mary Higgins Clark are filled with implausibilities, the events are not sheer impossibilities. Historical mysteries are mysteries; *historical* here is the adjective.

This said, one must also agree that there are several types of historical mysteries. For a book to be set in the past does not make it a historical mystery. Many writers of spy thrillers, faced with the end of the Evil Empire (the Soviet Union), have turned to settings in Nazi Germany. Daniel Silva's *The Unlikely Spy* (1996) uses historical realities as a backdrop for an otherwise good but rather conventional thriller. Philip Kerr has set three of his very good detective novels—such they are, since they involve German police—in 1930s and 1940s Germany and Austria (published as a trilogy, *Berlin Noir*, in 1993); the backdrop is lovingly realized but not essential. Walter Mosley's series on Easy Rawlins is set in the 1940s: see, for example, *A Red Death* (1991). Joseph Kanon has written, in *Los Alamos* (1997), a fine book about sexual, political, and scientific betrayal in the Manhattan Project that includes the director at Los Alamos, Robert Oppenheimer, as a key figure and brilliantly portrays the atomic test at Trinity Site in the New Mexican desert. From these novels, a reader will learn much history; yet the history is worn so lightly, the story might take place on a spaceship created by film director Stanley Kubrick. John Lawton, in *Black Out* (1995), tells us what it was like to live in London during the Blitz. Charles Todd sets *A Test of Wills* (1996) and *Wings of Fire* (1998) in post–World War I Britain. The historical backgrounds are authentic, accurate, and not irrelevant, and yet they function much as the expertise in an Emma Lathen novel about big business, or snow lore in Peter Hoeg's *Smilla's Sense of Snow* (in English, 1993), or in Dale Brown and Clive Cussler thrillers about flying: they provide vicarious experiences for the reader, a sense of being inside an enterprise—in this case, inside the past—but they do not much use this enterprise, the past, to purposeful intent.

There must be more to a historical mystery than being set at some point in the past. Indeed, perhaps the historical mystery must be set far enough into the past that no reader will have any personal recollection or experience of that past, so that the whole of the reader's experience must be provided by the writer. For many readers this would place George Baxt's novels set in the glory days of Hollywood (*The Clark Gable and Carole Lombard Murder Case*, 1997; *The Noel Coward Murder Case*, 1992) or Stuart M. Kaminsky's Toby Peters series, set in Hollywood in the 1940s, outside the subgenre; the same would be true of Elliott Roosevelt's numerous mysteries in which his mother, Eleanor Roosevelt, is the solver of crimes (of which *Murder at Mid-*

night, 1997, is the sixteenth and representative).

One could, but must not, use the historian's standard fifty-year rule and conclude that a historical mystery must be set more than fifty years in the past. Thus, Carola Dunn's British Daisy Dalrymple books, which take place in the 1920s, would qualify but Thomas H. Cook's *The Chatham School Affair* (1996) would not. Clearly, so arbitrary a line may meet the needs of archivists and historical plaque makers, but no such straitjacket can be placed on fiction.

Another type of book often called a historical mystery is the pastiche novel, most frequently using Sherlock Holmes as the lead figure, or at times giving John H. Watson full credit, or using Holmes's "smarter brother" Mycroft. Often these purport to be the real thing, new manuscripts found in a trunk belonging (generally) to Dr. Watson. Marvin Kaye's collections of the stories of others, *Resurrected Holmes* (1996) and *The Confidential Casebook of Sherlock Holmes* (1998), are representative. Often other figures, literary or historical, are turned into detectives, a practice said to have begun with Lillian de la Torre's *Dr. Sam Johnson, Detector* (1946). This is nicely illustrated by a series of mysteries featuring Benjamin Franklin by Robert Lee Hall (who first tried his hand with a Holmes pastiche), as in *Benjamin Franklin and a Case of Artful Murder* (1994). More recently, Stephanie Barron (pseudonym of Francine Mathews) has made a detective of Jane Austen in *Jane and the Unpleasantness at Scargrave Manor* (1996) and subsequent mystery novels. Generally, history is used as background only, and the real challenge to the reader is to attend to the authors' efforts to faithfully capture the style of the writers they are seeking to imitate (Doyle, for example) or the diction and thought of the historical figures they wish to parade before us. As a rule these are not very successful, though de la Torre had her admirers, especially Anthony Boucher, the authoritative reviewer for the *New York Times,* and Stephanie Barron is praised for her ability to capture Jane Austen's

concerns for pride and prejudice in the early nineteenth century. A few turn their stories upon historically rooted issues or historical events that propel the pastiche, and when successful—as Laurie R. King has been in her work—they are without doubt historical mysteries; but in general, the past does not drive the story, and we are only most temporarily in another country.

Laurie King has entered two quite different worlds and yet shows their similarities. One series, about Inspector Kate Martinelli of the San Francisco Police Department, and set in the present, features a lesbian; the other—focusing on Mary Russell, a highly intelligent young woman who becomes the wife of Sherlock Holmes and attracts to herself, because of her independence (and her learning, for she is a theology scholar at Oxford), much mutedly hostile attention—brilliantly reshapes the concept of the outsider precisely because Russell is seen in the context of history, of her times. *The Beekeeper's Apprentice* (1994) is a fine overture to *A Monstrous Regiment of Women* (1995), but it is *A Letter of Mary* (1996) that truly denotes this series as a triumphantly successful expression of the historical mystery at its best. Here a woman who may have proof that Mary Magdalene was fully admitted as an apostle is killed, and Mary Russell (with Holmes's help) must confront the period's attitudes toward women, sex, motherhood, religion, and much else. These attitudes are not merely historical background; they are of the essence of the novel, Mary being, as a historian must be, virtually a watcher in the shadows to the events of the time, until moved at last to action.

Yet another form of the historical mystery is represented by Peter Lovesey's *The False Inspector Dew* (1982), subtitled *A Murder Mystery Aboard the S.S. Mauritania, 1921;* some of the novels of Peter Dickinson; and, perhaps most tellingly, *Thrones, Dominations* by Dorothy L. Sayers (see separate essay) and Jill Paton Walsh (1997). These mysteries review the past from knowledge in the present; were they histories, they would instantly be found guilty of the sin of presentism—reading the meaning of the past in terms of the present—but this, of course, is inherent in the nature of the mystery novel. *Thrones, Dominations* is based on six chapters of manuscript left by Sayers at her death and found in the Sayers Papers at Wheaton College in Illinois. Walsh reorganized the original manuscript, blended her own voice to Sayers', and produced a Sayers novel that reads very like a book written in the 1930s, not one reconstructed in the 1990s. Sayers abandoned the novel, it is variously said, because her theatrical career was developing rapidly; because she wanted to devote more time to writing Christian apologetics and preparing her translation of Dante; because she was tired of the dominance of Lord Peter Wimsey in her life; or because, with the approach of war in Europe, she thought her talents should be used for purposes other than writing mysteries for money.

All these reasons for abandoning *Thrones, Dominations* appear in the book itself, for the novel is much concerned with the death of George V, the accession of Edward VIII, the approaching abdication crisis, and the movements of Hitler on the Continent; with the excitement of the theater, some of the book's principal figures being producers, playwrights, and actresses; and with Christian themes (the title is from Milton) concerning love, duty, and marriage. It is the tension between these matters that gives the novel its weight.

The mystery itself is classical Sayers. There is a murder and there is a death; much indirection; some fine laying down of clues; and all turns on character and human misunderstanding. One feels Walsh has carried the story to a conclusion that Sayers would have approved. There are some minor set pieces, a revelation about how Lord Peter helps a Jewish singer to escape from Austria, a few attitudes struck that one suspects Sayers would not have included, since she could have been little aware of the desirability of them at the time. The give-and-take between Lord Peter and Harriet Vane (Lady to Peter's Lord, since the action begins immediately after their honeymoon) will irritate or please to the same degree that they do when one reads vintage Say-

ers. There are some sharply done scenes involving Lord Peter's family; the duchess of Denver and Bunter are nicely recaptured for the reader; and the role of sexual passion is well handled, though in the restrained language of the 1930s.

In a way this is the best kind of historical mystery, for the reader grasps both the reality of the past and the revelations of the present: that is, genuine historical change occurs both *in* the novel and in the manner in which the reader (and author) *adjusts* to the past in awareness of what has taken place since. Harriet and Peter have three sons, not the five children Sayers had apparently projected for them, perhaps in recognition that in wartime so much birthing would have been difficult; sexual tension is heightened, revealed more openly despite discreet language, than Sayers would likely have permitted herself; while this past is another country, we are aware that it is so by virtue of our perspective on it.

There is yet another type of historical mystery, though it is more akin to science fiction: the counterfactual novel. Such books turn on events we know did not occur: Richard III survives Bosworth Field, Hitler's Germany invades and occupies Britain in Len Deighton's *SS-GB* (1978), Germany wins World War II in Robert Harris' *The Fatherland* (1992). Sometimes such books are based on true crimes, with modern solutions worked into past circumstances, as in the collection of short stories edited by Peter Lovesey as *The Black Cabinet* (1989). At other times a real institution from the past is given a new twist in order to support the mystery formula, as in Michael Pearce's Mamur Zapt series, set in Cairo in the early 1900s, and Elizabeth Peters' series set in nineteenth-century Egypt, of which *Crocodile on the Sandbank* (1975) is both the first and the best.

Irreducibly, however, it seems appropriate to insist that a historical mystery must arise from the realities of the past, not thrust attitudes or language of the present into that past, and must turn upon activities deemed criminous in the past and solutions that arise from the ethics and morality of the past. There must be a mystery. Wonderfully close research, as in the work of Sharan Newman—see *Death Comes as Epiphany* (1993) or *The Wandering Arm* (1995)—must be worn lightly, lest the book become a text; and above all, the story must grow from inside the past outward. The critic Henry Louis Gates, Jr., put this distinction well in writing of Elmore Leonard's *Cuba Libre* (1998), set in Havana at the outbreak of the Spanish-American War: history writ small (which is what he says Leonard has successfully done in the novel) evokes all the "plausible particulars" of narrow streets and closed shutters, but history writ large eludes Leonard, for he feels he must have someone explain the significance of events even before anyone at the time could know they would be significant (*The New Yorker*, 26 January 1998, p. 84). The didactic nature of much that passes for history in a historical mystery is simply teacherly; few would have remarked at the time on the event described.

This range of types of historical mysteries demonstrates that there is no one formula, any more than there is a single formula for the private eye novel. Examined from a sufficient distance, all may look quite similar; as with history itself, at close range one quickly realizes that pure formula, like unthinkingly applied theory, is unproductive of sound history. The range of types within the subgenre generally is nicely laid out in collections of short stories, such as Janet Hutchings' anthology *Once upon a Crime* (1994), all drawn from *Ellery Queen's Mystery Magazine*, or Miriam Grace Monfredo and Sharan Newman's *Crime Through Time* (1997), the editorial product of two writers of historical mysteries and an able introduction to some writers mentioned here (and several who are not). Yet precisely because the historical mystery is a growth field, one may anticipate new variations and, in time, new settings and periods.

Ancient, Medieval, Victorian

Still, at the end of the 1990s the historical mystery is quantitatively dominated by those who write on ancient Greece or Rome, on the Middle Ages (largely in England), and on Victorian Britain. Each period has its dominant writer: Lindsey Davis, Ellis Peters, and Anne Perry, respectively, three British authors. Peters has attracted the greatest number of imitators.

Perhaps the first into antiquity was Margaret Doody, whose *Aristotle Detective* (1978) was modeled on the approach of Lillian de la Torre. Doody chose 332 B.C. for a novel that unfolded fully to the formula: a family member is accused of murder; to free him, the real murderer must be unmasked; a young man acting as detective enlists the help of Aristotle; the two work against sinister opponents; a trial ensues; and at trial's end, a dramatic confrontation leads to the unmasking of the murderer who (there being little truly hard evidence) attempts to flee and drowns. But Doody's interests turned elsewhere, to writing of ancient intelligence and espionage, and Lindsey Davis occupied the vacancy.

Lindsey Davis' *The Silver Pigs* (1989) introduced Marcus Didius Falco, tough guy private eye in first-century Rome. Falco comes upon a plot to overthrow the emperor. He disguises himself as a slave and is taken to Britain. He wisecracks his way through every dangerous situation, ogling the girls, fussing with his "ma," tying everything up neatly in the end. Reviewers hailed Falco as ancient Rome's Philip Marlowe, and though he lacks the streak of romanticism and melancholy so essential to Marlowe's persona, the comparison stuck. Through successive novels, all very readable, to *A Dying Light in Corduba* (1998), Davis earned, after the death of Ellis Peters, the dust jacket title Queen of the Historical Whodunit. Yet except for *Time to Depart* (1995), one might reasonably argue that aside from time and setting, Falco and some lesser private eye of the present—Andrew Bergman's Jack LeVine, as in *Hollywood and LeVine* (1975), for example—are interchangeable. Still, there is sound social history here, especially in the romance between Falco and Helena Justina, the daughter of a wealthy senator; marriage is not possible for them until

Falco becomes a rich man. And some of Davis' books (*Venus in Copper*, 1991, for example) contain set scenes that are both instructive and great fun.

Steven Saylor, an American, has been less productive though somewhat more careful in constructing his historical settings. *Roman Blood* (1991) introduced Gordianus the Finder, who, across seven more novels, ages, retires, and is brought back into harness to oppose the great Cicero. The entire series is entitled *Rome sub Rosa*; each individual book wears its learning lightly and effectively; any reader will be pleased with the way in which real time and real events unfold before Gordianus' eyes. When Saylor moves an event—as in the previously mentioned Lucretian oration—he tells the reader so, and why. Saylor's sense of how corruption, power, and sexual licentiousness brought Rome to its knees is woven into the fabric of the books with great skill and conviction, so much so that historians of ancient Greece and Rome have praised him for his work. Interestingly, in 1997 Saylor drew together his Gordianus short stories, which bridge the gap between *Roman Blood* and the second novel, *Arms of Nemesis* (1992), as *The House of the Vestals.* These stories read so well that they quickly took their chronological place in the developing saga. When compared with the books of John M. Roberts, who also writes of ancient Rome—see *SPQR* (1990)—Saylor's integration of history with plot stands out.

Non-Western societies are also the subject of historical mysteries, of course. Sometimes, as with Robert van Gulik's (see separate essay) Judge Dee series, set in seventh-century China, these are reconstructions based to some extent on existing manuscripts, but generally they are woven freshly from a careful reading of secondary materials. Lynda S. Robinson has made ancient Thebes her own, pressing the historical mystery back to Egypt in the 1370s B.C. In *Murder in the Place of Anubis* (1994), an able debut, a priest dies in a fall from a statue of Tutankhamen, then only fourteen years old. As with Saylor's Gordianus, Robinson's Lord Meren, a "confidential inquiry agent," there is both fictional and real growth as the series progresses.

Still, all the historical mysteries set in the ancient world are but a sigh in the night set against the incredible burst of interest in medieval history. Or so it would seem from the many authors in the field. Clearly, the success of Edith Pargeter, who launched her highly popular Brother Cadfael in *A Morbid Taste for Bones* in 1977, is responsible for much of this. As Ellis Peters, she wrote seventeen novels about this Benedictine monk, and, despite a well-established reputation under her real name for moving and thoughtful mysteries, as in *Death and the Joyful Woman* (1961), Peters virtually re-created the post-Tey historical mystery.

Pargeter was remarkably productive. She wrote forty mystery novels, over thirty "straight" novels, and many short stories, and translated many works from Czech. Born and educated in Shropshire, recipient of a British Empire Medal for services in World War II, she died in 1995, by then the focus of fan clubs, critical studies, and great affection. Cadfael was given a television series with Sir Derek Jacobi playing the ever-observant Benedictine (though the films were badly marred by weak production values and never took hold as did John Thaw's Inspector Morse, Jeremy Brett's Sherlock Holmes, Roy Marsden's Adam Dalgleish, or David Suchet's Hercule Poirot). Peters had the good judgment to set Cadfael in the twelfth century, on which there is extensive scholarship, to provide only a light background of medieval reality; and to allow Cadfael a slowly revealed prior life that unfolds across the novels. His first case, she reported, developed from her contemplation of how the bones of one body might be hidden with another in a preforensic age. The bones of St. Winifred are to be moved to the abbey of Shrewsbury; a group of monks is sent to Wales to obtain the relics; Cadfael, after a life as a soldier, crusader, and enjoyer of the flesh, has found his calling; and by the end of *A Morbid Taste for Bones*, Brother Cadfael has burst full-born upon the reader.

Apparently, Peters did not intend a series

until she again began to contemplate the problem of bones and bodies. In *One Corpse Too Many* (1979), Cadfael prepares the bodies of ninety-four executed prisoners for burial, and finds ninety-five. This carefully constructed mystery, with its echoes of the classics in the genre, led to the series that expanded the historical mystery to a vast reading public. Cadfael's sense of humor, Peters' lightly worn learning, the occasional insights into the life and labors of the time, and a lively, straightforward style ensured a steady readership and the annual appearance of a new installment.

If one is to understand a time, one must enter into the minds of the people of that time. Peters knew this, but on the whole she shied away from truly doing so, for she apparently believed that the religiosity and superstition of the society in which Cadfael lived would be repellent to many readers. For this she may, as a historical novelist, be faulted. Yet in *The Heretic's Apprentice* (1989), she led the reader through the true meaning of heresy as carefully and dramatically as the historian Carlo Ginzburg did in his classic *The Cheese and the Worms* (1976, in English), hailed as a triumph of the post-*annaliste* school of historiography. In *The Potter's Field* (1989), Peters presented a conclusion that was, as Sue Feder remarked in the *St. James Guide to Crime and Mystery Writers* (1996, p. 840), to the modern mind, "completely incomprehensible, and yet totally justifiable in its context"—a powerful reminder that history requires one to enter into what people believe to be true, not to criticize their beliefs from the perspective of the present. If one is to study witches, as one historian has remarked, one must, during the time of the study, believe in witches.

Dozens of writers followed in Ellis Peters' footsteps. Paul Harding has been the most prolific, writing of thirteenth- and fourteenth-century England as P. C. Doherty and deriving plots from medieval classics, including Chaucer's *Canterbury Tales*. (As Michael Clynes, Harding has also written of sixteenth-century England and, as Anne Dukthas, of other periods as well.) The writing is that of a journeyman: clear, unencumbered, brief. As noted, Doherty has investigated *The Fate of Princes* (1990), to Ricardian conclusion; has examined the legend of Robin Hood in *The Assassin in the Greenwood* (1993), one of his Hugh Corbett series; and in two of his best books, *An Ancient Evil* (1994) and *A Tournament of Murders* (1997), gives us new versions of a Franklin's Tale while on pilgrimage from London to Canterbury, a device also used by Margaret Frazer.

Edward Marston (a pseudonym for Keith Miles, who under his real name writes golf and tennis mysteries) draws upon the Domesday Book, that great eleventh-century document that provided perhaps the most remarkable census the Western world has ever known. Marston has created a committee, consisting of a soldier, a lawyer, and others, to inquire into dubious Domesday entries. Foils to each other, the two men function as a medieval brain-and-brawn pair who confound murderers, set wrongs aright, and uphold the canons of the twentieth-century search or Grail novel in a time more appropriate to it. *The Wolves of Savernake* (1993), *The Ravens of Blackwater* (1994), and *The Dragons of Archenfield* (1995) are effective historical mysteries that show quite substantial growth from earlier Marston novels, set in Elizabethan England.

Sharan Newman's careful research is applied to twelfth-century France, and Candace Robb uses equally skillful research for fourteenth-century England. The latter has been more explicit than any other writer of historical mysteries in setting out how she does her research and why she feels it matters (in *The Apothecary Rose*, 1993, for example). Her series figure, Owen Archer, is a well-realized person, especially in *The Lady Chapel* (1994) and *The Nun's Tale* (1995). Robb accompanies her work with bibliographies, author's notes, maps, and glossaries, and is stylistically closest to Anne Perry in her writing.

The burst of medieval attention, which includes such writers as Ian Morson, C. L. Grace, Susanna Gregory, and Domini Highsmith, as well as Kate Sedley, has carried through the Renaissance, as in the work of Elizabeth Eyre and George Herman, using Italy for their settings, to th. seventeenth and eighteenth centuries. Peter Tremayne has written of a seventh-century nun, Sister Fidelma, using knowledge of Celtic history to advantage, as in *The Subtle Serpent* (1998). These periods have not attracted anything like the interest in the nineteenth century, however, with its apparent closeness to ourselves, its easily recognizable gaslight scenes, and its many resonating relationships arising from classics read or attempted in school.

Anne Perry is to the English nineteenth century what P. D. James and Ruth Rendell are to the twentieth: the embodiment of mystery and crime fiction. One tends to think of Sherlock Holmes as Victorian, but he was, essentially, Edwardian. Nevertheless, the rhythms of his speech can be heard in most historical novelists who choose the nineteenth century for their focus, and especially so in Perry.

Anne Perry was born in London in 1938. Her parents took her to New Zealand as a child. In 1954, she was convicted of helping a schoolgirl friend murder the friend's mother, for which she served over five years in prison. Perry settled quietly in Scotland and in 1979 began to write mysteries, all of which are about either Charlotte Pitt, a woman who has married below herself, and her husband, Thomas, of the London police; or a detective, William Monk. Perry alternates the two series and has averaged well over a novel a year. In 1994, after the release of the New Zealand film *Heavenly Creatures* and the revelation that Perry had been convicted of murder, critics and readers rushed to find evidence in her novels of contrition, suffering, or other autobiographical insights, but her writing remained as it had always been: clear, a little didactic, concerned with Victorian social mores, and nonjudgmental. From *The Cater Street Hangman* (1979), which introduced the Pitts, to *Brunswick Gardens* (1998), also about the Pitts, Perry has explored the almost claustrophobic nature of Victorian society os-

tensibly through her male figures; yet, as a reader becomes increasingly aware, almost obliquely the female characters reveal the most. Despite a tendency, diminishing across time, to weave in tidbits of information needlessly, Perry is a first-rate novelist. Her work varies from the excellent, as in *Cardington Crescent* (1987) or *Silence in Hanover Close* (1988), to the perfunctory: *Traitor's Gate* (1995). There is no sign of decline, however, merely some inconsistency at the margins.

No one has successfully challenged Anne Perry. There are other—indeed, many other—historical mystery novelists who have chosen the Victorian period as their own. Some, like Emily Brightwell or Robin Paige (a pseudonym for Susan and Bill Albert), view the period in lighter colors than Perry does. Kate Ross has written of a gentleman-detective, Julian Kestrel, who moves in the highest circles of English society; these lush books are poised between novels of romance and novels of mystery, and the uneasy mix does not threaten Anne Perry's dark dominance.

There was an American Victorian period, of course, though no writer has dominated the scene as Davis, Peters, and Perry have dominated their chosen periods. Maan Meyers, a pseudonym for Annette and Martin Meyers, has written a series tracing life in New York from the 1660s to the nineteenth century. Despite wearing their research on their sleeves, the Meyerses have created enjoyable characters and, in *The High Constable* (1994), a genuine whodunit. James D. Brewer writes of the Civil War and Reconstruction era (see *No Bottom*, 1994, and *No Virtue*, 1995, for the establishment of his series figures), and Miriam Monfredo has taken the pre–Civil War years as her arena, writing of the women's suffrage movement in *The Seneca Falls Inheritance* (1992), the Underground Railroad in *North Star Conspiracy* (1993), the temperance movement in *Blackwater Spirits* (1995)—much the best—and the abolition movement in *Through a Golden Eagle* (1996). Her work is undoubtedly feminist, as is that of Dianne Day and Barbara Hambly, and all make many sound points for their respective periods. In

The Stalking Horse, Monfredo (1998) moved to the outbreak of the Civil War and the founding of the Pinkerton Agency, also the subject of *Eye of the Agency* (1997), by Richard Moquist. Best received of all, by critics and purchasers, has been Caleb Carr, for *The Alienist* (1994).

Still, the Victorian and Edwardian periods—Dianne Day's work is set in the latter—really belong to the British. It was, after all, their monarchs who gave their names to the periods. And the writer who, after the Sherlockians, best added to developing the canon was Peter Lovesey, who in *Wobble to Death* (1970), which depicts a continuous walking contest, introduced all the elements discussed here. Carefully researched, written from the inside out, depicting crimes that arose from the times and their conditions, at once dark and amusing, his series featuring Sergeant Cribb and Constable Thackeray were ahead of their time, hailed as innovations before the subgenre of "historical mystery" was even known. Seven more Victorian mysteries followed, from *The Detective Wore Silk Drawers* (1971) to *Waxwork* (1978), before Lovesey moved on to Inspector Dew, Dr. Crippin, and 1921. He created a second historical series, featuring King Edward VII, the quintessential Edwardian, and a police procedural series set in Bath; the last sold substantially better than the adventures of Sergeant Cribb did. Lovesey was truly ahead of his time, for he is among a small group of authentic begetters of the historical mystery. Still, he abandoned his first series at the end of the 1970s, turning to Bertie, as the king was known, and to Peter Diamond of the contemporary Bath murder squad; thus, most students of the genre mark the true establishment of the contemporary historical mystery with Brother Cadfael in 1977 and Anne Perry's first novel in 1979.

New Directions

In the end one must not judge a historical mystery by how accurate its history is but by how good the story is: how well told, how entertaining, how revealing of character, and, yes, how mystifying. Writers of historical mysteries face a somewhat unfair disadvantage: their readers can check up on them relatively easily, while most readers cannot verify whether a pathologist in a Patricia Cornwell novel has used precisely the right instrument to examine a bit of human tissue. When an error is detected in a contemporary mystery or spy thriller, most readers are irritated—a computer expert will not tolerate a techno-thriller that is simply wrong in its programming, and a nurse will be quick to criticize a Mary Kittredge nursing mystery if hospital routine is set out implausibly. If a mystery is to be convincing, it must be accurate in all the particulars in which it can be accurate, and above all, in all the particulars that matter to the crime, its causes, its investigation, and its solution. A reader will tolerate errors around the edges but not in matters of centrality. Most readers do not know how to question the choice of a saw during an autopsy; they do know how to look up a date, even if they do not do it.

Most historical mysteries are, like most mysteries of any kind, often unsatisfying in their solution, and many are written far too hurriedly, as are many novels of any kind. But the best historical mysteries, like the best novels that use a sense of place and social scene powerfully to reveal the inner tensions of a society, as James McClure does in his superlative series set in apartheid-era South Africa, are good stories, and in a society and time not greatly given to reading history as written by academics and other professionals, who often shut readers out rather than embracing them, the historical mystery is at the least a good surrogate.

An Instance of the Fingerpost (1998), by Iain Pears, may well be, to date, the best "historical mystery" ever written. Pears' political thriller is set in Restoration Oxford. Charles II has just ascended the throne. England is rife with conspiracy theories, with accusations about political, religious, and sexual misconduct. The countryside has been ravaged by war, and the English hardly know how miserable they are or should be in their damp, muddy country. The monarchy is insecure, striving for stability. New ideas from the Continent are discussed at high table in the university city. An Oxford don is murdered, and Pears begins his chase.

The novel is constructed around four narratives, each person testifying to a version of the truth, each misleading the reader. Real figures, taken directly from the historical record, crowd the novel. The reader sees the events through the words of a Venetian visitor alert to the oddities of the English; a student obsessed with clearing his father's name of treason who is alert to nuance; a mathematician and codebreaker who obviously is not to be trusted; and a compassionate, observant historian who has the strengths and the weaknesses of his discipline. This novel requires much of the reader, and it makes a good name for the historical mystery. (Another Restoration mystery, *Invitation to a Funeral*, by Molly Brown, also published in 1998, suggests a possible trend to post-Commonwealth England.) Pears, an art historian by training, has an acute eye; an Oxford doctorate himself, he sees university life plain. Restoration England comes alive in this book, which surely ought to enjoy the success accorded Umberto Eco's *The Name of the Rose* (see also discussion of Eco in essay on "The Metaphysical Mystery"). This is classic mystery-making, but it is also exquisitely well-crafted history.

In 1997 *Publisher's Weekly*, the bible of the American publishing industry, authoritatively confirmed that the historical mystery was the fastest-growing branch of the mystery genre. Given the rapid growth of the parent field, this means that more writers are turning to the field, as, presumably, are more readers than ever before. Perhaps a book like Pears's *An Instance of the Fingerpost* will, like Umberto Eco's *The Name of the Rose*, published to acclamation and great financial success in 1980 (and in English in 1983), propel the historical mystery toward greater complexity, greater honesty, better writing. Eco's success turned in some measure on the "coffee table"

mentality of those who try to demonstrate their taste by displaying a book that remains unread; in part on the strange rise of semiotics into a kind of public popularity; in part because the period in which it was set was remote, even forbidding, yet intensely colorful and strange.

Still, such facile explanations cannot account for the phenomenal sales of Eco's book. A popular film, released in 1986 and starring Sean Connery, a major draw at the box office, no doubt buoyed sales further, though *The Name of the Rose* may still have remained the most-bought, least-read book of the decade. Eco's next book, *Foucault's Pendulum* (1988), was equally ambitious, elaborate, and historically rooted—anything by Eco constitutes "heavy history" as distinct from "light history," in the revealing language of reviewers for the many mystery review newsletters and magazines that have sprung up in the 1980s and 1990s—but it did not sell nearly as well. *Pendulum* was about (to the extent that anything versed in semiotic structure can be said to be "about" anything) conspiracies abstract and real, ancient and modern, and Eco employed virtually every plot device known to the mystery and thriller genre. Both these books were well translated into English, so their readability does not account for the relative difference in reception.

Perhaps the best explanation for the success of *The Name of the Rose* is that it was equally pleasing to more than one audience: historians liked it, and sophisticated modern readers finished it, in part (we might imagine) because the book is a whodunit in the classic sense, set in a time of great fascination to the present, when everything—morals, state formation, urban life, daily customs—seemed set in stone while in fact being under constant assault and undergoing constant change. Above all, Eco synthesized the main intellectual themes of the day and mirrored them for our time. His work was both historical and presentist, deeply researched and provocatively postmodern, despite, or even because of, that research. Above all, one would like to think, Eco's success turned in some measure on the recognition that history, and thus the historical mystery, must in fact be as complex as all of life, and not filled with cardboard characters who sound as though they had traveled by time machine from a demotically speaking present to a simplified past. Historical mysteries were once, rather like Mark Twain's *A Connecticut Yankee in King Arthur's Court*, about little more than modern-day events transposed onto past settings; but somewhere between Tey and Lovesey, or Eco and Pears, the historical mystery has taken on the qualities of secrecy, silence, and cunning associated not only with the best mystery fiction but with the best fiction of all.

Selected Bibliography

Bedell, Jeanne F. "Peter Lovesey's Sergeant Cribb and Constable Thackeray." In *Cops and Constables: American and British Fictional Policemen*. Edited by George N. Dove and Earl F. Bargainnier. Bowling Green, Ohio: Bowling Green State University Popular Press, 1986.

Cooper-Clark, Diana. "An Interview with Peter Lovesey." *Armchair Detective* 14: 210–212, 214–217 (summer 1981).

———. "An Interview with Anne Perry." *Clues: A Journal of Detection* 3: 52–65 (winter 1982).

Kelly, R. Gordon. *Mystery Fiction and Modern Life.* Jackson: University Press of Mississippi, 1998.

Leaker, Cathy, and Julie Anne Taddeo. "Defend and Preserve: Imminent Nostalgia in the Victorian Mysteries of Anne Perry." *Clues: A Journal of Detection* 17: 77–108 (summer 1996).

Lovesey, Peter. "Doctor Crippen and the Real Inspector Dew." *Armchair Detective* 17: 244–248 (summer 1984).

Lowenthal, David. *Possessed by the Past.* New York: Free Press, 1996.

Martin, Murray S. "Classical Times, Classical Crimes." *Clues: A Journal of Detection* 18: 147–156 (winter 1997).

Mystery Readers Journal: The Journal of Mystery Readers International. Two issues devoted to "History Mystery," 9 (summer, fall, 1993).

Roy, Sandra. *Josephine Tey.* Boston: Twayne, 1980.

THE LEGAL CRIME NOVEL

JON L. BREEN

IN THE LEGAL crime novel, or legal thriller, the workings of the law and the activities of lawyers—whether in courtrooms, conference rooms, or the intrigue-filled corridors of courthouses and law firms—are the focus of the action. By that definition, a great many works of fiction of the last century and a half (or even longer) seem to qualify, but legal crime novels, having never before appeared in such great numbers as in the past decade, have only recently come to be regarded as their own subgenre. Thus, the emergence of the legal thriller as a separate category of crime fiction could be regarded more as a commercial than a literary phenomenon, but this view is not entirely accurate. Although there is much crossover in attitude and subject matter, the focus and intent of current legal crime novels are significantly different from those of past crime novels with legal settings.

The new category is generally dated from the late 1980s and early 1990s, with the advent of lawyer-novelists Scott Turow and John Grisham. The extreme popularity of these writers was partially responsible for the entrance of a large number of others, mostly lawyers but including some law-savvy laypersons, into the fiction field.

From the beginning of mystery and detective fiction as a distinct genre in the middle nineteenth century, it is likely more authors have been drawn from the ranks of lawyers than of any other profession. Wilkie Collins, author of *The Woman in White* (1860) and *The Moonstone* (1868), was law trained. He was followed from the bar to the fiction shelves by such writers as M. McDonnell Bodkin, Octavus Roy Cohen, Erle Stanley Gardner, Lawrence Treat, Henry Kane, Michael Gilbert, and Harold Q. Masur. Most of these lawyer-writers used their knowledge of the law as incidental or supporting detail, and did not produce what are now called legal crime novels. Gilbert's *Smallbone Deceased* (1950), set in a solicitor's office, may be an exception, and of course Gardner's Perry Mason novels usually include courtroom climaxes. The novels of Eleazar Lipsky, notably *The People Against O'Hara* (1950), share many characteristics with the contemporary legal crime novel. But it probably never occurred to most of these writers that their readers would be interested in how real lawyers pursue their personal and professional lives.

Not even the authors most interested in explicating the law for a popular audience, like Melville Davisson Post and Arthur Train, were writing legal crime fiction in the contemporary sense. Post's "criminal" lawyer Randolph Mason used loopholes in the law to help his clients subvert justice in two short story collections, *The Strange Schemes of Randolph Mason* (1896) and *The Man of Last*

Resort (1897), and reformed somewhat to help the cause of justice in a third, *The Corrector of Destinies* (1908). Train's New York attorney Ephraim Tutt appeared in a long series of *Saturday Evening Post* stories, collected in a number of volumes from *Tutt and Mr. Tutt* (1920) to *Mr. Tutt Finds a Way* (1945). Generally, in both these series, though the stories turn on specific, often esoteric points of law, the problems of the clients carry more interest than the lives of the lawyers.

Of course, trials have always been popular subjects for fiction. Many of the major names in detective fiction—Agatha Christie, Dorothy L. Sayers, Margery Allingham, John Dickson Carr, Ellery Queen, and Anthony Berkeley—included a trial scene occasionally. The big-trial novel, in which a substantial part of the action is spent watching a major case (usually murder) unfold in court, dates back at least as far as James Fenimore Cooper's *The Ways of the Hour* (1850). Behind all its tangential argument and long-windedness, Cooper's novel has the same basic structure as its twentieth-century equivalents, moving from crime to accusation through the full course of the trial, from jury selection to verdict and sentencing, with a final revelation. (In its attacks on the jury system and on trial by press, the novel sounds almost contemporary, but some of the other views Cooper espouses—proslavery and antifeminist—clearly belong to another time.)

Throughout the twentieth century, periodic best-sellers have created surges of popularity for the big-trial form. Theodore Dreiser's *An American Tragedy* (1925), a large-canvas classic, spends more than sixty pages recounting murder defendant Clyde Griffith's testimony about the rowboat drowning of his pregnant girlfriend. Other examples include Frances Noyes Hart's *The Bellamy Trial* (1927), a still-enthralling all-courtroom novel based on the author's experience covering the Hall-Mills murder case; Robert Hichens' *The Paradine Case* (1933), an Old Bailey soap opera that holds up much less well today; James Gould Cozzens' *The Just and the Unjust* (1942), a leisurely novel nearly as negative toward juries as Cooper's; Meyer Levin's

Compulsion (1956), a masterful fictionalization of the 1924 trial of Nathan Leopold, Jr., and Richard Loeb, two wealthy Chicago youths saved by Clarence Darrow from execution for the "thrill killing" of a fourteen-year-old boy; and, most influential of all, Robert Traver's *Anatomy of a Murder* (1958). Traver, pseudonym of Michigan Supreme Court Justice John Donaldson Voelker, showed how much extra value in detail and authenticity a legal insider could bring to the fictional courtroom in his account of the trial of an army lieutenant for the murder of his wife's alleged rapist.

In the wake of Traver's enormous success, other outstanding examples of the big-trial novel found a ready public. Among the best was Al Dewlen's *Twilight of Honor* (1961), in which a burned-out criminal defender faces a classic situation: representing a feckless drifter accused of murdering the most prominent citizen in a Texas Panhandle town. The way Texas law and procedure differ from those of most other states adds to the interest of a novel that, like Traver's, is solidly in the tradition of the contemporary legal crime novel.

Many of the perennial best-selling writers of the time (though not themselves lawyers) turned to the courtroom for at least one book, sometimes eschewing homicide for a variety of other causes of action. Evan Hunter's *The Paper Dragon* (1966) is an outstanding novel about a plagiarism trial; Irving Wallace's *The Seven Minutes* (1969) is a well-researched if artistically undistinguished account of an obscenity case; and Leon Uris' *QB VII* (1970) concerns a British libel trial stemming from accusations of Nazi war crimes.

In addition to the plentitude of fictional trials, there have always been lawyer-detectives, created by lawyers and nonlawyers alike. Some of them, like Gardner's Perry Mason and Sara Woods's Antony Maitland, regularly make courtroom appearances, while others (Masur's Scott Jordan, Craig Rice's John J. Malone, and, more recently, William G. Tapply's Brady Coyne) usually stay out of court and function more like private eyes.

What Is a Legal Crime Novel?

What is the difference between most of these earlier examples and what is termed the legal crime novel or legal thriller? There are several factors. To begin with, the emphasis in earlier fictional court cases is on the parties to the case rather than on the lawyers. Even when the lawyer is the protagonist, as with Perry Mason, the emphasis is on the mystery, specific points of law, and the facts of the case itself, not on how Mason runs his law practice—nor on his legal ethics, since (thin as the ice he sometimes skates on) the courtroom hero defends only innocent clients and thus is always on the side of the angels. The legal system is used in most crime novels as were police activities before the advent of the police procedural: as a necessary piece of background detail that the reader might be expected to take for granted.

There is also a greater degree of confidence in the legal system and in those who carry out its mandates. Perry Mason's nemesis, District Attorney Hamilton Burger, is an honest public servant with an unfortunate habit of prosecuting the wrong person. If he gets the right suspect, his constituents can rest easy: he surely will get his conviction. For the system to work and justice to prevail, assume these novels, all it takes is for the right miscreant to be brought to the bar, and most trial stories are concerned with correcting the balance on the rare occasions that does not happen.

Not suprisingly, much of the legal procedure in crime novels was designed more for dramatic effect than for accuracy. As with police procedure, writers without inside knowledge sometimes patterned their view of the system on other fiction rather than on real life. An advocate would break off in the middle of the examination of a witness to argue to the jury; witnesses would appeal in an order that made sense dramatically but not procedurally; nonsensical objections would be made while obvious ones were missed; all sorts of things would happen in court (or on the way there) that would be impossible in

real life. Even the lawyer-novelists sometimes sacrificed the reality of the law and the courtroom for those elements that seemed best to serve the interests of a good story. Trials in fiction (as they still are in television and film adaptations) were full of angry outbursts from the defendant or the gallery, as if the trial situation in itself were not sufficiently dramatic to keep the reader's attention.

The world of the latter-day American legal thriller is quite different, and a number of factors combined to create it. One stems from the hostility of the public toward lawyers. Rightly or wrongly, the public blames the legal profession for the destructive litigiousness it perceives in the civil sphere and for the ineffectiveness of the criminal justice system in dealing with serious crime. Paradoxically, this hostility has worked in favor of law-trained novelists who can satisfy increased curiosity about how the system really works. Recent legal novelists have been less likely than their predecessors to glorify the system, more likely to show the law and lawyers, warts and all. The televising of high-profile trials, most notoriously that of O. J. Simpson, has educated the public about procedure and fed its doubts about the system's efficacy.

In earlier trial fiction, the central figure was almost always a defense attorney. If the prosecutor was the hero, particularly in detective novels like Gardner's Doug Selby series, writers had to find ways to keep him on the right side while retaining the element of surprise. In more recent trial fiction, more and more heroic prosecutors appear, as the hostility to defense attorneys, again at least partly as a result of the widely unpopular Simpson verdict, has grown stronger than to lawyers generally. In her novel *False Witness* (1996), Patricia D. Benke, whose protagonist is a prosecutor, quotes Supreme Court Justice Byron White, in a dissenting opinion in the 1967 case *United States* v. *Wade*, on the misunderstood role of the defender:

> Law enforcement officers have the obligation to convict the guilty and to make sure they do not convict the innocent. They must be

dedicated to making the criminal trial a procedure for the ascertainment of the true facts surrounding the commission of the crime. . . . But defense counsel has no comparable obligation to ascertain or present the truth. Our system assigns him a different mission. . . . Defense counsel need present nothing, even if he knows what the truth is. . . . If he can confuse a witness, even a truthful one, or make him appear at a disadvantage, unsure or indecisive, that will be his normal course. . . . In this respect, . . . we countenance or require conduct which in many instances has little, if any, relation to the search for truth. (p. 266)

Despite this clear accounting of their special role, defenders continue to be blamed for doing their jobs too well. While many leading characters of legal crime novels continue to be on the defense side, their role is often much more ambiguous than in past times.

The legal thriller is really a kind of legal procedural, in which the details of behind-the-scenes maneuvering are seen along with the public face of the trial, and in which the infighting and intrigues of law firms carry as much interest as any of the cases they handle. Sometimes, as in the police procedural, several different cases are covered rather than just one, providing a more realistic idea of what a busy advocate's or judge's life is like. Authors of legal crime fiction, though still depending on the element of surprise, moved away from the pure whodunit to more complex and ambiguous considerations of law and punishment.

The first and best novel of the most commercially successful lawyer-novelist of the 1990s illustrates many of the modern legal crime novel's defining characteristics.

John Grisham

Born in Jonesboro, Arkansas, in 1955, John Grisham received his law degree from the University of Mississippi and practiced criminal law in that state from 1981 to 1990, also serving in the Mississippi House of Representatives from 1984 to 1990. Introducing a 1992 reprint, Grisham recounts his inspiration for his first novel, *A Time to Kill* (1989):

> One day I stumbled upon a horrible trial in which a young girl testified against the man who brutally raped her. It was a gut-wrenching experience for me, and I was only a spectator. One moment she was courageous, the next pitifully frail. I was mesmerized. I could not imagine the nightmare she and her family had been through. I wondered what I would do if she were my daughter. As I watched her suffer before the jury, I wanted personally to shoot the rapist. For one brief yet interminable moment, I wanted to be her father. I wanted justice. There was a story there. (pp. ix–x)

White Mississippi lawyer Jake Brigance in many ways represents the familiar figure of the stalwart liberal defender, belonging to a line that includes Atticus Finch of Harper Lee's *To Kill a Mockingbird* (1960) and Gavin Stevens of William Faulkner's *Intruder in the Dust* (1948). Brigance willingly takes on the defense of Carl Lee Hailey, an African-American who, believing the two white rednecks who raped his young daughter would not get their due from the Mississippi justice system, shot them to death in the courthouse. But Brigance acts differently from earlier noble defenders in a number of ways. He forcefully emphasizes to his impoverished client the need for money, he fights off the attempts of other lawyers to get the case away from him, and he takes recourse to a somewhat sleazy expert witness in his effort to get Carl Lee off on an insanity defense. He is not a knee-jerk liberal—at one point, he shocks the female law student who offers to help him by asserting a belief in capital punishment. Whatever his views, Brigance certainly remains a hero, sticking with his client despite threats and attacks on himself and his family and ultimately prevailing with an eloquent plea to the white jurors.

The character of Brigance was closely based on Grisham himself, as he explains in his introduction:

> I no longer practice law, but for ten years I did so in a manner very similar to Jake Brigance. I represented people, never banks or insurance companies or big corporations. I was a street lawyer. Jake and I are the same age. I played quarterback in high school, though not very well. Much of what he says and does is what I think I would say and do under the circumstances. We both drive Saabs. We've both felt the unbearable pressure of murder trials, which is something I try to capture in the story. We've both lost sleep over clients and vomited in courthouse restrooms. (pp. xi–xii)

How personal this first novel obviously was may explain why *A Time to Kill* is so far superior to most of its successors. Grisham's first novel has many of the standard big-trial elements—the drunken former law partner who assists Brigance is another of them—but he gives them a fresh treatment. The presence of a sympathetically depicted vigilante as Brigance's client struck a responsive cord in many readers, who had come to believe like Carl Lee that they could not depend on receiving justice from the system and may have to take the law into their own hands. *A Time to Kill* is not only representative of the new-style legal novel but is one of the classics of courtroom fiction from any period.

Grisham's first book was not a notable commercial success on its initial publication. According to his introduction to the reprint, the 5,000 copies Wynwood printed "sold well within a hundred miles of home, but was neglected by the rest of the world" (p. xi). But his second and most famous novel, *The Firm* (1991), was an immediate major best-seller, as all its successors have been. *The Firm*, written by the author's own account according to a suspense novel formula gleaned from a *Writer's Digest* magazine article, is a prime example of another trend in the legal thriller, showing the inner workings and politics of a law firm, an area that would not have occurred to most of the early legal crime nov-

elists to explore. Harvard law graduate Mitchell McDeere, heavily recruited to join a large Memphis firm, gradually finds out its real nature as a front for organized crime and, like several Grisham protagonists to follow, becomes a target from all sides, crooks and law enforcers alike.

By the author's own admission, each of Grisham's early best-sellers, including *The Firm*, *The Pelican Brief* (1992), and *The Client* (1993), drops in quality from its predecessor. While his mastery of pace and plot accounts for their popularity, their characters often tend to be flat, and they often make better films than novels. *The Pelican Brief*, about a female law student who has suspicions concerning the murder of two Supreme Court justices, follows the chase-and-menace pattern of *The Firm* very closely. In *The Client*, eleven-year-old Mark Sway, who has witnessed the murder of a lawyer and has dangerous knowledge about a political assassination, has forces of both law and organized crime after him, much like the protagonists of the two previous books. Both Mark and the lawyer he consults, maverick female child-advocate Reggie Love, come to life more fully in the film version. The novel has a strong plot and some good courtroom action but is weakened by padding and the marginal credibility of the young hero.

The Chamber (1994) is a conscious attempt, and largely a successful one, to return to the quality level of *A Time to Kill*. Its treatment of capital punishment, including the atmosphere of death row, the appeals process leading up to an execution, and the mechanics of the execution itself, is among the most thorough in fiction. Although Grisham implied a favorable view of the death penalty through the hero of his first novel, his sentiments in this book are more ambiguous. Most of his characters, including protagonist Adam Hall, twenty-six-year-old associate of the third largest law firm in Chicago, view the death penalty with distaste. Adam is surprised when he learns from his firm's death-row appeals specialist that the prison warden opposes the death penalty. He is told,

You're about to learn something, Adam—the death penalty may be very popular in our country, but the people who are forced to impose it are not supporters. You're about to meet these people: the guards who get close to the inmates; the administrators who must plan for an efficient killing; the prison employees who rehearse for a month beforehand. It's a strange little corner of the world, and a very depressing one. (p. 42)

On the other side of the ledger, the inmate Adam is trying to save, his grandfather Sam Cayhall, is a bigoted white supremacist who was responsible for the deaths, in a law-office bombing, of the twin five-year-old sons of a Jewish civil rights lawyer. Grisham's sensitive treatment of Adam and Sam, together with his delineation of the process and his usual constructional mastery, shows what a good novelist he is capable of being.

Another of Grisham's better novels is *The Rainmaker* (1995), partly because he eschews his usual third-person narrative for the humorously cynical voice of recent law grad Rudy Baylor, who is involved with several cases over the course of the story. In a typical Grisham situation of one man outnumbered by a better-equipped enemy, Baylor takes on an insurance company's army of lawyers in his representation of a dying leukemia victim who was denied coverage for a bone marrow transplant from his twin brother.

The Runaway Jury (1996), with its trendy subject matter of a tobacco company liability trial, represents both Grisham's virtues and his limitations. The complicated jury-fixing scenario at the center of the plot is fascinating, if only marginally credible, and the crosscutting maintains suspense masterfully. But if the storytelling is strong, the characterization is weak, leaving the impression, as with *The Client,* that the film version, if well cast, could actually be an improvement.

As much as Grisham has become synonymous with the legal thriller, a less prolific best-selling writer who preceded him by two years has been at least as important in the genre's popularity and development.

Scott Turow

The novel that really started the new vogue for lawyer-written legal crime novels in the United States was Scott Turow's *Presumed Innocent* (1987). Although he has been surpassed by Grisham in purely commercial terms, he is a more skilled, versatile, and substantial writer, producing thrillers that are also formidable mainstream novels. If John Grisham is the Ian Fleming of the legal thriller, striking just the right note with the public to ensure outstanding commercial success, Turow is its John le Carré, bringing to the genre literary ambition and value beyond pure entertainment.

Turow was born in Chicago in 1949 and received a bachelor's degree from Amherst College and a master's degree from Stanford University. His first published book was nonfiction, *One L: An Inside Account of Life in the First Year at Harvard Law School* (1977), published the year before he received his juris doctor's degree from Harvard.

In introducing *Guilty as Charged* (1996), a Mystery Writers of America anthology of courtroom stories, Turow appropriately denies having invented the legal thriller, pointing to early examples by Plato (the trial of Socrates) and Shakespeare (*The Merchant of Venice*) as well as works of Herman Melville, Charles Dickens, Robert Traver, Harper Lee, and James Gould Cozzens. But the description of his intent in his first novel underlines the difference between the contemporary legal crime novel and most of its predecessors:

To my mind, the legal stories being written today differ . . . only in one significant regard, and that is the extent to which they dwell on legal detail. The longtime theory of storytellers—Hollywood screenwriters were the worst offenders—was that a popular audience would find the rigmarole of the law tiresome. But, generally speaking, the legal thriller is a chockablock [*sic*] with intricate renderings of the mechanics of the courtroom, lawyers' stratagems, and the rationales of judges' decisions. . . . In [*Presumed Innocent*], the questions asked, objections offered, and rulings made were, to the best of my ability, accurate, typical, and in conformance with the rules of evidence. When the novel was published, most readers seemed, rather than bored by this precision, enthralled by it. (pp. 2–3)

Strictly as a crime or mystery novel, *Presumed Innocent* remains Turow's masterpiece. It is narrated in the present tense by Rusty Sabich, small-town prosecutor in the fictitious midwestern Kindle County. It is obvious throughout, especially to experienced readers of detective fiction, that Sabich is not telling the reader everything he knows—in fact, the reader is bound to consider the possibility that he is actually guilty of the crime for which he is tried: the bludgeoning murder of his D.A.'s office colleague Carolyn Polhemus, with whom he once had an affair. The structure is in the grand tradition of deceptive but amply clued detective fiction, and the charges of unfairness leveled by some reviewers—notably Robert Towers, who felt so outraged at Turow's misdirection that he felt justified in revealing the solution in the *New York Review of Books* (28 June 1987)—were unjustified. The present tense, an affectation imitated by some other legal thriller writers with less apparent reason, works well here in creating a sense of immediacy and uncertainty.

Turow's trial scenes are some of the best in fiction, their procedural accuracy and dramatic give-and-take complemented by the vivid characterizations of the players: prosecutor Nico Della Guardia, Latin American–born defender Alejandro (Sandy) Stern, and African-American Judge Larren Lyttle. The finishing twist is expertly handled. In a way, the novel's literary quality and its excellence as a piece of detective fiction work against each other, at least according to its critical response. Turow wrote so well, some writers (including Anne Rice in the *New York Times Book Review*, 28 June 1987) seemed to resent the fact he was writing a mystery puzzle as well as an excellent novel.

Sandy Stern takes center stage in Turow's second novel, *The Burden of Proof* (1990),

which may be even better than its predecessor as a work of general fiction, though less notable as a legal thriller or detective novel. Adjusting to the shocking suicide of his wife, Clare, Stern probes family secrets to understand her motives, while defending his wealthy brother-in-law on charges of financial impropriety. Stern's personal quest to rebuild his life provides the novel's principal appeal.

The third Turow novel, *Pleading Guilty* (1993), another novel-cum-puzzle in which corporate lawyer Mack Malloy tries to find his firm's missing top litigator, is probably his least impressive novel to date, but the one to follow is his finest and most ambitious. *The Laws of Our Fathers* (1996) is a masterful large-canvas saga that alternates between a present-day drive-by shooting case in Kindle County and events years before, in the student antiwar protest period, involving some of the same characters. The alternating narrators are Judge Sonia (Sonny) Klonsky, presiding in the present-day case, and, in the sixties flashbacks, journalist Seth Weissman, Sonny's lover in her hippie days. The staggeringly ambitious novel manages to be a diverting detective story and courtroom drama along with a probing consideration of some major issues and social trends of the twentieth century, including the Holocaust, the student peace movement of the sixties, and street gangs of the nineties, as well as courtroom tactics and ethics.

John Mortimer and the British

For whatever reason, British writers have produced few successful legal thrillers in the American pattern—barrister Dexter Dias, author of *False Witness* (1995) and *Error of Judgment* (1996), is one of the few to try, without notable success. John Mortimer, in the short-story adaptations of scripts for his television series *Rumpole of the Bailey*, though in many ways closer to a British tradition of legal comedy, follows the legal crime novel pattern in several respects.

Mortimer, born in London in 1923, attended Brasenose College, Oxford, and became a barrister in 1948. His first novel, *Charade*, was published in 1947; his first and most famous stage play, the courtroom comedy *The Dock Brief*, was produced in 1958 after being broadcast in Britain a year earlier. His relationship with his blind father, also a barrister, was memorably depicted in *A Voyage Round My Father*, broadcast in 1963 and staged in 1970. During most of Mortimer's prolific writing career, during which he has produced screenplays, teleplays, radio plays, drama criticism, a ballet scenario, and memoirs as well as novels and plays, he continued to argue cases in British courts, taking silk as a Queen's Counsel in 1966.

How do the droll, seriocomic adventures of the elderly, poetry-quoting Horace Rumpole, different as they are in tone and structure from the thrillers of Grisham, Turow, and their colleagues, represent the legal crime novel? For one thing, the barristers' chambers in which Rumpole works is a constant scene of action, and the way the various lawyers and their clerks interact is an important element of the story. The politics involved in taking silk and becoming a judge are also explored. The cases addressed are full of legal ambiguity, with a situation in Rumpole's private life, either in chambers or at home with wife Hilda ("She Who Must Be Obeyed"), often reflecting the issues of the case at hand. This technique is best illustrated by "Rumpole and the Honourable Member" (from the collection *Rumpole of the Bailey*, 1978), a fine story in which his defense in court of a Labour M.P. accused of rape parallels his defense in chambers of senior clerk Albert, accused of robbing the petty cash. In another example, "Rumpole and the Fascist Beast" (from *The Trials of Rumpole*, 1979), an Indian barrister comes into chambers while a right-winger is being charged for rabble-rousing under the Race Relations Act.

The first two collections of Rumpole stories were followed by seven more through *Rumpole and the Angel of Death* (1996). The single novel in the series, *Rumpole's Return* (1980), concerning an ill-advised and short-lived retirement to Florida, is less successful than the shorter cases.

Occasionally, events in legal fiction become so outrageous, one doubts they have an equivalent in real life. Given that British courtrooms apparently allow more muttered comments and adversarial byplay than do American ones, Rumpole's sly comments and outright rudeness to the judge sometimes strain credulity. However, in a letter to the present writer, Mortimer claimed the artistic license taken was minimal: "The truth is that brave advocates (and Rumpole is *very* brave) can *almost* get away with what he does, and I have got very near it myself. . . . As for being rude to the Judge, F. E. Smith (later Lord Birkenhead) was much ruder to Judges than ever Rumpole was."

It may seem unusual to pay serious attention to prose adaptations of stories originally written for television. True, the Rumpole stories sometimes have a situation-comedy aura around them. Occasionally, a character must act in a way wildly *out* of character in order to suit the plot, as when an unlikely infatuation makes Rumpole temporarily give up wine and turn vegetarian in "Rumpole and the Eternal Triangle" (from *Rumpole on Trial*, 1992). But the literate first-person narration of Rumpole, together with the fact that the original writer is the one doing the adapting, makes the stories a special case. They could give pleasure and enlightenment even to a reader who had never seen the television version and did not imagine the remarkable Leo McKern reading every line in the leading role.

For whatever reason, humor has always been a stronger presence in British than in American legal fiction. Mortimer the courtroom humorist belongs to a tradition that includes such earlier authors as A. P. Herbert, Henry Cecil, and Michael Underwood. Cecil, the pseudonym of Henry Cecil Leon, was himself a judge, and though his humor makes comparison to P. G. Wodehouse more likely than to legal crime novelists, his determination to depict how the various personalities of the legal world behave, while detailing how the system, in all its ambiguity, really works, makes him a forerunner of the legal crime writers. He may be best known for the purely comic *Brothers in Law* (1955) and its sequels, but he is at his best as a crime novelist in books like *According to the Evidence* (1954) and *Settled Out of Court* (1959).

Introducing a reprint edition of the latter novel, the present writer speculates on the reasons for the greater incidence of humor in British legal fiction:

> Perhaps those archaic wigs and gowns seen in British courts have something to do with encouraging risibility. The more elaborate the trappings of outward dignity in an institution, the more fun for humorists to deflate them. That the wig-and-gown tradition persists bespeaks not only the British love of ceremony but also the British tolerance for eccentricity and absurdity, which is another key to the British sense of humor.

If they are not prominent among writers of the present-day legal crime novel, British writers have produced some of the classics of trial fiction; examples include Cyril Hare's *Tragedy at Law* (1942), which follows a High Court judge on circuit in wartime England; Edgar Lustgarten's *A Case to Answer* (1947; U.S. title: *One More Unfortunate*), a true-crime specialist's exhaustive account of an accused serial killer's trial; and Raymond Postgate's *Verdict of Twelve* (1940), one of the finest novels to focus on the jury.

Other Notable Writers

Several other writers deserve special note among the many contemporary legal fiction specialists. In *Rampage* (1985), a novel that preceded the debuts of Turow and Grisham, William P. Wood produced perhaps the first landmark in the new-style big-trial novel, where the emphasis has shifted from saving the innocent accused to making a case against the dangerous defendant. Beginning with a graphic account of a revolting triple murder, the novel follows the efforts of prosecutor Tony Fraser to get blood-drinking defendant Charlie Reece the death penalty he deserves. Wood, a former prosecutor in Sacramento, has written several other novels set in the fictitious Santa Maria County, California. *Court of Honor* (1991), with its interesting examination of the ethics of undercover operations, is another strong example.

Texan Jay Brandon has written some of the best trial scenes extant since establishing a legal specialty with *Fade the Heat* (1990). He usually takes the trial to a verdict, which makes his books most satisfactory to courtroom buffs, and he gathers strength from book to book. The small-town mystery *Local Rules* (1995) is impressive in its courtroom legerdemain as well as its gradual revelation through various characters' points of view of a golden girl victim who never appears alive in the story. Even better is *Defiance County* (1996), another small-town case in which a special prosecutor is brought in to make a case for murder against the brother of the D.A. Although some of his books have a San Antonio setting, smaller communities seem to bring out the best in Brandon.

Another former Sacramento advocate, Steve Martini, writes novels about lawyer Paul Madriani set in the thinly disguised Capitol City. Like Brandon, he writes expert courtroom scenes. In both *Compelling Evidence* (1992) and *Prime Witness* (1993), Martini, who himself turned from law practice to journalism, includes some lawyers and judges so incompetent they strain reader credibility; but the publicity-loving defenders toting book contracts seem perfectly true to contemporary life. Along with the realistic legal background, Martini provides some of the most devious formal puzzle plots among the legal crime novelists. *The Judge* (1996) is especially impressive in its reader misdirection.

Robert K. Tanenbaum uses his background as an assistant district attorney in New York in the 1970s to create the Butch Karp series, which shows how avoidance of trial, entailing routine plea bargaining, is the only thing that allows the overloaded criminal justice system to work at all. The Karp novels are usually of the modular kind, with several cases operating on parallel tracks but not necessarily intersecting. Insider details and a screenwriter's sense of action make the novels work, though overly movieish touches occasionally undercut the realism inherent in the narrative. *No Lesser Plea* (1987) was the first of the series, while *Reversible Error* (1992) is much the best. *Corruption of Blood* (1995), an enthralling but not completely successful fact/fiction hybrid, puts Karp to work investigating the JFK assassination for a congressional committee, drawing on the author's own experience in that role. Several of Tanenbaum's novels credit Michael Gruber as a collaborator.

An American approximation of the British tradition of legal comedy occurs in the works of Paul Levine. In *To Speak for the Dead* (1990), the first novel about Florida advocate Jake Lassiter, we meet a judge who might seem outrageous even in a Henry Cecil novel: a horseplayer who studies his racing form while on the bench, he carefully alternates between favoring the prosecution and the defense in his rulings on objections. In *Night Vision* (1991), one lawyer sings a song from the musical *The Fantasticks* in the course of arguing for privacy rights while representing a computer dating service. Despite the humorous tone, Lassiter's cases have their serious side, exploring ethical problems and Floridian mores in a manner reminiscent of John D. MacDonald. *Mortal Sin* (1994) is an especially strong example of Levine's work.

William Bernhardt, whose Oklahoma lawyer Ben Kincaid first appears in *Primary Justice* (1992), also includes some comic courtroom scenes in his novels, usually as a curtain-raiser before the main event. He also shares with Steve Martini a gift for classical puzzle plotting.

Philip Friedman, whose *Reasonable Doubt* (1990) and *Inadmissible Evidence* (1992) were well received courtroom novels, made his greatest contribution to the legal thriller in *Grand Jury* (1996), the most far-reaching fictional explication of the titular entity.

A number of mystery-writing lawyers do not really belong to the legal crime novel tradition. Francis M. Nevins Jr. and Michael Bowen specialize more in classical puzzles, though Nevins' principal series character, Loren Mensing, is a law professor. Jeremiah Healy's novels are in the private eye tradition, while the attorney furthest removed from the legal thriller may be Kate Ross, who writes classical historical novels set in Regency England.

Women Specialists

For a long time legal fiction, like the legal profession itself, appeared—notable exceptions like Frances Noyes Hart and Sara Woods apart—to be primarily a male preserve. However, as more and more women entered the legal profession in the late twentieth century, a number of them joined their male colleagues in turning to the legal thriller. By the late 1990s the most commercially successful female writer in the form was Nancy Taylor Rosenberg, whose first and best book was *Mitigating Circumstances* (1993), but a number of others produced far superior work.

Philadelphian Lisa Scottoline's first novel was *Everywhere That Mary Went* (1993), a paperback original. Graduating to hardcover in her third novel, she showed increasing mastery of the form. Her *Rough Justice* (1997) features a female defense lawyer who discovers after the jury has been charged that her client is actually guilty. The revelations send her and some of her colleagues around snowbound Philadelphia trying to find out the truth—and a way to reveal it without violating the ethics of their profession. As well as creating considerable suspense, it is a better jury-fixing novel than Grisham's *The Runaway Jury*.

Californian Lia Matera features two series lawyers in her novels, Willa Jansson, who first appeared in *Where Lawyers Fear to Tread* (1987), and Laura DiPalma, whose first case was *The Smart Money* (1988). Soaked in legal atmosphere, her novels are also characterized by their humor and sharp social observation.

Carolyn Wheat introduced her Brooklyn lawyer-sleuth Cass Jameson in two novels published before the advent of Turow and Grisham: *Dead Men's Thoughts* (1983) and *Where Nobody Dies* (1986). When she returned after a nine-year hiatus with *Fresh Kills* (1995), she revealed an even sharper eye for character and detail than before. Improving with each book, she received an Edgar nomination for *Mean Streak* (1996) and topped it with *Troubled Waters* (1997), which looks back on 1960s radicalism more briefly but nearly as tellingly as does Scott Turow's *Laws of Our Fathers*.

Patricia D. Benke, a California appellate judge, introduces San Diego Assistant District Attorney Judith Thornton in a fine paperback original, *Guilty by Choice* (1995). Two women writing as Perri O'Shaughnessy (Paula and Mary O'Shaughnessy) feature Lake Tahoe defender Nina Reilly in *Motion to Suppress* (1995), an excellent specimen of courtroom fiction, while at least one nonlawyer, science-fiction writer Kate Wilhelm, has developed a new courtroom specialty, featuring Oregon lawyer Barbara Holloway in a series of novels beginning with *Death Qualified* (1991). Margaret Maron, though her novels are more traditional mysteries than legal thrillers, wrote an outstanding series about North Carolina Judge Deborah Knott, beginning with *Bootlegger's Daughter* (1992).

Predecessors and Beneficiaries

Carolyn Wheat is not the only lawyer-novelist already established before the Turow/Grisham revolution to be numbered among the important legal crime novelists. Several writers who began their careers earlier either left the field or moved to other kinds of fiction before turning to the legal thriller in the welcoming market of the 1980s and 1990s.

William J. Coughlin, a U.S. administrative judge who achieved best-selling success only shortly before his death in 1992, started with other varieties of crime fiction but produced his best work in the legal thriller category. His best books are *Shadow of a Doubt* (1991) and *Death Penalty* (1992), both featuring alcoholic Detroit lawyer Charley Sloan.

Colorado lawyer Warwick Downing published some crime fiction in the earliest 1970s and then was not heard from for more than a decade. His novels about the National Association of Special Prosecutors, beginning with *A Clear Case of Murder* (1990), deserve more critical attention than their paperback original format affords. They are of astonishing quality. Of special merit is *Choice of Evils* (1994), with its surprisingly evenhanded treatment of the differences between American and Arab justice systems.

William Harrington wrote one of the greatest of all trial novels in *Which the Justice, Which the Thief* (1963), a novel designed like Traver's *Anatomy of a Murder* to counter the general public misunderstanding of trial procedure as gathered in other fictional presentations. Told in the first person by a retired judge of more than ninety years, the novel manages to rivet the reader's attention to a relatively mundane trial: the case of a man and woman accused of jewelry store armed robbery. After another outstanding trial novel, *The Power* (1964; U.K. title: *The Gospel of Death*), in which a faith-healing evangelist is accused of manslaughter when a "healed" diabetic dies after discontinuing her use of insulin, Harrington produced a wide variety of crime and espionage fiction. He occasionally returned to a legal setting, as in two novels centered on women lawyers, *Partners* (1980) and *For the Defense* (1988). *Town on Trial* (1994) successfully recaptures the small-town Ohio setting and the judge's-eye viewpoint of his first novel, though the crime (a high-profile murder case), the narrator (a sitting judge this time), and the times (with court TV in evidence) are quite different.

Joe L. Hensley, for many years an Indiana judge, published his first courtroom novel, *The Color of Hate*, in 1960. It was revised and published in hardcover for the first time as

Color Him Guilty in 1987, coincidentally the year of Turow's advent. Donald Robak, the series lawyer of most of Hensley's other books, sometimes performs in the courtroom and always deals with legal procedures and small-town politics. His best case is *Robak's Cross* (1985), but the author's best novel may be the nonseries *Grim City* (1994), set in Kentucky and based (according to the author) on a combination of Indiana, Kentucky, and made-up law.

Stephen Greenleaf began as a writer of private eye novels about San Franciscan John Marshall Tanner; his first legal novel, *The Ditto List* (1985), concerning divorce law, predated Grisham and Turow. Closer to the legal crime novel is *Impact* (1989), which takes on aviation law and aircraft personal injury cases.

Richard North Patterson's *Private Screening* (1985) was his first venture into the legal crime novel following some widely admired general thrillers. In recent years he has returned to the form with the best-sellers *Degree of Guilt* (1993) and *Eyes of a Child* (1995). Phillip Margolin, whose first novel, *Heartstone* (1978), was a courtroom novel, also benefited from the new vogue with novels like *Gone but Not Forgotten* (1993) and *After Dark* (1995). Nonlawyer Clifford Irving, author of the notorious unpublished Howard Hughes "autobiography," entered the field impressively with *Trial* (1990).

The Future of the Legal Crime Novel

By the late 1990s the public appetite for legal crime novels and the availability of talented lawyer-writers to produce them showed no sign of waning. It was too soon to estimate how much fiction directly inspired by the O. J. Simpson case would be written, but it was expected to continue well into the new millennium. Whether legal crime novels are used to attack the justice system, to defend it, or merely to depict it in all its bewildering variety, the inherent drama of adversarial give-and-take will keep the category vital for years to come.

Selected Bibliography

WORKS OF MAJOR WRITERS

JOHN GRISHAM

A Time to Kill. New York: Wynwood, 1989. Repr. with new intro. New York: Island, 1992.
The Firm. New York: Doubleday, 1991.
The Pelican Brief. New York: Doubleday, 1992.
The Client. New York: Doubleday, 1993.
The Chamber. New York: Doubleday, 1994.
The Rainmaker. New York: Doubleday, 1995.
The Runaway Jury. New York: Doubleday, 1996.
The Partner. New York: Doubleday, 1997.

SCOTT TUROW

One L: An Inside Account of Life in the First Year at Harvard Law School. New York: Putnam, 1977. Nonfiction.
Presumed Innocent. New York: Farrar, 1987.
The Burden of Proof. New York: Farrar, 1990.
Pleading Guilty. New York: Farrar, 1993.
The Laws of Our Fathers. New York: Farrar, 1996.
Guilty as Charged: A Mystery Writers of America Anthology. Edited by Scott Turow. New York: Pocket, 1996.

JOHN MORTIMER (RUMPOLE SERIES ONLY)

Rumpole of the Bailey. Harmondsworth, Eng.: Penguin, 1978.
The Trials of Rumpole. Harmondsworth, Eng.: Penguin, 1979.
Rumpole's Return. Harmondsworth, Eng.: Penguin, 1980. Novel.
Regina v. Rumpole. London: Allen Lane, 1981. U.S.: *Rumpole for the Defence*. New York: Penguin, 1984.
Rumpole and the Golden Thread. London and New York: Penguin, 1983.
Rumpole's Last Case. London: Penguin, 1987.
Rumpole and the Age of Miracles. London: Penguin, 1988.
Rumpole à la Carte. London and New York: Viking Penguin, 1990.
Rumpole on Trial. London and New York: Viking Penguin, 1992.
Rumpole and the Angel of Death. London and New York: Viking Penguin, 1996.

CRITICAL STUDIES

Breen, Jon L. Introduction to *Settled Out of Court* by Henry Cecil. New York: International Polygonics, 1991.

————. *Novel Verdicts: A Guide to Courtroom Fiction.* Metuchen, N.J.: Scarecrow, 1984.

Pederson, Jay P., ed. *St. James Guide to Crime and Mystery Writers*, 4th ed. Detroit: St. James, 1996.

Wright, Charles Alan. "The Fictional Lawyer." See issues of *The Practical Lawyer.*

THE POLICE PROCEDURAL

JON L. BREEN

CRITICS AND HISTORIANS of mystery fiction are nearly as unanimous in proclaiming Lawrence Treat's *V as in Victim* (1945) the first police procedural novel as in crediting Edgar Allan Poe's "The Murders in the Rue Morgue" (1841) as the first detective story. As is true of the crime story before Poe, however, the police procedural form has a long and complicated prehistory. It is not unreasonable to wonder why the police procedural should be considered a separate category of crime and mystery fiction at all. With very rare exceptions, mystery novels include police as characters—with murder and other criminal acts being committed, it would be difficult to keep them out. And if the central purpose of the tale is to arrive at the solution of the crime, are not police in the best position to do that, and are not their methods thus an inevitable driving force in the story? Not necessarily.

Many writers, bored by fingerprints, ballistics, and other tools of scientific detection and certainly without interest in departmental politics or the everyday lives of law enforcement personnel, would like nothing better than to keep official police and their doings out. The snowbound-house-party school of whodunit, where an official investigator cannot even get to the scene, is one extreme measure used to achieve such an exclusion, as is the practice, usually in romantic suspense novels, of burying the subject mystery deep in the past. The writer who does not want details of police routine cluttering up the narrative can always find ways of avoiding it. A scrap of authentic procedural information here and there is fine for establishing verisimilitude, but most detective stories of any period get away from the crime scene and the station house as expeditiously as they can. Not so the police procedural.

Definitions

In his *Encyclopedia Mysteriosa*, William L. DeAndrea defines "procedural" as "an approach to telling a story of a crime and its detection, offering a heightened illusion of reality by building the story as closely as possible around the actual techniques professionals use in real life" (p. 403). Although noting that the term is most often heard in the phrase "police procedural," DeAndrea also offers examples of journalistic, private eye, and medical examiner procedurals. Introducing Ed McBain's 1959 omnibus *The 87th Precinct*, Anthony Boucher wrote, "The story of police procedure . . . sticks closely to factual routine (including irrelevancy and boredom) and seeks to portray both cops and criminals as many-sided and often contradictory human beings" (p. vii).

In the course of a lengthier definition in his landmark study *The Police Procedural* (1982), George N. Dove noted:

[T]he detective in the procedural story does those things ordinarily expected of policemen, like using informants, tailing suspects, and availing himself of the resources of the police laboratory. . . . [T]he policemen in the procedurals almost always work in teams, sharing the responsibilities and the dangers, and also the credit, of the investigation, with the result that the resolution of the mystery is usually the product of the work of a number of people instead of the achievement of a single protagonist. . . . The conventions of a popular fiction demand that there be a main-character detective in the procedural, but he or she does not solve the crime without the collaborative efforts of other police. (p. 2)

Hillary Waugh, writing in John Ball's essay anthology *The Mystery Story,* contrasted the police detective with his fictional predecessors, the classical sleuth and the private eye, who

shared certain common traits. Both . . . were virtually free of legal restraint; both were laws unto themselves; both operated alone and kept their own counsel.

The police procedural changes all that. The police procedural thrusts the detective into the middle of a working police force, full of rules and regulations. Instead of bypassing the police, as did its predecessors, the procedural takes the reader inside the department and shows how it operates. (pp. 166–167)

In an essay in H. R. F. Keating's *Whodunit?,* the versatile Michael Gilbert, some of whose novels and stories belong to the procedural school, extends the definition by stressing the differing priorities of real life and fiction. Procedural novels often cast doubt on the assumption implicit in most detective fiction that once a case is solved, justice will be done:

[O]ne sometimes has the feeling that in a murder investigation the police have two adversaries to contend with: the criminal; and the great British public, who first confuse the issue by trampling on footprints and concealing clues; and then, when the police have arrested the murderer and have persuaded the Director of Public Prosecutions that they

have a case which will stand up in Court, become members of the jury, all too willing to be beguiled by silver-tongued counsel for the defence. In a true-life murder story it might be said that a quarter of the difficulty is identifying and charging the murderer; three-quarters of it is securing a conviction. (p. 50)

Thus, a police procedural is a specialized kind of crime fiction in which the problems, attitudes, and methods of police detectives are realistically depicted, and authentic (or at least ostensibly authentic) investigative procedures and teamwork are applied to the solution of the crime; it is a novel or story where realistic details of police work, including its practical frustrations as well as its criminalistic science, are central, not peripheral, to the action. Although this definition implies a higher degree of realism than other forms of crime fiction, a feeling of reality need only be sought, not necessarily achieved. A true duplication of reality would be fatal to a detective story, perhaps to any work of fiction, and once artistic license is taken, the result in a procedural may be as far removed from reality as the most elaborate and artificial cozy or the most operatic mean-streets bloodletting.

Writers whose fictional detectives are professional police are not necessarily writing procedurals. Ruth Rendell, the creator of Inspector Wexford, has expressed a lack of interest in police procedure and does a fine job of avoiding it in her novels. Robert Barnard, whose detectives are usually official police, told interviewer Adrian Muller that a writer of crime novels should have the motto "BUGGER POLICE PROCEDURE. . . . If you make a mistake that flies in the face of common sense of police procedure, then that is another matter, but the actual minutiae of police procedure? Who cares?!" (p. 43).

Many fictional detectives belong to what George Dove has called the Great Policeman school, in which the detective genius who solves the crime, aside from his official standing, might as well be Sherlock Holmes. No one would accuse Ngaio Marsh's Roderick Alleyn, Michael Innes' John Appleby, or Earl

Derr Biggers' Charlie Chan, for all their professional police credentials, of inhabiting procedurals, and the same is true of contemporary characters like H. R. F. Keating's Inspector Ghote, Barnard's Perry Trethowan, or even P. D. James's Adam Dalgliesh. It takes a considerable stretch to apply the procedural label even to the cases of Georges Simenon's Maigret, whose methods may have bordered on genuine police procedure but who essentially acted as a lone wolf.

Introducing a volume of *Best Police Stories,* editor Roy Vickers (1888–1965), whose Department of Dead Ends short stories are sometimes cited as early examples of the procedural, demonstrated why they, along with many works of his contemporaries, were not truly procedurals. He notes that among the reactions of real-life police to crime fiction was an observation

> that, in depicting the police at work, we telescope a complex process of investigation into a single scene—often crediting the ingenuity of the inspector with work done by other departments.
>
> We do and we are unrepentant. What concern have we with the details of police procedure? . . . We ourselves absorb an amount of solid information in order to avoid misrepresentation of what the police can and cannot accomplish—but we try not to unload it on the reader. (pp. 9–10)

Thus, like Barnard, Vickers denies what other writers of police stories have affirmed: that how the police do their jobs, including both investigative methods and administrative or bureaucratic barriers to effective work, can be made interesting to the reader for its own sake. Vickers comes closer to defining what we understand as a police procedural when he goes on to note:

> The police detective has no need to be gifted with an intelligence superior to that of the most intelligent criminal. Certainly, he must be an able man who misses nothing he ought not to miss. The dramatic value of him lies in the recognition that he is a unit in the collective brain which is the police force. (p. 11)

The recognition of teamwork and the nonsupersleuth status of the detective are two characteristics that define the police procedural. A few other characteristics often identified as necessities of the subgenre, including the multiplicity of cases and the revolving nature of investigative stardom, may or may not hold up under close scrutiny. Before considering them, some early history is in order.

Nineteenth-Century Roots

From the point in the nineteenth century when the detective story began to emerge as a separate genre, at least one of its ostensible appeals was in satisfying the curiosity of readers about how police did their jobs. Many of the most popular early books were fictionalized, sometimes totally fictional, police memoirs. Even before Poe came the anonymously published *Richmond; or, Scenes from the Life of a Bow Street Runner* (1827) and the memoirs of the French criminal-turned-Paris-police-chief Eugène-François Vidocq, first published in the late 1820s. Under the pseudonym Waters, William Russell produced such volumes as *The Recollections of a Policeman* (1852), *Recollections of a Sheriff's Officer* (1860), *The Experiences of a French Detective Officer* (1861), and *Autobiography of an English Detective* (1863). James M'Govan (pseudonym of William Crawford Honeyman) was the author of titles like *Brought to Bay; or, Experiences of a City Detective* (1878) and *Strange Clues; or, Chronicles of a City Detective* (1881).

Charles Dickens' forays into crime and detection, beginning with a series of articles in *Household Words* about the Detective Office, were based on his study of the methods of a policeman friend, Inspector Field, who provided the inspiration for Inspector Bucket of *Bleak House* (1853). Bucket, wrote Boucher, "is a genuine attempt . . . to represent a man of the Metropolitan Police at work, and a man, too, with a family and a nonworking life" (p. vii). In this recognition of a policeman's life apart from the job, Dickens anticipated one of the defining characteristics of the procedural, but Bucket is only one character in a large-canvas work.

Although professional police were central figures in much nineteenth-century crime fiction, their exploits seldom resemble those of the modern police procedural. Their adventures were based less on real procedural knowledge than on the imaginative action conventions of melodrama, including an excessive dependence on that dime-novel staple, disguise. Even when understood by the fiction writer, the police procedure of the time was less highly developed and scientific than latter-day practice. And, as later, writers tended to emphasize the efforts of a single central hero to the disadvantage of teamwork. Early detective characters like Anna Katharine Green's Ebenezer Gryce, introduced in *The Leavenworth Case* (1878), and Wilkie Collins' Sergeant Cuff of *The Moonstone* (1868) fit far more neatly into Dove's Great Policeman category than into the police procedural school as we understand it today.

For much of the nineteenth century, the public attitude toward police was different from what it became early in the twentieth. Because many of the early thief-takers had been drawn from the ranks of criminals, there was often a thin dividing line in the public mind (and in reality) between cops and robbers. The idea of a professional police force as we understand it today was slow to take hold. With the emergence of Arthur Conan Doyle's Sherlock Holmes in 1887, consulting (that is, private) detectives came into prominence, and the police detective hero went out of fashion for several decades.

Twentieth-Century Prehistory

Crime fiction entered the twentieth century with the real cops in eclipse. Professional private investigators like Holmes, gifted amateurs like G. K. Chesterton's Father Brown, and quasi-official scientific consultants like

R. Austin Freeman's Dr. Thorndyke and Arthur B. Reeve's Craig Kennedy were in the ascendancy, and the usual role of the official police officer was as dim-witted foil in the mold of Doyle's Lestrade and Gregson, though often even stupider.

By the 1920s, as the scientific methods of police advanced, so did public respect and interest, and writers again began trying to satisfy readers' interest in how the police really work. In Great Britain, police detectives reappeared as heroes. Freeman Wills Crofts's *Inspector French's Greatest Case* (1925) was the first of a long series about a relatively colorless Scotland Yard sleuth, while G. D. H. and M. I. Cole's similarly bland Superintendent Wilson first appeared in *The Brooklyn Murders* (1923, signed by G. D. H. Cole alone). Even though in their determined ordinariness they represent a signpost on the road to the true procedural, both characters belonged more to the Great Policeman tradition in their methods and behavior, and the problems they solved were firmly in the classical puzzle school that procedural fiction would subvert.

The most successful American detective novelist of the 1920s was S. S. Van Dine (pseudonym of Willard Huntington Wright). Phil and Karen McArdle, writing in *Fatal Fascination: Where Fact Meets Fiction in Police Work*, make a case for *The "Canary" Murder Case* (1927) as an early example of the procedural. The dust jackets of the Van Dine novels depict authentic-looking police index cards, making a realistic view of procedure a selling point, and the team and specialization aspects of police work are at least paid lip service. But the stupidity of Sergeant Heath combined with the eccentric genius of amateur sleuth Philo Vance rule out Van Dine as a real procedural pioneer. The early novels by Ellery Queen, beginning with *The Roman Hat Mystery* (1929), also include realistic depiction of police methods through the activities of Inspector Richard Queen, but son Ellery, a mystery-writing amateur, does the real (that is, successful) detecting.

Paradoxically, the police procedural pretended to exist before it actually did. Has any novel been more pointedly advanced as a procedural, for example, than Helen Reilly's *McKee of Centre Street* (1934)? The jacket blurb, as quoted by Ellen Nehr in *Doubleday Crime Club Compendium*, reads, "The lineup, the radio room, the morgue, the mysterious depths of the fingerprint department—all the varied and exciting activities of one of the greatest police departments in the world are in this startling new mystery" (p. 80), and a corpse's hand with identification tag appears on the endpapers and opposite the title page. The promise is borne out in the first two chapters, with a description of the headquarters radio room followed by various police specialists doing their jobs at a speakeasy crime scene. And consider this quote from *McKee of Centre Street*: "The effortless functioning of a perfect police machine relieves wear and tear on the individual and permits each man to work at the highest degree of efficiency" (p. 64).

Once the character of Inspector Christopher (the "Scotsman") McKee appears, however, it is clear we are closer to Van Dine or Queen territory than to the true procedural. McKee, with his literary allusions and esoteric knowledge, belongs to the Great Policeman school, along with 1930s American contemporaries like Rufus King's Lieutenant Valcour, Milton M. Propper's Tommy Rankin, Anthony Abbot's (Fulton Oursler's) Thatcher Colt, and George Bagby's (Aaron Marc Stein's) Inspector Schmidt. Some police characters in pulp magazines, such as Frederick Nebel's Steve McBride or MacKinlay Kantor's Nick and Dave Glennan, came closer than these hardcover sleuths to foreshadowing the modern procedural novel. Another precursor was William MacHarg's O'Malley, featured in a long series of cop vignettes collected in *The Affairs of O'Malley* (1940). But all of these series were more closely related to the hardboiled school than to the real procedural.

The British writer of the thirties who may have come closest to the modern procedural was retired police official Sir Basil Thomson, whose *P. C. Richardson's First Case* (1933) is praised by Jacques Barzun and Wendell Hertig Taylor in *A Catalogue of Crime* for ways in which it does not resemble the latter-day procedural; they call it "early police routine *minus* the contrived bickering, stomach ulcers, and pub-crawling with which later writers have masked poverty of invention and the dullness of repetitious questioning" (p. 503). While none of the short stories in the 1936 anthology *Six Against the Yard* (U.S. title, *Six Against Scotland Yard*) could be considered police procedurals, each of them is followed by an essay from ex–Scotland Yard Superintendent Cornish, explaining how the police actually would have investigated the crime and why the perfect murders advanced by Margery Allingham, Dorothy L. Sayers, and four others would have proved imperfect.

Then there were the crime dossiers of the thirties, works like *Murder off Miami* (1936; U.S. title, *The File on Bolitho Blane*) by the team of Dennis Wheatley and J. G. Links. In this somewhat gimmicky series, actual physical clues were included in the album-style books along with authentic-looking police forms and reports. Despite the documentary flavor, though, they belonged more to the classic puzzle tradition than to the police procedural. Also sometimes cited as a pioneer of the procedural field is Chester Gould's comic-strip character Dick Tracy, initially known as Plainclothes Tracy, who first appeared in newspapers in 1931. He may have made police heroes attractive to a wider public, but his credentials for both realism and teamwork are dubious. Some of his innovations, like the two-way wrist radio, belong more to science fiction than mystery fiction.

Lawrence Treat

With all this early interest in procedure, including the publication of novels that apparently claimed to be police procedurals, how can we so confidently trace the category's origin to Lawrence Treat? Treat introduced enough of the characteristics of the post–World War II procedural, elements that were practically unknown earlier, for his work to turn the corner into a new type of detective story, though others would add their refinements to the recipe.

Lawrence Treat (1903–1998) is the name adopted first as a pseudonym and later as a legal name by Lawrence Arthur Goldstone, a New Yorker who graduated from Dartmouth in 1924 and attained a law degree from Columbia in 1927. He practiced law briefly before embarking on a writing career. His earliest contributions to mystery fiction were picture puzzles, some of which were collected in notepad form in *Bringing Sherlock Home* (1930). He returned to this specialty in the 1980s after several decades producing a wide variety of crime fiction, both in short stories and book-length works.

When Treat began to write detective novels in the forties, he hit upon an alphabet title pattern that anticipated latter-day best-seller Sue Grafton, whose method differs from Treat's only in replacing "as in" with "is for" in her titles and using the letters in consecutive alphabetical order. Treat's first four books using this title pattern—*B as in Banshee* (1940), *D as in Dead* (1941), *H as in Hangman* (1942), and *O as in Omen* (1943)—feature amateur sleuth Carl Wayward, a professor of psychology. Standard puzzle mysteries of the time, they are not highly regarded by critics and historians. But when Treat produced *V as in Victim*, he created the police procedural as we know it and cemented his place in crime-fiction history.

In introducing the 1970 short-story collection *P as in Police*, Ellery Queen offers this account of how Treat came to write police procedurals:

> In the summer of 1942 a young woman living in New York City received some obscene anonymous telephone calls. She told her friend, Lawrence Treat, and at his urging they reported the crime to the 24th Precinct police station. The detective on duty was a chesty man of medium height, with short stiff hair, a tenorish voice, and deep brown eyes. After listening sympathetically, the detective persuaded them not to go ahead with a formal complaint. His reasons were convincingly organized—the emotional strain on the young woman, the danger to her if the caller should prove to be violent, and so on.... [I]t was not until years later that Treat realized they had been cleverly conned. All the detective wanted to do was to avoid making an investigation and being saddled with the necessary paper work.
>
> That short interview was the origin of Mr. Treat's procedurals; and that detective, physically and temperamentally, was the prototype of Mitch Taylor, one of Treat's three main characters. (pp. 7–8)

As the genius of Dr. Joseph Bell inspired Sherlock Holmes, the self-serving expediency of a lazy cop inspired Mitch Taylor. The anecdote helps illustrate one of the main differences between police procedurals and other detective fiction: supersleuths are in short supply, and bureaucratic administrative considerations share the stage with the mystery.

As *V as in Victim* opens, Mitch Taylor is sitting in the Twenty-First Precinct station house bemoaning the policeman's lot:

> Only a jackass ever got himself into the department. You worked every day of the week and you didn't get overtime and you never went anywhere except in bad weather and if anything happened you were supposed to take over, no matter what.... You were wide open to every crank civilian who didn't like the angle of your hat. All he had to do was write a letter to the commissioner and then you were considered guilty until proved innocent. So you even lost your constitutional rights. (p. 2)

A call to the site of a fatal hit-and-run accident interrupts Mitch's lament. As the investigation proceeds, Mitch has more concern for how his report will look to his superiors, and how it might improve his chances of promotion, than for the merits of the case itself. He surprises a patrolman by asking him to call the crime laboratory for help in identifying the vehicle—street cops resist science, but Mitch thinks the fact that he called the lab will favorably impress those upstairs.

Thus is introduced Treat's second main character in the series, Detective Jub Freeman, the easygoing lab man who is expected to do magic with "a collection of paint scrapings and half a pound of glass fragments" (p. 11). But he can't quite deliver what Mitch expects of him: tracing the car from headlight fragments. Told it was identified by witnesses as a late-model car, Jub says, "That's too bad. . . . Ever since 1939 when they put in the sealed-beam unit, headlights don't help much. Now with the older cars, you could match up the headlight and sometimes even find the serial numbers, and then you'd know something" (p. 12). According to Queen, Freeman had more distinguished real-life models than Taylor: Charles O'Hara and James Osterburg of the New York Police Department laboratory, whom Treat met in 1943 and who would later become authors of standard texts on criminalistics.

It became clear early that Treat's police novels not only were based on solid research into real police work but also offered a new viewpoint toward it. In an essay in *St. James Guide to Crime and Mystery Writers*, George Dove identifies several procedural conventions introduced by Treat: "the cop with family problems . . . , the hostile public . . . , the inter- and intra-departmental rivalries (detectives versus patrolmen, conventional cops versus the police lab), and the perennially under-staffed and over-worked squad . . ." (pp. 984–985). These are matters the Great Policeman of earlier years seldom if ever had to worry about. As Dove also points out, though, *V as in Victim* has at least as much in common with the Golden Age fair-play detective novel as it does with latter-day procedurals. One central case is followed to a conclusion in which the killer is identified from a circle of suspects and the clues elucidated in a flurry of exposition. This allegiance to the formal pattern continued in the subsequent novels in the series.

Treat's greatest contribution is the sense of teamwork, with the focus shifting among old-style bulldog Taylor, scientific cop Freeman, and in later books Commander Bill Decker.

The three take turns in the spotlight: Freeman appears alone in *H as in Hunted* (1946); Decker is introduced in *F as in Flight* (1948); only in *Big Shot* (1951) do all three share the stage.

Treat deployed many of the main characteristics of the police procedural, but he never abandoned the formal pattern of the whodunit. It was left to another American to take the next step in the development of the procedural and in doing so produce its first classic—but first a nonliterary account of police work became the real catalyst in the procedural form's popularity.

Dragnet

The often-noted drawback to crediting Lawrence Treat as "father" of the police procedural has been the failure of *V as in Victim* to have an immediate influence on other writers. A far clearer precursor of the flood of procedurals in the fifties and sixties was not a literary source at all but a radio/television series, *Dragnet*, created by its star, Jack Webb (1920–1982), a broadcast all-rounder as actor, writer, producer, and director. Sergeant Joe Friday and his Los Angeles Police Department colleagues first appeared on radio in 1949 and moved to television in 1952. The clipped, low-key dialogue practiced by cops, witnesses, and suspects; the references not only to realistic police routine but also to actual named members of the Los Angeles Police Department; and the assurance that each program was based on an actual case (its outcome revealed at the end of the program) combined to create an unprecedented sense of verisimilitude in a broadcast medium that generally had presented crime stories even more artificial and formulaic than print sources. It could be countered that no program was more formulaic than *Dragnet*, but it was a new formula and one the public was ready to embrace.

The series became a sensational success. Tag lines like "Just the facts, ma'am" and "only the names have been changed to protect the innocent" invited the compliment of parody. The back cover of the September 1953 issue of the influential crime-fiction digest *Manhunt* uses the term "Dragnet" in hyping stories by Richard Marsten (also known as Evan Hunter and Ed McBain) and Richard Deming, making it clear whence sprang the new vogue for police stories. Leaving the radio air in 1956, *Dragnet* survived on television until 1959 and then returned for a brief run in the late 1960s, by which time it had become a virtual public relations and propaganda arm of the Los Angeles Police Department and had lost much of its original impact.

Anthony Boucher contended in his introduction to *The 87th Precinct* that writers of the early 1950s "were trying to recapture the effects" of *Dragnet* but that "these effects had been shrewdly calculated precisely for broadcast; too closely imitated on the printed page, they seemed (particularly in a pair of authorized novelizations of *Dragnet*) wearisome and self-conscious" (p. viii). Actually, the *Dragnet* cops appeared in three paperback originals. Richard S. Prather, writing as David Knight, produced *Dragnet: Case No. 561* (1956), and Richard Deming followed with *The Case of the Courteous Killer* (1958) and *The Case of the Crime King* (1959).

Dragnet's creator and star, Jack Webb, is often confused with the mystery novelist Jack Webb, who featured Sergeant Sammy Golden along with sleuthing priest Father Shanley in a series beginning with *The Big Sin* (1952). The novelist Webb also wrote for *Manhunt* a series of stories about a specialized police unit, the Airport Detail, beginning with "Broken Doll" (May 1954). Tagging the series with the name of the unit rather than with the name of a particular sleuth was an early example of another procedural characteristic, which was most successfully developed by Ed McBain. That the two Webbs were different people was repeatedly made clear from the beginning, but they continue to be confused to this day.

British television is also sometimes credited with furthering the procedural, though its *Dragnet* equivalents came much later. Julian Symons in his history *Mortal Consequences* states that *Z Cars* (which debuted in 1960) and others "showed that the routine of police investigation could be fascinating as a thing in itself" and speculates that "because the British series were more firmly centered upon the day-to-day activities of a police station or department, leaving (as writers may have felt) little for them to add, the police novel has been developed principally by Americans" (p. 204).

Hillary Waugh

Like Lawrence Treat, Hillary Waugh (b. 1920) has written various types of crime and mystery fiction and began with more conventional work before turning to the police procedural. Born in Connecticut and a graduate of Yale University, he began his writing career after leaving the Navy at the end of World War II. In his *Mystery Story* article, he describes his first novel, *Madam Will Not Dine Tonight* (1947), and its two successors featuring Sheridan Wesley as "private-eye-cute-young-couple novels" (p. 163).

Reading a paperback true-crime book, Charles Boswell's *They All Died Young* (1949), a collection of accounts of the murders of young women, changed the course of Waugh's mystery writing and resulted in his fourth book, *Last Seen Wearing* (1952). Waugh wanted to get into his own fiction the kind of impact he found in the true-crime essays. The opening lines of his first chapter, headed "Friday, March 3, 1950," establish the matter-of-fact, semidocumentary, true-crime style he brought to the novel:

> Marilyn Lowell Mitchell, pretty eighteen-year-old freshman at Parker College in Bristol, Massachusetts, attended her noon history class on Friday, March 3, 1950. At its conclusion she went to the desk to speak to the teacher, Harlan P. Seward. She left the building a few moments later and walked back to

her room in Lambert Annex, unaccompanied as far as can be determined. (p. 11)

With Waugh's novel, the procedural took another step away from standard detective fiction. Unlike Treat, Waugh was not writing a classical detective story with realistic police as the central characters. He was writing a whole new form, one that was calculated to resemble a true-crime account more than a work of fiction and that could adapt or even ignore at least some of the rules and conventions that had governed the detective story since the twenties, when writers like Father Ronald Knox and S. S. Van Dine (with varying degrees of seriousness) laid down the law for writers in the genre.

In the classic detective story, the criminal, when revealed, is expected to be a reasonably prominent character who has been introduced to the reader in the course of the story, and there are supposed to be clues fairly laid for the reader to anticipate the solution. In life, the criminal may be somebody who never enters the case before the point of discovery, and even the police breaking the case may not be (indeed, probably are not) guided by clues in the detective-story sense. The police procedural, though still a work of fiction and obliged as such to satisfy the reader, tries to approximate life more than fiction. As he follows Chief of Police Frank Ford's investigation step by step, Waugh does introduce possible suspects in the murder of Marilyn Mitchell, but the murderer, more in line with a real-life investigation, does not actually appear as a character before being revealed.

In response to this trifling with the rules, Anthony Boucher, the *New York Times* critic who had complimented Treat's first procedural effort, had some discouraging words about Waugh's, as quoted in the Mystery Library edition of *Last Seen Wearing:*

> Plausible and convincing, yes; fictional entertainment, no. It rather resembles a blow-up to ten times normal size of the duller type of fact-crime article, which places all its emphasis on the minutiae of police work and

none on the characters. (In this case, the murderer never even appears on stage.) (p. 272)

On the other hand, the same book quotes Julian Symons, in selecting *Last Seen Wearing* as one of the "Sunday Times 100 Best Crime Stories," as finding the criminal's nonappearance "the neatest of many nice touches" (p. 278).

Rather than make a continuing character of Chief Frank Ford, Waugh wrote a variety of nonseries crime fiction through the 1950s before introducing in 1959 another small-town chief of police, Chief Fred Fellows of Stockford, Connecticut, not as similar a character as the similarity of jobs and initials might suggest. Fellows, a chewer of tobacco, is more low-key, less irascible, and fatter than the cigar-smoking Ford, and he always has a story to tell to make his point. *Sleep Long, My Love* (1959) is the first of eleven Fellows novels. The eighth of them, *The Missing Man* (1964), is nearly as successful in the documentary vein of faux true crime as *Last Seen Wearing.* Later Waugh moved from small-town police work to New York City in a series of three novels about Detective Frank Sessions—*"30" Manhattan East* (1968), *The Young Prey* (1969), and *Finish Me Off* (1970)—before abandoning the procedural for romantic suspense, private-eye novels, courtroom drama, and even Golden Age–style pure detection.

Maurice Procter

When Roy Vickers edited his anthology of police stories, he included a challenge to the reader. Noting that "[o]ne of our contributors was himself a member of the regular police force for nineteen years before his success as a novelist caused him to resign," Vickers asks, "Does one story in this collection stand out as the work of an author who obviously knows much more about police work than any of the others?" (p. 13). The answer Vickers was probably looking for was no, but many readers must already have been aware that the police officer-author was Maurice Procter (1906–1973).

While Procter (whose name in Vickers' anthology is misspelled Proctor) was not the first police officer to turn to crime writing—see Sir Basil Thomson, discussed earlier—he was the first of the genuine police procedural writers with actual law enforcement experience and also the major British writer in the early 1950s development of the procedural form. A native of Lancashire, Procter became a member of the Halifax Borough Police at the age of twenty-one. When his first novels were accepted for publication in 1946, he resigned from the force to write full-time. Procter featured two continuing police detectives, beginning with Detective Superintendent Philip Hunter in *The Chief Inspector's Statement* (1951; U.S. title, *The Pennycross Murders*, 1953) and *I Will Speak Daggers* (1956; U.S. title, *The Ripper*). Closer to the modern procedural are the books about the better-known Detective Chief Inspector Henry Martineau, who appears in fourteen novels beginning with *Hell Is a City* (1954; U.S. title, *Somewhere in This City*). Like the American cop Joseph Wambaugh twenty years later, Procter wrote a mainstream novel about police work before writing a police procedural per se. The apparently autobiographical *Each Man's Destiny* (1947) is a saga set in the Depression 1930s. The protagonist, policeman Marny Phillan, shares his creator's literary aspirations as well as his initials.

Procter's essay for the collection *Crime in Good Company*, edited by Michael Gilbert, shows how much his firsthand knowledge of police work contrasts with the image of the Great Policeman:

> Policemen are not usually intellectuals. They have a simple belief that the punishment should fit the crime. They think that violence can be checked by lawful counter-violence. They believe that prison life should not be pleasant. They *don't* believe that they can reform criminals by talking to them. Policemen don't hate these people. They merely want to put them in their place, which is in prison or on the scaffold. (p. 41)

Although Waugh and Procter advanced the police procedural's illusion of reality, they did not anticipate two innovations that some have tried to incorporate into the definition of the form: the modular (or multi-case) structure and the attempt to make the whole squad the hero, with no central character in the spotlight of each story. An Englishman accomplished the first, and an American at least tried to achieve the second, but both approaches, while not rare, have been far from obligatory in subsequent procedurals.

J. J. Marric and the Modular Procedural

Most detective novels, including most police procedurals, concentrate on one central mystery. If seemingly separate mysteries are introduced, convention generally dictates they must be shown at the end of the book to be connected. However, real police work obviously is not like that. The real-life cop works on several cases at once, some of which are satisfactorily resolved, others not. Some procedural writers have tried to add a greater sense of reality to their work in recognizing the not-so-neat multiplicity of cases by writing modular procedurals, in which several unrelated cases are addressed. The novelist Jack Webb, in the Father Shanley/Detective Sammy Golden novels, anticipates this trend in part, introducing multiple, seemingly unconnected investigations in books like *The Naked Angel* (1953), but he ultimately hews to convention by connecting them. Writers of the modular school usually keep the stories unconnected, and while the majority of the cases usually are resolved to the reader's satisfaction, loose ends may remain, again stressing their similarity to real life.

The first to make a specialty of the modular style of procedural was the incredibly prolific British author John Creasey (1908–1973), writing as J. J. Marric. *Gideon's Day* (1955), a landmark of the British police procedural, introduces Commander George Gideon, a high-ranking Scotland Yard officer. Each of the novels in which he appears has a theme that unites a variety of crimes and mysteries. At first, the common thread is a particular time period, *Gideon's Day* being followed by *Gideon's Week* (1956), *Gideon's Night* (1957), and *Gideon's Month* (1958). Later, the crimes are unified by their subject matter in titles like *Gideon's Fire* (1961), *Gideon's Vote* (1964), *Gideon's River* (1968), *Gideon's Sport* (1970), and *Gideon's Art* (1971).

In the most successful modular procedurals, and certainly in the Gideons, the exploration of character rather than the solution of crime is the key. In the final (and posthumously published) novel of the series, *Gideon's Drive* (1976), the police problems include an escaped rapist, food hijackers, and a ptomaine scare, but Mrs. Gideon's midlife crisis carries equal or greater interest. Often the Gideon novels are not so much about solving crimes as about how a high officer in a complex organization, which might as well be a university or a department store as a police department, applies interpersonal skills to his administrative job.

Few other series have been as faithfully modular as the Gideons. Forming the most consistent American equivalent are the various police series of Elizabeth Linington (also known as Dell Shannon and Leslie Egan), who always took the modular approach, beginning with Shannon's *Case Pending* (1960), first of a long series about the independently wealthy Los Angeles cop Luis Mendoza, and continuing with Linington's *Greenmask!* (1964), the first about Sergeant Ivor Maddox, and Egan's *The Borrowed Alibi* (1962), in which Los Angeles Detective Vic Varallo takes center stage. Linington, an outspoken political conservative, may not have offered the gritty realism of some of her contemporaries but had a particular knack for sympathetically depicted victims of crime. The Hong Kong procedurals of William Marshall, beginning with *Yellowthread Street* (1975), are among the most farcical, even surrealistic, of police novels. They are consistently modular and also follow Ed McBain's 87th Precinct series in sharing the spotlight among several continuing cops.

The modular format is tricky and should be attempted only by an unusually gifted writer. Switching among story lines runs the risk of losing the reader, especially if the characters are not sufficiently compelling. While Linington's earlier novels are quite successful in juggling the multiple investigations, a few of the later ones lapse into monotony.

Today, as always, modular procedurals are in the minority, but the existence of the option gives devious writers another way of playing with readers' expectations. Now a reader of a procedural has no way of knowing for sure whether seemingly unrelated investigations will prove to be connected. This added note of mystery can add to the reader's enjoyment, but it can be exasperating to those who are averse to the modular form. Although it has been used in private-eye fiction by writers like Joe Gores, Bill Pronzini, Lawrence Block, and George Chesbro and in legal thrillers by writers like Robert K. Tanenbaum, the modular approach is essentially a police procedural phenomenon.

Ed McBain and the 87th Precinct

Evan Hunter (b. 1926), born Salvatore A. Lombino in New York, is one of the most versatile and prolific writers of fiction of the twentieth century. After several years' apprenticeship writing mystery and science fiction, adult and juvenile, under a variety of pseudonyms, Hunter burst into prominence with the 1954 best-seller *The Blackboard Jungle*, in which he drew on his own experience as a teacher in a tough inner-city school. Through the fifties, he made frequent contributions to *Manhunt*, including some stories that exploited the new popularity of police procedural fiction. As Richard Marsten, he wrote "Accident Report" (September 1953) and "Classification: Dead" (November 1953), both of which anticipated his more famous later work in including reproduced police forms as a device for verisimilitude.

In 1956 Hunter adopted a new pseudonym for a series of police procedural novels in paperback original. Eventually, the fame of the chosen byline, Ed McBain, surpassed that of the best-selling Evan Hunter. McBain, also the author of a nonprocedural series about Florida lawyer Matthew Hope, has done so much to define, perfect, and popularize the police procedural form with his 87th Precinct series, he is sometimes credited by superficial commentators with inventing it. As we have seen, the form was already well established when *Cop Hater* (1956) appeared, but as Anthony Boucher wrote in introducing the 1959 omnibus volume, "Actually McBain's performance was something possibly even more valuable than invention: at exactly the right historical moment he managed to write, with more striking effect than anyone before him, what readers were hungering for with already whetted appetites" (p. vi).

The cover of the first 87th Precinct novel features a group of black-and-white photographs suggesting a television cop series or a true-crime magazine. Opposite the first page of text is the same statement that appears in *Nocturne* (1997) and all the intervening novels in the series: "The city in these pages is imaginary. The people, the places are all fictitious. Only the police routine is based on established investigatory technique." *Cop Hater* opens with a typical McBain description of his city, clearly based on New York but fictionalized to allow for variations in police procedure:

> The city lay like a sparkling nest of rare gems, shimmering in layer upon layer of pulsating intensity.
> The buildings were a stage set.
> They faced the river, and they glowed with man-made brilliance, and you stared up at them in awe, and you caught your breath.
> Behind the buildings, behind the lights, were the streets.
> There was garbage in the streets.

All that is missing in this cityscape is McBain's later proclivity to compare the city to a woman.

The first cop to be introduced in the series, Mike Reardon, is not around for long, becoming the first victim of a serial killer of cops whom Steve Carella, best known and most frequently featured of the 87th Precinct detectives, goes after. Other continuing figures are introduced: the commander, Lieutenant Byrnes; Teddy Franklin, the young deaf woman who will become Mrs. Carella; the young patrolman Bert Kling, later to be promoted to detective; the racist cop Roger Havilland; and Hal Willis, who barely meets the minimum height requirement. Forms and documents are reproduced at intervals to heighten the sense of reality: a pistol license application, a ballistics report on a bullet, an arrest report. The story is told in straightforward prose and clipped dialogue.

The second volume of the series, *The Mugger* (1956), opens with a signature city-as-woman riff:

> She is big and sprawling and dirty sometimes, and sometimes she shrieks in pain, and sometimes she moans in ecstasy.
> But she could be nothing but a woman, and that's good because your business is women.
> You are a mugger.

With Carella on his honeymoon, only to return in the final two pages, other cops share the leading role: Kling, Willis, and in his first appearance, the whimsically named Meyer Meyer, balding, patient, and thirty-seven years old throughout the series. The absence of Carella, clearly the hero of the first book, shows the fresh idea for the series McBain explains in Otto Penzler's essay collection *The Great Detectives*:

> The original concept . . . was to use a squadroom full of detectives as a conglomerate hero. I would try to portray accurately the working day of a big-city cop, but I would do so in terms of a handful of men whose diverse personalities and character traits, when combined, would form a single hero—the 87th Squad. To my knowledge, this had never been done before, and I felt it was unique. . . . [T]he concept would enable me to bring new men

into the squadroom as needed, adding their particular qualities or defects to the already existing mix, while at the same time disposing of characters who no longer seemed essential to the mix. (pp. 90–91)

Thus, it seemed perfectly reasonable to McBain that Carella should be severely wounded in the third book of the series, *The Pusher* (1956), which would finish:

Outside the hospital, the church bells tolled.
It was Christmas day, and all was right with the world.
But Steve Carella was dead. (p. 90)

Informed by his editor that despite his absence in the second book, Carella was the "star of the series," McBain rewrote the ending, sparing Carella's life. Later, he intended to replace Carella in the star spot with Cotton Hawes, introduced in *Killer's Choice* (1957), but reconsidered because the womanizing Hawes operated more like a private eye than a cop. The concept of the squad as a hero continued, though Carella has always been slightly more prominent overall than any of his colleagues. Few writers have attempted to emulate the squad-as-star concept of McBain's series, but William Marshall's Hong Kong cops in the Yellowthread Street series and Peter Turnbull's Glasgow P Division are in the tradition. The approach has been more memorably applied in television, notably in the long-running series *Hill Street Blues*, whose nighttime soap opera structure lent itself both to a multi-case format and to shifting protagonists.

Most mystery series give the reader the mixture as before in every outing. Stylistically at least, this is true of the 87th Precinct series: the pages of rapid-fire dialogue, the not-quite-over-the-top cityscapes, the little sidebar commentaries on police work and other aspects of modern life exist from the first novels in 1956 to the most recent more than forty years later. Within the series format, however, the 87th Precinct books have provided unusual variety in content and approach, sometimes leaving the realistic expectations of police procedurals behind to provide elements of other types of mystery fiction. For example, *Killer's Wedge* (1959), the first novel after the series shifted to hardcover (a progression now commonplace but almost unprecedented at the time), includes a locked-room murder. A whole series within a series, beginning with *The Heckler* (1960), recounts the squad's duels with a Moriarty-like master criminal known as the Deaf Man. (Other titles are *Fuzz*, 1968; *Let's Hear it for the Deaf Man*, 1973; and *Eight Black Horses*, 1985.) *Hail to the Chief* (1973), a self-indulgent and not very successful experiment, uses the first-person voice of a juvenile gang leader to satirize President Nixon. *Ghosts* (1980) entered the realm of the supernatural, causing Stephen King to proclaim it the best of the series (though few readers would probably agree).

The fine novel *Long Time No See* (1977), about the search for the killer of three seemingly inoffensive blind people, was the series' best in several years as well as the longest to that point. It signaled a trend toward more thematically complex entries. As the series entered the 1980s, the novels continued to get longer and more ambitious, their one-word titles suggesting a commonality of theme. One of the best is *Ice* (1983), in which three apparently unrelated murders (of a pusher, a dancer, and a diamond dealer) are all committed with the same gun. The novel is larded with literal and metaphoric meanings of the title word, the challenge to spot them all becoming a kind of game between author and reader. In *Vespers* (1990), the theme is religion, both Christian and satanic, as Steve Carella looks back on his Catholic boyhood in the course of investigating the murder of a priest.

There is a sense that the gifted McBain can spin out a story to whatever length is required, mostly through the use of that hypnotically captivating dialogue, sometimes one word to a line. Readability never flags, even when the whole process seems too easy and the authorial manipulation too blatant. McBain sometimes indulges in running jokes, as with all the references in *Nocturne* to Alfred Hitchcock "writing" *The Birds*—a 1963 film whose script was actually the work of Evan Hunter (McBain's alter ego).

Asked his own opinion of the 87th Precinct series in 1984, McBain indicated that his favorite was *Sadie When She Died*, which exists both as a novel (1972) and in a novella version published in *Alfred Hitchcock's Mystery Magazine* (January 1973). Beginning with a trial lawyer's expression of glee that his wife has been murdered, the story builds to one of the author's best shock endings. McBain also recommended *Blood Relatives* (1975), *Long Time No See*, and *Ice* but voiced less fondness for *So Long as You Both Shall Live* (1976).

Other Proceduralists of the 1950s and 1960s

Jonathan Craig (Frank E. Smith), who featured Manhattan detective Pete Selby in several Gold Medal originals of the fifties, has not received his full due as a procedural pioneer. The first Selby book, *The Dead Darling* (1955), beat the first 87th Precinct novel to the post by a year, and for *Manhunt* Craig was writing the "Police Files" series—like Jack Webb's Airport Detail, an early effort to star the squad rather than the individual detective.

John Ball's black Pasadena cop Virgil Tibbs, whose debut appearance in *In the Heat of the Night* (1965) became an Oscar-winning film starring Sidney Poitier, belongs, thanks to his Sherlock Holmes–style deductions and supersleuth aura, to the Great Policeman school. Still, Ball worked as a part-time Los Angeles County Sheriff's deputy and took great pains to get his police procedure right. The series about Jack Tallon, beginning with *Police Chief* (1977), and the nonseries novels *The Murder Children* (1979) and *The Van* (1989), are more clearly in the procedural category. Like the *Dragnet* cops, Ball's police are models of rectitude, giving his novels an occasional aura of public relations copy. Ball's wife, Nan Hamilton, also made a contribution

to the procedural with two novels about Japanese American policeman Isamu (Sam) Ohara, *Killer's Rights* (1984) and *The Shape of Fear* (1986).

The first of Joseph Harrington's three novels about New York cop Francis X. Kerrigan, *The Last Known Address* (1965), is often cited as a classic for its account of the painstaking search for a missing witness. Anthony Boucher, as quoted in *Encyclopedia of Mystery and Detection*, was "tempted to call [Harrington] the most truly procedural of all police-procedure novelists" (p. 191).

The versatile novelist Robert L. Fish, writing under the punning pseudonym Robert L. Pike, wrote three novels about New York City's Lieutenant Clancy, beginning with *Mute Witness* (1963), which was made into the successful film *Bullitt* (1968), its locale changed to San Francisco. Denied permission to use the name Bullitt, Pike started a new four-book series about a San Francisco police detective, beginning with *Reardon* (1970).

The police procedural form can be a vehicle for incisive social and political criticism, whether subtle or overt. The Swedish husband-and-wife team of Maj Sjöwall and Per Wahlöö, both Communists, wrote ten novels about Martin Beck and his Stockholm police colleagues, beginning with *Roseanna* (1965; first English translation, 1967) and ending with *Terroristerna* (1975; translated as *The Terrorists*, 1976). In *St. James Guide to Crime and Mystery Writers*, Bo Lundin quotes Wahlöö as asserting that the series was designed to "use the crime novel as a scalpel cutting open the belly of an ideologically pauperized and morally debatable so-called welfare state of the bourgeois type" (p. 1014). Although muted in the first few novels, the message was delivered more and more forcefully as the series went on. Whether despite or because of the politics, the well-crafted series was very well received in the English-reading world.

The Swedish team apart, most urban police procedurals in this period were set in London or a few major American cities. One of the first writers of English to break that mold was the Australian Jon Cleary, best known as author of *The Sundowners* (1952), who featured Sydney detective Scobie Malone in *The High Commissioner* (1966) and many later novels.

Joseph Wambaugh and the Cop Writers

Joseph Wambaugh was not the first American police officer to write police fiction. Dorothy Uhnak, who served with New York's Transit Police from 1953 to 1967, introduced Christie Opara, the first realistic woman cop to headline a procedural series, in a trilogy of novels: *The Bait* (1968), *The Witness* (1969), and *The Ledger* (1970). As Carol Cleveland writes in *St. James Guide to Crime and Mystery Writers*, Uhnak "makes the real pressures of police work clear: the struggle to develop the emotional shell that is absolutely necessary protection against constant exposure to the worst in human behavior, and the struggle to keep compassion and a modified idealism alive inside the shell" (p. 993).

The most famous and successful cop novelist, and the one who began the flood of would-be successors, though, is Wambaugh (b. 1937), who scored an immediate success in 1970 with *The New Centurions*, which follows the careers of three police recruits over a five-year period, culminating in the Los Angeles riots. Wambaugh continued to work for the Los Angeles Police Department through the publication of his second novel, *The Blue Knight* (1972), which shifted the focus to Bumper Morgan, a jaded old-timer on the force going through his last days on the job. Wambaugh retired in 1974 prior to the publication of the controversial *The Choirboys* (1975), which graphically depicts the very dark humor and sometimes self-destructive behavior police officers employ to keep them going in their grim job. Here is his description of the cops' MacArthur Park "choir practice," whose founder

always maintained that they shouldn't have married men in the group because they were

quite likely to go home early, and early dropouts were the death of any good choir practice.

"The songs must go on!" was the way Harold always put it.

Of course no one ever really sang at choir practice. Their "songs" were of a different genus but served much the same function as a rousing choral work. . . . It was merely an off duty meeting, usually in a secluded hideaway, for policemen who, having just finished their tour of duty, were too tense or stimulated or electrified to go to a silent sleeping house and lie down like ordinary people while nerve ends sparked. One hadn't always enough money to go to a policemen's bar. Still one felt the need to uncoil and have a drink and talk with others who had been on the streets that night. To reassure oneself. (pp. 18–19)

Technically, Wambaugh's early police novels are ancillary to a discussion of the police procedural since they are not really mysteries—in fact, one element of George Dove's definition of procedurals is that they concern police detectives, not uniformed patrolmen as in Wambaugh's first two. Beginning with his fifth book, *The Black Marble* (1978), Wambaugh's identification with mystery and detective fiction, already present in the public mind, grew more accurate. *The Delta Star* (1983) is a good example of his contributions to the procedural, offering the gallows humor of *The Choirboys*, the artistic use of obscenity associated with the playwright David Mamet, and a standard procedural structure that includes one main case (with an inventive murder weapon and an ingenious motive) and several minor ones.

According to an anecdote retold by H. R. F. Keating, writing on *The Glitter Dome* (1981) in *The Fine Art of Murder*, Wambaugh did not leave the police department because he wearied of police work:

He left the L.A.P.D. only when he found that his celebrity as a writer—his works were tremendous best sellers—was interfering with the work he loved. One evening, called to the scene of an armed robbery, he asked the barman victim, who had blood streaming from his pistol-whipped face, which hand the gunman had used. Instead of answering, the man asked Wambaugh in his turn what George C. Scott . . . was really like. Next day Wambaugh resigned. (p. 216)

Like steeplechase jockey turned novelist Dick Francis, another writer who made his reputation using professional expertise gathered in a dramatically intriguing career, Wambaugh emphasized specialized backgrounds in addition to police work in his later works: the dog show world in *The Black Marble*, the Hollywood studio scene in *The Glitter Dome*, and the America's Cup yacht race in *Floaters* (1996).

Wambaugh has also written nonfiction novels about police work, in the pattern of Truman Capote's *In Cold Blood* (1966), beginning with *The Onion Field* (1973). Since they include invented dialogue and other fictional storytelling techniques, some believe these works cross the line between fact and fiction based on fact.

Other Los Angeles cops who followed Wambaugh into the field include Dallas Barnes, author of *See the Woman* (1973) and other novels, and Paul Bishop, whose first novel was *Citadel Run* (1988). Retired New York police lieutenant William Caunitz wrote a number of large-canvas procedurals beginning with *One Police Plaza* (1984). One of the most notable officers from other jurisdictions, and certainly the highest ranking, is Hugh Holton, a commander in the Chicago Police Department and author of *Presumed Dead* (1994) and subsequent books.

American writers from other areas of law enforcement have exploited their professional expertise for fictional purposes. Former Federal Bureau of Investigation agent Gordon Gordon used that background in several of the novels he wrote with his wife, Mildred Gordon (as the Gordons), beginning with *FBI Story* (1950). U.S. Treasury agent Gerald Petievich wrote of counterfeiting investigators in a series beginning with *Money Men* (1981)

and *One Shot Deal* (1983) (both first published in one volume in 1981) and also produced a classic big-city police procedural in *To Live and Die in L.A.* (1984).

Britain's major cop writer after Maurice Procter is the very prolific John Wainwright. The mini-essays on police work, as well as the highly charged emotional style, in novels like *Pool of Tears* (1977) recall McBain. *Brainwash* (1979), a novel covering the events of one night as Detective Inspector Lyle questions a suspected child-rapist, is notable for its insights into police interrogation methods as well as its ambivalence about the workings of law and order. The fictional cop biography of *Blayde, R.I.P.* (1982) may be his best work in the procedural vein. In it, he takes one of the corniest old-movie situations—two brothers, one a cop, one a crook—and turns it into a near classic. In *All on a Summer's Day* (1981) and *All Through the Night* (1985), Wainwright emulates the fixed-time-period procedural pioneered in J. J. Marric's Gideon series.

Janwillem van de Wetering, a former Dutch policeman who now lives in the United States, writes his novels about the Amsterdam cops in English. From the beginning, with *Outsider in Amsterdam* (1975), they have had plots and structures similar to standard police procedurals, but the style, humor, and philosophical asides make them unique. The quirky characters, cops and crooks alike, are almost all likable, and the empathy that exists between the police and their criminal quarry, particularly in the earlier books in the series, is remarkable.

Albert Cornelis Baantjer, whose byline in the tradition of Simenon is his surname only, is also a former Amsterdam policeman. His long series about Inspector DeKok, more conventional than van de Wetering's, has been a major success in the Netherlands for more than thirty years but was first translated into English only in the mid-1990s.

The most famous fictional Amsterdam policeman, at least in the English-speaking world, is the creation of a British writer whose professional background is as a chef rather than a police officer. Nicolas Freeling's Van der Valk first appeared in *Love in Amsterdam* (1962; U.S. title, *Death in Amsterdam*, 1964). In defiance of the normal commercial considerations attending a successful series, Freeling killed off his famous character in *A Long Silence* (1972; U.S. title, *Auprès de ma Blonde*), briefly reviving him in *Sand Castles* (1989). Both author and character are mavericks in the procedural world: Freeling chafes at being labeled a crime writer, and Van der Valk often operates outside his urban home ground, sometimes investigating crime while on vacation, amateur detective style. Van der Valk properly belongs in the Great Policeman category with Maigret, with whom he and his successor, French policeman Henri Castang, are constantly compared. Although George Dove does cover Van der Valk in *The Police Procedural*, he admits "very few cops can quote Baudelaire, or would undertake to wear down a suspect by means of a series of social calls, or would refuse to call the lab boys to a murder site because police technology isn't his style" (p. 211).

Other Writers of the 1970s and 1980s

William McIlvanney's *Laidlaw* (1977) made an immediate critical impact on its first appearance. Abrasive but compassionate Glasgow policeman Jack Laidlaw, the creation of a Scottish writer already well known as an award-winning mainstream novelist and poet, has appeared in only two subsequent novels, *The Papers of Tony Veitch* (1983) and *The Big Man* (1985). But his first appearance put him immediately in the league of the giants, able to create crisp and vivid scenes with a feel of reality and make points about the human condition in a poet's prose. Even the sex scenes have an original touch.

Another writer to use Glasgow to good effect for a procedural series is Peter Turnbull, whose very 87th Precinct-like series about P Division began with *Deep and Crisp and Even* (1981), an excellent account of the

search for a serial killer in a city covered by snow. Turnbull is one of very few procedural writers (Lawrence Treat is another) who features his detectives in a series of short stories, beginning with "The Sort of Man He Was" (*Ellery Queen's Mystery Magazine*, August 1986). Like McBain's Steve Carella, P Division Chief Inspector Fabian Donogue emerges as somewhat "more equal" than his colleagues.

As rare as short stories in police procedural fiction is first-person narration. In part because he narrates most of his own cases, San Francisco's Lieutenant Frank Hastings, who first appeared in Collin Wilcox's *The Lonely Hunter* (1969), sometimes seems more like a lone wolf private eye than a member of a procedural team. But as the series goes on, teamwork is more manifest, and other officers play important roles. Writing in *St. James Guide to Crime and Mystery Fiction*, Bill Pronzini says Wilcox shares with McBain "the ability to combine the portrayal of investigative police work with incisive psychological and sociological examinations of the people who live, love, and die in a major metropolitan city" (p. 1056).

Many writers of police series, not all of them in the true procedural category, write about seemingly mismatched "odd couple" detecting teams. Examples from outside the true procedural tradition include Colin Dexter's Morse and Lewis and Ruth Rendell's Wexford and Burden. Joyce Porter exploited this kind of relationship with her comic team of obnoxious Chief Inspector Dover and long-suffering Sergeant MacGregor, introduced in *Dover One* (1964), but the best examples of the breed to occupy real procedural novels are Reginald Hill's Yorkshire cops Superintendent Dalziel and Sergeant Pascoe, old school and university educated, respectively, who first appeared in *A Clubbable Woman* (1970). Although often rich in humor, their relationship is not played for laughs—Dalziel is less purely offensive than Dover, Pascoe is far more formidable and assertive than Mac-Gregor, and both are fully fleshed, complex figures. Hill had explored the characters of his police team in increasing depth, reaching new levels of achievement in *Bones and Silence* (1990) and *Recalled to Life* (1992). Under his own name and various pseudonyms, most prominently Patrick Ruell, the extremely versatile Hill also has written spy fiction, romantic suspense, private-eye capers, war novels, and swashbuckling historicals.

The similarly versatile American, Lawrence Sanders, has written many types of mysteries in his long, best-selling career, but his greatest achievement is the series about Edward X. Delaney of the New York Police Department, who first appeared as a secondary character in the Edgar-winning documentary-style novel *The Anderson Tapes* (1970) and then in *The First Deadly Sin* (1973). The latter book pioneered a type of procedural that has become almost a cliché but that still provides some of the best books in the subgenre when done well: the novel about a big city cop versus a crazy serial killer. After a whodunit, *The Second Deadly Sin* (1977), Sanders returned to the inverted structure in *The Third Deadly Sin* (1981), pitting Delaney, frequently recalled from retirement, against the Hotel Ripper. The depiction of a female serial killer, while inventive and involving, ultimately proves hard to believe.

The cop-versus-serial-killer novels tend to be longer than the average mystery and do not always concern series detectives. Among key practitioners are William Bayer, whose first novel about New York detective Frank Janek, *Peregrine* (1981), won an Edgar award, and Thomas H. Cook, beginning with his paperback original, *Blood Innocents* (1980), whose aging and recently bereaved homicide detective Reardon has much in common with Sanders' Delaney.

Another trend is represented by Katharine V. Forrest, most prominent of the lesbian mystery writers who have flourished, primarily with smaller specialist publishers, in the seventies and eighties. Los Angeles policewoman Kate Delafield, introduced in *Amateur City* (1984), is a closeted lesbian, whose battle with the prejudices of her own department as well as the agents of crime creates an additional layer of tension. *Murder by Tradi-*

tion (1991) is a good example of the latter-day police novel's emphasis on making the case as well as solving it.

Susan Dunlap, creator of a straight policewoman, Berkeley's Jill Smith, in a series beginning with *Karma* (1984), exemplifies many series that have taken on characteristics of the procedural while in their plots remaining more in the tradition of pure detection. How a police department operates depends in many ways on the nature of its citizens and the government organization that oversees it. Dunlap's colorful depiction of Berkeley, a very liberal university town, demonstrates that procedurals can be as varied as the jurisdictions they depict.

The latter statement certainly applies to two Moscow-based series by American writers, both of which began in 1981. Martin Cruz Smith's major best-seller *Gorky Park* introduced homicide cop Arkady Renko in a long, complex examination of the Soviet criminal justice system and other aspects of the society. Renko reappears in *Polar Star* (1989) and *Red Square* (1992), the latter set in the post–Soviet Russia of Boris Yeltsin and organized crime. The modular-style novels of Stuart Kaminsky, beginning with *Rostnikov's Corpse* (1981; U.S. title, *Death of a Dissident*), form a longer series in which Porfiry Petrovich Rostnikov and his colleagues first do their police work under Soviet communism and later face the very different challenges of fighting crime under the new Russia's virtually unfettered capitalism.

Another very different jurisdictional background appears in James McClure's series about South African police Lieutenant Tromp Kramer (Afrikaner) and Sergeant Mickey Zondi (Bantu), introduced in *The Steam Pig* (1971). The way the biracial team works together and establishes grudging respect in a society based on racism is as fascinating as the criminal problems they confront.

The Mario Balzic novels of K. C. Constantine, beginning with *The Rocksburg Railroad Murders* (1972), follow the career of the Rocksburg, Pennsylvania, police chief to retirement and beyond. Despite very realistic demonstrations of the frustration of police work, the personality-centered novels may be no more true procedurals than the Maigret books. In whatever subcategory, they are among the best crime fiction being written today.

The Stars of the 1990s

Of the writers to come to prominence in the twentieth century's last decade, one Briton, one Canadian, and one American seem most likely to be numbered among the procedural masters in years to come. English-born Canadian Peter Robinson's first novel about Yorkshire's Inspector Alan Banks, *The Gallows View*, appeared in Toronto and London in 1987 but was not published in the United States until 1990. Some of Banks's cases, notably the Edgar-nominated *Wednesday's Child* (1992), about the search for the kidnapper of a seven-year-old, capture the dogged nature of police work in a manner reminiscent of Waugh's *Last Seen Wearing*. He is also more successful than most in balancing the professional and private lives of his detective hero, as shown in *Blood at the Root* (1997). Like William McIlvanney, Robinson was a poet before turning to crime fiction, a background that gives an extra distinction to his prose.

Another poet drawn to the procedural form is the very prolific British novelist John Harvey, who wrote westerns and other types of popular fiction under at least ten pseudonyms before introducing Nottingham policeman Charlie Resnick in *Lonely Hearts* (1989). In the *St. James Guide to Crime and Mystery Fiction*, Harvey indicates that the influence of Elmore Leonard and Ross Thomas led him to apply an American style to a British milieu:

> [T]he narrative would be character-based and dialogue-driven and . . . it would be possible for the tone to shift between the quirkily humorous and the highly dramatic. . . . American crime writers seemed to be able to convey a strong sense of a specific place and atmosphere . . . without resorting to the rather lengthy descriptive writing employed by some of their British counterparts. (p. 496)

Harvey also identifies McBain and Wambaugh, as well as closer-to-home writers like Dickens, Alan Sillitoe, and D. H. Lawrence, as influences. *Hill Street Blues*, which inspired Harvey in writing *Hard Cases*, a British television series about Nottingham probation officers, he valued for its "multi-strand narrative . . . , fast pace and off-the-wall humour" (p. 496). While the subject matter of the Resnick books is solidly British, Harvey's fascination with and firm grasp of American idiom are demonstrated in *Living Proof* (1995), set at Nottingham's annual mystery convention, Shots on the Page, in which an American woman private eye writer is the targeted victim and some of her writings are quoted.

Michael Connelly, who worked as a police reporter for the *Los Angeles Times* and other papers specifically to gather expertise in investigative procedure, introduced Los Angeles cop Hieronymus (Harry) Bosch in *The Black Echo* (1992). Vietnam veteran Bosch is a gifted misfit whose superiors, as well as the department's Internal Affairs division, prove nearly as troublesome opponents as the criminals. Connelly's Edgar-winning debut was followed by *The Black Ice* (1993); by the appearance of the third novel in the series, he was firmly established as one of the most highly praised new crime writers of the nineties. *The Concrete Blonde* (1994), a complex and multifaceted novel notable for vivid style, depth of character, and traditional puzzle plotting, depicts a situation familiar in recent police history: the widow of a supposed serial killer Harry shot is suing him for wrongful death. Connelly's first novel outside the Bosch series, *The Poet* (1996), centers on FBI procedure and concerns a series of ostensible police suicides.

Conclusion

As crime novels have grown longer and (sometimes) more complex, the dividing lines separating one subgenre from another and the whole crime fiction field from the mainstream have become increasingly blurred. If this trend continues, there may be fewer novels that can be handily pegged as police procedurals. At the same time, thanks to growing public awareness of the practical nature of police work, the wide spectrum of crime fiction categories provides a more informed depiction of how the criminal justice system operates. Just as lawyer novelists and *Court TV* have brought a new realism to courtroom fiction, writers with police experience have combined with television documentaries and "reality shows" to raise public knowledge of their work, though always (one hopes) without sacrificing the artifice (subtle or otherwise) that makes for good fiction.

Selected Bibliography

POLICE PROCEDURALS

ED McBAIN (PSEUDONYM OF EVAN HUNTER)

87th Precinct series:

Cop Hater. New York: Permabooks, 1956.
The Mugger. New York: Simon & Schuster, 1956.
The Pusher. New York: Simon & Schuster, 1956.
The Con Man. New York: Permabooks, 1957.
Killer's Choice. New York: Simon & Schuster, 1957.
Killer's Payoff. New York: Simon & Schuster, 1958.
Lady Killer. New York: Simon & Schuster, 1958.
Killer's Wedge. New York: Simon & Schuster, 1959.
'Til Death. New York: Simon & Schuster, 1959.
King's Ransom. New York: Simon & Schuster, 1959.
The 87th Precinct (with an introduction by Anthony Boucher). New York: Simon & Schuster, 1959. Omnibus volume: contains *Cop Hater, The Mugger,* and *The Pusher.*
Give the Boys a Great Big Hand. New York: Simon & Schuster, 1960.
The Heckler. New York: Simon & Schuster, 1960.
See Them Die. New York: Simon & Schuster, 1960.
Lady, Lady, I Did It! New York: Simon & Schuster, 1961.
The Empty Hours. New York: Simon & Schuster, 1962. Novella collection.
Like Love. New York: Simon & Schuster, 1962.
Ten Plus One. New York: Simon & Schuster, 1963.
Ax. New York: Simon & Schuster, 1964.
He Who Hesitates. New York: Delacorte, 1965.
Doll. New York: Delacorte, 1965.
Eighty Million Eyes. New York: Delacorte, 1966.

Fuzz. New York: Doubleday, 1968.
Shotgun. New York: Doubleday, 1969.
Jigsaw. New York: Doubleday, 1970.
Hail, Hail, the Gang's All Here! New York: Doubleday, 1971.
Sadie When She Died. New York: Doubleday, 1972.
Let's Hear It for the Deaf Man. New York: Doubleday, 1973.
Hail to the Chief. New York: Random House, 1973.
Bread. New York: Random House, 1974.
Blood Relatives. New York: Random House, 1975.
So Long As You Both Shall Live. New York: Random House, 1976.
Long Time No See. New York: Random House, 1977.
Calypso. New York: Viking, 1979.
Ghosts. New York: Viking, 1980.
Heat. New York: Viking, 1981.
Ice. New York: Arbor House, 1983.
Lightning. New York: Arbor House, 1984.
Eight Black Horses. New York: Arbor House, 1985.
Poison. New York: Arbor House, 1987.
Tricks. New York: Arbor House, 1987.
Lullaby. New York: Arbor House, 1989.
Vespers. New York: Morrow, 1990.
Widows. New York: Morrow, 1991.
Kiss. New York: Morrow, 1992.
Mischief. New York: Morrow, 1993.
And All Through the House. New York: Warner, 1994.
Romance. New York: Warner, 1995.
Nocturne. New York: Warner, 1997.

J. J. MARRIC (PSEUDONYM OF JOHN CREASEY)

Gideon series:

Gideon's Day. London: Hodder and Stoughton, 1955; New York: Harper, 1955.
Gideon's Week. London: Hodder and Stoughton, 1956; New York: Harper, 1956.
Gideon's Night. London: Hodder and Stoughton, 1957; New York: Harper, 1957.
Gideon's Month. London: Hodder and Stoughton, 1958; New York: Harper, 1958.
Gideon's Staff. London: Hodder and Stoughton, 1959; New York: Harper, 1959.
Gideon's Risk. London: Hodder and Stoughton, 1960; New York: Harper, 1960.
Gideon's Fire. London: Hodder and Stoughton, 1961; New York: Harper, 1961.
Gideon's March. London: Hodder and Stoughton, 1962; New York: Harper, 1962.
Gideon's Ride. London: Hodder and Stoughton, 1963; New York: Harper, 1963.
Gideon's Vote. London: Hodder and Stoughton, 1964; New York: Harper, 1964.
Gideon's Lot. New York: Harper, 1964; London: Hodder and Stoughton, 1965.
Gideon's Badge. London: Hodder and Stoughton, 1966; New York: Harper, 1966.

Gideon's Wrath. London: Hodder and Stoughton, 1967; New York: Harper, 1967.

Gideon's River. London: Hodder and Stoughton, 1968; New York: Harper, 1968.

Gideon's Power. London: Hodder and Stoughton, 1969; New York: Harper, 1969.

Gideon's Sport. London: Hodder and Stoughton, 1970; New York: Harper, 1970.

Gideon's Art. London: Hodder and Stoughton, 1971; New York: Harper, 1971.

Gideon's Men. London: Hodder and Stoughton, 1972; New York: Harper, 1972.

Gideon's Press. London: Hodder and Stoughton, 1973; New York: Harper, 1973.

Gideon's Fog. New York: Harper, 1974; London: Hodder and Stoughton, 1975.

Gideon's Drive. London: Hodder and Stoughton, 1976; New York: Harper, 1976.

MAURICE PROCTER

Each Man's Destiny. London: Longman, 1947.

Philip Hunter series:

The Chief Inspector's Statement. London: Hutchinson, 1951. U.S.: *The Pennycross Murders.* New York: Harper, 1953.

I Will Speak Daggers. London: Hutchinson, 1956. U.S.: *The Ripper.* New York: Harper, 1956.

Harry Martineau series:

Hell Is a City. London: Hutchinson, 1954. U.S. *Somewhere in This City.* New York: Harper, 1954.

The Midnight Plumber. London: Hutchinson, 1957; New York: Harper, 1958.

Man in Ambush. London: Hutchinson, 1958.

Killer at Large. London: Hutchinson, 1959; New York: Harper, 1959.

Devil's Due. London: Hutchinson, 1960; New York: Harper, 1960.

The Devil Was Handsome. London: Hutchinson, 1961; New York: Harper, 1961.

A Body to Spare. London: Hutchinson, 1962; New York: Harper, 1962.

Moonlight Flitting. London: Hutchinson, 1963. U.S.: *The Graveyard Rolls.* New York: Harper, 1964.

Two Men in Twenty. London: Hutchinson, 1964; New York: Harper, 1964.

Death Has a Shadow. London: Hutchinson, 1965. U.S.: *Homicide Blonde.* New York: Harper, 1965.

His Weight in Gold. London: Hutchinson, 1966; New York: Harper, 1966.

Rogue Running. London: Hutchinson, 1967; New York: Harper, 1967.

Exercise Hoodwink. London: Hutchinson, 1967; New York: Harper, 1967.

Hideaway. London: Hutchinson, 1968; New York: Harper, 1968.

LAWRENCE TREAT

V as in Victim. New York: Duell, 1945.

H as in Hunted. New York: Duell, 1946.

Q as in Quicksand. New York: Duell, 1947.

T as in Trapped. New York: Morrow, 1947.

F as in Flight. New York: Morrow, 1948.

Over the Edge. New York: Morrow, 1948.

Big Shot. New York: Harper, 1951.

Weep for a Wanton. New York: Ace, 1956.

Lady, Drop Dead. New York and London: Abelard, 1960.

P as in Police: 16 Procedural Short Stories. Edited and with intro. by Ellery Queen. New York: Davis, 1970.

JOSEPH WAMBAUGH

The New Centurions. Boston: Little, Brown, 1970.

The Blue Knight. Boston: Little, Brown, 1972.

The Choirboys. New York: Delacorte, 1975.

The Black Marble. New York: Delacorte, 1978.

The Glitter Dome. New York: Morrow, 1981.

The Delta Star. New York: Morrow, 1983.

The Secrets of Harry Bright. New York: Morrow, 1985.

The Golden Orange. New York: Morrow, 1990.

Fugitive Nights. New York: Morrow, 1992.

Finnegan's Week. New York: Morrow, 1993.

Floaters. New York and London: Bantam, 1996.

HILLARY WAUGH

Last Seen Wearing. New York: Doubleday, 1952. Repr. with accompanying editorial and bibliographic material. Del Mar, Calif.: Publisher's, 1978.

Fred Fellows series:

Sleep Long, My Love. New York: Doubleday, 1959.

Road Block. New York: Doubleday, 1960.

That Night It Rained. New York: Doubleday, 1961.

The Late Mrs. D. New York: Doubleday, 1962.

Born Victim. New York: Doubleday, 1962.

Death and Circumstance. New York: Doubleday, 1963.

Prisoner's Plea. New York: Doubleday, 1963.

The Missing Man. New York: Doubleday, 1964.

End of a Party. New York: Doubleday, 1965.

Pure Poison. New York: Doubleday, 1966.

The Con Game. New York: Doubleday, 1968.

Frank Sessions series:

"30" Manhattan East. New York: Doubleday, 1968.

The Young Prey. New York: Doubleday, 1969.

Finish Me Off. New York: Doubleday, 1970.

BIOGRAPHICAL AND CRITICAL STUDIES

Ball, John, ed. *The Mystery Story.* San Diego: University of California Extension, 1976.

Barzun, Jacques, and Wendell Hertig Taylor. *A Catalogue of Crime,* rev. ed. New York: Harper, 1989.

Brean, Herbert, ed. *The Mystery Writer's Handbook.* New York: Harper, 1956.

Carr, John C. *The Craft of Crime: Conversations with Crime Writers.* Boston: Houghton, 1983.

DeAndrea, William L. *Encyclopedia Mysteriosa.* New York: Prentice Hall, 1994.

Dove, George N. *The Police Procedural.* Bowling Green, Ohio: Bowling Green State University Popular Press, 1982.

———, *The Boys from Grover Avenue: Ed McBain's 87th Precinct Novels.* Bowling Green, Ohio: Bowling Green State University Popular Press, 1985.

Dove, George N., and Earl Bargainnier, eds. *Cops and Constables: American and British Fictional Policemen.* Bowling Green, Ohio: Bowling Green State University Popular Press, 1986.

Gilbert, Michael, ed. *Crime in Good Company.* London: Constable, 1959.

———. "The British Police Procedural." In *Whodunit?: A Guide to Crime, Suspense, and Spy Fiction.* Edited by H. R. F. Keating. New York: Van Nostrand Reinhold, 1982.

Gorman, Ed, Martin H. Greenberg, and Larry Segriff, eds., with Jon L. Breen. *The Fine Art of Murder.* New York: Carroll & Graf, 1993.

Haycraft, Howard. *Murder for Pleasure.* New York: Appleton, 1941.

Hubin, Allen J. *Crime Fiction II: A Comprehensive Bibliography, 1749–1990,* 2 vols. New York: Garland, 1994.

McArdle, Phil, and Karen McArdle. *Fatal Fascination: Where Fact Meets Fiction in Police Work.* Boston: Houghton, 1988.

Muller, Adrian. Interview with Robert Barnard. *Mystery Scene* (January/February 1996): 32 ff.

Nehr, Ellen. *Doubleday Crime Club Compendium, 1928–1991.* Martinez, Calif.: Offspring, 1992.

Ousby, Ian. *Bloodhounds of Heaven: The Detective in English Fiction from Godwin to Doyle.* Cambridge and London: Harvard University Press, 1976.

Pederson, Jay P., ed. *St. James Guide to Crime and Mystery Writers,* 4th ed. Detroit: St. James, 1996.

Penzler, Otto, ed. *The Great Detectives.* Boston: Little, Brown, 1978.

Steinbrunner, Chris, and Otto Penzler, eds. *Encyclopedia of Mystery and Detection.* New York: McGraw-Hill, 1976.

Stewart, R. F. *And Always a Detective: Chapters on the History of Detective Fiction.* Newton Abbot, Devon, and North Pomfret, Vt.: David & Charles, 1980.

Symons, Julian. *Mortal Consequences: A History—From the Detective Story to the Crime Novel.* New York: Harper, 1972.

Vickers, Roy. Intro. to his *Best Police Stories.* London: Faber, 1966.

Winn, Dilys, ed. *Murderess Ink.* New York: Workman, 1979.

———, ed. *Murder Ink,* rev. ed. New York: Workman, 1984.

REGIONALIZATION OF THE MYSTERY AND CRIME NOVEL

J. K. VAN DOVER

A SENSE OF PLACE, narrowly defined, is as fundamental in mystery fiction as are the essential formulas of plot and character, but the formula for setting requires only that the author construct a plausible physical environment that is functional for the commission of a crime that is both initially mysterious and ultimately explicable. The crime novel is always realistic: it is that realism that enables the reader to enter into the investigation fairly. With the exception of science-fiction crime novels such as Isaac Asimov's series featuring Elijah "Lije" Baley, that realism requires a worldly setting. The specific scene is often diagrammed in circumstantial detail—doors and windows, teacups and wine glasses, cigarette ashes and unfinished phrases scrawled in blood—the better to conceal the crucial items that are the clues to the true solution. These pragmatic considerations in staging can be met without providing any depiction of the larger natural and social environment that surrounds the crime. Indeed, in founding the genre, Edgar Allan Poe (see also separate essay) went to an extreme to avoid any broader setting by placing Dupin in a Paris that Poe never visited and never troubled himself to read much about; Dupin's Paris is, as "The Mystery of Marie Rogêt" makes clear, an amphibious Paris–New York. A sense of Paris (or of New York) would, Poe

evidently felt, distract from what he took to be the core of the detective story: the puzzling obscurity of the problem and the brilliance of the method of the detective.

Poe's first two important heirs, Émile Gaboriau and Sir Arthur Conan Doyle, conscientiously repaired his omission (see separate essays on Doyle and Gaboriau). Gaboriau, with Honoré de Balzac in mind, elevated a larger sense of place to the highest position; Lecoq's Paris is perhaps more fully evoked than Lecoq himself or his method. Conan Doyle established the balance, which has made Sherlock Holmes the quintessential detective: in the Holmes saga, the character of Holmes, of his method, and of his London contribute equally to the lasting appeal of the stories. London by gaslight (or Dartmoor by moonlight) is as much a fixture of the Holmes myth as the detective's bohemian habits and scientific method. After Holmes, mystery and crime writers had a precedent for concentrating their energies as much on the detective's world as on his cases. And so one can speak of the London of Richard Austin Freeman, the Chicago of William Riley Burnett, the San Francisco of Dashiell Hammett, or the New York of Mickey Spillane. A dedicated regionalist might even speak of the Virginia of Melville Davisson Post, or the Mississippi of William Faulkner. But generally, the place of the crime novel was the big city, and the big city, in the twentieth century especially, is not a region.

A "region" is a place that has resisted homogenization into a national culture. It retains its own peculiar human and natural identity, and both it and its surrounding territories are aware of these peculiarities, which may express themselves in regional prejudices, institutions, dialects, religious and social affiliations, ethnic distinctions, and so on. Regional characters are usually the result of historical evolution and natural boundaries (rivers, mountains, oceans). In the modern metropolis, history and nature are all too easily erased, though the argument can be made that neighborhoods within a large city, with their peculiar histories and marked boundaries, do qualify as distinctive regions. Thus, the Harlem of Chester Himes's Grave Digger Jones and Coffin Ed Johnson novels (see essay on "The Black Detective") or the Tenderloin of Lawrence Block's Matt Scudder novels may indeed constitute genuine regions. For the purposes of the survey, however, "region" will retain its traditional association with the peripheral provinces of the modern state.

No novel set in London, Paris, New York, Chicago, or Los Angeles is regional. These metropolitan centers may embody national characters, but they cannot claim to represent regions. Thus, none of the great names of the Golden Age of the mystery—G. K. Chesterton, S. S. Van Dine, Dorothy L. Sayers, Agatha Christie, Ellery Queen, Margery Allingham, Rex Stout, Georges Simenon, and so forth—qualify as regionalists. Any novel that is set outside of the metropolises, but pays little attention to the concrete past and present milieu of the city-town-countryside, is not regional. Therefore, the large class of British vicarage and seaside-resort mysteries are excluded: the author is very rarely interested in the quiddities of this particular parish or that particular resort. (On the other hand, a novel such as Dorothy L. Sayers' *The Nine Tailors*, which is set in the fen country of East Anglia, would qualify as regional.) Although the district in which Reginald Hill sets his Dalziel

and Pascoe novels appears on no map, the Yorkshire landscape and customs he depicts are rooted in Yorkshire reality, and the novels qualify as regional. The invented Calleshire of Catherine Aird's C. D. Sloan series is, however, a miniature of England, not of any particular English region. Finally, although Tony Hillerman's mysteries are firmly set in the topography and ethnography of the American Southwest and surely qualify as regional, they also qualify as "ethnic," and it is under that rubric that they (and comparable series such as Arthur Upfield's) are treated in this volume.

Although Philip Marlowe operates primarily in metropolitan Los Angeles, the novels of Raymond Chandler (see separate essay) may nonetheless be regarded as among the earliest and best exercises in detective regionalism. Chandler was not a deliberate regionalist; his project was an anatomy of the dead end of the American (not of the Californian or Los Angelean) Dream. But the local landscape and history of the Los Angeles region is, in the end, the central matter of Chandler's nine novels. Though born in Chicago and raised in England, Chandler caught Los Angeles at the moment it was becoming a nonregional metropolis—what James Ellroy called *The Big Nowhere* (1988) and what Marlowe himself, in *The Little Sister* (1949), called "a big hard-boiled city with no more personality than a paper cup" (1976 ed., p. 181). Chandler could still, with some nostalgia, sense the lingering presence of the Ghost of Region Past. Even from the all-American mean streets down which he must walk, Philip Marlowe can still smell the eucalyptus and wild sage; he can remember Los Angeles before Hollywood.

In his awareness of a lost local paradise, Chandler conforms to a common regionalist spirit: the original Regionalist movement in American literature rose to prominence as an offshoot of realism in the 1890s, precisely at the historical moment when America was making the transition from a rural polity to an urban one. Self-conscious regionalism often appeals most to writers and readers when they sense that the local colors are fading under the pressure of external historical forces. This may, indeed, be a motive for many of the regional crime writers today. Some are merely looking to exploit outsider curiosity, but some of the best, like Chandler, doubtless are moved to record and analyze what seems to be an endangered individuality, as mass media and mass transportation threaten to homogenize all regions.

The rise of the regional mystery is one of the most conspicuous of recent trends in the genre. Beginning in the 1970s, the hegemony of the metropolitan cities—London, Paris, New York, Chicago, and Los Angeles—began to yield to the provinces. Most crime-novel series are still set in cities for the same reason that they began in cities: that is where the crime is; at least, that is where there is enough crime to sustain with some degree of probability a detective's career. But the cities are now often secondary cities—Glasgow, New Orleans, Cincinnati, Barcelona—cities with distinct local cultures. Often, the detective's city is small indeed: Sechelt, British Columbia, or Meriwether, Montana, or "Rocksburg," Pennsylvania. Whereas the metropolitan crime novel tends to take the national character as its matter, the regional crime novel tends to focus on the historical, geographical, and social peculiarities of its locale. (This trend is, of course, equally evident in popular nongenre fiction such as that of William Kennedy, Mary Lee Settle, or John Edgar Wideman.)

Before examining a few of the prominent regions receiving attention from crime writers today, a few general observations can be made. The regionalists do not constitute a formal school. The artistic and financial success of an early quasi regionalist like John D. MacDonald certainly encouraged both writers and publishers to risk stories set in unmetropolitan locales, but the primary motive seems to be internal and individual. Crime writers seem to want to explore the specific world in which they were raised or to which they have since been drawn, and the crime novel, as Frederic Jameson observes in his essay "On Raymond Chandler," is the perfect vehicle for

such an exploration. The detective is by profession an inquirer, and his inquiries lead him through all the levels, all the neighborhoods, homes, and offices, of his city or countryside. The detective traverses time as well as space: his investigation almost always moves backward from the present into the past; by an easy transition the analysis of the past of the crime can slide into an analysis of the past of the region. Faulkner's Gavin Stevens stories illustrate this possibility. Though Faulkner acknowledged his envy of the pot-boiling success of mystery writers as a principal motive for turning to the genre in the 1930s, the Gavin Stevens stories of *Knight's Gambit,* and especially the Gavin Stevens novel, *Intruder in the Dust,* clearly use the investigation of the crime at hand as an occasion for Faulkner to reflect upon the larger crimes of Southern society.

Faulkner's exploitation of the detective-story formula in his regional fiction suggests a couple of further points. The first is a reminder that although the mystery genre attracts hack writers (including some really first-rate hacks), it also attracts what are widely recognized as major writers. Regional crime novels have been written by Ernest Hemingway (*To Have and Have Not*), Harper Lee (*To Kill a Mockingbird*), Truman Capote (*In Cold Blood*), Walker Percy (*The Thanatos Syndrome*), Peter Mathiessen (*Killing Mister Watson*), and others. Writers such as Chandler and George V. Higgins surely belong in the same class, and the status of novelists such as James Lee Burke, Carl Hiaasen, Loren Estleman, and Laurali R. Wright may well rise to that level.

Faulkner also exemplifies the value of being born to the region one writes about. Many regional crime writers are natives of their region, but there are important nonnative regional crime novelists like MacDonald, who was born in Pennsylvania and moved to Florida as an adult. An outsider may be intensely devoted to his adopted region and, though he misses some motes, may see the beams that the native overlooks. MacDonald became an acute critic of Florida's self-destructive appetite for development and, in his life as well as his fiction, a passionate defender of its endangered natural environments. Charles Willeford, Elmore Leonard, and Edna Buchanan are some other nonnative Floridians who have written excellent novels about a region they have come to know thoroughly and care about greatly. James Crumley was born in Texas and raised in the South, but he writes with conviction about the mountain West where he now lives.

Regional novels narrated by the detective may achieve a different effect from those narrated in the third person. A third-person narrative may comprehend more aspects of a social reality, and may, in the dialogue of its characters, shape emotional responses to that reality. But the first-person, native-son or native-daughter narrator is in a strong position to draw the sharpest portrait of his or her time and place. Chandler and MacDonald are the principal models here: their use of the filter of the detective's moral and aesthetic sensibility to shape a response to events and environments lies directly behind the first-person technique of some of the best contemporary writers. Chandler, for instance, appears immediately behind the fiction of Loren Estleman and James Crumley, and MacDonald evidently influenced Jeremiah Healy and Jonathan Valin.

Women writers are less likely to manifest such patriarchal affiliations. This suggests another useful distinction: male versus female regionalists. This was an important contrast in the original Regionalist movement. Although it had important male practitioners such as Hamlin Garland and Charles W. Chestnutt, many of the best of the local-color writers were women: Sarah Orne Jewett, Mary Wilkins Freeman, Kate Chopin, Alice Dunbar-Nelson, Mary Austin, Willa Cather. Regionalism, with its focus on domestic scenes and the nuances of morals and manners, allowed women to probe the worlds of their immediate experience. The modern detective story has welcomed women into all of its subgenres, and there are metropolitan successes such as Sue Grafton (Santa Teresa/ southern California), Marcia Muller (San Francisco), and Sara Paretsky (Chicago). Regional crime fiction has also profited from the number of women—such as Julie Smith, Sharyn McCrumb, Joan Hess, and Laurali R. Wright—who have seized the opportunity to have a detective (often a woman detective) investigate the ways their local worlds work.

Another historical connection between the regionalist crime writers of the late-twentieth century and the local-color writers of the late nineteenth century is the issue of dialect. Dialect narration and dialogue were staples of the earlier movement. Although it is less significant in the later one, partly because the mass media have diminished the strains of dialect in society, some of the best crime writers still find local speech patterns an effective device in depicting a regional sensibility. James Lee Burke's Cajun inflections are perhaps most distinctive in this regard, but George V. Higgins and K. C. Constantine have shown a generation of writers how idiom and even syntax can carry a plot as well as reveal character. Those who exploit an ethnic dimension to their detective's world have this advantage. There is, for example, a Hispanic accent in the Denver novels of Rex Burns and Manuel Ramos.

Another curious division in regional crime writing is that most of the writers seem to come from one of two backgrounds: academia (Burke, John William Corrington, Willeford, James W. Hall, Robert B. Parker, Valin, Crumley, Burns) or journalism (Smith, Hiaasen, Buchanan, Higgins, Estleman, Wright) or, occasionally, law (Higgins, Healy).

Finally, a contrast can be drawn between the regional police procedural and the regional private-eye novel. The police procedural encourages multiple plots (or, at least, subplots) as the realistic police detective handles his load of cases, and this encourages a broader depiction of the social character of the region, but the procedural form does tend, not surprisingly, to press attention toward the procedures by which the detectives pursue their cases, and these procedures are rarely regional. The private investigator—perhaps precisely because he does not have this procedural anchor in realism—may allow the writer to place more emphasis on realizing the scene of the crime.

Regionalism has become such a popular category in the contemporary detective story that it is impossible to survey all regions, let alone all regional detectives. There is, for example, the ten-volume "Old Beach P.I." series by Wade B. Fleetwood: the action is set in the thirty-mile stretch of coastal resorts in Delaware and Maryland. The books are sponsored by local businesses, and the characters frequently find themselves staying at a motel whose name, address, and phone number are listed under "Patrons" at the back of the book. Tish McWhinney, the seventy-five-year-old amateur sleuth in Barbara Comfort's series of novels set in Vermont, represents a somewhat more ambitious type of detective, but her adventures too are directed toward a local market. These are certainly regional mysteries; they are scrupulous in their depiction of their neighborhoods, but they cannot be considered in a short survey. What follows is a selective account of some of the main regions explored by some of the main contemporary writers of crime fiction.

The American South: New Orleans and Miami

Gertrude Stein famously dismissed her native Oakland with the line, "There is no there there." Of all American regions, the one that has possessed the most there-ness for more than two centuries, in its own eyes and in the eyes of outsiders, has been the South. It is not surprising, therefore, that the South has spawned the largest variety of regional crime writers. From Virginia to Florida to New Orleans to Maggody, Arkansas, local authors have imagined local detectives solving local crimes. The geographical range of "the South" is a reminder, however, that within a region there are many regions. There are many Souths: Tidewater, Piedmont, and Deep; old

and new (and post-new); white and black; Episcopalian, Baptist, and Creole Catholic; urban, rural, and really rural. The two preeminent Souths of the contemporary regionalist movement in mystery and crime fiction are the peculiar New Orleans South and the deracinated Miami South.

Once Edgar Allan Poe's Legrand abandoned New Orleans for his island near Charleston, the Big Easy went relatively undetected for more than a century. Since the 1980s, however, it has enjoyed an embarrassment of riches: a large number of very good writers have chosen New Orleans and the nearby bayou country as the scene for crime and detection. These include James Lee Burke, Julie Smith, John William Corrington and Joyce Corrington, James Sallis, Tony Fennelly, Chris Wiltz, Sarah Shankman, Dick Lochte, John Lutz, Tony Dunbar, D. J. Donaldson, M. K. Shuman, Rex Dancer, and Brian Tobin. Only the first six can be discussed here.

Though he was born in Texas, James Lee Burke (b. 1936) was raised in the New Iberia, Louisiana–east Texas region in which he plants his hero, Dave Robicheaux. In the first Robicheaux novel, *The Neon Rain* (1987), the detective is a member of the New Orleans Police Department living (like John D. MacDonald's Travis McGee) on a houseboat, but he resigns from the force at the novel's end, and in the next book, *Heaven's Prisoners* (1988), Burke has placed him back in his native Cajun parish of New Iberia, from which he can, when necessary, foray back into the dark violence of the Crescent City, but which also allows Burke to envelop Robicheaux in the landscapes and peoples of Cajun Louisiana.

Robicheaux evolves a complex personal life: in *Heaven's Prisoners*, his first wife, Annie, is murdered and he adopts a Salvadoran orphan whose life he has saved; in *A Morning for Flamingos* (1990), he marries his high-school sweetheart Bootsie, beginning a second deeply satisfying marriage. In several novels, Dave talks to his dead Cajun father. Dave's NOPD partner, the extra-hard-boiled, semimaniacal Clete Purcel, reappears frequently and represents his primary male bond. Since leaving the NOPD, Robicheaux has maintained his livelihood by running a bait shop and boat rental. He reemerges as a very tough investigator only when outside troubles intrude upon his peace, as they regularly do. Often the troubles are linked to figures from Robicheaux's personal past: men and women whose lives have taken them from New Iberia into all sorts of difficulties. In some novels, the larger past of his region also plays a role in the action. In *Burning Angel* (1995) the South's peculiar history of race relations affects the plot. *In the Electric Mist with the Confederate Dead* (1993) places Robicheaux in an ongoing dialogue with the ghost of Confederate General John Bell Hood. The two men discuss the meaning of integrity and the necessity of violence then and now.

Burke's greatest strengths as a writer lie in his responsiveness to the natural world and in his ability to drive his narratives forward from confrontation to confrontation. Few writers since John Buchan have been as successful at evoking the sensory pleasures of a landscape. Burke vividly describes the sights, sounds, smells, and tastes of Cajun Louisiana. The action frequently pauses as Dave Robicheaux savors a sunset or a rainstorm; these moments constitute a natural aesthetic respite from the moral corruptions that pollute the human environment. When he is not pausing, Robicheaux is racing from one encounter to another. More than most hard-boiled writers, Burke advances his narrative through a sequence of explosive confrontations. These are sometimes physically violent; they are usually rhetorically violent, as the characters exercise their bravado with an almost Elizabethan linguistic creativity. Burke picks up the local rhythms and idioms of his low characters with the same sure grasp as he depicts the environment. He is so successful in these aspects of his art that the reader overlooks the thinness of some of the plots and the dubiousness of some of the morality. Dave Robicheaux asserts that he is right after he has beaten a bad guy into unconsciousness with a pool stick or pistol-whipped an uncooperative thug, and he frequently hears from spouses,

partners, priests, lesbians, and dry cleaners that he is indeed right. But the preemptiveness with which he sometimes resorts to violence keeps the question open.

Aside from his predilection for violence, all Robicheaux's sentiments are proper: he has been profoundly troubled by his experiences in Vietnam; he opposes American interventions in Central America; he disparages racism, sexism, homophobia, and other popular forms of intolerance. In this sense, Robicheaux is representative of the genre. Although presidential election results since 1980 suggest that regional America tends to be quite conservative indeed, there are no conservative regional detectives at all. Nearly all of the post-1975 male detectives are troubled by their experiences in Vietnam, and disparagement of all forms of intolerance is a ubiquitous phenomenon.

Julie Smith (b. 1944) began her career as a crime writer in the 1980s with two series set in San Francisco, which, if it is defiantly not Los Angeles, is still more a metropolis than a region. But in 1990 she inaugurated a third series set in New Orleans. Although she was born in Maryland, went to college at the University of Mississippi, and worked as a journalist in San Francisco, Smith had, for a year in the mid-1960s, worked as a reporter in New Orleans. Her Skip Langdon novels exhibit an authenticity that evidently derives from personal experience as well as from the careful research acknowledged in the prefaces to the novels.

Smith is not an original stylist in the manner of James Lee Burke—her dialogue and her descriptions are sufficient—but she does display a sensitivity to nuances of relationships in the highly stratified society of middle- and upper-class New Orleans. Her detective, Skip Langdon, is herself a refugee from an established family; in choosing to be a cop, Langdon has repudiated the manner to which she was born, but she maintains contact with her well-connected peers. She is both an insider and an outsider in her family, her class, and her city. This ambivalent status secures her initial appointment to the homicide squad, and it becomes the device through which Smith can examine a wide variety of familial and class relationships in the world of New Orleans.

Skip Langdon situates herself in a social network. Having rebelled against the elite network into which she was born, she constructs her own alternative community, consisting of, among others, a gay landlord, an outsider boyfriend, and a black girlfriend. Her cases typically involve people trapped in destructive familial networks. The self-destructive dynamics of the eminent St. Amant family (the father is Rex of the Mardi Gras) are the matter of the first Langdon novel, *New Orleans Mourning* (1990), and psychological studies of functional and dysfunctional families are important in the novels that follow. *New Orleans Beat* (1994), for example, focuses on the family of Marguerite Terry: her husbands, her son, her daughter, and her mother. But two other unconventional "families" are also involved: a "virtual community" and a coven. The first exists in cyberspace; the second is a New Age, semi-feminist group of women who meet to engage in empowering rituals. The support of these ad hoc families stands in contrast to the devastating effects engendered by the "natural" family of Marguerite Terry.

Before Burke and Smith, a husband-and-wife team of writers had begun to use New Orleans as the setting for a series of novels. John William Corrington (1932–1988) had already established himself as a scholar of the South and was a significant voice in serious Southern literature when he began to collaborate with his wife, Joyce Corrington, on a series of novels featuring a cluster of detectives: John Wesley Colvin, who, as a native of Shreveport, Louisiana (the city with which John William Corrington identified himself), is an upstate outsider in New Orleans; Ralph "Rat" Trapp, a very tough black cop; and Denise Lemoyne, a well-connected debutante who eventually applies herself to becoming an assistant district attorney. The three are friends, and each serves as narrator of one of the three first novels. (The fourth novel, evi-

dently written primarily by Joyce Corrington, reprises Rat Trapp as narrator, but it is set in nonregional Los Angeles.) The three very different points of view make the series a uniquely interesting one. The novels betray a solid knowledge of the social terrain, and the Corringtons make essential use of historical background. The plot of *So Small a Carnival* (1986) turns in part upon the "deduct box" in which the notorious Huey Long stored his slush funds.

James Sallis (b. 1944) was the author of an important study of blues and jazz guitar before he turned to crime fiction in *The Long-Legged Fly* (1992). Sallis' detective is the hard-boiled black private eye, Lew Griffin. Griffin, like his author, is a native of Arkansas who has transplanted himself to New Orleans. His black New Orleans is a violent place, and Sallis gives Griffin an impressively tough rhetoric to suit his tough-guy actions, but the Griffin novels are also characterized by a high level of literary allusion (to Albert Camus, Chandler, Chester Himes, Miguel de Cervantes, James Baldwin, Herman Melville, Poe, Jorge Luis Borges, and many others). In fact, Griffin is an aspiring author himself, composing stories about a crazy Cajun detective named Boudleaux (close to Robicheaux). On the last page of *The Long-Legged Fly*, Griffin suggests that he may write a new book about a new detective, "someone I've named Lew Griffin." The complex, jazzlike structure of motifs in the novels and these self-referential comments suggest that Sallis has metafictional ambitions.

Another vivid writer to take up New Orleans as a scene is Tony Fennelly (b. 1945). Neither a scholar nor a journalist, Fennelly worked as an exotic dancer in New Orleans clubs before turning to fiction. Her detective Matt Sinclair is a well-born native of the city, a gay antiques dealer, and a former prosecutor. The novels embrace a wide range of characters, gay and straight, black and white, male and female, rich and not so rich; Sinclair's urbane manner extends a witty tolerance to all. Partly in response to publisher pressure to move beyond a homosexual-centered series, in 1994 Fennelly began a new detective series featuring the more acceptable gossip columnist and ex-topless dancer, Margo Fortier.

If New Orleans and south Louisiana have more there-ness than any other region in America, surely no region has less there-ness than Miami and south Florida. Even Los Angeles seems rich in local history and culture by comparison to the city that Henry M. Flagler virtually created in 1896 to provide a terminal for his railroad. Four years later, the population had increased six-fold, and advances in air-conditioning would soon make Miami into a metropolis full of retirees, tourists, exiles, drug dealers, and a vast underclass in the late twentieth century. It is a city full of ethnicity and empty of heritage.

As late as the 1940s and 1950s, when Brett Halliday (1904–1977) placed his moderately hard-boiled detective Mike Shayne in Miami, the city was merely a Bigtown, USA: not New York–Chicago–Los Angeles. The Shayne novels are not in any serious sense regional. Halliday is never much concerned with what made Miami Miami, or with what makes Miami Miami. (The writers who inherited the Shayne brand name have, in fact, often moved toward including local color.) There are essentially two places in Halliday's Shayne novels: Miami, where Shayne operates and where the decent cop Will Gentry runs things; and Miami Beach, where the mean, dumb cop Peter Painter runs things. Halliday emerged from the pulps where such simple moral geographies took precedence over any effort to re-create local color.

The next important writer to take up south Florida as a scene was the much more ambitious John D. MacDonald (1916–1986; see separate essay). MacDonald also trained in the pulps, but even in his novels of the 1950s he pushed toward an intelligent analysis of the way things are done in business and in small towns, frequently small Florida towns. By the early seventies, MacDonald had established Travis McGee in Fort Lauderdale, and while continuing his study of the way things get done, he had added an increasing interest in what doing things was doing to the south Florida environment. Travis McGee became perhaps the most influential character in regional crime fiction in the last quarter of the century: his sensibility, his voice, his ethics—all were widely imitated by detectives in other parts of the country.

Oddly enough, they have not been so widely imitated by Florida writers. MacDonald's environmentalism has been adopted as a central theme by perhaps the best of the new Florida writers, Carl Hiaasen, but the difference between Hiaasen's manner and MacDonald's could not be greater. The tone of the best late-twentieth-century south Florida crime novelists borders on the hysterical: hysterical in the sense of both wildly funny and wildly out of control. Though he often sees his values threatened, Travis McGee provides a stable moral center in MacDonald's novels. Things tend to fall apart in the worlds of his successors. As Hiaasen writes in *Double Whammy* (1987), "Living in Miami tended to recalibrate one's view of sanity" (Warner ed., p. 37). Lunacy seems to be the norm in the novels of Elmore Leonard, Charles Willeford, Hiaasen, and Edna Buchanan. Leonard (b. 1925) is a latecomer to Miami, having first established himself as a Detroit novelist. His careful re-creations of the southern Florida cityscape are partly the result of personal observation and partly the result of Leonard's famously rigorous preliminary research into the matter of his fiction.

Charles Willeford (1919–1988) was another nonnative who moved in the early 1960s to Miami, where he worked as a college instructor and a journalist. His novel *The Burnt Orange Heresy* (1971) is a provocative crime-story fable about the meaning of art, but Willeford's most noteworthy Florida mysteries are the four novels featuring Miami Police Department homicide detective Hoke Moseley. Moseley is an uncharismatic detective; with his dentures and his general passivity, Moseley is almost the antithesis of Burke's hard-driving Robicheaux. Moseley tends to roll with the bizarre events that life in Miami presents to him, but he retains a core of integrity and that dogged persistence that are essential qualities of the hard-boiled detective. His cases often involve psychopaths who have been drawn to the comforts and opportunities provided in modern south Florida, but they also take him through all levels of his society: elderly Jewish fugitives from the North, exploited Haitian farm workers, runaway crackers, refugees from Castro's Cuba. Willeford's rootless pyschopaths belong in the sunny city without roots; with great intensity they attempt to fix a place for themselves, sometimes constructing very strange surrogate families. Moseley, whom Willeford makes a native Conch, provides a perspective upon the strangenesses, but he too acquires his own peculiar menage, as he absorbs the daughters abandoned by his ex-wife and, for a time, takes on his pregnant homicide partner.

Carl Hiaasen (b. 1953) is a native Floridian, and as a prize-winning columnist for the Miami *Herald*, he has made a career of observing his native region. Beginning in 1986 he began to publish the best-selling novels in which he portrays, in slightly exaggerated form, the madnesses endemic to the region. Hiaasen's novels focus on some of the major events and pastimes of the region: the Orange Parade, bass fishing, evangelism, retirement living, Disney-like resorts, hurricanes, sugar growing, corrupt politics, ecological degradation. The last is perhaps the most persistent theme: Hiaasen seems to care greatly about the rape of the environment. One of his recurring characters is Skink, a former governor of the state who, shocked by the deviousness of developers and politicians who profit from unregulated development, abdicates his office and becomes a feral loner who obtains his protein from roadkill and who, with considerable violence, avenges himself on those depredators whom he can lay hands on.

Though Hiaasen's first three novels actually feature detectives, none of them are detective stories in the traditional sense. The novels are burlesque satires of the craziness that passes for normal in south Florida. There is no coherent progress from problem to solution, and no stable intelligence to provide a reliable moral perspective on the action. Instead, the events always spin out of the control of the good guys, the bad guys, and even the bystanders. In the end, a rough justice is achieved, but while the extremely venal madmen who pose the immediate threat to the world of south Florida are eliminated, the venality and madness remain.

Though a nonnative who moved to Miami in 1961, Edna Buchanan (b. 1939) is, like Hiaasen, a longtime journalist—a prize-winning crime reporter who turned to fiction to evoke the world she had come to know. Her first crime novel, *Nobody Lives Forever* (1990), was a well-plotted thriller with a psychopathic killer, but in 1992 she began the Britt Montero series of detective stories with *Contents Under Pressure*. Her novels are not as thickly populated with lunatics as those of Willeford and Hiaasen, but her Miami also tends to recalibrate one's view of insanity. Buchanan's novels follow a more traditional mystery form, with a definite villain and a definite progress toward the villain's identification and elimination; and in Britt Montero, she introduces a detective who does provide an ethical perspective on the action. Britt Montero is, like her author, a crime reporter; she has roots in both the Anglo community and the Cuban community; and like Julie Smith's Skip Langdon, Britt Montero maintains an ambivalent relationship to both of her worlds. She too manages to connect herself to a network of supportive friends. The most important is the news photographer, Lotte Dane. Montero's most dependable adversary is also a woman, however: the assistant city editor, Gretchen Platt. The novels have much to say about women's issues, and the journalistic realism that Buchanan brings to her series makes it especially interesting.

Southern Florida has attracted a large number of other crime writers who have found it a useful stage for detection. They have often chosen scenes at a distance from Miami. The Florida Keys appealed to James W. Hall, who has written popular series of Hemingway-esque novels about Thorn, "the Gandhi of Key Largo." In 1977 Ed McBain published *Goldilocks*, his first novel about the Calusa,

Florida, lawyer Matthew Hope. In 1986 John Lutz began a well-written series of novels about the central Florida (Del Moray) private investigator, Fred Carver. Mickey Friedman's novels set in the Florida panhandle offer portraits of life in backwater, un-deracinated Florida. Other Florida detective writers include Kevin Robinson, Janice Law, Randy Wayne White, and Barbara Parker.

The Rest of the South

Southern Louisiana and southern Florida may be densely populated with detectives, but crime seems to flourish elsewhere in the region as well. Virginia's chief medical examiner, Kay Scarpetta, is the protagonist of the well-written, best-selling series of novels by Patricia Cornwell (b. 1956). The emphasis in the series is upon Scarpetta's character and technical competence, and the primary scene is the morgue. But the morgue is in Richmond, Virginia, not New York, Chicago, or Los Angeles. Cornwell places her crimes in the carefully observed settings of Virginia and North Carolina. Two other popular series involving Southern women detectives have been developed by Sharyn McCrumb (Virginia and Tennessee) and Joan Hess (Arkansas). There was a strong line of comic writing in the earliest local-color writing (Augustus Baldwin Longstreet, Mark Twain, Bret Harte, Joel Chandler Harris, Charles W. Chestnutt); McCrumb and Hess carry on that tradition of regional literature in the mystery genre. Both also focus upon the experience of women, as detectives, but also as victims, suspects, and onlookers.

McCrumb's most popular detective is Elizabeth MacPherson, a student of forensic anthropology at a Virginia university. McCrumb (b. 1948) herself has roots in the Appalachian area of western Virginia and eastern Tennessee and has studied and taught at Virginia Tech in Blacksburg. Though she is sometimes transported beyond her region (as far away as Scotland), MacPherson finds her cases at home as well, and McCrumb, who identifies herself as "a regional scholar" (in the author's note to *Highland Laddy Gone*, 1986), says she takes care to get such elements as cultural patterns and dialect right. McCrumb plays the MacPherson mysteries with a light touch; there is a great deal of humorous banter to sugarcoat the investigation. Much of the interest inevitably lies in the entertaining character of Elizabeth MacPherson and the friends and adversaries with whom she exchanges witticisms. A second series of novels, with titles drawn from Appalachian ballads, takes a more serious approach to the crimes and to the Appalachian culture that spawns them. The "Ballad Books," which began with *If Ever I Return, Pretty Peggy-O* (1990), are set in fictional Wake County, Tennessee, near the North Carolina border. Sheriff Spencer Arrowood is the series protagonist, but the novels are more about the people and the isolated mountain environment they inhabit than about the investigator and his work. As a result, the Ballad Books offer a richer reward to readers interested in the scene of the crime.

Joan Hess (b. 1949) has developed two series set in Arkansas: the Claire Malloy series, set in Farberville, a version of Hess's hometown of Fayetteville, and the Arly Hanks series, set in small-town Maggody, population 755. The first series follows the conventional formula for cozy mysteries: Claire Malloy is a bookshop owner whose cleverness, sympathy, and persistence lead her into criminal matters and enable her to detect solutions. The Maggody novels are primarily comic in form; there is always a mystery to be solved, but Hess devotes most of each novel to the laughable schemes of Mayor Jim Bob Buchanon and others. Hess exploits the stereotypes of the small-minded, inbred, backwoods South. There are no Southern aristocrats in the Ozarks vicinity of Maggody, only the white trash Buchanons—and they are played entirely for fun. Sheriff Arly Hanks, who has been to New York City, is the voice of normalcy as well as of detective intelligence in the community. The women of Maggody, though often as caricatured as the men, do constitute a bedrock of common sense in the village.

Two other writers have established significant mystery series set in the South. Margaret Maron began her Deborah Knott novels with *Bootlegger's Daughter* (1992). Knott, like Maron, is a North Carolinian; she practices law in the fictional town of Dobbs. Though Maron sometimes plays for a light, comic touch, Deborah Knott, as a lawyer and as a judge, finds herself looking into serious crimes that give occasion for reflection on serious social issues such as child abuse or the changing status of women and homosexuals in the modern South.

Kathy Hogan Trocheck (b. 1954) places her detective, J. Callahan Garrity, in the capital of the new South, Atlanta. Like Deborah Knott, Callahan Garrity is a single woman, conscious of her ambivalent status in the evolving South. She leaves the Atlanta Police Department as a result of what she regards as discrimination, and she combines her career as a private investigator with management of her professional housecleaning service, House Mouse. Trocheck is uncommonly scrupulous in establishing Garrity as a businesswoman; Deborah Knott's law practice (and, for that matter, Dave Robicheaux's bait shop) are much less tangible. Trocheck is also conscientious in her presentation of the various milieus of Atlanta to which Garrity's cases take her.

At least one other Atlanta crime writer merits mention. Stuart Woods (b. 1938) enjoyed a great success with his ambitious novel *Chiefs* (1981), which chronicles three generations (1919–1963) of the small Georgia town of Delano. A single killer commits a series of murders; three different police chiefs representing three different Southern generations undertake the investigation of the homicides. Woods uses this situation to examine the evolution of the South in the twentieth century, especially with regard to matters of race. The success of *Chiefs* led Woods to follow it with other novels that do not make up a traditional series but that do employ some of the characters and the scenes featured in *Chiefs*.

New England

Though it once aspired to be *the* American metropolis, and there are probably still Bostonians who cannot imagine their town as a regional city, Boston is, at best, the center of New England. It certainly was never a central city in mystery fiction. George Harmon Coxe (1901–1984), a member of *Black Mask*'s strong second team, wrote a number of Boston mysteries featuring photographer Jack (Flash) Casey, private eye Jack Fenner, and others. And Phoebe Atwood Taylor (1909–1976) published twenty-five Asey Mayo novels between 1931 and 1951. These certainly qualify as local color; the scene is Cape Cod, and Asey is a quintessential Yankee; Taylor portrays Mayo's world with careful attention to the concrete details of everyday life. But it was not until the early 1970s that the Boston area entered the main arena of crime fiction. In 1972 George V. Higgins (b. 1939; see separate essay) published *The Friends of Eddie Coyle*, and in 1973 Robert B. Parker (b. 1932; see separate essay) published *The Godwulf Manuscript.*

Higgins may be the most important writer since Raymond Chandler to work in the genre of crime fiction, though, with some justice, he does not regard himself as defined by formulas. Only the series of novels featuring the lawyer Jerry Kennedy can really be classified as formula fiction, and even they are written a level above the usual lawyer novel. Like Chandler, Higgins grounds his novels in an intense awareness of the ways of his region. Higgins' first book, *The Friends of Eddie Coyle*, was something genuinely new: Higgins chose to tell about the life and death of a small-time crook in the spoken language of small-time crooks. There is very little descriptive prose in any of his novels; they are almost entirely narrated in conversations and monologues, as the reader overhears the characters talking to each other. They speak a convincing idiom that might be called New England Tough. The result is a brilliant authenticity in realizing the characters and their worlds. This stylistic innovation has been very influential, but Higgins is also important for the accuracy with which he depicts the petty lives of his petty criminals and for the seriousness of his themes, which center on the ways men (and sometimes women) acquire power (or what they take to be power). Higgins has been a journalist and a lawyer; he knows how things work in America generally and in Boston specifically: how guns are sold, or fires set, or influence peddled; and he knows how the men and women who do these things think and talk about what they do. In his later fiction, he has expanded his world to include politicians and lawyers as types of men engaged in complex struggles to exercise or add to their power.

Higgins' novels have been popular, but Robert B. Parker's Spenser novels have been even more popular. Spenser has been, since 1973, the preeminent Boston private eye. Like Higgins, Parker is a native of the region, and the early Spenser novels make a strong effort to apply the Chandlerian model of detective-observer to the Boston region. In the novels of the 1980s, Parker's focus was on his characters—Spenser, Susan, and Hawk—rather than on their city. But in the 1990s, Parker has returned almost programmatically to examining social environments in the Boston area: African American (*Double Deuce*, 1992), Chinese American (*Walking Shadow*, 1994), Hispanic American (*Thin Air*, 1995). So meticulous is Parker's setting that it in fact lent itself to the 1989 publication of a volume of photographs, a travel book entitled *Spenser's Boston*.

Boston's other private eye is John Francis Cuddy in the novels of Jeremiah Healy (b. 1948). Healy is not native to the region; he evidently converted to Bostonism as a result of his experience at Harvard Law School, where he earned his J.D. in 1973. In 1984 he decided that Spenser needed competition and launched his John Francis Cuddy series with *Blunt Darts*. Healy never challenges Parker's facility for snappy dialogue, but in other respects his novels are quite creditable examples of the regional private eye. Cuddy has been scarred by his experiences in Vietnam (like his author, he was an MP); he is altruistic in a Travis McGee way; he despises intolerance; his cases involve him in helping the helpless and confronting the callous or corrupt authorities who run the town/state/nation. The plots are sometimes improbably complicated and the solutions sometimes improbably neat, but never so improbable as to distract from the pleasure of a well-paced narrative. Healy began with the sentimental but effective device of having Cuddy regularly visit the grave of his young wife, Beth. He was unable to sustain the conceit over a long series, however, and Cuddy, like Spenser and like most detectives of the 1980s, enters into a steady emotional relationship with an independent professional woman, Assistant District Attorney Nancy Meagher. (With Beth's blessing, he commits to Nancy in *Swan Dive*, 1988.) Steady emotional relationships with independent professional women became a staple of the male private-eye novel series in the 1980s.

The year of Cuddy's first case also saw the debut of William G. Tapply's Boston lawyer-detective, Brady Coyne, in *Death at Charity's Point* (1984). Tapply (b. 1940) fashions smooth, well-paced cases for his hero. Coyne, like Spenser and Cuddy, is an attractive figure; as a lawyer to the rich, he tends to inhabit a somewhat more elevated social milieu. Tapply exploits his own interest in outdoor sports by making Coyne an avid fisherman.

Concord, Massachusetts, can claim two detectives, both amateurs. Jane Langton (b. 1922) published the first novel featuring the erudite Homer Kelly in 1964, but she did not begin to issue sequels until 1975. Langton's books are distinguished by the line drawings with which she illustrates their literate locales. Rick Boyer (b. 1943) makes his detective a prosperous oral surgeon, Dr. Charles Adams. Like Langton, Boyer sets his plots firmly in the terrain of eastern Massachusetts (including Cape Cod). Farther north, in Brattleboro, Vermont, Lieutenant Joe Gunther investigates crime in the series by Archer Mayor (b. 1950).

The Midwest

"The Midwest" is, of course, more a convenient rubric than a coherent region. It covers the rustbelt that extends west of the Appalachians to the Great Plains, and north of the Ohio River to Canada. Chicago is its metropolis, and until Michael Z. Lewin placed his detective in Indianapolis in 1971, Chicago was the principal scene of crime from Pittsburgh to Kansas City (or even from the Hudson to the Mojave). In the the years since, most cities of the region have found themselves investigated by at least one detective. The authors range from the prolific professional John Lutz, who assigned his steady private eye, Alo Nudger, to St. Louis, to the "One-Eyed Mack" series set in Oklahoma by television newsman Jim Lehrer. Indianapolis, "Rocksburg," Cincinnati, and Detroit have, however, been the primary scenes of regional midwestern crime.

Lewin (b. 1942) made a deliberate decision to place his detective, the small-time Albert R. Samson, in Indianapolis, not in New York, Chicago, or Los Angeles. Both the detective and his city are deliberately portrayed as pedestrian versions of Philip Marlowe and his Los Angeles. Samson has Marlowe's ethics but not his sophisticated sensibility; Indianapolis has the same upper-, middle-, and lower-class types as Los Angeles but none of the sexiness of Hollywood. Samson narrates his investigations, but without the elaborate pose and language employed by Marlowe. It would seem a formula for deliberately second-rate fiction; Lewin's success lies in his ability to make his undistinguished detective and his undistinguished city interesting. In part, this is due precisely to his premise: what happens when the mean streets down which a man must go are Ohio Street and Pennsylvania Avenue, not Hollywood and Vine? What happens when the man who is not himself mean nor tarnished nor afraid is a non-chess-playing joe who does not spout similes and whose mother runs a diner called Bud's Dugout? Lewin makes it work.

Though he began writing his novels after he had transplanted himself to England, Lewin was born and raised in Indianapolis. And Indianapolis, not Albert Samson, became the center of his fictional world. Although Samson appears in *Night Cover* (1976), the fourth Indianapolis novel, the narration shifts to third person and features Lieutenant Leroy Powder in a police procedural investigation. *Night Cover* also introduces social worker Adele Buffington, who, it turns out, is the anonymous "my woman" whom Samson has been courting. Lewin regards Samson, Powder, and Buffington as his "Indianapolis family." They provide three different perspectives on Lewin's city. All of the novels are carefully researched, and all are set precisely in the city's history. The first novel, *Ask the Right Question* (1971) opens precisely on 14 October 1970, and Lewin keeps track of the changing face of the city in the novels that follow.

There is no city called Rocksburg thirty miles from Pittsburgh in western Pennsylvania, and there is no person named K. C. Constantine, so it is difficult to classify Constantine's novels as authentically regional. (The pseudonymous author evidently admits to being born in 1934 near Pittsburgh.) Nonetheless, the books, which feature police chief Mario Balzic (who, in *Good Sons*, 1996, continues in an advisory role after being forced from office), constitute a very strong study of the ways people live and die in a small town with a decaying economy. Constantine, even more than the celebrated Elmore Leonard, is George V. Higgins' primary competition in the use of vivid speech as a device for advancing his narratives. Constantine began with *The Rocksburg Railroad Murders* in 1972 and, far from exhausting his vein, continues to write rich portraits of the people of Rocksburg.

Jonathan Valin (b. 1948), a native of Cincinnati, began writing his Harry Stoner novels in 1980, after several years of teaching college. Stoner, like Healy's John Cuddy, is a private eye clearly in the tradition of Travis McGee. He is cast in the knight-errant mold; he defies authorities who abuse their power; he com-

REGIONALIZATION OF THE MYSTERY AND CRIME NOVEL

mands a solid knowledge of the ways of his world; he consults experts when he lacks specific knowledge; he is tolerant (though in *Missing*, 1995, he admits to an initial uneasiness in dealing with homosexuals). Like Cuddy, he is a somewhat troubled Vietnam vet. In his predilection for good sex with a different girl in every novel, Stoner is more like McGee than Cuddy is. As in the McGee series, characters and situations in earlier novels echo in later ones. The names of several characters in the first novel in the series, *The Lime Pit* (1980), are explicit tributes to MacDonald (Preston LaForge) and to Chandler (Red Bannion, Bernie Olson).

Harry Stoner cannot be dismissed as a McGee sans houseboat. Valin's plots tend to be focused and well crafted; the prose is fluent, and the themes often develop serious moral issues. (In a novel such as *The Music Lovers*, 1993, Valin also shows a lighter tone). Stoner's character and narrative voice are attractive (the voice is often closer to Marlowe than McGee), and the plots he finds himself unraveling are sufficiently complicated to be interesting without being artificially byzantine. Cincinnati and its environs (including the Bay City–like suburb of Newport) seem to be accurately depicted in the course of the series.

Loren D. Estleman (b. 1952) began his Detroit series of Amos Walker novels with *Motor City Blue* in 1980, the same year that Harry Stoner began detecting in Cincinnati. Estleman is a Michigan native (Ann Arbor) who began working as a journalist in the region in 1973, and his knowledge of Detroit and its environs is evident in every novel. He has called Detroit the "co-star" of the Walker series, and more than any of the other midwestern crime novelists, Estleman devotes as much art to depicting his city in his time as to the character and the morality of his detective and his clients. In this regard, Estleman is perhaps the most direct heir of Raymond Chandler. Amos Walker is not quite the sophisticated filter of experience that Philip Marlowe is, but he is cast in Marlowe's tough, wisecracking mode, and he investigates the

Detroit of the 1980s and 1990s with the same thoroughness and responsiveness that Marlowe applied to the Los Angeles of the 1940s and 1950s.

Walker is another Vietnam vet, though unlike Dave Robicheaux, John Francis Cuddy, and Harry Stoner, Walker has not been scarred by the experience. Or rather, like Philip Marlowe, he has been so scarred by his encounters with the injustices of his region that his war wounds are relatively unimportant. Like Marlowe, Walker prides himself on his integrity. He is a knowing observer of the degeneration of his city, but he is not afflicted with Marlowe's world-weariness. He launches himself from the same sort of unadorned private eye's office, but he goes with a resilient energy.

The centrality of Detroit in Estleman's imagination is indicated in his two other crime-novel series. The first features Peter Macklin, a Detroit mob enforcer. The second is the ambitious "Detroit series," which has consumed most of Estleman's energy in the 1990s. Walker's moral intelligence is missing in both series, but the Detroit series emphasizes Estleman's seriousness as a regional writer. Each novel is set in an important decade in Detroit history: the 1920s in *Whiskey River* (1990), the 1950s in *Edsel* (1995), the 1960s in *Motown* (1991), the 1970s in *Stress* (1996), and the 1990s in *King of the Corner* (1992). Each uses a crime plot to reflect the character of Detroit life in that era. Detroit's declining industrial infrastructure and racial and ethnic conflicts may stand for the broader reality of late-twentieth-century America, but Estleman, like Chandler, roots his fiction in the concrete realities of his region.

The West

The American West is more naturally associated with the Western than the mystery novel. Aside from the Continental Op's excursion to Personville in Hammett's *Red Harvest* (1929), the mountain states seem to have required few criminal investigators. Beginning in the 1980s, however, the West from Santa Fe to Montana began to see local crime detected by local detectives. They constitute a very diverse lot. The most prominent have been Tony Hillerman's Navajo policemen, Joe Leaphorn and Jim Chee, who operate in the Four Corners region of the Southwest (see "The Ethnic Detective"). Hillerman has been acclaimed for the authenticity of his descriptions of the Navaho way of life and of the harsh terrain in which that way evolved. Other fine writers have also been attracted to the desert Southwest. Martin Cruz Smith (b. 1942) set two important novels in the region: *Nightwing* (1977), which features a Hopi detective, and *Stallion Gate* (1986), which contrasts the atomic project at Los Alamos with Native American culture. Jake Page (b. 1936) has written extensively about the peoples (especially the Hopi) and the environments of the Southwest. With *Knotted Strings* (1995), he began a series of detective novels featuring the blind Santa Fe sculptor Mo Bowdre. Walter Satterthwait's Santa Fe detectives, Joshua Croft and Rita Mondragon, are somewhat less focused on the Native American world of the Four Corners, but in a novel such as *At Ease with the Death* (1990), Croft finds the mysterious Navaho figure, Daniel Begay, playing a central role. Croft is a private eye with a narrative voice that owes something to Travis McGee, but Satterthwait (b. 1946) presents him as a distinctive hero in a well-paced series.

Rex Burns (Raoul Stephen Sehler, b. 1935) has produced the most substantial series featuring a Denver detective. Burns is a college professor who came to Denver in 1975 and in the same year began his Denver police-procedural series featuring the half-Hispanic homicide detective Sergeant Gabriel Wager. The novels concentrate Wager's investigations. As in most procedurals, Wager pursues several cases simultaneously; the main plot is sometimes quite melodramatic: in *Endangered Species* (1993), a militant environmentalist plans a suicide mission to blow up the Rocky Flats atomic weapons plant. As the series progresses, Wager, like so many 1980s

detectives, develops a steady relationship with a professional woman, in his case, city councilwoman Elizabeth Voss. Another Denver Hispanic detective—Hispanic on both sides—is the lawyer Luis Montez in the series of novels begun by Manuel Ramos in 1993 with *The Ballad of Rocky Ruiz*. With *Death on the Rocks* (1987), Michael Allegretto (b. 1944) began a series of novels featuring the Chandlerian detective Jacob Lomax. Allegretto's own father was a detective on the Denver police force, and the series reflects the author's intimate knowledge of Denver and its environs.

Farther north, western writers have begun to exploit the terrain of Montana as the scene of crime. Most of James Lee Burke's *Black Cherry Blues* (1989) finds Dave Robicheaux driving the rugged roads of Montana. A. B. Guthrie, famous for his panoramic novels of the settlement of the West (*The Big Sky*, 1947; *The Way West*, 1949; *These Thousand Hills*, 1956), adopted the detective format for a series of novels featuring Sheriff Chick Charleston and his assistant, Jason Beard. The first Chick Charleston novel, *Wild Pitch*, appeared in 1973.

The detectives featured in the crime fiction of James Crumley (b. 1939) are neither ethnic nor policemen; they are disaffected sons of the 1960s. In 1966 Crumley moved to Missoula, Montana, to teach at the university; his crime novels are set in the wilderness of western Montana. Both of Crumley's investigators, Milton Chester Milodragovitch and Chauncy Wayne Shugrue, are natives of the small town of Meriwether, Montana. Milo is an alienated heir who works as a detective in the agency of the improbably tolerant Colonel Haliburton; Shugrue is a Chandleresque private eye. Both men are products of the 1960s: antiestablishment Vietnam vets, they are the gonzo sons of Jack Kerouac, infatuated with speed, landscapes, and highly charged experiences. Both indulge in drugs and violence, and both find themselves involved in long, highly complicated plots that take them on the road throughout the West, from Montana, south to Texas, and west to California.

Crumley has described Milo as "the nicer guy" of the two; indeed, he is, at times, improbably nice. Milo's adventures tend to move in surprising, seemingly random directions. Shugrue's too is a wild spirit, but in his debut novel, *The Last Good Kiss* (1978), Crumley set him in a brilliant variation on Chandler's *The Long Good-bye* (1953). Crumley's version of Chandler's self-destructive novelist, Roger Wade, is Abraham Trahearne; like Marlowe, Shugrue is hired to bring the errant writer home but finds himself drawn into a strange and volatile set of relationships with Trahearne, Trahearne's mother, and Trahearne's wives. The assignment involves Shugrue in a long odyssey that takes him to the Sonoma Valley, San Francisco, and Bakersfield in California; Denver and Fort Collins in Colorado; a commune in Oregon; and several small towns in Montana, but the novel achieves a sort of thematic coherence and culminates in some genuine and effective surprises.

With *The Edge of the Crazies* (1995), Jamie Harrison brings the crime novel to the plains of eastern Montana. The scene is Blue Deer, population 3,872, elevation 4,500 feet. Her detective is Jules Clement, who spent his first seventeen years in Blue Deer, then traveled through Europe as an archaeologist before finally returning to run for the sheriff's office once held by his father. Clement's biography suggests a certain strain toward originality; by the 1990s, merely exploring a new region seems an insufficient draw. The plot of the novel is also highly complicated, with a large cast of characters, but there is a strong effort to realize the distinctive environment in which Harrison sets her mysteries.

The Northwest

California continues to spawn detectives of all persuasions, but although California can be classified as a region (or two) unto itself, its popularity renders it untreatable here. The Northwest, especially the trendy Boeing-Microsoft-Starbucks world of Seattle, however, is emerging as a distinctive region.

Earl W. Emerson (b. 1948), a native of Tacoma, has produced two significant series set in the Seattle region. The Thomas Black novels, which began with *The Rainy City* in 1985, are straightforward private-eye novels. Black is a decent man, averse to violence. He is something of a northwestern Spenser: he too engages in a multinovel evolving relationship with a professional woman, lawyer Kathy Birchfield, which occupies much of his attention. The banter between the two is perhaps less snappy than that between Spenser and Susan, and perhaps less fulsome as well. Emerson tends to devote more care to his plots; they are generally elaborate but coherent. *The Million Dollar Tattoo* (1996) develops some genuine surprises, but it also involves an improbably indirect billionaire and an improbably sleazy private eye. Emerson is a lieutenant in the Seattle Fire Department; his second series features Mac Fontana, fire chief of Staircase, a small town in the foothills of the Cascade Mountains, an hour east of Seattle. Fontana's cases are less compact, less focused than Black's, but they are full of inside know-how about professional firefighting.

Judith A. Jance (b. 1944) has established a popular series of novels about the Seattle police detective J. P. Beaumont. His cases tend to be well plotted; Jance emphasizes Beaumont's personal relationships with his ex-wives, his ex-partner, and others. Richard Hoyt (b. 1941), a native Oregonian, has also developed a detective series praised for its cleverness and its evocation of the landscapes of the Pacific Northwest. The series debuted with *Decoys* (1980) and features private eye John Denson, who, with his shaman ally, Willie Prettybird, covers a wide range of the region.

Canada

Canada is, of course, regions, not a region. Toronto may qualify as a nonregional metropolis, which would eliminate private eyes such as Howard Engel's (b. 1931) venerable protagonist Benny Cooperman (actually based in "Grantham") or police detectives such as Margaret Millar's (b. 1915) Inspector Sands, Eric Wright's (b. 1929) Inspector Charlie Salter, and Medora Sale's Inspector John Sanders. It might even exclude Ted Wood's (b. 1931) Reid Bennett novels, set in "Murphy's Harbor" north of Toronto. Wood seems to have consciously conceived of Bennett as typically Canadian, not typically Murphy's Harborian or Ontarian. He even gives him a French-Canadian mother to nationalize his character.

At least one specific region of Canada has nonetheless found a most articulate investigator: Karl Alberg of the Royal Canadian Mounted Police patrols the Sunshine Coast of British Columbia north of Vancouver from the small town of Sechelt. Laurali R. Wright was born in British Columbia and worked as a reporter and columnist in Calgary for a decade before turning to fiction at the end of the 1970s. In 1985 she introduced her middle-aged, divorced Staff Sergeant Alberg in *The Suspect.* As the series develops, Alberg's cases grow more psychologically complex. Alberg is always the central investigator, and his reactions to events are important, but he is not a controlling intelligence in the manner of most fictional detectives. His point of view rarely commands more than half of the narrative. Wright narrates from a variety—sometimes a bewildering variety—of perspectives. The actual criminal is often not the only disturbed mind reacting to the violent events. The narrative may slip from present to past and from place to place as the pieces of the puzzle are fitted together. The crucial relationships are often familial, involving parents, siblings, and surrogates. They are often generational, between a mother and daughter. The final resolution is often ambivalent; the violent crime in *Strangers Among Us* (1996) is committed and the criminal apprehended at the beginning of the book; most of the narrative concerns the noncriminal activities of people disturbed by the crime, and at the end nothing seems to have been resolved.

If he does not command the order of the plot, Alberg is nonetheless a center of attention. His relationships often echo the stresses that underlie his cases. Like so many detectives who debuted in the 1980s, he too is in an evolving relationship with a professional woman, but it is not a matter of good sex and snappy lines. Alberg and the librarian Cassandra Mitchell are adults in their forties, and they slowly work out the terms of their emotional engagement, which began with his response to an advertisement (Alberg proposes marriage in *Prized Possessions*, 1993; Mitchell proposes in *Mother Love*, 1995). Alberg also has to deal with his ex-wife and daughters in Calgary and with his parents in Ontario (his father dies in *Prized Possessions*). The precision with which Wright depicts Alberg's not always competent dealings with all of these complicated relationships typifies her approach to all her characters, who find themselves in webs of difficult and sometimes intolerable connections. Alberg is a hero less because of his detective genius than because of his ability to maintain his integrity and his decency, while the criminals are driven to destroy themselves and others. Wright's novels present complex portraits of the lives people live in the small towns set in the beautiful land and seascapes of the Sunshine Coast.

The Rest of the World

Although writers from Gaboriau to Simenon insisted the detective could speak French, in fact he mostly spoke English until, in the wake of Hammett and Chandler, writers around the world discovered that he could be an inherently popular vehicle for serious social criticism, and the detective began to flourish everywhere. In *Crimes of the Scene* (1997), Nina King and Robin Winks catalog dozens of prominent detectives of Europe, from Spain to Scandinavia to Russia, and throughout the third world: Africa, South and

East Asia, Latin America. The writers are sometimes Anglo-American tourists, such as James Melville (b. 1931) in Japan or H. R. F. Keating (b. 1926) in India, but they are more and more often native writers, such as Shizuko Natsuki (b. 1938), the "Agatha Christie of Japan," or Satyajat Ray (b. 1921), with his novellas about the Bengali detective Feluda.

James McClure (b. 1939, see "The Ethnic Detective"), for example, is a South African whose series of novels featuring the white Lieutenant Kramer and the Zulu Sergeant Zondi represents an accurate depiction and a strong indictment of life under apartheid. Maj Sjöwall (b. 1935) and Per Wahlöö (1926–1975) planned the ten-volume Martin Beck novels as a programmatic analysis of the ways Swedes lived their lives under what the authors regarded as the insufficient experiment of Swedish socialism in the period 1965–1975. The series is a remarkable achievement, but its matter is more national than regional. Less overtly ideological but similarly national are the Van der Valk novels of Nicholas Freeling (b. 1927) that portray the ways the Dutch live their lives. Or, for a Zen perspective on the same Dutch ways, one might look at the early Amsterdam novels of Janwillem van de Wetering (b. 1931). Poul Ørum (b. 1919) has published Danish mysteries that have been translated into English, but the Greenland scenes of Peter Høeg's (b. 1957) *Smilla's Sense of Snow* (English translation, 1993) make it a genuinely regional novel.

Georges Simenon (b. 1903) is now widely regarded as a major writer; his Maigret novels constitute a definitive portrait of Simenon's Paris. If Paris is far from a regional scene, there are still the half dozen Maigret novels set in Brittany or the seven set in Provence to qualify Simenon as a regionalist. William McIlvanney (b. 1936, see "The Police Procedural") had established a reputation as a novelist and poet when he began his probing series of novels about Glasgow detective inspector Jack Laidlaw. Manuel Vásquez Montalbán (b. 1939) is another serious writer who has used the hard-boiled detective formula to convey his social criticism. The first

novel in his series, written in 1977 and translated in 1990 as *The Angst-Ridden Executive*, has Barcelona private eye José (Pepe) Carvalho Larios investigate how a small group of idealistic anti-Franco leftists grew in different directions over the following decades. With *Study in Lilac* (1985), Maria-Antonia Oliver (b. 1946) has more recently set another politically conscious detective series in Barcelona; originally composed in Catalan, it features the Mallorcan feminist private eye Appolònia Lònià Guiu.

Several important Latin American detectives appear in the fiction of major Latin American writers, but although the influence of Chandler has been great, the metafictional example of Jorge Luis Borges has also been great, and in the detective novels of the Uruguayan Hiber Conteris (b. 1933) or the Peruvian Mario Vargas Llosa (b. 1936) or the Mexican Paco Ignacio Taibo II (b. 1949) there are as often as much philosophy and literary pyrotechnics as there is realistic portrayal of local scenes. The quality of these Latin American novels is a reminder of how the crime novel can be used as a vehicle for high literary achievement.

Selected Bibliography

THE AMERICAN SOUTH: NEW ORLEANS AND MIAMI

For John D. MacDonald and Elmore Leonard, see separate entries.

JAMES LEE BURKE'S DAVE ROBICHEAUX NOVELS

The Neon Rain. New York: Holt, 1987.
Heaven's Prisoners. New York: Holt, 1988.
Black Cherry Blues. Boston: Little, Brown, 1989.
A Morning for Flamingoes. Boston: Little, Brown, 1990.
A Stained White Radiance. New York: Hyperion, 1992.
In the Electric Mist with the Confederate Dead. New York: Hyperion, 1993.
Dixie City Iam. New York: Hyperion, 1994.
Burning Angel. New York: Hyperion, 1995.
Cadillac Jukebox. New York: Hyperion, 1996.

JULIE SMITH'S SKIP LANGDON NOVELS

New Orleans Mourning. New York: St. Martin's Press, 1990.

The Axeman's Jazz. New York: St. Martin's Press, 1991.
Jazz Funeral. New York: Fawcett, 1993.
New Orleans Beat. New York: Fawcett, 1994.
The House of Blues. New York: Fawcett, 1995.
The Kindness of Strangers. New York: Fawcett, 1996.

JOHN WILLIAM CORRINGTON AND
JOYCE CORRINGTON

So Small a Carnival. New York: Viking, 1986.
A Project Named Desire. New York: Viking, 1987.
A Civil Death. New York: Viking, 1987.
The White Zone. New York: Viking, 1990.

JAMES SALLIS' LEW GRIFFIN NOVELS

The Long-Legged Fly. New York: Carroll & Graf, 1992.
Moth. New York: Carroll & Graf, 1993.
The Black Hornet. New York: Carroll & Graf, 1994.
Eye of the Cricket. New York: Walker, 1997.

TONY FENNELLY'S MATT SINCLAIR AND
MARGO FORTIER NOVELS

The Glory Hole. New York: Carroll & Graf, 1986.
The Closet Hanging. New York: Carroll & Graf, 1987.
Kiss Yourself Goodbye. London: Arlington, 1989.
The Hippie in the Wall. New York: St. Martin's Press, 1994.
1 (900) D-E-A-D. New York: St. Martin's Press, 1997.

BRETT HALLIDAY'S MICHAEL SHAYNE NOVELS

Dividend on Death. New York: Holt, 1939.
The Private Practice of Michael Shayne. New York: Holt, 1940.
The Uncomplaining Corpses. New York: Holt, 1940.
Tickets for Death. New York: Holt, 1941.
Bodies Are Where You Find Them. New York: Holt, 1941.
The Corpse Came Calling. New York: Dodd Mead, 1942.
Murder Wears a Mummer's Mask. New York: Dodd Mead, 1943.
Blood on the Black Marker. New York: Dodd Mead, 1943. Revised as *Heads You Lose.* New York: Dell, 1958.
Michael Shayne's Long Chance. New York: Dodd Mead, 1944.
Murder and the Married Virgin. New York: Dodd Mead, 1944.
Murder Is My Business. New York: Dodd Mead, 1945.
Marked for Murder. New York: Dodd Mead, 1945.
Dead Man's Diary and Dinner at Dupre's. New York: Dodd Mead, 1945.
Blood on Biscayne Bay. Chicago: Ziff Davis, 1946.
Counterfeit Wife. Chicago: Ziff Davis, 1947.
Blood on the Stars. New York: Dodd Mead, 1948.
Michael Shayne's Triple Mystery. New York: Ziff Davis, 1948. Includes *A Taste for Cognac.*
A Taste for Violence. New York: Dodd Mead, 1949.
Call for Michael Shayne. New York: Dodd Mead, 1949.

This Is It, Michael Shayne. New York: Dodd Mead, 1950.
Framed in Blood. New York: Dodd Mead, 1951.
When Dorinda Dances. New York: Dodd Mead, 1951.
What Really Happened. New York: Dodd Mead, 1952.
One Night with Nora. New York: Torquil, 1953.
She Woke to Darkness. New York: Torquil, 1954.
Death Has Three Lives. New York: Torquil, 1955.
Stranger in Town. New York: Torquil, 1955.
The Blonde Cried Murder. New York: Torquil, 1956.
Weep for a Blonde. New York: Torquil, 1957.
Shoot the Works. New York: Torquil, 1957.
Murder and the Wanton Bride. New York: Torquil, 1958.

CHARLES WILLEFORD

The Burnt Orange Heresy. Berkeley, Calif.: Black Lizard, 1971.
Miami Blues. New York: St. Martin's Press, 1984.
New Hope for the Dead. New York: St. Martin's Press, 1985.
Sideswipe. New York: St. Martin's Press, 1987.
The Way We Die Now. New York: Random House, 1988.

CARL HIAASEN

Tourist Season. New York: Putnam, 1986.
Double Whammy. New York: Putnam, 1987. New York: Warner Books, 1989.
Skin Tight. New York: Putnam, 1989.
Native Tongue. New York: Knopf, 1991.
Strip Tease. New York: Knopf, 1993.
Stormy Weather. New York: Knopf, 1995.
Lucky You. New York: Knopf, 1997.

EDNA BUCHANAN

Nobody Lives Forever. New York: Random House, 1990.
Contents Under Pressure. New York: Hyperion, 1992.
Miami, It's Murder. New York: Hyperion, 1994.
Suitable for Framing. New York: Hyperion, 1995.
Act of Betrayal. New York: Hyperion, 1996.
Margin of Error. New York: Hyperion, 1997.

THE REST OF THE SOUTH

For Patricia Cornwell, see entry.

SHARYN MCCRUMB'S ELIZABETH MACPHERSON
NOVELS AND THE "BALLAD BOOKS"

Sick of Shadows. New York: Avon, 1984.
Lovely in Her Bones. New York: Avon, 1985.
Highland Laddie Gone. New York: Avon, 1986.
Paying the Piper. New York: Ballantine, 1988.
If Ever I Return, Pretty Peggy-O. New York: Scribners, 1990.
The Windsor Knot. New York: Ballantine, 1990.
Missing Susan. New York: Ballantine, 1991.
The Hangman's Beautiful Daughter. New York: Scribners, 1992.
MacPherson's Lament. New York: Ballantine, 1992.

She Walks These Hills. New York: Scribners, 1994.

If I'd Killed Him When I Met Him. New York: Ballantine, 1995.

The Rosewood Casket. New York: Dutton, 1996.

JOAN HESS'S CLAIRE MALLOY AND ARLY HANKS NOVELS

Strangled Prose. New York: St. Martin's Press, 1986.

Murder at the Murder at the Mimosa Inn. New York: St. Martin's Press, 1986.

Dear Miss Demeanor. New York: St. Martin's Press, 1987.

Malice in Maggody. New York: St. Martin's Press, 1987.

Mischief in Maggody. New York: St. Martin's Press, 1988.

A Really Cute Corpse. New York: St. Martin's Press, 1988.

A Diet to Die For. New York: St. Martin's Press, 1989.

Much Ado in Maggody. New York: St. Martin's Press, 1989.

Madness in Maggody. New York: St. Martin's Press, 1991.

Mortal Remains in Maggody. New York: St. Martin's Press, 1991.

Roll Over and Play Dead. New York: St. Martin's Press, 1991.

Death by the Light of the Moon. New York: St. Martin's Press, 1992.

Maggody in Manhattan. New York: Dutton, 1992.

O Little Town of Maggody. New York: Dutton, 1993.

Poisoned Pins. New York: Dutton, 1993.

Martians in Maggody. New York: Dutton, 1994.

Tickled to Death. New York: Dutton, 1994.

Busy Bodies. New York: Dutton, 1995.

Miracles in Maggody. New York: Dutton, 1995.

Closely Akin to Murder. New York: Dutton, 1996.

The Maggody Militia. New York: Dutton, 1997.

MARGARET MARON'S DEBORAH KNOTT NOVELS

Bootlegger's Daughter. New York: Mysterious Press, 1992.

Southern Discomfort. New York: Mysterious Press, 1993.

Shooting at Loons. New York: Mysterious Press, 1994.

Up Jumps the Devil. New York: Mysterious Press, 1996.

Killer Market. New York: Mysterious Press, 1997.

KATHY HOGAN TROCHECK'S CALLAHAN GARRITY NOVELS

Every Crooked Nanny. New York: HarperCollins, 1992.

To Live and Die in Dixie. New York: HarperCollins, 1993.

Homemade Sin. New York: HarperCollins, 1994.

Happy Never After. New York: HarperCollins, 1995.

Heart Trouble. New York: HarperCollins, 1996.

Strange Brew. New York: HarperCollins, 1997.

STUART WOODS

Chiefs. New York: Norton, 1981.

NEW ENGLAND

GEORGE V. HIGGINS

The Friends of Eddie Coyle. New York: Knopf, 1972.

The Digger's Game. New York: Knopf, 1973.

Cogan's Trade. New York: Knopf, 1974.

A City on a Hill. New York: Knopf, 1975.

The Judgment of Deke Hunter. Boston: Little, Brown, 1976.

Dreamland. Boston: Little, Brown, 1977.

A Year or So with Edgar. New York: Harper, 1979.

Kennedy for the Defense. New York: Knopf, 1980.

The Rat on Fire. New York: Knopf, 1981.

The Patriot Game. New York: Knopf, 1982.

A Choice of Enemies. New York: Knopf, 1984.

Penance for Jerry Kennedy. New York: Holt, 1985.

Imposters. New York: Holt, 1986.

Outlaws. New York: Holt, 1987.

The Sins of Their Father. London: Deutsch, 1988. New York: Holt, 1988.

Wonderful Years, Wonderful Years. New York: Holt, 1988.

Trust. New York: Holt, 1989.

Victories. New York: Holt, 1990.

The Mandeville Talent. New York: Holt, 1991.

Defending Billy Ryan. New York: Holt, 1992.

Bomber's Law. New York: Holt, 1993.

Swan Boats at Four. New York: Holt, 1995.

ROBERT B. PARKER

For additional works, see entry.

The Godwulf Manuscript. New York: Dell, 1973.

Double Deuce. New York: Putnam, 1992.

Walking Shadow. New York: Putnam, 1994.

Thin Air. New York: Putnam, 1995.

JEREMIAH HEALY'S JOHN FRANCIS CUDDY NOVELS

Blunt Darts. New York: Walker, 1984.

The Staked Goat. New York: Harper, 1986.

So Like Sleep. New York: Harper, 1987.

Swan Dive. New York: Harper, 1988.

Yesterday's News. New York: Harper, 1989.

Right to Die. New York: Pocket Books, 1991.

Shallow Graves. New York: Pocket Books, 1992.

Foursome. New York: Pocket Books, 1993.

Act of God. New York: Pocket Books, 1994.

Rescue. New York: Pocket Books, 1995.

Invasion of Privacy. New York: Pocket Books, 1996.

MIDWEST

MICHAEL Z. LEWIN'S SAMSON/POWDER NOVELS

Ask the Right Question. New York: Putnam, 1971.

The Way We Die Now. New York: Putnam, 1973.

The Enemies Within. New York: Knopf, 1974.
Night Cover. New York: Knopf, 1976.
The Silent Salesman. New York: Knopf, 1978.
Missing Woman. New York: Knopf, 1981.
Hard Line. New York: Morrow, 1982.
Out of Season. New York: Morrow, 1984.
Late Payments. New York: Morrow, 1986.
Called by a Panther. New York: Mysterious Press, 1991.

K. C. CONSTANTINE

For additional works, see entry.

The Rocksburg Railroad Murders. New York: Saturday Review Press, 1972.
Good Sons. New York: Mysterious Press, 1996.

JONATHAN VALIN'S HARRY STONER NOVELS

The Lime Pit. New York: Dodd Mead, 1980.
Final Notice. New York: Dodd Mead, 1980.
Dead Letter. New York: Dodd Mead, 1981.
Day of Wrath. New York: Congdon and Lattès, 1982.
Natural Causes. New York: Congdon and Weed, 1983.
Life's Work. New York: Delacorte, 1986.
Fire Lake. New York: Delacorte, 1987.
Extenuating Circumstances. New York: Delacorte, 1989.
Second Chance. New York: Delacorte, 1991.
The Music Lovers. New York: Delacorte, 1993.
Missing. New York: Delacorte, 1995.

LOREN ESTLEMAN'S AMOS WALKER AND DETROIT NOVELS

Motor City Blue. Boston: Houghton Mifflin, 1980.
Angel Eyes. Boston: Houghton Mifflin, 1981.
The Midnight Man. Boston: Houghton Mifflin, 1982.
The Glass Highway. Boston: Houghton Mifflin, 1983.
Sugartown. Boston: Houghton Mifflin, 1984.
Every Brilliant Eye. Boston: Houghton Mifflin, 1986.
Lady Yesterday. Boston: Houghton Mifflin, 1987.
Downriver. Boston: Houghton Mifflin, 1988.
General Murders: Ten Amos Walker Mysteries. Boston: Houghton Mifflin, 1988.
Silent Thunder. Boston: Houghton Mifflin, 1989.
Sweet Women Lie. Boston: Houghton Mifflin, 1990.
Whiskey River. New York: Bantam, 1990.
Motown. New York: Bantam, 1991.
King of the Corner. New York: Bantam, 1992.
Edsel. New York: Mysterious Press, 1995.
Stress. New York: Bantam, 1996.
Never Street. New York: Mysterious Press, 1997.

THE WEST

For Tony Hillerman, see essay on "The Ethnic Detective."

REX BURNS'S GABRIEL WAGER NOVELS

The Alverez Journal. New York: Harper, 1975.
The Farnsworth Score. New York: Harper, 1977.

Speak for the Dead. New York: Harper, 1978.
Angle of Attack. New York: Harper, 1979.
The Avenging Angel. New York: Viking, 1983.
Ground Money. New York: Viking, 1986.
Suicide Season. New York: Viking, 1987.
The Killing Zone. New York: Viking, 1988.
Endangered Species. New York: Viking, 1993.
Bloodline. New York: Walker, 1995.
The Leaning Land. New York: Walker, 1997.

MANUEL RAMOS

The Ballad of Rocky Ruiz. New York: St. Martin's Press, 1993.
The Ballad of Gato Guerrero. New York: St. Martin's Press, 1994.
The Last Client of Luis Montez. New York: St. Martin's Press, 1996.

JAMES CRUMLEY'S MILODRAGOVITCH AND SHUGRUE NOVELS

The Wrong Case. New York: Random House, 1975.
The Last Good Kiss. New York: Random House, 1978.
Dancing Bear. New York: Random House, 1983.
The Mexican Tree Duck. New York: Mysterious Press, 1993.

JAMIE HARRISON

The Edge of the Crazies. New York: Hyperion, 1995.
Going Local. New York: Hyperion, 1996.

THE NORTHWEST

EARL W. EMERSON'S THOMAS BLACK AND MAC FONTANA NOVELS

The Rainy City. New York: Avon, 1985.
Poverty Bay. New York: Avon, 1985.
Nervous Laughter. New York: Avon, 1986.
Fat Tuesday. New York: Morrow, 1987.
Black Hearts and Slow Dancing. New York: Morrow, 1988.
Deviant Behavior. New York: Morrow, 1988.
Help Wanted: Orphans Preferred. New York: Morrow, 1990.
Yellow Dog Party. New York: Morrow, 1991.
Morons and Madmen. New York: Morrow, 1993.
The Portland Laugher. New York: Ballantine, 1994.
The Vanishing Smile. New York: Ballantine, 1995.
The Million Dollar Tattoo. New York: Ballantine, 1996.
The Dead Horse Paint Company. New York: Morrow, 1997.

CANADA

LAURALI R. WRIGHT'S ALBERG/MITCHELL NOVELS

The Suspect. New York: Viking, 1985.
Sleep While I Sing. New York: Viking, 1986.

Love in the Temperate Zone. New York: Viking, 1988.
A Chill Rain in January. New York: Viking, 1990.
Fall from Grace. New York: Viking, 1991.
Prized Possessions. New York: Viking, 1993.
A Touch of Panic. New York: Scribners, 1994.
Mother Love. New York: Scribners, 1995.
Strangers Among Us. New York: Scribners, 1996.

EUROPE, ASIA, AND ELSEWHERE

For Georges Simenon, see separate entry; for H. R. F. Keating and James McClure, see "The Ethnic Detective"; for William McIlvanney, see "The Police Procedural."

Høeg, Peter, *Smilla's Sense of Snow.* Translated by Tiina Nunnally. New York: Farrar, Straus & Giroux, 1993.
Montalbán, Manuel Vásquez. *The Angst-Ridden Executive.* Translated by Ed Emery. London: Serpent's Tail, 1990.
Oliver, Maria-Antonia. *Study in Lilac.* Translated by Kathleen McNerney. Seattle: Seal, 1987.

CRITICAL STUDIES

Glassman, Steve, and Maurice O'Sullivan, eds. *Crime Fiction in the Sunshine State: Florida Noir.* Bowling Green, Ohio: Bowling Green State University Popular Press, 1987.
Jameson, Frederic. "On Raymond Chandler." *Southern Review* 6, no. 3: 624–650 (1970).
King, Nina, Robin Winks, et al. *Crimes of the Scene.* New York: St. Martin's Press, 1997.
Van Dover, J. K., and John F. Jebb. *Isn't Justice Always Unfair? The Detective in Southern Literature.* Bowling Green, Ohio: Bowling Green University Popular Press, 1996.
Willett, Ralph. *The Naked City: Urban Crime Fiction in the USA.* Manchester: Manchester Univ. Press, 1996.
Williams, John. *Into the Badlands.* London: Paladin Grafton, 1991.

RELIGIOUS MYSTERIES

WILLIAM DAVID SPENCER

IN HER WELL-KNOWN introduction to *The Omnibus of Crime*, Dorothy L. Sayers traces the roots of mystery literature to a variety of ancient sources, including Greek, Roman, Indian, and German folktales. Chief among these sources she highlights two books in the Apocrypha, "Bel and the Dragon," and "Susanna." These short thrillers are embellishments on the canonical story of Daniel in the Hebrew Bible. In the first, the earlier tale, young Daniel pits his wisdom against priests of Baal (Bel) who claim their idol becomes animate each night and consumes a sizable ration of food left before it. Through dusting the floor with ashes and then securely locking the temple, Daniel demonstrates by the resulting footprints that the priests themselves have slipped in by a secret passage during the night and feasted, thereby defrauding the gullible Babylonians into worshiping a false god. In the second story, Daniel rescues the innocent Susanna, who has been unjustly accused of infidelity by two supposedly irreproachable elders, by separating the witnesses against her and tripping them up in their false accusations. In each case the discernment of God fills Daniel and enables him to penetrate and solve each temporal mystery.

This seminal religious component provided several essential elements that were included when mystery literature began to appear in the latter half of the 1700s: the undeniable existence of "thou shalt nots" in human behavior, the inevitable fact that "one's sin will find

one out," and the absolute conviction that the Creator fashioned and ordered a good world that sin/crime disrupts. The duty of the detective, as moral agent of the good, is to put that world right again.

Defining the Mystery's Religious Subgenre

As their genesis reveals, mystery stories have been intensely religious from the beginning. The word "*mysterium*" itself, from which the genre derived its name, is a Greek religious term referring to the secret holiness of the divine that transcends human sense perception. After fusing with other words and their concepts in Latin, Old French, and Middle English, the cognate term "mystery" has come to describe a secularized obscuring secret that shuts truth off from perception. While the quest of the religious seeker is to penetrate God's *mysterium*, what mystics call the cloud of unknowing, to find the face and heart of the deity, the quest of the secular detective is to penetrate the cloud of secrecy to discover the heart of a mystery and uncover the face of its perpetrator. However, penetrate any secular mystery deeply enough, enter into its dimensions of justice and morality, and one arrives at the *mysterium*, the province of God.

One of the earliest precursors to the modern mystery demonstrated the presence of the

1161

sacred *mysterium* in the secular mystery. Matthew Gregory Lewis' 1795 gothic thriller, *The Monk,* a melange of rudimentary detective tale and supernatural melodrama, contains a detecting nun—one Mother St. Ursula—the offending title character, and an evil prioress. Despite a lack of literary quality, this tale followed the apocryphal lead, establishing a set of divine "thou shalt nots" that are violated, then fielding a religiously oriented heroine who receives divine discernment and is enabled by God to expose the evil of priest and prioress. Employing a technique similar to that of the two tales of Daniel, having lying religious superiors exposed by a young but divinely inspired religious detective, Lewis ensured not only that reality in the mystery would be revealed as differing from what it initially appears to be but also that no aspect, not even overtly religious characters, would be sacrosanct.

When the Golden Age of the modern mystery was budding at the beginning of the twentieth century, G. K. Chesterton (see separate essay) drew from these ancient elements to develop "The Blue Cross," the first entry in a series that has since become the standard against which all religious crime stories are judged. Chesterton introduced his own detecting Daniel or Mother St. Ursula in Father Brown, who was, like the ancient prototypes, an initially unassuming, nearly peripheral character. Chesterton made his Father Brown a seemingly ineffectual man: small, archaic in habit, and traditional in style. He is first introduced merely as a source of amusement, while Valentin, the Parisian police chief (who is the reader's window into the story), is concerned with another "priest," the masquerading archcriminal Flambeau. The story turns, as in the ancient models, on which representative of God is the true moral agent and which is false.

"The Blue Cross" is a rather whimsical as well as archetypal religious mystery. The story traces the odd antics of Chesterton's bumbling little priest, who announces to all and sundry that he is transporting a valuable jeweled cross to a gathering of clergy. He at-

tracts the attention of both master criminal and master detective and sets up the conditions where the latter arrests the former. The tale came under the guns of University of Puerto Rico (Rio Piedras) English professor Kenneth Gavrell, who termed it "the worst 'great' detective story" (p. 39), pointing out a wealth of coincidences and inconsistencies.

Despite any shortcomings, "The Blue Cross" and the subsequent series set a model for the religiously oriented detectives that were to follow. Like the church, Father Brown appeared marginalized, vague, archaic, and no longer effectual. But, also like the church, he represented the indispensable moral agent missing from the modern scene. In tale after tale, Chesterton pits his protagonist against the lethal, atheistic, "scientific" methods of detection of the modern, secularized age. Father Brown even tackles and defeats a lie detector and the "cadaverous, careful-spoken Yankee philosopher" who relied on it in "The Mistake of the Machine" (*The Father Brown Omnibus* [1951], p. 299). In short, under Chesterton's influence, the overtly religious mystery saw itself as providing the divine element missing from scientific detection.

In England, Chesterton's example was followed by Canon Victor Lorenzo Whitechurch, who created a young Anglican country cleric, Vicar Westerham, "an energetic parish priest," whose parishioners and the local constabulary "little guessed" what "a particularly shrewd and capable man" he was with his keen "habit of observation" until he steps in and solves *The Crime at Diana's Pool* (1927; pp. 72–73). The Dean of Durham, C. A. Alington, employed a similar technique, having his detecting archdeacons at first undervalued by their surrounding culture. He introduces them as incognito among their unsuspecting traveling companions until they are called on to save the day.

In the highly skeptical France of the mid–twentieth century, Henri Catalan's detecting nun, Soeur Angèle, is not only shunted aside but even roundly despised by the other characters, appearing as obsolete to modern France as the church she represents. Greater, then, is the impact when the constituted secular authority mocks her capabilities, sneering, in *Soeur Angèle and the Embarrassed Ladies* (1955):

> Okay. Tell me where you've got to. You've pursued inquiries, no doubt interrogated masses of witnesses, interviewed your highly virtuous ladies, made brilliant deductions, fooled the police, redressed the scales of justice, and discovered the murderer all by yourself.

With great satisfaction she can reply with Father Brownish simplicity, "Yes . . . that's exactly what I've done" (pp. 131–132).

In the United States, William Anthony Parker White, most famous under the pen name Anthony Boucher, but writing under another pseudonym, H. H. Holmes, placed his detecting nun, Sister Ursula, in a convent, while Margaret Ann Hubbard enrolled her Sister Simon on the staff of a Catholic school, and Matthew Head (John Canaday) shunted his Protestant team of doctor and evangelist, Mary Finney and Emily Collins, off to the mission field. All, while appearing to the police as peripheral as the religious outlook they represent appears in modern life, are revealed as holding the indispensable perspective to solve the mystery of evil, when the police are baffled and stymied by the mystery.

On through the century, past the world wars, and into the rise of the 1950s, when Jack Kerouac took the mutterings of a Times Square addict that he felt "beat" and fueled the propelling of bohemian counterculture into middle-class imagination, these detecting religious figures quietly served as their own kind of countercultural agents, preserving moral concern while standing in counterpoint to the growing relativistic confusion of a technological culture capable of accomplishing more than sanity prescribes. Readers began to notice the quiet contribution of the detecting clerics and increasingly wanted more mysteries featuring them. Not since Chesterton had the demand been greater.

Leonard Holton's Father Bredder

Where one to four novels seemed to satiate writers' and readers' interest in Vicar Westerham, Sister Simon, Sister Ursula, Soeur Angèle, the archdeacons, and the missionaries, Richard Goyne's The Padre became the first clerical sleuth since Father Brown to break the four-book limit and enjoy five books. His contemporary, Montana state legislator Margaret Scherf's ironic Father Buell, achieved seven, and the most faithful of all of Father Brown's successors (though his creator liked to deny that), Leonard Holton's Father Bredder, appeared in a whopping eleven novels. Like many of the creations of his illustrious author, Father Bredder, like Father Brown, seemed best able to incarnate the religious dimensions of the mystery's message and contextualize it to the particular concerns of his time.

Leonard Holton is a name largely forgotten today, but like "H. H. Holmes," "Matthew Head," and "Monica Quill," it was a pseudonym for someone who is still very well known. Leonard Patrick O'Connor Wibberley was a prolific writer of novels, essays, children's books, and the enduring classic *The Mouse That Roared* (1955), which spawned a movie series, featuring the great British comedian Peter Sellers. In the religious mystery genre, Wibberley as Holton nourished his series with the same key elements that had been staples before him. As he explained (in the same chapter in which he distances Father Bredder from Father Brown) in Otto Penzler's compilation *The Great Detectives:*

> From the point of view of a priest, a crime is not merely an offense against the laws of Man. It is (infinitely more important) an offense against the laws of God. "Thou shalt not Kill," "Thou shalt not Steal" are not, after all, reckoned man-made laws in their origin. When a criminal is caught and brought to justice, nothing at all has been achieved from the priestly point of view unless the offender acknowledges his offense against his Creator

and repents it. Indeed, if the crime is murder and the culprit is executed unrepentant, he faces a sentence of eternal damnation. (p. 28)

Herein is that simple, life-sustaining diet served up again: the existence of eternal and immutable "thou shalt nots," the assurance that offenses are not simply trespasses against transitory human courts but against the justice of almighty God, and the explanation that miscreants need their crimes to be uncovered and brought to justice for their own eternal well-being.

The first helping of Father Bredder's eleven-course feast was served in 1959. Like the suffering servant in Isaiah 53, Father Bredder had been through slaughter. A Marine in World War II, decorated by three countries, he shares the anomie, the sense of being caught between cultures, of all returning veterans and finds safe harbor at last on the shores of the church. His opening tale, *The Saint Maker* (1959), is, however, rather jarring: Father Bredder finds a severed head in his church building and must become a "policeman of God" (p. 136) in order to rescue those falsely accused by the police and discover the real murderer. What he uncovers is sobering for any religious professional: the theology he has been teaching has been misapprehended. Ignoring the church's message of grace and forgiveness, a crazed parishioner has inculcated only its rules and become a self-appointed "saint maker," a *homo necans* who ensures sinners' holiness by personally helping them over the border into sacred eternity with the aid of an ax.

That evil is subtle and can masquerade as holiness as it perverts the truth is the same lesson taught two millennia earlier by the example of the lying elders of "Susanna" and two centuries earlier by the perfidious title character of *The Monk*. A chastened and wiser Father Bredder employs in his subsequent outings a refined discernment when explaining a wide variety of subtle challenges, including taking on a "Jonah Curse" (*A Touch of Jonah*, 1968), a supposed instance of spon-

taneous immolation (*A Pact with Satan*, 1960), and even a purported attack by werewolves (*Deliver Us from Wolves*, 1963) in the fascinating series that follows.

Further, Holton's mysteries, as they span the sixties and seventies, take Bredder through the byways of countercultural California. He ministers to prizefighters, Latinos, and dispossessed Japanese immigrants, all the victims of midcentury culture. Two messages that permeate all the Father Bredder books are stated almost as premises in the first. They are that humanity must be affirmed in victim as well as perpetrator and that God's solution to dealing with the evil that bounds the human condition is the right one, no matter how obsolete it may seem.

Why is Bredder so certain of the first? He discovers truths within himself that extend to all humans, created and now fallen along the same lines. As he explains in *The Saint Maker*, "Priests are human, just like bus drivers . . . detectives. We are consecrated to God, but we are not angels. Not even saints. Just humans" (p. 21). Ironically, the nearer one draws to God, the more one discovers the essential humanity of God's creation and its continuing need for God's inexhaustible forgiveness. That is why Father Bredder can assure the astounded:

If a man steals in a church, he is stealing in the presence of God and will, even in the act of sin, be reminded that his Creator knows of his misdeed and so may repent it. . . . It isn't an odd point of view. . . . It is a Christian point of view, and if it strikes you as odd, it is only because Christianity has become odd. (p. 23)

Father Bredder's success, aided by lamentably minor appearances by delightful sleuths like Alice Scanlan Reach's Father Crumlish, preserved the overtly Roman Catholic religious mystery through the middle years of the century until the rise of the big three detecting priests: Ralph McInerny's Father Dowling, William Kienzle's Father Koesler, and Andrew Greeley's Monsignor Blackie Ryan.

The Golden Age of the Religious Mystery

The early years of the century, especially in England, are regularly labeled the Golden Age of the mystery genre, but the religious mystery, particularly in North America, experienced its ascendancy in the middle years, with the great booming of clerical detectives in the two decades from the mid-1970s to the mid-1980s. I term that its true Golden Age, because the impact of the religious awakening of the revival referred to as the Jesus Movement had not yet been annulled by the indiscretions of media-publicized religious figures (as we will shortly see reflected in the next phase of the development of the religious mystery).

In Great Britain, the secularizing of the culture was already stilling the proliferation of Judeo-Christian clerical detectives. While many in the culture seemed to be experiencing a general loss of contact with the religious perspective, a concordant rise among a few alternative religious movements, like atavistic neopaganism, was by 1977 already being reflected in the subgenre, for example, by Stephen Chance (pseudonym of an Anglican cleric, the Reverend Philip Turner) in his harrowing Father Septimus Treloar mystery, *The Stone of Offering*. In this tale, Anglican Father Septimus, on a visit to Wales, is confronted by a revival of the old nature religion. The book becomes part apologetic, as the unfolding of the story reminds readers why Christianity was so welcomed by those suffering under the blood demands of traditional paganism. It becomes part horror story as Septimus discovers fresh sacrifices found on an ancient altar are echoing an old Druidic rite—a white bird, a silver fish, and a black lamb. Realizing the final entry in the rune is a "white child," he must apply his spiritually oriented detecting to the task if he is to find the kidnapper of a five-year-old child and avert the rite's lethal fulfillment. The struggle between Christianity and a revival of neopagan sensibility in Great Britain is reflected microcosmically in this fictional battle.

ELLIS PETERS' BROTHER CADFAEL

While the United Kingdom was downsizing its mysteries featuring detecting Anglican clerics, ironically, Americans like Barbara Ninde Byfield with her Anglican Father Simon Bede and the husband-wife team writing as E. M. A. Allison with their Brother Barnabas were filling the gap by creating British clerical sleuths or setting mysteries in England. But the true receiver of the torch of Britain's religious mystery was the award-winning historian and translator of Czech poetry, Edith Pargeter, writing under the pseudonym Ellis Peters. Abandoning the present era, she set her superior mysteries in the Middle Ages, a time when Christianity had common currency among the populace.

Peters' simple yet divinely profound protagonist, Brother Cadfael, became her indictment of the pretension crippling both church and state. From the moment that Cadfael exposes the vaunting ambition that counterfeits miracles and misleads the people in the first novel, *A Morbid Taste for Bones* (1977), he becomes as much a sanctuary to the modern religious sensibility as the little herbarium he cultivates becomes a sanctuary for the innocent. The success of the Cadfael stories, which filled a score of volumes and enjoyed a series of television films featuring esteemed actor Derek Jacobi, signified that the appeal of the Judeo-Christian religious mystery was still very much alive.

In the novels, Cadfael is presented as a survivor. A veteran of the Crusades, the Welsh Cadfael is a small, squat, square, sturdy, "thickset fellow who rolls from one leg to the other like a sailor" (*Bones*, p. 6). He brings all his worldly wisdom to the Benedictine monastery, where he serves as apothecary, doctor, herbalist, and healer, a convenient position from which to apply ancient forensics to the crimes that visit him with the regularity of vespers and matins. Outside the abbey walls the political turmoil of Britain's twelfth-century civil war between King Stephen and the Empress Maud festers, while inside wage other sorts of competition, at times as deadly.

In the first story, competition between a Cluniac monastery and Cadfael's Benedictine abbey turns lethal in an escalating quest to secure the relics of a bona fide "spare" Welsh saint (unclaimed by any other order). Murder brings grasping religiosity under fire, when Cadfael, like Daniel, finds himself inspired by the divine to detect, convict, and prescribe justice. As he explains his ability to perceive what others do not, "God aids me with some new thought—for never forget God is far more deeply offended than you or I by this great wrong!" (*Bones*, p. 145). Through the series, God works within the sphere of human interaction, inspiring insights and ideas in Brother Cadfael (and sometimes acting quite independently to bring about justice).

UMBERTO ECO'S *THE NAME OF THE ROSE*

Cadfael's novels act in counterpart to another remarkable mystery set in the Middle Ages: Umberto Eco's *The Name of the Rose* (1980; English translation, 1983). What sets the Cadfael stories and *The Name of the Rose* off from each other, in their theological aspect, is the fact that God remains inscrutable, perhaps even absent, in the latter. *The Name of the Rose* is set in the 1300s, some two hundred years after the Cadfael series. As an exercise in literature, the book, even in translation, is a remarkable achievement. Italian semiotics professor Umberto Eco attempts a postmodern approach to the mystery; that is, he adopts the form, but with a contemporary twist. He uses his tale as a vehicle to explore some of his theories of semiotics, the study of "signs," symbols that are employed to trigger meaning and thereby convey information to those who read them. The microcosmic question upon which the story turns is this: Does the murderer leave signs in the style of each murder as a kind of bloody text to be read by the detective? In macrocosm the book asks, Does God place intelligible signs in the world to be read and understood by all of us human creatures who are both victims of inevitable death and detectives searching out the meaning of our own existence?

Eco sets his Franciscan, Sherlock Holmes–based, English detective within a tension of doubt until, in protomodern style, Eco has him exclaim, "As a philosopher I doubt the world has order" (p. 394), while affirming as a scholastic theologian, "reasoning about causes and effects is a very difficult thing, and I believe the only judge of that can be God" (p. 30). As Eco puts his detective through an escalating series of brutal murders—monks drop like ripe bananas, and so fast they are almost in bunches—William of Baskerville (whose names suggest a blending of Franciscan philosopher William of Ockham [1285?–1349?] and Sherlock Holmes) lags one frustrated length behind the perpetrator. Finally, he corners his quarry in a dizzying labyrinth of knowledge, the sealed-off tower library of an abbey, only to have this world go up in flames. Although he has solved the temporary mystery, having discovered the murderer, the monastery library (as a conduit to deeper meaning) is lost.

In the final pages, Eco leaves William's assistant, who has been the reader's entry point into the novel, contemplating the remains of the abbey several decades later. He finds the great library in scattered fragments. What remains is either rotted by water or termite-eaten. The assistant is left wondering whether the chronicle he has composed of the events has any hidden meaning. For him, neither that nor knowledge of God's true character is apprehensible. The book ends in an expression of perplexity and doubt. (See also essay on "The Metaphysical Mystery.")

RALPH MCINERNY'S FATHER DOWLING

Ralph McInerny's Father Dowling novels stand in contrast to Eco's vision. Father Dowling, like Cadfael, enjoyed a long-running television series with character actor Tom Bosley transforming the ascetic, postalcoholic Dowling into an optimistic, cuddly, "Father knows best" kind of priest. But the Dowling of Ralph

McInerny's series is actually a vehicle for the author's Thomist approach to questions of justice and morality. (Thomism, named for philosopher Thomas Aquinas [1225–1274] is a theological system that emphasizes God's revelation and human reason working together to bring truth.) This is not to say that in investing Dowling with a hefty dose of Thomism, professor McInerny has turned his novels into extensive allegories—a kind of Platonic play with a lethal component. McInerny is too fine a writer for that and decisively one of the masters of the religious mystery. In both his pseudonymous Monica Quill tales of Sister Mary Teresa and his Father Dowling series, McInerny goes to great lengths to bridge the gap of verisimilitude and present a world constructed on modern lines. Among the philandering husbands, dishonest contractors, and depressed police officers reflected from contemporary life, however, each novel contains at least one workaday next-door neighbor whose lack of moral principles precipitates murder.

While writing most of these novels, McInerny served as Michael P. Grace Professor of Medieval Studies and director of the Jacques Maritain Center at the University of Notre Dame in Indiana. Author of a number of college textbooks on Thomism, he used the series to flesh out his ideas in parabolic form. In the first Dowling novel, *Her Death of Cold* (1977), only by discerning the intent of a murderer can Dowling explain to the puzzled police why a widow has been found locked in a freezer in her own house. The concern of Father Dowling in this and in all his stories is that of all detecting religious protagonists: that satisfying the law of God is as crucial (and perhaps more so because it has eternal ramifications) as satisfying the demands of human law. In the religious mystery novel, the detective never forgets that (s)he serves as an agent of God's justice first.

Father Dowling also continues the tradition of the peripheral-appearing religious protagonist, while anticipating the "wounded" categorization of the postscandal religious professional. He is a dried-out alcoholic, once a promising mover and shaker on the marriage tribunal, now relegated to a back-eddy parish like so many other failed priests. In the great reversal of positions that so characterizes the "foolishness" of God viewed from the "wisdom" of humans (see 1 Corinthians 1), however, he finally finds his lost vocation there. Out of the corrupting politics of the church, Father Dowling finds his redemption, ministering to the lives of common people. All the truths of the faith rekindle for him, and he is able to light up the belief of others as the embers of his own stir into flame.

Attempting to explain the phenomenally popular Father Dowling in his chapter on the "Catholic Mystery" in *The Fine Art of Murder*, McInerny himself commented:

> When I began the Father Dowling stories, I wanted a priest to represent the contrast of sin and forgiveness and a cop, Captain Keegan, to represent that between crime and punishment. The novels exhibit the way these two overlap, interlock, and play off against each other. (p. 149)

The Dowling novels work because McInerny has done such a skillful job in drawing these contrasts. In doing so, he has articulated something foundationally true about the human condition within an entertaining vehicle. One is nourished, and the hearty meal tastes delicious. Therein lies a good deal of Dowling's recipe for success; his servings are well done as entertainment and edification.

WILLIAM KIENZLE'S FATHER KOESLER

In a similar fashion, ex-priest William X. Kienzle's Father Koesler serves an urban parish that takes him into all the back alleys of contemporary life in stories that are well constructed and executed and do not spare often heavy ladlings of the most ferocious ingredients of life in a fallen world. In his stories anything that can happen does, and in volume: nuns are raped and murdered, Vodun priestesses help solve crimes, disappointed parishioners commit serial murder, the world is revealed in near total turmoil. Mass murder seems to many of his characters the regular solution to tension in relationships. Some killers, like the serial murderer of *Sudden Death* (1985), give a theological rationale for their violence, but often enough murder is reactive, predicated by disappointment with the church and its representatives.

Father Koesler fights a rearguard battle, but he does so in the hope that is the constant of biblical revelation. As he explains in *Sudden Death*, the murderer

> has been judged by God . . . by an all-loving and forgiving and understanding God. We mustn't lose faith that Henry has found that God can find ways unknown to humans to forgive. We leave Henry to our Father in heaven with great confidence and hope. It's all we can do. (p. 197)

While humanity in the Koesler series lives at times in near chaos, the power of the series is to retreat finally to the God who can tame chaos. While God's mercy never sets aside God's justice and human perpetrators must suffer for their crimes, still the living hope is that forgiveness can lie on the other side of punishment and that restoration is the ultimate goal for repentant humanity.

These themes are largely present in Koesler's first explosive novel, *The Rosary Murders* (1979), a best-seller that became a motion picture featuring Donald Sutherland and Charles Durning. The tale explores the burden placed on priests by the vow each confessor makes that what he hears in the confessional will remain in sacred confidence. What if he hears a mass murderer confess he has killed and will kill again? Contemporary expediency would dictate a quick 911 call and a welcoming party from the gray-bar hotel to greet the absolved perp as he emerges shriven from the confessional. But the church's adherence to its vows remains a firm rock in a shifting world, and Koesler, caught in this dilemma, must detect without reference to what he has received in sacred confidence in order to stop a disappointed Catholic from wreaking vengeance on the church.

ANDREW GREELEY'S MONSIGNOR BLACKIE RYAN

This kind of angst between one's calling and the exigencies of ministry does not appear to plague Monsignor Blackie Ryan, the creation of the most successful Roman Catholic clerical crime writer who was himself active as a cleric. In fact, Blackie Ryan's creator is perhaps the most well-known figure in transmillennial Roman Catholicism next to the Pope. Best-selling author, winner of such prestigious awards as the Mark Twain Award and the Carl Sandberg Award for distinguished contributions to Midwestern American literature, sociologist and Chicago priest Andrew Greeley is a sardonic Fulton Sheen—a popular Roman Catholic television preacher and author in the mid–twentieth century—for the latter half of the twentieth century. His Blackie Ryan is an upbeat ecclesiastical leprechaun who is a repository of Vatican II futurism. While certainly not Matthew Fox—a controversial former Roman Catholic priest silenced by the Vatican for mixing many religions in with his Christianity—he does like to refer to God as "she" and infuriate the church's conservative wing. He is a rebel in a collar in an age when rebels are international fare in Catholicism. Yet, beneath all his new theo-speak, his creator is trying to preserve, even if repackaged, the key Christian message of God's love.

As Father Greeley explained to Christianity's watchdog humor magazine, *The Wittenburg Door:*

> I think we need to preach what Jesus preached. God loves us. The Kingdom of Heaven is the kingdom of mercy in which there are all kinds of surprises. The most powerfully effective image of God is God as a lover. People today need to hear that God is a God of overwhelming grace, a God whose grace is so awesome that if humans behaved like God, they'd be thought mad. (pp. 19–20)

This is the same hope-filled message that fuels the delightful Martha Williamson–produced television series, *Touched by an An-*

gel. The assurance that my parent loves me no matter how bad I have been is the ardent hope of every child.

Similarly, in Blackie Ryan, Greeley consciously preserves the tradition handed on by Chesterton, by fielding a character initially ignored but ultimately an effective and self-assured representative of God's view toward lethal human sin. Blackie Ryan's first appearance was in one of Greeley's best novels, the blood-curdling *Virgin and Martyr* (1985). As one onlooker in *Virgin and Martyr* describes him:

> Blackie looks like a modern Father Brown, short, pudgy, cherubic, with curly brown hair, apple cheeks and an expression of impenetrable composure. He is the kind of utterly unimportant-appearing person that you wouldn't even notice if he was on an elevator when the door opened and you walked in. He is also the brightest man I know, ruthlessly loyal, and as much a pixie as his cousin, though he hides that last attribute behind his guise of mordant cynicism. (p. 64)

In a sense, Blackie Ryan might be considered a postmodern Father Brown, reintroducing the form with an ironic twist. In the first book of Ryan's series, whose titles are built on the Beatitudes in Christ's Sermon on the Mount, Greeley also reintroduces the overtly supernatural element of *The Monk. Happy Are the Meek* (1985) playfully nods to a number of other precursing sources, among them H. H. Holmes's *Nine Times Nine* (1940), Chesterton's "The Eye of Apollo," and Leonard Holton's *A Pact with Satan,* to create a story about a defrocked priest who has introduced a new form of lethal paganism: Lucifer worship. Like another nonseries tale in which Blackie Ryan appears, *Angels of September* (1986), which features a painting with telekinetic powers, *Happy Are the Meek* includes some poltergeist manifestations. The mystery is in the locked-room tradition. A character who has angered the cult leader is found dead in his locked study. Responsibility is claimed by the defrocked priest, who, at the time of death, was appearing before his congregants. To explode the false claim of miraculous murder by astral projection, Blackie Ryan must point out the mundane solution, but not before encountering some genuinely preternatural events—objects whizzing around the room, possibly indicating, the story implies, that the deceased is making a posthumous bid for a good-old consecrated Catholic burial.

CAROL ANNE O'MARIE'S SISTER MARY HELEN

Monsignor Blackie Ryan proved to be the Roman Catholic Church's last major priestly detective to jut his chin out, rear his shoulders back, and wield with bold authority an ecclesiastical sword, sharpened with a double-millennial edge. The future of the Roman Catholic ministerial mystery would belong to the wounded and doubting clerics who make up the postscandal period of the clerical mystery and to the daughters of Mother Ursula, Sister Ursula, Sister Simon, and Dorothy Gilman's Sisters John and Hyacinthe of *A Nun in the Closet* (1975). The bridge for these in the latter part of the twentieth century was real-life sister Carol Anne O'Marie's sprightly septuagenarian, Sister Mary Helen, of a continuing series.

As is Father Andrew Greeley, Sister Carol Anne O'Marie is still under orders. A member of the sisters of St. Joseph of Carondolet, she has edited a diocesan newspaper and served as teacher, principal, and director of a Catholic high school. Her frail, semiretired Sister Mary Helen is an educator also, who from her first adventure, *A Novena for Murder* (1984), uses her divinely inspired discernment, sharpened by years of spotting miscreants in her classrooms, to identify the more deadly miscreants of adult life. In *A Novena for Murder,* the mystery even penetrates a contemporary sanctuary of the *mysterium,* the chapel of Sister Mary Helen's own nunnery. To have the mystery and *mysterium* meet so blatantly in Sister Mary Helen's world is not so unthinkable to her author. Reflecting on her choice of a character in the *Mystery Readers of America Journal*, O'Marie mused:

> Picking a religious as a series sleuth, especially if that religious happens to be a nun is, to my mind, like picking a winner. Why? Because nuns are inherently mysterious. . . . As women, they are accustomed to dealing with the human condition and well able to understand human behavior. As religious, they are concerned, not only with holiness, good works and the needs of people, but they have a professional interest in sin and the sinner which makes them especially suited to solving crimes. Put their womanhood and their religious calling together and you come up with a dynamite combination for a series detective. (*Synod*, pp. 131–133)

Like Jesus, to whom they have made a vow, nuns, in O'Marie's perspective, stand in the gap between the human mystery of struggling with evil and the divine *mysterium* of dispensing grace. Sister Mary Helen has no difficulty assuming her place in that gap with divinely anchored assurance. As she reasons, " 'If God is for you, who can be against?' St. Paul's letter to the Romans. And Paul was so right. Furthermore, whose side could God possibly be on but hers?" (*Novena*, p. 66). Shortly, in its attempt to reflect what was going on in real life, that question would not be so easily answered by the clerical detectives.

The Postscandal Catholic and Protestant Antiheroes

In the late-twentieth century the popular religion of the United States was rocked by a series of well-publicized scandals. Several Protestant televangelists were found to be hiring prostitutes or fraudulently overselling leases to retirement homes on land they were developing commercially, while in the Roman Catholic Church dark revelations were emerging of priestly molestation of children. Once again the truly devout were reminded of the words of the very first Christian sermon

outside the New Testament, the second century's 2 Clement, where Jesus chides:

> "My name is continually scoffed at by all peoples"; and again, "Alas for him through whom my name is scoffed at!" How is it scoffed at? By your failing to do what I want. For when the heathen hear God's oracles on our lips they marvel at their beauty and greatness. But afterwards, when they mark that our deeds are unworthy of the words we utter, they turn from this to scoffing. (13:2–3)

With the media image of the religious hero's toppling, like positive and negative images in art, the shadow remained when the light temporarily failed. The image of God had been defaced but not erased. In mystery fiction the shadow became the new religious antihero. New clerical sleuths created for the 1990s were not drawn simply as peripheral to society but as antiheroic.

The opening processional of this new order of the antiheroic clerical sleuth began in 1990 with William F. Love's Auxiliary Bishop Francis X. Regan, the first clerical sleuth who is permanently damaged physically as well as emotionally. According to *The Chartreuse Clue* (1990), Regan is wheelchair-bound owing to a shooting. A troubled genius with an IQ of 220, he is given to fierce fits of periodic depression and needs the stimulus of a mystery from time to time to "blast" him out (p. 14). Spiteful and childish, he has the appearance of the "serenity of a man of God" but is "about as peaceful as Mount Vesuvius" (p. 46). He requires five hours of prayer a day, but must stop at that point since, as he puts it, "I doubt that even God could tolerate that much of my company" (p. 19). And even at that he is still "foul-tempered" (p. 18).

Regan's style is half Nero Wolfe, half Father Shanley, but the plots of his tales are built on contemporary themes. For example, *The Chartreuse Clue* involves an Unamuno-spoiled, alcoholic "priest without faith" (p. 114) who confesses, "I don't believe in God, Jesus, the Church, any of it" (p. 113), and whose resulting double life wakes him up one morning in the apartment of a murdered heiress. Unlike the Father Browns and Bredders who preceded him, Bishop Regan cannot confine his concern simply to what is best for the errant priest. "My inclination is to say a prayer for the deceased young woman, send Father William packing, report the matter to the police and let the law take its rightful course," he snarls, except that "the publicity would be horrendous. Undoubtedly, every priest of this Archdiocese would be besmirched by the publicity . . . All because of this man's idiotic lack of judgment!" (pp. 23–24).

In this postscandal era foci have changed. The church's reputation is in survival mode— "We need to protect the good name of the two thousand priests of this Archdiocese, if that is still possible" (p. 24)—so housecleaning becomes the agenda of the tough-love nineties clerics. Similarly, Love's 1991 *The Fundamentals of Murder* was another sex-and-the-faithful foray involving the killing of prostitutes and the indictment of a pornography-addicted fundamentalist lay evangelist. Both the mainline and the independent church came onto the cleanup schedule for ex-Benedictine monk William F. Love's wounded healer.

Immediately behind Auxiliary Bishop Regan in the new processional loped a dissipating preacher created by *Eating Well* magazine editor Barry Estabrook. In *Bahama Heat* (1991), his Reverend Miles Farnsworth, televangelist and coinheritor of the Savior Network's multimillion-dollar "ministry," first appears in "the haze of a full-blown rum hangover" (p. 8). While he is a regulation Graham Greene whisky priest, Farnsworth has become disgusted by the crass materialism of his ministry and is trying desperately to redeem his soul by running a small mission in the Bahamas. In the meantime he keeps an emergency ration of rum under the life jackets and lines of his cabin cruiser (called "Come to Jesus") and fornicates from time to time. His explanation is quintessential to his time:

"You ever heard of the Savior Network?"

"That the outfit where the guy got caught in the sack with his secretary?"

"No. Not so large as that one. But the same idea. Television evangelism. I used to preach there. Reached millions of viewers—"

"So what happened? Caught diddling a choirboy?"

"No. More mundane than all that. Just got tired of the commercial side of the whole thing: millions of dollars' worth of equipment, state-of-the-art studios, executive offices and bureaucrats to fill them, enough BMWs to start a dealership. It's going to sound corny to you, but it seemed we had gotten so far from the original purpose . . . You just have to look at Christ and the disciples. You do remember who they are?" (p. 46)

By the end of *Bahama Heat*, Farnsworth frustrates a drug deal, saves his mission, salvages his father's ministry, and is severely physically beaten in a rough kind of cleansing penance.

A similar penance is required of Professor Paul Harding's (P. C. Doherty) Brother Athelstan of *The Nightingale Gallery* (1991), when he is sent to the seamiest parish in London in order to atone for his role in his brother's death: "I had to do private and public penance, take a solemn vow that, after I was ordained, I would accept whatever duties my superiors gave me" (p. 129). While Brother Cadfael, after a life of adventures, had washed up on his monastic shore to wear his faith like a survivor's blanket, a warm, secure symbol of safe harbor at last obtained, a twenty-eight-year-old Athelstan is presented as still fighting his storms, wearing his faith like a humble gown, showing all of his gaping wounds. Grieving for his brother, despairing for the prostitutes and ruffians of his congregation, his chief agony is the sexual yearning he himself feels for an attractive, widowed parishioner:

Although he might have a woman as a friend, he could not lust, he could not desire or covet any woman, whether she be free or not. Athelstan steeled himself. . . . Nevertheless, Athelstan felt a growing rage at his condition. (p. 214)

1171

So overpowering is his envy that it almost immobilizes his attempts to solve his book's mystery. But if this flirtation causes him tension, think how he would fare if he were catapulted across the centuries into a topless bar!

That is the predicament in which D. Keith Mano places his devastated Episcopal priest, Father Mike Wilson, in the well-crafted polemical novel *Topless* (1991), a systematic fictional analysis of the spiritual and physical deterioration of a Christian man, driven into and then out of the priesthood by sexual guilt. Summoned from a dull Nebraskan assistantship to wild-side New York City by his brother's sudden disappearance, Wilson is thrust into the (unlikely) temporary proprietorship of his brother's topless bar and consequently into a war between flesh and spirit where "all the resonance of Christian symbolism—cross and crucifixion, bread and wine—is gathered, it would seem, to counteract and answer the image of a single naked woman. . . . Christians aren't naive about this: we respect the body's power" (pp. 46–47).

Bit by bit he is overpowered by the body, as his book presents in graphic depiction "the whole mincing, perverse charade . . . the routine humiliation of women. Topless has always been about that: profitable humiliation" (p. 210). Confronted by a system that turns every man into victimizer, every woman into victim, he concludes:

> I took over The Smoking Car for reasons that I thought were extenuating. Good reasons. Charitable reasons. But you cannot employ sin in the service of good. And no one, believe me, should tempt the devil. I have sinned. I have alienated people I love. I have brought suspicion of murder on myself. And, most of all, I have embarrassed my priesthood. Which I now resign . . . You see a man devastated. But he is still a Christian man. I have resigned my priesthood, I have not renounced my faith. (pp. 184–185)

With his resignation, the novel turns a chastising focus on the Church itself. The problem, he snaps back at an ex-cop who cites the case of repressed priests, is that "the Episcopal Church doesn't repress its priests *enough*" (p. 209). A sage and disgusted bishop agrees, "A priest in a topless bar—you're nothing more than the absurd but logical result of my church's outreach to permissiveness and extremism. In fact, I've been expecting someone like you for some time" (p. 215).

A former contributing editor to *Playboy* magazine, Mano spun the book from research he did for an article on topless bars. He has his protagonist conclude:

> A case can be made for nudity as art. A case can be made for dancing as art. But, let's face it, they're shoddy cases, pretty much. Between the topless dancer and her admirer there exists a sexual charge that both insults and cheapens the human soul. IT IS NOT HARMLESS, no matter what apologists may tell you. It grinds the affections and stupefies those who seek beauty. It is not something Christians should countenance. It is certainly not something priests should countenance. (p. 184)

Luridly packaged and graphic, *Topless* dissects the effect of the moral decay that forces priests out of ministry.

Also out of the ministry is Lee Harris' Christine Marie Bennett of *The Good Friday Murder* (1992). Three weeks out of a Franciscan convent after fifteen years as a nun, Bennett neither prays nor seeks divine guidance in solving her book's mystery (only speaking about the latter in the past tense). For her the convent is like an alma mater from which she has graduated:

> I wanted to move on. I found that what I loved in the church was the ritual, all that I had grown up with, that I was comfortable with. I will never be anything but a Catholic, but my faith was no longer the center of my life. (p. 159)

The shift here from nearly all the clerical crime novels that preceded is striking. In the past, the religious professional represented a faith that appeared marginal to society, now that faith is marginal even to the religious professional. And it does not affect her decision making. She decides not to bed the book's love interest not for reasons of faith or morality, but because it was "something I didn't really want to happen so soon" (p. 159). Fifteen years in the nunnery have slipped away fast. On learning she has left the convent, one priest sadly reflects, "I'm sorry. We lose so many of our best" (p. 59)—a comment that can be taken largely as a reflection on the whole postscandal focus of the religious mystery.

In this period, mysteries featuring fallen religious figures seemed to center on a troop of ribald reverends, libidinous lectors, promiscuous priests who needed to have their zippers turned around along with their collars, for, as John Calvin termed the baptizing bandits of his day, they had become the "apes of the Apostles." And as Søren Kierkegaard commented, when an ape looks into a mirror, it does not see a bishop looking out. In my extensive analysis of detecting priests, pastors, nuns, rabbis, and missionaries, *Mysterium and Mystery: The Clerical Crime Novel*, I suggested that "the clerical crime novel, two-thirds of whose writers are lay people and one-third religious professionals, might be of interest to churches as one gauge of the current state of attitudes within and without the churches" (p. 317).

As gauges of the 1990s, these novels honor the ideal of Christianity but construct religious professionals who, like philandering televangelists and molesting priests, cannot measure up to that ideal. Three of the five protagonists just discussed drop out of formal ministry. In that sense, these books present a prescription for therapy: clean up (Regan, Athelstan) or drop out (Farnsworth, Wilson, Bennett). If a mirror exists in this literature, it is a glass in a hospital emergency ward or the back window of a hearse. A genre can only rehearse its own death for so long, however, for the book-buying public, like Almighty God, finally invests most in the living, not the dead. And, as is always the case when the great celestial gardener is at work, in the late

twentieth century other models were also appearing in the religious mystery.

Christian "Housecleaning" Clerics

While the heirs of religious tradition were despairing to reveal faith as relevant to the contemporary age, a certain undercurrent was already working with new models. At first glance, Methodist cleric Charles Merrill Smith's Reverend Randollph may have appeared like any other detecting cleric, but his figure owed more to Leslie Charteris' the Saint than it did to Father Brown. The Reverend Randollph (the second *l* is an affectation) is a high-living, former football quarterback (also known as "Con" Randollph), who dresses well, marries a television host, and makes sure he discovers which lethal religious fanatic is disturbing his comfortable existence as pastor of the powerful Good Shepherd Church, a wealthy urban parish in Chicago that rents out most of its building to high-paying corporate offices. When negotiating his salary, Randollph is a liberal version of what every cleric would be, if guilt and the desire to preach freely did not intercede (and what some parish budget committees suspect they hear when any cleric asks for a raise). He is certainly not Father Brown. While his lionized approach may have appeared as a last Protestant muscle flexing before a temporary eclipse, it was something much more futuristic. Randollph the righteous knew how to use the media. In real life mainly the wolves among the sheep seem to know.

His first novel, *Reverend Randollph and the Wages of Sin* (1974), though his least interesting from a religious perspective, reflects the internecine war between religious conservatives and liberals. When one of his female parishioners is found naked and strangled in the choir room, Randollph is plunged into the deadly side of disapproval of profligate behavior. As in *The Saint Maker*, the crime is found to have been committed by a devout parishioner whose revulsion has turned homicidal. Randollph finds he must dig as deeply into the religious conflicts in the church as into the sordid details of the woman's nineteen affairs to discover her executioner.

The Randollph novels often feature a former believer who has gone on a terminal tangent. In that sense they continue the housecleaning theme, a constant in the religious mystery, which began in the Apocrypha's "Susanna" when Daniel exposed the lying elders, continued in *The Monk*, traveled through Chesterton's "The Hammer of God" (where Father Brown exposed a cleric who stops a sinner from sinning by dropping a hammer on him from a great height), on through *The Saint Maker* and *The Rosary Murders*, and intensified in the postscandal novels. But if Randollph represented the liberal Protestant reaction to the missteps of conservative Christianity, among a spate of conservative offerings, James Johnson's Sebastian series was chastening both sides.

While ostensibly spy thrillers, the adventures of Reverend Raymond Sebastian actually contain a strong detecting component. They stand in the tradition of the conservative Christian hard-boiled tales of Lon Woodrum. Johnson's intense and unjustly overlooked series was dealing with questions of authenticity and sacrifice in ministry long before these topics were of general notice, forging a proactive cleric stripped of any security but God's grace. Reliance on God certainly proves to be what Sebastian needs most, for in each tale nothing is ever as it appears to be.

In Johnson's first novel, *Code Name Sebastian* (1967), burned-out parish minister Raymond Sebastian is packed off to Israel by his despairing congregation in hopes that he can refind his faith. When his plane is sabotaged and crashes in the wilderness, Sebastian discovers that the surviving party is filled with spies. Desperately seeking someone to trust, he serendipitously meets God in the desert and is shocked to discover:

> He knew nothing of the God in crisis, the God of the Negev, the God of the impossible—he

had reshaped God to his own form of Santa Claus and Easter bunny who could deliver gaily wrapped packages and chocolate eggs but who couldn't be counted on to alter the agony of the human condition. How then could he pray to God here, a different God in his mind altogether, a God he had never tried, proved, or seen work anywhere? (p. 172)

Likewise, he discovers a new Jesus, not the "Christ who died a neat, sophisticated death on a church steeple with the organ playing" (p. 181), but a suffering servant who challenges the church "to participate in the sufferings of God at the hands of a godless world" (p. 268).

Sebastian's emergence from the "cloister ... into the world" (p. 268) plunges him deeply in love with an Israeli spy, and in succeeding novels he is blown up at the Berlin Wall (in the best novel of the series—another story that blends detection and intrigue—*A Handful of Dominoes* [1970]), depth-bombed by the United States in the waters off Cuba, frozen at the North Pole, and shelled by Soviets after a howling southwester off the coast of Australia. Issued intermittently from 1967 to the year of Johnson's death in 1987, the novels anticipated the need for postmodern clerics by creating a model minister who preserves the key elements of faith while serving in a totally secularized setting.

Female Cleric Detectives

The need for new models shook off the focus on male Protestant protagonists that had set in after Canaday's Dr. Mary Finney/Emily Collins novels. Romance writer Isabelle Holland introduced a provocative alternative in the first clearly ordained Episcopal female sleuth, the Reverend Dr. Claire Aldington, a pastoral counselor who must penetrate the depths of a mystery while confronting the frailty of her own relationship with an anorexic daughter.

Holland's first tale, *A Death at St. Anselm's* (1984), is itself a material parable of what was happening spiritually in the religious milieu. The confused vestry of New York's St. Anselm's parish hires a homicidal lunatic as a new minister. Bodies begin to drop, and pastoral counselor Aldington must step in as reluctant detective and rid the church of this menace. Perhaps no story illustrates more strongly the distrust of power-oriented white male leadership in the U.S. Christian Church at the end of the twentieth century, or the desire for new clerical models.

A spate of writers on both sides of the Atlantic began turning, like Ellis Peters, to the Middle Ages to construct protomodels of detecting female religious figures. Medieval historian Sharan Newman put her detecting novice Catherine LeVendeur of *Death Comes as Epiphany* (1993) into the twelfth-century abbey of Mother Superior Heloise, former love of medieval theologian Peter Abelard. Margaret Frazer enrolled Sister Frevisse of *The Novice's Tale* (1992) into the era of Chaucer, and Peter Tremayne his Sister Fidelma of *Absolution by Murder* (1996) far back into the 600s.

Of Roman Catholic detecting nuns in contemporary settings, British author Maureen Peters, writing as "Veronica Black," preserved the best of the past in her Sister Joan mysteries, beginning in 1990 with *A Vow of Silence.* In this interesting mix of old traditions and new concerns, her detecting nun remains pure, while a convent's entire leadership succumbs to a rather deadly brand of goddess worship. Britain's age-old battle between Christianity and paganism is still being fought in contemporary microcosm.

The most futuristic adaptation appears to be Winona Sullivan's clever series beginning with *A Sudden Death at the Norfolk Cafe* (1993). The author, a former C.I.A. intelligence analyst, answers the problem of the relevance of fielding a full-fledged clerical detective by hybridizing her Sister Cecile as an heiress whose wealthy father stands in for the contemporary agnostic. Disapproving of her vocation, he leaves her his fortune on the understanding that none should be spent on the church. The clever Cecile takes her vows,

then sets up shop as a private eye, living off her fortune and donating her fees to her order. A fulfillment of Jesus' prayer for his future disciples in John 17, she is "in the world but not of it." She has taken to the final refuge of the faithful: out of the cloister and onto the battlefield.

The success of Sister Cecile—her first entry won the 1991 Best First Private Eye Novel contest and was subsequently published in 1993—recalls the success of all true reform movements that come before the jury of the people, like Jeremiah out of the council of prophets, Jesus out of the Temple, Saint Francis out of the Vatican, and Martin Luther out onto the front door of the Wittenberg castle church. Each becomes a living manifesto that religious faith bursts institutional wineskins that are allowed to grow decrepit. Active faith stays sweet and fresh.

How revolutionary are these living manifestos? While each of them, along with other detecting nuns, were under vows, they, like the Reverend Claire Aldington, were still limited in ministry. Even though ordained, Aldington was confined to her position as counseling staff member under a senior male minister. She is radical as a bridging figure, yet she is constructed to reflect her times by expressing discomfort with a title such as "mother" to meet the male appropriation of the term "father."

By 1995, however, the model had developed to the point where Kate Gallison could field a female Episcopal cleric who was thoroughly comfortable with the term "mother." In engaging novels like *Bury the Bishop* (1995), Gallison gives us Mother Lavinia Grey, a thirty-five-year-old straight-talking widow who is patronized because she is slight and delicate in appearance. She is in fact a stubborn idealist who goes doggedly about the task of rescuing the dying parish dumped upon her. Presented as vulnerably human, Mother Grey treats the reader to a hilarious take on her fellow characters ("Father Bingley is as close to a low-grade moron as anyone I have seen in the priesthood," p. 26). The loneliness that threatens her vows to sexual purity, her occasional "self medicating" that leaves her befuddled by sherry (p. 85), and other such touches reveal her fallenness. But within that fallenness she is redeemed and called to represent God; this call emerges powerfully, as we witness an innate spiritual strength that preserves her convictions and forges a potent ministry for her out of a dying parish.

As metaphor, Mother Grey is the ideal 1990s postmodern cleric. Small like Father Brown, detoured into a dying church, this widowed, marginalized female alternative takes that church into the center of ministry to the equally marginalized—the homeless, the suicidal, the abused—and wins the respect of all. Lest any reader suppose she is simply trying to prove a point by filling what was formerly a predominantly male job slot, rather than fulfilling a vocation, we soon discover that even her decision to solve the book's mystery is done as much to protect the people to whom she ministers as to clear her own name. In eucatastrophe (a catastrophic action that brings good), she ends with her building full, her ministry sanctioned by the citizens of the city, and legitimacy accorded to herself and the formerly voiceless victims of society she represents. She is one of the new successful examples of a model that reinvents the clerical sleuth.

Jewish Detecting Clerics

While housecleaning was happening in the Christian religious mystery, a burgeoning subgenre of modern Jewish mysteries also developed. At the apex, since his first appearance in *Friday the Rabbi Slept Late* (1964), was a direct heir of the detecting Daniel of the Apocrypha, the astute Rabbi Small of Harry Kemelman's excellent series. The Rabbi Small novels ignited the contemporary Jewish mystery, which has been so well developed by the Kellermans (particularly Faye) and taken in another, more orthodox, direction by Rabbi Joseph Telushkin in his poignant Rabbi Daniel Winter series.

Rabbi David Small, both in the novels and in the dialogical exercise *Conversations with Rabbi Small* (1981), is the apologia of contemporary Judaism, its defense in the modern world. In his detecting rabbi, Kemelman infused a humanity recognizable to all while still contextualized in Jewish customs. While the bulk of the stories turn on an interesting, historically significant premise—Jews are blamed for murders Gentiles commit—Rabbi Small becomes Kemelman's contribution to the "never again" stance of contemporary Judaism. Now the agent of good is very much in the world, ferreting out true guilt and succoring the innocent, so that both they and the people they represent will not suffer.

Harry Kemelman himself brought a rich background to his books. Since 1947 he had been publishing detective stories in *Ellery Queen's Mystery Magazine* but wanted to expand into a study of "the sociological situation of the Jew in suburbia" (*The Nine Mile Walk*, 1967; p. 11). When an editor suggested he blend his two interests, Rabbi Small was born. Also interested in education, having written a book called *Common Sense in Education* (1970), Kemelman made his rabbi a scholar and judge. As Rabbi Small explains, "One of the rabbi's functions [is] to sit in judgment" (*Friday*, p. 12). When a young governess is murdered and her body left in Rabbi Small's car in *Friday the Rabbi Slept Late*, he must use a scholar's skill to discern truth and a judge's acumen to bring it to bear on the culprit. But as a diasporan Jew he must deal with his congregation's overriding concern not to look bad before the Gentile neighbors while quelling continual movements within that congregation to remove him from office and replace him with a rabbi who looks more like a Roman Catholic priest or Protestant minister. Kemelman uses that tension as a vehicle to educate the reader on the distinctives of current Conservative and Reform Judaism. As he explains through Rabbi Small, "With us, however, faith in the Christian sense is almost meaningless, since God is by definition unknowable . . . Our religion is a code of ethical behavior" (*Wednesday the Rabbi Got Wet*, 1976; p. 277).

While Rabbi Small and Rabbi Winter are the most prominent of the Jewish religious professional detectives, a number of mysteries feature detectives in secular occupations who are Jewish. While they are not rabbis or religious professionals (or even religiously observant in some cases), these detectives work a cultural Judaism into their perspectives. Readers interested in a thorough analysis of these "secularized" Jewish detectives may consult James Yaffe's critique of a wide variety of detectives, from Claire Boothe's Moe Finkelstein of *Margin for Error* (1940) through David Delman's Jacob Horowitz of *Sudden Death* (1972), in Jon L. Breen and Martin H. Greenberg's splendid volume *Synod of Sleuths: Essays on Judeo-Christian Detective Fiction*. Mystery writer Serita Stevens, creator of Fanny Zindel (*Red Sea, Dead Sea*, 1991; *Bagels for Tea*, 1993) has also written an interesting insider's view of what makes a Jewish mystery in *The Fine Art of Murder*.

Other Religious Voices

The religious mystery has also expanded as a vehicle for "other voices" to gain a hearing. Hinduism is most associated in many readers' minds with H. R. F. Keating's Inspector Ghote of the Bombay police force, who fulfilled the promise of the Indian folktales that Dorothy L. Sayers pointed out served as precursors to the modern mystery when he began his long series of investigations in *The Perfect Murder* (1965), by tracking down the seemingly "perfect" crime of the murder of a man named Perfect. Among the witnesses the inspector interrogates are a sacred bull of Lord Siva, who points out a thief with its inspired horn. A more recent example is Paul Mann's *The Burning Ghats* (1996), which pits Bombay attorney George Sansi against a lethal chemical company whose discharge is burning the bodies of bathing pilgrims.

Even earlier in melding the East in a positive (not largely negative, à la Sax Rhomer) manner into the mystery was Earl Derr Biggers' Charlie Chan, who ended many of his tales with some Taoist-type maxim: "The Emperor Shi Hwang-ti, who built the Great Wall of China, once said: 'He who squanders to-day talking of yesterday's triumph, will have nothing to boast of to-morrow'" (*Charlie Chan Carries On*, 1930; p. 333). Buddhism is the background for mysteries like William D. Montalbano and Carl Hiaasen's *A Death in China* (1984). When a young American Mormon missionary is stabbed to death in a Shinto shrine in James Melville's *A Haiku for Hanae* (1989), Japanese police superintendent Otani must negotiate the depth of East/West religious differences:

> Like the vast majority of his fellow countrymen and women Otani was a casual Buddhist in the sense that he expected his funeral to be conducted in due course by a Buddhist priest . . . Again, like most of his compatriots he visited Shinto shrines on appropriate occasions . . . Otani knew about Christianity, of course, and was acquainted with one or two Japanese Christians. He regarded them as harmless eccentrics. . . . It seemed that the dead man had been a particular kind of Christian: a Mormon, whatever that might be. (pp. 22–23)

What it might be both superintendent and reader will learn.

Many times the religious element in the mystery seems to be part of the backdrop. Sometimes this component comes with place like the Latin paganism of Stephen Saylor's mysteries set in first-century Rome in his "Roma Sub Rosa" series beginning with *Roman Blood* (1991). The Egyptian religious perspective is worked into the adventures of Elizabeth Peters' Victorian Egyptologist/detective Amelia Peabody, as in *Crocodile on the Sandbank* (1988), *The Curse of the Pharaohs* (1981), and *The Mummy Case* (1985), and in Lynda S. Robinson's *Murder in the Place of Anubis* (1994), set during the fifth year of the rule of Pharaoh Tutankhamen.

Amerindian religion is increasingly appearing in such mysteries as Tony Hillerman's commanding novels following the exploits of his Navajo detecting team. *A Thief of Time* (1990), for example, deals with the desecration of sacred Native American burial cliffs, with one subtext involving the varying ways traditional and Christian Navajos view death. Terry Mullins' "People of Peace," published in *Ellery Queen's Mystery Magazine,* turns its intriguing plot on the impact of Hopi Indian mythology to define a tribal member's cultural understanding. When a Hopi rids the tribe of a murderer, he finds that his culture demands he must deal with his own "snake" side of evil. Cherokee Mardi Oakley Medawar has created a Kiowa healer, Tay-bodal, as protagonist for her *Death at Rainy Mountain* (1996). Although not himself religiously inclined, he works with medicine men who are. Respecting the psychological power of religion, at one point he even creates a prayer song to have "at least made an effort to seem a bit spiritual while I dealt with the physical." As reward, his patient mutters, "Do shut up. You have a terrible voice" (p. 36).

Even when it is not obviously central, a religious component is imbedded in many mysteries that feature Native American identity issues or deal with overt Amerindian and African-American power religions. These range from mysteries with characters who assume their heritage, like Gary Alexander's Mayan detective Luis Balam in *Blood Sacrifice* (1993); those who flee their heritage, like Jerome Charyn's Nez Percé descendant Joe Barbarossa in *Montezuma's Man* (1993); or those who separate their inherited racial identity from traditional religion's lethal underside, as Alex Abella's Cuban American, Charlie Morell, does in the Santeria-propelled novel *The Killing of the Saints* (1991). Even in mysteries with Anglo protagonists, like Gregory McDonald's *Carioca Fletch* (1984), for example, the Brazilian power religion Candomblé is central to the plot owing to the impact it exerts on the minds of the Brazilian characters.

Mostly, though, power religions like San-teria or the voodoo cults of numerous mysteries set in New Orleans (Allen Hubin lists sixty-four, sixty-seven more in Louisiana) or the threats of Satanists, as in Marilyn Wallace's chilling *Lost Angel* (1996), are there to color the plot. Sometimes, as in Peter Tremayne's mélange of mystery and monster horror tale, *Swamp* (1985), everything gets an outing, including voodoo, generic Amerindian faith—"I am at one with the Great Spirit and do his will," says one character (p. 142)—and even some fortuitous natural providence that strikes down with lightning at the penultimate moment a monster with the annoying habit of lunching on passersby in the Everglades. Wicca, too, figures regularly in mysteries. Some novels, like Susan Wittig Albert's *Witches' Bane* (1993), go to great lengths to separate New Age belief, witchcraft, and Satanism into distinct categories. Sax Rhomer's *The Dream-Detective* (1920), which incarnated Arthur Conan Doyle's fascination with the occult into an Edgar Cayce–like somnambulist who solved crimes as he exposed his "mind, a sensitive blank, to the etheric waves created here by mental emotion" (1925 ed., p. 145), is no longer such an oddity, despite the parabolic warnings of Dennis Wheatley's cautionary mysteries. Even religious manifestations that in the past might have served simply as lurid backdrops to a mystery, like the snake-handling cult of Ronald Levitsky's *The Wisdom of Serpents* (1992), receive a more thoughtful contemporary handling.

Exotic religious themes often pulsate on the far borders of the mystery, as in the appearance of Prester John and the Holy Grail in Charles Williams' *War in Heaven* (1930), the first created matter in his *Many Dimensions* (1931); sword and sorcery syncretism in Neal Stephenson's futuristic cyberspace sci-fi mystery hybrid about tracking down a lethal computer virus, *Snow Crash* (1992); and even a detecting nun, Sister Mary Magdalene of the Sisters of the Holy Nativity, investigating a murder among extraterrestrials in Randall Garrett's short story "A Little Intelligence." But even when the supernatural element appears to be all hoax, as in Hillary Waugh's "ghost" story *The Shadow Guest* (1971), still the mystery attests to one great supernatural message that is indispensable to the mundane: God, the Creator, is just and will demand an accounting for blood shed.

The Function of the Religious Mystery

An organization called Parents of Murdered Children has begun a letter-writing campaign entitled "Murder Is Not Entertainment." It challenges whether the vehicle of the mystery has become detrimental, searing the sensibility, just as theater, where women were forced to prostitute themselves and men to die in reality, wallowed in depravity in the last decadent ages of Rome. The organization was founded by a clergyman and a laywoman, after the bludgeoning death of their daughter. Introduced to other grieving parents of murder victims by a Roman Catholic counselor, Father Ken Czillinger, Lutheran minister Robert Hullinger and psychotherapist Charlotte Hullinger organized what today is a national group that supports surviving family members; advocates for lasting legal sanctions against murderers; and targets "businesses that exploit murder for profit," such as slasher-style motion pictures, murder-themed popular music, serial killer trading cards, murder mystery weekends, games like "How to Host a Murder," and murder mystery novels.

As current executive director Nancy Ruhe-Munch told Eric Schlosser, in "A Grief like No Other," "Can you imagine having a child-abuse game? Can you imagine having a rape mystery game? Everyone has to guess who's the serial rapist?" (p. 72). Parents of Murdered Children's challenge is one that every writer and reader of mystery novels needs to consider seriously in our increasingly violent contemporary age. Does the fiction we write and read serve to move the reader toward a repulsion to evil or toward attraction to its perversion? Does it provide a serious moral examination that edifies by detailing the ramifications of a violent act and moving the reader to act in ways that eliminate murder and protect other human beings or does it trivialize or glorify the horror of sin/crime, titillating the reader with a lurid attraction that makes the possibility of committing a similar act not so unthinkable?

In the late 1940s, Dr. Fredric Wertham, senior psychiatrist for the New York Department of Hospitals, levied a similar charge at crime comics. He concluded they impaired "the ethical development of children" (p. 72). Drawing from comic books supplied by his patients from their children's reading, he calculated that by the age of sixteen, reading an estimated average of eighteen comic books per week, a child in 1948 had "absorbed a minimum of 18,000 pictorial beatings, shootings, stranglings, and blood puddles and torturing to death from comic books alone" (p. 72).

Mike Benton, in an excellent chapter, "Guilty, Guilty, Guilty: Crime Comics on Trial," in his *Crime Comics: The Illustrated History*, quotes Wertham reflecting nearly thirty years later that his campaign was fueled by his experiences at a free psychiatric service for disturbed and delinquent youth he had founded in 1946. He noticed that violent impulses were stimulated by the social conditions surrounding the children with whom he worked and by the stabbings, beheadings, fatal beatings, and other depictions of slaughter that had become regular features of media like comics, "which feature all these kinds of cruelty and brutality." Children, he noticed, "lose their sense of the dignity of human life and the suffering of other people" (p. 72). The result of his campaign, and a wealth of corroborating testimony, was a congressional action that determined "this country cannot afford the calculated risk involved in feeding its children, through comic books, a concentrated diet of crime, horror, and violence" (p. 83).

Parents of Murdered Children is currently asking whether society can afford any diet of murder—whether made graphic in slasher films, lionized in trading cards, or luridly detailed in murder mystery novels—at any age level. If art is to govern itself, without the aid of governmental intervention, it needs to ask searching questions about its treatments of this ultimate affront to the Creator's gift of life and the sanctity of human existence.

In its best moments, the religious mystery attempts to reflect God at work in the present age, by imaging God's emissaries in the act of sorting sin from crime, meting out responsibility, and bringing justice, punishment, repentance, and restoration. These constructed figures serve different functions. Sometimes they champion faith as still intensely relevant in the indivisible moral dimension of our technological world. At other times they critique the worthiness of reflected religious custodians to perform the offices they have assumed. Further, the religious mystery serves as a continually reforming tool, taking the notion of God back again and again to be reexamined in the life and death crucible of capital crime. Murder is the antithesis to the creative act. It redefines the Creator by gauging creation's reaction.

When it achieves its intentions, the correct assurance of the religious dimension of the mystery is that God, who is just, is totally, eternally opposed to the unjust taking of human life. And God, who is merciful, is always relevant to and suffering with the agony of the human condition. Moreover, religious mysteries stand for humanity, blending a cry for caution against unbridled zeal, for tolerance, for humanization in an often dehumanizing world and, particularly, for looking beyond the power struggle of human greed and all the misery that comes from crushing, defrauding, or eliminating others for one individual's sordid, self-centered ends, to glimpse a higher divine intention for human existence. The message and motivating force of the religious mystery is simple yet profound. It is the assurance that God exists and has created this world for a purpose. God has set rules for life and will surely expose to justice those who break those rules, even though they disguise their actions behind innocence or righteousness so that nothing is as it appears.

Finally, it assures us by depiction that the one in tune with God's intentions should be counted on to point out truth and set things right. Jesus said that no one can serve two masters—God and murderous gain are not compatible. The religious mystery is often an extended illustration of that truth. In essence, the religious mystery is a parabolic exercise in rediscovering the true human priority: to live as God intended in peace with God and one's fellow human beings. If we do not, it assures us, either in a temporal or an eternal sense, justice will follow.

Selected Bibliography

RELIGIOUS MYSTERIES

JEWISH MYSTERIES

"Bel and the Dragon" and "Susanna." Apocrypha.

Kellerman, Faye. *The Ritual Bath.* New York: Arbor House, 1986.

Kemelman, Harry. *Friday the Rabbi Slept Late.* New York: Crown, 1964.

———. *The Nine Mile Walk.* New York: Putnam, 1967. Short stories.

———. *Wednesday the Rabbi Got Wet.* New York: Morrow, 1976.

Telushkin, Joseph. *The Unorthodox Murder of Rabbi Wahl.* New York: Bantam, 1987.

ROMAN CATHOLIC MYSTERIES

Allison, E. M. A. *Through the Valley of Death.* Garden City, N.Y.: Doubleday, 1983.

Black, Veronica. *A Vow of Silence.* New York: St. Martin's Press, 1990.

Catalan, Henri. *Soeur Angèle and the Embarrassed Ladies.* New York: Sheed & Ward, 1955.

Chesterton, G. K. *The Father Brown Omnibus.* New York: Dodd, Mead, 1951.

Eco, Umberto. *The Name of the Rose.* New York: Harcourt Brace Jovanovich, 1983.

Frazer, Margaret. *The Novice's Tale.* New York: Berkley, 1992.

Gilman, Dorothy. *A Nun in the Closet.* Garden City, N.Y.: Doubleday, 1975.

Goyne, Richard. *The Crime Philosopher.* London: Routledge and Kegan Paul, 1945.

Greeley, Andrew M. *Virgin and Martyr.* New York: Warner, 1985.

Harding, Paul. *The Nightingale Gallery*. New York: Morrow, 1991.

Harris, Lee. *The Good Friday Murder*. New York: Fawcett, 1992.

Holmes, H. H. *Nine Times Nine*. New York: Duell, 1940.

Holton, Leonard. *The Saint Maker*. New York: Dodd, Mead, 1959.

Hubbard, Margaret Ann. *Sister Simon's Murder Case*. Milwaukee: Bruce, 1959.

Kienzle, William. *The Rosary Murders*. Kansas City: Andrews and McMeel, 1979.

———. *Sudden Death*. Kansas City: Andrews and McMeel, 1985.

Love, William F. *The Chartreuse Clue*. New York: Finc, 1990.

McInerny, Ralph. *Her Death of Cold*. New York: Vanguard, 1977.

Moore, Brian. *The Color of Blood*. New York: Dutton, 1987.

Newman, Sharan. *Death Comes as Epiphany*. New York: Tor, 1993.

O'Marie, Carol Anne. *A Novena for Murder*. New York: Scribners, 1984.

Peters, Ellis. *A Morbid Taste for Bones*. London: Macmillan, 1977; New York: Morrow, 1978.

Quill, Monica. *Not a Blessed Thing*. New York: Vanguard, 1981.

Reach, Alice Scanlon. "Father Crumlish Celebrates Christmas." In *The Twelve Crimes of Christmas*. Edited by Carol-Lynn Rössel Waugh, Martin Harry Greenberg, and Isaac Asimov. New York: Avon, 1981.

Sullivan, Winona. *A Sudden Death at the Norfolk Cafe*. New York: St. Martin's Press, 1993.

Tremayne, Peter. *Absolution by Murder*. New York: St. Martin's Press, 1996.

PROTESTANT MYSTERIES

Alington, C. A. *Archdeacons Afloat*. London: Faber and Faber, 1946.

Chance, Stephen. *Septimus and the Danedyke Mystery*. London: Bodley, 1971; New York: Nelson, 1973.

Estabrook, Barry. *Bahama Heat*. New York: St. Martin's Press, 1991.

Fager, Chuck. *Murder Among Friends*. Falls Church, Va.: Kimo Press, 1993.

Gallison, Kate. *Bury the Bishop*. New York: Dell, 1995.

Head, Matthew. *The Cabinda Affair*. New York: Simon & Schuster, 1949.

Holland, Isabelle. *A Death at St. Anselm's*. Garden City, N.Y.: Doubleday, 1984.

Johnson, James. *Code Name Sebastian*. Philadelphia: Lippincott, 1967.

Mano, D. Keith. *Topless*. New York: Random House, 1991.

Martin, Robert E. *Vengeance Is Mine*. Newport, Vt.: REM, 1995.

Owens, Virginia Stem. *Congregation*. Grand Rapids, Mich.: Baker, 1992.

Scherf, Margaret. *Always Murder a Friend*. New York: Doubleday, 1948.

Smith, Charles Merrill. *Reverend Randollph and the Wages of Sin*. New York: Putnam, 1974.

Whitechurch, Victor Lorenzo. *The Crime at Diana's Pool*. New York: Duffield, 1927.

Williams, Charles. *War in Heaven*. London: Victor Gollancz, 1930; Grand Rapids, Mich.: Eerdmans, 1949.

OTHER RELIGIOUS VOICES AND OTHER SELECTED MYSTERIES

Abella, Alex. *The Killing of the Saints*. New York: Crown, 1991.

Albert, Susan Wittig. *Witches' Bane*. New York: Scribners, 1993.

Alexander, Gary. *Blood Sacrifice*. New York: Doubleday, 1993.

Biggers, Earl Derr. *Charlie Chan Carries On*. Indianapolis: Bobbs Merrill, 1930.

Charyn, Jerome. *Montezuma's Man*. New York: Mysterious Press, 1993.

Hillerman, Tony. *A Thief of Time*. New York: Harper & Row, 1988; 1990.

Keating, H. R. F. *The Perfect Murder*. London: Collins, 1964; New York: Dutton, 1965.

Levitsky, Ronald. *The Wisdom of Serpents*. New York: Scribners, 1992.

Lewis, Matthew Gregory. *The Monk*. New York: Grove, 1952; 1993.

Mann, Paul. *The Burning Ghats*. New York: Fawcett Columbine, 1996.

McDonald, Gregory. *Carioca Fletch*. New York: Warner, 1984.

Medawar, Mardi Oakley. *Death at Rainy Mountain*. New York: St. Martin's Press, 1996.

Melville, James. *A Haiku for Hanae*. New York: Scribners, 1989.

Montalbano, William D., and Carl Hiaasen. *A Death in China*. New York: Atheneum, 1984.

Mullins, Terry. "People of Peace." *Ellery Queen's Mystery Magazine* 96, no. 2: 103–114 (August 1990).

Peters, Elizabeth. *Crocodile on the Sandbank*. New York: Dodd, Mead, 1975; Mysterious Press, 1988.

Rhomer, Sax. *The Dream-Detective*. London: Jarrolds, 1920; New York: Doubleday, 1925.

Robinson, Lynda S. *Murder in the Place of Anubis*. New York: Walker, 1994.

Saylor, Stephen. *Roman Blood*. New York: St. Martin's Press, 1991.

Stephenson, Neal. *Snow Crash*. New York: Bantam, 1992.

Tremayne, Peter. *Swamp*. Surrey, England: Severn House, 1985.

Wallace, Marilyn. *Lost Angel*. New York: Doubleday, 1996.

Waugh, Hillary. *The Shadow Guest.* Garden City, N.Y.: Doubleday, 1971.

CRITICAL STUDIES

Aird, Catherine. "The Devout: Vicars, Curates, and Relentlessly Inquisitive Clerics." In *Murder Ink.* Edited by Dilys Winn. New York: Workman, 1984.

Bargainnier, Earl F. *Comic Crime.* Bowling Green, Ohio: Bowling Green State University Popular Press, 1987.

———. "Matthew Head's Dr. Mary Finney and Hooper Taliaferro Novels." In *Mysteries of Africa.* Edited by Eugene Schleh. Bowling Green, Ohio: Bowling Green State University Popular Press, 1991.

Barzun, Jacques, and Wendell Hertig Taylor. *A Catalogue of Crime.* New York: Harper, 1971.

Basney, Lionel. "Detective Stories." *Christianity Today,* 30 August 1974.

Benton, Mike. *Crime Comics: The Illustrated History.* Dallas: Taylor, 1993.

Breen, Jon L., and Martin H. Greenberg. *Synod of Sleuths: Essays on Judeo-Christian Detective Fiction.* Metuchen, N.J.: Scarecrow, 1990.

———. "Introduction." In *The Fine Art of Murder.* Edited by Ed Gorman, Martin H. Greenberg, Larry Segriff, and Jon L. Breen. New York: Carroll & Graf, 1993.

Cleary, Maryell. "Contemporary Clergy-Detectives." *The Mystery Fancier* 9, no. 3 (May/June 1987).

Dove, George N. *The Police Procedural.* Bowling Green, Ohio: Bowling Green State University Popular Press, 1982.

Eco, Umberto. *Postscript to* The Name of the Rose. New York: Harcourt Brace Jovanovich, 1984.

Gavrell, Kenneth. "The Worst 'Great' Detective Story." *Clues* 18: 39–43 (spring/summer 1997).

Haycraft, Howard. *Murder for Pleasure: The Life and Times of the Detective Story.* New York: Appleton Century, 1941.

Holton, Leonard. "Father Bredder." In *The Great Detectives.* Edited by Otto Penzler. Boston: Little, Brown, 1978.

Hubin, Allen J. *Crime Fiction: 1749–1980.* New York: Garland, 1984.

McInerny, Ralph. "Saints Preserve Us: The Catholic Mystery." In *The Fine Art of Murder.* Edited by Ed Gorman, Martin H. Greenberg, Larry Segriff, and Jon L. Breen. New York: Carroll & Graf, 1993.

O'Marie, Carol Anne. "A Habit for Murder." *Mystery Readers of America Journal* (spring 1987). Quoted in *Synod of Sleuths.* Edited by Jon L. Breen and Martin H. Greenberg. Metuchen, N.J.: Scarecrow, 1990.

Packer, J. I. "'Tecs, Thrillers, and Westerns." *Christianity Today,* 8 November 1985.

Sayers, Dorothy L. "Introduction." In *The Omnibus of Crime.* New York: Payson and Clarke, 1929.

Schlosser, Eric. "A Grief like No Other." *The Atlantic Monthly,* 1 September 1997: 37–76.

Siegel, Jeff. *The American Detective: An Illustrated History.* Dallas: Taylor, 1993.

Spencer, William David. *Mysterium and Mystery: The Clerical Crime Novel.* Carbondale: Southern Illinois Univ. Press, 1989. Includes a bibliography of clerical crime novels.

———. "Lady Justice." *Priscilla Papers* 3, no. 3: 12–13 (summer 1989).

———. "The Clerical Crime Novel's Cinematic Struggle." *Clues* 15, no. 1: 3–21 (spring/summer 1994).

Stevens, Serita. "The Jewish Mystery." In *The Fine Art of Murder.* Edited by Ed Gorman, Martin H. Greenberg, Larry Segriff, and Jon L. Breen. New York: Carroll & Graf, 1993.

Tani, Stefano. *The Doomed Detective: The Contribution of the Detective Novel to Postmodern American and Italian Literature.* Carbondale: Southern Illinois Univ. Press, 1984.

Winks, Robin, ed. *Detective Fiction.* Englewood Cliffs, N.J.: Prentice-Hall, 1980.

———. *Modus Operandi: An Excursion into Detective Fiction.* Boston: Godine, 1982.

"Door Interview: Andrew Greeley." *The Wittenburg Door* (June/July 1982).

Yaffe, James. "Is This Any Job for a Nice Jewish Boy?" In *Synod of Sleuths.* Edited by Jon L. Breen and Martin H. Greenberg. Metuchen, N.J.: Scarecrow, 1990.

THE ROMANTIC SUSPENSE MYSTERY

JENNIFER CRUSIE SMITH

ROMANTIC SUSPENSE IS a balanced hybrid of two powerful genres, the mystery story and the romance novel, so intertwined that neither can be removed without fundamental damage to both plot and theme. The classic mystery plot question, "Who is the killer?" complements the classic romance plot question, "Who is the right man?" increasing the consequences for both. For if the heroine mistakenly identifies the hero as the killer, she loses his love, and if she mistakenly identifies the killer as the right man, she loses her life. Although this genre is often ignored by scholars (many encyclopedias and historical studies of mystery fiction refuse to admit it exists), and when not ignored denigrated (as Gothics, Had-I-But-Known [HIBK] stories, Girl-Gets-House books, and, worst of all, romance novels), the romantic suspense novel has been popular for over two hundred years because of the elasticity of its conventions and because of the continuing relevance of its basic premise: women in patriarchal culture have a lot to fear, particularly from the men they marry.

Conventions

The conventions of the genre evolve across time as women's changing social position demands, but because they combine to create the archetypal dilemma for the heroine, most of them occur in some form in romantic suspense stories. These conventions include a heroine, usually young and naive, and always vulnerable because of inexperience (she is a virgin), lack of protectors (she is an orphan), class position (she is a governess), money (she is penniless), or all of the above. In eighteenth- and nineteenth-century gothics, she is a supporting character meant to arouse pity and horror by her plight, as the males in the text act as protagonist and antagonist; in most modern romantic suspense, she is the protagonist, often claiming the entire story as her own with her first-person point of view.

The hero is usually older but not old, often Byronic, and always posing a danger to the heroine because of experience (he is a rake), family position (he is heir to the mansion or already owns it, his family has been in the county for generations and can get away with murder), class position (he has a title), money (he is rolling in it), or all of the above. In twentieth-century romantic suspense, he often appears as a false antagonist because he is condescending, rude, remote, or sexually demanding of the heroine.

Imposing, confining architecture, usually belonging to the hero or to the mentor-father defined below, frames the stories. Theoretically a reflection of the strength and security of the social structure within which the heroine moves, these abbeys, castles, and mansions are complex, dangerous structures controlled by the men who have built and inherited them, most of whom are almost pathologically dedicated to their preservation. The house is the most powerful symbol of the romantic suspense novel, which explains why the derogatory term "Girl-Gets-House" actually reflects one of the most important symbolic moves in the genre: the heroine assuming control of her society and environment.

Hostile natural conditions in the form of storms, barren moors, wild forests, and foreign settings (foreign to the heroine, that is) add to the mood of the books and are often accompanied by supernatural elements that may or may not be logically explained at the end of the book. These conditions symbolize the sexuality in the conflict and prevent the heroine from escaping the confining architecture: it may be bad inside but it is a jungle outside. The climax of a romantic suspense novel is sometimes precipitated when the heroine decides to leave because the wilderness, wildness, and sexuality she does not know is preferable to the prison that is suffocating her.

Often, a much older male character implicitly or explicitly offers himself as a mentor or substitute father to the heroine, then betrays her by pursuing her sexually or trying to destroy her in order to obtain or retain property. This means the sexual advances often have incestuous undertones, a subtext common in the romantic literature that first inspired the genre. A variation on this is the older female character who offers herself as a substitute mother to the heroine, then fails her because of lack of knowledge or power, or betrays her because the mother figure has aligned herself with the male elements in the story, particularly the betraying father. This failure of parenting often precipitates the heroine's growth from child-woman to adult.

A child, even more vulnerable than the heroine, may reflect the heroine's persona and ultimately inspire her to assume an adult role in order to save him or her. This character becomes more prevalent as society begins to devalue the childlike woman and privilege strong, independent heroines; the child then becomes the strong heroine's Achilles heel, for she cannot desert the child as parent figures have deserted her, even though she is now capable of extricating herself from the dangerous situation by leaving.

Taken together, these conventions make the romantic suspense novel a bildungsroman for women, an archetypal story of the Other who moves from innocence to experience and masters her environment through her growth. The mocking HIBK label ignores the fact that "Had I but known . . ." implies the rest of the line: ". . . what I know now," the premise of every rite-of-passage story since time began. Therefore, although the quality of the work in this subgenre varies wildly from author to author, its pull upon the female reader remains constant as it reinvents its archetypal premise across decades. A closer look at how the genre has evolved shows not only its infinite variety but also its complexity.

The Forerunners

The roots of romantic suspense lie in the gothic novel of the late-eighteenth and early-nineteenth centuries. Horace Walpole's *The Castle of Otranto* (1765) named the genre with its subtitle, *A Gothic Story*, which referred to the medieval setting, but "gothic" quickly came to mean macabre stories of terror and the supernatural set in large, eerie buildings in which helpless virgins were preyed upon by powerful, corrupt men. The symbols were there from the beginning: emotional and sexual turmoil and mystery were reflected in the stormy weather and the supernatural elements; the villains represented perversions of protective roles such as fathers and priests; and the architecture, usually castles and abbeys, symbolized the imprisoning powers of the male-dominated social structure. Gothic fiction was born in a world where women could not vote or own property, a world in which they were instead the property of their fathers and husbands, and therefore utterly at the mercy of the men in their lives. Small wonder, then, that the stories that blatantly acted out their very real fears became so popular with women readers.

Walpole's *Otranto* is a classic in the genre: a young noblewoman, Isabella, is pursued by Manfred, the lascivious father of her dead fiancé, and tries to escape by fleeing through the vault of his castle, where she is aided by a mysterious young man. In the climax, Manfred tries to stab her to death and instead kills his own daughter, and the mysterious young man is revealed to be not only highborn but the true owner of the castle, which becomes Isabella's when she marries him. The social mores that are supposed to protect women are clearly absent or reversed: Manfred murders his daughter; breaks his marriage vows and discards his wife to pursue Isabella; and threatens his daughter-in-law who, left unprotected by her absent father, is forced to rely on a stranger for her survival. With *Otranto*, Walpole set up the central premise of romantic suspense—choose the men in your life wisely or die—and other gothic novels soon followed.

Ann Radcliffe's *The Mysteries of Udolpho* (1794) features another virginal noblewoman, the orphaned and therefore unprotected Emily, who is carried off to a remote castle by the nearest thing she has to a father figure, her aunt's husband. Emily is rescued and finds true love. But sometimes the betrayal is so complete that the woman's struggles are to no avail. In M. G. Lewis's *The Monk* (1796), the virginal Antonia is raped in a vaulted tomb and murdered by her confessor and spiritual father. The Monk gets his retribution in the end, first from the Inquisition and then from the Devil, but the central message is still the same as Walpole's and the same as all romantic suspense novels for the next two centuries.

These early gothics were wildly popular, but they were often derided because of their theatricality and lack of realism. Jane Austen took this criticism to task in *Northanger Ab-*bey (1818), the first feminist gothic, in which she moves the gothic heroine from the role of supporting character-victim to center stage in her own rite-of-passage plot. Austen's protagonist, Catherine, a passionate reader of gothics, is invited to the home of her potential suitor, Henry, and there she meets Henry's father, the General, a remote and forbidding widower. Catherine adds together the abbey, the missing wife-mother, and the cruel patriarch, and decides the old man murdered his wife or, at the very least, has her locked up somewhere. Unwisely sharing this theory with Henry, she is told in no uncertain terms that this is England, the General is an Englishman, and she has been reading too many trashy novels. Properly chastised, Catherine backs off, only to find herself evicted and abandoned seventy miles from her home by the General when he discovers she is not an heiress. Although *Northanger Abbey* is often cited as a satire of the genre, Austen clearly demonstrates the truth of the central theme of the gothic, as she has Catherine realize that "in suspecting General Tilney of either murdering or shutting up his wife, she had scarcely sinned against his character or magnified his cruelty." Only when she discards the lessons she has learned from her novels and trusts the male authority of Henry and his father does Catherine become a victim; clearly Catherine's reading of romantic suspense has taught her the truth about her world.

Two other nineteenth-century masterpieces also used the gothic tradition to warn of the perfidy of patriarchal culture. Charlotte Brontë's *Jane Eyre* and Emily Brontë's *Wuthering Heights* (both published in 1847) built on existing gothic conventions and utilized Austen's female protagonist and modern English realistic setting, but they enriched the complexity of the genre by incorporating the Byronic hero into the mix. Although the absent or incompetent father is still in the picture (not surprising, given the Brontës' own patriarch), the real menace now comes from the hero, who may rescue or betray the heroine, depending on how his day has gone.

The Byronic hero has always been dangerous—Byron's dramatic poem *Manfred* is the cry of a man tormented forever because he killed his sister-lover—but in the romantic suspense story he becomes the Devil himself, the sexual fate to which the heroine dares not succumb, but to which she is inexorably drawn. Selfish, remote, and sexually predatory, he is driven by passion to terrible betrayals that the heroine must withstand because he is the hero, the man she is meant to love. In *Jane Eyre,* Rochester imprisons his wife in his attic and tries to lure Jane into a bigamous marriage; in *Wuthering Heights,* Heathcliff brutalizes his wife, persecutes his daughter-in-law, and pursues his great love, Catherine, even after her death. There is no one to rescue these women because the men who should save them, their heroes, are also their tormentors. Therefore, the Brontës' contribution to the genre was to fuse the hero and the villain so that the heroine must rescue both herself and him, redeeming the hero by defeating the villain within him and thereby making him safe for her to love: Jane denies Rochester while he is powerful and patriarchal and accepts him only when he is broken, humble, and respectful of women; Catherine's placeholder, her namesake daughter, redeems the boy whom Heathcliff has perverted in his own image and coaches him until he is safe for her to marry.

The romantic suspense novel continued to be wildly popular, drawing writers like Wilkie Collins to its success (see separate essay). Collins' *The Woman in White* (1860) is the story of a brave woman, Marian Halcombe, who with the aid of the noble Walter, rescues her sister Laura from the hands of her lethal husband. Collins deals with the oxymoron of the powerful Victorian female character by splitting his heroine: strong and noble Marian defeats the villains and good but wimpy Laura gets Walter. In Collins' *The Moonstone* (1868), Rachel Verinder is much more passive than Marian. She sees Franklin, the man she loves, steal a valuable jewel from her room but says and does nothing in the hopes that everything will work out well. She is therefore worthy to be married to Franklin once he has saved her and his innocence is made clear. Both novels feature young frightened women, uncommunicative heroes, confining structures, supernatural terrors that turn out to have rational explanations, and threatening authority figures, and both also heighten the subliminal sexuality that infuses most gothics; the repressed sexuality in *The Moonstone* is almost hysterical in its intensity.

Equally intense in repressed sexuality, but infinitely more complex psychologically, is Henry James's great novel, *The Turn of the Screw* (1898). James chose a classic gothic heroine, a governess, and sent her to a classic gothic house, Bly, owned by a classic gothic hero who is both sexually compelling and distant and who wants the heroine to care for his orphaned niece and nephew. Something is gothically wrong at Bly; ghosts appear, the children are threatened, and the governess digs in her heels to save her charges and win the esteem of her employer. But James is much more interested in what the gothic story means to the governess than he is in following out the cathartic plot. Are the ghosts something the governess has imagined? If they are real, has she conjured them up through her repressed sexuality? And are the children possessed or simply evil, particularly the little boy Miles who draws the governess' sexual energy to himself? James later wrote that of course the ghosts were real, but even this does not answer all the questions he raised about the gothic heroine's psychology, particularly in the realms of sexuality and possession.

These gothic novels of the nineteenth century are clearly the ancestors of the modern romantic suspense novel. The conventions they established shifted and evolved but the essential theme of the genre remained relevant and powerful throughout the next century, reflecting changing social roles for women while staying true to the premise that all love stories are also potentially death stories.

The Golden Age

The Golden Age of mystery fiction was also a golden age for romantic suspense. Although social conditions had improved for women—their place in the outside world was strengthened by their contributions during the wars—the basic inequities between women and men were still in place, and the same dangerous tension remained: a woman without a man was still terribly vulnerable, and a woman with the wrong man could still end up terribly dead. The Golden Age romantic suspense writer told stories of innocent and unworldly women who wised up and became worldly so they could go on breathing, but who did so subversively so they would not be punished for being too pushy. Known in the early-twentieth century as the Had-I-But-Known school after its protagonists' annoying habit of saying "Had I but known what lurked in the attic, I would never have gone up those stairs," romantic suspense was sneered at just as its gothic precursors had been reviled, but the nickname was a good reflection of what these stories were about: experience, regret, and education. Although the Golden Age gothics usually end with the female protagonist saved by and married to the hero, she also clearly and subversively acts and grows within her own plot, and the mystery she solves is often thematically more important than the romance she achieves.

The first great romantic suspense novelist of the Golden Age was Mary Roberts Rinehart (1876–1958). Like her classic romantic heroines, Rinehart's life was inspired and formed by the men in her life. Her uncle encouraged her to write fiction, her short-story editor encouraged her to write a novel, the difficult pregnancies and births of her three sons gave her the time to imagine and the background for her hospital stories, and her husband's speculation with their money gave her the reason to do what women of her class and time rarely did, pursue a career and make money. She wrote three suspense novels at the beginning of her career; her editor first

published the best, *The Circular Staircase* (1908), and she became an instant success. Hardworking, prolific, and absolutely traditional in her values and gender roles, Mary Roberts Rinehart was a good writer who entertained millions of readers and a "good" woman who was successful without threatening the status quo.

The Circular Staircase is the finest example of her work. It begins with spinster Rachel Innes' voice: "This is the story of how a middle-aged spinster lost her mind," and goes on to showcase Rachel's awakening to the potential of life through the threatening events she encounters in a large old house she rents for the summer with her niece and nephew. Middle-aged Rachel is not allowed a romance plot (although one is there subtextually anyway); that is reserved for the young people. But Rachel does become fully aware of her strength and independence as an adult through her exertions to protect her family (after a midnight trip to a graveyard to exhume a body, proper Rachel wonders if she has ever really experienced life), and she ends up triumphant on the roof of the house having foiled the killer and saved herself. Rachel can do this and retain her independence because she is not young: as an older spinster Rachel is outside the restrictions that would prevent a young heroine from experiencing that kind of growth and insisting on that kind of independence. She never appeared in another book, but her literary sister is Letitia Carberry who became one of Rinehart's series characters. Rinehart continued to write best-sellers, firmly establishing the genre of romantic suspense in its twentieth-century popular incarnation. For that she is universally recognized as the mother of modern romantic suspense.

Like a good mother, Rinehart inspired others to follow her. Writers like Mabel Seeley (b. 1903) wrote well-received romantic suspense that reflected the new freedoms and old restrictions for women. Seeley's *The Listening House* (1938), for example, changes the architecture from a male-controlled power structure to the female-controlled community of Mrs. Garr's boarding house, but heroine Gwynne is young, divorced (without protection), jobless, and stuck in a threatening environment: she fantasizes that the house is alive, listening for something, and wakes one night to find someone's hands around her throat. Dorothy MacCardle (b. 1889) also drew on the powerful gothic form for *The Uninvited* (1942), in which a young invalid (male this time) is haunted by two ghostly maternal figures, Mary and Carmen, who are struggling from beyond the grave for the soul of the childlike woman he loves. The haunted house, vulnerable protagonist (both hero and heroine this time), and failed parent figures are not the only gothic elements: he also faces the classic decision of whom to love and whom to reject as he investigates the two dead women to discover which is the deserving mother and which is the soul-sucking demon. The climax is a chilling confrontation between the hero and the malevolent mother as they struggle for possession of the girl who can only achieve adulthood through leaving her mother for marriage.

Seeley and MacCardle were joined by Doris Miles Disney (see "Women of Mystery" article) Mignon Eberhart (see separate article), Dorothy Eden, and Leslie Ford in writing classic Golden Age romantic fiction, but the strengths of the genre can most easily be seen in the work of three authors who took advantage of the genre's elasticity by playing with the conventions to explore new aspects of its theme.

Georgette Heyer Rougier (1902–1974) wrote brilliantly funny Regency romances as Georgette Heyer, but between 1932 and 1953 she also wrote twelve equally brilliant Golden Age mystery novels with strong romantic subplots that were the bright-young-thing interpretation of the gothic novel. Heyer was a bright-young-thing herself: Elaine Bander describes her as "attractive, unusually tall, intellectually arrogant, and caustic," with an "acerbic wit," a description that also fits some of her heroines and all her heroes (p. 157). The Heyer romantic suspense novel features an intelligent, exasperated young woman who struggles to protect those she loves while she is alternately blocked and aided by the hero, best described as Byronic Lite, who uses cunning and misdirection to manipulate events and save the day without ever breaking a sweat. So Stella in *Behold, Here's Poison* (1936) is stuck in the family home protecting her dysfunctional and unworthy family after her despicable uncle is poisoned, while her cousin Randall, whom Stella describes as "an amiable snake . . . smooth and fanged," works behind the scenes to save her and in front of the scenes to annoy her, leaving her as torn as any Eve in her quandary about trusting him (p. 34). Heyer's fast pacing and ironic dialogue mask this central sexual conflict, melding mystery and romance under increasing pressure until at roughly the same time that the masks and deceptions of her killers break down, so do the masks and deceptions of her lovers. Heyer's smart, slick style took the gothic gloom out of the genre and demonstrated its excellent and hitherto explored potential for comedy and satire.

Vera Caspary (1899–1987) also tweaked the genre in her greatest novel, *Laura* (1943). A self-made woman who skipped college to spare her father the expense, Caspary worked her way up from stenographer to advertising copywriter (her heroine Laura's profession) to New York editor of *Dance* magazine by the time she was twenty-four. She published her first novel four years later, followed by three others by the time she was thirty-one. She then turned to plays for stage and screen, including the hit screenplays *Les Girls* (1957), *A Letter to Three Wives* (1949), and *I Can Get It for You Wholesale* (1951). During this period she also began writing mysteries, the first and best of which was *Laura*, a multi-viewpoint modern gothic that owes much to Caspary's cinematic experience.

As Caspary's novel begins, her heroine Laura is dead, her face mutilated in a savage shooting at the door to her apartment, and her story is being told by an urbane older man, Waldo Lydecker, Laura's mentor in New York society. Lydecker describes Laura to the coldly skeptical detective on the case, Mark

MacPherson, as a fawn-like innocent; Mac-Pherson, drawing on his own investigations, describes her as a two-timing dame. Together they reverse the romantic suspense convention of hero and heroine, giving Laura the duality of the Byronic hero, the dangerous, unknowable, yet irresistible Other. As Lydecker puts it: "the activities of crooks and racketeers . . . seem simple in comparison with the motives of a modern woman" (p. 17). Caspary also plays with the convention of the male-dominated house that confines the heroine. Here the architecture that obsesses is Laura's apartment: Lydecker walks by every night, while MacPherson with the advantage of police access enters her space, sits before her portrait, reads her books, and listens to her music. Yet they also assume the classic roles of betraying older mentor and cynical younger hero, adding a generational jealousy that enriches the conflict: Lydecker watches MacPherson's attempts to catch Laura's killer, saying of the detective, "he was the man I should have been, the hero of the story" (p. 21).

In part two, no-nonsense MacPherson takes over the narrative as he goes back to Laura's apartment after her funeral, falls asleep, and wakes to find her standing in front of him. There has been a huge mistake, Laura is not dead, an enemy of hers has been killed instead. Here the story becomes male gothic, as MacPherson is caught in the classic dilemma: is she the right woman or is she the killer? Part three is a brief stenographer's report in which Laura's ne'er-do-well fiancé implicates her in the murder, an odd stylistic interruption, which Caspary seems to have added for plot purposes more than effect. Part four reverts to classic romantic suspense as Laura narrates her struggle to determine which of the men in her life, mentor or detective, she can trust. Laura's narrative is inextricably tied to her gender; like any good heroine of romantic suspense, she mixes her mystery plot equally with her romance plot as she chooses the detective:

When they ask me, "Did you return on Friday night to kill her, Laura?" I shall answer, "He hasn't the face of a man who would lie and flirt to get a confession" and when they ask me about ringing the bell and waiting at the door for her to come and be killed, I shall tell them that I wish, more than anything in the world, that I had met him before this happened. (p. 198)

Part five is climax and denouement, which belongs to MacPherson, who narrates a classic obligatory scene of romantic suspense, the struggle between younger hero and older authority figure for possession of the heroine.

Laura owes much of its success to clever plotting and tight cinematic structure, but the aspect that most makes it a classic is the vivid handling of the voices of the heroine, hero, and villain, as each struggles through the gothic plot of gender betrayal and darkness. Caspary seems to be arguing that all relationships are romantic suspense, and the beleaguered protagonist is determined not by gender but by the narrator. But Caspary and Heyer were not the only Golden Age writers to explore the alternatives inherent in the romantic suspense form; Daphne du Maurier (b. 1907; see separate essay) put such a distinctive stamp on the genre that her novel has become the Ur-gothic of the twentieth century.

Du Maurier's *Rebecca* (1938) is the first romantic suspense novel based on the premise that the danger is not without but within. Du Maurier's family included her grandfather George, who wrote the enormously successful novel *Trilby*, and her father Gerald, a very popular actor whom she adored. The weight of the name links her to her heroine in *Rebecca*. Although the first-person narrator-heroine never gives her name to the reader, she does to Maxim de Winter, her future husband, who tells her, "You have a very lovely and unusual name." She replies, "My father was a lovely and unusual person." That du Maurier was proud of her history is undeniable; she wrote her father's biography and a history of the family. That she also was haunted by it is reflected in her heroine who is oppressed, not by her Byronic hero, but by the memory of one who died before her.

Although de Winter's first wife, Rebecca, is dead before the book opens, psychically she is more alive than the nameless heroine. The story is classic romantic suspense in its premise: a young penniless woman is swept off her feet by a brooding, dark aristocrat, Maxim de Winter, who proposes by saying, "I'm asking you to marry me, you little fool," and when she confesses her love in return, tells her, "It's a pity you have to grow up." He takes his child-bride to his mansion in equally brooding Cornwall, giving her one of the greatest first lines in twentieth-century literature: "Last night I dreamt I went to Manderley again." But once the heroine gets to gothic Manderley, she finds not a betraying father figure but a punishing mother figure, the housekeeper, Mrs. Danvers, who loves the drowned Rebecca, the last Mrs. de Winter, with a passion that death cannot obliterate. Maxim has rescued the heroine from her living burial as a paid companion, but in marrying her buries her again, entombed not by a silly, stupid rich woman but by the relentless memory of the full-blooded Rebecca.

Thus du Maurier's version of the gothic conflict shifts the struggle from male versus female to female versus female. Although de Winter is Byronic, he is softened by his guilt and his love for the heroine, and while the heroine often feels reviled and neglected by him, she does not feel endangered by him. The danger comes from Rebecca, who makes her feel inferior from beyond the grave. For in Rebecca, du Maurier created the perfect woman that every real woman knows she is not, a sort of gothic Martha Stewart in the face of whom the heroine can only throw up her hands and admit defeat. Thus, in that struggle from innocence to experience that every heroine has to make, du Maurier's heroine must break through not the barrier of male bias, but that of her own internalized female bias. The enemy, du Maurier argues, is not the easily defeated male without (de Winter is much more victim than aggressor in this story) but the overwhelming sense of inferiority within.

Unfortunately, this independent premise is undercut by the agency by which du Maurier's heroine achieves full adulthood. Although she collects enough anecdotal evidence to know that there was something terribly wrong about Rebecca, she is not set free until de Winter confesses that he not only loathed Rebecca but also murdered her. The combination of the knowledge that Rebecca does not hold her loved one's heart and the threat of her husband's imminent arrest catapults the heroine to the adulthood that must climax the romantic suspense story. She dominates and defeats the malevolent Mrs. Danvers and becomes a maternal support to her husband, telling him, "I've grown up, Maxim, in twenty-four hours. I'll never be a child again" (p. 318). De Winter is not completely thrilled with this—"It's gone forever, that funny, young, lost look that I loved. . . . You are so much older"—but he leans on her anyway as she cements their partnership by telling him to shut up and quit confessing: "We are the only two people in the world to know, Maxim. You and I." When his only reply to this is a passive and reiterated "Yes," the heroine takes possession of what was once Rebecca's and thereby assumes adulthood, admitting in a *Jane Eyre*–like reflective moment, "I suppose it is his dependence upon me that has made me bold at last" (p. 10).

Left here, *Rebecca* would be an interesting variation on the psychology of the romantic suspense novel, directly addressing for the first time the danger within, but du Maurier incorporates one last twist that elevates this novel to another plane entirely. The book ends as the weary and now fully exonerated lovers drive home and notice an odd glow to the west, and her husband drives faster, telling her, "That's Manderley," as the wind blows ashes toward them in the last sentence. This ending would seem abrupt were it not for that famous beginning, "Last night I dreamed I went to Manderley again," making the novel a circle, the story of a woman who must psychically return again and again to the place she never quite occupied and to the woman who represents the side of herself she will never accept. For Rebecca is a name, a place, a passion, and a history that the reflective narrator can never claim, subsumed as she is in her husband's desperation for an uncomplicated woman and a quiet life: "our little hotel is dull, and the food indifferent, and . . . day after day dawns very much the same," adding to this dismal category, "yet we would not have it otherwise" (p. 6). Du Maurier's heroine has a superficially happy ending, but because she must repress a part of herself to achieve it, she must return to her story again, trying to claim the house she has lost and the self she will not recognize.

The gothic plot was so well established by the time du Maurier wrote *Rebecca* that a plagiarism suit against her was thrown out of court because of the ubiquity of the plot. Had they but known what lay ahead, the plaintiffs would never have brought the suit at all, because the boom in romantic suspense was only beginning.

The Gothic Revival

The questions the best of the Golden Age romantic suspense writers raised were all but forgotten in the complacency of the mid-twentieth century, as political changes in the lives of women spurred the return of the genre to its gothic roots. In the conservative backlash of the postwar period, women were returned to the home and encouraged to be feminine instead of independent, a loss of freedom that made those old stories about women trapped in castles suddenly relevant again. Although the novels in this genre were still referred to as HIBKs, the continued importance of the architecture and the heroines' propensity for taking possession of the castle through marriage led to a new nickname, "Girl-Gets-House," a tag that was meant to belittle but actually pinpoints the theme. For in taking possession of the house in which she is terrorized, the heroine takes control over her world and becomes mistress of her own life in a conservatively accepted way; after all, women were *supposed* to be in their houses.

Although most of the romantic suspense of this time hewed closely to classic form, there was one important addition, the threatened child, prompted in part by the growing importance of children in the culture, and even more by the wider although still limited freedom women retained. For romantic suspense writers now had a new problem; by the 1950s, there was no reason for the gothic heroine not to look around and say, "This place is dangerous and I'm gone." The addition of the child to the plot meant she could not leave without becoming an abandoning mother figure, so the child becomes part of the house that holds her, and in rescuing the child, the romantic suspense heroine makes her own transition from child-woman to adult by assuming maternal responsibility. This alliance with a helpless child was powerful because it increased reader identification, made the heroine more of an active and selfless player in the text, and insured that the denouement would find the heroine not only in possession of a house and a husband but also, automatically, a family, the prefeminist utopia.

Because it played out this fantasy for its female readers, the gothic revival was huge: in 1973, gothics accounted for five percent of all paperback fiction sold. The big names in the field included Victoria Holt, Jane Aiken Hodge, Dorothy B. Hughes, Velda Johnston, and Phyllis Whitney, all writing variations on the gothic plot that put a woman in a nightgown running away from a big house at midnight on the cover of millions of books. The most skilled and most influential of all was Mary Stewart.

Mary Stewart (b. 1916) did not begin writing until 1949, when she realized "this I could do, this I must do," and began her career as a gothic novelist. Her bachelor's degree with honors and her later master's degree provided first a job as a lecturer at her alma mater, Durham University, and later the foundation for the effortless prose and warm characterization of her novels. She resisted categorizing her work, not from any lack of respect for the gothic genre but because she preferred to write the stories and let others categorize them. Her first ten novels, however, are clearly romantic suspense, a form she returned to after writing several children's books and while finishing her popular Arthurian trilogy. Stewart's lack of interest in formula and her canonical education, in combination with her innate interest in escapist literature—she said that she did not want anyone made troubled or unhappy by her stories—led her to write classic romantic suspense without becoming a gothic factory. Her books generally feature the same spirited, intelligent heroine in her twenties in a foreign land, who aids a stranger and in doing so finds herself drawn into his troubles. All her books are well written and engaging; *Nine Coaches Waiting* (1958) is representative of her work.

The heroine of *Coaches* is Linda Martin, an intelligent, orphaned young woman who longs to return to France, her home before her parents were killed. Hired by Madame de Valmy, a wealthy French aristocrat, to be governess to her orphaned nephew, Linda is taken to a beautiful mansion that turns out to be owned not by de Valmy but by her nephew, a seven-year-old named Phillipe. Madame's husband, Leon, a once vital man now confined to a wheel chair, is a failed parent, treating Phillipe with coldness and disdain, and as the plot unfolds, the heroine begins to suspect that he is trying to kill her charge. Into the mix comes Leon's son Raoul, driving a car too fast and almost running the heroine down. He is the archetypal Byronic hero—when he has kissed the heroine against her will and she protests, he laughs it off with "Don't be so Sabine, darling"—too like his father to be trusted and too attractive to ignore. As Linda moves through her plot, she falls in love with Raoul, but when she is told that he is part of the plot to kill Phillipe, she abandons love to protect the boy, breaking the chain of absent or abusive parents and moving into an adult role. Her courage and her maternal success win her the devotion of the hero after all, and the denouement of the book promises that hero, heroine, and child will be secure together as a family.

Stewart's early patterns in romantic suspense in the fifties and sixties are echoed in the book she wrote when she returned to the genre in 1988, but *Thornyhold* shows some radical and important departures. Stewart's heroine Geillis has the requisite deprived childhood, but Stewart now dwells on this aspect directly in the narrative instead of in revealed back story, showing the combination of circumstances, history, and parenting that made Geillis the complicated and haunted creature she is when she inherits Thornyhold, the house of her fey aunt. The bone-deep satisfaction that Geillis feels as she takes possession carefully but thoroughly of several rooms of her own is reinforced by the pride she feels as she also takes possession of her aunt's legacy of healing and mystery. Her reward for claiming her place and herself comes when she meets the hero for the first time, more than halfway through the narrative. Instead of discovering herself through the agency of the hero and being rewarded with the house, she discovers herself through the agency of the house and her matriarchal tradition and is rewarded with the hero, his charming son, and children of her own. In both *Thornyhold* and her earlier romantic suspense novels, Stewart's writing skill and her variation of the catalyst for her heroines' maturation plots make her the best of the revival novelists.

Another romantic suspense author who continues to write past the gothic revival is Barbara Michaels, a pseudonym of Barbara Mertz (b. 1927), who also writes series detective novels as Elizabeth Peters. Michaels has cited both H. P. Lovecraft and *The Woman in White* as influences, which may account for the realistic supernatural and horror elements in her work that are often spurred by repressed or perverted sexuality caused by unresolved gothic conflicts in the past. In books like *Ammie, Come Home* (1968), Michaels uses parallel conflicts in the present to address ancient wrongs, drawing on romantic suspense conventions to make those conflicts universal.

In *Ammie*, Michaels' middle-aged heroine Ruth has taken her beautiful young niece, Sara, into her home. All of Ruth's repressed maternal instincts are unleashed on Sara, who has fallen in love with the unacceptable hippie Bruce, and when Sara brings home Patrick, one of her professors, Ruth's long buried sexual instincts are unleashed, too. Coping with her history of abuse by a long dead husband, her passionate need to defend Sara from whatever danger might lurk, and her strong feelings for Patrick, Ruth stumbles on another problem: her beautiful Georgetown house is haunted by a malevolent spirit. As the four characters deal with the threat, they begin to fall into the patterns of a Revolutionary War–era gothic story: a girl who tries to escape her house, a passionate suitor, an absent mother, and a controlling and sexually predatory father. Just as Michaels' characters are possessed by the dead spirits and must break free of them, so Michaels herself creates the traditional gothic plot and then breaks free of it.

Michaels wrote of this same house and recurring characters in two more novels, *Shattered Silk* (1986), and *Stitches in Time* (1995). *Stitches* has the classic Michaels' plot—wrongs done to women in the past are recognized and understood if not avenged in the present—but Michaels has grown in the thirty years between this book and *Ammie,* and *Stitches* brings a new complexity to the mix. There is still the trapped young female, the sexually predatory male, and the failed female mother figure, but this time the malevolent spirit is working through one of the most powerful of all female artifacts, the quilt, and her revenge has worked not only on those for whom she intended it, but also on those who have inherited the quilt. The resolution of *Stitches* is less tidy than that of *Ammie,* but the crimes it deals with and the consequences of those crimes are complex; by ending the vengeance through the destruction of the quilt, Michaels implies that redemption cannot be bought without sacrifice and loss, and her ending is more elegiac than triumphant.

In spite of Michael's skill and influence (many modern romantic suspense writers rank her after Stewart in influence), the second most famous romantic suspense writer of this period was the prolific Eleanor Alice Burford Hibbert (1906–1993) who wrote under the pseudonym Victoria Holt. Holt began her career with an historical novel in 1947 writing as Jean Plaidy, and achieved her first great success with *Mistress of Mellyn* (1960) after her agent convinced her to try romantic suspense because it was a hot seller. *Mellyn* has all the elements of classic gothic revival fiction: her heroine Martha comes reluctantly to Mount Mellyn to act as a governess for the neglected and motherless Alvean, daughter of the handsome, distant Connan TreMellyn. A varied cast of characters, a fairly complex plot, and a gruesome twist at the end make this a classic romantic suspense novel, but the humorless protagonist who is almost Mrs. Danvers–like in her devotion to duty hampers any real identification in the plot. Like most gothic revival novels, *Mellyn* is told in first-person point of view, and it is hard to spend much time there without being weighed down by Martha's rigid sense of duty, her class consciousness, and her almost unbearable piousness.

By the time Holt died in 1993, she had written more than two hundred novels under seventeen different pseudonyms, which may account for the unevenness of her work. Her gothics cling close to form, but unfortunately also ignore psychological complexity and thematic subtlety, and her later books became plot-driven rather than character-driven, providing ample ammunition for critics who have argued that romantic suspense is essentially a silly genre. Her *Seven for a Secret* is a good example of the blandness of much of the work of the gothic revival even though it was published in 1992.

Seven begins as a study in poor parenting: the heroine Frederica has a crazed and neglectful mother; her absent father dumped her aunt to marry her mother, whom he left for another woman after Frederica was born; her friend Rachel was orphaned and is now living with her perverted uncle and helpless aunt; and her friend Tamarisk was raised by nannies, at first because her parents were too interested in parties, and then, after her father's death, because her mother was too exhausted by self-pity and selfishness to take an interest in her. Not content with that, Holt adds a careless nanny who kills a baby, and a man who refuses to love his coming child because he is not the biological father. At this point, the reader is tempted to say, "Can't anybody here raise kids?" and Holt seems to feel the same because she abandons the theme, tidying everything up with a relentless and convenient illogic: the heroine's whiny mother dies; the pervert hangs himself from guilt; the helpless aunt remarries an excessively healthy man who is always smiling; the expectant father changes his mind when the baby is born; the heroine forgives her father's abandonment when it turns out he is charming and blind; in short, everything works out just *fine* without anyone breaking a psychological sweat.

Instead, Holt shifts to the duplicity of man: knowing that Frederica's aunt has always been in love with him, Frederica's father leaves her with the task of raising Frederica; a rogue impregnates Rachel and marries Tamarisk for her money; and the hero, like Rochester in *Jane Eyre*, plans to marry Frederica even though he is married to another woman. This seems to inconvenience the characters more than truly move them, and everything is resolved satisfactorily when the only insane character in the story kills the rogue, the heroine's aunt insists she is happy with twenty years of letters to weep over, and the hero finds out he was not married after all. At no point does the heroine turn to father and say, "You bastard, I haven't seen you for twenty years, you emotionally abuse the only good mother in this story, and *now* you want a daughter?" nor does she hit the hero with a critical eye and say, "So the bigamy thing doesn't bother you, huh?" Holt's later characters have no inner lives; they go wherever she shoves them in order to arrive at a completely implausible happy ending.

At the other end of the spectrum from Holt was Shirley Jackson (1919–1965) whose *Haunting of Hill House* (1959) is a magnificent inversion of the romantic suspense story in which once again a poor woman who is the victim of abysmal parenting comes to a powerful old house. Because of an experience with poltergeists in her childhood, Eleanor Vance is invited by the academic Dr. Montague to participate in a psychic experience at troubled Hill House. Like every other gothic heroine, isolated Eleanor is looking for a home and a community, and at first she thinks she has found it with her pseudofather Montague and the two other subjects he brings along, the bohemian Theodora and the charming ne'er-do-well Luke. But Montague fails as father figure–hero because he is dabbling in things he cannot understand, Luke is shallow (in this case the careless Byronic figure really is a loser), and Eleanor's relationship with the house takes a decidedly unromantic turn when it begins to call to her. In a standard gothic, Eleanor would be reclaimed by her love for Luke or Montague and establish her power over the house by giving it a good cleaning; in Jackson's reversal, the house takes Eleanor, giving her that home and community she has longed for as she kills herself in order to haunt the house forever. Her fate hearkens back to the dark gothics of the eighteenth century, but her twisted psychology is pure mid-twentieth century anxiety and alienation. Jackson's sensibility was ahead of her time in many ways and foreshadows the edgier romantic suspense of the late-twentieth century by refusing to provide a glossy happy ending.

Regardless of their quality, the novels of gothic revival share the classic romantic suspense premise: they are about women trapped by their cultures, failed by their parental figures, and anxious about love. As a reflection of the repressed anger and malaise women felt in the time after the wars and before the liberation movement, they played out a promise of salvation and security through love that sold millions of books. The boom had to end, and in the 1980s the bottom finally dropped out of the gothic market, probably precipitated by the vast quantities of abysmal prose the demand had produced and the new security and independence the feminist liberation movement offered women. But if the gothic variation of the romantic suspense novel dropped into a coma for awhile, the genre itself, with its infinite capacity for reinventing itself around its universal theme, was still going strong.

The Inheritors

In the latter part of the twentieth century, women had more power than ever before, but that power, while it did adjust the inequalities somewhat, did not make women particularly safe. The tension between the sexes was just as great if not greater as a result of the feminist revolution, and when that tension erupted, the woman was still the most likely to end up in the emergency room or the morgue. The freedom women had in society made the gothic mansion, castle, and abbey out of date, but the increasing violence they faced made the Byronic hero even more appropriate as the genre began to deal deliberately with child abuse, spousal abuse, and rape. In this fertile atmosphere, the romantic suspense novel began to broaden in its approaches even as it retained its basic theme, and as the genre broadened, so did its writer base. Authors like Stewart, Holt, and Michaels continued to write gothic revival novels during this time, but new authors also claimed the romantic suspense genre for their own.

Mary Higgins Clark (b. 1929) is considered by many to be the queen of the contemporary romantic suspense novel. Although Clark does not stray far from the classic plot, she does return repeatedly to themes that reflect her own life experience. Clark's father died when she was ten, and her family was left penniless. Her mother managed to hold the family together, but five years later her brother died. At eighteen she married the love of her life, Warren Clark, but Clark died of a heart attack fifteen years later and left her and their five children penniless. During the next ten years, Clark worked to keep her family together and put her children through school as first her mother-in-law, then her mother, and finally her younger brother died. Given this background, it is not surprising that Clark seems obsessed by the motifs of single motherhood, dead relatives, and endangered children. In fact, her first novel, *Where Are the Children?* (1975), was turned down by two publishers because it dealt with not only endangered children but murdered children.

Clark's heroine, Nancy Eldridge, has a gothic past: she had married an older Byronic suitor only to find him cold and abusive to her and their two children. Then one day the children are found drowned, and Nancy's husband accuses her of murder before he drowns himself from grief. Nancy is acquitted and begins life over again, marrying a gentle man this time and giving birth to two more children. Clark has done several interesting things with this premise, including moving the heroine into actual jeopardy instead of threatened peril by having her marry the wrong man in back story, and undercutting the Byronic or "alpha" hero and replacing him with a more humane or "beta" hero. She has also made the heroine pay a high price for being a child-woman at the beginning of her story: she loses her children because she fails to protect them.

On the day the story takes place, Nancy loses her children again, and the old nightmare begins once more. Nancy must break through the passivity of her childlike existence, go to the kidnapper's apartment in a large house, claim the space for her own by rescuing the children, and in the climax, save her children by not only risking her own life but also trusting in the strength and love of her second husband. It is a huge character journey, based on the shift from the heroine's rescue and well-being to that of her children. Nancy's rescue is particularly powerful because it reverses the pattern of abusive or absent parenting seeded throughout the text, not only because Nancy risks everything to rescue her children, but because the man she rescues them from turns out to be her abusive ex-husband, the real murderer of her children. Clark's plot is horrific and her villain despicable just as in romantic suspense of old; what is new is the emphasis on completed evil instead of just the threat, and the movement of children to center stage. Another of Clark's novels, *Pretend You Don't See Her* (1997), makes use of the dislocation of the Witness Protection Program to isolate her protagonist. Clark's heroine Lacey is on the run from a professional killer who has murdered a mother and daughter previously, and her life is endangered by her family ties, which she cannot break (especially her tie to her young niece), and by her mother's innocent chatter. Clark's fascination with family and failure give her romantic suspense novels a classic depth even while they break new ground.

Clark is not alone in the modernization of the genre, however. Her daughter, Carol Higgins Clark (b. 1956?), has followed in her footsteps with books like *Iced* (1995). Others have taken the romantic suspense novel to darker places: Anne Stuart (b. 1948), in books like *Nightfall* (1995), writes heroes whose actions cross the line into abuse, while her heroines remain classically steadfast, often protecting children as they struggle. Another master of the form is Nora Roberts (b. 1950); in novels like *Carnal Innocence* (1991), her damaged, orphaned heroines meet Byronic heroes in the midst of crimes so perverse as to be almost supernatural; their love for and belief in these heroes redeem them while exorcising the ghosts of failed parenting that have clouded their lives.

Still grittier writers like Eileen Dreyer have rejected that redemption to write stories of strong women who defeat the Byronic male, which in their interpretations are murderous mentors, would-be lovers, or ex-spouses. Where the classic romantic heroine civilizes the Byronic hero, the modernist heroine blows him away to make room for a man who can commit without bodily harm. Dreyer's *A Man to Die For* (1991) is a fine example.

Dreyer's expertise as a former emergency-room nurse infuses this story of an emotionally distressed young woman haunted by her abusive childhood and burdened with an emotionally disturbed mother. Casey Mc-

Donough finds comfort and connection in her work as an ER nurse until a heroic surgeon comes to town. He is skilled, brilliant, and sexually magnetic—Byronic to the teeth—but Casey is no dummy; she first suspects and then knows that he is a serial killer. Her logical efforts to bring him to justice bring her in contact with the low-key burned-out hero of the piece, a police detective who believes in her and stands by her, even though her story seems ludicrous, because he recognizes a kindred spirit in her; in this he resembles the patient, faithful heroine of the earlier genre. Unfortunately, these same efforts also backfire on her because of the surgeon's Machiavellian manipulation of the community in which he is an aristocrat and she is a commoner; he takes over first the emergency room then, in the climax, her house; her struggle to control these spaces is a classic gothic conflict that she solves not by marrying him but by defeating him.

Although Dreyer writes with a blackly comic voice, she shuns the glossy happily-ever-after of the gothic revival; Casey's antagonist is a brutal killer, but he shares her abusive past, and his death at the end is an assault not only on her sense of justice but also on her sense of self. Dreyer's heroines are often victims of absent or neglectful parents, her villains often male authority figures run amok, and she takes a gleeful joy in destroying traditional power figures: in *Bad Medicine* (1995), lawyers die like flies; in *Nothing Personal* (1994), her killer targets officious hospital administrators. Dreyer thus writes feminist romantic suspense with a vengeance, modernizing the form while attacking patriarchal institutions. In this she is joined by writers like Lisa Gardner, whose *Perfect Husband* (1998) features a Byronic ex-husband who turns out to be a homicidal maniac threatening not only the heroine but also her young daughter, and Tami Hoag (b. 1959), whose *Night Sins* (1995) features a killer who preys on children.

Thus romantic suspense lives on, encompassing ever more radical variations on its theme. An exciting, elastic form of mystery fiction, it is the only form that is intrinsically feminine, because of the tensions at the heart of it. The Had-I-But-Known story continues to thrive because it questions, tests, and usually reassures without ever denying the dangers of the institutions it examines or the tragedy and hope of the knowledge it imparts, and because its conventions continue to reflect the anxieties of women who want to believe that love is not lethal in spite of the evidence around them.

Selected Bibliography

WORKS OF ROMANTIC SUSPENSE

Austen, Jane. *Northanger Abbey.* London: John Murray, 1818.

Brontë, Charlotte. *Jane Eyre.* London: Smith, Elder, and Co., 1847.

Brontë, Emily. *Wuthering Heights.* London: T. C. Newby, 1847.

Caspary, Vera. *Laura.* Boston: Houghton Mifflin, 1943.

Clark, Carol Higgins. *Iced.* New York: Warner, 1995.

Clark, Mary Higgins. *Where Are the Children?* New York: Simon & Schuster, 1975.

———. *Pretend You Don't See Her.* New York: Simon & Schuster, 1997.

Collins, Wilkie. *The Woman in White.* (1860) New York: Bantam, 1985.

———. *The Moonstone.* London: Tinsley Brothers, 1868.

Dreyer, Eileen. *A Man to Die For.* New York: Harper, 1991.

———. *Nothing Personal.* New York: Harper, 1994.

———. *Bad Medicine.* New York: Harper, 1995.

Du Maurier, Daphne. *Rebecca.* New York: Doubleday, Doran and Company, 1938.

Gardner, Lisa. *The Perfect Husband.* New York: Bantam, 1998.

Heyer, Georgette. *Behold, Here's Poison.* London: Hodder & Stoughton, 1936.

———. *A Blunt Instrument.* London: Hodder & Stoughton, 1938.

———. *Envious Casca.* London: Hodder & Stoughton, 1941.

Hoag, Tami. *Night Sins.* New York: Bantam, 1995.

Holt, Victoria. *Mistress of Mellyn.* Garden City, N.Y.: Doubleday, 1960.

———. *Seven for a Secret.* Garden City, N.Y.: Doubleday, 1992.

Jackson, Shirley. *The Haunting of Hill House.* New York: Viking, 1959.

James, Henry. *The Turn of the Screw.* New York: Macmillan, 1898.

Lewis, M. G. *The Monk.* London: J. Bell, 1796.

MacCardle, Dorothy. *The Uninvited.* Garden City, N.Y.: Doubleday, 1942.

Michaels, Barbara. *Ammie, Come Home.* New York: Meredith, 1968.

———. *Stitches in Time.* New York: Harper, 1995.

Radcliffe, Ann. *The Mysteries of Udolpho.* London: G. G. and J. Robinson, 1794.

Rinehart, Mary Roberts. *The Circular Staircase.* New York: Grosset & Dunlap, 1908.

Roberts, Nora. *Carnal Innocence.* New York: Bantam, 1991.

Seeley, Mabel. *The Listening House.* New York: Doubleday, Doran, 1938.

Stewart, Mary. *Nine Coaches Waiting.* New York: Fawcett Crest, 1958.

———. *The Ivy Tree.* New York: Ballantine, 1961.

———. *Thornyhold.* New York: Morrow, 1988.

Stuart, Anne. *Nightfall.* New York: Onyx, 1995.

Walpole, Horace. *The Castle of Otranto.* London: Thomas Lownds, 1765.

BIOGRAPHICAL AND CRITICAL STUDIES

Bander, Elaine. "Georgette Heyer." In *Great Women Mystery Writers.* Edited by Kathleen Gregory Klein. Westport, Conn.: Greenwood Press, 1994. Pp. 157–160.

Budd, Elaine. "Mary Higgins Clark." In her *Thirteen Mistresses of Murder.* New York: Ungar, 1986. Pp. 1–11.

Cohn, Jan. "Mary Roberts Rinehart." In *Ten Women of Mystery.* Edited by Earl F. Bargainnier. Bowling Green, Ohio: Bowling Green State University Popular Press, 1981. Pp. 183–220.

Dance, James C. "Spinsters in Jeopardy." *The Armchair Detective* (winter 1989): 28–37.

Grape, Jan, Dean James, and Ellen Nehr. *Deadly Women.* New York: Carroll & Graf, 1998.

Mussell, Kay. *Fantasy and Reconciliation: Contemporary Formulas of Women's Romance Fiction.* Westport, Conn.: Greenwood Press, 1984.

———. *Women's Gothic and Romantic Fiction.* Westport, Conn.: Greenwood Press, 1981.

Swanson, Jean, and Dean James. *By a Woman's Hand.* New York: Berkley, 1994.

———. *Killer Books.* New York: Berkley, 1998.

THE SPY THRILLER

WESLEY K. WARK

GRAHAM GREENE, one of the acknowledged masters of the spy thriller, dedicated his classic anthology, *The Spy's Bedside Book* (1957), to "the immortal memory of William Le Queux and John Buchan." Forty years later, the immortality of Le Queux seems doubtful, while Buchan is only holding his own. Spy fiction has new writers in its pantheon. But Greene was hailing two pioneers of the genre and also reminding us about the spy thriller's roots. These were to be found precisely in the Le Queux–Buchan years, amid the turbulent drama of the first decades of the twentieth century. Greene's dedication, and *The Spy's Bedside Book* itself, were reminders that the spy novelist and the reader both operate within a long-established literary tradition. This sense of tradition, carrying with it a rich stock of motifs, plots, locales, and character types, is crucial to the emergence and flourishing of any distinct literary genre. Le Queux and Buchan, as well as Graham Greene, were to contribute mightily to the tradition. The cultural work of the spy novel spans the twentieth century and shows no signs of letup as the twenty-first century dawns. Its earliest configurations, as Greene hinted, were to prove extremely influential.

The Birth of the Spy Thriller

The spy thriller, though it burst forth with great suddenness, had antecedents, including the anarchist/terrorist fiction of the late nineteenth century and Victorian pornography, with its locked rooms, secrets, and general odor of threat to established values. There was one early experiment in the genre, *The Spy: A Tale of the Neutral Ground* (1821), by the American writer James Fenimore Cooper. But it failed to generate any literary succession. When the spy thriller emerged, it did so from a firmly British base, and British writers were to hold a near monopoly on the genre for many decades. This was a tribute to the power of the London publishing industry, to Britain's status as a world power, and, just as important, to the popular fears that attached themselves to a nation beginning to suffer from imperial overstretch.

The contours of this new literary genre were first suggested by two key works, Rudyard Kipling's *Kim* (1901) and Erskine Childers' *The Riddle of the Sands* (1903). Both novels wedded tales of adventure to visions of Britain's political standing, mediated by the figure of the spy.

Kipling's tale features the exploits of the Anglo-Indian orphan boy Kim, who becomes a player in the Great Game, a loyal servant of a shadowy but extensive system of British surveillance and espionage on the frontiers of India. Kipling (1865–1936) depicted espionage as a form of patriotic adventure that put a premium on disguise, cleverness, and individual heroics. Kim proves a natural and nimble spy, but his exploits are abetted by other native players of the Great Game, principally a Bengali clerk and a Pathan horse dealer. Such a supporting cast, as Edward Said suggests, allowed Kipling to map and affirm the structures of British imperial control of India. The novel opens with Kim astride the great bronze cannon, Zam-Zammah, in the town square of Lahore, engaged in a winning game of king-of-the-castle with a Hindu and a Muslim boy.

Kipling gave to English literature a heady invocation of empire. He gave to the spy thriller suggestive pieces of a formula in which exotic locales, travelogue, heroic action, caricatured depiction of the enemy (inept French and Russian spies), and ultimately political affirmation could all be set to work.

Erskine Childers (1870–1922) offered an equally suggestive, but differently constituted, formula. His only spy thriller, *The Riddle of the Sands*, tells the story of two Englishmen, a bored and frowzy Foreign Office clerk, Carruthers, and his more vital friend, the yachtsman Arthur Davies, who stumble on and foil a vast German plan to mount a surprise naval assault on Great Britain. There is a great deal of lovingly detailed nautical action in the novel, as Davies and Carruthers pilot the little, spartanly equipped yacht *Dulcibella* through the treacherous waters of the inshore Baltic Sea. But at the novel's heart there is something much more didactic. Carruthers' slow awakening to the German threat and to his own manhood, as he shakes off the corrupting skin of London society, is an emblematic device that drives the novel's action. His personal regeneration operates as a call for the regeneration of Britain, for the renewal of patriotism, individual action, and a keen-eyed appreciation of the German threat. The key moment of renewal comes when Carruthers decides to engage in "a little secret service on the high seas." The effect on him is potent, a metaphoric draft described as "the purest of her pure vintages, instilling the ancient inspiration which, under many guises, quickens thousands of better brains than mine, but whose essence is always the same: the gay pursuit of a perilous quest" (p. 82).

But Carruthers' quest was no ordinary romance; it was a spy quest. The novel's heroes needed some armor against the conventions of the day, which decried espionage as ungentlemanly. Patriotism was that armor. Childers also made the spy story function as a redemptive morality tale through the use of a narrative ploy that lacked elegance but did the trick. In the epilogue, an "editor" suddenly appears to lecture the reader on the realities of a damaged cipher message, outlining the German invasion plan, which Carruthers has managed to snatch. This is no "baseless romance," the reader is sternly warned (p. 260). Crude or not, Childers' experiment with what has come to be called "faction" (the deceptive blending of fact and fiction) was wildly successful. The British Naval Intelligence Division felt compelled to investigate the novel's claims, and the author himself fell under the sway of his own invention. Faction would be taken up in many guises by the legions of spy novelists who came to the genre in the years after *Riddle of the Sands*.

Formula Fiction

The political and imaginative work of the spy thriller had begun. Kipling equated espionage with imperial security; Childers made the link between spying and individual and national regeneration. Two contemporary writers saw the potential of what Kipling and Childers had wrought and moved quickly to fill out the formula of the spy thriller and to fill up the shelves of home and circulating libraries. E. Phillips Oppenheim and William Le Queux were men of remarkably similar and, it must be said, subliterary talent. But they were ready to seize the spy thriller and make it their own at just the right moment in time. These men were the first makers of mass-produced spy fiction, and without them perhaps the literary spark lit by the solo novels of Kipling and Childers would never have caught with a wide audience.

E. Phillips Oppenheim (1866–1946) began

his novelistic career in 1882, a decade before Le Queux. He is credited by Donald McCormick with having written 115 novels and 39 books of short stories but, as McCormick adds, "never a polished one" (1979, p. 174). As early as 1898, in *The Mysterious Mr. Sabin*, espionage emerges as a theme. But it was the growing apprehension of the German threat to Britain in the years before 1914 that helped concentrate Oppenheim's mind and set his fiction firmly in the groove of the spy thriller. In novels like *The Maker of History* (1905) and *The Great Secret* (1907), amateur British agents uncover dastardly German plots designed to fulfill a German lust for power and conquest at the expense of Britain and its newfound ally, France. *The Great Secret* exposes a German spy ring some thirty thousand strong operating in Britain under the innocent guise of the Waiters Union and preparing to wreak havoc in support of an all-out invasion of the British Isles.

Oppenheim's energy scarcely flagged with the outbreak of war in Europe in 1914. He immediately volunteered for duty with the British secret service, only to have his application rejected. But Oppenheim swallowed his disappointment and quickly returned to writing, producing a dozen novels in the course of the war. Tapping the popular mood of spy fever and anti-German hysteria stirred up by the sinking of the passenger liner *Lusitania* in May 1915, Oppenheim published in the following year what came to be regarded as his best novel, *The Kingdom of the Blind*. Its themes are the war-charged issues of loyalty and power, with a sideline in romance. Surgeon-Major Thomson, in reality a director of the British secret service, tracks down a conspiracy at the heart of the British government involving a wealthy financier, Sir Alfred Anselman. Anselman is in reality loyal to the German nation of his birth but plays a watching game and is finally too powerful to expose. Instead, his son, the German agent Captain Thanet, takes the fall, betrayed by his weakness for the woman who is also the love object of the austere Major Thomson. The novel played on many of the new conventions of the spy thriller—the sense of sinister conspiracy, underwritten by scarcely disguised xenophobia, the heroic work of the lone agent, and fast-paced action. But what really gave this novel its cachet was its psychological attunement to the spirit of the day and, in particular, the sense that Britain's war fortunes were fragile and were being undermined from within, while overhead the Zeppelin bombers that Captain Thanet was so treacherously directing to their targets were wreaking a new and terrifying destruction.

Oppenheim, though he had an earlier start, was eventually overtaken by William Le Queux (1864–1927) in terms of sheer quantity of output. Le Queux first took up the pen as a journalist, and it was not until the 1890s that he began writing novels. His early efforts involved depictions of intrigue in foreign capitals and, moving closer still to the spy thriller, invasion-scare novels like *The Great War in England in 1897* (1894). Le Queux first shot to fame in 1906, when he published *The Invasion of 1910*. This novel was part publicity stunt, part propaganda broadsheet and more in the tradition of the invasion-scare literature than of the spy novel. Le Queux does have a small force of German spies undertake sabotage in Britain as the invasion flotilla sets sail, but its activity is only a prelude to the main event.

By 1909, Le Queux was ready to present an even bigger bombshell novel, *Spies of the Kaiser*. German spying is now at the forefront, while the threat of invasion lurks in the background. *Spies of the Kaiser* is full of fast-paced action, makes no bones about the German threat and Britain's peril, and is contemptuous of foreigners, sinister or otherwise. The novel offers a romantic vision of civilization rescued by the inspired action of amateur secret agents Ray Raymond and John James Jacox, with Vera Vallance, "pretty, fair-haired daughter of Admiral Sir Charles Vallance," in the inevitable supporting role. The novel is, in other words, steeped in the political work and xenophobia of the early spy thriller. It does make one innovative contribution (an early prefiguring of the techno-spy novels of writers like Tom Clancy), by spicing up the action with frequent revelations of technological secrets and new gadgets—fast cars, motorcycles, submarines, and airplanes all fill the pages. But what is vital to the novel's construction is its claim to authenticity. Le Queux took Childers' epilogue and thrust it to the very front, literally, of his novel. *Spies of the Kaiser* opens with the screed "If England Knew," which lays out in detail the facts of German espionage in Britain (more than five thousand German spies are at work) and the spinelessness of the authorities in dealing with them. Le Queux stakes out the novel's claims (and his own motives) baldly: "I have no desire to create undue alarm. I am an Englishman, and, I hope, a patriot. What I have written in this present volume in the form of fiction is based upon serious facts within my own personal knowledge" (p. xxxiii).

In case this declamatory statement of fact and loyalty was not enough, Le Queux gave his readers an intimate mental picture of his secret work, a snapshot of his writing desk, with pen poised above paper: "As I write, I have before me a file of amazing documents, which plainly show the feverish activity with which this advance guard of our enemy is working. . . . These documents have already been placed before the Minister for War, who returned them without comment!" (p. xxxiv).

What is remarkable is that the War Office had done no such thing. Le Queux had a close ally and friend in Lieutenant Colonel Edmonds, head of MO5 of the War Office, in charge of secret-service work. Edmonds and Le Queux were on the same mental wavelength—they both had the German invasion threat and spies on the brain. Colonel Edmonds risked his career by pestering the authorities with evidence (some of it directly from Le Queux) about the German spy threat. The government, prompted in part by a spy panic created by Le Queux's writing, eventually succumbed, created a commission of inquiry, and bought the fictional story of German spies in its midst. The result of this hilarious metamorphosing of fiction into fact

was the creation in 1909 of the modern British secret service, with its domestic-security and foreign-intelligence branches. No greater tribute can be imagined for the new power of the spy-thriller formula, and, in particular, its experiment with faction.

Spy fiction was firmly established by 1914, when World War I was unleashed. The pioneering work of Kipling, Childers, Oppenheim, and Le Queux had created a new genre that was firmly plugged into the popular psyche of its British readership. Indeed, spy fiction acquired an almost oracular quality with the outbreak of fighting in the summer of 1914, German naval raids on the coast of Britain, and the intensive manhunt conducted by MI5 for German spies.

Creators of Clubland Heroes

Le Queux and Oppenheim continued to mass-produce their thrillers, but the writer who came to dominate the spy genre during the war and for many years thereafter was a newcomer, John Buchan (1875–1940), the future Lord Tweedsmuir. Buchan's Richard Hannay novels, beginning in 1915 with the publication of *The Thirty-Nine Steps*, looked for formulaic inspiration more to Oppenheim and Kipling than to Le Queux. For one thing, Buchan set a higher literary standard for the spy novel, something that only Joseph Conrad (1857–1924), operating on the edges of the genre with novels such as *The Secret Agent* (1907) and *Under Western Eyes* (1911), had achieved before the war. But the crude politics of the mainstream spy thriller of prewar days were not those of Conrad, who was more interested in limning the nature of terrorism and revolutionary fervor than in telling stories of German spy plots. Conrad's characters were outsiders, as he himself was; they were also more fully developed psychologically than the likes of Ray Raymond and John James Jacox.

Buchan may have been less psychologically penetrating than Conrad, but he possessed a stylistic talent well in excess of Le Queux and Oppenheim. He was also more self-aware of the writerly tricks the thriller formula required, especially its pushing chance and happenstance to the outer limits of probability—what Alfred Hitchcock was later to refer to as the "McGuffin." But while there are improbable moments in the action of the Hannay novels, Buchan took care to stress their topicality. *The Thirty-Nine Steps* involves a German plot to steal British naval secrets. *Greenmantle* (1916) takes Hannay on a dangerous mission to the Near East to foil a German-backed jihad, reflecting the fears that Turkey's entry into the war had created. *Greenmantle* also moved the spy thriller out of its geographic absorption with Britain and the Continent and reawakened the imperial adventure story that Kipling had fostered. *Mr. Standfast* (1919), perhaps the best of the Hannay novels, paints a dramatic story of the climax of the war on the western front, the German spring 1918 offensive, in which Brigadier Hannay plays a leading role by foiling a German spy plot before returning to his army division to see the war to its conclusion. With Buchan, the cruder tactics of faction—the deliberate alerting of the reader to the spy novel as a vessel for secret truths—begin to be replaced by the more subtle design of apparent realism. Authenticity is conveyed not through the narrator's insistence but through setting fictional plots amid real-life events, characters, and topical concerns.

Buchan's creation, Richard Hannay, became the very model of the "clubland hero"—the denizen of the elite male clubs of London who could turn his good breeding, talents, and leisure time to the pursuit of patriotic espionage. As Richard Usborne remarks in his study, *Clubland Heroes* (1953), many secret warriors of Usborne's acquaintance during World War II began the conflict imagining themselves in the mode of Hannay or his companion, Sandy Arbuthnot.

Geoffrey Household (1900–1988) was one of the secret warriors who marched off to war (in his case on a mission to blow up the oil wells at Ploesti in Romania), but before he did

so he produced a marvelous variant on the Buchan hero in *Rogue Male* (1939). The novel was, as Household remarked in his autobiography, "Buchan without his coincidences" (*Against the Wind*, p. 209). Looking back, this startling tale of an English aristocrat bent on a mission to assassinate Hitler but forced to go into hiding like a burrowing animal to escape his German pursuers reads like a metaphor of the age of appeasement. The hero of the novel can, in the beginning, barely acknowledge to himself the reality of his self-imposed mission, so far outside the code of gentlemanly conduct does it lie. His escape, pursuit by the German secret service, and underground existence are all treated vividly and with psychological penetration. The novel, in its middle passages, is an extended discourse on fear and survival, significant motifs of the 1930s. The hero's eventual breakout from his hiding place, his triumph against his German nemesis, and the resumption of his quest to destroy Hitler read like a commentary on the new mood of post-Munich Britain. *Rogue Male* was Household's second novel; he went on to write another dozen novels, including a sequel, *Rogue Justice* (1982). None matched the achievement of *Rogue Male*, which was sustained in the public imagination by two film treatments, a Fritz Lang Hollywood production, *Man Hunt* (1941), and a BBC TV production, starring Peter O'Toole, which appeared in 1976.

A very different sort of clubland spy hero emerged in the writing of Sapper, the nom de plume of Lieutenant Colonel Herman Cyril McNeile (1888–1937). Sapper's best-known literary creation was a muscular hero, "Bulldog" Drummond, good with his fists and with no time for foreigners, Bolshies, and Jews. Drummond featured in a series of novels that began in 1920 with *Bull-Dog Drummond* and lasted until 1937 with the appropriately named *Bulldog Drummond Hits Out*, written in the year of McNeile's death.

Sapper's *The Black Gang* (1922) gives everything of the flavor of his style. The novel opens with a "huge man covered from head to foot in black" who breaks in on a conspiratorial meeting led by the Russian Zaboleff and proceeds to dish out summary British justice to a collection of sniveling clerks, working-class types, and overdressed Jews. He has two revolvers, but boots, a whip, and a stern warning are mainly applied to the malefactors. The Jews get special treatment. The mystery man tells them: "My friends and I do not like your trade, you swine. It is well that we have come provided with the necessary implement for such a case. Fetch the cat" (p. 18). The man dressed in black with this rough sense of justice and social caste is none other than Bulldog Drummond himself.

The Sapper novels spoke to the same anxiety as had the prewar novels of Le Queux and Oppenheim. The enemy had changed, at least superficially, with the Bolshevik threat replacing the German menace. But underneath that, Colonel McNeile, with his barrack-room political philosophy, could see only a nation undermined from within by too great a tolerance of foreigners, Jews, and the socially ambitious lower classes. Sapper represented the darker potential always present in the spy-thriller formula—its crude politics of conservative, authoritarian reassurance, its xenophobia and racism, and its reliance on individual heroes operating outside the law (in Bulldog Drummond's case, quite a way outside). Bulldog Drummond was kept alive after McNeile's death by his close friend Gerard Fairlie, who kept Drummond bashing away until 1951.

Sapper's real heir, however, was Peter Cheyney (1896–1951), who created the character Lemmy Caution in 1936 in *This Man Is Dangerous.* Caution shared Drummond's delight in fisticuffs and right-wing politics but was not of the manor born. Cheyney's innovation was to take his hero out of clubland and into the streets. Lemmy Caution also came equipped with a hard-boiled dialogue borrowed straight from the fast-rising genres of the American crime novel and Hollywood gangster movie. Cheyney, prefiguring Mickey Spillane, caught on and enjoyed enormous sales, especially during World War II, when the violence of his spies and detectives paled

into insignificance amid the casualty lists and harsh realities of war. By this time, Cheyney's own past as a member of Oswald Mosley's British Union of Fascists had been buried under the mantle of popular fame. His novels were especially well received in the United States and France, where Lemmy Caution became the improbable hero of Jean-Luc Godard's cult science-fiction film *Alphaville* (1965).

Challenges to the Genre's Conventions

Fortunately, the spy-thriller formula had avenues of development open to it other than this descent from prewar Germanophobia to postwar celebration of freelance rough justice, dished up with a taste of British-style fascism. One such avenue was parody.

Almost from the beginning, the spy thriller had faced a comedic counterattack, a spoofing of the spies. A. A. Milne (1882–1956), the creator of the Winnie-the-Pooh stories, had a very funny swipe at Le Queux in a parodic story he published in *Punch* in 1909, "The Secret of the Army Aeroplane." In 1908 G. K. Chesterton (1874–1936), author of the Father Brown detective series, penned a lone classic, *The Man Who Was Thursday: A Nightmare,* a comic exploration of double agentry and the futility of espionage.

But perhaps the funniest of all novels to take espionage in vain was published in 1933. Its author, Compton Mackenzie (1883–1972), was sure there was much black comedy to espionage, not least because he had witnessed it in full himself. Mackenzie, a Scot by birth, had served with the British army at Gallipoli, and then been invalided out to join the British secret service as head of its operations in Athens. That experience furnished the material for a couple of competent spy thrillers, *Extremes Meet* (1928) and *The Three Couriers* (1929). There was better still to come.

Mackenzie developed a taste for memoir writing, to which he turned in the early

1930s. *Greek Memories* (1932), the third volume of his life saga, got him into serious trouble with the British government, which brought down the full force of the Official Secrets Act on his head for revealing wartime operations, treating the espionage establishment to a good deal of criticism, and, sin of sins, revealing the real name of the wartime *C.* Mackenzie, thinking it all a bit of a joke, decided to plead guilty and was given a minimum fine by the judge in the much-publicized trial that was held in camera at the Old Bailey in London. However, he found himself deeply in debt to his lawyers. Noting that the government had made no move against him for his earlier spy novels, which were in the style of romans à clef, he decided to exact his revenge by publishing a satirical, fictional version of *Greek Memories*, which became the celebrated *Water on the Brain* (1933). Major "Bunny" Blenkinsop, retired cavalryman and henpecked spouse, is recruited by the director general of extraordinary espionage and sent to Mendacia, where he operates under cover as a banana importer. The novel gently decapitates His Majesty's Secret Service, making fun of the secrecy, eccentricity, gullibility, and silliness of the military types then in charge. It is wildly over the top but must have been delicious revenge for the harassed Mackenzie. Only one other parodic spy novel, Graham Greene's *Our Man in Havana* (1958)—in which a hard-up businessman fools the British secret service with his fake drawings of vacuum-cleaner parts made to look like the latest missile technology—is in its class.

Parody and satire were means to challenge the dominant mode of the spy thriller by playing with its conventions and stock characters. A still more radical challenge was mounted in the late 1920s and 1930s. The principal contributors to what emerged as a new school of spy-fiction writing were Eric Ambler, Somerset Maugham, and Graham Greene. Collectively, they were responsible for casting down the clubland hero and putting in his place more psychologically complex characters. These authors were also interested in using the spy thriller to probe more deeply into the troubled political environment between the two world wars. Ambler, Maugham, and Greene took turns at moving the spy novel in the direction of greater verisimilitude, literary and aesthetic seriousness, and (in the case of Ambler and Greene) left-wing politics. Michael Denning, author of a sophisticated, materialist study of the spy novel, *Cover Stories* (1987), regards the new political landscape of the 1930s spy thriller as its "central mutation" (p. 60).

Eric Ambler (b. 1909) mounted an assault on clubland by fastening on a "merchants of death" theme. Arms dealers and industrialists were widely credited in the early 1930s with pursuing profits at the expense of peace and thereby spawning World War I. The onset of the Depression gave further credence to the vision of the capitalist and industrialist as forces not of order and stability but of threat, their greed and moral nullity a danger. Ambler described his inspiration: "I looked around for something I could change and decided it was the thriller-spy story. . . . I decided to turn that upside down and make the heroes left wing and popular front figures" (quoted in Stafford, *The Silent Game*, p. 133).

Ambler produced six novels between 1936 and 1940. From *The Dark Frontier* (1936) to *Journey into Fear* (1940), they feature a new sort of spy protagonist, one who begins as an innocent and finds himself slowly trapped and sometimes crushed by the forces of politics, espionage, and the incomprehensibility of life beyond the frontiers of Britain, especially life in the strife-ridden Balkans.

Ambler's spy fiction never had the public reception it deserved. World War II intervened, and when it was over Ambler went to Hollywood to write film scripts. Only after a considerable hiatus did he return to writing thrillers in the early 1950s. Soon there was new competition on the scene, most notably from Ian Fleming and John le Carré. Two of Ambler's books—*The Mask of Dimitrios* (1939; U.S. title, *A Coffin for Dimitrios*) and *Journey into Fear*—were made into films, but these were wartime productions and were quickly forgotten in the tidal wave of Bond films.

Somerset Maugham's contribution to the new political orientation of the spy thriller was different from that of Ambler and Greene. Maugham (1874–1965), in his one major contribution to the spy genre, the linked stories of *Ashenden* (1928), had no interest in the anticapitalist musings of Ambler or the popular front and left-wing politics of Greene. What he wanted to examine was the morality of espionage, a sore spot first explored by Childers in *The Riddle of the Sands.* Rather than searching for a patriotic justification for espionage as something a British gentleman could do if done first by the enemy, Maugham took a much grittier view, informed by his experiences with intelligence work in Switzerland and Russia during World War I. In *Ashenden,* espionage is repeatedly the subject of cold, Machiavellian calculations rooted in *raison d'état.* The principal exponent of the new Machiavellianism is R, the colonel who heads British intelligence and plays the game with grim relish. At the very outset of the first *Ashenden* story, R's hard-bitten view of espionage is made clear. Ashenden, a writer, is recruited by R into the secret service and sent to Geneva to keep a watch on German spies. The first interview between R and his new agent ends in this manner: "The last words that R said to him, with a casualness that made them impressive, were: 'There's just one thing I think you ought to know before you take on this job. And don't forget it. If you do well you'll get no thanks and if you get into trouble you'll get no help. Does that suit you?' " (p. 13). Ashenden replies, "Perfectly," and the deal is done. But as the stories unfold, the sangfroid of his answer will be tested by murder, cruel mishap, deception, and failure.

Maugham claimed that his *Ashenden* stories were written for no purpose other than entertainment and that, as he put it in the preface, "fact is a poor story-teller" (p. 5). He may have been reacting to the crudities of the Le Queux–Oppenheim style of thriller fiction, but there was much beyond "entertainment" in *Ashenden.* The stories have an undeniable didactic function, reminding the reader constantly about what Maugham regarded as the realities of espionage and the dubious morality that spying entails.

Entertainment was also the ostensible purpose of Graham Greene's initial forays into the spy thriller. But, as with Maugham, "entertainment" is a deceptive label. Greene (1904–1991) shared with Maugham a desire to alter the aesthetics of the spy thriller. He shared with Ambler a desire to shift its political sights away from clubland heroes and conservative affirmation. Ultimately, he contributed a great deal more to the spy-thriller genre than either of his contemporaries. His longevity enabled him to experiment with many variations on the spy thriller, from the prewar treatment of the Spanish Republican agent in *The Confidential Agent* (1939), to the wartime fifth-column theme of *The Ministry of Fear* (1943), to the spoof, *Our Man in Havana,* and on to what is perhaps his finest achievement in the spy-thriller form, the psychological portrait of the double agent Maurice Castle in *The Human Factor* (1978). Such range and experimentation were no accident. The character of the spy was to prove a central figure in "Greeneland," the tortured world made and remade by its author. And Greene was more conscious than any of his predecessors of the traditions of the spy thriller and of the alternate strategies it offered.

The writing of John Buchan, whom Greene described as an "early hero of mine," exerted a strong pull on him. Greene knew his Le Queux also. He paid tribute to the impact of Le Queux's thrillers in *The Ministry of Fear* during a dream sequence in which an innocent man on the run, Arthur Rowe, takes shelter in the London underground and imagines what his long-dead mother would have made of the world above his head, a London torn apart by the Blitz, in which the adventures of Le Queux have somehow become reality. "The world," Rowe muses, "has been remade by William Le Queux" (1979 ed., p. 65). And when Greene set sail for Freeport, Sierra Leone, in December 1941, on his way to an assignment with the British Secret Intelligence Service, Eric Ambler's *Mask of Dimitrios* was among his reading. *Ministry of Fear* was actually written in West Africa, while Greene kept a watch on pro-Axis espionage activities.

Greene's spy thrillers were informed by his knowledge of the genre, by his experiences in wartime intelligence, and, perhaps most sharply, by his closeness to one of the most significant real-life spy dramas of the century—the unmasking of Kim Philby as a double agent. Greene had worked for Philby in the British Secret Intelligence Service during the latter stages of World War II and was to add a controversial, exculpatory foreword to Philby's memoir, *My Silent War* (1968), written from exile in Moscow. The Philby case provided a touchstone for the kinds of issues that drew Greene toward the spy thriller—private loyalties in conflict with public duties, belief and betrayal, a corrupting political world. Forty years after writing his first spy "entertainment," Greene published his last and most accomplished spy novel, *The Human Factor*, which is permeated by the ghost of Kim Philby.

New Directions for the Postwar Novel

Greene, among the most talented, productive, and knowledgeable writers in the spy-thriller form, made an essential contribution to the genre's postwar renaissance. But for all his achievements, it was not Greene who set the postwar spy novel on a new course of popularity and established its dominant tones. This work instead was accomplished by three newcomers—Ian Fleming, Len Deighton, and John le Carré. Each author mined the spy-thriller tradition in unique ways; and each pointed the thriller in different directions as an instrument of political and social commentary.

Ian Fleming's contribution to the postwar spy novel is the one we take most for granted, and thus underestimate. Fleming (1908–1964)

became a formulaic writer, indeed one trapped and ultimately wearied by his own creation, James Bond. The style of his novels was to be overshadowed by that of the subsequent film versions, which increasingly tipped over into extremes of parody, self-caricature, gadgetry, and thrill seeking. But for all that, Fleming helped establish one of the two dominant modes of the Cold War spy thriller by repackaging, and renewing, it. In Fleming's work, the traditional elements of heroic and patriotic adventure were given new Cold War clothes. Fleming possessed an essential faith in British power and prestige, despite the erosion of the British empire. He was also steeped in the mythology of the British secret service's supremacy, derived from his wartime service as personal assistant to the director of naval intelligence.

Yet while Fleming clearly drew on the tradition set down by Le Queux, Buchan, and the hard-hitting, numskull heroes of Sapper, he refashioned the spy novel for the 1950s. From the appearance of *Casino Royale* in 1953 until his death in 1964, Fleming churned out Bond novels almost yearly, and they caught on with British and American audiences.

The Fleming novels offered a world of adventurous fun seemingly just around the corner from the dingier reality of the 1950s. Bond operated just a step—a safe step—beyond the moral and social conventions of the day. The novels also offered a reassuring political message. The Cold War could be lived with; it had not changed the essential realities of power. Political power was still exercised by wise (British) officials and their unbeatable agents, who were capable of foiling the most dastardly plots of atomic-bomb terrorists (*Thunderball*, 1961), Chinese missile freaks (*Dr. No*, 1958), and those who would disturb the equanimity of the capitalist order (*Goldfinger*, 1959).

Many competent spy-thriller writers labored in the shadow of the Bond phenomenon. One such was William Haggard (1907–1993), the pseudonym of former Indian army officer and civil servant Richard Henry Michael Clayton, who began writing the serial adventures of his very tough-minded hero, Colonel Charles Russell of the British Security Executive, in 1958. Haggard's Colonel Russell had a certain affinity with Fleming's spy chief M, but Haggard's stories lacked a Bond, were more cerebral, and at the same time were avowedly conservative and nostalgic for a lost order. Just to be sure that readers knew where he stood, Colonel Russell was given to occasional political asides. In *The Antagonists* (1964), for instance, we learn that he "was paid to frustrate the formidable apparatus of international communism, but it was an enemy which he feared and respected equally. . . . His hatred he saved for futile compromise, for the creaking bones of a calcified community. An Anglo-Irishman, he could look at the English impersonally. What was contemptible about their establishment wasn't its power, but its inefficiency" (p. 51).

While Haggard offered genuine insights into the realities of Whitehall decision making, it was Fleming's fantasies of a resurgent Britannia and its libidinous agent that dominated the market during the 1950s and early 1960s, especially in the United States. Ian Fleming's thrillers were even endorsed from the new "Camelot" of the Kennedy administration as among the favorite novels of the president and his First Lady. But Bond's adventures were ill suited to some of the more ominous realities of the Cold War, which was driven home by the tense confrontation over Soviet deployment of nuclear missiles in Cuba in 1962. There was another spy-thriller tradition waiting in the wings to be rediscovered and reinvented, as Fleming had done with the older heroic and clubland spy stories. Starting in the early 1960s, the Fleming stories found a riposte in a very different style of spy thriller offered up by two emerging writers—Len Deighton and John le Carré—who would come to dominate the genre for the next thirty years. Both men refurbished the spy-novel tradition of the years between the world wars, with its stock of antiestablishment motifs and revelations of Machiavellian intrigue, duplicity, and treachery. The 1960s, with its Cold War shocks, Vietnam War, rise of politi-

cal protest, and growing disenchantment with big government, provided the perfect setting for an anti-Bond spy thriller.

Len Deighton (b. 1929) was the first to challenge the Bond formula, with his novel *The Ipcress File* (1962). The novel features an unnamed, bemused, but hardy protagonist (later called Harry Palmer and played by Michael Caine in the film version), who operates in a world in which the threats are obscure and the evildoers rather invisible. It is a far cry from the world of Bond. The novel opens with the briefing of a cabinet minister on the latest espionage case; the protagonist acknowledges at the outset: "It's a confusing story . . . I'm in a very confusing business" (Triad/Panther paperback ed., p. 10). *The Ipcress File*, in fact, revels in confusion and a persistent mockery of the spy and military establishments of Britain and the United States. The hero, a man at odds with his masters, must puzzle out a plot that involves defecting atomic scientists, brainwashing, and treachery from within. He does so only after suffering confinement and brainwashing himself. He even has an "insurance policy," a little unpatriotic trafficking with the enemy, in case his own untrustworthy chiefs turn on him.

The insouciance of Deighton's antiestablishment spy was an early trademark and signaled a new course for the spy novel, one in which writer and reader refused to be gulled by the tricks and sham certainties, the hidden appeal to order and patriotism, of the Bond novels. There's an edge of sharp repartee and class-consciousness in the novel's dialogue. Deighton's new approach delighted a formidable student of the genre, Julian Symons, who called him "a kind of poet of the spy novel" (*Bloody Murder*, p. 249). But Deighton also became an exemplar of what Symons regarded as the potential for exhaustion in the spy-thriller formula. Having written his first spy novel at the age of thirty-three, Deighton proved to be in the tradition of the mass-production thriller writer, first exemplified by Le Queux and Oppenheim. The classic Deighton spy novels were written in the early to mid-1960s—*The Ipcress File, Funeral in Ber-*

lin (1964), and *Billion Dollar Brain* (1966) (all of which were made into films starring Michael Caine). Beyond these works lies the sprawling and seemingly endless saga of Bernard Samson, starting in 1983 with *Berlin Game.*

A more formidable challenger to the Bond phenomenon was John le Carré (b. 1931), the pseudonym of David John Moore Cornwell. Le Carré's first major venture into spy-fiction writing was *The Spy Who Came in from the Cold* (1963). The success of the novel encouraged le Carré to resign from the British Foreign Office and leave behind his days in the British embassy in Bonn and the consulate in Hamburg, where he worked under cover for the British secret service. But his experience serving in the front lines of the Cold War in Germany sharply marked *The Spy Who Came in from the Cold.* The novel provided the mold for what would become some of the standard features of le Carré–land. Alec Leamas, former head of the Berlin station of the British secret service, finds himself drawn into a devious plot to sustain a British mole in the East German intelligence apparatus. He becomes, in the end, the unintended victim of the plot and dies on the Berlin Wall in a sacrificial moment in which he chooses not to carry on with the spy game but to join his dead lover, Liz, in the no-man's-land of the Wall itself. The novel is dark in tone, full of anger and passion, and characterization and plot are skillfully developed. In these ways, *The Spy Who Came in from the Cold* was a literary challenge to Fleming, and indeed to Len Deighton. The challenge was further extended in the 1965 film version directed by Martin Ritt, with Richard Burton playing the role of Leamas.

But le Carré's contribution to the genre, and his eventual and unparalleled dominance of it, went well beyond raising the aesthetic qualities of the spy novel. Le Carré refashioned the spy thriller's apparent realism. In doing so, he was simultaneously turning away from Fleming and building on the work of his predecessors: Buchan had discarded the strident tactic of faction employed by Le

Queux and relied instead on topicality as an authenticating device; Maugham had imbued the spy story with a darker morality; Ambler had altered its politics; and Greene had deepened its psychology. Le Carré added to all this by the simple but masterful stroke of inventing for the spy thriller a new vocabulary. His language—of safe houses, watchers, the Circus, the Nursery, baby-sitters, lamplighters, and so on—invested the familiar with a parallel and more sinister meaning. This language game mirrored the distorting effects that espionage has, in le Carré's fiction, on everything from public politics to the private love between individuals.

Le Carré's spy novels, from *The Spy Who Came in from the Cold* to *The Tailor of Panama* (1996), are all commentaries on the politics of intelligence understood in a new way. This is not the familiar thriller politics of good and evil, white hats and black hats, us and them. It is, rather, the politics of power and of profession. Spy services become, in le Carré–land, archetypal bureaucracies and microcosms of the societies in which they furtively operate. They have hierarchical structures and access to secrets, both of which define power. But the power that resides in intelligence services carries its own corruption. Leamas denounces British intelligence to his doomed lover, Liz, in *The Spy Who Came in from the Cold* as "a squalid procession of vain fools, traitors too, yes . . . people who play cowboys and Indians to brighten their rotten little lives" (p. 231).

Leamas is destroyed at the Berlin Wall because he begins by knowing too little and ends by knowing too much. The final novel of the so-called Karla trilogy, *Smiley's People* (1980), commences with British spymaster George Smiley being brought out of his "dubious retirement" (without information or power) and ends with him at the German frontier, grimly measuring a surfeit of knowledge about his enemy and himself. In *The Tailor of Panama,* Harry Pendel moves from the humbleness of his trade (in which he possesses no real secrets) and his deliberately obscured past into the suicidal embrace of a fireball caused by an

American invasion of which he was a secret instigator. Pendel shares Alec Leamas' end, for he, too, comes to know too much. *The Tailor of Panama* is a riposte to Graham Greene's more playful story in *Our Man in Havana*. But whereas Greene's character Wormold can get away with inventing knowledge, and even profit by it, Pendel is burned for trying the same game.

The reinvention of the spy thriller achieved by le Carré and Deighton drew many new writers to the genre. One of the first was Adam Hall (b. 1920), the pseudonym of Elleston Trevor, who created the figure of the rumpled, contrary spy Quiller in *The Quiller Memorandum* (1965; U.K. title, *The Berlin Memorandum*). This novel set Quiller, a lone-wolf agent at perpetual odds with his masters in London, against a murderous neo-Nazi organization. Hall later explained that he was inspired to write the first Quiller novel by the excitement that surrounded the publication of *The Spy Who Came in from the Cold.* But his novels operate more in the Deighton mode. Eighteen subsequent Quiller novels have appeared over the years, as Hall, like Deighton, settled into a formula.

The Spy Thriller at Century's End

Fleming's tales of adventure, perpetuated long after his death by sequel writers and an endless stream of Bond films, Deighton's agents with little love of the spy establishment, and le Carré's meditations seem to dominate the literary landscape of the spy thriller at century's end. They all partake of the genre's now-deep literary roots: Fleming and his successors looking back to the heroic tales of spying of the first generation of thriller writers and to the clubland era; Deighton and le Carré reawakening the elements of thriller writing of the 1930s. Does this mean the spy thriller faces closure as a genre? Is it writing itself into dreary repetition?

The answer is no. The spy thriller has a solid history and a proven ability imaginatively to recycle itself. It long ago ceased to be a fledgling literary form dependent on a handful of writers to sustain its production. Nowadays, it attracts legions of authors. One standard bibliography, *Cloak and Dagger Fiction* (3d ed., 1995), edited by Myron J. Smith and Terry White, lists more than five thousand spy thrillers written between 1940 and 1995. This sheer quantity of production guarantees variety. The spy thriller has also proved capacious in another sense. Many writers have swooped in and out of the genre from crime and adventure fiction, providing cross-fertilization. Berkely Mather, the pseudonym of John E. W. Davies, is a good example, writing adeptly in all three genres and often taking his spies into unusual geographic locales, as in *A Spy for a Spy* (1968), set in Hong Kong, and *With Extreme Prejudice* (1975), set at the Suez Canal. Some authors, not writing wholly within the genre, defy its prevailing conventions. Lionel Davidson (b. 1922), in his tale of an innocent young man thrust unexpectedly behind the Iron Curtain and into the midst of a case of nuclear secrets in *The Night of Wenceslas* (1960), brought to the Cold War thriller a comic sense. Blockbuster writers like Hammond Innes (b. 1913) and Alistair Maclean (b. 1923), in their occasional forays into the genre, undoubtedly brought new readers with them. Innes' contributions date back to his Battle of Britain novel, *Attack Alarm* (1941), while Maclean's first venture into spy fiction was *The Last Frontier* (1959; U.S. title, *The Secret Ways*), which features an American agent paid by British intelligence to spirit a defector from Hungary.

Spy fiction is clearly expansive, but it has also been subject to change. Beneath the wings of the current set of dominant spy stories, three remarkable developments have taken place. Some 150 years after James Fenimore Cooper's first essay in the form, the spy thriller has finally recrossed the Atlantic and taken on new vitality as an American genre. The spy novel survived the end of the Cold War and attendant doomsaying about public apathy. Finally, it has shown signs of escaping beyond the walls of the genre itself.

The emergence of a distinctly American spy story—one written by American authors using American voices, characters, settings, and plots—had its roots in a crisis of political confidence remarkably similar to that which helped give birth to the turn-of-the-century spy novel in Britain. First came the Vietnam War and the shock of an unattainable victory, then political protest at home on a massive scale matched by slippage in America's image and leadership abroad. Then, during the early and mid-1970s, a very public spotlight was thrown on U.S. intelligence by congressional investigations into wrongdoing by the Central Intelligence Agency (CIA). Those investigations engendered fierce public debate over the rights and wrongs of U.S. intelligence that scarcely diminished in the decades that followed. In the political turbulence of the era, which also witnessed Watergate and a widespread loss of public faith in the institutions of government, British treatments of American espionage inevitably lost some of their resonance with American readers.

One of Ian Fleming's more egregious acts of fictional imperialism was to have the American spy service, in the shape of Felix Leiter, play a willing second string to Her Majesty's Secret Service. An American author, E. Howard Hunt (b. 1918), a longtime CIA officer, later exposed for his part in the Watergate affair, tried to create an American version of James Bond in his Peter Ward stories, penned under the pseudonym David St. John. Such a belated erasure of American colonial status was, however, sufficient for neither the political mood nor the realities of the 1970s.

Another, and darker, American response to Bond was penned by Donald Hamilton (b. 1916) in his serial Matt Helm stories, the first of which was issued in 1960 in paperback as *Death of a Citizen*. Helm is an agent, indeed a trained assassin, who works for a tight-lipped boss, Mac, and a secret government agency of exterminators, the Wrecking Crew. Matt Helm handles violence easily and has no scruples about gunning down his enemies.

The struggle with the morality of espionage, a feature of the spy thriller since its inception, troubles neither hero nor author. The Matt Helm series was extraordinarily successful for Hamilton; it blended Western shootist action with a fast-paced plot and can be regarded as a conservative backlash against the implied snobbery of the Bond novels, and later the antiestablishment ethos of Deighton and le Carré. But curiously, Hamilton began his exploration of the spy-fiction genre in an entirely different key with two postwar novels, *Date with Darkness* (1947) and *The Steel Mirror* (1948), both of which feature more sophisticated narratives and protagonists who are by no means simply automatons of violence. An interlude of writing Westerns in the 1950s and his publisher's suggestion that he try to match the success of Edward S. Aarons' *Assignment* series, which featured the exploits of hard-boiled operative Sam Durell, turned Hamilton in the direction of the killer spy.

Conservative pundit William F. Buckley, Jr. (b. 1925), was among those who came along in the 1970s to write an American spy story with a new sort of American hero, one freed from hard-boiled mannerisms and capable of carrying a political message. Buckley created the figure of Blackford Oakes and invested him with what he regarded as distinctively American male qualities. Oakes is a man who, in Buckley's words, "believed"—in the American way—in the Cold War struggle and the need for victory. Buckley also set out to write a spy story that would restore moral and political simplicity to the genre by showing that the CIA was the good guys and the KGB the bad.

Buckley, like Hunt before him, brought a degree of practical experience to the American spy story, thereby mirroring a long British tradition. In fact, Buckley had worked for Hunt as an undercover officer in Mexico for nine months before resigning from the CIA—out of boredom, he later claimed. There is an autobiographical flavor to his account of CIA training school in his first Blackford Oakes novel, *Saving the Queen* (1976). But for the most part, he looked to the Buchanesque device of topicality to anchor his novels. This can be seen in the intertwining of his fictional plots with real-life events and characters, notable especially in *Marco Polo, If You Can* (1982), which is set during the 1960 U-2 shootdown, and *Mongoose, R.I.P.* (1987), which takes place in Cuba against a background of CIA plots to assassinate Castro.

Other notable American spy novelists set to work in the same period as Buckley, also with career experience in intelligence. Charles McCarry (b. 1930), who served for a decade between the late 1950s and late 1960s with the CIA, published his first spy novel, *The Miernik Dossier*, in 1973. This novel is built around the device of an intelligence dossier, the individual documents of which are laid out before the reader in epistolary style. Miernik is a mysterious Pole, whom American intelligence, in the shape of agent Paul Christopher, is anxious to identify as either an innocent or a deep-cover Soviet agent. The dossier on Miernik is full of beguiling evidence, which is slowly revealed to the reader as the plot unfolds. It is also incomplete; the final mystery of Miernik is never solved.

McCarry continued to write stories featuring Paul Christopher, including *The Tears of Autumn* (1974), *The Secret Lovers* (1977), *The Last Supper* (1983), and *Second Sight* (1991). All the novels in the series are marked by apparent realism and are highly competent, but none matches the inventiveness of *The Miernik Dossier.*

The presence of American spy novelists in significant numbers since the 1970s has widened the range of and enlivened the spy thriller without necessarily challenging its central motifs. Robert Littell (b. 1939) is a good example of an American author skilled at turning the established motifs of the spy thriller to his own uses. In his first novel, *The Defection of A. J. Lewinter* (1973), Littell muses on the theme of the mole, but this time the mole is an American inventor, and neither the KGB nor the CIA is quite sure of his bona fides. In *The Amateur* (1981), Littell provides an imaginative twist to the old convention of the amateur spy able to foil the misdeeds of his country's enemies—a tradition that dates back to Erskine Childers—by having a quiet CIA scholar transform into an avenging assassin who tracks down the terrorists who murdered his wife. In *The Once and Future Spy* (1990), Littell tells the story of a rogue operation and its unraveling, an American take on the spy novel's habit, first advanced by Somerset Maugham in the 1920s, of exploring the Machiavellian dictates of intelligence practice and morality.

When Tom Clancy (b. 1947) burst on the scene with *The Hunt for Red October* in 1984, he not only completed Buckley's work of fashioning an American hero acceptable to the needs of conservatism but also proved beyond a shadow of a doubt that an American spy thriller could appeal to a mass audience. There is plenty of action and gadgetry in Clancy's novels and an explicit political agenda. Although he is noted for the technical detail that suffuses his novels, this is an old device in the spy thriller, one that stretches back to Le Queux. *The Hunt for Red October* was followed by several other spy novels featuring the multitalented Jack Ryan, a man capable not only of foiling an IRA plot while on vacation and making friends with the British royal family (*Patriot Games,* 1987) but also of running a successful war against the Medellín drug cartel (*Clear and Present Danger,* 1989).

David Ignatius (b. 1950) brought his own version of the highly charged politics of American intelligence to the spy novel. In *Agents of Innocence* (1987), he tells the story of an effort by the CIA to penetrate the Palestine Liberation Organization and the backlash that follows. Many read this novel as a thinly disguised roman à clef that revealed something of the secret background to the bombing of the Marine barracks in Beirut in 1980. Ignatius was, at the time, the Middle East bureau chief for the *Wall Street Journal.* His next novel, *Siro* (1991), is also set in the Middle East and features a rogue CIA operation. In *A Firing Offense* (1997), Ignatius takes up the controversy over whether journalists and journalistic cover should be used by U.S. intelligence agencies. Eric Truell, the hero of the story, finds himself drawn into collaboration with the CIA, for patriotic and private reasons, but pays a high price in the foundering of his career as a reporter.

The arrival of an American story at the heart of the spy thriller, with all it promised of potent mass-market forces, undoubtedly helped to sustain the genre's momentum after the demise of the Cold War, which had provided the bulk of the spy thriller's settings, characters, plots, and political tension after 1945. Commentators naturally wondered whether the disappearance of the Soviet threat would deprive the spy thriller of material, audience, and relevance. Similar views were floated about the future of spy agencies themselves. In each case, the pundits were wrong, failing to see the long historical roots of both the spy thriller and the real-life practice of espionage and mistaking their persistence.

Some veterans of the genre, it is true, went into retirement with the end of the Cold War. Following *A Very Private Plot* (1994), Buckley decided that "the time had come to pack it in" (*The Blackford Oakes Reader*, p. xxx). And Frederick Forsyth (b. 1938) threatened to do the same. "I do not want to write any more political thrillers," he said in 1997. "Nothing else interests me, there are no other subjects that need to be covered—the Cold War is well over" (*The Independent*, London, 21 October 1997, p. 2). Ennui and exhaustion are understandable in a novelist, and Forsyth, who shot to fame with *The Day of the Jackal* (1971), had made a sustained effort to fashion post–Cold War politics into topical spy thrillers in *The Deceiver* (1991), *The Fist of God* (1994), and *Icon* (1996).

But Buckley and Forsyth seem atypical. The industry has instead followed le Carré, who shrugged off the end of the Cold War as something that would have little impact on the spy thriller. During a publicity tour for his novel *The Russia House* (1989), le Carré stated, "So long as there are nation states, trade competition and statesmen who do not quite tell the truth, spying will go on"—and he and others will continue to fictionalize it.

Le Carré has been as good as his word. Following on *The Russia House*, he has kept up an extraordinary production, with the appearance of *The Secret Pilgrim* (1991), a reverie of times past in British espionage narrated by a George Smiley protégé, Ned; *The Night Manager* (1993), whose villain is an international arms and drug dealer; *Our Game* (1995), in which the North Caucasus beckons as a new realm for old espionage and rekindled idealism; and *The Tailor of Panama*, in which British intelligence, still peopled by recognizably Thatcherite types, has a go at destabilizing Panama.

Le Carré has been matched in productivity by another veteran writer, Ted Allbeury (b. 1917), whose first spy novel, *A Choice of Enemies*, appeared in 1973. The end of the Cold War has stimulated a burst of writing from Allbeury, with novels appearing almost yearly. His *Beyond the Silence* (1995) and *The Long Run* (1996) both use the Cold War as a pool of hidden secrets with a nasty habit of coming back to life. *Beyond the Silence* concerns a backtracking investigation of Lord Carling, who is suspected of being a classic double agent. In *The Long Run* highly damaging STASI files on eminent British politicians come to light.

For some, the post–Cold War years even sparked a return to the spy genre. Gavin Lyall (b. 1932), who left it while the Cold War was still going strong, produced a quartet of well-crafted espionage novels, starting with *The Secret Servant* (1980), featuring the exploits of Major Harry Maxim. The Maxim series came to an end with *Uncle Target* in 1988, by which time reviewers were using the usual le Carré benchmarks to assess Lyall's fiction. After a hiatus of several years, Lyall suddenly reappeared with two new spy thrillers, *Spy's Honour* (1993) and *Flight from Honour* (1996), both set in the very early, pre–World War I days of British intelligence.

In short, no extinction of the post–Cold War spy novel seems at hand. The genre persists. There has been no mass defection of its veteran authors or of its readers. But what directions might the spy thriller take in the future?

One mark of the genre's success, and a pointer to the future, is its recent export into the realm of the literary novel. Notable works such as John Banville's *The Untouchable* (1997), James Buchan's *Heart's Journey in Winter* (1995), Don DeLillo's *Libra* (1988), Ian MacEwan's *The Innocent* (1990), Norman Mailer's *Harlot's Ghost* (1991), Michael Ondaatje's *The English Patient* (1992), and M. G. Vassanji's *The Book of Secrets* (1994) all contain spy stories. This infiltration into the literary novel suggests a fascination with clandestinity and the potency of the mythology of espionage. It also confirms that the figure of the spy has become what it was not at the beginning of the twentieth century—namely, a common trope.

Fascination with the spy theme in the literary novel has brought with it degrees of experimentation that are bound to influence future genre writing. Much of this experimentation uses a documentary mode in which the story revolves around the contemplation of secret evidence. There was an inkling of this technique in the spy thriller as long ago as Le Queux, but the literary novel has deeper uses for the documentary mode than for the stridency of Le Queux's device of faction. Victor Maskell, the exposed double agent of Banville's *The Untouchable,* is writing his memoirs and is the subject of vague journalistic probings by a female reporter, Serena Vandeleur. Maskell's memoir is a device for reconstructing his identity in a world certain of the truth about the exposed spy. A found diary is at the heart of Vassanji's *The Book of Secrets,* which is set in East Africa and spans the colonial and postcolonial years. The diary offers a hidden history of the region and profoundly changes the lives of those who come to understand its contents. One of the main characters in DeLillo's *Libra* is a retired CIA official writing the secret history of the Kennedy assassination. His documents become the storehouse for the novel—"Nicholas Branch sits in the book-filled room, the room of documents, the room of theories and dreams"

(Penguin paperback ed., p. 14). The storehouse hums with secrets, all of which are ambiguous.

The Future of the Genre

The most finely crafted of literary novels and the most formulaic genre thriller alike share the spy story's promise of secrets revealed. Oppenheim, a self-confessed formula writer, understood well the appeal of the spy story: "So long as the world lasts, its secret international history will . . . suggest the most fascinating of all material for the writing of fiction" (quoted in David Stafford, *The Silent Game,* p. 37). Oppenheim's predecessors, Kipling and Childers, were aware of the power of secret history at the very birth of the genre. The secret, often an apocalyptic one, is to the spy thriller what the corpse is to the detective novel. But the secret is only part of the spy story's appeal. The narrative must tell how the secret came to be, who controls or competes for it, and what ruin it might bring. Secret history is the result, and secret history is different. The spy novel's alternative history has its terrifying dimensions—in everything from human corruption to weapons of mass destruction. But it also has a comforting face. What spy fiction offers is a story in which the individual spy, even one caught up in the "confusing business" of a Deighton novel, can still master his or her own destiny or at least make knowledgeable choices. The spy thriller is the last bastion of the "great man" theory of history; it offers a parable of individual decisiveness in the face of the terrible heaviness of international politics. Both James Bond and George Smiley can change history, though they come from opposite traditions of the spy thriller. For an alternative version of the Gulf conflict, we can read Forsyth's *The Fist of God* and marvel at just how close we came to nuclear war and just how well we were served by a hero of truly epic proportions from the British Special Air Service.

As the Forsyth novel suggests, the spy thriller's alternative secret history is usually a commentary on the present. But while topicality is likely to persist as a motif, the spy thriller is poised to spread its alternative secret histories over a broader time span and move closer in form to the historical novel. In the days of Childers and Le Queux, there was not much history to confront. A twenty-first-century thriller writer will have plenty. Robert Harris (b. 1957) enjoyed enormous success with *Enigma* (1995), a well-researched novel that takes us into the heart of British code breaking against Nazi Germany during World War II. Anthony Price (b. 1928) has taken a different tack by setting the action of his novels within a historical mystery and by featuring the exploits of a trained historian and academic turned spymaster, the always clever David Audley. In Price's *The Old Vengeful* (1982), the mystery concerns the interest of Soviet intelligence in a British frigate sunk during the Napoleonic Wars. *The Hour of the Donkey* (1980) is a first-rate thriller set during the Battle of France and the retreat to Dunkirk. Audley has to crack the mystery of a senior British officer seen passing secrets to the Germans. But good historical spy fiction is not a monopoly of the British. Alan Furst, an American expatriate journalist who lives in Paris, has also written most effectively in a historical vein. In a series of novels, including *Night Soldiers* (1988), *Dark Star* (1991), *The Polish Officer* (1995), and *The World at Night* (1996), Furst has brilliantly captured the ambience of espionage and politics in Europe during the 1930s and World War II. The spy thriller may well follow the lead of Harris, Price, and Furst and feast on the rich history of intelligence services in the expired twentieth century.

Yet there are problems that may dim the spy thriller's future. Perhaps the most obvious is that it remains a resolutely masculinist genre. Its principal authors are male, its fictional characters are mostly male, and the world of high politics and covert operations that it describes is male. Spy fiction has not experienced a wave of feminist writing, as has occurred in detective and crime fiction. But this resistance may break down if a turn is made in the direction of the historical novel, where stories of female agents and resistance fighters await their fictional recapitulation. Even without recourse to historical fiction, the spy thriller may still prove malleable at the hands of women writers bent on exploring the world of politics. Joan Didion, in *The Last Thing He Wanted* (1996), has offered a highly suggestive motif in which a female protagonist, Elena McMahon, finds herself enmeshed in a shadowy plot that features gunrunning, covert operations, and assassinations. In the murk of this Iran contra–inspired novel, nobody is empowered. Through the depiction of Elena McMahon's powerlessness, Didion found an exit from the difficulty of writing women into traditional spy-thriller plots. But whatever the way forward for the spy thriller, it urgently needs compelling female characters and a female readership.

The spy thriller has also missed the energizing presence of black authors and characters. Sam Greenlee's *The Spook Who Sat by the Door* (1969), whose plot revolves around a token movement for racial integration at the CIA, and John A. Williams' *The Man Who Cried I Am* (1967), with its imaginary plan for a vast surveillance and roundup of blacks in America, together revealed the kind of political edge and agenda that black writers might bring to the spy thriller. But the writing of Greenlee and Williams stands outside the mainstream spy thriller.

The politics of the spy thriller was, and is, a matter for concern. Eric Ambler rightly noted that some of the genre's early practitioners were peddling a barely disguised fascism. The Cold War had the effect of damping down the kinds of politically aware, left-wing thrillers that were a brief feature of the 1930s. The didactic functions of warning and reassurance that have been features of the spy thriller from its birth have tended to keep its political spectrum narrow and in the main conservative. Without greater political range, the spy thriller is threatened with stagnation and a loss of readership.

The frontiers of the spy thriller also need adjustment. Traditionally, the genre has operated on the front lines of European power politics (between 1900 and 1945) and on the fissures of the U.S.-Soviet Cold War. Voyeuristic agents such as James Bond have traveled outward from this geopolitical space, it is true. But the post–Cold War world requires a rethinking of the geopolitical setting of the spy thriller. The world of international politics is no longer Eurocentric, or bipolar, or indeed easily described as a world of competing nation-states, where dangerous secrets are monopolized by government institutions. So long as the spy thriller maintains its ambition to write an alternative secret history of world politics, it will have to accommodate itself to the new realities. But these offer a wealth of new settings and a wealth of new fictional threats to civilization, including international crime, terrorism, weapons proliferation, global corporate power, business corruption, and ecological degradation. Even the Internet and the information revolution, touted as threatening the future of the novel itself, are likely to provide a new frontier for the spy thriller.

Oppenheim was right about the enduring appeal of "secret international history." What he could not predict was just how appealing this history would prove to be and the massive popular cultural production that would result. Nor could he predict how the history itself would change and throw up new challenges for its fictional shapers and seers.

Selected Bibliography

WORKS CITED

Aarons, Edward S. *Assignment to Disaster.* Greenwich, Conn.: Fawcett, 1955.

Allbeury, Ted. *A Choice of Enemies.* London: P. Davies, 1973.

———. *Beyond the Silence.* London: Hodder and Stoughton, 1995.

———. *The Long Run.* London: Hodder and Stoughton, 1996.

Ambler, Eric. *The Dark Frontier.* London: Hodder and Stoughton, 1936.

———. *The Mask of Dimitrios.* London: Hodder and Stoughton, 1939. U.S.: *A Coffin for Dimitrios.* New York: Knopf, 1939.

———. *Journey into Fear.* New York: Knopf, 1940.

Banville, John. *The Untouchable.* New York: Knopf, 1997.

Buchan, John. *The Four Adventures of Richard Hannay,* with an introduction by Robin Winks. Boston: David R. Godine, 1988. Omnibus edition of *The Thirty-Nine Steps, Greenmantle, Mr. Standfast,* and *The Three Hostages.*

Buckley, William F., Jr. *Saving the Queen.* Garden City, N.Y.: Doubleday, 1976.

———. *Marco Polo, If You Can.* Garden City, N.Y.: Doubleday, 1982.

———. *Mongoose, R. I. P.* New York: Random House, 1987.

———. *A Very Private Plot.* New York: Morrow, 1994.

———. *The Blackford Oakes Reader.* Kansas City, Mo.: Andrews and McMeel, 1995.

Chesterton, G. K. *The Man Who Was Thursday.* New York: Dodd, Mead, 1908. New York: Carroll & Graf, 1986.

Cheyney, Peter [Reginald Southouse Cheyney]. *This Man Is Dangerous.* New York: Dodd, Mead, 1936.

Childers, Erskine. *The Riddle of the Sands.* London: Smith, Elder, 1903. Oxford: Oxford University Press, 1995, with an introduction by David Trotter.

Clancy, Tom. *The Hunt for Red October.* Annapolis, Md.: Naval Institute Press, 1984.

———. *Patriot Games.* New York: Putnam, 1987.

———. *Clear and Present Danger.* New York: Putnam, 1989.

Conrad, Joseph. *The Secret Agent.* London: Methuen, 1907.

———. *Under Western Eyes.* London: Methuen, 1911.

Cooper, James Fenimore. *The Spy: A Tale of the Neutral Ground.* New York: Wiley & Halsted, 1821.

Davidson, Lionel. *The Night of Wenceslas.* New York: Harper, 1960. Harmondsworth, Eng.: Penguin Books, 1962.

Deighton, Len. *The Ipcress File.* London: Hodder and Stoughton, 1962.

———. *Funeral in Berlin.* London: Jonathan Cape, 1964.

———. *Billion Dollar Brain.* New York: Putnam, 1966.

———. *Berlin Game.* London: Hutchinson, 1983.

DeLillo, Don. *Libra.* New York: Viking Penguin, 1988.

Didion, Joan. *The Last Thing He Wanted.* New York: Knopf, 1996.

Fleming, Ian. *Casino Royale.* London: Jonathan Cape, 1953.

———. *Dr. No.* London: Jonathan Cape, 1958.

———. *Goldfinger.* London: Jonathan Cape, 1959.

———. *Thunderball.* London: Jonathan Cape, 1961.

Forsyth, Frederick. *The Day of the Jackal.* New York: Viking Press, 1971.

———. *The Deceiver*. 1991. Rpt. New York: Bantam Books, 1995.

———. *The Fist of God*. New York: Bantam Books, 1994.

———. *Icon*. 1996. Rpt. New York: Bantam Books, 1997.

Furst, Alan. *Night Soldiers*. Boston: Houghton Mifflin, 1988.

———. *Dark Star*. Boston: Houghton Mifflin, 1991.

———. *The Polish Officer*. London: HarperCollins, 1995.

———. *The World at Night*. New York: Random House, 1996.

Greene, Graham. *The Confidential Agent*. London: Heinemann, 1939.

———. *The Ministry of Fear*. London: Heinemann, 1943; Harmondsworth, Eng.: Penguin, 1979.

———. *Our Man in Havana*. London: Heinemann, 1958.

———. *The Human Factor*. London: Bodley Head, 1978.

Greene, Graham, and Hugh Greene, eds. *The Spy's Bedside Book*. London: Rupert Hart-David, 1957.

Greenlee, Sam. *The Spook Who Sat by the Door*. London: Allison and Busby, 1969.

Haggard, William [Richard Henry Michael Clayton]. *The Antagonists*. London: Cassell, 1964. Harmondsworth, Eng.: Penguin Books, 1968.

Hall, Adam [Elleston Trevor]. *The Quiller Memorandum*. New York: Simon & Schuster, 1965. U.K.: *The Berlin Memorandum*. London: Collins, 1965.

Hamilton, Donald. *Date with Darkness*. New York: Rinehart, 1947.

———. *The Steel Mirror*. New York: Rinehart, 1948.

———. *Death of a Citizen*. Greenwich, Conn.: Fawcett, 1960.

Harris, Robert. *Enigma*. London: Hutchinson, 1995.

Household, Geoffrey. *Rogue Male*. London: Chatto & Windus, 1939. Harmondsworth, Eng.: Penguin Books, 1982.

———. *Against the Wind*. London: Michael Joseph, 1958. Autobiography.

———. *Rogue Justice*. London: Michael Joseph, 1982. Harmondsworth, Eng.: Penguin Books, 1984.

Ignatius, David. *Agents of Innocence*. New York: Norton, 1987.

———. *Siro*. New York: Farrar, Straus & Giroux, 1991.

———. *A Firing Offense*. New York: Random House, 1997.

Innes, Hammond [Ralph Hammond-Innes]. *Attack Alarm*. London: Collins, 1941.

Kipling, Rudyard. *Kim*. London: Macmillan, 1901. Harmondsworth, Eng.: Penguin Classics, 1987, with an introduction by Edward Said.

le Carré, John [David John Moore Cornwell]. *The Spy Who Came in from the Cold*. London: Gollancz, 1963.

———. *Smiley's People*. London: Hodder and Stoughton, 1980.

———. *The Russia House*. New York: Knopf, 1989.

———. *The Secret Pilgrim*. New York: Knopf, 1991.

———. *The Night Manager*. New York: Knopf, 1993.

———. *Our Game*. New York: Viking Penguin, 1995.

———. *The Tailor of Panama*. New York: Knopf, 1996.

Le Queux, William. *The Great War in England in 1897*. London: Tower, 1894.

———. *The Invasion of 1910*. London: Nash, 1906.

———. *Spies of the Kaiser*. London: Hurst & Blackett, 1909. London: Frank Cass, 1996, with an introduction by Nicholas Hiley.

Littell, Robert. *The Defection of A. J. Lewinter*. Boston: Houghton Mifflin, 1973.

———. *The Amateur*. New York: Simon & Schuster, 1981.

———. *The Once and Future Spy*. New York: Bantam, 1990.

Lyall, Gavin. *The Secret Servant*. London: Hodder and Stoughton, 1980.

———. *Uncle Target*. London: Hodder and Stoughton, 1988.

———. *Spy's Honour*. London: Hodder and Stoughton, 1993.

———. *Flight from Honour*. London: Hodder and Stoughton, 1996.

McCarry, Charles. *The Miernik Dossier*. New York: Saturday Review Press, 1973.

———. *The Tears of Autumn*. New York: Saturday Review Press, 1974.

———. *The Secret Lovers*. New York: Dutton, 1977.

———. *The Last Supper*. New York: Dutton, 1983.

———. *Second Sight*. New York: Dutton, 1991.

Mackenzie, Compton. *Extremes Meet*. London: Cassell, 1928.

———. *The Three Couriers*. London: Cassell, 1929.

———. *Greek Memories*. London: Cassell, 1932. London: Chatto & Windus, 1939.

———. *Water on the Brain*. London: Cassell, 1933.

Maclean, Alistair. *The Last Frontier*. London: Collins, 1959. U.S.: *The Secret Ways*. Garden City, N.Y.: Doubleday, 1959.

Mather, Berkely [John E. W. Davies]. *A Spy for a Spy*. New York: Scribners, 1968.

———. *With Extreme Prejudice*. London: Collins, 1975.

Maugham, Somerset. *Ashenden; or, the British Agent*. London: Heinemann, 1928. Harmondsworth, Eng.: Penguin Books, 1977, with original preface.

Milne, A. A., "The Secret of the Army Aeroplane." *Punch*, May 1909.

Oppenheim, E. Phillips. *The Mysterious Mr. Sabin*. London: Ward, Lock, 1898.

———. *The Maker of History*. London: Ward, Lock, 1905.

———. *The Great Secret*. Boston: Little, Brown, 1907.

———. *The Kingdom of the Blind*. Boston: Little, Brown, 1916. London: Frank Cass, 1998, with an introduction by David Stafford.

Philby, Kim. *My Silent War*, with a foreword by Graham Greene. New York: Grove Press, 1968.

Price, Anthony. *The Hour of the Donkey*. London: Gollancz, 1980.

———. *The Old Vengeful*. London: Gollancz, 1982.

Sapper [Herman Cyril McNeile]. *Bull-Dog Drummond.* London: Hodder and Stoughton, 1920.

———. *The Black Gang.* London: Hodder and Stoughton, n.d., but 1922.

———. *Bulldog Drummond Hits Out.* London: Hodder and Stoughton, 1937.

Vassanji, M. G. *The Book of Secrets.* Toronto: McClelland and Stewart, 1994.

Williams, John A. *The Man Who Cried I Am.* Boston: Little, Brown, 1967.

BIOGRAPHICAL AND CRITICAL STUDIES

Ambler, Eric. *Here Lies: An Autobiography.* London: Weidenfeld & Nicolson, 1985.

Andrew, Christopher. *Secret Service: The Making of the British Intelligence Community.* London: Heinemann, 1985.

Atkins, John. *The British Spy Novel: Styles in Treachery.* London: Calder, 1984.

Barley, Tony. *Taking Sides: The Fiction of John le Carré.* Milton Keynes, U.K.: Open Univ. Press, 1986.

Bennett, Tony, and Janet Woollacott. *Bond and Beyond: The Political Career of a Popular Hero.* New York: Methuen, 1987.

Bold, Alan, ed. *The Quest for le Carré.* London: Vision Press, 1988.

Cawelti, John G., and Bruce A. Rosenberg. *The Spy Story.* Chicago: Univ. of Chicago Press, 1987.

Daniell, David. *The Interpreter's House: A Critical Assessment of John Buchan.* London: Thomas Nelson, 1975.

Davis, Earle. "Howard Hunt and the Peter Ward–CIA Spy Novels." *Kansas Quarterly* 10, no. 4: 85–95 (1978).

Denning, Michael. *Cover Stories: Narrative and Ideology in the British Spy Thriller.* London: Routledge and Kegan Paul, 1987.

Eco, Umberto, and Oreste del Buono, eds. *The Bond Affair.* Translated by Robert Angus Downie. London: Macdonald, 1966.

Fletcher, Katy. "Evolution of the Modern American Spy Novel." *Journal of Contemporary History* 22, no. 2: 319–331 (1987).

Hixson, Walter L. " 'Red Storm Rising': Tom Clancy Novels and the Cult of National Security." *Diplomatic History* 17, no. 4: 599–613 (1993).

Hopkins, Joel. "An Interview with Eric Ambler." *Journal of Popular Culture* 9 (fall 1975).

Lycett, Andrew. *Ian Fleming.* London: Weidenfeld & Nicolson, 1995.

McCormick, Donald. *17F: The Life of Ian Fleming.* London: Peter Owen, 1993.

———. *Who's Who in Spy Fiction.* London: Sphere Books, 1979.

McCormick, Donald, and Katy Fletcher. *Spy Fiction: A Connoisseur's Guide.* New York: Facts on File, 1990.

Morgan, Ted. *Somerset Maugham.* London: Jonathan Cape, 1980.

Palmer, Jerry. *Thrillers: Genesis and Structure of a Popular Genre.* London: Edward Arnold, 1978.

Panek, LeRoy. *The Special Branch: The British Spy Novel, 1890–1980.* Bowling Green, Ohio: Bowling Green State Univ. Popular Press, 1981.

Pearson, John. *The Life of Ian Fleming.* London: Jonathan Cape, 1966.

Sarchett, Barry W. "Unreading the Spy Thriller: The Example of William F. Buckley, Jr." *Journal of Popular Culture* 26: 127–139 (fall 1992).

Sauerberg, Lars Ole. *Secret Agents in Fiction: Ian Fleming, John le Carré, and Len Deighton.* New York: St. Martin's Press, 1984.

Smith, Myron J., and Terry White, eds. *Cloak and Dagger Fiction: An Annotated Guide to Spy Thrillers,* 3d ed. Westport, Conn.: Greenwood Press, 1995.

Stafford, David. *The Silent Game: The Real World of Imaginary Spies.* Toronto: Lester and Orpen Dennys, 1988.

Standish, Robert. *The Prince of Storytellers: The Life of E. Phillips Oppenheim.* London: Peter Davies, 1957.

Symons, Julian. *Bloody Murder: From the Detective Story to the Crime Novel: A History.* London: Faber, 1972.

Usborne, Richard. *Clubland Heroes.* London: Constable, 1953.

Wark, Wesley K., ed. *Spy Fiction, Spy Films and Real Intelligence.* London: Frank Cass, 1991.

Winks, Robin. *Modus Operandi: An Excursion into Detective Fiction.* Boston: David R. Godine, 1982.

———. "The Sordid Truth: Donald Hamilton." *New Republic,* 26 July 1975. Pp. 21–24.

———. "William Haggard." In *Dictionary of Literary Biography Yearbook.* 1993.

WOMEN OF MYSTERY:
Helen McCloy (1904–1994)
Doris Miles Disney (1907–1976)
Dorothy Salisbury Davis (b. 1916)

ROBERT ALLEN PAPINCHAK

HELEN MCCLOY, Doris Miles Disney, and Dorothy Salisbury Davis are three female mystery writers deserving of renewed attention. While the best of their novels appeared in the 1940s and 1950s, ideas, themes, and concepts they dealt with became staples of a category of mysteries that remains popular. Though they might easily be overlooked as minor practitioners of the art, each helped to develop a subgenre which linked eerie suspense with domestic violence tempered by romance. They explore the desperate lives of lonely widows, the moral isolation of passionately committed prelates, and the claustrophobic confines of socially condemned prostitutes. They peel off the veneer of small towns to reveal populations of little minds natty with murder. They introduced the first psychiatric detective in American mystery fiction and created one of the early female amateur detectives who sought personal fulfillment with an independent career. All of this was accomplished in three writing careers that spanned almost fifty years, more than ninety novels, several Edgars, and two Grand Master awards.

Helen McCloy

Helen Worrell Clarkson McCloy, born in New York City on 6 June 1904, to editor William Conrad and writer Helen Worrell McCloy, was the first female president (1950) of Mystery Writers of America. Educated at Brooklyn Friends School and the Sorbonne, Paris, she lived abroad from 1923 to 1932, becoming a staff correspondent for the Hearst Universal Service in Paris from 1927 to 1932. She served as Paris art critic for *International Studio* (1930–1931) and as London art critic for the *New York Times* (1930–1931). She married Davis Dresser, a writer known as Brett Halliday, on 13 October 1946; they had one daughter, Chloe McCloy, and divorced in 1961. Along with Dresser, she founded Torquil Publishing Company and Halliday and McCloy Literary Agency (1953–1964). She received an Edgar nomination for best short story in 1952, was awarded an Edgar for criticism in 1954, and was named Grand Master in 1990. She died in 1994.

SOCIETY'S FAILED PROMISES

McCloy introduced America's first psychiatrist detective, Dr. Basil Willing, in her first novel, *Dance Of Death* (1938). He appeared in eleven more books, including McCloy's last novel, *Burn This* (1980). Anthony Boucher's introduction to *Cue for Murder* (1942; Willing's fifth case) recalls the praise the first novel received with reviewers "stumb[ling] over each other to proclaim her a genuine find." Comparisons were drawn to Margery Allingham and Ngaio Marsh. He claims that the only reason the book did not win an Edgar was because Mystery Writers of America did not yet exist.

In the best tradition of the classic detective story, McCloy introduces Dr. Basil Willing to the puzzling beginning of a mystery he must solve. Two snow removal workers on East Seventy-eighth Street in New York face a conundrum when they uncover the body of a young woman buried in the snow. Her corpse, however, is so hot that it appears she has died of heatstroke. As forensic psychiatric assistant to the district attorney, Basil asserts that "every criminal leaves psychic fingerprints." Basil recognizes the woman as Catharine Jocelyn, a debutante who endorsed a weight-reduction product, Sveltis, on the back cover of a magazine. The difficulty with his identification of the deceased is that the young woman appears to be very much alive, attending her coming-out party and appearing at the opera.

McCloy waltzes through the echelon of the upper crust as she moves Basil through his paces. A cousin, Ann Jocelyn Claude, claims she was forced to exchange places with Catharine when she fell ill the night of her party. Since sixty thousand dollars was spent on the affair, her stepmother, Rhoda Jocelyn, refuses to cancel the party because it would be a social embarrassment. When it appears that Catharine may have drunk a poisoned cocktail, Basil rounds up nine suspects, those persons who were in the room when the drink was served. In classic Freudian fashion, Basil attempts to sort out unconscious blunders, "messages in code," the criminal would commit to reveal guilt. With his scientific background, he discovers that the yellow tinge to Catharine's flesh came from dinitrophenol

(a.k.a. thermol) in the formula for Sveltis. An overdose of thermol would cause an internal heatstroke, leading to death. Basil's investigation is stymied when he learns that even though Catharine endorsed Sveltis, she never took the product. Clue after classic clue—an inexpensive black coat from Paris, a diamond ring, a stolen sapphire-studded cigarette case, a missigned check—finally lead Basil to a logical conclusion. He finds that while "[m]ost crimes are due to the failure of the individual to adapt himself to society . . . this crime is due to the failure of society to fulfill its obligations to the individual." The murderer was avenging the death of her daughter who died taking Sveltis; since her death was caused by a dishonest endorsement of patent medicine containing a dangerous drug, she vowed to murder all those who endorsed it.

McCloy's acknowledged masterpiece is the eighth Basil Willing novel, *Through a Glass, Darkly* (1950). Basil faces one of his most terrifying and compelling cases when he encounters what appears to be paranormal behavior involving the teacher at a girls' school in Connecticut. Five weeks into her first term at Brereton School for Girls, art teacher Faustina Crayle is dismissed without reason or reference and given six months advance salary. The only hint at the cause of the firing is that her presence would ruin the school by the atmosphere she created. Basil is brought into the case when he receives a letter from his fiancée Gisela Von Hohenems, the German instructor at the school. Basil's investigation is compounded by the fact that this has apparently happened to Faustina before, when she was employed at the Maidstone School in Virginia.

Testimony reveals that Faustina frequently appears in two places at the same time. Two teenagers, Meg Vining and Beth Chase, detail seeing Faustina outside sketching on the lawn at the same time they supposedly see her inside sitting in a blue chair. A maid shudders at having seen Faustina simultaneously on the back stairs and in the kitchen. Even the headmistress asserts she passed Faustina at the top of the stairs and the bottom of the stairs. This evidence allows McCloy to introduce the legend of the doppelgänger as Basil pursues the mystery of two Faustinas.

The possible ominous presence of a double in the novel allows the terror to escalate as the story unfolds. Gisela finds the drama teacher, Alice Aitchison, dead at the foot of the garden steps after a board of trustees meeting. Beth says that she saw Faustina push Alice but Faustina has an alibi—she had just phoned Gisela from New York. Meanwhile, Basil learns of Faustina's past, which includes a deceased mother who had been a courtesan in Europe and who was named the corespondent in a famous divorce case. Since her father is also dead, Faustina has inherited a beach cottage in New Jersey and, when she turns thirty, a number of priceless jewels. If Faustina dies before then, the jewels, part of her mother's estate from her various lovers, are to be returned to the heirs of the original owners.

The chilling climax of the novel culminates at the Brightsea cottage when Gisela decides to visit Faustina. Although Gisela is certain that she saw Faustina on the road to the dunes and almost ran into her, when she arrives at the cottage, Faustina is on the floor. Basil rushes to the seashore. The ending of the story entails further discussion of the doppelgänger theory, which involves an association with death, the history of the double with regard to the body and the spirit, and a complicated series of images and reflections. When the murderer is pitted against Basil, the resolution is ingenious but plausible with a clever conclusion that leaves a conviction in doubt.

There is no doubt about the future of Dr. Basil Willing. Having met Gisela in *The Man in the Moonlight* (1940), he becomes engaged to her in *Through a Glass, Darkly*. They marry and have a daughter named Gisela. Willing's career includes stints in Naval Intelligence. In subsequent stories, he moves to Boston, writes books, and lectures at Harvard.

One other McCloy novel of note, *A Change of Heart* (1973), does not feature Willing. This later book is closer to a psychological thriller than it is to a pure detective mystery. A schoolboy friendship which includes a blood pledge stretches over thirty-six years to end in betrayal and death. In May 1936, at a Massachusetts boys' school, thirteen-year-old Parmalee Graeme (Lee) and Percival Leicester Laurence (Laurie) vow to meet again on 5 June 1972 (at age fifty) and prove they have not turned into stuffed shirts. Their password will be a secret French phrase, "*Un canon bien tenu en vaut deux.*" Lee goes on to become a translator and cryptographer during World War II; Laurie, a paratrooper.

Though they have had no contact since the war, the reunion does occur on the site of the Crane Club, now a diner, in New York City. Lee is anxious about the meeting because his past includes an academic scandal which lost him his linguistics professorship. What he does not know is that Laurie has an even more criminal history—he has become a jewel thief. Laurie enlists Lee's help when he claims he wants to return the Claudian amethyst (a carved jewel dating back to the Claudian invasion of England) to the Museum of Classic Art. In the midst of what should have been a resolution of the blood pledge, the caper goes awry, and the curator of the museum is killed. McCloy's double theme from *Through a Glass, Darkly* appears again when Lee learns that Laurie supposedly died in Normandy during the war and the man he met at the club was not his schoolboy chum. Eventually, the mystery of the false double is resolved through another series of betrayed friendships and reprisals for an unrequited love. There is a reversal of fortune for Lee and his daughter, Girzel, who aids in the solution, and a romantic "L'Envoi" chapter which ties up all the loose ends.

Doris Miles Disney

Like McCloy, Doris Miles Disney found subjects of romantic suspense buried in past lives, cozy New England villages, and the listlessness of rudderless marriages. She was born 8 March 1907, in Glastonbury, Connecticut, to Edward Lucas and Elizabeth Malone Miles. She married George Disney on 19 June 1936;

they had one daughter, Elizabeth. After attending public schools in Glastonbury, Disney worked in an insurance office and did publicity for a number of social agencies before becoming a full-time writer. Her extensive writing career spanned thirty-three years. In that time, she published forty-seven books, three of which were adapted for movies and television. She had three series characters, Jim O'Neill, David Madden, and, the best known, Jefferson DiMarco. Her mysteries are often set in her native New England and usually contain some element of romance. She died 8 March 1976.

SECRETS AND LIES

Two of Disney's best novels are early ones published the same year (1946), *Dark Road* and *Who Rides a Tiger*. *Dark Road* introduces the insurance agent DiMarco. *Who Rides a Tiger* focuses on the diaries of a deceased, elderly woman and the secrets in her past, a frequent subject for Disney.

Jefferson DiMarco's debut novel is distinctive because the criminal gets away with murder and the amateur detective falls in love with her. It's apparent from the opening chapter of the novel that discontented Hazel Lindsey Clements wants her older husband, Ralph, a partner in a specialty shop, dead. Her controlling, interfering sister-in-law, Esther Clements Olney, a widow, lives next door and uses the Clementses' house as if it were her own. One June evening, Hazel encounters a former lover, wealthy Eugene Hurd, in a parking lot. They have not seen each other for sixteen years. Hazel resumes a relationship with him, despite the fact that he is married to Rachel Carey and has a seven-year-old son.

By July, Hazel is plotting to kill Ralph, but she can't find a suitable method. One occurs to her when they are visiting their cottage on Lake Moquin. Just before the entrance to the cabin is a logging road that leads to a deserted sawmill and the lake. Certain that Eugene will seek a divorce and marry her, Hazel visits the library seeking books on car accidents. Though there are no specific details on how

to arrange death by automobile, Hazel keeps the book, *The Chevrolet Car*, hoping to find enough information to give her some ideas about how to arrange an accident. A torrential rainstorm in October gives Hazel the idea she needs. She will exchange the signs that mark the separate entrances to their cottage and to the lake, assuming Ralph will take a wrong turn on the dark road. Since she knows Ralph's habits so well, she knows she will be able to convince him to drive back into town to buy some liquor, then, already drunk, he will drive onto the incorrectly marked road and drown in the lake.

For the most part, Hazel's scheme works. She switches the signs, stages alibis with Esther, the police, and the salesperson at the liquor store. But she hasn't planned on Jefferson DiMarco entering her life. As the claims adjuster for Commonwealth Assurance Company in Boston, Jeff investigates the partnership insurance claim filed by Ralph's business partner, Ernie Woodruff. Jeff's superior suspects Hazel and Woodruff may have planned what looks like an alcohol-related accident and sends Jeff to sort out the truth of the validity of the claim.

Jeff is thorough. Although his focus is supposed to remain on Woodruff, all roads lead to Hazel. The liquor store owner claims Ralph told him Hazel was waiting in the car while he was shopping for whiskey. Jeff thinks Hazel could have misdirected Ralph, jumped out of the car at the last minute, and watched as the car sank. Esther assures Jeff that it was Hazel's idea to drive to the cottage on the rainy night and she is certain that Hazel planned to kill Ralph that night. After talking with Hazel, Jeff follows her to a rendezvous with Eugene where he sees them having sex in Eugene's car.

Meanwhile, Hazel is still trying to plan her future with Eugene, to the point of going to Rachel and detailing their affair. While at the Hurd house, Hazel covets a blue Chinese box which she assumes will be hers once the divorce is final and she has married Eugene. Rachel decides not to let Eugene know what Hazel has told her and asks him to leave. Eugenc, however, is having second thoughts. When he and Hazel meet, not at their usual place, the shabby, secluded Red Mill, but, instead, at the upscale White Swan Inn, Hazel's fantasy life continues. She imagines going back to her hometown with proper social status and living in the Hurd house. She lets it slip that she admired a blue Chinese box, thereby revealing to Eugene that she has been at his house and probably passed the information about the adultery on to Rachel. He storms out of the restaurant, leaving Hazel with shattered dreams. When he returns to Rachel, Jeff is there with the incriminating facts he has discovered about Hazel. When Eugene warns Hazel by going back to her house, she storms out, encountering Esther in the driveway. In a rage, she shouts out a confession in one word and drives to the train station in an attempt to get away. Jeff is watching the house from across the street and follows her to the station, where he watches her diversionary maneuvers of escape. Having become enchanted by her devices, he lets her get away. Disney makes the ending plausible becasue she has created a taut thriller which exposes several layers of deception on the part of many of the characters. Once the false images are revealed and the facades broken, escape from those hypocrisies seems a reasonable resolution.

Uniformly regarded as one of Disney's best early works, *Who Rides a Tiger* is also about domestic secrets and lies. Like *Dark Road*, the novel meticulously depicts a character vying for love, killing for it, and losing it. This time, however, the consequences of the duplicities follow the participants for more than eighty years.

When her unmarried, irascible great-aunt Harriet Lowden dies at age eighty-three, it falls upon Susan to sort through the old magazines, discarded clothes, and abandoned trunks that fill the attic of her old house. Susan's discovery of fourteen volumes of diaries (beginning on 1 January 1877) helps her find answers to why Harriet hated Susan's grandparents. All Harriet would say on her deathbed was that they ruined her life. It is a tes-

tament to Disney's narrative skill that what could have been a minor example of the romantic suspense genre turns into a spellbinding gothic mystery when the past impinges on the present and the present reclaims the past.

As Susan reads the diaries, Disney subtly moves from that present moment into vividly re-creating the moments the diaries record. Pink satin evening dresses and dance cards dissolve into a ballroom dance scene (6 July 1879) where Harriet accepts a proposal from her first love, Lieutenant Roger Devitt. But Harriet has some competition from her cousin Rose, who is two years older and from the distaff side of the family. With the wedding pending, Rose appears unhappy and apparently disappears in New York City. Soon, however, Harriet's great joy turns to grief when Roger's mother writes to say that he has been killed in the Indian Territories. When her mourning period goes on far too long (over sixteen months), Susan's grandmother Sophie berates Harriet into joining life again. By 1885 Harriet has met and almost married another soul mate, Philip Speare, a painter who has been abroad for ten years. His father, Asahel, is an eminent portrait painter who asks to paint Harriet. When Asahel is not satisfied with how he captured her eyes, he asks to do a second portrait. She declines because she knows that Asahel has told Philip that he saw a certain madness in her eyes. By the end of 1885, Harriet has broken her engagement to Philip, claiming she will always love Roger. Though he finds it hard to accept that explanation, he moves on to another marriage, and he and Harriet don't meet again for ten years.

Susan, too, is dumbfounded by the strange turn of events. Her great-aunt Harriet has been engaged to two men; one has died, the other has been rejected in favor of the deceased fiancé. She turns to Major Philip Speare, the painter's son, and shares her story with him. She admits she has an ulterior motive for reading the diaries. Except for a small legacy to her housekeeper, Aunt Harriet has left her entire estate (over $250,000) to the Sumner Congregational Church. The will seems unbreakable, but Susan's ailing father,

Dwight, Harriet's nephew, could benefit from an inheritance. Philip agrees to read the diaries from his own viewpoint. He suspects that everything hinges on the orphan cousin, Rose, and a mysterious birthmark on Harriet's back. By the time Susan and Philip travel to New York to try to find Rose, it is obvious that they have a mutual attraction for each other. What they find out from an aging wardrobe mistress leads them back to the cellar of the shuttered house. The gothic trappings of the novel are pulled full stop when they exhume a body buried in a quilt and unearth the brown diamond ring that Roger had given Harriet, a ring that never fit Rose's finger. Philip suspects Rose killed Harriet and took her place in order to marry Roger when he sees the diaries misrepresent the false Harriet's age. The diaries refer to Harriet as being seventy-five when she should have been seventy-three, two years younger than Rose. The horrific irony is that when Roger died, Rose was trapped in the lie she created. Having killed Harriet, she had to live out the rest of her life as Harriet, losing two loves in the process. When the false Harriet told Susan that her grandparents had ruined her life, she was really speaking as Rose. Though the plot is intricate and convoluted, Disney succeeds in fulfilling the promise of the old Eastern proverb referred to in the title, "Who rides a tiger dare not dismount." Once Rose mounted the tiger, she could never get off.

Another novel which bears attention in Disney's canon is *No Next of Kin* (1959). Once again a number of lives are altered by a decade-old indiscretion. A double secret haunts Andrea Langdon. When the novel starts (September 1954), she is picking up her five-year-old son, Greg, from a farm couple, Walt and Effie Horbal, in rural Connecticut. Andrea and Greg stop at an annual fair and are caught in a fire that kills the boy along with eighty-eight others. He is never identified, and Andrea leaves the area without recovering his body. Four years later, she is serving as her widowed father's hostess while he runs for a congressional seat. During a television interview, she is spotted by Seymour Boyd, a ter-

rorizing menace who knew Andrea ten years earlier when she was at Miss Merrivale's School for Girls in Washington, D.C. She had gotten pregnant by Boyd and claimed she had an abortion. When he uncovers the truth about the boy and the fire, he sees his chance for blackmail. A series of violent events escalate to a cover-up story involving a gambling ring concocted to protect Andrea, leaving her the only survivor of a lie perpetrated when she was almost eighteen.

Dorothy Salisbury Davis

Born 26 April 1916, in Chicago, Illinois, Dorothy Salisbury Davis was raised by her adoptive parents, Alfred Joseph Salisbury, a midwestern farmer, and Margaret Jane Greer Salisbury. After attending Holy Child High School in Waukegan, Illinois, she matriculated at Barat College in Lake Forest, graduating in 1938 with a degree in English. Her first job was as a booking agent for Kestone the Magician and the girl he sawed in half. In an interview in *Publishers Weekly* (13 June 1980), Davis indicated that the loneliness and desolation of those travel days transferred into some of her later fiction, particularly *The Clay Hand* (1950).

By 1940 Davis had taken a more permanent job with Swift & Company in Chicago. She was a research librarian and editor for *The Merchandiser*. During World War II, she worked in industrial relations, writing letters and sending gifts to servicemen. She met her husband, Harry Davis, an actor, in Chicago in 1945. They married on 25 April 1946 and moved to New York when Harry was offered a position as stage manager for *The Glass Menagerie*.

In 1956 Davis served as president of Mystery Writers of America. Among Davis' most significant professional recognitions as a writer are seven Edgar nominations from Mystery Writers of America, four for best novel and three for best short story. In 1985 she was given the Grand Master award from

MWA for lifelong achievement and contribution in the field of mystery writing. In 1989 the Bouchercon convention granted her a Lifetime Achievement award. As a founding director of Sisters in Crime, she encouraged the development of women writers. Since 1982 she has been a member of the Adams Roundtable. This group of mystery writers meets monthly to discuss writing experiences. They have published four anthologies; short stories by Davis have appeared in each volume.

A SENSE OF COMMUNITY: PRIESTS, PROSTITUTES, POETRY, AND PERSONAL CRISES

Davis' second novel, *The Clay Hand* (after *The Judas Cat*, 1949), established her as a writer concerned with a sense of community and the mitigating circumstances of the environment. She also introduced themes of loneliness and personal crises of faith, threads which run through many of her later works.

Philip McGovern, a Rockland, Illinois, sports editor, is filing a basketball game report at the Chicago Press Club when he gets word of the death of a college friend, Pulitzer Prize–winning investigative reporter Dick Coffee. Coffee's body was found at the bottom of a cliff in the small coal-mining town of Winston (population 1,092) on the borders of Ohio, Kentucky, and West Virginia. When McGovern and Coffee's widow, Margaret, arrive in Winston, they eventually learn that Coffee had followed a lead on a story about a California prison break, discovered dangerous gases in a mine shaft, and stumbled onto a bootlegging racket. In the process, McGovern and Margaret unravel the fabric of small-town life.

Gossip creates scandal, which leads to death for several members of the community. When a miner is crushed by a loading car after his wife enters the mine, the town is certain that the mine is cursed forever. A feisty, jealous landlady blames Margaret for Dick's death because she seemingly abandoned him, leading him to have an affair with a married woman in town. This, along with Margaret's past as a prostitute, introduces a Mary Magdalene theme, which appears in several of Davis' later works. Dick left notes that indicated that "loneliness makes desperate wooers of us all." Margaret, however, has told Philip that she, too, was lonely as she traveled with Dick and he filed his stories while she sat in empty hotel rooms. The sheriff recognizes the disconsolate nature of Dick's notes, suggesting that he had lost his faith and perhaps committed suicide. Dick's death, however, proves to have been an accident occasioned by the geological conformation of the hills in the town which created a false echo, disorienting him as he stood on the cliff. When the illegal bootlegging trade is revealed, Margaret, too, becomes a victim of the town, taken to her death by the vengeful landlady.

Davis' third novel, *A Gentle Murderer* (1951), carried through several of the themes in *The Clay Hand* but developed them more fully, moving her into the top ranks of mystery writers. Her introduction boldly states that the book is "about loneliness." Discussing the inception of the novel, she recounts a story of sitting with Harry on cottage steps at a camp and hearing the clack of an unidentified woman's heels. She filed the image away until weeks later when what she calls the "dramatic intruder" sat beside her on a New York subway and became a key character in the book.

Though the identity of the murderer is known to the reader from the early chapters, it is a testament to Davis' narrative skills that suspense never lags as other characters have to discover who the murderer is. The central protagonist is Father Duffy, a former army chaplain now an assistant pastor in a New York City church. Duffy is one of Davis' several priest characters who form a core of her theme of religious faith. He faces his own moral crisis when, on a late August night, he hears someone confess to a murder but does not know the identity of the murderer or the victim. Nor is Duffy certain that the confessor will not kill again before he can be found. The organizational structure of the novel provides three alternating viewpoints which include Duffy, the gentle murderer of the title, and the professional detectives.

Davis admits an inordinate fondness for her criminals. She recognizes them as fallible human beings. As the gentle murderer, Tim Brandon is a sympathetic villain. Duffy sees him in the guise of St. Francis. Tim sees himself trapped in a goldfish bowl. He writes poetry. In his youth, he attended a seminary and aspired to the priesthood. Kate Galli, daughter of his landlady, is in love with him. She sees him as the "one clean thing . . . in a world very much in need of scrubbing."

As she did in *The Clay Hand*, Davis adeptly maneuvers her story through several layers of social stratification. Tim lives in a boardinghouse on West Twelfth Street. When Norah Flaherty, a housekeeper from the West Sixties, discovers the battered body of her employer, prostitute Dolly Gebhardt, it is in an apartment hotel in the East Sixties. Several story lines come together in the venue of the church. Norah attends services in Father Duffy's parish. Detective Sergeant Ben Goldsmith follows a paper trail of one of Tim's published poems, "The Mother," an unflattering portrait of an abusive parent. The poem provides additional evidence about Tim's background—he comes from a violent setting with an alcoholic father and a mother who abandoned him. Since he sees women as either madonnas or whores, his motive in killing them is to save their souls by "getting them out of the world." According to Goldsmith, he confesses to Father Duffy because he believes that Duffy, too, is on a crusade to free New York of prostitutes. Tim seeks love and redemption, finally receiving absolution in the violent conclusion to the novel.

Davis returns to the subject of murder and its effects on a small midwestern community in her fourth mystery, *A Town of Masks* (1952). Campbell's Cove, on the shore of Lake Michigan, has a population of 15,000. Once a prosperous fishing village, the town now profits from a wood industry that manufactures furniture, boxes, and boats. On the surface, its inhabitants join together to support the library and prepare a simulated air raid and mock invasion for Campbell's Cove Day. Under the surface, it is a town without pity, a town of "half-friend, half-foe—with smiles on foes and scowls on friends." It is a place where "old friends aren't always good ones."

Lifelong resident forty-seven-year-old Hannah Blake has been the cashier at the Loan and Savings Bank for fifteen years. She was appointed by her now deceased father who had been the president of the bank. Her childhood friend, Maria Adams Verlaine, is now her bitter enemy, competing for social standing by using the library board as a fulcrum for the enmity. Hannah is certain she will become the next president of the board; Maria publicly excoriates the men in the community for not participating in literary endeavors. She trumps Hannah's nomination by endorsing and electing the only man on the board, plumber Ed Baker. Hannah thinks she has outwitted Maria when she anonymously proposes a thousand-dollar poetry prize to be awarded on Campbell's Cove Day. Hannah's candidate to win the award is twenty-four-year-old Dennis Keogh, a gardener whose love poetry Hannah discovers when she is hunting for a trowel in a toolshed. Maria, however, gets the upper hand again when she puts forward Andrew Sykes, her own favorite poet, to judge the contest. The final blow to Hannah's sense of empowerment and place in the community occurs when she spies Dennis and the twenty-year-old librarian, Elizabeth Merritt, to whom she confided her support of the poetry award, in the throes of passion on the beach. Hannah's interest in Dennis goes beyond her affection for his poetry. Traumatized by the sight of the couple, Hannah confronts Maria, claiming she and Sykes are responsible for stealing Dennis from her, as a poet and as a possible life partner. Maria reveals that she knows who has sponsored the poetry contest. In a fit of rage, Hannah strangles Maria with a silk bell cord.

What might have turned into pure melodrama in other hands Davis turns into a finely drawn exposé of hypocrisy driven by loneliness and a conspiracy of silence. In *Colloquium on Crime* (1986), Davis characterizes

Hannah as a person who "cannot set her own worth independent of the imagined disdain of others." Hannah views the murder as a profound accomplishment. A cache of jewelry has disappeared and is considered the motive for the murder. Hannah decides that if she can find the jewels and dispose of them, they will remain a distracting issue to everyone except herself. She searches Maria's house, finds the gems in a false book appropriately titled *Jewels of the Madonna*, and plans to drop them in the waterfront during the false invasion planned for Campbell's Cove Day.

Hannah's cover-up almost succeeds until the results of the poetry contest are announced. When only five entries are submitted, the library board agrees that announcing the lack of community support for the contest would defame the town. They decide to keep the number of entries a secret, claiming 105 poems were entered. They also pick a winner Hannah cannot endorse so she changes the name to be announced at the celebration. In the midst of rousing patriotism, Hannah spots Dennis, Elizabeth, and Police Chief Matheson in the crowd. Sykes and the board have become aware of Hannah's deception and give the poetry award to the original recipient. Elizabeth confronts Hannah about the night on the beach and deduces Hannah's involvement in the other events that have altered the peaceful sense of community. Hannah somewhat hastily confesses everything, then, feeling the pressures of loneliness and the presence of doom surrounding her, she hangs herself, leaving a note which incriminates the town for her actions.

In *The Pale Betrayer* (1965), Davis tackles the world of the espionage thriller. As with *A Gentle Murderer* and *A Town of Masks*, the villain is known. Eric Mather, an English professor in New York City is enlisted by two nefarious individuals known to him only as Tom and Jerry to inveigle his friend Peter Bradley, a high-energy physicist, to unknowingly bring secret microfilm information into the United States in his briefcase after attending an international conference on particle physics in Athens. When Bradley is subse-

quently murdered, Mather is wracked with guilt until he disassembles all the conspiracies and counterconspiracies which led to Bradley's death. The novel demonstrates Davis' diverse ability to range from pure detective fiction to suspense thriller.

Priests and prostitutes return as the major characters in two other important novels in the Davis canon, *Where the Dark Streets Go* (1969) and *A Death in the Life* (1976). The first is significant because it returns Davis to the New York scene after two novels set in Europe. It also deals with a "clash of environments" in a manner similar to the exploration of the subcultures of Manhattan in *A Gentle Murderer*. The second novel introduces one of Davis' efforts at a series, Julie Hayes (the other is Mrs. Norris, who appeared in three books).

Like Father Duffy before him, Father Joseph McMahon faces a spiritual crisis when he becomes embroiled in a murder case in his diverse neighborhood. While Father McMahon is in the midst of preparing a Sunday sermon on brotherhood, "a matter of getting close enough to recognize one another," a young Puerto Rican, Carlos Morales, brings him to a man with a knife wound, Gust Muller. Muller lives in Priscilla Phelan's rooming house. Priscilla has confided in Father McMahon that her husband, a stagehand named Dan, has no sexual interest in her. When Father McMahon finds Dan in a gay bar in Greenwich Village, he knows why. Dan explains to Father MacMahon that his mother had wanted him to be a priest and he still wants to try life in the seminary again. At the same time that Father McMahon is trying to help his parishioners and trying to solve the murder, he faces his own temptations. His faith in the church has faltered; he has become cynical about his position in the neighborhood; he covets material goods like Muller's art books. When Muller's real identity (he is a well known painter, Thomas Stuart Chase) is uncovered, Father McMahon realizes that everyone has "dark corners" in their lives, including himself, and he must begin to face the demons that haunt him. He retreats to an island in Maine to contemplate his future.

Next to *A Gentle Murderer, A Death in the Life* was one of the best received of Davis' novels. It incorporates many of the characters, themes, and settings of her previous work. Priests, poets, and prostitutes; abandonment, isolation, and the loneliness of city living; and personal crisis all enter into the book.

A despondent twenty-five-year-old Julie Hayes is married to a controlling husband, a forty-year-old reporter named Jeff. He has suggested Julie seek psychiatric counseling. Her female psychiatrist, Dr. Callahan, advises her to find some kind of job that interests her. As Julie is walking on Fifth Avenue near the Plaza Hotel, a man hands her a flyer advertising psychic readings by Madame Tozares. Though Tozares' reading is somewhat standard fare—including mention of big changes in Julie's life—the tarot reader does recognize "something rotten, decadent" and hints at marital separation. When a friend suggests that Julie become a reader herself, she learns that it is a short walk from psychiatrist to psychic, and a fine line between being a victim and being a savior.

The sense of community that is a hallmark of Davis' fiction pervades the nature of the Broadway and Forty-fourth Street neighborhood where "Friend Julie" sets up shop. She soon becomes friends with many of the residents and passersby. Chief among them is Rita Morgan, a teenager who wants out of "the life" of the street. When Julie's friend Peter Mallory, a stage designer for Actors Forum whom Julie has known a long time, is stabbed in Rita's apartment, Julie must juggle her newfound friendship with Rita and her desire to solve Peter's murder. In the process, she must deal with a belligerent pimp, Goldie, who thinks Julie has moved in on his territory; a rival pimp, Mack; her upstairs neighbor, Rose Rodriguez, who wants Julie to pimp for her; and an electrical repairman, Philip Bourke, who is trying to hide his homosexuality. Everyone's skin is pulled back, finally revealing the dark secrets that have motivated their actions. Most significantly, Julie con-

fronts the harrowing events of her childhood so that she can move on with her life.

Davis wrote three more novels featuring Julie Hayes (*Scarlet Night*, 1980; *Lullaby of Murder*, 1984; *The Habit of Fear*, 1987) in which she traces her development from tarot reader to gossip columnist. In *The Habit of Fear*, Davis touches on a subject closest to her own life when Julie goes to Dublin in an attempt to solve the mystery of her past, seeking an Irish father she never knew.

Of the collected crime stories in *Tales for a Stormy Night* (1984), several are notable, particularly the three nominated for Edgars, and two others. Edgar nominations went to "Backward, Turn Backward," "The Purple Is Everything," and "Old Friends." Also deserving recognition are "Born Killer" and "Spring Fever."

"Spring Fever" (1952) starts as a seemingly poignant portrait of loneliness in a country setting, then turns into a hauntingly terrifying tale of terror when what looks like a tender seduction turns to murder. "Born Killer" (1953) creates a psychological portrait of a country character born in violence and unable to escape that birthright. Patricide dominates "Backward, Turn Backward" (1954) in the aftermath of a failed love relationship. Urban ironies and the world of art inhabit the life of wallpaper designer Mary Gardner when she finds herself the accidental owner of a Monet painting that she rescues from a fire at the Institute of Modern Art in New York and then cannot return in "The Purple Is Everything" (1963). "Old Friends" (1975) touches on earlier Davis themes of skewed relationships when innocent lies between lifelong friends lead to rape.

Conclusion

Taken together, McCloy's precursory foray into psychology and psychiatry, Disney's fervid exploration of marital vicissitudes, and Davis' revealing exposure of rural and urban hypocrisy establish a significant watermark for future mystery writers working with the subject of domestic violence. Though grounded in their respective time periods, they were able to break out from the field of ordinary writers by creating characters with distinctive personalities, use settings to reveal the environmental and social impact on their protagonists, and find inventive plots that make their signature novels timeless.

Selected Bibliography

HELEN McCLOY

NOVELS

Dance of Death. New York: Morrow, 1938.
The Man in the Moonlight. New York: Morrow, 1940.
The Deadly Truth. New York: Morrow, 1941.
Who's Calling. New York: Morrow, 1942.
Cue for Murder. New York: Morrow, 1942.
Do Not Disturb. New York: Morrow, 1943.
The Goblin Market. New York: Morrow, 1943.
Panic. New York: Morrow, 1944.
The One that Got Away. New York: Morrow, 1945.
She Walks Alone. New York: Random House, 1948.
Through a Glass, Darkly. New York: Random House, 1950.
Better Off Dead. New York: Dell, 1951.
Alias Basil Willing. New York: Random House, 1951.
Unfinished Crime. New York: Random House, 1954.
The Long Body. New York: Random House, 1955.
Two-Thirds of a Ghost. New York: Random House, 1956.
The Slayer and the Slain. New York: Random House, 1957.
Before I Die. New York: Torquil, 1963.
The Further Side of Fear. New York: Dodd, Mead, 1967.
Mr. Splitfoot. New York: Dodd, Mead, 1968.
A Question of Time. New York: Dodd, Mead, 1971.
A Change of Heart. New York: Dodd, Mead, 1973.
The Sleepwalker. New York: Dodd, Mead, 1974.
Minotaur Country. New York: Dodd, Mead, 1975.
The Changeling Conspiracy. New York: Dodd, Mead, 1976.
The Imposter. New York: Dodd, Mead, 1977.
The Smoking Mirror. New York: Dodd, Mead, 1979.
Burn This. New York: Dodd, Mead, 1980.

SHORT STORIES

The Singing Diamonds and Other Stories. New York: Dodd, Mead, 1965.

DORIS MILES DISNEY

A Compound for Death. New York: Doubleday, 1943.
Murder on a Tangent. New York: Doubleday, 1945.
Dark Road. New York: Doubleday, 1946; as *Dead Stop*, New York, Dell, 1956.
Who Rides a Tiger. New York: Doubleday, 1946.
Appointment at Nine. New York: Doubleday, 1947.
Enduring Old Charms. New York: Doubleday, 1947.
Testimony by Silence. New York: Doubleday, 1948.
That Which Is Crooked. New York: Doubleday, 1948.
Count the Ways. New York: Doubleday, 1949.
Family Skeleton. New York: Doubleday, 1949.
Fire at Will. New York: Doubleday, 1950.
Look Back on Murder. New York: Doubleday, 1951.
Straw Man. New York: Doubleday, 1951.
Heavy, Heavy Hangs. New York: Doubleday, 1952.
Do unto Others. New York: Doubleday, 1953.
Prescription: Murder. New York: Doubleday, 1953.
The Last Straw. New York: Doubleday, 1954.
Room for Murder. New York: Doubleday, 1955.
Trick or Treat. New York: Doubleday, 1955.
Unappointed Rounds. New York: Doubleday, 1956.
Method in Madness. New York: Doubleday, 1957.
My Neighbor's Wife. New York: Doubleday, 1957.
Black Mail. New York: Doubleday, 1958.
Did She Fall or Was She Pushed? New York: Doubleday, 1959.
No Next of Kin. New York: Doubleday, 1959.
Dark Lady. New York: Doubleday, 1960.
Mrs. Meeker's Money. New York: Doubleday, 1961.
Find the Woman. New York: Doubleday, 1962.
Should Auld Acquaintance. New York: Doubleday, 1962.
Here Lies. New York: Doubleday, 1963.
The Departure of Mr. Gaudette. New York: Doubleday, 1964.
The Hospitality of the House. New York: Doubleday, 1964.
Shadow of a Man. New York: Doubleday, 1964.
At Some Forgotten Door. New York: Doubleday, 1966.
The Magic Grandfather. New York: Doubleday, 1966.
Night of Clear Choice. New York: Doubleday, 1967.
Money for the Taking. New York: Doubleday, 1968.
Voice from the Grave. New York: Doubleday, 1968.
Two Little Children and How They Grew. New York: Doubleday, 1969.
Do Not Fold, Spindle, or Mutilate. New York: Doubleday, 1970.
The Chandler Pony. New York: Putnam, 1971.
Three's a Crowd. New York: Doubleday, 1971.
The Day Miss Bessie Lewis Disappeared. New York: Doubleday, 1972.
Only Couples Need Apply. New York: Doubleday, 1973.
Don't Go into the Woods. New York: Doubleday, 1974.
Cry for Help. New York: Doubleday, 1975.
Winifred. New York: Doubleday, 1976.

DOROTHY SALISBURY DAVIS

NOVELS

The Judas Cat. New York: Scribners, 1949.
The Clay Hand. New York: Scribners, 1950.
A Gentle Murderer. New York: Scribners, 1951.
A Town of Masks. New York: Scribners, 1952.
Men of No Property. New York: Scribners, 1956.
Death of an Old Sinner. New York: Scribners, 1957.
A Gentleman Called. New York: Scribners, 1958.
Old Sinners Never Die. New York: Scribners, 1959.
Black Sheep, White Lamb. New York: Scribners, 1963.
The Pale Betrayer. New York: Scribners, 1965.
Enemy and Brother. New York: Scribners, 1966.
God Speed the Night, with Jerome Ross. New York: Scribners, 1968.

Where the Dark Streets Go. New York: Scribners, 1969.
Shock Wave. New York: Scribners, 1972.
The Little Brothers. New York: Scribners, 1973.
A Death in the Life. New York: Scribners, 1976.
Scarlet Night. New York: Scribners, 1980.
Lullaby of Murder. New York: Scribners, 1984.
The Habit of Fear. New York: Scribners, 1987.

SHORT STORIES

Tales for a Stormy Night: The Collected Crime Stories. Woodstock, Vt.: Countryman Press, 1984.

INTERVIEW

Colloquium on Crime: Eleven Renowned Mystery Writers Discuss Their Work. Edited by Robin W. Winks. New York: Scribners, 1986.

APPENDIX 1

Pseudonyms and Series Characters

Mystery writers have published under a bewildering variety of pseudonyms, often achieving fame in several different roles. The genre personae of "Nicholas Blake" and "Amanda Cross" are no less famous than the poetic and scholarly incarnations of Cecil Day Lewis and Carolyn Heilbrun. The present work generally identifies writers by the name used for their genre fiction, here listed in the left column. Unless otherwise specified, the author is treated in a full essay under this name. Succeeding columns list the writer's actual name, the most important pseudonyms, and the principal recurring characters that have populated their books. Consult the index for fuller cross-referencing and for the minority of authors who have employed neither pseudonyms nor series characters.

Name Used in This Work	Actual Name	Pseudonyms	Principal Recurring Series Characters
Adams, Harriet Stratemeyer (in *The Female Detective*)	Harriet Stratemeyer Adams	Carolyn Keene	Nancy Drew
Allingham, Margery	Margery Louise Allingham	Maxwell March	Albert Campion
Ambler, Eric	Eric Ambler	Eliot Reed	
Asimov, Isaac (in *The Armchair Detective*)	Isaac Asimov	Paul French	The Black Widowers
Baker, Nikki (in *The Black Detective; The Female Detective; Gay and Lesbian Mystery Fiction*)	Nikki Baker		Virginia Kelley
Barnard, Robert	Robert Barnard	Bernard Bastable	Perry Trethowan
Barron, Stephanie (in *The Historical Mystery*)	Francine Mathews	Stephanie Barron	Jane Austen
Beal, M. F. (in *The Female Detective*)	M. F. Beal		Kat Guerrera
Bentley, E. C.	E(dmund) C(lerihew) Bentley	E. Clerihew	Philip Trent
Blake, Nicholas	Cecil Day Lewis	Nicholas Blake	Nigel Strangeways
Bland, Eleanor Taylor (in *The Female Detective*)	Eleanor Taylor Bland		Marti MacAlister
Block, Lawrence	Lawrence Block	William Ard Chip Harrison Paul Kavanaugh	Leo Haig, Chip Harrison, Bernie Rhodenbarr, Matt Scudder, Evan Tanner

Name Used in This Work	Actual Name	Pseudonyms	Principal Recurring Series Characters
Borges, Jorge Luis	Jorge Luis Borges	Herbert Quain	Erik Lönnrot
Bramah, Ernest (in *The Armchair Detective*)	Ernest Bramah Smith	Ernest Bramah	Max Carrados
Buchan, John	John Buchan, Baron Tweedsmuir		Richard Hannay
Burke, James Lee (in *Regionalization of the Mystery and Crime Novel*)	James Lee Burke		Dave Robicheaux
Carr, John Dickson	John Dickson Carr	Carr Dickson Carter Dickson	Henri Bencolin, Dr. Gideon Fell, Colonel March, Sir Henry Merrivale
Chandler, Raymond	Raymond Chandler		Philip Marlowe
Charteris, Leslie	Leslie Charteris (born Leslie Charles Bowyer Yin		The Saint (Simon Templar)
Chesterton, G. K.	G(ilbert) K(eith) Chesterton		Father Brown
Christie, Agatha	Dame Agatha Mary Clarissa Miller Christie Mallowan	Mary Westmacott	Tuppence and Tommy Beresford, Jane Marple, Hercule Poirot, Parker Pyne, Mr. Satterthwaite
Cody, Liza (in *The Female Detective*)	Liza Nassim	Liza Cody	Anna Lee, Eva Wylie
Collins, Wilkie	(William) Wilkie Collins		Sergeant Cuff
Constantine, K. C.	?	K. C. Constantine	Mario Balzic
Cornwell, Patricia	Patricia D(aniels) Cornwell		Dr. Kay Scarpetta
Coryell, John Russell (in *The Nick Carter Stories*)	John Russell Coryell	Milton Quarterly *Various others*	Nick Carter
Creasey, John (in *The Police Procedural*)	John Creasey	J. J. Marric Gordon Ashe	Patrick Dawlish, George Gideon
Crispin, Edmund	(Robert) Bruce Montgomery	Edmund Crispin	Gervase Fen
Crofts, Freeman Wills	Freeman Wills Crofts		Inspector Joseph French
Cross, Amanda	Carolyn Gold Heilbrun	Amanda Cross	Kate Fansler

Daly, Carroll John	Carroll John Daly	Vee Brown, Satan Hall, Race Williams
Davis, Dorothy Salisbury (in *Women of Mystery*)	Dorothy Salisbury Davis	Julie Hayes, Jasper Tully, Mrs. Norris
Davis, Frederick William (in *The Nick Carter Stories*)	Frederick William Davis	Nick Carter, Felix Boyd, Harrison Keith, Sheridan Keene, Steve Manley
Davis, Lindsey (in *The Historical Mystery*)	Lindsey Davis	Marcus Didius Falco
de la Torre, Lillian (in *The Historical Mystery*)	Lillian McCue	Dr. Sam Johnson
Deighton, Len (in *The Spy Thriller*)	Len Deighton	Bernard Samson
Dexter, Colin	(Norman) Colin Dexter	Inspector Morse, Sergeant Lewis
Dey, Frederic Merrill van Rensselaer (in *The Nick Carter Stories*)	Frederic Merrill Van Rensselaer Dey	Marmaduke Dey, Varick Vanardy, Nick Carter
Doyle, Sir Arthur Conan	Sir Arthur Conan Doyle	Sherlock Holmes, Dr. John H. Watson
Dunlap, Susan (in *The Female Detective*)	Susan Dunlap	Jill Smith, Vejay Haskell, Kieran O'Shaughnessy
Dunn, Carola (in *The Historical Mystery*)	Carola Dunn	Daisy Dalrymple
Ellin, Stanley	Stanley Bernard Ellin	John Milano
Estleman, Loren (in *Regionalization of the Mystery and Crime Novel*)	Loren D. Estleman	Amos Walker, Peter Macklin
Fast, Howard (in *The Ethnic Detective*)	Howard Fast	E. V. Cunningham, Walter Ericson, Masao Masuto
Fleming, Ian	Ian Fleming	James Bond
Forrest, Katherine V. (in *The Female Detective; Gay and Lesbian Mystery Fiction*)	Katherine V. Forrest	Kate Delafield

1233

Name Used in This Work	Actual Name	Pseudonyms	Principal Recurring Series Characters
Francis, Dick	Richard Stanley Francis		Sid Halley
Gaboriau, Émile	Émile Gaboriau		Monsieur Lecoq, Père Tabaret
Gardner, Erle Stanley	Erle Stanley Gardner	A. A. Fair Carleton Kendrake Charles J. Kenney	Bertha Cool, Donald Lam, Perry Mason, D.A. Doug Selby
Gilbert, Michael	Michael Gilbert		Inspector Hazelrigg, Sgt. Patrick Petrella
Grafton, Sue	Sue Grafton		Kinsey Millhone
Grandower, Elissa (in *The Police Procedural*)	Hillary Waugh	Elissa Grandower	Simon Kaye, Fred Fellows, Frank Sessions
Greeley, Andrew (in *The Religious Mystery*)	Andrew M. Greeley		Blackie Ryan
Green, Anna Katharine	Anna Katharine Green		Ebenezer Gryce, Violet Strange
Hager, Jean (in *The Ethnic Detective*)	Jean Hager		Chief Busyhead, Iris House, Molly Bearpaw
Hall, Robert Lee (in *The Historical Mystery*)	Robert Lee Hall		Benjamin Franklin
Hammett, Dashiell	Samuel Dashiell Hammett	Peter Collinson	Nick and Nora Charles, Sam Spade, the Continental Op
Hansen, Joseph (in *Gay and Lesbian Mystery Fiction*)	Joseph Hansen		Dave Brandstetter
Harding, Paul (in *The Historical Mystery*)	Paul Harding	Michael Clynes Anne Dukthas	Hugh Corbett
Higgins, George V.	George V. Higgins		Jerry Kennedy
Highsmith, Patricia	Mary Patricia Plangman	Patricia Highsmith	Tom Ripley
Hillerman, Tony (in *The Ethnic Detective; Regionalization of the Mystery and Crime Novel; The Religious Mystery*)	Tony Hillerman		Sergeant Jim Chee, Lieutenant Joe Leaphorn

Himes, Chester (in *The Black Detective*)	Chester Himes	Grave Digger Jones, Coffin Ed Johnson
Holt, Victoria (in *The Historical Mystery*; *The Romantic Suspense Mystery*)	Eleanor Alice Hibbert	Philippa Carr Victoria Holt Jean Plaidy *Many others*
Holton, Leonard (in *The Religious Mystery*)	Leonard Patrick O'Connor Wibberley	Father Bredder
Hunter, Evan	Evan Hunter (b. Salvatore Lombino)	Curt Cannon, Matthew Hope, the 87th Precinct Ezra Hannon Ed McBain Richard Marsten
Innes, Michael	J(ohn) I(nnes) M(ackintosh) Stewart	Sir John Appleby Michael Innes
James, P. D.	P(hyllis) D(orothy) James	Adam Dalgliesh, Cordelia Gray
Kaminsky, Stuart M. (in *The Historical Mystery*)	Stuart M. Kaminsky	Toby Peters
Keating, H. R. F. (in *The Ethnic Detective*)	H(enry) R(edmond) F(itzwalter) Keating	Inspector Ganesh Ghote
Kemelman, Harry (in *The Armchair Detective*)	Harry Kemelman	Rabbi David Small, Nicky Welt
Kienzle, William X. (in *The Religious Mystery*)	William X. Kienzle	Father Robert Koesler
King, Laurie R. (in *The Historical Mystery*)	Laurie R. King	Kate Martinelli, Mary Russell
Knox, Ronald A.	Ronald A(rbuthnott) Knox	Miles Bredon
Komo, Colores (in *The Black Detective*)	Dolores Komo	Clio Browne
le Carré, John	David John Moore Cornwell	George Smiley John le Carré
Love, William F. (in *The Religious Mystery*)	William F. Love	Francis X. Regan
Lovesey, Peter (in *The Historical Mystery*)	Peter Lovesey	Peter Lear	Sergeant Cribb, Constable Thackeray, Inspector Dew, Dr. Cripping, Bertie (King Edward VII), Peter Diamond

Name Used in This Work	Actual Name	Pseudonyms	Principal Recurring Series Characters
Ludlum, Robert	Robert Ludlum	Jonathan Ryder Michael Shepherd	Jason Bourne
MacDonald, John D.	John D(ann) MacDonald		Travis McGee
Macdonald, Ross	Kenneth Millar	John Macdonald John Ross Macdonald Ross Macdonald	Lew Archer, Chet Gordon
Marsh, Ngaio	Dame Edith Ngaio Marsh		Inspector Roderick Alleyn
McCarry, Charles (in The The Spy Thriller)	Charles McCarry		Paul Christopher
McCloy, Helen (in Women of Mystery)	Helen Worrell Clarkson McCloy	Helen Clarkson	Dr. Basil Willing
McClure, James (in The Ethnic Detective)	James McClure		Lieutenant Tromp Kramer, Sergeant Mickey Zondi
McInerny, Ralph (in The Religious Mystery)	Ralph McInerny	Monica Quill	Father Dowling, Sister Mary Teresa
Mertz, Barbara (in The Romantic Suspense Mystery)	Barbara Mertz	Barbara Michaels Elizabeth Peters	
Miles, Keith (in The Historical Mystery)	Keith Miles	Edward Marston	
Millar, Margaret	Margaret Ellis Sturm Millar		Tom Aragon, Paul Prye, Inspector Sands
Mortimer, John	John (Clifford) Mortimer		Horace Rumpole
Mosley, Walter (in The Black Detective; The Historical Mystery)	Walter Mosley		Easy Rawlins
Muller, Marcia (in The Female Detective)	Marcia Muller		Sharon McCone, Elena Oliverez, Joanna Stark
Nava, Michael (in Gay and Lesbian Mystery Fiction)	Michael Nava		Henry Rios

Author	Real name	Pen name(s)	Character(s)
Neely, Barbara (in *The Female Detective; The Black Detective*)	Barbara Neely	Barbara Neely	Blanche White
Orczy, Baroness (in *The Armchair Detective*)	Emma Magdalena Rosalia Maria Josefa Barbara Orczy	Baroness Orczy	The Old Man (Bill Owen), Lady Molly Robertson-Kirk, The Scarlet Pimpernel (Sir Percy Blakeney)
Paretsky, Sara	Sara Paretsky		V. I. Warshawski
Parker, Robert B.	Robert B[rown] Parker		Spenser, Jesse Stone
Perry, Anne (in *The Historical Mystery*)	Anne Perry		Charlotte Pitt, Thomas Pitt, William Monk
Peters, Ellis (in *The Historical Mystery; The Religious Mystery*)	Edith Pargeter	Ellis Peters	Brother Cadfael
Poe, Edgar Allan	Edgar Allan Poe		C. Auguste Dupin
Procter, Maurice (in *The Police Procedural*)	Maurice Procter		Harry Martineau, Philip Hunter
Queen, Ellery	Frederic Dannay (b. Daniel Nathan) and Manfred Bennington Lee (b. Manford Lepofsky). Later Anthony Boucher and numerous ghostwriters.	Ellery Queen Barnaby Ross Daniel Nathan	Ellery Queen, Drury Lane
Rendell, Ruth	Ruth Rendell (b. Ruth Barbara Grasemann)	Ruth Rendell Barbara Vine	Chief Inspector Reginald Wexford
Robb, Candace (in *The Historical Mystery*)	Candace Robb		Owen Archer
Robinson, Lynda S. (in *The Historical Mystery*)	Lynda S. Robinson		Lord Meren
Rohmer, Sax	Arthur Henry Sarsfield Ward	Sax Rohmer Michael Furey	Dr. Fu Manchu, Sumuru
Roosevelt, Elliott (in *The Historical Mystery*)	Elliott Roosevelt		Eleanor Roosevelt
Ross, Kate (in *The Historical Mystery*)	Kate Ross		Julian Kestrel
Sapper (in *The Spy Thriller*)	H(erman) C(yril) McNeile	Sapper	Bulldog Drummond

Name Used in This Work	Actual Name	Pseudonyms	Principal Recurring Series Characters
Sayers, Dorothy L.	Dorothy L(eigh) Sayers		Lord Peter Wimsey, Harriet Vane
Saylor, Steven (in *The Historical Mystery*)	Steven Saylor		Gordianus the Finder
Shiel, Mathew Phipps (in *The Armchair Detective*)	Mathew Phipps Shiel		Prince Zaleski
Simenon, Georges	Georges (Joseph Christian) Simenon		Inspector Jules Maigret
Sjöwall, Maj	Maj Sjöwall		Martin Beck
Smith, Julie (in *Regionalization of the Mystery and Crime Novel*)	Julienne Drew Smith		Skip Langdon, Rebecca Schwartz, Paul MacDonald
Spaulding, Samuel Charles (in *The Nick Carter Stories*)	Samuel Charles Spaulding		Nick Carter
Spillane, Mickey	Frank Morrison Spillane	Mickey Spillane	Mike Hammer, Tiger Mann
Stabenow, Dana (in *The Ethnic Detective*)	Dana Stabenow		Kate Shugak
Stevenson, Richard (in *Gay and Lesbian Mystery Fiction*)	Richard Lipez	Richard Stevenson	Don Strachey
Stout, Rex	Rex Todhunter Stout		Tecumseh Fox, Nero Wolfe
Stratemeyer, Edward (in *The Female Detective*)	Edward Stratemeyer	Carolyn Keene	Nancy Drew
Symons, Julian	Julian Gustave Symons		Francis Quarles
Tey, Josephine	Elizabeth Mackintosh	Gordon Daviot	Inspector Alan Grant
Treat, Lawrence (in *The Police Procedural*)	Lawrence Treat (b. Lawrence Arthur Goldstone)		Carl Wayward, Mitch Taylor, Jub Freeman
Upfield, Arthur W. (in *The Ethnic Detective*)	Arthur W(illiam) Upfield		Inspector Napoleon ("Bony") Bonaparte

Van Dine, S. S.	Willard Huntington Wright	S. S. Van Dine	Philo Vance
van Gulik, Robert	Robert Hans van Gulik		Judge Dee
Vassch, Andrew (in *Crime Noir*)	Andrew Vassch		Burke
Wahlöö, Per	Per Wahlöö		Martin Beck
Wallace, Edgar	(Richard Horatio) Edgar Wallace		J. G. Reeder, Inspector Elk, Superintendent Minter, The Sooper, T. B. Smith
Westlake, Donald E.	Donald E(dwin) Westlake	Curt Clark Tucker Coe Timothy J. Culver Samuel Holt Richard Stark	Mitch Tobin
Woolrich, Cornell	Cornell George Hopley Woolrich	George Hopley William Irish	
Wright, L. R. (in *Regionalization of the Mystery and Crime Novel*)	L(aurali) R(ose) Wright		Sergeant Karl Alberg
Yaffe, James (in *The Armchair Detective*)	James Yaffe		Mom

Some Mystery and Suspense Subgenres with a Selection of Practitioners

The number of mystery subgenres is legion, and the fields are endlessly divisible. The "caper" novel is in some ways distinct from the hard-boiled, the humorous, or the procedural, but it draws upon the traditions of all three. The legal subgenre can be broken down into trial novels, lawyer-as-detective novels, and psychological-legal novels. Many writers have created a "master detective," though some of them are not remembered for having done so. Any list of subgenres is arbitrary and incomplete. The present selection may nonetheless help users to chart future reading by identifying figures with some generic likeness to a known favorite.

Most of the authors listed below are the subjects of individual essays. The thematic essays in Volume 2 treat many additional writers, only a few of whom can be listed here. For additional authors consult the index.

Academic
Robert Barnard
Nicholas Blake
G. K. Chesterton
Edmund Crispin
Amanda Cross
Michael Innes
Ronald A. Knox
Dorothy L. Sayers

Adventure
John Buchan
Dick Francis
Michael Gilbert
Hammond Innis
Alistair McLean
Sax Rohmer
Edgar Wallace

Crime Noir
James Lee Burke
James M. Cain
Raymond Chandler
Carroll John Daly
Patricia Highsmith
Chester Himes
Elmore Leonard
Cornell Woolrich

English "Cozy"
Margery Allingham
E. C. Bentley

Agatha Christie
Anna Katharine Green
Ronald A. Knox
Josephine Tey

Ethnic
Tony Hillerman
Chester Himes
H. R. F. Keating
James McClure
Walter Mosley
Sax Rohmer
Arthur Upfield

Hard-boiled
Lawrence Block
Raymond Chandler
K. C. Constantine
Carroll John Daly
Sue Grafton
Dashiell Hammett
George V. Higgins
Chester Himes
Evan Hunter
Elmore Leonard
John D. MacDonald
Ross Macdonald
Sara Paretsky
Robert B. Parker
Mickey Spillane
Edgar Wallace
Donald E. Westlake

Historical
John Dickson Carr
Daphne du Maurier
Umberto Eco
Anne Perry
Ellis Peters
Josephine Tey
Robert van Gulik

Humorous
Robert Barnard
Lawrence Block
Elmore Leonard
Robert B. Parker
Rex Stout
Donald E. Westlake

Legal
Erle Stanley Gardner
Michael Gilbert
John Grisham
John Mortimer
Scott Turow
Robert van Gulik

Master Detective
Margery Allingham
Nicholas Blake
The Nick Carter Stories
Leslie Charteris
Agatha Christie

Arthur Conan Doyle
Émile Gaboriau
Erle Stanley Gardner
P. D. James
Harry Kemelman
John D. MacDonald
Ross Macdonald
Ngaio Marsh
Edgar Allan Poe
Dorothy L. Sayers
Georges Simenon
Rex Stout
Josephine Tey
S. S. Van Dine
Robert van Gulik

Medical
Patricia Cornwell
Ngaio Marsh
Helen McCloy
Edgar Allan Poe

Metaphysical
Jorge Luis Borges
G. K. Chesterton
Graham Greene
P. D. James
Ronald A. Knox
Ruth Rendell
Dorothy L. Sayers

Police Procedural
K. C. Constantine
Colin Dexter
Émile Gaboriau
Michael Gilbert
Tony Hillerman
Evan Hunter (Ed McBain)
P. D. James
Maurice Procter
Georges Simenon
Maj Sjöwall and Per Wahlöö
Josephine Tey
Joseph Wambaugh
Hillary Waugh

Psychological
Robert Barnard
Nicholas Blake
James Lee Burke
Dorothy Salisbury Davis
Doris Miles Disney
Daphne du Maurier
Mignon Eberhart
Stanley Ellin
Helen McCloy
Margaret Millar
Ruth Rendell
Georges Simenon
Julian Symons
Cornell Woolrich

Puzzle
E. C. Bentley
Nicholas Blake
John Dickson Carr
Agatha Christie
Wilkie Collins
Edmund Crispin
Freeman Wills Crofts
Colin Dexter
Arthur Conan Doyle
Ronald A. Knox
Ellery Queen

Romantic Suspense
Mary Higgins Clark
Wilkie Collins
Daphne du Maurier
Mignon G. Eberhart
Helen MacInnes
Mary Roberts Rinehart

Spy
Eric Ambler
Lawrence Block
John Buchan
Ian Fleming
Michael Gilbert
Graham Greene
John le Carré
Robert Ludlum
Helen MacInnes
Baroness Orczy

Selected Awards

The Diamond Dagger

The Diamond Dagger is awarded by the Crime Writers of Great Britain for outstanding contributions to the genre.

1986 Eric Ambler
1987 P. D. James
1988 John le Carré
1989 Dick Francis
1990 Julian Symons
1991 Ruth Rendell

1992 Leslie Charteris
1993 Edith Pargeter (a.k.a. Ellis Peters)
1994 Michael Gilbert
1995 Reginald Hill
1996 H. R. F. Keating

The Crossed Red Herring Award for Best Crime Novel

Crime Writers of Great Britain

1955 Winston Graham, *The Little Walls*
1956 Edward Grierson, *The Second Man*
1957 Julian Symons, *The Colour of Murder*
1958 Margot Bennett, *Someone from the Past*
1959 Eric Ambler, *Passage of Arms*
1960 Lionel Davidson, *The Night of Wenceslas*
1961 Mary Kelly, *The Spoilt Kill*
1962 Joan Fleming, *When I Grow Rich*

1963 John le Carré, *The Spy Who Came in from the Cold*
1964 H. R. F. Keating, *The Perfect Murder*
1965 Ross Macdonald, *The Far Side of the Dollar*
1966 Lionel Davidson, *A Long Way to Shiloh*
1967 Emma Lathen, *Murder Against the Grain*
1968 Peter Dickinson, *Skin Deep*

The Gold Award for Best Crime Novel

Crime Writers of Great Britain

1969 Peter Dickinson, *A Pride of Heroes*
1970 Joan Fleming, *Young Man, I Think You're Dying*
1971 James McClure, *The Steam Pig*
1972 Eric Ambler, *The Levanter*
1973 Robert Littrell, *The Defection of A. J. Lewinter*
1974 Anthony Price, *Other Paths to Glory*
1975 Nicholas Meyer, *The Seven Per Cent Solution*
1976 Ruth Rendell, *A Demon in My View*
1977 John le Carré, *The Honourable Schoolboy*

1978 Lionel Davidson, *The Chelsea Murders*
1979 Dick Francis, *Whip Hand*
1980 H. R. F. Keating, *The Murder of the Maharajah*
1981 Martin Cruz Smith, *Gorky Park*
1982 Peter Lovesey, *The False Inspector Dew*
1983 John Hutton, *Accidental Crimes*
1984 B. M. Gill, *The Twelfth Juror*
1985 Paula Gosling, *Monkey Puzzle*
1986 Ruth Rendell, *Live Flesh*

1987 Barbara Vine (a.k.a. Ruth Rendell), *A Fatal Inversion*
1988 Michael Dibdin, *Ratking*
1989 Colin Dexter, *The Wench Is Dead*
1990 Reginald Hill, *Bones and Silence*
1991 Barbara Vine (a.k.a. Ruth Rendell), *King Solomon's Carpet*
1992 Colin Dexter, *The Way Through the Woods*

1993 Patricia D. Cornwell, *Cruel and Unusual*
1994 Minetta Walters, *The Scold's Bridle*
1995 Val McDermid, *The Mermaids Singing*
1996 Ben Elton, *Popcorn*
1997 Ian Rankin, *Black & Blue*

The Grandmaster Award

The Grandmaster Award is given by the Mystery Writers of America in recognition of a history of contributions to the mystery field and of consistently high quality work.

1955 Agatha Christie
1958 Vincent Starrett
1959 Rex Stout
1961 Ellery Queen (Frederic Dannay and Manfred B. Lee)
1962 Erle Stanley Gardner
1963 John Dickson Carr
1964 George Harmon Coxe
1966 Georges Simenon
1967 Baynard Kendrick
1969 John Creasey
1970 James M. Cain
1971 Mignon G. Eberhart
1972 John D. MacDonald
1973 Judson Philips and Alfred Hitchcock
1974 Ross Macdonald
1975 Eric Ambler
1976 Graham Greene
1978 Daphne du Maurier, Dorothy B. Hughes, and Ngaio Marsh
1979 Aaron Marc Stein

1980 W. R. Burnett
1981 Stanley Ellin
1982 Julian Symons
1983 Margaret Millar
1984 John le Carré
1985 Dorothy Salisbury Davis
1986 Ed McBain
1987 Michael Gilbert
1988 Phyllis A. Whitney
1989 Hillary Waugh
1990 Helen McCloy
1991 Tony Hillerman
1992 Elmore Leonard
1993 Donald E. Westlake
1994 Lawrence Block
1995 Mickey Spillane
1996 Dick Francis
1997 Ruth Rendell
1998 Barbara Mertz (a.k.a. Elizabeth Peters and Barbara Michaels)

The Edgar Award for Best Novel

Mystery Writers of America

1954 Charlotte Jay, *Beat Not the Bones*
1955 Raymond Chandler, *The Long Goodbye*
1956 Margaret Millar, *Beast in View*
1957 Charlotte Armstrong, *A Dram of Poison*
1958 Ed Lacy, *Room to Swing*
1959 Stanley Ellin, *The Eighth Circle*

1960 Celia Fremlin, *The Hours Before Dawn*
1961 Julian Symons, *The Progress of a Crime*
1962 J. J. Marric, *Gideon's Fire*
1963 Ellis Peters, *Death and the Joyful Woman*
1964 Eric Ambler, *The Light of Day*

1965 John le Carré, *The Spy Who Came in from the Cold*
1966 Adam Hall, *The Quiller Memorandum*
1967 Nicolas Freeling, *The King of the Rainy Country*
1968 Donald E. Westlake, *God Save the Mark*
1969 Jeffrey Hudson, *A Case of Need*
1970 Dick Francis, *Forfeit*
1971 Maj Sjöwall and Per Wahlöö, *The Laughing Policeman*
1972 Frederick Forsyth, *The Day of the Jackal*
1973 Warren Kiefer, *The Lingala Code*
1974 Tony Hillerman, *Dance Hall of the Dead*
1975 Jon Cleary, *Peter's Pence*
1976 Brian Garfield, *Hopscotch*
1977 Robert B. Parker, *Promised Land*
1978 William H. Hallahan, *Catch Me: Kill Me*
1979 Kevin Follett, *The Eye of the Needle*
1980 Arthur Maling, *The Rheingold Route*

1981 Dick Francis, *Whip Hand*
1982 William Bayer, *Peregrine*
1983 Rick Boyer, *Billingsgate Shoal*
1984 Elmore Leonard, *La Brava*
1985 Ross Thomas, *Briarpatch*
1986 L. R. Wright, *The Suspect*
1987 Barbara Vine, *A Dark-Adapted Eye*
1988 Aaron Elkins, *Old Bones*
1989 Stuart M. Kaminsky, *A Cold Red Sunrise*
1990 James Lee Burke, *Black Cherry Blues*
1991 Julie Smith, *New Orleans Mourning*
1992 Lawrence Block, *A Dance at the Slaughterhouse*
1993 Margaret Maron, *Bootlegger's Daughter*
1994 Minette Walters, *The Sculptress*
1995 Mary Willis Walker, *The Red Scream*
1996 Dick Francis, *Come to Grief*
1997 Thomas A. Cook, *The Chatham School Affair*
1998 James Lee Burke, *Cimarron Rose*

CONTRIBUTORS

Robin W. Winks Randolph W. Townsend, Jr., Professor of History at Yale University. His academic work is largely in the history of the British Empire and in conservation history. Two of his books have been nominated for the Pulitzer Prize, and one, *Cloak & Gown*, about academics in intelligence work, won the 1988 award from the National Center for Intelligence Studies as best book of the year. His long-time avocation is mystery and spy thriller fiction, and he received a Dove Award in recognition of outstanding contributions to the serious study of mystery and crime fiction. Winks is an advisory editor and contributor to the forthcoming *Oxford Companion to Crime and Mystery Writing*, has edited *The Historian as Detective* and *Colloquium on Crime*, and has written (with Nina King) *Crime of the Scene*. He is the author of *Detective Fiction* and the Edgar-nominated *Modus Operandi*, and writes a regular column for the *Boston Globe*. He has recently completed a history of the genre, to be called *Secrecy, Exile, and Cunning*.
EDITOR IN CHIEF
THE HISTORICAL MYSTERY

Maureen Corrigan Adjunct Professor of English at Georgetown University. Among other courses, she teaches hard-boiled detective fiction as a popular form of American social criticism. Professor Corrigan is also the book critic for the NPR program, "Fresh Air," and a "Mystery Page" columnist for *The Washington Post*. Among the many prominent mystery writers Professor Corrigan has interviewed for NPR and *Newsday* and in programs for the Smithsonian Institution are P. D. James, Robert B. Parker, Colin Dexter, and Richard Stevenson. Professor Corrigan has taught a course on women's mysteries for the Smithsonian Institution entitled, "Sleuthing Spinsters and Dangerous Dames," and she has served as the study leader for the Smithsonian's "Mystery Tour of Great Britain." At present, she is working on a study to be called *Hard-Boiled Dreams: Detective Fiction and the Promise of America*. She has also written a Nancy Drew novel that was rejected by the publishers for being too sexually suggestive.
ASSOCIATE EDITOR
ROBERT B. PARKER

Walter Albert Retired professor of French. He edited *Detective and Mystery Fiction: An International Bibliography of Secondary Sources*, which was awarded an Edgar in 1985 by the Mystery Writers of America. The revised and expanded second edition was published in 1997. He has contributed to *Twentieth Century Crime and Mystery Writers*, the *St. James Guide to Crime and Mystery Writers*, *Anatomy of Wonder 4*, *British Fantasy and Science-Fiction Writers Before World War I*, and numerous other publications.
ÉMILE GABORIAU

David R. Anderson Vice President for Academic Affairs and Dean of the College at Luther College. He is the author of *Rex Stout* and numerous other scholarly works on detective fiction and eighteenth-century British literature.
REX STOUT

Charles Ardai Mystery writer and editor. His work has appeared in numerous publications including *Ellery Queen's Mystery Magazine*, *Alfred Hitchcock's Mystery Magazine*, and *Twilight Zone*, as well as in collections such as *The Year's Best Horror Stories XIX* and *Third Annual Best Mystery Stories of the Year*. A

summa cum laude graduate of Columbia University, Mr. Ardai was nominated for a Shamus Award in 1994 for his short fiction. He lost the award to Lawrence Block.
LAWRENCE BLOCK

Burl Barer Writer, director, and producer. Barer is an Edgar winner (*The Saint: A Complete History*) and a two-time Anthony Award nominee (*The Saint: A Complete History; Man Overboard: The Counterfeit Resurrection of Phil Champagne*). In addition to books on popular culture, religion, and true crime, Barer writes the Jeff Reynolds mystery series and the new adventures of Simon Templar, alias The Saint. Mr. Barer has written, produced, and/or directed thousands of radio and television commercials; garnered awards in radio, television, and print industries; provided creative services for such diverse artists as Frank Sinatra, Bob Dylan, Paul McCartney, and the Moody Blues; and been featured on numerous talk shows in America, Canada, and Great Britian.
LESLIE CHARTERIS

Melvyn Barnes Director of Libraries and Art Galleries for the Corporation of London. He has worked in

public libraries throughout England for forty years, and is a Past President of The Library Association (U.K.) and the International Association of Metropolitan City Libraries. In 1990 he was awarded the Order of the British Empire for services to public libraries. A lifelong interest in crime fiction led to the publication of three books—*Best Detective Fiction*, *Dick Francis*, and *Murder in Print*—and numerous articles and contributions to reference books. He has also written books and articles in the field of librarianship.
FREEMAN WILLS CROFTS

LynnDianne Beene Professor of English at the University of New Mexico. LynnDianne Beene is the author of *John le Carré*, co-author of *The Riverside Handbook of Rhetoric and Grammar*, and co-editor of *Solving Problems in Technical Writing*. When not writing, she teaches courses in espionage and detective fiction, classical rhetoric, grammar, and history of the English language.
JOHN LE CARRÉ

Ellen Bleiler Former Practice Management Editor at *Medical Economics* magazine, translator of various opera libretti, and author of several books about operas. She holds an A.B. from University of California, Berkeley, and an M.A. from New York University.
PATRICIA CORNWELL

Richard Bleiler Humanities Reference Librarian at the Homer Babbidge Library at the University of Connecticut.
EDGAR WALLACE

Lawrence Block Author of more than forty books of fiction and nonfiction. A four-time winner of the Edgar Award, he has also won four Shamus Awards, and was the first recipient of the Nero Wolfe Award. Named a Grand Master by the Mystery Writers of America, he is the author of several books on the business of writing, and has conducted a series of seminars for writers. His most recent works include *Hit Man* and *Everybody Dies*.
DONALD E. WESTLAKE

Jon L. Breen Professor of English at Rio Hondo College in Whittier, California. Author of six mystery novels and over eighty short stories, he is a book reviewer for *Ellery Queen's Mystery Magazine*, annually writes the introduction to *Year's 25 Finest Crime and Mystery Stories*, and has won Edgar Awards from Mystery Writers of America for *What About Murder?: A Guide to Books About Mystery and Detective Fiction* and *Novel Verdicts: A Guide to Courtroom Fiction*. His novel *Touch of the Past* was short-listed by the Crime Writers Association of Great Britain for their Dagger Awards.

ROBERT BERNARD; THE LEGAL CRIME NOVEL; THE POLICE PROCEDURAL

Robert E. Briney Professor of Computer Science and former Department Chairman at Salem State College in Salem, Massachusetts. Over the past thirty years he has contributed articles and bibliographies on various aspects of popular fiction to journals such as *The Armchair Detective*, *Journal of Popular Culture*, and *Views and Reviews*, and to numerous reference works, including *The Mystery Writer's Art*, *1001 Midnights*, *Twentieth Century Crime and Mystery Writers*, *Twentieth Century Science Fiction Writers*, *Twentieth Century Western Writers*, and *Twentieth Century Literary Criticism*. He was a Contributing Editor to the *Encyclopedia of Mystery and Detection* and the *Encyclopedia of Frontier and Western Fiction*.
SAX ROHMER

Ray B. Browne Chair Emeritus of the Popular Culture Department, Bowling Green State University. He founded and edits the *Journal of Popular Culture* and the *Journal of American Culture*. He founded the Bowling Green State University Popular Press. He co-created the Popular Culture Association and the American Culture Association and serves as Secretary-Treasurer to both. He has edited or authored more than sixty books.
THE ETHNIC DETECTIVE

Rex Burns Professor of American Literature and Chair of the English Department at the University of Colorado at Denver. He is the author of numerous books, articles, reviews, and stories, including *Success in America: The Yeoman Dream and the Industrial Revolution*. His police procedural *The Alvarez Journal* won an Edgar for best first mystery. *The Avenging Angel* was made into a feature movie starring Charles Bronson. He is also co-editor of an anthology, *Crime Classics*, and has published under the pen name "Tom Sehler." For several years Burns wrote a monthly mystery book review column for the *Rocky Mountain News*, and other of his reviews have appeared in the *Denver Post*, the *Miami Herald*, and *The Washington Post*. He is also an adviser and contributor to the forthcoming *Oxford Companion to Mystery*.
CARROLL JOHN DALY

Max Allan Collins Permanent staff member of the Mississippi Valley Writers Conference at Augustana College. Collins is a University of Iowa Writer's Workshop graduate and has taught at Muscatine Community College. He is a two-time winner of the Private Eye Writers of America Shamus Award for Best Novel for his Nathan Heller thrillers *True De-*

tective and *Stolen Away*, and was nominated for an Edgar for *Mickey Spillane: One Lonely Night*, co-authored with James Traylor. The author of over forty suspense novels, he was screenwriter and director of the films *Mommy* and *Mommy's Day*. His comics scripting credits include *Dick Tracy*, *Batman*, *Ms. Tree*, and *Mike Danger*.
IAN FLEMING; MICKEY SPILLANE

J. Randolph Cox Professor Emeritus and Reference Librarian at Saint Olaf College. Cox is the Editor-Publisher of *Dime Novel Round-up* and was Area Chair for Dime Novels, Series Books, and Pulp Magazines of the American Culture Association from 1987 to 1992. He has contributed articles on detective fiction and dime novels to *The Armchair Detective*, *Baker Street Journal*, *Dictionary of Literary Biography*, *Dime Novel Round-up*, *Oxford Companion to Crime and Mystery Writing*, *Yellowback Library*, and other journals and reference books. He is the author of bibliographic studies of detective fiction, the Nick Carter stories, H. G. Wells, and Walter B. Gibson, and is currently working on *The Dime Novel Companion*.
THE NICK CARTER STORIES

Mary Jean DeMarr Professor Emerita of English and Women's Studies at Indiana State University. DeMarr is a winner of the Dove Award given by the Mystery/Detection Caucus of the Popular Culture Association for "outstanding contribution to the serious study of mystery and crime fiction." She has also published in the areas of adolescent fiction and Midwestern American literature. Her most recent books are *In the Beginning: First Novels in Mystery Series* and *Colleen McCullough: A Critical Companion*. She is currently writing a book on Barbara Kingsolver.
MARGARET MILLAR

Brian Diemert Associate Professor at Brescia College in London, Ontario. He is the author of *Graham Greene's Thrillers and the 1930s*, which was short-listed for the 1997 Arthur Ellis Award (nonfiction). He has also written on Edgar Allan Poe and F. Scott Fitzgerald.
GRAHAM GREENE

Michael Dirda Writer and Editor for the *Washington Post Book World*. He holds a Ph.D. in comparative literature from Cornell University, where his checkered studies focused on medieval literature and European romanticism. At *Book World* he oversees the arts and letters coverage and writes about fiction and poetry, biography, intellectual history, classics in translation, and popular literature (children's books, science fiction, mysteries). In 1993 he received the Pulitzer Prize for criticism.
JOHN DICKSON CARR; EDMUND CRISPIN

Owen Dudley Edwards Professor of History at the University of Edinburgh. Born in Dublin, Ireland, on 27 July 1938 to academic parents, he studied with the Jesuits at Belvedere College, Dublin; was undergraduate at University College Dublin; and was a graduate student at The Johns Hopkins University. His *The Quest for Sherlock Holmes* (1982) established the Scottish and Jesuit roots of Arthur Conan Doyle's writing. He was General Editor of *The Oxford Sherlock Holmes*, the definitive edition of the Holmes stories in nine volumes. Edwards delights in being Robin Winks's Watson whenever they can meet. He is married to Bonnie Lee; they have three children, one a folklorist, one a theologian, one a geologist.
ARTHUR CONAN DOYLE

Erwin H. Ford II Professor of English at Morris Brown College/The Atlanta University Center in Atlanta, Georgia. Ford holds a B.A. in Philosophy, an M.A. in English, and a Ph.D. in English from the State University of New York, Buffalo. He has pursued advanced studies at the University of Tübingen and Yale University and is Syndicated Columnist for Cox Newspapers.
GEORGE V. HIGGINS

Jeffery Fraser Writer. Fraser lives in Pittsburgh. He worked as a reporter from 1975 to 1993 for several western Pennsylvania newspapers, including the *Jeanette News Dispatch*; the *Greensburg Tribune-Review*; and the *Pittsburgh Press*. Since 1993 he has written extensively about poverty, violence, and social welfare issues for the University of Pittsburgh Center for Social and Urban Research. In 1997 he was awarded a Pennsylvania Council of the Arts Screenwriting Fellowship. He graduated from Kent State University in 1975 with a B.A. in journalism.
K. C. CONSTANTINE

June M. Frazer Professor of English at Western Illinois University. Frazer received her B.A. from Stetson University in DeLand, Florida, and M.A. and Ph.D. degrees from the University of North Carolina at Chapel Hill. Her areas of academic specialization are nineteenth-century British literature and literature by women, especially Jane Austen. A secondary interest in mystery fiction led to the teaching of a course, "The Literature of Crime and Detection," at Western Illinois University, and the co-editing (with R. G. Walker) of a book, *The Cunning Craft. Original Essays on Detective Fiction and Contemporary Literary Theory*.
DAPHNE DU MAURIER

David Geherin Professor of English at Eastern Michigan University in Ypsilanti. He is the author of several articles and four books on mystery fiction:

Sons of Sam Spade; John D. MacDonald; The American Private Eye; Elmore Leonard. Geherin teaches courses in twentieth-century literature, mystery fiction, and murder in literature.
DASHIELL HAMMETT

Robert Gleason Editor at Tor/Forge Publishing Company who also works for Stephen Cannell Motion Pictures. Gleason is the acclaimed author of *Wrath of God* and is currently working on a prequel to that novel. He has been involved in publishing for thirty years.
ELMORE LEONARD

Roy S. Goodman Adjunct faculty member of Wayne State University. Goodman is an ear, nose, and throat physician in Michigan and the author of numerous medical publications. He has been an amateur critic since his college days, reviewing music, drama, and books ranging from *How to Pick up Girls* to *Headache Disorders.* He served on the editorial board of *The American Journal of Otolaryngology* and was Thriller Genre Specialist for *Rave Reviews* and a major contributor to *The Robert Ludlum Companion.* He is married and has two children.
ROBERT LUDLUM

Edward Gorman Suspense novelist, anthologist, and editorial director of *Mystery Scene Magazine.* His novels include *Night of Shadows, Cage of Night,* and *Blood Moon.* Among the many anthologies he has edited are *American Pulp* and *Dark Crimes One* and *Dark Crimes Two.*
ELMORE LEONARD

Douglas G. Greene Professor of History and Director of the Institute of Humanities at Old Dominion University. He has written or edited thirteen books, most recently *Detection by Gaslight: Fourteen Victorian Detective Stories.* He is the author of *John Dickson Carr: The Man Who Explained Miracles,* editor of *The Collected Short Fiction of Ngaio Marsh,* and co-editor of *Death Locked In.* He has written for *The Armchair Detective, The Baker Street Journal, The Poisoned Pen, Deadly Pleasure, CADS,* and other periodicals.
COLIN DEXTER

George Grella Professor of English and Film Studies at the University of Rochester. He is the author of hundreds of books and film reviews and scores of articles and essays on detective, crime, and mystery fiction and on individual writers—Arthur Conan Doyle, Edgar Allan Poe, Dashiell Hammett, Ian Fleming, Ross Macdonald, Georges Simenon, John le Carré. Grella is also the author of many articles and essays

on modern and contemporary American and British literatures, film, and baseball, and is a film critic for the *Rochester City Newspaper* and for WXXI-FM (Rochester).
GEORGES SIMENON

Bruce Harding Curator of the Ngaio Marsh House (Cashmere, Christchurch, New Zealand) and Fellow of The Macmillan Brown Centre for Pacific Studies at the University of Canterbury (New Zealand). Harding wrote the first academic thesis on Ngaio Marsh in 1979 at the Masterate level at the University of Canterbury. He was later awarded a Ph.D. in English from the University of Otago for a literary-historical study of fiction about criminality and social deviance in the Australian and New Zealand literary traditions.
NGAIO MARSH

David Hawkes Associate Professor of English at Lehigh University. His book, *Ideology,* was published in 1996.
AGATHA CHRISTIE

Michael Holquist Chair of Comparative Literature at Yale University. A charter member of the Yale Sherlock Holmes Society, Holquist has taught and published articles on Borges and the detective story since 1970. He has also published a number of volumes on the Russian thinker Mikhail Bakhtin, a book on Dostoevsky, and numerous articles on a wide variety of topics. He is currently at work on a book devoted to philology's war with magic languages.
JORGE LUIS BORGES AND
THE METAPHYSICAL MYSTERY

Wilt L. Idema Professor of Chinese Literature at Leiden University. He has studied Chinese Literature in Leiden, Sapporo, and Kyoto. He has also taught at the University of California, Berkeley, and at Harvard University and has published extensively on traditional Chinese fiction and drama, both in English and Dutch. One of his most recent publications is *A Guide to Chinese Literature.* For his Dutch translations of Chinese poetry he was awarded the Martinus Nijhoff Prize for 1991.
ROBERT VAN GULIK

H. R. F. Keating Former crime-books reviewer for the *Times of London.* He is the author of *Sherlock Holmes: The Man and His World; Crime and Mystery, the 100 Best Books;* and *Writing Crime Fiction.* In 1994 he was given the George N. Dove Award in recognition of his "outstanding contribution to the serious study of crime and mystery fiction."
JULIAN SYMONS

J. Gerald Kennedy William A. Read Professor of English at Louisiana State University and President of the Poe Studies Association. He has published two books on Poe, including *Poe, Death, and the Life of Writing* and *The Narrative of Arthur Gordon Pym and the Abyss of Interpretation*, as well as an edition of *The Narrative of Arthur Gordon Pym and Related Tales*. His many articles on Poe have appeared in the leading journals in American literature, and his 1982 essay on Roland Barthes and autobiography was a Pushcart Prize selection.
EDGAR ALLAN POE

Margaret H. Kinsman Senior Lecturer in English at South Bank University in London. Her research and teaching interests include early-twentieth-century women writers and crime and mystery fiction. She has contributed essays on women mystery writers to *Women Times Three*, the *St. James Guide to Crime and Mystery Writers*, and the forthcoming *Oxford Companion to Crime and Mystery Writing*. She is a member of the Popular Culture Association's crime and mystery fiction caucus and the British Crime Writers Association. She has given papers on feminism and crime fiction at international conferences. A longer work on Paretsky and women writers of Chicago is in progress.
SARA PARETSKY

Marvin S. Lachman Writer and critic. A mystery reader since 1943, Lachman contributed to the first issue of *The Armchair Detective* in 1967 and since then has written articles and reviews for virtually every mystery reference book and journal. He was co-author and co-editor of *Detectionary* and the Edgar-winning *Encyclopedia of Mystery and Detection*. He wrote *A Reader's Guide to the American Novel of Detection*, which was nominated for the Edgar, Anthony, Agatha, and Macavity Awards. In 1997, the Mystery Writers of America presented him with their Raven Award for his life-long achievements in the mystery field.
STANLEY ELLIN

Thomas M. Leitch Professor of English at the University of Delaware and Mystery Editor at *Kirkus Reviews*. He is the author of *What Stories Are: Narrative Theory and Interpretation*; *Find the Director and Other Hitchcock Games*; and *Lionel Trilling: An Annotated Bibliography*.
E. C. BENTLY; NICHOLAS BLAKE

Peter Lewis Reader (Emeritus) in English Studies at the University of Durham in England. For several years he was Executive Editor of *The Durham University Journal*, and is now in charge of Flambard Press, a small publishing house in the North of England devoted to poetry and fiction, especially mystery writing. He has also been Associate Editor of the major British literary quarterly *Stand*. As an eighteenth-century specialist, he has published books on John Gay and Henry Fielding, but he has also written widely on contemporary fiction, radio drama, and Anglo-Welsh poetry. His *John le Carré* won the Edgar Award in 1986 from the Mystery Writers of America, and his subsequent book, *Eric Ambler*, was short-listed for two American literary awards in 1991.
ERIC AMBLER

John Loughery Art critic for *The Hudson Review*. His biography of S. S. Van Dine, *Alias S. S. Van Dine: The Man Who Created Philo Vance*, won the 1993 Edgar Award for biography. His other books include *John Sloan: Painter and Rebel*, a finalist for the 1996 Pulitzer Prize in biography, and *The Other Side of Silence: Men's Lives and Gay Identities, a Twentieth-Century History*.
S. S. VAN DINE

Patricia D. Maida Professor of English at the University of the District of Columbia. She coordinates English composition courses and also teaches American literature. Recently she received a college award for outstanding teaching and scholarship. A former president of the College English Association, Middle Atlantic Group, she currently serves on the Executive Board.
ANNA KATHARINE GREEN

Noel Dorman Mawer Teacher of English and sociology at Edward Waters College in Jacksonville, Florida. Her Ph.D. dissertation at Bryn Mawr was on P. B. Shelley, about whom she has published essays in *Literature and Psychology*, *Prose Studies*, and *Essays in Literature*. While teaching in Philadelphia, she was given a copy of Highsmith's *This Sweet Sickness* and thenceforth found herself increasingly inhabiting Highsmith's world, at times confusing herself with Tom Ripley. In recent years Professor Mawer has, like Highsmith herself, turned to social and political concerns, both as a teacher and activist; in addition to teaching sociology, she serves as a union official and negotiator.
PATRICIA HIGHSMITH

Nancy C. Mellerski Professor of French at Dickinson College in Carlisle, Pennsylvania. She is the co-author, with Robert P. Winston, of *The Public Eye: Ideology and the Police Procedural* and of "The Detective in the Intertext: Freeling's Dialogue with Chandler" (in *Texas Studies in Literature and Language*). She has also published articles on the fantastic in literature, on the French *nouveau roman*, and, most recently, on the Occupation in French cinema since 1945.
MAJ SJÖWALL AND PER WAHLÖÖ

Dean A. Miller Emeritus Professor of History at the University of Rochester. He took his Ph.D. in Byzantine studies and has published in this and related fields for the past thirty years; his most recent work, *The Book of the Hero*, is to be published by The Johns Hopkins University Press. He read and enjoyed detective, police-procedural, and suspense fiction for decades before beginning to write critical analyses of the field, and has now published in the *St. James Guide to Crime and Mystery Writers* and in the forthcoming *Oxford Companion to Crime and Mystery Writing*. He is also interested in the historical novel and in that strange growth, the historical mystery.
EVAN HUNTER

Lewis D. Moore Professor of English at the University of the District of Columbia. He has taught there for twenty-four years. He received his Ph.D. from American University in 1974. In addition to publishing articles on John D. MacDonald, John Dryden, George Gissing, and Jean Toomer, he has published *Meditations on America: John D. MacDonald's Travis McGee Series and Other Fiction* and has given talks at various academic conferences on MacDonald and other writers. He lives in Washington, D.C., with his wife, Barbara.
JOHN D. MACDONALD

Robert F. Moss Ph.D. candidate at the University of South Carolina. He has published articles on Raymond Chandler, Ross Macdonald, F. Scott Fitzgerald, Mark Twain, Stephen Crane, and American social history.
ROSS MACDONALD

Francis M. Nevins Professor at St. Louis University School of Law. He is the author of five mystery novels: *Publish and Perish, Corrupt and Ensnare, The 120-Hour Clock, The Ninety Million Dollar Mouse,* and *Into the Same River Twice*. He has also written about forty short stories, which have appeared in *Ellery Queen, Alfred Hitchcock,* and other national magazines, and many of which have been reprinted in leading anthologies. He has edited more than fifteen mystery collections and has written a number of nonfiction books on the genre. Two of these, *Royal Bloodline: Ellery Queen, Author and Detective* and *Cornell Woolrich: First You Dream, Then You Die* have won Edgars from Mystery Writers of America. He has written articles and reviews on mystery fiction for newspapers, magazines, and reference works. During 1994 he served as Awards Chair for Mystery Writers of America.
ELLERY QUEEN; CORNELL WOOLRICH

William F. Nolan Critic, historian, novelist, and screenwriter. Nolan's books include *The Black Mask Boys, Hammet: A Life at the Edge,* and *The Marble Orchard,* the latest in his Black Mask Mystery series. His crime-based movies of the week include *Melvin Purvis, G-Man, The Kansas City Massacre, The Norliss Tapes, Sky Heist,* and *Terror at London Bridge*. Nolan attended the Kansas City Art Institute and San Diego State College and has lectured widely, taught a creative writing seminar at Bowling Green State University, and contributed to over 240 magazines and newspapers worldwide. Twice winner of the Mystery Writers of America's Edgar Special Award, Nolan's output includes 65 books, 135 short stories, 600 nonfiction magazine pieces, and 40 screenplays. His works have been selected for some 250 anthologies and textbooks. He is recognized as a major authority in the genre of hard-boiled fiction.
ERLE STANLEY GARDNER

George O'Brien Professor of English at Georgetown University in Washington, D.C. He is the author of *The Village of Longing,* which won the autobiographical trilogy Irish Book Awards Silver Medal in 1988, *Dancehall Days,* and *Out of Our Minds,* as well as two books on the playwright Brian Friel. He edited *The Irish Anthology*.
JOHN BUCHAN

Susan Oleksiw Writer and scholar. She received her doctorate in Sanskrit from the University of Pennsylvania. Her articles have appeared in *Clues, The Drood Review of Mystery, Adyar Library Bulletin, Journal of the American Oriental Society,* and other journals, and her short fiction has appeared in numerous literary journals. She was a consulting editor for the *Oxford Companion to Crime and Mystery Writing* and an adviser to the *St. James Guide to Crime and Mystery Fiction*. She is the author of the Mellingham series of mysteries and of *A Reader's Guide to the Classic British Mystery*.
RONALD A. KNOX

LeRoy Lad Panek Professor of English at Western Maryland College. In addition to articles on Shakespeare, Emerson, Poe, and Graham Greene, he is the author of *Watteau's Shepherds: The Detective Novel in Britain; The Special Branch: The Spy Novel in Britain; An Introduction to the Detective Story;* and *Probable Cause: Crime Fiction in America*. For his work, he has received an Edgar Award from the Mystery Writers of America, and the George N. Dove Award from the Popular Culture Association of America.
MIGNON G. EBERHART

Robert Allen Papinchak Writer and educator. He received his Ph.D. in English from the University of Wisconsin, Madison, with a dissertation on the American short story, and has taught creative writing, literature, film, and composition at the university level for over twenty years. Papinchak has received Pushcart Prize nominations for his short stories and has published nonfiction, critical work (*Sherwood Anderson: A Study of the Short Fiction*), and poetry in numerous journals and magazines.
DOROTHY L. SAYERS; WOMEN OF MYSTERY

Audrey Peterson Former Professor of English at California State University, Long Beach. Peterson was born in Los Angeles, received her B.A. from the University of California, Los Angeles, and her Ph.D. from the University of Southern California. As a professor, her course offerings have included Victorian literature and occasional classes in mystery fiction. After publishing articles on nineteenth-century literature and a book, *Victorian Masters of Mystery: From Wilkie Collins to Conan Doyle*, she turned to writing mystery fiction. Her nine novels all feature an academic background and are set in England, where she frequently visits. She now makes her home in Bellingham, Washington.
WILKIE COLLINS

B. A. Pike Writer and editor. Pike is the author of *Campion's Career*, a study of Margery Allingham, and co-author of two editions of *Detective Fiction: The Collector's Guide* and of *Artists in Crime*, a survey of dustwrapper art from the Golden Age to 1960. He has contributed to *CADS*, *The Armchair Detective*, and a number of reference works, including all four editions of *Twentieth Century Crime and Mystery Writers* (now *The St. James Guide*). He is a Consultant Editor for the forthcoming *Oxford Companion to Crime and Mystery Writing*. He edited *Murder in Miniature*, the collected stories of Leo Bruce, and is active in the Dorothy L. Sayers Society. He also edits *The Bottle Street Gazette* for the Margery Allingham Society.
MICHAEL GILBERT

Dennis Porter Germaine Brée Professor of French and Comparative Literature at the University of Massachusetts, Amherst. He has been an NEH and an ACLS Research Fellow, and a Research Fellow at the Center for Advanced Studies in the Humanities in Canberra. He is the author of *The Pursuit of Crime*; *Haunted Journeys: Transgression and Desire in European Travel Writing*; and *Rousseau's Legacy: Emergence and Eclipse of the Writer in France*. He is also the translator of Jacques Lacan's *The Ethics of Psychoanalysis*.
P. D. JAMES

B. J. Rahn Professor in the English Department at Hunter College of the City University of New York. She has been teaching, researching, and writing about crime fiction for over a decade. Professor Rahn has published numerous articles in the field, and in 1995 she edited a collection of essays celebrating the centenary of Ngaio Marsh entitled, *Ngaio Marsh: The Woman and Her Work*. She is Co-founder and Editor of *Murder Is Academic*, a newsletter for teachers of crime fiction at colleges and universities. She is a member of the Mystery Writers of America, the Crime Writers Association of Great Britain, the Agatha Christie Society, the Ngaio Marsh Society International, the Dorothy L. Sayers Society, and the Sherlock Holmes Society of London.
RUTH RENDELL; THE ARMCHAIR DETECTIVE

Maureen T. Reddy Professor of English and Director of the Women's Studies Program at Rhode Island College in Providence. Reddy's first book, *Sisters in Crime: Feminism and the crime Novel*, was nominated for an Edgar Award for best biographical or critical book of 1988. She is currently working on a book for Rutgers University Press, tentatively titled *Traces, Codes, and Clues: Reading Race in Genre Fiction*.
THE FEMALE DETECTIVE

Rachel Schaffer Professor in the Department of English and Philosophy at Montana State University, Billings. She earned a Ph.D. in linguistics from the Ohio State University. Schaffer has taught linguistics, English as a second language, composition, and literature since 1983 and has won several Montana State University faculty awards. Her current research focuses on mystery fiction, in particular on the work of Dick Francis. She has presented papers and published articles about his novels, as well as those of mystery writers Sue Grafton, Liza Cody, and others.
DICK FRANCIS

George L. Scheper Professor of Humanities and Coordinator of the Interdisciplinary Humanities Program at Essex Community College in Baltimore County, Maryland and Adjunct Professor of Interdisciplinary Studies at The Johns Hopkins University School of Continuing Studies. Scheper holds a Ph.D. from Princeton University. He is the Director of four NEH summer institutes and the author of *Michael Innes* and articles in the *Oxford Companion to Crime and Mystery*, *Encyclopedia of Popular Culture*, *Dictionary of Biblical Tradition in English Literature*, *New England Quarterly*, *PMLA*, *Annalecta Husserliana*, *Semiotics 1990*, and *The Rhetoric of Vision: Essays on Charles Williams*.
MICHAEL INNES

Charles L. P. Silet Teacher of courses in contemporary literature and culture and film at Iowa State University. His essays, reviews, and interviews with crime and mystery writers have appeared in a wide variety of publications both in the United States and abroad. He has just edited a book of critical materials on Chester Himes and is preparing an edition of his interviews for publication. He is an Advisory Editor to *The Armchair Detective.*
CRIME NOIR

Robert Skinner University Librarian at Xavier University of Louisiana in New Orleans. He is a critic and fiction writer whose novels include *Skin Deep, Blood Red, Cat-Eyed Trouble,* and *Daddy's Gone A-Hunting.* Among his critical works are *Two Guns from Harlem: The Detective Fiction of Chester Himes, The New Hard-Boiled Dicks: Heroes for a New Urban Mythology,* and *Conversations with Chester Himes.*
ELMORE LEONARD

Anthony Slide Author and editor. Slide has written more than sixty volumes on the history of popular entertainment, including *Early American Cinema, The Silent Feminists: America's First Women Directors, The New Historical Dictionary of the American Film Industry,* and *The Encyclopedia of Vaudeville.* He is also the author of *Gay and Lesbian Characters and Themes in Mystery Novels.* In 1990, in recognition of his work on the history of popular culture, Slide was awarded an honorary doctorate of letters by Bowling Green State University.
GAY AND LESBIAN MYSTERY FICTION

Jennifer Crusie Smith Writer and scholar. She holds an M.A. in feminist criticism and an M.F.A. in fiction, and she is currently completing her dissertation on romance fiction at the Ohio State University. Her critical work includes *Anne Rice: A Critical Companion* and essays for anthologies and journals such as *Paradoxa.* She is also the author of ten novels; her eleventh, *Crazy for You,* is forthcoming.
THE ROMANTIC SUSPENSE MYSTERY

Stephen F. Soitos Teacher of writing, literature, and film at Springfield College, Massachusetts. Soitos has written three mystery novels as well as his *Blues Detective: A Study of African-American Detective Fiction.*
BLACK DETECTIVE FICTION

William David Spencer Adjunct Professor of Theology at Gordon-Conwell Theological Seminary (Hamilton, Massachusetts) and the Caribbean Graduate School of Theology (Kingston, Jamaica) and the Pastor of Encouragement at Pilgrim Church (Beverly, MA). He is a Presbyterian Church (USA) minister. His

books include *Mysterium and Mystery: The Clerical Crime Novel, Chanting Down Babylon: The Rastafari Reader, God Through the Looking Glass: Glimpses from the Arts, Dread Jesus, The Global God: Multicultural Evangelical Views of God, The Prayer Life of Jesus, The Goddess Revival, Joy Through the Night: Biblical Resources for Suffering People,* and *2 Corinthians: A Commentary.*
RELIGIOUS MYSTERIES

Mary Rose Sullivan Professor Emerita at the University of Colorado, Denver. She has taught courses in Victorian literature and mystery fiction, edited collections of letters and poetry by Elizabeth Barrett Browning, and co-edited, with Rex Burns, *Crime Classics: The Mystery Story From Poe to the Present.* She wrote the entry on detective fiction for the *Women's Studies Encyclopedia.*
AMANDA CROSS

Jean Swanson Member of the library faculty at the University of Redlands in southern California. With co-author Dr. Dean James, she has written *By a Woman's Hand: A Guide to Mystery Fiction by Women.* It won both Agatha and Macavity awards for best nonfiction and was nominated for an Edgar. A second edition was published in 1996, and it was nominated for Agatha and Anthony awards. Swanson and James have also written *Killer Book: A Reader's Guide to Exploring the Popular World of Mystery and Suspense.*
SUE GRAFTON

John C. Tibbetts Assistant Professor of Film at the University of Kansas. He holds a Ph.D. from Kansas in Multi-Disciplinary Studies—art history, theater, photography and film. He has hosted his own television show, *A.M. Live* (Kansas City, Mo.), worked as a news reporter and commentator for CBS Television and CNN, produced fine arts programming for radio, and written or illustrated four books and numerous articles and short stories. From 1976 to 1985 he edited *American Classic Screen.* A regular contributor to the *Christian Science Monitor, he is also* a Senior Editor for the annual *Movie/Video Guides* from Ballantine Books and has been a Senior Consultant and Contributor to several major reference works, including *The New Film Index, Encyclopedia of the Twentieth Century, Oxford Companion to Mystery and Crime Writing,* and *American Cultural Biography.* His newest book is *Dvorak in America.*
G. K. CHESTERTON

J. K. Van Dover Professor of English at Lincoln University of Pennsylvania. He has served as a Fulbright Professor in Germany in 1980 and again in 1988. He is the author of several books, including *Murder in the Millions, At Wolfe's Door, Understanding Wil-*

liam Kennedy, You Know My Method, and *Isn't Justice Always Unfair?* (with John Jebb), and the editor of *The Critical Response to Raymond Chandler*.
REGIONALIZATION OF THE MYSTERY
AND CRIME NOVEL

Sharon Villines Professor Emeritus, State University of New York, Empire State College and Director of the Archives of Detective Fiction, Mercantile Library of New York. Villines is a publisher and editor at Deadly Serious Press, which publishes the *Deadly Directory*, an annual, international guide to mystery fiction related businesses, organizations, and publications. She is co-author with Elizabeth Steltenpohl and Jane Shipton of the text *Orientation to College: A Reader on Becoming an Educated Person* as well as numerous papers and articles on the education of the artist.
JOHN MORTIMER

Alexandra von Malottke Roy Assessment Specialist at Harcourt Brace. She is a former college and university professor, and her interests now include writing and editing. She has published several college textbooks, articles on direct marketing, and a book on Josephine Tey.
JOSEPHINE TEY

Priscilla L. Walton Associate Professor of English at Carleton University. She is the author of *Patriarchal Desire and Victorian Discourse: A Lacanian Reading of Anthony Trollope's Palliser Novels* and *The Disruption of the Feminine in Henry James*. She has also published articles in such journals as *Narrative, Genre, Henry James Review, Literature/Interpretation/Theory, Commonwealth, World Literature Written in English, Victorian Review*, and *Ariel*. Her *Detective Agency: Women Re-Writing the Hardboiled Tradition*, co-authored with Manina Jones, is forthcoming. She is a member of the Advisory Council of the *PMLA* and co-editor of the *Canadian Review of American Studies*.
HELEN MacINNES

Wesley K. Wark Associate Professor of History at the University of Toronto. His publications include *The Ultimate Enemy: British Intelligence and Nazi Germany 1933–1939* and three edited books dealing with intelligence, including *Security and Intelligence*

in a Changing World: New Perspectives for the 1990s (with A. Stuart Farson and David Stafford); *Spy Fiction, Spy Films and Real Intelligence;* and *Espionage: Past, Present, Future?* He serves as editor of the journal *Intelligence and National Security* and as series editor for *Classics for Espionage*. He is currently working on a study of the popular culture of espionage during the cold war.
THE SPY THRILLER

Robert P. Winston Professor of English at Dickinson College in Carlisle, Pennsylvania. He is the co-author, with Nancy C. Mellerski, of *The Public Eye: Ideology and the Police Procedural* and of "The Detective in the Intertext: Freeling's Dialogue with Chandler" (in *Texas Studies in Literature and Language*). In addition to a two-part interview with the contemporary American detective novelist J. S. Borthwick, in *Clues*, he has also published articles on eighteenth- and nineteenth-century American literature.
MAJ SJÖWALL AND PER WAHLÖÖ

Paula M. Woods Lecturer in English at Baylor University. She teaches nondramatic literature of the sixteenth and seventeenth centuries, specializing in the works of early women writers. From 1993 to 1995 she served as Chair of Mystery/Detective Fiction Area of the Popular Culture Association and the Texas/Southwest Popular Culture Association. She has presented papers on Margery Allingham and other women mystery writers at Popular Culture Association conferences. Her publications include articles on Allingham in *Great Women Mystery Writers* and *In the Beginning: First Novels in Mystery Series*.
MARGERY ALLINGHAM

Joan Zseleczky Writer and editor. Born in Fort Belvoir, Virginia and a graduate of Barnard College, she has lectured widely on writing and publishing since 1980 and has taught graduate seminars at Harvard Graduate School of Education and the Radcliffe Publishing Procedures course. Her first published poetry, "Dream," appeared in 1967, and her first work of fiction, the novella *Henry Swan*, in 1977. Since 1979 she has published fiction and poetry under a pseudonym. She is currently completing a collection of elegies, *What Spring Is Like*. She lives in Manhattan and in Palm Harbor, Florida.
RAYMOND CHANDLER

INDEX

Page citations in **boldface** indicate extended discussion of subject.